THEME AND VARIATIONS

(handwritten notes):

By 140⁰⁰

Rent 20 94 per month

New Down 49⁰⁰   16.25 GAS
              timo

9 54

17
12
34
170
204
44
5 53

Other Scott, Foresman/Little, Brown books by Laurence Behrens
and Leonard J. Rosen

Writing and Reading Across the Curriculum (Third Edition, 1987)
Writing Papers in College (1986)
Reading for College Writers (1987)

THEME AND VARIATIONS

The Impact of Great Ideas

Laurence Behrens
UNIVERSITY OF CALIFORNIA, SANTA BARBARA

Leonard J. Rosen
BENTLEY COLLEGE

Scott, Foresman/Little, Brown College Division
Scott, Foresman and Company
Glenview, Illinois   Boston   London

Library of Congress Cataloging-in-Publication Data

Theme and variations.

Includes bibliographies.
1. Learning and scholarship — History.   2. Learning
and scholarship — History — Sources.   3. Intellectual
life — History.   4. Intellectual life — History —
Sources.   5. Civilization, Occidental — History.
6. Civilization, Occidental — History — Sources.
I. Behrens, Laurence.   II. Rosen, Leonard J.
AZ221.T45   1987   001   87–23361
ISBN 0–673–39707–6

1 2 3 4 5 6 7 8 9 10 – RRC – 93 92 91 90 89 88 87

Printed in the United States of America

Credits

Photo Credits

    II. Copernicus: Culver Pictures.
    III. Hobbes: Culver Pictures.
    IV. Condorcet: The Bettmann Archive.
    V. Darwin: Culver Pictures.
    VI. Marx: The Bettmann Archive.
    VII. Freud: Photo Researchers.
    Dali paintings: Dismal Sport, 1929. Oil and collage on canvas. Private collection. *The
First Days of Spring,* 1929. Oil and collage on panel. Private collection. *The Great Masturbator,* 1929. Oil on canvas. Private collection. *The Enigma of Desire,* 1929. Oil on canvas. Oskar
R. Schlag. Zurich. *Portrait of Paul Eluard,* 1929. Oil on cardboard. Private collection. *Accommodations of Desire,* 1926. Oil on panel. Private collection. *Illumined Pleasures,* 1929. Oil and
collage on panel. The Sidney and Harriet Janis Collection. Gift to the Museum of Modern
Art, New York.

Text Credits

COPERNICUS AND THE NEW UNIVERSE

    Thomas Kuhn: Excerpted by permission of the publishers from *The Copernican Revolu-
tion: Planetary Astronomy and the Development of Western Thought* by Thomas S. Kuhn, Cambridge, Mass.: Harvard University Press. Copyright © 1985 by Thomas S. Kuhn.

(Continues on p. 845)

Preface

"Theme and Variations" is a musical term, referring to a type of composition in which a musical theme is first stated in its basic, unadorned form and then, in a series of varied repetitions, adapted, enhanced, speeded up, slowed down, re-orchestrated, set in a new key or to a new rhythm or to a counterpoint, or otherwise modified. At its most humble, the theme and variations form is an academic exercise for fledgling composers, helping them develop their musical skill and versatility. At its most exalted — as in Bach's "Passacaglia and Fugue in C Minor" or the final movements of Beethoven's "Eroica" and Brahms's Fourth Symphonies — the theme and variations can stir the soul to its depths. Sometimes, as in Gershwin's "'I Got Rhythm' Variations," composers will write variations on their own themes; sometimes, as in Brahms's "Variations on a Theme by Haydn" and Rachmaninoff's "Variations on a Theme by Paginini," on themes composed by others.

It is in this latter sense that we use the term to describe this book. Instead of musical themes, we begin with great ideas as expressed by six of the most influential thinkers of Western civilization during the past four hundred years. Following the statement of each idea is a series of variations upon it by other thinkers, variations adapted to the times and to the cultures of origin, as well as to the particular temperaments and intellectual orientations of the thinkers. *Theme and Variations* is thus intended not only to acquaint students with some of the most important ideas in our Western intellectual tradition, but also to show the effects of these ideas, and to show how they have been applied (and in some cases, misapplied) in a variety of fields. We hope that these themes and variations will frequently stir the mind, if not the soul, since they go to the heart of our own relationship to the universe, to our past and to our future, to our society and to our government, to our fellow creatures, and to our own human natures.

More immediately — for this text is designed primarily for writing and humanities courses — *Theme and Variations* is designed to stimulate discussion and writing. It begins with a "Critical Introduction," which helps students pose and respond to questions about what they read and that considers the ways in which theories are developed and applied in various fields. The body of the text consists of six parts, each focusing on a major thinker and the impact of his central idea upon others.

The first selection in each part presents a seminal statement of this idea: the "theme." For example, "Darwin and the Survival of the Fittest" begins with Darwin's own statement of this idea, as expressed in *The Origin of the Species*. Subsequent selections reveal the impact of this idea on other thinkers. Thus, the statement by Charles Darwin is followed by statements from such social Darwinists as Herbert Spencer, William Graham Sumner, and Andrew Carnegie, as well as by those (Josiah Strong and Adolf Hitler) who adapted Darwin's biological ideas to support racist thinking. We have tried to select passages that reflect the impact of ideas on a wide array of fields. Sigmund Freud, for example, was a psychoanalyst, but both he and those he influenced have employed his insights on the unconscious to explore such fields as history, art, literature, and anthropology. In fact, one of the qualities that makes an idea "great" is that it has an impact not only in its own particular field, but in many fields — so many, that it affects the very ways in which we perceive the world and our own selves.

Each part begins with a brief essay in which we explore some of the issues raised by the idea in question. Each selection is preceded by a headnote that provides an intellectual context for the subject matter to follow (often a context that includes previous selections) and that also provides biographical information about the author. Each selection is followed by two kinds of questions: Review Questions, focusing upon recall of information and ideas, and Discussion and Writing Questions, focusing upon the implications of the ideas expressed in the article and the inferences than can be drawn from them. Some questions require students to write essays drawing upon multiple sources in the part, relating the ideas to one another. Other questions call for personal reflections upon single readings. At the end of the book is a brief list of additional readings on each subject. An instructor's manual is available that provides strategies for classroom discussion of the material in *Theme and Variations*, as well as additional writing assignments.

As we progressed with the research on this book, we were struck by the number of times that our key authors — particularly Copernicus, Darwin, Marx, and Freud — were cited in relationship to one another. Together, these thinkers appear to trace the evolution of humanity's sense of itself over the past several hundred years, an evolution that explains a great deal of what poet W. H. Auden called "the age of anxiety." Copernicus displaced humanity from the center of the universe and, by extension, from the center of God's attention. Darwin demonstrated that humans evolved from apes and other lower creatures, attributing human supremacy not to moral superiority, but rather to a superior ability to adapt to the environment. Marx placed humanity in the grip of historical determinism, forces that individuals might help guide, but not control. Freud argued that we even lack ultimate control over our own personal behavior; much of what we do and say, he claimed, is at the mercy of powerful psychic forces buried deep below the level of consciousness.

We were also intrigued to discover that the influences and relationships between one thinker and another often crossed the boundaries of individual ideas. For example, there are striking similarities in their conceptions of human nature between the industrialist Andrew Carnegie (whose essay appears in Part V, "The Survival of the Fittest") and ex-socialist Max Eastman (whose essay appears in Part VI, "The Class Struggle"). Feminists of two centuries, Charlotte Perkins Gilman (who employs Darwinist thought) and Angela Davis (a Marxist), have similar views on the social evolution of women. The Marxist psychologist Joseph Nahem ("Class Struggle") has some acid comments on B. F. Skinner and his behaviorist school ("Power of the Unconscious"). Marx himself is treated as the chief exponent of the theory of class struggle, but of course his ideas on history and on the relationship of individuals to the government tie in directly to both Part IV on "The Progress of Civilization" and Part III on "The Social Contract." Two writers appear in more than one part: T. H. Huxley in "The New Universe" and "The Survival of the Fittest;" Herbert Spencer in both "The Survival of the Fittest" and "The Social Contract." Thus, for the great ideas, diversity and unity are often two sides of the same coin.

From a pedagogical standpoint, we believe that the close relationship among the ideas in this text will both facilitate students' comprehension and deepen their understanding. Comprehension and understanding are generally cumulative processes; and the particular structure of *Theme and Variations* — a series of different yet related themes, each explored from a variety of angles — is designed to provide the kind of cumulative intellectual experience from which provocative discussions and thoughtful essays are generated.

ACKNOWLEDGMENTS

We would like to acknowledge the invaluable contributions of the many people who assisted us in this project. *Theme and Variations* was conceived during after-dinner conversations with Annabel K. Nelson (History, Los

Angeles Unified School District) and Richard B. Nelson (Engineering, UCLA). For their advice in the early stage of this book, we thank Robert L. Crouch (Economics), Jeffrey B. Russell (History), Roger A. Freedman (Physics), Howard H. Kendler (Psychology), Hubert Schwyzer (Philosophy), Stephen M. Weatherford (Political Science), and Laura Manning (Law and Society), all of the University of California, Santa Barbara, and Robert Dallek (History), of UCLA. Thanks also to Barry Chabot (English) of Miami University for his suggestions on the writings of Freud. For their assistance during the later stages of the project, thanks to Porter Abbott, Sheridan Blau, James Campbell, Marie Foley, Patrick McCarthy, Muriel Ridland, and Tom Steiner (English), Muriel Zimmerman (Interdisciplinary Writing Program), Jane Burbank, Frank A. Dutra, and Immanuel C. Y. Hsu (History), Robert F. Renehan (Classics), and Lieselotte Fajardo, Research Librarian, all of U.C.S.B. Our appreciation to Badri Aghassi, of Bentley College, for his kind and patient tutorial on Copernican astronomy; to Edward Zlotkowski, also of Bentley College, for his translations from the Latin; and to John Atteberry, of Boston College Library, for suggesting references to Vatican documents bearing on the trial of Galileo. Thanks also to those who read and commented upon the manuscript during its various stages, including Robert Schwegler of the University of Rhode Island, Patricia Bizzell of the College of the Holy Cross, Michael G. Moran of the University of Rhode Island, and Lucille M. Schultz of McMicken College.

We owe a special debt of gratitude to Carol Galletly (English) and Jeanine Mendoza (History), of the University of California, Santa Barbara, who researched and wrote the bulk of the non-credited textual glosses, to Leonard J. Tourney, also of U.C.S.B., who wrote the Instructor's Manual (available upon request from the publisher), and to those who wrote the "perspective" essays appearing in the Critical Introduction and the Appendix: Jeffrey Chin (Sociology, Le Moyne College), Lawrence Badash (History of Science, U.S.C.B.), and Dorion Sagan and Lynn Margulis (Biology), Boston University. Our thanks also to the thoroughly professional staff assistance from the U.C.S.B., Bentley College, Boston College, and Ventura College libraries. Finally, this project would not have begun without the initial suggestions of Carolyn Potts, nor could it have been brought successfully to completion without the editorial and production skills of Joseph Opiela, Amy L. Johnson, Nan Upin, Janice Friedman, and Susan McIntyre.

Contents

THEME AND
VARIATIONS

Part I

CRITICAL
INTRODUCTION

Posing and Responding to Questions About What You Read

The selections in this book are not light reading. They will challenge you to the limits of your understanding. They will often frustrate you; but they will just as often (we hope) reward you — surprise you, make you think, make you understand. What is the best way to approach them? In the following critical introduction, we'll consider this question.

UNDERSTAND WHAT YOU READ

In college, most learning is based upon written material. Your professors assign texts; you read. Research takes you to the library; you read. How can you be sure that you've understood? This question affects everyone in a college community, students and professors alike; for we each have certain capacities and we each regularly encounter material that extends and challenges us, that on a first reading is bound to confuse. Confusion, however, is very much a part of the process of understanding, and so one should develop strategies for contending with it and for using it as a springboard to knowledge. Thus, the very first task of a critical reading is to distinguish between what you do and do not understand.

Summary

An excellent way to gauge the extent of your understanding is to write a summary — a brief restatement, in your own words, of the essential content of a passage. A summary should be brief, complete, and objective. Every article you read will present a different challenge as you work to summarize it, and you'll soon discover that being able to say in a few words what has taken someone else a great many can be difficult. But the ability to summarize improves with practice. We recommend the following technique to get you thinking systematically about what you read:

- *Consider your purpose.* Ask yourself these questions: Why are you reading this passage? Do you need to summarize it at all? In whole? In part? Will the summary stand by itself, or is it to be part of a larger paper? If part of a larger paper, what information in the passage does your audience need to know in order to follow your overall discussion? (The following steps are based on the assumption that you are going to summarize the entire passage. If this is not the case, you will need to modify these procedures accordingly.)

- *Read the passage carefully.* Determine its structure. Identify the author's purpose in writing. (This will help you to distinguish between more important and less important information.)

- *Reread.* This time divide the passage into sections or stages of thought. The author's use of paragraphing will often be a useful guide. *Label,* on the passage itself, each section or stage of thought. *Underline* key ideas and terms.

- *Write one-sentence summaries,* on a separate sheet of paper, of each stage of thought.

- *Write a thesis: a one-sentence summary of the entire passage.* The thesis should express the central idea of the passage, as you have determined it from the preceding steps. You may find it useful to keep in mind the information contained in the lead sentence or paragraph of most newspaper stories — the *what, who, why, where, when,* and *how* of the matter. For persuasive passages, summarize in a sentence the author's conclusion. For descriptive passages, indicate the subject of the description and its key feature(s). *Note:* in some cases *a suitable thesis may be found in the original passage.* If so, you may want to quote it directly in your summary.

- *Write the first draft of your summary* by (1) combining the thesis with your list of one-sentence summaries or (2) combining the thesis with one-sentence summaries *plus* significant details from the passage. In either case, eliminate repetition. Eliminate less important information. Disregard minor details, or generalize them (e.g., Nixon, Ford, and Carter might be generalized as "recent presidents"). Use as few words as possible to convey the main ideas.

- *Check your summary against the original passage,* and make whatever adjustments are necessary for accuracy and completeness.

- *Revise your summary,* inserting transitional words and phrases where necessary to ensure coherence. Check for style. *Avoid a series of short, choppy sentences.* Combine sentences for a smooth, logical flow of ideas. Check for grammatical correctness, punctuation, and spelling.

If You Don't Understand a Piece, What Exactly Is the Reason? What Will You Do to Address the Problem?

If you do not understand the author's main point, determine as clearly as possible the source of the misunderstanding. There are at least two possibilities:

The piece is not written clearly.   To know that a piece is not written clearly is to imply that you know what a clearly written article or essay looks like. Do you? This is not the place to write at length on the subject: you have taken or are taking an entire course on effective writing; suffice it to say that for a piece to be well written, its purpose must be clear; it must be structured so that component parts of the reading flow logically from one to the next and support a main point; it must contain no extraneous information; its paragraphs within sections must likewise be carefully structured; its sentences must be grammatical. In sum, there must be a tight and carefully crafted fit between the whole — the purpose of the work — and its parts. If some or all of these conditions aren't met and you don't clearly understand the piece, then try to determine where the problems lie.

The level of discussion has given you difficulty.   When you encounter material you don't understand, consider responding as follows:

1. In the library, find articles and books that treat the same topic more accessibly. Hunt for information until you find a source that sheds light on the original selection. As you are working, create a glossary in which you note new terms; consult specialized dictionaries, if necessary.

2. Find reviews of the author's work, either in the *Book Review Digest* or in the cumulative indexes of appropriate journals. (Reviews are generally written from six months to two years following publication of a book.) Reviewers will often precede their evaluations with summaries; both sum-

mary and evaluation can be of use. Take notes as you read and identify important issues.

3. Reread the original article. Given the benefit of your research, the article should now make more sense to you. Underline and make marginal notations. On two sheets of paper, one of which has a question mark at the top, list what you do and do not understand about the selection. Identify as clearly as possible what you have not understood. At this point, you've made *informed* distinctions. You can return to the library with your set of questions and begin a more narrowly defined search; you can also in good conscience seek out your professor for help, now that you've done as much work as possible on your own.

Demonstration

Following is an excerpt from the preface to an epoch-making book: *On the Revolution of Heavenly Spheres* (1543), by Nicolaus Copernicus, taken from an extended passage in Part II. Throughout this introduction we will provide example passages from "Copernicus and the New Universe" as we demonstrate various techniques for critical reading. In effect, we'll present a microchapter that will provide an occasion to discuss a few of the skills important to the process of inquiry. We choose Copernicus for our first reading because it is likely that you'll understand some sections of his discussion and fail to understand others. For this reason, the preface to *On the Revolution of Heavenly Spheres* is representative of much of the material you'll read during your college career. Upon encountering material you don't understand, you'll need to be patient; note questions carefully so that you can go to the library and conduct appropriate research. In this case, such a trip would clarify for you the terminology of Renaissance astronomy. Portions of the following will not make much sense; but our bet is that you will generally understand the thrust of the passage:

TO THE MOST HOLY LORD, POPE PAUL III

The Preface of Nicolaus Copernicus
to the Books of the Revolutions

I may well presume, most Holy Father, that certain people, as soon as they hear that in this book about the Revolutions of the Spheres of the Universe I ascribe movement to the earthly globe [around the sun], will cry out that, holding such views, I should at once be hissed off the stage. For I am not so pleased with my own work that I should fail duly to weigh the judgment which others may pass thereon; and though I know that the speculations of a philosopher are far removed from the judgment of the multitude — for his aim is to seek truth in all things as far as God has permitted human reason so to do — yet I hold that opinions which are quite erroneous should be avoided.

Thinking therefore within myself that to ascribe movement to the Earth must indeed seem an absurd performance on my part to those who know that many centuries have consented to the establishment of the contrary judgment, namely that the Earth is placed immovably as the central point in the middle of the Universe, I hesitated long whether, on the one hand, I should give to the light these my Commentaries written to prove the Earth's motion, or whether, on the other hand, it were better to follow the example of the Pythagoreans and others who were wont to impart their philosophic mysteries only to intimates and friends, and then not in writing but by word of mouth, as the letter of Lysis to Hipparchus witnesses. In my judgment they did so not, as some would have it, through jealousy of sharing their doctrines, but as fearing lest these so noble and hardly won discoveries of the learned should be despised by such as either care not to study aught save for gain, or — if by the encouragement and example of others they are stimulated to philosophic liberal pursuits — yet by reason of the dullness of their wits are in the company of philosophers as drones among bees. Reflecting thus, the thought of the scorn which I had to fear on account of the novelty and incongruity of my theory, well-nigh induced me to abandon my project. 2

These misgivings and actual protests have been overcome by my friends . . . [one of whom] often urged and even importuned me to publish this work which I had kept in store not for nine years only, but to a fourth period of nine years. . . . They urged that I should not, on account of my fears, refuse any longer to contribute the fruits of my labors to the common advantage of those interested in mathematics. They insisted that, though my theory of the Earth's movement might at first seem strange, yet it would appear admirable and acceptable when the publication of my elucidatory comments should dispel the mists of paradox. Yielding then to their persuasion I at last permitted my friends to publish that work which they have so long demanded. 3

That I allow the publication of these my studies may surprise your Holiness the less in that, having been at such travail to attain them, I had already not scrupled to commit to writing my thoughts upon the motion of the Earth. How I came to dare to conceive such motion of the Earth, contrary to the received opinion of the Mathematicians and indeed contrary to the impression of the senses, is what your Holiness will rather 4 expect to hear. So I should like your Holiness to know that I was induced to think of a method of computing the motions of the spheres by nothing else than the knowledge that the Mathematicians are inconsistent in these investigations.

For, first, the Mathematicians are so unsure of the movements of the   5
Sun and Moon that they cannot even explain or observe the constant length of the seasonal year. Secondly, in determining the motions of these and of the other five planets, they use neither the same principles and hypotheses nor the same demonstrations of the apparent motions and revolutions. So some use only homocentric circles, while others [employ] eccentrics and epicycles. Yet even by these means they do not completely attain their ends. Those who have relied on homocentrics, though they have proven that some different motions can be compounded therefrom, have not thereby been able fully to establish a system which agrees with the phenomena. Those again who have devised eccentric systems, though they appear to have well-nigh established the seeming motions by calculations agreeable to their assumptions, have yet made many admissions which seem to violate the first principle of uniformity in motion. Nor have they been able thereby to discern or deduce the principal thing — namely the shape of the Universe and the unchangeable symmetry of its parts. With them it is as though an artist were to gather the hands, feet, head and other members for his images from diverse models, each part excellently drawn, but not related to a single body, and since they in no way match each other, the result would be monster rather than man. So in the course of their exposition, which the mathematicians call their system, . . . we find that they have either omitted some indispensable detail or introduced something foreign and wholly irrelevant. This would of a surety not have been so had they followed fixed principles; for if their hypotheses were not misleading, all inferences based thereon might be surely verified. Though my present assertions are obscure, they will be made clear in due course.

We have glossed every reading in the main body of *Theme and Variations*, so you will not have to contend with obscure names and terms as you work through the chapters. We nonetheless ask that you read a passage without glosses to demonstrate how a reading of a difficult text might be organized. We suggest that you read with pen in hand so that you can raise questions and summarize points as need be in the margins. During an initial reading, limit your remarks to identifying points that you do and do not understand. Other responses come later; for the moment, work paragraph by paragraph, making notes as follows:

What you know	*Questions*
PARAGRAPH 1	
Preface addressed to Pope Paul III	Why is a book on astronomy dedicated to a pope?
In this book Copernicus (C) will state that the earth moves.	"speculations of a philosopher" In 1543, was astronomy considered a branch of philosophy?
Certain critics will denounce C, and C is sensitive to the opinions of others. C will also denounce "erroneous" views.	What are "Spheres of the Universe"?
PARAGRAPH 2	
Given the apparent absurdity of his views, C debated whether or not it would be better to withhold his work from publication.	Who were Lysis and Hipparchus? Who were the Pythagoreans?
PARAGRAPH 3	
Friends persuaded C to write his book for "the common advantage of those interested in mathematics." Apparent incongruities would be explained and the theory admired.	"a fourth period of nine years" What does this mean?
PARAGRAPH 4	
C led to proposing motion of the Earth because the accounts given by mathematicians for "computing the motions of the spheres" were inconsistent.	What are "motions of the spheres"? First sentence difficult, especially ". . . I had already not scrupled to commit to writing. . . ."
PARAGRAPH 5	
Mathematicians cannot with certainty "explain or observe" length of the year.	Mathematicians considered astronomers? And, from par. 1, astronomers considered philosophers? How was inquiry divided among disciplines in the Renaissance? (Certainly not like today.)

What you know	*Questions*
Mathematicians use inconsistent means to determine motions of planets; none of their accounts fully conforms to observed phenomena.	What is a homocentric circle? What is an epicycle? What is an eccentric? C apparently expected a theory of planetary motion to explain shape of universe. Do modern astronomers know shape? C apparently believed in an unchanging symmetry to all parts of universe. Do modern astronomers?

This is typical of the mix of comments, both statements and questions, that we either wonder to ourselves or that we write in the margins of books as we read. In the preface by Copernicus, there are a number of obscure references to be tracked down in the library. Straightforward identifications (who was Lysis?) and definitions (what is an epicycle?) are the easiest to find. Other questions, while matters of information, require a bit more work. For instance, in determining whether modern astronomers believe that the universe has an unchanging symmetry, we first need to define the "symmetrical universe"; understand how Copernicus used the term; and discover whether the term is still current in astronomy.

To understand a passage *thoroughly,* you should answer all the questions that occur to you while reading it. Of course, this can be time-consuming. Depending on the purpose of your reading, you might decide that chasing down a response to every question is not warranted — which is fine as long as you are careful to appreciate the potential significance of questions you are discarding. If you planned to write on the philosophical impact of the Copernican Revolution, you could probably forgo identifying Lysis. But you would be unwise to discard the question: How was inquiry divided among disciplines in the Renaissance? It may turn out that the division of knowledge pre- and post-Copernicus reveals an important legacy of the Copernican Revolution, and you would therefore find the question important to your research. This is all to say that the thoroughness of your reading must be a matter of judgment. Our advice is to explore a question well enough to appreciate its potential importance before you discard it and move on to another, or you may overlook some reference that could provide a key to later understanding.

Though there was a good deal we did not understand when reading these five paragraphs from *On the Revolution of Heavenly Spheres,* we were nevertheless able to follow the gist of Copernicus's thinking. If we had to write a summary of the passage, we would offer something like this:

> In his preface addressed to Pope Paul III, Copernicus states that in the book to follow he will propose a theory of the earth's motion that will, to many, appear absurd. He then shares the misgivings he had about publication and explains how his friends prevailed upon him to allow his work into print. Copernicus says that the motive for conceiving the idea of the earth's motion came from the many errors committed by mathematicians who could not properly calculate the motions of the sun, moon, and planets.

In writing this summary we followed the same steps we suggested to you. Basically, we combined information from the eight sentences appearing in the left-hand column of our notes — which we could have just as easily done from notes scribbled in the margins of a book. Certainly we could add more information if we needed a more extensive summary; but this one will do for general purposes.

In this exercise we've demonstrated what will often be the case when you're reading college-level material: you'll understand some sections of a passage and fail to understand others. Your response should be to make clear distinctions between what you know and don't know so that you can respond appropriately.

RESPOND TO WHAT YOU READ

Once you've determined what you do and do not understand about a piece, you can continue with the next stage of critical reading: that is, begin to develop responses. The *category* of question that you pose at this point in your reading changes. Instead of asking "Do I understand?" — a question that calls for a yes or no answer, you ask: "What is the purpose of this piece? Has the author achieved this purpose? With what ideas do I agree or disagree? *Why* have I reacted in this way?" Questions such as these call for interpretations and evaluations; and answers are judged not according to correctness, but according to persuasiveness. Recall that we posed fifteen questions about the preface to *On the Revolution of Heavenly Spheres;* fourteen of these (e.g., "What is an epicycle?") required informational responses: we could go to the library, locate an appropriate reference, and find a definition. An epicycle has a definite meaning about which we can be correct or incorrect. But what of the question: "Why is a book on astronomy dedicated to a pope?" There are several possible answers, all of which may have merit. As long as there exists no direct statement by Copernicus explaining his decision to dedicate the book as he did, the question calls for *interpretation.* Consider two possibilities:

Copernicus admired Pope Paul III and therefore dedicated the preface of his book to him.

Realizing how potentially explosive his theory of the earth's movement was, realizing also that without at least the Pope's tacit approval the work would be vehemently denounced by theologians, Copernicus sought to calm the political and theological waters before launching his new enterprise.

Both answers are speculative — and their validity is determined by how well they are developed. If we were responding to the question "Who were the Pythagoreans?" the validity of the answer would be determined by an appeal to historical fact; the answer would be correct or incorrect. In the case of a speculative answer, by contrast, no such appeal can be made because an *interpretation* is called for. An interpretation is more or less persuasive, not correct or incorrect.

Develop Your Responses to Interpretive and Evaluative Questions

One dependable way of developing a response to an evaluative or interpretive question is to question yourself. Usually, questions like *how?*, *why?*, and *for what reasons?* will be very useful. Notice how we developed the following:

Copernicus sought to calm the political and theological waters before launching his new enterprise.

The answer is serviceable but could be made more convincing by asking, in this case, *why*. Our question requires that we elaborate:

Copernicus sought to calm the waters because he realized how potentially explosive his theory of the earth's movement was.

Copernicus sought to calm the waters because he also realized that without at least the Pope's tacit approval the work would be vehemently denounced by theologians.

By responding to the question *why*, we can develop our initial answer:

Realizing how potentially explosive his theory of the earth's movement was, realizing also that without at least the Pope's tacit approval the work would be vehemently denounced by theologians, Copernicus sought to calm the political and theological waters before launching his new enterprise.

You might develop and make the following statement more convincing by asking *for what reasons?*

Copernicus admired Pope Paul III and therefore dedicated the preface of his book to him.

When you feel at a loss for developing an interpretive response, pose questions appropriate to the occasion. Questioning your initial answers, as above, is one way to develop your views. Another way is to infer the author's intentions for the piece: determine whether the author has written the selection to inform, to persuade, or to entertain. You can then respond by posing additional questions:

Is the Selection Intended to Inform?

A piece intended to inform will provide definitions, describe or report on a process, recount a history, or provide facts and figures. An informational piece responds to the following questions:

- What is _____ ?
- What happened?
- What is the pertinent information?
- How does _____ work?
- What were the results?

To the extent that an author answers these and related questions and the answers are a matter of verifiable record (i.e., you could check for accuracy if you had the time and inclination), the selection is informational. When you've determined this, you can organize your response by posing three questions:

Is the information accurate?   If you are going to use any of the information presented, you must be satisfied that it is reliable. Is it? One of your responsibilities as a critical reader is to find out.

Is the information significant?   A useful question that you can put to a reading is "So what?" In the case of a selection that attempts to inform, it is reasonable that you wonder whether what you've learned makes a difference. What does the information gain the person who is writing? How is knowledge advanced by the publication of this material? Is the information of importance to you? Why or why not? Elaborate.

Has the information been interpreted fairly?   At times you will read reports, the sole function of which is to relate raw data or information. In these cases you will build your response on the two questions above. More frequently, once an author has presented information, he or she will attempt to evelute it — which is only reasonable, since information that has not been evaluated is of little use. One of your jobs as a critical reader is to make a distinction between the author's presentation of facts and figures and the later attempt at evaluation. You may find that the information is valuable but the interpretation is not. Perhaps the author's conclusions are not justified. Could you offer a contrary explanation for the same facts? Does more information need to be gathered before conclusions can be drawn? Why? Elaborate.

Is the Selection Intended to Persuade?

Academic writing is most often intended to persuade — that is, to influence your thinking. To make a persuasive case, the writer must begin with an assertion that is arguable, some statement about which reasonable people could disagree. An example in keeping with the topic of Copernicus:

> The writing of Nicolaus Copernicus had a direct influence on philosophy and theology from the 16th century to the present.

A writer will organize an argument by arranging evidence that will favor one view and oppose another so that the reader — you — will be inclined to accept a certain conclusion. Once you realize that you are reading an argument, you can respond by putting a series of questions:

Has the author defined terms carefully?   The validity of an argument depends to a large extent on how carefully key terms have been defined. Take the example assertion: "The writing of Nicolaus Copernicus had a direct influence on philosophy and theology from the 16th century to the present." What constitutes a "direct" influence on philosophy and theology? Until the meaning of the term is clarified, an argument based upon any assertion using it could not progress very far, for on this definition rests the type of evidence that will be offered in support. If "direct" is taken to mean that theologians and philosophers since the 16th century have composed their works in *conscious* response to Copernicus, then the evidence for the argument would amount to references in important documents that mention Copernicus by name as the starting point for research. The evidence might be difficult to assemble; you may determine, in fact, that an author has assembled "indirect" evidence: references to theologians and philosophers who worked on problems associated with the Copernican world view but who infrequently, if at all, mentioned the astronomer by name. In this case, the success of the argument — its ability to persuade you — hinges on the definition of a term. So when you begin responding to an argument, make certain that you are clear, and the author is clear, on what exactly is being argued. Once you are satisfied that an author has defined terms carefully, you can respond to the logic of the argument, the use of evidence, and the author's opinions. Three questions will help you to organize your response:

Has the author used information fairly?   Information is used as evidence in support of arguments. When presented with such evidence, you do well to bear several concerns in mind. The first: "Is the information accurate?" A least a portion of an argument is rendered invalid if the information used to support it is inaccurate. A second question: "Has the author cited *representative* information?" The evidence used in an argument must be presented in a spirit of fair play. An author is less than ethical who presents only evidence favoring his views when he is well aware that contrary evidence exists. For instance, it would be dishonest to argue that an economic recession is imminent and to cite as evidence only those indicators of economic well-being that have taken a decided turn for the worse — while ignoring and failing to cite contrary (positive) evidence.

Has the author argued logically?   At some point you will need to respond to the logic of the argument itself. Though this is not the place to present a detailed account of the rules of argumentation, we can point out that arguments *are* rule governed and, in order to be convincing, must abide by the rules. Here are four common errors you can watch for:

1. *Arguing ad hominem:*   In an *ad hominem* argument the writer rejects opposing views by attacking the person who holds them. By calling opponents names, an author avoids the issue: "The chief of police, my opponent, disagrees with me, but then he is a dissolute, boozing scoundrel, so his opinions can't be trusted." It could well be that the police chief has raised excellent arguments, but they are lost in the attack against the man himself. Such an attack violates the rules of logic. A writer must make his points by citing convincing evidence and by challenging directly opposing evidence.

2. *Faulty cause and effect:*   The fact that one event precedes another in time does not mean that the first event has caused the second. An example: You receive a phone call and accept an invitation to a dinner dance. Five minutes later you break out in hives. Are the two events related merely because one has preceded the other? To take up the economic example: a recession strikes; weeks before the event a major oil company goes bankrupt. Is a general recession due to one company's insolvency? It would be faulty cause-and-effect reasoning to argue so. The causes of an event are usually complex and not traceable to a single instance. Carefully examine cause-and-effect reasoning whenever a writer uses it.

3. *Either/or reasoning:*   Either/or reasoning also results from an unwillingness to recognize complexity. If an author analyzes a problem and offers

only two explanations, one of which he refutes, then you are entitled to object; for usually a third or fourth explanation (at the very least) would be possible. For whatever reason, the author has chosen to overlook these. An example: You are reading a selection on genetic engineering and the author builds an argument on the basis of the following:

> Research in gene splicing is at a crossroads: either scientists will be carefully monitored by civil authorities and their efforts limited to acceptable applications, such as disease control; or, lacking regulatory guidelines, scientists will set their own ethical standards and begin programs in embryonic manipulation that, however well intended, exceed the proper limits of human knowledge.

Certainly other possibilities for genetic engineering exist beyond the two mentioned here. But the author limits debate by establishing an either/or choice. Such limitation is artificial and does not allow for complexity. As a critical reader, you should be on the alert for either/or reasoning.

4. *Faulty generalization:* A list of facts reported or numbers assembled means little without an accompanying interpretation, and we rely on authors to generalize from or to interpret information they've assembled. At the same time, we want to be certain that the generalizations are warranted. A troubling example: In February 1987 the Department of Health in the state of Massachusetts reported that infant mortality rose 32 percent from 1984 to 1985. Moreover, the major part of the rise was attributable to the death of black infants. How does one respond to this statistic? The first order of business is to establish the validity of the numbers, and this has been done. What generalizations can be drawn? (1) Given the strong link between prenatal care and postnatal infant health, one can surmise that black women in Massachusetts do not receive the prenatal attention of their white counterparts. (2) A second generalization one could make is that the health care system in the state of Massachusetts is selectively ineffective, or racist. The first generalization is certainly warranted; the second generalization, however, is problematic. The attack is a broadside: it pinpoints no specific reasons for the rise in mortality among black infants and assumes, in addition, that only one reason is possible: racism. This second generalization may eventually prove to be correct, but the proof must be based on additional, supporting facts — two examples of which might be the age and income levels of the mothers delivering in the years 1984 and 1985, and a comparison among the fifty states of infant mortality based not only on race but also on age and income. Certainly information is assembled so that we can generalize from it; but the process of generalization is complex, and as a reader you must watch to see that an author has generalized fairly.

To what extent do you agree with the author? Once you have reviewed the validity of an argument, determining the extent to which an author has argued fairly and logically, respond to the author's opinions. Of course, you may do this first and attend to matters of argumentation later. Whichever — when responding to an author's opinions, you'll want to keep two concerns in mind:

1. *Identify points of agreement and disagreement:* Be precise in identifying points of agreement and disagreement with an author. You should state as clearly as possible what *you* believe, and an effective way of doing this is to define your position against the author's. Whether you agree enthusiastically, disagree, agree with reservations, accept some points as valid and others as not, you can organize your reactions in two parts: first, summarize the author's position; second, state your own position and elaborate on your reasons for holding it. The elaboration, in effect, becomes an argument itself, and this is true regardless of the position you take. An opinion is effective when you validate it by supplying evidence. Without such evidence, opinions cannot be authoritative. "I thought the article on inflation was lousy." Why? "I just thought so, that's all." The opinion is flawed on two accounts: the individual expressing it has not carefully analyzed the article; neither has he been precise in explaining the reasons for his criticism.

2. *Explore the reasons for agreement and disagreement: Evaluate assumptions.*   One way of elaborating your reactions to a reading is to explore the *reasons* for agreement and disagreement. Your reactions are based largely on assumptions that you hold and how these assumptions compare with the author's. An assumption is a fundamental statement about the world and its operations that you take to be true. A writer's assumptions may be explicitly stated; but just as often assumptions are implicit and you will have to infer them. Here's an example you've already seen:

> Research in gene splicing is at a crossroads: either scientists will be carefully monitored by civil authorities and their efforts limited to acceptable applications, such as disease control; or, lacking regulatory guidelines, scientists will set their own ethical standards and begin programs in embryonic manipulation that, however well intended, exceed the proper limits of human knowledge.

We've shown how the either/or reasoning of this sentence is flawed. Now, notice also the *implicit* assumptions behind the sentence. Note the phrases "acceptable applications" and "proper limits of human knowledge." Both phrases imply that standards of acceptability are available to the author but not, without rigidly enforced guidelines, to scientists. What are these standards? What is an acceptable application of genetic engineering? What are the limits of human knowledge? How has the author defined them? On what authority has the author defined them? Answers to these questions constitute the author's assumptions. As a reader you will need to identify these as best you can, for ultimately the extent to which you agree with the views expressed in the piece will depend on the congruence between your assumptions and the author's.

Is the Selection Intended to Entertain?

Authors write not only to inform and persuade but also to entertain. One response to good entertainment is a hearty laugh; yet a good book or play or poem might also cause you to ruminate, grow wistful or elated — a whole range of reactions is possible. Once you have realized that the purpose of a piece is to entertain, read and enjoy. But when the time comes to articulate your response, you'll need to distance yourself from the piece. As with a response to an argument or an attempt to evaluate information, your responses to an essay, poem, story, play, or novel designed to entertain should be precisely stated and carefully elaborated. Again, develop ideas by questioning yourself: You didn't care for the portrayal of a certain character in a novel? Why? State as carefully as possible which elements of the portrayal did not work for you and give your reasons. Offer an overall assessment, again carefully elaborating your views.

Write a Critique

A well-crafted piece of writing can simultaneously inform, persuade, and entertain: but usually the primary purpose will be one of these; and on the basis of this purpose you can develop a response along the lines we've suggested. An excellent way to clarify your ideas on a reading and to get yourself thinking systematically is to write a formal review, or critique. One method for doing so is as follows:[1]

- Introduce both the piece under analysis and the author. State the author's main argument and the point(s) you intend to make about it.

- Provide for your reader background information that will help him or her to understand the nature of the passage. Background information might include responses to one or more of the following:

  Is there biographical information or, perhaps, a comment concerning the circumstances under which the passage was written, that would aid the reader's understanding?

---

[1]We gratefully acknowledge the assistance of two colleagues in preparing these recommendations for writing a critique, as well as parts of the definition of critique: William Leap, professor of anthropology at The American University; Yvonne Yaw, professor of English at Bentley College.

Is the passage part of a book or a magazine with a specialized audience?

Is there a controversy surrounding either the passage or the subject that it concerns?

What aspect of the subject matter is of current interest?

- Briefly summarize the author's main arguments, and state his or her key assumptions.

- State the criteria by which you will evaluate the passage. (That is, to the extent possible, state your assumptions.) Then analyze the passage in light of your criteria. You may wish to critique the author's purpose, the author's method for achieving that purpose, the author's assumptions. Having written the summary, you may wish to state and analyze the author's assumptions one at a time.

- State your conclusions about the overall validity of the passage. Remind the reader of the weaknesses and strengths of the passage you've critiqued. Discuss the implications of your analysis.

Demonstration

Consider the following, an excerpt of a long letter that the astronomer Galileo wrote to the Grand Duchess of Tuscany in 1615. Galileo was a confirmed believer in the Copernican account of planetary motion. As you read, attempt first to understand the points Galileo is making. Then (or simultaneously, if you're able) respond to the presentation. If you were writing a critique of the piece, you'd want to infer the reason it was written (to inform, to persuade, to entertain); you'd need to state the main arguments and key assumptions; and you'd need to present your own criteria for assessment, followed by the assessment itself. Test your skills and then compare the response that you've developed against ours.

> The reason produced for condemning the opinion that the earth moves and the sun stands still is that in many places in the Bible one may read that the sun moves and the earth stands still. Since the Bible cannot err, it follows as a necessary consequence that anyone takes an erroneous and heretical position who maintains that the sun is inherently motionless and the earth movable.
>
> With regard to this argument, I think in the first place that it is very pious to say and prudent to affirm that the holy Bible can never speak untruth — whenever its true meaning is understood. But I believe nobody will deny that

it is often very abstruse, and may say things which are quite different from what its bare words signify. Hence in expounding the Bible if one were always to confine oneself to the unadorned grammatical meaning, one might fall into error. Not only contradictions and propositions far from true might thus be made to appear in the Bible, but even grave heresies and follies. Thus it would be necessary to assign to God feet, hands, and eyes, as well as corporeal and human affections, such as anger, repentance, hatred, and sometimes even the forgetting of things past and ignorance of those to come. These propositions uttered by the Holy Ghost were set down in that manner by the sacred scribes in order to accommodate them to the capacities of the common people, who are rude and unlearned. For the sake of those who deserve to be separated from the herd, it is necessary that wise expositors should produce the true senses of such passages, together with the special reasons for which they were set down in these words. This doctrine is so widespread and so definite with all theologians that it would be superfluous to adduce evidence for it.

Hence I think that I may reasonably conclude that whenever the Bible has occasion to speak of any physical conclusion (especially those which are very abstruse and hard to understand), the rule has been observed of avoiding confusion in the minds of the common people which would render them contumacious toward the higher mysteries. Now the Bible, merely to condescend to popular capacity, has not hesitated to obscure some very important pronouncements, attributing to God himself some qualities extremely remote from (and even contrary to) His essence. Who, then, would positively declare that this principle has been set aside, and the Bible has confined itself rigorously to the bare and restricted sense of its words, when speaking but casually of the earth, of water, of the sun, or of any other created thing? Especially in view of the fact that these things in no way concern the primary purpose of the sacred writings, which is the service of God and the salvation of souls — matters infinitely beyond the comprehension of the common people.

This being granted, I think that in discussions of physical problems we ought to begin not from the authority of scriptural passages, but from sense-experiences and necessary demonstrations; for the holy Bible and the phenomena of nature proceed alike from the divine Word, the former as the dictate of the Holy Ghost and the latter as the observant executrix of God's commands. It is necessary for the Bible, in order to be accommodated to the understanding of every man, to speak many things which appear to differ from the absolute truth so far as the bare meaning of the words is concerned. But Nature, on the other hand, is inexorable and immutable; she never transgresses the laws imposed upon her, or cares a whit whether her abstruse reasons and methods of operation are understandable to men. For that reason it appears that nothing physical which sense-experience sets before our eyes, or which necessary demonstrations prove to us, ought to be called in question (much less condemned) upon the testimony of biblical passages which may have some different meaning beneath their words. For the Bible is not chained in every expression to conditions as strict as those which govern all physical effects; nor is God any less excellently revealed in Nature's actions than in the sacred statements of the Bible.

How Do You Respond?

We'll organize our responses to this excerpt from Galileo's letter as though we were preparing to write a formal evaluation, or critique. The first order of business is to determine the author's purpose. What has Galileo intended to do in this section of his letter? Clearly, the answer is to *persuade* the Grand Duchess that when considering physical problems, such as the motion of the earth, one should rely on "sense-experience" — not on the Bible — to arrive at explanations.

Galileo's argument includes these main points:

1. The argument against the earth's movement around the sun is that such movement contradicts the testimony of the Bible — which, being divinely inspired, "cannot err."

2. The Bible, however, is very abstruse; on difficult points it offers accounts designed to avoid "confusion in the minds of the common people." Literal interpretations of abstruse points can lead to error — for instance, the assigning of bodily parts to God. "Wise expositors" have therefore understood the need to develop figurative interpretations.

3. When the Bible speaks of difficult physical conclusions, the rule has been to obscure complexity for the sake of keeping people's attention on the primary purpose of Scripture: the salvation of souls.

4. Thus, in exploring complexities of the physical world, one should proceed not on biblical authority but on the authority of sense experience and demonstration.

5. A study of Nature based on sense experience complements, and does not contradict, a study of the Bible; for Nature, organized as it is according to God's immutable laws, also reveals the miracle of the divine Word.

In his argument Galileo works hard to persuade the Grand Duchess that, in matters concerning the physical world, the authority of science (demonstrated by sense experience) does not contradict the authority of Scripture. He is trying to reconcile opposing assumptions: first, that truth — the Word of God — is revealed in the Bible; and second, that truth can be *discovered* through human inquiry. Because Galileo wants to be both a man of science and a man of religion, he needs to make the argument he does. The argument is understandable. But is it convincing? To the Renaissance church it wouldn't have been, for the idea of God's being revealed in any way other than through Scripture was at the time considered heretical. From a 20th-century perspective, however, someone who wants to believe in God but also to support scientific inquiry might find in Galileo's position an appealing way to reconcile faith and science. A modern-day atheist would reject Galileo's logic altogether and see in the letter a rationalization — evidence of a noble mind not yet free from the fetters of superstition.

Our first job in writing a formal critique of Galileo's letter would be to review the occasion for which he wrote to the Grand Duchess. (In the chapters of *Theme and Variations* we provide such a context for the readings.) We would then summarize the argument and work with one of the responses outlined above: sympathetic to what Galileo was attempting, we (benefiting from a permissive religious environment) would accept his rationale; as atheists we would reject it, at the same time appreciating his predicament; and if, along with the Renaissance church, we believed that the Divine word was revealed *only* in the Bible, we would also reject the arguments. Whether or not we write a formal critique of the letter, we profit from thinking systematically about it. Do we agree with Galileo? It is not enough simply to say so; we must explain our reactions. We must elaborate.

APPLY WHAT YOU READ

The process of critical reading is completed when, having understood and responded to single sources, you apply what you've observed, inferring relationships from your own experiences to the sources, and among the sources themselves. Already, you've read a section of the preface to Copernicus's *On the Revolution of Heavenly Spheres* and a justification by Galileo on the need to explain the physical world by appeals to the senses. We'll now add several more passages to the mix and create an occasion for drawing inferences among sources. Having read the excerpts, you will achieve on a micro scale what you would achieve in devoting yourself to any systematic study: a knowledge of different authors writing on the same topic. The challenge you face is to understand as best you are able the principal features of this topic and then to construct a conversation among authors.

What Other Authors Have Written on the Same Topic? What Positions Have They Taken?

In each of the six parts in *Theme and Variations*, we have assembled eight to ten readings that bear directly and indirectly on the work of a single author. The challenge that you will face there is the one that we create for you in miniature, here. Assume that in response to the question, What other authors have written on the same topic? you've located four additional passages. The first comes from a pamphlet published in 1696 by

John Edwards, a fellow of St. John's College in Cambridge. (The author is no relation to the American theologian, Jonathan Edwards.)

> The Copernican opinion seems to confront a higher opinion than that of reason. If we will speak like men of religion, and such as own the Bible, we must acknowledge that their assertion is against the plain history of the Holy Book; for there we read that the Sun stood still in Joshua's time, and went back in King Hezekiah's. Now, this relation is either true or false, (it must be one of them): If it be the latter, then the Inspired Scripture is false, which I take to be as great an absurdity as any man can be reduced to: If it be the former, i.e. if the relation be really true, then the Sun hath a diurnal motion about the Earth; for the Sun's standing still could not be a strange and wonderful thing (as it is here represented) unless its general course was to move. This any man of sense will grant. And so likewise the Sun's going back doth necessarily imply that it went forward before: And if it did so, surely it moved. This I think no man can deny, and consequently it is evident that the Sun hath a progressive motion, and goes from one part of the Heavens to the other. If it be said (as it is suggested by some) that the sun only seemed to stand or to go backward, then farewell to all Miracles, for they may be only seeming ones according to this answer: Which is as much to say, There are no such things in truth and reality. If it be said (as I know it is) that this manner of speaking is in compliance with the speech and notion of the vulgar, I grant indeed that Scripture speaks so very often (as I have elsewhere shew'd from several instances both in the Old and New Testament): yea even when it makes mention of some of the heavenly bodies, the expressions are according to the capacity and common apprehension of men, and not according to the accuracy of the thing. So that I do not think that a body of natural philosophy, or a system of astronomy, is to be composed out of the Bible; this being designed for a far greater and higher purpose: Yet this I say, that whenever the Scripture speaks after the foresaid manner, concerning these things and several others, it doth it in the manner that we may plainly see that the words are not to be taken strictly and properly, but only in a popular way. . . . But it is not so here, for in the forenamed places we have matter[s] of fact plainly and directly set down; we are told what Prodigious Things happened in those days, *viz.* that upon the request of Joshua the Sun stood still (as well as the Moon stayed): And that we might not think that this is spoken popularly, and merely according to the common notion of men, the very same words are repeated, and others are added to convince us that they must be meant in the plain and proper sense of them. So the Sun stood still, yea in the midst of Heaven, and hastened not to go down about a whole day. All this is said to let us know that it was a reality, and not an appearance; that what is here said is spoken properly, and not in conformity to a receiv'd opinion.[2]

The next passage is found in the sentence read by the Holy Inquisition in its condemnation of Galileo for holding, along with Copernicus, that the

---

[2]John Edwards. *A Demonstration of the Existence and Providence of God, From the Contemplation of the Visible Structure of the Greater and Lesser World.* London: Printed by J. D. for Jonathan Robinson at the Golden Lion, and John Wyat at the Rose in St. Paul's Church-yard 1696.

earth revolves about the sun. Copernicus's treatise, *On the Revolution of Heavenly Spheres*, was condemned by the Congregation of the Index in 1616 (just after Galileo wrote his letter to the Grand Duchess Christina); Galileo was advised at that time to cease publication of documents supporting the Copernican theory. He did not and was brought to trial in 1633.

> Invoking, therefore, the most holy name of our Lord Jesus Christ and of His most glorious Mother, and ever Virgin Mary, by this our final sentence, which sitting in judgment, with the counsel and advice of the Reverend Masters of sacred theology and Doctors of both Laws, our assessors, we deliver in these writings, in the cause and causes presently before us between the magnificent Carlo Sinceri, Doctor of both Laws, Proctor Fiscal of this Holy Office, of the one part, and you Galileo Galilei, the defendant, here present, tried and confessed as above, of the other part, — we say, pronounce, sentence, declare, that you, the said Galileo, by reason of the matters adduced in process, and by you confessed as above, have rendered yourself in the judgment of this Holy Office vehemently suspected of heresy, namely, of having believed and held the doctrine — which is false and contrary to the sacred and divine Scriptures — that the sun is the centre of the [universe] and does not move from east to west, and that the earth moves and is not the centre of the [universe]; and that an opinion may be held and defended as probable after it has been declared and defined to be contrary to Holy Scripture; and that consequently you have incurred all the censures and penalties imposed and promulgated in the sacred canons and other constitutions, general and particular, against such delinquents. From which we are content that you be absolved, provided that first, with a sincere heart, and unfeigned faith, you abjure, curse, and detest the aforesaid errors and heresies, and every other error and heresy contrary to the Catholic and Apostolic Roman Church in the form to be prescribed by us.

The third passage related to Copernicus is found in *Conversations on the Plurality of Worlds* (1686) by Bernard de Fontenelle, a French philosopher and popularizer of science who gained attention for his speculations on the structure of the universe. In this passage, Fontenelle mentions "vortexes," which you can take to mean "solar systems."

> . . . I have long entertained an opinion that each Star may very probably be a *Sun* to enlighten other Worlds. I will not, however, swear that this is true; but I hold it for true, because it gives me pleasure to believe it. It is an idea which pleases me, and which is very agreeably fixed in my mind. According to my opinion, the agreeable is necessary even to truth itself.
>
> . . . When the Heavens appeared to me as only a blue vault, where the Stars were fixed like nails, the Universe appeared little, and confined within narrow bounds, I seemed oppressed: presently they give an infinite extent and profoundity to this blue vault, in dividing it into a thousand and a thousand Vortexes, it now seems to me that I breath[e] with more liberty, that I am in a much greater extent of Air, and that the Universe is far more magnificent.

The final passage is taken from the *Pensées* (1662) of French mathematician and religious philosopher Blaise Pascal.

When I consider the short duration of my life, swallowed up in the eternity before and after, the little space which I fill, and even can see, engulfed in the infinite immensity of spaces of which I am ignorant, and which know me not, I am frightened, and am astonished at being here rather than there; for there is no reason why here rather than there, why now rather than then. Who has put me here? By whose order and direction have this place and time been allotted to me? . . .

The eternal silence of these infinite spaces frightens me.

What Relationships Can You Infer Among Your Sources?

Now that you have assembled (or have had assembled for you) a series of readings that bear on a single topic, you have an opportunity to apply information and ideas from one source to others. Your goal is to make inferences that will allow you to create and to participate in a conversation among authors. The process involves three steps:

Summarize your source materials.   This step is crucial, for the reasons we've discussed earlier. Unless you understand your sources (and this includes an awareness of what you *don't* know about them), you can't hope to comment intelligently or to make inferences among sources. We recommend that you jot down a sentence or two about each of your sources if you have not already written formal summaries.

1. *The preface to* On the Revolution of Heavenly Spheres: In the section of the preface that we've excerpted, Copernicus states that in his book he will propose a theory of the earth's motion that will, to many, appear absurd. He then shares the misgivings he had about publication and explains how his friends prevailed upon him to allow his work into print. Copernicus says that the motive for conceiving the idea of the earth's motion came from the many errors committed by mathematicians who could not properly calculate the motions of the sun, moon, and planets.

2. *Galileo's letter to the Grand Duchess Christina:*   In this excerpt from the letter, Galileo argues that in exploring complexities of the physical world, one should proceed on the authority of sense experience and demonstration, not on biblical authority.

3. *John Edwards, from* A Demonstration of the Existence and Providence of God: Edwards argues against the Copernican theory through an analysis of a biblical passage in which Joshua commands the sun to stand still. Either the biblical account is false, which Edwards cannot accept; or it is true — in which case if the sun stopped it must have had (and continues to have) motion around the earth — thus disproving the Copernican theory.

4. *From the sentence of the Inquisition:* The Holy Inquisition condemns Galileo for having held the doctrine that the sun, and not the earth, lies at "the centre of the [universe]." The basis of the condemnation is that the belief contradicts the teachings of the Holy Scripture.

5. *Bernard de Fontenelle, from* Conversations on the Plurality of Worlds: Fontenelle speculates that every star may be a sun around which other worlds revolve; the thought leads Fontenelle to reflect on the enormity of the universe, a thought that cheers him.

6. *Blaise Pascal, from the* Pensées: Pascal despairs at "being engulfed" in an infinite, indifferent universe. He is frightened by the immensity of space and does not understand why he happened to be born in a particular place, at a particular time.

Respond to your source materials. The quality of the relationships you infer among sources depends first upon your ability to understand single sources and next upon your ability to respond to them, individually. It is not necessary that you write a formal summary and critique of every source; but at the same time you must understand and develop a critical response to each *as though* you were writing a summary and critique. This means that for each source you will need to understand main ideas; distinguish between what you do and do not know; identify an author's key assumptions; *react* to those assumptions; evaluate the validity of an argument; and develop an overall assessment. Once you're satisfied that you've responded thoroughly to each of your sources, you've prepared yourself for the next stage of inquiry.

Infer relationships among your sources. It would be discouraging if there existed as many relationships among source materials as there were sources. Happily, this is not the case. Though the number of sources you may assemble when researching a topic may be great, the ways in which they are related will fall into a few patterns used time and again in academic writing. We'll review four of the principal relationships in light of the selections you've read.

EXAMPLE: Frequently an author in one of your sources will make a general statement that is illustrated in another source. Recall that Copernicus wrote in his preface how some critics would find his ideas absurd:

> I may well presume, most Holy Father, that certain people, as soon as they hear that in this book about the Revolutions of the Spheres of the Universe I ascribe movement to the earthly globe, will cry out that, holding such views, I should at once be hissed off the stage.

Two examples of critics "hissing" the Copernican theory off the stage come to mind: First, there is John Edwards arguing from the Bible that if the story of Joshua's ordering the sun to stand still is true, then the motion of the sun must also be true, since only things in motion can come to a halt. The Copernican opinion, therefore, is mistaken (according to Edwards). A second example is found in the sentence against Galileo. Here, the church uses strong language to condemn both the Copernican theory and Galileo, who has endorsed it.

We can infer two other examples, this time illustrating a statement that we (not one of the authors) have made: On reading the passages by Galileo and Edwards, we've concluded that though they reach different conclusions on the matter of the Copernican theory, both illustrate the predicament of those whose faith requires that they create elaborate rationales to explain apparent errors in the Bible. We illustrate our observation by quoting from Galileo and Edwards:

> *Galileo:* ". . . whenever the Bible has occasion to speak of any physical conclusion (especially those which are very abstruse and hard to understand), the rule has been observed of avoiding confusion in the minds of the common people. . . ."

> *Edwards:* ". . . when [Scripture] makes mention of some of the heavenly bodies, the expressions are according to the capacity and common apprehension of men, and not according to the accuracy of the thing. So I do not think that a body of natural philosophy, or a system of astronomy, is to be composed out of the Bible. . . ."

Though both Galileo and Edwards allow that biblical accounts are abstruse and written down to the level of the common man, neither is willing, based on apparent contradictions between statements of the Bible and sense impressions, to admit that the Bible may be *wrong.* Rather, they avoid the issue of biblical authority altogether and conclude that any misstatements in Scripture are made for higher reasons.

We've inferred two instances of examples: the first illustrates a statement made by one of the authors we've read; the second illustrates a conclusion we've drawn based on our understanding of two sources.

CAUSE AND EFFECT: When you infer a cause-and-effect relationship among sources, your responsibility is to establish that a certain event (which would include a piece of writing) has led to and explains the occurrence of a second event. We've noted elsewhere (page 16) that unambiguous links of cause and effect are difficult to establish, given the usually complex nature of things. Nonetheless, inferring cause and effect is an important component of understanding. We wish to know why events happen as they do, and we trace out causes as best we're able, bearing in mind that the process can be complicated. We have inferred two instances of cause and effect among our sources. The first is direct:

Galileo wrote in support of the Copernican theory and argued for the acceptance of an authority equal to (and complementary to) the Bible. The church, which had repudiated the Copernican teaching, also repudiated those who held it: in this case, Galileo. The links of cause and effect — statement (by Galileo) and counterstatement (by the church) are direct and unambiguous.

The second instance is less obvious but, we feel, warranted: Copernicus, along with others who followed him, believed that the sun and not the earth lay at the center of creation. One effect of this belief was to render the earth "just another planet," no more favored than the others revolving around the sun. The earth and the human beings presiding on it had lost a privileged status, one consequence of which was a feeling of displacement. People could no longer be sure of where they stood in relation to the immensities of the universe. Our inference is this: Pascal's lament about being swallowed up in eternity was caused by the psychological displacement resulting from the acceptance of Copernican theory. The links in this second cause-and-effect relationship are not direct as in the first — one reason being that some one hundred years had elapsed between the cause (publication of *On the Revolution of Heavenly Spheres*) and the effect (publication of the *Pensées*). Necessarily, more links are involved in the chain, so a more elaborate explanation is called for. Moreover, the effect we have inferred is psychological — which is inherently a more difficult relation to infer than a *physical* effect (a ball is kicked, it rolls). Psychological processes are hidden. Still, we feel that the causal relationship between Copernicus and Pascal can be made.

Most cause-and-effect inferences will be complex, so proceed with care. Identify as many links as you can in the chain of causal reasoning; only then determine if it is valid to claim that one event accounts for the occurrence of another.

EXTENSION: Frequently, a conclusion will be reached by one author that is then taken up and extended by another — perhaps even into areas that the first had not thought possible. When applied to new circumstances, the conclusion is tested and, if it is found wanting, will be changed. When you observe one author applying the views of another, you want to be sure that the conclusion is restated accurately; you will also want to establish that the new circumstance is analogous to the one in which the original conclusion was reached: the stronger the analogy, the more compelling will be the application. Then observe the (new) author's results. To what extent does the first conclusion hold up? How successfully does it illuminate the new circumstance? To what use has the (second) author put the application?

We have observed Galileo extending one of Copernicus's implicit conclusions — that important problems of the physical world can be understood through direct sense experience and demonstration. Galileo applies this conclusion in his attempt to drive a wedge between the subjects on which the Bible can speak with authority and the subjects on which it cannot. While the conclusion was radical in its time and posed a threat to the church, today it seems well founded, so much so that skeptics would extend *Galileo's* conclusion and argue that the Bible has no authority to speak on *any* subject.

Bernard de Fontenelle has extended the explicit Copernican conclusion (on the earth's motion) to a new circumstance. He's claimed that stars function in an analogous fashion to our sun. If the earth and the other planets revolve around the sun, why is it not possible that other stars are suns with planets revolving around them? The result of this application of Copernicus is startling, for if Fontenelle is correct, the earth is even less privileged than it was when Copernicus moved it from the center of the heavens. Fontenelle is charmed by the prospect. For our part, the application seems fair enough: though Fontenelle offers no evidence (he is merely speculating) his reasoning appears sound. Other solar systems in the universe do seem possible — even likely.

COMPARISON AND CONTRAST: The comparison-and-contrast essay enables you to examine two subjects in terms of each other. In this way, both subjects receive a comparative analysis, suggesting subtleties that otherwise might not have come to your attention. To organize a comparative analysis, you must carefully read passages in order to discover *significant criteria* for comparison and contrast. A criterion is a specific point to which both of your authors refer and about which they may agree or disagree. (For example, in a comparative report on compact cars, criteria for comparison and contrast might be road handling, fuel economy, and comfort of ride.) The best criteria are those which allow you to account for obvious similarities and differences between passages but then let you plumb "deeper," to more subtle and perhaps more significant similarities and differences.

There are two basic approaches to organizing a comparison and contrast: organization by summary of sources and organization by criteria. (Assume for purposes of discussion that you have read two articles, A and B, which you want to compare and contrast.)

ORGANIZING BY SUMMARY: You can organize a comparative analysis as two summaries of your sources, followed by a discussion in which you point out significant similarities and differences between passages. Having read the summaries and become familiar with the distinguishing features of each passage, your readers will most likely be able to appreciate the more obvious similarities and differences. Follow up on these summaries by discussing both the obvious and the subtle comparisons and contrasts, focusing on the most significant.

Organization by summary is best saved for passages that are briefly summarized. If the summary becomes too long, your audience might forget the remarks you made in the first summary while they read the second. A comparison-and-contrast synthesis organized by summary might follow this format:

    I. Introduction, leading to the thesis.
   II. Summary of passage A, discussing its significant features.
  III. Summary of passage B, discussing its significant features.
  IV. A paragraph (or two) in which you discuss the significant points of comparison and contrast between passages A and B.

ORGANIZING BY CRITERIA: Instead of summarizing entire passages one at a time with the intention of comparing them later, you could discuss two passages simultaneously, examining the views of each author point by point (criterion by criterion), comparing and contrasting these views in the process. The criterion approach is best used when you have a number of points to discuss or when passages are long and/or complex. A synthesis organized by criteria might take this form:

    I. Introduction, leading to the thesis.
   II. Criterion 1
      A. Discuss what author A says about this point.
      B. Discuss what author B says about this point.
  III. Criterion 2
      A. Discuss what author A says about this point.
      B. Discuss what author B says about this point.

And so on. Proceed criterion by criterion until you have completed your discussion. Be sure to arrange criteria with a clear method. Knowing how the discussion of one criterion leads to the next will ensure smooth transitions throughout your paper. End with a conclusion in which you summarize your points and, perhaps, raise and respond to pertinent questions.

We can infer three comparisons and contrasts among the readings. The first is between the views of Pascal, who finds the prospect of a vast universe frightening, and Fontenelle, who finds such a prospect liberating. A comparative analysis could also be based on the views of Galileo and the church with respect to the Bible's authority to speak on matters of physical phenomena. And a comparative analysis could be based on the views of John Edwards and Galileo with respect to the explanations for apparent errors in the Bible.

Given that we are working with excerpts of pieces only, the possibilities for comparison and contrast are limited; our suggestions represent single criteria on the basis of which we could develop an analysis. With lengthier selections (of the sort you'll find throughout *Theme and Varia-*

tions), you would be able to develop an extended comparison and contrast, identifying several criteria by which to examine the selections at hand.

The relationships of *example, cause and effect, extension,* and *comparison and contrast* that you infer among readings can be observed *within* readings themselves; just as you have assembled sources on a single topic and have drawn relationships among them, so too authors assemble sources and infer relationships. The process of inference making is fundamental to critical activity, for both readers and writers. We've noted four of the several relationships that you can use in attempting to understand your sources in light of one other.

How Will You Put to Use the Relationships You've Inferred?

Just as reading to understand and reading to respond are associated with particular forms of writing — the summary and the critique — so too the process of making inferences among sources is associated with a particular form: the synthesis. To *synthesize* means to combine and to make coherent. You have assembled several sources that bear in various ways on a topic — in this case, the thesis of the earth's motion. The challenge of a synthesis is to create a conversation among sources in which you can participate. You observe what one author would say on a topic; what another author would say; and then you provide your analysis, joining the conversation. If the effort is to be coherent, then it must be carefully focused. To this end, you should begin with a well-crafted thesis.

Develop a thesis.   A thesis, essentially a one- or two-sentence summary of your paper, provides an organizing principle on the basis of which you can select sources. There is a direct relationship between the complexity of a paper, or conversation, and the complexity of its thesis. Like any sentence, a thesis includes a subject and predicate — an assertion about the subject. What distinguishes a thesis from any other sentence is the level of generality of the subject and the care with which you choose the assertion. The subject needs to present the right balance between the general and specific to allow for a thorough discussion within the allotted length of a paper. The more general the subject, the longer the paper will be, since you will have to provide more details in your efforts at explanation. The predicate of a thesis must also be carefully crafted: you want to make a specific and *reasonable* claim that, again, can be demonstrated within the allotted length of the paper.

At this stage in the process of critical reading and writing, you could create several conversations: you've inferred a number of relationships among sources and you could organize a paper based on any one inference or on a combination of them. What is needed now is a decision. How will you organize your own ideas, along with the source materials, into a coherent whole? Your choice will be shaped by a single statement, a thesis that expresses your purpose and that will guide you in organizing material.

Use sources according to your thesis.   Consider the following seven statements. Each is a potential thesis, narrowly defining the scope of a conversation. We have noted which sources we would use in conjunction with these statements; we have noted also the principal inferences we would make in developing them.

1. In his preface to *On the Revolution of Heavenly Spheres*, Nicolaus Copernicus anticipated the furor that would be caused by his theory of the earth's motion; he was largely right.

    The paper would refer to selections by Copernicus, the Holy Inquisition, and Edwards. Primary inference: *example*.

2. Science's displacement of the earth from the center of creation was accompanied by a psychological displacement: before Copernicus, men could locate themselves in the universe and could be confident of their importance; after Copernicus, both the location and the confidence were open to doubt.

    The paper would refer to selections by Copernicus and Pascal. Primary inference: *cause and effect*.

3. Galileo and Bernard de Fontenelle extended the conclusions of Copernicus in ways that might have alarmed the Polish astronomer.

    The paper would refer to selections by Copernicus, Galileo, and Fontenelle. Primary inference: *extension*.

4. The pronouncements of the Catholic church are based upon an authority that directly opposes the authority of science.

    The paper would refer to selections by the Holy Inquisition and Galileo. Primary inference: *comparison and contrast*.

5. Galileo's effort to reconcile the contradictory authorities of faith and science set a precedent for many scientists who followed.

    The paper would refer to the selection by Galileo. Primary inference: *extension*.

6. A glass is half-empty or half-full; the enormity of the universe is debilitating or liberating: whether he views the most pedestrian of events or the most cosmic, the optimist, like the pessimist, is a consistent thinker.

    The paper would refer to selections by Pascal and Fontenelle. Primary inference: *comparison and contrast*.

7. In the 17th century, belief in the divine authority of the Bible severely constrained the ways in which scientists and nonscientists approached the discussion of the physical world.

> The paper would refer to selections by Galileo and Edwards. Primary inference: *example.*

Each of these statements would work to organize a conversation; each limits the sources to which you would refer; each allows you an opportunity to participate in the conversation by expressing your own views; each is built upon a primary inference that is to be developed: example, cause and effect, comparison and contrast, or extension.

Write a Synthesis

The final written object that comes of critical inquiry is the *synthesis,* a paper in which you develop an original idea by making reference to selected sources. When the synthesis succeeds, you create a conversation in which you participate, along with the authors of your source materials. The various ways in which you construct a synthesis will be a topic to which you'll devote a great deal of attention in your composition course. We offer the following general advice:

- *Consider your purpose in writing.* What are you trying to accomplish in your essay? How will this purpose shape the way that you approach your sources?

- *Select and carefully read your sources,* according to your purpose. Then reread the passages, mentally summarizing each one. Identify those aspects or parts of your sources that will help you in fulfilling your purpose. When rereading, *label* or *underline* the passages for main ideas, key terms, and any details you want to use in the synthesis.

- *Formulate a thesis.* Your thesis is the main idea that you want to present in your synthesis. It should be expressed as a complete sentence. Sometimes the thesis is the first sentence, but more often it is the *final sentence of the first paragraph.* If you are writing an inductively arranged synthesis, the thesis sentence may not appear until the final paragraphs.

- *Decide how you will use your source material.* How will the information and the ideas in the passages help you to fulfill your purpose? To what extent can you fulfill your purpose by inferring certain relationships among source materials: *example, extension, comparison and contrast, cause and effect?*

- *Develop an organizational plan,* according to your thesis. How will you arrange your material? It is not necessary to prepare a formal outline. But you should have some plan that will indicate the order in which you will present your material and that will indicate the relationships among your sources.

- *Write the first draft* of your synthesis, following your organizational plan. Be flexible with your plan, however. Frequently, you will use an outline to get started. As you write, you may discover new ideas and make room for them by adjusting the outline. When this happens, reread your work frequently, making sure that your thesis still accounts for what follows, and that what follows still logically supports your thesis.

- *Document your sources.* You may do this by crediting them within the body of the synthesis or by footnoting them.

- *Revise* your synthesis, inserting transitional words and phrases where necessary. Make sure that the synthesis reads smoothly, logically, and clearly from beginning to end. Check for grammatical correctness, punctuation, and spelling.

Note: The writing of syntheses is a recursive process, and you should accept a certain amount of backtracking and reformulating as inevitable. For instance, in developing an organizational plan (step 5), you may discover a gap in your presentation, which will send you scrambling for another source — back to step 2. You may find that steps 3 and 4 (formulating a thesis and making inferences among sources) occur simultaneously. Indeed, inferences are often made before a thesis is formulated. Our recommendations for writing syntheses will give you a structure; they will get you started. But be flexible in your approach: expect discontinuity and, if possible, be comforted that through backtracking and reformulating you will eventually produce a coherent, well-crafted essay.

Bear in mind, when organizing a particular conversation among sources, that the "participants" you choose will sometimes fail to acknowledge others who are writing on the same topic. The participants may not be aware of one another's work (often because of the passage of time); they may also disagree so completely that they have little or nothing to say directly to one another, aside from the obvious — that each believed the other was wrong. You will often encounter examples of profound disagreement. In this text, an example would be the work of Sigmund Freud and B. F. Skinner. Freud believed that much neurotic behavior was the result of unconscious conflict and could be changed only through prolonged psychoanalytic probing into the sources of the neurosis. Skinner believed that neurotic behavior could be changed through techniques of behavior modification, without bothering with the unconscious. The operating assumptions of these two thinkers could not have differed more. Your job as a critical reader and writer is to note such differences and, if appropriate, to bring them to bear on a conversation you are preparing. The fact that writers do not acknowledge one another (for whatever reason) should not limit you as you work to develop a coherent response to sources.

SUMMARY

Here in outline form are the activities discussed in this overview:

I. Understand what you read.
   A. What is the main point of the reading?
      Write a summary.
   B. If you don't understand a piece, what is the reason? What will you do to address the problem?
      1. The piece is not written clearly.
      2. The level of discussion is giving you difficulty.
         a. Find more accessible treatments of the same topic.
         b. Find reviews of the author's work.
         c. Reread the selection and distinguish between what you do and do not understand.
II. Respond to what you read.
   A. Develop initial responses to interpretive and evaluative questions by asking *why, how, for what reason*, etc.
   B. Is the selection intended to inform?
      1. Is the information accurate?
      2. Is the information significant?
      3. Has the information been interpreted fairly?
   C. Is the selection intended to persuade?
      1. Has the author defined terms carefully?
      2. Has the author used information fairly?
      3. Has the author argued logically?
         a. Arguing *ad hominem*
         b. Faulty cause and effect
         c. Either/or reasoning
         d. Faulty generalization

    4. To what extent do you agree with the author?
      a. Identify points of agreement and disagreement.
      b. Explore reasons for agreement and disagreement: Evaluate assumptions.
  D. Is the selection intended to entertain?
  E. Write a critique.
III. Apply what you read.
  A. What other authors have written on the same topic? What positions have they taken?
  B. What relationships can you infer among your sources?
    1. Summarize your source materials.
    2. Respond to your source materials.
    3. Infer relationships among your sources.
      a. Example
      b. Cause and effect
      c. Extension
      d. Comparison and contrast
  C. How will you put to use the relationships you've inferred?
    1. Develop a thesis.
    2. Use sources according to your thesis.
  D. Write a synthesis.

Understand, respond, apply: These are activities that form the core of critical thinking. The chapters of this book will challenge you to do what, in summary fashion, we have done in this overview. Questions that follow each of the selections will help you to organize your reading: Review Questions test your understanding; Discussion Questions stimulate your response to single sources and ask that you consider applications to other sources and to your own experience.

DISCIPLINARY PERSPECTIVES: HOW THEORIES ARE DEVELOPED AND APPLIED

    When you can understand, respond to, and apply the material you read, you will have come a long way toward joining the academic community, where rules are in effect that govern the way people talk and write to one another. When you can step back and follow the development and impact of an idea as it has gained currency, your initiation will be still more complete: for at that point you are observing how knowledge gets created, extended, and changed over time. To help you appreciate this broader enterprise, we have asked three practicing academics to discuss theory construction and application in their disciplines. A sociologist, historian of science, and biologist have written essays in which they respond to the following:

1. What would you want a student to know about your discipline after taking an introductory course in the field?

2. What are some of the assumptions that underlie the thinking of practitioners in your field? How do these assumptions distinguish your field from related ones?

3. What kinds of (research) questions do you ask?

4. What are some of the theories that characterize inquiry in your field? How do these theories reflect general assumptions? How are theories applied? How do they change over time?

We've included here the first of these essays, written by sociologist Jeffrey Chin. The remaining essays appear in the Appendix, pages 825–838. We urge that you read each to gain a sense of the ways in which theory development and application — theme and variation — proceeds in disciplines across the curriculum. You'll find that some significant features of inquiry remain the same, while others change. Our hope is that your appreciation of both similarities and differences will stimulate response to the readings in this book. Important thinkers tend to span disciplinary perspectives in their writing — or, failing that, will prompt discussion outside of the disciplines in which they practice. Thus, Darwin (a biologist) caused a stir among theologians and philosophers and had his ideas applied — and misapplied — by social engineers; Marx combined the perspectives of history, economics, and sociology when he collaborated with Engels to write *The Communist Manifesto*. We urge that you approach the selections in *Theme and Variations* from as many perspectives as the pieces themselves will allow. For a single reading, pose the questions that a sociologist, historian, and psychologist would ask and see how multiple perspectives can aid your understanding. Some of these perspectives may clash; others will certainly be compatible. All can stimulate your thinking about the selections.

Finally, we note that an understanding of the similarities and differences among disciplines will enhance your appreciation of inquiry at the college level. It is useful, when sitting down on the first day of a new course, to ask: What are the assumptions underlying this course? What sort of questions will the professor ask? How are theories developed and applied? What adaptations to *my* working assumptions are required in order for me to follow the discussion? These are some of the broadest possible questions you can pose: by asking them you demonstrate an interest in the ways that knowledge gets created and applied, an interest that characterizes you as a careful thinker open to new learning.

THE SOCIOLOGICAL PERSPECTIVE: ASSUMPTIONS UNDERLYING THEORIES OF SOCIAL LIFE

by Jeffrey Chin[3]

INTRODUCTION

Earlier in this section, the authors suggested that the crucial building blocks needed for the development of a solid foundation in critical thinking include an ability to take the points made in classic works and to see how these ideas have been extended by subsequent thinkers. It is usually clear how the ideas in these essays have had an impact on an author's own discipline, in part because most college students have some preconceptions about academic areas and the contribution made by classic work to that field. For example, virtually everyone knows something about psychology, whether accurate or not, and of the monumental impact of Freud's work on that area of study. What is considerably less obvious is the impact of Freud's work on other disciplines.

The application of ideas to related disciplines is made more difficult by the fact that some academic areas share common ground with others: in the social sciences, for example, both psychologists and sociologists concern themselves with the effects of social influence on individual behavior, but the concerns — the sorts of questions posed, the answers expected — lead in widely different directions depending upon the approach taken. Nonetheless, both disciplines can justifiably claim the turf of social psychology as their own (House, 1977).

It is the purpose of this essay and two others (found in the Appendix, pages 825–838) to provide some background on how practitioners in the fields of sociology, history of science, and biology view the world. What assumptions do they bring to their work? How do they generate theories and then apply them to teaching, research, and policy-making? These discussions — brief as they are and obviously no substitute for a thorough immersion into the various disciplines — will provide you with some tools to aid in your critical reading of the selections in *Theme and Variations*. It will be useful to know, for instance, in reading *The Communist Manifesto* how an economist would view and *use* the document according to the assumptions of that discipline while a literary critic would respond to and

---

[3]Dr. Jeffrey C. Chin is an Assistant Professor of Sociology at Le Moyne College, Syracuse, New York.

use the *Manifesto* in an entirely different way, consistent with the assumptions of literary criticism. Familiarity with the assumptions underlying the various academic disciplines is an important component of the critical reading you will be expected to do.

In the following essay, you will be introduced to the field of sociology. The attentive student will gain a passing knowledge of what sociologists look for and the models that underlie their thinking in their attempts to understand the social world in which we live. The term "sociological perspective" will be used to describe the underlying commonalities that all sociologists share.

THE ASSUMPTIONS OF THE
SOCIOLOGICAL PERSPECTIVE

Sociologists like to think that they have a unique way of viewing the world. C. Wright Mills called it the sociological imagination (1959); most sociologists today call it the sociological perspective. All practitioners of sociology — teachers, researchers, and applied sociologists — share this perspective; for this reason, it will be useful for your reading in this book and any other time you come across sociological writing to acquire a working understanding of the term.

All social scientists — those individuals trained in sociology, psychology, economics, political science, or a hybrid discipline which draws on some combination of the above (such as social psychology) — share an interest in studying social phenomena and trying to explain them. However, social scientists will generally disagree on the factors they feel are most important in explaining the phenomenon being studied. If we were to construct a long list of reasons to explain a social occurrence, most sociologists could agree on reasons that they felt were the most important in understanding the occurrence, while most psychologists would agree on other items, economists on others, and political scientists on still others.

Take the notion of deviance. Sociologists define deviance as a behavior that (1) runs counter to the rules of society, whether these rules are formal or informal; or (2) elicits negative reactions from a significant segment of a community. Most behaviors fit both criteria: for example, child molestation not only is a violation of criminal code but is also considered by virtually all segments of society to be criminal. (This is supported by the fact that in prison societies child molesters occupy the lowest rung in that social order.) However, some activities are not deviant by both definitions. Behaviors that break rules but that are generally not considered deviant include driving faster than 55 miles per hour and cheating on taxes, while men who wear women's underwear break no formal rules but are generally viewed as deviant. Social scientists will advocate reasons for why people engage in these behaviors, reasons that are consistent with their disciplinary training.

When it comes to deviance, a sociologist would examine a behavior, determine whether or not the behavior was in fact deviant by the criteria described above, and attempt to explain the behavior using reasons founded in social structure. This is because sociologists assume that individuals are socially interconnected in significant ways and that behavior is more often influenced by situational factors than by an individual's characteristics. Sociologists, by virtue of their concern with social structural explanations, would say that deviant behavior is the product of perfectly normal, average individuals being placed in abnormal, unusual situations rather than abnormal people being placed in normal settings.

By comparison, other disciplines would look elsewhere to explain deviance. Individuals trained in the area of psychology, including psychiatric social workers, clinical psychologists, and psychiatrists, would examine the individual, looking for aberrations in individual personality constructs. Anthropologists would examine the behavior in terms of the context of the culture in which it occurs. Political scientists might examine the laws regulating the deviant behavior. Economists might be interested in the effects of deviance on economic trends. But no discipline other than sociology attempts to analyze the occurrence of deviant behavior, or any other social issue, using social structure as the primary set of explanatory factors.

Consensus within sociology will more likely be the rule rather than the exception, although disagreement within any discipline is common. For example, some criminologists with sociological training believe that the scientific study of crime should provide social reasons for why individuals commit criminal acts such as burglary, assault, and murder. Some of these reasons include a lack of financial resources or legitimate employment opportunities, or associating and being influenced by the "wrong" people. Other sociologists involved in the study of crime believe that the focus of criminology should be on social institutions such as the criminal justice system and its role in criminal behavior, for example, in studying the concept of recidivism. The focus of these two groups is distinctively sociological since both look at social structure in explaining crime, but each has quite different substantive concerns.

It is also possible that practitioners from different areas may be more alike than they are to people in their own fields. The first group of criminologists described above — those who study street crime — would posit *social* reasons for the commission of these crimes, but the policy concerns would be on changing *individual* circumstances that lead a person to crime. Criminologists who adopt nonsociological approaches, e.g., psychologists and biogeneticists, would suggest different *reasons* for why criminals engage in illegal activity, but they would agree with sociologists who argued that certain *individuals* should be targeted for treatment of some kind in order to make any substantial changes in criminal behavior.

THEORY CONSTRUCTION AND APPLICATION

Sociologists concern themselves with many subjects. A partial list would include the following: poverty, racism, sexism; problems within institutions such as the family and the church; crime and deviance such as prostitution, homosexuality, pornography, mental illness, suicide, and substance abuse; street crime, white collar crime, corporate and government crimes; and problems with the criminal justice system. While none of these areas is by any means the exclusive domain of sociology, the contributions made by sociologists in addressing these issues have been substantial and distinctive. One illustration would be the sociologist's discussion of poverty.

Poverty is one of many pressing social issues facing American society — an ironic and sad state of affairs given the wealth of our resources in raw materials, technology, and labor. The American economy is vital enough to provide subsistence materials — food, shelter, adequate health care — for every man, woman, and child in the country; yet we find indigents living in every corner of every American city and town. Despite the efforts by government, voluntary, and philanthropic organizations to diminish its impact, poverty continues to leave large numbers of people homeless, people who must frequent charitable agencies for a square meal, for clothing, or for basic health care, or who must rely on general assistance programs funded by the federal government. Moreover, some research indicates that poverty has been getting worse in a polarized, 1980s society rather than better.

What causes poverty? A common belief — though one that is inconsistent with the sociological perspective — is that the answer lies within poor individuals themselves. This belief is consistent with an assumption basic to American thinking: that individuals have a great deal of control over their destinies. The "rags-to-riches" myth follows from this assumption, as does its converse: a person rises or falls according to his own wits. The poor suffer from their poverty because they lack qualities found in those who are not poor: intelligence, drive, determination, etc. Poverty is thus the product of an individual's inability to integrate himself into the mainstream of American society. If we can change some of these traits and characteristics, we will at least be able to solve the problem for individuals. This is the approach traditionally used by social work, a valid and effective strategy for dealing with select segments of the population, but one that in Ryan's (1976) terms, "blames the victim" because it ignores social structural, systemic reasons that may come into play.

How does the sociologist explain the problem of poverty? The sociological perspective directs our attention to elements of social structure and assumes that they are largely responsible for the problem: the most obvious of these elements is that poor people are disadvantaged by a lack of resources, both financial and political. The maldistribution of resources is a system-level, social structural condition: it is not simply the coincidental by-product of all participants playing the game as best they can with the result of some rising to the top and some sinking to the bottom. Rather, the inequitable access to resources allows some to play the game with an advantage, an outcome that is often manipulated and usually exploited.

Sociologists argue that the rags-to-riches stories we hear so often are very much the exception rather than the rule. Instead, important factors in determining success include characteristics over which we have very little control, such as sex, race or ethnicity, family background — including financial resources, choice of schools, social and work-related contacts, etc. How much effort one puts into one's life does make a difference; but it makes a very small difference in terms of the big picture. Acknowledging the inefficacy of individual factors compared to social structural factors is a first step fundamental to the sociological perspective. Based on this assumption, sociologists have constructed theories of social stratification that account for both individual success and failure in American society. These theories state that both upward and downward mobility are determined by social structural factors more than by individual ones.

A good example of a sociological explanation would be the classic Marxist analysis of poverty: that it is in the nature of a capitalist political economy to have poverty (see *The Communist Manifesto*, pages 554–574). Indeed, such an approach would argue that poverty is an essential element for a capitalist society to function smoothly and that wealthy and powerful individuals will ensure that there are always poor and disenfranchised individuals to fulfill the unglamorous but necessary jobs of society. For Marxists, to "blame the system" (Ryan, 1976) would be to identify the capitalist political economy as the source of conditions that cause poverty.

Both the individual and social structural approaches to poverty have their merits. There can be no single answer to the question of poverty and, as a result, no single or simple solution. In most cases, poverty is the product of both individual shortcomings and social structural inadequacies. For sociologists, however, the proportion of weight given to structural reasons for social problems is greater than that given to individual reasons.

How does one reconcile the differences presented by competing theories? In the natural sciences, the issue of validity is more easily tested than in the social sciences. For example, in the area of astronomy, Copernicus argued that the old Aristotelian theory of a geocentric universe was incorrect; subsequent research has shown indisputably that the earth does indeed revolve around the sun. Only one theory about the earth's relationship to the sun could be right: it was up to scientists to demonstrate that the heliocentric model was the correct one. (See Kuhn, 1962, for a fascinating discussion of how scientists determine what is "truth.") In the social sciences, there can be no indisputable truths; there will always be anomalies. This is because social scientists study people and their institutions, and therefore the conclusions derived from social scientific research will reflect human inconsistencies. The value of social science theory lies in its explanatory power rather than in its "correctness." Social scientists in general and sociologists in particular contend with this problem by talking about their conclusions in terms of probabilities and likelihoods. This is where statistics become indispensable. When competing theories produce results where the differences are small, social scientists must rely on universally accepted cut-off points to determine which theory to use: if the results of a theory do not meet a standard level of statistical significance, the theory is rejected. Thus, one measure of a theory's explanatory power is when it is statistically significant. A powerful theory is also applicable in a greater variety of situations than a rival theory.

There are certainly objective criteria that a theory must meet in order to be considered effective. When these criteria are met, one chooses between theories according to personal philosophy. Are you inclined to focus on individual achievement? Then the individualist explanation of poverty will most likely appeal to you. Are you given to analyzing problems in a systemic fashion? Then a sociological account would seem the more attractive. Which of these accounts is correct? If you have followed this discussion, then you know the answer must be neither, for each theory has its strengths that in no way purport to deny the strengths of the other.

SUMMARY

In this essay I have described a way of looking at the world, one that is common to all sociological enterprises: the sociological perspective. The sociological perspective is characterized by the ability to analyze a social issue by identifying social structural factors that influence social outcomes. Social structural determinants differ from individualistic determinants: the former consider the influence that people and their institutions have on a given situation, while the latter focus on forces within the individual that determine the same.

REFERENCES

House, James. 1977. "The Three Faces of Social Psychology." *Sociometry*. 40:2: 161–177.

Kuhn, Thomas. 1962. *The Structure of Scientific Revolutions*, 2e. Chicago: University of Chicago Press.

Mills, C. Wright. 1959. *The Power Elite*. New York: Oxford University Press.
————. 1959. *The Sociological Imagination*. New York: Oxford University Press.
Ryan, William. 1976. *Blaming the Victim*, 2e. New York: Vintage.

(The above references follow the conventions of the American Sociological Association.)

Part II

COPERNICUS AND THE NEW UNIVERSE

Nicolaus Copernicus

Galileo Galilei

Suppression of On the Revolution of Heavenly Spheres

Sentence of the Holy Inquisition, pronounced on Galileo Galilei

Blaise Pascal

Bernard Le Bovier de Fontenelle

Alexander Pope

T. H. Huxley

Jorge Luis Borges

The great mystery is not that we should have been thrown
down here at random between the profusion of matter and
that of the stars; it is that from our very prison we should
draw, from our own selves, enough to deny our
nothingness.

— André Malraux, *Man's Fate*

What do you think about when standing alone at night, looking at the sky? If you have a scientific disposition, what questions do you ask? If you're a poet, how do you react? Are you religious — do you see evidence of a Divinity in the stars? Perhaps you see only the stars, or feel nothing so much as your own loneliness and insignificance and an aching need to know more than we can presently know.

From the moment we as a species emerged with a consciousness that distinguished us from other creatures, we were able to wonder at creation. What is the sun? What have we to do with it, or with the stars? Where *are* we? What is this place we call home? As far as historians and anthropologists can tell, all civilizations have developed answers to these and similar questions; that is, all civilizations have developed *cosmologies*, or theories on the origin and structure of the universe. Necessarily, there exists a relationship between such theories and the ways in which civilizations have understood themselves. In the Western world, the earliest cosmology placed the earth at the center of a universe that was finite in extent. Given naked-eye observations, it seemed natural to describe the universe as did the Greek astronomer Ptolemy in his *Almagest* (2d century A.D.):

> We have to state that the heavens are spherical and move spherically; that the earth, in figure, is sensibly spherical also when taken as a whole; in position, lies right in the middle of the heavens, like a geometrical centre; in magnitude and distance, has a ratio of a point with respect to the sphere of the fixed stars, having itself no local motion at all.

This *geocentric*, earth-centered model persisted for fifteen centuries, offering those who accepted it an assurance that the earth was located in a knowable place — that is, the center; and that all of Creation, both here below and in the heavens above was made for the delight of man.

But gradually, evidence mounted against the geocentric view. Observers realized that the planets did not move across the night sky in ways that could be explained by the reigning astronomy. According to Aristotle, the planets and stars were affixed to a series of concentric spheres that revolved around the earth; all heavenly movement was supposedly uniform and circular (the circle explaining recurrent patterns traced by the sun, the stars, and the planets). Observers noted that the planets appeared to have variable speeds and to actually retrogress, or move backward, as seen against the uniform movement of the distant stars. This "problem of the planets" led Ptolemy to modify Aristotle's system by adding complex secondary motions to the spheres, called "epicycles." Soon, revisions of Ptolemy were needed. These revisions were in turn revised until, by the 16th century, the old cosmology was ungainly and, for all its modifications, still incapable of giving a satisfactory account of heavenly motion. (See figure on next page.)

Rather than revise the old system yet again, Nicolaus Copernicus in 1543 proposed a heliocentric model — a model that displaced the earth from the center of the universe and placed the sun in its stead. Copernicus did not believe that the earth was stationary: he thought it revolved about the sun every three hundred and sixty-five days and also spun on its own axis once every twenty-four hours — conclusions that were for the time radical and even now contradict the senses. Nonetheless, taking the sun as the center of the orbital spheres, he could explain both the sun's apparent motion and the apparently nonuniform, retrograde motions of the planets.

To be sure, Copernicus made mistakes: he believed that the sun lay very near the center of the universe; he also believed that the planets revolved in *circular* orbits (whereas now we think their orbits are elliptical). Yet on an essential point — the dual motion of the earth, Copernicus was correct, and for this a revolution bears his name. Historian of science Thomas Kuhn notes that astronomers who followed Copernicus inherited a new system in which the earth moved. From that beginning discoveries would be made by Kepler, Galileo, Newton, and others that would lead eventually to our present view of the heavens.

We now know that our sun is one star among billions; that, in fact, it lies nowhere near the center of our galaxy, let alone the center of the universe; and that our place, astronomically speaking, is far from privileged. Just as a world view followed from the old geocentric model — the security of knowing that one occupied a central position in the heavens — so too a world view followed from heliocentrism. With the displacement of the earth came a corresponding displacement of the human spirit. In theology, philosophy, and literature, certainties had vanished. So shaken was the foundation of knowledge that by 1611, in his poem *An Anatomy of the World*, John Donne could write:

> And new philosophy calls all in doubt,
> The element of fire is quite put out;
> The sun is lost, and the earth, and no man's wit

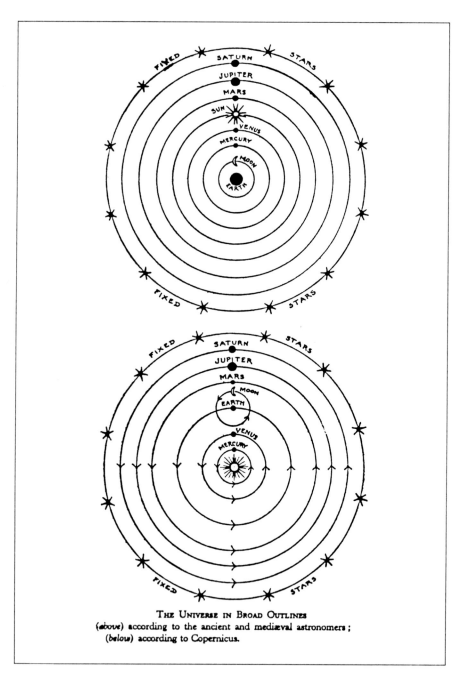

THE UNIVERSE IN BROAD OUTLINES
(*above*) according to the ancient and mediæval astronomers;
(*below*) according to Copernicus.

Diagram appears courtesy of Henry Schuman, New York, in Angus Armitage, *Copernicus and the Reformation of Astronomy*. Published for The Historical Association. London: George Philip & Son, Ltd., 32 Fleet Street, E.C.4., 1950, p. 17.

Can well direct him where to look for it.
And freely men confess that this world's spent,
When in the planets and the firmament
They seek so many new; they see that this
Is crumbled out again to his atomies.
'Tis all in pieces, all coherence gone;
All just supply, and all relation . . .

The philosophical and spiritual displacement to which Donne refers is our topic in this chapter. We begin with the first book from Copernicus's *On the Revolution of Heavenly Spheres,* that section of the treatise written to the lay person. Next comes a selection by Galileo, an ardent supporter of the heliocentric model whose support earned him the condemnation of the church; this is followed by key documents from his trial before the Holy Inquisition. Next come two selections from the *Pensées* of Blaise Pascal, reflecting his fear and confusion over human insignificance in the face of a universe perceived to be infinite. Then, in a charming dialogue, Bernard de Fontenelle speculates on the possibility that every star in the heavens is a sun, about which other worlds revolve; unlike Pascal, Fontenelle's reaction to the immensity of the universe is one of wonder and delight. In his *Essay on Man,* Alexander Pope considers the same immensities that annihilated Pascal, and he reaches a different conclusion: his faith in God's order is confirmed. Next, T. H. Huxley argues forcefully that our ignorance of the universe and the despair that can follow as a consequence is in principle a temporary condition that will be corrected. With the advancement in natural knowledge will one day come an explanation of *all* phenomena, at which point a recourse to God will no longer be necessary (a position that neither Copernicus nor Galileo would have sanctioned). Finally, we hear from Jorge Luis Borges, the late Latin American writer in whose fanciful "Library of Babel" the universe becomes an "indefinite and perhaps infinite" collection of books that cannot be understood, though this fact does not keep "librarians" from trying.

The selections that follow the passage from Copernicus's treatise all speak in some way to the tension that exists between being located in a universe that is knowable and benign — the universe of Aristotle and Ptolemy; and being lost in a universe that is infinite in extent and, with respect to human beings, utterly indifferent — the universe we inherited, eventually, from Copernicus. Chiefly at stake in this tension is the degree to which over the past 450 years we humans have felt important, purposeful, and at home on our planet. The impact of the Copernican revolution has been, and continues to be, enormous.

As a prelude to this unit, we offer here a brief essay by Angus Armitage, author of several books on Copernicus. Armitage discusses in detail a number of the important developments in astronomy, dating from the ancient world and continuing through to the 16th century — the age of

Copernicus. The essay provides an excellent historical introduction to *On the Revolution of Heavenly Spheres.*

From COPERNICUS AND THE REFORMATION OF ASTRONOMY [1]

The classic problem to which Copernicus made his decisive contribution was that of interpreting the complicated motions which the heavenly bodies are observed to perform. Before the beginning of history, men had learnt to identify the principal celestial objects. They conceived them at first vaguely as animated beings journeying freely across the sky, and later more precisely as luminaries revolving daily about the centrally situated observer. The Sun, Moon, and planets were found to share with the stars in the diurnal motion of rising in the east and setting in the west; but they were distinguished from the stars by their individual movements in relation to the general background of the constellations. It was found that they performed periodic circuits of the heavens in the opposite direction to the common daily motion, but that their rates of travel from day to day were not uniform, that they did not all move in the same plane, and that the general eastward progress of the five planets through the field of stars was halted and reversed at regular intervals of time. Further, the Sun and Moon showed variations in apparent size, and the planets showed fluctuations in brightness, which suggested that a heavenly body does not always keep the same distance from the terrestrial observer.

Among the ancient Babylonians, and in larger measure among the Greeks, there were men who felt the scientific impulse to reduce the courses of the planets to an orderly rule serving to systematize the observed behaviour of these bodies and to predict their future positions. Hence arose the earliest of the *planetary theories* of which the system of Copernicus was to afford a classic example. For their part, the Greek philosophers sought to connect the observed phenomena with speculative doctrines concerning the nature of the celestial bodies. By the prevailing majority of these thinkers, the central position in the Universe was assigned to the Earth, round which all the heavenly bodies were thought to revolve. This conclusion was dictated, partly by the direct testimony of the senses, and partly by a philosophy of nature which was itself based upon superficial observations of how things behave, or even upon pre-conceptions as to how they ought to behave.

---

[1]Angus Armitage. *Copernicus and the Reformation of Astronomy.* Published for The Historical Association. London: George Philip & Son, Ltd., 32 Fleet Street, E.C. 4., 1950, pp. 3–8.

The doctrine of the Earth-centred, or *geocentric,* Universe was transmitted from the ancient world to mediæval Christendom by several currents of literary tradition which entered the main stream of Western thought at widely separated parts of its course. The conception of the Earth as a sphere at rest in the centre of the Universe originated (so far as we can tell) with the Pythagoreans of the sixth century B.C. It passed from them into the cosmology of Plato in the fourth century B.C., and thence to Aristotle and his school. In the third century A.D., Plato's philosophy was revived and combined with alien admixtures to form the system known as Neo-Platonism, which preserved much of the Pythagorean tradition. This school exercised a dominant influence on Christian thought in the early Middle Ages, partly through the debt of St. Augustine to its leader, Plotinus, and partly through such works as the commentary of Chalcidius on Plato's cosmological Dialogue, the *Timæus,* which largely coloured Western conceptions of the Universe down to the twelfth century. The preponderantly Platonic phase of European thought was eventually transformed by the indirect recovery, through the Arabic tradition, of the scientific works of Aristotle and of the Alexandrian astronomer Ptolemy. These two great figures of antiquity gave their names and authority to two geocentric systems of cosmology which, although strictly inconsistent one with another, had yet come to play complementary rôles in the scheme of the Universe generally accepted in the sixteenth century. Copernicus re-fashioned this scheme, assigning the central position in the Universe, in principle, to the Sun instead of to the Earth, so that we describe his system as a *heliocentric,* or Sun-centred, one. But he felt bound to relate his new hypothesis to the general principles of cosmology accepted in his day. And, for his opponents, these principles formed the basis of their continuing opposition to his views. Hence, by way of introduction to our study of the Copernican theory and its fortunes, we must devote some attention to the growth and essence of the traditional cosmology.

At the head of one stream of the tradition stood Aristotle (fourth century B.C.). He conceived the whole physical world as comprised within a solid sphere of vast but not infinite radius, of which the Earth, itself a motionless sphere, occupied the centre. He followed his older contemporary, the mathematician Eudoxus of Cnidos, in supposing the heavenly bodies to be carried round the Earth by combinations of concentric spheres. The several rotations of these, when compounded together, gave to each orb the characteristic motion we observe it to possess. The sphere which carried round the Moon enclosed within itself the central portion of the Universe, which we inhabit; this was filled with the four corruptible elements, *earth* (forming the dry land), *water* (the ocean), the atmospheric *air,* and an upper layer of *fire.* The heavenly bodies, stars and planets, and the spheres which carried them round, were composed of a fifth element, the *æther.* The motion of an element, according to Aristotle, could be *nat-*

ural, or it could be *unnatural* (i.e. violent, or forced). The four terrestrial elements moved naturally in straight lines — earth and water down towards the centre of the Universe, air and fire up towards the Moon's sphere — and such motion ceased when the element reached its *natural place*. On the other hand, the æther, composing the heavenly bodies, had, as its natural motion, revolution in a circle about the centre of the Universe. This motion, as it could be maintained for ever, was judged to be superior to the rectilinear motion of the corruptible elements, and so it befitted the incorruptible æther. Thus the uniform circulation of the celestial spheres about the central Earth was physically established. So also was the geocentric theory; for any displacement or motion of the Earth away from the centre was *unnatural*, as brought about by an external agent, and so it could not be eternal, since that agent must some time cease to act.

Aristotle's physical principles and his broad structural plan of the Universe were generally adopted wherever they became known. However, to represent the motions of the planets with numerical accuracy under the restrictions of the Aristotelian scheme would have required an intolerably complicated machinery of revolving spheres; and even then there could have been no recognition of the obvious variations in the distances of these bodies from the Earth. Hence, about the beginning of the third century B.C., the Greek astronomers (now beginning to form a separate class from the pure philosophers) originated a largely independent tradition by attempting an alternative treatment of the planetary problem. They postulated geometrical schemes expressly designed to represent the individual motions of the Sun, Moon, and planets, and to serve for the construction of numerical tables predicting the future behaviour of these bodies. The astronomers started out from the orthodox conception of a planet as revolving at a uniform rate in a circle about the Earth, which was still supposed to occupy a stationary, central position. They then sought to represent the complications in the planet's course by modifying this basic theory in certain conventional ways, while still preserving, as far as possible, the restriction to uniform circular motion. Thus they accounted for variations in the observed distance and rate of angular motion of a planet by supposing the centre of the planet's revolution to be displaced from the Earth, so that the body described what was called an *excentric circle*. Or they supposed that the planet described a small circle (an *epicycle*) about its mean position, while the latter revolved in a larger circle (a *deferent*) about the Earth. These devices were refined upon and combined in various ways; the planetary theories were thus made to fit the observations, broadly speaking, to within the limits of uncertainty of the latter.

The geometrical astronomy of the ancients received its classic exposition in the *Syntaxis* (or 'Almagest') of Ptolemy, who flourished about the middle of the second century A.D. Ptolemy based all his calculations upon the geocentric assumption, and the enduring authority of his great book played an important part in ensuring the survival of this doctrine down to the sixteenth century.

It was towards the end of the twelfth century that the scientific writings of Aristotle and Ptolemy began to be introduced into Western Christendom. They were at first translated into Latin from the Arabic in which they had been preserved and studied during the great age of Islamic science and philosophy. Subsequent versions were made from the original tongue, and, by the beginning of the sixteenth century, the Greek texts themselves had become generally known to scholars. In the thirteenth century, the Dominican St. Thomas Aquinas achieved a partial synthesis of the Aristotelian doctrines with Christian theology. There thus arose the system of thought known as Scholasticism which constituted the backbone of the subsequent opposition to the establishment of the heliocentric theory.

To the mediæval mind, however, the bleak, impersonal cosmos of the ancients, uncreated and everlasting, had become transformed into a mere dissolving background against which the Christian drama was working to its climax. The outermost sphere of heaven was the Empyreal abode of God and the saints, while the Devil and his angels dwelt in the heart of the Earth. Mediæval thought was also deeply coloured by the ancient Eastern superstition of astrology. All the parts of creation were supposed to interact, the disposition of the planets influencing man's life and destiny. The human body was even regarded as being itself a Universe in little — a *microcosm* — between whose various organs and 'humours' and the several luminaries and divisions of the great world — the *macrocosm* — a mystic sympathy existed.

It had all along been recognized that the planetary motions postulated by Ptolemy could not be strictly reconciled with the physical principles of Aristotle. This conflict remained unresolved throughout the later Middle Ages. The details of planetary motion were represented by means of the intricate geometrical devices of Ptolemy, often conceived at this period as celestial machinery made of ætherial matter. On the other hand, the Universe, in its broad outlines, was conceived, following Aristotle, as built up of concentric spheres one inside the other like the skins of an onion.

By the beginning of the sixteenth century, however, this composite cosmology was beginning to break up under the impact of ideas brought to light through the literary revival of the Renaissance. Doctrines which Aristotle had condemned or ignored now came again into the field of discussion, among them those of the Pythagoreans, favoured by the Neo-Platonist philosophers of fifteenth century Italy. The later Pythagoreans had conceived the Earth as revolving about the centre of the Universe (though not about the Sun), and, on that account, they have often been credited undeservedly with having anticipated the Copernican system. The Greek world had also produced other would-be reformers of astronomy whose systems could not compete with the prejudices of their day, but whom Copernicus expressly includes among those who helped to inspire his own speculations. Heraclides of Pontus, in the fourth century B.C., developed the Pythagorean revolution of the Earth into a daily rotation of the Earth on its axis; and he made a limited application of the heliocentric theory by supposing the planets Mercury and Venus to revolve about the Sun. A century later, Aristarchus of Samos completely anticipated, in broad outlines, the Copernican system with its revolving and rotating Earth. Another long submerged idea of the Greek Atomists, that the Universe is infinite in extent, was revived in the fifteenth century by Nicolaus de Cusa. He inferred that the Universe could therefore have no centre or fixed landmarks, and that the Earth, like all other cosmic bodies, must have a motion of its own, imperceptible to us. Thus by the end of the fifteenth century, the recovery of the non-Aristotelian elements in Greek natural philosophy had brought the supremacy of the geocentric theory into dispute. Other forces, too, were at work, breaking down long-standing intellectual inhibitions — the widening of the geographical horizon through ocean navigation, the reforming movement in religion, and the rise of national ideas. The art of printing, rapidly multiplying copies of the classics and favouring the diffusion of new ideas, also acted as a powerful solvent.

At this crisis in cosmological speculation, a new turn was given to the course of development by the work of a great astronomer. The emergence of Nicolaus Copernicus marks the close of the era covered by this introductory survey.

NICOLAUS COPERNICUS *(1473–1543)*

By his own word, Nicolaus Copernicus was not the first to believe that the planets revolved about the sun. Several ancient Greek astronomers had proposed that (Aristarchus chief among them) as well as later medieval and Renaissance astronomers, whose work Copernicus probably knew. Nonetheless, it is Copernicus who is credited with overthrowing the geocentric model, for it was he who argued for heliocentrism — not merely as a hypothesis that could be used to improve planetary calculations but as an actual description of heavenly motion that could be presented in mathematical terms.

Niklas Koppernigk was born the youngest of four children in what is now eastern Poland, in the town of Torun, on February 19, 1473. His father was a businessman and magistrate and his mother the daughter of a prosperous merchant. In 1483, the child's father died; his maternal uncle, later to be bishop of Ermeland (an area of Prussia), assumed responsibility for educating the children and sent Nicolaus to school in Torun and, eventually, to the University of Cracow, famed for its instruction in the sciences. From there Copernicus (his Latin name) traveled to the University of Bologna, where he studied further in astronomy and mathematics and where he also learned Greek, which was later to be of great use in reading ancient texts.

While in Italy, Copernicus was elected to the post of canon at the Frauenburg Cathedral; he returned home for a time to conduct services and generally assist the bishop — his uncle — in management of the diocese. When he resumed his studies in Italy, he took a degree in canon law and studied medicine. His uncle died in 1512; but with his special training in mathematics, medicine, theology, and astronomy acknowledged by church authorities, Copernicus retained a position of influence at Frauenburg. It was at about this time that he circulated a preliminary sketch of his planetary theory, entitled *Commentariolus*. Two years later, with his reputation in astronomy solidly established, he was asked to advise the Lateran Council on reforming the ecclesiastical calendar. He declined, however, stating that until the motions of the sun and moon could be calculated precisely, reforms would not be successful. He later justified the publication of his masterwork, *De Revolutionibus Orbium Coelestium (On the Revolution of Heavenly Spheres)*, in part based on the continued need for calendar reform.

Copernicus continued to study planetary and solar movement; at the same time he attended to the indigent sick of Frauenburg and, during a brief monetary crisis, advised authorities on how best to manage the minting of coins. By 1515, he was writing *On the Revolution of Heavenly Spheres*, which he would withhold from publication for thirty years, fearing ridicule "on account of the novelty and incongruity" of his theory. Still, scholarly interest in the *Commentariolus* led in 1533 to a presentation on heliocentrism before Pope Clement VII. Cardinal Schonberg, who had attended the lecture given by a papal secretary and who himself was Clement's ambassador to Poland and Prussia, wrote Copernicus and urged that he publish a full account of his theories.

In 1539, a young German mathematician named Rheticus traveled to Frauenburg to study with Copernicus. At the urging of Rheticus and an old friend, the Bishop of Kulm, along with the urging of Cardinal Schonberg, Copernicus at last agreed to publication; *On the Revolution of Heavenly Spheres* was published in 1543, the year of his death. He is said to have briefly seen and held an advance copy of the book hours before he died.

There are historians who regard Copernicus as a conservative, an apparently odd description for one we associate with a revolution in Western thought. Yet a reading of *On the Revolution of Heavenly Spheres* substantiates the claim: though Copernicus placed the sun at the center of our planetary system, he nonetheless subscribed to what Herbert Butterfield has called "the celestial machinery" of Ptolemy. In Copernicus's model, the planets and the stars are still affixed to spheres that revolve in circular paths; and though the earth has been displaced from the center of the universe, it continues to lie (with respect to the fixed stars) very near the center. And rather than make his own extensive observations of the planets, Copernicus trusted the observations of Ptolemy, which in many cases were incorrect.

Yet this "conservative" was the same man who created an extensive mathematical account of how a heliocentric universe would work. (Strictly speaking, Copernicus's system is not heliocentric but *heliostatic*; he locates the sun near, *not at*, the center of the universe.) He recognized as had none before him that only a mathematically coherent challenge to Ptolemy could shake geocentrism from its preeminence. And, in fact, it was that mathematics that allowed Kepler, Newton, and others to modify the heliocentric model and, at last, confirm it as true. So was Copernicus a conservative, the last of the Ptolemaic astronomers? Or was he one of our first modern scientists? Thomas Kuhn, in his *Copernican Revolution*, argues that the very fact of the debate is telling:

> Copernicus is neither an ancient nor a modern but rather a Renaissance astronomer in whose work the two traditions merge. To ask whether his work is really ancient or modern is rather like asking whether a bend in an otherwise straight road belongs to the section of the road that precedes the bend or to the portion that comes after it. From the bend both sections of the road are visible, and its continuity is apparent. . . . The bend belongs equally to both sections, or it belongs to neither. It marks a turning point in the direction of the road's progress, just as *De Revolutionibus* marks a shift in the direction in which astronomical thought developed.

On the Revolution of Heavenly Spheres consists of six books, the first of which was written for the lay reader. Several translations from the Latin are available, and we've chosen the one used (and also glossed) by Kuhn in his *Copernican Revolution*. We do not expect you to understand all or even most of the technical aspects of Copernicus's discussion; yet a good part of his general presentation in these first ten chapters from Book I can be appreciated without reference to formal astronomy. Read for the main ideas and you will gain understanding enough; you will also achieve the point of reference necessary for reading further in the chapter.

We present, then, the Preface and excerpts from the first book of *On the Revolution of Heavenly Spheres*. Copernicus dedicated the work to Pope Paul III, Clement's successor — a respected reformer of the church and a patron of the arts. It was Paul III who commissioned Michelangelo to paint the *Last Judgment* in the Sistine Chapel. It was also Paul who excommunicated Henry VIII of England and who, ironically, reestablished the Roman Inquisition (in 1542) that would condemn Galileo for his support of heliocentrism ninety years later.

The following excerpt is from Thomas Kuhn's *The Copernican Revolution*. It contains Kuhn's selections from *On the Revolution of Heavenly Spheres* as modified by him and with his bracketed comments, plus Kuhn's own explanatory text. Occasionally, we've provided explanatory notes.

ON THE REVOLUTION OF HEAVENLY SPHERES [De Revolutionibus]

To the Most Holy Lord, Pope Paul III[1]

THE PREFACE OF NICOLAUS COPERNICUS TO THE BOOKS OF THE REVOLUTIONS

I may well presume, most Holy Father, that certain people, as soon as   1
they hear that in this book about the Revolutions of the Spheres of the Universe I ascribe movement to the earthly globe, will cry out that, holding such views, I should at once be hissed off the stage. For I am not so pleased with my own work that I should fail duly to weigh the judgment which others may pass thereon; and though I know that the speculations of a philosopher are far removed from the judgment of the multitude — for his aim is to seek truth in all things as far as God has permitted human reason so to do — yet I hold that opinions which are quite erroneous should be avoided.

Thinking therefore within myself that to ascribe movement to the Earth   2

Explanatory text from Thomas Kuhn. *The Copernican Revolution: Planetary Astronomy and the Development of Western Thought*. Cambridge: Harvard UP, 1957, pp. 136–154, 176–181. Essay selections from Nicolaus Copernicus. *De Revolutionibus Orbium Caelestium* (1543). Trans. John F. Dobson and Selig Brodetsky, as cited in Kuhn. Published as *Occasional Notes of the Royal Astronomical Society*, vol. 2, no. 10. London: Royal Astronomical Society, 1947.

[1]"As a typical Renaissance Pope, Paul III was a patron of arts and learning who restored the Roman university and commissioned Michelangelo to paint the 'Last Judgment' in the Sistine Chapel. As such, he was an appropriate person for Copernicus to address. Ironically, however, he was also, times being what they were, the reformer who revived the Roman Inquisition, approved the formation of the Society of Jesus, established the censorship, and summoned the Council of Trent. Born in 1468, he became Pope in 1534 and died in 1549." [Note by A.M. Duncan, from his translation of *On the Revolution of Heavenly Spheres*. New York: Barnes and Noble, 1976.]

must indeed seem an absurd performance on my part to those who know that many centuries have consented to the establishment of the contrary judgment, namely that the Earth is placed immovably as the central point in the middle of the Universe, I hesitated long whether, on the one hand, I should give to the light these my Commentaries written to prove the Earth's motion, or whether, on the other hand, it were better to follow the example of the Pythagoreans[2] and others who were wont to impart their philosophic mysteries only to intimates and friends, and then not in writing but by word of mouth, as the letter of Lysis to Hipparchus witnesses. [This letter, which Copernicus had at one time intended to include in the *De Revolutionibus*, describes the Pythagorean and Neoplatonic injunction against revealing nature's secrets to those who are not initiates of a mystical cult. Reference to it here exemplifies Copernicus' participation in the Renaissance revival of Neoplatonism[3]. . . .] In my judgment they did so not, as some would have it, through jealousy of sharing their doctrines, but as fearing lest these so noble and hardly won discoveries of the learned should be despised by such as either care not to study aught save for gain, or — if by the encouragement and example of others they are stimulated to philosophic liberal pursuits — yet by reason of the dullness of their wits are in the company of philosophers as drones among bees. Reflecting thus, the thought of the scorn which I had to fear on account of the novelty and incongruity of my theory, well-nigh induced me to abandon my project.

These misgivings and actual protests have been overcome by my friends   3
. . . [one of whom] often urged and even importuned me to publish this work which I had kept in store not for nine years only, but to a fourth period of nine years. . . .[4] They urged that I should not, on account of my fears, refuse any longer to contribute the fruits of my labors to the common advantage of those interested in mathematics. They insisted that, though my theory of the Earth's movement might at first seem strange, yet it would appear admirable and acceptable when the publication of my elucidatory comments should dispel the mists of paradox. Yielding then to their persuasion I at last permitted my friends to publish that work which they have so long demanded.

That I allow the publication of these my studies may surprise your Holi-   4
ness the less in that, having been at such travail to attain them, I had already not scrupled to commit to writing my thoughts upon the motion of the Earth.

---

[2]"The Pythagoreans were the followers of the philosopher Pythagoras who emigrated from Samos in about 530 B.C. and taught at Croton, a Greek colony in Southern Italy. They recognised that the Earth was a sphere, and believed that the Earth, together with a similar but unseen Counter-Earth and the other heavenly bodies including the Sun, revolved round the unseen Central Fire in perfect circles. The quotation is from Plutarch, *De Placitis Philosophorum*, III, 13." [Duncan]

[3]*Neoplatonism:* The philosophical movement developed from the skeptics in the third century A.D., which interpreted Plato's philosophy. Neoplatonism became the philosophical foundation for Western Christianity as well as Islamic philosophy. During the Italian Renaissance, Neoplatonism experienced a revival after having been ignored in the thirteenth century in favor of the works of Aristotle. The Romantic poets of the nineteenth century were also greatly influenced by the metaphysical thought of Neoplatonism.

[4]That is, four times nine years, or thirty-six years.

[Some years before the publication of the *De Revolutionibus* Copernicus had circulated among his friends a short manuscript called the *Commentariolus*, describing an earlier version of his sun-centered astronomy. A second advance report of Copernicus' major work, the *Narratio Prima* by Copernicus' student, Rheticus, had appeared in 1540 and again in 1541.] How I came to dare to conceive such motion of the Earth, contrary to the received opinion of the Mathematicians and indeed contrary to the impression of the senses, is what your Holiness will rather expect to hear. So I should like your Holiness to know that I was induced to think of a method of computing the motions of the spheres by nothing else than the knowledge that the Mathematicians are inconsistent in these investigations.

For, first, the mathematicians are so unsure of the movements of the Sun and Moon that they cannot even explain or observe the constant length of the seasonal year. Secondly, in determining the motions of these and of the other five planets, they use neither the same principles and hypotheses nor the same demonstrations of the apparent motions and revolutions. So some use only homocentric circles[5] [the Aristotelian system, derived by Aristotle from Eudoxus and Callippus, and revived in Europe shortly before Copernicus' birth by the Italian astronomers Frascatoro and Amici], while others [employ] eccentrics[6] and epicycles.[7] Yet even by these means they do not completely

5

---

[5]That is, a series of concentric spheres revolving about a central earth. [Behrens & Rosen]
[6]A planetary body describes an eccentric circle when the center of its revolution is displaced, or moved away from, the earth — as in the diagram that follows. [Diagram by Vincent Edward Smith in "The New Sciences." *Science and Philosophy*. Milwaukee: The Bruce Publishing Co., 1965, p. 34.]:

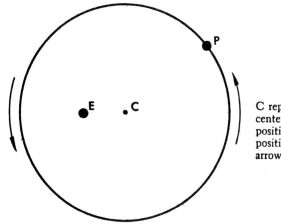

C represents the geometrical center of the circle; E, the position of the earth; P, the position of the planet; and the arrows, the direction of rotation.

[7]A planet describes an epicycle when it revolves in a small circle about a point, which itself is revolving around a central Earth. This larger circle (the revolution of the point about the

attain their ends. Those who have relied on homocentrics, though they have proven that some different motions can be compounded therefrom, have not thereby been able fully to establish a system which agrees with the phenomena. Those again who have devised eccentric systems, though they appear to have well-nigh established the seeming motions by calculations agreeable to their assumptions, have yet made many admissions [like the use of the equant] which seem to violate the first principle of uniformity in motion.[8,9] Nor have

---

Earth) is called a deferent. The following diagram illustrates this process [Diagram by Vincent Edward Smith]:

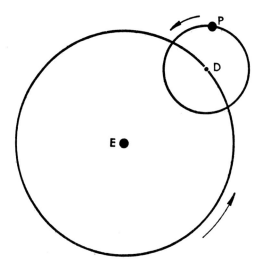

E represents the earth as the center of the deferent; D, the center of the epicycle; P, the position of the planet; and the arrows, the direction of rotation.

---

[8]*the first principle of uniformity in motion:* In the cosmology of Aristotle, the motion of a planet in a circle occurred at a constant rate and was the most perfect kind of motion in that it could continue indefinitely.

[9]Ptolemy's solution to the "problem of the planets," that is, their retrograde motion, is summarized in the following diagram and accompanying text, excerpted from George O. Abell, *Exploration of the Universe,* 3e. [New York: Holt, 1975, pp. 28–29.] *Equant* is defined in relation to the terms just discussed.

Ptolemy solved the problem [of the planets] by having a planet *P* revolve in an epicyclic orbit about *C*. The center of the epicycle *C* in turn revolved in the deferent about the earth. When the planet is at position *x*, it is moving in its epicyclic orbit in the same direction as the point *C* moves about the earth, and the planet appears to be moving eastward. When the planet is at *y*, however, its epicyclic motion is in the opposite direction to the motion of *C*. By choosing the right combination of speeds and distances, Ptolemy succeeded in having the planet moving westward at the right speed at *y* and for the correct interval of time. However, because the planets, as does the earth, travel about the sun in elliptical orbits, their actual behavior cannot be represented accurately by so simple a scheme of uniform circular motions. Conse-

they been able thereby to discern or deduce the principal thing — namely the shape of the Universe and the unchangeable symmetry of its parts. With them it is as though an artist were to gather the hands, feet, head and other members for his images from diverse models, each part excellently drawn, but not related to a single body, and since they in no way match each other, the result would be monster rather than man. So in the course of their exposition, which the mathematicians call their system, . . . we find that they have either omitted some indispensable detail or introduced something foreign and wholly irrelevant. This would of a surety not have been so had they followed fixed principles; for if their hypotheses were not misleading, all inferences based thereon might be surely verified. Though my present assertions are obscure, they will be made clear in due course.

An honest appraisal of contemporary astronomy, says Copernicus, shows that the earth-centered approach to the problem of the planets is

6

---

quently, Ptolemy made the deferent an eccentric, centered not on the earth, but slightly away from the earth at *A*. Furthermore, he had the center of the epicycle, *C*, move at a uniform angular rate, not around *A*, or *E*, but at point *B*, called the *equant*, on the opposite side of *A* from the earth.

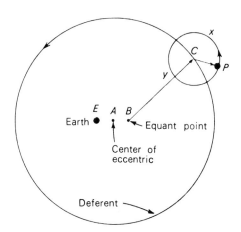

It is a tribute to the genius of Ptolemy as a mathematician that he was able to conceive such a complex system to account successfully for the observations. His hypothesis, with some modifications, was accepted as absolute authority throughout the Middle Ages, until it finally gave way to the heliocentric theory in the seventeenth century.

hopeless. The traditional techniques of Ptolemaic astronomy have not and will not solve that problem; instead they have produced a monster; there must, he concludes, be a fundamental error in the basic concepts of traditional planetary astronomy. For the first time a technically competent astronomer had rejected the time-honored scientific tradition for reasons internal to his science, and this professional awareness of technical fallacy inaugurated the Copernican Revolution. A felt necessity was the mother of Copernicus' invention. But the feeling of necessity was a new one. The astronomical tradition had not previously seemed monstrous. By Copernicus' time a metamorphosis had occurred, and Copernicus' preface brilliantly describes the felt causes of that transformation.

Copernicus and his contemporaries inherited not only the *Almagest* but also the astronomies of many Islamic and a few European astronomers who had criticized and modified Ptolemy's system. These are the men to whom Copernicus refers as "the mathematicians." One had added or subtracted a few small circles; another had employed an epicycle to account for a planetary irregularity that Ptolemy had originally treated with an eccentric; still another had invented a means unknown to Ptolemy of accounting for small deviations from the motion predicted by a one-epicycle one-deferent system;[10] others had, with new measurements, altered the rates at which the compounded circles of Ptolemy's system rotated. There was no longer one Ptolemaic system, but a dozen or more, and the number was multiplying rapidly with the multiplication of technically proficient astronomers. All these systems were modeled on the system of the *Almagest*, and all were therefore "Ptolemaic." But because there were so many variant systems, the adjective "Ptolemaic" had lost much of its meaning. The astronomical tradition had become diffuse; it no longer fully specified the techniques that an astronomer might employ in computing planetary position, and it could not therefore specify the results that he would obtain from his computations. Equivocations like these deprived the astronomical tradition of its principal source of internal strength. 7

Copernicus' monster has other faces. None of the "Ptolemaic" systems which Copernicus knew gave results that quite coincided with good naked-eye observations. They were no worse than Ptolemy's results, but they were also no better. After thirteen centuries of fruitless research a perceptive astronomer might well wonder, as Ptolemy could not have, whether further attempts within the same tradition could conceivably be successful. Besides, the centuries that had intervened between Ptolemy and Copernicus had magnified the errors of the traditional approach, thus providing an additional source of discontent. The motions of a system of epicycles 8

---

[10]*one-epicycle one-deferent system:* That is, the system described by the diagram in footnote 9.

and deferents are not unlike those of the hands of a clock, and the apparent error of a clock increases with the passage of time. If a clock loses, say, 1 second per decade, its error may not be apparent at the end of a year or the end of ten. But the error can scarcely be evaded after a millennium, when it will have increased to almost 2 minutes. Since Copernicus and his contemporaries possessed astronomical data extending over a time span thirteen centuries longer than that covered by Ptolemy's data, they could impose a far more sensitive check upon their systems. They were necessarily more aware of the errors inherent in the ancient approach.

The passage of time also presented the sixteenth-century astronomer with a counterfeit problem which ironically was even more effective than the real motion of the planets in fostering recognition of the errors in the Ptolemaic method. Many of the data inherited by Copernicus and his colleagues were bad data which placed the planets and stars in positions that they had never occupied. Some of the erroneous records had been collected by poor observers; others had once been based upon good observations but had been miscopied or misconstrued during the process of transmission. No simple planetary system — Ptolemy's, Copernicus', Kepler's, or Newton's — could have reduced to order the data that Renaissance astronomers thought they had to explain. The complexity of the problem presented by Renaissance data transcended that of the heavens themselves. Copernicus was himself a victim of the data that had originally aided him in rejecting the Ptolemaic system. His own system would have given far better results if he had been as skeptical about his predecessors' observations as he was about their mathematical systems.

Diffuseness and continued inaccuracy — these are the two principal characteristics of the monster described by Copernicus. In so far as the Copernican Revolution depended upon explicit changes within the astronomical tradition itself, these are its major sources. But they are not the only ones. We may also ask why Copernicus was able to recognize the monster. Some of the tradition's apparent metamorphosis must have been in the eye of the beholder, for the tradition had been diffuse and inaccurate before. In fact we have already considered this question. Copernicus' awareness of monstrosity depended upon [a] larger climate of philosophical and scientific opinion. . . . From the state of contemporary astronomy a man without Copernicus' Neoplatonic bias might have concluded merely that the problem of the planets could have no solution that was simultaneously simple and precise. Similarly, an astronomer unacquainted with the tradition of scholastic criticism might have been unable to develop parallel criticisms for his own field. These and other novelties . . . are main currents of Copernicus' time. Though he seems unaware of them, Copernicus was carried by these philosophical currents, as his contemporaries were unwittingly carried by the motion of the earth. Copernicus' work remains incomprehensible unless viewed in its relation to both the internal state of astronomy and the larger intellectual climate of the age. Both together produced the monster.

Discontent with a recognized monster was, however, only the first *11* step toward the Copernican Revolution. Next came a search whose beginnings are described in the remaining portions of Copernicus' prefatory letter:

> I pondered long upon this uncertainty of mathematical tradition in estab- *12* lishing the motions of the system of the spheres. At last I began to chafe that philosophers could by no means agree on any one certain theory of the mechanism of the Universe, wrought for us by a supremely good and orderly Creator, though in other respects they investigated with meticulous care the minutest points relating to its circles. [Note how Copernicus equates "orderly" with "mathematically neat," an aspect of his Neoplatonism from which any good Aristotelian would have vehemently dissented. There are other sorts of orderliness.] I therefore took pains to read again the works of all the philosophers on whom I could lay hand to seek out whether any of them had ever supposed that the motions of the spheres were other than those demanded by the mathematical schools. I found first in Cicero[11] that Hicetas [of Syracuse, fifth century B.C.] had realized that the Earth moved. Afterwards I found in Plutarch[12] that certain others had held the like opinion. I think fit here to add Plutarch's own words, to make them accessible to all:
>
> "The rest hold the Earth to be stationary, but Philolaus the Pythagorean *13* [fifth century B.C.] says that she moves around the [central] fire on an oblique circle like the Sun and Moon. Heraclides of Pontus and Ecphantus the Pythagorean [fourth century B.C.] also make the Earth to move, not indeed through space but by rotating her own center as a wheel on an axle from West to East."
>
> Taking advantage of this I too began to think of the mobility of the Earth; *14* and though the opinion seemed absurd, yet knowing now that others before me had been granted freedom to imagine such circles as they chose to explain the phenomena of the stars, I considered that I also might easily be allowed to try whether, by assuming some motion of the Earth, sounder explanations than theirs for the revolution of the celestial spheres might so be discovered.
>
> Thus assuming motions, which in my work I ascribe to the Earth, by long *15* and frequent observations I have at last discovered that, if the motions of the rest of the planets be brought into relation with the circulation of the Earth and be reckoned in proportion to the circles of each planet, not only do their phenomena presently ensue, but the orders and magnitudes of all stars and spheres, nay the heavens themselves, become so bound together that nothing in any part thereof could be moved from its place without producing confusion of all the other parts and of the Universe as a whole. . . . [Copernicus here

---

[11]*Cicero:* Marcus Tullius Cicero (106–43 B.C.) was a Roman statesman and scholar who advocated republican principles. He is also known as one of the greatest orators of all time as well as a prolific writer.

[12]*Plutarch:* Plutarch (46 A.D.–119 ?) is known for his approximately 227 works, including essays on ethical, political, and physical topics.

points to the single most striking difference between his system and Ptolemy's. In the Copernican system it is no longer possible to shrink or expand the orbit of any one planet at will, holding the others fixed. Observation for the first time can determine the order and the relative dimensions of all the planetary orbits without resort to the hypothesis of space-filling spheres. . . .]

I doubt not that gifted and learned mathematicians will agree with me if *16* they are willing to comprehend and appreciate, not superficially but thoroughly, according to the demands of this science, such reasoning as I bring to bear in support of my judgment. But that learned and unlearned alike may see that I shrink not from any man's criticism, it is to your Holiness rather than anyone else that I have chosen to dedicate these studies of mine, since in this remote corner of Earth in which I live you are regarded as the most eminent by virtue alike of the dignity of your Office and of your love of letters and science. You by your influence and judgment can readily hold the slanderers from biting, though the proverb hath it that there is no remedy against a sycophant's tooth. It may fall out, too, that idle babblers, ignorant of mathematics, may claim a right to pronounce a judgment on my own work, by reason of a certain passage of Scripture basely twisted to suit their purpose. Should any such venture to criticize and carp at my project, I make no account of them; I consider their judgment rash, and utterly despise it. I well know that even Lactantius,[13] a writer in other ways distinguished but in no sense a mathematician, discourses in a most childish fashion touching the shape of the Earth, ridiculing even those who have stated the Earth to be a sphere. Thus my supporters need not be amazed if some people of like sort ridicule me too.

Mathematics are for mathematicians, and they, if I be not wholly deceived, *17* will hold that these my labors contribute somewhat even to the Commonwealth of the Church, of which your Holiness is now Prince. For not long since, under Leo X, the question of correcting the ecclesiastical calendar was debated in the Council of the Lateran. It was left undecided for the sole cause that the lengths of the years and months and the motions of the Sun and Moon were not held to have been yet determined with sufficient exactness. From that time on I have given thought to their more accurate observation, by the advice of that eminent man Paul, Lord Bishop of Sempronia, sometime in charge of that business of the calendar. What results I have achieved therein, I leave to the judgment of learned mathematicians and of your Holiness in particular. And now, not to seem to promise your Holiness more than I can perform with regard to the usefulness of the work, I pass to my appointed task.

"Mathematics are for mathematicians." There is the first essential in- *18* congruity of the *De Revolutionibus*. Though few aspects of Western thought were long unaffected by the consequences of Copernicus' work, that work itself was narrowly technical and professional. It was mathematical plan-

---

[13]*Lactantius:* An early Christian Apologist who lived in the late third century A.D. His *Divinae Institutiones* (Divine Precepts) was the first Latin account of Christian ethics and attitudes.

etary astronomy, not cosmology or philosophy, that Copernicus found monstrous, and it was the reform of mathematical astronomy that alone compelled him to move the earth. If his contemporaries were to follow him, they would have to learn to understand his detailed mathematical arguments about planetary position, and they would have to take these abstruse arguments more seriously than the first evidence of their senses. The Copernican Revolution was not primarily a revolution in the mathematical techniques employed to compute planetary position, but it began as one. In recognizing the need for and in developing these new techniques, Copernicus made his single original contribution to the Revolution that bears his name.

Copernicus was not the first to suggest the earth's motion, and he did   *19* not claim to have rediscovered the idea for himself. In his preface he cites most of the ancient authorities who had argued that the earth was in motion. In an earlier manuscript he even refers to Aristarchus, whose sun-centered universe very closely resembles his own. Although he fails, as was customary during the Renaissance, to mention his more immediate predecessors who had believed that the earth was or could be in motion, he must have known some of their work. He may not, for example, have known of Oresme's contributions, but he had probably at least heard of the very influential treatise in which the fifteenth-century Cardinal, Nicholas of Cusa, derived the motion of the earth from the plurality of worlds in an unbounded Neoplatonic universe. The earth's motion had never been a popular concept, but by the sixteenth century it was scarcely unprecedented. What was unprecedented was the mathematical system that Copernicus built upon the earth's motion. With the possible exception of Aristarchus, Copernicus was the first to realize that the earth's motion might solve an existing astronomical problem or indeed a scientific problem of any sort. Even including Aristarchus, he was the first to develop a detailed account of the astronomical consequences of the earth's motion. Copernicus' mathematics distinguish him from his predecessors, and it was in part because of the mathematics that his work inaugurated a revolution as theirs had not.

COPERNICUS' PHYSICS AND COSMOLOGY

For Copernicus the motion of the earth was a by-product of the prob-   *20* lem of the planets. He learned of the earth's motion by examining the celestial motions, and, because the celestial motions had to him a transcendent importance, he was little concerned about the difficulties that his innovation would present to normal men whose concerns were predominantly terrestrial. But Copernicus could not quite ignore the problems that the earth's motion raised for those whose sense of values was less exclusively astronomical than his own. He had at least to make it possible for his contemporaries to conceive the earth's motion; he had to show that the consequences of this motion were not so devastating as they were commonly supposed to be. Therefore Copernicus opened the *De Revolutionibus* with a nontechnical sketch of the universe that he had constructed to house a moving earth. His introductory First Book was directed to laymen, and it included all the arguments that he thought he could make accessible to those without astronomical training.

Those arguments are profoundly unconvincing. Except when they de-   *21* rive from mathematical analyses that Copernicus failed to make explicit in the First Book, they were not new, and they did not quite conform to the details of the astronomical system that Copernicus was to develop in the later books. Only a man who, like Copernicus, had other reasons for supposing that the earth moved could have taken the First Book of the *De Revolutionibus* entirely seriously.

But the First Book is not unimportant. Its very weaknesses foreshadow   *22* the incredulity and ridicule with which Copernicus' system would be greeted by those who could not follow the detailed mathematical discussion of the subsequent books. Its repeated dependence upon Aristotelian and scholastic concepts and laws shows how little even Copernicus was able to transcend his training and his times except in his own narrow field of specialization. Finally, the incompleteness and incongruities of the First Book illustrate again the coherence of traditional cosmology and traditional astronomy. Copernicus, who was led to revolution by astronomical motives only and who inevitably tried to restrict his innovation to astronomy, could not evade entirely the destructive cosmological consequences of the earth's motion.

BOOK ONE

1. That the Universe is Spherical.

In the first place we must observe that the Universe is spherical. This is   *23* either because that figure is the most perfect, as not being articulated but whole and complete in itself; or because it is the most capacious and therefore best suited for that which is to contain and preserve all things [of all solids with a given surface the sphere has the greatest volume]; or again because all the perfect parts of it, namely, Sun, Moon and Stars, are so formed; or because all things tend to assume this shape, as is seen in the case of drops of water and liquid bodies in general if freely formed. No one doubts that such a shape has been assigned to the heavenly bodies.

2. That the Earth also is Spherical.

The Earth also is spherical, since on all sides it inclines [or falls] toward   *24* the center. . . . As we pass from any point northward, the North Pole of the daily rotation gradually rises, while the other pole sinks correspondingly and more stars near the North Pole cease to set, while certain stars in the South do not rise. . . . Further, the change in altitude of the pole is always proportional to the distance traversed on the Earth,[14] which could not be save on a spherical figure. Hence the Earth must be finite and spherical. . . . [Copernicus concludes the chapter with a few more arguments for the earth's sphericity typical of . . . classical sources. . . .]

3. How Earth, with the Water on it, forms one Sphere.

The waters spread around the Earth form the seas and fill the lower declivities. The volume of the waters must be less than that of the Earth, else they would swallow up the land (since both, by their weight, press toward the same center). Thus, for the safety of living things, stretches of the Earth are left uncovered, and also numerous islands widely scattered. Nay, what is a continent, and indeed the whole of the Mainland, but a vast island? . . .   25

[Copernicus wishes, in this chapter, to show both that the terrestrial globe is predominantly made of earth and that water and earth together are required to make the globe a sphere. Presumably he is looking ahead. Earth breaks up less easily than water when moved; motion of a solid globe is more plausible than of a liquid one. Again, Copernicus will finally say that the earth moves naturally in circles because it is a sphere (see Chapter 8 of his First Book, below). He therefore needs to show that both earth and water are essential to the composition of the sphere, in order that both will participate together in the sphere's natural motion. The passage is of particular interest, because in documenting his view of the structure of the earth Copernicus displays his acquaintance with the recent voyages of discovery and with the corrections that must consequently be made in Ptolemy's geographical writings. For example, he says: 26

If the terrestrial globe were predominantly water,] the depth of Ocean would constantly increase from the shore outwards, and so neither island nor rock nor anything of the nature of land would be met by sailors, how far soever they ventured. Yet, we know that between the Egyptian Sea and the Arabian Gulf, well-nigh in the middle of the great land-mass, is a passage barely 15 stades wide. On the other hand, in his *Cosmography* Ptolemy would have it that the habitable land extends to the middle circle [of the earth, that is, through a hemisphere extending 180° eastward from the Canary Islands] with   27

---

[14]Here, Copernicus reproduces one of Aristotle's arguments that the earth is spherical. "Aristotle explained that northbound travelers observed hitherto invisible stars to appear above the northern horizon and other stars to disappear behind the southern horizon. Southbound travelers observed the opposite effect. The only possible explanation is that the travelers' horizons had tipped to the north or south, respectively, which indicates that they must have moved over a curved surface of the earth." [George O. Abell. *Exploration of the Universe*, 3e. New York: Holt, 1975, pp. 19–20.]

a *terra incognita* beyond where modern discovery has added Cathay and a very extensive region as far as 60° of longitude.[15] Thus we know now that the Earth is inhabited to a greater longitude than is left for Ocean.

This will more evidently appear if we add the islands found in our own   *28* time under the Princes of Spain and Portugal, particularly America, a land named after the Captain who discovered it and, on account of its unexplored size, reckoned as another Mainland — besides many other islands hitherto unknown. We thus wonder the less at the so-called Antipodes or Antichthones [the inhabitants of the other hemisphere]. For geometrical argument demands that the Mainland of America on account of its position be diametrically opposite to the Ganges basin in India. . . .

4. That the Motion of the Heavenly Bodies is Uniform, Circular, and Perpetual, or Composed of Circular Motions.

We now note that the motion of heavenly bodies is circular.[16] Rotation is   *29* natural to a sphere and by that very act is its shape expressed. For here we deal with the simplest kind of body, wherein neither beginning nor end may be discerned nor, if it rotate ever in the same place, may the one be distinguished from the other.

Because there are a multitude of spheres, many motions occur. Most evi-   *30* dent to sense is the diurnal rotation . . . marking day and night. By this motion the whole Universe, save Earth alone, is thought to glide from East to West. This is the common measure of all motions, since Time itself is numbered in days. Next we see other revolutions in contest, as it were, with this daily motion and opposing it from West to East. Such opposing motions are those of Sun and Moon and the five planets. . . .

But these bodies exhibit various differences in their motion. First their axes   *31* are not that of the diurnal rotation, but of the Zodiac, which is oblique thereto. Secondly, they do not move uniformly even in their own orbits; for are not Sun and Moon found now slower, now swifter in their courses? Further, at times the five planets become stationary at one point and another and even go

---

[15]Ptolemy had calculated that the world was only 180 degrees in longitude. This area included the Mediterranean, Europe, Asia, and Africa. It was not until the seventeenth century that the continental mass of Australia was discovered. Cathay was the name given in the Middle Ages to Northern China. Marco Polo's famous voyage made Cathay famous in medieval Europe, and Columbus thought that he was heading toward Cathay in his voyage to the New World.

[16]"According to the Aristotelian tradition, the natural motion of the heavenly bodies was circular, and quite different from that of terrestrial bodies, which was vertically up or down [or rectilinear]. It is a bold step on the part of Copernicus to attribute the same motion to any sphere, whether it is one of the heavenly spheres or the sphere of the Earth; but it also provides the only physical argument for his theory that the Earth revolves." [Duncan]

backward. . . . Furthermore, sometimes they approach Earth, being then in *Perigee*, while at other times receding they are in *Apogee*.

Nevertheless, despite these irregularities, we must conclude that the motions of these bodies are ever circular or compounded of circles. For the irregularities themselves are subject to a definite law and recur at stated times, and this could not happen if the motions were not circular, for a circle alone can thus restore the place of a body as it was. So with the Sun which, by a compounding of circular motions, brings ever again the changing days and nights and the four seasons of the year. Now therein it must be that divers motions are conjoined, since a simple celestial body cannot move irregularly in a single circle. For such irregularity must come of unevenness either in the moving force (whether inherent or acquired) or in the form of the revolving body. Both these alike the mind abhors regarding the most perfectly disposed bodies. 32

It is then generally agreed that the motions of Sun, Moon, and Planets do but seem irregular either by reason of the divers directions of their axes of revolution, or else by reason that Earth is not the center of the circles in which they revolve, so that to us on Earth the displacements of these bodies [along their orbits] seem greater when they are near [the earth] than when they are more remote (as is demonstrated in optics [or in everyday observation — boats or carriages always seem to move by more quickly when they are closer]). Thus, equal [angular] motions of a sphere, viewed from different distances, will seem to cover different distances in equal times. It is therefore above all needful to observe carefully the relation of the Earth toward the Heavens, lest, searching out the things on high, we should pass by those nearer at hand, and mistakenly ascribe earthly qualities to heavenly bodies. 33

Copernicus here provides the fullest and most forceful version that we have yet examined of the traditional argument for restricting the motions of celestial bodies to circles. Only a uniform circular motion, or a combination of such motions, can, he thinks, account for the regular recurrence of all celestial phenomena at fixed intervals of time. So far every one of Copernicus' arguments is Aristotelian or scholastic, and his universe is indistinguishable from that of traditional cosmology. In some respects he is even more Aristotelian than many of his predecessors and contemporaries. He will not, for example, consent to the violation of the uniform and symmetric motion of a sphere that is implicit in the use of an equant. 34

The radical Copernicus has so far shown himself a thoroughgoing conservative. But he cannot postpone the introduction of the earth's motion any longer. He must now take account of his break with tradition. And strangely enough, it is in the break that Copernicus shows his dependence on the tradition most clearly. In dissent he still remains as nearly as possible an Aristotelian. Beginning in the fifth chapter, below, and culminating in the general discussion of motion in the eighth and ninth chapters, Copernicus suggests that because the earth is a sphere, like the celestial bodies, it too must participate in the compounded circular motions which, he says, are natural to a sphere. 35

5. Whether Circular Motion belongs to the Earth; and concerning its position.

Since it has been shown that Earth is spherical, we now consider whether *36*
her motion is conformable to her shape and her position in the Universe. Without these we cannot construct a proper theory of the heavenly phenomena.
Now authorities agree that Earth holds firm her place at the center of the Universe, and they regard the contrary as unthinkable, nay as absurd. Yet if we
examine more closely it will be seen that this question is not so settled, and
needs wider consideration.

A seeming change of place may come of movement either of object or *37*
observer, or again of unequal movements of the two (for between equal and
parallel motions no movement is perceptible). Now it is Earth from which the
rotation of the Heavens is seen. If then some motion of Earth be assumed it
will be reproduced in external bodies, which will seem to move in the opposite
direction.

Consider first the diurnal rotation. By it the whole Universe, save Earth *38*
alone and its contents, appears to move very swiftly. Yet grant that Earth revolves from West to East, and you will find, if you ponder it, that my conclusion is right. It is the vault of Heaven that contains all things, and why should
not motion be attributed rather to the contained than to the container, to the
located than the locater? The latter view was certainly that of Heraclides and
Ecphantus the Pythagorean and Hicetas of Syracuse (according to Cicero). All
of them made the Earth rotate in the midst of the Universe, believing that the
Stars set owing to the Earth coming in the way, and rise again when it has
passed on.

If this [possibility of the earth's motion] is admitted, then a problem no *39*
less grave arises about the Earth's position, even though almost everyone has
hitherto held that the Earth is at the center of the Universe. [Indeed, if the
earth can move at all, it may have more than a simple axial motion about the
center of the Universe. It may move away from the center altogether, and there
are some good astronomical reasons for supposing that it does.] For grant that
Earth is not at the exact center but at a distance from it which, while small
compared [with the distance] to the starry sphere, is yet considerable compared with [the distances to] the spheres of the Sun and the other planets.
Then calculate the consequent variations in their seeming motions, assuming
these [motions] to be really uniform and about some center other than the
Earth's. One may then perhaps adduce a reasonable cause for the irregularity
of these variable motions. And indeed since the Planets are seen at varying
distances from the Earth, the center of Earth is surely not the center of their
circles. Nor is it certain whether the Planets move toward and away from
Earth, or Earth toward and away from them. It is therefore justifiable to hold
that the Earth has another motion in addition to the diurnal rotation. That the
Earth, besides rotating, wanders with several motions and is indeed a Planet,
is a view attributed to Philolaus the Pythagorean, no mean mathematician, and
one whom Plato is said to have sought out in Italy.

Copernicus is here pointing to the most immediate advantage for as- *40*
tronomers of the concept of a moving earth. If the earth moves in an orbital

circle around the center as well as spinning on its axis, then, at least qualitatively, the retrograde motions and the different times required for a planet's successive journeys around the ecliptic can be explained without the use of epicycles. In Copernicus' system the major irregularities of the planetary motions are only apparent. Viewed from a moving earth a planet that in fact moved regularly would appear to move irregularly. For this reason, Copernicus feels, we should believe in the orbital motion of the earth. But, strangely enough, in the parts of his work accessible to the lay reader, Copernicus never demonstrates this point any more clearly than he has above. Nor does he demonstrate the other astronomical advantages that he cites elsewhere. He asks the nonmathematical reader to take them for granted, though they are not difficult to demonstrate qualitatively. Only in the later books of the *De Revolutionibus* does he let the real advantages of his system show, and since he there deals, not with retrograde motions in general, but with the abstruse quantitative details of the retrograde motions of each individual planet, only the astronomically initiate were able to discover what the earlier references to astronomical advantages meant. Copernicus' obscurity may have been deliberate, for he had previously referred with some approval to the Pythagorean tradition which dictated withholding nature's secrets from those not previously purified by the study of mathematics (and by other more mystical rites). In any case, the obscurity helps explain the way in which his work was received. . . .

Omitting for the moment Chapter 6,[17] *Of the Vastness of the Heavens* 41 *compared with the Size of the Earth,* we proceed to the central chapters in which Copernicus, having asked indulgent readers to assume that astronomical arguments necessitate the earth's motion around the center, attempts to make that motion physically reasonable.

7. Why the Ancients believed that the Earth is at rest, like a Center, in the Middle of the Universe.

The ancient Philosophers tried by divers . . . methods to prove Earth fixed 42 in the midst of the Universe. The most powerful argument was drawn from the doctrine of the heavy and the light. For, they argue, Earth is the heaviest

---

[17][In Chapter 6,] Copernicus' argument is essentially that an observer on the surface of the Earth always appears to be at the centre of the celestial sphere, so that the distance from the surface of the Earth to its centre must be negligible in comparison with the size of the celestial sphere. He emphasises the immense size of the universe much more than Ptolemy, as it is essential to his case. If the stars were not at a vast distance from the Earth, the Earth's annual motion should make each star appear to an observer on the Earth to move relatively to the celestial sphere. Such motions are indeed observable, but only with powerful telescopes; and they were not available until long after the time of Copernicus. [Duncan]

element, and all things of weight move towards it, tending to its center. Hence since the Earth is spherical, and heavy things move vertically to it, they would all rush together to the center if not stopped at the surface. Now those things which move towards the center must, on reaching it, remain at rest. Much more than will the whole Earth remain at rest at the center of the Universe. Receiving all falling bodies, it will remain immovable by its own weight.

Another argument is based on the supposed nature of motion. Aristotle says that motion of a single and simple body is simple. A simple motion may be either straight, or circular. Again a straight motion may be either up or down. So every simple motion must be either toward the center, namely downward, or away from the center, namely upward, or round the center, namely circular. [That is, according to Aristotelian and scholastic physics, natural motions, the only motions that can occur without an external push, are caused by the nature of the body that is in motion. The natural motion of each of the simple bodies (the five elements — earth, water, air, fire, and aether) must itself be simple, because it is a consequence of a simple or elementary nature. And, finally, there are only three (geometrically) simple motions within the spherical universe: up, down, circularly about the center.] Now it is a property only of the heavy elements earth and water to move downward, that is, to seek the center. But the light elements air and fire move upward away from the center. Therefore we must ascribe rectilinear motion[18] to these

───────────────

[18]In the Aristotelian system the elementary bodies constituting the earth and filling the whole region within the moon's sphere differed from the ethereal bodies forming the surrounding heavens not only in their substance but also in their natural modes of motion. Thus it was supposed that, whereas elementary bodies moved naturally in straight lines [i.e., rectilinearly], outward from the center of the universe, or inward toward the center, celestial bodies revolved eternally in circles round the center. These celestial motions were supposed to be maintained by virtue of an incorporeal "unmoved mover," or by a plurality of such movers, inspiring the spheres to an activity represented by their uniform rotation. The rectilinear motions of the terrestrial elements, on the other hand, were attributed to a sifting agency of space itself, whereby these elements were relegated by "natural motions" to their "natural places," i.e., to the layers in which they were respectively supposed to congregate. Such laws of motion were not derived from intelligent experimentation, but were suggested by mere appearances, support for them being sought in plausible deductions from very general statements about the supposed nature of things (many of them little more than popular maxims), or sometimes even from the etymology of the terms employed.

Thus, in this matter of natural motions, Aristotle lays it down (*De caelo*, I, 2) that every motion must be either rectilinear or circular, or compounded of the two, and that the most excellent motion is that which can go on unaltered forever. Now rectilinear motion cannot be indefinitely maintained in a finite universe without sooner or later being stopped at the boundary of that universe; it is hence inferior to circular motion, which can be so maintained. But the natural motion of each terrestrial element is manifestly rectilinear — fire and air move straight upward, earth and water straight downward. Hence there must be some superior element to which circular motion is natural, and this is readily identified with the ether composing the heavens and the heavenly bodies.

Now Copernicus so far belonged to his age as not to find any fault with mechanical principles of this sort, which indeed were not effectively challenged until about a century

four elements. The celestial bodies however have circular motion. So far
Aristotle.[19]

If then, says Ptolemy, Earth moves at least with a diurnal rotation, the   44
result must be the reverse of that described above. For the motion must be of
excessive rapidity, since in 24 hours it must impart a complete rotation to the
Earth. Now things rotating very rapidly resist cohesion or, if united, are apt to
disperse, unless firmly held together. Ptolemy therefore says that Earth would
have been dissipated long ago, and (which is the height of absurdity) would
have destroyed the Heavens themselves; and certainly all living creatures and
other heavy bodies free to move could not have remained on its surface, but
must have been shaken off. Neither could falling objects reach their appointed
place vertically beneath, since in the meantime the Earth would have moved
swiftly from under them. Moreover clouds and everything in the air would
continually move westward.

8. The Insufficiency of these Arguments, and their Refutation.[20]

For these and like reasons, they say that Earth surely rests at the center of   45
the Universe. Now if one should say that the Earth *moves*, that is as much as
to say that the motion is natural, not violent [or due to an external push]; and
things which happen according to nature produce the opposite effects to those
which occur by violence. Things subjected to any force or impetus, gradual or
sudden, must be disintegrated, and cannot long exist. But natural processes
being adapted to their purpose work smoothly. [That is, if the earth moves at
all, it does so because it is of the nature of earth to move, and a natural motion
cannot be disruptive.]

Idle therefore is the fear of Ptolemy that Earth and all thereon would be   46
distintegrated by a natural rotation, a thing far different from an artificial act.
Should he not fear even more for the Universe, whose motion must be as much
more rapid as the Heavens are greater than the Earth? Have the Heavens become so vast because of their vehement motion, and would they collapse if
they stood still? If this were so the Heavens must be of infinite size. For the
more they expand by the force of their motion, the more rapid will become the
motion because of the ever increasing distance to be traversed in 24 hours.
And in turn, as the motion waxes, must the immensity of the Heavens wax.
Thus velocity and size would increase each the other to infinity. . . .

---

after his death. His concern was only to rebut Aristotle's and Ptolemy's application of such
principles to prove that the earth must be at rest. For his own part, he employs closely
similar, and to a modern mind equally artificial and worthless, mechanical arguments to
prove that the earth is more probably in motion. [Angus Armitage, *Copernicus: The Founder
of Modern Astronomy*. New York: A.S. Barnes and Co., 1957, pp. 74–75.]

[19]That is, Aristotle's theory. [Duncan]

[20]Copernicus here replies to one of the stock arguments against the motion of the Earth in
terms of purely Aristotelian concepts. Although he refutes some of the conclusions of
Aristotelian physics, he gives no indication that his theory invalidates the whole basis of
the Aristotelian world picture. [Duncan]

They say too that outside the Heavens is no body, no space, nay not even　*47*
void, in fact absolutely nothing, and therefore no room for the Heavens to
expand [as we have suggested above that they would]. Yet surely it is strange
that something can be held by nothing. Perhaps indeed it will be easier to
understand this nothingness outside the Heavens if we assume them to be
infinite, and bounded internally only by their concavity, so that everything, however great, is contained in them, while the Heavens remain
immovable. . . .

Let us then leave to Natural Philosophers the question whether the Uni-　*48*
verse be finite or no, holding only to this that Earth is finite and spherical.[21]
Why then hesitate to grant Earth that power of motion natural to its [spherical]
shape, rather than suppose a gliding round of the whole universe, whose limits are unknown and unknowable? And why not grant that the diurnal rotation
is only apparent in the Heavens but real in the Earth? It is but as the saying of
Aeneas in Virgil — "We sail forth from the harbor, and lands and cities retire."
As the ship floats along in the calm, all external things seem to have the motion
that is really that of the ship, while those within the ship feel that they and all
its contents are at rest.

It may be asked what of the clouds and other objects suspended in the air,　*49*
or sinking and rising in it? Surely not only the Earth, with the water on it,
moves thus, but also a quantity of air and all things so associated with the
Earth. Perhaps the contiguous air contains an admixture of earthy or watery
matter and so follows the same natural law as the Earth, or perhaps the air
acquires motion from the perpetually rotating Earth by propinquity and absence of resistance. . . .

We must admit the possibility of a double motion of objects which fall and　*50*
rise in the Universe, namely the resultant of rectilinear and circular motion.[22]

---

[21]Since in Copernicus' system the universe is bounded by the celestial sphere, it is presumably finite. However, his argument in Chapter VI suggests that it is very much larger than
had generally been supposed. He carefully avoids committing himself on the question
whether it is finite or not, which had theological implications. The idea that it might be
infinite was not new. For instance Cardinal Nicholas of Cusa had suggested in the fifteenth
century that it was impossible to conceive a boundary to space. The Copernicus system
did not logically require that the stars should all be fastened to the same sphere, and the
Englishman Thomas Digges in expounding the system later in the sixteenth century suggested that the stars were scattered through space up to distances infinitely distant from
the earth. Giordano Bruno revived the notion that there are many worlds inhabited like
our own in the universe. An apostate from the Dominican Order, he was burnt at the stake
in Rome in 1600 for refusing to abandon such notions. [Duncan]

[22]Aristotelian physics generally took the common sense view that an object could not have
two different motions at the same time. It was Galileo who showed how the path of an
ordinary moving body could be represented as the resultant of more than one motion,
which is a fundamental part of modern mechanics. However, mathematical astronomy had
even in Aristotle's time represented the motion of heavenly bodies as being compounded
of more than one circular motion, though some might believe that this was merely a device
to enable their paths to be calculated and did not represent physical reality. Copernicus is
boldly applying the notion that two different motions might be compounded to ordinary
terrestrial objects, and to the combination of a motion in a straight line with a circular
motion. [Duncan]

[This is the analysis advocated earlier by Oresme.] Thus heavy falling objects, being specially earthy, must doubtless retain the nature of the whole to which they belong. . . . [Therefore a stone, for example, when removed from the earth will continue to move circularly with the earth and will simultaneously fall rectilinearly toward the earth's surface. Its net motion will be some sort of spiral, like the motion of a bug that crawls straight toward the center of a rotating potter's wheel.]

That the motion of a simple body must be simple is true then primarily of   51
circular motion, and only so long as the simple body rests in its own natural place and state. In that state no motion save circular is possible, for such motion is wholly self-contained and similar to being at rest. But if objects move or are moved from their natural place rectilinear motion supervenes. Now it is inconsistent with the whole order and form of the Universe that it should be outside its own place. Therefore there is no rectilinear motion save of objects out of their right place, nor is such motion natural to perfect objects, since [by such a motion] they would be separated from the whole to which they belong and thus would destroy its unity. . . . [Copernicus' argument shows how quickly the traditional distinction between the terrestrial and the celestial regions must disappear when the earth becomes a planet, for he is here simply applying a traditional argument about celestial bodies to the earth. Circular motion, whether simple or compound, is the nearest thing to rest. It can be natural to the earth just as it has always been natural to the heavens, because it cannot disrupt the observed unity and regularity of the universe. Linear motion, on the other hand, cannot be natural to any object that has achieved its own place, for linear motion is disruptive and a natural motion that destroys the universe is absurd.]

Further, we conceive immobility to be nobler and more divine than change   52
and inconstancy, which latter is thus more appropriate to Earth than to the Universe. Would it not then seem absurd to ascribe motion to that which contains or locates, and not rather to that contained and located, namely the Earth?

Lastly, since the planets approach and recede from the Earth, both their   53
motion round the center, which is held [by Aristotelians] to be the Earth, and also their motion outward and inward are the motion of one body. [And this violates the very laws from which Aristotelians derive the central position of the earth, for according to these laws the planets should have only a single motion.] Therefore we must accept this motion round the center in a more general sense, and must be satisfied provided that every motion has a proper center. From all these considerations it is more probable that the Earth moves than that it remains at rest. This is especially the case with the diurnal rotation, as being particularly a property of the earth.

9. Whether more than one Motion can be attributed to the Earth, and of the center of the Universe.

Since then there is no reason why the Earth should not possess the power   54
of motion, we must consider whether in fact it has more motions than one, so as to be reckoned as a Planet.

That Earth is not the center of all revolutions is proved by the apparently   *55*
irregular motions of the planets and the variations in their distances from the
Earth. These would be unintelligible if they moved in circles concentric with
Earth. Since, therefore, there are more centers than one [that is, a center for
all the orbital motions, a center of the earth itself, and perhaps others besides],
we may discuss whether the center of the Universe is or is not the Earth's
center of gravity.

Now it seems to me gravity is but a natural inclination, bestowed on the   *56*
parts of bodies by the Creator so as to combine the parts in the form of a sphere
and thus contribute to their unity and integrity. And we may believe this property present even in the Sun, Moon, and Planets, so that thereby they retain
their spherical form notwithstanding their various paths. If, therefore, the
Earth also has other motions, these must necessarily resemble the many outside [planetary] motions having a yearly period [since the earth now seems
like a planet in so many other respects]. For if we transfer the motion of the
Sun to the Earth, taking the Sun to be at rest, then morning and evening ris-
ings and settings of Stars will be unaffected, while the stationary points, retrogressions, and progressions of the Planets are due not to their own motions,
but to that of the Earth, which their appearances reflect. Finally we shall place
the Sun himself at the center of the Universe. All this is suggested by the
systematic procession of events and the harmony of the whole Universe, if
only we face the facts, as they say, "with both eyes open."

In these last three chapters we have Copernicus' theory of motion, a   *57*
conceptual scheme that he designed to permit his transposing the earth
and sun without tearing apart an essentially Aristotelian universe in the
process. According to Copernicus' physics all matter, celestial and terrestrial, aggregates naturally into spheres, and the spheres then rotate of their
own nature. A bit of matter separated from its natural position will continue to rotate with its sphere, simultaneously returning to its natural place
by a rectilinear motion. It is a singularly incongruous theory . . . and, in
all but its most incongruous portions, it is a relatively unoriginal one. Copernicus may possibly have reinvented it for himself, but most of the essential elements in both his criticism of Aristotle and his theory of motion
can be found in earlier scholastic writers, particularly in Oresme. Only
when applied to Oresme's more limited problem, they are less implausible.

Failure to provide an adequate physical basis for the earth's motion   *58*
does not discredit Copernicus. He did not conceive or accept the earth's
motion for reasons drawn from physics. The physical and cosmological
problem treated so crudely in the First Book are of his making, but they
are not really his problems; he might have avoided them altogether if he
could. But the inadequacies of Copernicus' physics do illustrate the way in
which the consequences of his astronomical innovation transcend the astronomical problem from which the innovation was derived, and they do
show how little the author of the innovation was himself able to assimilate
the Revolution born from his work. The moving earth is an anomaly in a
classical Aristotelian universe, but the universe of the *De Revolutionibus* is

classical in every respect that Copernicus can make seem compatible with the motion of the earth. As he says himself, the motion of the sun has simply been transferred to the earth. The sun is not yet a star but the unique central body about which the universe is constructed; it inherits the old functions of the earth and some new ones besides. As we shall soon discover, Copernicus' universe is still finite, and concentric nesting spheres still move all planets, even though they can no longer be driven by the outer sphere, which is now at rest. All motions must be compounded of circles; moving the earth does not even enable Copernicus to dispense with epicycles. The Copernican Revolution, as we know it, is scarcely to be found in the *De Revolutionibus*. . . .

10. Of the Order of the Heavenly Bodies.[23]

No one doubts that the Sphere of the Fixed Stars is the most distant of visible things. As for the order of the planets, the early Philosophers wished to determine it from the magnitude of their revolutions. They adduce the fact that of objects moving with equal speed, those farther distant seem to move more slowly (as is proved in Euclid's *Optics*). They think that the Moon describes her path in the shortest time because, being nearest to the Earth, she revolves in the smallest circle. Farthest they place Saturn, who in the longest time describes the greatest circuit. Nearer than he is Jupiter, and then Mars. *59*

Opinions differ as to Venus and Mercury which, unlike the others, do not altogether leave the Sun. Some place them beyond the Sun, as Plato in *Timaeus*; others nearer than the Sun, as Ptolemy and many of the moderns. Alpetragius [a twelfth-century Moslem astronomer] makes Venus nearer and Mercury farther than the Sun. If we agree with Plato in thinking that the planets are themselves dark bodies that do but reflect light from the Sun, it must follow, that if nearer than the Sun, on account of their proximity to him they would appear as half or partial circles; for they would generally reflect such light as they receive upwards, that is toward the Sun, as with the waxing or waning Moon. Some think that since no eclipse even proportional to their size is ever caused by these planets, they can never be between us and the Sun. . . . [Copernicus proceeds to note many difficulties in the arguments usually used to determine the relative order of the sun and the inferior planets. Then he continues:] *60*

Unconvincing too is Ptolemy's proof that the Sun moves between those bodies that do and those that do not recede from him completely [that is, between the superior planets which can assume any angle of elongation and the inferior planets whose maximum elongation is limited].[24] Consideration of the *61*

---

[23]One of the merits of the Copernican system was that it produced evidence for the order of the orbits of the planets, which in the older system could only be conjectural. [Duncan]

[24]Planets whose orbits fall between the earth's orbit and the sun (i.e., Mercury and Venus) are termed "inferior." Planets whose orbits lie beyond the earth's orbit (i.e., Mars, Jupiter, Saturn, Uranus, Neptune, and Pluto) are termed "superior."

case of the Moon, which does so recede, exposes its falseness. Again, what cause can be alleged, by those who place Venus nearer than the Sun, and Mercury next, or in some other order? Why should not these planets also follow separate paths, distinct from that of the Sun, as do the other planets [whose deferents are not tied to the sun's]? And this might be said even if their relative swiftness and slowness did not belie their alleged order. Either then the Earth cannot be the center to which the order of the planets and their Spheres is related, or certainly their relative order is not observed, nor does it appear why a higher position should be assigned to Saturn than to Jupiter, or any other planet.

Therefore I think we must seriously consider the ingenious view held by *62* Martianus Capella [a Roman encyclopedist of the fifth century who recorded a theory of the inferior planets probably first suggested by Heraclides] . . . and certain other Latins, that Venus and Mercury do not go round the Earth like the other planets but run their courses with the Sun as center, and so do not depart from him farther than the convexity of their Spheres allows. . . . What else can they mean than that the center of these Spheres is near the Sun? So certainly the circle of Mercury must be within that of Venus, which, it is agreed, is more than twice as great.

We may now extend this hypothesis to bring Saturn, Jupiter and Mars also *63* into relation with this center, making their Spheres great enough to contain those of Venus and Mercury and the Earth. . . . These outer planets are always nearer to the Earth about the time of their evening rising, that is, when they are in opposition to the Sun, and the Earth between them and the Sun. They are more distant from the Earth at the time of their evening setting, when they are in conjunction with the Sun and the Sun between them and the Earth. These indications prove that their center pertains rather to the Sun than to the Earth, and that this is the same center as that to which the revolutions of Venus and Mercury are related.

[Copernicus' remarks do not actually "prove" a thing. The Ptolemaic sys- *64* tem explains these phenomena as completely as the Copernican, but the Copernican explanation is again more natural, for, like the Copernican explanation of the limited elongation of the inferior planets, it depends only on the geometry of a sun-centered astronomical system, not on the particular orbital periods assigned to the planets. . . .]

But since all these [Spheres] have one center it is necessary that the space *65* between the convex side of Venus's Sphere and the concave side of Mars's must also be viewed as a Sphere concentric with the others, capable of receiving the Earth with her satellite the Moon and whatever is contained within the Sphere of the Moon — for we must not separate the Moon from the Earth, the former being beyond all doubt nearest to the latter, especially as in that space we find suitable and ample room for the Moon.

We therefore assert that the center of the Earth, carrying the Moon's path, *66* passes in a great circuit among the other planets in an annual revolution round the Sun; that near the Sun is the center of the Universe; and that whereas the Sun is at rest, any apparent motion of the Sun can be better explained by motion of the Earth. Yet so great is the Universe that though the distance of the Earth from the Sun is not insignificant compared with the size of any other planetary path, in accordance with the ratios of their sizes, it is insignificant compared with the distances of the Sphere of the Fixed Stars.

I think it easier to believe this than to confuse the issue by assuming a vast *67* number of Spheres, which those who keep Earth at the center must do. We thus rather follow Nature, who producing nothing vain or superfluous often prefers to endow one cause with many effects. Though these views are difficult, contrary to expectation, and certainly unusual, yet in the sequel we shall, God willing, make them abundantly clear at least to mathematicians.

Given the above view — and there is none more reasonable — that the *68* periodic times are proportional to the sizes of the Spheres, then the order of the Spheres, beginning from the most distant is as follows. Most distant of all is the Sphere of the Fixed Stars, containing all things, and being therefore itself immovable. It represents that to which the motion and position of all the other bodies must be referred. . . . Next is the planet Saturn, revolving in 30 years. Next comes Jupiter, moving in a 12-year circuit; then Mars, who goes round in 2 years. The fourth place is held by the annual revolution [of the Sphere] in which the Earth is contained, together with the Sphere of the Moon as on an epicycle. Venus, whose period is 9 months, is in the fifth place, and sixth is Mercury, who goes round in the space of 80 days.

In the middle of all sits Sun enthroned. In this most beautiful temple could *69* we place this luminary in any better position from which he can illuminate the whole at once? He is rightly called the Lamp, the Mind, the Ruler of the Universe; Hermes Trismegistus[25] names him the Visible God, Sophocles' Electra calls him the All-seeing. So the Sun sits as upon a royal throne ruling his children the planets which circle round him. The Earth has the Moon at her service. As Aristotle says, in his *On [the Generation of] Animals*, the Moon has the closest relationship with the Earth. Meanwhile the Earth conceives by the Sun, and becomes pregnant with an annual rebirth.

So we find underlying this ordination an admirable symmetry in the Uni- *70* verse, and a clear bond of harmony in the motion and magnitude of the Spheres such as can be discovered in no other wise. For here we may observe why the progression and retrogression appear greater for Jupiter than Saturn, and less than for Mars, but again greater for Venus than for Mercury; and why such oscillation appears more frequently in Saturn than in Jupiter, but less frequently in Mars and Venus than in Mercury [the earth will lap a slowly moving superior planet more frequently than it laps a rapid one, and conversely for an inferior planet]; moreover why Saturn, Jupiter and Mars are nearer to the Earth at opposition to the Sun than when they are lost in or emerge from the Sun's rays. Particularly Mars, when he shines all night [and is therefore in opposition], appears to rival Jupiter in magnitude, being only distinguishable by his ruddy color; otherwise he is scarce equal to a star of the second magnitude, and can be recognized only when his movements are care-

---

[25]Hermes Trismegistus, a legendary figure derived from the ancient Egyptian god Thoth, was supposed to be the author of a number of works in Greek on Platonic and Stoic philosophy, astrology and alchemy. [Duncan]

fully followed. All these phenomena proceed from the same cause, namely Earth's motion.

That there are no such phenomena for the fixed stars proves their im-   71
measurable distance, because of which the outer sphere's [apparent] annual motion or its [parallactic][26] image is invisible to the eyes. For every visible object has a certain distance beyond which it can no more be seen, as is proved in optics. The twinkling of the stars, also, shows that there is still a vast distance between the farthest of the planets, Saturn, and the Sphere of the Fixed Stars [for if the stars were very near Saturn, they should shine as he does], and it is chiefly by this indication that they are distinguished from the planets. Further, there must necessarily be a great difference between moving and non-moving bodies. So great is this divine work of the Great and Noble Creator!

Throughout this crucially important tenth chapter Copernicus' empha-   72
sis is upon the "admirable symmetry" and the "clear bond of harmony in the motion and magnitude of the Spheres" that a sun-centered geometry imparts to the appearances of the heavens. If the sun is the center, then an inferior planet cannot possibly appear far from the sun; if the sun is the center, then a superior planet must be in opposition to the sun when it is closest to the earth; and so on and on. It is through arguments like these that Copernicus seeks to persuade his contemporaries of the validity of his new approach. Each argument cites an aspect of the appearances that can be explained by *either* the Ptolemaic *or* the Copernican system, and each then proceeds to point out how much more harmonious, coherent, and natural the Copernican explanation is. There are a great many such arguments. The sum of the evidence drawn from harmony is nothing if not impressive.

But it may well be nothing. "Harmony" seems a strange basis on which   73
to argue for the earth's motion, particularly since the harmony is so obscured by the complex multitude of circles that make up the full Copernican system. Copernicus' arguments are not pragmatic. They appeal, if at all, not to the utilitarian sense of the practicing astronomer but to his aesthetic sense and to that alone. They had no appeal to laymen, who, even when they understood the arguments, were unwilling to substitute minor celestial harmonies for major terrestrial discord. They did not necessarily appeal to astronomers, for the harmonies to which Copernicus' arguments pointed did not enable the astronomer to perform his job better. New harmonies did not increase accuracy or simplicity. Therefore they could and did appeal primarily to that limited and perhaps irrational subgroup of

---

[26]*parallax:* Any alteration in the relative apparent positions of objects produced by a shift in the position of the observer. Stellar parallax is the apparent displacement of a nearby star against the background of more distant stars resulting from the motion of the earth in its orbit around the sun. [*The Concise Columbia Encyclopedia.* New York: Avon, 1983.]

mathematical astronomers whose Neoplatonic ear for mathematical harmonies could not be obstructed by page after page of complex mathematics leading finally to numerical predictions scarcely better than those they had known before. Fortunately, . . . there were a few such astronomers. Their work is also an essential ingredient of the Copernican Revolution.

Revolution by Degrees. Because he was the first fully to develop an 74 astronomical system based upon the motion of the earth, Copernicus is frequently called the first modern astronomer. But, as the text of the *De Revolutionibus* indicates, an equally persuasive case might be made for calling him the last great Ptolemaic astronomer. Ptolemaic astronomy meant far more than astronomy predicated on a stationary earth, and it is only with respect to the position and motion of the earth that Copernicus broke with the Ptolemaic tradition. The cosmological frame in which his astronomy was embedded, his physics, terrestrial and celestial, and even the mathematical devices that he employed to make his system give adequate predictions are all in the tradition established by ancient and medieval scientists.

Though historians have occasionally grown livid arguing whether 75 Copernicus is really the last of the ancient or the first of the modern astronomers, the debate is in principle absurd. Copernicus is neither an ancient nor a modern but rather a Renaissance astronomer in whose work the two traditions merge. To ask whether his work is really ancient or modern is rather like asking whether the bend in an otherwise straight road belongs to the section of road that precedes the bend or to the portion that comes after it. From the bend both sections of the road are visible, and its continuity is apparent. But viewed from a point before the bend, the road seems to run straight to the bend and then to disappear; the bend seems the last point in a straight road. And viewed from a point in the next section, after the bend, the road appears to begin at the bend from which it runs straight on. The bend belongs equally to both sections, or it belongs to neither. It marks a turning point in the direction of the road's progress, just as the *De Revolutionibus* marks a shift in the direction in which astronomical thought developed.

REVIEW QUESTIONS

1. For what two reasons did Copernicus consider withholding publication of *On the Revolution of Heavenly Spheres*?
2. What reasons does Copernicus give Pope Paul III for beginning his investigations into the motion of the planets?
3. What, according to Kuhn, inaugurated the Copernican Revolution?

4. According to Kuhn, what was Copernicus's "single original contribution to the Revolution that bears his name"?
5. What is diurnal motion?
6. According to Copernicus, why must the motion of the planets, the moon, and the sun be circular?

DISCUSSION AND WRITING QUESTIONS

1. What is the purpose of Copernicus's analogy, comparing his contemporaries' system of the universe and an artist's assemblage of a "monster"? How does the analogy work to help establish (and validate) his motives for writing *On the Revolution of Heavenly Spheres*?
2. What do you make of Copernicus's dedicating his book to the pope? Why does Copernicus say he's done it? Why do you believe he's done it?
3. Kuhn speaks of the argument in Copernicus's "First Book" as "profoundly unconvincing." Take any three statements from Copernicus's work and discuss the ways in which they are unconvincing.
4. Consider the strategy of addressing the first of the six books in *On the Revolution of Heavenly Spheres* to the lay reader. If, as he says, Copernicus believes that "mathematics are for mathematicians," and he gives five of the six books of his treatise to detailed, mathematical accounts, why do you suppose he addresses the lay reader at all?
5. Using the chapter titles in Book I of *On the Revolution of Heavenly Spheres*, as well as a summary of each chapter (as best you can manage it), trace the development of Copernicus's argument that the planets, including the earth, revolve about the sun.

GALILEO GALILEI *(1564–1642)*

Galileo Galilei was the first to use a telescope in exploring the heavens. With his discovery of sunspots, he confirmed the Copernican "hypothesis" as the true account of planetary motion. Galileo's fame rests not only on his observations with the telescope but also on his experiments in hydrostatics (the study of fluids), the motion of pendulums, and the motion of falling bodies. It is doubtful that he ever climbed the tower of Pisa to conduct his experiment on the acceleration of falling bodies, but it was he who predicted and eventually proved that bodies of differing weights will accelerate (toward the ground) at the same rate of speed. He is credited as the first to use closely controlled experiments for testing the accuracy of mathematically derived, theoretical predictions. He led a distinguished life inside the academy, where as both student and professor he attacked the received opinions of Aristotle, and outside, where he attained fame with a public for whom he wrote in the vernacular Italian.

Galileo was born in 1564, at Pisa, son of Vincenzo Galilei, a cloth merchant who was also a musician, composer, and author on musical matters. The young Galileo was educated at the convent of Vollombrose, where he read thoroughly in the classics. Later, he was to write essays on Dante and a portion of a play, demonstrating a love for and virtuosity of language that was to win him acclaim — and condemnation — in the decades to follow. At seventeen, he began his studies (intending to become a physician) at the University of Pisa, where he soon irritated his professors by challenging the authority of Aristotle and Galen. He left the university without taking his degree and pursued the study of mathematics in Florence. There, at the age of twenty-two, he published an enthusiastically received essay on hydrostatics. By 1589, he had won a post as lecturer in mathematics at the University of Pisa. Three years later, he assumed the chair of mathematics at Padua, where he lived for eighteen years and made his most important discoveries. Galileo's research in astronomy brought him into contact with Johannes Kepler, a fellow Copernican. Kepler had just written his *Mysterium cosmographicum* (in support of heliocentric theory) and had a copy sent to Galileo, who responded as follows:

Padua, August 4th, 1597

I count myself happy, in the search after truth, to have so great an ally as yourself, and one who is so great a friend of the truth itself. It is really pitiful

---

Galileo Galilei. "Letter to Kepler" (August 4, 1597) in Karl Von Gebler, *Galileo Galilei and the Roman Curia*. Trans. Mrs. George Sturge. Merrick, New York: Richwood Publishing Co., 1977, p. 13. (Reprint of the 1879 ed., published by C. K. Paul, London.)

that there are so few who seek truth, and who do not pursue a perverse method of philosophising. But this is not the place to mourn over the miseries of our times, but to congratulate you on your splendid discoveries in confirmation of truth. I shall read your book to the end, sure of finding much that is excellent in it. I shall do so with the more pleasure, because *I have been for many years an adherent of the Copernican system,* and it explains to me the causes of many of the appearances of nature which are quite unintelligible on the commonly accepted hypothesis. *I have collected many arguments for the purpose of refuting the latter;* but I do not venture to bring them to the light of publicity, for fear of sharing the fate of our master, Copernicus, who, although he has earned immortal fame with some, yet with very many (so great is the number of fools) has become an object of ridicule and scorn.[1] I should certainly venture to publish my speculations if there were more people like you. But this not being the case, I refrain from such an undertaking.

> Yours in sincere friendship,
> Galilaeus Galilaeus
> Mathematician at the Academy of Padua

In his reply, Kepler urged Galileo to publicize the results of his studies:

> Graz, October 13th, 1597

I received your letter of August 4th on September 1st. It was a double pleasure to me. First, because I became friends with you, the Italian, and second because of the agreement in which we find ourselves concerning Copernican cosmography. As you invite me kindly at the end of your letter to enter into correspondence with you, and I myself feel greatly tempted to do so, I will not let pass the occasion of sending you a letter with the present young nobleman. For I am sure, if your time has allowed it, you have meanwhile obtained a closer knowledge of my book. And so a great desire has taken hold of me, to learn your judgment. For this is my way, to urge all those to whom I have written to express their candid opinion. Believe me, the sharpest criticism of one single understanding man means much more to me than the thoughtless applause of the great masses.

I would, however, have wished that you who have such a keen insight [into everything] would choose another way [to reach your practical aims]. By the strength of your personal example you advise us, in a cleverly veiled manner, to go out of the way of general ignorance and [warn us against exposing ourselves to] the furious attacks of the scholarly crowd. (In this you are follow-

---

Johannes Kepler. "Letter to Galileo" (October 13, 1597) in *Johannes Kepler: Life and Letters.* Ed. Carol Baumgardt. New York: Philosophical Library, 1956, pp. 40–42.

[1]Copernicus himself realized that the novelty of his theory would invite "ridicule and scorn" from those not prepared to see the earth displaced from the center of creation. Philosophers (citing Aristotle and Ptolemy) argued for a stationary earth, along with theologians (who cited passages from the Bible — chiefly the Book of Joshua). The matter was far from academic. In 1600, Giordano Bruno was burned at the stake in Rome for his defense of the Copernican doctrine.

ing the lead of Plato and Pythagoras, our true masters.) But after the beginning of a tremendous enterprise has been made in our time, and furthered by so many learned mathematicians, and after the statement that the earth moves can no longer be regarded as something new, would it not be better to pull the rolling wagon to its destination with united effort. . . . For it is not only you Italians who do not believe that they move unless they feel it, but we in Germany, too, in no way make ourselves popular with this idea. Yet there are ways in which we protect ourselves against these difficulties. . . .

Be of good cheer, Galileo, and appear in public. If I am not mistaken there are only a few among the distinguished mathematicians of Europe who would dissociate themselves from us. So great is the power of truth. If Italy seems less suitable for your publication and if you have to expect difficulties there, perhaps Germany will offer us more freedom. But enough of this. Please let me know, at least privately if you do not want to do so publicly, what you have discovered in favor of Copernicus. . . .

Galileo would indeed publish his findings, but not before he secured a telescope and trained it on the heavens, where he discovered the presence of sunspots, an irregular lunar terrain, and the existence of moons in orbit around Saturn. His discoveries proved for him the correctness of the Copernican system, and he published his results in *The Starry Messenger* (1610), writing in a vernacular Italian that won him popular support. Academics who subscribed to the Aristotelian and Ptolemaic models of the universe were alarmed and mounted an attack by alerting church authorities and denouncing Copernicanism as running contrary to the teaching of Holy Scripture that the sun revolved around the earth, as evidenced in the Book of Joshua. (Religious objections to Copernicanism are treated more fully in the introduction to "The Church Responds," p. 100.)

Concerned by these attacks, Galileo — who was himself a devoted Catholic — began to write letters in which he defended himself and his position, claiming that a distinction should be maintained between truth revealed by Scripture and truth discovered through scientific inquiry. One such letter, written in 1615, was addressed to "Madame Christina of Lorraine, Grand Duchess of Tuscany" and mother of Galileo's patron, the Grand Duke. (Galileo had left Padua to return to his birthplace, Pisa, and conduct research free from the responsibilities of teaching.) The first part of Galileo's long letter to the Grand Duchess is presented below. The discoveries to which he alludes in the first paragraph are the ones announced in his *Starry Messenger*.

LETTER TO THE GRAND DUCHESS CHRISTINA

Some years ago, as Your Serene Highness well knows, I discovered in the heavens many things that had not been seen before our own age. The novelty of these things, as well as some consequences which followed from them in contradiction to the physical notions commonly held among academic philosophers, stirred up against me no small number of professors — as if I had placed these things in the sky with my own hands in order to upset nature and overturn the sciences. They seemed to forget that the increase of known truths stimulates the investigation, establishment, and growth of the arts; not their diminution or destruction.

Showing a greater fondness for their own opinions than for truth, they sought to deny and disprove the new things which, if they had cared to look for themselves, their own senses would have demonstrated to them. To this end they hurled various charges and published numerous writings filled with vain arguments, and they made the grave mistake of sprinkling these with passages taken from places in the Bible which they had failed to understand properly, and which were ill suited to their purposes.

These men would perhaps not have fallen into such error had they but paid attention to a most useful doctrine of St. Augustine's, relative to our making positive statements about things which are obscure and hard to understand by means of reason alone. Speaking of a certain physical conclusion about the heavenly bodies, he wrote: "Now keeping always our respect for moderation in grave piety, we ought not to believe anything inadvisedly on a dubious point, lest in favor to our error we conceive a prejudice against something that truth hereafter may reveal to be not contrary in any way to the sacred books of either the Old or the New Testament."[1]

Well, the passage of time has revealed to everyone the truths that I previously set forth; and, together with the truth of the facts, there has come to light the great difference in attitude between those who simply and dispassionately refused to admit the discoveries to be true, and those who combined with their incredulity some reckless passion of their own. Men who were well grounded in astronomical and physical science were

Galileo Galilei. "Letter to the Grand Duchess Christina" in *Discoveries and Opinions of Galileo.* Trans. Stillman Drake. Garden City: Doubleday, 1957, pp. 175–188.

[1]*De Genesi ad literam,* end of bk. ii. (Citations of theological works are taken from Galileo's marginal notes, without verification.) [Drake] All other footnotes have been prepared by the translator of Galileo's "Letter," Stillman Drake. [Behrens and Rosen]

persuaded as soon as they received my first message. There were others who denied them or remained in doubt only because of their novel and unexpected character, and because they had not yet had the opportunity to see for themselves. These men have by degrees come to be satisfied. But some, besides allegiance to their original error, possess I know not what fanciful interest in remaining hostile not so much toward the things in question as toward their discoverer. No longer being able to deny them, these men now take refuge in obstinate silence, but being more than ever exasperated by that which has pacified and quieted other men, they divert their thoughts to other fancies and seek new ways to damage me.

I should pay no more attention to them than to those who previously   4
contradicted me — at whom I always laugh, being assured of the eventual outcome — were it not that in their new calumnies and persecutions I perceive that they do not stop at proving themselves more learned than I am (a claim which I scarcely contest), but go so far as to cast against me imputations of crimes which must be, and are, more abhorrent to me than death itself. I cannot remain satisfied merely to know that the injustice of this is recognized by those who are acquainted with these men and with me, as perhaps it is not known to others.

Persisting in their original resolve to destroy me and everything mine   5
by any means they can think of, these men are aware of my views in astronomy and philosophy. They know that as to the arrangement of the parts of the universe, I hold the sun to be situated motionless in the center of the revolution of the celestial orbs while the earth rotates on its axis and revolves about the sun. They know also that I support this position not only by refuting the arguments of Ptolemy and Aristotle, but by producing many counterarguments; in particular, some which relate to physical effects whose causes can perhaps be assigned in no other way. In addition there are astronomical arguments derived from many things in my new celestial discoveries that plainly confute the Ptolemaic system while admirably agreeing with and confirming the contrary hypothesis. Possibly because they are disturbed by the known truth of other propositions of mine which differ from those commonly held, and therefore mistrusting their defense so long as they confine themselves to the field of philosophy, these men have resolved to fabricate a shield for their fallacies out of the mantle of pretended religion and the authority of the Bible. These they apply, with little judgment, to the refutation of arguments that they do not understand and have not even listened to.

First they have endeavored to spread the opinion that such proposi-   6
tions in general are contrary to the Bible and are consequently damnable and heretical. They know that it is human nature to take up causes whereby a man may oppress his neighbor, no matter how unjustly, rather than those from which a man may receive some just encouragement. Hence they have had no trouble in finding men who would preach the

damnability and heresy of the new doctrine from their very pulpits with unwonted confidence, thus doing impious and inconsiderate injury not only to that doctrine and its followers but to all mathematics and mathematicians in general. Next, becoming bolder, and hoping (though vainly) that this seed which first took root in their hypocritical minds would send out branches and ascend to heaven, they began scattering rumors among the people that before long this doctrine would be condemned by the supreme authority. They know, too, that official condemnation would not only suppress the two propositions which I have mentioned, but would render damnable all other astronomical and physical statements and observations that have any necessary relation or connection with these.

In order to facilitate their designs, they seek so far as possible (at least among the common people) to make this opinion seem new and to belong to me alone. They pretend not to know that its author, or rather its restorer and confirmer, was Nicolaus Copernicus; and that he was not only a Catholic, but a priest and a canon. He was in fact so esteemed by the church that when the Lateran Council under Leo X took up the correction of the church calendar, Copernicus was called to Rome from the most remote parts of Germany to undertake its reform. At that time the calendar was defective because the true measures of the year and the lunar month were not exactly known. The Bishop of Culm,[2] then superintendent of this matter, assigned Copernicus to seek more light and greater certainty concerning the celestial motions by means of constant study and labor. With Herculean toil he set his admirable mind to this task, and he made such great progress in this science and brought our knowledge of the heavenly motions to such precision that he became celebrated as an astronomer. Since that time not only has the calendar been regulated by his teachings, but tables of all the motions of the planets have been calculated as well. *7*

Having reduced his system into six books, he published these at the instance of the Cardinal of Capua[3] and the Bishop of Culm. And since he has assumed his laborious enterprise by order of the supreme pontiff, he dedicated this book *On the celestial revolutions* to Pope Paul III. When printed, the book was accepted by the holy Church, and it has been read and studied by everyone without the faintest hint of any objection ever being conceived against its doctrines. Yet now that manifest experiences and necessary proofs have shown them to be well grounded, persons exist who would strip the author of his reward without so much as looking at his book, and add the shame of having him pronounced a heretic. All this they would do merely to satisfy their personal displeasure conceived with- *8*

---

[2]Tiedmann Giese, to whom Copernicus referred in his preface as "that scholar, my good friend."

[3]Nicholas Schoenberg, spoken of by Copernicus as "celebrated in all fields of scholarship."

out any cause against another man, who has no interest in Copernicus beyond approving his teachings.

Now as to the false aspersions which they so unjustly seek to cast upon 9
me, I have thought it necessary to justify myself in the eyes of all men, whose judgment in matters of religion and of reputation I must hold in great esteem. I shall therefore discourse of the particulars which these men produce to make this opinion detested and to have it condemned not merely as false but as heretical. To this end they make a shield of their hypocritical zeal for religion. They go about invoking the Bible, which they would have minister to their deceitful purposes. Contrary to the sense of the Bible and the intention of the holy Fathers, if I am not mistaken, they would extend such authorities until even in purely physical matters — where faith is not involved — they would have us altogether abandon reason and the evidence of our senses in favor of some biblical passage, though under the surface meaning of its words this passage may contain a different sense.

I hope to show that I proceed with much greater piety than they do, 10
when I argue not against condemning this book, but against condemning it in the way they suggest — that is, without understanding it, weighing it, or so much as reading it. For Copernicus never discusses matters of religion or faith, nor does he use arguments that depend in any way upon the authority of sacred writings which he might have interpreted erroneously. He stands always upon physical conclusions pertaining to the celestial motions, and deals with them by astronomical and geometrical demonstrations, founded primarily upon sense experiences and very exact observations. He did not ignore the Bible, but he knew very well that if his doctrine were proved, then it could not contradict the Scriptures when they were rightly understood. And thus at the end of his letter of dedication, addressing the pope, he said:

"If there should chance to be any exegetes ignorant of mathematics 11
who pretend to skill in that discipline, and dare to condemn and censure this hypothesis of mine upon the authority of some scriptural passage twisted to their purpose, I value them not, but disdain their unconsidered judgment. For it is known that Lactantius — a poor mathematician though in other respects a worthy author — writes very childishly about the shape of the earth when he scoffs at those who affirm it to be a globe. Hence it should not seem strange to the ingenious if people of that sort should in turn deride me. But mathematics is written for mathematicians, by whom, if I am not deceived, these labors of mine will be recognized as contributing something to their domain, as also to that of the Church over which Your Holiness now reigns."[4]

---

[4]*De Revolutionibus* (Nuremberg, 1543), f. iiii. [See page 67, paragraphs 16 & 17.]

Such are the people who labor to persuade us that an author like Copernicus may be condemned without being read, and who produce various authorities from the Bible, from theologians, and from Church Councils to make us believe that this is not only lawful but commendable. Since I hold these to be of supreme authority, I consider it rank temerity for anyone to contradict them — when employed according to the usage of the holy Church. Yet I do not believe it is wrong to speak out when there is reason to suspect that other men wish, for some personal motive, to produce and employ such authorities for purposes quite different from the sacred intention of the holy Church.   *12*

Therefore I declare (and my sincerity will make itself manifest) not only that I mean to submit myself freely and renounce any errors into which I may fall in this discourse through ignorance of matters pertaining to religion, but that I do not desire in these matters to engage in disputes with anyone, even on points that are disputable. My goal is this alone; that if, among errors that may abound in these considerations of a subject remote from my profession, there is anything that may be serviceable to the holy Church in making a decision concerning the Copernican system, it may be taken and utilized as seems best to the superiors. And if not, let my book be torn and burnt, as I neither intend nor pretend to gain from it any fruit that is not pious and Catholic. And though many of the things I shall reprove have been heard by my own ears, I shall freely grant to those who have spoken them that they never said them, if that is what they wish, and I shall confess myself to have been mistaken. Hence let whatever I reply be addressed not to them, but to whoever may have held such opinions.   *13*

The reason produced for condemning the opinion that the earth moves and the sun stands still is that in many places in the Bible one may read that the sun moves and the earth stands still. Since the Bible cannot err, it follows as a necessary consequence that anyone takes an erroneous and heretical position who maintains that the sun is inherently motionless and the earth movable.   *14*

With regard to this argument, I think in the first place that it is very pious to say and prudent to affirm that the holy Bible can never speak untruth — whenever its true meaning is understood. But I believe nobody will deny that it is often very abstruse, and may say things which are quite different from what its bare words signify. Hence in expounding the Bible if one were always to confine oneself to the unadorned grammatical meaning, one might fall into error. Not only contradictions and propositions far from true might thus be made to appear in the Bible, but even grave heresies and follies. Thus it would be necessary to assign to God feet, hands, and eyes, as well as corporeal and human affections, such as anger, repentance, hatred, and sometimes even the forgetting of things past and ignorance of those to come. These propositions uttered by the Holy Ghost   *15* were set down in that manner by the sacred scribes in order to accommodate them to the capacities of the common people, who are rude and unlearned. For the sake of those who deserve to be separated from the herd, it is necessary that wise expositors should produce the true senses of such passages, together with the special reasons for which they were set down in these words. This doctrine is so widespread and so definite with all theologians that it would be superfluous to adduce evidence for it.

Hence I think that I may reasonably conclude that whenever the Bible   16
has occasion to speak of any physical conclusion (especially those which are very abstruse and hard to understand), the rule has been observed of avoiding confusion in the minds of the common people which would render them contumacious toward the higher mysteries. Now the Bible, merely to condescend to popular capacity, has not hesitated to obscure some very important pronouncements, attributing to God himself some qualities extremely remote from (and even contrary to) His essence. Who, then, would positively declare that this principle has been set aside, and the Bible has confined itself rigorously to the bare and restricted sense of its words, when speaking but casually of the earth, of water, of the sun, or of any other created thing? Especially in view of the fact that these things in no way concern the primary purpose of the sacred writings, which is the service of God and the salvation of souls — matters infinitely beyond the comprehension of the common people.

This being granted, I think that in discussions of physical problems we   17
ought to begin not from the authority of scriptural passages, but from sense-experiences and necessary demonstrations; for the holy Bible and the phenomena of nature proceed alike from the divine Word, the former as the dictate of the Holy Ghost and the latter as the observant executrix of God's commands. It is necessary for the Bible, in order to be accommodated to the understanding of every man, to speak many things which appear to differ from the absolute truth so far as the bare meaning of the words is concerned. But Nature, on the other hand, is inexorable and immutable; she never transgresses the laws imposed upon her, or cares a whit whether her abstruse reasons and methods of operation are understandable to men. For that reason it appears that nothing physical which sense-experience sets before our eyes, or which necessary demonstrations prove to us, ought to be called in question (much less condemned) upon the testimony of biblical passages which may have some different meaning beneath their words. For the Bible is not chained in every expression to conditions as strict as those which govern all physical effects; nor is God any less excellently revealed in Nature's actions than in the sacred statements of the Bible. Perhaps this is what Tertullian meant by these words:

"We conclude that God is known first through Nature, and then again,   18 more particularly, by doctrine; by Nature in His Works, and by doctrine in His revealed word."[5]

From this I do not mean to infer that we need not have an extraordi- *19*
nary esteem for the passages of holy Scripture. On the contrary, having arrived at any certainties in physics, we ought to utilize these as the most appropriate aids in the true exposition of the Bible and in the investigation of those meanings which are necessarily contained therein, for these must be concordant with demonstrated truths. I should judge that the authority of the Bible was designed to persuade men of those articles and proposi-tions which, surpassing all human reasoning, could not be made credible by science, or by any other means than through the very mouth of the Holy Spirit.

Yet even in those propositions which are not matters of faith, this au- *20*
thority ought to be preferred over that of all human writings which are supported only by bare assertions or probable arguments, and not set forth in a demonstrative way. This I hold to be necessary and proper to the same extent that divine wisdom surpasses all human judgment and conjecture.

But I do not feel obliged to believe that that same God who has en- *21*
dowed us with senses, reason, and intellect has intended to forgo their use and by some other means to give us knowledge which we can attain by them. He would not require us to deny sense and reason in physical mat-ters which are set before our eyes and minds by direct experience or nec-essary demonstrations. This must be especially true in those sciences of which but the faintest trace (and that consisting of conclusions) is to be found in the Bible. Of astronomy, for instance, so little is found that none of the planets except Venus are so much as mentioned, and this only once or twice under the name of "Lucifer." If the sacred scribes had had any intention of teaching people certain arrangements and motions of the heavenly bodies, or had they wished us to derive such knowledge from the Bible, then in my opinion they would not have spoken of these matters so sparingly in comparison with the infinite number of admirable conclu-sions which are demonstrated in that science. Far from pretending to teach us the constitution and motions of the heavens and the stars, with their shapes, magnitudes, and distances, the authors of the Bible intentionally forbore to speak of these things, though all were quite well known to them. Such is the opinion of the holiest and most learned Fathers, and in St. Augustine we find the following words:

"It is likewise commonly asked what we may believe about the form *22*
and shape of the heavens according to the Scriptures, for many contend much about these matters. But with superior prudence our authors have

---

[5]*Adversus Marcionem*, ii, 18. [Galileo]

forborne to speak of this, as in no way furthering the student with respect to a blessed life — and, more important still, as taking up much of that time which should be spent in holy exercises. What is it to me whether heaven, like a sphere, surrounds the earth on all sides as a mass balanced in the center of the universe, or whether like a dish it merely covers and overcasts the earth? Belief in Scripture is urged rather for the reason we have often mentioned; that is, in order that no one, through ignorance of divine passages, finding anything in our Bibles or hearing anything cited from them of such a nature as may seem to oppose manifest conclusions, should be induced to suspect their truth when they teach, relate, and deliver more profitable matters. Hence let it be said briefly, touching the form of heaven, that our authors knew the truth but the Holy Spirit did not desire that men should learn things that are useful to no one for salvation."[6]

 The same disregard of these sacred authors toward beliefs about the phenomena of the celestial bodies is repeated to us by St. Augustine in his next chapter. On the question whether we are to believe that the heaven moves or stands still, he writes thus:

 "Some of the brethren raise a question concerning the motion of heaven, whether it is fixed or moved. If it is moved, they say, how is it a firmament? If it stands still, how do these stars which are held fixed in it go round from east to west, the more northerly performing shorter circuits near the pole, so that heaven (if there is another pole unknown to us) may seem to revolve upon some axis, or (if there is no other pole) may be thought to move as a discus? To these men I reply that it would require many subtle and profound reasonings to find out which of these things is actually so; but to undertake this and discuss it is consistent neither with my leisure nor with the duty of those whom I desire to instruct in essential matters more directly conducing to their salvation and to the benefit of the holy Church."[7]

 From these things it follows as a necessary consequence that, since the Holy Ghost did not intend to teach us whether heaven moves or stands still, whether its shape is spherical or like a discus or extended in a plane, nor whether the earth is located at its center or off to one side, then so much the less was it intended to settle for us any other conclusion of the same kind. And the motion or rest of the earth and the sun is so closely linked with the things just named, that without a determination of the one, neither side can be taken in the other matters. Now if the Holy Spirit has purposely neglected to teach us propositions of this sort as irrelevant to

23

24

25

---

[6] *De Genesi ad literam* ii, 9. Galileo has noted also: "The same is to be read in Peter the Lombard, master of opinions."

[7] *Ibid.*, ii, 10. [Galileo]

the highest goal (that is, to our salvation), how can anyone affirm that it is obligatory to take sides on them, and that one belief is required by faith, while the other side is erroneous? Can an opinion be heretical and yet have no concern with the salvation of souls? Can the Holy Ghost be asserted not to have intended teaching us something that does concern our salvation? I would say here something that was heard from an ecclesiastic of the most eminent degree: "That the intention of the Holy Ghost is to teach us how one goes to heaven, not how heaven goes."[8]

But let us again consider the degree to which necessary demonstrations and sense experiences ought to be respected in physical conclusions, and the authority they have enjoyed at the hands of holy and learned theologians. From among a hundred attestations I have selected the following: 26

"We must also take heed, in handling the doctrine of Moses, that we altogether avoid saying positively and confidently anything which contradicts manifest experiences and the reasoning of philosophy or the other sciences. For since every truth is in agreement with all other truth, the truth of Holy Writ cannot be contrary to the solid reasons and experiences of human knowledge."[9]   27

And in St. Augustine we read: "If anyone shall set the authority of Holy Writ against clear and manifest reason, he who does this knows not what he has undertaken; for he opposes to the truth not the meaning of the Bible, which is beyond his comprehension, but rather his own interpretation; not what is in the Bible, but what he has found in himself and imagines to be there."[10]   28

This granted, and it being true that two truths cannot contradict one another, it is the function of wise expositors to seek out the true senses of scriptural texts. These will unquestionably accord with the physical conclusions which manifest sense and necessary demonstrations have previously made certain to us. Now the Bible, as has been remarked, admits in many places expositions that are remote from the signification of the words for reasons we have already given. Moreover, we are unable to affirm that all interpreters of the Bible speak by divine inspiration, for if that were so there would exist no differences between them about the sense of a given passage. Hence I should think it would be the part of prudence not to permit anyone to usurp scriptural texts and force them in some way to maintain any physical conclusion to be true, when at some future time the senses and demonstrative or necessary reasons may show the contrary.   29

---

[8]A marginal note by Galileo assigns this epigram to Cardinal Baronius (1538–1607). Baronius visited Padua with Cardinal Bellarmine in 1598, and Galileo probably met him at that time.

[9]Pererius on Genesis, near the beginning.

[10]In the seventh letter to the Marcellinus.

Who indeed will set bounds to human ingenuity? Who will assert that everything in the universe capable of being perceived is already discovered and known? Let us rather confess quite truly that "Those truths which we know are very few in comparison with those which we do not know."

We have it from the very mouth of the Holy Ghost that God delivered   30
up the world to disputations, *so that man cannot find out the work that God hath done from the beginning even to the end.*[11] In my opinion no one, in contradiction to that dictum, should close the road to free philosophizing about mundane and physical things, as if everything had already been discovered and revealed with certainty. Nor should it be considered rash not to be satisfied with those opinions which have become common. No one should be scorned in physical disputes for not holding to the opinions which happen to please other people best, especially concerning problems which have been debated among the greatest philosophers for thousands of years. One of these is the stability of the sun and mobility of the earth, a doctrine believed by Pythagoras and all his followers, by Heracleides of Pontus[12] (who was one of them), by Philolaus the teacher of Plato,[13] and by Plato himself according to Aristotle. Plutarch writes in his *Life of Numa* that Plato, when he had grown old, said it was most absurd to believe otherwise.[14] The same doctrine was held by Aristarchus of Samos,[15] as Archimedes tells us; by Seleucus the mathematician, by Nicetas the philosopher (on the testimony of Cicero), and by many others. Finally this opinion has been amplified and confirmed with many observations and demonstrations by Nicolaus Copernicus.

---

[11]Ecclesiastes 3:11.

[12]Heracleides was born about 390 B.C. and is said to have attended lectures by Aristotle at Athens. He believed that the earth rotated on its axis, but not that it moved around the sun. He also discovered that Mercury and Venus revolve around the sun, and may have developed a system similar to that of Tycho.

[13]Philolaus, an early follower of Pythagoras, flourished at Thebes toward the end of the fifth century B.C. Although a contemporary of Socrates, the teacher of Plato, he had nothing to do with Plato's instruction. According to Philolaus the earth revolved around a central fire, but not about the sun.

[14]"Plato held opinion in that age, that the earth was in another place than in the very middest, and that the centre of the world, as the most honourable place, did appertain to some other of more worthy substance than the earth." (Trans. Sir Thomas North.) This tradition is no longer accepted.

[15]Aristarchus (ca. 310–230 B.C.) was the true forerunner of Copernicus in antiquity, and not the Pythagoreans as was generally believed in Galileo's time.

REVIEW QUESTIONS

1. Why has Galileo written to the Grand Duchess?
2. According to Galileo, what was the foundation upon which Copernicus built his theories? In what ways does Galileo find Copernicus's method of proceeding exemplary?
3. Cite statements in the letter that demonstrate Galileo's desire to be both a man of science and a man of religion.
4. How, according to Galileo, did the "rude and unlearned" state of the "common people" affect the way in which the Bible was recorded? How is explanation important to Galileo's argument?
5. In what ways does Galileo believe a discussion of physical problems should proceed?
6. Nature and the Bible both "proceed from the divine word," according to Galileo. Yet the two differ. How? And how does this difference bear on Galileo's argument?
7. The letter to the Grand Duchess is an argument. In your own words, state what you take to be the thesis of the argument and, in outline form, trace the argument through its development.

DISCUSSION AND WRITING QUESTIONS

1. Galileo complains bitterly about critics who "have resolved to fabricate a shield for their fallacies out of the mantle of pretended religion and the authority of the Bible." Can you name any 20th century figures against whom Galileo might make the same criticism? On what basis?
2. Discuss the ways in which Galileo argues for an allegorical interpretation of the Bible. Given Galileo's position, why *must* he argue in this way?
3. Galileo clearly wants to be both a man of science and a man of religion. (See your answer to Review Question 3.) Do you believe that there exists an opposition between the two pursuits? Attempt to explain how a scientist, committed to discovering truth through direct inquiry, can also be religious — that is, accept certain truths as a matter of faith.
4. Galileo believed that the Bible cannot err. What is your view? Explain.

THE CHURCH RESPONDS

Two official church documents follow, the first condemning the views of Copernicus, the second condemning the man who supported those views: Galileo. Over 350 years later, we read the condemnations and wonder why authorities in Rome would have bothered to dispute so obvious a fact as the earth's motion. It is helpful to remember that in the early 17th century, what we take to be a fact was a novel idea; moreover, it was an idea that, if accepted, undermined the received truth of the Bible. We realize now that a battle was being fought for the freedom to explore the natural world on the basis of what Galileo called "sense-experiences and necessary demonstrations." The following documents are as much an account of that battle as they are condemnations of the heliocentric model.

SUPRESSION OF *ON THE REVOLUTION OF HEAVENLY SPHERES* (1616)

Albert Einstein found in Galileo's manner the "heavenly maliciousness" of one who derived "instinctive pleasure from [doing] battle with others." Some have described that same manner as pugnacious, some as brilliantly witty and satirical. However one characterizes the man, there is no denying that Galileo publicized his views and attacked his enemies with vigor. He often wrote his treatises in the vernacular Italian (instead of Latin, the standard academic language) so as to reach as wide an audience as possible.

Having posted his letter to the Grand Duchess, Galileo traveled to Rome in 1616 to make his case personally that the church allow for the discovery of truth through science. Where such truth conflicted with Scripture, Scripture would need a new, allegorical interpretation. Some church authorities were sympathetic to these arguments, though the Vatican's chief theologian, Cardinal Bellarmine, was not. The Cardinal and his allies wanted to suppress the challenge of Copernicanism; they not only denied Galileo his requests, they convened the Congregation of the Index and formally prohibited Catholics from reading *On the Revolution of Heavenly Spheres* until such time as certain "errors" in the document were corrected.

What were the church's objections to a heliocentric universe? First, the Copernican account of the planets directly contradicted passages from the Scriptures, most flagrantly the one in which Joshua makes his famous command: "Sun, stand thou still, stand thou still" (Joshua: 10:12). Implicit in the command is the belief that the sun *moves* — that it revolves around the earth. If divinely inspired Scripture could be wrong on this point, then the truth of other points might be challenged as well, and this the church would not allow. From Rome, a friend of Galileo's, Giovanni Ciampoli, wrote and warned him as follows:

Cardinal Barberini, who, as you know from experience, has always admired your worth, told me only yesterday evening that with respect to these opinions he would like greater caution in not going beyond the arguments used by Ptolemy and Copernicus, and finally in not exceeding the limitations of physics and mathematics. For to explain the Scriptures is claimed by theologians as their field, and if new things are brought in, even by an admirable mind, not everyone has the dispassionate faculty of taking them just as they are said. One man amplifies, the next one alters, and what came from the author's own mouth becomes so transformed in spreading that he will no longer recognize it as his own. And I know what he means. Your opinion regarding the phenomena of light and shadow in the bright and dark spots of the moon creates some analogy between the lunar globe and the earth; somebody expands on this, and says that you place human inhabitants on the moon; the next fellow starts to dispute how these can be descended from Adam, or how they can have come off Noah's ark, and many other extravagances you never dreamed of. Hence to declare frequently that one places oneself under the authority of those who have jurisdiction over the minds of men in the interpretation of Scripture is to remove this pretext for other people's malice. . . .

Cardinal Bellarmine, the Vatican's chief theologian, had also expressed his views:

I have always believed Copernicus [spoke hypothetically].[1] For to say that assuming the earth moves and the sun stands still saves all the appearances better than eccentrics and epicycles is to speak well. This has no danger in it, and it suffices for mathematicians. But to wish to affirm that the sun is really fixed in the center of the heavens and merely turns upon itself without traveling from east to west, and that the earth is situated in the third sphere and revolves very swiftly around the sun, is a very dangerous thing, not only by irritating all the theologians and scholastic philosophers, but also by injuring our holy faith and making the sacred Scripture false. . . .

Second. I say that, as you know, the Council [of Trent] would prohibit expounding the Bible contrary to the common agreement of the holy Fathers. And if Your Reverence would read not only all their works but the commentaries of modern writers on Genesis, Psalms, Ecclesiastes, and Joshua, you would find that all agree in expounding literally that the sun is in the heavens and travels swiftly around the earth, while the earth is far from the heavens

---

Giovanni Ciampoli. "Letter to Galileo" in *Discoveries and Opinions of Galileo*. Trans. Stillman Drake. Garden City: Doubleday, 1957, pp. 158–159.

Cardinal Bellarmine. "Letter to Foscarini" in *Discoveries and Opinions of Galileo*. Trans. Stillman Drake. Garden City: Doubleday, 1957, pp. 163–164.

[1]Bellarmine could reasonably assume this because of an anonymous introduction to *On the Revolution of Heavenly Spheres*, written by the sympathetic Andreas Osiander, who assisted in the publication of the book and sought to disarm criticism by stating that Copernicus's discussion amounted to so many hypotheses that were never intended "to persuade anyone of their truth but only [to] . . . provide a correct basis for calculation." Osiander was later identified by Johannes Kepler as author of the introduction.

and remains motionless in the center of the [universe]. Now consider whether, in all prudence, the Church could support the giving to Scripture of a sense contrary to the holy Fathers and all the Greek and Latin expositors. Nor may it be replied that this is not a matter of faith, since if it is not so with regard to the subject matter, it is with regard to those who have spoken. Thus that man would be just as much a heretic who denied that Abraham had two sons and Jacob twelve, as one who denied the virgin birth of Christ, for both are declared by the Holy Ghost through the mouths of the prophets and apostles.

Third. I say that if there were a true demonstration that the sun was in the center of the universe and the earth in the third sphere, and that the sun did not go around the earth but the earth went around the sun, then it would be necessary to use careful consideration in explaining the Scriptures that seemed contrary, and we should rather have to say that we do not understand them than to say that something is false which had been proven. But I do not think there is any such demonstration, since none has been shown to me. To demonstrate that the appearances are saved by assuming the sun at the center and the earth in the heavens is not the same thing as to demonstrate that in fact the sun is in the center and the earth in the heavens. I believe that the first demonstration may exist, but I have very grave doubts about the second; and in case of doubt one may not abandon the Holy Scriptures as expounded by the holy Fathers. I add that the words *The sun also riseth, and the sun goeth down, and hasteth to the place where he ariseth*[2] were written by Solomon, who not only spoke by divine inspiration, but was a man wise above all others, and learned in the human sciences and in the knowledge of all created things, which wisdom he had from God; so it is not very likely that he would affirm something that was contrary to demonstrated truth, or truth that might be demonstrated. And if you tell me that Solomon spoke according to the appearances, and that it seems to us that the sun goes round when the earth turns, as it seems to one aboard ship that the beach moves away, I shall answer thus. Anyone who departs from the beach, though to him it appears that the beach moves away, yet knows that this is an error and corrects it, seeing clearly that the ship moves and not the beach; but as to the sun and earth, no sage has needed to correct the error, since he clearly experiences that the earth stands still and that his eye is not deceived when it judges the sun to move, just as he is likewise not deceived when it judges that the moon and the stars move. And that is enough for the present.

Galileo's observations with his telescope and his open support of the Copernican system helped heliocentrism to gain currency — not as a hypothesis, but as the truth — the implications of which for the church were enormous: if Copernicus and Galileo were correct and the earth was, like Venus, Mars, Mercury, and Jupiter, a planet, then what was to prevent these other heavenly bodies, holding the same planetary status as the earth, from having their *own* inhabitants? And if they were inhabited, what then was God's relationship with those beings? If intelligent life elsewhere in the universe were allowed, then the salvation of souls on earth — the principal business of the church — could no longer be assumed as having a privi-

---

[2]Ecclesiastes 1:5.

leged significance in the larger scheme of things. Just possibly, God had created the universe for some reason other than providing for the delight and ultimate salvation of man. As Karl von Gebler put it in *Galileo Galilei and the Roman Curia,* "the bare possibility of a number of inhabited worlds could but imperil the first principles of Christian philosophy."

With so much at stake for both sides in the argument, the battle lines were clearly drawn. Already in 1600, the Copernican philosopher Giordano Bruno had been burned at the stake in Rome for having declared the universe to be infinite, populated with an infinity of worlds. With the passage of time, Galileo had hoped for a more enlightened reception; but on March 5, 1616, the Holy Congregation of the Index, charged with protecting the faithful from ideas that would endanger their spiritual well-being, condemned *On the Revolution of Heavenly Spheres:*

> And whereas it has also come to the knowledge of the said Congregation, that the Pythagorean doctrine — which is false and altogether opposed to Holy Scripture — of the motion of the earth, and the quiescence of the sun, which is also taught by Nicolaus Copernicus in *De Revolutionibus orbium Cœlestium,* and by Diego di Zuñiga in (his book on) Job, is now being spread abroad and accepted by many — as may be seen from a certain letter of a Carmelite Father, entitled, *Letter of the Rev. Father Paolo Antonio Foscarini, Carmelite, on the opinion of the Pythagoreans and of Copernicus concerning the motion of the earth, and the stability of the sun, and the new Pythagorean system of the world, at Naples, printed by Lazzaro Scorriggio,* 1615: wherein the said father attempts to show that the aforesaid doctrine of the quiescence of the sun in the centre of the world, and of the earth's motion, is consonant with truth and is not opposed to Holy Scripture. Therefore, in order that this opinon may not insinuate itself any further to the prejudice of Catholic truth, the Holy Congregation has decreed that the said Nicolaus Copernicus, *De Revolutionibus orbium,* and Diego di Zuñiga, on Job, be suspended until they be corrected; but that the book of the Carmelite Father, Paolo Antonio Foscarini, be altogether prohibited and condemned, and that all other works likewise, in which the same is taught, be prohibited, as by this present decree it prohibits, condemns, and suspends them all respectively. In witness whereof the present decree has been signed and sealed with the hands and with the seal of the most eminent and Reverend Lord Cardinal of St. Cecilia, Bishop of Albano, on the 5th day of March, 1616.

SENTENCE OF THE HOLY INQUISITION, PRONOUNCED ON GALILEO GALILEI (1633)

One week before the condemnation of Copernicus's treatise, Cardinal Bellarmine summoned Galileo to inform him of the coming action and to warn, in effect, that he cease and desist from publicly supporting the Copernican system. There is

Catholic Church. "The Decree of the Congregation of the Index on Writings and Books Treating the Copernican System" (March 5, 1616); "The Sentence Against Galileo and the Recantation" (June 22, 1633) in Karl Von Gebler, *Galileo Galilei and the Roman Curia.* Trans. Mrs. George Sturge. Merrick, New York: Richwood Publishing Co., 1977, pp. 84, 230–234, 243–244. (Reprint of the 1879 ed., published by C. K. Paul, London.)

some confusion as to the wording of Bellarmine's injunction. Vatican documents reveal two accounts, one dated Febrary 25, 1616, and the other February 26. The first account has Bellarmine summon Galileo and ask that he recant his belief in Copernicanism. The second account has Bellarmine issue a binding order that Galileo not "hold, teach, or defend [the Copernican system] in any way whatsoever, verbally or in writing" — to which Galileo is reported to have agreed. Historians now believe that the second account was spurious and planted by Galileo's enemies.

Seventeen years later, in 1633, the great scientist was summoned to Rome because he had written a new book in which he supported the heliocentric universe, in direct violation of the alleged prohibition of February 26, 1616. Galileo maintained that he never received such a prohibition. But the Inquisition disagreed, and cited his *Dialogue Concerning the Two Chief World Systems — Ptolemaic and Copernican* as contrary to Holy Scripture. The dialogue, ostensibly a neutral trading of views on the competing world systems, did in fact favor Copernicanism. Galileo had written the work with impressive rhetorical flourish, and his book was instantly acclaimed as a masterpiece in both scientific and literary circles throughout Europe. The church was incensed and summoned him to face Vatican authorities. He was tried by the Inquisition in Rome and convicted of being "vehemently suspected of heresy."

The text of the Inquisition's sentence follows, along with Galileo's recantation — delivered while on his knees in the Dominican Convent of St. Maria sopra la Minerva.

Galileo Galilei spent the remainder of his life under house arrest. In 1634, he published what many take to be his crowning achievement, the *Dialogue Concerning Two New Sciences,* in which he summarized his life's work in the field of mechanics. He lost his sight in 1638, and though blind for his remaining years he maintained an enthusiasm for science, dictating observations to disciples until the very end. He died in his villa at Arcetri on January 8, 1642, the same year in which Isaac Newton was born.

SENTENCE OF THE HOLY INQUISITION

WE, Gasparo del titolo di S. Croce in Gierusalemme Borgia;   *1*
   Fra Felice Centino del titolo di S. Anastasia, detto d'Ascoli;
   Guido del titolo di S. Maria del Popolo Bentivoglio;
   Fra Desiderio Scaglia del titolo di S. Carlo detto di Cremona;
   Fra Antonio Barberino detto di S. Onofrio;
   Laudivio Zacchia del titolo di S. Pietro in Vincola detto di S. Sisto;
   Berlingero del titolo di S. Agostino, Gessi;

Fabricio del titolo di S. Lorenzo in pane e perna, Verospi, chiamato
   Prete;
Francesco di S. Lorenzo in Damaso Barberino, e
Martio di S. Maria Nuova Ginetti Diaconi;

by the grace of God, cardinals of the Holy Roman Church, Inquisitors General, by the Holy Apostolic see specially deputed, against heretical depravity throughout the whole Christian Republic.

Whereas you, Galileo, son of the late Vincenzo Galilei, Florentine, aged seventy years, were in the year 1615 denounced to this Holy Office for holding as true the false doctrine taught by many, that the sun is the centre of the [universe] and immovable, and that the earth moves, and also with a diurnal motion; for having disciples to whom you taught the same doctrine; for holding correspondence with certain mathematicians of Germany concerning the same; for having printed certain letters, entitled "On the Solar Spots," wherein you developed the same doctrine as true; and for replying to the objections from the Holy Scriptures, which from time to time were urged against it, by glossing the said Scriptures according to your own meaning: and whereas there was thereupon produced the copy of a document in the form of a letter, purporting to be written by you to one formerly your disciple, and in this divers propositions are set forth,[1] following the hypothesis of Copernicus, which are contrary to the true sense and authority of Holy Scripture: 2

This Holy Tribunal being therefore desirous of proceeding against the disorder and mischief thence resulting, which went on increasing to the prejudice of the Holy Faith, by command of his Holiness and of the most eminent Lords Cardinals of this supreme and universal Inquisition, the two propositions of the stability of the sun and the motion of the earth were by the theological "Qualifiers" qualified as follows: 3

The proposition that the sun is the centre of the [universe] and does not move from its place is absurd and false philosophically and formally heretical, because it is expressly contrary to the Holy Scripture. 4

The proposition that the earth is not the centre of the [universe] and immovable, but that it moves, and also with a diurnal motion, is equally absurd and false philosophically, and theologically considered, at least erroneous in faith. 5

But whereas it was desired at that time to deal leniently with you, it was decreed at the Holy Congregation held before his Holiness on the 25th February, 1616, that his Eminence the Lord Cardinal Bellarmine should order you to abandon altogether the said false doctrine, and, in the event of your refusal, that an injunction should be imposed upon you by the 6

---

[1]Galileo's letter to Castelli of 21st December, 1613. [Von Gebler]

Commissary of the Holy Office, to give up the said doctrine, and not to teach it to others, nor to defend it, nor even discuss it; and failing your acquiescence in this injunction, that you should be imprisoned. And in execution of this decree, on the following day, at the Palace, and in the presence of his Eminence, the said Lord Cardinal Bellarmine, after being gently admonished by the said Lord Cardinal, the command was intimated to you by the Father Commissary of the Holy Office for the time before a notary and witnesses, that you were altogether to abandon the said false opinion, and not in future to defend or teach it in any way whatsoever, neither verbally nor in writing; and upon your promising to obey you were dismissed.

And in order that a doctrine so pernicious might be wholly rooted out   7
and not insinuate itself further to the grave prejudice of Catholic truth, a decree was issued by the Holy Congregation of the Index, prohibiting the books which treat of this doctrine, and declaring the doctrine itself to be false and wholly contrary to sacred and divine Scripture.

And whereas a book appeared here recently, printed last year at Flo-   8
rence, the title of which shows that you were the author, this title being: "Dialogue of Galileo Galilei on the Two Principal Systems of the World, the Ptolemaic and the Copernican"; and whereas the Holy Congregation was afterwards informed that through the publication of the said book, the false opinion of the motion of the earth and the stability of the sun was daily gaining ground; the said book was taken into careful consideration, and in it there was discovered a patent violation of the aforesaid injunction that had been imposed upon you, for in this book you have defended the said opinion previously condemned and to your face declared to be so, although in the said book you strive by various devices to produce the impression that you leave it undecided, and in express terms as probable: which however is a most grievous error, as an opinion can in no wise be probable which has been declared and defined to be contrary to Divine Scripture:

Therefore by our order you were cited before this Holy Office, where,   9
being examined upon your oath, you acknowledged the book to be written and published by you. You confessed that you began to write the said book about ten or twelve years ago, after the command had been imposed upon you as above; that you requested licence to print it, without however intimating to those who granted you this licence that you had been commanded not to hold, defend, or teach in any way whatever the doctrine in question.

You likewise confessed that the writing of the said book is in various   10
places drawn up in such a form that the reader might fancy that the arguments brought forward on the false side are rather calculated by their cogency to compel conviction than to be easy of refutation; excusing yourself for having fallen into an error, as you alleged, so foreign to your intention, by the fact that you had written in dialogue, and by the natural compla-

cency that every man feels in regard to his own subtleties, and in showing himself more clever than the generality of men, in devising, even on behalf of false propositions, ingenious and plausible arguments.

And a suitable term having been assigned to you to prepare your de- *11* fence, you produced a certificate in the handwriting of his Eminence the Lord Cardinal Bellarmine, procured by you, as you asserted, in order to defend yourself against the calumnies of your enemies, who gave out that you had abjured and had been punished by the Holy Office; in which certificate it is declared that you had not abjured and had not been punished, but merely that the declaration made by his Holiness and published by the Holy Congregation of the Index, had been announced to you, wherein it is declared that the doctrine of the motion of the earth and the stability of the sun is contrary to the Holy Scriptures, and therefore cannot be defended or held. And as in this certificate there is no mention of the two articles of the injunction, namely, the order not "to teach" and "in any way," you represented that we ought to believe that in the course of fourteen or sixteen years you had lost all memory of them; and that this was why you said nothing of the injunction when you requested permission to print your book. And all this you urged not by way of excuse for your error, but that it might be set down to a vainglorious ambition rather than to malice. But this certificate produced by you in your defence has only aggravated your delinquency, since although it is there stated that the said opinion is contrary to Holy Scripture, you have nevertheless dared to discuss and defend it and to argue its probability; nor does the licence artfully and cunningly extorted by you avail you anything, since you did not notify the command imposed upon you.

And whereas it appeared to us that you had not stated the full truth *12* with regard to your intention, we thought it necessary to subject you to a rigorous examination, at which (without prejudice, however, to the matters confessed by you, and set forth as above, with regard to your said intention) you answered like a good Catholic. Therefore, having seen and maturely considered the merits of this your cause, together with your confessions and excuses above mentioned, and all that ought justly to be seen and considered, we have arrived at the underwritten final sentence against you: —

Invoking, therefore, the most holy name of our Lord Jesus Christ and *13* of His most glorious Mother, and ever Virgin Mary, by this our final sentence, which sitting in judgment, with the counsel and advice of the Reverend Masters of sacred theology and Doctors of both Laws, our assessors, we deliver in these writings, in the cause and causes presently before us between the magnificent Carlo Sinceri, Doctor of both Laws, Proctor Fiscal of this Holy Office, of the one part, and you Galileo Galilei, the defendant, here present, tried and confessed as above, of the other part, — we say, pronounce, sentence, declare, that you, the said Galileo, by reason of the matters adduced in process, and by you confessed as above, have rendered yourself in the judgment of this Holy Office vehemently suspected of heresy, namely, of having believed and held the doctrine — which is false and contrary to the sacred and divine Scriptures — that the sun is the centre of the [universe] and does not move from east to west, and that the earth moves and is not the centre of the [universe]; and that an opinion may be held and defended as probable after it has been declared and defined to be contrary to Holy Scripture; and that consequently you have incurred all the censures and penalties imposed and promulgated in the sacred canons and other constitutions, general and particular, against such delinquents. From which we are content that you be absolved, provided that first, with a sincere heart, and unfeigned faith, you abjure, curse, and detest the aforesaid errors and heresies, and every other error and heresy contrary to the Catholic and Apostolic Roman Church in the form to be prescribed by us.

And in order that this your grave and pernicious error and transgression may not remain altogether unpunished, and that you may be more cautious for the future, and an example to others, that they may abstain from similar delinquencies — we ordain that the book of the *"Dialogues of Galileo Galilei"* be prohibited by public edict.   14

We condemn you to the formal prison of this Holy Office during our pleasure, and by way of salutary penance, we enjoin that for three years, to come you repeat once a week the seven penitential Psalms.   15

Reserving to ourselves full liberty to moderate, commute, or take off, in whole or in part, the aforesaid penalties and penance.   16

And so we say, pronounce, sentence, declare, ordain, condemn and reserve, in this and any other better way and form which we can and may lawfully employ.   17

So we the undersigned Cardinals pronounce.   18

> F. Cardinalis de Asculo.
> G. Cardinalis Bentiuolus.
> Fr. Cardinalis de Cremona.
> Fr. Antonius Cardinalis S. Honuphrij.
> B. Cardinalis Gypsius.
> Fr. Cardinalis Verospius.
> M. Cardinalis Ginettus.

THE RECANTATION OF GALILEO

I, Galileo Galilei, son of the late Vincenzo Galilei, Florentine, aged seventy years, arraigned personally before this tribunal, and kneeling before you, most Eminent and Reverend Lord Cardinals, Inquisitors general against heretical depravity throughout the whole Christian Republic, having before my eyes and touching with my hands, the holy Gospels — swear that I have always believed, do now believe, and by God's help will for the future believe, all that is held, preached, and taught by the Holy Catholic and Apostolic Roman Church. But whereas — after an injunction had been judicially intimated to me by this Holy Office, to the effect that I must altogether abandon the false opinion that the sun is the centre of the [universe] and immovable, and that the earth is not the centre of the [universe], and moves, and that I must not hold, defend, or teach in any way whatsoever, verbally or in writing, the said doctrine, and after it had been notified to me that the said doctrine was contrary to Holy Scripture — I wrote and printed a book in which I discuss this doctrine already condemned, and adduce arguments of great cogency in its favour, without presenting any solution of these; and for this cause I have been pronounced by the Holy Office to be vehemently suspected of heresy, that is to say, of having held and believed that the sun is the centre of the [universe] and immovable, and that the earth is not the centre and moves: — *1*

Therefore, desiring to remove from the minds of your Eminences, and of all faithful Christians, this strong suspicion, reasonably conceived against me, with sincere heart and unfeigned faith I abjure, curse, and detest the aforesaid errors and heresies, and generally every other error and sect whatsoever contrary to the said Holy Church; and I swear that in future I will never again say or assert, verbally or in writing, anything that might furnish occasion for a similar suspicion regarding me; but that should I know any heretic, or person suspected of heresy, I will denounce him to this Holy Office, or to the Inquisitor and ordinary of the place where I may be. Further, I swear and promise to fulfil and observe in their integrity all penances that have been, or that shall be, imposed upon me by this Holy Office. And, in the event of my contravening, (which God forbid!) any of these my promises, protestations, and oaths, I submit myself to all the pains and penalties imposed and promulgated in the sacred canons and other constitutions, general and particular, against such delinquents. So help me God, and these His holy Gospels, which I touch with my hands. *2*

I, the said Galileo Galilei, have abjured, sworn, promised, and bound myself as above; and in witness of the truth thereof I have with my own hand subscribed the present document of my abjuration, and recited it *3* word for word at Rome, in the Convent of Minerva, this twenty-second day of June, 1633.

I, Galileo Galilei, have abjured as above with my own hand.   *4*

REVIEW QUESTIONS

1. In list form, point by point, reconstruct the offenses committed by Galileo, according to the Holy Office.
2. Examine the structure of the sentence read to Galileo. Of what parts does the sentence consist? Identify transitions and explain their function within the document.
3. Make a list of twenty words in the sentence that captures for you its tone. Compare the list with those assembled by classmates.

DISCUSSION AND WRITING QUESTIONS

1. What accounts for the authoritative tone of the document? Respond in two ways: First, consider the position taken by the church with regard to the heliocentric model. How does the church establish its authority to speak on the subject? (By contrast, when Galileo speaks on the subject, how does he establish *his* authority?) Second, consider the sentence structures along with the use of pronouns, verbs, and legal-sounding vocabulary.
2. What, exactly, is Galileo's crime? You've summarized the Inquisition's views in Review Question 1. How do you define the crime? What are the issues on trial, here? And what is your opinion of the affair?
3. We've included the text of Galileo's recantation. Knowing as you do that the Inquisition had (and, within Galileo's lifetime, exercised) the authority to burn heretics; knowing also that Galileo's views were ultimately vindicated (even by the Church itself); and knowing that in his final years Galileo produced one of his most famous works; what is your response to the recantation? Should he have recanted?
4. Take the side of the Holy Inquisition and in a letter argue why it is necessary that an official body of the church defend "against heretical depravity throughout the whole Christian Republic."
5. Examine Galileo's use of quotations. How does he use them, given the context of the larger letter? Why has he chosen these particular sources?
6. The letter to the Grand Duchess can be described as an extended discussion on authority: scientific and ecclesiastical. What distinctions do you make between these kinds of authority? When do you rely on one more than (or possibly to the exclusion of) the other? Why?

BLAISE PASCAL (1623–1662)

Blaise Pascal lived a brief but extraordinarily prolific life during which his genius for mathematics, physics, religious thought, and *belles lettres* gained him recognition throughout Europe. He was a sickly man who searched with passion for
absolute knowledge. Despite brilliant successes in science, he concluded that no
such knowledge lay in that pursuit; so he turned to religion, which he believed
could explain the mysteries of the Infinite. Pascal held that man without God, even
the man of science, lives in misery.

He was born on June 19, 1623, in the French province of Auvergne. Three years
later his mother died, and his father, Etienne, devoted himself to the education of
his three children. At an early age both Blaise and his sister, Jacqueline, proved
exceptionally gifted students. When twelve, Pascal deduced elements of Euclidean
geometry without instruction; when sixteen, he wrote his *Treatise on Conic Sections*,
which was received with acclaim by (among others) the great philosopher René
Descartes; when nineteen, in order to relieve his father from the tedium of figuring
tax calculations (Etienne was a collector of taxes and government administrator),
he invented a mechanical computing device that could add, subtract, and divide
with accuracy — earning him still more recognition, this time internationally.

In 1646, his father fell and suffered a broken hip. Two men, both associated
with the Jansenist convent of Port Royal, nursed Etienne back to health and, for
their trouble, won a convert in his son. Blaise in turn converted the family. The
pursuit of science had left him strangely incomplete, and he looked for guidance
to the austere Jansenists, who believed that life was preordained and that salvation
followed more from the humble acceptance of divine grace than from good deeds.
Though dedicated to Jansenist doctrines, Pascal continued to pursue experiments
in atmospheric pressure, the results of which led to the development of the barometer. During this period, as during most of his life, he remained sickly. At one point
he was stricken with a paralysis and lay bedridden as his brother-in-law carried
out his experiments. Even thus limited, the successes continued: the invention of
the syringe; several more treatises on mathematics; exploration into the principles
of hydrostatics and pneumatics, which yielded Pascal's law of pressure and the
invention of the hydraulic press.

In response to her father's death in 1651, Jacqueline entered the Jansenist convent, to be followed several years later by her brother. This time, Pascal's conversion was complete. At Port Royal he experienced a mystical conversion that led
him to renounce worldly pursuits, including his scientific explorations, which he
would not resume until the last years of his life. Pascal devoted himself to contemplation and prayer, and at the request of Port Royal theologians wrote a series of
pseudonymous letters in support of Monsieur Arnauld, a Jansenist who had been
put on trial by the Jesuits. The *Provincial Letters* were published separately between
January 1656 and March 1657, winning an enthusiastic readership impressed by

the writer's wit, finely reasoned arguments, and eloquence. Long after Arnauld's cause was forgotten, the *Provincial Letters* have been read as models of exemplary prose — as have the *Pensées sur la Religion,* Pascal's *Thoughts on Religion.*

The plan for the *Pensées* began at Port Royal as an apologia — or a justification — of the Christian religion. It was to be an extended argument that would persuade skeptics to abandon their skepticism and embrace the faith. Pascal never completed the work, dying at the age of 39 in the home of his sister, Gilberte. Friends organized his notes and published them posthumously as the *Pensées,* in which we find the reflections of one in search of peace in an infinite universe. Humans are constituted such that they want to know more than they can know, says Pascal. We all aspire to Infinite, Godlike knowledge but can never achieve that wisdom — and can never escape the torment of our failure without the aid of faith. The knowledge of the Infinite reduces us, belittles us beyond reclaiming, unless we turn to God, who in the incarnation of Christ allowed the Infinite briefly to become finite and within human reach.

Whether or not one accepts Pascal's conclusions, one marvels at the searing honesty and the beauty and the depth of feeling he brings to his *Pensées.* He gives us a portrait of human consciousness once it has recognized the infinities of nature. Nowhere does he refer directly to the Polish astronomer, Copernicus; but everywhere — and especially in the *pensées* to follow — one senses the *effects* of the Copernican Revolution at work. In the Middle Ages one supposes it was possible to live in peace with a universe that was finite and with the role of human beings well defined in the scheme of Creation. Writing in the late Renaissance, Pascal realized the price of advances in science and of burgeoning individualism: the universe was now infinite and man's privileged place lost. Rational inquiry had destroyed the old peace by providing knowledge enough to expose man's insignificance but not nearly knowledge enough to let him reclaim his privileged status. In response, Pascal turned to God. As we shall see, some of those who followed him dispensed altogether with the need for God on the grounds that science would eventually explain natural phenomena so completely (the infinity of the universe included) that any recourse to God would be unnecessary. Still others maintained that the presence or absence of God had no bearing on the essential human predicament, that of being alone and claiming one's existence from that aloneness.

But to Pascal: *Pensées* 205 and 206 appear in the section titled "On the Necessity of the Wager," where Pascal attempts to win the skeptic over to belief. The argument is that the skeptic has nothing to lose in wagering his soul on faith: if there is no God, he has surrendered nothing; and if there *is* a God, he has gained eternal salvation. Pensée 72, on man's disproportion, follows and appears in the section titled "The Misery of Man Without God."

PENSÉES

205

When I consider the short duration of my life, swallowed up in the eternity before and after, the little space which I fill, and even can see, engulfed in the infinite immensity of spaces of which I am ignorant, and which know me not, I am frightened, and am astonished at being here rather than there; for there is no reason why here rather than there, why now rather than then. Who has put me here? By whose order and direction have this place and time been allotted to me? *Memoria hospitis unius diei prætereuntis.*[1]

206

The eternal silence of these infinite spaces frightens me.

72

Man's disproportion.   — [This is where our innate knowledge leads us. If it be not true, there is no truth in man; and if it be true, he finds therein great cause for humiliation, being compelled to abase himself in one way or another. And since he cannot exist without this knowledge, I wish that, before entering on deeper researches into nature, he would consider her both seriously and at leisure, that he would reflect upon himself also, and knowing what proportion there is . . .] Let man then contemplate the whole of nature in her full and grand majesty, and turn his vision from the low objects which surround him. Let him gaze on that brilliant light, set like an eternal lamp to illumine the universe; let the earth appear to him a point in comparison with the vast circle described by the sun; and let him wonder at the fact that this vast circle is itself but a very fine point in comparison with that described by the stars in their revolution round the firmament.[2] But if our view be arrested there, let our imagination pass beyond; it will sooner exhaust the power of conception than nature that of supplying material for conception. The whole visible world is only an imperceptible atom in the ample bosom of nature. No idea approaches it. We

Blaise Pascal. "Pensées 72, 205, and 206" in *Pensées and The Provincial Letters*. Trans. W. F. Trotter. New York: Modern Library (Random House), 1941, pp. 21–28, 74–75.

[1]Latin, literally: The memory of a guest passing by one day.

[2]Pascal seems to be working with a Ptolemaic view of the universe here; nonetheless, note the displacement he feels living on an earth that exists in a centerless universe, as an "imperceptible atom in the . . . bosom of nature."

may enlarge our conceptions beyond all imaginable space; we only produce atoms in comparison with the reality of things. It is an infinite sphere, the centre of which is everywhere, the circumference nowhere. In short it is the greatest sensible mark of the almighty power of God, that imagination loses itself in that thought.

Returning to himself, let man consider what he is in comparison with   2
all existence; let him regard himself as lost in this remote corner of nature; and from the little cell in which he finds himself lodged, I mean the universe, let him estimate at their true value the earth, kingdoms, cities, and himself. What is a man in the Infinite?

But to show him another prodigy equally astonishing, let him examine   3
the most delicate things he knows. Let a mite be given him, with its minute body and parts incomparably more minute, limbs with their joints, veins in the limbs, blood in the veins, humours in the blood,[3] drops in the humours, vapours in the drops. Dividing these last things again, let him exhaust his powers of conception, and let the last object at which he can arrive be now that of our discourse. Perhaps he will think that here is the smallest point in nature. I will let him see therein a new abyss. I will paint for him not only the visible universe, but all that he can conceive of nature's immensity in the womb of this abridged atom. Let him see therein an infinity of universes, each of which has its firmament, its planets, its earth, in the same proportion as in the visible world; in each earth animals, and in the last mites, in which he will find again all that the first had, finding still in these others the same thing without end and without cessation. Let him lose himself in wonders as amazing in their littleness as the others in their vastness. For who will not be astounded at the fact that our body, which a little while ago was imperceptible in the universe, itself imperceptible in the bosom of the whole, is now a colossus, a world, or rather a whole, in respect of the nothingness which we cannot reach? He who regards himself in this light will be afraid of himself, and observing himself sustained in the body given him by nature between those two abysses of the Infinite and Nothing, will tremble at the sight of these marvels; and I think that, as his curiosity changes into admiration, he will be more disposed to contemplate them in silence than to examine them with presumption.

For in fact what is man in nature? A Nothing in comparison with the   4
Infinite, an All in comparison with the Nothing, a mean between nothing and everything. Since he is infinitely removed from comprehending the

---

[3]*humours in the blood:* Body fluids thought by ancient and medieval scientists to determine personality and temperament. It was believed that there were four main humors (blood, phlegm, choler, and melancholy) which corresponded with the four natural elements (fire, earth, air, and water). If all the humors were in the correct proportions, they would result in a healthy, well-balanced person.

extremes, the end of things and their beginning are hopelessly hidden from him in an impenetrable secret; he is equally incapable of seeing the Nothing from which he was made, and the Infinite in which he is swallowed up.

What will he do then, but perceive the appearance of the middle of things, in an eternal despair of knowing either their beginning or their end. All things proceed from the Nothing, and are borne towards the Infinite. Who will follow these marvellous processes? The Author of these wonders understands them. None other can do so.

Through failure to contemplate these Infinites, men have rashly rushed into the examination of nature, as though they bore some proportion to her. It is strange that they have wished to understand the beginnings of things, and thence to arrive at the knowledge of the whole, with a presumption as infinite as their object. For surely this design cannot be formed without presumption or without a capacity infinite like nature.

If we are well informed, we understand that, as nature has graven her image and that of her Author on all things, they almost all partake of her double infinity. Thus we see that all the sciences are infinite in the extent of their researches. For who doubts that geometry, for instance, has an infinite infinity of problems to solve? They are also infinite in the multitude and fineness of their premises; for it is clear that those which are put forward as ultimate are not self-supporting, but are based on others which, again having others for their support, do not permit of finality. But we represent some as ultimate for reason, in the same way as in regard to material objects we call that an indivisible point beyond which our senses can no longer perceive anything, although by its nature it is infinitely divisible.

Of these two Infinites of science, that of greatness is the most palpable, and hence a few persons have pretended to know all things. "I will speak of the whole," said Democritus.

But the infinitely little is the least obvious. Philosophers have much oftener claimed to have reached it, and it is here they have all stumbled. This has given rise to such common titles as *First Principles, Principles of Philosophy,* and the like, as ostentatious in fact, though not in appearance, as that one which blinds us, *De omni scibili.*[4]

We naturally believe ourselves far more capable of reaching the centre of things than of embracing their circumference. The visible extent of the world visibly exceeds us; but as we exceed little things, we think ourselves more capable of knowing them. And yet we need no less capacity for attaining the Nothing than the All. Infinite capacity is required for both, and it seems to me that whoever shall have understood the ultimate principles of being might also attain to the knowledge of the Infinite. The one de-

[4]Latin, literally: Concerning everything knowable.

pends on the other, and one leads to the other. These extremes meet and reunite by force of distance, and find each other in God, and in God alone.

Let us then take our compass; we are something, and we are not every-   *11* thing. The nature of our existence hides from us the knowledge of first beginnings which are born of the Nothing; and the littleness of our being conceals from us the sight of the Infinite.

Our intellect holds the same position in the world of thought as our   *12* body occupies in the expanse of nature.

Limited as we are in every way, this state which holds the mean be-   *13* tween two extremes is present in all our impotence. Our senses perceive no extreme. Too much sound deafens us; too much light dazzles us; too great distance or proximity hinders our view. Too great length and too great brevity of discourse tend to obscurity; too much truth is paralysing (I know some who cannot understand that to take four from nothing leaves nothing). First principles are too self-evident for us; too much pleasure disagrees with us. Too many concords are annoying in music; too many benefits irritate us; we wish to have the wherewithal to over-pay our debts. *Beneficia eo usque læta sunt dum videntur exsolvi posse; ubi multum antevenere, pro gratia odium redditur.*[5] We feel neither extreme heat nor extreme cold. Excessive qualities are prejudicial to us and not perceptible by the senses; we do not feel but suffer them. Extreme youth and extreme age hinder the mind, as also too much and too little education. In short, extremes are for us as though they were not, and we are not within their notice. They escape us, or we them.

This is our true state; this is what makes us incapable of certain knowl-   *14* edge and of absolute ignorance. We sail within a vast sphere, ever drifting in uncertainty, driven from end to end. When we think to attach ourselves to any point and to fasten to it, it wavers and leaves us; and if we follow it, it eludes our grasp, slips past us, and vanishes for ever. Nothing stays for us. This is our natural condition, and yet most contrary to our inclination; we burn with desire to find solid ground and an ultimate sure foundation whereon to build a tower reaching to the Infinite. But our whole groundwork cracks, and the earth opens to abysses.

Let us therefore not look for certainty and stability. Our reason is al-   *15* ways deceived by fickle shadows; nothing can fix the finite between the two Infinites, which both enclose and fly from it.

If this be well understood, I think that we shall remain at rest, each in   *16* the state wherein nature has placed him. As this sphere which has fallen to us as our lot is always distant from either extreme, what matters it that

---

[5]Latin, literally: Kindnesses up to that point of time are delightful while they seem to be; hatred is returned in place of gratitude.

man should have a little more knowledge of the universe? If he has it, he but gets a little higher. Is he not always infinitely removed from the end, and is not the duration of our life equally removed from eternity, even if it lasts ten years longer?

In comparison with these Infinites all finites are equal, and I see no 17 reason for fixing our imagination on one more than on another. The only comparison which we make of ourselves to the finite is painful to us.

If man made himself the first object of study, he would see how inca- 18 pable he is of going further. How can a part know the whole? But he may perhaps aspire to know at least the parts to which he bears some proportion. But the parts of the world are all so related and linked to one another, that I believe it impossible to know one without the other and without the whole.

Man, for instance, is related to all he knows. He needs a place wherein 19 to abide, time through which to live, motion in order to live, elements to compose him, warmth and food to nourish him, air to breathe. He sees light; he feels bodies; in short, he is in a dependent alliance with everything. To know man, then, it is necessary to know how it happens that he needs air to live, and, to know the air, we must know how it is thus related to the life of man, etc. Flame cannot exist without air; therefore to understand the one, we must understand the other.

Since everything then is cause and effect, dependent and supporting, 20 mediate and immediate, and all is held together by a natural though imperceptible chain, which binds together things most distant and most different, I hold it equally impossible to know the parts without knowing the whole, and to know the whole without knowing the parts in detail.

[The eternity of things in itself or in God must also astonish our brief 21 duration. The fixed and constant immobility of nature, in comparison with the continual change which goes on within us, must have the same effect.]

And what completes our incapability of knowing things, is the fact that 22 they are simple, and that we are composed of two opposite natures, different in kind, soul and body. For it is impossible that our rational part should be other than spiritual; and if any one maintain that we are simply corporeal, this would far more exclude us from the knowledge of things, there being nothing so inconceivable as to say that matter knows itself. It is impossible to imagine how it should know itself.

So if we are simply material, we can know nothing at all; and if we are 23 composed of mind and matter, we cannot know perfectly things which are simple, whether spiritual or corporeal. Hence it comes that almost all philosophers have confused ideas of things, and speak of material things in spiritual terms, and of spiritual things in material terms. For they say boldly that bodies have a tendency to fall, that they seek after their centre, that they fly from destruction, that they fear the void, that they have inclinations, sympathies, antipathies, all of which attributes pertain only to mind. And in speaking of minds, they consider them as in a place, and attribute to them movement from one place to another; and these are qualities which belong only to bodies.[6]

Instead of receiving the ideas of these things in their purity, we colour   24
them with our own qualities, and stamp with our composite being all the simple things which we contemplate.

Who would not think, seeing us compose all things of mind and body,   25
but that this mixture would be quite intelligible to us? Yet it is the very thing we least understand. Man is to himself the most wonderful object in nature; for he cannot conceive what the body is, still less what the mind is, and least of all how a body should be united to a mind. This is the consummation of his difficulties, and yet it is his very being. *Modus quo corporibus adhærent spiritus comprehendi ab hominibus non potest, et hoc tamen homo est. . . ."*[7]

---

[6]Here, Pascal is referring to Aristotle.

[7]Latin, literally: The manner by which spirits cling (adhere) to bodies, this way is not able to be grasped by men; nevertheless, this thing is human.

REVIEW QUESTIONS

1. For Pascal, how does the analysis or dissection of a mite, a tiny insect, reveal the same immensities as exist in the universe?
2. Humanity is sustained between "those two abysses of the Infinite and Nothing." What does Pascal mean?
3. Summarize Pascal's views on the relation of parts (of creation) to the whole.
4. How is it that our being composed of both soul and body inhibits our ability to know things?
5. Why does Pascal believe that mankind is presumptuous?

DISCUSSION AND WRITING QUESTIONS

1. In *Pensée* 205, Pascal says that he fears the infinite immensity of spaces of which he is ignorant and which *"know me not."* How does this one clause, "which know me not," signal a radical change from the pre-Copernican cosmology?
2. In the beginning of *Pensée* 72, Pascal says that our innate knowledge leads inevitably to an awareness of our disproportion and that *that* awareness leads to humiliation and self-abasement. Do you agree?
3. "What is man in the infinite?" Pascal poses the question rhetorically; that is, he asks, having already established an answer for himself and the reader. What is his answer? And if the same prodigious question were put to you, how would you answer?
4. See paragraph 3, in which Pascal says that he who regards himself as poised between the Infinite and Nothing will tremble, will be afraid of himself. What

does he mean by this? What is the process by which "curiosity changes into admiration"? And how does admiration lead to one's contemplating the universe in silence? Finally, what is the distinction Pascal makes between silence and presumption?

5. Pascal believes that "the end of things and their beginning are hopelessly hidden from us," that we are incapable of certain knowledge and yet at the same time avoid absolute ignorance. Which is to say, we drift with uncertainty. Uncertainty "is our natural condition."

How does Pascal's view of our potential for knowledge contrast with the assumptions that underlie scientific inquiry?

6. Based on your reading of Galileo's letter to the Grand Duchess and Pascal's two *pensées*, write a dialogue between the two men concerning the possibilities and limitations of knowing. Consider, as you are constructing the dialogue, the ways in which the two use the word *knowledge*. Appreciate that Galileo was a devoutly religious Catholic (ample evidence for which exists in his letter) and Pascal a brilliant mathematician.

7. "If man made himself the first object of study, he would see how incapable he is of going further." What is your response to this sentence from paragraph 18?

BERNARD LE BOVIER
DE FONTENELLE *(1657–1757)*

Bernard Le Bovier de Fontenelle was an accomplished philosopher and popularizer of science. He wrote numerous books in his long life, among them *Dialogues of the Dead* (1683), in which he had figures of antiquity conversing with one another; *Digressions on the Ancients and the Moderns* (1688), in which he mirrored the sentiment of leading figures of his age by rejecting the supremacy of classical ideas to modern, in this way foreshadowing the attack that was to follow in the Enlightenment against all forms of received opinion. Fontenelle enjoyed a position as permanent secretary of the French Academy of Sciences; throughout his life he remained conversant with scientific theories of the day and, given his considerable literary talents, was well positioned to write his famous *Conversations on the Plurality of Worlds* [*Entretiens sur la pluralité des mondes* (1686)], in which he explores the implications of the Copernican system.

Fontenelle states his intentions for the work in its Preface:

> I have been desirous to treat of Philosophy in a manner that is not philosophical: I have endeavoured to lead to a certain point, without being too dry for people of pleasure, nor too trifling for the Learned.

The effect, happily, is a conversation witty and charming in its own right and, in matters of scientific speculation, most provocative. Fontenelle's *Conversations* were read widely and did much to popularize the Copernican system. The author was sensitive to criticism from religious readers who might be offended by speculations on the plurality of worlds. For them he saved the final part of his Preface:

> There only remains one thing to be mentioned . . . which is, that there are a sort of persons who are the most difficult to satisfy, not but that very good reasons might be given them, but because they have the privilege of not submitting to them if they please, the best will not be sufficient. These are those scrupulous people, who may imagine that religion is in some danger, by placing inhabitants elsewhere than on the *Earth*. I respect even their excessive delicacy on the subject of religion; and that respect I carry so far as not willingly to shock their delicacy on this article in the following Work, if it was contrary to my sentiments; but that which will appear more surprising is, I speak not only of inhabitants in this system (that is, the system of our universe), or collection of Planetary Bodies: but, I have mentioned an infinite number of other worlds that are inhabited. . . . [I]f you are ever so little of a Theologian, you find in the idea infinite difficulties. The posterity of Adam have never extended themselves so far as the *Moon*, nor have we ever sent colonies into that coun-

try: the men who are in the *Moon* are not the children of Adam. Now, in Theology, it is an embarrassing point that there are men who have not descended from him. . . .

If you find Fontenelle smirking behind his solicitude for the religious reader, your instincts are correct; for as an advocate of reason and a forerunner of the Enlightenment, he held a strong, if playful, bias against religious thinking that was evident in several of his other works.

Fontenelle divided his book into a series of evening conversations with an imaginary Marchioness (the wife of a marquis). The excerpts that follow are taken from the first and fifth evenings. Note that when Fontenelle mentions the term *vortex*, he refers to Descartes's theory of a substance, such as air, spinning around a fixed star and accounting for planetary motion. The theory was disproved by Newton in 1687.

CONVERSATIONS ON THE PLURALITY OF WORLDS

FIRST EVENING

That the Earth is a planet, which turns round on its axis, and also revolves round the Sun.

One evening after supper, we went out, and walked in the Park. The fresh air was delicious, and recompensed us for a very hot day, that had greatly fatigued us. The *Moon* had been risen, perhaps, about an hour; and her rays, which came to us through the branches of the trees, made an agreeable mixture of a very lively white, with all the surrounding green, which appeared of a dark colour. There was not a cloud which deprived us of a ray, or which obscured the least star: they were all like pure and shining gold; which was yet relieved by the blue arch in which they were set. This scene threw me into a reverie; and, had it not been for the Marchioness, I might not have awaked from it for a long time; but the presence of a Lady so amiable, would not permit me long to continue in it, and wholly to abandon myself to the *Moon* and the Stars. Don't you think, Madam, said I, that the day itself is not so fine as a fine night? Yes, she answered, the beauty of the day is like a fair beauty which hath in it more

1

Bernard de Fontenelle. *Conversations on the Plurality of Worlds* (1686). "A New Translation . . . by a Gentleman of the Inner Temple." Printed for R. Withy, at the Dunciad in Cornhill; H. Woodgate and S. Brookes in Pater-noster Road; and J. Cook in May-Fair. 1760, Preface and pp. 4–10, 264–267.

of the brilliant; but the beauty of the night is like a brown beauty, which is more touching, and has a greater effect. You are very generous, replied I, to give this preference to the brunettes, you who are not a brunette. It is, however, true, that day hath the greatest beauty in Nature; and, that the heroines of romances, which are the produce of the finest imaginations, are almost always fair. This beauty is not any thing replied she, if it affects not. Acknowledge, that the day hath not ever thrown you into a reverie, so sweet as that into which I saw you ready to fall, but a moment since, at the sight of this fine night. I agree, answered I; but, in return, a fair one, like you, will cast me into a reverie sooner than the finest night in the world, with all its brown beauty. Whether this is true, or not, replied she, I will not contend: I would have the day, (because the fair ought to be in its interests) have the same effect. Wherefore do lovers, who are the best judges of that which affects, never address themselves to the day, but to the night, in all their songs, and all their elegies, that I have ever read? Certainly the night ought to yield them many thanks, said I to her. But, replied she, to the night they make all their complaints; the day never gains their confidence: What is the reason of this? It appears to me, answered I, that it does not inspire them with that kind of sorrow and passion, which I know not how to describe, that the night inspires them with. It seems, that during the night, every thing is in repose: they imagine, that the Stars march with more silence than the *Sun,* the objects that the Heavens present are more engaging, the sight is more easily attracted: in short, they think better, because they suppose themselves to be, at that time, the only persons in Nature employed in reveries: perhaps also, day hath too much uniformity; there is only one *Sun,* and one blue vault: but, perhaps, the view of all the Stars, confusedly mixed, and disposed as if by chance, into a thousand different figures, may favour their reveries, and a certain disorder of thought, into which they fall, not without pleasure. I have always thought the same, replied the Marchioness; I love the Stars, and I readily and freely complain of the *Sun,* who deprives me of the sight of them. Ah! cried I, I cannot pardon him for depriving us of the sight of all these Worlds. What do you call all these Worlds? said she, looking at me, and turning towards me. I beg your pardon, answered I; you have occasioned me to be guilty of a folly, and immediately my imaginations have escaped me. What then is this folly? replied she. To this I answered, I am sorry, Madam, that you oblige me to confess my folly, but I have long entertained an opinion that each Star may very probably be a *Sun* to enlighten other Worlds. I will not, however, swear that this is true; but I hold it for true, because it gives me pleasure to believe it. It is an idea which pleases me, and which is very agreeably fixed in my mind. According to my opinion, the agreeable is necessary even to truth itself. Very well, replied the Lady; and, I desire, if your folly is so very agreeable, you will impart it to me: with regard to the Stars, I will believe whatever you please, provided I find a pleasure in it. Ah! Madam, answered I very shortly; it is not a pleasure such as you would enjoy from a representation of one of Molière's Comedies: it is a pleasure, which is, I know not how, founded in reason, and which only makes the mind laugh. And do you, replied she, suppose I am incapable of tasting pleasures founded on reason? I will instantly convince you of the contrary, learn me your Doctrine of the Stars. No, replied I, it shall never be said by way of reproach on me, that, in a wood at ten in the evening, I have spoke of Philosophy to the most amiable person that I know. You must search elsewhere for your Philosophers.

I had resolution enough to defend myself for some time in this manner, but was at length obliged to submit. I made her at least promise, for my honour, that she would keep the secret; and, when every objection was removed, and I was willing to speak, I knew not where to begin my discourse; for, with a person like this Lady, who was not, in any manner, acquainted with Philosophical Subjects, I must take things from afar, proving to her that the *Earth* might be a *Planet*, the *Planets* so many *Earths*, and all the *Stars* so many *Suns*, which enlightened other Worlds. I could not avoid saying to her, that we had better discourse on other subjects, as all reasonable people in our situation would: at length, however, for giving her a general idea of this part of Philosophy, I made use of the following method.

The whole of Philosophy, said I to her, is founded upon these two things: That *our minds are curious, and our eyes bad:* for, if you have the best eyes you can possibly have, you cannot discover whether the Stars are Suns that enlighten other Worlds, or whether they are not; and if, on the other side, you are less curious, you will not wish to know; which will be just the same; but we wish to know more than we can see; this is the difficulty: yet if that which we see, we saw well, it would always be so much known; but we see things very different from what they really are. Thus do true Philosophers pass their lives, in not believing that which they see, and in endeavoring to divine that which they see not: and this condition, as it appears to me, is not greatly to be envied. On this occasion, I always represent to myself, that Nature is a great spectacle, which resembles that of an opera. When you are at an opera, you do not see the theatre as it is in reality made; they, in a particular manner, dispose the decorations and machines, for causing, at a great distance, an agreeable effect; and they conceal from your view the springs, and wheels, etc. which give motion to the whole machinery: it will embarrass you to discover how the whole is made to act: there is, perhaps, behind the theatre, some mechanic concealed, who disquiets himself to discover the machinery of the whole, and which to him appears very extraordinary. You see, that this mechanic is like our Philosophers: but that which, with regard to Philosopher's augments, the difficulty is, that in the machinery which Nature represents to our eyes, the springs are perfectly concealed. . . .

FIFTH EVENING

That the Fixed Stars are so many Suns, each of which enlighten other Worlds.

The Marchioness expressed great impatience to know what would be- 4
come of the Fixed Stars. Shall they be inhabited as the Planets are? Said
she. Or shall they not be inhabited? In short, what do you make of them?
You will guess, perhaps, if you have a great desire to know, answered I.
The Fixed Stars cannot be less distant from the Earth, than twenty-seven
thousand six hundred and fifty times the distance from hence to the *Sun*,
which is thirty three millions of leagues, and if you displease an Astronomer, he will place them yet farther off. The distance from the *Sun* to *Saturn*,
which is the most remote planet, is only three hundred and thirty millions
of leagues;[1] this is not any thing with relation to the distance from the *Sun*
or from the *Earth* to the Fixed Stars, they take not the trouble to count it.
Their light as we see, is lively and bright enough. If they receive it from
the *Sun*, they must receive it very weak, after passing so far; by reflection
it must be much weaker, they are then to send it to us at this great distance.
It is impossible that reflected light, and which hath twice passed so far
should have the force and vivacity that the light of the Fixed Stars have.
They are therefore, luminous of themselves, and all of them, in one word,
so many Suns.

If I am not deceived, said the Marchioness, I already see to what you 5
are leading. You are going to say; *The Fixed Stars are so many Suns, our* Sun
*is the centre of a Vortex, which turns round him, for why therefore shall not
each* Fixed Star *be also the centre of a Vortex, which shall have a motion round
it? Our* Sun *hath Planets that he enlightens, for why therefore should not each*
Fixed Star *have Planets that he enlightens?* I have not any thing to answer,
said I to her, than that which Phaedrus said to Enone, *It is thee who hath
named it.*

But replied she, I see the Universe so great, that I am lost in it: I no 6
longer know where I am: I no longer know any thing. What, shall all be
divided into Vortexes thrown confusedly one amongst another? Shall each
Fixed Star be the centre of a Vortex, as great perhaps as that in which we
are situated? Shall all this immense space, which comprehends our *Sun*
and our Planets, be only a little parcel of the Universe? Shall there be as
many such spaces as there are Fixed Stars? This confounds me, troubles
me, frights me. And as for me, answered I, I am very easy about it. When
the Heavens appeared to me as only a blue vault, where the Stars were
fixed like nails, the Universe appeared little, and confined within narrow
bounds, I seemed oppressed: presently they give an infinite extent and

---

[1]The most distant known planets in the solar system, Uranus, Neptune, and Pluto, were
discovered in 1781, 1846, and 1930, respectively. A league equals three miles.

profoundity to this blue vault, in dividing it into a thousand and a thousand Vortexes, it now seems to me that I breath with more liberty, that I am in a much greater extent of Air, and that the Universe is far more magnificent. Nature hath not spared any thing in producing it, she hath every where shewn a profusion of riches, wholly worthy of her. Not any thing can be so fine as to represent to ourselves this prodigious number of Vortexes, the middle of each of which is occupied by a Sun, which causes divers Planets to turn round him. The Inhabitants of a Planet of one of these infinite number of Vortexes, sees on all sides the Suns of these Vortexes, with which they are surrounded, but they cannot see the Planets, who have only a weak light, which they borrow from their respective Suns, and which they cannot send beyond their own Vortex.

You offer me, said she, a kind of perspective so long, that the sight cannot discover the end: I see clearly the Inhabitant of the *Earth,* then you shew me those of the *Moon,* and of other Planets of our Vortex clearly enough, indeed, but less so than those of the *Earth;* after them come the Inhabitants of the Planets of other Vortexes. But I acknowledge they are thrown at so vast, so infinite a distance, that whatever effort I make for seeing then, I can scarce perceive them. And in fact, are they not almost annihilated even by the expressions you have been obliged to make use of, when speaking of them? You have been obliged to call them Inhabitants of one of the Planets of one of those Vortexes, whose number is infinite. We ourselves, with whom the same expression agrees, acknowledge, that we scarce know where we are in the midst of so many Worlds. As to me, I begin to see the *Earth* so excessively small, that I believe I shall not hereafter have a very great desire for any thing. Certainly, if we have so much ardor for grandeur, if we form designs upon designs, if we give ourselves so much pain, it is because we know not these Vortexes. I now hope that my laziness will profit from my new light, and when I am reproached with my indolence, I shall answer, *Ah! if you did but know what the Fixed Stars are!*

REVIEW QUESTIONS

1. Briefly state Fontenelle's thesis on the plurality of worlds.
2. Fontenelle uses the analogy of the opera in his discussion of philosophers. Explain the analogy.
3. The Marchioness responds to thoughts on the immensity of the heavens as Pascal does: with confusion and fear. Fontenelle's view is different. How so?
4. The Marchioness believes that "we have so much ardor for grandeur" and "form designs upon designs" because we do *not* appreciate the immensity of the universe. Explain her position. How is it reminiscent of Pascal's?

DISCUSSION AND WRITING QUESTIONS

1. Fontenelle makes a distinction between types of pleasures. What is this distinction, and does it hold up for you — that is, by reference to your own experience of pleasure? Explain.
2. "The whole of philosophy," says Fontenelle, "is founded upon these two things: That *our minds are curious, and our eyes bad.*" Now that astronomers have at their disposal powerful telescopes, how do you respond to Fontenelle's observation?
3. Does the idea that there exists life on other planets seem tenable to you? How does the media — movies, for instance — help to influence popular opinion?
4. In what ways does the theory on the plurality of worlds discussed by Fontenelle represent a further displacement of the medieval cosmology that the heavens revolve around the earth?
5. Fontenelle sees nature as an elaborate mechanism whose "springs are perfectly concealed." How does viewing the universe as a mechanism, something akin to an elaborate watch, help to define what is possible through scientific inquiry?

ALEXANDER POPE *(1688–1744)*

Alexander Pope is remembered for his masterly poetic satires and his transla-tions of Homer. As a successful young poet, Pope went on to make a profession of the literary life, the only poet of his period who could support himself in this way. Success also earned him the scorn of detractors, who attacked him freely and for their trouble became targets of sometimes venomous rebuttals. But more often, as a satirist, Pope took as his subject the lax morals of the day, writing poetical com-mentaries with force and wit.

He was born a Roman Catholic in London on May 21, 1688, the same year in which Parliament deposed the Catholic king, James II. An anti-Catholic sentiment prevailed under the new monarchs, William and Mary, and Pope's family moved from London to Binfield in Windsor Forest, the rural setting in which he reached maturity and where he developed the sensitivity to nature so well evidenced in his early work. The rustic environment notwithstanding, the young Pope was sickly, afflicted with a spinal condition that left him four and a half feet tall at full maturity. He was of noble bearing, however; his portrait was painted and his features were sculpted by the leading artists of the day.

Pope achieved his first great critical success at the age of twenty-three with his *Essay on Criticism*, a poem in which he presented traditional principles of literary criticism in memorable, verse form. Samuel Johnson believed it "a work which displays such extent of comprehension, such nicety of distinction, such acquain-tance with mankind, and such knowledge both of ancient and modern learning, as are not often attained by the maturest age and longest experience." But Pope's attacks in his poetry on many of his contemporaries earned him their lifelong en-mity. Throughout his career, Pope would be attacked vigorously (his enemies were not above penning cruel references to his physical deformities), and he often met the challenge by writing verses in which he would excoriate detractors with refer-ences that, for many, would be the only immortality they would receive.

Pope wrote his mock epic, *The Rape of the Lock* (1714), at the request of a friend who wished to reconcile two families that were feuding over a locket of hair (snipped by the son of one family from the head of a daughter of another). The poem treated the affair in all mock seriousness as the equivalent of some ancient battle and is written in the style of a Homeric epic. Pope soon turned to *bona fide* epics as translator of the *Iliad* (1720) and *Odyssey* (1726), for which subscriptions were taken (by, among other notables, Jonathan Swift). The translations earned him money enough to secure both his and his mother's leisure (his father having died in 1717).

Taking up residence in a country estate at Twickenham on the Thames, Pope continued his work, in addition becoming a devoted gardener and entertaining his distinguished friends. Jonathan Swift stayed at Twickenham while seeing *Gulliver's*

Travels through to publication. Lord Bolingbroke was a neighbor and close friend, and it was to him that the poet dedicated *An Essay on Man*, a work in which he turned philosopher in order to examine, and justify, the works of God. There are four Epistles to the poem: the first, reproduced below, is entitled "Of the Nature and State of Man, With Respect to the Universe." Here Pope reviews the works of creation in a way that will recall to you the writing of Fontenelle, who saw in the universe an enormous mechanism, the designer of which was God. Pope will also recall to you the reflections of Pascal, who wonders why he exists "here rather than there, why now rather than then." Pascal's loneliness and despair are for Pope a negative way of stating a case that could be put otherwise. As you will see, Pope along with Pascal and Fontenelle appreciates the immensity of Creation. But he is not at all forlorn that we cannot understand our place in the immensities. It is enough merely for him to observe them and to know implicitly that an order exists, albeit one that is unavailable to human understanding. The plan of creation is to be trusted and celebrated; in Pope's words, "Whatever is, is right." His mood accords perfectly with the optimism of the 18th century, which received its ultimate expression in the writing of Condorcet. (See pages 293–314 and the part on "Condorcet and the Progress of Civilization.")

As in Pascal, the effects of Copernican thought are at work in *An Essay on Man*; the universe referred to is the one proposed first by Copernicus and modified by Kepler and Newton. Note that Pope's narrator is one who can

> See worlds on worlds compose one universe,
> Observe how system into system runs,
> What other planets circle other suns,
> What varied Being peoples every star,
> May tell why Heaven has made us as we are.

Faced with the same immensity, Pascal looked for comfort to God; and Fontenelle, with piquant mocking, dismissed religious concerns and welcomed the extra room this enlarged universe gave him. Pope looks to the immensities with a different eye, suggesting both Fontenelle's optimism and Pascal's dependence on faith.

The remaining three Epistles of the poem treat, in turn, human nature and self-love; the mutual dependence of man and society; and the possibilities for human happiness. The metrical scheme (used here and in many of Pope's works) is the "heroic couplet," the lines written in iambic pentameter with rhyming line pairs.

From *AN ESSAY ON MAN*

To Henry St. John, Lord Bolingbroke

EPISTLE I. OF THE NATURE AND STATE OF MAN, WITH RESPECT TO THE UNIVERSE

Awake, my St. John! leave all meaner things
To low ambition, and the pride of kings.
Let us (since life can little more supply
Than just to look about us and to die)
Expatiate free[1] o'er all this scene of man;   5
A mighty maze! but not without a plan;
A wild, where weeds and flowers promiscuous shoot,
Or garden, tempting with forbidden fruit.
Together let us beat this ample field,
Try what the open, what the covert yield;   10
The latent tracts, the giddy heights, explore
Of all who blindly creep, or sightless soar;
Eye Nature's walks, shoot folly as it flies,
And catch the manners living as they rise;
Laugh where we must, be candid[2] where we can;   15
But vindicate the ways of God to man.[3]

    1. Say first, of God above, or man below,
What can we reason, but from what we know?
Of man, what see we but his station here,
From which to reason, or to which refer?   20
Through worlds unnumbered though the God be known,
'Tis ours to trace him only in our own.
He, who through vast immensity can pierce,
See worlds on worlds compose one universe,
Observe how system into system runs,   25
What other planets circle other suns,
What varied Being peoples every star,
May tell why Heaven has made us as we are.

Alexander Pope. *An Essay on Man.* "Epistle I: On the Nature and State of Man, With Respect to the Universe" in *The Norton Anthology of English Literature,* 4th ed., Vol. 1. New York: Norton, 1979, pp. 2243–2250. All notes provided by Samuel Holt Monk and Lawrence Lipking, W. W. Norton's editors for the Restoration and the Eighteenth Century.
[1]Range freely.
[2]Kindly.
[3]Pope deliberately echoes *Paradise Lost* I.26.

But of this frame the bearings, and the ties,
The strong connections, nice dependencies,   30
Gradations just, has thy pervading soul
Looked through? or can a part contain the whole?
    Is the great chain, that draws all to agree,
And drawn supports, upheld by God, or thee?

    2. Presumptuous man! the reason wouldst thou find,   35
Why formed so weak, so little, and so blind?
First, if thou canst, the harder reason guess,
Why formed no weaker, blinder, and no less!
Ask of thy mother earth, why oaks are made
Taller or stronger than the weeds they shade?   40
Or ask of yonder argent fields above,
Why Jove's satellites[4] are less than Jove?
    Of systems possible, if 'tis confessed
That Wisdom Infinite must form the best,
Where all must full or not coherent be,   45
And all that rises, rise in due degree;
Then, in the scale of reasoning life, 'tis plain,
There must be, somewhere, such a rank as man:
And all the question (wrangle e'er so long)
Is only this, if God has placed him wrong?   50
    Respecting man, whatever wrong we call,
May, must be right, as relative to all.
In human works, though labored on with pain,
A thousand movements scarce one purpose gain;
In God's, one single can its end produce;   55
Yet serves to second too some other use.
So man, who here seems principal alone,
Perhaps acts second to some sphere unknown,
Touches some wheel, or verges to some goal;
'Tis but a part we see, and not a whole.   60
    When the proud steed shall know why man restrains
His fiery course, or drives him o'er the plains;
When the dull ox, why now he breaks the clod,
Is now a victim, and now Egypt's god:
Then shall man's pride and dullness comprehend   65
His actions', passions', being's use and end;
Why doing, suffering, checked, impelled; and why
This hour a slave, the next a deity.

---

[4]In his *Dictionary* Johnson notes and condemns Pope's giving his word four syllables, as in Latin.

Then say not man's imperfect, Heaven in fault;
Say rather, man's as perfect as he ought: 70
His knowledge measured to his state and place,
His time a moment, and a point his space.
If to be perfect in a certain sphere,[5]
What matter, soon or late, or here or there?
The blest today is as completely so,   75
As who began a thousand years ago.

    3. Heaven from all creatures hides the book of Fate,
All but the page prescribed, their present state:
From brutes what men, from men what spirits know:
Or who could suffer Being here below?   80
The lamb thy riot dooms to bleed today,
Had he thy reason, would he skip and play?
Pleased to the last, he crops the flowery food,
And licks the hand just raised to shed his blood.
O blindness to the future! kindly given,   85
That each may fill the circle marked by Heaven:
Who sees with equal eye, as God of all,
A hero perish, or a sparrow fall,
Atoms or systems[6] into ruin hurled,
And now a bubble burst, and now a world.   90
    Hope humbly then; with trembling pinions soar;
Wait the great teacher Death, and God adore!
What future bliss, he gives not thee to know,
But gives that hope to be thy blessing now.
Hope springs eternal in the human breast: 95
Man never is, but always to be blest:
The soul, uneasy and confined from home,
Rests and expatiates in a life to come.
    Lo! the poor Indian, whose untutored mind
Sees God in clouds, or hears him in the wind;   100
His soul proud Science never taught to stray
Far as the solar walk, or milky way;
Yet simple Nature to his hope has given,
Behind the cloud-topped hill, an humbler heaven;
Some safer world in depth of woods embraced,   105
Some happier island in the watery waste,
Where slaves once more their native land behold,
No fiends torment, no Christians thirst for gold!

---

[5]I.e., in one's "state and place."
[6]Solar systems.

To be, contents his natural desire,
He asks no angel's wing, no seraph's fire;   *110*
But thinks, admitted to that equal sky,
His faithful dog shall bear him company.

      4. Go, wiser thou! and, in thy scale of sense,
Weigh thy opinion against Providence;
Call imperfection what thou fancy'st such,   *115*
Say, here he gives too little, there too much;
Destroy all creatures for thy sport or gust,[7]
Yet cry, if man's unhappy, God's unjust;
If man alone engross not Heaven's high care,
Alone made perfect here, immortal there: *120*
Snatch from his hand the balance and the rod,
Rejudge his justice, be the God of God!
In pride, in reasoning pride, our error lies;
All quit their sphere, and rush into the skies.
Pride still is aiming at the blest abodes,   *125*
Men would be angels, angels would be gods.
Aspiring to be gods, if angels fell,
Aspiring to be angels, men rebel:
And who but wishes to invert the laws
Of order, sins against the Eternal Cause.   *130*

      5. Ask for what end the heavenly bodies shine,
Earth for whose use? Pride answers, "'Tis for mine:
For me kind Nature wakes her genial power,
Suckles each herb, and spreads out every flower;
Annual for me, the grape, the rose renew   *135*
The juice nectareous, and the balmy dew;
For me, the mine a thousand treasures brings;
For me, health gushes from a thousand springs;
Seas roll to waft me, suns to light me rise;
My footstool earth, my canopy the skies."   *140*
      But errs not Nature from this gracious end,
From burning suns when livid deaths descend,
When earthquakes swallow, or when tempests sweep
Towns to one grave, whole nations to the deep?
"No," 'tis replied, "the first Almighty Cause   *145*
Acts not by partial, but by general laws;
The exceptions few; some change since all began,
And what created perfect?" — Why then man?

---

[7]"Sense of tasting" (Johnson's *Dictionary*).

If the great end be human happiness,
Then Nature deviates; and can man do less?   *150*
As much that end a constant course requires
Of showers and sunshine, as of man's desires;
As much eternal springs and cloudless skies,
As men forever temperate, calm, and wise.
If plagues or earthquakes break not Heaven's design,   *155*
Why then a Borgia, or a Catiline?[8]
Who knows but he whose hand the lightning forms,
Who heaves old ocean, and who wings the storms,
Pours fierce ambition in a Caesar's mind,
Or turns young Ammon[9] loose to scourge mankind?   *160*
From pride, from pride, our very reasoning springs;
Account for moral, as for natural things:
Why charge we Heaven in those, in these acquit?
In both, to reason right is to submit.

    Better for us, perhaps, it might appear,   *165*
Were there all harmony, all virtue here;
That never air or ocean felt the wind;
That never passion discomposed the mind:
But ALL subsists by elemental strife;
And passions are the elements of life.   *170*
The general ORDER, since the whole began,
Is kept in Nature, and is kept in man.

    6. What would this man? Now upward will he soar,
And little less than angel, would be more;
Now looking downwards, just as grieved appears   *175*
To want the strength of bulls, the fur of bears.
Made for his use all creatures if he call,
Say what their use, had he the powers of all?
Nature to these, without profusion, kind,
The proper organs, proper powers assigned;
Each seeming want compénsated of course,   *180*
Here with degrees of swiftness, there of force;
All in exact proportion to the state;
Nothing to add, and nothing to abate.

---

[8]The Renaissance Italian family of the Borgias were notorious for their crimes: ruthless lust for power, cruelty, rapaciousness, treachery, and murder (especially by poisoning); Cesare Borgia (1476–1507), son of Pope Alexander VI, is here referred to. Lucius Sergius Catiline (ca. 108–62 B.C.), an ambitious, greedy, and cruel conspirator against the Roman state, was denounced in Cicero's famous orations before the senate and in the Forum.

[9]Alexander the Great.

Each beast, each insect, happy in its own;   *185*
Is Heaven unkind to man, and man alone?
Shall he alone, whom rational we call,
Be pleased with nothing, if not blessed with all?
        The bliss of man (could pride that blessing find)
Is not to act or think beyond mankind;   *190*
No powers of body or of soul to share,
But what his nature and his state can bear.
Why has not man a microscopic eye?
For this plain reason, man is not a fly.
Say what the use, were finer optics given,   *195*
To inspect a mite, not comprehend the heaven?
Or touch, if tremblingly alive all o'er,
To smart and agonize at every pore?
Or quick effluvia[10] darting through the brain,
Die of a rose in aromatic pain?   *200*
If nature thundered in his opening ears,
And stunned him with the music of the spheres,
How would he wish that Heaven had left him still
The whispering zephyr, and the purling rill?
Who finds not Providence all good and wise,   *205*
Alike in what it gives, and what it denies?

    7. Far as creation's ample range extends,
The scale of sensual,[11] mental powers ascends:
Mark how it mounts, to man's imperial race,
From the green myriads in the peopled grass: *210*
What modes of sight betwixt each wide extreme,
The mole's dim curtain, and the lynx's beam:[12]
Of smell, the headlong lioness between,
And hound sagacious[13] on the tainted green:
Of hearing, from the life that fills the flood,   *215*
To that which warbles through the vernal wood:
The spider's touch, how exquisitely fine!
Feels at each thread, and lives along the line:

---

[10]According to the philosophy of Epicurus (adopted by Robert Boyle, the chemist, and other 17th-century scientists), the senses are stirred to perception by being bombarded through the pores by steady streams of "effluvia," incredibly thin and tiny — but material — images of the objects which surround us.

[11]Sensory.

[12]One of several early theories of vision held that the eye casts a beam of light which makes objects visible.

[13]Quick of scent.

In the nice[14] bee, what sense so subtly true
From poisonous herbs extracts the healing dew: *220*
How instinct varies in the groveling swine,
Compared, half-reasoning elephant, with thine!
'Twixt that, and reason, what a nice barrier;[15]
Forever separate, yet forever near!
Remembrance and reflection how allied;   *225*
What thin partitions sense from thought divide:
And middle natures, how they long to join,
Yet never pass the insuperable line!
Without this just gradation, could they be
Subjected, these to those, or all to thee?   *230*
The powers of all subdued by thee alone,
Is not thy reason all these powers in one?

    8. See, through this air, this ocean, and this earth,
All matter quick, and bursting into birth.
Above, how high progressive life may go!   *235*
Around, how wide! how deep extend below!
Vast Chain of Being! which from God began,
Natures ethereal, human, angel, man,
Beast, bird, fish, insect, what no eye can see,
No glass can reach! from Infinite to thee,   *240*
From thee to nothing. — On superior powers
Were we to press, inferior might on ours:
Or in the full creation leave a void,
Where, one step broken, the great scale's destroyed:
From Nature's chain whatever link you strike,   *245*
Tenth or ten thousandth, breaks the chain alike.
    And, if each system in gradation roll
Alike essential to the amazing Whole,
The least confusion but in one, not all
That system only, but the Whole must fall.   *250*
Let earth unbalanced from her orbit fly,
Planets and suns run lawless through the sky,
Let ruling angels from their spheres be hurled,
Being on being wrecked, and world on world,
Heaven's whole foundations to their center nod,   *255*
And Nature tremble to the throne of God:

---

[14]Exact, accurate.
[15]Pronounced *ba-réer.*

All this dread ORDER break — for whom? for thee?
Vile worm! — oh, madness, pride, impiety!

   9. What if the foot, ordained the dust to tread,
Or hand, to toil, aspired to be the head?   *260*
What if the head, the eye, or ear repined
To serve mere engines to the ruling Mind?[16]
Just as absurd for any part to claim
To be another, in this general frame:
Just as absurd, to mourn the tasks or pains,   *265*
The great directing MIND OF ALL ordains.
   All are but parts of one stupendous whole,
Whose body Nature is, and God the soul;
That, changed through all, and yet in all the same,
Great in the earth, as in the ethereal frame,   *270*
Warms in the sun, refreshes in the breeze,
Glows in the stars, and blossoms in the trees,
Lives through all life, extends through all extent,
Spreads undivided, operates unspent,
Breathes in our soul, informs our mortal part,   *275*
As full, as perfect, in a hair as heart;
As full, as perfect, in vile man that mourns,
As the rapt seraph that adores and burns;
To him no high, no low, no great, no small;
He fills, he bounds, connects, and equals all.   *280*

   10. Cease then, nor ORDER imperfection name:
Our proper bliss depends on what we blame.
Know thy own point: this kind, this due degree
Of blindness, weakness, Heaven bestows on thee.
Submit — In this, or any other sphere,   *285*
Secure to be as blest as thou canst bear:
Safe in the hand of one disposing Power,
Or in the natal, or the mortal hour.
All Nature is but art, unknown to thee;
All chance, direction, which thou canst not see;   *290*
All discord, harmony not understood;
All partial evil, universal good:
And, spite of pride, in erring reason's spite,
One truth is clear: WHATEVER IS, IS RIGHT.

---

[16]Cf. I Corinthians xii.14–26.

REVIEW QUESTIONS

1. Paraphrase the eleven verses of the poem.
2. Review your paraphrase and write in four or five sentences what you take to be Pope's view of man in the universe. Include in your answer Pope's considerations of human presumptuousness, limits to human knowledge, and divine order.
3. Cite lines to the poem in answering Review Questions 3–6. For what reasons does Pope feel we should be hopeful?
4. How does Pope account for unhappiness? (See verse 5.)
5. What is man's proper place, according to Pope? In what way does man exist properly in his sphere just as the animals do in theirs?
6. How do humans risk breaking the "Vast Chain of Being" if they overstep their bounds? (See lines 233–258.)

DISCUSSION AND WRITING QUESTIONS

1. In what ways does Pope believe we are presumptuous? In order to justify this charge of presumption, what views must Pope hold about a deity and a divine plan? Are these your views?
2. Reread lines 69–76. Then reread Pascal, *Pensée* 205. What relationship between the two authors do you infer here? Characterize the conversation that is taking place. Whose side do you take on the issue? (See also Pope, lines 189–206, and Pascal, paragraph 3, on the mite.)
3. How does the Indian's view of the world differ from that of the Christian to whom the lessons of science are available, according to Pope? Are there any ways in which you find Pope's characterization of the Indian unrealistic, or even patronizing?
4. Pope says:

   > In pride, in reasoning pride, our error lies;
   > All quit their sphere, and rush into the skies.

   Fontenelle says:

   > "we wish to know more than we can see; this is the difficulty."

   Pascal says:

   > It is strange that [men] have wished to understand the beginnings of things, and thence to arrive at the knowledge of the whole, with a presumption as infinite as their object.

   What is this impulse about which the three authors are speaking? How is this impulse related to the activities of Copernicus and Galileo? Is this the same impulse that is the subject of condemnation by the Holy Inquisition?
5. "Submit — In this, or any other sphere. . . ." What, in the context of the poem, does Pope mean? Do you agree with Pope? Explain.
6. Reread the last twelve lines of the poem. What is Pope's rationale for the statement, "Whatever is, is right"? Do you agree (especially in light of contemporary history) with his conclusions?

T. H. HUXLEY *(1825–1895)*

As a biologist, physician, educator, and supporter of Darwin's theories, Thomas Henry Huxley was a voice respected and heard often — on many subjects — in Victorian England. Not surprisingly, his work is also included in another chapter in this book. For a biographical sketch of Huxley, turn to page 363, our introduction to an excerpt from his *Evolution and Ethics.*

Huxley wrote and delivered the following essay to a London audience in 1866, by which time the Copernican account of planetary motion had long been accepted as factual — at least within the scientific community. But as recently as 1821 the governing bodies of the Catholic church had resisted endorsing the heliocentric view. Then, in the following year, responding to pressures arising from the publication of a textbook, the Holy Inquisition amended its position on Copernicus, agreeing that

> the printing and publication of works treating of the motion of the earth and the stability of the sun, in accordance with the general opinion of modern astronomers, is permitted at Rome.

Not until Huxley was ten years old (in 1835) did the Inquisition expunge from the Index of prohibited books *On the Revolution of Heavenly Spheres,* along with Galileo's *Dialogue Concerning the Two Chief World Systems* and Kepler's *Epitome of Copernican Astronomy.* Almost immediately following this resolution of the Copernican affair, a new attack on church doctrine was underway. In 1859, Charles Darwin published *The Origin of Species* and rocked the scientific and theological worlds with his thesis that humans are descended from primates and that, evolutionarily speaking, they are no more privileged than the other species.

One can well imagine the church's response to the challenge. Already the earth had lost its privileged position in the cosmos. Before Darwin, theologians could console their loss with the knowledge that on earth, at least, man and woman retained their unique status — if not with respect to the heavens then at least with respect to the lower animals. With Darwin even this distinction was threatened, and the church responded with a fight. A series of well-publicized debates took place between theologians and Darwinians. Huxley argued eloquently for the theory of evolution and, more generally, for the spirit of rational inquiry. There is little wonder that he should call himself an "agnostic," the term he coined to establish his position as one for whom truth does not exist without the support of direct, clearly observable evidence. His creed extended to all fields, especially theology: until evidence for the existence of God could be provided, he believed, it is logically untenable for one to have faith. In his essay "Agnosticism and Christianity," he wrote on the implications of this belief:

> It was inevitable that a conflict should arise between Agnosticism and Theology; or rather, I ought to say, between Agnosticism and Ecclesiasticism. For

138

Theology, the science, is one thing; and Ecclesiasticism, the championship of a foregone conclusion as to the truth of a particular form of Theology, is another. With scientific Theology, Agnosticism has no quarrel. On the contrary, the Agnostic, knowing too well the influence of prejudice and idiosyncrasy, even on those who desire most earnestly to be impartial, can wish for nothing more urgently than that the scientific theologian should not only be at perfect liberty to thresh out the matter in his own fashion; but that he should, if he can, find flaws in the Agnostic position; and, even if demonstration is not to be had, that he should put, in their full force, the grounds of the conclusions he thinks probable. The scientific theologian admits the Agnostic principle, however widely his results may differ from those reached by the majority of Agnostics.

But, as between Agnosticism and Ecclesiasticism, or, as our neighbours across the Channel call it, Clericalism, there can be neither peace nor truce. The Cleric asserts that it is morally wrong not to believe certain propositions, whatever the results of a strict scientific investigation of the evidence of these propositions. He tells us "that religious error is, in itself, of an immoral nature."[1] He declares that he has prejudged certain conclusions, and looks upon those who show cause for arrest of judgment as emissaries of Satan. It necessarily follows that, for him, the attainment of faith, not the ascertainment of truth, is the highest aim of mental life. And, on careful analysis of the nature of this faith, it will too often be found to be, not the mystic process of unity with the Divine, understood by the religious enthusiast; but that which the candid simplicity of a Sunday scholar once defined it to be. "Faith," said this unconscious plagiarist of Tertullian, "is the power of saying you believe things which are incredible."

Now I, and many other Agnostics, believe that faith, in this sense, is an abomination; and though we do not indulge in the luxury of self-righteousness so far as to call those who are not of our way of thinking hard names, we do feel that the disagreement between ourselves and those who hold this doctrine is even more moral than intellectual. . . .

It was the development of just such a philosophy for discovering truth through direct, positive knowledge (as opposed to discovery through revelation) that the Holy Office foresaw in its condemnation of Galileo and tried to suppress. But the spirit of rational inquiry had taken hold, and the church, for all its authority, was powerless to stop it. In the essay that follows we see the logical extension of the scientific optimism expressed (in germinal form) in the writings of Copernicus and Galileo — and (in more developed form) in the writings of the Enlightenment philosophers.[2]

T. H. Huxley lived during an age in which the engines of science and technol-

---

Thomas Henry Huxley. From "Agnosticism and Christianity" (1889) in *Collected Essays: Science and Christian Tradition*, Vol. 5. London, Macmillan and Co., 1897, pp. 312–314.

[1]Dr. Newman, *Essay on Development*, p. 357. [Huxley]

[2]For example, see selections by Locke, Rousseau, and Condorcet — pages 194, 221, and 293. For a second 19th-century view, see the essay by Macaulay on page 347.

ogy gave one good cause for optimism. In Europe, infant mortality was on the decline; the ravages of the plague had been defeated and life expectancy prolonged; a revolution in sociological thinking had given rise to representative governments that seemed to work; industry flourished and the accumulation of great wealth was possible. Would successive advances in science lead to further and kindred achievements? The answer was *yes*, so far as Huxley was concerned; but then he did not live to see technology applied so expertly to the killing of human beings in the First World War. What would Huxley have said to a devastation in which the "improvement of natural knowledge" had played so great a part?

No such question needed be asked in the middle and late 19th century, since grand demonstrations of brutality (rivaling that of World War I) had yet to tarnish the intellectual's view of the human enterprise. Prospects for achieving a salvation on earth — without assistance from God — seemed promising. And, as no proof existed for an afterlife, there was apparently little need felt by the agnostic for eternal salvation. God was dispensable; humanity could care for itself. The scientific view of the world now offered an impressive, rival system to religious faith and through the efforts of Huxley and others was attacking the need to "believe things which are incredible." When viewed from the 1980s, this development seems an inevitable consequence of the work begun by Copernicus in 1543. As you will see, the agnostic Huxley extends Copernicus to regions where the Polish astronomer would never have ventured. Yet Huxley's faith in the "advisableness of improving natural knowledge" finds its roots in the same spirit of inquiry that led to the discovery of planetary motion.

ON THE ADVISABLENESS OF IMPROVING NATURAL KNOWLEDGE

This time two hundred years ago — in the beginning of January, 1666 — those of our forefathers who inhabited this great and ancient city, took breath between the shocks of two fearful calamities: one not quite past, although its fury had abated; the other to come.   1

Within a few yards of the very spot on which we are assembled, so the tradition runs, that painful and deadly malady, the plague, appeared in the latter months of 1664; and, though no new visitor, smote the people of England, and especially of her capital, with a violence unknown before, in the course of the following year. The hand of a master has pictured what happened in those dismal months; and in that truest of fictions, "The His-   2

Thomas Henry Huxley. "On the Advisableness of Improving Natural Knowledge" in *Collected Essays: Method and Results*, Vol. 1. London, Macmillan and Co., 1894, pp. 18–41.

tory of the Plague Year," Defoe[1] shows death, with every accompaniment of pain and terror, stalking through the narrow streets of old London, and changing their busy hum into a silence broken only by the wailing of the mourners of fifty thousand dead; by the woful denunciations and mad prayers of fanatics; and by the madder yells of despairing profligates.

But, about this time in 1666, the death-rate had sunk to nearly its or-   3 dinary amount; a case of plague occurred only here and there, and the richer citizens who had flown from the pest had returned to their dwellings. The remnant of the people began to toil at the accustomed round of duty, or of pleasure; and the stream of city life bid fair to flow back along its old bed, with renewed and uninterrupted vigour.

The newly-kindled hope was deceitful. The great plague, indeed, re-   4 turned no more; but what it had done for the Londoners, the great fire, which broke out in the autumn of 1666,[2] did for London; and, in September of that year, a heap of ashes and the indestructible energy of the people were all that remained of the glory of five-sixths of the city within the walls.

Our forefathers had their own ways of accounting for each of these   5 calamities. They submitted to the plague in humility and in penitence, for they believed it to be the judgment of God. But, towards the fire they were furiously indignant, interpreting it as the effect of the malice of man, — as the work of the Republicans,[3] or of the Papists,[4] according as their pre-possessions ran in favour of loyalty or of Puritanism.[5]

It would, I fancy, have fared but ill with one who, standing where I   6 now stand, in what was then a thickly-peopled and fashionable part of London, should have broached to our ancestors the doctrine which I now propound to you — that all their hypotheses were alike wrong; that the plague was no more, in their sense, Divine judgment, than the fire was

---

[1]Refers to English writer Daniel Defoe (1660–1731), best known for his novels *Robinson Crusoe* and *Moll Flanders*. His *Journal of the Plague Year* was first published in 1722. [N.B.: The title is "Journal," not "History," as mentioned by Huxley.]

[2]*the great fire of 1666:* The "great fire" refers to the worst fire in London's history, lasting from September 2 to 5 of that year. It began with an accidental fire in the house of the king's baker on Pudding Lane. Because of a particularly strong wind that day, it spread rapidly throughout most of the City of London, destroying most civic buildings, old St. Paul's Cathedral, and some 13,000 houses.

[3]*Republicans:* Those in England who advocated political power by vote rather than by monarchical rule.

[4]*Papists:* Generally considered a pejorative epithet used from the sixteenth century on to describe Roman Catholics or those who believed in the supremacy of the Pope.

[5]*Puritanism:* The religious reform movement of the sixteenth and seventeenth centuries that attempted to recover from the Church of England remnants of Roman Catholic ritual. This attempt at church reform ultimately led to civil war in England and to the founding of colonies in America.

the work of any political, or of any religious, sect; but that they were themselves the authors of both plague and fire, and that they must look to themselves to prevent the recurrence of calamities, to all appearance so peculiarly beyond the reach of human control — so evidently the result of the wrath of God, or of the craft and subtlety of an enemy.

And one may picture to one's self how harmoniously the holy cursing   7
of the Puritan of that day would have chimed in with the unholy cursing and the crackling wit of the Rochesters and Sedleys,[6] and with the revilings of the political fanatics, if my imaginary plain dealer had gone on to say that, if the return of such misfortunes were ever rendered impossible, it would not be in virtue of the victory of the faith of Laud,[7] or of that of Milton;[8] and, as little, by the triumph of republicanism, as by that of monarchy. But that the one thing needful for compassing this end was, that the people of England should second the efforts of an insignificant corporation, the establishment of which, a few years before the epoch of the great plague and the great fire, had been as little noticed, as they were conspicuous.

Some twenty years before the outbreak of the plague a few calm and   8
thoughtful students banded themselves together for the purpose, as they phrased it, of "improving natural knowledge." The ends they proposed to attain cannot be stated more clearly than in the words of one of the founders of the organisation: —

"Our business was (precluding matters of theology and state affairs)   9
to discourse and consider of philosophical enquiries, and such as related thereunto: — as Physick, Anatomy, Geometry, Astronomy, Navigation, Staticks, Magneticks, Chymicks, Mechanicks, and Natural Experiments; with the state of these studies and their cultivation at home and abroad. We then discoursed of the circulation of the blood, the valves in the veins,

---

[6] *Rochesters and Sedleys:* Huxley is using as examples of quintessential seventeenth century satire the two most popular court wits of the day, John Wilmont, second earl of Rochester, and Sir Charles Sedley. Wilmont (1647–1680) received his M.A. at Oxford in 1661. He soon became known as one of the most educated of court wits and is generally considered one of the most original of English satirists to have emerged from the Restoration period. Sedley (1639–1701) was also a court wit for king Charles II and a respected Restoration poet and dramatist.

[7] *Laud:* William Laud (1573–1645) was the archbishop of Canterbury and religious advisor to king Charles I of Great Britain. He was tried and executed by the House of Commons for his violent persecution of Puritans and other religious dissidents.

[8] *Milton:* John Milton (1608–1674) is considered one of the greatest poets of the English language and is best known for his epic poem, *Paradise Lost*. Aside from his literary career, he was also a respected historian and pamphleteer who devoted much of his life to the Puritan cause in England. He also worked as a civil servant for the Puritan Commonwealth.

the venæ lacteæ, the lymphatic vessels, the Copernican hypothesis, the nature of comets and new stars, the satellites of Jupiter, the oval shape (as it then appeared) of Saturn, the spots on the sun and its turning on its own axis, the inequalities and selenography[9] of the moon, the several phases of Venus and Mercury, the improvement of telescopes and grinding of glasses for that purpose, the weight of air, the possibility or impossibility of vacuities and nature's abhorrence thereof, the Torricellian experiment in quicksilver,[10] the descent of heavy bodies and the degree of acceleration therein, with divers other things of like nature, some of which were then but new discoveries, and others not so generally known and embraced as now they are; with other things appertaining to what hath been called the New Philosophy, which from the times of Galileo at Florence, and Sir Francis Bacon (Lord Verulam) in England, hath been much cultivated in Italy, France, Germany, and other parts abroad, as well as with us in England."

The learned Dr. Wallis, writing in 1696, narrates in these words, what happened half a century before, or about 1645. The associates met at Oxford, in the rooms of Dr. Wilkins, who was destined to become a bishop; and subsequently coming together in London, they attracted the notice of the king. And it is a strange evidence of the taste for knowledge which the most obviously worthless of the Stuarts shared with his father and grandfather, that Charles the Second was not content with saying witty things about his philosophers, but did wise things with regard to them. For he not only bestowed upon them such attention as he could spare from his poodles and his mistresses, but, being in his usual state of impecuniosity, begged for them of the Duke of Ormond;[11] and, that step being without effect, gave them Chelsea College,[12] a charter, and a mace: crowning his favours in the best way they could be crowned, by burdening them no further with royal patronage or state interference.

Thus it was that the half-dozen young men, studious of the "New Philosophy," who met in one another's lodgings in Oxford or in London, in the middle of the seventeenth century, grew in numerical and in real strength, until, in its latter part, the "Royal Society for the Improvement of Natural Knowledge" had already become famous, and had acquired a

---

[9]*selenography:* The study of the physical features of the moon.

[10]*Torricellian experiment in quicksilver:* Italian physicist Evangelista Torricelli (1608–1674) was the first man to create a sustained vacuum by filling a long tube with mercury (quicksilver), inverting the tube into a dish and observing that some of the mercury remained in the tube, thus creating a vacuum above it. Torricelli is also known for his invention of the barometer and his work in geometry.

[11]*Duke of Ormond:* James Butler, the twelfth earl and first duke of Ormonde, was an Anglo-Irish Protestant who supported the authority of the king in Ireland from the English Civil War to the Revolution of 1688.

[12]*Chelsea College:* A college of the University of London.

claim upon the veneration of Englishmen, which it has ever since retained, as the principal focus of scientific activity in our islands, and the chief champion of the cause it was formed to support.

It was by the aid of the Royal Society that Newton published his "Principia." If all the books in the world, except the "Philosophical Transactions,"[13] were destroyed, it is safe to say that the foundations of physical science would remain unshaken, and that the vast intellectual progress of the last two centuries would be largely, though incompletely, recorded. Nor have any signs of halting or of decrepitude manifested themselves in our own times. As in Dr. Wallis's days, so in these, "our business is, precluding theology and state affairs, to discourse and consider of philosophical enquiries." But our "Mathematick" is one which Newton would have to go to school to learn; our "Staticks, Mechanicks, Magneticks, Chymicks, and Natural Experiments" constitute a mass of physical and chemical knowledge, a glimpse at which would compensate Galileo for the doings of a score of inquisitorial cardinals; our "Physick" and "Anatomy" have embraced such infinite varieties of being, have laid open such new worlds in time and space, have grappled, not unsuccessfully, with such complex problems, that the eyes of Vesalius and Harvey might be dazzled by the sight of the tree that has grown out of their grain of mustard seed.[14]

The fact is perhaps rather too much, than too little, forced upon one's notice, nowadays, that all this marvellous intellectual growth has a no less wonderful expression in practical life; and that, in this respect, if in no other, the movement symbolised by the progress of the Royal Society stands without a parallel in the history of mankind.

A series of volumes as bulky as the "Transactions of the Royal Society" might possibly be filled with the subtle speculations of the Schoolmen; not improbably, the obtaining a mastery over the products of mediæval thought might necessitate an even greater expenditure of time and of energy than the acquirement of the "New Philosophy"; but though such work engrossed the best intellects of Europe for a longer time than has elapsed since the great fire, its effects were "writ in water," so far as our social state is concerned.

12

13

14

---

[13]*"Philosophical Transactions":* The published transactions of the Royal Society of London for the Promotion of Natural Knowledge. The Royal Society is the oldest scientific society in Great Britain, founded in 1660 by royal charter. Its publication, "Philosophical Transactions," began in 1665 and included papers by famous scientists such as Isaac Newton and Francis Bacon.

[14]Huxley is referring to the pioneering scientific exploration and discoveries of early scientists like Andreas Vesalius and William Harvey. Vesalius, a Renaissance Greek physician, revolutionized the study of medicine with his observations on dissections and his textbook of anatomy, the first ever to be published. Harvey was an English physician who demonstrated the nature of the circulatory system and the function of the heart.

On the other hand, if the noble first President of the Royal Society   15
could revisit the upper air and once more gladden his eyes with a sight of
the familiar mace, he would find himself in the midst of a material civilisation more different from that of his day, than that of the seventeenth was
from that of the first century. And if Lord Brouncker's[15] native sagacity had
not deserted his ghost, he would need no long reflection to discover that
all these great ships, these railways, these telegraphs, these factories, these
printing-presses, without which the whole fabric of modern English society would collapse into a mass of stagnant and starving pauperism, — that
all these pillars of our State are but the ripples and the bubbles upon the
surface of that great spiritual stream, the springs of which only he and his
fellows were privileged to see; and seeing, to recognise as that which it
behoved them above all things to keep pure and undefiled.

It may not be too great a flight of imagination to conceive our noble   16
revenant[16] not forgetful of the great troubles of his own day, and anxious to
know how often London had been burned down since his time, and how
often the plague had carried off its thousands. He would have to learn that,
although London contains tenfold the inflammable matter that it did in
1666; though, not content with filling our rooms with woodwork and light
draperies, we must needs lead inflammable and explosive gases into every
corner of our streets and houses, we never allow even a street to burn
down. And if he asked how this had come about, we should have to explain that the improvement of natural knowledge has furnished us with
dozens of machines for throwing water upon fires, any one of which
would have furnished the ingenious Mr. Hooke,[17] the first "curator and
experimenter" of the Royal Society, with ample materials for discourse before half a dozen meetings of that body; and that, to say truth, except for
the progress of natural knowledge, we should not have been able to make
even the tools by which these machines are constructed. And, further, it
would be necessary to add, that although severe fires sometimes occur and
inflict great damage, the loss is very generally compensated by societies,
the operations of which have been rendered possible only by the progress
of natural knowledge in the direction of mathematics, and the accumulation of wealth in virtue of other natural knowledge.

But the plague? My Lord Brouncker's observation would not, I fear,   17
lead him to think that Englishmen of the nineteenth century are purer in

---

[15]Huxley is commenting on the changes that have taken place since the days of Sir William
Brouncker, the first president of the Royal Society. A mace is a staff used by leaders to
symbolize their authority.

[16]*revenant:* A person who returns after a long absence.

[17]*Mr. Hooke:* Robert Hooke (1635–1703) was the famous English physicist who discovered
the law of elasticity. In 1662 he was appointed curator of experiments to the Royal Society.

life, or more fervent in religious faith, than the generation which could produce a Boyle,[18] an Evelyn,[19] and a Milton. He might find the mud of society at the bottom, instead of at the top, but I fear that the sum total would be as deserving of swift judgment as at the time of the Restoration.[20] And it would be our duty to explain once more, and this time not without shame, that we have no reason to believe that it is the improvement of our faith, nor that of our morals, which keeps the plague from our city; but, again, that it is the improvement of our natural knowledge.

We have learned that pestilences will only take up their abode among those who have prepared unswept and ungarnished residences for them. Their cities must have narrow, unwatered streets, foul with accumulated garbage. Their houses must be ill-drained, ill-lighted, ill-ventilated. Their subjects must be ill-washed, ill-fed, ill-clothed. The London of 1665 was such a city. The cities of the East, where plague has an enduring dwelling, are such cities. We, in later times, have learned somewhat of Nature, and partly obey her. Because of this partial improvement of our natural knowledge and of that fractional obedience, we have no plague; because that knowledge is still very imperfect and that obedience yet incomplete, typhoid is our companion and cholera our visitor. But it is not presumptuous to express the belief that, when our knowledge is more complete and our obedience the expression of our knowledge, London will count her centuries of freedom from typhoid and cholera, as she now gratefully reckons her two hundred years of ignorance of that plague which swooped upon her thrice in the first half of the seventeenth century.

Surely, there is nothing in these explanations which is not fully borne out by the facts? Surely, the principles involved in them are now admitted among the fixed beliefs of all thinking men? Surely, it is true that our countrymen are less subject to fire, famine, pestilence, and all the evils which result from a want of command over and due anticipation of the course of Nature, than were the countrymen of Milton; and health, wealth, and well-being are more abundant with us than with them? But no less certainly is the difference due to the improvement of our knowledge of Nature, and the extent to which that improved knowledge has been incorporated with

18

19

---

[18]*Boyle:* Robert Boyle (1627–1691) was an Anglo-Irish chemist who became famous for his experiments on the properties of gasses. As for his exemplary religious faith, he was a devout Protestant who promoted missionary efforts to Christianize the "infidels" abroad and donated large sums of money to translate the New Testament into Irish and Turkish.

[19]*Evelyn:* John Evelyn (1620–1706) was a member of the English gentry who wrote some thirty books on various topics ranging from the fine arts to forestry. He is also known for his essays on religion.

[20]*Restoration:* Refers to the restoration of the monarchy in England in 1660 after the fall of the republican Commonwealth and Protectorate. King Charles II was restored to power after a period of exile on condition that he guarantee religious tolerance.

the household words of men, and has supplied the springs of their daily actions.

Granting for a moment, then, the truth of that which the depreciators   20 of natural knowledge are so fond of urging, that its improvement can only add to the resources of our material civilisation; admitting it to be possible that the founders of the Royal Society themselves looked for no other reward than this, I cannot confess that I was guilty of exaggeration when I hinted, that to him who had the gift of distinguishing between prominent events and important events, the origin of a combined effort on the part of mankind to improve natural knowledge might have loomed larger than the Plague and have outshone the glare of the Fire; as a something fraught with a wealth of beneficence to mankind, in comparison with which the damage done by those ghastly evils would shrink into insignificance.

It is very certain that for every victim slain by the plague, hundreds of mankind exist and find a fair share of happiness in the world by the aid of the spinning jenny.[21] And the great fire, at its worst, could not have burned the supply of coal, the daily working of which, in the bowels of the earth, made possible by the steam pump, gives rise to an amount of wealth to which the millions lost in old London are but as an old song.

But spinning jenny and steam pump are, after all, but toys, possessing   21 an accidental value; and natural knowledge creates multitudes of more subtle contrivances, the praises of which do not happen to be sung because they are not directly convertible into instruments for creating wealth. When I contemplate natural knowledge squandering such gifts among men, the only appropriate comparison I can find for her is, to liken her to such a peasant woman as one sees in the Alps, striding ever upward, heavily burdened, and with mind bent only on her home; but yet without effort and without thought, knitting for her children. Now stockings are good and comfortable things, and the children will undoubtedly be much the better for them; but surely it would be shortsighted, to say the least of it, to depreciate this toiling mother as a mere stocking-machine — a mere provider of physical comforts?

However, there are blind leaders of the blind, and not a few of them,   22 who take this view of natural knowledge, and can see nothing in the bountiful mother of humanity but a sort of comfort-grinding machine. According to them, the improvement of natural knowledge always has been, and always must be, synonymous with no more than the improvement of the material resources and the increase of the gratifications of men.

Natural knowledge is, in their eyes, no real mother of mankind, bring-   23 ing them up with kindness, and, if need be, with sternness, in the way

---

[21]*spinning jenny:* An early form of spinning machine developed in the 1760s.

they should go, and instructing them in all things needful for their welfare; but a sort of fairy godmother, ready to furnish her pets with shoes of swiftness, swords of sharpness, and omnipotent Aladdin's lamps, so that they may have telegraphs to Saturn, and see the other side of the moon, and thank God they are better than their benighted ancestors.

If this talk were true, I, for one, should not greatly care to toil in the service of natural knowledge. I think I would just as soon be quietly chipping my own flint axe, after the manner of my forefathers a few thousand years back, as be troubled with the endless malady of thought which now infests us all, for such reward. But I venture to say that such views are contrary alike to reason and to fact. Those who discourse in such fashion seem to me to be so intent upon trying to see what is above Nature, or what is behind her, that they are blind to what stares them in the face in her.   24

I should not venture to speak thus strongly if my justification were not to be found in the simplest and most obvious facts, — if it needed more than an appeal to the most notorious truths to justify my assertion, that the improvement of natural knowledge, whatever direction it has taken, and however low the aims of those who may have commenced it — has not only conferred practical benefits on men, but, in so doing, has effected a revolution in their conceptions of the universe and of themselves, and has profoundly altered their modes of thinking and their views of right and wrong. I say that natural knowledge, seeking to satisfy natural wants, has found the ideas which can alone still spiritual cravings. I say that natural knowledge, in desiring to ascertain the laws of comfort, has been driven to discover those of conduct, and to lay the foundations of a new morality.   25

Let us take these points separately; and first, what great ideas has natural knowledge introduced into men's minds?   26

I cannot but think that the foundations of all natural knowledge were laid when the reason of man first came face to face with the facts of Nature; when the savage first learned that the fingers of one hand are fewer than those of both; that it is shorter to cross a stream than to head it; that a stone stops where it is unless it be moved, and that it drops from the hand which lets it go; that light and heat come and go with the sun; that sticks burn away in a fire; that plants and animals grow and die; that if he struck his fellow savage a blow he would make him angry, and perhaps get a blow in return, while if he offered him a fruit he would please him, and perhaps receive a fish in exchange. When men had acquired this much knowledge, the outlines, rude though they were, of mathematics, of physics, of chemistry, of biology, of moral, economical, and political science, were sketched. Nor did the germ of religion fail when science began   27 to bud. Listen to words which, though new, are yet three thousand years old: —

> . . . When in heaven the stars about the moon
> Look beautiful, when all the winds are laid,
> And every height comes out, and jutting peak
> And valley, and the immeasurable heavens
> Break open to their highest, and all the stars
> Shine, and the shepherd gladdens in his heart.[22]

If the half savage Greek could share our feelings thus far, it is irrational to doubt that he went further, to find as we do, that upon that brief gladness there follows a certain sorrow, — the little light of awakened human intelligence shines so mere a spark amidst the abyss of the unknown and unknowable; seems so insufficient to do more than illuminate the imperfections that cannot be remedied, the aspirations that cannot be realised, of man's own nature. But in this sadness, this consciousness of the limitation of man, this sense of an open secret which he cannot penetrate, lies the essence of all religion; and the attempt to embody it in the forms furnished by the intellect is the origin of the higher theologies.   *28*

Thus it seems impossible to imagine but that the foundations of all knowledge — secular or sacred — were laid when intelligence dawned, though the superstructure remained for long ages so slight and feeble as to be compatible with the existence of almost any general view respecting the mode of governance of the universe. No doubt, from the first, there were certain phænomena which, to the rudest mind, presented a constancy of occurrence, and suggested that a fixed order ruled, at any rate, among them. I doubt if the grossest of Fetish worshippers[23] ever imagined that a stone must have a god within it to make it fall, or that a fruit had a god within it to make it taste sweet. With regard to such matters as these, it is hardly questionable that mankind from the first took strictly positive and scientific views.   *29*

But, with respect to all the less familiar occurrences which present themselves, uncultured man, no doubt, has always taken himself as the standard of comparison, as the centre and measure of the world; nor could he well avoid doing so. And finding that his apparently uncaused will has a powerful effect in giving rise to many occurrences, he naturally enough ascribed other and greater events to other and greater volitions, and came   *30*

---

[22]Need it be said that this is Tennyson's English for Homer's Greek? [Huxley]

[23]*Fetish worshippers:* Those who attach magical powers to inanimate objects and make them the subject of religious worship.

to look upon the world and all that therein is, as the product of the volitions of persons like himself, but stronger, and capable of being appeased or angered, as he himself might be soothed or irritated. Through such conceptions of the plan and working of the universe all mankind have passed, or are passing. And we may now consider what has been the effect of the improvement of natural knowledge on the views of men who have reached this stage, and who have begun to cultivate natural knowledge with no desire but that of "increasing God's honour and bettering man's estate."

For example, what could seem wiser, from a mere material point of   31
view, more innocent, from a theological one, to an ancient people, than that they should learn the exact succession of the seasons, as warnings for their husbandmen; or the position of the stars, as guides to their rude navigators? But what has grown out of this search for natural knowledge of so merely useful a character? You all know the reply. Astronomy, — which of all sciences has filled men's minds with general ideas of a character most foreign to their daily experience, and has, more than any other, rendered it impossible for them to accept the beliefs of their fathers. Astronomy, — which tells them that this so vast and seemingly solid earth is but an atom among atoms, whirling, no man knows whither, through illimitable space; which demonstrates that what we call the peaceful heaven above us, is but that space, filled by an infinitely subtle matter whose particles are seething and surging, like the waves of an angry sea; which opens up to us infinite regions where nothing is known, or ever seems to have been known, but matter and force, operating according to rigid rules; which leads us to contemplate phænomena the very nature of which demonstrates that they must have had a beginning, and that they must have an end, but the very nature of which also proves that the beginning was, to our conceptions of time, infinitely remote, and that the end is as immeasurably distant.

But it is not alone those who pursue astronomy who ask for bread and   32
receive ideas. What more harmless than the attempt to lift and distribute water by pumping it; what more absolutely and grossly utilitarian? Yet out of pumps grew the discussions about Nature's abhorrence of a vacuum; and then it was discovered that Nature does not abhor a vacuum, but that air has weight; and that notion paved the way for the doctrine that all matter has weight, and that the force which produces weight is co-extensive with the universe, — in short, to the theory of universal gravitation and endless force. While learning how to handle gases led to the discovery of oxygen, and to modern chemistry, and to the notion of the indestructibility of matter.

Again, what simpler, or more absolutely practical, than the attempt to   33
keep the axle of a wheel from heating when the wheel turns round very fast? How useful for carters and gig drivers to know something about this; and how good were it, if any ingenious person would find out the cause

of such phænomena, and thence educe a general remedy for them. Such an ingenious person was Count Rumford;[24] and he and his successors have landed us in the theory of the persistence, or indestructibility, of force. And in the infinitely minute, as in the infinitely great, the seekers after natural knowledge of the kinds called physical and chemical, have everywhere found a definite order and succession of events which seem never to be infringed.

And how has it fared with "Physick" and Anatomy? Have the anatomist, the physiologist, or the physician, whose business it has been to devote themselves assiduously to that eminently practical and direct end, the alleviation of the sufferings of mankind, — have they been able to confine their vision more absolutely to the strictly useful? I fear they are the worst offenders of all. For if the astronomer has set before us the infinite magnitude of space, and the practical eternity of the duration of the universe; if the physical and chemical philosophers have demonstrated the infinite minuteness of its constituent parts, and the practical eternity of matter and of force; and if both have alike proclaimed the universality of a definite and predicable order and succession of events, the workers in biology have not only accepted all these, but have added more startling theses of their own. For, as the astronomers discover in the earth no centre of the universe, but an eccentric speck, so the naturalists find man to be no centre of the living world, but one amidst endless modifications of life; and as the astronomer observes the mark of practically endless time set upon the arrangements of the solar system so the student of life finds the records of ancient forms of existence peopling the world for ages, which, in relation to human experience, are infinite.

Furthermore, the physiologist finds life to be as dependent for its manifestation on particular molecular arrangements as any physical or chemical phenomenon; and wherever he extends his researches, fixed order and unchanging causation reveal themselves, as plainly as in the rest of Nature.

Nor can I find that any other fate has awaited the germ of Religion. Arising, like all other kinds of knowledge, out of the action and interaction of man's mind, with that which is not man's mind, it has taken the intellectual coverings of Fetishism or Polytheism; of Theism or Atheism; of Superstition or Rationalism. With these, and their relative merits and demerits, I have nothing to do; but this it is needful for my purpose to say, that if the religion of the present differs from that of the past, it is because the

---

[24]*Count Rumford:* Sir Benjamin Thompson, count of Rumford, (1753–1814), was an American-born British physicist and a founder of the Royal Institution of Great Britain who helped to establish the modern theory that heat is a type of motion rather than a liquid, as previously thought.

theology of the present has become more scientific than that of the past; because it has not only renounced idols of wood and idols of stone, but begins to see the necessity of breaking in pieces the idols built up of books and traditions and fine-spun ecclesiastical cobwebs: and of cherishing the noblest and most human of man's emotions, by worship "for the most part of the silent sort" at the altar of the Unknown.

Such are a few of the new conceptions implanted in our minds by the improvement of natural knowledge. Men have acquired the ideas of the practically infinite extent of the universe and of its practical eternity; they are familiar with the conception that our earth is but an infinitesimal fragment of that part of the universe which can be seen; and that, nevertheless, its duration is, as compared with our standards of time, infinite. They have further acquired the idea that man is but one of innumerable forms of life now existing on the globe, and that the present existences are but the last of an immeasurable series of predecessors. Moreover, every step they have made in natural knowledge has tended to extend and rivet in their minds the conception of a definite order of the universe — which is embodied in what are called, by an unhappy metaphor, the laws of Nature —and to narrow the range and loosen the force of men's belief in spontaneity, or in changes other than such as arise out of that definite order itself. 37

Whether these ideas are well or ill founded is not the question. No one can deny that they exist, and have been the inevitable outgrowth of the improvement of natural knowledge. And if so, it cannot be doubted that they are changing the form of men's most cherished and most important convictions. 38

And as regards the second point — the extent to which the improvement of natural knowledge has remodelled and altered what may be termed the intellectual ethics of men, — what are among the moral convictions most fondly held by barbarous and semi-barbarous people. 39

They are the convictions that authority is the soundest basis of belief; that merit attaches to a readiness to believe; that the doubting disposition is a bad one, and scepticism a sin; that when good authority has pronounced what is to be believed, and faith has accepted it, reason has no further duty. There are many excellent persons who yet hold by these principles, and it is not my present business, or intention, to discuss their views. All I wish to bring clearly before your minds is the unquestionable fact, that the improvement of natural knowledge is effected by methods which directly give the lie to all these convictions, and assume the exact reverse of each to be true. 40

The improver of natural knowledge absolutely refuses to acknowledge authority, as such. For him, scepticism is the highest of duties; blind faith the one unpardonable sin. And it cannot be otherwise, for every great advance in natural knowledge has involved the absolute rejection of author- 41 ity, the cherishing of the keenest scepticism, the annihilation of the spirit of blind faith; and the most ardent votary of science holds his firmest convictions, not because the men he most venerates hold them; not because their verity is testified by portents and wonders; but because his experience teaches him that whenever he chooses to bring these convictions into contact with their primary source, Nature — whenever he thinks fit to test them by appealing to experiment and to observation — Nature will confirm them. The man of science has learned to believe in justification, not by faith, but by verification.

Thus, without for a moment pretending to despise the practical results   42
of the improvement of natural knowledge, and its beneficial influence on material civilisation, it must, I think, be admitted that the great ideas, some of which I have indicated, and the ethical spirit which I have endeavoured to sketch, in the few moments which remained at my disposal, constitute the real and permanent significance of natural knowledge.

If these ideas be destined, as I believe they are, to be more and more   43
firmly established as the world grows older; if that spirit be fated, as I believe it is, to extend itself into all departments of human thought, and to become co-extensive with the range of knowledge; if, as our race approaches its maturity, it discovers, as I believe it will, that there is but one kind of knowledge and but one method of acquiring it; then we, who are still children, may justly feel it our highest duty to recognise the advisableness of improving natural knowledge, and so to aid ourselves and our successors in our course towards the noble goal which lies before mankind.

REVIEW QUESTIONS

1. What charge does Huxley make against Londoners of 1666 and how does this charge relate directly to his thesis?
2. What is Huxley's position (as compared with Pascal's and Pope's) concerning subjects we do not yet understand?
3. What relationship does Huxley infer between the prevalence of the plague in 17th century London and that of cholera and typhoid two hundred years later?
4. What is the position of the critics, or depreciators, of natural knowledge? What does materialism (the accumulation of goods and the development of techniques to ease our physical condition) have to do with this critique?
5. In what ways has "natural knowledge, seeking to satisfy natural wants, . . . found the ideas which can alone still spiritual cravings"?
6. What, according to Huxley, are the origins of secular knowledge?
7. How does Huxley explain the emergence of religions?
8. What is it that "constitutes the real and permanent significance of natural knowledge"?

DISCUSSION AND WRITING QUESTIONS

1. What advantages, for the purpose of his essay, does Huxley gain in beginning with two events in 1666?

2. Huxley uses a word to which other authors in this part have spoken: "presumptuous." (See paragraph 18.) Huxley believes that it is not presumptuous to forecast the betterment of the human lot when one considers advances in natural knowledge. What do you infer are the limits to human learning, according to Huxley? In the sense of Pope's "Essay" and Pascal's "Pensées," how is Huxley being presumptuous? What do *you* feel are the limits to human understanding, present and future?

3. Reread paragraph 23. How is this criticism of natural knowledge reminiscent of the Holy Inquisition's condemnation of Galileo? Is there any sense in which you agree with the critics? Explain.

4. Huxley believes that natural knowledge, in "seeking to satisfy natural wants, has found the ideas which can alone still spiritual cravings." Consider the spiritual cravings addressed by Pascal. Do you believe that advancements in knowledge, in Huxley's time or our own, can still these cravings? Explain.

5. Whereas Pascal looks to the infinite and the minute (i.e., to the universe and to the mite) and sees an abyss, Huxley looks and sees everywhere "a definite order and succession of events which seem never to be infringed." Try to account for those two reactions to the infinite and minute. Do you think it possible that Pascal's remarks could be made with equal validity in 1866 (the time of Huxley's writing) and in 1660 (the time of Pascal's writing)? What do advances in natural knowledge have to do with Pascal's question?

6. In response to Question 5, write a dialogue between Pascal and Huxley.

7. Reread paragraph 34. Observe the ways in which Huxley synthesizes discoveries in astronomy and biology. (If you've read selections in the part on Darwin in this book, you'll be particularly aware of this synthesis.) What is the effect of this synthesis on you — that the earth, with respect to the universe, is but an infinitesimal atom; and the human form, with respect to the other animals of creation, is just one more modification of life in the natural world? Not that you have a choice, but would you rather have lived in an age wherein the status of both the earth and the human form was privileged? Explain your answer.

8. In paragraph 40, Huxley directly assaults the principles underlying belief in the world's greatest religions. Paraphrase this attack. Then evaluate the validity of the attack. To what extent do you agree that the methods by which natural knowledge is advanced "directly give lie to" — that is, directly undermine — the principles of faith and belief in authority that provide the basis for religion?

9. Write a dialogue between Huxley and Pope, exploring the issues touched on by both men. Recall that for Huxley, "scepticism is the highest of duties." For Pope, submission to God's unknowable order is the highest duty.

10. Reread the final paragraph of the essay. Huxley can be read as predicting the end of religion. Certainly, this has not happened as of 1988. Do you foresee it happening ever — as a consequence of successive advances in natural knowledge? Explain, and in your answer refer to the issues raised by Pascal.

JORGE LUIS BORGES *(1899–1986)*

Short-story writer, poet, and essayist Jorge Luis Borges was largely unknown outside his native Argentina before winning the Prix Formentor — the International Publisher's Prize — in 1961 (along with the playwright Samuel Beckett). From that point on, Borges — already 61 years old and blind from a hereditary condition — gained worldwide stature as one of Latin America's greatest writers. Borges was a master of fantasy, whose ingenious weavings of the real and the fictive puzzled and delighted his readers. He created arcane, labyrinthine worlds in which attempts at making order and understanding cosmic significances were futile.

Borges was born on August 24, 1899, in Buenos Aires, Argentina, to a literary family: his father was a teacher of psychology and a disciple of Herbert Spencer; his mother was a translator (into Spanish) of Nathaniel Hawthorne and Herman Melville. As a child of weak constitution, Borges spent a great deal of time in the library of his parents, reading books in English and Spanish. In 1914, the family moved to Europe and with the outbreak of World War I remained in Geneva for a time, where Borges and his sister attended school.

Having spent several years after the war in Spain, the family returned to Argentina in 1921, the year Borges published his first collection of poems, *Fervor de Buenos Aires (Passion for Bueno Aires)*. Between 1921 and 1930, he published seven more books; but it was not until he turned to short fiction in the 1940s and 1950s that his reputation solidified. During these years he worked as a municipal librarian and as a teacher of English literature, publishing two important works — *Ficciones, 1935–1944,* and *El Aleph* (1949). From 1955 (the year in which the Peron government fell) to 1973, Borges was director of the National Library. Advancing age and blindness did not diminish his enthusiasm for writing. In his later years he concentrated on poetry and published *In Praise of Darkness* (1969), *The Gold of Tigers* (1972), and *History of Night* (1977). Borges also translated selections from Virginia Woolf, Franz Kafka, Herman Melville, and Walt Whitman. He won awards the world over — including the Gran Premio de Honor (Argentina), 1945; the Jerusalem Prize, 1971; the Gold Medal (France), 1979; and the Miguel de Cervantes Award (Spain), 1980. Borges died of liver cancer at the age of 86.

Many literary critics have written on the complexities and puzzles of Borges's work, which shows an affinity for labyrinths, mirrors, stories within stories, doubles, dreamworlds, and accounts (such as book reviews) that would be considered essays were it not that the items under consideration did not exist. Scholarly references within stories are often elaborate; many are fictional. Traditional narrative elements are often suppressed in favor of ideas. Paradoxes abound. Without doubt, Borges's fiction is puzzling. And yet its evocative fantasy, its humor, its concern for important philosophical problems have for twenty years delighted an international audience.

"The Library of Babel" is representative of Borges's fiction: it will certainly confuse on a first reading; but then it is short enough that you can have a go at it a number of times. Your understanding of specific symbols in the story is less important than your appreciation of the more general concerns, such as the narrator's perplexity at living in an infinite, unintelligible universe. "The Library of Babel" raises in its own puzzling way many of the issues addressed in this chapter. It is a rich, difficult story that will reward your effort.

THE LIBRARY OF BABEL[1]

> By this art you may contemplate
> the variation of the 23 letters . . .
> *The Anatomy of Melancholy,*[2]
> part 2, sect. II, mem. IV

The universe (which others call the Library) is composed of an indefinite and perhaps infinite number of hexagonal galleries, with vast air

1

Jorge Luis Borges. "The Library of Babel." Trans. James E. Irby. *Labyrinths: Selected Stories and Other Writings.* Eds. Donald A. Yates and James E. Irby. New York: New Directions, 1964, pp. 51–58.

Editor's note: All footnotes not marked [Behrens & Rosen] are provided by Borges and are to be considered part of the story.

[1]*Babel* is the name of a city mentioned in *Genesis* 11: 1–9:

> In the days when the earth had one language and one vocabulary, there was a migration from the east, and men came upon a plain in the land of Shinar, where they settled. Then they said to one another, "Come on, let us make bricks, and give them a good burning." Then, as they had bricks for stone and asphalt for mortar, they said: "Come on, let us make a name for ourselves by building a city and a tower whose top reaches to heaven; it will keep us from being scattered all over the wide earth."
> Down came the Eternal to see the city and the tower which human beings had built. "They are one people," said the Eternal, "and they have one language; if this is what they do, to start with, nothing that they ever undertake will prove too hard for them. Come, let us go down and make a babble of their language on the spot, so that they cannot understand one another's speech." Thus did the Eternal scatter them all over the wide earth; they gave up building the city. Hence it was called Babylon because it was there that the Eternal made a babble of the language of the whole earth, and there that the Eternal scattered men all over the wide earth.
> (James Moffatt, trans. *The Bible.* New York: Harper and Brothers, 1935.) [Behrens & Rosen]

[2]The life's work of English scholar and clergyman Robert Burton (1577–1640), *The Anatomy of Melancholy* was an encyclopedic study of melancholia — severe depression and withdrawal, which according to medieval learning was thought to be caused by an excess of black bile, one of the four humours. [Behrens & Rosen]

shafts between, surrounded by very low railings. From any of the hexagons one can see, interminably, the upper and lower floors. The distribution of the galleries is invariable. Twenty shelves, five long shelves per side, cover all the sides except two; their height, which is the distance from floor to ceiling, scarcely exceeds that of a normal bookcase. One of the free sides leads to a narrow hallway which opens onto another gallery, identical to the first and to all the rest. To the left and right of the hallway there are two very small closets. In the first, one may sleep standing up; in the other, satisfy one's fecal necessities. Also through here passes a spiral stairway, which sinks abysmally and soars upwards to remote distances. In the hallway there is a mirror which faithfully duplicates all appearances. Men usually infer from this mirror that the Library is not infinite (if it really were, why this illusory duplication?); I prefer to dream that its polished surfaces represent and promise the infinite . . . Light is provided by some spherical fruit which bear the name of lamps. There are two, transversally placed, in each hexagon. The light they emit is insufficient, incessant.

Like all men of the Library, I have traveled in my youth; I have wandered in search of a book, perhaps the catalogue of catalogues; now that my eyes can hardly decipher what I write, I am preparing to die just a few leagues from the hexagon in which I was born. Once I am dead, there will be no lack of pious hands to throw me over the railing; my grave will be the fathomless air; my body will sink endlessly and decay and dissolve in the wind generated by the fall, which is infinite. I say that the Library is unending. The idealists argue that the hexagonal rooms are a necessary form of absolute space or, at least, of our intuition of space. They reason that a triangular or pentagonal room is inconceivable. (The mystics claim that their ecstasy reveals to them a circular chamber containing a great circular book, whose spine is continuous and which follows the complete circle of the walls; but their testimony is suspect; their words, obscure. This cyclical book is God.) Let it suffice now for me to repeat the classic dictum: *The Library is a sphere whose exact center is any one of its hexagons and whose circumference is inaccessible.*[3]

There are five shelves for each of the hexagon's walls; each shelf contains thirty-five books of uniform format; each book is of four hundred and ten pages; each page, of forty lines, each line, of some eighty letters which are black in color. There are also letters on the spine of each book; these letters do not indicate or prefigure what the pages will say. I know that this incoherence at one time seemed mysterious. Before summarizing the

[3]In 1584 Giordano Bruno wrote: "We can assert with certitude that the universe is all center, or that the center of the universe is everywhere and the circumference nowhere." In 1600 Bruno was burned at the stake for heresy. Borges discusses Bruno, Pascal, and "Copernican space" in his essay "The Fearful Sphere of Pascal." See *Labyrinths*. New York: New Directions, 1962. [Behrens & Rosen]

solution (whose discovery, in spite of its tragic projections, is perhaps the capital fact in history) I wish to recall a few axioms.

First: The Library exists *ab aeterno*.[4] This truth, whose immediate corollary is the future eternity of the world, cannot be placed in doubt by any reasonable mind. Man, the imperfect librarian, may be the product of chance or of malevolent demiurgi; the universe, with its elegant endowment of shelves, of enigmatical volumes, of inexhaustible stairways for the traveler and latrines for the seated librarian, can only be the work of a god. To perceive the distance between the divine and the human, it is enough to compare these crude wavering symbols which my fallible hand scrawls on the cover of a book, with the organic letters inside: punctual, delicate, perfectly black, inimitably symmetrical.

Second: *The orthographical symbols are twenty-five in number.*[5] This finding made it possible, three hundred years ago, to formulate a general theory of the Library and solve satisfactorily the problem which no conjecture had deciphered: the formless and chaotic nature of almost all the books. One which my father saw in a hexagon on circuit fifteen ninety-four was made up of the letters MCV, perversely repeated from the first line to the last. Another (very much consulted in this area) is a mere labyrinth of letters, but the next-to-last page says *Oh time thy pyramids.* This much is already known: for every sensible line of straightforward statement, there are leagues of senseless cacophonies, verbal jumbles and incoherences. (I know of an uncouth region whose librarians repudiate the vain and superstitious custom of finding a meaning in books and equate it with that of finding a meaning in dreams or in the chaotic lines of one's palm . . . They admit that the inventors of this writing imitated the twenty-five natural symbols, but maintain that this application is accidental and that the books signify nothing in themselves. This dictum, we shall see, is not entirely fallacious.)

For a long time it was believed that these impenetrable books corresponded to past or remote languages. It is true that the most ancient men, the first librarians, used a language quite different from the one we now speak; it is true that a few miles to the right the tongue is dialectal and that ninety floors farther up, it is incomprehensible. All this, I repeat, is true, but four hundred and ten pages of inalterable MCV's cannot correspond to any language, no matter how dialectal or rudimentary it may be. Some insinuated that each letter could influence the following one and that the value of MCV in the third line of page 71 was not the one the same series

---

[4]Latin: from eternity. [Behrens & Rosen]

[5]The original manuscript does not contain digits or capital letters. The punctuation has been limited to the comma and the period. These two signs, the space and the twenty-two letters of the alphabet are the twenty-five symbols considered sufficient by this unknown author.

may have in another position on another page, but this vague thesis did not prevail. Others thought of cryptographs; generally, this conjecture has been accepted, though not in the sense in which it was formulated by its originators.

Five hundred years ago, the chief of an upper hexagon[6] came upon a book as confusing as the others, but which had nearly two pages of homogeneous lines. He showed his find to a wandering decoder who told him the lines were written in Portuguese; others said they were Yiddish. Within a century, the language was established: a Samoyedic Lithuanian dialect of Guarani, with classical Arabian inflections. The content was also deciphered: some notions of combinative analysis, illustrated with examples of variation with unlimited repetition. These examples made it possible for a librarian of genius to discover the fundamental law of the Library. This thinker observed that all the books, no matter how diverse they might be, are made up of the same elements: the space, the period, the comma, the twenty-two letters of the alphabet. He also alleged a fact which travelers have confirmed: *In the vast Library there are no two identical books.* From these two incontrovertible premises he deduced that the Library is total and that its shelves register all the possible combinations of the twenty-odd orthographical symbols (a number which, though extremely vast, is not infinite): in other words, all that it is given to express, in all languages. Everything: the minutely detailed history of the future, the archangels' autobiographies, the faithful catalogue of the Library, thousands and thousands of false catalogues, the demonstration of the fallacy of those catalogues, the demonstration of the fallacy of the true catalogue, the Gnostic gospel of Basilides, the commentary on that gospel, the commentary on the commentary on that gospel, the true story of your death, the translation of every book in all languages, the interpolations of every book in all books.

When it was proclaimed that the Library contained all books, the first impression was one of extravagant happiness. All men felt themselves to be the masters of an intact and secret treasure. There was no personal or world problem whose eloquent solution did not exist in some hexagon. The universe was justified, the universe suddenly usurped the unlimited dimensions of hope. At that time a great deal was said about the Vindications: books of apology and prophecy which vindicated for all time the acts of every man in the universe and retained prodigious arcana for his future. Thousands of the greedy abandoned their sweet native hexagons and rushed up the stairways, urged on by the vain intention of finding their

7

8

---

[6]Before, there was a man for every three hexagons. Suicide and pulmonary diseases have destroyed that proportion. A memory of unspeakable melancholy: at times I have traveled for many nights through corridors and along polished stairways without finding a single librarian.

Vindication. These pilgrims disputed in the narrow corridors, proffered dark curses, strangled each other on the divine stairways, flung the deceptive books into the air shafts, met their death cast down in a similar fashion by the inhabitants of remote regions. Others went mad . . . The Vindications exist (I have seen two which refer to persons of the future, to persons who perhaps are not imaginary) but the searchers did not remember that the possibility of a man's finding his Vindication, or some treacherous variation thereof, can be computed as zero.

At that time it was also hoped that a clarification of humanity's basic   9
mysteries — the origin of the Library and of time — might be found. It is verisimilar that these grave mysteries could be explained in words: if the language of philosophers is not sufficient, the multiform Library will have produced the unprecedented language required, with its vocabularies and grammars. For four centuries now men have exhausted the hexagons . . . There are official searchers, *inquisitors*. I have seen them in the performance of their function: they always arrive extremely tired from their journeys; they speak of a broken stairway which almost killed them; they talk with the librarian of galleries and stairs; sometimes they pick up the nearest volume and leaf through it, looking for infamous words. Obviously, no one expects to discover anything.

As was natural, this inordinate hope was followed by an excessive   10
depression. The certitude that some shelf in some hexagon held precious books and that these precious books were inaccessible, seemed almost intolerable. A blasphemous sect suggested that the searches should cease and that all men should juggle letters and symbols until they constructed, by an improbable gift of chance, these canonical books. The authorities were obliged to issue severe orders. The sect disappeared, but in my childhood I have seen old men who, for long periods of time, would hide in the latrines with some metal disks in a forbidden dice cup and feebly mimic the divine disorder.

Others, inversely, believed that it was fundamental to eliminate use-   11
less works. They invaded the hexagons, showed credentials which were not always false, leafed through a volume with displeasure and condemned whole shelves: their hygienic, ascetic furor caused the senseless perdition of millions of books. Their name is execrated, but those who deplore the "treasures" destroyed by this frenzy neglect two notable facts. One: the Library is so enormous that any reduction of human origin is infinitesimal. The other: every copy is unique, irreplaceable, but (since the Library is total) there are always several hundred thousand imperfect facsimiles: works which differ only in a letter or a comma. Counter to general opinion, I venture to suppose that the consequences of the Purifiers' depredations have been exaggerated by the horror these fanatics produced. They were urged on by the delirium of trying to reach the books in the Crimson Hexagon: books whose format is smaller than usual, all-powerful, illustrated and magical.

We also know of another superstition of that time: that of the Man of ⟨12⟩
the Book. On some shelf in some hexagon (men reasoned) there must exist
a book which is the formula and perfect compendium *of all the rest:* some
librarian has gone through it and he is analogous to a god. In the language
of this zone vestiges of this remote functionary's cult still persist. Many
wandered in search of Him. For a century they exhausted in vain the most
varied areas. How could one locate the venerated and secret hexagon
which housed Him? Someone proposed a regressive method: To locate
book A, consult first a book B which indicates A's position; to locate book
B, consult first a book C, and so on to infinity . . . In adventures such as
these, I have squandered and wasted my years. It does not seem unlikely
to me that there is a total book on some shelf of the universe;[7] I pray to the
unknown gods that a man — just one, even though it were thousands of
years ago! — may have examined and read it. If honor and wisdom and
happiness are not for me, let them be for others. Let heaven exist, though
my place be in hell. Let me be outraged and annihilated, but for one instant, in one being, let Your enormous Library be justified. The impious
maintain that nonsense is normal in the Library and that the reasonable
(and even humble and pure coherence) is an almost miraculous exception.
They speak (I know) of the "feverish Library whose chance volumes are
constantly in danger of changing into others and affirm, negate and confuse everything like a delirious divinity." These words, which not only
denounce the disorder but exemplify it as well, notoriously prove their
authors' abominable taste and desperate ignorance. In truth, the Library
includes all verbal structures, all variations permitted by the twenty-five
orthographical symbols, but not a single example of absolute nonsense. It
is useless to observe that the best volume of the many hexagons under my
administration is entitled *The Combed Thunderclap* and another *The Plaster
Cramp* and another *Axaxaxas mlö.* These phrases, at first glance incoherent,
can no doubt be justified in a cryptographical or allegorical manner; such
a justification is verbal and, *ex hypothesi,* already figures in the Library. I
cannot combine some characters

dhcmrlchtdj

which the divine Library has not foreseen and which in one of its secret
tongues do not contain a terrible meaning. No one can articulate a syllable
which is not filled with tenderness and fear, which is not, in one of these
languages, the powerful name of a god. To speak is to fall into tautology.
This wordy and useless epistle already exists in one of the thirty volumes

---

[7] I repeat: it suffices that a book be possible for it to exist. Only the impossible is excluded.
For example: no book can be a ladder, although no doubt there are books which discuss
and negate and demonstrate this possibility and others whose structure corresponds to
that of a ladder.

of the five shelves of one of the innumerable hexagons — and its refutation as well. (An *n* number of possible languages use the same vocabulary; in some of them, the symbol *library* allows the correct definition *a ubiquitous and lasting system of hexagonal galleries*, but *library* is *bread* or *pyramid* or anything else, and these seven words which define it have another value. You who read me, are You sure of understanding my language?)

The methodical task of writing distracts me from the present state of 13 men. The certitude that everything has been written negates us or turns us into phantoms. I know of districts in which the young men prostrate themselves before books and kiss their pages in a barbarous manner, but they do not know how to decipher a single letter. Epidemics, heretical conflicts, peregrinations which inevitably degenerate into banditry, have decimated the population. I believe I have mentioned the suicides, more and more frequent with the years. Perhaps my old age and fearfulness deceive me, but I suspect that the human species — the unique species — is about to be extinguished, but the Library will endure: illuminated, solitary, infinite, perfectly motionless, equipped with precious volumes, useless, incorruptible, secret.

I have just written the word "infinite." I have not interpolated this 14 adjective out of rhetorical habit; I say that it is not illogical to think that the world is infinite. Those who judge it to be limited postulate that in remote places the corridors and stairways and hexagons can conceivably come to an end — which is absurd. Those who imagine it to be without limit forget that the possible number of books does have such a limit. I venture to suggest this solution to the ancient problem: *The Library is unlimited and cyclical.* If an eternal traveler were to cross it in any direction, after centuries he would see that the same volumes were repeated in the same disorder (which, thus repeated, would be an order: the Order). My solitude is gladdened by this elegant hope.[8]

---

[8]Letizia Álvarez de Toledo has observed that this vast Library is useless: rigorously speaking, *a single volume* would be sufficient, a volume of ordinary format, printed in nine or ten point type, containing an infinite number of infinitely thin leaves. (In the early seventeenth century, Cavalieri said that all solid bodies are the superimposition of an infinite number of planes.) The handling of this silky vade mecum would not be convenient: each apparent page would unfold into other analogous ones; the inconceivable middle page would have no reverse.

DISCUSSION AND WRITING QUESTIONS

1. It might be helpful, in starting, to note all the aspects of the story that confuse you. (We trust that, along with us, you've been perplexed.) Having made your list, take two or three items similar in nature, and pose a question based on

them. Then reread the story and attempt to make a response. Share your questions with others in the class. Generate a list of questions and use them as a guide for subsequent readings of the story.

2. The story of Babel is to be found in *Genesis* 11: 1–9. (See footnote 1.) Respond to the passage from *Genesis*. Why did God make a babble of the language?

   According to the biblical story, Babel was a city in which no one could understand the speech of another. What use would Babel have for a library? What would you expect of a collection of books assembled in such a library?

3. In what ways does it make sense to equate the universe with a library? In following out the analogy, if books comprise the Library, what (corresponding to books) comprises the universe? And who, with respect to the universe, would correspond with the librarians?

4. "Like all men of the Library, I have traveled in my youth; I have wandered in search of a book, perhaps the catalogue of catalogues. . . ." What has become of the narrator's search? How has it ended, now that he is preparing to die?

5. "When it was proclaimed that the Library contained all books, the first impression was one of extravagant happiness" (paragraph 8). Why?

6. A vindication is a defense that justifies an action or condition. (Alexander Pope undertakes to "vindicate the ways of God to man" in his *Essay on Man*. See pages 129–136.) In "The Library of Babel," vindications are said to exist for every man in the universe; but no one seems to be able to locate the book of his own vindication — the book that would justify his existence. What is the significance of this?

7. Horrors have been committed in an effort to "reach the books in the Crimson Hexagon" (paragraph 11). What is this Crimson Hexagon? Why might horrors be committed in its name? And *why* would horrors be committed in its name if it had not yet been found?

8. In paragraph 12, the narrator loses his scholarly reserve and grows emotional with the thought of some person, the Man of the Book, who has located and read the one book in the Library that gives an account of all the rest. It is a comfort for the narrator to believe that if he is not that man, then at least some such man and some such book exist — and thus justify the Library. To shift vocabularies: if the Library is also the universe, then who — or what — is this Man of the Book? And what is this book?

9. Many sentences in the story are pregnant with meaning. These seem especially so. What do you make of them?

   "I pray to the unknown gods that a man — just one, even though it were thousands of years ago! — may have examined and read it. If honor and wisdom and happiness are not for me, let them be for others. Let heaven exist, though my place be in hell." [Paragraph 12]

   "You who read me, are You sure of understanding my language?" [Paragraph 12]

   "The Library is unlimited and cyclical. If an eternal traveler were to cross it in any direction, after centuries he would see that the same volumes were repeated in the same disorder (which, thus repeated, would be an order: the Order). My solitude is gladdened by this elegant hope." [Paragraph 14]

10. While we can speculate at length on the meanings of various symbols in "The Library of Babel," we can be confident that the story concerns man's place in the universe and the possibilities of understanding. Other authors in this chapter have had definite emotional and intellectual responses to the issue: Pascal, Fontenelle, Pope, Huxley. What have these others had to say? How do their conclusions compare with those of Borges?

11. Having considered the progression of readings in this chapter, explain the ways in which "The Library of Babel" can be seen as a contribution to the continuing legacy of the Copernican Revolution.

Part III

HOBBES AND THE SOCIAL CONTRACT

Thomas Hobbes

John Locke

Jean-Jacques Rousseau

*Political Declarations of the
Social Contract*
  The Declaration of Independence
  The Virginia Resolutions of 1798
  *Declaration of the Rights of Man
  and Citizen*

Herbert Spencer

John W. Gough

He who is unable to live in society or who has no need
because he is sufficient for himself, must be either a beast or
a god; he is no part of a state.

— Aristotle, *Politics*

The Social Contract is nothing more or less than a vast
conspiracy of human beings to lie to and humbug themselves
and one another for the general Good. Lies are the mortar
that bind the savage individual man into the social masonry.

— H. G. Wells, *Love and Mr. Lewisham*

In Plato's dialogue *Crito* the philosopher Socrates has been sentenced
to death by an Athenian court for corrupting the young with his teachings.
His friend and student Crito urges him to escape from prison and from his
sentence. Socrates refuses. To Crito's pleas that escape would not be dishonorable, since both the laws under which he was condemned and the
sentence were unjust, Socrates personifies the laws and imagines what
they would say to him if they knew he were contemplating escape:

Consider, Socrates . . . that in your present attempt you are going to do us
wrong. For, after having brought you into the world, and nurtured you and
educated you, and given you and every other citizen a share in every good
that we had to give, we further proclaim and give the right to every Athenian,
that if he does not like us when he has come of age and has seen the ways of
the city, and made our acquaintance, he may go where he pleases and take his
goods with him, and none of us laws will forbid him or interfere with him.
Any of you who does not like us and the city, and who wants to go to a colony
or to any other city, may go where he likes, and take his goods with him. But
he who has experience of the manner in which we order justice and administer
the state, and still remains, has entered into an implied contract that he will
do as we command him. And he who disobeys us is, as we maintain, thrice
wrong; first, because in disobeying us he is disobeying his parents; secondly,
because we are the authors of his education, thirdly, because he has made an
agreement with us that he will duly obey our commands; and he neither obeys
them nor convinces us that our commands are wrong; and we do not rudely
impose them, but give them the alternative of obeying or convincing us; that
is what we offer, and he does neither. . . . You, Socrates, are breaking the
covenants and agreements which you made with us at your leisure, not in any
haste or any compulsion or deception, but having had seventy years to think
of them, during which time you were at liberty to leave the city, if we were

not to your mind, or if our covenants appeared to you to be unfair. . . . And now you run away and forsake your agreements.[1]

Could not this same type of argument — based on contracts made and broken — be made today? Suppose a person refused to pay taxes on what he considers moral grounds: taxes help support war. A representative of the state could argue as follows: "Since your birth, you have enjoyed the benefits of citizenship. You have been educated by the state; you have used its libraries, its highways, its parks and public lands; your personal safety and property have been protected by the police and fire departments; you have been protected from foreign conquest by the military. In return for these benefits, you are obliged by the terms of the social contract to support the state by obeying its laws and by paying taxes. If you did not wish to enter into such a contract, or to keep it in force once you came of age, you should have given up all claim to the benefits of citizenship and gone to live elsewhere. Your electing to remain here indicates that you intend to continue receiving these benefits; therefore, it is only just that you continue to fulfill your part of the contract by helping to pay for the benefits you receive." If the person then says that he doesn't object to paying all taxes, only those that help support certain weapons, the state could respond that to allow each citizen to pay taxes on only those services of which he or she personally approves would cause chaos and ultimately lead to the collapse of the state.

Such a debate goes to the very heart of the relationship between a government and the citizens it governs. Among the issues raised: Why do governments exist? From whom do they derive their powers? What are the responsibilities of the government to the citizens? Of citizens to the government? What powers does government possess? What rights accrue to citizens? Under what circumstances do citizens have the right to disobey the government? To change or overthrow it? Such questions lead inevitably to social contract theory — the type of theory that postulates an agreement (on paper or not) between government and citizens.

Although, as we have just seen, social contract theory can be traced as far back as ancient Greece, we will focus on the modern flowering of the social contract that began in the 17th century with Thomas Hobbes and continued into the next century with John Locke and Jean-Jacques Rousseau. According to these thinkers, before governments existed, people lived in a state of nature. This state may have been a beneficent one, as in the Garden of Eden, or it may have been a savage and dangerous one, where the law of the jungle prevailed. Eventually people began to realize

---

[1]Translated by Benjamin Jowett.

that for their own safety and welfare they would have to band together. In doing so, they would have to turn over part of the control over their own lives to a government — or perhaps to one person — a sovereign. In return, the government would protect the citizens' lives and property from threats both within and without the community. Thus, the people made a contract (or a "covenant" or a "compact") with the government. Written, oral, or tacitly understood, the contract stipulated the rights and obligations of each party — citizens and government — to the agreement.

Most discussions of the social contract are at heart justifications of the exercise of political authority, either by the state, by the citizens, or both. Some theorists use the contract to justify absolute rule, others to justify rebellion against absolutism. The state of nature is postulated less for historical reasons than as a rhetorical device to point up the advantages of organized government and civil authority (as opposed to anarchy), and to help persuade people that it is in their own interest to enter voluntarily into a social contract from which their rights and obligations as citizens would derive.

Modern historians no longer accept the idea that there is such a clear dividing line between the state of nature and the age of governments, or that social contracts were formed in such a deliberate manner. Nevertheless, the idea of the social contract remains a powerful one. It is of particular importance to the United States because it directly inspired our two most important political documents — the Declaration of Independence and the Constitution. In fact, because the idea of the social contract — as it evolved in the writings of Locke and Rousseau — is so firmly embodied in our political tradition, we tend to take our particular type of social contract for granted. But many of the world's governments are established on social contracts of considerably harsher type: the government agrees to protect life and property (and often reneges on even this basic consideration) in return for the citizens' surrendering almost total control over their own lives. One way of looking at the popular unrest and the revolutionary movements of recent years (for example, in Chile, Haiti, the Philippines, and even in Communist China) is to view them as attempts by citizens to work out more equitable social contracts with their governments — or, failing that, to change the governments with whom they enter into a contract.

The chapter begins with a selection from Thomas Hobbes's *Leviathan* (1651). Hobbes, as we shall see, is the least democratic of modern theorists on the social contract, vesting far more rights in the sovereign than in the citizenry. Next is a selection from John Locke's *Second Treatise on Government* (1690), which argues that citizens do have a right to overthrow the sovereign if the terms of the contract are violated. Jean-Jacques Rousseau is the figure most closely identified today with the social contract, and we include next a crucial section of his *On the Social Contract* (1762). Next is included the *Declaration of Independence,* by Thomas Jefferson, who drew on the work of Locke and Rousseau; an exercise includes preambles from the constitutions of New Jersey (1776) and Massachusetts (1780) which reflect similar thought. The *Resolutions of Virginia* of 1798 demonstrate a variation of social contract thinking — a contract between the state and federal governments. The *Declaration of the Rights of Man* (1798), drawn up at the time of the French Revolution, presents interesting parallels to the *Declaration of Independence.* Next, the British philosopher Herbert Spencer, in "The Great Political Superstition" (1881) explains why there must be severe restrictions on social contracts. Finally, a British scholar, J. W. Gough, who has written an extended study of the social contract, questions the very need for such a concept.

THOMAS HOBBES *(1588–1679)*

Thomas Hobbes was born in 1588, the year the Spanish Armada was launched against England. A man of timid disposition, despite his absolutist political inclinations, Hobbes enjoyed telling his friends that "Fear and I were born twins." His father, a "choleric" vicar, fled the county after striking another clergyman at his own church door, and Hobbes was left to the care of his uncle, a glove maker in the town of Malmesbury. Schooled in the classics, he entered Magdalen Hall, Oxford, at the age of 15, and devoted most of his studies to books of travel and maps. After graduating in 1608, Hobbes became a private tutor to the eldest son of William Cavendish, later the Earl of Devonshire. His lifelong association with the Cavendish family gave him access to libraries, foreign travel, and persons of political influence and literary and scientific fame.

A trip to France and Italy with his pupil, who was about the same age, inspired him upon his return to become a classical scholar. Eventually, he produced a translation of the ancient Greek historian Thucydides, explaining to his readers that the fate of Greece served as a warning on the dangers of democracy. During another tour of the continent, around 1630, Hobbes became acquainted with Euclid's *Elements,* a treatise on geometry, and was greatly struck with the logic and clarity of Euclid's demonstrations, by which ironclad proofs were derived from sequences of propositions. Hobbes's own studies into geometry led him to produce his first philosophical treatise, *A Short Tract on First Principles.* During another trip abroad, Hobbes became fascinated by the laws of motion, which, he became convinced, accounted for all reality. He began formulating a three-part philosophical treatise that would explain how motion provides the basis of (1) all physical phenomena; (2) all operations of human perception, motivation, and behavior; and (3) all operations of human society. During this period, he visited the astronomer Galileo in Italy and joined a circle of scholars and scientists in Paris who congregated around a friar named Marin Mersenne and held philosophical discussions.

By the time of his return to England in 1637, politics was fast intruding into Hobbes's philosophical preoccupations. The country was heading toward Civil War between the Royalists (supporters of King Charles I) and the Parliamentarians, who were largely Puritans. (War did break out in 1642; the Royalists were eventually defeated by Oliver Cromwell's forces; Cromwell became Lord Protector, governing England as a military dictator; and in 1649 King Charles was executed. Two years after Cromwell died in 1658, the monarchy was restored under Charles II, son of the executed king.) In 1640, Hobbes wrote a brief political treatise, *The Elements of Law, Natural and Politique,* which supported the absolute authority of the king. When a key royal supporter, Sir Thomas Wentworth, Earl of Strafford, was impeached by Parliament, Hobbes, fearful for his own safety because of the views he had expressed, fled to France, where he again joined Mersenne's circle.

Soon afterward, Hobbes began work on what was to become his most famous work, *Leviathan*, which was published in 1651. *Leviathan* supported the absolute authority of the king, not on the basis of divine right, heredity, or fitness to govern, but because an absolute sovereign was the only practical alternative to anarchy, the only force that could keep warring factions of men in awe and thus assure peace and security. As Hobbes explained in his introduction, the creation of an artificial entity, the state, is parallel to the creation by God of a natural creature, the human animal:

> For by art is created that great LEVIATHAN called a COMMONWEALTH, or STATE . . . which is but an artificial man; though of greater stature and strength than the natural, for whose protection and defense it was intended; and in which the *sovereignty* is an artificial *soul*, as giving life and motion to the whole body. . . .

Unfortunately for Hobbes, *Leviathan* was a work that offended everyone: Parliament, ignoring his insistence that government is a matter of popular consent, resented the idea that the monarch must be an absolute ruler; the Royalists, on the other hand, resented Hobbes's dismissal of the divine right of monarchy; Christians were angered that he had dismissed the doctrine of free will, basing the actions of humanity on mechanical laws; Puritans and Catholics were outraged by his dismissal of individual conscience, on the one hand, and the authority of the church, on the other; lawyers and scholars were furious at Hobbes's scorn for their precedents and experiments.

Though Hobbes sent a fine manuscript copy of *Leviathan* to the Royalist court in exile in Paris, Charles II (whom Hobbes had at one time tutored) refused to see him. In addition to the causes already mentioned, the Royalists were upset by those parts of *Leviathan* that implied that the people were not bound to a ruler who could not assure their peace (for the establishment of peace was the main purpose of the covenant). Indeed, they could submit themselves to *any* sovereign authority capable of assuring their security. Hobbes's enemies charged him with trying to curry favor with Cromwell's Puritan government, which was certainly one such authority. Although this charge was untrue, Hobbes found his position in Paris untenable and returned to England late in 1651, throwing himself upon the mercy of the Commonwealth. His submission was accepted, and he settled in London, where he spent most of the rest of his life.

After the Restoration, Charles II again received Hobbes into his favor and granted him a pension of 100 pounds a year. The clergy, however, was less forgiving, publicly burning his books at Oxford and threatening him with charges of heresy. Hobbes was so alarmed that he wrote a treatise to prove that he could not legally be tried as a heretic and burned. The parliamentary charges were dropped, but on condition that Hobbes not publish any future works on human conduct. (*Behemoth*, his history of the Civil War, was banned by the censor and not published until 1682, after his death.)

Hobbes returned to his philosophical treatises but never did complete his great projected work on the influence of motion (though parts of it were published). Still vigorous in his later years (he played tennis until he was seventy), Hobbes engaged in numerous disputes with academicians and theologians. Priding himself on his mathematical skill, he at one point claimed to have solved the ancient problem of squaring the circle — a solution that was quickly refuted by abler mathematicians than he. Toward the end of his life, in 1672, he composed a short autobiography in Latin verse, and in 1675 and 1676 he produced English verse translations of *The Odyssey* and *The Iliad*. In 1675, Hobbes left London, to spend his remaining years at Chatsworth and Hardwick, where the Cavendish family lived. He died in 1679 at the age of ninety-one.

Although Hobbes considered himself as much a scientist as a philosopher (largely because of his extensive researches into optics), his reputation rests upon his great insight as a political thinker. His realistic, even cynical observations about human nature swept away a great many sentimental and idealistic assumptions, and have helped explain much in human history. Men are basically selfish and grasping, he argued, and inclined to go to war not only to protect what they have, but to gain even more. In the state of nature, therefore, life is "solitary, poor, nasty, brutish, and short." But men do fear death, and so to avoid death (the inevitable result of unrestricted warfare in the state of nature) they enter into a covenant to create an artificial entity — a commonwealth — of which they can stand in awe, and which will protect them from one another's avarice and hatred. They agree to submit to the absolute authority of this commonwealth, vested in the sovereign. All rights and powers are vested in the sovereign, and none in the people (except the ultimate right of self-defense). Few social thinkers, either in Hobbes's time or subsequently (as we shall see, in the cases of Locke and Rousseau) have been able to accept such an extreme doctrine; but its originality and power is undeniable. In analyzing political — and human — behavior, Hobbes's ideas may be disputed, but they cannot be ignored.

Our selection from *Leviathan* is excerpted from Chapters 13, 17, and 18.

OF COMMONWEALTH

OF THE NATURAL CONDITION OF MANKIND AS CONCERNING THEIR FELICITY AND MISERY

Men by nature equal.   Nature hath made men so equal, in the faculties   1
of the body, and mind; as that though there be found one man sometimes manifestly stronger in body, or of quicker mind than another; yet when all is reckoned together, the difference between man, and man, is not so considerable, as that one man can thereupon claim to himself any benefit, to which another may not pretend, as well as he. For as to the strength of

Thomas Hobbes. Of Commonwealth [1651]. Rpt. in *Leviathan*. London: George Routledge and Sons, 1885.

body, the weakest has strength enough to kill the strongest, either by secret machination, or by confederacy with others, that are in the same danger with himself.

And as to the faculties[1] of the mind, setting aside the arts grounded upon words, and especially that skill of proceeding upon general, and infallible rules, called science; which very few have, and but in few things; as being not a native faculty, born with us; nor attained, as prudence, while we look after somewhat else, I find yet a greater equality amongst men, than that of strength. For prudence, is but experience; which equal time, equally bestows on all men, in those things they equally apply themselves unto. That which may perhaps make such equality incredible, is but a vain conceit of one's own wisdom, which almost all men think they have in a greater degree, than the vulgar[2]; that is, than all men but themselves, and a few others, whom by fame, or for concurring with themselves, they approve. For such is the nature of men, that howsoever they may acknowledge many others to be more witty, or more eloquent, or more learned; yet they will hardly believe there be many so wise as themselves; for they see their own wit[3] at hand, and other men's at a distance. But this proveth rather that men are in that point equal, than unequal. For there is not ordinarily a greater sign of the equal distribution of any thing, than that every man is contented with his share. 2

From equality proceeds diffidence. From this equality of ability, ariseth equality of hope in the attaining of our ends. And therefore if any two men desire the same thing, which nevertheless they cannot both enjoy, they become enemies; and in the way to their end, which is principally their own conservation,[4] and sometimes their delectation[5] only, endeavour to destroy, or subdue one another. And from hence it comes to pass, that where an invader hath no more to fear, than another man's single power; if one plant, sow, build, or possess a convenient seat,[6] others may probably be expected to come prepared with forces united, to dispossess, and deprive him, not only of the fruit of his labour, but also of his life, or liberty. And the invader again is in the like danger of another. 3

From diffidence war. And from this diffidence of one another, there is no way for any man to secure himself, so reasonable, as anticipation; that 4

---

[1]*faculties:* Mental abilities or aptitudes.

[2]*vulgar:* People of average intelligence or talent.

[3]*wit:* Ability to think and reason: intelligence, understanding, good sense.

[4]*conservation:* Preservation of life and health.

[5]*delectation:* Pleasure, enjoyment.

[6]*seat:* A residence and its surroundings.

is, by force, or wiles, to master the persons of all men he can, so long, till he see no other power great enough to endanger him: and this is no more than his own conservation requireth, and is generally allowed. Also because there be some, that taking pleasure in contemplating their own power in the acts of conquest, which they pursue farther than their security requires; if others, that otherwise would be glad to be at ease within modest bounds, should not by invasion increase their power, they would not be able, long time, by standing only on their defence, to subsist. And by consequence, such augmentation of dominion over men being necessary to a man's conservation, it ought to be allowed him.

Again, men have no pleasure, but on the contrary a great deal of grief,   5
in keeping company, where there is no power able to over-awe them all. For every man looketh that his companion should value him, at the same rate he sets upon himself: and upon all signs of contempt, or undervaluing, naturally endeavours, as far as he dares, (which amongst them that have no common power to keep them in quiet, is far enough to make them destroy each other), to extort a greater value from his contemners, by damage; and from others, by the example.

So that in the nature of man, we find three principal causes of quarrel.   6
First, competition; secondly, diffidence; thirdly, glory.

The first, maketh men invade for gain; the second, for safety; and the   7
third, for reputation. The first use violence, to make themselves masters of other men's persons, wives, children, and cattle; the second, to defend them; the third, for trifles, as a word, a smile, a different opinion, and any other sign of undervalue, either direct in their persons, or by reflection in their kindred, their friends, their nation, their profession, or their name.

Out of civil states, there is always war of every one against every   8
one.   Hereby it is manifest, that during the time men live without a common power to keep them all in awe, they are in that condition which is called war; and such a war, as is of every man, against every man. For WAR, consisteth not in battle only, or the act of fighting; but in a tract of time, wherein the will to contend by battle is sufficiently known: and therefore the notion of *time,* is to be considered in the nature of war; as it is in the nature of weather. For as the nature of foul weather, lieth not in a shower or two of rain; but in an inclination thereto of many days together: so the nature of war, consisteth not in actual fighting; but in the known disposition thereto, during all the time there is no assurance to the contrary. All other time is PEACE.

The incommodities of such a war.   Whatsoever therefore is consequent to   9
a time of war, where every man is enemy to every man; the same is consequent to the time, wherein men live without other security, than what their own strength, and their own invention shall furnish them withal. In such condition, there is no place for industry; because the fruit thereof is uncertain: and consequently no culture of the earth; no navigation, nor use

of the commodities that may be imported by sea; no commodious building; no instruments of moving, and removing, such things as require much force; no knowledge of the face of the earth; no account of time; no arts; no letters; no society; and which is worst of all, continual fear, and danger of violent death; and the life of man, solitary, poor, nasty, brutish, and short.

It may seem strange to some man, that has not well weighed these things; that nature should thus dissociate, and render men apt to invade, and destroy one another: and he may therefore, not trusting to this inference, made from the passions, desire perhaps to have the same confirmed by experience. Let him therefore consider with himself, when taking a journey, he arms himself, and seeks to go well accompanied; when going to sleep, he locks his doors; when even in his house he locks his chests; and this when he knows there be laws, and public officers, armed, to revenge all injuries shall be done him; what opinion he has of his fellow-subjects, when he rides armed; of his fellow citizens, when he locks his doors; and of his children, and servants, when he locks his chests. Does he not there as much accuse mankind by his actions, as I do by my words? But neither of us accuse man's nature in it. The desires, and other passions of man, are in themselves no sin. No more are the actions, that proceed from those passions, till they know a law that forbids them: which till laws be made they cannot know: nor can any law be made, till they have agreed upon the person that shall make it. 10

It may peradventure be thought, there was never such a time, nor condition of war as this; and I believe it was never generally so, over all the world: but there are many places, where they live so now. For the savage people in many places of America, except the government of small families, the concord whereof dependeth on natural lust, have no government at all; and live at this day in that brutish manner, as I said before. Howsoever, it may be perceived what manner of life there would be, where there were no common power to fear, by the manner of life, which men that have formerly lived under a peaceful government, use to degenerate into, in a civil war. 11

But though there had never been any time, wherein particular men were in a condition of war one against another; yet in all times, kings, and persons of sovereign authority, because of their independency, are in continual jealousies, and in the state and posture of gladiators; having their weapons pointing, and their eyes fixed on one another; that is, their forts, garrisons, and guns upon the frontiers of their kingdoms; and continual spies upon their neighbours; which is a posture of war. But because they uphold thereby, the industry of their subjects; there does not follow from it, that misery, which accompanies the liberty of particular men. 12

In such a war nothing is unjust.   To this war of every man, against every man, this also is consequent; that nothing can be unjust. The notions of 13 right and wrong, justice and injustice have there no place. Where there is no common power, there is no law: where no law, no injustice. Force, and fraud, are in war the two cardinal virtues. Justice, and injustice are none of the faculties neither of the body, nor mind. If they were, they might be in a man that were alone in the world, as well as his senses, and passions. They are qualities, that relate to men in society, not in solitude. It is consequent also to the same condition, that there be no propriety, no dominion, no *mine* and *thine* distinct; but only that to be every man's, that he can get: and for so long, as he can keep it. And thus much for the ill condition, which man by mere nature is actually placed in; though with a possibility to come out of it, consisting partly in the passions, partly in his reason.

The passions that incline men to peace. The passions that incline men to   14
peace, are fear of death; desire of such things as are necessary to commodious living; and a hope by their industry to obtain them. And reason suggesteth convenient articles of peace, upon which men may be drawn to agreement. . . .

OF THE CAUSES, GENERATION, AND DEFINITION OF A COMMONWEALTH

The end of commonwealth, particular security. The final cause, end, or   15
design of men, who naturally love liberty, and dominion over others, in the introduction of that restraint upon themselves, in which we see them live in commonwealths, is the foresight of their own preservation, and of a more contented life thereby; that is to say, of getting themselves out from that miserable condition of war, which is necessarily consequent, as hath been shown, to the natural passions of men, when there is no visible power to keep them in awe, and tie them by fear of punishment to the performance of their covenants,[7] and observation of laws of nature.

---

[7]*covenants:* Agreements made by people who enter into a contract that those involved in the contract will honor its terms in the future. In the previous part, Hobbes distinguished between contracts and covenants, as follows:

> *Contract what.* The mutual transferring of right, is that which men call CONTRACT.
> There is difference between transferring of right to the thing; and transferring, or tradition, that is delivery of the thing itself. For the thing may be delivered together with the translation of the right; as in buying and selling with ready-money; or exchange of goods, or lands: and it may be delivered some time after.
> *Covenant what.* Again, one of the contractors, may deliver the thing contracted for on his part, and leave the other to perform his part at some determinate time after, and in the mean time be trusted; and then the contract on his part, is called PACT, or COVENANT: or both parts may contract now, to perform hereafter: in which cases, he that is to perform in time to come, being trusted, his performance is called *keeping of promise,* or faith; and the failing of performance, if it be voluntary, *violation of faith.*

Which is not to be had from the law of nature. For the laws of nature, as   16
justice, equity, modesty, mercy, and, in sum, *doing to others, as we would be
done to,* of themselves, without the terror of some power, to cause them to
be observed, are contrary to our natural passions, that carry us to partial-
ity, pride, revenge, and the like. And covenants, without the sword, are
but words, and of no strength to secure a man at all. Therefore notwithstanding the laws of nature (which every one hath then kept, when he has
the will to keep them, when he can do it safely) if there be no power
erected, or not great enough for our security; every man will, and may
lawfully rely on his own strength and art, for caution against all other men.
And in all places, where men have lived by small families, to rob and spoil
one another, has been a trade, and so far from being reputed against the
law of nature, that the greater spoils they gained, the greater was their
honour; and men observed no other laws therein, but the laws of honour;
that is, to abstain from cruelty, leaving to men their lives, and instruments
of husbandry. And as small families did then; so now do cities and kingdoms which are but greater families, for their own security, enlarge their
dominions, upon all pretences of danger, and fear of invasion, or assistance that may be given to invaders, and endeavour as much as they can,
to subdue, or weaken their neighbours, by open force, and secret arts, for
want of other caution, justly; and are remembered for it in after ages with
honour.

Nor from the conjunction of a few men or families. Nor is it the joining   17
together of a small number of men, that gives them this security; because
in small numbers, small additions on the one side or the other, make the
advantage of strength so great, as is sufficient to carry the victory; and
therefore gives encouragement to an invasion. The multitude sufficient to
confide in for our security, is not determined by any certain number, but
by comparison with the enemy we fear; and is then sufficient, when the
odds of the enemy is not of so visible and conspicuous moment, to determine the event of war, as to move him to attempt.

Nor from a great multitude, unless directed by one judgment. And be there   18
never so great a multitude; yet if their actions be directed according to their
particular judgments, and particular appetites, they can expect thereby no
defence, nor protection, neither against a common enemy, nor against the
injuries of one another. For being distracted in opinions concerning the
best use and application of their strength, they do not help but hinder one
another; and reduce their strength by mutual opposition to nothing:
whereby they are easily, not only subdued by a very few that agree together; but also when there is no common enemy, they make war upon
each other, for their particular interests. For if we could suppose a great
multitude of men to consent in the observation of justice, and other laws

of nature,[8] without a common power to keep them all in awe; we might as well suppose all mankind to do the same; and then there neither would be, nor need to be any civil government, or commonwealth at all; because there would be peace without subjection.

And that continually.   Nor is it enough for the security, which men de-   19
sire should last all the time of their life, that they be governed, and directed by one judgment, for a limited time; as in one battle, or one war. For though they obtain a victory by their unanimous endeavour against a foreign enemy; yet afterwards, when either they have no common enemy, or he that by one part is held for an enemy, is by another part held for a friend, they must needs by the difference of their interests dissolve, and fall again into a war amongst themselves.

Why certain creatures without reason, or speech, do nevertheless live in society,   20
without any coercive power.   It is true, that certain living creatures, as bees, and ants, live sociably one with another, which are therefore by Aristotle[9] numbered amongst political creatures; and yet have no other direction, than their particular judgments and appetites; nor speech, whereby one of them can signify to another, what he thinks expedient for the common benefit: and therefore some man may perhaps desire to know, why mankind cannot do the same. To which I answer.

First, that men are continually in competition for honour and dignity,   21
which these creatures are not; and consequently amongst men there ariseth on that ground, envy and hatred, and finally war; but amongst these not so.

Secondly, that amongst these creatures, the common good differeth   22
not from the private; and being by nature inclined to their private, they procure thereby the common benefit. But man, whose joy consisteth in comparing himself with other men, can relish nothing but what is eminent.

Thirdly, that these creatures, having not, as man, the use of reason,   23
do not see, nor think they see any fault, in the administration of their

---

[8]*laws of nature:* Earlier in *Leviathan* (Book I, Chapter 14), Hobbes has defined a law of nature as "a precept or general rule, found out by reason, by which a man is forbidden to do that which is destructive of his life, or taketh away the means of preserving the same; and to omit that, by which he thinketh it may be preserved." The first and fundamental law of Nature, according to Hobbes, is to seek peace and to defend oneself. The second law, derived from the first, is for a man to give himself as much liberty in dealing with others as he would allow them in dealing with him — as long as he is not thereby prevented from seeking peace and defending himself.

[9]*Aristotle:* (384–322 B.C.) Greek philosopher, student of Plato, teacher of Alexander the Great. In his history of animals, *Historia Animalia,* Aristotle classifies ants and bees as political creatures because they live socially in groups, working together for the survival of the group as a whole.

common business; whereas amongst men, there are very many, that think themselves wiser, and abler to govern the public, better than the rest; and these strive to reform and innovate, one this way, another that way; and thereby bring it into distraction and civil war.

Fourthly, that these creatures, though they have some use of voice, in making known to one another their desires, and other affections; yet they want that art of words, by which some men can represent to others, that which is good, in the likeness of evil; and evil, in the likeness of good; and augment, or diminish the apparent greatness of good and evil; discontenting men, and troubling their peace at their pleasure.   24

Fifthly, irrational creatures cannot distinguish between *injury*, and *damage*; and therefore as long as they be at ease, they are not offended with their fellows: whereas man is then most troublesome, when he is most at ease: for then it is that he loves to shew his wisdom, and control the actions of them that govern the commonwealth.   25

Lastly, the agreement of these creatures is natural; that of men, is by covenant only, which is artificial: and therefore it is no wonder if there be somewhat else required, besides covenant, to make their agreement constant and lasting; which is a common power, to keep them in awe, and to direct their actions to the common benefit.   26

The generation of a commonwealth. The definition of a commonwealth. The only way to erect such a common power, as may be able to defend them from the invasion of foreigners, and the injuries of one another, and thereby to secure them in such sort, as that by their own industry, and by the fruits of the earth, they may nourish themselves and live contentedly; is, to confer all their power and strength upon one man, or upon one assembly of men, that may reduce all their wills, by plurality of voices, unto one will: which is as much as to say, to appoint one man, or assembly of men, to bear their person; and every one to own, and acknowledge himself to be author of whatsoever he that so beareth their person, shall act, or cause to be acted, in those things which concern the common peace and safety; and therein to submit their wills, every one to his will, and their judgments, to his judgment. This is more than consent, or concord; it is a real unity of them all, in one and the same person, made by covenant of every man with every man, in such manner, as if every man should say to every man, *I authorize and give up my right of governing myself, to this man, or to this assembly of men, on this condition, that thou give up thy right to him, and authorize all his actions in like manner.* This done, the multitude so united in one person, is called a COMMONWEALTH, in Latin CIVITAS. This is the generation of that great LEVIATHAN, or rather, to speak more reverently, of that *mortal god,* to which we owe under the *immortal God,* our peace and defence. For by this authority, given him by every particular man in the commonwealth, he hath the use of so much power and strength conferred on   27 him, that by terror thereof, he is enabled to form the wills of them all, to peace at home, and mutual aid against their enemies abroad. And in him consisteth the essence of the commonwealth; which, to define it, is *one person, of whose acts a great multitude, by mutual covenants one with another, have made themselves every one the author, to the end he may use the strength and means of them all; as he shall think expedient, for their peace and common defence.*

Sovereign, and subject, what.   And he that carrieth this person is called   28
SOVEREIGN, and said to have *sovereign power*; and every one besides, his SUBJECT.

The attaining to this sovereign power, is by two ways. One by natural   29
force; as when a man maketh his children, to submit themselves, and their children to his government, as being able to destroy them if they refuse; or by war subdueth his enemies to his will, giving them their lives on that condition. The other, is when men agree amongst themselves, to submit to some man, or assembly of men, voluntarily, on confidence to be protected by him against all others. This latter, may be called a political commonwealth, or commonwealth by *institution*; and the former, a commonwealth by *acquisition*. And first, I shall speak of a commonwealth by institution.

OF THE RIGHTS OF SOVEREIGNS BY INSTITUTION

The act of instituting a commonwealth, what.   A *commonwealth* is said to   30
be *instituted*, when a *multitude* of men do agree, and *covenant, every one, with every one*, that to whatsoever *man*, or *assembly of men*, shall be given by the major part, the *right* to *present* the person of them all, that is to say, to be their *representative*; every one, as well he that *voted for it*, as he that *voted against it*, shall *authorize* all the actions and judgments, of that man, or assembly of men, in the same manner, as if they were his own, to the end, to live peaceably amongst themselves, and be protected against other men.

The consequences to such institutions, are: From this institution of a com-   31
monwealth are derived all the *rights*, and *faculties* of him, or them, on whom the sovereign power is conferred by the consent of the people assembled.

1. *The subjects cannot change the form of government.*   First, because they   32
covenant, it is to be understood, they are not obliged by former covenant to any thing repugnant hereunto. And consequently they that have already instituted a commonwealth, being thereby bound by covenant, to own the actions, and judgments of one, cannot lawfully make a few covenant, amongst themselves, to be obedient to any other, in any thing whatsoever, without his permission. And therefore, they are subjects to a monarch, cannot without his leave cast off monarchy, and return to the confusion of a disunited multitude; nor transfer their person from him that

beareth it, to another man, or other assembly of men: for they are bound, every man to every man, to own, and be reputed author of all, that he that already is their sovereign, shall do, and judge fit to be done: so that any one man dissenting, all the rest should break their covenant made to that man, which is injustice: and they have also every man given the sovereignty to him that beareth their person; and therefore if they depose him, they take from him that which is his own, and so again it is injustice. Besides, if he that attempteth to depose his sovereign, be killed, or punished by him for such attempt, he is author of his own punishment, as being by the institution, author of all his sovereign shall do: and because it is injustice for a man to do any thing, for which he may be punished by his own authority, he is also upon that title, unjust. And whereas some men have pretended for their disobedience to their sovereign, a new covenant, made, not with men, but with God; this also is unjust: for there is no covenant with God, but by mediation of somebody that representeth God's person; which none doth but God's lieutenant, who hath the sovereignty under God. But this pretence of covenant with God, is so evident a lie, even in the pretenders' own consciences, that it is not only an act of an unjust, but also of a vile, and unmanly disposition.

2. *Sovereign power cannot be forfeited.*   Secondly, because the right of bearing the person of them all, is given to him they make sovereign, by covenant only of one to another, and not of him to any of them; there can happen no breach of covenant on the part of the sovereign; and consequently none of his subjects, by any pretence of forfeiture, can be freed from his subjection. That he which is made sovereign maketh no covenant with his subjects beforehand, is manifest; because either he must make it with the whole multitude, as one party to the covenant; or he must make a several covenant with every man. With the whole, as one party, it is impossible; because as yet they are not one person: and if he make so many several covenants as there be men, those covenants after he hath the sovereignty are void; because what act soever can be pretended by any one of them for breach thereof, is the act both of himself, and of all the rest, because done in the person, and by the right of every one of them in particular. Besides, if any one, or more of them, pretend a breach of the covenant made by the sovereign at his institution; and others, or one other of his subjects, or himself alone, pretend there was no such breach, there is in this case, no judge to decide the controversy; it returns therefore to the sword again; and every man recovereth the right of protecting himself by his own strength, contrary to the design they had in the institution. It is therefore in vain to grant sovereignty by way of precedent covenant. The opinion that any monarch receiveth his power by covenant, this is to say, on condition, proceedeth from want of understanding this easy truth, that covenants being but words and breath, have no force to oblige, contain,

constrain, or protect any man, but what it has from the public sword; that is, from the untied hands of that man, or assembly of men that hath the sovereignty, and whose actions are avouched by them all, and performed by the strength of them all, in him united. But when an assembly of men is made sovereign; then no man imagineth any such covenant to have passed in the institution; for no man is so dull as to say, for example, the people of Rome made a covenant with the Romans, to hold the sovereignty on such or such conditions; which not performed, the Romans might lawfully depose the Roman people. That men see not the reason to be alike in a monarchy, and in a popular government, proceedeth from the ambition of some, that are kinder to the government of an assembly, whereof they may hope to participate, than of monarchy, which they despair to enjoy.

3. *No man can without injustice protest against the institution of the sovereign declared by the major part.* Thirdly, because the major part hath by consenting voices declared a sovereign; he that dissented must now consent with the rest; that is, be contented to avow all the actions he shall do, or else justly be destroyed by the rest. For if he voluntarily entered into the congregation of them that were assembled, he sufficiently declared thereby his will, and therefore tacitly covenanted, to stand to what the major part should ordain: and therefore if he refuse to stand thereto, or make protestation against any of their decrees, he does contrary to his covenant, and therefore unjustly. And whether he be of the congregation, or not; and whether his consent be asked, or not, he must either submit to their decrees, or be left in the condition of war he was in before; wherein he might without injustice be destroyed by any man whatsoever.   34

4. *The sovereign's actions cannot be justly accused by the subject.*   Fourthly, because every subject is by this institution author of all the actions, and judgments of the sovereign instituted; it follows, that whatsoever he doth, it can be no injury to any of his subjects; nor ought he to be by any of them accused of injustice. For he that doth anything by authority from another, doth therein no injury to him by whose authority he acteth: but by this institution of a commonwealth, every particular man is author of all the sovereign doth: and consequently he that complaineth of injury from his sovereign, complaineth of that whereof he himself is author; and therefore ought not to accuse any man but himself; no nor himself of injury; because to do injury to one's self, is impossible. It is true that they that have sovereign power may commit iniquity; but not injustice, or injury in the proper signification.   35

5. *Whatsoever the sovereign doth is unpunishable by the subject.*   Fifthly, and consequently to that which was said last, no man that hath sovereign power can justly be put to death, or otherwise in any manner by his subjects punished. For seeing every subject is author of the actions of his sovereign; he punisheth another for the actions committed by himself.   36

6. *The sovereign is judge of what is necessary for the peace and defence of his* 37
subjects. And because the end of this institution, is the peace and defence
of them all; and whosoever has right to the end, has right to the means; it
belongeth of right, to whatsoever man, or assembly that hath the sovereignty, to be judge both of the means of peace and defence, and also of the
hindrances, and disturbances of the same; and to do whatsoever he shall
think necessary to be done, both beforehand, for the preserving of peace
and security, by prevention of discord at home, and hostility from abroad;
and, when peace and security are lost, for the recovery of the same. And
therefore,

And judge of what doctrines are fit to be taught them. Sixthly, it is annexed 38
to the sovereignty, to be judge of what opinions and doctrines are averse,
and what conducing to peace; and consequently, on what occasions, how
far, and what men are to be trusted withal, in speaking to multitudes of
people; and who shall examine the doctrines of all books before they be
published. For the actions of men proceed from their opinions; and in the
well-governing of opinions, consisteth the well-governing of men's actions, in order to their peace, and concord. And though in matter of doctrine, nothing ought to be regarded but the truth; yet this is not repugnant
to regulating the same by peace. For doctrine repugnant to peace, can no
more be true, than peace and concord can be against the law of nature. It
is true, that in a commonwealth, where by the negligence, or unskilfulness
of governors, and teachers, false doctrines are by time generally received;
the contrary truths may be generally offensive. Yet the most sudden, and
rough busling in of a new truth, that can be, does never break the peace,
but only sometimes awake the war. For those men that are so remissly
governed, that they dare take up arms to defend, or introduce an opinion,
are still in war; and their condition not peace, but only a cessation of arms
for fear of one another; and they live, as it were, in the precincts of battle
continually. It belongeth therefore to him that hath the sovereign power,
to be judge, or constitute all judges of opinions and doctrines, as a thing
necessary to peace; thereby to prevent discord and civil war.

7. *The right of making rules; whereby the subjects may every man know what* 39
is so his own, as no other subject can without injustice take it from
him. Seventhly, is annexed to the sovereignty, the whole power of prescribing the rules, whereby every man may know, what goods he may
enjoy, and what actions he may do, without being molested by any of his
fellow-subjects; and this is it men call *propriety.* For before constitution of
sovereign power, as hath already been shown, all men had right to all
things; which necessarily causeth war: and therefore this propriety, being
necessary to peace, and depending on sovereign power, is the act of that
power, in order to the public peace. These rules of propriety, or *meum and*

tuum,[10] and of *good, evil, lawful,* and *unlawful* in the actions of subjects, are the civil laws; that is to say, the laws of each commonwealth in particular; though the name of civil law be now restrained to the ancient civil laws of the city of Rome[11]; which being the head of a great part of the world, her laws at that time were in these parts the civil law.

8. *To him also belongeth the right of judicature and decision of contro-*   40
versy.   Eighthly, is annexed to the sovereignty, the right of judicature; that is to say, of hearing and deciding all controversies, which may arise concerning law, either civil, or natural; or concerning fact. For without the decision of controversies, there is no protection of one subject, against the injuries of another; the laws concerning *meum* and *tuum* are in vain; and to every man remaineth, from the natural and necessary appetite of his own conservation, the right of protecting himself by his private strength, which is the condition of war, and contrary to the end for which every commonwealth is instituted.

9. *And of making war, and peace, as he shall think best.*   Ninthly, is an-   41
nexed to the sovereignty, the right of making war and peace with other nations, and commonwealths; that is to say, of judging when it is for the public good, and how great forces are to be assembled, armed, and paid for that end; and to levy money upon the subjects, to defray the expenses thereof. For the power by which the people are to be defended, consisteth in their armies; and the strength of an army, in the union of their strength under one command; which command the sovereign instituted, therefore hath; because the command of the *militia*, without other institution, maketh him that hath it sovereign. And therefore whosoever is made general of an army, he that hath the sovereign power is always generalissimo.

10. *And of choosing all counsellors and ministers, both of peace and*   42
war.   Tenthly, is annexed to the sovereignty, the choosing of all counsellors, ministers, magistrates, and officers, both in peace, and war. For seeing the sovereign is charged with the end, which is the common peace and defence, he is understood to have power to use such means, as he shall think most fit for his discharge.

11. *And of rewarding and punishing, and that (where no former law hath*   43
determined the measure of it) arbitrarily.   Eleventhly, to the soverign is com-

---

[10]*meum and tuum:* Literally, mine and thine, or my property and your property — a reference to the property rights of Roman law.

[11]*ancient civil laws of Rome:* Roman laws relating to commerce and domestic matters. Originally these laws pertained only to the citizens of the city of Rome, and not to others in the empire. Later, when Roman citizenship was granted to everyone in the empire, Roman civil law was extended to all citizens.

mitted the power of rewarding with riches, or honour, and of punishing with corporal or pecuniary punishment, or with ignominy, every subject according to the law he hath formerly made; or if there be no law made, according as he shall judge most to conduce to the encouraging of men to serve the commonwealth, or deterring of them from doing disservice to the same.

12. *And of honour and order.*   Lastly, considering what value men are   44 naturally apt to set upon themselves; what respect they look for from others; and how little they value other men; from whence continually arise amongst them, emulation, quarrels, factions, and at last war, to the destroying one of another, and diminution of their strength against a common enemy; it is necessary that there be laws of honour, and a public rate of the worth of such men as have deserved, or are able to deserve well of the commonwealth; and that there be force in the hands of some or other, to put those laws in execution. But it hath already been shown, that not only the whole *militia,* or forces of the commonwealth; but also the judicature of all controversies, is annexed to the sovereignty. To the sovereign therefore it belongeth also to give titles of honour; and to appoint what order of place, and dignity, each man shall hold; and what signs of respect, in public or private meetings, they shall give to one another.

These rights are indivisible.   These are the rights, which make the es-   45 sence of sovereignty; and which are the marks, whereby a man discern in what man, or assembly of men, the sovereign power is placed, and resideth. For these are incommunicable, and inseparable. The power to coin money; to dispose of the estate and persons of infant heirs; to have præemption[12] in markets; and all other statute prerogatives, may be transferred by the sovereign; and yet the power to protect his subjects be retained. But if he transfer the *militia,* he retains the judicature in vain, for want of execution of the laws: or if he grant away the power of raising money; the *militia* is in vain; or if he give away the government of doctrines, men will be frighted into rebellion with the fear of spirits. And so if we consider any one of the said rights, we shall presently see, that the holding of all the rest will produce no effect, in the conservation of peace and justice, the end for which all commonwealths are instituted. And this division is it, whereof it is said, *a kingdom divided in itself cannot stand:* for unless this division precede, division into opposite armies can never happen. If there had not first been an opinion received of the greatest part of England, that these powers were divided between the King, and the Lords,

---

[12]*præemption:* Literally, the first buying of a thing; it refers to a law giving the crown the right to buy articles for use by the royal household without consideration of other buyers' needs or desires, and without the owner's consent.

and the House of Commons,[13] the people had never been divided and fallen into this civil war[14]; first between those that disagreed in politics; and after between the dissenters[15] about the liberty of religion; which have so instructed men in this point of sovereign right, that there be few now in England that do not see, that these rights are inseparable, and will be so generally acknowledged at the next return of peace; and so continue, till their miseries are forgotten; and no longer, except the vulgar be better taught than they have hitherto been.

And can by no grant pass away without direct renouncing of the sovereign   46
power.   And because they are essential and inseparable rights, it follows necessarily, that in whatsoever words any of them seem to be granted away, yet if the sovereign power itself be not in direct terms renounced, and the name of sovereign no more given by the grantees to him that grants them, the grant is void: for when he has granted all he can, if we grant back the sovereignty, all is restored, as inseparably annexed thereunto.

The power and honour of subjects vanisheth in the presence of the power sov-   47
ereign.   This great authority being indivisible, and inseparably annexed to the sovereignty, there is little ground for the opinion of them, that say of sovereign kings, though they be *singulis majores,*[16] of greater power than every one of their subjects, yet they be *universis minores,*[17] of less power than them all together. For if by *all together,* they mean not the collective body as one person, then *all together,* and *every one,* signify the same; and the speech is absurd. But if by *all together,* they understand them as one person, which person the sovereign bears, then the power of all together, is the same with the sovereign's power; and so again the speech is absurd: which absurdity they see well enough, when the sovereignty is in an assembly of the people; but in a monarch they see it not; and yet the power of sovereignty is the same in whomsoever it be placed.

---

[13]*the Lords, and the House of Commons:* The two houses of Britain's bicameral Parliament. The House of Lords consists of hereditary nobility appointed by the monarch; the House of Commons consists of popularly elected commoners. Because the House of Commons has authority over matters of taxation and the allocation of money, it can exert financial pressure on the King; hence, Hobbes's reference to divided powers.

[14]*civil war:* See the introduction to this selection. The English civil war started in 1642 because of conflicts between Parliamentarians and supporters of the monarchy over matters of national religion and governmental authority. During the war, Parliament deposed and later executed King Charles I.

[15]*dissenters:* Protestants who refused to conform to the doctrines and practices of the Anglican Church, the established Church of England.

[16]*singulis majores:* Literally, one great person alone; a ruler with absolute power.

[17]*universus minores:* Literally, citizens together; a ruling body of citizens.

And as the power, so also the honour of the soverign, ought to be greater, than that of any, or all the subjects. For in the sovereignty is the fountain of honor. The dignities of lord, earl, duke, and prince are his creatures. As in the presence of the master, the servants are equal, and without any honour at all; so are the subjects, in the presence of the sovereign. And though they shine some more, some less, when they are out of his sight; yet in his presence, they shine no more than the stars in the presence of the sun. [48]

Sovereign power not so hurtful as the want of it, and the hurt proceeds for the greatest part from not submitting readily to a less. But a man may here object, that the condition of subjects is very miserable; as being obnoxious to the lusts, and other irregular passions of him, or them that have so unlimited a power in their hands. And commonly they that live under a monarch, think it the fault of monarchy; and they that live under the government of democracy, or other sovereign assembly, attribute all the inconvenience to that form of commonwealth; whereas the power in all forms, if they be perfect enough to protect them, is the same: not considering that the state of man can never be without some incommodity or other; and that the greatest, that in any form of government can possibly happen to the people in general, is scarce sensible in respect of the miseries, and horrible calamities, that accompany a civil war, or that dissolute condition of masterless men, without subjection to laws, and a coercive power to tie their hands from rapine and revenge: nor considering that the greatest pressure of sovereign governors, proceedeth not from any delight, or profit they can expect in the damage or weakening of their subjects, in whose vigour, consisteth their own strength and glory; but in the restiveness of themselves, that unwillingly contributing to their own defence, make it necessary for their governors to draw from them what they can in time of peace, that they may have means on any emergent occasion, or sudden need, to resist, or take advantage on their enemies. For all men are by nature provided of notable multiplying glasses, that is their passions and self-love, through which, every little payment appeareth a great grievance; but are destitute of those prospective glasses, namely moral and civil science, to see afar off the miseries that hang over them, and cannot without such payments be avoided. [49]

REVIEW QUESTIONS

1. What are the causes of conflicts between men? What are the motives behind such causes? How does Hobbes define war?
2. How does Hobbes respond to those who might object to his low opinion of

humanity? Why does Hobbes claim that in the state of nature nothing is unjust and that there is no right or wrong?

3. Why do men who love liberty and who seek power over others agree to give up their liberty and rein in their aggressive tendencies? Why can a small, common enemy sometimes overpower a much greater number of opponents?

4. Some argue that if some nonhuman species, such as insects, can live together without war, humanity should be able to do the same. Why is this impossible, according to Hobbes?

5. How and why are commonwealths formed? Among what parties is the covenant made? How does Hobbes define "commonwealth"? In what two ways can a person achieve sovereign power?

6. By what reasoning does Hobbes argue that the sovereign cannot justly be deposed by his subjects? Why does Hobbes also reject the idea that people can reject their ruler's sovereign authority for God's?

7. Why is it impossible, in Hobbes's view, for the sovereign to breach the covenant? What obligations do the minority (i.e., those who did not agree to the covenant) have to the sovereign and to each other?

8. How does Hobbes justify censorship in a commonwealth? Why, according to Hobbes, is the sovereign the best judge of which opinions and doctrines can be promulgated and which must be suppressed?

9. At what point does Hobbes appear to blame the English civil war upon a violation of the social covenant? Specifically, what principle was violated?

DISCUSSION AND WRITING QUESTIONS

1. To what extent do you believe Hobbes's analysis of the cause of war remains valid today? In particular, which contemporary wars and conflicts arise from the kind of motives he discusses? You may wish to begin by looking at a particular conflict and then determining the extent to which each of Hobbes's "principal" causes accounts for it.

2. Evaluate Hobbes's doctrines. From your own knowledge of human history and human nature, how accurate are his analyses? At what points are his arguments strongest? At what points, weakest? Why are they strong (or weak)? What kind of factors, for example, do you believe that Hobbes has *not* sufficiently taken into account?

3. In the first part of this selection, Hobbes presents the "problem" — the situation that leads to people warring among themselves. His "solution" is an absolute monarchy (or some other form of totalitarian government). If you disagree that this solution is the only possible — and effective — one for the problem, point out the flaws in his reasoning. Anticipate the argument that democracies cannot effectively deal with violent crime, civil strife, or terrorism (all forms of persons warring against one another), and be prepared to respond.

4. Trace the logic by which Hobbes argues that a sovereign cannot be justly deposed, punished, or even accused of injustice. Do you find a flaw in this reasoning? Explain.

5. Select an example of a country that is today governed by the kind of absolute

sovereign postulated by Hobbes. Research the recent history of this country, particularly the conditions that led up to the installation of the present dictatorship, and the conditions of social stability in the country since that time. To what extent do you find that Hobbes's doctrines account for what has happened in this country? What alternatives do you see for this country? At what point were opportunities to act upon these alternatives missed?

JOHN LOCKE *(1632–1704)*

Theories on the social contract are often devised and cited when people wish to support or attack existing governmental authority. As such, these theories generally reflect the prevailing political situation. What we might today call conservative social contract theories support the monarch or other executive authority; liberal theories support the legislative (or parliamentary) authority, when this authority is a genuine reflection of the popular will. As we have seen, Hobbes's theory supported the supremacy of the monarch, although the Royalists objected to Hobbes's assumption that the source of sovereign power lay in the people, and even more to his suggestion that the sovereign's subjects could, in perilous times, shift their allegiance to a more able protector (since protection from the perils of war was the very basis of the social contract). Presumably, such thinking could justify the shift in popular allegiance from King Charles I, then to Oliver Cromwell in the 1640's when the Parliamentary forces defeated and later executed the king, and then back to Charles II in 1660 when the monarchy was restored. Such wavering of popular support leaves in considerable doubt the theory of the divine right of kings.

The social contract theory of John Locke was very much the product of the political situation in England during the second half of the 17th century. Locke's father, an attorney, had fought on the Parliamentary side in the Civil War. Born in 1632 in Wrington, Somerset, Locke was educated at the Westminster school (controlled by a Parliamentary committee) and then at Oxford, where he took his B.A. in 1656 and his M.A. in 1658. Two years later he became a tutor at Christ Church college at Oxford and for several years taught philosophy and rhetoric to undergraduates. During this period he became interested in natural science and medicine and made the acquaintance of many eminent scientists, including Robert Boyle (one of the founders of modern chemistry) and Isaac Newton. In 1668, he became a fellow of the Royal Society, a group dedicated to the furtherance of scientific knowledge. Locke studied medicine himself, earning a medical degree in 1674, and subsequently joined the household of Anthony Ashley Cooper (later Lord Shaftesbury) as family physician.

Through Shaftesbury, Locke became directly involved in the political struggles of the day. Once an influential adviser to Charles II, Shaftesbury (who favored a constitutional monarchy, a strong parliament, guaranteed civil liberties, and religious toleration) fell out with the King over the matter of succession. Charles's son James was a staunch Catholic, and Shaftesbury (along with the majority in Protestant England) wanted to exclude James from the succession, fearing that once king, he would try to return England to the Catholic fold and discriminate against Protestants. (In fact, when James did become king, he tried to do exactly that.) Shaftesbury was imprisoned for a time, and in 1682 he fled to Holland, where he died in 1683. As a close friend of Shaftesbury, Locke (who had returned to England after four years in France) was closely watched by government spies, and the following year he too sailed for Holland. Soon after this, he was expelled from Christ Church by royal decree.

Locke stayed in Holland for five years, pursuing his philosophical, theological, and scientific interests. During this period, James II became king (1685), but his blundering attempts to restore Catholicism to England led to the bloodless "Glorious Revolution" of 1688, and he was forced to flee to France. James was succeeded by the Protestant William of Orange (an aristocratic family of Holland); and Locke himself accompanied back to England the Princess of Orange, who became Queen Mary II. During the remaining fifteen years of his life, he continued to pursue his scientific and intellectual interests and to publish most of his most well-known works, the product of a lifetime of thought.

Locke's writings were not confined to politics. Two of his important works on religious belief were *A Letter Concerning Toleration* (1689) and *The Reasonableness of Christianity* (1695). His *Essay Concerning Human Understanding* (1690) was a major contribution to the theory of epistemology, or the acquisition of knowledge; and his treatise, *Some Thoughts Concerning Education* (1693), originally written with a particular child in mind, have much broader application. The work that most directly concerns the subject of this chapter, however, is his *Two Treatises of Government* (1690). Its liberal views have led some to conclude that it was written to justify the Glorious Revolution of 1688, but modern scholarship has established that much of the *Two Treatises* was written between 1679 and 1683. As a contribution to social contract theory, this work may be contrasted with Hobbes's, in terms of its assumptions about human nature (during and subsequent to the state of nature); in its insistence that the government is responsible to the people (rather than the other way around); in its emphasis on the importance of private property; in its division of government into executive, legislative, and judicial authorities; and, perhaps most important, in its assumption of the right of the people to rebel against and overthrow the government when the government acts tyrannically. These ideas are of clear significance in the founding of the American republic almost a century later. Although Locke's ideas (along with the ideas of most other social contract theorists) can be attacked on both historical and intellectual grounds, their power and importance derive less from their accuracy as history or their logical validity than from their appeal to the ultimate dignity of human beings in their social and political relations.

The following passage is derived from Chapters 8, 9, 10, 11, and 19 of the *Second Treatise on Government*. Earlier in this treatise, Locke has described the state of nature in a manner quite different from that of Hobbes ("the life of man [was] solitary, poor, nasty, brutish, and short"). For Locke, the "state of Nature has a law of Nature to govern it, which obliges everyone; and reason, which is that law, teaches mankind . . . that being all equal and independent, no one ought to harm another in his life, health, liberty, or possessions." Thus, the state of nature does not have to be a Hobbesian state of continuous warfare; what distinguishes the state of nature from the civil society is the lack of a common authority to which people agree to submit themselves.

OF THE ENDS OF POLITICAL SOCIETY AND GOVERNMENT

CHAP. VIII.

Of the Beginning of Political Societies.

Men being, as has been said, by Nature, all free, equal and independent, no one can be put out of this Estate,[1] and subjected to the Political Power of another, without his own *Consent*. The only way whereby any one devests himself of his Natural Liberty, and *puts on the bonds of Civil Society* is by agreeing with other Men to joyn and unite into a Community, for their comfortable, safe, and peaceable living one amongst another, in a secure Enjoyment of their Properties, and a greater Security against any that are not of it. This any number of Men may do, because it injures not the Freedom of the rest; they are left as they were in the Liberty of the State of Nature. When any number of Men have so *consented to make one Community* or Government, they are thereby presently incorporated, and make *one Body Politick*, wherein the *Majority* have a Right to act and conclude the rest.

    For when any number of Men have, by the consent of every individual, made a *Community*, they have thereby made that *Community* one Body, with a Power to Act as one Body, which is only by the will and determination of the *majority*. For that which acts any Community, being only the consent of the individuals of it, and it being necessary to that which is one body to move one way; it is necessary the Body should move that way whither the greater force carries it, which is the *consent of the majority*: or else it is impossible it should act or continue one Body, *one Community*, which the consent of every individual that united into it, agreed that it should; and so every one is bound by that consent to be concluded by the *majority*. And therefore we see that in Assemblies impowered to act by positive Laws where no number is set by that positive Law which impowers them, the *act of the Majority* passes for the act of the whole, and of course determines, as having by the Law of Nature and Reason, the power of the whole.

    And thus every Man, by consenting with others to make one Body

1

2

3

John Locke. Of the Ends of Political Society and Government [1690]. Rpt. in *Two Treatises on Government: A Critical Edition with an Introduction and Apparatus Criticus*. Peter Laslett. Cambridge University Press, 1960.

[1]*estate:* One's state of being. Here it refers to the condition of being free, equal, and independent.

Politick under one Government, puts himself under an Obligation to every one of that Society, to submit to the determination of the *majority*, and to be concluded by it; or else this *original Compact*, whereby he with others incorporates into *one Society*, would signifie nothing, and be no Compact, if he be left free, and under no other ties, than he was in before in the State of Nature. For what appearance would there be of any Compact? What new Engagement if he were no farther tied by any Decrees of the Society, than he himself thought fit, and did actually consent to? This would be still as great a liberty, as he himself had before his Compact, or any one else in the State of Nature hath, who may submit himself and consent to any acts of it if he thinks fit.[2]

For if *the consent of the majority* shall not in reason, be received, as *the act of the whole*, and conclude every individual, nothing but the consent of every individual can make any thing to be the act of the whole: But such a consent is next impossible ever to be had, if we consider the Infirmities of Health, and Avocations of Business, which in a number, though much less than that of a Common-wealth, will necessarily keep many away from the publick Assembly. To which if we add the variety of Opinions, and contrariety of Interests, which unavoidably happen in all Collections of Men, the coming into Society upon such terms, would be only like *Cato's* coming into the Theatre, only to go out again.[3] Such a Constitution as this would make the mighty *Leviathan* of a shorter duration, than the feeblest Creatures; and not let it outlast the day it was born in[4]: which cannot be suppos'd, till we can think, that Rational Creatures should desire and constitute Societies only to be dissolved. For where the *majority* cannot conclude the rest, there they cannot act as one Body, and consequently will be immediately dissolved again.

Whosoever therefore out of a state of Nature unite into a *Community*, must be understood to give up all the power, necessary to the ends for which they unite into Society, to the *majority* of the Community, unless they expressly agreed in any number greater than the majority. And this   5

---

[2]The effect, if not the sense and phraseology, of paragraph 3 is very close to that of Hobbes, *Leviathan*, chapter 18, headed *No man can without injustice protest against the Institution of the Soveraigne declared by the major part* (Hobbes, paragraph 34). [Peter Laslett, ed. *Two Treatises of Government*, by John Locke (Cambridge University Press, 1960).]

[3]Martial, *Epigrammaton*, I, Praef.: "Cur in theatrum, Cato severe, venisti/An ideo tantum veneras, ut exires?" ["Why, stern Cato, did you come into the theatre? Did you come only in order to leave?"] A common anecdote about Cato of Utica; information from E. J. Kenney. [Laslett]

[4]A deliberate invocation of the language of Hobbes, clearly sarcastic and not intended as a critical comment on the theory of *Leviathan*, nor on any particular passage in it. . . . Locke and Hobbes were agreed on the necessity of the consent of the majority being taken for the act of the whole. [Laslett]

is done by barely agreeing to *unite into one Political Society*, which is *all the Compact* that is, or needs be, between the Individuals, that enter into, or make up a *Common-wealth*. And thus that, which begins and actually *constitutes any Political Society*, is nothing but the consent of any number of Freemen[5] capable of a majority to unite and incorporate into such a Society. And this is that, and that only, which did, or could give *beginning* to any *lawful Government* in the World. . . .

Every Man being, as has been shewed, *naturally free*, and nothing being 6 able to put him into subjection to any Earthly Power, but only his own Consent; it is to be considered, what shall be understood to be *a sufficient Declaration of* a Mans *Consent, to make him subject* to the Laws of any Government. There is a common distinction of an express and a tacit consent, which will concern our present Case. No body doubts but an *express Consent*, of any man, entering into any Society, makes him a perfect Member of that Society, a Subject of that Government. The difficulty is, what ought to be look'd upon as a *tacit Consent*, and how far it binds, *i.e.* how far any one shall be looked on to have consented, and thereby submitted to any Government, where he has made no Expressions of it at all. And to this I say, that every Man, that hath any Possession, or Enjoyment, of any part of the Dominions of any Government, doth thereby give his *tacit Consent*, and is as far forth obliged to Obedience to the Laws of that Government, during such Enjoyment, as any one under it; whether this his Possession be of Land, to him and his Heirs for ever, or a Lodging only for a Week; or whether it be barely travelling freely on the Highway; and in Effect, it reaches as far as the very being of any one within the Territories of that Government.

To understand this the better, it is fit to consider, that every Man, when 7 he, at first, incorporates himself into any Commonwealth, he, by his uniting himself thereunto, annexed also, and submits to the Community those Possessions, which he has, or shall acquire, that do not already belong to any other Government. For it would be a direct Contradiction, for any one, to enter into Society with others for the securing and regulating of Property: And yet to suppose his Land, whose Property is to be regulated by the Laws of the Society, should be exempt from the Jurisdiction of that Government, to which he himself the Proprietor of the Land, is a Subject. By the same Act therefore, whereby any one unites his Person, which was before free, to any Commonwealth; by the same he unites his Possessions, which were before free, to it also; and they become, both of them, Person and Possession, subject to the Government and Dominion of that Commonwealth, as long as it hath a being. *Whoever* therefore, from thenceforth,

---

[5]*freemen:* Men free to unite under a new political system because they have no obligations to another system.

by Inheritance, Purchase, Permission, or otherways *enjoys any part of the Land,* so annext to, and under the Government *of that Commonwealth, must take it with the Condition* it is under; that is, *of submitting to the Government of the Commonwealth,* under whose Jurisdiction it is, as far forth, as any Subject of it.

But since the Government has a direct Jurisdiction only over the Land,   8
and reaches the Possessor of it, (before he has actually incorporated himself in the Society) only as he dwells upon, and enjoys that: *The Obligation* any one is under, by Virtue of such Enjoyment, *to submit to the Government, begins and ends with the Enjoyment;* so that whenever the Owner, who has given nothing but such a *tacit Consent* to the Government, will, by Donation, Sale, or otherwise, quit the said Possession, he is at liberty to go and incorporate himself into any other Commonwealth, or to agree with others to begin a new one, *in vacuis locis,*[6] in any part of the World, they can find free and unpossessed: Whereas he, that has once, by actual Agreement, and any *express* Declaration, given his *Consent* to be of any Commonweal, is perpetually and indispensably obliged to be and remain unalterably a Subject to it, and can never be again in the liberty of the state of Nature; unless by any Calamity, the government, he was under, comes to be dissolved; or else by some publick Act cuts him off from being any longer a Member of it.

But submitting to the Laws of any Country, living quietly, and enjoy-   9
ing Priviledges and Protection under them, *makes not a Man a Member of that Society:* This is only a local Protection and Homage due to, and from all those, who, not being in a state of War, come within the Territories belonging to any Government, to all parts whereof the force of its Law extends. But this no more *makes a Man a Member of that Society,* a perpetual Subject of that Commonwealth, than it would make a Man a Subject to another in whose Family he found it convenient to abide for some time; though, whilst he continued in it, he were obliged to comply with the Laws, and submit to the Government he found there. And thus we see, that *Foreigners,* by living all their Lives under another Government, and enjoying the Priviledges and Protection of it, though they are bound, even in Conscience, to submit to its Administration, as far forth as any Denison[7]; yet do not thereby come to be *Subjects or Members of that Commonwealth.* Nothing can make any Man so, but his actually entering into it by positive Engagement, and express Promise and Compact. This is that, which I think, concerning the beginning of Political Societies, and that *Consent which makes any one a Member* of any Commonwealth.

---

[6]*in vacuis locis:* Literally, in an empty region; Locke uses this to say that men have the right to start a new commonwealth in any location not already occupied by another community.

[7]*denison:* An actual citizen of a state as opposed to a foreigner living in the state.

CHAP. IX.

Of the Ends of Political Society and Government.

If Man in the State of Nature be so free, as has been said; If he be   *10*
absolute Lord of his own Person and Possessions, equal to the greatest,
and subject to no Body, why will he part with his Freedom? Why will he
give up this Empire, and subject himself to the Dominion and Controul of
any other Power? To which 'tis obvious to Answer, that though in the state
of Nature he hath such a right, yet the Enjoyment of it is very uncertain,
and constantly exposed to the Invasion of others. For all being Kings as
much as he, every Man his equal, and the greater part no strict Observers
of Equity and Justice, the enjoyment of the property he has in this state is
very unsafe, very unsecure. This makes him willing to quit a Condition,
which however free, is full of fears and continual dangers: And 'tis not
without reason, that he seeks out, and is willing to joyn in Society with
others who are already united, or have a mind to unite for the mutual
Preservation of their Lives, Liberties and Estates, which I call by the general
Name, *Property*.[8]

The great and *chief end* therefore, of Mens uniting into Common-   *11*
wealths, and putting themselves under Government, *is the Preservation of
their Property*. To which in the state of Nature there are many things
wanting.

First, There wants an *establish'd*, settled, known *Law*, received and al-   *12*
lowed by common consent to be the Standard of Right and Wrong, and
the common measure to decide all Controversies between them. For
though the Law of Nature be plain and intelligible to all rational Creatures;
yet Men being biassed by their Interest, as well as ignorant for want of
study of it, are not apt to allow of it as a Law binding to them in the application of it to their particular Cases.

Secondly, In the State of Nature there wants *a known and indifferent Judge*,   *13*
with Authority to determine all differences according to the established
Law. For every one in that state being both Judge and Executioner of the
Law of Nature, Men being partial to themselves, Passion and Revenge is
very apt to carry them too far, and with too much heat, in their own Cases;
as well as negligence, and unconcernedness, to make them too remiss, in
other Mens.

Thirdly, In the state of Nature there often wants *Power* to back and   *14*
support the Sentence when right, and to *give* it due *Execution*.[9] They who
by any Injustice offended, will seldom fail, where they are able, by force

---

[8]This whole paragraph should be compared and contrasted with the first paragraph of
Leviathan, chapter 17. [Hobbes, paragraph 15] [Laslett]

[9]*execution*: The carrying out of what the law sentences.

to make good their Injustice: such resistance many times makes the punishment dangerous, and frequently destructive, to those who attempt it.

Thus Mankind, notwithstanding all the Priviledges of the state of Nature, being but in an ill condition, while they remain in it, are quickly driven into Society. Hence it comes to pass, that we seldom find any number of Men live any time together in this State. The inconveniences, that they are therein exposed to, by the irregular and uncertain exercise of the Power every Man has of punishing the transgressions of others, make them take Sanctuary under the establish'd Laws of Government, and therein seek *the preservation of their Property*. 'Tis this makes them so willingly give up every one his single power of punishing to be exercised by such alone as shall be appointed to it amongst them; and by such Rules as the Community, or those authorised by them to that purpose, shall agree on. And in this we have the original *right and rise* of both *the Legislative and Executive Power*, as well as of the Governments and Societies themselves.   15

For in the State of Nature, to omit the liberty he has of innocent Delights, a Man has two Powers.   16

The first is to do whatsoever he thinks fit for the preservation of himself and others within the permission of the *Law of Nature:* by which Law common to them all, he and all the rest of *Mankind are one Community*, make up one Society distinct from all other Creatures. And were it not for the corruption, and vitiousness of degenerate Men, there would be no need of any other; no necessity that Men should separate from this great and natural Community, and by positive agreements combine into smaller and divided associations.   17

The other power a Man has in the State of Nature, is the *power to punish the Crimes* committed against that Law. Both these he gives up, when he joyns in a private, if I may so call it, or particular Political Society, and incorporates into any Commonwealth, separate from the rest of Mankind.   18

The first *Power, viz.*[10] *of doing whatsoever he thought fit for the Preservation of himself,* and the rest of Mankind, *he gives up* to be regulated by Laws made by the Society, so far forth as the preservation of himself, and the rest of that Society shall require; which Laws of the Society in many things confine the liberty he had by the Law of Nature.   19

Secondly, the *Power of punishing* he wholly *gives up,* and engages his natural force, (which he might before imploy in the Execution of the Law of Nature, by his own single Authority, as he thought fit) to assist the Executive Power of the Society, as the Law thereof shall require. For being now in a new State, wherein he is to enjoy many Conveniences, from the labour, assistance, and society of others in the same Community, as well   20

---

[10]*viz.*: Namely. . . .

as protection from its whole strength; he is to part also with as much of his natural liberty in providing for himself, as the good, prosperity, and safety of the Society shall require: which is not only necessary, but just; since the other Members of the Society do the like.

But though Men when they enter into Society, give up the Equality,   *21*
Liberty, and Executive Power they had in the State of Nature, into the hands of the Society, to be so far disposed of by the Legislative, as the good of the Society shall require; yet it being only with an intention in every one the better to preserve himself his Liberty and Property; (For no rational Creature can be supposed to change his condition with an intention to be worse) the power of the Society, or *Legislative* constituted by them, *can never be suppos'd to extend farther than the common good*; but is obliged to secure every ones Property by providing against those three defects above-mentioned, that made the State of Nature so unsafe and uneasie. And so whoever has the Legislative or Supream Power of any Common-wealth, is bound to govern by establish'd *standing Laws,*[11] promulgated and known to the People, and not by Extemporary Decrees[12]; by *indifferent*[13] and upright *Judges,* who are to decide Controversies by those Laws; And to imploy the force of the Community at home, *only in the Execution of such Laws,* or abroad to prevent or redress Foreign Injuries, and secure the Community from Inroads and Invasion. And all this to be directed to no other *end,* but the *Peace, Safety,* and *publick good* of the People.[14]

CHAP. X.

Of the Forms of a Common-wealth.

The Majority having, as has been shew'd, upon Mens first uniting into   *22*
Society, the whole power of the Community, naturally in them, may imploy all that power in making Laws for the Community from time to time, and Executing those Laws by Officers of their own appointing; and then the *Form* of the Government is a perfect *Democracy*: Or else may put the power of making Laws into the hands of a few select Men, and their Heirs or Successors; and then it is an *Oligarchy*[15]: Or else into the hands of one

---

[11]*standing laws:* Laws that have already been agreed upon and recorded. These laws are fixed; they are applied consistently to all persons in all similar situations.

[12]*extemporary decrees:* Laws created spontaneously to serve a particular situation.

[13]*indifferent:* Unbiased.

[14]These statements . . . seem likely to be a reference to the actions of James II and the view he took of his position, for they are less appropriate than the political judgments which Locke implies elsewhere to the actions of Charles II. [Laslett]

[15]*oligarchy:* A system of government in which only a few persons have the power to take part in the legislation and the execution of laws.

Man, and then it is a *Monarchy*: If to him and his Heirs, it is an *Hereditary Monarchy*: If to him only for Life, but upon his Death the Power only of nominating a Successor to return to them; an *Elective Monarchy*. And so accordingly of these the Community may make compounded and mixed Forms of Government, as they think good. And if the Legislative Power be at first given by the Majority to one or more Persons only for their Lives, or any limited time, and then the Supream Power to revert to them again, when it is so reverted, the Community may dispose of it again anew into what hands they please, and so constitute a new Form of Government. For the *Form of Government depending upon the placing* the Supreme Power, which is the *Legislative*, it being impossible to conceive that an inferiour Power should prescribe to a Superiour, or any but the Supreme make Laws, according as the Power of making Laws is placed, such is *the Form of the Common-wealth.*

By *Common-wealth*, I must be understood all along to mean, not a De-   23
mocracy, or any Form of Government, but *any Independent Community* which the *Latines*[16] signified by the word *Civitas*, to which the word which best answers in our Language, is *Commonwealth*, and most properly expresses such a Society of Men, which Community or City in *English* does not, for there may be Subordinate Communities in a Government; and City amongst us has a quite different notion from Commonwealth: And therefore to avoid ambiguity, I crave leave to use the word *Commonwealth* in that sense, in which I find it used by King *James the First*,[17] and I take it to be its genuine signification; which if any Body dislike, I consent with him to change it for a better.

CHAP. XI.

Of the Extent of the Legislative Power.

The great end of Mens entring into Society, being the enjoyment of   24
their Properties in Peace and Safety, and the great instrument and means of that being the Laws establish'd in that Society; the *first and fundamental positive Law* of all Commonwealths, *is the establishing of the Legislative* Power; as the *first and fundamental natural Law*, which is to govern even the Legislative it self, is *the preservation of the Society*, and (as far as will consist with the publick good) of every person in it. This *Legislative* is not only *the supream power* of the Common-wealth, but sacred and unalterable in the

---

[16]*Latines:* Speakers of Latin living in the Roman Empire.
[17]*King James I:* King James I ruled England from 1603 to 1625. It appears that the king used the word "commonwealth" in speeches to the English people in 1603 and 1607 to refer to a community of people who had agreed to live together under common laws.

hands where the Community have once placed it; nor can any Edict of any Body else, in what Form soever conceived, or by what Power soever backed, have the force and obligation of a *Law,* which has not its *Sanction from* that *Legislative,* which the publick has chosen and appointed. For without this the Law could not have that, which is absolutely necessary to its being a *Law, the consent of the Society,* over whom no Body can have a power to make Laws, but by their own consent, and by Authority received from them; and therefore all the *Obedience,* which by the most solemn Ties any one can be obliged to pay, ultimately terminates in this *Supream Power,* and is directed by those Laws which it enacts: nor can any Oaths to any Foreign Power whatsoever, or any Domestick Subordinate Power, discharge any Member of the Society from his *Obedience to the Legislative,* acting pursuant to their trust, nor oblige him to any Obedience contrary to the Laws so enacted, or farther than they do allow; it being ridiculous to imagine one can be tied ultimately to *obey* any *Power* in the Society, which is not *the Supream.*

Though the *Legislative,* whether placed in one or more, whether it be   25 always in being, or only by intervals, tho' it be the *Supream* Power in every Common-wealth; yet,

First, It is *not,* nor can possibly be absolutely *Arbitrary* over the Lives   26 and Fortunes of the People. For it being but the joynt power of every Member of the Society given up to that Person, or Assembly, which is Legislator, it can be no more than those persons had in a State of Nature before they enter'd into Society, and gave up to the Community. For no Body can transfer to another more power than he has in himself; and no Body has an absolute Arbitrary Power over himself, or over any other, to destroy his own Life, or take away the Life or Property of another. A Man, as has been proved, cannot subject himself to the Arbitrary Power of another; and having in the State of Nature no Arbitrary Power over the Life, Liberty, or Possession of another, but only so much as the Law of Nature gave him for the preservation of himself, and the rest of Mankind; this is all he doth, or can give up to the Common-wealth, and by it to the *Legislative Power,* so that the Legislative can have no more than this. Their Power in the utmost Bounds of it, is *limited to the publick good* of the Society. It is a Power, that hath no other end but preservation, and therefore can never have a right to destroy, enslave, or designedly to impoverish the Subjects. The Obligations of the Law of Nature, cease not in Society, but only in many Cases are drawn closer, and have by Humane Laws known Penalties annexed to them, to inforce their observation. Thus the Law of Nature stands as an Eternal Rule to all Men, *Legislators* as well as others. The *Rules* that they make for other Mens Actions, must, as well as their own and other Mens Actions, be conformable to the Law of Nature, *i.e.* to the Will of God, of which that is a Declaration, and the *fundamental Law of Nature* being *the preservation of Mankind,* no Humane Sanction can be good, or valid against it.

Secondly, The *Legislative,* or Supream Authority, cannot assume to its self a power to Rule by extemporary Arbitrary Decrees, but is *bound to dispense Justice,* and decide the Rights of the Subject *by promulgated standing Laws, and known Authoris'd Judges.* For the Law of Nature being unwritten, and so no where to be found but in the minds of Men, they who through Passion or Interest shall mis-cite, or misapply it, cannot so easily be convinced of their mistake where there is no establish'd Judge: And so it serves not, as it ought, to determine the Rights, and fence the Properties of those that live under it, especially where every one is Judge, Interpreter, and Executioner of it too, and that in his own Case: And he that has right on his side, having ordinarily but his own single strength, hath not force enough to defend himself from Injuries, or to punish Delinquents. To avoid these Inconveniences which disorder Mens Properties in the state of Nature, Men unite into Societies, that they may have the united strength of the whole Society to secure and defend their Properties, and may have *standing Rules* to bound it, by which every one may know what is his. To this end it is that Men give up all their Natural Power to the Society which they enter into, and the Community put the Legislative Power into such hands as they think fit, with this trust, that they shall be govern'd by *declared Laws,* or else their Peace, Quiet, and Property will still be at the same uncertainty, as it was in the state of Nature. 27

Absolute Arbitrary Power, or Governing without *settled standing Laws,* can neither of them consist with the ends of Society and Government, which Men would not quit the freedom of the state of Nature for, and tie themselves up under, were it not to preserve their Lives, Liberties and Fortunes; and by *stated Rules* of Right and Property to secure their Peace and Quiet. It cannot be supposed that they should intend, had they a power so to do, to give to any one, or more, an *absolute Arbitrary Power* over their Persons and Estates, and put a force into the Magistrates hand to execute his unlimited Will arbitrarily upon them: This were to put themselves into a worse condition than the state of Nature, wherein they had a Liberty to defend their Right against the Injuries of others, and were upon equal terms of force to maintain it, whether invaded by a single Man, or many in Combination. Whereas by supposing they have given up themselves to the *absolute Arbitrary Power* and will of a Legislator, they have disarmed themselves, and armed him, to make a prey of them when he pleases. He being in a much worse condition who is exposed to the Arbitrary Power of one Man, who has the Command of 100000. than he that is expos'd to the Arbitrary Power of 100000. single Men: no Body being secure, that his Will, who has such a Command, is better, than that of other Men, though his Force be 100000. times stronger. And therefore whatever 28

Form the Common-wealth is under, the Ruling Power ought to govern by *declared* and *received Laws*, and not be extemporary Dictates and undetermined Resolutions. For then Mankind will be in a far worse condition, than in the State of Nature, if they shall have armed one or a few Men with the joynt power of a Multitude, to force them to obey at pleasure the exorbitant and unlimited Decrees of their sudden thoughts, or unrestrain'd, and till that moment unknown Wills without having any measures set down which may guide and justifie their actions. For all the power the Government has, being only for the good of the Society, as it ought not to be *Arbitrary* and at Pleasure, so it ought to be exercised by *established and promulgated Laws*: that both the People may know their Duty, and be safe and secure within the limits of the Law, and the Rulers too kept within their due bounds, and not to be tempted, by the Power they have in their hands, to imploy it to such purposes, and by such measures, as they would not have known, and own not willingly.

Thirdly, The *Supream Power cannot take* from any Man any part of his *Property* without his own consent. For the preservation of Property being the end of Government, and that for which Men enter into Society, it necessarily supposes and requires, that the People should *have Property*, without which they must be suppos'd to lose that by entring into Society, which was the end for which they entered into it, too gross an absurdity for any Man to own. *Men* therefore *in Society having Property,* they have such a right to the goods, which by the Law of the Community are theirs, that no Body hath a right to take their substance, or any part of it from them, without their own consent; without this, they have no *Property* at all. For I have truly no *Property* in that, which another can by right take from me, when he pleases, against my consent. Hence it is a mistake to think, that the Supream or *Legislative Power* of any Commonwealth, can do what it will, and dispose of the Estates of the Subject *arbitrarily,* or take any part of them at pleasure. This is not much to be fear'd in Governments where the *Legislative* consists, wholly or in part, in Assemblies which are variable,[18] whose Members upon the Dissolution of the Assembly, are Subjects under the common Laws of their Country, equally with the rest.[19] But in Governments, where the *Legislative* is in one lasting Assembly always in being, or in one Man, as in Absolute Monarchies, there is danger still, that they will think themselves to have a distinct interest, from the rest of the Community; and so will be apt to increase their own Riches and Power, by taking,

---

[18]*assemblies which are variable:* A legislative body comprised of average citizens who, before and after serving in the assembly, have no special rights or privileges. Locke contrasts this type of legislative body with ruling bodies whose members inherit their positions or are appointed by persons currently in power, instead of being appointed by the majority.

[19]The government of England is obviously meant. . . . [Laslett]

what they think fit, from the People. For a Man's *Property* is not at all secure, though there be good and equitable Laws to set the bounds of it, between him and his Fellow Subjects, if he who commands those Subjects, have Power to take from any private Man, what part he pleases of his *Property*, and use and dispose of it as he thinks good.

But *Government* into whatsoever hands it is put, being as I have before   30
shew'd, intrusted with this condition, and *for this end*, that Men might have and secure *their Properties*, the Prince or Senate, however it may have power to make Laws for the regulating of *Property* between the Subjects one amongst another, yet can never have a Power to take to themselves the whole or any part of the Subjects *Property*, without their own consent. For this would be in effect to leave them no *Property* at all. And to let us see, that even *absolute Power*, where it is necessary, is *not Arbitrary* by being absolute, but is still limited by that reason, and confined to those ends, which required it in some Cases to be absolute, we need look no farther than the common practice of Martial Discipline. For the Preservation of the Army, and in it of the whole Commonwealth, requires an *absolute Obedience* to the Command of every Superiour Officer, and it is justly Death to disobey or dispute the most dangerous or unreasonable of them: but yet we see, that neither the Serjeant, that could command a Souldier to march up to the mouth of a Cannon, or stand in a Breach,[20] where he is almost sure to perish, can command that Soldier to give him one penny of his Money; nor the *General*, that can condemn him to Death for deserting his Post, or for not obeying the most desperate Orders, can yet with all his absolute Power of Life and Death, dispose of one Farthing of that Soldiers Estate, or seize one jot of his Goods; whom yet he can command any thing, and hang for the least Disobedience. Because such a blind Obedience is necessary to that end for which the Commander has his Power, *viz.* the preservation of the rest; but the disposing of his Goods has nothing to do with it.

'Tis true, Governments cannot be supported without great Charge,   31
and 'tis fit every one who enjoys his share of the Protection, should pay out of his Estate his proportion for the maintenance of it. But still it must be with his own Consent, *i.e.* the Consent of the Majority, giving it either by themselves, or their Representatives chosen by them.[21] For if any one shall claim a *Power to lay* and levy *Taxes* on the People, by his own Authority, and without such consent of the People, he thereby invades the *Fundamental Law of Property*, and subverts the end of Government. For what

---

[20]*breach:* A gap in fortification along a battle line. A person standing in a breach would be left wide open for enemy attack.

[21]Here Locke's individual doctrine of property and his assumption about majorities and representation are joined with traditional English constitutionalism. [Laslett]

property have I in that which another may by right take, when he pleases to himself?

Fourthly, The *Legislative cannot transfer the Power of Making Laws* to any 32 other hands. For it being but a delegated Power from the People, they, who have it, cannot pass it over to others. The People alone can appoint the Form of the Commonwealth, which is by Constituting the Legislative, and appointing in whose hands that shall be. And when the People have said, We will submit to rules, and be govern'd by *Laws* made by such Men, and in such Forms, no Body else can say other Men shall make *Laws* for them; nor can the people be bound by any *Laws* but such as are Enacted by those, whom they have Chosen, and Authorised to make *Laws* for them. The power of the *Legislative* being derived from the People by a positive voluntary Grant and Institution, can be no other, than what that positive Grant conveyed, which being only to make *Laws,* and not to make *Legislators,* the *Legislative* can have no power to transfer their Authority of making Laws, and place it in other hands.

These are the *Bounds* which the trust that is put in them by the Society, 33 and the Law of God and Nature, have *set to the Legislative* Power of every Commonwealth, in all Forms of Government.

First, They are to govern by *promulgated establish'd Laws,* not to be var- 34 ied in particular Cases, but to have one Rule for Rich and Poor, for the Favourite at Court, and the Country Man at Plough.

Secondly, These *Laws* also ought to be designed *for* no other end ulti- 35 mately but *the good of the People.*

Thirdly, they must *not raise Taxes* on the Property of the People, *without* 36 *the Consent of the People,* given by themselves, or their Deputies. And this properly concerns only such Governments where the *Legislative* is always in being, or at least where the People have not reserv'd any part of the Legislative to Deputies, to be from time to time chosen by themselves.

Fourthly, The *Legislative* neither must *nor can transfer the Power of making* 37 *Laws* to any Body else, or place it any where but where the People have. . . .

CHAP. XIX.

Of the Dissolution of Government.[22]

He that will with any clearness speak of the *Dissolution of Government,* 38 ought, in the first place to distinguish between the *Dissolution of the Society,* and the *Dissolution of the Government.* That which makes the Community, and brings Men out of the loose State of Nature, into *one Politick Society,* is

---

[22]This chapter contains those statements of Locke's which associate his book most closely with the events of 1688–9. [Laslett]

the Agreement which every one has with the rest to incorporate, and act as one Body, and so be one distinct Commonwealth. The usual, and almost only way whereby *this Union is dissolved*, is the Inroad of Foreign Force making a Conquest upon them. For in that Case, (not being able to maintain and support themselves, as *one intire* and *independent Body*) the Union belonging to that Body which consisted therein, must necessarily cease, and so every one return to the state he was in before, with a liberty to shift for himself, and provide for his own Safety as he thinks fit in some other Society.[23] Whenever the *Society is dissolved*, 'tis certain the Government of that Society cannot remain. Thus Conquerours Swords often cut up Governments by the Roots, and mangle Societies to pieces, separating the subdued or scattered Multitude from the Protection of, and Dependence on that Society which ought to have preserved them from violence. The World is too well instructed in, and too forward to allow of this way of dissolving of Governments to need any more to be said of it: and there wants not much Argument to prove, that where the *Society is dissolved*, the Government cannot remain; that being as impossible, as for the Frame of an House to subsist when the Materials of it are scattered, and dissipated by a Whirlwind, or jumbled into a confused heap by an Earthquake.

Besides this over-turning from without, *Governments are dissolved from within*,   39

First, When the *Legislative* is *altered*. Civil Society being a State of Peace,   40 amongst those who are of it, from whom the State of War is excluded by the Umpirage,[24] which they have provided in their Legislative, for the ending all Differences, that may arise amongst any of them, 'tis in their *Legislative*, that the Members of a Commonwealth are united, and combined together into one coherent living Body. This *is the Soul that gives Form, Life, and Unity* to the Commonwealth: From hence the several Members have their mutual Influence, Sympathy, and Connexion: And therefore when the *Legislative* is broken, or *dissolved*, Dissolution and Death follows.[25] For

---

[23]Compare Hobbes's *Leviathan*, chapter 29: "When in a warre (forraign or intestine,) the enemies get a finall Victory; so as . . . there is no farther protection of Subjects in their loyalty; then is the Common-wealth DISSOLVED, and every man at liberty to protect himselfe by such courses as his own discretion shall suggest to him." Locke equates rebellion with foreign conquest in a similar way. [Laslett]

[24]*umpirage*: A body in the legislature which is set up to hear and settle any disputes between persons within the commonwealth.

[25]Compare Hobbes, *Leviathan*, chapter 29, continuation of passage quoted in footnote of paragraph 38: "For the Sovereign is the publique Soule, giving Life and Motion to the Common-wealth," and when it departs death follows. Locke seems to be deliberately putting his legislative in the place of the sovereign, and though there are very similar passages to this one in *Leviathan* about sovereignty and the soul of a political society in Grotius and Pufendorf . . . it may be that Locke had the words of Hobbes specifically in mind here. [Laslett]

the *Essence and Union of the Society* consisting in having one Will, the Legislative, when once established by the Majority, has the declaring, and as it were keeping of that Will. The *Constitution of the Legislative* is the first and fundamental Act of Society, whereby provision is made for the *Continuation of their Union*, under the Direction of Persons, and Bonds of Laws made by persons authorized thereunto, by the consent and Appointment of the People, without which no one Man, or number of Men, amongst them, can have Authority of making Laws, that shall be binding to the rest. When any one, or more, shall take upon them to make Laws, whom the People have not appointed so to do, they make Laws without Authority, which the People are not therefore bound to obey; by which means they come again to be out of subjection, and may constitute to themselves a *new Legislative*, as they think best, being in full liberty to resist the force of those, who without Authority would impose any thing upon them. Every one is at the disposure of his own Will, when those who had by the delegation of the Society, the declaring of the publick Will, are excluded from it, and others usurp the place who have no such Authority or Delegation.

This being usually brought about by such in the Common-wealth who   *41*
misuse the Power they have: It is hard to consider it aright, and know at whose door to lay it, without knowing the Form of Government in which it happens. Let us suppose then the Legislative placed in the Concurrence of three distinct Persons.

1. A single hereditary Person having the constant, supream, executive Power, and with it the Power of Convoking and Dissolving the other two within certain Periods of Time.

2. An Assembly of Hereditary Nobility.

3. An Assembly of Representatives chosen *pro tempore*,[26] by the People: Such a Form of Government supposed, it is evident.

First, That when such a single Person or Prince sets up his own Arbi-   *42*
trary Will in place of the Laws, which are the Will of the Society, declared by the Legislative, then the *Legislative is changed.* For that being in effect the Legislative whose Rules and Laws are put in execution, and required to be obeyed; when other Laws are set up, and other Rules pretended, and inforced, than what the Legislative, constituted by the Society, have enacted, 'tis plain, that the *Legislative is changed.* Whoever introduces new Laws, not being thereunto authorized by the fundamental Appointment of the Society, or subverts the old, disowns and overturns the Power by which they were made, and so sets up a *new Legislative.*

---

[26]*pro tempore:* Literally, as the occasion demands; it refers to the term of office set by a commonwealth for its representatives. When this term is over, the authority bestowed on these persons goes back to the commonwealth as a whole, which then chooses other representatives for another term.

Secondly, When the Prince hinders the Legislative from assembling in *63*
its due time, or from acting freely, pursuant to those ends, for which it was
Constituted, the *Legislative is altered.* For 'tis not a certain number of Men,
no, nor their meeting, unless they have also Freedom of debating, and
Leisure of prefecting, what is for the good of the Society wherein the Legislative consists: when these are taken away or altered, so as to deprive the
Society of the due exercise of their Power, the *Legislative* is truly *altered.* For
it is not Names, that Constitute Governments, but the use and exercise of
those Powers that were intended to accompany them; so that he who takes
away the Freedom, or hinders the acting of the Legislative in its due seasons, in effect *takes away the Legislative,* and *puts an end to the Government.*

Thirdly, When by the Arbitrary Power of the Prince, the Electors, or *44*
ways of Election are altered, without the Consent, and contrary to the common Interest of the People, there also the *Legislative is altered.* For if others,
than those whom the Society has authorized thereunto, do chuse, or in
another way, than what the Society hath prescribed, those chosen are not
the Legislative appointed by the People.[27]

Fourthly, The delivery also of the People into the subjection of a Foreign *45*
Power, either by the Prince, or by the Legislative, is certainly a *change of
the Legislative,* and so a *Dissolution of the Government.* For the end why People entered into Society, being to be preserved one intire, free, independent Society, to be governed by its own Laws; this is lost, whenever they
are given up into the Power of another.[28]

Why in such a Constitution as this, the *Dissolution of the Government* in *46*
these Cases is to be imputed to the Prince, is evident: because he having
the Force, Treasure, and Offices of the State to imploy, and often perswad-
ing himself, or being flattered by others, that as Supream Magistrate he is
uncapable of controul; he alone is in a Condition to make great Advances
toward such Changes, under pretence of lawful Authority, and has it in
his hands to terrifie or suppress Opposers, as Factious, Seditious, and Enemies to the Government: Whereas no other part of the Legislative, or People is capable by themselves to attempt any alteration of the Legislative,
without open and visible Rebellion, apt enough to be taken notice of;
which when it prevails, produces Effects very little different from Foreign

---

[27]Paragraph 44 seems to refer to the attempt of both Charles II and James II to alter the
parliamentary franchise by remodelling the charters of boroughs. . . . Although the Bill of
Rights of 1689 declared that James II had "violated the freedom of election of members"
and claimed that "Election of Members of Parliament ought to be free," Locke's words and
meaning here do not seem to be as close to that document as is so often assumed. [Laslett]

[28]Locke may have had in mind here the possibility of a Catholic king submitting his country
to the Pope, which was provided against by the Bill of Rights. [Laslett]

Conquest. Besides the Prince in such a Form of Government, having the Power of dissolving the other parts of the Legislative, and thereby rendering them private Persons, they can never in opposition to him, or without his Concurrence, alter the Legislative by a Law, his Consent being necessary to give any of their Decrees that Sanction. But yet so far as the other parts of the Legislative any way contribute to any attempt upon the Government, and do either promote, or not, what lies in them, hinder such designs, they are guilty, and partake in this, which is certainly the greatest Crime Men can be guilty of one towards another.[29]

There is one way more whereby such a Government may be dissolved, 47 and that is, when he who has the Supream Executive Power, neglects and abandons that charge, so that the Laws already made can no longer be put in execution. This is demonstratively to reduce all to Anarchy, and so effectually to *dissolve the Government.* For Laws not being made for themselves, but to be by their execution the Bonds of the Society, to keep every part of the Body Politick in its due place and function, when that totally ceases, the *Government* visibly *ceases,* and the People become a confused Multitude, without Order or Connexion. Where there is no longer the administration of Justice, for the securing of Mens Rights, nor any remaining Power within the Community to direct the Force, or provide for the Necessities of the publick, there certainly is *no Government left.* Where the Laws cannot be executed, it is all one as if there were no Laws, and a Government without Laws, is, I suppose, a Mystery in Politicks, unconceivable to humane Capacity, and inconsistent with humane Society.[30]

In these and the like Cases, *when the Government is dissolved,* the People 48 are at liberty to provide for themselves, by erecting a new Legislative, differing from the other, by the change of Persons, or Form, or both as they shall find it most for their safety and good. For the *Society* can never, by the fault of another, lose the Native and Original Right it has to preserve it self, which can only be done by a settled Legislative, and a fair and impartial execution of the Laws made by it. But the state of Mankind is not so miserable that they are not capable of using this Remedy, till it be too late to look for any. To tell *People* they *may provide for themselves,* by erecting a new Legislative, when by Oppression, Artifice, or being delivered over

---

[29]It seems quite unlikely that even the cautious and devious Locke can have written this paragraph (46) after the events of 1688–9. . . . [Laslett]

[30]This paragraph (47) . . . must have been written in 1689 to refer to James II having "abdicated the government . . . and withdrawn himself out of the kingdom" so "that the throne is thereby vacant," which were the words used in the Parliamentary resolutions. . . . The fact that these statements are difficult to reconcile with what Locke says elsewhere about the dissolution of government as opposed to the dissolution of society . . . may mark the passage as a subsequent insertion. [Laslett]

to a Foreign Power, their old one is gone, is only to tell them they may expect Relief, when it is too late, and the evil is past Cure. This is in effect no more than to bid them first be Slaves, and then to take care of their Liberty; and when their Chains are on, tell them, they may act like Freemen. This, if barely so, is rather Mockery than Relief; and Men can never be secure from Tyranny, if there be no means to escape it, till they are perfectly under it: And therefore it is, that they have not only a Right to get out of it, but to prevent it.

There is therefore, secondly, another way whereby *Governments are dissolved*, and that is; when the Legislative, or the Prince, either of them act contrary to their Trust. 49

First, The *Legislative acts against the Trust* reposed in them, when they endeavour to invade the Property of the Subject, and to make themselves, or any part of the Community, Masters, or Arbitrary Disposers of the Lives, Liberties, or Fortunes of the People. 50

The Reason why Men enter into Society, is the preservation of their Property; and the end why they chuse and authorize a Legislative, is, that there may be Laws made, and Rules set as Guards and Fences to the Properties of all the Members of the Society, to limit the Power, and moderate the Dominion of every Part and Member of the Society. For since it can never be supposed to be the Will of the Society, that the Legislative should have a Power to destroy that, which every one designs to secure, by entering into Society, and for which the People submitted themselves to the Legislators of their own making; whenever the *Legislators endeavour to take away, and destroy the Property of the People*, or to reduce them to Slavery under Arbitrary Power, they put themselves into a state of War with the People, who are thereupon absolved from any farther Obedience, and are left to the common Refuge, which God hath provided for all Men, against Force and Violence. Whensoever therefore the *Legislative* shall transgress this fundamental Rule of Society; and either by Ambition, Fear, Folly or Corruption, *endeavour to grasp* themselves, *or put into the hands of any other an Absolute Power* over the Lives, Liberties, and Estates of the People; By this breach of Trust they *forfeit the Power*, the People had put into their hands, for quite contrary ends, and it devolves to the People, who have a Right to resume their original Liberty, and, by the Establishment of a New Legislative (such as they shall think fit) provide for their own Safety and Security, which is the end for which they are in Society. What I have said here, concerning the Legislative, in general, holds true also concerning the *supreame Executor*, who having a double trust put in him, both to have a part in the Legislative, and the supreme Execution of the Law, Acts against both, when he goes about to set up his own Arbitrary Will, as the Law of the Society. He *acts* also *contrary to his Trust*, when he either imploys the Force, Treasure, and Offices of the Society, to corrupt the *Representatives*, 51

and gain them to his purposes: or openly pre-ingages the *Electors,* and
prescribes to their choice, such, whom he has by Sollicitations, Threats,
Promises, or otherwise won to his designs; and imploys them to bring in
such, who have promised before-hand, what to Vote, and what to Enact.
Thus to regulate Candidates and *Electors,* and new model the ways of *Election,* what is it but to cut up the Government by the Roots, and poison the
very Fountain of publick Security? For the People having reserved to themselves the Choice of their *Representatives,* as the Fence to their Properties,
could do it for no other end, but that they might always be freely chosen,
and so chosen, freely act and advise, as the necessity of the Commonwealth, and the publick Good should, upon examination, and mature debate, be judged to require. This, those who give their Votes before they
hear the Debate, and have weighed the Reasons on all sides, are not capable of doing. To prepare such an Assembly as this, and endeavour to set
up the declared Abettors of his own Will, for the true *Representatives* of the
People, and the Law-makers of the Society, is certainly as great a *breach of
trust,* and as perfect a Declaration of a design to subvert the Government,
as is possible to be met with. To which, if one shall add Rewards and Punishments visibly imploy'd to the same end, and all the Arts of perverted
Law made use of, to take off and destroy all that stand in the way of such
a design, and will not comply and consent to betray the Liberties of their
Country, 'twill be past doubt what is doing. What Power they ought to
have in the Society, who thus imploy it contrary to the trust went along
with it in its first Institution, is easie to determine; and one cannot but see,
that he, who has once attempted any such thing as this, cannot any longer
be trusted.[31]

To this perhaps it will be said, that the People being ignorant, and   52
always discontented, to lay the Foundation of Government in the unsteady
Opinion, and uncertain Humour of the People, is to expose it to certain
ruine; and *no Government will be able to subsist,* if the People may set up a
new Legislative, whenever they take offence at the old one. To this, I Answer: Quite the contrary. People are not so easily got out of their old
Forms, as some are apt to suggest. They are hardly to be prevailed with to
amend the acknowledg'd Faults, in the Frame they have been accustom'd
to. And if there be any Original defects, or adventitious ones introduced
by time, or corruption; 'tis not an easie thing to get them changed, even
when all the World sees there is an opportunity for it. This slowness and
aversion in the People to quit their old Constitutions, has, in the many

---

[31]Here Locke seems to have James II's attempts to control the electorate specifically in
mind. . . . The final lines can only refer to James II, and it seems likely that the whole
passage was added in 1689, making the paragraph the longest in the book. [Laslett]

Revolutions which have been seen in this Kingdom, in this and former Ages, still kept us to, or, after some interval of fruitless attempts, still brought us back again to our old Legislative of King, Lords and Commons[32]: And whatever provocations have made the Crown be taken from some of our Princes Heads, they never carried the People so far, as to place it in another Line.

But 'twill be said, this *Hypothesis* lays a *ferment* for frequent *Rebellion*.   53
To which I Answer,

First, No more than any other *Hypothesis*. For when the *People* are made   54
miserable, and find themselves *exposed to the ill usage of Arbitrary Power*, cry up their Governours, as much as you will for Sons of *Jupiter*,[33] let them be Sacred and Divine, descended or authoriz'd from Heaven; give them out for whom or what you please, the same will happen, *The People generally ill treated*, and contrary to right, will be ready upon any occasion to ease themselves of a burden that sits heavy upon them. They will wish and seek for the opportunity, which, in the change, weakness, and accidents of humane affairs, seldom delays long to offer it self. He must have lived but a little while in the World, who has not seen Examples of this in his time; and he must have read very little, who cannot produce Examples of it in all sorts of Governments in the World.

Secondly, I Answer, such *Revolutions happen* not upon every little mis-   55
management in publick affairs. *Great mistakes* in the ruling part, many wrong and inconvenient Laws, and all the *slips* of humane frailty will be *born by the People*, without mutiny or murmur. But if a long train of Abuses, Prevarications, and Artifices, all tending the same way,[34] make the design visible to the People, and they cannot but feel, what they lie under, and see, whither they are going; 'tis not to be wonder'd, that they should then rouze themselves, and endeavour to put the rule into such hands, which may secure to them the ends for which Government was at first erected; and without which, ancient Names, and specious Forms, are so far from being better, that they are much worse, than the state of Nature, or pure Anarchy; the inconveniences being all as great and as near, but the remedy farther off and more difficult.

---

[32]*Lords and Commons:* The House of Lords and the House of Commons is the traditional division of the British parliament. Though this division of parliamentary power has been disputed at different times during Britain's history, the system still prevails and has done so, with few exceptions, since the 13th century.

[33]*Sons of Jupiter:* The sons of the all-powerful Latin god Jupiter, who was thought to be the king of all gods and the embodiment of governmental authority and national unity. Locke uses this reference to suggest that pleas, even to the greatest political inspiration and authority, will not stop the rebellion of people whose rights have been abused.

[34]The American Declaration of Independence has: "But when a long train of abuses and usurpations pursuing invariably the same object . . ." (paragraph 2). [Laslett]

Thirdly, I Answer, That *this Doctrine* of a Power in the People of pro-   56
viding for their safety a-new by a new Legislative, when their Legislators
have acted contrary to their trust, by invading their Property, is *the best
fence against Rebellion,* and the probablest means to hinder it. For Rebellion
being an Opposition, not to Persons, but Authority, which is founded only
in the Constitutions and Laws of the Government; those, whosever they
be, who by force break through, and by force justifie their violation of
them, are truly and properly *Rebels.* For when Men by entering into Society
and Civil Government, have excluded force, and introduced Laws for the
preservation of Property, Peace, and Unity amongst themselves; those
who set up force again in opposition to the Laws, do *Rebellare,*[35] that is,
bring back again the state of War, and are properly Rebels: Which they
who are in Power (by the pretence they have to Authority, the temptation
of force they have in their hands, and the Flattery of those about them)
being likeliest to do; the properest way to prevent the evil, is to shew them
the danger and injustice of it, who are under the greatest temptation to
run into it.

In both the forementioned Cases, when either the Legislative is   57
changed, or the Legislators act contrary to the end for which they were
constituted; those who are guilty are *guilty of Rebellion.* For if any one by
force takes away the establish'd Legislative of any Society, and the Laws
by them made pursuant to their trust, he thereby takes away the Umpirage, which every one had consented to, for a peaceable decision of all their
Controversies, and a bar to the state of War amongst them. They, who
remove, or change the Legislative, take away this decisive power, which
no Body can have, but by the appointment and consent of the People; and
so destroying the Authority, which the People did, and no Body else can
set up, and introducing a Power, which the People hath not authoriz'd,
they actually *introduce a state of War,* which is that of Force without Authority: And thus by removing the Legislative establish'd by the Society
(in whose decisions the People acquiesced and united, as to that of their
own will) they unty the Knot, and *expose the People a new to the state of War.*
And if those, who by force take away the Legislative, are *Rebels,* the *Legislators* themselves, as has been shewn, can be no less esteemed so; when
they, who were set up for the protection, and preservation of the People,
their Liberties and Properties, shall by force invade, and indeavour to take
them away; and so they putting themselves into a state of War with those,

---

[35]*rebellare:* Literally, to rebel; Locke uses this word to refer to persons who either disregard
or abuse the laws of the commonwealth for their own purposes.

who made them the Protectors and Guardians of their Peace, are properly, and with the greatest aggravation, *Rebellantes*[36] Rebels.

But if they, who say it *lays a foundation for Rebellion,* mean that it may 58 occasion Civil Wars, or Intestine Broils, to tell the People they are absolved from Obedience, when illegal attempts are made upon their Liberties or Properties, and may oppose the unlawful violence of those, who were their Magistrates, when they invade their Properties contrary to the trust put in them; and that therefore this Doctrine is not to be allow'd, being so destructive to the Peace of the World. They may as well say upon the same ground, that honest Men may not oppose Robbers or Pirates, because this may occasion disorder or bloodshed. If any *mischief* come in such Cases, it is not *to be charged* upon him, who defends his own right, but *on him,* that *invades* his Neighbours. If the innocent honest Man must quietly quit all he has for Peace sake, to him who will lay violent hands upon it, I desire it may be consider'd, what a kind of Peace there will be in the World, which consists only in Violence and Rapine; and which is to be maintain'd only for the benefit of Robbers and Oppressors. Who would not think it an admirable Peace betwixt the Mighty and the Mean, when the Lamb, without resistance, yielded his Throat to be torn by the imperious Wolf? *Polyphemus's* Den[37] gives us a perfect Pattern of such a Peace, and such a Government, wherein *Ulysses* and his Companions had nothing to do, but quietly to suffer themselves to be devour'd. And no doubt *Ulysses,* who was a prudent Man, preach'd up *Passive Obedience,* and exhorted them to a quiet Submission, by representing to them of what concernment Peace was to Mankind; and by shewing the inconveniencies might happen, if they should offer to resist *Polyphemus,* who had now the power over them.

The end of Government is the good of Mankind, and which is *best for* 59 *Mankind,* that the People should be always expos'd to the boundless will of Tyranny, or that the Rulers should be sometimes liable to be oppos'd, when they grow exorbitant in the use of their Power, and imploy it for the destruction, and not the preservation of the Properties of their People?

---

[36]*rebellantes:* Persons who rebel against the laws of the commonwealth. Locke uses this word to signify a wrongful rebellion, in contrast to people who rebel rightfully against persons in authority when these persons abuse the laws of the commonwealth.

[37]*Polyphemus's Den:* Polyphemus, a cyclops (one-eyed giant) in Homer's *Odyssey,* captured and held Odysseus (Ulysses) and his men in his cave, devouring a number of them. For a time, Odysseus could do nothing to stop Polyphemus because of the giant's superior strength. Locke sarcastically asks his readers whether Odysseus urged his men to submit to Polyphemus in the interests of not disturbing the peace. That kind of peace, Locke suggests, is nothing more than meek submission to injustice; upright citizens have a right to fight, if necessary, to protect their rights.

Nor let any one say, that mischief can arise from hence, as often as it shall please a busie head, or turbulent spirit, to desire the alteration of the Government. 'Tis true, such Men may stir, whenever they please, but it will be only to their own just ruine and perdition. For till the mischief be grown general, and the ill designs of the Rulers become visible, or their attempts sensible to the greater part, the People, who are more disposed to suffer, than right themselves by Resistance, are not apt to stir.[38] The examples of particular Injustice, or Oppression of here and there an unfortunate Man, moves them not. But if they universally have a perswasion, grounded upon manifest evidence, that designs are carrying on against their Liberties, and the general course and tendency of things cannot but give them strong suspicions of the evil intention of their Governors, who is to be blamed for it? Who can help it, if they, who might avoid it, bring themselves into this suspicion? Are the People to be blamed, if they have the sence of rational Creatures, and can think of things no otherwise than as they find and feel them? And is it not rather *their fault*, who puts things in such a posture that they would not have them thought, to be as they are? I grant, that the Pride, Ambition, and Turbulency of private Men have sometimes caused great Disorders in Commonwealths, and Factions have been fatal to States and Kingdoms. But whether the *mischief* hath *oftner* begun *in the Peoples Wantonness*, and a Desire to cast off the lawful Authority of their Rulers; or *in the Rulers Insolence*, and Endeavours to get, and exercise an Arbitrary Power over their People; whether Oppression, or Disobedience gave the first rise to the Disorder, I leave it to impartial History to determine. This I am sure, whoever, either Ruler or Subject, by force goes about to invade the Rights of either Prince or People, and lays the foundation for *overturning* the Constitution and Frame of any *Just Government*, is guilty of the greatest Crime, I think, a Man is capable of, being to answer for all those mischiefs of Blood, Rapine, and Desolation, which the breaking to pieces of Governments bring on a Countrey. And he who does it, is justly to be esteemed the common Enemy and Pest of Mankind; and is to be treated accordingly.

That *Subjects*, or *Foreigners* attempting by force on the Properties of any People, may be *resisted* with force, is agreed on all hands. But that *Magistrates* doing the same thing, may be *resisted*, hath of late been denied: As if those who had the greatest Priviledges and Advantages by the Law, had thereby a Power to break those Laws, by which alone they were set in a better place than their Brethren: Whereas their Offence is thereby the greater, both as being ungrateful for the greater share they have by the

---

[38]Parallel in the *American Declaration of Independence* (paragraph 2): "mankind are more disposed to suffer, while evils are sufferable, than to right themselves." [Laslett]

Law, and breaking also that Trust, which is put into their hands by their Brethren.

REVIEW QUESTIONS

1. According to Locke, when and how are commonwealths constituted? What is the chief restriction on liberty which individuals who agree to make up a commonwealth place upon themselves? What argument does Locke urge for the necessity of this restriction? Why is it impractical for a commonwealth to require unanimous consent to its laws?
2. What is the difference between *tacit consent* and *express consent?* In what ways do the rights and responsibilities differ between those who live in a commonwealth under tacit consent and those who live in it under express consent?
3. In what ways are conditions in the state of nature inadequate to protect property? What liberties do people give up when they leave the state of nature to enter into society and under the laws of government? Into whose hands do these liberties pass? What are the obligations of the new holders of these liberties?
4. What does Locke consider to be the supreme power in a commonwealth? What is the ultimate source of this power? What is its ultimate purpose? What are its limits? In what form must it be dispensed? What are the special limitations placed upon taxation? Why is arbitrary power vested in the government of a commonwealth a basic violation of the social contract? What is the alternative to such arbitrary power?
5. Under what circumstances are governments dissolved from within? In what ways may the legislative power be altered? Where does the blame generally lie for such alterations? What does Locke consider "the greatest crime men can be guilty of one towards another"? Why?
6. Under what conditions do the obligations of the people to support and obey the government cease? In what particular ways may the executive forfeit the right to popular support? What objections does Locke acknowledge can be made to this right to change the government? What are his answers to such objections? In what way can legislators and magistrates (and not just subjects) be considered rebels?

DISCUSSION AND WRITING QUESTIONS

1. How does Locke's description of the origin of the social contract differ from that of Hobbes? Which description seems to you a more plausible explanation of the founding of commonwealths? How do Hobbes's and Locke's discussions represent opposing views of human nature?
2. In what way might Locke's comments in paragraph 31 have given aid and comfort to the American colonists who were protesting the various injustices of the British Crown? Cite other passages that throw light upon the American revolution and explain why they apply.

3. In paragraphs 48 and following, Locke discusses the circumstances under which governments may be legitimately overthrown. Do you agree with these arguments? Which of the objections that Locke considers do you believe are the most valid? Cite specific historical (or contemporary) developments in support of either the objections or the answers to these objections.

4. It is well acknowledged that the ideas of Locke (and Rousseau and other Enlightenment thinkers) were instrumental in founding the American republic. Now that the United States is entering its third century, how well do you believe that Locke's ideas continue to form the philosophical basis not only of the American government itself but also of the way that Americans regard their government? Suppose, for example, that Locke's ideas were expressed in modern English in contemporary newspaper editorials and columns. To what extent do you think that these ideas would be controversial? Do you see evidence that some people might like to return to what Locke would consider the state of nature? Or that Locke's ideas might be considered seditious?

JEAN-JACQUES ROUSSEAU *(1712–1778)*

The idea of the social contract is more closely associated with Jean-Jacques Rousseau than with any other individual. But as we have seen, Rousseau was far from being the first — or the last — to make use of the idea. Aside from the fact that he entitled one of his major works *On the Social Contract,* he was a great popularizer of philosophical ideas, and he cut a heroic figure through late 18th century Europe, coming in some ways to symbolize the ideal of romantic individualism breaking decisively with the tradition-bound past. Rousseau — fairly or not — is also associated with the idea of romantic primitivism — the idea that people in their natural state are good (honest and altruistic) but have been corrupted by social, political, and educational institutions. In his attack on social, religious, and literary conventions, he employed a variety of forms: philosophical treatise, novel, autobiography, opera, and drama. In his prime he was, perhaps, the most celebrated intellect in Europe, and one of the inspirational forces behind the French Revolution of 1789. (During that revolution his remains were moved to the Pantheon in Paris.)

Born in Geneva, Switzerland, in 1712, Rousseau was brought up by his father, a watchmaker (his mother died a few days after his birth), and later by his uncle, for whom he worked briefly as a clerk. He was self-educated, reading widely in fiction, classical history, and ethics from books in his father's library. For a short time he was apprenticed to an engraver but was badly treated; and at the age of 16, he fled Geneva and went to Italy, where he converted from Calvinism to Catholicism. For the next 20 years, he led a picaresque existence in Italy and France, entering a seminary but finding he had no aptitude for the priesthood, working as an engraver, as a tutor, in a tax office, on a farm, and as secretary to the French ambassador (a job that gave him his first close look at the workings of political institutions). During these years he continued his wide reading and began to write, producing both dramatic and philosophical works. In 1745, he began living with Thérèse Levasseur, a chambermaid in the hotel where he stayed; they had five children — all of whom he placed in an institution for foundlings. Also in 1745, he met Denis Diderot, a young philosopher (also to become a spiritual father of the French Revolution) and editor of the Encyclopédie, a new compendium of knowledge, for which Rousseau was to contribute several articles on music.

Rousseau first broke into public attention — and began his lifelong notoriety — with a prize-winning essay called *Discourse on the Science and the Arts* (1750). The contestants had been asked to discuss how science and the arts had improved human morals; Rousseau argued with passionate intensity that science and the arts had, in fact, corrupted and degraded morals. This work was followed some years later with his *Discourse on the Origins of Inequality,* in which he distinguished natural inequality (differences in talent and other personal endowments) from unnatural inequality (differences in social station and wealth), maintaining that the former were desirable but the latter were evil and the source of numerous injustices. In particular, Rousseau objected to private property, asserting that "The first man who, having enclosed a piece of ground, bethought himself of saying 'This is mine,' and found people simple enough to believe him, was the real founder of civil society." Even before this time, he had backed up the sincerity of his words by refusing to accept a royal pension for a successful opera he had written, selling off his valuables, resigning from a position as cashier at a bank, and henceforth earning his living by copying music. Previously, he had been living in comfort, entertained in the houses of the great; now he decided to live the simple life, retiring to l'Ermitage, a country house (with which he had been provided by a wealthy patroness) near the forest of Montmorency.

At l'Ermitage and later at a nearby house, Montlouis, Rousseau composed several of his masterpieces: *The New Héloïse* (1761), a romantic and philosophical novel; *Émile, or Education* (1762), a novelistic treatise on the education of children; and *On the Social Contract; or the Principles of Political Right* (1762). The principles expressed particularly in the latter two works struck at the heart of contemporary government and religion. Rousseau's earlier works had already gotten him into trouble with the authorities (he had been under police surveillance since 1753); now *Émile* was condemned by the Parliament in Paris, and Rousseau was forced to flee to Switzerland, where he was received no more kindly than in France. Rousseau was especially devastated by a stinging personal attack (in the form of an anonymous pamphlet) from a fellow iconoclast, the philosopher Voltaire. At about this time, he became mentally unstable as a result of his misfortunes; and for the rest of his life, he was subject to delusions, paranoia, and (it was alleged) even insanity. He moved restlessly from place to place. At the invitation of the philosopher David Hume, he visited England in 1766, but suspecting Hume of treachery and openly quarreling with him, Rousseau fled back to France the following year. In 1768, he finally married Thérèse Levasseur. During the next few years, he worked on his masterful autobiography, *Confessions* (published posthumously in 1783), reading sections of the manuscript in Parisian salons until asked to desist by the authorities. In the last two years of his life, he achieved a measure of serenity, living in seclusion with Thérèse and concluding his autobiographical writings with *Reveries of a Solitary Walker*. He died in Ermenonville in 1778.

The Social Contract opens with a famous sentence that epitomizes Rousseau's sentiments: "Man was born free, and everywhere he is in chains." Rousseau is particularly concerned with the forces that allow some people to dominate and tyrannize over others. Like Hobbes and Locke, he acknowledges the need for authority in the name of safety and security; but he insists that all such authority derives from the consent of the governed, a consent that may be legitimately withdrawn for sufficient cause. This was not an idea calculated to appeal to those who held the reins of authority in 1762. Possibly to avoid the political dangers of overexplicitness, however, Rousseau wrote in general and often ambiguous terms. Commentators have long argued over exactly what he meant by such statements as: "Find a form of association that defends and protects the person and goods of each associate with all the common force, and by means of which each one, uniting with all, nevertheless obeys only himself and remains as free as before." How, critics have asked, can one enter into an association while still obeying only oneself and remaining "as free as before"? But this is only to point out that Rousseau's ideas on the social contract are as subject to illogicality and ambiguity as the ideas of almost every other thinker on the subject. What remains, when all the contradictions have been pointed out, is the play of a powerful mind on a subject of enduring importance: the legitimate and illegitimate exercise of political authority over the individual will.

The following passage comprises Book I of *The Social Contract.*

THE SOCIAL CONTRACT

I want to inquire whether there can be a legitimate and reliable rule of administration in the civil order, taking men as they are and laws as they can be. I shall try always to reconcile in this research what right permits with what interest prescribes, so that justice and utility are not at variance.   1

I start in without proving the importance of my subject. It will be asked if I am a prince or a legislator to write about politics. I reply that I am neither, and that is why I write about politics. If I were a prince or a legislator, I would not waste my time saying what has to be done. I would do it, or keep silent.   2

Born a citizen of a free State, and a member of the sovereign, the right to vote there is enough to impose on me the duty of learning about public affairs, no matter how feeble the influence of my voice may be. And I am happy, every time I meditate about governments, always to find in my research new reasons to love that of my country![1]   3

CHAPTER I: SUBJECT OF THIS FIRST BOOK

Man was born free, and everywhere he is in chains. One who believes himself the master of others is nonetheless a greater slave than they. How did this change occur? I do not know. What can make it legitimate? I believe I can answer this question.   4

Jean-Jacques Rousseau. The Social Contract [1762]. Rpt. in *On The Social Contract.* Ed. Roger D. Masters. Trans. Judith R. Masters. New York: St. Martin's, 1978.

[1]Despite this praise, Rousseau [has an] ambivalent attitude toward his native Geneva. . . . This ambivalence is not, however, merely a logical contradiction. Since Geneva's republican regime is superior to monarchies, it deserves to be a model for French readers whereas, for Genevan readers, the issue is the extent to which one can slow down the inevitable decline of all governments toward despotism. [Roger D. Masters, ed. *On the Social Contract,* by Jean-Jacques Rousseau (New York: St. Martins, 1978).]

If I were to consider only force and the effect it produces, I would say   5
that as long as a people is constrained to obey and does so, it does well;
as soon as it can shake off the yoke and does so, it does even better. For
in recovering its freedom by means of the same right used to steal it, either
the people is justified in taking it back, or those who took it away were not
justified in doing so. But the social order is a sacred right that serves as a
basis for all the others. However, this right does not come from nature; it
is therefore based on conventions. The problem is to know what these
conventions are. Before coming to that, I should establish what I have just
asserted.

CHAPTER II: ON THE FIRST SOCIETIES

The most ancient of all societies, and the only natural one, is that of   6
the family. Yet children remain bound to the father only as long as they
need him for self-preservation. As soon as this need ceases, the natural
bond dissolves. The children, exempt from the obedience they owed the
father, and the father, exempt from the care he owed the children, all return equally to independence. If they continue to remain united, it is no
longer naturally but voluntarily, and the family itself is maintained only by
convention.

This common freedom is a consequence of man's nature. His first law   7
is to attend to his own preservation, his first cares are those he owes himself; and as soon as he has reached the age of reason, as he alone is the
judge of the proper means of preserving himself, he thus becomes his own
master.

The family is therefore, so to speak, the prototype of political societies.   8
The leader is like the father, the people are like the children; and since all
are born equal and free, they only alienate their freedom for their utility.
The entire difference is that in the family, the father's love for his children
rewards him for the care he provides; whereas in the State, the pleasure of
commanding substitutes for this love, which the leader does not have for
his people.

Grotius[2] denies that all human power is established for the benefit of   9

---

[2]*Grotius:* (1583–1645) A Dutch political and legal philosopher, Hugo Grotius is the author
of *The Right of War and Peace,* one of the first great works in what later became our modern
international law. Here Rousseau is questioning Grotius's assertion that human power
naturally benefits the persons in authority rather than the persons governed. Rousseau
disagrees with Grotius because the latter uses current experience as the basis for his generalization on the nature of government, rather than basing his generalization on what a
governing system could ideally be.

those who are governed. He cites slavery as an example. His most persistent mode of reasoning is always to establish right by fact.[3] One could use a more rational method, but not one more favorable to tyrants.

It is therefore doubtful, according to Grotius, whether the human race 10 belongs to a hundred men, or whether these hundred men belong to the human race; and throughout his book he appears to lean toward the former view. This is Hobbes's sentiment as well. Thus the human species is divided into herds of livestock, each with its leader, who tends it in order to devour it.[4]

As a herdsman's nature is superior to that of his herd, so the shepherds 11 of men, who are their leaders, are also superior in nature to their peoples. The emperor Caligula[5] reasoned thus, according to Philo,[6] concluding rather logically from this analogy that the kings were Gods or that people were beasts.

Caligula's reasoning amounts to the same thing as that of Hobbes and 12 Grotius. Before any of them, Aristotle[7] too had said that men are not naturally equal, but that some are born for slavery and others for domination.

Aristotle was right, but he mistook the effect for the cause. Every man 13 born in slavery is born for slavery; nothing could be more certain. Slaves lose everything in their chains, even the desire to be rid of them. They love

---

[3]"Learned research on public right is often merely the history of ancient abuses, and people have gone to a lot of trouble for nothing when they have bothered to study it too much." *Treatise on the Interests of France in Relation to her Neighbors,* by M. le Marquis d'Argenson (printed by Rey in Amsterdam). This is exactly what Grotius has done. [Rousseau]

[4]Rousseau seems to refer to Hobbes's argument that "whatsoever he [the sovereign] doth, it can be no injury to any of his subjects; nor ought he to be by any of them accused of injustice." Thomas Hobbes, *Leviathan,* Part 2, chap. 18 (ed. Oakeshott [Oxford: Blackwell, 1960], p. 115). For the origin of the comparison between a leader and a shepherd, see Thrasymachus' speech in Plato's *Republic,* I, 343a–344c (ed. Bloom, pp. 21–22). [Masters]

[5]*Caligula:* Also known as Gaius Caesar, he was the Roman Emperor from A.D. 37 to 41. An extremely unpopular leader, Caligula was tyrannical in his attempts to exercise and maintain absolute authority. He was said to have used sentences of expropriation, exile, and even execution to deter those who opposed him.

[6]*Philo:* Judaeus Philo (10–15 B.C. to A.D. 40–45) was a Greek-speaking Jewish philosopher. Rousseau is referring here to his work, *On the Embassy to Gaius,* written as an attack on Emperor Caligula after he refused Philo's request that Jewish rights be reinstated in the empire.

[7]*Aristotle:* A Greek philosopher (384–322 B.C.) who wrote on a variety of subjects, from politics to biology. Rousseau is referring here to a passage in Aristotle's *Politics,* a book containing ideas that were later to become the foundation for modern constitutional governments.

their servitude as the companions of Ulysses[8] loved their brutishness.[9] If there are slaves by nature, therefore, it is because there have been slaves contrary to nature. Force made the first slaves; their cowardice perpetuated them.

I have said nothing about king Adam[10] or emperor Noah,[11] father of three great monarchs who divided up the universe among themselves, as did the children of Saturn[12] who have been identified with them. I hope this moderation will be appreciated, for as I am a direct descendant of one of these princes, and perhaps of the eldest branch, how am I to know whether, through the verification of titles, I would not discover that I am the legitimate king of the human race? However that may be, it cannot be denied that Adam was sovereign of the world, like Crusoe[13] of his island, as long as he was its only inhabitant. And what was convenient in that

14

---

[8]*Ulysses:* The Roman title for Odysseus, the hero of Homer's epics the *Iliad* and the *Odyssey*. Rousseau uses this passage from the *Odyssey* to emphasize his point that men naturally adapt to their social positions. He believes that the security of familiarity will often lead men to see only the positive aspects of their present conditions, even when these conditions are abominable.

[9]"See a short treatise by Plutarch entitled *That Animals Reason.*" [Rousseau] This short dialogue in Plutarch's *Moralia* is worth reading: in reply to Ulysses' request that the Greeks turned into animals be released in human form, Circe [the sorceress who transformed them into swine] asks him to persuade one of them, named Gryllus, that this would be desirable. Gryllus then explains why "man is the most miserable and most calamitous animal in the world" whereas "the soul of animals is better disposed and more perfected for producing virtue, since without being forced, or commanded, or taught, . . . it produces and nourishes the virtue which, according to nature, suits each one." Hence, instead of proving that slavery is unnatural — as the text leads one to expect — Plutarch's dialogue suggests that human *civilization* is unnatural and corrupt. [Masters]

[10]*King Adam:* According to the biblical account of the creation of the earth and its inhabitants, Adam was the first human being created by God. Adam's wife, Eve, was created from his own rib, which makes Adam the first and primary progenitor of the entire human race. Rousseau uses this biblical passage to undermine doctrines supporting the legitimacy of kings by hereditary succession: technically, we are all descendants of Adam and thus we might all be kings.

[11]*Emperor Noah:* In the biblical account of The Great Flood, God created a flood to destroy life on earth, instructing Noah beforehand to build a great ark in order to save himself, his wife, and a mating pair of every species on earth. Rousseau uses this biblical account to undermine, once again, doctrines on the hereditary legitimacy of kings. Since the flood destroyed all human life except for Noah and his wife, the entire human race after the flood descends from Noah; therefore, any of us might be king.

[12]*Saturn:* The Roman mythological god who fathered the god Jupiter, who later became the ruler of all gods and men. Since Saturn sired Jupiter who then became king, Saturn is another "first king," like Adam and Noah.

[13]*Crusoe:* In Daniel Defoe's novel *Robinson Crusoe* (1719), the character Crusoe is shipwrecked on a deserted island and sets up a home there.

empire was that the monarch, secure on his throne, had neither rebellions, nor wars, nor conspirators to fear.

CHAPTER III: ON THE RIGHT OF THE STRONGEST

The strongest is never strong enough to be the master forever unless he transforms his force into right and obedience into duty.[14] This leads to the right of the strongest, a right that is in appearance taken ironically and in principle really established. But won't anyone ever explain this word to us? Force is a physical power. I do not see what morality can result from its effects. Yielding to force is an act of necessity, not of will. At most, it is an act of prudence. In what sense could it be a duty? 15

Let us suppose this alleged right for a moment. I say that what comes of it is nothing but inexplicable confusion. For as soon as force makes right, the effect changes along with the cause. Any force that overcomes the first one succeeds to its right. As soon as one can disobey without punishment, one can do so legitimately, and since the strongest is always right, the only thing to do is to make oneself the strongest. But what is a right that perishes when force ceases? If it is necessary to obey by force, one need not obey by duty, and if one is no longer forced to obey, one is no longer obligated to do so. It is apparent, then, that this word right adds nothing to force. It is meaningless here. 16

Obey those in power. If that means yield to force, the precept is good, but superfluous; I reply that it will never be violated. All power comes from God, I admit, but so does all illness. Does this mean it is forbidden to call the doctor? If a brigand takes me by surprise at the edge of a woods, must I not only give up my purse by force; am I obligated by conscience to give it even if I could keep it away? After all, the pistol he holds is also a power. 17

Let us agree, therefore, that might does not make right, and that one is only obligated to obey legitimate powers. Thus my original question still remains. 18

---

[14]Rousseau's insistence that "might does not make right" deserves more emphasis than it is usually given, since it means that "legitimate authority" must be freely accepted "in *conscience*" even by those who are being punished for violating the rules. . . . The second sentence contains an untranslatable play on words: when Rousseau speaks of the "right of the strongest" as a right that is *"réellement établi en principe"* he could mean either that this right is "in principle really established" in the works of political theorists like Grotius or Hobbes, or that this right was "really established *in the beginning*" (i.e., that human history was originally based only on the right of the strongest). [Masters]

CHAPTER IV: ON SLAVERY

Since no man has any natural authority over his fellow man, and since   *19*
force produces no right, there remain only conventions as the basis of all
legitimate authority among men.

If a private individual, says Grotius, can alienate his freedom and en-   *20*
slave himself to a master, why can't a whole people alienate its freedom
and subject itself to a king? There are many equivocal words in this that
need explaining, but let us limit ourselves to the word *alienate*. To alienate
is to give or to sell. Now a man who makes himself another's slave does
not give himself, he sells himself, at the least for his subsistence. But why
does a people sell itself? Far from furnishing the subsistence of his subjects,
a king derives his own only from them, and according to Rabelais[15] a king
does not live cheaply. Do the subjects give their persons, then, on condition that their goods will be taken too? I do not see what remains for them
to preserve.

It will be said that the despot guarantees civil tranquillity to his sub-   *21*
jects. Perhaps so, but what have they gained if the wars that his ambition
brings on them, if his insatiable greed, if the harassment of his ministers
are a greater torment than their dissensions would be? What have they
gained, if this tranquillity is one of their miseries? Life is tranquil in jail
cells, too. Is that reason enough to like them? The Greeks lived tranquilly
shut up in the Cyclops'[16] cave as they awaited their turn to be devoured.[17]

To say that a man gives himself gratuitously is to say something absurd   *22*
and inconceivable. Such an act is illegitimate and null, if only because he

---

[15]*Rabelais:* François Rabelais (1490–1553), French author and classical scholar.

[16]*Cyclops:* In Homer's epic, the *Odyssey* (IX, 216–436), the cyclops Polyphemus held Odysseus and his men captive in his cave, devouring a number of them. Because Odysseus and
his men had no resources with which to stop the giant and escape, they were forced to
accept their captive state. Rousseau uses this passage to highlight a possible flaw in the
argument that subjects give themselves to their kings in order to gain peace. In this case,
Odysseus and his men were forced by terror to remain passive; thus, their peaceful state
was not a benefit provided them by their ruler, but a product of the ruler's abuse.

[17]Compare *État de Guerre*, where Rousseau first uses this example: "I open the books on
right and morality, I listen to the scholars and jurists and, touched by their insinuating
discourses, I admire the peace and justice established by the civil order, I bless the wisdom
of public institutions, and I console myself for being a man by seeing myself as a citizen.
Well taught concerning my duties and my happiness, I close the book, leave the classroom,
and look around me. I see unfortunate peoples groaning under an iron yoke, the human
race crushed by a handful of oppressors, a starving crowd worn out by difficulty and
hunger whose blood and tears the rich drink in peace, and everywhere the strong armed
against the weak with the fearsome power of the laws. All that is done peacefully and
without resistance; it is the tranquillity of Ulysses' companions trapped in the Cyclops'
cave, waiting to be devoured." (Pléiade, III, 608–609). Rousseau emphatically denies
Hobbes's argument that it is rational to abandon one's natural freedom to enter any society

who does so is not in his right mind. To say the same thing about an entire people is to suppose a people of madmen. Madness does not make right.

Even if everyone could alienate himself, he could not alienate his children. They are born men and free. Their freedom belongs to them; no one but themselves has a right to dispose of it. Before they have reached the age of reason, their father can, in their name, stipulate conditions for their preservation, for their well-being; but he cannot give them irrevocably and unconditionally, because such a gift is contrary to the ends of nature and exceeds the rights of paternity. For an arbitrary government to be legitimate, it would therefore be necessary for the people in each generation to be master of its acceptance or rejection. But then this government would no longer be arbitrary.   23

To renounce one's freedom is to renounce one's status as a man, the rights of humanity and even its duties. There is no possible compensation for anyone who renounces everything. Such a renunciation is incompatible with the nature of man, and taking away all his freedom of will is taking away all morality from his actions. Finally, it is a vain and contradictory convention to stipulate absolute authority on one side and on the other unlimited obedience. Isn't it clear that one is in no way engaged toward a person from whom one has the right to demand everything, and doesn't this condition alone — without equivalent and without exchange — entail the nullification of the act? For what right would my slave have against me, since all he has belongs to me, and his right being mine, my right against myself is a meaningless word?   24

Grotius and others derive from war another origin of the alleged right of slavery. As the victor has the right to kill the vanquished, according to them, the latter can buy back his life at the cost of his freedom — a convention all the more legitimate in that it is profitable for both of them.   25

But it is clear that this alleged right to kill the vanquished in no way results from the state of war. Men are not naturally enemies, if only because when living in their original independence, they do not have sufficiently stable relationships among themselves to constitute either the state of peace or the state of war. It is the relationship between things, not between men, that constitutes war; and as the state of war cannot arise from simple, personal relations, but only from proprietary relations, private war between one man and another can exist neither in the state of nature, where there is no stable property, nor in the social state, where everything is under the authority of the laws.   26

Individual combats, duels, encounters are not acts that constitute a   27

---

as long as it is peaceful and quiet. Compare *Leviathan*, Part 2, chap. 18 (ed. Oakeshott, p. 120) [paragraph 37, this edition] and Locke, *Second Treatise*, chap. xix, paragraph 228 (ed. Laslett, pp. 434–435) [paragraph 58, this edition]. [Masters]

state. And with regard to private wars, authorized by the establishments of King Louis IX of France[18] and suspended by the peace of God, they are abuses of feudal government, an absurd system if there ever was one, contrary to the principles of natural right and to every good polity.

War is not, therefore, a relation between man and man, but between *28* State and State, in which private individuals are enemies only by accident, not as men, nor even as citizens,[19] but as soldiers; not as members of the homeland but as its defenders. Finally, each State can have only other States, and no men, as enemies, since no true relationship can be established between things of different natures.

This principle even conforms with the established maxims of all ages *29* and with the constant practice of all civilized peoples. Declarations of war are not so much warnings to those in power as to their subjects. The foreigner — whether he be king, private individual, or people — who robs, kills, or imprisons subjects without declaring war on the prince, is not an enemy, but a brigand. Even in the midst of war, a just prince may well seize everything in an enemy country that belongs to the public, but he respects the person and goods of private individuals. He respects rights on which his own are based. The end of war being the destruction of the enemy State, one has the right to kill its defenders as long as they are armed. But as soon as they lay down their arms and surrender, since they cease to be enemies or instruments of the enemy, they become simply men once again, and one no longer has a right to their lives. Sometimes it is possible to kill the State without killing a single one of its members. War confers no right that is not necessary to its end. These principles are not those of Grotius; they are not based on the authority of poets, but are derived from the nature of things, and are based on reason.

---

[18]*King Louis IX of France:* . . . The king of France from 1226 to 1270, he engaged his men in an unpopular and unsuccessful crusade (the Seventh Crusade) to save Jerusalem from Muslim invaders. Rousseau apparently sees Louis' use of state soldiers in the Crusades as an abuse of the men's feudal obligation to remain loyal to their king in war: the soldiers didn't necessarily have any personal interests in the Crusades; they fought because their king called them to fight.

[19]The Romans, who understood and respected the right of war better than any nation in the world, were so scrupulous in this respect that a citizen was not allowed to serve as a volunteer unless he had expressly engaged himself against the enemy, and against the particular enemy by name. When a legion in which Cato the Younger was serving for the first time under Popilius had been reorganized, Cato the Elder wrote to Popilius that if he wanted his son to continue to serve under him, Popilius would have to have him take the military oath again, because the first oath being annulled, he could no longer bear arms against the enemy. And the same Cato wrote his son to be careful not to appear in combat without swearing this new oath. I know that the siege of Clusium and other specific events can be raised in contradiction to this, but I cite laws and practices. The Romans were the people who least often transgressed their laws, and they are the only people who had such fine ones. [Rousseau]

With regard to the right of conquest, it has no basis other than the law   30
of the strongest. If war does not give the victor the right to massacre the
vanquished peoples, this right he does not have cannot establish the right
to enslave them. One only has the right to kill the enemy when he cannot
be made a slave. The right to make him a slave does not come, then, from
the right to kill him. It is therefore an iniquitous exchange to make him
buy his life, over which one has no right, at the cost of his freedom. By
establishing the right of life and death on the right of slavery, and the right
of slavery on the right of life and death, isn't it clear that one falls into a
vicious circle?

Even assuming this terrible right to kill everyone, I say that a man   31
enslaved in war or a conquered people is in no way obligated toward his
master, except to obey for as long as he is forced to do so. In taking the
equivalent of his life, the victor has not spared it; rather than to kill him
purposelessly, he has killed him usefully. Therefore, far from the victor
having acquired any authority over him in addition to force, the state of
war subsists between them as before; their relation itself is its effect, and
the customs of the right of war suppose that there has not been a peace
treaty. They made a convention, true; but that convention, far from destroying the state of war, assumes its continuation.

Thus, from every vantage point, the right of slavery is null, not merely   32
because it is illegitimate, but because it is absurd and meaningless. These
words *slavery* and *right* are contradictory; they are mutually exclusive.
Whether it is said by one man to another or by a man to a people, the
following speech will always be equally senseless: *I make a convention with
you that is entirely at your expense and entirely for my benefit; that I shall observe
for as long as I want, and that you shall observe for as long as I want.*

CHAPTER V: THAT IT IS ALWAYS NECESSARY
TO GO BACK TO A FIRST CONVENTION

Even if I were to grant everything I have thus far refuted, the propo-   33
nents of despotism would be no better off. There will always be a great
difference between subjugating a multitude and governing a society. If
scattered men, however many there may be, are successively enslaved by
one individual, I see only a master and slaves; I do not see a people and
its leader. It is an aggregation, if you wish, but not an association. It has
neither public good nor body politic. That man, even if he had enslaved
half the world, is nothing but a private individual. His interest, separate
from that of the others, is still nothing but a private interest. If this same
man dies, thereafter his empire is left scattered and without bonds, just as
an oak tree disintegrates and falls into a heap of ashes after fire has consumed it.

A people, says Grotius, can give itself to a king. According to Grotius,   34
a people is therefore a people before it gives itself to a king. This gift itself

is a civil act; it presupposes a public deliberation. Therefore, before examining the act by which a people elects a king, it would be well to examine the act by which a people becomes a people. For this act, being necessarily prior to the other, is the true basis of society.

Indeed, if there were no prior convention, what would become of the   *35*
obligation for the minority to submit to the choice of the majority, unless the election were unanimous; and where do one hundred who want a master get the right to vote for ten who do not? The law of majority rule is itself an established convention, and presupposes unanimity at least once.[20]

CHAPTER VI: ON THE SOCIAL COMPACT

I assume that men have reached the point where obstacles to their self-   *36*
preservation in the state of nature prevail by their resistance over the forces each individual can use to maintain himself in that state. Then that primitive state can no longer subsist and the human race would perish if it did not change its way of life.

Now since men cannot engender new forces, but merely unite and   *37*
direct existing ones, they have no other means of self-preservation except to form, by aggregation, a sum of forces that can prevail over the resistance; set them to work by a single motivation; and make them act in concert.

This sum of forces can arise only from the cooperation of many. But   *38*
since each man's force and freedom are the primary instruments of his self-preservation, how is he to engage them without harming himself and without neglecting the cares he owes to himself? In the context of my subject, this difficulty can be stated in these terms.

"Find a form of association that defends and protects the person and   *39*
goods of each associate with all the common force, and by means of which each one, uniting with all, nevertheless obeys only himself and remains as free as before." This is the fundamental problem which is solved by the social contract.

The clauses of this contract are so completely determined by the nature   *40*
of the act that the slightest modification would render them null and void. So that although they may never have been formally pronounced, they are

---

[20]This passage criticizes Hobbes, who admits that each individual has "tacitly covenanted" to accept a majority vote *before* the assembly "hath by consenting voices declared a sovereign": *Leviathan*, Part 2, chap. 18 (ed. Oakeshott, p. 115) [paragraph 34, this edition]. Rousseau insists that the "true basis of society" is Hobbes's "tacit covenant," whereas Hobbes had treated the subsequent election of the sovereign or ruler as the social contract. In other words, Rousseau's definition of the social contract can be treated as the logic which leads any assembly to accept the principle of majority rule. [Masters]

everywhere the same, everywhere tacitly accepted and recognized, until the social compact is violated, at which point each man recovers his original rights and resumes his natural freedom, thereby losing the conventional freedom for which he renounced it.[21]

Properly understood, all of these clauses come down to a single one, *41* namely the total alienation of each associate, with all the rights, to the whole community. For first of all, since each one gives his entire self, the condition is equal for everyone, and since the condition is equal for everyone, no one has an interest in making it burdensome for the others.

Furthermore, as the alienation is made without reservation the union *42* is as perfect as it can be, and no associate has anything further to claim. For if some rights were left to private individuals, there would be no common superior who could judge between them and the public. Each man being his own judge on some point would soon claim to be so on all; the state of nature would subsist and the association would necessarily become tyrannical or ineffectual.

Finally, as each gives himself to all, he gives himself to no one; and *43* since there is no associate over whom one does not acquire the same right one grants him over oneself, one gains the equivalent of everything one loses, and more force to preserve what one has.

If, then, everything that is not of the essence of the social compact is *44* set aside, one will find that it can be reduced to the following terms. *Each of us puts his person and all his power in common under the supreme direction of the general will; and in a body we receive each member as an indivisible part of the whole.*

Instantly, in place of the private person of each contracting party, this *45* act of association produces a moral and collective body, composed of as many members as there are voices in the assembly, which receives from this same act its unity, its common *self*, its life, and its will. This public person, formed thus by the union of all the others, formerly took the name *City*,[22] and now takes that of *Republic* or *body politic*, which its members call

---

[21]This paragraph, added in the final version, implies that Rousseau's definition of the social contract is analogous to the law of gravity. "Everywhere the same" even if "never" stated, like Newton's law, Rousseau's principle is also self-enforcing: if "the social contract is violated," it follows immediately that "each man recovers his original rights and resumes his natural freedom." [Masters]

[22]The true meaning of this word has been almost entirely lost among modern men. Most of them mistake a town for a City, and a bourgeois for a citizen. They do not know that houses make the town, but that citizens make the City. This same error was very costly to the Carthaginians long ago. I have not read that the title *cives* has ever been given to the subjects of any prince — even in ancient times to the Macedonians or currently to the English, although they are closer to freedom than all others. Only the French use the name *citizens* with complete familiarity, because they have no true idea of its meaning, as can be

State when it is passive, *Sovereign* when active, *Power* when comparing it to similar bodies. As for the associates, they collectively take the name *people*; and individually are called *Citizens* as participants in the sovereign authority, and *Subjects* as subject to the laws of the State. But these terms are often mixed up and mistaken for one another. It is enough to know how to distinguish them when they are used with complete precision.

CHAPTER VII: ON THE SOVEREIGN

This formula shows that the act of association includes a reciprocal   46
engagement between the public and private individuals, and that each individual, contracting with himself so to speak, finds that he is doubly engaged, namely toward private individuals as a member of the sovereign and toward the sovereign as a member of the State. But the maxim of civil right that no one can be held responsible for engagements toward himself cannot be applied here, because there is a great difference between being obligated to oneself, or to a whole of which one is a part.

It must further be noted that the public deliberation that can obligate   47
all of the subjects to the sovereign — due to the two different relationships in which each of them is considered — cannot for the opposite reason obligate the sovereign toward itself; and that consequently it is contrary to the nature of the body politic for the sovereign to impose on itself a law it cannot break. Since the sovereign can only be considered in a single relationship, it is then in the situation of a private individual contracting with himself. It is apparent from this that there is not, nor can there be, any kind of fundamental law that is obligatory for the body of the people, not even the social contract. This does not mean that this body cannot perfectly well enter an engagement toward another with respect to things that do not violate this contract. For with reference to the foreigner, it becomes a simple being or individual.

But the body politic or the sovereign, deriving its being solely from the   48
sanctity of the contract, can never obligate itself, even toward another, to do anything that violates that original act, such as to alienate some part of itself or to subject itself to another sovereign. To violate the act by which it exists would be to destroy itself, and whatever is nothing, produces nothing.

---

seen from their dictionaries. If this were not the case, in usurping it they would be guilty of the crime of high treason. For the French, this name expresses a virtue and not a right. When Bodin wanted to talk about our citizens and bourgeois, he made a gross blunder in taking one for the other. M. d'Alembert did not confuse them, and in his article *Geneva* carefully distinguished the four orders of men (even five counting simple foreigners) who are in our town, and of whom only two compose the Republic. No other French author, to my knowledge, has understood the true meaning of the word *citizen*. [Rousseau]

As soon as this multitude is thus united in a body, one cannot harm   *49*
one of the members without attacking the body, and it is even less possible
to harm the body without the members feeling the effects. Thus duty and
interest equally obligate the two contracting parties to mutual assistance,
and the same men should seek to combine in this double relationship all
the advantages that are dependent on it.

Now the sovereign, formed solely by the private individuals compos-   *50*
ing it, does not and cannot have any interest contrary to theirs. Consequently, the sovereign power has no need of a guarantee toward the subjects, because it is impossible for the body ever to want to harm all its
members, and we shall see later that it cannot harm any one of them as an
individual. The sovereign, by the sole fact of being, is always what it ought
to be.

But the same is not true of the subjects in relation to the sovereign,   *51*
which, despite the common interest, would have no guarantee of the subjects' engagements if it did not find ways to be assured of their fidelity.

Indeed, each individual can, as a man, have a private will contrary to   *52*
or differing from the general will he has as a citizen. His private interest
can speak to him quite differently from the common interest. His absolute
and naturally independent existence can bring him to view what he owes
the common cause as a free contribution, the loss of which will harm others less than its payment burdens him. And considering the moral person
of the State as an imaginary being because it is not a man, he might wish
to enjoy the rights of the citizen without wanting to fulfill the duties of a
subject, an injustice whose spread would cause the ruin of the body
politic.[23]

Therefore, in order for the social compact not to be an ineffectual for-   *53*
mula, it tacitly includes the following engagement, which alone can give
force to the others: that whoever refuses to obey the general will shall be
constrained to do so by the entire body; which means only that he will be
forced to be free.[24] For this is the condition that, by giving each citizen to
the homeland, guarantees him against all personal dependence; a condi-

---

[23]Note that since the State *is* a "moral person" and thus, in a sense, "an imaginary being,"
Rousseau's principles of political right could increase injustice if they are taught to selfish
or corrupted men. "The democratic constitution is certainly the masterpiece of political
art: but the more admirable its artifice, the less it belongs to all eyes to penetrate it." *Lettres
Écrites de la Montagne*, VIII (Pléiade, III, 838). [Masters]

[24]The last phrase seems a puzzling contradiction in terms, and has led some to call Rousseau a "totalitarian": for example, J. L. Talmon, *The Origins of Totalitarian Democracy* (New
York: Praeger, 1960), pp. 38–49; Lester G. Crocker, "Rousseau et la voi du totalitarisme,"
Rousseau et la Philosophie Politique (Paris: Presses Universitaires, 1965), pp. 99–136. In context, however, the sentence concerns the means by which each individual can have an
obligation, in *conscience*, to obey the laws he has previously enacted. Rousseau applied

tion that creates the ingenuity and functioning of the political machine, and alone gives legitimacy to civil engagements which without it would be absurd, tyrannical, and subject to the most enormous abuses.

CHAPTER VIII: ON THE CIVIL STATE

This passage from the state of nature to the civil state produces a re- 54 markable change in man, by substituting justice for instinct in his behavior and giving his actions the morality they previously lacked. Only then, when the voice of duty replaces physical impulse and right replaces appetite, does man, who until that time only considered himself, find himself forced to act upon other principles and to consult his reason before heeding his inclinations. Although in this state he deprives himself of several advantages given him by nature, he gains such great ones, his faculties are exercised and developed, his ideas broadened, his feelings ennobled, and his whole soul elevated to such a point that if the abuses of this new condition did not often degrade him beneath the condition he left, he ought ceaselessly to bless the happy moment that tore him away from it forever, and that changed him from a stupid, limited animal into an intelligent being and a man.

Let us reduce the pros and cons to easily compared terms. What man 55 loses by the social contract is his natural freedom and an unlimited right to everything that tempts him and that he can get; what he gains is civil freedom and the proprietorship of everything he possesses. In order not to be mistaken about these compensations, one must distinguish carefully between natural freedom, which is limited only by the force of the individual, and civil freedom, which is limited by the general will; and between possession, which is only the effect of force or the right of the first occupant, and property, which can only be based on a positive title.

To the foregoing acquisitions of the civil state could be added moral 56 freedom, which alone makes man truly the master of himself. For the impulse of appetite alone is slavery, and obedience to the law one has prescribed for oneself is freedom. But I have already said too much about this topic, and the philosophic meaning of the word *freedom* is not my subject here.

---

precisely this reasoning in defending his works against the charges brought by the Magistrates of Geneva: "an accuser must convince the accused before the judge. To be treated as a wrongdoer, it is necessary that I be convinced of being one." *Letters Écrites de la Montagne*, I (Pléiade, III, 693). For a brilliant psychological analysis of the phrase "forced to be free," see John Plamenatz, "Ce qui ne signifie autre chose sinon qu'on le forcera d'être libre," in *Hobbes and Rousseau*, ed. Cranston and Peters, pp. 318–332. [Masters]

CHAPTER IX: ON REAL ESTATE

Each member of the community gives himself to it at the moment of   57
its formation, just as he currently is — both himself and all his force, which
includes the goods he possesses. It is not that by this act possession, in
changing hands, changes its nature and becomes property in the hands of
the sovereign. But as the force of the City is incomparably greater than that
of a private individual, public possession is by that very fact stronger and
more irrevocable, without being more legitimate, at least as far as foreigners are concerned. For with regard to its members, the State is master of
all their goods through the social contract, which serves within the State
as the basis of all rights. But with regard to other powers, it is master only
through the right of the first occupant, which it derives from the private
individuals.

The right of the first occupant, although more real than the right of the   58
strongest, becomes a true right only after the establishment of the right of
property. Every man naturally has a right to everything he needs; but the
positive act that makes him the proprietor of some good excludes him from
all the rest. Once his portion is designated, he should limit himself to it,
and no longer has any right to the community's goods. That is why the
right of the first occupant, so weak in the state of nature, is respectable to
every civilized man. In this right, one respects not so much what belongs
to others as what does not belong to oneself.

In general, the following conditions are necessary to authorize the   59
right of the first occupant to any land whatsoever. First, that this land not
yet be inhabited by anyone. Second, that one occupy only the amount
needed to subsist. Third, that one take possession not by a vain ceremony,
but by labor and cultivation, the only sign of property that others ought to
respect in the absence of legal titles.

Indeed, by granting the right of the first occupant to need and labor,   60
hasn't it been extended as far as possible? Is it impossible to establish limits
to this right? Will setting foot on a piece of common ground be sufficient
to claim on the spot to be its master? Will having the force to disperse other
men for a moment be sufficient to take away forever their right to return?
How can a man or a people seize an immense territory and deprive the
whole human race of it except through punishable usurpation, since this
act takes away from the remaining men the dwelling place and foods that
nature gives them in common? When Nuñez Balboa,[25] standing on the

---

[25]*Nuñez Balboa:* (1475–1519) A Spanish conquistador and explorer, Balboa in the autumn of
1513 reached the Gulf of San Miguel and took possession of what he called the South Sea
(now called the Pacific Ocean) in the name of Ferdinand II, King of Castile.

shore, took possession of the South Sea[26] and all of South America in the name of the crown of Castile,[27] was this enough to dispossess all the inhabitants and exclude all the princes of the world? On that basis such ceremonies multiplied rather ineffectually, and all the Catholic King[28] had to do was to take possession of the entire universe all at once from his study, subsequently eliminating from his empire what had previously been possessed by other princes.

It is understandable how the combined and contiguous lands of private   *61* individuals become public territory, and how the right of sovereignty, extending from the subjects to the ground they occupy, comes to include both property and persons, which places those who possess land in a greater dependency and turns even their force into a guarantee of their loyalty. This advantage does not appear to have been well understood by ancient kings who, only calling themselves Kings of the Persians, the Scythians, the Macedonians,[29] seem to have considered themselves leaders of men rather than masters of the country. Today's kings more cleverly call themselves Kings of France, Spain, England, etc. By thus holding the land, they are quite sure to hold its inhabitants.

What is extraordinary about this alienation is that far from plundering   *62* private individuals of their goods, by accepting them the community thereby only assures them of legitimate possession, changes usurpation into a true right, and use into property. Then, since the possessors are considered as trustees of the public goods, and since their rights are respected by all the members of the State and maintained with all its force against foreigners, through a transfer that is advantageous to the public and even more so to themselves, they have, so to speak, acquired all they have given. This paradox is easily explained by the distinction between the rights of the sovereign and of the proprietor to the same resource, as will be seen hereafter.

It can also happen that men start to unite before possessing anything   *63* and that subsequently taking over a piece of land sufficient for all, they use it in common or divide it among themselves, either equally or according to proportions established by the sovereign. However this acquisition

---

[26]*South Sea:* The Pacific Ocean.

[27]*Crown of Castile:* The succession of rulers of Castile who united Spain in the 15th century through a series of conquests and political unions.

[28]*The Catholic King:* Rousseau is apparently referring to Ferdinand II, the King of Castile, who amassed a great deal of land through explorations and political unions. Rousseau is against the practice of foreign kings claiming ownership of lands through foreign expeditions, while disclaiming the rights of natives of the land.

[29]*Scythians and Macedonians:* Two ancient Greek tribes whose kings identified themselves by the lineage of their peoples instead of by the land they occupied.

is made, the right of each private individual to his own resources is always subordinate to the community's right to all, without which there would be neither solidity in the social bond nor real force in the exercise of sovereignty.

I shall end this chapter and this book with a comment that ought to serve as the basis of the whole social system. It is that rather than destroying natural equality, the fundamental compact on the contrary substitutes a moral and legitimate equality for whatever physical inequality nature may have placed between men, and that although they may be unequal in force or in genius, they all become equal through convention and by right.[30]

64

---

[30]Under bad governments, this equality is only apparent and illusory. It serves merely to maintain the poor man in his misery and the rich in his usurpation. In fact, laws are always useful to those who have possessions and harmful to those who have nothing. It follows from this that the social state is only advantageous to men insofar as they all have something and none of them has anything superfluous. [Rousseau]

REVIEW QUESTIONS

1. In what ways is the government of the family similar to the government of society? In what ways is it different? Why does Rousseau reject the idea that citizens are duty bound to obey their rulers? How does he argue against the idea that "might makes right"?
2. Why does Rousseau maintain that victors in war have no right to enslave the conquered people? What rules does he specify should be observed during and after warfare between states?
3. State, in Rousseau's own words, the "fundamental problem which is solved by the social contract." State, in his own words, the "essence of the social compact." What (in contrast to Hobbes) are the essential conditions of Rousseau's social contract? What rights and obligations does the contract confer upon the individual? In what respect does Rousseau's social contract have a moral dimension?
4. What rights and limitations does Rousseau place on ownership of real estate by individuals? In what way do modern kings appear to Rousseau to hold a different view of their right to real estate than former rulers? Why is it a good thing for individuals to surrender their lands to the state and for them to act, in effect, as trustees, rather than sole owners, of these lands?

DISCUSSION AND WRITING QUESTIONS

1. Unlike Locke, Rousseau attacks Hobbes by name. In what ways do his ideas (particularly those expressed in the sections headed "On the First Societies" and "On the Right of the Strongest") directly contradict the doctrines of Hobbes?

2. In the section entitled "On the Sovereign," Rousseau argues (paragraph 52) that the citizen can, against his will, "be forced to be free." By what reasoning does Rousseau arrive at such a paradox? What do you think he means by it? What might it mean in contemporary, American terms? Some critics claim to have found authoritarian, even totalitarian tendencies in Rousseau, and have cited such passages as evidence. Do you believe this charge is a fair one? (Be sure to consider Rousseau's distinction between "private interest" and "common interest.")

3. Write a personal essay focusing on the convergence and conflict of your "private interest" with your "common interest." (These terms may be roughly synonymous with the terms "rights" and "responsibilities," respectively.) At what points do the two interests coincide? At what points do they diverge? On what occasions must one (as far as you are concerned) give way to the other?

4. Summarize the losses and gains to the individual of entering into the social contract (according to Rousseau). Compare and contrast these losses and gains to the corresponding losses and gains specified by Hobbes and by Locke. Finally, include your own assessment of the losses and gains entailed in the social contract. (If you have already read the unit on "The Survival of the Fittest," you may wish to consider some of the sentiments of the social Darwinists in responding to this question.)

5. In paragraph 58 Rousseau states that "Every man . . . has a right to everything that he needs, but . . . once his portion is designated, he should limit himself to it, and no longer has any right to the community's goods." Discuss this idea. Do you consider it communist? (If you have read Marx's "The Communist Manifesto" in the unit on "The Class Struggle," you might wish to consider Rousseau's ideas in this section in light of Marx's.)

6. Rousseau concludes this passage with one of his paradoxes: the social contract does not destroy equality but rather creates it; the unequal become equal. Discuss the implications of this idea with particular reference to the social and political conditions prevailing in the contemporary United States, as compared with the conditions that would prevail were people residing on the American continent still living in the "state of nature."

7. Of the three social contract theorists you have read thus far in this chapter, which one seems to you to have the most perceptive view of human nature? Why? Which one describes conditions that most closely approximate conditions that currently exist in American society? What are these conditions?

Political Declarations
of the Social Contract

The social contract continues to exercise a powerful influence in the free world today by virtue of its enshrinement, not in academic debates, but in such political documents as declarations and constitutions. The ideas that lie behind the Declaration of Independence and the United States Constitution are — in significant degree — the ideas of Locke and Rousseau, ideas that had become the intellectual currency of Europe and America during the 18th century. We hear the echoes of the social contract in the ringing Preamble to the U.S. Constitution:

> We the people of the United States, in order to form a more perfect Union, establish justice, insure domestic tranquility, provide for the common defense, promote the general welfare, and secure the blessings of liberty to ourselves and our posterity, do ordain and establish this Constitution for the United States of America.

The long phrase, "in order to . . .", rehearses the time-honored reasons for the necessity of a social contract; and the main clause of the sentence itself constitutes the agreement.

The U.S. Constitution, inspired by Locke's and Rousseau's theories of the social contract, has itself inspired similar documents around the world. For instance, the first sentence of the Constitution of the Republic of India (adopted in 1949) reads:

> We, the people of India, having solemnly resolved to constitute India into a sovereign democratic republic and to secure to all its citizens: JUSTICE, social, economic and political; LIBERTY of thought, expression, belief, faith and worship; EQUALITY of status and of opportunity; and to promote among them all FRATERNITY assuring the dignity of the individual and the unity of the

Nation; in our Constituent Assembly this 26th day of November 1949 do hereby adopt, enact and give to ourselves this Constitution.

Other important political documents incorporating social contract theory include the Declaration of Independence, the Virginia Resolution of 1798, and the Declaration of the Rights of Man.

THE DECLARATION OF INDEPENDENCE *(1776)*

The Declaration of Independence did not lead to the Revolutionary War; the battles of Lexington, Bunker Hill, and Concord ("the shot heard round the world") had already been fought a year earlier, in 1775. Rather, the Declaration was issued to announce and justify to the world the decision of the Continental Congress to break the political bonds with England, to rally Americans to the cause of independence, and equally important, to certify the United States as an independent nation to which other independent nations like France could now legitimately give financial and military assistance. The war had been started not to gain independence but rather to obtain relief from King George III's oppressive colonial policies and to gain for the colonies a greater degree of self-governing authority. In fact, a substantial portion of the American populace was opposed to complete independence, and before the onset of hostilities British authorities and soldiers had acted with considerably more restraint than such American radicals as Samuel Adams and Thomas Paine had led their countrymen to believe. Nevertheless, both the colonial and British governments had maneuvered themselves into positions from which they could not easily retreat, and by the end of 1774, it was clear to both sides that war was inevitable.

In the Continental Congress the movement for independence began in 1776. On June 7 of that year, Richard Henry Lee, a delegate from Virginia, offered a resolution asserting "that these united colonies are, and of right ought to be, free and independent states." Subsequently, a committee of five congressmen (John Adams, Benjamin Franklin, Roger Sherman, Robert Livingston, and Thomas Jefferson) was appointed to draft a Declaration of Independence. None of the five wanted to do the actual writing; and in a letter to his wife, John Adams explains how he persuaded the reluctant Jefferson to do the job:

> The subcommittee met. Jefferson proposed to me to make the draft. I said, "I will not." [Jefferson:] "You should do it." [Adams:] "Oh! no." [Jefferson:] "Why will you not? You ought to do it." [Adams:] "I will not." [Jefferson:] "Why?" [Adams:] "Reasons enough." [Jefferson:] "What can be your reasons?" [Adams:] "Reason first, you are a Virginian, and a Virginian ought to appear at the head of this business. Reason second, I am obnoxious, suspected, and unpopular. You are very much otherwise. Reason third, you can write ten times better than I can." "Well," said Jefferson, "if you are decided, I will do as well as I can." [Adams:] "Very well. When you have drawn it up, we will have a meeting."

Elsewhere, Adams had asserted that Jefferson had "a happy talent for composition and a remarkable felicity of expression"; these abilities were necessary, for the purpose of the declaration was "to place before mankind the common sense of the subject in terms so plain and firm as to command their assent."

When the first draft of the declaration came before the Congress, it was debated for three days. Scores of changes were made, in deference to particular interests and sensibilities; and the southern delegates insisted that Jefferson drop a paragraph in which King George was accused of promoting slavery in the colonies and which called for the abolition of this "infamous practice." When the declaration was finally adopted, John Dickinson of Pennsylvania, the leader of the anti-independence forces, refused to sign the document; but, asserting his loyalty to America, he then enlisted as a private in the Delaware Militia.

Thomas Jefferson, born in Virginia in 1743, was trained as a lawyer but was also fascinated by science, philosophy, education, music, and architecture. After his term in the Continental Congress he served in the Virginia House of Delegates. He became governor of Virginia in 1779; but after the British invaded the state in 1781, he retired to his estate at Monticello. Called back to the government in 1783, he served first in the U.S. Congress, then as minister to France, then as Washington's Secretary of State. Growing differences with the administration over the role of the central government led to his resignation (Jefferson, fearing the reestablishment of monarchy or despotism in America by Alexander Hamilton and his followers, believed in agrarian democracy and a federal government of limited strength). He was elected vice president in 1786 and president in 1801, serving two terms as chief executive. He retired to Monticello in 1809, where he pursued his interest in education by designing and founding the University of Virginia. Jefferson died at Monticello on July 4, 1826, fifty years to the day after the signing of the Declaration.

The intellectual heritage of the declaration will be readily apparent to those who have read in social contract theory. That the government is formed by compact, that all men are created equal, that they have unalienable (natural) rights, that governments derive their power from the consent of the governed, that the people have a right to overthrow oppressive governments: all these ideas were familiar to Locke, Rousseau, and their intellectual followers. The bulk of the declaration — a long list of specific grievances against King George III (not all of which were fair or accurate) — was intended to serve as the justification for the act of rebellion. To modern readers, however, the great power of the declaration derives from its unmatched eloquence in asserting the sovereignty of the people over their government.

THE DECLARATION OF INDEPENDENCE

w rituns for allies, the people, parliment-
for posterity (himself)   In Congress, July 4, 1776
The Unanimous Declaration of the
Thirteen United States of America

When in the Course of human events it becomes necessary for one   1
people to dissolve the political bands which have connected them with

[Handwritten annotations at top: "To persude the people that they / He the right to overthrow / the government. / apeal to toutns like, liberty / (pointing out faults)"]

another, and to assume among the powers of the earth, the separate and equal station to which the Laws of Nature and of Nature's God entitle them, a decent respect to the opinions of mankind requires that they should declare the causes which impel them to the separation.

We hold these truths to be self-evident, that all men are created equal, that they are endowed by their Creator with certain unalienable Rights, that among these are Life, Liberty and the pursuit of Happiness. That to secure these rights, Governments are instituted among Men, deriving their just powers from the consent of the governed. That whenever any Form of Government becomes destructive to these ends, it is the Right of the People to alter or to abolish it, and to institute new Government, laying its foundation on such principles and organizing its powers in such form, as to them shall seem most likely to affect their Safety and Happiness. Prudence, indeed, will dictate that Governments long established should not be changed for light and transient causes; and accordingly all experience hath shewn that mankind are more disposed to suffer, while evils are sufferable, than to right themselves by abolishing the forms to which they are accustomed. But when a long train of abuses and usurpations, pursuing invariably the same Object envinces a design to reduce them under absolute Despotism, it is their right, it is their duty, to throw off such Government, and to provide new Guards for their future security. Such has been the patient sufferance of these Colonies; and such is now the necessity which constrains them to alter their former Systems of Government. The history of the present King of Great Britain is a history of repeated injuries and usurpations, all having in direct object the establishment of an absolute Tyranny over these States. To prove this, let Facts be submitted to a candid world.

[Margin annotations: "2" beside second paragraph; "These" beside "Such has been"; "3" "4" "5" "6" "7" "8" in right margin beside following paragraphs; "King D…" and "Kings D…" partial annotations]

He has refused his Assent to Laws, the most wholesome and necessary for the public good.

He has forbidden his Governors to pass laws of immediate and pressing importance, unless suspended in their operation till his Assent should be obtained; and when so suspended, he has utterly neglected to attend to them.

He has refused to pass other Laws for the accommodation of large districts of people, unless those people would relinquish the right of Representation in the Legislature, a right inestimable to them and formidable to tyrants only.

He has called together legislative bodies at places unusual, uncomfortable, and distant from the depository of their Public Records, for the sole purpose of fatiguing them into compliance with his measures.

He has dissolved Representative Houses repeatedly, for opposing with manly firmness his invasions on the rights of the people.

He has refused for a long time, after such dissolutions, to cause others to be elected; whereby the Legislative Powers, incapable of Annihilation, have returned to the People at large for their exercise; the State remaining in the mean time exposed to all the dangers of invasion from without, and convulsions within.

He has endeavored to prevent the population of these States; for that purpose obstructing the Laws for Naturalization of Foreigners; refusing to pass others to encourage their migration hither, and raising the conditions of new Appropriations of Lands.   9

He has obstructed the Administration of Justice, by refusing his Assent to Laws for establishing Judiciary Powers.   10

He has made Judges dependent on his Will alone, for the tenure of their offices, and the amount and payment of their salaries.   11

He has erected a multitude of New Offices, and sent hither swarms of Officers to harass our people, and eat out their substance.   12

He has kept among us, in times of peace, Standing Armies without the Consent of our legislatures.   13

He has affected to render the Military independent of and superior to the Civil Power.   14

He has combined with others to subject us to a jurisdiction foreign to our constitution, and unacknowledged by our laws; giving his Assent to their Acts of pretended Legislation: For quartering large bodies of armed troops among us: For protecting them, by a mock Trial, from punishment for any Murders which they should commit on the Inhabitants of these States: For cutting off our Trade with all parts of the world: For imposing Taxes on us without our Consent: For depriving us in many cases, of the benefits of Trial by Jury; For transporting us beyond Seas to be tried for pretended offenses: for abolishing the free System of English Laws in a neighboring Province, establishing therein an Arbitrary government, and enlarging its Boundaries so as to render it at once an example and fit instrument for introducing the same absolute rule into these Colonies: For taking away our Charters,[1] abolishing our most valuable Laws and altering fundamentally the Forms of our Governments: For suspending our own Legislatures, and declaring themselves invested with power to legislate for us in all cases whatsoever.   15

He has abdicated Government here, by declaring us out of his Protection and waging War against us.   16

He has plundered our seas, ravaged our Coasts, burnt our towns, and destroyed the lives of our people.   17

---

[1]*our Charters:* Documents from the King of England which gave the separate colonies individual rights. A charter is much like a constitution except that charters are granted by a sovereign to his people, whereas constitutions are drawn up by the people (or their representatives) for themselves.

He is at this time transporting large Armies of foreign Mercenaries[2] to complete the works of death, desolation and tyranny, already begun with circumstances of Cruelty & Perfidy scarcely paralleled in the most barbarous ages, and totally unworthy the Head of a civilized nation.

He has constrained our fellow Citizens taken Captive on the high Seas to bear Arms against their Country, to become the executioners of their friends and Brethren, or to fall themselves by their Hands.

He has excited domestic insurrections amongst us, and has endeavored to bring on the inhabitants of our frontiers, the merciless Indian Savages, whose known rule of warfare, is an undistinguished destruction of all ages, sexes, and conditions.

In every stage of these Oppressions We have Petitioned for Redress in the most humble terms: Our repeated Petitions have been answered only by repeated injury. A Prince, whose character is thus marked by every act which may define a Tyrant, is unfit to be the ruler of a free people.

Nor have We been wanting in attention to our British brethren. We have warned them from time to time of attempts by their legislature to extend an unwarrantable jurisdiction over us. We have reminded them of the circumstances of our emigration and settlement here. We have appealed to their native justice and magnanimity, and we have conjured them by the ties of our common kindred to disavow these usurpations, which would inevitably interrupt our connections and correspondence. They too have been deaf to the voice of justice and of consanguinity. We must, therefore, acquiesce in the necessity, which denounces our Separation, and hold them, as we hold the rest of mankind, Enemies in War, in Peace Friends.

We, THEREFORE, the Representatives of the UNITED STATES OF AMERICA, in General Congress, Assembled, appealing to the Supreme Judge of the world for the rectitude of our intentions, do, in the Name, and by Authority of the good People of these Colonies, solemnly publish and declare, That these United Colonies are, and of Right ought to be FREE AND INDEPENDENT STATES; that they are Absolved from all Allegiance to the British Crown, and that all political connection between them and the State of Great Britain, is and ought to be totally dissolved; and that as Free and Independent States, they have full Power to levy War, conclude Peace, contract Alliances, establish Commerce, and to do all other Acts and Things which Independent States may of right do. And for the support of this Declaration, with a firm reliance on the protection of Divine Providence, we mutually pledge to each other our Lives, our Fortunes, and our sacred Honor.

---

[2]*large armies of foreign mercenaries:* The British armies were assisted by almost 30,000 mercenaries — many of them from the German principality of Hesse (hence, Hessians).

REVIEW QUESTIONS

1. What reason does Jefferson give for the composition of the Declaration of Independence? Under what circumstances does he declare that governments can be altered or abolished? Under what circumstances should governments *not* be altered or abolished?
2. Summarize the offenses of King George III which, for Jefferson, justify his being labeled a tyrant.
3. What steps does Jefferson claim the colonists have taken to resolve their grievances peaceably and to avoid conflict? Why have these steps failed?
4. Analyze the structure of the declaration. Into how many main parts is it divided? What is the function of each part in relation to the other parts and to the whole?

DISCUSSION AND WRITING QUESTIONS

1. Identify the separate components of social contract theory discussed in paragraph 2 of the declaration; show how these ideas derive from concepts discussed by Hobbes, Locke, and Rousseau.
2. Is the Declaration of Independence itself a social contract? If not, what is its relationship to the social contract?
3. Printed below are the preambles to the Constitution of New Jersey (1776) and the Constitution of the Commonwealth of Massachusetts (1780). Compare and contrast the ideas expressed in these constitutions to the ideas expressed in the Declaration of Independence. Trace the derivations of these ideas in the social contract theory of Hobbes, Locke, and Rousseau.

CONSTITUTION OF NEW JERSEY — 1776

WHEREAS all the constitutional authority ever possessed by the kings of Great Britain over these colonies, or their other dominions, was, by compact, derived from the people, and held of them, for the common interest of the whole society; allegiance and protection are, in the nature of things, reciprocal ties, each equally depending upon the other, and liable to be dissolved by the others being refused or withdrawn. And whereas George the Third, king of Great Britain, has refused protection to the good people of these colonies; and, by assenting to sundry acts of the British parliament, attempted to subject them to the absolute dominion of that body; and has also made war upon them, in the most cruel and unnatural manner, for no other cause, than asserting their just rights — all civil authority under him is necessarily at an end, and a dissolution of government in each colony has consequently taken place.

And whereas, in the present deplorable situation of these colonies, exposed to the fury of a cruel and relentless enemy, some form of government is absolutely necessary, not only for the preservation of good order, but also the more effectually to unite the people, and enable them to exert their whole force in their own necessary defence; and as the honorable the continental congress, the supreme council of the American colonies, has advised such of the colonies as have not yet gone into measures, to adopt for themselves, respectively, such government as shall best conduce to their own happiness and safety, and the well-being of America in general.

CONSTITUTION OR FORM OF GOVERNMENT FOR THE COMMONWEALTH OF MASSACHUSETTS — 1780

Preamble

The end of the institution, maintenance, and administration of government, is to secure the existence of the body politic, to protect it and to furnish the individuals who compose it with the power of enjoying in safety and tranquillity their natural rights, and the blessings of life: and whenever these great objects are not obtained, the people have a right to alter the government, and to take measures necessary for their safety, prosperity, and happiness.

The body politic is formed by a voluntary association of individuals: it is a social compact, by which the whole people covenants with each citizen, and each citizen with the whole people, that all shall be governed by certain laws for the common good. It is the duty of the people, therefore, in framing a constitution of government, to provide for an equitable mode of making laws, as well as for an impartial interpretation and a faithful execution of them; that every man may, at all times, find his security in them.

We, therefore, the people of Massachusetts, acknowledging, with grateful hearts, the goodness of the great Legislator of the universe, in affording us, in the course of His providence, an opportunity, deliberately and peaceably, without fraud, violence, or surprise, of entering into an original, explicit, and solemn compact with each other; and of forming a new constitution of civil government, for ourselves and posterity; and devoutly imploring His direction in so interesting a design, do agree upon, ordain, and establish, the following *Declaration of Rights, and Frame of Government,* as the CONSTITUTION OF THE COMMONWEALTH OF MASSACHUSETTS.

4. The Declaration of Independence grew out of a particular set of historical circumstances, but its ideals have much broader application. Discuss how the ideals expressed in the declaration might be used by particular peoples today who wish to gain independence from tyrannical governments. Are there some principles that would no longer apply? How do the particular abuses of the contemporary government on which you are focusing parallel the particular abuses cited by Jefferson against George III?

5. Journalists and political scientists have conducted experiments in which the Bill of Rights (the first ten amendments to the Constitution) is typed up and presented as a petition to people on the street. Alarmingly high numbers of Americans have refused to sign such petitions, sometimes accusing the petitioners of being Communists! Suppose that the principles of the Declaration of Independence (particularly those expressed in the second and final paragraphs) were rephrased in modern English and presented as a petition. What kind of objections do you think some people would have? What kind of people would they be? What kind of arguments would they make? Try to support your assertions with evidence from your own reading and observations.

THE VIRGINIA RESOLUTIONS OF 1798

In 1798, in an attempt to shore up declining support for President John Adams, the leaders of the Federalist party rushed two laws through Congress — the Alien and Sedition Acts. The Alien Act allowed the President to expel from the country any alien who was deemed "dangerous to the peace and safety of the United States," and the Sedition Act authorized fines or imprisonment for anyone found guilty of "combining and conspiring to oppose the execution of the laws, or publishing false, scandalous, or malicious writings against the President, Congress or the government of the United States." No alien was actually deported under the Alien Act, but about seventy opposition (Republican) newspaper editors were fined or imprisoned under the Sedition Act for criticizing the President. The Alien and Sedition Acts were widely condemned as outrageous assaults upon American civil liberties. In particular, the Sedition Act was rightly seen as a violation of the First Amendment protection of the right of freedom of speech and of the press.

The passage of these acts confirmed Jefferson's worst fears about the despotic tendencies of the Federalist party. To counter them, he and James Madison drafted a series of resolutions. Jefferson's resolutions were adapted by the newly admitted state of Kentucky, which called upon the other states to declare the Alien and Sedition Acts unconstitutional, "null and void." When other states refused to go along, the Kentucky legislature passed another set of resolutions declaring that states, as parties to a "compact," had the authority to nullify unconstitutional federal laws that reached beyond the scope of the compact. The milder Virginia Resolutions, authored by Madison, claimed no such right of "nullification" for states but also asserted that by passing and enforcing the Alien and Sedition Acts, the federal government had violated its compact with the states.

Jefferson and Madison had no intention of encouraging the dissolution of the union, and in fact Jefferson rebuked a "hyper-Republican" from Virginia who proposed that his state should secede. Their purpose, rather, was to discredit the Alien and Sedition Acts and, by extension, the Federalist party. In this purpose, they succeeded. John Adams was defeated for reelection in 1800, and Jefferson became president. The Alien and Sedition Acts had already expired with the end of Adams's term; Jefferson now fulfilled a campaign pledge by releasing all who had been imprisoned under the Sedition Act and by returning the money of those who had been fined.

The Virginia Resolutions of 1798 show the continuing influence of social contract theory, in a somewhat new form: instead of a contract (or compact) involving individuals and their government, we have a contract involving two levels of government — state and federal.

RESOLUTIONS OF VIRGINIA

of December 21, 1798, and Debate and Vote Thereon.

Resolutions as Adopted by Both Houses of Assembly.

1. *Resolved,* That the General Assembly of Virginia doth unequivocally express a firm resolution to maintain and defend the Constitution of the United States, and the Constitution of this State, against every aggression, either foreign or domestic, and that it will support the government of the United States in all measures warranted by the former.

2. That this Assembly most solemnly declares a warm attachment to the union of the States, to maintain which, it pledges all its powers; and that for this end it is its duty to watch over and oppose every infraction of those principles, which constitute the only basis of that union, because a faithful observance of them can alone secure its existence, and the public happiness.

3. That this Assembly doth explicitly and peremptorily declare that it views the powers of the Federal Government as resulting from the compact, to which the States are parties, as limited by the plain sense and intention of the instrument constituting that compact; as no further valid than they are authorized by the grants enumerated in that compact; and that in case of a deliberate, palpable, and dangerous exercise of other powers not granted by the said compact, the States, who are the parties thereto, have the right, and are in duty bound, to interpose for arresting the progress of the evil, and for maintaining within their respective limits, the authorities, rights, and liberties appertaining to them.

4. That the General Assembly doth also express its deep regret that a spirit has in sundry instances been manifested by the Federal Government, to enlarge its powers by forced constructions of the constitutional charter which defines them; and that indications have appeared of a design to expound certain general phrases (which, having been copied from the very limited grant of powers in the former articles of confederation, were the less liable to be misconstrued), so as to destroy the meaning and effect of the particular enumeration, which necessarily explains and limits the general phrases, and so as to consolidate the States by degrees into one sovereignty, the obvious tendency and inevitable result of which would be to

James Madison. The Virginia Resolutions [1798]. Rpt. in *The Virginia Report of 1799–1800, Together with the Virginia Resolutions of December 21, 1798.* New York: Da Capo Press, 1970.

transform the present republican system of the United States into an absolute, or at best, a mixed monarchy.

5. That the General Assembly doth particularly protest against the palpable and alarming infractions of the Constitution, in the two late cases of the "alien and sedition acts," passed at the last session of Congress, the first of which exercises a power nowhere delegated to the Federal Government; and which by uniting legislative and judicial powers to those of executive, subverts the general principles of free government, as well as the particular organization and positive provisions of the federal Constitution; and the other of which acts exercises in like manner a power not delegated by the Constitution, but on the contrary expressly and positively forbidden by one of the amendments thereto; a power which more than any other ought to produce universal alarm, because it is levelled against that right of freely examining public characters and measures, and of free communication among the people thereon, which has ever been justly deemed the only effectual guardian of every other right.

6. That this State having by its convention which ratified the federal Constitution, expressly declared, "that among other essential rights, the liberty of conscience and of the press cannot be cancelled, abridged, restrained, or modified by any authority of the United States," and from its extreme anxiety to guard these rights from every possible attack of sophistry or ambition, having with other States recommended an amendment for that purpose, which amendment was in due time annexed to the Constitution, it would mark a reproachful inconsistency and criminal degeneracy, if an indifference were now shown to the most palpable violation of one of the rights thus declared and secured, and to the establishment of a precedent which may be fatal to the other.

7. That the good people of this commonwealth having ever felt, and continuing to feel the most sincere affection to their brethren of the other States, the truest anxiety for establishing and perpetuating the union of all, and the most scrupulous fidelity to that Constitution which is the pledge of mutual friendship, and the instrument of mutual happiness, the General Assembly doth solemnly appeal to the like dispositions of the other States, in confidence that they will concur with this commonwealth in declaring, as it does hereby declare, that the acts aforesaid are unconstitutional, and that the necessary and proper measure will be taken by each, for co-operating with this State in maintaining unimpaired the authorities, rights, and liberties reserved to the States respectively, or to the people.

8. That the Governor be desired to transmit a copy of the foregoing resolutions to the executive authority of each of the other States, with a request that the same may be communicated to the legislature thereof. And that a copy be furnished to each of the senators and representatives representing this state in the Congress of the United States.

REVIEW QUESTIONS

1. Summarize the Virginia Resolutions, devoting no more than one or two sentences of your own words to each section.
2. Paragraph 3 refers to the "instrument" that constitutes the compact to which the states have agreed. What is that "instrument"?
3. What general and particular charges do the resolutions make against the federal government? What steps to remedy the situation are proposed toward the end of the resolutions?

DISCUSSION AND WRITING QUESTIONS

1. Identify and discuss the elements of social contract theory enunciated in the Virginia Resolutions. Compare and contrast these elements to the principles expressed by John Locke. Do you think Locke would have approved of the Virginia Resolutions? Would Hobbes?
2. Madison presents a highly logical, step-by-step argument in this document. Trace the steps of his reasoning. What premises are first established? What conclusions follow from these premises? What evidence is provided to support these conclusions?
3. Suppose circumstances had worked out differently, that Adams had been re-elected president, and that the Alien and Sedition Acts had continued in force. What do you think might have happened if the Virginia Resolutions had gained wide favor and support? What, exactly, is called for in the resolutions? Develop a chain of events that might have ensued if people had acted in support of the principles and sentiments expressed in this document. You might wish to consider both "best" and "worst" scenarios.
4. At heart, this document is one of many that favor states' rights over what is often seen as the excessive power of the federal government. Select another, more recent issue that also turns upon states' rights and discuss that issue in some of the terms employed by Madison in the Virginia Resolutions. How appropriate are those terms? Who is to decide that the federal government has overly "enlarged" its powers, and at what point does this enlargement violate the Constitution? At what point, on the other hand, does the insistence upon states' rights endanger the national union (as occurred during the American Civil War)? What do you think is a reasonable balance of power between the states and the federal government?

DECLARATION OF THE RIGHTS OF MAN AND CITIZEN *(1789)*

The Declaration of the Rights of Man and Citizen was produced in the early days of the French Revolution. One of the great political, social, and military convulsions of the modern age, the French Revolution transformed not only France but also the rest of Europe in ways that are still being felt. It was the beginning of the end of the *ancien régime,* the political and social order by which an absolute monarch, a landed aristocracy, and a powerful clergy exercised total control over the affairs of the nation. (What was left of the *ancien régime* in Europe ended once and for all in the devastation of World War I.)

The revolution was precipitated by a combination of economic and political crises beginning in 1787. Initially, it was a revolution of aristocrats who demanded a sharing of power with the king, Louis XVI; such a revolution would have not substantially altered the political structure of society. The democratic revolution that followed in reaction, however, was far more radical. Inspired by the thinkers of the French Enlightenment and by the success of the American revolution, the democratic revolutionaries strove to establish a regime in which distinctions of birth were abolished, in which the will of the people (as expressed through their elected representatives) was sovereign, in which the rights of the individual were protected, and in which there would be equal justice under law.

The revolution passed through several stages, from the storming of the Bastille prison in July 1798 to the defeat of Napoleon in 1814. During this period, a constitutional monarchy was established, the nobility was abolished, the Catholic Church was reformed, the king was executed, a new democratic constitution was set aside, a Reign of Terror was instituted in which thousands of accused counter-revolutionaries (including former directors of the revolution) were guillotined, war was waged with most of the rest of Europe and with Russia, and a military dictatorship was established under Napoleon Bonaparte, who had declared himself Emperor of France. In both England and the United States, supporters of the revolution, who had initially cheered its egalitarian ideals, became disillusioned by its excesses, and finally recoiled in horror at the Reign of Terror. Still, in post-Napoleonic Europe, it was impossible to return to the *ancien régime;* many of the political and social reforms of the revolution remained in place to influence future generations in France and elsewhere, and its original egalitarian and libertarian ideals have continued to exercise a powerful influence.

Those ideals were nowhere more eloquently expressed than in the Declaration of the Rights of Man and Citizen. In this document, adopted by the governing National Assembly on August 26, 1789, we see not only echoes of the American Declaration of Independence but also the continuing force of social contract theory, as it had been interpreted by thinkers like Locke and Rousseau.

DECLARATION OF THE RIGHTS OF MAN AND CITIZEN

The representatives of the French people, organized in National Assembly, considering that ignorance, forgetfulness, or contempt for the rights of man are the only causes of the public miseries and of the corruption of governments, have resolved to set out in a solemn declaration the natural, inalienable, and sacred rights of man, so that this declaration, ever present to all the members of the body social, may remind them unceasingly of their rights and their duties; so that the acts of the legislative power and those of the executive power can at each moment be compared with the aim of every political institution, and thus be more respected; so that the demands of the citizens, based henceforth on simple and incontestable principles, may turn always toward the preservation of the Constitution and the welfare of all. *1*

Therefore, the National Assembly recognizes and declares, in the presence and under the auspices of the Supreme Being, the following rights of Man and of the Citizen. *2*

1. Men are born and remain free and equal in rights. Social distinctions can be founded only on the common utility. *3*

2. The object of every political association is the conservation of the natural and imprescriptible rights of man. These rights are liberty, property, security, and resistance to oppression. *4*

3. The principle of all sovereignty resides essentially in the Nation. No body, no individual can exercise authority that is not expressly derived from it. *5*

4. Liberty consists in the power of doing anything that does not injure others; accordingly, the exercise of the natural rights of each man has no limits other than those that insure other members of the society the enjoyment of those same rights. Those limits can only be determined by the Law. *6*

5. The Law has the right to forbid only actions injurious to society. Whatever is not forbidden by the Law can not be obstructed, and no one can be constrained to do that which it does not decree. *7*

6. The Law is the expression of the general will. All the citizens have the right to contribute personally, or by their representatives, to its for- *8*

Declaration of the Rights of Man and Citizen [1789]. Rpt. in *The Constitutions of Europe.* Ed., E.A. Goerner. Chicago: Henry Regnery, 1967.

mation. It must be the same for all, whether it protects, or whether it punishes. All citizens are equal in its eyes and are equally eligible for all public dignities, offices, and employments, according to their abilities and without other distinction than that of their virtues and their talents.

7. No man may be accused, arrested, or detained except in cases determined by the Law and according to the forms that it has prescribed. Those who solicit, expedite, execute, or cause to be executed arbitrary orders should be punished; but every citizen summoned or seized by virtue of the Law should obey instantly: he makes himself guilty by resistance.   9

8. The Law should not establish penalties except those strictly and evidently necessary, and no one may be punished except by virtue of a law established and promulgated before the crime and legally applied.   10

9. Every man being presumed innocent until he has been declared guilty, if it is judged indispensable to arrest him, all severity that may not be necessary to secure his person should be severely repressed by law.   11

10. No one should be disturbed because of his opinions, even religious, provided their manifestation does not disturb the public order established by law.   12

11. The free communication of thoughts and opinions is one of the most precious rights of man: every citizen, therefore, may freely speak, write, and print, subject to responsibility for the abuse of that liberty in cases determined by law.   13

12. The guarantee of the rights of man and of the citizen requires a public force: that force is, therefore, instituted for the advantage of all, and not for the private use of those to whom it is entrusted.   14

13. For the maintenance of the public force and for the expenses of administration, a general tax is indispensable: it ought to be equally apportioned among all the citizens, in accordance with their abilities.   15

14. All the citizens have the right to decide, by themselves or by their representatives, the necessity of the public tax, to consent to it freely, to follow the use of it, and to determine the quota, the assessment, the collection, and the duration of it.   16

15. Society has the right to demand an accounting from every public agent of his administration.   17

16. Every society in which the guarantee of rights is not assured, or the separation of powers not determined, has no constitution whatever.   18

17. Property being an inviolable and sacred right, no one may be deprived of it, except when the public necessity, legally established, evidently demands it, and under the condition of a just and prior indemnification.   19

REVIEW QUESTIONS

1. Summarize the stated purpose of the Declaration of the Rights of Man and Citizen. To what is attributed the cause of "public miseries and . . . the corruption of governments"?
2. In terms of the social contract thinking of the Declaration of the Rights of Man and Citizen, why do people band together in political associations?
3. Based on the declaration, summarize in two lists (1) the rights and (2) the obligations of citizens.

DISCUSSION AND WRITING QUESTIONS

1. Compare and contrast both the content and the form of the Declaration of the Rights of Man and Citizen with the content and the form of the Declaration of Independence. To what extent do you think the Declaration of the Rights of Man and Citizen applies to the United States?
2. Identify and discuss those elements of social contract theory most prominent in the Declaration of the Rights of Man and Citizen. If possible, relate these particular elements to passages in the writings of Locke and Rousseau.
3. In what ways are the principles of the Declaration of the Rights of Man and Citizen most opposed to the principles of Hobbes?
4. The declaration states in Section 4 that "Liberty consists in the power of doing anything that does not injure others . . .". Evaluate this idea. Be sure to consider it in the context of the rest of Section 4.
5. The declaration gives certain powers to the law but also provides for certain restrictions. Evaluate the wisdom of these powers and restrictions. How effective, in your judgment, would such powers and restrictions be in the contemporary United States?
6. Infer from the Declaration of the Rights of Man and Citizen some of the worst abuses of the *ancien régime.*

HERBERT SPENCER *(1820–1903)*

If this part of *Theme and Variations* has traced an evolution of the social contract, from that of Hobbes to that of Rousseau and his disciples, it is an evolution from executive to legislative supremacy. The constant of social contract theory is that people join together for mutual protection, agreeing to surrender some of their individual liberties to the state in return for the improved security of their lives and property. A variable of social contract theory is the identity of the new holder (and withholder) of those liberties. To whom has power been transferred? For Hobbes, it is an all-powerful sovereign. For Locke and Rousseau, the people are sovereign and they have transferred their power to their elected representatives who sit in the legislature. If their elected representatives do not follow the popular will — as this will is expressed by majority vote — they can be voted out of office.

In the meantime, it is the duty of the minority to submit to the majority. And if a citizen in the minority refuses to submit to one or more particular measures? As Rousseau declared, that citizen may then be "forced to be free." Locke and other advocates of democracy did not put the matter quite so strongly (indeed, the writers of the U.S. Constitution clearly foresaw the dangers of the tyranny of the majority); but they too recognized that the balance of power in democratic states had shifted to the legislature. The danger of an increasing powerful legislative authority is that it appears on the surface to be less oppressive than a powerful executive authority (since legislative power is less concentrated and since the people are still — at least in theory — "sovereign"). Nevertheless, an intrusive and meddlesome legislature is capable of trampling just as heavily on individual rights — and may be just as capable of violating the social contract — as an absolute monarch.

Such was the fervent belief of Herbert Spencer, an English sociologist and philosopher, who stood, above all, for natural rights of the individual against the incursions of the state. Born in Derby, England, in 1820, the son of a schoolmaster, Spencer turned down the opportunity to matriculate at Cambridge University, preferring to plan his own broad course of study. At seventeen he became, briefly, a schoolteacher himself and then was apprenticed as a railway civil engineer in London. During the 1840s he began writing on government and natural rights, and in 1848 (a year after abandoning the profession of railway engineer) he became a subeditor of the journal, *The Economist*. His first book, *Social Statics* (1850), contained many of the laissez-faire themes that were to preoccupy him throughout life. A legacy from his uncle, beginning in 1852, allowed him thenceforth to devote himself full time to writing. In 1855, he published his second book, *The Principles of Psychology*, in which he applied the principles of evolution (his second chief intellectual concern) to the life of the mind.

At about this time, his health began to break down; he suffered the first of several heart attacks and became subject for the rest of his life to hypochondria.

Nevertheless, he undertook, at age forty, a massive project: a projected, 10-volume work, *The Synthetic Philosophy,* which was to cover not only psychology but also biology, sociology, and ethics. Spencer was attempting nothing less than a synthesis of all human knowledge. Aided by public and private subscriptions (Spencer was perhaps the most widely read and discussed of English philosophers in the second half of the 19th century) and his own iron determination, he succeeded in completing this enormous project, while continuing to write other essays, as well as his *Autobiography,* published in 1904, a year after this death.

The following essay, "The Great Political Superstition," was collected into his *The Man versus the State* (1881). Throughout this book, Spencer vehemently argues against government interference and for the cause of individual rights. As you read, note which elements of social contract theory Spencer accepts (or, it might be more accurate to say, he is willing to concede) and which he rejects. Note also that Spencer's thought over the years was so consistent that (as in another of his writings reprinted in the unit on "Darwin and the Survival of the Fittest"), he supports his views by quoting from one of his own essays written decades earlier.

THE GREAT POLITICAL SUPERSTITION

The great political superstition of the past was the divine right of kings. The great political superstition of the present is the divine right of parliaments. The oil of anointing seems unawares to have dripped from the head of the one on to the heads of the many, and given sacredness to them also and to their decrees.   1

However irrational we may think the earlier of these beliefs, we must admit that it was more consistent than is the latter. Whether we go back to times when the king was a god, or to times when he was a descendant of a god, or to times when he was god-appointed, we see good reason for passive obedience to his will. When, as under Louis XIV,[1] theologians like   2

Herbert Spencer. The Great Political Superstition [1881]. *The Man Versus the State.* London: Williams and Norgate, 1884.

[1]*Louis XIV:* Also known as Louis the Great, Louis XIV (1638–1715) was the King of France from 1643 to 1715. He was known for being an unusually strong monarch, personally overseeing and directing all aspects of government in his kingdom. He was also noted for his unique interpretation of the role of a dictator by divine right: he saw himself personally as God's representative; therefore, he saw his decisions as directly inspired and nearly infallible, and he saw all acts of rebellion against him as sin. (For the more traditional interpretation of the doctrine of the divine right of kings, see footnote 2 on Bossuet.)

Bossuet[2] taught that kings "are gods, and share in a manner the Divine independence," or when it was thought, as by our own Tory party in old days, that "the monarch was the delegate of heaven;" it is clear that, given the premise, the inevitable conclusion was that no bounds could be set to governmental commands. But for the modern belief such a warrant does not exist. Making no pretension to divine descent or divine appointment, a legislative body can show no supernatural justification for its claim to unlimited authority; and no natural justification has ever been attempted. Hence, belief in its unlimited authority is without that consistency which of old characterized belief in a king's unlimited authority.

It is curious how commonly men continue to hold in fact, doctrines which they have rejected in name — retaining the substance after they have abandoned the form. In Theology an illustration is supplied by Carlyle,[3] who, in his student days, giving up, as he thought, the creed of his fathers, rejected its shell only, keeping the contents; and was proved by his conceptions of the world, and man, and conduct, to be still among the sternest of Scotch Calvinists.[4] Similarly, Science furnishes an instance in one who united naturalism in Geology with supernaturalism in Biology — Sir Charles Lyell.[5] While, as the leading expositor of the uniformitarian theory in Geology, he ignored wholly the Mosaic cosmogony,[6] he long defended that belief in special creations of organic types, for which no other source than the Mosaic cosmogony could be assigned; and only in the lat-

---

[2]*Bossuet:* A Catholic bishop known for his arbitration on conflicts arising between the division of church and state power, Bossuet (1627–1704) developed the doctrine of the divine right of kings. Generally, this doctrine states that it is the will of God that men live peaceably under governments; therefore, the authority of the government is sacred (as long as it doesn't violate other sacred laws), and acts of rebellion against the government are criminal.

[3]*Carlyle:* Thomas Carlyle (1795–1881), Scottish historian and essayist.

[4]*Scotch Calvinists:* Followers of John Calvin (1509–1564), a French Protestant reformer who emphasized the depravity of man and the necessity for strict moral codes.

[5]*Sir Charles Lyell:* Lyell (1797–1875) was a Scottish geologist whose most famous book, *Principles of Geology*, helped to popularize the theory of uniformitarianism in geology. The theory of uniformitarianism basically states that the development of the earth can be explained by natural phenomena that are occurring presently and have been occurring since the beginnings of the earth. This theory, and Darwin's ensuing theory of evolution in biology, were (and to some extent still are) controversial because they do not support the literal accuracy of the earth's history as recorded in the Bible.

[6]*Mosaic cosmogony:* A theory of the universe that suggests that the earth's organisms and geological features have developed at an irregular rate over time, instead of at the regular rate that uniformitarian principles suggest. In Lyell's era (and to some extent in our own) this irregular rate in development is thought to be planned and directed by a primary creative force such as God.

ter part of his life surrendered to the arguments of Mr. Darwin. In Politics, as above implied, we have an analogous case. The tacitly-asserted doctrine, common to Tories, Whigs, and Radicals, that governmental authority is unlimited, dates back to times when the law-giver was supposed to have a warrant from God; and it survives still, though the belief that the law-giver has God's warrant has died out. "Oh, an Act of Parliament can do anything," is the reply made to a citizen who questions the legitimacy of some arbitrary State-interference; and the citizen stands paralyzed. It does not occur to him to ask the how, and the when, and the whence, of this asserted omnipotence bounded only by physical impossibilities.

Here we will take leave to question it. In default of the justification, once logically valid, that the ruler on Earth being a deputy of the ruler in Heaven, submission to him in all things is a duty, let us ask what reason there is for asserting the duty of submission in all things to a ruling power, constitutional or republican, which has no Heaven-derived supremacy. Evidently this inquiry commits us to a criticism of past and present theories concerning political authority. To revive questions supposed to be long since settled, may be thought to need some apology; but there is a sufficient apology in the implication above made clear, that the theory commonly accepted is ill-based or unbased.

The notion of sovereignty is that which first presents itself; and a critical examination of this notion, as entertained by those who do not postulate the supernatural origin of sovereignty, carries us back to the arguments of Hobbes.

Let us grant Hobbes's postulate that, "during the time men live without a common power to keep them all in awe, they are in that condition which is called war . . . . of every man against every man;"[7] though this is not true, since there are some small uncivilized societies in which, without any "common power to keep them all in awe," men maintain peace and harmony better than it is maintained in societies where such a power exists. Let us suppose him to be right, too, in assuming that the rise of a ruling power over associated men, results from their desires to preserve order among themselves; though, in fact, it habitually arises from the need for subordination to a leader in war, defensive or offensive, and has originally no necessary, and often no actual, relation to the preservation of order among the combined individuals. Once more, let us admit the indefensible assumption that to escape the evils of chronic conflicts, which must otherwise continue among them, the members of a community enter into a "pact or covenant," by which they all bind themselves to surrender their primitive freedom of action, and subordinate themselves to the will

---

[7]Hobbes, paragraph 8, this edition.

of a ruling power agreed upon: accepting, also, the implication that their descendants for ever are bound by the covenant which remote ancestors made for them. Let us, I say, not object to these data, but pass to the conclusions Hobbes draws. He says: —

> For where no covenant hath preceded, there hath no right been transferred, and every man has right to every thing; and consequently, no action can be unjust. But when a covenant is made, then to break it is *unjust*: and the definition of INJUSTICE, is no other than *the not performance of covenant.* . . . Therefore before the names of just and unjust can have place, there must be some coercive power, to compel men equally to the performance of their covenants, by the terror of some punishment, greater than the benefit they expect by the breach of their covenant.[8]

Were people's characters in Hobbes's day really so bad as to warrant   7
his assumption that none would perform their covenants in the absence of a coercive power and threatened penalties? In our day "the names of just and unjust can have place" quite apart from recognition of any coercive power. Among my friends I could name half a dozen whom I would implicitly trust to perform their covenants without any "terror of some punishment;" and over whom the requirements of justice would be as imperative in the absence of a coercive power as in its presence. Merely noting, however, that this unwarranted assumption vitiates Hobbes's argument for State-authority, and accepting both his premises and conclusion, we have to observe two significant implications. One is that State-authority as thus derived, is a means to an end, and has no validity save as subserving that end: if the end is not subserved, the authority, by the hypothesis, does not exist. The other is that the end for which the authority exists, as thus specified, is the enforcement of justice — the maintenance of equitable relations. The reasoning yields no warrant for other coercion over citizens than that which is required for preventing direct aggressions, and those indirect aggressions constituted by breaches of contract; to which, if we add protection against external enemies, the entire function implied by Hobbes's derivation of sovereign authority is comprehended.

Hobbes argued in the interests of absolute monarchy. His modern ad-   8
mirer, Austin[9] had for his aim to derive the authority of law from the unlimited sovereignty of one man, or of a number of men, small or large compared with the whole community. Austin was originally in the army;

---

[8]*Leviathan,* Chapter 15.

[9]*Austin:* An English jurist who committed his career primarily to the study of jurisprudence or the philosophy of law, John Austin (1790–1859) believed that laws by nature were a type of command created and carried out by a sovereign who was not himself subject to these laws.

and it has been truly remarked that "the permanent traces left" may be seen in his *Province of Jurisprudence*. When, undeterred by the exasperating pedantries — the endless distinctions and definitions and repetitions — which serve but to hide his essential doctrines, we ascertain what these are, it becomes manifest that he assimilates civil authority to military authority: taking for granted that the one, as the other, is above question in respect of both origin and range. To get justification for positive law, he takes us back to the absolute sovereignty of the power imposing it — a monarch, an aristocracy, or that larger body of men who have votes in a democracy; for such a body also, he styles the sovereign, in contrast with the remaining portion of the community which, from incapacity or other cause, remains subject. And having affirmed, or, rather, taken for granted, the unlimited authority of the body, simple or compound, small or large, which he styles sovereign, he, or course, has no difficulty in deducing the legal validity of its edicts, which he calls positive law. But the problem is simply moved a step further back and there left unsolved. The true question is — Whence the sovereignty? What is the assignable warrant for this unqualified supremacy assumed by one, or by a small number, or by a large number, over the rest? A critic might fitly say — "We will dispense with your process of deriving positive law from unlimited sovereignty: the sequence is obvious enough. But first prove your unlimited sovereignty."

To this demand there is no response. Analyze his assumption, and the doctrine of Austin proves to have no better basis than that of Hobbes. In the absence of admitted divine descent or appointment, neither single-headed ruler nor many-headed ruler can produce such credentials as the claim to unlimited sovereignty implies.   *9*

"But surely," will come in deafening chorus the reply, "there is the unquestionable right of the majority, which gives unquestionable right to the parliament it elects."   *10*

Yes, now we are coming down to the root of the matter. The divine right of parliaments means the divine right of majorities. The fundamental assumption made by legislators and people alike, is that a majority has powers to which no limits can be put. This is the current theory which all accept without proof as a self-evident truth. Nevertheless, criticism will, I think, show that this current theory requires a radical modification.   *11*

In an essay on "Railway Morals and Railway Policy," published in the *Edinburgh Review* for October, 1854, I had occasion to deal with the question of a majority's powers as exemplified in the conduct of public companies; and I cannot better prepare the way for conclusions presently to be drawn, than by quoting a passage from it: —   *12*

> "Under whatever circumstances, or for whatever ends, a number of men co-operate, it is held that if difference of opinion arises among them, justice requires that the will of the greater number shall be executed rather than that of

the smaller number; and this rule is supposed to be uniformly applicable, be the question at issue what it may. So confirmed is this conviction, and so little have the ethics of the matter been considered, that to most this mere suggestion of a doubt will cause some astonishment. Yet it needs but a brief analysis to show that the opinion is little better than a political superstition. Instances may readily be selected which prove, by *reductio ad absurdum*, that the right of a majority is a purely conditional right, valid only within specific limits. Let us take a few. Suppose that at the general meeting of some philanthropic association, it was resolved that in addition to relieving distress the association should employ home-missionaries to preach down popery.[10] Might the subscriptions of Catholics, who had joined the body with charitable views, be rightfully used for this end? Suppose that of the members of a book-club, the greater number, thinking that under existing circumstances rifle-practice was more important than reading, should decide to change the purpose of their union, and to apply the funds in hand for the purchase of powder, ball, and targets. Would the rest be bound by this decision? Suppose that under the excitement of news from Australia, the majority of a Freehold Land Society[11] should determine, not simply to start in a body for the gold-diggings, but to use their accumulated capital to provide outfits. Would this appropriation of property be just to the minority? and must these join the expedition? Scarcely anyone would venture an affirmative answer even to the first of these questions; much less to the others. And why? Because everyone must perceive that by uniting himself with others, no man can equitably be betrayed into acts utterly foreign to the purpose for which he joined them. Each of these supposed minorities would properly reply to those seeking to coerce them: — 'We combined with you for a defined object; we gave money and time for the furtherance of that object; on all questions thence arising we tacitly agreed to conform to the will of the greater number; but we did not agree to conform on any other questions. If you induce us to join you by professing a certain end, and then undertake some other end of which we were not apprised, you obtain our support under false pretences; you exceed the expressed or understood compact to which we committed ourselves; and we are no longer bound by your decisions.' Clearly this is the only rational interpretation of the matter. The general principle underlying the right government of every incorporated body, is, that its members contract with each other severally to submit to the will of the majority in all matters concerning the fulfilment of the objects for which they are incorporated; but in no others. To this extent only can the contract hold. For as it is implied in the very nature of a contract, that those entering into it must know what they contract to do; and as those who unite with others for a specified object, cannot contemplate all the unspecified objects which it is hypothetically possible for the union to undertake; it follows that the contract entered into cannot extend to such unspecified objects. And if

---

[10]*popery:* Catholicism.

[11]*Freehold Land Society:* Groups of British investors who collectively held tenure to parcels of Australian land and the resources of that land.

there exists no expressed or understood contract between the union and its members respecting unspecified objects, then for the majority to coerce the minority into undertaking them, is nothing less than gross tyranny."

Naturally, if such a confusion of ideas exists in respect of the powers of a majority where the deed of incorporation tacitly limits those powers, still more must there exist such a confusion where there has been no deed of incorporation. Nevertheless the same principle holds. I again emphasize the proposition that the members of an incorporated body are bound "severally to submit to the will of the majority *in all matters concerning the fulfilment of the objects for which they are incorporated; but in no others.*" And I contend that this holds of an incorporated nation as much as of an incorporated company.

"Yes, but," comes the obvious rejoinder, "as there is no deed by which the members of a nation are incorporated — as there neither is, nor ever was, a specification of purposes for which the union was formed, there exist no limits; and, consequently, the power of the majority is unlimited."

Evidently it must be admitted that the hypothesis of a social contract, either under the shape assumed by Hobbes or under the shape assumed by Rousseau, is baseless. Nay more, it must be admitted that even had such a contract once been formed, it could not be binding on the posterity of those who formed it. Moreover, if any say that in the absence of those limitations to its powers which a deed of incorporation might imply, there is nothing to prevent a majority from imposing its will on a minority by force, assent must be given — an assent, however, joined with the comment that if the superior force of the majority is its justification, then the superior force of a despot backed by an adequate army, is also justified: the problem lapses. What we here seek is some higher warrant for the subordination of minority to majority than that arising from inability to resist physical coercion. Even Austin, anxious as he is to establish the unquestionable authority of positive law, and assuming, as he does, an absolute sovereignty of some kind, monarchic, aristocratic, constitutional, or popular, as the source of its unquestionable authority, is obliged, in the last resort, to admit a moral limit to its action over the community. While insisting, in pursuance of his rigid theory of sovereignty, that a sovereign body originating from the people "is *legally* free to abridge their political liberty, at its own pleasure or discretion," he allows that "a government may be hindered by *positive morality* from abridging the political liberty which it leaves or grants to its subjects."[12] Hence, we have to find, not a physical justification, but a normal justification, for the supposed absolute power of the majority.

13

14

15

---

[12]*The Province of Jurisprudence* (second edition), p. 241. [Spencer]

This will at once draw for the rejoinder — "Of course, in the absence   16
of any agreement, with its implied limitations, the rule of the majority is
unlimited; because it is more just that the majority should have its way
than that the minority should have its way." A very reasonable rejoinder
this seems until there comes the re-rejoinder. We may oppose to it the
equally tenable proposition that, in the absence of an agreement, the supremacy of a majority over a minority does not exist at all. It is co-operation
of some kind, from which there arise these powers and obligations of majority and minority; and in the absence of any agreement to co-operate,
such powers and obligations are also absent.

Here the argument apparently ends in a dead lock. Under the existing   17
condition of things, no moral origin seems assignable either for the sovereignty of the majority or for the limitation of its sovereignty. But further
consideration reveals a solution of the difficulty. For if, dismissing all
thought of any hypothetical agreement to co-operate heretofore made, we
ask what would be the agreement into which citizens would now enter
with practical unanimity, we get a sufficiently clear answer; and with it a
sufficiently clear justification for the role of the majority inside a certain
sphere, but not outside that sphere. Let us first observe a few of the limitations which at once become apparent.

Were all Englishmen now asked if they would agree to co-operate for   18
the teaching of religion, and would give the majority power to fix the creed
and the forms of worship, there would come a very emphatic "No" from
a large part of them. If, in pursuance of a proposal to revive sumptuary
laws,[13] the inquiry were made whether they would bind themselves to
abide by the will of the majority in respect of the fashions and qualities of
their clothes, nearly all of them would refuse. In like manner if (to take an
actual question of the day) people were polled to ascertain whether, in
respect of the beverages they drank, they would accept the decision of the
greater number, certainly half, and probably more than half, would be unwilling. Similarly with respect to many other actions which most men now-
a-days regard as of purely private concern. Whatever desire there might
be to co-operate for carrying on, or regulating, such actions, would be far
from a unanimous desire. Manifestly, then, had social co-operation to be
commenced by ourselves, and had its purposes to be specified before consent to co-operate could be obtained, there would be large parts of human
conduct in respect of which co-operation would be declined; and in respect
of which, consequently, no authority by the majority over the minority
could be rightfully exercised.

---

[13]*sumptuary laws:* Laws regulating private life and morality.

Turn now to the converse question — For what ends would all men   *19*
agree to co-operate? None will deny that for resisting invasion the agreement would be practically unanimous. Excepting only the Quakers,[14] who,
having done highly useful work in their time, are now dying out, all would
unite for defensive war (not, however, for offensive war); and they would,
by so doing, tacitly bind themselves to conform to the will of the majority
in respect of measures directed to that end. There would be practical unanimity, also, in the agreement to co-operate for defence against internal
enemies as against external enemies. Omitting criminals, all must wish to
have person and property adequately protected. In short, each citizen desires to preserve his life, to preserve those things which conduce to maintenance of his life and enjoyment of it, and to preserve intact his liberties
both of using these things and getting further such. It is obvious to him
that he cannot do all this if he acts alone. Against foreign invaders he is
powerless unless he combines with his fellows; and the business of protecting himself against domestic invaders, if he did not similarly combine,
would be alike onerous, dangerous, and inefficient. In one other co-operation all are interested — use of the territory they inhabit. Did the primitive
communal ownership survive, there would survive the primitive communal control of the uses to be made of land by individuals or by groups of
them; and decisions of the majority would rightly prevail respecting the
terms on which portions of it might be employed for raising food, for making means of communication, and for other purposes. Even at present,
though the matter has been complicated by the growth of private land-
ownership, yet, since the State is still supreme owner (every landowner
being in law a tenant of the Crown) able to resume possession, or authorize
compulsory purchase, at a fair price; the implication is that the will of the
majority is valid respecting the modes in which, and conditions under
which, parts of the surface or sub-surface, may be utilized: involving certain agreements made on behalf of the public with private persons and
companies.

Details are not needful here; nor is it needful to discuss that border   *20*
region lying between these classes of cases, and to say how much is included in the last and how much is excluded with the first. For present
purposes, it is sufficient to recognize the undeniable truth that there are
numerous kinds of actions in respect of which men would not, if they were
asked, agree with anything like unanimity to be bound by the will of the
majority; while there are some kinds of actions in respect of which they

---

[14]*Quakers:* Members of the Religious Society of Friends, founded in 17th century England
by George Fox. Quakers refuse to bear arms, even to defend themselves from attack. In
the United States they settled primarily in Rhode Island and Pennsylvania.

would almost unanimously agree to be thus bound. Here, then, we find a definite warrant for enforcing the will of the majority within certain limits, and a definite warrant for denying the authority of its will beyond those limits.

But evidently, when analyzed, the question resolves itself into the further question — What are the relative claims of the aggregate and of its units? Are the rights of the community universally valid against the individual? or has the individual some rights which are valid against the community? The judgment given on this point underlies the entire fabric of political convictions formed, and more especially those convictions which concern the proper sphere of government. Here, then, I propose to revive a dormant controversy, with the expectation of reaching a different conclusion from that which is fashionable. . . .

Though mere love of companionship prompts primitive men to live in groups, yet the chief prompter is experience of the advantages to be derived from co-operation. On what condition only can co-operation arise? Evidently on condition that those who join their efforts severally gain by doing so. If, as in the simplest cases, they unite to achieve something which each by himself cannot achieve, or can achieve less readily, it must be on the tacit understanding, either that they shall share the benefit (as when game is caught by a party of them) or that if one reaps all the benefit now (as in building a hut or clearing a plot) the others shall severally reap equivalent benefits in their turns. When, instead of efforts joined in doing the same thing, different things are effected by them — when division of labour arises, with accompanying barter of products, the arrangement implies that each, in return for something which he has in superfluous quantity, gets an approximate equivalent of something which he wants. If he hands over the one and does not get the other, future proposals to exchange will meet with no response. There will be a reversion to that rudest condition in which each makes everything for himself. Hence the possibility of co-operation depends on fulfilment of contract, tacit or overt.

Now this which we see must hold of the very first step towards that industrial organization by which the life of a society is maintained, must hold more or less fully throughout its development. Though the militant type of organization, with its system of *status* produced by chronic war, greatly obscures these relations of contract, yet they remain partially in force. They still hold between freemen, and between the heads of those small groups which form the units of early societies; and, in a measure, they still hold within these small groups themselves; since survival of them as groups, implies such recognition of the claims of their members, even when slaves, that in return for their labours they get sufficiencies of food, clothing, and protection. And when, with diminution of warfare and growth of trade, voluntary co-operation more and more replaces compul-

21

22

23

sory co-operation, and the carrying on of social life by exchange under agreement, partially suspended for a time, gradually re-establishes itself; its re-establishment makes possible that vast elaborate industrial organization by which a great nation is sustained.

For in proportion as contracts are unhindered and the performance of them certain, the growth is great and the social life active. It is not now by one or other of two individuals who contract, that the evil effects of breach of contract are experienced. In an advanced society, they are experienced by entire classes of producers and distributors, which have arisen through division of labour; and, eventually, they are experienced by everybody. Ask on what condition it is that Birmingham[15] devotes itself to manufacturing hardware, or part of Staffordshire[16] to making pottery, or Lancashire[17] to weaving cotton. Ask how the rural people who here grow wheat and there pasture cattle, find it possible to occupy themselves in their special businesses. These groups can severally thus act only if each gets from the others in exchange for its own surplus product, due shares of their surplus products. No longer directly effected by barter, this obtainment of their respective shares of one another's products is indirectly effected by money; and if we ask how each division of producers gets its due amount of the required money, the answer is — by fulfilment of contract. If Leeds[18] makes woollens and does not, by fulfilment of contract, receive the means of obtaining from agricultural districts the needful quantity of food, it must starve, and stop producing woollens. If South Wales smelts iron and there comes no equivalent agreed upon, enabling it to get fabrics for clothing, its industry must cease. And so throughout, in general and in detail. That mutual dependence of parts which we see in social organization, as in individual organization, is possible only on condition that while each part does the particular kind of work it has become adjusted to, it receives its proportion of those materials required for repair and growth, which all the other parts have joined to produce: such proportion being settled by bargaining. Moreover, it is by fulfilment of contract that there is effected a balancing of all the various products to the various needs — the large manufacture of knives and the small manufacture of lancets[19]; the great growth of wheat and the little growth of mustard-seed. The check on undue production of each commodity, results from finding that after a certain quantity, no one will agree to take any further quantity on terms

24

---

[15]*Birmingham:* An industrial city in central England.

[16]*Staffordshire:* A county in central England.

[17]*Lancashire:* A county in northwest England.

[18]*Leeds:* A city in Yorkshire County in northern England.

[19]*lancets:* Surgical knives.

that yield an adequate money equivalent. And so there is prevented a useless expenditure of labour in producing that which society does not want.

Lastly, we have to note the still more significant fact that the condition under which only, any specialized group of workers can grow when the community needs more of its particular kind of work, is that contracts shall be free and fulfilment of them enforced. If when, from lack of material, Lancashire failed to supply the usual quantity of cotton-goods, there had been such interference with contracts as prevented Yorkshire from asking a greater price for its woollens, which it was enabled to do by the greater demand for them, there would have been no temptation to put more capital into the woollen manufacture, no increase in the amount of machinery and number of artizans employed, and no increase of woollens: the consequence being that the whole community would have suffered from not having deficient cottons replaced by extra woollens. What serious injury may result to a nation if its members are hindered from contracting with one another, was well shown in the contrast between England and France in respect of railways. Here, though obstacles were at first raised by classes predominant in the legislature, the obstacles were not such as prevented capitalists from investing, engineers from furnishing directive skill, or contrators from undertaking works; and the high interest originally obtained on investments, the great profits made by contractors, and the large payments received by engineers, led to that drafting of money, energy, and ability, into railway-making, which rapidly developed our railway-system, to the enormous increase of our national prosperity. But when M. Thiers, then Minister of Public works, came over to inspect, and having been taken about by Mr. Vignoles, said to him when leaving: — "I do not think railways are suited to France,"[20] there resulted, from the consequent policy of hindering free contract, a delay of "eight or ten years" in that material progress which France experienced when railways were made.

What do all these facts means? They mean that for the healthful activity and due proportioning of those industries, occupations, professions, which maintain and aid the life of a society, there must, in the first place, be few restrictions on men's liberties to make agreements with one another, and there must, in the second place, be an enforcement of the agreements which they do make. As we have seen, the checks naturally arising to each man's actions when men become associated, are those only which result from mutual limitation; and there consequently can be no resulting check to the contracts they voluntarily make: interference with these is interference with those rights to free action which remain to each when the rights of others are fully recognized. And then, as we have seen, en-

---

[20]Address of C. B. Vignoles, Esq., F.R.S. on his Election as President of the Institution of Civil Engineers, Session 1869–70, p. 53 [Spencer]

forcement of their rights implies enforcement of contracts made; since breach of contract is indirect aggression. If, when a customer on one side of the counter asks a shopkeeper on the other for a shilling's worth of his goods, and, while the shopkeeper's back is turned, walks off with the goods without leaving the shilling he tacitly contracted to give, his act differs in no essential way from robbery. In each such case the individual injured is deprived of something he possessed, without receiving the equivalent something bargained for; and is in the state of having expended his labour without getting benefit — has had an essential condition to the maintenance of life infringed.

Thus, then, it results that to recognize and enforce the rights of individuals, is at the same time to recognize and enforce the conditions to a normal social life. There is one vital requirement for both.   27

Before turning to those corollaries which have practical applications, let us observe how the special conclusions drawn converge to the one general conclusion originally foreshadowed — glancing at them in reversed order.   28

We have just found that the pre-requisite to individual life is in a double sense the pre-requisite to social life. The life of a society, in whichever of two senses conceived, depends on maintenance of individual rights. If it is nothing more than the sum of the lives of citizens, this implication is obvious. If it consists of those many unlike activities which citizens carry on in mutual dependence, still this aggregate impersonal life rises or falls according as the rights of individuals are enforced or denied.   29

Study of men's politico-ethical ideas and sentiments, leads to allied conclusions. Primitive peoples of various types show us that before governments exist, immemorial customs recognize private claims and justify maintenance of them. Codes of law independently evolved by different nations, agree in forbidding certain trespasses on the persons, properties, and liberties of citizens; and their correspondences imply, not an artificial source for individual rights, but a natural source. Along with social development, the formulating in law of the rights pre-established by custom, becomes more definite and elaborate. At the same time, Government undertakes to an increasing extent the business of enforcing them. While it has been becoming a better protector, Government has been becoming less aggressive — has more and more diminished its intrusions on men's spheres of private action. And, lastly, as in past times laws were avowedly modified to fit better with current ideas of equity; so now, law-reformers are guided by ideas of equity which are not derived from law but to which law has to conform.   30

Here, then, we have a politico-ethical theory justified alike by analysis and by history. What have we against it? A fashionable counter-theory which proves to be unjustifiable. On the one hand, while we find that individual life and social life both imply maintenance of the natural relation   31 between efforts and benefits; we also find that this natural relation, recognized before Government existed, has been all along asserting and reasserting itself, and obtaining better recognition in codes of law and systems of ethics. On the other hand, those who, denying natural rights, commit themselves to the assertion that rights are artificially created by law, are not only flatly contradicted by facts, but their assertion is self-destructive: the endeavour to substantiate it, when challenged, involves them in manifold absurdities.

Nor is this all. The re-institution of a vague popular conception in a   32
definite form on a scientific basis, leads us to a rational view of the relation between the wills of majorities and minorities. It turns out that those co-operations in which all can voluntarily unite, and in the carrying on of which the will of the majority is rightly supreme, are co-operations for maintaining the conditions requisite to individual and social life. Defence of the society as a whole against external invaders, has for its remote end to preserve each citizen in possession of such means as he has for satisfying his desires, and in possession of such liberty as he has for getting further means. And defence of each citizen against internal invaders, from murderers down to those who inflict nuisances on their neighbours, has obviously the like end — an end desired by every one save the criminal and disorderly. Hence it follows that for maintenance of this vital principle, alike of individual life and social life, subordination of minority to majority is legitimate; as implying only such a trenching[21] on the freedom and property of each, as is requisite for the better protecting of his freedom and property. At the same time it follows that such subordination is not legitimate beyond this; since, implying as it does a greater aggression upon the individual than is requisite for protecting him, it involves a breach of the vital principle which is to be maintained.

Thus we come round again to the proposition that the assumed divine   33
right of parliaments, and the implied divine right of majorities, are superstitions. While men have abandoned the old theory respecting the source of State-authority, they have retained a belief in that unlimited extent of State-authority which rightly accompanied the old theory, but does not rightly accompany the new one. Unrestricted power over subjects, rationally ascribed to the ruling man when he was held to be a deputy-god, is now ascribed to the ruling body, the deputy-godhood of which nobody asserts. . . .

Here, then, we reach the ultimate interdict against meddling legisla-   34
tion. Reduced to its lowest terms, every proposal to interfere with citizens' activities further than by enforcing their mutual limitations, is a proposal

---

[21]*trenching:* Encroaching.

to improve life by breaking through the fundamental conditions to life. When some are prevented from buying beer that others may be prevented from getting drunk, those who make the law assume that more good than evil will result from interference with the normal relation between conduct and consequences, alike in the few ill-regulated and the many well-regulated. A government which takes fractions of the incomes of multitudinous people, for the purpose of sending to the colonies[22] some who have not prospered here, or for building better industrial dwellings, or for making public libraries and public museums, &c., takes for granted that, not only proximately but ultimately, increased general happiness will result from transgressing the essential requirement to general happiness — the requirement that each shall enjoy all those means to happiness which his actions, carried on without aggression, have brought him. In other cases we do not thus let the immediate blind us to the remote. When asserting the sacredness of property against private transgressors, we do not ask whether the benefit to a hungry man who takes bread from a baker's shop, is or is not greater than the injury inflicted on the baker: we consider, not the special effects, but the general effects which arise if property is insecure. But when the State exacts further amounts from citizens, or further restrains their liberties, we consider only the direct and proximate effects, and ignore the indirect and distant effects which are caused when these invasions of individual rights are continually multiplied. We do not see that by accumulated small infractions of them, the vital conditions to life, individual and social, come to be so imperfectly fulfilled that the life decays.

Yet the decay thus caused becomes manifest where the policy is pushed to an extreme. Any one who studies, in the writings of MM. Taine[23] and de Tocqueville,[24] the state of things which preceded the French Revolution, will see that that tremendous catastrophe came about from so excessive a regulation of men's actions in all their details, and such an enormous drafting away of the products of their actions to maintain the regulating organization, that life was fast becoming impracticable. The empirical utilitarianism[25] of that day, like the empirical utilitarianism of our

35

---

[22]*colonies:* The American colonies.

[23]*MM. Taine:* Hippolyte Adolphe Taine (1828–1893), a French historian and literary critic.

[24]*de Tocqueville:* Alexis Charles de Tocqueville (1805–1859), French statesman and writer, author of *Democracy in America.*

[25]Utilitarianism is the philosophy that holds that the goodness or badness of actions depends upon the goodness or badness of the effect(s) of these actions. *Empirical* utilitarianism focuses on particular actions; *rational* utilitarianism focuses on general or multiple actions, or actions considered in the abstract.

day, differed from rational utilitarianism in this, that in each successive case it contemplated only the effects of particular interferences on the actions of particular classes of men, and ignored the effects produced by a multiplicity of such interferences on the lives of men at large. And if we ask what then made, and what now makes, this error possible, we find it to be the political superstition that governmental power is subject to no restraints.

When that "divinity" which "doth hedge a king," and which has left   36
a glamour around the body inheriting his power, has quite died away —
when it begins to be seen clearly that, in a popularly-governed nation, the government is simply a committee of management; it will also be seen that this committee of management has no intrinsic authority. The inevitable conclusion will be that its authority is given by those appointing it; and has just such bounds as they choose to impose. Along with this will go the further conclusion that the laws it passes are not in themselves sacred; but that whatever sacredness they have, it is entirely due to the ethical sanction — an ethical sanction which, as we find, is derivable from the laws of human life as carried on under social conditions. And there will come the corollary that when they have not this ethical sanction they have no sacredness, and may rightly be challenged.

The function of Liberalism in the past was that of putting a limit to the   37
powers of kings. The function of true Liberalism in the future will be that of putting a limit to the powers of Parliaments.

REVIEW QUESTIONS

1. Why does Spencer argue that belief in the divine right of kings is more consistent (though just as irrational) as belief in the divine right of parliaments? How does he account for the fact that people believe in such an irrational doctrine as the divine right of parliaments?
2. Concerning which aspects of Hobbes's social contract theory does Spencer express skepticism? What are the reasons for his skepticism? Which aspects of Hobbes's theory does he accept? What are the implications of those aspects that he accepts?
3. Summarize in a sentence or two the main point of the quoted passage in paragraph 12 and Spencer's discussion immediately following. To what extent is the will of the majority limited? What is the moral basis for the sovereignty of the majority?
4. In what areas is the majority morally justified in imposing its will on all individuals? In what areas is it not justified?
5. Why are contracts essential in the evolution of society from one form to another? How *has* society evolved, in Spencer's view? Why is the free and unrestricted use of contracts, and the enforcement of these contracts, necessary for the economic vitality of a society? What does Spencer mean when he says that "breach of contract is indirect aggression"?

6. What role does Spencer assign to government, at the conclusion of his essay? What is the source of the government's authority? Upon what basis are its laws to be obeyed?

DISCUSSION AND WRITING QUESTIONS

1. Before reading this essay, what were your own beliefs about the moral basis of majority rule? Has Spencer changed your thinking on this issue? If so, how? If not, why not? What, in your judgment, constitute the proper limits of majority rule? What are the proper limits of individual rights?

2. Spencer's essay proceeds in an extremely logical and systematic manner, as he considers and examines the validity of each side of the matter at hand, and concludes that a particular position is tenable or untenable. Focusing on a particular part of this essay, examine the logical process by which Spencer tries to convince us that his own position is the only reasonable one.

3. In paragraph 22 Spencer declares that "the possibility of co-operation depends on fulfilment of contract, tacit or overt." Use this as the thesis of an essay dealing with politics, business, social, or domestic relations, or some combination of these. Be sure to explain what you understand by such key terms as "co-operation" and "tacit contract." *Alternate assignment*: Use as the thesis of an essay Spencer's sentence in paragraph 29: "The life of a society . . . depends on maintenance of individual rights." Use evidence from your own reading and experience.

4. Toward the end of his essay (see especially paragraph 37) Spencer takes the position that individuals should not be taxed to support welfare programs, government subsidized housing for workers, or such public services as libraries and museums. Do you agree with him? If not, explain how and why your own position on individual rights and the proper role of government differs from his.

5. Research a paper on the subject of how political debate in this country since the New Deal of President Franklin D. Roosevelt has turned on the axes of government regulation (on the one hand) and individual rights (on the other). Begin your thinking on this subject by surveying what you already know about the personal inclinations and the programs of presidents like Lyndon B. Johnson and Ronald Reagan. Discuss the shifts of thinking in terms of Spencer's discussion. As part of your research you may want to get information on the Libertarian Party in the United States. (See also the writings of Robert J. Ringer, particularly his *Restoring the American Dream*.) How does the philosophy of the Libertarian party compare and contrast with the philosophy of Spencer?

JOHN W. GOUGH *(1900–1976)*

Modern political theorists no longer discuss the reciprocal obligations of individual and state in terms of the social contract. They argue that the social contract is a historically inaccurate idea because at no time have people ever actually come together, agreed by mutual consent to form a society, and thereby surrendered to society some of their natural rights as individuals. Society, these theorists argue, is a natural growth, not an artificial construction. As such, society (an association of individuals) must be distinguished from government (the political authority that administers or controls these associations). Individuals create or destroy governments, but they can no more agree to form a society than they can decide to withdraw from society — and thus terminate the contract. We are, whatever our individual circumstances, social creatures. Furthermore, the concept of natural rights in the state of nature is a logical absurdity, because rights cannot exist except in a social context. An individual's rights exist only in relation to other people, who must recognize these rights. If the social contract has any contemporary meaning, the theorists conclude, it is only as a metaphor or an analogy to help clarify the mutual rights and duties of individuals and governments.

Among those who have articulated such objections to the idea of the social contract is the British political scientist, John W. Gough. Educated in history and political philosophy at Merton College of Oxford, Gough taught from 1922 to 1931 at Bristol University and subsequently was appointed Fellow and Tutor, and then University Lecturer in Modern History, at Oriel College, Oxford University, where he remained until his retirement in 1967. Particularly interested in 17th century England, Gough edited several works of Locke and wrote *John Locke's Political Philosophy* (1950), *English Constitutional History* (1955), and *The Rise of the Entrepreneur* (1970). His most well-known work is *The Social Contract: A Critical Study of Its Development* (1936). A starting point for any detailed study of the subject, this work traces social contract theory from the ancient Greeks to the 19th century. In the conclusion to his study, reprinted below, Gough acknowledges the impact of the social contract theory but raises serious questions about its validity.

A CRITIQUE OF THE SOCIAL CONTRACT

We have now reached the end of the history of the social contract the-   *1*
ory, and it has been suggested more than once that, though open to serious
objections, and inadequate by itself as an explanation of the state, it nevertheless contains some elements of truth. It would indeed be surprising if a
theory which had commanded such widespread support for so many centuries was wholly erroneous. The end of this book is hardly the place to
embark on the construction of a complete political philosophy, but we
must at least attempt to disentangle the truth that lies concealed beneath
the apparatus of the contract, and decide what justification there really was
for the support the theory has received.

The contract theory in each of its forms has usually had two purposes;
on the one hand it was an historical account of the origin of government,
or of the state, or of society itself; on the other hand it was a theory of
political obligation, to explain the nature and limits of the duty of allegiance owed by subjects to the state, and of the right on the part of the
state or its government to control the lives of its citizens. There is no need
to dwell further on the first of these two purposes, for as an historical
theory the contract has now long been discredited, and its more recent
adherents have wisely confined themselves to the claim that a contract is
the philosophical basis of the state. This claim itself has taken various
forms. It may be argued, as by Kant,[1] that the contract, though historically
a fiction, is valid as an "idea of reason"; and this, we saw, meant that
political rights and duties should be ordered "as if" political obligation
were founded on a contract, although really it is not. This theory was
doubtless intended as a guarantee of justice and a safeguard against
oppression; but it seems to reduce the contract to a merely pragmatic reality, and we may wonder whether in that case it retains much value or
efficacy.

Or there is Fouillée's[2] theory, who, like Kant, admitted that many ex-   *2*
isting states govern tyrannically, and believed that contract ought to be the
basis of government. Fouillée's contract, however, unlike Kant's, was to be
real not in idea only but in fact; but while he abandoned the theory that a

J.W. Gough. A Critique of the Social Contract [1936]. In *The Social Contract: A Critical Study of its Development.* Oxford: Oxford UP, 1936.
[1]*Kant:* Immanual Kant (1724–1804), a German philosopher, argued thus in *On the Saying, 'That May Be Right in Theory but Has No Value in Practice'* (1793).
[2]*Fouillée:* Alfred Fouillée, in *La Science Sociale Contemporaine* (1890).

contract had been made in the past, he projected it instead into the future, suggesting that the contract could be realized in practice by establishing a democratic constitution with universal suffrage. But little gain and much risk of confusion may arise from the really quite groundless identification of representative institutions with contract, and if what is really meant is that democracy should be the goal of political evolution, it would be much better to say so directly without misleading allusions to the social contract.

More often, however, and perhaps more defensibly, it may be argued   *3* that while the state is obviously not the product of any formal or express contract, yet political obligation is essentially contractual; or, if it be objected that the word contract has a legal connotation which is inadmissible, that the mutual relationship of citizens is sufficiently analogous to contract to justify the use of the word in some metaphorical or qualified sense. A member of society is aware that in return for the security, protection, and opportunity for development afforded him by political organization, he is bound to obey the laws, pay the taxes, and share the risks of defence, while society recognizes that if it makes these claims on its members it must in return provide the benefits that they can rightly expect of it. The rights and duties of the state and its citizens, in other words, are reciprocal, and the recognition of this reciprocity constitutes a relationship which by analogy can be called a social contract. This kind of theory may, as in Herbert Spencer, be associated with an extreme individualism which seeks to reduce the claims of the state to a minimum; but there is no logical reason why the claims of the state or of individuals should be fixed at any particular level, and in principle the contract theory is compatible with a far more reasonable attitude than Spencer's to the duties of citizenship and the functions of the state.

A good example of this kind of qualified contract theory may be found   *4* in Nettleship.

> "The conception of an original contract upon which society is based," he writes, "is, emphatically, unhistorical (in some writers, who have used it, it is avowedly fictitious), but it has been not the less influential. It is one of the most striking examples of the reflexion of an idea into the past to give it apparent solidity and concreteness. . . . It is based upon a very important fact, that every civilized community, perhaps any real community, requires, in order that it may exist at all, a mutual recognition of rights on the part of its members, which is a tacit contract. It becomes unhistorical if one goes on to say that at a certain period in the world's history people met together and said, Let us come to an understanding, and make society on the basis of contract. This has never taken place, but the potency of the idea lies not in the fictitious historical account it gives of the matter, but in the real present truth it expresses."[3]

---

[3]R. L. Nettleship, *Lectures on the Republic of Plato* (2nd edn., 1901), pp. 52, 53. [Gough]

Farther on he repeats his belief in "the truth that the existence of society does in the last resort depend on a mutual understanding; all the institutions of the state and of society are forms of mutual understanding, and, as they are emphatically creations of man, there is no reason why he should not dispense with them if he wished. If the theory of contract is understood in this sense, it is not profitable to dismiss it by saying it is unhistorical. That does not invalidate the fact, for it is a fact, that society is based upon contract." It is equally true, he continues, "that the existence of society implies that the individual members of it agree to sacrifice a part of their individuality, or to sacrifice a part of their rights, if we call what a man *can* do his rights."[4]

What a man *can* do, however, can only be called his rights in the peculiar sense which Hobbes gave to that word, and it is entirely fictitious to suggest that men could dispense with the institutions of society if they wished. Nettleship, in fact, rightly rejects the extreme individualism which such a contention would involve,[5] and his fundamental position, though his statement of it is not altogether consistent, really approximates to that of T. H. Green. For if an agreement to dissolve society and return to a "state of nature" is ruled out as not a practical possibility, his remark that the institutions of the state are "forms of mutual understanding" amounts in the end to no more than the foundation of government on consent, in the sense in which Green argued that "will, not force, is the basis of the State."[6] Apart from this, it will be observed that Nettleship equates his "mutual recognition of rights" with a "tacit contract," and this is a formula that we have often met with in tracing the history of the contract theory. Alternatively, we have sometimes read that there is an implied contract in membership of the state, and that political obligation is implicitly though not explicitly contractual. Both of these formulae, however, are open to the objection that the recognition of reciprocal obligations, which, it is argued, is involved in the structure of society, is not in fact a contract; but if we say that there is a tacit or implied contract, we must mean, if we mean any-

---

[4]Ibid., p. 55. [Gough]

[5]"Two people cannot live and work together," he points out, "without surrendering something which they would do if separate, for joint action is not the same as separate action." But it is absurd, he continues, to represent "the results of this mutual understanding not only as conventional but as *merely* conventional, contrasting them with something natural which has a deeper authority." A "natural" man in this sense would only be "himself *minus* everything that he is by convention, and that means *minus* everything in him which the existence of society implies. Such a 'natural' man does not exist." (Ibid., pp. 55, 56.) [Gough]

[6]T. H. Green, *Principles of Political Obligation*, §§ 80–136. Green himself is really, though perhaps unconsciously, admitting a contractual element into his political thought in so far as he maintains that rights depend for their existence on recognition by society. [Gough]

thing precise at all, that what is understood or implied is a genuine contract.

The variety of phrases — tacit contract, implied contract, quasi-contract, and so on — by which different writers have tried to express themselves, is largely due, indeed, to vagueness of thought. Aware that political obligation does not rest on a legal contract properly so called, they clung to the belief that nevertheless there was some kind of contractual element in the composition of the state, and so they attached to the word contract some vaguely qualifying epithet. If we could dismiss from our minds the technical meaning of quasi-contract in Roman Law; and the elaborate and rather absurd erection that was built on M. Léon Bourgeois's use of it,[7] we might perhaps be inclined to feel that quasi-contract was the least objectionable of the possible alternative phrases, for it at any rate avoids confusing implication and analogy. Its attractiveness, however, is insidious by the very reason of its vagueness, and we ought really to define it more exactly. If we attempt to do this, I think we shall be forced to admit that what we really mean is not that political obligation implies a contract properly so called, but that it involves a relationship which resembles or is analogous to contract in some respects but not in others.[8] In other words, it has some features in common with contract, but others which are not contractual at all. If the phrase "social contract" is to be retained, therefore, it had probably best be interpreted as an abbreviation for the idea that political obligation involves a relationship analogous to contract.

This, I think, is the maximum that could be conceded to the contract theory. Whether even this is tenable remains to be considered, but before pursuing this inquiry any further let us pause a moment to examine briefly the question of natural rights. The social contract theory has often been attacked on account of its association with this idea, and it is true that contractarians have often held that society is a contractual union of unrelated individuals, each claiming the enjoyment of certain rights which belong to him as a man. We are not considering here the historical idea that society was ever actually formed in such a way out of such elements, though we may notice in passing that the objection that society is not an

---

[7]M. Léon Bourgeois, French politician, began a debate on the scope of the "quasi-contract," that, according to Gough, led to the postulation of "three quasi-contracts enclosed within one another — that of individuals between each other, of governors with the governed, and of living men with past and future generations — and these constitute the whole legal structure of public life." [Gough]

[8]Similarly, if we say that society is an organism, we are using another analogy which also is appropriate in some respects but not in others. To some extent these two analogies supply each other's deficiencies, and it will be remembered that Fouillée proposed to combine them. [Gough]

artificial construction but a natural growth can only carry weight against the contract theory in its historical sense. History apart, however, it may be held that if society, as it is, is subjected to a logical analysis into its component parts, those parts will be found to be right-possessing individuals mutually related in a manner analogous to contract. The great objection to natural rights as ordinarily understood is that if any man possesses rights, he must possess them against or in relation to somebody else; that it is therefore meaningless to attribute rights to isolated individuals, and that in fact rights necessarily involve society. But if you admit this, it is argued, why drag in a social contract to explain society and guarantee your rights, seeing that unless society already existed there could be no rights to guarantee? This argument, however, really introduces the historical factor once more, which we have agreed to disregard; in a logical analysis, on the other hand, there is no question of *pre-social* natural rights or the *creation* of society, for we never supposed that the individual units into which we were analysing society existed or had rights before or apart from society; on the contrary, they were admittedly members of society all the time.

It is sometimes maintained, however, not only that there can be no rights apart from society, but also that there can be no rights apart from their recognition by society, and indeed that rights can be created only by such recognition. Legal rights, needless to say, can only be created by and exist within the legal fabric of the state; but moral rights, it seems to me, while necessarily involving society, do not necessarily involve recognition by society — certainly not by any particular society; and they can only be said to be constituted by society in the sense that society is the necessary medium within which alone they can exist.[9]

This brings us to the position from which the most serious attacks on natural rights and the social contract have been delivered, whether it be the philosophy of Plato and Aristotle that man is naturally political, or the Hegelian idealism which attributes to the state all that men are and can become. We may admit that this philosophy "can ennoble the individual and lift him above self-centred concern in his own immediate life,"[10] that a one-sided individualism is inadequate as an explanation of the varied manifestations of social life, and that the "police theory" of the state, which reduces its functions to the mere protection of life and property, is not only insufficient but unworkable. Yet the political consequences of Hegelianism can be dangerous and repulsive. It may lead to a virtual deification of the

9

10

---

[9]This is not to say that any particular list of the "rights of man" can be defended as "natural rights." [Gough]

[10]E. Barker, Introduction to his translation of Gierke's *Natural Law and the Theory of Society*, p. xvii. [Gough]

nation or the folk or the race (perhaps quite mythical in reality), which so engulfs and enslaves the individual that he loses all independence of mind and action; while in the international sphere the state may be led to cast aside all considerations of law and morality and embark on a naked career of aggression and conquest. "Individualism is often used as a word of reproach," as Professor Barker remarks, "but it is good to see simple shapes of 'men as trees, walking,' and to think in simple terms of human persons. . . . If we hold that individual personality is the one intrinsic value of human life, we shall have no very great reason to fling stones at a theory which rested on a similar basis." We can fully agree with the idealists that it is only in society that rights can have any meaning and that individual personality can develop its potentialities, but with these qualifications we may well feel that there is more to be said for the natural rights of individuals than their critics have allowed.

Professor Barker, it seems, goes further, and declares that "there is still a case to be made for the view that the State, as distinct from Society, is a legal association which fundamentally rests on the presuppositions of contract."[11] The refusal to distinguish the political from other aspects of society, and the consequent identification of society and the state, is a dangerous error which a true political philosophy does well to avoid, but does this distinction really entitle us to rest political obligation on contract, or anything analogous to contract? For the purposes of a philosophical analysis of the implications of our social life this distinction between society and the state is a valuable one, but we shall go astray if we imagine that either can really be separated from the other.[12]

The political and legal aspects of society — the government and laws of the state —, though they do not include the whole of social life, are indispensable to its cohesion and very existence, and while politically organized society has a duty to respect the individuals of which it is composed, individuals have a duty to support the organization on which social life depends, quite irrespective of any agreement to do so. This duty is not necessarily unlimited or unconditional, but if there are occasions when resistance or revolution is justified, its justification will arise, not from the terms of any contract, but from the greater general good to be attained by resistance than by continued submission.[13] The state indeed involves a rec-

---

[11]Ibid., p. xlix. "The presuppositions of contract" is another vague phrase (cf. above, p. 227), and I am not sure exactly what Professor Barker means by it. Does it differ materially from the *implication* of contract? [Gough]

[12]Cf. the similar distinction for philosophical purposes of the objects of knowledge into universals and particulars, neither of which is found in reality apart from the other. [Gough]

iprocity of rights and duties, but if we translate this reciprocity into a social contract, however modified, we are introducing as a motive for obedience to the laws an element which is quite imaginary. Valid and important as are the principles which contractarians have striven to uphold, we must conclude that it is a mistake to regard the language of contract as either necessary or helpful for the explanation of them. Respect for individuality can be held to justify belief in what we may call natural rights, but the duty of obedience to the laws can be explained, without any recourse to the social contract, in terms of the responsibilities and duties to our fellow men which are the necessary correlatives of their rights.[14] It is this reciprocity which is the truth that underlies the contract theory, but there seems no good reason for expressing it as the product of a mutual agreement. To do so is only to confuse once more the existence of rights and duties with the recognition of them.

---

[13]What my behaviour should be in any particular political circumstances, what claims the government can rightly make on me in this or that situation, what, if any, are the rights and duties of conscientious objectors — questions like these must be met by a systematic political philosophy, but we are concerned here only with the general principles with which an answer to them must cohere. In practice the answer would have to be guided largely by circumstances and experience. [Gough]

[14]Our theory, in short, would put political obligation on the same footing as moral obligation, and treat political obligation as a special kind of moral obligation. But while contract, on this view, is not necessary as the general ground of political obligation, there may be particular political obligations, just as there may be particular moral obligations, which are definitely contractual. Such, for example, would be the special duties which a soldier undertakes to perform when he enlists. [Gough]

REVIEW QUESTIONS

1. According to Gough, what are the two purposes of social contract theory? Which of these purposes is no longer taken seriously? With which view of social contract thinking does Gough associate Herbert Spencer? Upon what basis does Gough finally accept the idea of a "contract" to describe political obligations between individual and state?

2. Upon what basis can we attack the concept of "natural rights" — i.e., those rights supposedly possessed by humans in the state of nature? In view of the fact that the concept of natural rights is related to the concept of individualism, what dangers lie in attacking the concept of natural rights?

3. Why does Gough conclude that there is no need for the concept of a social contract? What does he believe is the best way to consider the relationship between individuals and the state?

DISCUSSION AND WRITING QUESTIONS

1. Do you agree with Gough's conclusion that ultimately we do not need the concept of a social contract? If so, how would Gough's thinking modify the kind of relationships between individual and state that have been discussed by Hobbes, Locke, and Rousseau? For example, would the absence of a social contract affect the relationship between Hobbes's all-powerful sovereign and the sovereign's subjects? How would the absence of a social contract affect Locke's ideas about justified revolution? How would the absence of a social contract affect Rousseau's ideas about the majority's right to coerce the unwilling minority to fall in line?

2. After reading Gough, as well as the other writers in this part, write an essay explaining how you view your own relationship to the state. Consider both your obligations to the state and the state's obligations to you. Does the idea of a social contract help you to define or clarify this relationship? If not, why not? If so, how? Does the relationship you have with the state vary to any degree, depending upon whether you are considering local or national government? Wherever possible, cite specific issues or activities to illustrate your points.

Part IV

CONDORCET AND THE PROGRESS OF CIVILIZATION

Marquis de Condorcet

Thomas Robert Malthus

William Godwin

Robert Southey

Thomas Babington Macaulay

Karl Marx

George Bernard Shaw

Aldous Huxley

Reinhold Niebuhr

Robert L. Heilbroner

Progress will doubtless vary in speed, but it will never be reversed as long as the earth occupies its present place in the system of the universe.

— Condorcet, *Sketch for a Historical Picture of the Progress of the Human Mind*

All history treats almost exclusively of wicked men who in the course of time have come to be looked upon as good men. All progress is the result of successful crime.

— Friedrich Nietzsche, Aphorism 20, *The Dawn*

Our earliest ancestors emerged some 1.5 million years ago; but not until 6,000 years ago did humans think to record their activities. From the beginning of those first records until now, according to historian Arnold Toynbee, nineteen civilizations have arisen; fourteen have died; five currently flourish — ours (what Toynbee has termed "Western Christendom") being one of the five. It is somewhat humbling to take the historian's view of the human enterprise and see civilizations rise and fall, as if according to some cycle of nature. We pause to wonder: will *our* civilization go the way of the Egyptian dynasties? Given our capacity for reason and bolstered by an understanding of the past, should we not be able to manage our affairs such that we flourish and avoid calamity?

In 1794, Marie Jean Antoine Nicolas Caritat, marquis de Condorcet, along with other philosophers of the Enlightenment, believed that progress was not only possible but inevitable since laws of nature were at work ensuring the advancement of civilization. As Condorcet put it so enthusiastically in his *Sketch for a Historical Picture of the Progress of the Human Mind*:

nature has set no term to the perfection of human faculties; . . . the perfectibility of man is truly indefinite; and . . . the progress of this perfectibility, from now onwards independent of any power that might wish to halt it, has no other limit than the duration of the globe upon which nature has cast us.

From our vantage point we can see that the idea of progress arose at a particular moment in history — according to some, in the 16th century; according to others, in the 17th. Historians do agree that during the greater part of the 6,000 years for which we have records (and certainly for the millennia preceding), humankind did *not* look to the future with a hopeful eye. As late as the age of Copernicus the belief in a future that could offer an improvement over present conditions was yet to be conceived. For that belief to become possible, three historical conditions had to be met: "First there was needed the power to alter man's subservience before nature to a mastery of it. Second, there was required a belief in the legitimacy of the idea of human betterment. And last there was missing a framework of social institutions which would combine power and hope, and which would then permit this fruitful combination to achieve its own sponta-neous growth."[1] These conditions were met in the 17th century — initially, when achievements in science were applied to technology: machines were invented that could ease the burden of physical labor and, by the time of the Industrial Revolution 200 years later, achieve a mastery over nature. Then a revolution in political thinking, the belief in the inalienable rights of the common man and woman, allowed for the possibility that all people — not just the nobility — might improve their fortunes.[2] And finally, the change in Europe from a feudal to a capitalist economy enabled entrepre-neurs to act on their dreams of prosperity. Forces at work in technology, politics, and economics converged to give men and women of the 17th century their first glimpse of a future that held out a promise of improved fortunes. Barriers to change that had been in place since the emergence of human life were now removed. The idea of progress was born.

Progress is a relative term that depends for its meaning on an assess-ment of the past as well as of the future. Clearly, if we are to improve tomorrow, we do so as judged against some less satisfactory yesterday. Famous contributors to the idea of progress have thus developed theories of history. For instance, Condorcet saw the growth of reason as a natural law that, working through successive epochs in human development (which Condorcet himself defined), had liberated man from barriers that kept him from achieving perfectibility. Writing fifty years later, Karl Marx and Friedrich Engels saw "the history of all hitherto existing society [as] the history of class struggles." Humanity, for Marx and Engels, was di-vided into two camps: the exploiters and the exploited. The inevitable ten-sion between them led to revolutions in ancient and feudal societies and would lead to revolution in the modern industrial world — this last revolt ending in a classless society free of exploitation. Both Condorcet and Marx predicted that the lot of humankind would improve in specific ways: the laws of progress, every bit as fixed as the laws of nature, required it.

At this point in the 20th century, we are in a position to judge the extent to which conditions actually have improved — at least since the late

---

[1] Robert Heilbroner. *The Future as History.* New York: Harper, 1960, p. 21.
[2] For a related discussion, see Part III on "Hobbes and the Social Contract."

18th and middle 19th centuries, when Condorcet and Marx developed their ideas. If we take progress in science as our measure, our conclusion must be unqualified: *yes*, we have progressed. From the time of the Enlightenment to the present, greater accomplishments have been made in medicine, industry, agriculture, and related fields than in the thousands of years preceding. The rate of infant mortality in developed countries has been lowered and life expectancies lengthened. Steam power has been harnessed along with electric, solar, and nuclear power. Distances have shrunk with the inventions of the train, the automobile, and the airplane. Truly, the progress of science in 200 brief years has been astounding, and the quality of life for millions has improved. But this is only part of the story.

For it is equally true that if progress in human affairs has occurred at all, it has been fitful. World War I provided a great jolt to the optimistic fervor that man, the *rational* animal, would perfect his nature along with his technology. In four short years (1914–1918), ten million died and thirty million were wounded in a conflict revolting for its use of poison gas and of automatic weaponry trained on wave after wave of largely defenseless infantrymen. In the Second World War (1939–1945), 24.5 million combatants died, along with an estimated 30 million civilians — two hundred thousand of whom were killed in single bomb blasts at Hiroshima and Nagasaki. The grisly portrait of our century is completed by the massacres of Armenians, Jews, and Cambodians, and by the image of children whose malnourished faces stare vacantly from the pages of weekly news magazines. In spite of our capacity to reason, wrongs that we have not merely suffered to exist but have actively helped to create continue, and we have shocked ourselves with our own capacity for indifference — and evil. As early as the 18th century, Jonathan Swift charged (speaking through one of his Houyhnhnms — or talking horses — in *Gulliver's Travels* [1728]) that humans were "animals to whose share . . . some small pittance of reason had fallen, whereof we made no other use than by its assistance to aggravate our natural corruptions, and to acquire new ones which Nature had not given us."

Among other lessons, the 20th century has taught us to distrust predictions regarding the perfectibility of man. We read Condorcet and wonder how he could have so misjudged the darker side of human nature. And we would indict him as a propagandist were it not for the fact that his naïveté continues to seduce us. The truth is we *want* to improve human nature, and we wonder why, despite our best intentions, we cannot. Perhaps Condorcet and Marx were wrong and the Law of Progress is no law, but merely an idea that has had its time and is now expired. Historian J. B. Bury calls the belief in progress an act of faith belonging "to the same order of ideas as Providence or personal immortality. [The notion of progress as a law] is true or it is false, and like [Providence or immortality] cannot be proved either true or false."[3]

Do we, then — can we — still believe in progress, knowing what we do? This we take to be the central question of the readings that follow. As with other ideas organizing selections in this book, the idea of progress cuts to the heart of what we think about ourselves. Nothing less is at stake then the position in which we stand with respect to the future. To paraphrase Robert Heilbroner, what *is* the human prospect? Is it still possible to have hope?

The discussion begins with the tenth section of Condorcet's *Sketch for a Historical Picture of the Progress of the Human Mind*, the classic statement of Enlightenment optimism. Thomas Malthus, writing five years after Condorcet, takes immediate exception to the proposition that the potential for human prosperity is unlimited. Malthus raises a problem: if Condorcet's program succeeds, world population will grow and eventually exhaust the earth's resources — triggering mass starvation. William Godwin responds directly to Malthus, accusing him of a philosophy that blots out "the unlimited power we possess to remedy our evils." If the population grows, says Godwin, we shall respond to meet that challenge — and, in a larger sense, to meet all challenges. Next, Robert Southey surveys the 19th century industrial towns of his native England to discover a depressing aspect, a sign perhaps that progress comes not without costs. This conclusion infuriates the great spokesman of Victorian optimism, Thomas Babington Macaulay, who was as enthusiastic about the perfectibility of man in the 19th century as Condorcet was in the 18th. You will then be referred to a selection in another part of the book, "The Class Struggle"; in *The Communist Manifesto* Marx and Engels, writing in the spirit of those who take progress to be a law of nature, lay out a pattern to history along class lines and then offer a prediction for an enlightened future. A short essay by George Bernard Shaw follows in which the dramatist calls the idea of progress an illusion, reasoning that individual human nature is flawed and that net progress, necessarily dependent on individuals, is therefore unlikely. The next three selections were written after the great conflagration of World War I, and we find in them a view of human potential profoundly changed from Condorcet's. This section begins with an excerpt from Aldous Huxley's *Brave New World*, a novel in which many of the predictions of the Enlightenment philosophers have been achieved, yet in a world that few would describe as idyllic. Theologian Reinhold Niebuhr follows with as doubtful a view of progress as G. B. Shaw, though for different reasons: whereas Shaw de-

---

[3]J. B. Bury. *The Idea of Progress: An Inquiry into Its Origin and Growth*. London: Macmillan and Co., 1921, p. 4.

nied the individual's capacity for improving his human nature, Niebuhr believed that individuals are capable of improvement but that the societies in which they live are manifestly *in*capable. We conclude with Robert Heilbroner's "Final Reflections on the Human Prospect," a 20th century response to Condorcet. Like the French philosopher, Heilbroner takes stock of the past, measures it against what we have achieved and failed to achieve in the present, and offers a prognosis for the future — a future considerably different from the hopeful one imagined during the Enlightenment.

MARQUIS DE CONDORCET
(1743–1794)

Marie Jean Antoine Nicolas Caritat, marquis de Condorcet, was born on September 17, 1743. Raised a pious Catholic, he later declared himself an atheist and held that the salvation of the human race lies not in the hands of Providence but in *mortal* hands. In his fifty-one years he led a distinguished life in mathematics, political theory, and social reform — the culmination of his work occurring with key events of the French Revolution, which he believed would usher in an age of progressive reform. Condorcet was the biographer and friend of Voltaire and Turgot — an influential economist and statesman charged (briefly) by Louis XVI to reform the ailing administration of the monarchy. Condorcet was also a protégé of Jean d'Alembert, principal editor of the *Encyclopédie* — an essential document of Enlightenment literature that helped to advance the cause of skeptical and rational inquiry. Condorcet's abilities in mathematics earned him, with the help of d'Alembert, an appointment as permanent secretary to the prestigious Academy of Sciences. He is best remembered for his *Sketch for a Historical Picture of the Progress of the Human Mind,* written while in hiding from the directors of the revolution.

The French Revolution was a long and tumultuous struggle to break free of the *ancien régime* — the feudal power sharing of monarch, landed aristocracy, and clergy — and establish an egalitarian society in which the privileges of birth were abolished. Under the reign of Louis XVI, deep antagonisms destabilized the French government: nobility began agitating for greater political power; the rising middle class, impressed with the success of the American Revolution, was growing restless with monarchial incompetence; peasants in the countryside chafed against continued poverty. By 1787, opposition united against the King and the *ancien régime*. The writers of the French Enlightenment called for a society founded on reason, in which the people — equal under the eye of the law — would be sovereign.

As a pamphleteer, Condorcet supported these objectives. In *On the Influence of the American Revolution on Europe* (1786), he wrote enthusiastically for inalienable rights guaranteed by a written declaration. Condorcet is regarded as a father of modern social science because he attempted to apply the exactitude of the natural sciences (mathematics, in particular) to the social affairs of men and women — specifically, in the area of government. In 1792, with the revolution fully under way, he was elected to a committee responsible for drafting a constitution. Condorcet set to work, attempting to apply lifelong commitments to equality and the virtues of rational thought to a document that could guide the French nation. But in the political wranglings that followed, the plan he devised (allowing for local assemblies and a national, unicameral assembly) was defeated by the Jacobins, who soon condemned Condorcet as an outlaw for vehemently protesting their rise to power and suspecting them of an extremism that would itself become a new tyranny for the people.

Condorcet's suspicions were all too prescient. He went into hiding and, within a year, was discovered. Two days after his arrest he was found dead in his prison cell, perhaps poisoned by his own hand. Condorcet did not live to see the revolution completed. As it turned out, the critics who had united in their opposition against the *ancien régime* could not create an effective replacement. In 1791, a constitution was written, only to be discarded a year later. Louis XVI was executed in 1793, and there followed a Reign of Terror in which alleged counterrevolutionaries (some of whom were champions of earlier reform) were arrested and murdered. To divert attention from domestic woes, wars were waged against the rest of Europe and Russia. Napoleon rose to power and established a military dictatorship. And those who had initially supported the revolution, applauding its rationalist sentiments and soaring defense of equality, turned away in horror at the prospect of an enterprise begun so nobly and ended so murderously.

Condorcet did not see these excesses, and his *Sketch for a Historical Picture of the Progress of the Human Mind,* written while he was in hiding from the Jacobins, does not reflect the darker nature of man evidenced through their later acts. Rather, the *Sketch* was written in the spirit of the "Declaration of the Rights of Man and Citizen" (see pages 253–254) adopted by the French National Assembly in 1789. Condorcet believed that the French Revolution could be guided by the rational principles of the Enlightenment and begin a new epoch in world history. In establishing a basis for this belief, he sought to sketch a history of human life to the present. Based upon lessons drawn from the past, he could extrapolate to the future. His *Sketch* was written in ten sections, or epochs, each corresponding to a stage of human history. The Tenth Stage is reproduced below. A rationale of the preceding nine stages is offered by a modern translator and biographer of Condorcet, Keith Michael Baker:

> The aim of the *Sketch for a Historical Picture of the Progress of the Human Mind* was to reclaim man's past in order to demonstrate his power to control the future. This meant that it was necessary to see history as a truly human past, which is to say a secular past, the product of human action and interaction rather than of divine intervention and inspiration. This meant, too, that it was necessary to find a principle of order that would reveal an intelligible past, the orderly creation of men rather than the haphazard product of chance and circumstance. . . . The aim of the *Sketch* was less to explain the growth of reason itself — that growth was posited as natural — than to point to the destruction of the obstacles which had inhibited or distorted that growth. It was to demonstrate man's progressive emancipation, first from the arbitrary domination of his physical environment and then from the historical bondage of his own making.[1]

We begin with a section from the introduction to the *Sketch for a Historical Picture of the Progress of the Human Mind,* along with the complete final chapter of that

[1]Keith Michael Baker. *Condorcet: Selected Writings.* Indianapolis: Bobbs-Merrill, 1976, pp. xxxv–xxxvi.

work: "The Tenth Stage: The Future Progress of the Human Mind." As you are reading, realize that Condorcet completed only a sketch of the more detailed book he intended to write. This explains his use of the constructions "We shall prove" or "We shall show." His death six months after he had completed the *Sketch* obviously made such proofs impossible.

SKETCH FOR A HISTORICAL PICTURE OF THE PROGRESS OF THE HUMAN MIND

INTRODUCTION

Man is born with the ability to receive sensations; to perceive them and to distinguish between the various simple sensations of which they are composed; to remember, recognize and combine them; to compare these combinations; to apprehend what they have in common and the ways in which they differ; to attach signs to them all in order to recognize them more easily and to allow for the ready production of new combinations.   *1*

This faculty is developed in him through the action of external objects, that is to say, by the occurrence of certain composite sensations whose constancy or coherence in change are independent of him; through communication with other beings like himself; and finally through various artificial methods which these first developments have led him to invent.   *2*

Sensations are attended by pleasure or pain; and man for his part has the capacity to transform such momentary impressions into permanent feelings of an agreeable or disagreeable character, and then to experience these feelings when he either observes or recollects the pleasures and pains of other sentient beings.   *3*

Finally, as a consequence of this capacity and of his ability to form and combine ideas, there arise between him and his fellow-creatures ties of interest and duty, to which nature herself has wished to attach the most precious portion of our happiness and the most painful of our ills.   *4*

Marie Jean Antoine Nicolas Caritat, Marquis de Condorcet. "Introduction and The Tenth Stage: The Future Progress of the Human Mind" from *Sketch for a Historical Picture of the Progress of the Human Mind.* In *Condorcet: Selected Writings.* Ed., Keith Michael Baker. Indianapolis: Bobbs-Merrill, 1976, pp. 210–211, 258–281.

If one confines oneself to the study and observation of the general facts   5
and laws about the development of these faculties, considering only what
is common to all human beings, this science is called metaphysics. But if
one studies this development as it manifests itself in the inhabitants of a
certain area at a certain period of time and then traces it on from generation
to generation, one has the picture of the progress of the human mind. This
progress is subject to the same general laws that can be observed in the
development of the faculties of the individual, and it is indeed no more
than the sum of that development realized in a large number of individuals
joined together in society. What happens at any particular moment is the
result of what has happened at all previous moments, and itself has an
influence on what will happen in the future.

So such a picture is historical, since it is a record of change and is based   6
on the observation of human societies throughout the different stages of
their development. It ought to reveal the order of this change and the influence that each moment exerts upon the subsequent moment, and so
ought also to show, in the modifications that the human species has undergone, ceaselessly renewing itself through the immensity of the centuries,
the path that it has followed, the steps that it has made toward truth or
happiness.

Such observations upon what man has been and what he is today, will   7
instruct us about the means we should employ to make certain and rapid
the further progress that his nature allows him still to hope for.

Such is the aim of the work that I have undertaken, and its result will   8
be to show by appeal to reason and fact that nature has set no term to the
perfection of human faculties; that the perfectibility of man is truly indefinite; and that the progress of this perfectibility, from now onwards independent of any power that might wish to halt it, has no other limit than
the duration of the globe upon which nature has cast us. This progress will
doubtless vary in speed, but it will never be reversed as long as the earth
occupies its present place in the system of the universe, and as long as the
general laws of this system produce neither a general cataclysm nor such
changes as will deprive the human race of its present faculties and its present resources.

THE TENTH STAGE: THE FUTURE PROGRESS
OF THE HUMAN MIND

If man can, with almost complete assurance, predict phenomena when   9
he knows their laws, and if, even when he does not, he can still, with great
expectation of success, forecast the future on the basis of his experience of
the past, why, then, should it be regarded as a fantastic undertaking to
sketch, with some pretense to truth, the future destiny of man on the basis
of his history? The sole foundation for belief in the natural sciences is this

idea, that the general laws directing the phenomena of the universe, known or unknown, are necessary and constant. Why should this principle be any less true for the development of the intellectual and moral faculties of man than for the other operations of nature? Since beliefs founded on past experience of like conditions provide the only rule of conduct for the wisest of men, why should the philosopher be forbidden to base his conjectures on these same foundations, so long as he does not attribute to them a certainty superior to that warranted by the number, the constancy, and the accuracy of his observations?

Our hopes for the future condition of the human race can be subsumed 10 under three important heads: the abolition of inequality between nations, the progress of equality within each nation, and the true perfection of mankind. Will all nations one day attain that state of civilization which the most enlightened, the freest, and the least burdened by prejudices, such as the French and the Anglo-Americans, have attained already? Will the vast gulf that separates these peoples from the slavery of nations under the rule of monarchs, from the barbarism of African tribes, from the ignorance of savages, little by little disappear?

Is there on the face of the earth a nation whose inhabitants have been 11 debarred by nature herself from the enjoyment of freedom and the exercise of reason?

Are those differences which have hitherto been seen in every civilized 12 country in respect of the enlightenment, the resources, and the wealth enjoyed by the different classes into which it is divided, is that inequality between men which was aggravated or perhaps produced by the earliest progress of society, are these part of civilization itself, or are they due to the present imperfections of the social art? Will they necessarily decrease and ultimately make way for a real equality, the final end of the social art, in which even the effects of the natural differences between men will be mitigated and the only kind of inequality to persist will be that which is in the interests of all and which favors the progress of civilization, of education, and of industry, without entailing either poverty, humiliation, or dependence? In other words, will men approach a condition in which everyone will have the knowledge necessary to conduct himself in the ordinary affairs of life, according to the light of his own reason, to preserve his mind free from prejudice, to understand his rights and to exercise them in accordance with his conscience and his creed; in which everyone will become able, through the development of his faculties, to find the means of providing for his needs; and in which at last misery and folly will be the exception, and no longer the habitual lot of a section of society?

Is the human race to better itself, either by discoveries in the sciences 13 and the arts, and so in the means to individual welfare and general prosperity; or by progress in the principles of conduct or practical morality; or by a true perfection of the intellectual, moral, or physical faculties of man, an improvement which may result from a perfection either of the instruments used to heighten the intensity of these faculties and to direct their use or of the natural constitution of man?

In answering these three questions we shall find in the experience of *14* the past, in the observation of the progress that the sciences and civilization have already made, in the analysis of the progress of the human mind and of the development of its faculties, the strongest reasons for believing that nature has set no limit to the realization of our hopes.

If we glance at the state of the world today we see first of all that in *15* Europe the principles of the French constitution are already those of all enlightened men. We see them too widely propagated, too seriously professed, for priests and despots to prevent their gradual penetration even into the hovels of their slaves; there they will soon awaken in these slaves the remnants of their common sense and inspire them with that smoldering indignation which not even constant humiliation and fear can smother in the soul of the oppressed.

As we move from nation to nation, we can see in each what special *16* obstacles impede this revolution and what attitudes of mind favor it. We can distinguish the nations where we may expect it to be introduced gently by the perhaps belated wisdom of their governments, and those nations where its violence intensified by their resistance must involve all alike in a swift and terrible convulsion.

Can we doubt that either common sense or the senseless discords of *17* European nations will add to the effects of the slow but inexorable progress of their colonies, and will soon bring about the independence of the New World? And then will not the European population in these colonies, spreading rapidly over that enormous land, either civilize or peacefully remove the savage nations who still inhabit vast tracts of its land?

Survey the history of our settlements[1] and commercial undertakings in *18* Africa or in Asia, and you will see how our trade monopolies, our treachery, our murderous contempt for men of another color or creed, the insolence of our usurpations, the intrigues or the exaggerated proselytic zeal of our priests, have destroyed the respect and good-will that the superiority of our knowledge and the benefits of our commerce at first won for us in the eyes of the inhabitants. But doubtless the moment approaches when, no longer presenting ourselves as always either tyrants or corrupters, we shall become for them the beneficent instruments of their freedom.

The sugar industry, establishing itself throughout the immense conti- *19*

---

[1]*History of our settlements:* The practice of colonizing foreign territories to take advantage of abundant resources and inexpensive labor became increasingly popular in the 18th century as Europeans developed a taste for imported goods. France established a number of colonies in Africa and Asia, funding and overseeing the production of sugar, coffee, tobacco, and cotton cloth. Though these settlements brought great profit to their foreign investors, they typically exploited the native work force and indigenous cultures.

nent of Africa, will destroy the shameful exploitation which has corrupted and depopulated that continent for the last two centuries.

Already in Great Britain, friends of humanity have set us an example; and if the Machiavellian government of that country has been restrained by public opinion from offering any opposition, what may we not expect of this same spirit, once the reform of a servile and venal constitution has led to a government worthy of a humane and generous nation? Will not France hasten to imitate such undertakings dictated by philanthropy and the true self-interest of Europe alike? Trading stations have been set up in the French islands, in Guiana, and in some English possessions, and soon we shall see the downfall of the monopoly that the Dutch have sustained with so much treachery, persecution, and crime. The nations of Europe will finally learn that monopolistic companies are nothing more than a tax imposed upon them in order to provide their governments with a new instrument of tyranny.

So the peoples of Europe, confining themselves to free trade, understanding their own rights too well to show contempt for those of other peoples, will respect this independence, which until now they have so insolently violated. Their settlements, no longer filled with government hirelings hastening, under the cloak of place or privilege, to amass treasure by brigandry and deceit, so as to be able to return to Europe and purchase titles and honor, will now be peopled with men of industrious habit, seeking in these propitious climates the wealth that eluded them at home. The love of freedom will retain them there, ambition will no longer recall them, and what have been no better than the counting-houses of brigands will become colonies of citizens propagating throughout Africa and Asia the principles and the practice of liberty, knowledge, and reason that they have brought from Europe. We shall see the monks who brought only shameful superstition to these peoples and aroused their antagonism by the threat of yet another tyranny, replaced by men occupied in propagating among them the truths that will promote their happiness and in teaching them about their interests and their rights. Zeal for the truth is also one of the passions, and it will turn its efforts to distant lands, once there are no longer at home any crass prejudices to combat, any shameful errors to dissipate.

These vast lands are inhabited partly by large tribes who need only assistance from us to become civilized, who wait only to find brothers among the European nations to become their friends and pupils; partly by races oppressed by sacred despots or dull-witted conquerors, and who for so many centuries have cried out to be liberated; partly by tribes living in a condition of almost total savagery in a climate whose harshness repels the sweet blessings of civilization and deters those who would teach them its benefits; and finally, by conquering hordes who know no other law but force, no other profession but piracy. The progress of these two last classes of people will be slower and stormier; and perhaps it will even be that, reduced in number as they are driven back by civilized nations, they will finally disappear imperceptibly before them or merge into them.

We shall point out how these events will be the inevitable result not merely of the progress of Europe but also of the freedom that the French and the North American Republics can, and in their own real interest should, grant to the trade of Africa and Asia; and how they must of necessity be born either of a new-found wisdom on the part of the European nations, or of their obstinate attachment to mercantilist prejudices. [23]

We shall show that there is only one event, a new invasion of Asia by the Tartars,[2] that could prevent this revolution, and that this event is now impossible. Meanwhile everything forecasts the imminent decadence of the great religions of the East, which in most countries have been made over to the people, and, not uncontaminated by the corruption of their ministers, are in some already regarded by the ruling classes as mere political inventions; in consequence of which they are now powerless to retain human reason in hopeless bondage, in eternal infancy. [24]

The progress of these peoples is likely to be more rapid and certain than our own because they can receive from us everything that we have had to find out for ourselves, and in order to understand those simple truths and infallible methods which we have acquired only after long error, all that they need to do is to follow the expositions and proofs that appear in our speeches and writings. If the progress of the Greeks was lost to later nations, this was because of the absence of any form of communication between the different peoples, and for this we must blame the tyrannical domination of the Romans. But when mutual needs have brought all men together, and the great powers have established equality between societies as well as between individuals and have raised respect for the independence of weak states and sympathy for ignorance and misery to the rank of political principles, when maxims that favor action and energy have ousted those which would compress the province of human faculties, will it then be possible to fear that there are still places in the world inaccessible to enlightenment, or that despotism in its pride can raise barriers against truth that are insurmountable for long? [25]

The time will therefore come when the sun will shine only on free men who know no other master but their reason; when tyrants and slaves, priests and their stupid or hypocritical instruments will exist only in works of history and on the stage; and when we shall think of them only to pity their victims and their dupes; to maintain ourselves in a state of vigilance by thinking on their excesses; and to learn how to recognize and so to [26]

---

[2]*Tartars:* Called Tartars by Europeans (meaning "hordes of death" from the Greek Tartarus), these Turkish-speaking peoples followed the conquests of the famed warriors Attila the Hun (406?–453) and Genghis Khan (1167?–1227). Today the Tartars form a small, autonomous Soviet Socialist Republic on the north shore of the Black Sea.

destroy, by force of reason, the first seeds of tyranny and superstition, should they ever dare to reappear among us.

In looking at the history of societies we shall have had occasion to observe that there is often a great difference between the rights that the law allows its citizens and the rights that they actually enjoy, and, again, between the equality established by political codes and that which in fact exists among individuals: and we shall have noticed that these differences were one of the principal causes of the destruction of freedom in the ancient republics, of the storms that troubled them, and of the weakness that delivered them over to foreign tyrants.   *27*

These differences have three main causes: inequality in wealth; inequality in status between the man whose means of subsistence are hereditary and the man whose means are dependent on the length of his life, or, rather, on that part of his life in which he is capable of work; and, finally, inequality in education.   *28*

We therefore need to show that these three sorts of real inequality must constantly diminish without however disappearing altogether: for they are the result of natural and necessary causes which it would be foolish and dangerous to wish to eradicate; and one could not even attempt to bring about the entire disappearance of their effects without introducing even more fecund sources of inequality, without striking more direct and more fatal blows at the rights of man.   *29*

It is easy to prove that wealth has a natural tendency to equality, and that any excessive disproportion could not exist or at least would rapidly disappear if civil laws did not provide artificial ways of perpetuating and uniting fortunes; if free trade and industry were allowed to remove the advantages that accrued wealth derives from any restrictive law or fiscal privilege; if taxes on covenants, the restrictions placed on their free employment, their subjection to tiresome formalities, and the uncertainty and inevitable expense involved in implementing them did not hamper the activity of the poor man and swallow up his meager capital; if the administration of the country did not afford some men ways of making their fortune that were closed to other citizens; if prejudice and avarice, so common in old age, did not preside over the making of marriages; and if, in a society enjoying simpler manners and more sensible institutions, wealth ceased to be a means of satisfying vanity and ambition, and if the equally misguided notions of austerity, which condemn spending money in the cultivation of the more delicate pleasures, no longer insisted on the hoarding of all one's earnings.   *30*

Let us turn to the enlightened nations of Europe, and observe the size of their present populations in relation to the size of their territories. Let us consider, in agriculture and industry the proportion that holds between labor and the means of subsistence, and we shall see that it would be impossible for those means to be kept at their present level and consequently   *31* for the population to be kept at its present size if a great number of individuals were not almost entirely dependent for the maintenance of themselves and their family either on their own labor or on the interest from capital invested so as to make their labor more productive. Now both these sources of income depend on the life and even on the health of the head of the family. They provide what is rather like a life annuity, save that it is more dependent on chance; and in consequence there is a very real difference between people living like this and those whose resources are not at all subject to the same risks, who live either on revenue from land, or on the interest on capital which is almost independent of their own labor.

Here then is a necessary cause of inequality, of dependence, and even 32 of misery, which ceaselessly threatens the most numerous and most active class in our society.

We shall point out how it can be in great part eradicated by guarantee- 33 ing people in old age a means of livelihood produced partly by their own savings and partly by the savings of others who make the same outlay, but who die before they need to reap the reward; or, again, on the same principle of compensation, by securing for widows and orphans an income which is the same and costs the same for those families which suffer an early loss and for those which suffer it later; or again by providing all children with the capital necessary for the full use of their labor, available at the age when they start work and found a family, a capital which increases at the expense of those whom premature death prevents from reaching this age. It is to the application of the calculus to the probabilities of life and the investment of money that we owe the idea of these methods which have already been successful, although they have not been applied in a sufficiently comprehensive and exhaustive fashion to render them really useful, not merely to a few individuals, but to society as a whole, by making it possible to prevent those periodic disasters which strike at so many families and which are such a recurrent source of misery and suffering.

We shall point out that schemes of this nature, which can be organized 34 in the name of the social authority and become one of its greatest benefits, can also be the work of private associations, which will be formed without any real risk, once the principles for the proper working of these schemes have been widely diffused and the mistakes which have been the undoing of a large number of these associations no longer hold terrors for us.

[We shall reveal other methods of ensuring this equality, either by 35 seeing that credit is no longer the exclusive privilege of great wealth, but that it has another and no less sound foundation; or by making industrial progress and commercial activity more independent of the existence of the great capitalists. And once again, it is to the application of the calculus that we shall be indebted for such methods.]

The degree of equality in education that we can reasonably hope to 36 attain, but that should be adequate, is that which excludes all dependence, either forced or voluntary. We shall show how this condition can be easily attained in the present state of human knowledge even by those who can study only for a small number of years in childhood, and then during the rest of their life in their few hours of leisure. We shall prove that, by a suitable choice of syllabus and of methods of education, we can teach the citizen everything that he needs to know in order to be able to manage his household, administer his affairs, and employ his labor and his faculties in freedom; to know his rights and to be able to exercise them; to be acquainted with his duties and fulfill them satisfactorily; to judge his own and other men's actions according to his own lights and to be a stranger to none of the high and delicate feelings which honor human nature; not to be in a state of blind dependence upon those to whom he must entrust his affairs or the exercise of his rights; to be in a proper condition to choose and supervise them; to be no longer the dupe of those popular errors which torment man with superstitious fears and chimerical hopes; to defend himself against prejudice by the strength of his reason alone; and, finally, to escape the deceits of charlatans who would lay snares for his fortune, his health, his freedom of thought, and his conscience under the pretext of granting him health, wealth, and salvation.

From such time onwards the inhabitants of a single country will no longer be distinguished by their use of a crude or refined language; they will be able to govern themselves according to their own knowledge; they will no longer be limited to a mechanical knowledge of the procedures of the arts or of professional routine; they will no longer depend for every trivial piece of business, every insignificant matter of instruction on clever men who rule over them in virtue of their necessary superiority; and so they will attain a real equality, since differences in enlightenment or talent can no longer raise a barrier between men who understand each other's feelings, ideas, and language, some of whom may wish to be taught by others but, to do so, will have no need to be controlled by them, or who may wish to confide the care of government to the ablest of their number but will not be compelled to yield them absolute power in a spirit of blind confidence. 37

This kind of supervision has advantages even for those who do not exercise it, since it is employed for them and not against them. Natural differences of ability between men whose understanding has not been cultivated give rise, even in savage tribes, to charlatans and dupes, to clever men and men readily deceived. These same differences are truly universal, but now they are differences only between men of learning and upright men who know the value of learning without being dazzled by it; or between talent or genius and the common sense which can appreciate and benefit from them; so that even if these natural differences were greater, and more extensive than they are, they would be only the more influential in improving the relations between men and promoting what is advantageous for their independence and happiness. 38

These various causes of equality do not act in isolation; they unite, 39 combine, and support each other and so their cumulative effects are stronger, surer, and more constant. With greater equality of education there will be greater equality in industry and so in wealth; equality in wealth necessarily leads to equality in education: and equality between the nations and equality within a single nation are mutually dependent.

So we might say that a well-directed system of education rectifies nat-   40
ural inequality in ability instead of strengthening it, just as good laws remedy natural inequality in the means of subsistence, and just as in societies where laws have brought about this same equality, liberty, though subject to a regular constitution, will be more widespread, more complete than in the total independence of savage life. Then the social art will have fulfilled its aim, that of assuring and extending to all men enjoyment of the common rights to which they are called by nature.

The real advantages that should result from this progress, of which we   41
can entertain a hope that is almost a certainty, can have no other term than that of the absolute perfection of the human race; since, as the various kinds of equality come to work in its favor by producing ampler sources of supply, more extensive education, more complete liberty, so equality will be more real and will embrace everything which is really of importance for the happiness of human beings.

It is therefore only by examining the progress and the laws of this per-   42
fection that we shall be able to understand the extent or the limits of our hopes.

No one has ever believed that the mind can gain knowledge of all the   43
facts of nature or attain the ultimate means of precision in the measurement or in the analysis of the facts of nature, the relations between objects, and all the possible combinations of ideas. Even the relations between magnitudes, the mere notion of quantity or extension, taken in its fullest comprehension, gives rise to a system so vast that it will never be mastered by the human mind in its entirety, that there will always be a part of it, always indeed the larger part of it that will remain forever unknown. People have believed that man can never know more than a part of the objects that the nature of his intelligence allows him to understand, and that he must in the end arrive at a point where the number and complexity of the objects that he already knows have absorbed all his strength so that any further progress must be completely impossible.

But since, as the number of known facts increases, the human mind   44
learns how to classify them and to subsume them under more general facts, and, at the same time, the instruments and methods employed in their observation and their exact measurement acquire a new precision; since, as more relations between various objects become known, man is able to reduce them to more general relations, to express them more simply, and to present them in such a way that it is possible to grasp a greater

number of them with the same degree of intellectual ability and the same amount of application; since, as the mind learns to understand more complicated combinations of ideas, simpler formulae soon reduce their complexity; so truths that were discovered only by great effort, that could at first only be understood by men capable of profound thought, are soon developed and proved by methods that are not beyond the reach of common intelligence. If the methods which have led to these new combinations of ideas are ever exhausted, if their application to hitherto unsolved questions should demand exertions greater than either the time or the capacity of the learned would permit, some method of a greater generality or simplicity will be found so that genius can continue undisturbed on its path. The strength and the limits of man's intelligence may remain unaltered; and yet the instruments that he uses will increase and improve, the language that fixes and determines his ideas will acquire greater breadth and precision and, unlike mechanics where an increase of force means a decrease of speed, the methods that lead genius to the discovery of truth increase at once the force and the speed of its operations.

Therefore, since these developments are themselves the necessary con- 45 sequences of progress in detailed knowledge, and since the need for new methods in fact only arises in circumstances that give rise to new methods, it is evident that, within the body of the sciences of observation, calculation, and experiment, the actual number of truths may always increase, and that every part of this body may develop, and yet man's faculties be of the same strength, activity, and extent.

If we apply these general reflections to the various sciences, we can 46 find in each of them examples of progressive improvement that will remove any doubts about what we may expect for the future. We shall point out in particular the progress that is both likely and imminent in those sciences which prejudice regards as all but exhausted. We shall give examples of the manner and extent of the precision and unity which could accrue to the whole system of human knowledge as the result of a more general and philosophical application of the sciences of calculation to the various branches of knowledge. We shall show how favorable to our hopes would be a more universal system of education by giving a greater number of people the elementary knowledge which could awaken their interest in a particular branch of study, and by providing conditions favorable to their progress in it; and how these hopes would be further raised, if more men possessed the means to devote themselves to these studies, for at present even in the most enlightened countries scarcely one in fifty of the people who have natural talents, receives the necessary education to develop them; and how, if this were done there would be a proportionate increase in the number of men destined by their discoveries to extend the boundaries of science.

We shall show how this equality in education and the equality which 47 will come about between the different nations would accelerate the advance of these sciences whose progress depends on repeated observations over a large area; what benefits would thereby accrue to mineralogy, botany, zoology, and meteorology; and what a vast disproportion holds in all these sciences between the poverty of existing methods which have nevertheless led to useful and important new truths, and the wealth of those methods which man would then be able to employ.

We shall show how even the sciences in which discovery is the fruit of   48
solitary meditation would benefit from being studied by a greater number of people, in the matter of these improvements in detail which do not demand the intellectual energy of an inventor but suggest themselves to mere reflection.

If we turn now to the arts, whose theory depends on these same sci-   49
ences, we shall find that their progress, depending as it does on that of theory, can have no other limits; that the procedures of the different arts can be perfected and simplified in the same way as the methods of the sciences; new instruments, machines, and looms can add to man's strength and can improve at once the quality and the accuracy of his productions, and can diminish the time and labor that has to be expended on them. The obstacles still in the way of this progress will disappear, accidents will be foreseen and prevented, the insanitary conditions that are due either to the work itself or to the climate will be eliminated.

A very small amount of ground will be able to produce a great quantity   50
of supplies of greater utility or higher quality; more goods will be obtained for a smaller outlay; the manufacture of articles will be achieved with less wastage in raw materials and will make better use of them. Every type of soil will produce those things which satisfy the greatest number of needs; of several alternative ways of satisfying needs of the same order, that will be chosen which satisfies the greatest number of people and which requires least labor and least expenditure. So, without the need for sacrifice, methods of preservation and economy in expenditure will improve in the wake of progress in the arts of producing and preparing supplies and making articles from them.

So not only will the same amount of ground support more people, but   51
everyone will have less work to do, will produce more and satisfy his wants more fully.

With all this progress in industry and welfare which establishes a hap-   52
pier proportion between men's talents and their needs, each successive generation will have larger possessions, either as a result of this progress or through the preservation of the products of industry; and so, as a consequence of the physical constitution of the human race, the number of people will increase. Might there not then come a moment when these necessary laws begin to work in a contrary direction; when, the number of people in the world finally exceeding the means of subsistence, there will

in consequence ensue a continual diminution of happiness and population, a true retrogression, or at best an oscillation between good and bad? In societies that have reached this stage will not this oscillation be a perennial source of more or less periodic disaster? Will it not show that a point has been attained beyond which all further improvement is impossible, that the perfectibility of the human race has after long years arrived at a term beyond which it may never go?

There is doubtless no one who does not think that such a time is still   *53* very far from us; but will it ever arrive? It is impossible to pronounce about the likelihood of an event that will occur only when the human species will have necessarily acquired a degree of knowledge of which we can have no inkling. And who would take it upon himself to predict the condition to which the art of converting the elements to the use of man may in time be brought?

But even if we agree that the limit will one day arrive, nothing follows   *54* from it that is in the least alarming as far as either the happiness of the human race or its indefinite perfectibility is concerned; if we consider that, before all this comes to pass, the progress of reason will have kept pace with that of the sciences, and that the absurd prejudices of superstition will have ceased to corrupt and degrade the moral code by its harsh doctrines instead of purifying and elevating it, we can assume that by then men will know that, if they have a duty toward those who are not yet born, that duty is not to give them existence but to give them happiness; their aim should be to promote the general welfare of the human race or of the society in which they live or of the family to which they belong, rather than foolishly to encumber the world with useless and wretched beings. It is, then, possible that there should be a limit to the amount of food that can be produced, and, consequently, to the size of the population of the world, without this involving that untimely destruction of some of those creatures who have been given life, which is so contrary to nature and to social prosperity.

Since the discovery, or rather the exact analysis, of the first principles   *55* of metaphysics, morals, and politics is still recent and was preceded by the knowledge of a large number of detailed truths, the false notion that they have thereby attained their destination, has gained ready acceptance; men imagine that, because there are no more crude errors to refute, no more fundamental truths to establish, nothing remains to be done.

But it is easy to see how imperfect is the perfect analysis of man's moral   *56* and intellectual faculties; how much further the knowledge of his duties which presumes a knowledge of the influence of his actions upon the welfare of his fellow men and upon the society to which he belongs, can still be increased through a more profound, more accurate, more considered observation of that influence; how many questions have to be solved, how many social relations to be examined, before we can have precise knowledge of the individual rights of man and the rights that the state confers upon each in regard to all. Have we yet ascertained at all accurately the limits of the rights that exist between different societies in times of war, or that are enjoyed by society over its members in times of trouble and schism, or that belong to individuals, or spontaneous associations at the moment of their original, free formation or of their necessary disintegration?

If we pass on to the theory which ought to direct the application of *57* particular principles and serve as the foundation for the social art, do we not see the necessity of acquiring a precision that these elementary truths cannot possess so long as they are absolutely general? Have we yet reached the point when we can reckon as the only foundation of law either justice or a proved and acknowledged utility instead of the vague, uncertain, arbitrary views of alleged political expediency? Are we yet in possession of any precise rules for selecting out of the almost infinite variety of possible systems in which the general principles of equality and natural rights are respected, those which will best secure the preservation of these rights, which will afford the freest scope for their exercise and their enjoyment, and which will moreover insure the leisure and welfare of individuals and the strength, prosperity, and peace of nations?

The application of the calculus of combinations and probabilities to *58* these sciences promises even greater improvement, since it is the only way of achieving results of an almost mathematical exactitude and of assessing the degree of their probability or likelihood. Sometimes, it is true, the evidence upon which these results are based may lead us, without any calculation, at the first glance, to some general truth and teach us whether the effect produced by such-and-such a cause was or was not favorable, but if this evidence cannot be weighed and measured, and if these effects cannot be subjected to precise measurement, then we cannot know exactly how much good or evil they contain; or, again, if the good and evil nearly balance each other, if the difference between them is slight, we cannot pronounce with any certainty to which side the balance really inclines. Without the application of the calculus it would be almost impossible to choose with any certainty between two combinations that have the same purpose and between which there is no apparent difference in merit. Without the calculus these sciences would always remain crude and limited for want of instruments delicate enough to catch the fleeting truth, of machines precise enough to plumb the depths where so much that is of value to science lies hidden.

However, such an application, notwithstanding the happy efforts of *59* certain geometers, is still in its earliest stages: and it will be left to the generations to come to use this source of knowledge which is as inexhaustible as the calculus itself, or as the number of combinations, relations, and facts that may be included in its sphere of operation.

There is another kind of progress within these sciences that is no less 60 important; and that is the perfection of scientific language which is at present so vague and obscure. This improvement could be responsible for making the sciences genuinely popular, even in their first rudiments. Genius can triumph over the inexactitude of language as over other obstacles and can recognize the truth through the strange mask that hides or disguises it. But how can someone with only a limited amount of leisure to devote to his education master and retain even the simplest truths if they are distorted by an imprecise language? The fewer the ideas that he is able to acquire and combine, the more necessary is it that they should be precise and exact. He has no fund of knowledge stored up in his mind which he can draw upon to protect himself from error, and his understanding, not being strengthened and refined by long practice, cannot catch such feeble rays of light as manage to penetrate the obscurities, the ambiguities of an imperfect and perverted language.

Until men progress in the practice as well as in the science of morality, 61 it will be impossible for them to attain any insight into either the nature and development of the moral sentiments, the principles of morality, the natural motives that prompt their actions, or their own true interests either as individuals or as members of society. Is not a mistaken sense of interest the most common cause of actions contrary to the general welfare? Is not the violence of our passions often the result either of habits that we have adopted through miscalculation, or of our ignorance how to restrain them, tame them, deflect them, rule them?

Is not the habit of reflection upon conduct, of listening to the deliver- 62 ances of reason and conscience upon it, of exercising those gentle feelings which identify our happiness with that of others, the necessary consequence of a well-planned study of morality and of a greater equality in the conditions of the social pact? Will not the free man's sense of his own dignity and a system of education built upon a deeper knowledge of our moral constitution, render common to almost every man those principles of strict and unsullied justice, those habits of an active and enlightened benevolence, of a fine and generous sensibility which nature has implanted in the hearts of all and whose flowering waits only upon the favorable influences of enlightenment and freedom? Just as the mathematical and physical sciences tend to improve the arts that we use to satisfy our simplest needs, is it not also part of the necessary order of nature that the moral and political sciences should exercise a similar influence upon the motives that direct our feelings and our actions?

What are we to expect from the perfection of laws and public institu- 63 tions, consequent upon the progress of those sciences, but the reconciliation, the identification of the interests of each with the interests of all? Has the social art any other aim save that of destroying their apparent opposition? Will not a country's constitution and laws accord best with the rights of reason and nature when the path of virtue is no longer arduous and when the temptations that lead men from it are few and feeble?

Is there any vicious habit, any practice contrary to good faith, any   *64* crime, whose origin and first cause cannot be traced back to the legislation, the institutions, the prejudices of the country wherein this habit, this practice, this crime can be observed? In short will not the general welfare that results from the progress of the useful arts once they are grounded on solid theory, or from the progress of legislation once it is rooted in the truths of political science, incline mankind to humanity, benevolence, and justice? In other words, do not all these observations which I propose to develop further in my book, show that the moral goodness of man, the necessary consequence of his constitution, is capable of indefinite perfection like all his other faculties, and that nature has linked together in an unbreakable chain truth, happiness, and virtue?

Among the causes of the progress of the human mind that are of the   *65* utmost importance to the general happiness, we must number the complete annihilation of the prejudices that have brought about an inequality of rights between the sexes, an inequality fatal even to the party in whose favor it works. It is vain for us to look for a justification of this principle in any differences of physical organization, intellect, or moral sensibility between men and women. This inequality has its origin solely in an abuse of strength, and all the later sophistical attempts that have been made to excuse it are vain.

We shall show how the abolition of customs authorized, laws dictated   *66* by this prejudice, would add to the happiness of family life, would encourage the practice of the domestic virtues on which all other virtues are based, how it would favor the progress of education, and how, above all, it would bring about its wider diffusion; for not only would education be extended to women as well as to men, but it can only really be taken proper advantage of when it has the support and encouragement of the mothers of the family. Would not this belated tribute to equity and good sense put an end to a principle only too fecund of injustice, cruelty, and crime, by removing the dangerous conflict between the strongest and more irrepressible of all natural inclinations and man's duty or the interests of society? Would it not produce what has until now been no more than a dream, national manners of a mildness and purity, formed not by proud asceticism, not by hypocrisy, not by the fear of shame or religious terrors but by freely contracted habits that are inspired by nature and acknowledged by reason?

Once people are enlightened they will know that they have the right   *67* to dispose of their own life and wealth as they choose; they will gradually learn to regard war as the most dreadful of scourges, the most terrible of crimes. The first wars to disappear will be those into which usurpers have forced their subjects in defense of their pretended hereditary rights.

Nations will learn that they cannot conquer other nations without los-   *68*
ing their own liberty; that permanent confederations are their only means
of preserving their independence; and that they should seek not power
but security. Gradually mercantile prejudices will fade away: and a false
sense of commercial interest will lose the fearful power it once had of
drenching the earth in blood and of ruining nations under pretext of en-
riching them. When at last the nations come to agree on the principles of
politics and morality, when in their own better interests they invite foreigners to share equally in all the benefits men enjoy either through the
bounty of nature or by their own industry, then all the causes that produce
and perpetuate national animosities and poison national relations will disappear one by one; and nothing will remain to encourage or even to arouse
the fury of war.

Organizations more intelligently conceived than those projects of eter-   *69*
nal peace which have filled the leisure and consoled the hearts of certain
philosophers, will hasten the progress of the brotherhood of nations, and
wars between countries will rank with assassinations as freakish atrocities,
humiliating and vile in the eyes of nature and staining with indelible op-
probrium the country or the age whose annals record them.

When we spoke of the fine arts in Greece, Italy, and France, we ob-   *70*
served that it was necessary to distinguish in artistic productions between
what belonged properly to the progress of the art itself and what was due
only to the talent of the individual artist. We shall here indicate what progress may still be expected in the arts as a result of the progress in philosophy and the sciences, of the increasing number of observations made
about the aim, effects, and methods of the arts, of the destruction of those
prejudices which have formerly narrowed their sphere and even now hold
them within the shackles of authority, shackles that science and philosophy have broken. We shall ask, whether, as some have thought, these
means are exhausted, and the arts condemned to an eternal, monotonous
imitation of their first models since the most sublime and moving beauty
has already been apprehended, the happiest subjects treated, the simplest
and most arresting ideas used, the most marked or most generous characters delineated, the liveliest intrinsic passions and their truest or most
natural manifestations, the most striking truths and the most brilliant images already exploited.

We shall see that this opinion is a mere prejudice, born of the habit,   *71*
which is prevalent among artists and men of letters, of judging men, instead of enjoying their works. If the more reflective pleasure of comparing
the products of different ages and countries and admiring the success and
energy of the efforts of genius will probably be lost, the pleasure to be
derived from the actual contemplation of works of art as such will be just
as vivid as ever, even though the author may no longer deserve the same
credit for having achieved such perfection. As works of art genuinely wor-

thy of preservation increase in number, and become more perfect, each successive generation will devote its attention and admiration to those which really deserve preference, and the rest will unobtrusively fall into oblivion; the pleasure to be derived from the simpler, more striking, more accessible aspects of beauty will exist no less for posterity although they will be found only in the latest works.

The progress of the sciences ensures the progress of the art of educa- 72 tion which in turn advances that of the sciences. This reciprocal influence, whose activity is ceaselessly renewed, deserves to be seen as one of the most powerful and active causes working for the perfection of mankind. At the present time a young man on leaving school may know more of the principles of mathematics than Newton ever learned in years of study or discovered by dint of genius, and he may use the calculus with a facility then unknown. The same observation, with certain reservations, applies to all the sciences. As each advances, the methods of expressing a large number of proofs in a more economical fashion and so of making their comprehension an easier matter, advance with it. So, in spite of the prog- ress of science, not only do men of the same ability find themselves at the same age on a level with the existing state of science, but with every gen- eration, that which can be acquired in a certain time with a certain degree of intelligence and a certain amount of concentration will be permanently on the increase, and, as the elementary part of each science to which all men may attain grows and grows, it will more and more include all the knowledge necessary for each man to know for the conduct of the ordinary events of his life, and will support him in the free and independent exer- cise of his reason.

In the political sciences there are some truths that, with free people 73 (that is to say, with certain generations in all countries) can be of use only if they are widely known and acknowledged. So the influence of these sciences upon the freedom and prosperity of nations must in some degree be measured by the number of truths that, as a result of elementary in- struction, are common knowledge; the swelling progress of elementary in- struction, connected with the necessary progress of these sciences prom- ises us an improvement in the destiny of the human race, which may be regarded as indefinite, since it can have no other limits than that of this same progress.

We have still to consider two other general methods which will influ- 74 ence both the perfection of education and that of the sciences. One is the more extensive and less imperfect use of what we might call technical methods; the other is the setting up of a universal language.

I mean by technical methods the art of arranging a large number of 75 subjects in a system so that we may straightway grasp their relations, quickly perceive their combinations, and readily form new combinations out of them.

We shall develop the principles and examine the utility of this art, which is still in its infancy, and which, as it improves, will enable us, within the compass of a small chart, to set out what could possibly not be expressed so well in a whole book, or, what is still more valuable, to present isolated facts in such a way as to allow us to deduce their general consequences. We shall see how by means of a small number of these charts, whose use can easily be learned, men who have not been sufficiently educated to be able to absorb details useful to them in ordinary life, may now be able to master them when the need arises; and how these methods may likewise be of benefit to elementary education itself in all these branches where it is concerned either with a regular system of truths or with a series of observations and facts. [76]

A universal language is that which expresses by signs either real objects themselves, or well-defined collections composed of simple and general ideas, which are found to be the same or may arise in a similar form in the minds of all men, or the general relations holding between these ideas, the operations of the human mind, or the operations peculiar to the individual sciences, or the procedures of the arts. So people who become acquainted with these signs, the ways to combine them and the rules for forming them will understand what is written in this language and will be able to read it as easily as their own language. [77]

It is obvious that this language might be used to set out the theory of a science or the rules of an art, to describe a new observation or experiment, the invention of a procedure, the discovery of a truth or a method; and that, as in algebra, when one has to make use of a new sign, those already known provide the means of explaining its import. [78]

Such a language has not the disadvantages of a scientific idiom different from the vernacular. We have already observed that the use of such an idiom would necessarily divide society into two unequal classes, the one composed of men who, understanding this language, would possess the key to all the sciences, the other of men who, unable to acquire it, would therefore find themselves almost completely unable to acquire enlightenment. In contrast to this, a universal language would be learned, like that of algebra, along with the science itself; the sign would be learned at the same time as the object, idea, or operation that it designates. He who, having mastered the elements of a science, would like to know more of it, would find in books not only truths he could understand by means of the signs whose import he has learned, but also the explanation of such further signs as he needs in order to go on to other truths. [79]

We shall show that the formation of such a language, if confined to the expression of those simple, precise propositions which form the system of a science or the practice of an art, is no chimerical scheme; that even at the present time it could be readily introduced to deal with a large number of objects; and that, indeed, the chief obstacle that would prevent its exten- [80]

sion to others would be the humiliation of having to admit how very few precise ideas and accurate, unambiguous notions we actually possess.

We shall show that this language, ever improving and broadening its *81* scope all the while, would be the means of giving to every subject embraced by the human intelligence, a precision and a rigor that would make knowledge of the truth easy and error almost impossible. Then the progress of every science would be as sure as that of mathematics, and the propositions that compose it would acquire a geometrical certainty, as far, that is, as is possible granted the nature of its aim and method.

All the causes that contribute to the perfection of the human race, all *82* the means that ensure it must by their very nature exercise a perpetual influence and always increase their sphere of action. The proofs of this we have given and in the great work they will derive additional force from elaboration. We may conclude then that the perfectibility of man is indefinite. Meanwhile we have considered him as possessing the natural faculties and organization that he has at present. How much greater would be the certainty, how much vaster the scheme of our hopes if we could believe that these natural faculties themselves and this organization could also be improved? This is the last question that remains for us to ask ourselves.

Organic perfectibility or deterioration among the various strains in the *83* vegetable and animal kingdom can be regarded as one of the general laws of nature. This law also applies to the human race. No one can doubt that, as preventive medicine improves and food and housing become healthier, as a way of life is established that develops our physical powers by exercise without ruining them by excess, as the two most virulent causes of deterioration, misery and excessive wealth, are eliminated, the average length of human life will be increased and a better health and a stronger physical constitution will be ensured. The improvement of medical practice, which will become more efficacious with the progress of reason and of the social order, will mean the end of infectious and hereditary diseases and illnesses brought on by climate, food, or working conditions. It is reasonable to hope that all other diseases may likewise disappear as their distant causes are discovered. Would it be absurd then to suppose that this perfection of the human species might be capable of indefinite progress; that the day will come when death will be due only to extraordinary accidents or to the decay of the vital forces, and that ultimately the average span between birth and decay will have no assignable value? Certainly man will not become immortal, but will not the interval between the first breath that he draws and the time when in the natural course of events, without disease or accident, he expires, increase indefinitely? Since we are now speaking of a progress that can be represented with some accuracy in figures or on a graph, we shall take this opportunity of explaining the two meanings that can be attached to the word *indefinite.*

In truth, this average span of life which we suppose will increase in-   *84*
definitely as time passes, may grow in conformity either with a law such
that it continually approaches a limitless length but without ever reaching
it, or with a law such that through the centuries it reaches a length greater
than any determinate quantity that we may assign to it as its limit. In the
latter case such an increase is truly indefinite in the strictest sense of the
word, since there is no term on this side of which it must of necessity stop.
In the former case it is equally indefinite in relation to us, if we cannot fix
the limit it always approaches without ever reaching, and particularly if,
knowing only that it will never stop, we are ignorant in which of the two
senses the term "indefinite" can be applied to it. Such is the present condition of our knowledge as far as the perfectibility of the human race is
concerned; such is the sense in which we may call it indefinite.

So, in the example under consideration, we are bound to believe that   *85*
the average length of human life will forever increase unless this is prevented by physical revolutions; we do not know what the limit is which it
can never exceed. We cannot tell even whether the general laws of nature
have determined such a limit or not.

But are not our physical faculties and the strength, dexterity, and   *86*
acuteness of our senses, to be numbered among the qualities whose perfection in the individual may be transmitted? Observation of the various
breeds of domestic animals inclines us to believe that they are, and we can
confirm this by direct observation of the human race.

Finally may we not extend such hopes to the intellectual and moral   *87*
faculties? May not our parents, who transmit to us the benefits or disadvantages of their constitution, and from whom we receive our shape and
features, as well as our tendencies to certain physical affections, hand on
to us also that part of the physical organization which determines the intellect, the power of the brain, the ardor of the soul or the moral sensibility?
Is it not probable that education, in perfecting these qualities, will at the
same time influence, modify, and perfect the organization itself? Analogy,
investigation of the human faculties, and the study of certain facts, all seem
to give substance to such conjectures which would further push back the
boundaries of our hopes.

These are the questions with which we shall conclude this final stage.   *88*
How consoling for the philosopher who laments the errors, the crimes, the
injustices which still pollute the earth and of which he is often the victim
is this view of the human race, emancipated from its shackles, released
from the empire of fate and from that of the enemies of its progress, advancing with a firm and sure step along the path of truth, virtue, and happiness! It is the contemplation of this prospect that rewards him for all his
efforts to assist the progress of reason and the defense of liberty. He dares
to regard these strivings as part of the eternal chain of human destiny; and

in this persuasion he is filled with the true delight of virtue and the pleasure of having done some lasting good which fate can never destroy by a
sinister stroke of revenge, by calling back the reign of slavery and prejudice. Such contemplation is for him an asylum, in which the memory of
his persecutors cannot pursue him; there he lives in thought with man
restored to his natural rights and dignity, forgets man tormented and corrupted by greed, fear, or envy; there he lives with his peers in an Elysium
created by reason and graced by the purest pleasures known to the love of
mankind.

REVIEW QUESTIONS

1. In paragraphs 11, 12, and 13, Condorcet poses three questions. Paraphrase
   these questions.
2. What is Condorcet's opinion of missionaries, including priests and monks? Cite
   evidence for your answers.
3. What role did Condorcet believe European nations would play in spreading
   the lessons of the Enlightenment?
4. In the enlightened, future society, what will become of natural differences in
   intelligence?
5. What are the various causes of equality? How do they act in concert to achieve
   the great aims of the Enlightenment?
6. What is the faculty that allows the human mind, which is limited in its capacities, to assimilate ever-increasing amounts of knowledge?
7. Why is it that an increase in the world's population will not threaten "either
   the happiness of the human race or its perfectibility"?
8. What are Condorcet's views on the equality of the sexes?
9. What discoveries will lead to the cessation of wars and to a lasting peace among
   nations?
10. According to Condorcet, what (in his day) limited the development of a uni-
    versal language?

DISCUSSION AND WRITING QUESTIONS

1. In paragraph 41, Condorcet entertains "almost as a certainty" the idea that the
   human race will achieve perfection. Clearly the perfection he had in mind has
   not been achieved. Write a letter to Condorcet explaining why his program for
   perfectibility has not yet succeeded. Indicate whether or not you think it will
   ever succeed.
2. Take two of Condorcet's predictions. Explain how one of these was accurate,
   even inspired; explain how the other missed the mark. Then attempt to acount
   for the success and failure of these predictions.
3. Reread paragraphs 17–22. While Condorcet appears enlightened in one sense
   with respect to the influence of Europeans on non-European lands, he makes

several assumptions that would today be unacceptable to many. What are some of these assumptions?

4. Attempt to infer from Condorcet's writing just what the truth of the Enlightenment is that will spread around the world. In developing your answer, you may want to refer to paragraphs 25–26.

5. "It is easy to prove that wealth has a natural tendency to equality." What are Condorcet's reasons for making this statement? Given what you know of American history of the past 100 years, to what extent does the statement seem accurate?

6. In paragraph 33, Condorcet discusses a system that will ensure the elderly of a regular income. Compare Condorcet's system with the present social security system. Also compare Condorcet's thoughts on education (paragraph 36) with public education today. To what extent have we succeeded in meeting these two predictions?

7. Reread paragraph 61. To what extent do you think it feasible that a science of morality can be mastered and human motives understood? Take the additional step of speculating on teaching morality such that all people would develop habits of careful reflection and consideration for others. What complications can you imagine?

8. Reread paragraph 64, in which Condorcet declares his assumptions about the moral goodness of man. Discuss potential problems with this view.

9. "Nations will learn that they cannot conquer other nations without losing their own liberty" (paragraph 68). What does Condorcet mean here? Can you cite examples that prove his point?

10. Summarize Condorcet's ideas for a universal language. Do you find the concept desirable? Explain. Include in your answer the dangers that the designers of such a language would have to guard against. If time permits, research the efforts that have been made to achieve a universal language.

11. Condorcet's final image is one of an asylum, an Elysium in which the philosopher "forgets man tormented and corrupted by greed, fear, or envy. . . ." In what ways is Elysium a fitting metaphor for Condorcet's image of the future?

12. What is your final assessment of Condorcet's optimism?

THOMAS ROBERT MALTHUS
(1766–1834)

Thomas Robert Malthus, the British economist, is best known for *An Essay on the Principle of Population as It Affects the Future Improvement of Society* (1798). Written as a direct response to Condorcet's *Sketch for a Historical Picture of the Progress of the Human Mind* and William Godwin's similarly optimistic views on the perfectibility of man, Malthus's *Essay* explores the impact of population growth on the quality of life and reaches a startling conclusion: population tends to increase at a faster rate than the food supply; the future prospects for the human race, therefore, are bleak and will be characterized by famine, misery, and vice — that is, unless the population is held in check.

Malthus received his early education at home, near Guildford, Surrey, where his father and tutors prepared him for his entry into Jesus College, Cambridge. Excelling in Latin and Greek, he graduated with a degree in mathematics in 1788, the same year he was ordained as a clergyman of the Anglican church. Three years later he took a masters degree and in 1796 assumed the duties of a curate at Albury, Surrey.

Malthus gained immediate fame with the publication in 1798 of his *Essay on Population.* Prior to the *Essay,* economists had argued that an increase in population was beneficial to a country in that it would lead to expanded political power and to greater production and consumption — hence, to greater economic power. In addition, with the revolution in France under way, the air was filled with the optimistic fervor of Enlightenment philosophers such as Condorcet. And just five years before, William Godwin (an English philosopher) had written *Political Justice,* in which he expressed a faith similar to Condorcet's regarding the perfectibility of man. (See Godwin's biography and response to Malthus on pages 324–332.) Malthus doubted the basis for such optimism and responded with his argument on population: not only did he deny perfectibility, he predicted vice and misery. The law of increase was immutable and the prospect for humanity was necessarily bleak.

Little wonder that in attempting to refute the predictions of Condorcet and Godwin Malthus attracted considerable attention. In England, politicians began to invoke Malthus in their attacks on the poor laws, a system of state aid through which the poor received relief. According to the Malthusian argument, relief led to comfort, comfort to propagation, propagation to increased competition for scarce goods, and increased competition to greater misery. The surest remedy for these evils was to allow the afflicted to suffer and thereby convince themselves to decrease their numbers. In the Malthusian model, the poor were responsible for their own ills. Marx and Engels (among others) would later argue that poverty was institutional and that the capitalist system, *not* the indolence of individuals, was responsible for the plight of the poor. (See *The Communist Man.* 554–574.)

Another way in which Malthus influenced public debate was through the work of Charles Darwin, whose theories on the struggle for existence owed much to the *Essay on Population.* (See the section on Darwin, pages 414–435.) In our century, the influence of Malthus continues to be felt: the People's Republic of China, faced with certain famine if its population continues to grow, has mandated that no family can have more than one child. The modern assessment of Malthus is that he understood the pressures a burgeoning population would place on world resources but that he underestimated the ability of technology to increase agricultural yields.

The fame that his writing earned him gained Malthus the first chair of political economy at the East India College, where he spent the remainder of his career — revising the *Essay on Population* six times and publishing important new works: *An Inquiry into the Nature and Progress of Rent* (1815); and *Principles of Political Economy Considered with a View to Their Practical Applications* (1820). Malthus received numerous awards in his lifetime: he was elected a member of the Royal Society, the Political Economy Club, and the Royal Society of Literature. He died at the age of 68, in 1834.

The essential argument of *Essay on the Principles of Population as It Affects the Future Improvement of Society* is to be found in the first chapter, reprinted here.

AN ESSAY ON THE PRINCIPLE OF POPULATION

CHAPTER I

The great and unlooked for discoveries that have taken place of late years in natural philosophy, the increasing diffusion of general knowledge from the extension of the art of printing, the ardent and unshackled spirit of inquiry that prevails throughout the lettered and even unlettered world, the new and extraordinary lights that have been thrown on political subjects which dazzle and astonish the understanding, and particularly that tremendous phenomenon in the political horizon, the French revolution,[1] which, like a blazing comet, seems destined either to inspire with fresh life and vigour, or to scorch up and destroy the shrinking inhabitants of the earth, have all concurred to lead many able men into the opinion that we

Thomas Robert Malthus. "Chapter 1" in *An Essay on the Principle of Population* (A Norton Critical Edition). Ed., Phillip Appleman. New York: Norton, 1976, pp. 16–21.

[1]*The French Revolution:* (1789–1799) For information on the French Revolution, refer to the introduction to this chapter.

were touching on a period big with the most important changes, changes that would in some measure be decisive of the future fate of mankind.

It has been said that the great question is now at issue, whether man shall henceforth start forwards with accelerated velocity towards illimitable, and hitherto unconceived improvement, or be condemned to a perpetual oscillation between happiness and misery, and after every effort remain still at an immeasurable distance from the wished-for goal. 2

Yet, anxiously as every friend of mankind must look forwards to the termination of this painful suspense, and eagerly as the inquiring mind would hail every ray of light that might assist its view into futurity, it is much to be lamented that the writers on each side of this momentous question still keep far aloof from each other. Their mutual arguments do not meet with a candid examination. The question is not brought to rest on fewer points, and even in theory scarcely seems to be approaching to a decision. 3

The advocate for the present order of things is apt to treat the sect of speculative philosophers either as a set of artful and designing knaves who preach up ardent benevolence and draw captivating pictures of a happier state of society only the better to enable them to destroy the present establishments and to forward their own deep-laid schemes of ambition, or as wild and madheaded enthusiasts whose silly speculations and absurd paradoxes are not worthy the attention of any reasonable man. 4

The advocate for the perfectibility of man and of society retorts on the defender of establishments a more than equal contempt. He brands him as the slave of the most miserable and narrow prejudices; or as the defender of the abuses of civil society only because he profits by them. He paints him either as a character who prostitutes his understanding to his interest, or as one whose powers of mind are not of a size to grasp any thing great and noble, who cannot see above five yards before him, and who must therefore be utterly unable to take in the views of the enlightened benefactor of mankind. 5

In this unamicable contest the cause of truth cannot but suffer. The really good arguments on each side of the question are not allowed to have their proper weight. Each pursues his own theory, little solicitous to correct or improve it by an attention to what is advanced by his opponents. 6

The friend of the present order of things condemns all political speculations in the gross. He will not even condescend to examine the grounds from which the perfectibility of society is inferred. Much less will he give himself the trouble in a fair and candid manner to attempt an exposition of their fallacy. 7

The speculative philosopher equally offends against the cause of truth. With eyes fixed on a happier state of society, the blessings of which he paints in the most captivating colours, he allows himself to indulge in the most bitter invectives against every present establishment, without apply- 8 ing his talents to consider the best and safest means of removing abuses and without seeming to be aware of the tremendous obstacles that threaten, even in theory, to oppose the progress of man towards perfection.

It is an acknowledged truth in philosophy that a just theory will always   *9* be confirmed by experiment. Yet so much friction and so many minute circumstances occur in practice, which it is next to impossible for the most enlarged and penetrating mind to foresee, that on few subjects can any theory be pronounced just, that has not stood the test of experience. But an untried theory cannot fairly be advanced as probable, much less as just, till all the arguments against it have been maturely weighed and clearly and consistently refuted.

I have read some of the speculations on the perfectibility of man and   *10* of society with great pleasure. I have been warmed and delighted with the enchanting picture which they hold forth. I ardently wish for such happy improvements. But I see great, and, to my understanding, unconquerable difficulties in the way to them. These difficulties it is my present purpose to state, declaring, at the same time, that so far from exulting in them, as a cause of triumph over the friends of innovation, nothing would give me greater pleasure than to see them completely removed.

The most important argument that I shall adduce is certainly not new.   *11* The principles on which it depends have been explained in part by Hume,[2] and more at large by Dr. Adam Smith.[3] It has been advanced and applied to the present subject, though not with its proper weight, or in the most forcible point of view, by Mr. Wallace,[4] and it may probably have been stated by many writers that I have never met with. I should certainly therefore not think of advancing it again, though I mean to place it in a point of view in some degree different from any that I have hitherto seen, if it had ever been fairly and satisfactorily answered.

---

[2]*David Hume:* (1711–1776) A British philosopher, historian, and economist, his work in moral philosophy and the nature of knowledge led him to theorize on the self-regulating nature of world economies.

[3]*Adam Smith:* (1723–1790) A Scottish philosopher and political economist, author of the immensely popular *Wealth of Nations* (1776), Smith was one of the first major advocates of laissez-faire economies, believing that progress toward prosperity was a natural system and shouldn't be controlled by outside forces such as government. According to Smith, self-interest promoted the common good.

[4]*Alfred Russel Wallace:* (1823–1913) A British naturalist, his theory on evolution had remarkable parallels to Charles Darwin's theory, though it was developed independently. Malthus refers to Wallace here in support of the idea that a great disjunction between the rate of the increase of population and of subsistence will inevitably lead to the extinction of weaker or less prosperous parties. Applied to economics, this theory suggests that having both very poor and very rich citizens in the same society is inevitable, since the poor are less fit to survive and are thus on their way to extinction.

The cause of this neglect on the part of the advocates for the perfect-   *12*
ibility of mankind is not easily accounted for. I cannot doubt the talents of
such men as Godwin[5] and Condorcet. I am unwilling to doubt their can-
dour. To my understanding, and probably to that of most others, the difficulty appears insurmountable. Yet these men of acknowledged ability
and penetration scarcely deign to notice it, and hold on their course in such
speculations, with unabated ardour and undiminished confidence. I have
certainly no right to say that they purposely shut their eyes to such arguments. I ought rather to doubt the validity of them, when neglected by
such men, however forcibly their truth may strike my own mind. Yet in
this respect it must be acknowledged that we are all of us too prone to err.
If I saw a glass of wine repeatedly presented to a man, and he took no
notice of it, I should be apt to think that he was blind or uncivil. A juster
philosophy might teach me rather to think that my eyes deceived me and
that the offer was not really what I conceived it to be.

In entering upon the argument I must premise that I put out of the   *13*
question, at present, all mere conjectures, that is, all suppositions, the
probable realization of which cannot be inferred upon any just philosophical grounds. A writer may tell me that he thinks man will ultimately become an ostrich. I cannot properly contradict him. But before he can expect
to bring any reasonable person over to his opinion, he ought to shew that
the necks of mankind have been gradually elongating, that the lips have
grown harder and more prominent, that the legs and feet are daily altering
their shape, and that the hair is beginning to change into stubs of feathers.
And till the probability of so wonderful a conversion can be shewn, it is
surely lost time and lost eloquence to expatiate on the happiness of man
in such a state; to describe his powers, both of running and flying, to paint
him in a condition where all narrow luxuries would be contemned, where
he would be employed only in collecting the necessaries of life, and where,
consequently, each man's share of labour would be light, and his portion
of leisure ample.

I think I may fairly make two postulata.   *14*

First, That food is necessary to the existence of man.   *15*

Secondly, That the passion between the sexes is necessary and will   *16*
remain nearly in its present state.

These two laws, ever since we have had any knowledge of mankind,   *17*
appear to have been fixed laws of our nature, and, as we have not hitherto
seen any alteration in them, we have no right to conclude that they will
ever cease to be what they now are, without an immediate act of power in
that Being who first arranged the system of the universe, and for the ad-

---

[5]*William Godwin:* (1756–1836) For biographical information on William Godwin, refer to
Godwin's essay "Of Population" in this section.

vantage of his creatures, still executes, according to fixed laws, all its various operations.

I do not know that any writer has supposed that on this earth man will   18
ultimately be able to live without food. But Mr. Godwin has conjectured that the passion between the sexes may in time be extinguished. As, however, he calls this part of his work a deviation into the land of conjecture, I will not dwell longer upon it at present than to say that the best arguments for the perfectibility of man are drawn from a contemplation of the great progress that he has already made from the savage state and the difficulty of saying where he is to stop. But towards the extinction of the passion between the sexes, no progress whatever has hitherto been made. It appears to exist in as much force at present as it did two thousand or four thousand years ago. There are individual exceptions now as there always have been. But, as these exceptions do not appear to increase in number, it would surely be a very unphilosophical mode of arguing, to infer merely from the existence of an exception, that the exception would, in time, become the rule, and the rule the exception.

Assuming then, my postulata as granted, I say that the power of pop-   19
ulation is indefinitely greater than the power in the earth to produce subsistence for man.

Population, when unchecked, increases in a geometrical ratio. Subsis-   20
tence increases only in an arithmetical ratio. A slight acquaintance with numbers will shew the immensity of the first power in comparison of the second.[6]

By that law of nature which makes food necessary to the life of man,   21
the effects of these two unequal powers must be kept equal.

This implies a strong and constantly operating check on population   22
from the difficulty of subsistence. This difficulty must fall some where and must necessarily be severely felt by a large portion of mankind.

Through the animal and vegetable kingdoms, nature has scattered the   23
seeds of life abroad with the most profuse and liberal hand. She has been comparatively sparing in the room and the nourishment necessary to rear them. The germs of existence contained in this spot of earth, with ample food and ample room to expand in, would fill millions of worlds in the course of a few thousand years. Necessity, that imperious all pervading law of nature, restrains them within the prescribed bounds. The race of

---

[6]*Arithmetical and geometrical ratios:* Malthus compares the ratio of the average increase of population over a given period of time with the average increase of subsistence over the same period. These ratios show that population increases geometrically — that is, with each generation the number of persons doubles (1, 2, 4, 8, 16), whereas subsistence increases arithmetically — by an increase of one unit in each successive generation (1, 2, 3, 4, 5). Malthus's argument here is that population increases much more rapidly than the production of food and other means of subsistence.

plants and the race of animals shrink under this great restrictive law. And the race of man cannot, by any efforts of reason, escape from it. Among plants and animals its effects are waste of seed, sickness, and premature death. Among mankind, misery and vice. The former, misery, is an absolutely necessary consequence of it. Vice is a highly probable consequence, and we therefore see it abundantly prevail, but it ought not, perhaps, to be called an absolutely necessary consequence. The ordeal of virtue is to resist all temptation to evil.

This natural inequality of the two powers of population and of production in the earth and that great law of our nature which must constantly keep their effects equal form the great difficulty that to me appears insurmountable in the way to the perfectibility of society. All other arguments are of slight and subordinate consideration in comparison of this. I see no way by which man can escape from the weight of this law which pervades all animated nature. No fancied equality, no agrarian regulations in their utmost extent, could remove the pressure of it even for a single century. And it appears, therefore, to be decisive against the possible existence of a society, all the members of which should live in ease, happiness, and comparative leisure, and feel no anxiety about providing the means of subsistence for themselves and families.   24

Consequently, if the premises are just, the argument is conclusive against the perfectibility of the mass of mankind.   25

I have thus sketched the general outline of the argument, but I will examine it more particularly, and I think it will be found that experience, the true source and foundation of all knowledge, invariably confirms its truth.   26

REVIEW QUESTIONS

1. According to Malthus, what arguments do the defenders of the status quo and the prophets of progress level against one another? How do these arguments keep the important question at hand from being resolved?
2. In one or two sentences, state the crux of Malthus's argument. Be sure to include in your summary both of his postulates and his conclusions.

DISCUSSION AND WRITING QUESTIONS

1. Reread paragraph 8. To what extent can Malthus's criticism be applied to the ideas of Condorcet?
2. Explain Malthus's reference to the "glass of wine" in paragraph 12 and the ostrich in paragraph 13. How are these references appropriate to the content of the paragraphs and to the purpose of the essay as a whole?

3. Malthus believes that man cannot escape the all-pervading law of nature that limits the growth of seeds and, subsequently, of food. Have we since Malthus's day altered this restrictive law in any manner?
4. How does the invention of birth control affect the Malthusian argument?
5. The People's Republic of China has initiated a radical program designed to limit its enormous population: the government has mandated that no couple have more than one child — under the pain of losing state support for medical care and schooling. The government's arguments are essentially Malthusian: either population is drastically cut or the country faces famine at worst and, at best, a catastrophic reduction in its standard of living. What do you feel about a government's involvement in a couple's decision to have children? If you are against the idea, what solutions would you offer the People's Republic for avoiding famine?
6. Malthus feels that his argument is conclusive. Do you?
7. Which vision of the future do you find more convincing: Condorcet's or Malthus's? Why?

WILLIAM GODWIN *(1756–1836)*

William Godwin — English novelist and writer on social philosophy and politics — was born in Wisbech, Cambridgeshire, on March 3, 1756. Intending to follow the example of his father and devote himself to the ministry, he instead at the age of twenty-six turned to a life of social and political reform through writing. Godwin believed, along with the leading Enlightenment philosophers of France, in the importance of skepticism and rational inquiry as the tools necessary for reforming society. He distrusted the power of corrupting institutions (centralized governments being a primary offender) and believed that small communities should govern themselves. It was his famous work, *Inquiry Concerning Political Justice, and Its Influence on General Virtue and Happiness,* that (in part) prompted Malthus to write the *Essay on Population.* In his *Inquiry,* Godwin laid out an optimistic view of man: individuals were perfectible; social institutions were inherently flawed.

Only for a brief time in his adult life, during his marriage with Mary Wollstonecraft — famous author of *A Vindication of the Rights of Woman* — did it appear that Godwin was happy. Shortly after the birth of their daughter Mary (who would later write the novel *Frankenstein* and marry the poet Percy Shelley), his wife died. Years later, Godwin remarried, unhappily.

His writings include the novels *The Adventures of Caleb Williams* (1794) and *Fleetwood* (1805), the *Memoirs* (1798) of Mary Wollstonecraft Godwin, and a *History of the Commonwealth* (1824–1828). The present selection comprises the final chapter in *Of Population* (1820), Godwin's direct response to the arguments of Malthus.

OF POPULATION

An Enquiry Concerning the Power of Increase in the Numbers of Mankind

BEING AN ANSWER TO MR. MALTHUS'S ESSAY
ON THAT SUBJECT

There can be no conclusion more natural or more profitable to such an   *1*
enquiry as has formed the scope of the present volume, than an attempt
to fix a just estimate of the state of man upon earth.

Man is perhaps the only animal in the world endowed with the faculty   *2*
we call taste. Man is the only animal capable of persevering and premedi-
tated industry, with the fruits of which the land and even the water of our
globe are interspersed and adorned. Man is the only creature susceptible
of science and invention, and possessing the power of handing down his
thoughts in those permanent records, called books. Man has in him the
seeds of sentiment and virtue, and the principle of comprehensive affections, patriotism and philanthropy. The human species is capable of improvement from age to age, by means of which capacity we have arrived
at those refinements of mechanical production and science, which have
been gradually called into existence; while all other animals remain what
they were at first, and the young of no species becomes better or more
powerful by the experience of those that went before him.

It cannot be but that a being so gloriously endowed should be capable   *3*
of much enjoyment and happiness. Our tastes and our judgment are fitted
to add indefinitely to our pleasures: we admire the works of God and the
works of man. Our affections are to us a source of enjoyments, variegated
and exquisite. Self-approbation and self-complacency are main pillars of
human happiness. The consciousness of freedom and the pride of independence are inexhaustible sources of joy. There is a peculiar and an inex-
pressible delight which belongs to perseverance and a resolved constancy
in the operations of science, in the cultivation of mind, and in a course of
virtuous action. We are delighted with these things in solitude and intent
application; and society in such pursuits increases our delight. Indeed,
when we do but name the word society, we touch a magical chord which
introduces us at once to a whole volume of peculiar felicities.

Yet the state of man on earth is not a state of unmingled happiness.   *4*
We have many pains and infirmities. Every stage of our existence from the

---

William Godwin. "Conclusion (Chapter IX, Bk VI)" in *Of Population: An Enquiry Concerning the Power of Increase in the Numbers of Mankind, Being an Answer to Mr. Malthus's Essay on That Subject* (1820). New York: Augustus M. Kelley, 1964, pp. 612–626.

cradle to the grave, has its peculiar compartment in this magazine of ills. Our cares and anxieties are innumerable. All those things which, presented to us in one aspect, are sources of pleasure, may, if reversed, become equally sources of affliction. The generous ambition of the human heart, if disappointed, preys upon our vitals. Our affections, those conduits of exquisite enjoyment, are often turned into the means of agony. Man is an erring creature, and may become the victim of remorse; or, if his heart is hardened in this respect, he may be made the object of the resentment and vengeance of his fellow-creatures.

Beside all this, it is now time to add, that human institutions may be   5
the source of much mischief to those they were framed to control. There have been such things as despotism and as tyranny. Society is the source of innumerable pleasures; without society we can scarcely be said to live; yet in how many ways does society infringe upon the independence and peace of its members. Man delights to control and to inforce submission upon his fellow-man; human creatures desire to exercise lordship and to display authority. One class and division of the community, is taught to think its interests adverse to the interests of another class and division of the community. The institution of property has been the source of much improvement and much admirable activity to mankind; yet how many evils to multitudes of our species have sprung from the institution of property. The same may be said of the inequality of conditions.

All that is here stated is very much of the nature of common-place.   6
Every man has heard it; and every man knows it. Yet it is sometimes of great use that common-places should be recollected; and the author would deserve the name of absurdly fastidious, who should resolve upon all occasions to avoid them. Those which have been here introduced are particularly proper on the present occasion.

Between the advantages and disadvantages attendant on the state of   7
man on earth there is one thing that seems decisively to turn the balance in favour of the former. Man is to a considerable degree the artificer of his own fortune. We can apply our reflections and our ingenuity to the remedy
 of whatever we regret. Speaking in a general way, and within certain liberal and expansive limitations, it should appear that there is no evil under which the human species can labour, that man is not competent to cure. This is a source of unspeakable consolation to us in two ways: first, we can bear with some cheerfulness the ill which for ourselves or our posterity we have the power to remedy: and, secondly, this power inherent in our nature is the basis of that elasticity and exultation which are most congenial to the mind of man. "We are perplexed, but not in despair; we are persecuted, but not forsaken; we are cast down, but not destroyed." Man, in the most dejected condition in which a human being can be placed, has still something within him which whispers him, "I belong to a world that is worth living in."

Such was, and was admitted to be the state of the human species,   8

previously to the appearance of the Essay on Population. Now let us see how, under the ascendancy of Mr. Malthus's theory, all this is completely reversed.

The great error of those who sought to encourage and console their *9* fellow-beings in this vale of tears, was, we are told, in supposing that any thing that we could do, could be of substantial benefit in remedying the defects of our social existence. "Human institutions are light and superficial, mere feathers that float upon the surface." The enemy that hems us in, and reduces our condition to despair, is no other than "the laws of Nature, which are the laws of God."

Nor is this by any means the worst of the case. The express object of *10* Mr. Malthus's writing was to prove how pernicious was their error, who aimed at any considerable and essential improvement in human society. The only effectual checks upon that excess of population, which, if unchecked, would be sufficient in no long time to people all the stars, are vice and misery. The main and direct moral and lesson of the Essay on Population, is passiveness. Human creatures may feel that they are unfortunate and unhappy; but it is their wisdom to lie still, and rather "bear the ills they have, than fly to others that they know not of."

The two main propositions that are revealed to us by the Essay on *11* Population are, 1. the kind of mortality and massacre that is continually taking place in the midst of us, without our having been aware of it: and, 2. the conduct which it is our wisdom to adopt under the unhappy condition of man upon earth.

It has been already sufficiently proved in the proper place, that, ac- *12* cording to Mr. Malthus's principles, all the children in each generation on this side of the globe are born, that can be born. The difference between the population of Europe on the one hand, and of the United States on the other, is not that a smaller number of children are born in the former case, but that a greater number are cut off in their infancy. If the present population of England and Wales is ten millions, it would twenty-five years hence be twenty millions, and so on for ever, were it not for the hitherto unobserved destruction of the young of the human species on this side of the globe. That man is mortal we sufficiently knew; we had studied and rehearsed, time out of mind, the various accidents that waylay us in every stage of our existence; and the thought of this was sufficient to make us sober, if not to make us sad: but Mr. Malthus has discovered to us the hourly destruction of millions upon millions more, of which we had no previous knowledge. And how are they destroyed? "By all those causes, whether arising from vice or misery, which in various degrees and diversified manners contribute to shorten the natural duration of human life." "Every loss of a child from the consequences of poverty [and, were it not for these losses, the population of England and Wales would double every twenty-five years] must evidently be preceded and accompanied by great misery to various individuals."

The second of the two main propositions that are revealed to us by the   13
Essay on Population, is the conduct which it is our wisdom to adopt under
the unhappy condition of man upon earth. Vice and misery are the main
securities upon which we are to depend: it is they that make the condition
of man upon earth so tolerable as we find it. The most pernicious error
into which we can fall, and which is beyond all others to be deprecated,
would be the inconsiderate attempt materially to improve the state of society, to relieve the hardships under which the greater part of our species
at present labour, and to introduce equality, or any approach towards
equality, in the conditions of men. Since vice and misery are discovered to
be the *mala bene posita,* the indispensible evils, without which the pillars of
creation would tumble into ruins, we must be careful to touch them with
the utmost tenderness, or rather we must be careful not to touch them on
any account. They are the mysterious treasures, laid up in the sanctuary
of the covenant between God and his creatures.

Look now upon this picture and on this, the faithful representment of   14
two worlds![1] One is the world I was born in, and in which I lived for forty
years: the other is the world of Mr. Malthus.

In the Old World (if I may be allowed so to denominate it) there was   15
something exhilarating and cheerful. We felt that there was room for a
generous ambition to unfold itself. If we were under the cloud or the grief
of calamity, we had still something to console us. We might animate our
courage with reflections on the nature of man, and support our constancy

by recollecting the unlimited power we possess to remedy our evils, and
better our condition. We felt, as I said before, that we "belonged to a world
worth living in."

Mr. Malthus blots out all this with one stroke of his pen. By a statement   16
of six pages, or rather of six lines, he undertakes to shew us what a fool
the man is who should be idle enough to rejoice in such a world as this.
He tells us that our ills are remediless, and that human institutions, and
the resources of human ingenuity, are feathers, capable of doing little
harm, and no more competent to produce us benefit. We are fallen into

the hands of a remorseless stepmother, Nature: it is in vain that we struggle against her laws; the murderous principle of multiplication will be for
ever at work; the viper-brood of passion, the passion between the sexes,
the fruitful source of eternal mischiefs, we may condemn, but must never
hope to control. He forbids us to argue well of the general weal, for all is
despair; he forbids us to attempt to raise or improve our condition, for
every such attempt is destructive.

I can liken Mr. Malthus's world to nothing but a city under the severe   17

---

[1]Godwin is making an ironic reference to Hamlet's speech to his mother (Act III, sc. iv, 54):
"Look here upon this picture, and on this." (Hamlet is referring to two pictures — one of
his murdered father, and the other of the usurping murderer, Claudius.)

visitation of a pestilence. All philanthropy and benevolence are at an end. To serve our fellow-citizens is a hopeless undertaking. With hope, the very wish to serve them expires. We no longer love, where to benefit is impossible. "It were all one," as Shakespear says, "that I should love a bright particular star, and think to wed it." Our only refuge then is in pure self-indulgence, and an entire contempt for, and oblivion of our fellow-creatures. Boccaccio's description of some of his contemporaries in the great plague of Florence is excellently to this purpose.[2] "The reflections of these men," says he, "led them to a determination sufficiently cruel: and this was, to shun and fly from their unfortunate and suffering countrymen. They shut themselves up in houses free from the infection, and sought to forget the very existence of their fellow-citizens. They nourished themselves with the most delicate meats and the finest wines they could procure. Nay, they sung, they danced, they laughed, they jested, and considered this, as far as they were concerned, to be a sovereign remedy for every evil." It is wonderful how exactly this coincides with what is recommended in the Essay on Population, concerning the neglect to be shewn to the poor, and the wastefulness of the rich.

Till Mr. Malthus wrote, political writers and sages had courage. They   18
said, "The evils we suffer are from ourselves; let us apply ourselves with assiduity and fortitude to the cure of them." This courage was rapidly descending, by the progress of illumination and intellect, to a very numerous portion of mankind; and the sober and considerate began deliberately to say, "Let us endeavour to remedy the evils of political society, and mankind may then be free and contented and happy." Mr. Malthus has placed himself in the gap. He has proclaimed, with a voice that has carried astonishment and terror into the hearts of thousands, the accents of despair. He has said, The evils of which you complain, do not lie within your reach to remove: they come from the laws of nature, and the unalterable impulse of human kind.

But Mr. Malthus does not stop here. He presents us with a code of   19
morality conformable to his creed.

This code consists principally of negatives.   20

We must not preach up private charity. For charity, "if exerted at all,   21
will necessarily lead" to pernicious consequences.

We must not preach up frugality. For the "waste among the rich, and   22

---

[2]*Boccaccio's description:* The Italian poet and author Giovanni Boccaccio (1313–1375) is best known for his *Decameron* (1353), a collection of comic and tragic tales and songs written as an account of the adventures and pastimes of ten youths who are fleeing from Florence, Italy during the Great (bubonic) Plague of 1348. Godwin is focusing on the comic elements of the *Decameron* here, suggesting that the youths' flight and ensuing frolics during a time of plague reflect their rejection of moral responsibility in reaction to despair. Godwin believes that a similar moral rejection would be a logical reaction to Malthus's pessimism.

the horses kept by them merely for their pleasure, operate like granaries, and tend rather to benefit than to injure the lower classes of society."

We must deny that the poor, whatever may be the causes or degree of   23
their distress, "have a right to support."

We must maintain that every man "has a right to do what he will with   24
his own."

We must preach down marriage. We must affirm that no man has a   25
right to marry, without a fair "prospect of being able to support a family."
"They should not have families, if they cannot support them." And this
rule is strictly to govern our treatment of the married man in distress. "To
the punishment of Nature he should be left, the punishment of want. He
should be taught to know that the laws of Nature, which are the laws of
God, have doomed him and his family to suffer for disobeying their repeated admonitions."

What havock do these few maxims make with the old received notions   26
of morality![3]

It has not been enough attended to, how complete a revolution the   27
Essay on Population proposes to effect in human affairs. Mr. Malthus is
the most daring and gigantic of all innovators.

To omit all other particulars, if we embrace his creed, we must have a   28
new religion, and a new God.

Mr. Malthus's is not the religion of the Bible. On the contrary it is in   29
diametrical opposition to it.

> Increase and multiply, is Heaven's command.
> Who bids abstain, but our destroyer, foe
> To God and man?

Christianity is, and has always been called, a religion of charity and love.
It is rigorous in prescribing the duties of the rich, as well as of the poor. It
does not admit that we "have a right to do what we will with our own."
On the contrary, it teaches that we have nothing that we can strictly call
our own, that the rich are but stewards and administrators of the benefits
of Providence, and that we shall be austerely called to give an account of
every talent that is intrusted to us. We are taught to consider our fellow-
creatures in distress as our brothers, and to treat them accordingly. "Inasmuch as ye have done it to one of the least of these, ye have done it to
me."

But, if we embrace the creed of Mr. Malthus, we must not only have a   30
new religion, but a new God.

---

[3]For additional explanations and expressions of this dispute, see the section on "Darwin
and the Survival of the Fittest," particularly the general introduction and the selections by
Sumner and Spencer.

The God of the Essay on Population, the God, as we are there in- *31*
formed, of Nature, and the author of her laws, has given us laws, "the
deep-seated causes of evil," in comparison with which all that human ingenuity can effect of harm or of good, is but as a feather. These deep-seated
causes of evil we can never counteract, nor can any thing extract their
venom, unless we were capable of that moral restraint, which Mr. Malthus
has in one instance "allowed himself to suppose," but which he has no
expectation or belief that man ever will or can reduce into practice. Such
are the laws, according to him, in conformity to which God has built the
world, and such is the imbecil and impotent creature which he has planted
here to inhabit it. The irresistible strength of these laws, and the weakness
of man, are equally his work. It is his breath that has pronounced the fiat,
"Vice and misery shall be the concomitants of the human species as long
as they exist; I have made for them a law of multiplication so enormous,
that the action of these causes shall be regularly required to cut off the
excessive increase as fast as it appears." Lo now, and see, whether this is
the God, which any system of religion on earth has taught men to recognise. Lo now, and see, whether this is the God, which serious men in
enlightened Europe are prepared to praise and adore.

It is but just that those who adopt the creed of Mr. Malthus, should *32*
understand it in all its bearings, and be made aware of the full extent of
the conclusions into which it leads; while, on the other hand, those by
whom these conclusions are regarded with aversion, will perhaps feel
themselves indebted to a book, by which the premises on which they are
built are, I trust, fully refuted.

The general inferences from the statements and reasonings of the pre- *33*
ceding sheets are plainly these. There is in man, absolutely speaking, a
power of increasing the number of his species. Yet the numbers of mankind appear not to have increased on the whole within the limits of authentic profane history. To speak from the best authorities to which we
have access, the increase has never amounted to the rate of a doubling in
one hundred years, nor has ever proceeded at that rate for a hundred years
together. And, till human affairs shall be better and more auspiciously conducted than they have hitherto been under the best governments, there
will be no absolute increase in the numbers of mankind. This is enough
for Mr. Malthus, and the other adversaries of the dignity and honour of
human nature. For myself and those who hope better things, a doubling
of the numbers of mankind once in an hundred years, has nothing in it,
which can afford rational ground of alarm. We have but too cogent reasons
to believe, that a regular and uninterrupted progress of increase is a thing
that cannot for a long time be looked for. And, at all events, we may be as
well assured, as it is possible to be upon a subject of this sort, that the
progressive power of increase in the numbers of mankind, will never out-

run the progressive power of improvement which human intellect is en-abled to develop in the means of subsistence.

I am sensible that what I have written may be regarded in some re-   34
spects as a book about nothing. The proposition of which it treats appears
to have been established by universal consent from the days of Homer. I
may perhaps however be allowed the merit of having brought new arguments in aid of old truth. In these times of innovation (innovation, one of
the noblest characteristics of man) a pernicious novelty has been started,
and has obtained for the time a general success. It seemed necessary that
some one should stoop to the task of refuting it. Too happy, if I may flatter
myself with the fate hereafter that Swift predicates of Marvel, whose "Answer to Parker is still read with pleasure, though the positions it exposes
have long ceased to have any supporters."[4] I have accordingly endeavoured that my volume should contain some reflections and trains of thinking not unprofitable for other purposes than those for which they were
originally produced. Add to which, if I have contributed to place a leading
point of political economy on a permanent basis, my labour may not in
that respect be found altogether fugitive and nugatory.

REVIEW QUESTIONS

1. What quality, according to Godwin, argues in favor of mankind's reaping more
   advantages than disadvantages in its interactions with the world?
2. Describe, briefly, the two worlds to which Godwin refers in paragraphs 14–18.
   What are the principal competing assumptions in these views of the world?
3. What are the functions of misery and vice in Malthus's essay, according to
   Godwin?
4. Restate Godwin's critique of Malthus in paragraphs 15, 16, and 17.

DISCUSSION AND WRITING QUESTIONS

1. For what purpose does Godwin review humankind's virtues and faults in the
   first several paragraphs?
2. Godwin is more careful than Condorcet to admit the faults of man; yet he
   reaches the same conclusion that "there is no evil under which the human species can labour, that man is not competent to cure." Knowing what you do of
   human nature, state whether or not you agree with Godwin. Explain your
   position.

---

[4]*Swift predicates of Marvell:* The reference here is to a comment made by author and satirist
Jonathan Swift (1667–1745) in his "Apology" to *A Tale of the Tub*, regarding fellow author
Andrew Marvell (1621–1678). In *The Rehearsal Transposed,* Marvell chastises Bishop Mat-
thew Parker (1504–1575) for various treatises against religious dissenters.

3. Reread paragraph 7, noting especially Godwin's assessment of the human spirit and its essential optimism. Setting aside for the moment your agreement or disagreement with Godwin's faith in progress, do you think his description of the human spirit an accurate one?
4. Godwin claims that there are two worlds, his and Malthus's. How valid is this neat distinction between these worlds?
5. The clear differences that Godwin cites between his views and Malthus's represent, in extreme form, a divergence of views in contemporary America regarding the role of government in providing for the welfare of its citizens. Work out, if you can, the analogy. Today, whose views on the role of government support for the indigent most closely resemble the views of Malthus? the views of Godwin? What are the virtues of each position? the faults? With which position do you side? If with neither, then stake out your own position.
6. For what purpose does Godwin bring God and Christianity into the argument? How do you think Malthus would respond to this part of Godwin's critique? (Recall that Malthus was a clergyman.)
7. One hundred and sixty years after the debate between Godwin and Malthus, whose argument has held up better? Explain.
8. "The progressive power of increase in the numbers of mankind, will never outrun the progressive power of improvement which human intellect is enabled to develop in the means of subsistence." Your comments?

ROBERT SOUTHEY *(1774–1843)*

Robert Southey, Romantic poet, poet laureate of England, and author of many prose works, was born at Bristol, Gloucestershire, on August 12, 1774. Outspoken as a student, Southey was expelled from the Westminster School of London for protesting corporal punishment. Soon after (in 1792), while at Oxford, he wrote the long poem *Joan of Arc* in support of the French Revolution and its ideals. The poem earned him early literary fame. It was at Oxford that Southey met Samuel Taylor Coleridge and planned with him a project for founding a community in Pennsylvania based on utopian principles, where inhabitants would work toward moral and social perfection. The plan failed, however, and neither Southey nor Coleridge moved to the United States.

In the years that followed, having married the sister of Coleridge's wife, Southey moved to Greta Hall, Keswick, where he developed a friendship with William Wordsworth. Southey remained in Greta Hall for the remainder of his life. There he wrote three epic poems: *Madoc* (1805), *The Curse of Kehama* (1810), and *Roderick* (1814). He was appointed poet laureate of England in 1813. His prose works include *Life of Nelson; The Doctor,* in which one finds the nursery tale "The Three Bears"; and numerous political commentaries published over a span of three decades for the *Quarterly Review,* a forum from which he argued for improved public services.

The *Colloquies on The Progress and Prospects of Society* was published in 1829. A *colloquy* is a formal, written conversation or dialogue; in this case, Southey's participants are an imaginary poet, named Montesinos, and the ghostly spirit of Sir Thomas More (1478–1535), the English statesman and martyred author of *Utopia.* While Montesinos drifts between sleep and lethargic wakefulness one day, the spirit of Sir Thomas comes to him, and the two begin their discourse on a wide range of subjects, the general topic of which is the progress and prospects of society. In the excerpt that follows, Southey has these two figures discuss the virtues and faults of the British manufacturing system — the critique of which infuriated reviewer Thomas Babington Macaulay (see pages 345–352). Though Southey was an advocate of social progress (as evidenced in the articles he wrote for the *Quarterly Review*), he was sensitive to the abuses that followed from the introduction of new technology into the workplace during the Industrial Revolution. These sections from the *Colloquies* reflect Southey's misgivings.

THE PROGRESS AND PROSPECTS OF SOCIETY

From *Colloquy II. The Improvement of the World.*

MONTESINOS.[1] An excellent friend of mine, one of the wisest, best, and   *1*
happiest men whom I have ever known, delights . . . to trace the moral
order of Providence through the revolutions of the world; and in his historical writings keeps it in view as the pole-star of his course. I wish he
were present, that he might have the satisfaction of hearing his favourite
opinion confirmed by one from the dead.

SIR THOMAS MORE. His opinion requires no other confirmation than what   *2*
he finds for it in observation and scripture, and in his own calm judgement. I should differ little from that friend of yours concerning the past;
but his hopes for the future appear to me like early buds which are in
danger of March winds. He believes the world to be in a rapid state of sure
improvement; and in the ferment which exists every where he beholds
only a purifying process; not considering that there is an acetous as well
as a vinous fermentation; and that in the one case the liquor may be spilt,
in the other it must be spoilt.[2]

MONTESINOS. Surely you would not rob us of our hopes for the human   *3*
race! If I apprehended that your discourse tended to this end, I should
suspect you, notwithstanding your appearance, and be ready to exclaim,

---

Robert Southey. Sections from "Colloquy II: The Improvement of the World" and from
"Colloquy VII: The Manufacturing System" in *Sir Thomas More: Or Colloquies on the Progress
and Prospects of Society*. Vol. 1. London: John Murray (Albemarle Street), 1829, pp. 26–38,
158–174.

[1]*Montesinos:* The name Montesinos is a possible reference to a knight-errant of Charle-
magne named Montesinos who, after being insulted at the French court, retired to a cave
at La Mancha, Spain. In Cervantes's novel, *Don Quixote* (1605,1615), the hero visits Montesinos's cave, where he falls into a trance and imagines himself conversing with Montesinos and other knights.

[2]*Acetous as well as vinous fermentation:* Here fermentation refers to both the literal process
of fermentation by which grains and fruits are made into alcohol-based substances (such
as liquor or vinegar), and to fermentation as a general mood of excitement or commotion
occurring in a society that undergoes change. More is reminding Montesinos (who suggests that all change is for the better) that societal fermentation, like organic fermentation,
does not always produce positive results: acetous or bitter vinegar substances are produced by fermentation as well as vinous or wine products.

Avaunt, Tempter![3] For there is no opinion from which I should so hardly be driven, and so reluctantly part, as the belief that the world will continue to improve, even as it has hitherto continually been improving; and that the progress of knowledge and the diffusion of Christianity will bring about at last, when men become Christians in reality, as well as in name, something like that Utopian state of which philosophers have loved to dream, . . . like that millennium in which Saints as well as enthusiasts have trusted.

SIR THOMAS MORE.   Do you hold that this consummation must of necessity   4
come to pass; or that it depends in any degree upon the course of events, that is to say, upon human actions? The former of these propositions you would be as unwilling to admit as your friend Wesley,[4] or the old Welsh-man Pelagius[5] himself. The latter leaves you little other foundation for your opinion than a desire, which, from its very benevolence, is the more likely to be delusive. . . You are in a dilemma.

MONTESINOS.   Not so, Sir Thomas. Impossible as it may be for us to rec-   5
oncile the free will of man with the foreknowledge of God, I nevertheless believe in both with the most full conviction. When the human mind plunges into time and space in its speculations, it adventures beyond its sphere; no wonder, therefore, that its powers fail, and it is lost. But that my will is free, I know feelingly: it is proved to me by my conscience. And that God provideth all things, I know by his own word, and by that instinct which he hath implanted in me to assure me of his being. My answer to your question then is this: I believe that the happy consummation which I desire is appointed, and must come to pass; but that when it is to come depends upon the obedience of man to the will of God, that is, upon human actions.

SIR THOMAS MORE.   You hold then that the human race will one day attain   6
the utmost degree of general virtue, and thereby general happiness, of which humanity is capable. Upon what do you found this belief?

---

[3]*Avaunt Tempter:* Literally "away devil." This is an oath said to evil spirits or devils, com-manding them to depart. Montesinos responds with this exclamation to More's suggestion that change might not be for the better. More's pessimism, according to Montesinos, con-tradicts the Biblical prophecy of a forthcoming utopian world; hence, More could be seen as heretical or devilish.

[4]*John Wesley:* (1703–1791) The Anglican clergyman who, with his brother Charles, founded the Methodist movement in the Church of England, a Christian sect based on the tenet that only faith is necessary for humans to achieve salvation.

[5]*Pelagius:* (c.354–after 418) A monk and theologian who, in response to what he saw as moral laxities in the Christian church brought about by notions of divine grace, developed an unorthodox theology emphasizing the importance of human actions in attaining grace.

MONTESINOS. The opinion is stated more broadly than I should chuse to 7
advance it. But this is ever the manner of argumentative discourse: the
opponent endeavours to draw from you conclusions which you are not
prepared to defend, and which perhaps you have never before acknowledged even to yourself. I will put the proposition in a less disputable form.
A happier condition of society is possible than that in which any nation is
existing at this time, or has at any time existed. The sum both of moral and
physical evil may be greatly diminished by good laws, good institutions,
and good governments. Moral evil cannot indeed be removed, unless the
nature of man were changed; and that renovation is only to be effected in
individuals, and in them only by the special grace of God. Physical evil
must always, to a certain degree, be inseparable from mortality. But both
are so much within the reach of human institutions that a state of society
is conceivable almost as superior to that of England in these days, as that
itself is superior to the condition of the tattooed Britons, or of the Northern
Pirates from whom we are descended. Surely this belief rests upon a reasonable foundation, and is supported by that general improvement (always going on if it be regarded upon the great scale) to which all history
bears witness.

SIR THOMAS MORE. I dispute not this: but to render it a reasonable ground 8
of immediate hope, the predominance of good principles must be supposed. Do you believe that good or evil principles predominate at this
time?

MONTESINOS. If I were to judge by that expression of popular opinion 9
which the press pretends to convey, I should reply without hesitation that
never in any other known age of the world have such pernicious principles
been so prevalent.

> *Qua terra patet, fera regnat. Erinnys;*
> *In facinus jurasse putes.*[6]

SIR THOMAS MORE. Is there not a danger that these principles may bear 10
down every thing before them? and is not that danger obvious, . . . palpable, . . . imminent? Is there a considerate man who can look at the signs
of the times without apprehension, or a scoundrel connected with what is
called the public press, who does not speculate upon them, and join with
the anarchists as the strongest party? Deceive not yourself by the fallacious
notion that truth is mightier than falsehood, and that good must prevail
over evil! Good principles enable men to suffer, rather than to act. Think
how the dog, fond and faithful creature as he is, from being the most docile

---

[6]*Qua terra patet . . .:* Where the earth lies open there reigns savage Erinnys; [one of the
Greek furies or goddesses of vengeance]/You would think she had sworn herself to crime.

and obedient of all animals, is made the most dangerous, if he becomes mad; so men acquire a frightful and not less monstrous power when they are in a state of moral insanity, and break loose from their social and religious obligations. Remember too how rapidly the plague of diseased opinions is communicated, and that if it once gain head, it is as difficult to be stopt as a conflagration or a flood. The prevailing opinions of this age go to the destruction of every thing which has hitherto been held sacred. They tend to arm the poor against the rich; the many against the few: worse than this, . . . for it will also be a war of hope and enterprize against timidity, of youth against age.

MONTESINOS.   Sir Ghost, you are almost as dreadful an alarmist as our   11
Cumberland cow,[7] who is believed to have lately uttered this prophecy, delivering it with oracular propriety in verse:

> Two winters, a wet spring,
> A bloody summer, and no king.

SIR THOMAS MORE.   That prophecy speaks the wishes of the man, whoever   12
he may have been, by whom it was invented: and you who talk of the progress of knowledge, and the improvement of society, and upon that improvement build your hope of its progressive melioration, you know that even so gross and palpable an imposture as this is swallowed by many of the vulgar, and contributes in its sphere to the mischief which it was designed to promote. I admit that such an improved condition of society as you contemplate is possible, and that it ought always to be kept in view: but the error of supposing it too near, of fancying that there is a short road to it, is, of all the errors of these times, the most pernicious, because it seduces the young and generous, and betrays them imperceptibly into an alliance with whatever is flagitious and detestable.[8] The fact is undeniable that the worst principles in religion, in morals, and in politics, are at this time more prevalent than they ever were known to be in any former age. You need not be told in what manner revolutions in opinion bring about the fate of empires; and upon this ground you ought to regard the state of the world, both at home and abroad, with fear, rather than with hope.

MONTESINOS.   . . . I know that the world has improved; I see that it is   13
improving; and I believe that it will continue to improve in natural and certain progress. Good and evil principles are widely at work: a crisis is evidently approaching; it may be dreadful, but I can have no doubts con-

---

[7]*Cumberland cow:* Apparently a popular fictive creature, the origin of which is unclear.

[8]Southey here refers to the failed ideals of the French Revolution. Begun with the purest of hopes that the *ancien régime* could be replaced *quickly* with an egalitarian society founded on reason, the revolution stalled and subjected the French people to a Reign of Terror, shocking for its murderous excesses.

cerning the result. Black and ominous as the aspects may appear, I regard them without dismay. The common exclamation of the poor and helpless, when they feel themselves oppressed, conveys to my mind the sum of the surest and safest philosophy. I say with them, "God is above," and trust Him for the event.

SIR THOMAS MORE.   God is above, . . . but the devil is below. Evil princi- 14 ples are, in their nature, more active than good. The harvest is precarious, and must be prepared with labour, and cost, and care; weeds spring up of themselves, and flourish and seed whatever may be the season. Disease, vice, folly and madness are contagious; while health and understanding are incommunicable, and wisdom and virtue hardly to be communicated! . . . We have come however to some conclusion in our discourse. Your notion of the improvement of the world has appeared to be a mere speculation, altogether inapplicable in practice; and as dangerous to weak heads and heated imaginations as it is congenial to benevolent hearts. Perhaps that improvement is neither so general, nor so certain as you suppose. Perhaps, even in this country there may be more knowledge than there was in former times, and less wisdom, . . . more wealth and less happiness, . . . more display and less virtue. This must be the subject of future conversation. I will only remind you now, that the French had persuaded themselves this was the most enlightened age of the world, and they the most enlightened people in it, . . . the politest, the most amiable, the most humane of nations, . . . and that a new era of philosophy, philanthropy and peace was about to commence under their auspices, . . . when they were upon the eve of a revolution which, for its complicated monstrosities, absurdities and horrors, is more disgraceful to human nature than any other series of events in history. Chew the cud upon this, and farewell!

From *Colloquy VII. The Manufacturing System.*

SIR THOMAS MORE.   . . . The spirit which built and endowed monasteries 15 is gone. Are you one of those persons who think it has been superseded for the better by that which erects steam-engines and cotton mills?

MONTESINOS.   They are indeed miserable politicians who mistake wealth 16 for welfare in their estimate of national prosperity; and none have committed this great error more egregiously than some of those who have been called statesmen by the courtesy of England. Yet the manufacturing system is a necessary stage in the progress of society. Without it this nation could not have supported the long and tremendous conflict which has delivered Europe from the yoke of military despotism, . . . the worst of all evils. If England had not been enabled by the use of steam-engines to send out every year myriads of brave men, and millions of specie, . . . what had Europe, and what had England itself been now? This inestimable benefit we have seen and felt. And from the consequences of that skill in machinery which the manufacturing system alone could have produced, we may expect ultimately to obtain the greatest advantages of science and civilization at the least expense of human labour.

SIR THOMAS MORE.   Sir Poet, travel not so hastily in your speculations!   *17* There is a wide gulph between you and that point, and it is not to be crost by one of these flying leaps in seven-leagued boots. . . . Yonder children are on the way to a manufactory, where they pass six days out of the seven, from morning till night. Is it likely that the little they learn at school on the seventh, (which ought to be their day of recreation as well as rest,) should counteract the effects of such an education, when the moral atmosphere wherein they live and move and have their being, is as noxious to the soul, as the foul and tainted air which they inhale is to their bodily constitution?

MONTESINOS.   Yet the most celebrated minister of the age,[9] the only min-   *18* ister who for many generations has deserved to be called a Premier, the minister whom our best and wisest statesmen at this day profess entirely to admire and implicitly to follow, . . . he made his boast of this very evil, and congratulated Parliament that the nation had a new source of wealth and revenue in the labour of children: so completely had the political system in which he was trained up seared his heart and obscured his understanding.

SIR THOMAS MORE.   Confess that this is an evil which had no existence in   *19* former times! There are new things under the sun, . . . new miseries, . . . new enormities, . . . this portentous age produces them,

partimque figuras
Rettulit antiquas, partim nova monstra creavit.[10]

MONTESINOS.   This evil, however, existed long ago to a considerable de-   *20* gree in the Low Countries. It is Sueyro's remark that, when Count Baldwin the Young, in the tenth century, established the weavers and clothiers in Ghent, he laid the foundation of that city's wealth and prosperity; but prepared at the same time the seed-bed of those commotions which made it during some ages the most turbulent city in Christendom.

SIR THOMAS MORE.   The history of the Low Countries down to their fatal   *21* connection with the House of Austria, deserves to be treated by some one

---

[9]The reference is most probably to William Pitt (the Elder, 1708–1778), first earl of Chatham and Prime Minister of England.

[10]*partimque figuras . . . :* Partly it [industrialization] has brought back ancient figures and partly it has created new monsters.

who, with the minute diligence of an antiquary, should unite the comprehensiveness of a philosophic mind. Manufactures in those times produced more good than evil, . . . for the men whom they brutalized in one way, would have been brutalized in another and a worse by the warlike spirit of the age. They raised up a civic and pacific interest; and even their strong democratic tendency was favourable to the improvement of Europe. The modern system possesses this tendency in a much greater degree, when it has become altogether dangerous. It is also essentially different and essentially worse. Large properties were in former times carved out with the sword, and founded upon the right of conquest. Are those fortunes raised on a better foundation which are derived from a system like this? . . . from slavery direct or indirect, abroad or at home? . . . from the sweat and blood of black or brown slaves, working under the whip? or from the degradation in body and soul of those who, though white by complexion, and free by birth, are nevertheless in an actual state of servitude?

MONTESINOS.   Bad enough to serve the planter for a parallel and an excuse? There is a nation of warriors in Hindostan who call their deity All-Steel. Commercial nations, if they acknowledged the deity whom they serve, might call him All-Gold. And if the sum of their sacrifices were compared, Mammon[11] would be found a more merciless fiend than Moloch.[12] 22

SIR THOMAS MORE.   The servants of Mammon are however wiser in their generation than the children of light. They serve a master who rewards them. 23

MONTESINOS.   They pursue their object with steadiness and singleness of purpose, and rewarded they are abundantly with what they covet. Yet their power of creating wealth brings with it a consequence not dissimilar to that which Midas[13] suffered. The love of lucre is one of those base passions which 24

> harden all within,
> And petrify the feeling.

He who, at the beginning of his career, uses his fellow-creatures as bodily machines for producing wealth, ends not unfrequently in becoming an intellectual one himself, employed in continually increasing what it is impossible for him to enjoy.

---

[11]*Mammon:* A false god, as alluded to in the New Testament, the personification of worldly riches and greed.

[12]*Moloch:* In the Old Testament, the god to whom the Phoenicians sacrificed children.

[13]*Midas:* In Greek mythology, the king of Phrygia who, granted his wish of the "golden touch," turned everything — even his food — to gold, whereupon he repented his greed and washed away his powers in the river Pactolus.

SIR THOMAS MORE.   What then shall we say of a system which in its direct   25
consequences debases all who are engaged in it? a system that employs
men unremittingly in pursuits unwholesome for the body, and unprofitable for the mind, . . . a system in which the means are so bad, that any
result would be dearly purchased at such an expense of human misery and
degradation, and the end so fearful, that the worst calamities which society
has hitherto endured may be deemed light in comparison with it?

MONTESINOS.   Like the whole fabric of our society it has been the growth   26
of circumstances, not a system foreplanned, foreseen and deliberately chosen. Such as it is we have inherited it, . . . or rather have fallen into it, and
must get out of it as well as we can. We must do our best to remove its
evils, and to mitigate them while they last, and to modify and reduce it till
only so much remains as is indispensable for the general good.

SIR THOMAS MORE.   The facts will not warrant you in saying that it has   27
come upon the country unsought and unforeseen. You have prided yourselves upon this system, you have used every means for extending it; you
have made it the measure of your national prosperity. It is a wen, a fun-
gous excrescence from the body politic: the growth might have been
checked if the consequences had been apprehended in time; but now it has
acquired so great a bulk, its nerves have branched so widely, and the vessels of the tumour are so inosculated into some of the principal veins and
arteries of the natural system, that to remove it by absorption is impossible,
and excision would be fatal.

MONTESINOS.   Happily, this is but a metaphor; and the body politic, like   28
its crowned head, never dies.

SIR THOMAS MORE.   But as there are evils worse than death for individuals,   29
so are there calamities for a people worse than extermination. The Jews,
during a full millennium, might have envied the lot of the Carthaginians;
and even at this day the great body of that extraordinary and miraculously
preserved people would have cause to regret that a remnant had been
spared, were it not for the hope of Israel.[14]

---

[14]*Carthaginians and Jews:* When the city of Carthage were destroyed in the Punic Wars of
147, the vast majority of its citizens were killed, whereas in the Roman conquests of Jerusalem from 62 B.C., the Jewish people were allowed to survive, though they were forced
to live under foreign rule or in exile. Montesinos refers to these conquests and suggests
that though the Carthaginians appear to have suffered a worse fate in being annihilated,
in many ways the fate of the Jews was worse in that they suffered more and for a longer
period of time.

MONTESINOS.   We shall work our way through this evil, as we have done   *30*
through others. . . .

• • •

[Some time has passed, and Montesinos and Sir Thomas are walking
in the English countryside.] By this time we had reached the bank above
Applethwaite. The last question of my companion was one to which I
could make no reply, and as he neither talked for triumph, nor I endeavoured to elude the force of his argument, we remained awhile in silence,
looking upon the assemblage of dwellings below. Here, and in the adjoining hamlet of Millbeck, the effects of manufactures and of agriculture may
be seen and compared. The old cottages are such as the poet and the
painter equally delight in beholding. Substantially built of the native stone
without mortar, dirtied with no white-lime, and their long low roofs covered with slate, if they had been raised by the magic of some indigenous
Amphion's music, the materials could not have adjusted themselves more
beautifully in accord with the surrounding scene[15]; and time has still farther harmonized them with weather, stains, lichens and moss, short
grasses and short fern, and stone plants of various kinds. The ornamented
chimnies, round or square, less adorned than those which, like little turrets, crest the houses of the Portugueze peasantry, and yet not less happily
suited to their place; the hedge of clipt box beneath the windows, the rose
bushes beside the door, the little patch of flower ground with its tall hol-
yocks in front, the garden beside, the bee-hives, and the orchard with its
bank of daffodils and snowdrops, (the earliest and the profusest in these
parts,) indicate in the owners some portion of ease and leisure, some regard to neatness and comfort, some sense of natural and innocent and
healthful enjoyment. The new cottages of the manufacturers, are . . . upon
the manufacturing pattern . . . naked, and in a row.

How is it, said I, that every thing which is connected with manufac-   *32*
tures, presents such features of unqualified deformity? From the largest of
Mammon's temples down to the poorest hovel in which his helotry are
stalled, the edifices have all one character.[16] Time cannot mellow them;
Nature will neither clothe nor conceal them; and they remain always as
offensive to the eye as to the mind!

---

[15]*Amphion:* In Greek mythology, the player of a magic lyre whose music enabled stones of
the yet unbuilt walls of Thebes to be moved into place without effort.

[16]*Mammon's temples down to the poorest hovel:* More is suggesting that all that money or mammon creates, from the greatest mansions (temples) to the poorest shacks (hovels), is in
some way grotesque. Here "helotry" refers to peasants who are "stalled," living as cattle
do in domiciles resembling stalls.

REVIEW QUESTIONS

1. What is the interplay between fate and free will that will lead to the improvement of the world, according to Southey?
2. How does Montesinos modify Sir Thomas More's statement "that the human race will one day attain the utmost degree of general virtue, and thereby general happiness, of which humanity is capable"?
3. What are the dangers of supposing that an improved condition of society is too near?
4. According to Montesinos, what effects will follow from the emergence of the manufacturing system? How does Sir Thomas More challenge the point?
5. What are the offenses of the manufacturing system? In what way does this system debase those involved with it?

DISCUSSION AND WRITING QUESTIONS

1. Sir Thomas attacks the optimism of Montesinos by claiming that his "notion of the improvement of the world has appeared to be a mere speculation, altogether inapplicable in practice; and as dangerous to weak heads and heated imaginations as it is congenial to benevolent hearts." How fair is the criticism? To what extent can it be applied to Condorcet as well as Montesinos?
2. Consider your answer to Review Question 5. Conditions for laborers in the manufacturing houses of the Industrial Revolution were notoriously bad — prompting Southey, through the voice of Sir Thomas More, to claim that workers had become, in effect, free-born slaves. In the *Communist Manifesto* you will read much the same remark. Is there any way today in which you find wage laborers existing in a "state of servitude"? How do you define this servitude?
3. Attempt to explain the reaction of Montesinos to the cottages of the manufacturers — which, he says, present "features of unqualified deformity." In what ways does the manufacturing system present both an advance toward progress and a regression from it?

THOMAS BABINGTON MACAULAY
(1800–1859)

The history of England is emphatically the history of progress. It is the history of a constant movement of the public mind, of a constant change in the institutions of a great society. We see that society, at the beginning of the twelfth century, in a state more miserable than the state in which the most degraded nations of the East now are. We see it subjected to the tyranny of a handful of armed foreigners. We see a strong distinction of caste separating the victorious Norman from the vanquished Saxon. We see the great body of the population in a state of personal slavery. We see the most debasing and cruel superstition exercising boundless dominion over the most elevated and benevolent minds. We see the multitude sunk in brutal ignorance, and the studious few engaged in acquiring what did not deserve the name of knowledge. In the course of seven centuries the wretched and degraded race have become the greatest and most highly civilised people that ever the world saw, have spread their dominion over every quarter of the globe, have scattered the seeds of mighty empires and republics over vast continents of which no dim intimation had ever reached Ptolemy or Strabo, have created a maritime power which would annihilate in a quarter of an hour the navies of Tyre, Athens, Carthage, Venice, and Genoa together, have carried the science of healing, the means of locomotion and correspondence, every mechanical art, every manufacture, every thing that promotes the convenience of life, to a perfection which our ancestors would have thought magical, have produced a literature which may boast of works not inferior to the noblest which Greece has bequeathed to us, have discovered the laws which regulate the motions of the heavenly bodies, have speculated with exquisite subtilty on the operations of the human mind, have been the acknowledged leaders of the human race in the career of political improvement. The history of England is the history of this great change in the moral, intellectual, and physical state of the inhabitants of our own island.[1]

The vigorous optimism of this statement perfectly records what Thomas Babington Macaulay's contemporaries thought an ennobling and assured view of the English character; the passage also records what later critics would consider a smug assumption of English preeminence. Thomas Babington Macaulay was a man of great influence in 19th century England. He served in Parliament, where his gift

---

[1]Thomas Babington Macaulay. "Sir James Mackintosh's History of the Revolution," in *Critical, Historical, and Miscellaneous Essays*. New York: Sheldon and Co., Riverside Press, 1866, pp. 279–280.

for oratory gained him an influential circle of friends; he served the interests of the empire by sitting on the Supreme Council of India, in which capacity he instituted a penal code and system of Western education; for a brief time he served as secretary for war; and, at the end of his life, he was granted the title of Baron Macaulay of Rothley.

If Macaulay was excessive in his enthusiasm for the progress of the English character, he nonetheless is regarded as a master of language. His style set the standard for fifty years of English letters. He is best remembered for his five-volume *History of England from the Revolution of 1688*, the year in which Parliament deposed James II and wrested authority from the crown. Macaulay had intended to end his history in 1820 but, at the time of his death, had completed only the treatment of the revolution itself, through the life of William III (d. 1702).

Macaulay was born on October 25, 1800, at Rothley Temple, Leicestershire. He was educated at private schools and while at Trinity college, Cambridge, won prizes in poetry and, at the age of twenty-four, a fellowship that included a yearly stipend. Though trained as a lawyer, he did not practice; instead, he devoted himself to literary reviews and essays (on, among other topics, the need to abolish slavery). At the age of twenty-five he won general acclaim — which was to last a lifetime — for an essay on the poet Milton that appeared in the *Edinburgh Review*.

In 1830, Macaulay entered Parliament and worked for the passage of the Reform Act of 1832. Two years later he was an administrator in India, where he lived with his sister for a time (he never married) and, through his writing, influenced the development of Indian jurisprudence and education. On returning to England he resumed his political career and held a seat in the prime minister's cabinet. But he soon tired of politics and began work on his *History,* the first four volumes of which sold enormously well and were translated into ten languages. Before he could finish the fifth volume, he succumbed to illness and died on December 28, 1859. Macaulay was honored with burial at Westminster Abbey.

Among Macaulay's published letters, speeches, and essays are many reviews, one of which (in the *Edinburgh Review,* 1830) was devoted to Robert Southey's *Colloquies*. Though Southey was himself an optimist, he paused in the *Colloquies* to consider the negative effects of growth. Macaulay found the reflection unwarranted and unsubstantiated; he savaged Southey's work, especially the sections you have just read on the British manufacturing system. From a man who believed that "the history of England [was] emphatically the history of progress," such an attack could be expected. (N.B. Unless otherwise indicated, footnotes in this selection are provided by George H. Ford, editor of "The Victorian Age" in *The Norton Anthology of English Literature*, 4th edition, Volume 2, M. H. Abrams, general editor. New York: W. W. Norton, 1979, pp. 1631–1637.)

From *A REVIEW OF SOUTHEY'S* COLLOQUIES[1]

. . . Perhaps we could not select a better instance of the spirit which   *1*
pervades the whole book than the passages in which Mr. Southey gives
his opinion of the manufacturing system. There is nothing which he hates
so bitterly. It is, according to him, a system more tyrannical than that of
the feudal ages, a system of actual servitude, a system which destroys the
bodies and degrades the minds of those who are engaged in it. He expresses a hope that the competition of other nations may drive us out of
the field; that our foreign trade may decline; and that we may thus enjoy
a restoration of national sanity and strength. But he seems to think that
the extermination of the whole manufacturing population would be a
blessing, if the evil could be removed in no other way.

Mr. Southey does not bring forward a single fact in support of these   *2*
views; and, as it seems to us, there are facts which lead to a very different
conclusion. In the first place, the poor rate[2] is very decidedly lower in the
manufacturing than in the agricultural districts. If Mr. Southey will look
over the Parliamentary returns on this subject, he will find that the amount
of parochial relief required by the laborers in the different counties of England is almost exactly in inverse proportion to the degree in which the
manufacturing system has been introduced into those counties. The returns for the years ending in March, 1825, and in March, 1828, are now
before us. In the former year we find the poor rate highest in Sussex,[3]
about twenty shillings to every inhabitant. Then come Buckinghamshire,
Essex, Suffolk, Bedfordshire, Huntingdonshire, Kent, and Norfolk. In all
these the rate is above fifteen shillings a head. We will not go through the

---

Thomas Babington Macaulay. "A Review of Southey's *Colloquies*." [Published originally in
the *Edinburgh Review,* 1830]. Text and notes (unless otherwise indicated) appear in *The
Norton Anthology of English Literature,* 4th ed., Vol. 2. New York: Norton, pp. 1631–1637.

[1]Published in the *Edinburgh Review* (1830). In a book entitled *Colloquies on the Progress and
Prospects of Society* (1829), the poet and man of letters Robert Southey (1774–1843) had
sought to expose the evils of industrialism and to assert the superiority of the traditional
feudal and agricultural way of life of England's past. His romantic Toryism provoked Macaulay (1800–59) to review the book in a long and characteristic essay. As in his popular
History of England (1849–61), Macaulay seeks here to demolish his opponent with a bombardment of facts and figures demonstrating that industrialism and middle-class government have resulted in progress and increased comforts for mankind.

[2]Taxes on property, to provide food and lodging for the unemployed or unemployable.
The amount or rate of such taxes varied from district to district in England, depending
upon local conditions of unemployment.

[3]A predominantly agricultural district.

whole. Even in Westmoreland and the North Riding of Yorkshire, the rate is at more than eight shillings. In Cumberland and Monmouthshire, the most fortunate of all the agricultural districts, it is at six shillings. But in the West Riding of Yorkshire,[4] it is as low as five shillings: and when we come to Lancashire, we find it at four shillings, one-fifth of what it is in Sussex. The returns of the year ending in March, 1828, are a little, and but a little, more unfavorable to the manufacturing districts. Lancashire, even in that season of distress, required a smaller poor rate than any other district, and little more than one-fourth of the poor rate raised in Sussex. Cumberland alone, of the agricultural districts, was as well off as the West Riding of Yorkshire. These facts seem to indicate that the manufacturer is both in a more comfortable and in a less dependent situation than the agricultural laborer.

As to the effect of the manufacturing system on the bodily health, we must beg leave to estimate it by a standard far too low and vulgar for a mind so imaginative as that of Mr. Southey, the proportion of births and deaths. We know that, during the growth of this atrocious system, this new misery, to use the phrases of Mr. Southey, this new enormity, this birth of a portentous age, this pest which no man can approve whose heart is not seared or whose understanding has not been darkened, there has been a great diminution of mortality, and that this diminution has been greater in the manufacturing towns than anywhere else. The mortality still is, as it always was, greater in towns than in the country. But the difference has diminished in an extraordinary degree. There is the best reason to believe that the annual mortality of Manchester, about the middle of the last century, was one in twenty-eight. It is now reckoned at one in forty-five. In Glasgow and Leeds a similar improvement has taken place. Nay, the rate of mortality in those three great capitals of the manufacturing districts is now considerably less than it was, fifty years ago, over England and Wales, taken together, open country and all. We might with some plausibility maintain that the people live longer because they are better fed, better lodged, better clothed, and better attended in sickness, and that these improvements are owing to that increase of national wealth which the manufacturing system has produced. 3

Much more might be said on this subject. But to what end? It is not from bills of mortality and statistical tables that Mr. Southey has learned his political creed. He cannot stoop to study the history of the system which he abuses, to strike the balance between the good and evil which it has produced, to compare district with district, or generation with generation. We will give his own reason for his opinion, the only reason which he gives for it, in his own words: 4

---

[4] A manufacturing district.

"We remained a while in silence looking upon the assemblage of dwell-   5
ings below. Here, and in the adjoining hamlet of Millbeck, the effects of
manufactures and of agriculture may be seen and compared. The old cottages are such as the poet and the painter equally delight in beholding.
Substantially built of the native stone without mortar, dirtied with no
white lime, and their long low roofs covered with slate, if they had been
raised by the magic of some indigenous Amphion's[5] music, the materials
could not have adjusted themselves more beautifully in accord with the
surrounding scene; and time has still further harmonized them with
weather stains, lichens, and moss, short grasses, and short fern, and
stoneplants of various kinds. The ornamented chimneys, round or square,
less adorned than those which, like little turrets, crest the houses of the
Portuguese peasantry, and yet not less happily suited to their place;
the hedge of clipped box beneath the windows, the rose bushes beside the
door, the little patch of flower ground, with its tall hollyhocks in front; the
garden beside, the beehives, and the orchard with its bank of daffodils and
snowdrops, the earliest and profusest in these parts, indicate in the owners
some portion of ease and leisure, some regard to neatness and comfort,
some sense of natural, and innocent, and healthful enjoyment. The new
cottages of the manufacturers are upon the manufacturing pattern — naked, and in a row."

"'How is it,' said I, 'that everything which is connected with manufac-   6
tures presents such features of unqualified deformity? From the largest of
Mammon's temples down to the poorest hovel in which his helotry are
stalled, these edifices have all one character. Time will not mellow them;
nature will neither clothe nor conceal them; and they will remain always
as offensive to the eye as to the mind.'"

Here is wisdom. Here are the principles on which nations are to be   7
governed. Rosebushes and poor rates, rather than steam engines and independence. Mortality and cottages with weather stains, rather than
health and long life with edifices which time cannot mellow. We are told
that our age has invented atrocities beyond the imagination of our fathers;
that society has been brought into a state compared with which extermination would be a blessing; and all because the dwellings of cotton-spin-
ners are naked and rectangular. Mr. Southey has found out a way, he tells
us, in which the effects of manufactures and agriculture may be compared.
And what is this way? To stand on a hill, to look at a cottage and a factory,
and to see which is the prettier. Does Mr. Southey think that the body of
the English peasantry live, or ever lived, in substantial or ornamented cottages, with boxhedges, flower gardens, beehives, and orchards? If not,

---

[5]According to Greek mythology, Amphion's magical skill as a harp player caused the walls
of Thebes to be erected without human aid.

what is his parallel worth? We despise those mock philosophers,[6] who think that they serve the cause of science by depreciating literature and the fine arts. But if anything could excuse their narrowness of mind, it would be such a book as this. It is not strange that, when one enthusiast makes the picturesque the test of political good, another should feel inclined to proscribe altogether the pleasures of taste and imagination. . . .

It is not strange that, differing so widely from Mr. Southey as to the past progress of society, we should differ from him also as to its probable destiny. He thinks, that to all outward appearance, the country is hastening to destruction; but he relies firmly on the goodness of God. We do not see either the piety or the rationality of thus confidently expecting that the Supreme Being will interfere to disturb the common succession of causes and effects. We, too, rely on his goodness, on his goodness as manifested, not in extraordinary interpositions, but in those general laws which it has pleased him to establish in the physical and in the moral world. We rely on the natural tendency of the human intellect to truth, and on the natural tendency of society to improvement. We know no well-authenticated instance of a people which has decidedly retrograded in civilization and prosperity, except from the influence of violent and terrible calamities, such as those which laid the Roman Empire in ruins, or those which, about the beginning of the sixteenth century, desolated Italy. We know of no country which, at the end of fifty years of peace and tolerably good government, has been less prosperous than at the beginning of that period. The political importance of a state may decline, as the balance of power is disturbed by the introduction of new forces. Thus the influence of Holland and of Spain is much diminished. But are Holland and Spain poorer than formerly? We doubt it. Other countries have outrun them. But we suspect that they have been positively, though not relatively, advancing. We suspect that Holland is richer than when she sent her navies up the Thames,[7] that Spain is richer than when a French king was brought captive to the footstool of Charles the Fifth.[8]

History is full of the signs of this natural progress of society. We see in almost every part of the annals of mankind how the industry of individuals, struggling up against wars, taxes, famines, conflagrations, mischie-

8

9

---

[6]Presumably such Utilitarian philosophers as Jeremy Bentham, who had equated poetry with pushpin, a trifling game. It should be noted, however, that although Macaulay often attacked the Utilitarians for their narrow preoccupation with theory, his own position has much in common with theirs.

[7]In 1667 a Dutch fleet displayed its power by sailing up the river Thames without being challenged by the English navy.

[8]The Spanish king, Charles V, captured the king of France, Francis I, in the battle of Pavia (1525).

vous prohibitions, and more mischievous protections, creates faster than governments can squander, and repairs whatever invaders can destroy. We see the wealth of nations increasing, and all the arts of life approaching nearer and nearer to perfection, in spite of the grossest corruption and the wildest profusion on the part of rulers.

The present moment is one of great distress. But how small will that distress appear when we think over the history of the last forty years; a war,[9] compared with which all other wars sink into insignificance; taxation, such as the most heavily taxed people of former times could not have conceived; a debt larger than all the public debts that ever existed in the world added together; the food of the people studiously rendered dear; the currency imprudently debased, and imprudently restored. Yet is the country poorer than in 1790? We firmly believe that, in spite of all the misgovernment of her rulers, she has been almost constantly becoming richer and richer. Now and then there has been a stoppage, now and then a short retrogression; but as to the general tendency there can be no doubt. A single breaker may recede; but the tide is evidently coming in.

If we were to prophesy that in the year 1930[10] a population of fifty millions, better fed, clad, and lodged than the English of our time, will cover these islands, that Sussex and Huntingdonshire will be wealthier than the wealthiest parts of the West Riding of Yorkshire now are, that cultivation, rich as that of a flower garden, will be carried up to the very tops of Ben Nevis and Helvellyn,[11] that machines constructed on principles yet undiscovered will be in every house, that there will be no highways but railroads, no traveling but by steam, that our debt, vast as it seems to us, will appear to our great-grandchildren a trifling encumbrance, which might easily be paid off in a year or two, many people would think us insane. We prophesy nothing; but this we say: If any person had told the Parliament which met in perplexity and terror after the crash in 1720 that in 1830 the wealth of England would surpass all their wildest dreams, that the annual revenue would equal the principal of that debt which they considered as an intolerable burden, that for one man of ten thousand pounds then living there would be five men of fifty thousand pounds, that London would be twice as large and twice as populous, and that nevertheless the rate of mortality would have diminished to one-half of what it then was, that the post office would bring more into the exchequer than the excise and customs had brought in together under Charles the Second, that stage

---

[9]The wars against France and Napoleon, extending, with some interruptions, from 1792 to 1815.

[10]*1930:* That is, 100 years after the present essay was first published. [Behrens and Rosen]

[11]Mountains, in Scotland and in the English Lake District, respectively.

coaches would run from London to York in twenty-four hours,[12] that men would be in the habit of sailing without wind, and would be beginning to ride without horses, our ancestors would have given as much credit to the prediction as they gave to *Gulliver's Travels*.[13] Yet the prediction would have been true; and they would have perceived that it was not altogether absurd, if they had considered that the country was then raising every year a sum which would have purchased the fee-simple[14] of the revenue of the Plantagenets, ten times what supported the Government of Elizabeth, three times what, in the time of Cromwell,[15] had been thought intolerably oppressive. To almost all men the state of things under which they have been used to live seems to be the necessary state of things. We have heard it said that five per cent is the natural interest of money, that twelve is the natural number of a jury, that forty shillings is the natural qualification of a county voter. Hence it is that, though in every age everybody knows that up to his own time progressive improvement has been taking place, nobody seems to reckon on any improvement during the next generation. We cannot absolutely prove that those are in error who tell us that society has reached a turning point, that we have seen our best days. But so said all who came before us, and with just as much apparent reason. "A million a year will beggar us," said the patriots of 1640. "Two millions a year will grind the country to powder," was the cry in 1660. "Six millions a year, and a debt of fifty millions!" exclaimed Swift, "the high allies have been the ruin of us." "A hundred and forty millions of debt!" said Junius[16]; "well may we say that we owe Lord Chatham more than we shall ever pay, if we owe him such a load as this." "Two hundred and forty millions of debt!" cried all the statesmen of 1783 in chorus; "what abilities, or what economy on the part of a minister, can save a country so burdened?" We know that if, since 1783, no fresh debt had been incurred, the increased resources of the country would have enabled us to defray that debt at which Pitt, Fox, and Burke[17] stood aghast, nay, to defray it over and over again, and that with much lighter taxation than what we have actually borne. On what principle is it that, when we see nothing but improvement behind us, we are to expect nothing but deterioration before us?

---

[12]*London to York:* A distance of about 140 miles. [Behrens and Rosen]

[13]*Gulliver's Travels:* A satire by Jonathan Swift, 1726. [Behrens and Rosen]

[14]Absolute ownership of their estates. The Plantagenet family provided the monarchs of England from 1145 to 1485.

[15]*Cromwell:* The Puritan Oliver Cromwell (1599–1658) ruled England as a military dictator from 1653 until his death. [Behrens and Rosen]

[16]*Junius:* The pen name of an English political writer, who sent letters to a London newspaper from 1769 to 1772. [Behrens and Rosen]

[17]*Pitt, Fox, and Burke:* Liberal English statesmen — William Pitt (1708–1778), Charles James Fox (1749–1806), and Edmund Burke (1729–1797). [Behrens and Rosen]

It is not by the intermeddling of Mr. Southey's idol, the omniscient and omnipotent State, but by the prudence and energy of the people, that England has hitherto been carried forward in civilization; and it is to the same prudence and the same energy that we now look with comfort and good hope. Our rulers will best promote the improvement of the nation by strictly confining themselves to their own legitimate duties, by leaving capital to find its most lucrative course, commodities their fair price, industry and intelligence their natural reward, idleness and folly their natural punishment, by maintaining peace, by defending property, by diminishing the price of law, and by observing strict economy in every department of the State. Let the Government do this: the People will assuredly do the rest. *12*

REVIEW QUESTIONS

1. Macaulay is fond of using statistics. Cite two uses of statistics in his review. To what purpose does he put them?
2. Macaulay refers to general laws in the physical and moral worlds. What are these laws?
3. Macaulay asks on what principle it is that, when we see nothing but improvement behind us, we are to expect nothing but deterioration before us. What can you infer from this selection is Macaulay's answer to this question?

DISCUSSION AND WRITING QUESTIONS

1. Macaulay takes Southey to task for attacking the manufacturing system without citing proper evidence, such as statistics. You have noted (in Review Question 1) the uses to which Macaulay has put statistics. Do you agree that Southey's observations are weakened by his lack of quantifiable evidence? Are there aspects of Southey's argument that cannot be quantified?
2. In reading Macaulay's celebration of manufacturing, do you sense that he has overlooked evidence that might argue against his optimism? What statistics has he *not* cited?
3. Macaulay's contempt for Southey's *Colloquies* is plain. Find examples in Macaulay's use of language that reveal this contempt.
4. How accurate were Macaulay's predictions for 1930? Following his logic, how comfortable would you be in making the argument that despite our present difficulties (in the 1980s), conditions in one hundred years will be far superior to those of today?
5. "Though in every age everybody knows that up to his own time progressive improvement has been taking place, nobody seems to reckon on any improvement during the next generation." How accurate is this remark? Does it apply today?
6. What evidence does Macaulay give that the general laws to which he refers (see Review Question 2) are actually laws of nature — and not laws of Macaulay's invention?

KARL MARX *(1818–1883)*

At this point, we ask that you turn to *The Communist Manifesto*, written by Karl Marx and Friedrich Engels in 1848. First, read the general introduction to *The Class Struggle*, on pages 548–550. This will establish for you something of the philosophical and social contexts in which Marx and Engels were writing. Of particular note is the theory of history to which Marx subscribed, the Hegelian dialectic of progress achieved through conflict. Having read the introduction to Part VI, read the biographical sketch of Marx and then the *Manifesto* itself. You will readily see that the document is an important one in the literature of progress; though the engine that drives history, according to Marx, differs from the one described by Condorcet, both men accept implicitly the inevitability of progressive change. The advancement of the race proceeds not according to human law but according to natural, social law. For both Condorcet and Marx, the end is the same: an advanced state in which the ills of society are eliminated.

Separate questions for review and discussion are provided here so that you may reflect critically on *The Communist Manifesto* in relation to the other selections in this part of the book. While reading, you might want to keep in mind Marx's critique of industrial society and how it contrasts sharply with the views of Macaulay — and agrees, in part, with Southey's reservations. You may also want to observe similarities and differences between Marx and Condorcet. Both develop theories of history and then extrapolate from the past to the future. In spirit, the fundamental enterprises are quite similar, though the particular analyses of society differ markedly. (Turn, then, to page 548 for the introduction to *The Class Struggle*; to page 551 for the biographical sketch of Marx; and to page 554 for *The Communist Manifesto*.)

REVIEW QUESTIONS

1. What classes replaced the social gradations of feudal life?
2. What is the "bourgeoisie," and what role has it played in bringing about the fall of the feudal economy?
3. In paragraph 30, Marx and Engels sum up the contributions of the bourgeoisie. In helping to relieve abuses of feudal life, however, the bourgeoisie created new problems. What are these?
4. Recount the ways in which life for a worker in the 19th century manufacturing house was oppressive, according to Marx and Engels.
5. How is the proletariat recruited from all classes of the population?
6. Trace the stages of development of the proletariat.

7. In what relation do the Communists stand to the proletarians?
8. As you understand them, what are the goals of the Communist society with respect to the worker; private property; the family; education; national identity and international rivalry; class antagonisms?

DISCUSSION AND WRITING QUESTIONS

1. For Marx and Engels, economic forces in conflict are the engine of change in the world. According to Condorcet, human reason accounts for progressive change in the world. Marx and Engels and Condorcet regard progress to be law governed, yet they describe different laws. How do you account for the differences?
2. Reconsider the validity of Southey's observations in light of the attack on the manufacturing system by Marx and Engels. Do Macaulay's criticisms of Southey continue to hold up for you now that you've read *The Communist Manifesto?*
3. In paragraph 38, Marx and Engels use the language of military life to describe the conditions of a worker in a manufacturing house. To what effect?
4. Consider your answer to Review Question 8. To what extent are the goals of the Communists, as discussed in Part II of the *Manifesto,* compatible with the goals of Condorcet?
5. Find examples of the language that Marx and Engels use in the *Manifesto* to indicate that the class struggle operates as a *law* of social relations. One example would be item 2 in paragraph 64.
6. "The theoretical conclusions of the Communists are in no way based on ideas or principles that have been invented or discovered by this or that would-be universal reformer." What assumptions underlie this statement?

GEORGE BERNARD SHAW *(1856–1950)*

George Bernard Shaw lived a long and extraordinarily prolific life. Generally acknowledged as the most important English playwright since Shakespeare, Shaw is remembered also for his drama and music criticism, as well as for his pamphleteering on politics and matters of general social concern.

He was raised in Dublin, in a home of little affection. His father had failed in business and turned to drink; his mother was an opera singer and teacher of music who, while Shaw was a teenager, took his two sisters and moved to London. Shaw soon followed and, in his twenties, turned to a slow-aborning career in journalism. He wrote five novels, all rejected by the English publishing establishment. During this time, with no steady work, he spent a great deal of his time completing what was largely a process of self-education. He became a socialist (having read the works of Marx); joined the Fabian Society — a socialist organization dedicated to the reforming of British society through nonviolent means; discovered a genius for public speaking; and became a vegetarian. His journalism, chiefly reviews of drama, books, and music, began to sell. By 1892, Shaw had completed his first play, which, though unstaged, nonetheless began the career that was to earn him the Nobel Prize for Literature in 1925.

Among Shaw's most famous plays is *Man and Superman,* one long scene from which is entitled "Don Juan in Hell." In legend, Don Juan was a notorious lover who, having seduced the daughter of a military officer from Seville (in the Spanish rendering of the tale), kills the girl's father in a duel. Later, he has a statue of the slain man brought to a feast. The statue comes to life and drags Don Juan off to hell. Shaw describes his version of the legend as dealing "with sexual attraction . . . in a society in which the serious business of sex is left by men to women. . . ." The principal players are John Tanner (Don Juan), a socialist pamphleteer, and the woman who pursues him, Ann Whitefield (Dona Ana). Tanner flees to Spain and dreams of a descent into hell, where the mythic figures — Don Juan, Ana, the Devil, and Ana's slain father (as the statue) — gather in Shaw's words to discuss the "merits of the heavenly and hellish states, and the future of the world." The scene forms a major section of the play and is often staged by itself. In one memorable speech, the Devil (addressing Don Juan, Ana, and the statue) offers an unflattering view of Man, in direct counterpoint to the optimism of Macaulay.

And is Man any the less destroying himself for all this boasted brain of his? Have you walked up and down upon the earth lately? I have; and I have examined Man's wonderful inventions. And I tell you that in the arts of life man invents nothing; but in the arts of death he outdoes Nature herself, and produces by chemistry and machinery all the slaughter of plague, pestilence, and famine. The peasant I tempt today eats and drinks what was eaten and drunk by the peasants of ten thousand years ago; and the house he lives in has not altered as much in a thousand centuries as the fashion of a lady's bonnet in a score of weeks. But when he goes out to slay, he carries a marvel of mechanism that lets loose at the touch of his finger all the hidden molecular energies, and leaves the javelin, the arrow, the blowpipe of his fathers far behind. In the arts of peace Man is a bungler. I have seen his cotton factories and the like, with machinery that a greedy dog could have invented if it had wanted money instead of food. I know his clumsy typewriters and bungling locomotives and tedious bicycles: they are toys compared to the Maxim gun, the submarine torpedo boat. There is nothing in Man's industrial machinery but his greed and sloth: his heart is in his weapons. This marvellous force of Life of which you boast is a force of Death: Man measures his strength by his destructiveness. What is his religion? An excuse for hating me. What is his law? An excuse for hanging you. What is his morality? Gentility! an excuse for consuming without producing. What is his art? An excuse for gloating over pictures of slaughter. What are his politics? Either the worship of a despot because a despot can kill, or parliamentary cock-fighting. I spent an evening lately in a certain celebrated legislature, and heard the pot lecturing the kettle for its blackness, and ministers answering questions. When I left I chalked up on the door the old nursery saying "Ask no questions and you will be told no lies." I bought a sixpenny family magazine, and found it full of pictures of young men shooting and stabbing one another. I saw a man die: he was a London bricklayer's laborer with seven children. He left seventeen pounds club money; and his wife spent it all on his funeral and went into the workhouse with the children next day. She would not have spent sevenpence on her children's schooling: the law had to force her to let them be taught gratuitously; but on death she spent all she had. Their imagination glows, their energies rise up at the idea of death, these people: they love it; and the more horrible it is the more they enjoy it. Hell is a place far above their comprehension: they derive their notion of it from two of the greatest fools that ever lived, an Italian and an Englishman. The Italian described it as a place of mud, frost, filth, fire, and venomous serpents: all torture.[1] This ass, when he was not lying about me, was maundering about some woman whom he saw once in the street. The Englishman described me as being expelled from heaven by cannons and gunpowder; and to this day every Briton believes that the whole of his silly story is in the Bible.[2] What else he says I do not know; for it is all in a long poem which neither I nor anyone else ever succeeded in wading through. It is the same in everything. The highest form of literature is the tragedy, a play in which everybody is murdered at the end. In the old chronicles you read of earthquakes and pestilences, and are told that these shewed the power and majesty of God and the littleness of Man. Nowadays the chronicles describe battles. In a battle two bodies of men shoot at one another with bullets and explosive shells until one body runs away, when the others chase the fugitives on horseback and cut them to pieces as they fly. And this, the chron-

---

[1] Shaw is referring to *The Inferno*, by the Italian poet Dante Alighieri (1265–1321).

[2] *Paradise Lost*, by the English poet John Milton (1608–1674).

icle concludes, shews the greatness and majesty of empires, and the littleness of the vanquished. Over such battles the people run about the streets yelling with delight, and egg their Governments on to spend hundreds of millions of money in the slaughter, whilst the strongest Ministers dare not spend an extra penny in the pound against the poverty and pestilence through which they themselves daily walk. I could give you a thousand instances; but they all come to the same thing: the power that governs the earth is not the power of Life but of Death; and the inner need that has served Life to the effort of organising itself into the human being is not the need for higher life but for a more efficient engine of destruction. The plague, the famine, the earthquake, the tempest were too spasmodic in their action; the tiger and crocodile were too easily satiated and not cruel enough: something more constantly, more ruthlessly, more ingeniously destructive was needed; and that something was Man, the inventor of the rack, the stake, the gallows, the electric chair; of sword and gun and poison gas: above all, of justice, duty, patriotism, and all the other isms by which even those who are clever enough to be humanely disposed are persuaded to become the most destructive of all the destroyers.

Shaw is well known for introducing his plays with essay-length discussions not only on stagecraft but also on the themes of the work at hand. In *Man and Superman* he adds an appendix as well — a series of ten pamphlets representing the political thinking of his main character, John Tanner. The following essay, entitled "Progress an Illusion" (the seventh of the ten pamphlets), stands with the Devil's speech in marked contrast to Macaulay's optimism. While the tone of both essay and speech is pessimistic, even cynical, Shaw himself believed in "a purposeful and eternal movement toward ever higher organisms." Such a movement was for Shaw "a more satisfactory explanation of the nature of things than 'blind' Darwinian evolution, and one which restored a sense of divinity to the universe besides."[3] As you've already seen, Shaw's hope for what man could become did not deter him from offering candid and often withering views of what man was.

Shaw lived ninety-four years, through two world wars. He spent his youth in an age in which air travel had not yet been invented; he spent his last years in a postnuclear world. Surely the changes he saw in his long life were enormous; and as over twenty plays, five novels, and volumes of miscellaneous essays can attest, Shaw was a man who had something to say about his world. His most famous plays include *Man and Superman* (1905), *Pygmalion* (1913) — the basis for the popular musical *My Fair Lady*, *Heartbreak House* (1920), and *Saint Joan* (1923); these continue to be produced today. Shaw survived his wife of forty-five years; he died in 1950.

---

[3]Stanley Weintraub. *The Portable Bernard Shaw.* New York: Penguin, 1977, p. 13.

PROGRESS AN ILLUSION

Unfortunately the earnest people get drawn off the track of evolution *1* by the illusion of progress. Any Socialist can convince us easily that the difference between Man as he is and Man as he might become, without further evolution, under millennial conditions of nutrition, environment, and training, is enormous. He can shew that inequality and iniquitous distribution of wealth and allotment of labor have arisen through an unscientific economic system, and that Man, faulty as he is, no more intended to establish any such ordered disorder than a moth intends to be burnt when it flies into a candle flame. He can shew that the difference between the grace and strength of the acrobat and the bent back of the rheumatic field laborer is a difference produced by conditions, not by nature. He can shew that many of the most detestable human vices are not radical, but are mere reactions of our institutions on our very virtues. The Anarchist, the Fabian,[1] the Salvationist, the Vegetarian, the doctor, the lawyer, the parson, the professor of ethics, the gymnast, the soldier, the sportsman, the inventor, the political program-maker, all have some prescription for bettering us; and almost all their remedies are physically possible and aimed at admitted evils. To them the limit of progress is, at worst, the completion of all the suggested reforms and the levelling up of all men to the point attained already by the most highly nourished and cultivated in mind and body.

Here, then, as it seems to them, is an enormous field for the energy of *2* the reformer. Here are many noble goals attainable by many of those paths up the Hill Difficulty along which great spirits love to aspire. Unhappily, the hill will never be climbed by Man as we know him. It need not be denied that if we all struggled bravely to the end of the reformers' paths we should improve the world prodigiously. But there is no more hope in that If than in the equally plausible assurance that if the sky falls we shall all catch larks. We are not going to tread those paths: we have not sufficient energy. We do not desire the end enough: indeed in most cases we do not effectively desire it at all. Ask any man would he like to be a better man; and he will say yes, most piously. Ask him would he like to have a million of money; and he will say yes, most sincerely. But the pious citizen who would like to be a better man goes on behaving just as he did before. And the tramp who would like the million does not take the trouble to earn ten

George Bernard Shaw. "Devil's Speech," pp. 145–147; and "Progress an Illusion," pp. 236–242 in *Man and Superman*. Baltimore: Penguin, 1964.
[1]*Fabian:* A member of a nonrevolutionary socialist society founded in London in 1883–1884 by persons seeking to establish a democratic socialist state in England.

shillings: multitudes of men and women, all eager to accept a legacy of a million, live and die without having ever possessed five pounds at one time, although beggars have died in rags on mattresses stuffed with gold which they accumulated because they desired it enough to nerve them to get it and keep it. The economists who discovered that demand created supply soon had to limit the proposition to "effective demand," which turned out, in the final analysis, to mean nothing more than supply itself; and this holds good in politics, morals, and all other departments as well: the actual supply is the measure of the effective demand; and the mere aspirations and professions produce nothing. No community has ever yet passed beyond the initial phases in which its pugnacity and fanaticism enabled it to found a nation, and its cupidity to establish and develop a commercial civilization. . . .

Turn to Republican America. America has no Star Chamber, and no feudal barons. But it has Trusts; and it has millionaires whose factories, fenced in by live electric wires and defended by Pinkerton retainers with magazine rifles, would have made a Radical of Reginald Front de Bœuf.[2] Would Washington or Franklin have lifted a finger in the cause of American Independence if they had foreseen its reality?

No: what Cæsar, Cromwell, and Napoleon could not do with all the physical force and moral prestige of the State in their mighty hands, cannot be done by enthusiastic criminals and lunatics. Even the Jews, who, from Moses to Marx and Lassalle,[3] have inspired all the revolutions, have had to confess that, after all, the dog will return to his vomit and the sow that was washed to her wallowing in the mire; and we may as well make up our minds that Man will return to his idols and his cupidities, in spite of all "movements" and all revolutions, until his nature is changed. Until then, his early successes in building commercial civilizations (and such civilizations, Good Heavens!) are but preliminaries to the inevitable later stage, now threatening us, in which the passions which built the civilization became fatal instead of productive, just as the same qualities which make the lion king in the forest ensure his destruction when he enters a city. Nothing can save society then except the clear head and the wide purpose: war and competition, potent instruments of selection and evolution in one epoch, become ruinous instruments of degeneration in the next. In the breeding of animals and plants, varieties which have arisen by selection through many generations relapse precipitously into the wild type in a generation or two when selection ceases; and in the same way a civilization in which lusty pugnacity and greed have ceased to act as selec-

---

[2]*Reginald Front de Boeuf:* A tyrannical knight in Sir Walter Scott's *Ivanhoe* (1819).

[3]*Ferdinand Lassalle:* (1825–1864) A disciple of Karl Marx and a leading proponent of socialism in Germany, Lassalle was influential in founding the German Worker's Union.

tive agents and have begun to obstruct and destroy, rushes downwards and backwards with a suddenness that enables an observer to see with consternation the upward steps of many centuries retraced in a single lifetime. This has often occurred even within the period covered by history; and in every instance the turning point has been reached long before the attainment, or even the general advocacy on paper, of the levelling-up of the mass to the highest point attainable by the best nourished and cultivated normal individuals.

We must therefore frankly give up the notion that Man as he exists is   5
capable of net progress. There will always be an illusion of progress, because wherever we are conscious of an evil we remedy it, and therefore always seem to ourselves to be progressing, forgetting that most of the evils we see are the effects, finally become acute, of long-unnoticed retrogressions; that our compromising remedies seldom fully recover the lost ground; above all, that on the lines along which we are degenerating, good has become evil in our eyes, and is being undone in the name of progress precisely as evil is undone and replaced by good on the lines along which we are evolving. This is indeed the Illusion of Illusions; for it gives us infallible and appalling assurance that if our political ruin is to come, it will be effected by ardent reformers and supported by enthusiastic patriots as a series of necessary steps in our progress. Let the Reformer, the Progressive, the Meliorist then reconsider himself and his eternal ifs and ans[4] which never become pots and pans. Whilst Man remains what he is, there can be no progress beyond the point already attained and fallen headlong from at every attempt at civilization; and since even that point is but a pinnacle to which a few people cling in giddy terror above an abyss of squalor, a mere progress should no longer charm us.

---

[4]*ans:* Plural of *an,* an archaism for "if."

REVIEW QUESTIONS

1. According to Shaw, what account do socialists give of present human conditions? How do socialists explain the ills of society?
2. Why is it that man shall never climb up the "Hill Difficulty"?
3. Shaw refers to principles of evolution in this essay. For what purpose?
4. How does Shaw account for what he terms the illusion of progress?
5. "Whilst Man remains what he is, there can be no progress. . . ." Based on your answers to Review Questions 1–4 and on your consideration of the discussion questions, write a paragraph in which you take Shaw's position and define who — and what — man is.

DISCUSSION AND WRITING QUESTIONS

1. You've read the Devil's speech from "Don Juan in Hell." You've also read Macaulay's views on optimism. How do you account for such widely divergent views of human perfectibility?
2. Reread Shaw's first paragraph. How accurately has he summarized the views of Marx and Engels, as expressed in *The Communist Manifesto*?
3. "No community has ever yet passed beyond the initial phases in which its pugnacity and fanaticism enabled it to found a nation. . . ." Shaw applies this statement to Republican America. What conclusions does he draw? Do you agree with him?
4. Shaw believes that the passions that led to the building of modern civilization are the same passions that now threaten us. Marx and Engels make much the same point in their discussion of the bourgeoisie. In Shaw's case, to what passions do you believe he is referring? Do you agree with his assessment?
5. What evidence do you find that Shaw in his fashion — like Marx and Condorcet in theirs — operates with a theory of history? What is this theory?
6. Shaw gives us a bleak view. He holds out no hope for progress until man's nature changes. What changes do you think Shaw has in mind? What changes do you believe are called for? Do you think these changes possible? Explain.

ALDOUS HUXLEY *(1894–1963)*

Aldous Huxley, the grandson of T. H. Huxley (see pages 492 and 493), was born in Godalming, Surrey, in 1894. Other members of his distinguished family devoted careers to physiology, biology, and education; Aldous would have given his life to medicine had he not contracted a corneal disease that left him nearly blind and incapable of working with microscopes. He turned instead to literature and published his first novel, *Crome Yellow,* in 1921 and followed with *Antic Hay* in 1923. Both were successes, and his career was established. Numerous books followed, among them: *Point Counterpoint* (1928); *Eyeless in Gaza* (1936); and *Time Must Have a Stop* (1944). In 1936, Huxley moved to the United States and made a home in California. Increasingly, he tended to the mystical and experimented with naturally occurring, hallucinogenic drugs — the subject of his *Doors of Perception* (1954). Huxley died on November 22, 1963.

The selection that follows is taken from his anti-utopian novel *Brave New World* (1932), in which Huxley the satirist and cynic takes a hard look at the world he projects based on deficiencies of English life in the 1920s. The novel's ironic title comes from a line in Shakespeare's *The Tempest,* in which Miranda marvels in response to an enchanted island: "O brave new world that has such people in it!" The future that Huxley imagines is more nightmare than enchantment, for here life is controlled completely. The story takes place in 632 A.F. — "After Ford." (Henry Ford, 1863–1947, was the founder of the automotive assembly line.) Following a general upheaval called the Nine Years' War, the world Controllers established a new society (a Brave New World). To achieve order, the controllers give people whatever they need to keep them content: unlimited sex, tranquilizers, and carefully orchestrated experiences so that no one will suffer from hunger, either physical or spiritual. People are "happy"; but then one must examine the extent to which the inhabitants, mass-produced in a genetic hatchery, are people: up to ninety-six twins can be incubated from one fertilized egg. Alphas, Betas, Deltas, Gammas, and Epsilons form an intellectual caste system, and are created with intellects and emotions perfectly suited to their stations; thus no deformed Epsilon Semi Moron who does what an Alpha would consider "demeaning" work is capable of being frustrated with his lot. Love, art, and science are suppressed because they lead to instability, and instability threatens happiness. Idle reflection is suppressed for the same reason, and the inhabitants of the Brave New World are given regular doses of the powerful tranquilizer "soma"; they are titillated at movies that physically stimulate them ("feelies"); and they engage in casual and promiscuous sex without giving thought to procreation.

Early in the novel, we meet Bernard Marx, a bright but misanthropic Alpha who is unlike others of his kind in that he is physically unattractive — his dwarfism owing, perhaps, to a mistake in the recipe for his incubation. As an Alpha, Bernard is entitled to travel from the carefully controlled environment of the Brave New World to New Mexico, where he can study a reservation of "savages" whose lives have gone uncontrolled. There Bernard — and the woman who accompanies him, Lenina — find John, who turns out to be the naturally born son of the soon-to-be-deposed Director of the Hatcheries (Tomakin). John speaks a somewhat awkward English but quotes Shakespeare with effect; his mother, Linda, is herself a transplant from the controlled world who has been left to languish in the wilderness. Bernard and Lenina return to London with John and Linda. John is to become a "curiosity" and is referred to as the "Savage." All of London is excited by his presence, but John finds the mindless pleasure-seeking of this new world repugnant. His mother is spirited away and pumped into oblivion with soma. Eventually, she's given an overdose; when John learns that she is dying, he visits the hospital and finds children at play near her bed in order that they may be made insensitive to death. John reacts violently and, along with Bernard Marx and a poet friend — Helmholtz Watson, is brought before one of the world Controllers, Mustapha Mond, a once-brilliant scientist who is now responsible for shaping life in the Brave New World. This brings us to our excerpt, Chapters sixteen and seventeen of the novel.

In curious ways, Huxley's future world resembles the one Condorcet imagined, at least in its ends: there is apparently no suffering; there are no wars; people are happy and indulged. Yet this is not a world of reasoned happiness; or rather, it is a world in which a few can reason while the mass of humanity exists in a state of torpid, unthinking pleasure. But one who considers the pain and inordinate suffering of our own world might ask: would it be so terrible to have food enough, carnal pleasure enough, job satisfaction enough never to be unhappy? Could we not do worse (and haven't we)? What, after all, are we attempting to achieve with our programs for progress?

BRAVE NEW WORLD

Chapter Sixteen

The room into which the three were ushered was the Controller's study. 1

"His fordship will be down in a moment." The Gamma butler left them to themselves. 2

Helmholtz laughed aloud. 3

"It's more like a caffeine-solution party than a trial," he said, and let himself fall into the most luxurious of the pneumatic arm-chairs. "Cheer up, Bernard," he added, catching sight of his friend's green unhappy face. 4

Aldous Huxley. Chapters 16 & 17 of *Brave New World*. New York: Bantam, 1932, pp. 147–163.

But Bernard would not be cheered; without answering, without even looking at Helmholtz, he went and sat down on the most uncomfortable chair
in the room, carefully chosen in the obscure hope of somehow deprecating
the wrath of the higher powers.

The Savage meanwhile wandered restlessly round the room, peering   5
with a vague superficial inquisitiveness at the books in the shelves, at the
sound-track rolls and reading machine bobbins in their numbered pigeon-
holes. On the table under the window lay a massive volume bound in limp
black leather-surrogate, and stamped with large golden T's. He picked it
up and opened it. MY LIFE AND WORK, BY OUR FORD. The book had been
published at Detroit by the Society for the Propagation of Fordian Knowledge. Idly he turned the pages, read a sentence here, a paragraph there,
and had just come to the conclusion that the book didn't interest him,
when the door opened, and the Resident World Controller for Western
Europe walked briskly into the room.

Mustapha Mond shook hands with all three of them; but it was to the   6
Savage that he addressed himself. "So you don't much like civilization, Mr.
Savage," he said.

The Savage looked at him. He had been prepared to lie, to bluster, to   7
remain sullenly unresponsive; but, reassured by the good-humoured intelligence of the Controller's face, he decided to tell the truth, straightfor-
wardly. "No." He shook his head.

Bernard started and looked horrified. What would the Controller   8
think? To be labelled as the friend of a man who said that he didn't like
civilization — said it openly and, of all people, to the Controller — it was
terrible. "But, John," he began. A look from Mustapha Mond reduced him
to an abject silence.

"Of course," the Savage went on to admit, "there are some very nice   9
things. All that music in the air, for instance . . ."

"Sometimes a thousand twangling instruments will hum about my   10
ears and sometimes voices."[1]

The Savage's face lit up with a sudden pleasure. "Have you read it   11
too?" he asked. "I thought nobody knew about that book here, in
England."

"Almost nobody. I'm one of the very few. It's prohibited, you see. But   12
as I make the laws here, I can also break them. With impunity, Mr. Marx,"
he added, turning to Bernard. "Which I'm afraid you *can't* do."

Bernard sank into a yet more hopeless misery.   13

"But why is it prohibited?" asked the Savage. In the excitement of   14
meeting a man who had read Shakespeare he had momentarily forgotten
everything else.

---

[1] cf. *The Tempest*, Act III, sc. ii, 131–132.

The Controller shrugged his shoulders. "Because it's old; that's the   15
chief reason. We haven't any use for old things here."

"Even when they're beautiful?"   16

"Particularly when they're beautiful. Beauty's attractive, and we don't   17
want people to be attracted by old things. We want them to like the new
ones."

"But the new ones are so stupid and horrible. Those plays, where   18
there's nothing but helicopters flying about and you *feel* the people kiss-
ing." He made a grimace. "Goats and monkeys!" Only in Othello's word
could he find an adequate vehicle for his contempt and hatred.

"Nice tame animals, anyhow," the Controller murmured paren-   19
thetically.

"Why don't you let them see *Othello* instead?"   20

"I've told you; it's old. Besides, they couldn't understand it."   21

Yes, that was true. He remembered how Helmholtz had laughed at   22
Romeo and Juliet. "Well then," he said, after a pause, "something new that's
like *Othello,* and that they could understand."

"That's what we've all been wanting to write," said Helmholtz, break-   23
ing a long silence.

"And it's what you never will write," said the Controller. "Because, if   24
it were really like *Othello* nobody could understand it, however new it
might be. And if were new, it couldn't possibly be like *Othello.*"

"Why not?"   25

"Yes, why not?" Helmholtz repeated. He too was forgetting the un-   26
pleasant realities of the situation. Green with anxiety and apprehension,
only Bernard remembered them; the others ignored him. "Why not?"

"Because our world is not the same as Othello's world. You can't make   27
flivvers[2] without steel — and you can't make tragedies without social instability. The world's stable now. People are happy; they get what they
want, and they never want what they can't get. They're well off; they're
safe; they're never ill; they're not afraid of death; they're blissfully ignorant
of passion and old age; they're plagued with no mothers or fathers; they've
got no wives, or children, or lovers to feel strongly about; they're so conditioned that they practically can't help behaving as they ought to behave.
And if anything should go wrong, there's *soma.* Which you go and chuck
out of the window in the name of liberty, Mr. Savage. *Liberty!*" He laughed.
"Expecting Deltas to know what liberty is! And now expecting them to
understand *Othello!* My good boy!"

The Savage was silent for a little. "All the same," he insisted obsti-   28
nately, "*Othello's* good, *Othello's* better than those feelies."

"Of course it is," the Controller agreed. "But that's the price we have   29

---

[2]*flivver:* An old car.

to pay for stability. You've got to choose between happiness and what people used to call high art. We've sacrificed the high art. We have the feelies and the scent organ instead."

"But they don't mean anything."   30

"They mean themselves; they mean a lot of agreeable sensations to the   31
audience."

"But they're . . . they're told by an idiot."[3]   32

The Controller laughed. "You're not being very polite to your friend,   33
Mr. Watson. One of our most distinguished Emotional Engineers . . ."

"But he's right," said Helmholtz gloomily. "Because it *is* idiotic. Writ-   34
ing when there's nothing to say . . ."

"Precisely. But that requires the most enormous ingenuity. You're   35
making flivvers out of the absolute minimum of steel — works of art out
of practically nothing but pure sensation."

The Savage shook his head. "It all seems to me quite horrible."   36

"Of course it does. Actual happiness always looks pretty squalid in   37
comparison with the over-compensations for misery. And, of course, stability isn't nearly so spectacular as instability. And being contented has
none of the glamour of a good fight against misfortune, none of the pic-
turesqueness of a struggle with temptation, or a fatal overthrow by passion
or doubt. Happiness is never grand."

"I suppose not," said the Savage after a silence. "But need it be quite   38
so bad as those twins?" He passed his hand over his eyes as though he
were trying to wipe away the remembered image of those long rows of
identical midgets at the assembling tables, those queued-up twin-herds at
the entrance to the Brentford monorail station, those human maggots
swarming round Linda's bed of death, the endlessly repeated face of
his assailants. He looked at his bandaged left hand and shuddered.
"Horrible!"

"But how useful! I see you don't like our Bokanovsky Groups; but, I   39
assure you, they're the foundation on which everything else is built.
They're the gyroscope that stabilizes the rocket plane of state on its un-
swerving course." The deep voice thrillingly vibrated; the gesticulating
hand implied all space and the onrush of the irresistible machine. Mustapha Mond's oratory was almost up to synthetic standards.

"I was wondering," said the Savage, "why you had them at all —   40
seeing that you can get whatever you want out of those bottles. Why don't
you make everybody an Alpha Double Plus while you're about it?"

---

[3]cf. *Macbeth*, Act V, sc. v, 24–28: On hearing of his wife's death, a besieged and bitter
Macbeth says: "Life's but a walking shadow, a poor player/That struts and frets his hour
upon the stage/And then is heard no more. It is a tale/Told by an idiot, full of sound and
fury/Signifying nothing."

Mustapha Mond laughed. "Because we have no wish to have our   *41*
throats cut," he answered. "We believe in happiness and stability. A society of Alphas couldn't fail to be unstable and miserable. Imagine a factory
staffed by Alphas — that is to say by separate and unrelated individuals of
good heredity and conditioned so as to be capable (within limits) of making
a free choice and assuming responsibilities. Imagine it!" he repeated.

The Savage tried to imagine it, not very successfully.   *42*

"It's an absurdity. An Alpha-decanted, Alpha-conditioned man would   *43*
go mad if he had to do Epsilon Semi-Moron work — go mad, or start
smashing things up. Alphas can be completely socialized — but only on
condition that you make them do Alpha work. Only an Epsilon can be
expected to make Epsilon sacrifices, for the good reason that for him they
aren't sacrifices; they're the line of least resistance. His conditioning has
laid down rails along which he's got to run. He can't help himself; he's
foredoomed. Even after decanting, he's still inside a bottle — an invisible
bottle of infantile and embryonic fixations. Each one of us, of course," the
Controller meditatively continued, "goes through life inside a bottle. But
if we happen to be Alphas, our bottles are, relatively speaking, enormous.
We should suffer acutely if we were confined in a narrower space. You
cannot pour upper-caste champagne-surrogate into lower-caste bottles. It's
obvious theoretically. But it has also been proved in actual practice. The
result of the Cyprus experiment was convincing."

"What was that?" asked the Savage.   *44*

Mustapha Mond smiled. "Well, you can call it an experiment in rebot-   *45*
tling if you like. It began in A.F. 473. The Controllers had the island of
Cyprus cleared of all its existing inhabitants and re-colonized with a specially prepared batch of twenty-two thousand Alphas. All agricultural and
industrial equipment was handed over to them and they were left to manage their own affairs. The result exactly fulfilled all the theoretical predictions. The land wasn't properly worked; there were strikes in all the factories; the laws were set at naught, orders disobeyed; all the people
detailed for a spell of low-grade work were perpetually intriguing for high-
grade jobs, and all the people with high-grade jobs were counter-intriguing
at all costs to stay where they were. Within six years they were having a
first-class civil war. When nineteen out of the twenty-two thousand had
been killed, the survivors unanimously petitioned the World Controllers
to resume the government of the island. Which they did. And that was the
end of the only society of Alphas that the world has ever seen."

The Savage sighed, profoundly.   *46*

"The optimum population," said Mustapha Mond, "is modelled on the   *47*
iceberg — eight-ninths below the water line, one-ninth above."

"And they're happy below the water line?"   *48*

"Happier than above it. Happier than your friend here, for example."   *49*
He pointed.

"In spite of that awful work?" ₅₀

"Awful? *They* don't find it so. On the contrary, they like it. It's light, ₅₁
it's childishly simple. No strain on the mind or the muscles. Seven and a
half hours of mild, unexhausting labour, and then the *soma* ration and
games and unrestricted copulation and the feelies. What more can they
ask for? True," he added, "they might ask for shorter hours. And of course
we could give them shorter hours. Technically, it would be perfectly simple
to reduce all lower-caste working hours to three or four a day. But would
they be any the happier for that? No, they wouldn't. The experiment was
tried, more than a century and a half ago. The whole of Ireland was put
on to the four-hour day. What was the result? Unrest and a large increase
in the consumption of *soma*; that was all. Those three and a half hours of
extra leisure were so far from being a source of happiness, that people felt
constrained to take a holiday from them. The Inventions Office is stuffed
with plans for labour-saving processes. Thousands of them." Mustapha
Mond made a lavish gesture. "And why don't we put them into execution?
For the sake of the labourers; it would be sheer cruelty to afflict them with
excessive leisure. It's the same with agriculture. We could synthesize every
morsel of food, if we wanted to. But we don't. We prefer to keep a third of
the population on the land. For their own sakes — because it takes *longer*
to get food out of the land than out of a factory. Besides, we have our
stability to think of. We don't want to change. Every change is a menace
to stability. That's another reason why we're so chary of applying new
inventions. Every discovery in pure science is potentially subversive; even
science must sometimes be treated as a possible enemy. Yes, even science."

Science? The Savage frowned. He knew the word. But what it exactly ₅₂
signified he could not say. Shakespeare and the old men of the pueblo had
never mentioned science, and from Linda he had only gathered the vaguest hints: science was something you made helicopters with, something
that caused you to laugh at the Corn Dances, something that prevented
you from being wrinkled and losing your teeth. He made a desperate effort
to take the Controller's meaning.

"Yes," Mustapha Mond was saying, "that's another item in the cost of ₅₃
stability. It isn't only art that's incompatible with happiness; it's also science. Science is dangerous; we have to keep it most carefully chained and
muzzled."

"What?" said Helmholtz, in astonishment. "But we're always saying ₅₄
that science is everything. It's a hypnopædic platitude."

"Three times a week between thirteen and seventeen," put in Bernard. ₅₅

"And all the science propaganda we do at the College . . ." ₅₆

"Yes; but what sort of science?" asked Mustapha Mond sarcastically. ₅₇
"You've had no scientific training, so you can't judge. I was a pretty good
physicist in my time. Too good — good enough to realize that all our science is just a cookery book, with an orthodox theory of cooking that no-

body's allowed to question, and a list of recipes that mustn't be added to except by special permission from the head cook. I'm the head cook now. But I was an inquisitive young scullion once. I started doing a bit of cooking on my own. Unorthodox cooking, illicit cooking. A bit of real science, in fact." He was silent.

"What happened?" asked Helmholtz Watson.   58

The Controller sighed. "Very nearly what's going to happen to you   59
young men. I was on the point of being sent to an island."

The words galvanized Bernard into violent and unseemly activity.   60
"Send *me* to an island?" He jumped up, ran across the room, and stood gesticulating in front of the Controller. "You can't send *me*. I haven't done anything. It was the others. I swear it was the others." He pointed accusingly to Helmholtz and the Savage. "Oh, please don't send me to Iceland. I promise I'll do what I ought to do. Give me another chance. Please give me another chance." The tears began to flow. "I tell you, it's their fault," he sobbed. "And not to Iceland. Oh please, your fordship, please . . ." And in a paroxysm of abjection he threw himself on his knees before the Controller. Mustapha Mond tried to make him get up; but Bernard persisted in his grovelling; the stream of words poured out inexhaustibly. In the end the Controller had to ring for his fourth secretary.

"Bring three men," he ordered, "and take Mr. Marx into a bedroom.   61
Give him a good *soma* vaporization and then put him to bed and leave him."

The fourth secretary went out and returned with three green-uni-   62
formed twin footmen. Still shouting and sobbing, Bernard was carried out.

"One would think he was going to have his throat cut," said the Con-   63
troller, as the door closed. "Whereas, if he had the smallest sense, he'd understand that his punishment is really a reward. He's being sent to an island. That's to say, he's being sent to a place where he'll meet the most interesting set of men and women to be found anywhere in the world. All the people who, for one reason or another, have got too self-consciously individual to fit into community-life. All the people who aren't satisfied with orthodoxy, who've got independent ideas of their own. Every one, in a word, who's any one. I almost envy you, Mr. Watson."

Helmholtz laughed. "Then why aren't you on an island yourself?"   64

"Because, finally, I preferred this," the Controller answered. "I was   65
given the choice: to be sent to an island, where I could have got on with my pure science, or to be taken on to the Controllers' Council with the prospect of succeeding in due course to an actual Controllership. I chose this and let the science go." After a little silence, "Sometimes," he added, "I rather regret the science. Happiness is a hard master — particularly other people's happiness. A much harder master, if one isn't conditioned to accept it unquestioningly, than truth." He sighed, fell silent again, then

continued in a brisker tone, "Well, duty's duty. One can't consult one's own preference. I'm interested in truth, I like science. But truth's a menace, science is a public danger. As dangerous as it's been beneficent. It has given us the stablest equilibrium in history. China's was hopelessly insecure by comparison; even the primitive matriarchies weren't steadier than we are. Thanks, I repeat, to science. But we can't allow science to undo its own good work. That's why we so carefully limit the scope of its researches — that's why I almost got sent to an island. We don't allow it to deal with any but the most immediate problems of the moment. All other enquiries are most sedulously discouraged. It's curious," he went on after a little pause, "to read what people in the time of Our Ford used to write about scientific progress. They seemed to have imagined that it could be allowed to go on indefinitely, regardless of everything else. Knowledge was the highest good, truth the supreme value; all the rest was secondary and subordinate. True, ideas were beginning to change even then. Our Ford himself did a great deal to shift the emphasis from truth and beauty to comfort and happiness. Mass production demanded the shift. Universal happiness keeps the wheels steadily turning; truth and beauty can't. And, of course, whenever the masses seized political power, then it was happiness rather than truth and beauty that mattered. Still, in spite of everything, unrestricted scientific research was still permitted. People still went on talking about truth and beauty as though they were the sovereign goods. Right up to the time of the Nine Years' War. *That* made them change their tune all right. What's the point of truth or beauty or knowledge when the anthrax bombs are popping all around you? That was when science first began to be controlled — after the Nine Years' War. People were ready to have even their appetites controlled then. Anything for a quiet life. We've gone on controlling ever since. It hasn't been very good for truth, of course. But it's been very good for happiness. One can't have something for nothing. Happiness has got to be paid for. You're paying for it, Mr. Watson — paying because you happen to be too much interested in beauty. I was too much interested in truth; I paid too."

"But *you* didn't go to an island," said the Savage, breaking a long silence. 66

The Controller smiled. "That's how I paid. By choosing to serve happiness. Other people's — not mine. It's lucky," he added, after a pause, "that there are such a lot of islands in the world. I don't know what we should do without them. Put you all in the lethal chamber, I suppose. By the way, Mr. Watson, would you like a tropical climate? The Marquesas, for example; or Samoa? Or something rather more bracing?" 67

Helmholtz rose from his pneumatic chair. "I should like a thoroughly bad climate," he answered. "I believe one would write better if the climate were bad. If there were a lot of wind and storms, for example . . ." 68

The Controller nodded his approbation. "I like your spirit, Mr. Watson. I like it very much indeed. As much as I officially disapprove of it." He smiled. "What about the Falkland Islands?" 69

"Yes, I think that will do," Helmholtz answered. "And now, if you don't mind, I'll go and see how poor Bernard's getting on." 70

Chapter Seventeen

"Art, science — you seem to have paid a fairly high price for your happiness," said the Savage, when they were alone. "Anything else?" 71

"Well, religion, of course," replied the Controller. "There used to be something called God — before the Nine Years' War. But I was forgetting; you know all about God, I suppose." 72

"Well . . ." The Savage hesitated. He would have liked to say something about solitude, about night, about the mesa lying pale under the moon, about the precipice, the plunge into shadowy darkness, about death. He would have liked to speak; but there were no words. Not even in Shakespeare. 73

The Controller, meanwhile, had crossed to the other side of the room and was unlocking a large safe set into the wall between the bookshelves. The heavy door swung open. Rummaging in the darkness within, "It's a subject," he said, "that has always had a great interest for me." He pulled out a thick black volume. "You've never read this, for example." 74

The Savage took it. "*The Holy Bible, containing the Old and New Testaments*," he read aloud from the title-page. 75

"Nor this." It was a small book and had lost its cover. 76

"*The Imitation of Christ.*" 77

"Nor this." He handed out another volume. 78

"*The Varieties of Religious Experience. By William James.*" 79

"And I've got plenty more," Mustapha Mond continued, resuming his seat. "A whole collection of pornographic old books. God in the safe and Ford on the shelves." He pointed with a laugh to his avowed library — to the shelves of books, the rack full of reading-machine bobbins and sound-track rolls. 80

"But if you know about God, why don't you tell them?" asked the Savage indignantly. "Why don't you give them these books about God?" 81

"For the same reason as we don't give them *Othello*: they're old; they're about God hundreds of years ago. Not about God now." 82

"But God doesn't change." 83

"Men do, though." 84

"What difference does that make?" 85

"All the difference in the world," said Mustapha Mond. He got up again and walked to the safe. "There was a man called Cardinal Newman," 86 he said. "A cardinal," he exclaimed parenthetically, "was a kind of Arch-Community-Songster."

"'I Pandulph, of fair Milan, cardinal.' I've read about them in 87 Shakespeare."

"Of course you have. Well, as I was saying, there was a man called 88 Cardinal Newman. Ah, here's the book." He pulled it out. "And while I'm about it I'll take this one too. It's by a man called Maine de Biran. He was a philosopher, if you know what that was."

"A man who dreams of fewer things than there are in heaven and 89 earth," said the Savage promptly.

"Quite so. I'll read you one of the things he *did* dream of in a moment. 90 Meanwhile, listen to what this old Arch-Community-Songster said." He opened the book at the place marked by a slip of paper and began to read. "'We are not our own any more than what we possess is our own. We did not make ourselves, we cannot be supreme over ourselves. We are not our own masters. We are God's property. Is it not our happiness thus to view the matter? Is it any happiness or any comfort, to consider that we *are* our own? It may be thought so by the young and prosperous. These may think it a great thing to have everything, as they suppose, their own way — to depend on no one — to have to think of nothing out of sight, to be without the irksomeness of continual acknowledgment, continual prayer, continual reference of what they do to the will of another. But as time goes on, they, as all men, will find that independence was not made for man — that it is an unnatural state — will do for a while, but will not carry us on safely to the end . . .'" Mustapha Mond paused, put down the first book and, picking up the other, turned over the pages. "Take this, for example," he said, and in his deep voice once more began to read: "'A man grows old; he feels in himself that radical sense of weakness, of listlessness, of discomfort, which accompanies the advance of age; and, feeling thus, imagines himself merely sick, lulling his fears with the notion that this distressing condition is due to some particular cause, from which, as from an illness, he hopes to recover. Vain imaginings! That sickness is old age; and a horrible disease it is. They say that it is the fear of death and of what comes after death that makes men turn to religion as they advance in years. But my own experience has given me the conviction that, quite apart from any such terrors or imaginings, the religious sentiment tends to develop as we grow older; to develop because, as the passions grow calm, as the fancy and sensibilities are less excited and less excitable, our reason becomes less troubled in its working, less obscured by the images, desires and distractions, in which it used to be absorbed; whereupon God emerges as from behind a cloud; our soul feels, sees, turns towards the source of all light; turns naturally and inevitably; for now that all that gave to the world of sensations its life and charms has begun to leak away from us, now that phenomenal existence is no more bolstered up by impressions from within or from without, we feel the need to lean on something that abides, something that will never play us false — a reality, an absolute and everlasting truth. Yes, we inevitably turn to God; for this religious sentiment is of its nature so pure, so delightful to the soul that experiences it, that it makes up to us for all our other losses.'" Mustapha Mond shut the book and leaned back in his chair. "One of the numerous things in heaven and earth that these philosophers didn't dream about was this" (he waved his hand), "us, the modern world. 'You can only be independent of God while you've got youth and prosperity; independence won't take you safely to the end.' Well, we've now got youth and prosperity right up to the end. What follows? Evidently, that we can be independent of God. 'The religious sentiment will compensate us for all our losses.' But there aren't any losses for us to compensate; religious sentiment is superfluous. And why should we go hunting for a substitute for youthful desires, when youthful desires never fail? A substitute for distractions, when we go on enjoying all the old fooleries to the very last? What need have we of repose when our minds and bodies continue to delight in activity? of consolation, when we have *soma*? of something immovable, when there is the social order?

"Then you think there is no God?" 91

"No, I think there quite probably is one." 92

"Then why? . . ." 93

Mustapha Mond checked him. "But he manifests himself in different 94 ways to different men. In premodern times he manifested himself as the being that's described in these books. Now . . ."

"How does he manifest himself now?" asked the Savage. 95

"Well, he manifests himself as an absence; as though he weren't there 96 at all."

"That's your fault." 97

"Call it the fault of civilization. God isn't compatible with machinery 98 and scientific medicine and universal happiness. You must make your choice. Our civilization has chosen machinery and medicine and happiness. That's why I have to keep these books locked up in the safe. They're smut. People would be shocked if . . ."

The Savage interrupted him. "But isn't it *natural* to feel there's a God?" 99

"You might as well ask if it's natural to do up one's trousers with zip- 100 pers," said the Controller sarcastically. "You remind me of another of those old fellows called Bradley. He defined philosophy as the finding of bad reasons for what one believes by instinct. As if one believed anything by instinct! One believes things because one has been conditioned to believe them. Finding bad reasons for what one believes for other bad reasons — that's philosophy. People believe in God because they've been conditioned to believe in God."

"But all the same," insisted the Savage, "it is natural to believe in God   101
when you're alone — quite alone, in the night, thinking about death . . ."

"But people never are alone now," said Mustapha Mond. "We make   102
them hate solitude; and we arrange their lives so that it's almost impossible
for them ever to have it."

The Savage nodded gloomily. At Malpais he had suffered because they   103
had shut him out from the communal activities of the pueblo, in civilized
London he was suffering because he could never escape from those communal activities, never be quietly alone.

"Do you remember that bit in *King Lear?*" said the Savage at last. "'The   104
gods are just and of our pleasant vices make instruments to plague us; the
dark and vicious place where thee he got cost him his eyes,' and Edmund
answers — you remember, he's wounded, he's dying — 'Thou hast spoken
right; 'tis true. The wheel has come full circle; I am here.' What about that
now? Doesn't there seem to be a God managing things, punishing,
rewarding?"

"Well, does there?" questioned the Controller in his turn. "You can   105
indulge in any number of pleasant vices with a freemartin and run no risks
of having your eyes put out by your son's mistress. 'The wheel has come
full circle; I am here.' But where would Edmund be nowadays? Sitting in
a pneumatic chair, with his arm round a girl's wast, sucking away at his
sex-hormone chewing-gum and looking at the feelies. The gods are just.
No doubt. But their code of law is dictated, in the last resort, by the people
who organize society; Providence takes its cue from men."

"Are you sure?" asked the Savage. "Are you quite sure that the Ed-   106
mund in that pneumatic chair hasn't been just as heavily punished as the
Edmund who's wounded and bleeding to death? The gods are just.
Haven't they used his pleasant vices as an instrument to degrade him?"

"Degrade him from what position? As a happy, hard-working, goods-   107
consuming citizen he's perfect. Of course, if you choose some other standard than ours, then perhaps you might say he was degraded. But you've
got to stick to one set of postulates. You can't play Electro-magnetic Golf
according to the rules of Centrifugal Bumble-puppy."

"But value dwells not in particular will," said the Savage. "It holds his   108
estimate and dignity as well wherein 'tis precious of itself as in the prizer."[4]

---

[4]*'tis precious of itself . . . :* The reference is to Shakespeare's *Troilus and Cressida* (Act II, sc.
ii, 53–56). The Trojan warrior and prince, Hector, is arguing with Troilus, his brother, over
the return of Helen of Troy to the Greeks as a condition for ending the Trojan War. Hector
maintains that Helen is not worth what she is costing the Trojans. In response to Troilus's
question, "What's ought, but as 'tis valued?" Hector says, "But value dwells not in particular will;/It holds his estimate in dignity/As well wherein 'tis precious of itself/As in the
prizer."

"Come, come," protested Mustapha Mond, "that's going rather far,   *109*
isn't it?"

"If you allowed yourselves to think of God, you wouldn't allow your-   *110*
selves to be degraded by pleasant vices. You'd have a reason for bearing
things patiently, for doing things with courage. I've seen it with the
Indians."

"I'm sure you have," said Mustapha Mond. "But then we aren't Indi-   *111*
ans. There isn't any need for a civilized man to bear anything that's seriously unpleasant. And as for doing things — Ford forbid that he should
get the idea into his head. It would upset the whole social order if men
started doing things on their own."

"What about self-denial, then? If you had a God, you'd have a reason   *112*
for self-denial."

"But industrial civilization is only possible when there's no self-denial.   *113*
Self-indulgence up to the very limits imposed by hygiene and economics.
Otherwise the wheels stop turning."

"You'd have a reason for chastity!" said the Savage, blushing a little as   *114*
he spoke the words.

"But chastity means passion, chastity means neurasthenia. And pas-   *115*
sion and neurasthenia mean instability. And instability means the end of
civilization. You can't have a lasting civilization without plenty of pleasant
vices."

"But God's the reason for everything noble and fine and heroic. If you   *116*
had a God . . ."

"My dear young friend," said Mustapha Mond, "civilization has ab-   *117*
solutely no need of nobility or heroism. These things are symptoms of
political inefficiency. In a properly organized society like ours, nobody has
any opportunities for being noble or heroic. Conditions have got to be thoroughly unstable before the occasion can arise. Where there are wars,
where there are divided allegiances, where there are temptations to be resisted, objects of love to be fought for or defended — there, obviously,
nobility and heroism have some sense. But there aren't any wars nowadays. The greatest care is taken to prevent you from loving any one too
much. There's no such thing as a divided allegiance; you're so conditioned
that you can't help doing what you ought to do. And what you ought to
do is on the whole so pleasant, so many of the natural impulses are allowed free play, that there really aren't any temptations to resist. And if
ever, by some unlucky chance, anything unpleasant should somehow happen, why, there's always *soma* to give you a holiday from the facts. And
there's always *soma* to calm your anger, to reconcile you to your enemies,
to make you patient and long-suffering. In the past you could only accomplish these things by making a great effort and after years of hard moral
training. Now, you swallow two or three half-gramme tablets, and there
you are. Anybody can be virtuous now. You can carry at least half your

mortality about in a bottle. Christianity without tears — that's what *soma* is."

"But the tears are necessary. Don't you remember what Othello said? 'If after every tempest came such calms, may the winds blow till they have wakened death.' There's a story one of the old Indians used to tell us, about the Girl of Mátaski. The young men who wanted to marry her had to do a morning's hoeing in her garden. It seemed easy; but there were flies and mosquitoes, magic ones. Most of the young men simply couldn't stand the biting and stinging. But the one that could — he got the girl." 118

"Charming! But in civilized countries," said the Controller, "you can have girls without hoeing for them; and there aren't any flies or mosquitoes to sting you. We got rid of them all centuries ago." 119

The Savage nodded, frowning. "You got rid of them. Yes, that's just like you. Getting rid of everything unpleasant instead of learning to put up with it. Whether 'tis better in the mind to suffer the slings and arrows of outrageous fortune, or to take arms against a sea of troubles and by opposing end them . . . But you don't do either. Neither suffer nor oppose. You just abolish the slings and arrows. It's too easy." 120

He was suddenly silent, thinking of his mother. In her room on the thirty-seventh floor, Linda had floated in a sea of singing lights and perfumed caresses — floated away, out of space, out of time, out of the prison of her memories, her habits, her aged and bloated body. And Tomakin, ex-Director of Hatcheries and Conditioning, Tomakin was still on holiday — on holiday from humiliation and pain, in a world where he could not hear those words, that derisive laughter, could not see that hideous face, feel those moist and flabby arms round his neck, in a beautiful world . . . 121

"What you need," the Savage went on, "Is something *with* tears for a change. Nothing costs enough here." 122

("Twelve and a half million dollars," Henry Foster had protested when the Savage told him that. "Twelve and a half million — that's what the new Conditioning Centre cost. Not a cent less.") 123

"Exposing what is mortal and unsure to all that fortune, death and danger dare, even for an eggshell. Isn't there something in that?" he asked, looking up at Mustapha Mond. "Quite apart from God — though of course God would be a reason for it. Isn't there something in living dangerously?" 124

"There's a great deal in it," the Controller replied. "Men and women must have their adrenals stimulated from time to time." 125

"What?" questioned the Savage, uncomprehending. 126

"It's one of the conditions of perfect health. That's why we've made the V.P.S. treatments compulsory." 127

"V.P.S.?" 128

"Violent Passion Surrogate. Regularly once a month. We flood the whole system with adrenin. It's the complete physiological equivalent of 129 fear and rage. All the tonic effects of murdering Desdemona and being murdered by Othello, without any of the inconveniences."

"But I like the inconveniences."   130

"We don't," said the Controller. "We prefer to do things comfortably."   131

"But I don't want comfort. I want God, I want poetry, I want real dan-   132
ger, I want freedom, I want goodness. I want sin."

"In fact," said Mustapha Mond, "you're claiming the right to be   133
unhappy."

"All right then," said the Savage defiantly, "I'm claiming the right to   134
be unhappy."

"Not to mention the right to grow old and ugly and impotent; the right   135
to have syphilis and cancer; the right to have too little to eat; the right to
be lousy; the right to live in constant apprehension of what may happen
tomorrow; the right to catch typhoid; the right to be tortured by unspeakable pains of every kind." There was a long silence.

"I claim them all," said the Savage at last.   136

Mustapha Mond shrugged his shoulders. "You're welcome," he said.[5]   137

DISCUSSION AND WRITING QUESTIONS

1. What is the significance of the honorific, "His Fordship"? What relationship
   can you infer between Huxley's use of the title and the ideas of Marx and Niebuhr? (Reinhold Niebuhr has written the next selection in the chapter, "Man
   and Society: The Art of Living Together." See page 380.)
2. How savage is the Savage? With what do you usually associate the term? With
   what does Huxley associate the term?
3. Social instability does not exist in Huxley's brave new world. "People are
   happy. They get what they want and they never want what they can't get."
   Would Condorcet view the world of the Savage and the Controller as the realization of his dreams? Why or why not?
4. "You've got to choose between happiness and what people used to call high
   art." The Controller implies here that to produce high art one needs to be unhappy. He put it another way as well: "You can't make tragedies without social
   instability." Do happiness and high art seem mutually exclusive pursuits to
   you? If Condorcet's program were completely realized, do you think there
   would continue to be high art?

---

[5]The novel ends with John going off to live as a hermit, choosing hard physical labor and
tears over Mustapha Mond's program for bliss. In his lighthouse retreat, John becomes a
sensation for the curious. Goaded, made the subject of intrusive reports, observed like a
caged animal, he eventually whips and kills a woman. And then in an agony of remorse
— an emotion foreign to the soma-benumbed citizens of Huxley's world — John the Savage
hangs himself.

5. In the Brave New World the Controller argues that there must be inequality to ensure the smooth running of society — without the disruptions of workers who wish either to improve or escape their conditions. For this purpose, genetic engineers create humans perfectly suited both emotionally and intellectually to their jobs, in this way guaranteeing that there is no dissatisfaction. What advantages does such a world have over our present one? what disadvantages?

6. Argue against the genetic engineering described in Discussion Question 5. How would you defend, as the Savage puts it, the right to be unhappy? Refer to the Cyprus experiment.

7. The Controller says that the inhabitants of his society need "unexhausting labor, and then the soma [narcotic] ration and games and unrestricted copulation and the feelies" to make them happy. The Savage says, in effect, that he needs unhappiness to be happy. Discuss these differing definitions of happiness.

8. Science is often regarded as the one pursuit that has saved humanity from the so-called backward superstitions and unreasoning beliefs of primitive life. Such was the opinion of Huxley's grandfather, T.H. Huxley. (See his essay on "The Advisibleness of Improving Natural Knowledge," page 140.) Yet in the Brave New World, science along with art is seen to be incompatible with happiness. Why? (If you have read the section on the Copernican Revolution, try casting your answer in terms of what you learned from the readings there.)

9. The Controller is a man of obvious talents. He has made the decision not to go to an island but to remain in society and work to engineer its happiness. To what extent has he succeeded? Do you regard the Controller as someone to be despised? admired? Explain.

10. Whose side do you take in the debate on God — the Savage's or the Controller's? Why? If you take neither side, develop your own position.

11. "Nothing costs enough here," says the Savage. What does he mean? Do you agree with the Savage's choice, his *right*, to be unhappy?

REINHOLD NIEBUHR *(1892–1971)*

Reinhold Niebuhr was an important Protestant theologian whose writings extended to political philosophy. He believed that an essential tension existed between individuals, who could be and often were moral-minded, and social institutions, which are necessary but are by nature coercive and incapable of delivering a permanent peace. Individuals must exist within the larger, imperfect social order. However moral the individual's intentions, he cannot act alone to achieve goodness, and the attempt to do so represents for Niebuhr the original sin of pride — a sin that leads in dangerous directions: for a man never fully achieves goodness in his finite, limited state and is tempted to lust for power. All varieties of abuses follow, and in the process, both the initial intention is ruined and much harm is done. Niebuhr gravely distrusted the unexamined assumption that the progress of society was assured. For him, inherent, troubling tensions existed that placed society in a "perpetual state of war," the cessation of which seemed nowhere in sight. Condorcet's dream of lasting peace and perfectibility can never be fully realized, given the present nature of man. A far more humble agenda must be set.

Reinhold Niebuhr was born to German immigrants, Gustav and Lydia Niebuhr, in Wright City, Missouri, on June 21, 1892. He followed his father into the ministry, attending Elmhurst College, Eden Theological Seminary, and Yale University (1915). After his ordination, Niebuhr became pastor of the Bethel Evangelical Church in Detroit for thirteen years (1915–1928); many of his parishioners were assembly-line workers in the automotive industry, and it was in Detroit that Niebuhr grew to distrust capitalism, attacking its dehumanizing abuses. As you will see, part of his critique is available in the essay that follows: democracy, along with capitalism — the economic system that drives it — are in their ways just as coercive and abusive as the systems that preceded them.

Niebuhr left Detroit for a long and distinguished career at the Union Theological Seminary in New York, where he taught Christian ethics and philosophy and later served as vice-president. He was active politically, evidence of his belief that limited progressive change was possible. Following World War I, he became a pacifist; but faced with the threat of fascism in the 1930s, he resolutely opposed Hitler and endorsed the use of force to defeat him. Niebuhr's principal works include *Moral Man and Immoral Society* (1932), from which the present essay, "Man and Society: The Art of Living Together," is taken; *An Interpretation of Christian Ethics* (1935); *The Nature and Destiny of Man* (1941, 1943); and *The Irony of American History* (1952). Niebuhr also edited several journals. Though a stroke limited his activities in 1952, he continued to write and teach for many years. He died in 1971.

MAN AND SOCIETY: THE ART OF LIVING TOGETHER

Though human society has roots which lie deeper in history than the 1 beginning of human life, men have made comparatively but little progress in solving the problem of their aggregate existence. Each century originates a new complexity and each new generation faces a new vexation in it. For all the centuries of experience, men have not yet learned how to live together without compounding their vices and covering each other "with mud and with blood." The society in which each man lives is at once the basis for, and the nemesis of, that fulness of life which each man seeks. However much human ingenuity may increase the treasures which nature provides for the satisfaction of human needs, they can never be sufficient to satisfy all human wants; for man, unlike other creatures, is gifted and cursed with an imagination which extends his appetites beyond the requirements of subsistence. Human society will never escape the problem of the equitable distribution of the physical and cultural goods which provide for the preservation and fulfillment of human life.

Unfortunately the conquest of nature, and the consequent increase in 2 nature's beneficences to man, have not eased, but rather accentuated, the problem of justice. The same technology, which drew the fangs of nature's enmity of man, also created a society in which the intensity and extent of social cohesion has been greatly increased, and in which power is so unevenly distributed, that justice has become a more difficult achievement. Perhaps it is man's sorry fate, suffering from ills which have their source in the inadequacies of both nature and human society, that the tools by which he eliminates the former should become the means of increasing the latter. That, at least, has been his fate up to the present hour; and it may be that there will be no salvation for the human spirit from the more and more painful burdens of social injustice until the ominous tendency in human history has resulted in perfect tragedy.

Human nature is not wanting in certain endowments for the solution 3 of the problem of human society. Man is endowed by nature with organic relations to his fellowmen; and natural impulse prompts him to consider the needs of others even when they compete with his own. With the higher mammals man shares concern for his offspring; and the long infancy of the child created the basis for an organic social group in the earliest period of human history. Gradually intelligence, imagination, and the necessities of

Reinhold Niebuhr. "Man and Society: The Art of Living Together" in *Moral Man and Immoral Society*. New York: Scribner's, 1932, pp. 1–22.

social conflict increased the size of this group. Natural impulse was refined and extended until a less obvious type of consanguinity than an immediate family relationship could be made the basis of social solidarity. Since those early days the units of human cooperation have constantly grown in size, and the areas of significant relationships between the units have likewise increased. Nevertheless conflict between the national units remains as a permanent rather than a passing characteristic of their relations to each other; and each national unit finds it increasingly difficult to maintain either peace or justice within its common life.

While it is possible for intelligence to increase the range of benevolent   4
impulse, and thus prompt a human being to consider the needs and rights of other than those to whom he is bound by organic and physical relationship, there are definite limits in the capacity of ordinary mortals which makes it impossible for them to grant to others what they claim for themselves. Though educators ever since the eighteenth century have given themselves to the fond illusion that justice through voluntary co-operation waited only upon a more universal or a more adequate educational enterprise, there is good reason to believe that the sentiments of benevolence and social goodwill will never be so pure or powerful, and the rational capacity to consider the rights and needs of others in fair competition with our own will never be so fully developed as to create the possibility for the anarchistic millennium which is the social utopia, either explicit or implicit, of all intellectual or religious moralists.

All social co-operation on a larger scale than the most intimate social   5
group requires a measure of coercion. While no state can maintain its unity purely by coercion neither can it preserve itself without coercion. Where the factor of mutual consent is strongly developed, and where standardised and approximately fair methods of adjudicating and resolving conflicting interests within an organised group have been established, the coercive factor in social life is frequently covert, and becomes apparent only in moments of crisis and in the group's policy toward recalcitrant individuals. Yet it is never absent. Divergence of interest, based upon geographic and functional differences within a society, is bound to create different social philosophies and political attitudes which goodwill and intelligence may partly, but never completely, harmonise. Ultimately, unity within an organised social group, or within a federation of such groups, is created by the ability of a dominant group to impose its will. Politics will, to the end of history, be an area where conscience and power meet, where the ethical and coercive factors of human life will interpenetrate and work out their tentative and uneasy compromises. The democratic method of resolving social conflict, which some romanticists hail as a triumph of the ethical over the coercive factor, is really much more coercive than at first seems apparent. The majority has its way, not because the minority believes that the majority is right (few minorities are willing to grant the majority the

moral prestige of such a concession), but because the votes of the majority are a symbol of its social strength. Whenever a minority believes that it has some strategic advantage which outweighs the power of numbers, and whenever it is sufficiently intent upon its ends, or desperate enough about its position in society, it refuses to accept the dictates of the majority. Military and economic overlords and revolutionary zealots have been traditionally contemptuous of the will of majorities. Recently Trotsky[1] advised the German communists not to be dismayed by the greater voting strength of the fascists since in the inevitable revolution the power of industrial workers, in charge of the nation's industrial process, would be found much more significant than the social power of clerks and other petty bourgeoisie who comprised the fascist movement.

There are, no doubt, rational and ethical factors in the democratic process. Contending social forces presumably use the forum rather than the battleground to arbitrate their differences in the democratic method, and thus differences are resolved by moral suasion and a rational adjustment of rights to rights. If political issues were really abstract questions of social policy upon which unbiased citizens were asked to commit themselves, the business of voting and the debate which precedes the election might actually be regarded as an educational programme in which a social group discovers its common mind. But the fact is that political opinions are inevitably rooted in economic interests of some kind or other, and only comparatively few citizens can view a problem of social policy without regard to their interest. Conflicting interests therefore can never be completely resolved; and minorities will yield only because the majority has come into control of the police power of the state and may, if the occasion arises, augment that power by its own military strength. Should a minority regard its own strength, whether economic or martial, as strong enough to challenge the power of the majority, it may attempt to wrest control of the state apparatus from the majority, as in the case of the fascist movement in Italy. Sometimes it will resort to armed conflict, even if the prospects of victory are none too bright, as in the instance of the American Civil War, in which the Southern planting interests, outvoted by a combination of Eastern industrialists and Western agrarians, resolved to protect their peculiar interests and privileges by a forceful dissolution of the national union. The coercive factor is, in other words, always present in politics. If economic interests do not conflict too sharply, if the spirit of accommodation partially resolves them, and if the democratic process has achieved moral prestige

6

---

[1]*Leon Trotsky:* (1879–1940) The by-name of Lev Davidovich Bronstein, an agitator for the communist party in Russia and Germany. Though a leader in Russia's October Revolution and the Commissar of Foreign Affairs and War in the Soviet Union, Trotsky was later stripped of all power by Stalin and his supporters.

and historic dignity, the coercive factor in politics may become too covert to be visible to the casual observer. Nevertheless, only a romanticist of the purest water could maintain that a national group ever arrives at a "common mind" or becomes conscious of a "general will" without the use of either force or the threat of force. This is particularly true of nations, but it is also true, though in a slighter degree, of other social groups. Even religious communities, if they are sufficiently large, and if they deal with issues regarded as vital by their members, resort to coercion to preserve their unity. Religious organisations have usually availed themselves of a covert type of coercion (excommunication and the interdict) or they have called upon the police power of the state.

The limitations of the human mind and imagination, the inability of human beings to transcend their own interests sufficiently to envisage the interests of their fellowmen as clearly as they do their own, makes force an inevitable part of the process of social cohesion. But the same force which guarantees peace also makes for injustice. "Power," said Henry Adams, "is poison"; and it is a poison which blinds the eyes of moral insight and lames the will of moral purpose. The individual or the group which organises any society, however social its intentions or pretensions, arrogates an inordinate portion of social privilege to itself. The two most obvious types of power are the military and the economic, though in primitive society the power of the priest, partly because he dispenses supernatural benefits and partly because he establishes public order by methods less arduous than those of the soldier, vies with that of the soldier and the landlord. The chief difference between the agrarian civilisations, which lasted from the rise of ancient Babylon and Egypt to the fall of European feudalism, and the commercial and industrial civilisations of today is that in the former the military power is primary, and in the latter it has become secondary, to economic power. In agrarian civilisations the soldier becomes the landlord. In more primitive periods he may claim the land by his own military prowess. In later periods a grateful sovereign bestowed land upon the soldiers who defended his realm and consolidated his dominion. The soldier thus gained the economic security and the social prestige which could be exploited in further martial service to his sovereign. The business man and industrial overlord are gradually usurping the position of eminence and privilege once held by the soldier and the priest. In most European nations their ascendancy over the landed aristocrat of military traditions is not as complete as in America, which has no feudal traditions. In present-day Japan the military caste is still so powerful that it threatens to destroy the rising power of the commercial groups. On the pre-eminence of economic power in an industrial civilisation and its ability to make the military power its tool we shall have more to say later. Our interest at the moment is to record that any kind of significant social power develops social inequality. Even if history is viewed from other than equalitarian perspectives, and it is granted that differentials in economic rewards are morally justified and socially useful, it is impossible to justify the degree of inequality which complex societies inevitably create by the increased centralisation of power which develops with more elaborate civilisations. The literature of all ages is filled with rational and moral justifications of these inequalities, but most of them are specious.[2] If superior abilities and services to society deserve special rewards it may be regarded as axiomatic that the rewards are always higher than the services warrant. No impartial society determines the rewards. The men of power who control society grant these perquisites to themselves. Whenever special ability is not associated with power, as in the case of the modern professional man, his excess of income over the average is ridiculously low in comparison with that of the economic overlords, who are the real centres of power in an industrial society. Most rational and social justifications of unequal privilege are clearly afterthoughts. The facts are created by the disproportion of power which exists in a given social system. The justifications are usually dictated by the desire of the men of power to hide the nakedness of their greed, and by the inclination of society itself to veil the brutal facts of human life from itself. This is a rather pathetic but understandable inclination; since the facts of man's collective life easily rob the average individual of confidence in the human enterprise. The inevitable hypocrisy, which is associated with all of the collective activities of the human race, springs chiefly from this source: that individuals have a moral code which makes the actions of collective man an outrage to their conscience. They therefore invent romantic and moral interpretations of the real facts, preferring to obscure rather than reveal the true character of their collective behavior. Sometimes they are as anxious to offer moral justifications for the brutalities from which they suffer as for those which they commit. The fact that the hypocrisy of man's group behavior, about which we shall have much more to say later, expresses itself not only in terms of self-justification but in terms of moral justification of human behavior in general, symbolises one of the tragedies of the human spirit: its inability to conform its collective life to its individual ideals. As individuals, men believe that they ought to love and serve each other and establish justice between each other. As racial, economic and national groups they take for themselves, whatever their power can command.

The disproportion of power in a complex society which began with the transmutation of the pastoral to the agrarian economy, and which destroyed the simple equalitarianism and communism of the hunting and nomadic social organisation, has perpetuated social injustice in every form *8*

---

[2]*The literature of all ages . . . . :* For an example of such a justification, see Alexander Pope's "Essay on Man," pages 129–136, in the section on "Copernicus and the New Universe."

through all ages. Types of power have changed, and gradations of social inequality have varied, but the essential facts have remained unchanged. In Egypt the land was divided into three parts, respectively claimed by the king, the soldiers and the priests. The common people were landless. In Peru, where a rather remarkable despotic communism developed, the king owned all the land but gave the use of one third to the people, another third to the priests and kept one third for himself and his nobles. Needless to say, the commoners were expected to till not only their third but the other two thirds of the lands. In China, where the emperor maintained the right of eminent domain for many centuries, defeating the experiment in feudalism in the third century A.D., and giving each family inalienable rights in the soil which nominally belonged to him, there has probably been less inequality than in any other ancient empire. Nevertheless slavery persisted until a very recent day. In Japan the emperor gave the land to feudal princes, who again sublet it to the inferior nobility. The power of the feudal clans, originating in martial prowess and perpetuated through land ownership, has remained practically unbroken to this day, though the imperial power was ostensibly restored in the latter part of the last century, and growing industry has developed a class of industrial overlords who were partly drawn from the landed aristocracy. In Rome the absolute property rights of the *pater familias*[3] of the patrician class gave him power which placed him on top of the social pyramid. All other classes, beginning with his own women and children, then the plebeians and finally the slaves, took their places in the various lower rungs of the social ladder. The efforts of the Gracchi[4] to destroy the ever growing inequality, which resulted from power breeding more power, proved abortive, as did the land reforms of Solon and Lycurgus in Greece.[5] Military conquest gave the owners of the

---

[3]*pater familias:* The fundamental units of ancient Roman society (called "gens" or "familia") were groups of persons bonded by shared ancestors, customs, and beliefs. The *pater familia,* or head of a familia, had absolute power.

[4]*Gracchi:* Tiberius Gracchus (d. 133B.C.) and his brother Gaius Gracchus (d. 121B.C.) (collectively called the Gracchi) strove to solve urban problems in Rome by initiating reforms aimed at strengthening the class of small, independent farmers. Though their efforts resulted in temporary prosperity, basic flaws in the organization of Rome's government and economy inevitably led to regression.

[5]*Land reforms:* The Athenian statesman Solon (c. 630B.C.–c. 560B.C.) attempted to redistribute land in Greece, allowing peasants who had been forced to mortgage land, and thus work for subsistence without profit, to rightfully own their lands. The Spartan statesman Lycurgus (7th century B.C.) likewise initiated legislation aimed at allowing workers to share in the profits of the land they cultivated. Though both measures were initially successful, neither had lasting or widespread success due to resistance from more prosperous owners.

Roman *latifundia*[6] hundreds of slaves by the labor of which they reduced the small freeholders to penury. Thus the decay of the Roman Empire was prepared; for a state which has only lords and slaves lacks the social cement to preserve it from internal disintegration and the military force to protect it from external aggression.

All through history one may observe the tendency of power to destroy its very *raison d'être*.[7] It is suffered because it achieves internal unity and creates external defenses for the nation. But it grows to such proportions that it destroys the social peace of the state by the animosities which its exactions arouse, and it enervates the sentiment of patriotism by robbing the common man of the basic privileges which might bind him to his nation. The words attributed by Plutarch to Tiberius Gracchus[8] reveal the hollowness of the pretensions by which the powerful classes enlist their slaves in the defense of their dominions: "The wild beasts in Italy had at least their lairs, dens and caves whereto they might retreat; whereas the men who fought and died for that land had nothing in it save air and light, but were forced to wander to and fro with their wives and children, without resting place or house wherein they might lodge. . . . The poor folk go to war, to fight and to die for the delights, riches and superfluities of others."[9] In the long run these pretensions are revealed and the sentiment of patriotism is throttled in the breasts of the disinherited. The privileged groups who are outraged by the want of patriotism among modern proletarians could learn the cause of proletarian internationalism by a little study of history. "It is absurd," says Diodorus Siculus,[10] speaking of Egypt, "to entrust the defence of a country to people who own nothing in it,"[11] a reflection which has applicability to other ages and other nations than his own. Russian communists of pure water pour their scorn upon European socialists, among whom patriotism outweighed class loyalty in the World

9

---

[6]*Roman latifundia:* Large estates in ancient Rome owned by upper-class citizens who, having more capital than small freeholders, could invest in agricultural improvements and virtually monopolize smaller owners.

[7]*Raison d'être:* Literally "reason for being." Here, Niebuhr is saying that power eventually destroys those relationships and institutions it was initially intended to develop.

[8]*Plutarch to Tiberius Gracchus:* In his *Parallel Lives*, the biographer and author Plutarch (A.D.46?–c.120) chronicled the work of Tiberius Gracchus in agrarian reform and the redevelopment of the small, independent farming class.

[9]Plutarch, *The Parallel Lives*, see "Tiberius Gracchus," *Loeb Classical Library*, Vol. X. [Niebuhr]

[10]*Diodorus Siculus:* (1st century B.C.) A Greek historian and author of *Bibliotheca Historica*, one of the only continuous chronicles of history still existing.

[11]Quoted by C. J. M. Letourneau, *Property; Its Origins and Development*, p. 277. [Niebuhr]

War. But there is a very simple explanation for the nationalism of European socialists. They were not as completely, or at least not as obviously, disinherited as their Russian comrades.

The history of slavery in all ancient civilisations offers an interesting illustration of the development of social injustice with the growing size and complexity of the social unit. In primitive tribal organisation rights are essentially equal within the group, and no rights, or only very minimum rights are recognised outside of the group. The captives of war are killed. With the growth of agriculture the labor of captives becomes useful, and they are enslaved rather than destroyed. Since rightless individuals are introduced into the intimate life of the group, equality of rights disappears; and the inequality remains even after the slaves are no longer regarded as enemies and have become completely organic to the life of the group. The principle of slavery once established, is enlarged to include debt slaves, victims of the growing property system. The membership of the debt slaves in the original community at first guarantees them rights which the captive slaves do not enjoy. But the years gradually wipe out these distinctions and the captive slaves are finally raised to the status of debtor slaves. Thus the more humane attitudes which men practice within their social groups gain a slight victory over the more brutal attitudes towards individuals in other groups. But the victory is insignificant in comparison with the previous introduction of the morals of intergroup relations into the intimate life of the group by the very establishment of slavery. Barbarism knows little or nothing of class distinctions. These are created and more and more highly elaborated by civilisation. The social impulses, with which men are endowed by nature are not powerful enough, even when they are extended by a growing intelligence, to apply with equal force toward all members of a large community. The distinction between slave and freeman is only one of the many social gradations which higher societies develop. They are determined in every case by the disproportion of power, military and economic, which develops in the more complex civilisations and in the larger social units. A growing social intelligence may be affronted by them and may protest against them, but it changes them only slightly. Neither the prophets of Israel nor the social idealists of Egypt and Babylon, who protested against social injustice, could make their vision of a just society effective. The man of power, though humane impulse may awaken in him, always remains something of the beast of prey. He may be generous within his family, and just within the confines of the group which shares his power and privilege. With only rare exceptions, his highest moral attitude toward members of other groups is one of warlike sportsmanship toward those who equal his power and challenge it, and one of philanthropic generosity toward those who possess less power and privilege. His philanthropy is a perfect illustration of the curious compound of the brutal and the moral which we find in all human behavior;

for his generosity is at once a display of his power and an expression of his pity. His generous impulses freeze within him if his power is challenged or his generosities are accepted without grateful humility. If individual men of power should achieve more ethical attitudes than the one described, it remains nevertheless typical for them as a class; and is their practically unvarying attitude when they express themselves not as individuals but as a group.

The rise of modern democracy, beginning with the Eighteenth Century, is sometimes supposed to have substituted the consent of the governed for the power of royal families and aristocratic classes as the cohesive force of national society. This judgment is partly true but not nearly as true as the uncritical devotees of modern democracy assume. The doctrine that government exists by the consent of the governed, and the democratic technique by which the suffrage of the governed determines the policy of the state, may actually reduce the coercive factor in national life, and provide for peaceful and gradual methods of resolving conflicting social interests and changing political institutions. But the creeds and institutions of democracy have never become fully divorced from the special interests of the commercial classes who conceived and developed them. It was their interest to destroy political restraint upon economic activity, and they therefore weakened the authority of the state and made it more pliant to their needs. With the increased centralisation of economic power in the period of modern industrialism, this development merely means that society as such does not control economic power as much as social well-being requires; and that the economic, rather than the political and military, power has become the significant coercive force of modern society. Either it defies the authority of the state or it bends the institutions of the state to its own purposes. Political power has been made responsible, but economic power has become irresponsible in society. The net result is that political power has been made more responsible to economic power. It is, in other words, again the man of power or the dominant class which binds society together, regulates its processes, always paying itself inordinate rewards for its labors. The difference is that owners of factories, rather than owners of land, exert the power, and that it is more purely economic and less military than that which was wielded by the landed aristocrats. Needless to say, it is not completely divorced from military power. It may on occasion appropriate the police and the army of the state to defend its interests against internal and external foes. The military power has become the hired servant and is no longer the progenitor of economic ownership.

There will be opportunity to discuss these modern developments in the growth and use of power in society at greater length in another chapter. At the same time it will be possible to do justice to those aspects of the democratic creed which transcend the interests of the commercial and industrial classes and add a permanent contribution to the history of social life. At present it must suffice to discount a still widely held conviction that the democratic movement has given society a permanent solution for its vexing problems of power and justice.

Society is perennially harassed not only by the fact that the coercive factors in social life (which the limitations of human intelligence and imagination make inevitable) create injustice in the process of establishing peace; but also by the tendency of the same factors, which make for an uneasy peace within a social group, to aggravate intergroup conflict. Power sacrifices justice to peace within the community and destroys peace between communities. It is not true that only kings make war. The common members of any national community, while sentimentally desiring peace, nevertheless indulge impulses of envy, jealousy, pride, bigotry, and greed which make for conflict between communities. Neither is it true that modern wars are caused solely by the modern capitalistic system with its disproportion of economic power and privilege. Without an almost miraculous increase in human intelligence it will not be easy to resolve the conflicts of interest between various national communities even after the special privilege and the unequal power, which now aggravate international conflicts, have been destroyed. Nevertheless the whole history of mankind bears testimony to the fact that the power which prevents anarchy in intragroup relations encourages anarchy in intergroup relations. The kings of old claimed the loyalty and the sacrifices of their subjects in conflicts with other tyrants, in which the interests of the state and the welfare of the people were completely subordinated to the capricious purposes of the monarch. No personal whim, which a human being might indulge, is excluded from the motives, which have prompted monarchs to shed the blood of their unhappy subjects. Pride, jealousy, disappointed love, hurt vanity, greed for greater treasures, lust for power over larger dominions, petty animosities between royal brothers or between father and son, momentary passions and childish whims, these all have been, not the occasional but the perennially recurring, causes and occasions of international conflict. The growing intelligence of mankind and the increased responsibility of monarchs to their people have placed a check upon the caprice, but not upon the self-interest, of the men of power. They may still engage in social conflict for the satisfaction of their pride and vanity provided they can compound their personal ambitions with, and hallow them by, the ambitions of their group, and the pitiful vanities and passions of the individuals who compose the group. The story of Napoleon belongs to modern and not to ancient history. He could bathe Europe in blood for the sake of gratifying his overweening lust for power, as long as he could pose as the tool of French patriotism and as the instrument of revolutionary fervor. The fact that the democratic sentiment, opposed to the traditional absolutisms of Europe, could be exploited to create a tyranny more sanguinary and terrible than those which it sought ostensibly to destroy; and that the dream of equality, liberty and fraternity of the French Revolution could turn so quickly into the nightmare of Napoleonic imperialism is a tragic revelation of the inadequacies of the human resources with which men must try to solve the problems of their social life. The childish vanity of the German Emperor,[12] who wanted a large navy so that he could stand on equal footing with his royal English uncle at naval manœuvres, helped to make the World War inevitable.[13] He would not have been permitted to indulge this vanity however had it not seemed compatible with the prejudices of his people and the economic necessities of a growing empire. Theodore Roosevelt belonged to a little junta which foisted the Spanish-American War upon the American people. The ambition and vanity which prompted him could be veiled and exalted because the will-to-power of an adolescent nation and the frustrated impulses of pugnacity and martial ardor of the pitiful little "men in the street" could find in him symbolic expression and vicarious satisfaction. The need of the modern industrial overlord for raw materials and markets, and rivalry over control of the undeveloped and unexploited portions of the earth are the occasion of modern wars. Yet the ambitions and greed of dominant economic groups within each nation are not the only cause of international conflict. Every social group tends to develop imperial ambitions which are aggravated, but not caused solely, by the lusts of its leaders and privileged groups. Every group, as every individual, has expansive desires which are rooted in the instinct of survival and soon extend beyond it. The will-to-live becomes the will-to-power. Only rarely does nature provide armors of defense which cannot be transmuted into instruments of aggression. The frustrations of the average man, who can never realise the power and the glory which his imagination sets as the ideal, makes him the more willing tool and victim of the imperial ambitions of his group. His frustrated individual ambitions gain a measure of satisfaction in the power and the aggrandisement of his nation. The will-to-power of competing national groups is the cause of the international anarchy which the moral sense of mankind has thus far vainly striven to overcome. Since some nations are more powerful than others, they will at times prevent anarchy by effective imperialism, which in our industrial period has become more covert than overt. But the peace is gained by force and is always an uneasy and an unjust one. As powerful classes organise a nation, so powerful nations organise a crude society of nations. In each case the peace is a tentative

---

[12]*German Emperor:* Here Niebuhr is referring to Friedrich Wilhelm William II (1859–1941), the emperor of Germany and the King of Prussia prior to and during World War I. The strongly militaristic William II allowed the implementation of two German naval bills (1897 and 1900) that had the effect of challenging Britain's naval domination, exacerbating tensions and leading to World War 1.

[13]See *Memoirs of Prince Von Bülow*, Vol. III, p. 204. [Niebuhr]

one because it is unjust. It has been achieved only partially by a mutual accommodation of conflicting interests and certainly not by a rational and moral adjustment of rights. It will last only until those, who feel themselves too weak to challenge strength, will become, or will feel themselves, powerful enough to do so. It is not necessary to discount the moral influence of the League of Nations completely or to deny that it represents certain gains in the rational and moral organisation of society, to recognise that the peace of contemporary Europe is maintained by the force of French arms and that it will last only as long as the ingenuities of French statesmanship can maintain the combination of political and military forces which holds the people, who feel themselves defrauded by the Versailles Treaty,[14] in check. Significantly the same power, which prompts the fear that prevents immediate action, also creates the mounting hatred which guarantees ultimate rebellion.

Thus society is in a perpetual state of war. Lacking moral and rational   14
resources to organise its life, without resort to coercion, except in the most immediate and intimate social groups, men remain the victims of the individuals, classes and nations by whose force a momentary coerced unity is achieved, and further conflicts are as certainly created. The fact that the coercive factor in society is both necessary and dangerous seriously complicates the whole task of securing both peace and justice. History is a long tale of abortive efforts toward the desired end of social cohesion and justice in which failure was usually due either to the effort to eliminate the factor of force entirely or to an undue reliance upon it. Complete reliance upon it means that new tyrants usurp the places of eminence from which more traditional monarchs are cast down. Tolstoian pacifists[15] and other advocates of nonresistance, noting the evils which force introduces into society, give themselves to the vain illusion that it can be completely eliminated, and society organised upon the basis of anarchistic principles. Their conviction is an illusion, because there are definite limits of moral goodwill and social intelligence beyond which even the most vital religion and the most astute educational programme will not carry a social group, whatever may be possible for individuals in an intimate society. The problem which society faces is clearly one of reducing force by increasing the factors which make for a moral and rational adjustment of life to life; of bringing such

---

[14]*Versailles Treaty:* The Treaty of Versailles (1919) was the first treaty to be established in the Peace Conference at Paris after World War I. Though the treaty was designed to weaken Germany's power and was successful in doing so temporarily, in 1939 Germany rose again in war.

[15]*Tolstoian pacifists:* Persons following the philosophy of Russian author Leo Tolstoy (1828–1910) as conveyed in his novels, especially *War and Peace* (1865–1869), where war is characterized as absurd if not insane. Tolstoian pacifists believe that war is a product of social, not natural, flaws and can therefore be avoided by following the practice of nonresistance.

force as is still necessary under responsibility of the whole of society; of destroying the kind of power which cannot be made socially responsible (the power which resides in economic ownership for instance); and of bringing forces of moral self-restraint to bear upon types of power which can never be brought completely under social control. Every one of these methods has its definite limitations. Society will probably never be sufficiently intelligent to bring all power under its control. The stupidity of the average man will permit the oligarch, whether economic or political, to hide his real purposes from the scrutiny of his fellows and to withdraw his activities from effective control. Since it is impossible to count on enough moral goodwill among those who possess irresponsible power to sacrifice it for the good of the whole, it must be destroyed by coercive methods and these will always run the peril of introducing new forms of injustice in place of those abolished. There is, for instance, as yet no clear proof that the power of economic overlords can be destroyed by means less rigorous than communism has employed; but there is also no proof that communistic oligarchs, once the idealistic passion of a revolutionary period is spent, will be very preferable to the capitalistic oligarchs, whom they are to displace. Since the increasing complexity of society makes it impossible to bring all those who are in charge of its intricate techniques and processes, and who are therefore in possession of social power, under complete control, it will always be necessary to rely partly upon the honesty and self-restraint of those who are not socially restrained. But here again, it will never be possible to insure moral antidotes sufficiently potent to destroy the deleterious effects of the poison of power upon character. The future peace and justice of society therefore depend upon, not one but many, social strategies, in all of which moral and coercive factors are compounded in varying degrees. So difficult is it to avoid the Scylla of despotism and the Charybdis of anarchy that it is safe to hazard the prophecy that the dream of perpetual peace and brotherhood for human society is one which will never be fully realised.[16] It is a vision prompted by the conscience and insight of individual man, but incapable of fulfillment by collective man. It is like all true religious visions, possible of approximation but not of realisation in actual history. The vitality of the vision is the measure of man's rebellion against the fate which binds his collective life to the world of nature from which his soul recoils. The vision can be kept alive only by permitting it to overreach itself. But meanwhile collective man, operating on the historic and mundane scene, must content himself with a more

---

[16]*Scylla and Charybdis:* In Homer's *Odyssey* (Book XII), Scylla — a six-headed monster — inhabited a cave to one side of a sea channel (the Strait of Messina), across from the treacherous whirlpool of Charybdis. Sailors who ventured too near to either would perish. The modern reference suggests a difficult course steered between twin, though opposite, dangers.

modest goal. His concern for some centuries to come is not the creation of an ideal society in which there will be uncoerced and perfect peace and justice, but a society in which there will be enough justice, and in which coercion will be sufficiently non-violent to prevent his common enterprise from issuing into complete disaster. That goal will seem too modest for the romanticists; but the romanticists have so little understanding for the perils in which modern society lives, and overestimate the moral resources at the disposal of the collective human enterprise so easily, that any goal regarded as worthy of achievement by them must necessarily be beyond attainment.

REVIEW QUESTIONS

1. Niebuhr's first paragraph summarizes the essay. Take each of the six sentences in paragraph 1 and gloss them by making references to other parts of the essay. This exercise should lead to a six-paragraph summary. If time does not permit a complete summary, develop a gloss for sentence 4.
2. According to Niebuhr, what qualities are exhibited in a natural relationship among individuals? What are the very explicit limits to this relationship?
3. Niebuhr makes a glancing reference to Condorcet, among others, in paragraph 4. What is the reference? What is Niebuhr's point, here?
4. What are the competing forces in the democratic process?
5. According to Niebuhr, what are the chief differences between ancient/medieval agrarian civilizations and modern industrial civilizations? How does Niebuhr use this distinction in developing his essay?
6. What is the relationship between social power and social inequality? What are Niebuhr's views on this relationship?
7. According to Niebuhr, what is one of the tragedies of the human spirit?
8. How does the rise of slavery illustrate the development of social injustice? What function does the philanthropist play in the social equation?
9. How do forces that act to preserve peace within communities serve to aggravate hostilities between them?
10. In Napoleonic imperialism Niebuhr finds a "tragic revelation." What is it?
11. How can an individual's frustrated dreams of glory be satisfied through allegiance to a group? How does such a relationship exacerbate social conflict, according to Niebuhr?

DISCUSSION AND WRITING QUESTIONS

1. "Perhaps it is man's sorry fate, suffering from ills which have their source in the inadequacies of both nature and human society, that the task by which he eliminates the former should become the means of increasing the latter." This somewhat difficult concept is a key to understanding Niebuhr's essay — and much of the pessimistic thinking on the idea of progress. Recall that in "Progress an

Illusion," George Bernard Shaw wrote: "Early successes in building commercial civilizations . . . are but preliminaries to the inevitable later stages, now threatening us, in which the passions which built the civilization become fatal instead of productive, just as the same qualities which make the lion king of the forest ensure his destruction when he enters a city. . . . [W]ar and competition, potent instruments of selection and evolution in one epoch, become ruinous instruments of degeneration in the next." And Marx and Engels held that the bourgeoisie, responsible for relieving the hardships of feudal life through the exercise of newly discovered powers, created deep economic divisions in capitalist society through the extension of those same powers. Thus three authors share this single idea, though each applies it differently. How damning to the notion of progress is the observation that the same forces acting to build a civilization over time are the same ones acting to destroy it?

2. "Politics will, to the end of history, be an area where conscience and power meet, where the ethical and coercive factors of human life interpenetrate and work out their tentative and uneasy compromises." Explain Niebuhr's statement, giving one example from the political wranglings on some current event, as you have followed it in the news. Then comment on what Niebuhr is proposing as a law of human relations. Does the law seem correctly stated? Is it in fact a law? In developing your answer, take notice of how Niebuhr's law stands in relation to the other laws mentioned in the work of Condorcet and Marx.

3. Summarize Niebuhr's account of history. In what ways does it differ from the accounts offered by Shaw and Marx?

4. "Individuals have a moral code which makes the actions of collective man an outrage to their conscience." What is Niebuhr's justification for this statement? To what extent do you agree?

5. Niebuhr concludes that society is in a state of perpetual war, which he sees as necessary given the present state of human abilities. What are the competing forces at odds in this war? Why is the war necessary?

6. Niebuhr's hopes for civilization over the next few centuries are considerably more modest than those of Condorcet. Whose vision of human potential are you inclined to endorse? Why?

ROBERT L. HEILBRONER (b. 1919)

Robert Heilbroner is Norman Thomas Professor at the New School for Social Research in New York City. As an economist, he has been a consultant to government, business, labor, and educational groups. Heilbroner was born on March 24, 1919, in New York City. On graduating from Harvard University in 1940, he served with U.S. Army Intelligence during World War II. On returning, decorated with a Bronze Star, he earned his Ph.D. at the New School for Social Research.

Heilbroner has written texts on economics and provocative book-length examinations of economic theory and practice in America and elsewhere. A partial listing of his work includes *The Worldly Philosophers* (1953), *The Quest for Wealth* (1956), *The Future as History* (1960), *The Limits of American Capitalism* (1966), and *Marxism: For and Against* (1980). The present selection constitutes the final chapter of *An Inquiry into the Human Prospect* (1975).

Heilbroner is one in whom we sense a deep awe of the human enterprise and a hope that the peace we can imagine becomes the peace we shall one day achieve. Unlike Condorcet, Heilbroner writes in a nuclear, heavily industrialized age that has gained — and suffered — from 250 years of technical innovation. Given the record of history, it is no longer possible for him — or us — to hold what now amounts to a naive belief in the perfectibility of man. Where can we point for proof that conditions are improving? We take stock of the threats facing us and realize that poverty continues to be a problem of immense proportions. We are no nearer than was Condorcet to global peace; we are no nearer to an equitable distribution of wealth within or among nations; we are, by contrast, closer to exhausting the limits of our resources and closer to destroying all resources with agents of destruction undreamed of two centuries ago. So it is fair to ask: where are we headed, given that we, too, want peace and perfectibility? "What is needed now," says Heilbroner, "is a summing up of the human prospect, some last reflections on its implications for the present and future alike."

Heilbroner is well qualified to make this summation that is at once hopeful and foreboding. In his "Final Reflections" one sees the realism of Niebuhr managing to avoid the apparent cynicism of Shaw. The hopes of Condorcet, Godwin, and Macaulay are respected but soberly examined. Malthus is defended and Marxist analysis applied. Heilbroner's vision, like that of so many important thinkers, extends beyond the narrow range of disciplinary concerns. He is an economist who examines history and speaks of the human spirit with moving, poetic authority. His call for a stable society (for which we shall have to pay a price) will remind you of Huxley's *Brave New World*. And his view of ritual and tradition in the postindustrial age may be surprising: for Heilbroner implies that the program of "enlightened," rational thought that began in 18th century Europe has left us, at this late date, wanting. It is possible that we shall need to call on some pre-"enlightened," pre-rational faculty in order to achieve the happiness that Condorcet argued would follow naturally from the application of reason alone. Perhaps in our rush away from the primitive we have left a valuable heritage behind.

In the preceding four chapters of *Inquiry into the Human Prospect*, Heilbroner takes up the question, "Is there hope for man?" He assumes in his contemporaries (of 1974) a "pessimistic frame of mind" or "civilizational malaise," attributing this to three causes: confidence-shaking events such as the Vietnam War, an inability of middle-aged Americans to pass their values to the younger generation, and a general awareness that life as we have known it (economic, environmental, and spiritual life) is deteriorating, spinning out of control. Heilbroner next lays down the external challenges we face — a Malthusian rate of population growth, with the attendant problems of food production; nuclear war; and the destruction of natural resources. He reviews the individual and larger social responses we can mount in the face of these challenges, concluding that we must ease consumption of diminishing resources, avoid polluting the environment, redistribute wealth, and generally learn to forego immediate pleasures for the sake of humanity's long-term survival. Because individuals will not likely muster the self-sacrifice needed to achieve these ends, Heilbroner feels that "the passage through the gantlet ahead may be possible only under [authoritarian] governments capable of rallying obedience far more effectively than would be possible in a democratic setting." These sober considerations bring him to his final chapter, reprinted here.

FINAL REFLECTIONS ON THE HUMAN PROSPECT

What is needed now is a summing up of the human prospect, some last reflections on its implications for the present and future alike. 1

The external challenges can be succinctly reviewed. We are entering a period in which rapid population growth, the presence of obliterative weapons, and dwindling resources will bring international tensions to dangerous levels for an extended period. Indeed, there seems no reason for these levels of danger to subside unless population equilibrium is achieved and some rough measure of equity reached in the distribution of wealth among nations, either by great increases in the output of the under-developed world or by a massive redistribution of wealth from the richer to the poorer lands. 2

Robert L. Heilbroner. "Final Reflections on the Human Prospect" in *An Inquiry into The Human Prospect*. New York: Norton, 1974, pp. 127–144.

Whether such an equitable arrangement can be reached — at least   3
within the next several generations — is open to serious doubt. Transfers
of adequate magnitude imply a willingness to redistribute income internationally on a more generous scale than the advanced nations have evidenced within their own domains. The required increases in output in the
backward regions would necessitate gargantuan applications of energy
merely to extract the needed resources. It is uncertain whether the requisite energy-producing technology exists, and, more serious, possible that
its application would bring us to the threshold of an irreversible change in
climate as a consequence of the enormous addition of man-made heat to
the atmosphere.

It is this last problem that poses the most demanding and difficult of   4
the challenges. The existing pace of industrial growth, with no allowance
for increased industrialization to repair global poverty, holds out the risk
of entering the danger zone of climatic change in as little as three or four
generations. If that trajectory is in fact pursued, industrial growth will then
have to come to an immediate halt, for another generation or two along
that path would literally consume human, perhaps all, life. That terrifying
outcome can be postponed only to the extent that the wastage of heat can
be reduced, or that technologies that do not add to the atmospheric heat
burden — for example, the use of solar energy — can be utilized. The
outlook can also be mitigated by redirecting output away from heat-creat-
ing material outputs into the production of "services" that add only trivi-
ally to heat.

All these considerations make the designation of a timetable for indus-   5
trial deceleration difficult to construct. Yet, under any and all assumptions,
one irrefutable conclusion remains. The industrial growth process, so central to the economic and social life of capitalism and Western socialism
alike, will be forced to slow down, in all likelihood within a generation or
two, and will probably have to give way to decline thereafter. To repeat
the words of the text, "whether we are unable to sustain growth or unable
to tolerate it," the long era of industrial expansion is now entering its final
stages, and we must anticipate the commencement of a new era of stationary total output and (if population growth continues or an equitable sharing among nations has not yet been attained) declining material output per
head in the advanced nations.

These challenges also point to a certain time frame within which dif-   6
ferent aspects of the human prospect will assume different levels of importance. In the short run, by which we may speak of the decade immediately ahead, no doubt the most pressing questions will be those of the
use and abuse of national power, the vicissitudes of the narrative of political history, perhaps the short-run vagaries of the economic process, about
which we have virtually no predictive capability whatsoever. From our
vantage point today, another crisis in the Middle East, further Vietnams or

Czechoslovakias, inflation, severe economic malfunction — or their avoid-ance — are sure to exercise the primary influence over the quality of exis-tence, or even over the possibilities for existence.

In a somewhat longer time frame — extending perhaps for a period of   7
a half century — the main shaping force of the future takes on a different aspect. Assuming that the day-to-day, year-to-year crises are surmounted in relative safety, the issue of the relative resilience and adaptive capabili-ties of the two great socio-economic systems comes to the fore as the de-cisive question. Here the properties of industrial socialism and capitalism as ideal types seem likely to provide the parameters within which and by which the prospect for man will be formed. We have already indicated what general tendencies seem characteristic of each of these systems, and the advantages that may accrue to socialist — that is, planned and probably authoritarian social orders — during this era of adjustment.

In the long run, stretching a century or more ahead, still a different   8
facet of the human prospect appears critical. This is the transformational problem, centered in the reconstruction of the material basis of civilization itself. In this period, as indefinite in its boundaries but as unmistakable in its mighty dimensions as a vast storm visible on the horizon, the challenge devolves upon those deep-lying capabilities for political change whose roots in "human nature" have been the subject of our last chapter.

It is the challenges of the middle and the long run that command our   9
attention when we speculate about the human prospect, if only because those of the short run defy our prognostic grasp entirely. It seems unnec-essary to add more than a word to underline the magnitude of these still distant problems. No developing country has fully confronted the impli-cations of becoming a "modern" nation-state whose industrial develop-ment must be severely limited, or considered the strategy for such a state in a world in which the Western nations, capitalist and socialist both, will continue for a long period to enjoy the material advantages of their early start. Within the advanced nations, in turn, the difficulties of adjustment are no less severe. No capitalist nation has as yet imagined the extent of the alterations it must undergo to attain a viable stationary socio-economic structure, and no socialist state has evidenced the needed willingness to subordinate its national interests to supra-national ones.

To these obstacles we must add certain elements of the political pro-   10
pensities in "human nature" that stand in the way of a rational, orderly adaptation of the industrial mode in the directions that will become in-creasingly urgent as the distant future comes closer. There seems no hope for rapid changes in the human character traits that would have to be mod-ified to bring about a peaceful, organized reorientation of life styles. Men and women, much as they are today, will set the pace and determine the necessary means for the social changes that will eventually have to be made. The drift toward the strong exercise of political power — a move-

ment given its initial momentum by the need to exercise a much wider and deeper administration of both production and consumption — is likely to attain added support from the psychological insecurity that will be sharpened in a period of unrest and uncertainty. The bonds of national identity are certain to exert their powerful force, mobilizing men for the collective efforts needed but inhibiting the international sharing of burdens and wealth. The myopia that confines the present vision of men to the short-term future is not likely to disappear overnight, rendering still more difficult a planned and orderly retrenchment and redivision of output.

Therefore the outlook is for what we may call "convulsive change" — 11 change forced upon us by external events rather than by conscious choice, by catastrophe rather than by calculation. As with Malthus's much derided but all too prescient forecasts, nature will provide the checks, if foresight and "morality" do not. One such check could be the outbreak of wars arising from the explosive tensions of the coming period, which might reduce the growth rates of the surviving nation-states and thereby defer the danger of industrial asphyxiation for a period. Alternatively, nature may rescue us from ourselves by what John Platt has called a "storm of crisis problems."[1] As we breach now this, now that edge of environmental tolerance, local disasters — large-scale fatal urban temperature inversions, massive crop failures, resource shortages — may also slow down economic growth and give a necessary impetus to the piecemeal construction of an ecologically and socially viable social system.

Such negative feedbacks are likely to exercise an all-important damp- 12 ening effect on a crisis that would otherwise in all probability overwhelm the slender human capabilities for planned adjustment to the future. However brutal these feedbacks, they are apt to prove effective in changing our attitudes as well as our actions, unlike appeals to our collective foresight, such as the exhortations of the Club of Rome's *Limits to Growth*,[2] or the manifesto of a group of British scientists calling for an immediate halt to growth.[3] The problem is that the challenge to survival still lies sufficiently far in the future, and the inertial momentum of the present industrial order is still so great, that no substantial voluntary diminution of growth, much less a planned reorganization of society, is today even remotely imaginable. What leader of an underdeveloped nation, particularly one caught up in the exhilaration of a revolutionary restructuring of society, would call a halt to industrial activity in his impoverished land? What capitalist or so-

---

[1]John Platt, "What We Must Do," *Science,* November 28, 1969, p. 1115. [Heilbroner]

[2]*Club of Rome:* A scholarly organization or "think tank," the Club of Rome was established in 1968 in Rome to address emerging world problems. The club was famous for its predictions of world catastrophe in the year 2000 due to population increase.

[3]"Blueprint for Survival," *The Ecologist,* January 1972. [Heilbroner]

cialist nation would put a ceiling on material output, limiting its citizens to the well-being obtainable from its present volume of production?

Thus, however admirable in intent, impassioned polemics against   *13* growth are exercises in futility today. Worse, they may even point in the wrong direction. Paradoxically, perhaps, the priorities for the present lie in the temporary encouragement of the very process of industrial advance that is ultimately the mortal enemy. In the backward areas, the acute misery that is the potential source of so much international disruption can be remedied only to the extent that rapid improvements are introduced, including that minimal infrastructure needed to support a modern system of health services, education, transportation, fertilizer production, and the like. In the developed nations, what is required at the moment is the encouragement of technical advances that will permit the extraction of new resources to replace depleted reserves of scarce minerals, new sources of energy to stave off the collapse that would occur if present energy reservoirs were exhausted before substitutes were discovered, and, above all, new techniques for the generation of energy that will minimize the associated generation of heat.

Thus there is a short period left during which we can safely continue   *14* on the present trajectory. It is possible that during this period a new direction will be struck that will greatly ease the otherwise inescapable adjustments. The underdeveloped nations, making a virtue of necessity, may redefine "development" in ways that minimize the need for the accumulation of capital, stressing instead the education and vitality of their citizens. The possibilities of such an historic step would be much enhanced were the advanced nations to lead the way by a major effort to curtail the enormous wastefulness of industrial production as it is used today. If these changes took place, we might even look forward to a still more desirable redirection of history in a diminution of scale, a reduction in the size of the human community from the dangerous level of immense nation-states toward the "polis"[4] that defined the appropriate reach of political power for the ancient Greeks.

All these are possibilities, but certainly not probabilities. The revitali-   *15* zation of the polis is hardly likely to take place during a period in which an orderly response to social and physical challenges will require an increase of centralized power and the encouragement of national rather than communal attitudes. The voluntary abandonment of the industrial mode of production would require a degree of self-abnegation on the part of its beneficiaries — managers and consumers alike — that would be without parallel in history. The redefinition of development on the part of the

---

[4]*polis:* An ancient Greek city-state, the polis was a small, locally governed unit that included a central town and the surrounding countryside.

poorer nations would require a prodigious effort of will in the face of the envy and fear that Western industrial power and "affluence" will arouse.

Thus in all likelihood we must brace ourselves for the consequences of 16 which we have spoken — the risk of "wars of redistribution" or of "preemptive seizure," the rise of social tensions in the industrialized nations over the division of an ever more slow-growing or even diminishing product, and the prospect of a far more coercive exercise of national power as the means by which we will attempt to bring these disruptive processes under control.

From that period of harsh adjustment, I can see no realistic escape. 17 Rationalize as we will, stretch the figures as favorably as honesty will permit, we cannot reconcile the requirements for a lengthy continuation of the present rate of industrialization of the globe with the capacity of existing resources or the fragile biosphere to permit or to tolerate the effects of that industrialization. Nor is it easy to foresee a willing acquiescence of humankind, individually or through its existing social organizations, in the alterations of lifeways that foresight would dictate. If then, by the question "Is there hope for man?" we ask whether it is possible to meet the challenges of the future without the payment of a fearful price, the answer must be: No, there is no such hope.

At this final stage of our inquiry, with the full spectacle of the human 18 prospect before us, the spirit quails and the will falters. We find ourselves pressed to the very limit of our personal capacities, not alone in summoning up the courage to look squarely at the dimensions of the impending predicament, but in finding words that can offer some plausible relief in a situation so bleak. There is now nowhere to turn other than to those private beliefs and disbeliefs that guide each of us through life, and whose disconcerting presence was the first problem with which we had to deal in appraising the prospect before us. I shall therefore speak my mind without any pretense that the words I am about to write have any basis other than those subjective promptings from which I was forced to begin and in which I must now discover whatever consolation I can offer after the analysis to which they have driven me.

At this late juncture I have no intention of sounding a call for moral 19 awakening or for social action on some unrealistic scale. Yet, I do not intend to condone, much less to urge, an attitude of passive resignation, or a relegation of the human prospect to the realm of things we choose not to think about. Avoidable evil remains, as it always will, an enemy that can be defeated; and the fact that the collective destiny of man portends unavoidable travail is no reason, and cannot be tolerated as an excuse, for doing nothing. This general admonition applies in particular to the intellectual elements of Western nations whose privileged role as sentries for society takes on a special importance in the face of things as we now see them. It is their task not only to prepare their fellow citizens for the sacrifices that will be required of them but to take the lead in seeking to redefine the legitimate boundaries of power and the permissible sanctuaries of freedom, for a future in which the exercise of power must inevitably increase and many present areas of freedom, especially in economic life, be curtailed.

Let me therefore put these last words in a somewhat more "positive" frame, offsetting to some degree the bleakness of our prospect, without violating the facts or spirit of our inquiry. Here I must begin by stressing for one last time an essential fact. The human prospect is not an irrevocable death sentence. It is not an inevitable doomsday toward which we are headed, although the risk of enormous catastrophes exists. The prospect is better viewed as a formidable array of challenges that must be overcome before human survival is assured, before we can move *beyond doomsday.* These challenges can be overcome — by the saving intervention of nature if not by the wisdom and foresight of man. The death sentence is therefore better viewed as a contingent life sentence — one that will permit the continuance of human society, but only on a basis very different from that of the present, and probably only after much suffering during the period of transition.

What sort of society might eventually emerge? As I have said more than once, I believe the long-term solution requires nothing less than the gradual abandonment of the lethal techniques, the uncongenial lifeways, and the dangerous mentality of industrial civilization itself. The dimensions of such a transformation into a "post-industrial" society have already been touched upon, and cannot be greatly elaborated here: in all probability the extent and ramifications of change are as unforeseeable from our contemporary vantage point as present-day society would have been unimaginable to a speculative observer a thousand years ago.

Yet I think a few elements of the society of the post-industrial era can be discerned. Although we cannot know on what technical foundation it will rest, we can be certain that many of the accompaniments of an industrial order must be absent. To repeat once again what we have already said, the societal view of production and consumption must stress parsimonious, not prodigal, attitudes. Resource-consuming and heat-generating processes must be regarded as necessary evils, not as social triumphs, to be relegated to as small a portion of economic life as possible. This implies a sweeping reorganization of the mode of production in ways that cannot be foretold, but that would seem to imply the end of the giant factory, the huge office, perhaps of the urban complex.

What values and ways of thought would be congenial to such a radical reordering of things we also cannot know, but it is likely that the ethos of "science," so intimately linked with industrial application, would play a much reduced role. In the same way, it seems probable that a true post-industrial society would witness the waning of the work ethic that is also intimately entwined with our industrial society. As one critic has pointed out, even Marx, despite his bitter denunciation of the alienating effects of labor in a capitalist milieu, placed his faith in the presumed "liberating" effects of labor in a socialist society, and did not consider a "terrible secret" — that even the most creative work may be only "a neurotic activity that diverts the mind from the diminution of time and the approach of death."[5]

It is therefore possible that a post-industrial society would also turn in the direction of many pre-industrial societies — toward the exploration of inner states of experience rather than the outer world of fact and material accomplishment. Tradition and ritual, the pillars of life in virtually all societies other than those of an industrial character, would probably once again assert their ancient claims as the guide to and solace for life. The struggle for individual achievement, especially for material ends, is likely to give way to the acceptance of communally organized and ordained roles.   24

This is by no means an effort to portray a future utopia. On the contrary, many of these possible attributes of a post-industrial society are deeply repugnant to my twentieth-century temper as well as incompatible with my most treasured privileges. The search for scientific knowledge, the delight in intellectual heresy, the freedom to order one's life as one pleases, are not likely to be easily contained within the tradition-oriented, static society I have depicted. To a very great degree, the public must take precedence over the private — an aim to which it is easy to give lip service in the abstract but difficult for someone used to the pleasures of political, social, and intellectual freedom to accept in fact.   25

These are all necessarily prophetic speculations, offered more in the spirit of providing some vision of the future, however misty, than as a set of predictions to be "rigorously" examined. In these half-blind gropings there is, however, one element in which we can place credence, although it offers uncertainty as well as hope. This is our knowledge that some human societies have existed for millennia, and that others can probably exist for future millennia, in a continuous rhythm of birth and coming of age and death, without pressing toward those dangerous ecological limits, or engendering those dangerous social tensions, that threaten present-day "advanced" societies. In our discovery of "primitive" cultures, living out their timeless histories, we may have found the single most important object lesson for future man.   26

What we do not know, but can only hope, is that future man can rediscover the self-renewing vitality of primitive culture without reverting to its levels of ignorance and cruel anxiety. It may be the sad lesson of the future that no civilization is without its pervasive "malaise," each express-   27

---

[5] John Diggins, "Thoreau, Marx, and the Riddle of Alienation," *Social Research*, Winter 1973, p. 573. [Heilbroner]

ing in its own way the ineradicable fears of the only animal that contemplates its own death, but at least the human activities expressing that malaise need not, as is the case in our time, threaten the continuance of life itself.

All this goes, perhaps, beyond speculation to fantasy. But something 28 more substantial than speculation or fantasy is needed to sustain men through the long trials ahead. For the driving energy of modern man has come from his Promethean spirit,[6] his nervous will, his intellectual daring. It is this spirit that has enabled him to work miracles, above all to subjugate nature to his will, and to create societies designed to free man from his animal bondage.

Some of that Promethean spirit may still serve us in good stead in the 29 years of transition. But it is not a spirit that conforms easily with the shape of future society as I have imagined it; worse, within that impatient spirit lurks one final danger for the years during which we must watch the approach of an unwanted future. This is the danger that can be glimpsed in our deep consciousness when we take stock of things as they now are: the wish that the drama run its full tragic course, bringing man, like a Greek hero, to the fearful end that he has, however unwittingly, arranged for himself. For it is not only with dismay that Promethean man regards the future. It is also with a kind of anger. If after so much effort, so little has been accomplished; if before such vast challenges, so little is apt to be done — then let the drama proceed to its finale, let mankind suffer the end it deserves.

Such a view is by no means the expression of only a few perverse 30 minds. On the contrary, it is the application to the future of the prevailing attitudes with which our age regards the present. When men can generally acquiesce in, even relish, the destruction of their living contemporaries, when they can regard with indifference or irritation the fate of those who live in slums, rot in prison, or starve in lands that have meaning only insofar as they are vacation resorts, why should they be expected to take the painful actions needed to prevent the destruction of future generations whose faces they will never live to see? Worse yet, will they not curse these future generations whose claims to life can be honored only by sacrificing present enjoyments; and will they not, if it comes to a choice, condemn them to nonexistence by choosing the present over the future?

The question, then, is how we are to summon up the will to survive 31 — not perhaps in the distant future, where survival will call on those deep sources of imagined human unity, but in the present and near-term future,

---

[6]*Promethean spirit:* Prometheus, one of the four Titans in Greek mythology, was said to have endured terrible punishments for tricking and/or defying Zeus, the king of the Olympians, by daring to make a gift of fire to man. Promethean spirit here refers to daring and imaginative invention, often without regard to consequence.

while we still enjoy and struggle with the heritage of our personal liberties, our atomistic existences.

At this last moment of reflection another figure from Greek mythology   32
comes to mind. It is that of Atlas,[7] bearing with endless perseverance the weight of the heavens in his hands. If mankind is to rescue life, it must first preserve the very will to live, and thereby rescue the future from the angry condemnation of the present. The spirit of conquest and aspiration will not provide the inspiration it needs for this task. It is the example of Atlas, resolutely bearing his burden, that provides the strength we seek. If, within us, the spirit of Atlas falters, there perishes the determination to preserve humanity at all cost and any cost, forever.

But Atlas is, of course, no other but ourselves. Myths have their magic   33
power because they cast on the screen of our imaginations, like the figures of the heavenly constellations, immense projections of our own hopes and capabilities. We do not know with certainty that humanity will survive, but it is a comfort to know that there exist within us the elements of fortitude and will from which the image of Atlas springs.

---

[7]*Atlas:* In Greek mythology, the Titan Atlas was condemned to support the pillars of the heavens (or the heavenly sphere, as it is often depicted) on his shoulders.

REVIEW QUESTIONS

1. Why must the growth of industrialization slow down, according to Heilbroner? In the long run, what will replace industrial growth?
2. What forces will shape the human prospect during the next 50 years? the next 100?
3. Why is convulsive change, as opposed to change by conscious choice, likely to occur? Over the long run, what function is served by convulsive change?
4. In the second part of the essay, Heilbroner makes a strong case for *not* submitting to the "impending predicament." Briefly state his reasons.
5. What is the difference between a "death sentence" and a "contingent life sentence"? How is this distinction important in understanding Heilbroner's position on the human prospect?
6. How can "primitive" cultures serve as an important object lesson for post-industrial man?
7. Heilbroner refers to two figures from Greek mythology. Why?

DISCUSSION AND WRITING QUESTIONS

1. Heilbroner argues that human survival depends upon achieving a "viable stationary socio-economic structure," the attainment of which depends upon the inhabitants of capitalist countries curtailing extravagant lifestyles and subor-

dinating "national interests to supra-national ones." Heilbroner is saying that we must make sacrifices in order to achieve stability, even to the point of deemphasizing science and accepting "communally organized and ordained roles." Has he in mind a stability akin to the one Huxley describes in *Brave New World?* Explain your answer and discuss your response to Heilbroner's view of the future.

2. Compare and contrast the views of Heilbroner with those of Reinhold Niebuhr, especially with regard to the diminished expectations these men have. Note also that their differing analyses yield similar conclusions.

3. Consider the views of Malthus, G. B. Shaw, Niebuhr, and Heilbroner. Are these thinkers realistic? pessimistic? a combination of the two? Does realism necessarily lead to pessimism? Why or why not? Consider also the differences between pessimism and cynicism — the differences, say, between the views of Heilbroner and Shaw. Whose views are you more likely to endorse? Why?

4. In counterpoint to Discussion Question 3, discuss the extent to which you consider the optimism of Condorcet, Godwin, and Macaulay to be realistic. What are the differences between optimism and naïveté?

5. Is it possible to be a realist and *not* pessimistic?

6. Sum up *your* beliefs about the human prospect. How would you characterize your views — with what combination of realism, optimism, pessimism, naïveté, or cynicism?

7. If the president or some body of respected scientists argued much in the fashion of Heilbroner and said: "Restrain your lifestyles or our prospects for survival are dim 200 years hence," how would you respond? Heilbroner believes that such appeals to our collective conscience do not work and that people will not voluntarily forgo their pleasures. Do you agree? If not, explain what it would take to elicit such voluntary behavior, worldwide. If you agree with Heilbroner, do you see the need, eventually, for some authoritarian body to mandate and enforce the sorts of restraints mentioned in "Final Reflections on the Human Prospect"? How would this authoritarian body differ from the Controllers in Huxley's *Brave New World?*

8. Heilbroner writes of a "fearful price" that must be paid to ensure hope for humanity. The Controller also speaks of a price paid for stability. In *Brave New World,* science and high art are sacrificed for happiness. Heilbroner sees science, at least, being sacrificed. Do you agree with Huxley and Heilbroner? What sort of price do you think must be paid?

9. What is Heilbroner's critique of industrial society? Compare and contrast this critique with Marx's. Then compare and contrast the views of Heilbroner and Marx with those of Macaulay.

10. Heilbroner envisions a post-industrial society that is more inner-directed and more respectful of tradition than our contemporary society. How do his views represent a coming full circle, a return to the view of the world derided by philosophers of the Enlightenment?

11. In paragraph 30, we see an affinity that Heilbroner shares with Condorcet. What are the essential similarities between the two men? the essential differences?

Part V

DARWIN AND THE SURVIVAL OF THE FITTEST

Charles Darwin

William Graham Sumner

Herbert Spencer

Andrew Carnegie

Samuel Butler

T. H. Huxley

Charlotte Perkins Gilman

Josiah Strong

Adolf Hitler

The struggle for existence — which in extreme cases is a life and death struggle — is waged not only between different classes of society but also between individuals within these social groups. Everybody competes in some way against everyone else and consequently each individual tries to push aside anyone whose existence is a barrier to his own advancement.

— Friedrich Engels, *The Condition of the Working Class in England*

The growth of a large business is merely a survival of the fittest.

— John D. Rockefeller, Sunday school address

The survival of the fittest, a doctrine that derives from Charles Darwin, has become one of the most powerful ideas in the modern world. It has influenced the thinking of thousands who have only the vaguest notions of what Darwin actually wrote in *The Origin of Species.* Such diametrically opposed figures as the capitalist Andrew Carnegie and the fascist Adolf Hitler have drawn upon this doctrine to support their own ideas. And although the debate has considerably subsided since Darwin's time, there remain many "people in the street" who still wholeheartedly believe that only the fittest survive; indeed, for some, this belief motivates entire careers.

What does it mean — "the survival of the fittest"? Why did it become such an epoch-making idea? One way of viewing the intellectual history of the last several hundred years is to see it as a series of unpleasant and unsettling jolts to human beings and their sense of privileged status in the natural order. The Copernican revolution removed the earth from the center of the universe and made it simply another revolving planetary body, along with innumerable others. As the earth lost its special status, so did the humans who inhabited it. Still, the humans could claim they had a special status in relation to the rest of the animal kingdom — they were the culmination of God's creative efforts on earth. It fell to Darwin, like Copernicus before him, to smash such cherished illusions. Biologically, he argued, humans were no more special than beetles. Humans were not created, by divine will, as a special race of superior beings; they simply evolved from lower creatures through a process of natural selection. God (if indeed there was a God) had nothing to do with this process. Humans survived into the present because they could adapt themselves to their environment better than other classes of creatures with whom they were struggling for existence. Hence, the survival of the fittest.

The human race was subjected to more jolts from Karl Marx and Sigmund Freud. Marx argued that humans were not in control of their own collective destiny but were at the mercy of economic forces that determined the course of history. Freud maintained that humans were not even in control of their own personal behavior but were subject to powerful unconscious influences to which they could gain access only with the greatest difficulty. The net effect of these redefinitions of humanity from Copernicus to Freud was to displace men and women from their central and all-important position in the universe and to render them insignificant, powerless, purposeless, and removed from divine grace.

Still, humans are resilient and will often try to make the best of a new situation. In one sense the "survival of the fittest" is a depressing concept; for those who see themselves as "the fittest," however, there are compensations. Let's consider the meaning of the term in the popular mind. According to this meaning, those creatures who are fittest — strongest, smartest, even most devious — will triumph in conflict for supremacy (or living space) with fellow creatures who are less strong, less smart, less devious. Their survival may be physical, financial, national, or racial. The losers will fall by the wayside of history. There are at least two corollaries to this idea. One is that those who fall deserve to fall. Only the strong deserve to survive, and since the continuing good fortunes of society depend upon strength, weakness should certainly not be transmitted to the next generation. The other corollary is that since this process of the strong triumphing over the weak is inevitable —a law of nature —it is folly, indeed a perversion of nature, to attempt to do anything about it. Thus, any social programs or policies that artificially support the less fit (by, for instance, redistributing income or establishing welfare programs paid for with the taxes of the rich) are both futile and unnatural.

It is easy to see how this idea has given new life to a basic conflict in human attitudes, a conflict much older than Darwin. On the one hand are those who believe that people should not compete but should cooperate, that such doctrines as Christian charity should encourage or even require us to aid the less fortunate, and that the rich and strong should be prevented from enjoying the fruits of their unfair and sometimes unlawful struggle to the top. On the other hand are those who believe that individuals (or groups of individuals) should have unrestricted freedom to achieve whatever power, wealth, or other success they can, giving little or no thought to those who are less able to compete. (And there must be a competition, since many are competing for few prizes; there is much less space at the top than at the bottom.)

Thus, many of those who followed Darwin attempted to apply his theories concerning the evolution of the species to human society — to how it was constituted and to how it *ought* to be constituted. These thinkers became known as social Darwinists. Using Darwin's theories to give scientific respectability to their conservative ideas, social Darwinists strove to justify cutthroat competition and *laissez-faire* capitalism. They believed that a rigid class system (just like the biological hierarchy, from plants, to unintelligent animals, to intelligent animals) was part of the natural order of things. In this natural order, wealth was the visible sign of superiority; poverty was the sign of inferiority. Wealth, according to social Darwinism, was also a sign of superior moral attributes: industriousness, sobriety, thriftiness. This being the case, programs of social reform made no more sense than programs of biological reform. In fact, social reform was actually pernicious because the resources involuntarily transferred from those best able to survive to those least able to survive would eventually remove the competitive edge from the fittest, and then fit and unfit alike would eventually perish. The same kind of thinking could be employed along racial lines: by means of the process of natural selection, certain races had been selected by nature as superior to the others. It is then only one step from tolerating inferior races to destroying them, for fear of their corrupting the superior races.

In this chapter, we explore some of the aspects of the idea of the survival of the fittest. We begin with the seminal thinker, Charles Darwin. Darwin was a biologist, and he confined his theories of natural selection of the best-adapted species strictly to biology. As we will see, Darwin himself was no social Darwinist. Significantly, he did not invent the phrase "survival of the fittest," and it did not appear in the first edition of *Origin of Species*. (In later editions, Darwin adopted the term, devised by the English philosopher and scientist Herbert Spencer, and it appeared alongside the more truly Darwinist term "natural selection," in the title to Chapter 4 of *Origin of Species*.) Following the selection from *The Origin of Species* and *The Descent of Man* by Darwin, we include two passages from *What the Social Classes Owe to Each Other*, a tract by the chief American social Darwinist, William Graham Sumner. This is followed by an essay by Herbert Spencer, whose work we have already seen in Part III on the Social Contract; Spencer argues here, as in his other piece, for social *laissez-faire*, maintaining that indiscriminately giving money to the poor "favors the multiplication of those worst fitted for existence, and, by consequence, hinders the multiplication of those best fitted for existence. . . ." Next, we offer an article by the American industrialist Andrew Carnegie, who claims that while the law of competition "is sometimes hard for the individual, it is best for the race, because it insures the survival of the fittest in every department"; Carnegie then outlines the ways in which great wealth can best be administered. Following Carnegie's essay is a section of "The Book of the Machines," from Samuel Butler's utopian novel, *Erewhon,* about a place where machines once evolved to the point that they threatened to overtake humans. Against the social Darwinists, the biologist T. H. Huxley next argues that "what we call goodness or virtue . . . involves a course of conduct which, in all respects, is opposed to that which leads to success in the cosmic struggle for existence." Following Huxley is a selection by Charlotte Perkins Gilman, a turn-of-the-century feminist and sociologist who argues that natural selection has, up to the present point in history, favored excessive sex differentiation between men and women, but that in the future men and women will alter the economic environment so that such sexual differentiation will considerably lessen. The chapter concludes with two selections that indicate the perniciousness of social Darwinism when translated into racial terms: two very different men argue that natural selection favors certain nations and races over others. Josiah Strong makes the case for Anglo-Saxons in the United States, and Adolf Hitler makes a similar case for Aryans in Germany.

CHARLES DARWIN *(1809–1882)*

For a man who eventually revolutionized human knowledge, Charles Darwin had a remarkably unpromising youth. He was born in Shrewsbury, England, of a well-to-do family. His grandfather, Erasmus Darwin, was a famous physician and philosopher; his mother, Susannah Wedgwood, was the daughter of the famous potter, Josiah Wedgwood. Darwin attended Shrewsbury School but did so poorly that he was removed by his father, who told him, "You care for nothing but shooting, dogs, and rat catching, and you will be a disgrace to yourself and all your family." He then went to Edinburgh to study medicine, but he had no aptitude for the subject and became nauseated when watching operations. Leaving Edinburgh in 1827, he went to Cambridge to prepare for Holy Orders in the Church of England — another profession in which he showed no interest.

His going to Cambridge was a crucial turning point in his life, however, because there he met John Stevens Henslowe, a professor of botany, who stimulated Darwin's interest in natural history and helped restore his faltering self-esteem. Through Henslowe's recommendation, the otherwise unqualified Darwin was in 1831 appointed naturalist aboard the Royal Navy's *H.M.S. Beagle*, which was about to sail on a five-year scientific expedition to South America and some Pacific Islands. During this voyage, Darwin observed numerous natural phenomena at first hand, observations that were to become the basis of much of his later work, including his theory of evolution by natural selection. Also fascinated by geology, Darwin developed a theory about the formation of coral reefs (atolls), still accepted today. His book, *Journal of Researches into the Geology and Natural History of the Various Countries Visited by H.M.S. Beagle, 1832–36* (1839), is not only a scientific landmark but has been called one of the best books of travel ever written.

At the time Darwin made his voyage, the accepted scientific view was that the various species had been separately created, according to God's design, and were immutable. The idea that species can change over time — the central concept of evolution — was not conceived by Darwin; some evolutionary ideas had been mentioned by Darwin's own grandfather, Erasmus Darwin, and a theory developed in 1809 by the French biologist Lamarck, according to which an organism's acquired characteristics could be transmitted by heredity (a theory since discredited). But no one had developed a systematic account, with adequate evidence, of just how evolution occurred. Darwin's observations on the *Beagle* eventually formed the basis of this systematic account. For example, he observed the similarities between related species in different geographical areas, and the differences between related species in geographically adjacent areas. He wondered what accounted for the variations in species of Galapagos turtles on different islands on which the climactic conditions seemed identical.

But Darwin delayed more than twenty years before publishing his ideas. For one thing, he was sidetracked by work in other areas: on the taxonomy of barnacles, on volcanic islands, on comparative zoology. For another, his health had been ruined as a result of a disease he had contracted from an insect bite during his voyage. But mainly, he could not set down a satisfactory account of the evolution of the species until he knew *how* evolution worked. Gradually, however, he developed the central idea of evolution through natural selection. According to the theory of natural selection, because of the limited quantity of food more organisms of a given species are born than can survive (this part of the theory was influenced by Malthus's *Essay on the Principle of Population;* see pp. 316–322). Since there must be a high rate of mortality and since there are always variations among members of a species (the mechanisms behind these variations were later demonstrated by Mendelian genetics), those individual organisms that will survive and produce offspring represent the variations that are best adapted to their environment. These adaptations may take the form of protective coloration, of superior feeding ability (the ability to break small seeds, for example), of greater endurance, or of many other factors. The less well adapted individuals will perish. The offspring of the better adapted variations will, over several generations, form an increasing proportion of the species, and thus, over time, the species will change into a different, though related form. The less well adapted variants of the species will become extinct — or they will survive only in those geographical areas for which they continue to be adapted — possibly the next island, where the food conditions are different. Natural selection,[1] therefore, simply means that through a process of nature, those varieties that are best adapted to their environment are selected for survival. The term "natural selection" is perhaps unfortunate in that it suggests that there is a "selector" — possibly even a divine selector. But this is not the case: natural selection is an automatic process; no one is doing the selecting. Indeed, Darwin's theories encountered (and continue to encounter) their most violent opposition from those who object that Darwin has removed God and any other element of divine guidance and design from the natural world. (Another religious objection, of course, is that Darwin's account of the evolution of the species, taking place over eons of time, runs directly contrary to the account of the creation in the Book of Genesis. Finally, many could not tolerate the idea that man was not unique, that he was, in fact, descended from the apes.)

With his work known only to a few friends, Darwin began to write down his theories in 1856. Two years later, he was astonished and dismayed to receive a letter from the naturalist Alfred Russel Wallace, who had quite independently worked out his own theory of evolution by natural selection, almost identical to Darwin's own. A joint paper by Darwin and Wallace was hastily arranged and presented in mid-1858, but it was received without impact. Darwin immediately began working on an "abstract" of his theories, and the result, the epoch-making *Origin of Species,* was published on November 24, 1859 (the book went through six editions in Darwin's lifetime). Its influence quickly spread to almost all areas of human thought.

---

[1]"Natural" selection may be contrasted with the kind of artificial process by which humans attempt to improve plants or animals by selective breeding of parents with desirable traits.

As suggested above, Darwin's ideas were enormously controversial, particularly to the orthodox, but also to some other scientists, whose own ideas had been displaced. With time, Darwin's theories became generally accepted (even by the Church of England), but the process was a long and painful one. As late as 1925, in the notorious Scopes trial in Tennessee, a high school biology teacher was put on trial (and found guilty) of teaching Darwin's theory of evolution to his students. The teacher, John T. Scopes, had challenged a Tennessee law that forbade the teaching of anything that "denies the divine creation of man as taught in the Bible."

In 1871, Darwin published a companion volume to *The Origin of Species*, *The Descent of Man and the Selection in Relation to Sex*, which applied to principles of evolution to humanity. Darwin wrote many other books in his later life, including *On the Various Contrivances by Which British and Foreign Orchids are Fertilized by Insects* (1862), *Insectivorous Plants* (1875), *The Effects of Cross and Self Fertilization in the Vegetable Kingdom* (1876), and his last book, *The Formation of Vegetable Mould through the Action of Worms* (1881).

Darwin died in 1882 and was buried in Westminster Abbey; his funeral was attended by many of the greatest scientists and foreign dignitaries of the day.

The selection below comprises part of Chapter 4 ("Natural Selection; or The Survival of the Fittest") of *The Origin of Species* and part of Chapter 2 ("On the Manner of Development of Man from Some Lower Form") of *The Descent of Man*.

NATURAL SELECTION; OR THE SURVIVAL OF THE FITTEST

GEOMETRICAL RATIO OF INCREASE

A struggle for existence inevitably follows from the high rate at which   1
all organic beings tend to increase. Every being, which during its natural
lifetime produces several eggs or seeds, must suffer destruction during
some period of its life, and during some season or occasional year, otherwise, on the principle of geometrical increase, its numbers would quickly
become so inordinately great that no country could support the product.
Hence, as more individuals are produced than can possibly survive, there
must in every case be a struggle for existence, either one individual with
another of the same species, or with the individuals of distinct species, or

Charles Darwin. Natural Selection, or The Survival of the Fittest [6th ed., 1872]. Rpt. in *The Origin of Species* and *The Descent of Man*. New York: Modern Library [n.d.].

with the physical conditions of life. It is the doctrine of Malthus[1] applied with manifold force to the whole animal and vegetable kingdoms; for in this case there can be no artificial increase of food, and no prudential restraint from marriage. Although some species may be now increasing, more or less rapidly, in numbers, all cannot do so, for the world would not hold them.

There is no exception to the rule that every organic being naturally increases at so high a rate, that, if not destroyed, the earth would soon be covered by the progeny of a single pair. Even slow-breeding man has doubled in twenty-five years, and at this rate, in less than a thousand years, there would literally not be standing-room for his progeny. Linnæus[2] has calculated that if an annual plant produced only two seeds — and there is no plant so unproductive as this — and their seedlings next year produced two, and so on, then in twenty years there should be a million plants. The elephant is reckoned the slowest breeder of all known animals, and I have taken some pains to estimate its probable minimum rate of natural increase; it will be safest to assume that it begins breeding when thirty years old, and goes on breeding till ninety years old, bringing forth six young in the interval, and surviving till one hundred years old; if this be so, after a period of from 740 to 750 years there would be nearly nineteen million elephants alive, descended from the first pair.   2

But we have better evidence on this subject than mere theoretical calculations, namely, the numerous recorded cases of the astonishingly rapid increase of various animals in a state of nature, when circumstances have been favourable to them during two or three following seasons. Still more striking is the evidence from our domestic animals of many kinds which have run wild in several parts of the world; if the statements of the rate of increase of slow-breeding cattle and horses in South America, and latterly in Australia, had not been well authenticated, they would have been incredible. So it is with plants; cases could be given of introduced plants which have become common throughout whole islands in a period of less than ten years. . . .   3

In looking at Nature, it is most necessary to keep the foregoing consid-   4

---

[1] *the doctrine of Malthus:* The theories of Thomas Robert Malthus (1766–1834), an English economist and demographer best known for his theory that population growth will always tend to outrun the food supply and that betterment of the lot of mankind is impossible without stern limits on reproduction. Malthus was an economic pessimist, arguing that poverty is man's inescapable lot. (See pp. 317–322 for an excerpt from Malthus's essay.)

[2] *Linnaeus:* Carl Linnaeus (1707–1778), a Swedish botanist and explorer who was the first to frame principles for defining genera and species of organisms and to create a uniform system for naming them. His manuscripts, herbarium, and collections of insects and shells are preserved by the Linnean Society in London.

erations always in mind — never to forget that every single organic being may be said to be striving to the utmost to increase in numbers; that each lives by a struggle at some period of its life; that heavy destruction inevitably falls either on the young or old, during each generation or at recurrent intervals. Lighten any check, mitigate the destruction ever so little, and the number of the species will almost instantaneously increase to any amount. . . . When we reflect on this struggle, we may console ourselves with the full belief, that the war of nature is not incessant, that no fear is felt, that death is generally prompt, and that the vigorous, the healthy, and the happy survive and multiply.

NATURAL SELECTION

How will the struggle for existence, briefly discussed in the last [section], act in regard to variation? Can the principle of selection, which we have seen is so potent in the hands of man, apply under nature? I think we shall see that it can act most efficiently. Let the endless number of slight variations and individual differences occurring in our domestic productions, and, in a lesser degree, in those under nature, be borne in mind; as well as the strength of the hereditary tendency. Under domestication, it may be truly said that the whole organisation becomes in some degree plastic.[3] But the variability, which we almost universally meet with in our domestic productions, is not directly produced, as Hooker[4] and Asa Gray[5] have well remarked, by man; he can neither originate varieties, nor prevent their occurrence; he can preserve and accumulate such as do occur. Unintentionally he exposes organic beings to new and changing conditions of life, and variability ensues; but similar changes of conditions might and do occur under nature. Let it also be borne in mind how infinitely complex and close-fitting are the mutual relations of all organic beings to each other and to their physical conditions of life; and consequently what infinitely varied diversities of structure might be of use to each being under changing conditions of life. Can it, then, be thought improbable, seeing that variations useful to man have undoubtedly occurred, that other variations use-

[3]*plastic:* Capable of changing in form.

[4]*Hooker:* Sir Joseph Hooker (1817–1911) was an English botanist noted for his botanical travels and studies and for his encouragement of Darwin's theories. Hooker was among the first to demonstrate the importance of the evolutionary theory to botany in general.

[5]*Asa Gray:* A U.S. botanist (1810–1888) whose extensive studies of the flora of North America did more than the work of any other botanist to unify the taxonomic knowledge of plants of this region. His 1856 paper on plant distribution, "Statistics of the Flora of the Northern United States," was written partly in response to a request by Darwin for a list of American alpine plants.

ful in some way to each being in the great and complex battle of life, should occur in the course of many successive generations. If such do occur, can we doubt (remembering that many more individuals are born than·can possibly survive) that individuals having any advantage, however slight, over others, would have the best chance of surviving and of procreating their kind? On the other hand, we may feel sure that any variation in the least degree injurious would be rigidly destroyed. This preservation of favourable individual differences and variations, and the destruction of those which are injurious, I have called Natural Selection, or the Survival of the Fittest. Variations neither useful nor injurious would not be affected by natural selection, and would be left either a fluctuating element, as perhaps we see in certain polymorphic species,[6] or would ultimately become fixed, owing to the nature of the organism and the nature of the conditions.

Several writers have misapprehended or objected to the term Natural Selection. Some have even imagined that natural selection induces variability, whereas it implies only the preservation of such variations as arise and are beneficial to the being under its conditions of life. No one objects to agriculturists speaking of the potent effects of man's selection; and in this case the individual differences given by nature, which man for some object selects, must of necessity first occur. Others have objected that the term selection implies conscious choice in the animals which become modified; and it has even been urged that, as plants have no volition,[7] natural selection is not applicable to them! In the literal sense of the word, no doubt, natural selection is a false term; but who ever objected to chemists speaking of the elective affinities of the various elements? — and yet an acid cannot strictly be said to elect the base with which it in preference combines. It has been said that I speak of natural selection as an active power or Deity; but who objects to an author speaking of the attraction of gravity as ruling the movements of the planets? Every one knows what is meant and is implied by such metaphorical expressions; and they are almost necessary for brevity. So again it is difficult to avoid personifying the word Nature; but I mean by Nature, only the aggregate action and product of many natural laws, and by laws the sequence of events as ascertained by us. With a little familiarity such superficial objections will be forgotten.   6

We shall best understand the probable course of natural selection by taking the case of a country undergoing some slight physical change, for instance, of climate. The proportional numbers of its inhabitants will almost immediately undergo a change, and some species will probably be-   7

---

[6]*polymorphic species:* A species that passes through several markedly different forms in successive stages of development.

[7]*volition:* The power or faculty of using the will.

come extinct. We may conclude, from what we have seen of the intimate and complex manner in which the inhabitants of each country are bound together, that any change in the numerical proportions of the inhabitants, independently of the change of climate itself, would seriously affect the others. If the country were open on its borders, new forms would certainly immigrate, and this would likewise seriously disturb the relations of some of the former inhabitants. Let it be remembered how powerful the influence of a single introduced tree or mammal has been shown to be. But in the case of an island, or of a country partly surrounded by barriers, into which new and better adapted forms could not freely enter, we should then have places in the economy of nature[8] which would assuredly be better filled up, if some of the original inhabitants were in some manner modified; for, had the area been open to immigration, these same places would have been seized on by intruders. In such cases, slight modifications, which in any way favoured the individuals of any species, by better adapting them to their altered conditions, would tend to be preserved; and natural selection would have free scope for the work of improvement.

We have good reason to believe, as shown in the first chapter, that changes in the conditions of life give a tendency to increased variability; and in the foregoing cases the conditions have changed, and this would manifestly be favourable to natural selection, by affording a better chance of the occurrence of profitable variations. Unless such occur, natural selection can do nothing. Under the term of "variations," it must never be forgotten that mere individual differences are included. As man can produce a great result with his domestic animals and plants by adding up in any given direction individual differences, so could natural selection, but far more easily from having incomparably longer time for action. Nor do I believe that any great physical change, as of climate, or any unusual degree of isolation to check immigration, is necessary in order that new and unoccupied places should be left, for natural selection to fill up by improving some of the varying inhabitants. For as all the inhabitants of each country are struggling together with nicely balanced forces, extremely slight modifications in the structure or habits of one species would often give it an advantage over others; and still further modifications of the same kind would often still further increase the advantage, as long as the species continued under the same conditions of life and profited by similar means of subsistence and defence. No country can be named in which all the native inhabitants are now so perfectly adapted to each other and to the physical conditions under which they live, that none of them could be still better adapted or improved; for in all countries, the natives have been so

8

---

[8]*economy of nature:* Darwin believed that evolutionary change in general tended toward a maximum efficiency in the use of resources.

human selection vs Natural selection

far conquered by naturalised productions, that they have allowed some foreigners to take firm possession of the land. And as foreigners have thus in every country beaten some of the natives, we may safely conclude that the natives might have been modified with advantage, so as to have better resisted the intruders.

As man can produce, and certainly has produced, a great result by his methodical and unconscious means of selection, what may not natural selection effect? Man can act only on external and visible characters: Nature, if I may be allowed to personify the natural preservation or survival of the fittest, cares nothing for appearances, except in so far as they are useful to any being. She can act on every internal organ, on every shade of constitutional difference, on the whole machinery of life. Man selects only for his own good: Nature only for that of the being which she tends. Every selected character is fully exercised by her, as is implied by the fact of their selection. Man keeps the natives of many climates in the same country; he seldom exercises each selected character in some peculiar and fitting manner; he feeds a long and a short beaked pigeon on the same food; he does not exercise a long-backed or long-legged quadruped in any peculiar manner; he exposes sheep with long and short wool to the same climate. He does not allow the most vigorous males to struggle for the females. He does not rigidly destroy all inferior animals, but protects during each varying season, as far as lies in his power, all his productions. He often begins his selection by some half-monstrous form; or at least by some modification prominent enough to catch the eye or to be plainly useful to him. Under nature, the slightest differences of structure or constitution may well turn the nicely balanced scale in the struggle for life, and so be preserved. How fleeting are the wishes and efforts of man! how short his time! and consequently how poor will be his results, compared with those accumulated by Nature during whole geological periods! Can we wonder, then, that Nature's productions should be far "truer" in character than man's productions; that they should be infinitely better adapted to the most complex conditions of life, and should plainly bear the stamp of far higher workmanship?

It may metaphorically be said that natural selection is daily and hourly scrutinising, throughout the world, the slightest variations; rejecting those that are bad, preserving and adding up all that are good; silently and insensibly working, *whenever and wherever opportunity offers,* at the improvement of each organic being in relation to its organic and inorganic conditions of life. We see nothing of these slow changes in progress, until the hand of time has marked the lapse of ages, and then so imperfect is our view into long-past geological ages, that we see only that the forms of life are now different from what they formerly were.

In order that any great amount of modification should be effected in a species, a variety when once formed must again, perhaps after a long interval of time, vary or present individual differences of the same favourable nature as before; and these must be again preserved, and so onwards step by step. Seeing that individual differences of the same kind perpetually recur, this can hardly be considered as an unwarrantable assumption. But whether it is true, we can judge only by seeing how far the hypothesis accords with and explains the general phenomena of nature. On the other hand, the ordinary belief that the amount of possible variation is a strictly limited quantity is likewise a simple assumption.

Although natural selection can act only through and for the good of   12 each being, yet characters and structures, which we are apt to consider as of very trifling importance, may thus be acted on. When we see leaf-eating insects green, and bark-feeders mottled-grey; the alpine ptarmigan[9] white in winter, the red-grouse the colour of heather, we must believe that these tints are of service to these birds and insects in preserving them from danger. Grouse, if not destroyed at some period of their lives would increase in countless numbers; they are known to suffer largely from birds of prey; and hawks are guided by eyesight to their prey — so much so, that on parts of the Continent[10] persons are warned not to keep white pigeons, as being the most liable to destruction. Hence natural selection might be effective in giving the proper colour to each kind of grouse, and in keeping that colour, when once acquired, true and constant. Nor ought we to think that the occasional destruction of an animal of any particular colour would produce little effect: we should remember how essential it is in a flock of white sheep to destroy a lamb with the faintest trace of black. We have seen how the colour of the hogs, which feed on the "paint-root" in Virginia,[11] determines whether they shall live or die. In plants, the down on the fruit and the colour of the flesh are considered by botanists as characters of the most trifling importance: yet we hear from an excellent horticulturist, Downing,[12] that in the United States, smooth-skinned fruits suffer far more from a beetle, a Curculio,[13] than those with down; that purple plums suffer far more from a certain disease than yellow plums; whereas another disease attacks yellow-fleshed peaches far more than those with

---

[9]*alpine ptarmigan:* A partridge-like bird of cold regions that undergoes seasonal changes of plumage.

[10]*the Continent:* All of Europe except the British Isles.

[11]*"paint-root" in Virginia:* A plant of the bloodwort family, characterized by sword-shaped leaves and small, woolly, yellow flowers, found along the Atlantic coast of the United States.

[12]*Downing:* Andrew Jackson Downing (1815–1852), an American horticulturist, landscape gardener, and architect whose influences survive in the modern suburb and the large urban park.

[13]*Curculio:* Stout-bodied weevils of the beetle family Curculionidae. Among the best known is the plum curculio, which attacks plums, apples, peaches, and other fruit.

other coloured flesh. If, with all the aids of art, these slight differences make a great difference in cultivating the several varieties, assuredly, in a state of nature, where the trees would have to struggle with other trees, and with a host of enemies, such differences would effectually settle which variety, whether a smooth or downy, a yellow or purple fleshed fruit, should succeed.

In looking at many small points of difference between species, which, as far as our ignorance permits us to judge, seem quite unimportant, we must not forget that climate, food, &c., have no doubt produced some direct effect. It is also necessary to bear in mind that, owing to the law of correlation,[14] when one part varies, and the variations are accumulated through natural selection, other modifications, often of the most unexpected nature, will ensue. 13

As we see that those variations which, under domestication, appear at any particular period of life, tend to reappear in the offspring at the same period; — for instance, in the shape, size, and flavour of the seeds of the many varieties of our culinary and agricultural plants; in the caterpillar and cocoon stages of the varieties of the silk-worm; in the eggs of poultry, and in the colour of the down of their chickens; in the horns of our sheep and cattle when nearly adult; — so in a state of nature natural selection will be enabled to act on and modify organic beings at any age, by the accumulation of variations profitable at that age, and by their inheritance at a corresponding age. If it profit a plant to have its seeds more and more widely disseminated by the wind, I can see no greater difficulty in this being effected through natural selection, than in the cotton-planter increasing and improving by selection the down in the pods on his cotton-trees. Natural selection may modify and adapt the larva of an insect to a score of contingencies, wholly different from those which concern the mature insect; and these modifications may effect, through correlation, the structure of the adult. So, conversely, modifications in the adult may affect the structure of the larva; but in all cases natural selection will ensure that they shall not be injurious: for if they were so, the species would become extinct. 14

Natural selection will modify the structure of the young in relation to the parent, and of the parent in relation to the young. In social animals it will adapt the structure of each individual for the benefit of the whole community; if the community profits by the selected change. What natural selection cannot do, is to modify the structure of one species, without giving it any advantage, for the good of another species; and though statements to this effect may be found in works of natural history, I cannot find 15

---

[14]*the law of correlation:* The mutual relation of association between different characteristics. In studying the normal coincidence of one characteristic with another, Darwin observed that cats that are entirely white and have blue eyes are generally deaf.

one case which will bear investigation. A structure used only once in an animal's life, if of high importance to it, might be modified to any extent by natural selection; for instance, the great jaws possessed by certain insects, used exclusively for opening the cocoon — or the hard tip to the beak of unhatched birds, used for breaking the egg. It has been asserted, that of the best short-beaked tumbler-pigeons a greater number perish in the egg than are able to get out of it; so that fanciers[15] assist in the act of hatching. Now if nature had to make the beak of a full-grown pigeon very short for the bird's own advantage, the process of modification would be very slow, and there would be simultaneously the most rigorous selection of all the young birds within the egg, which had the most powerful and hardest beaks, for all with weak beaks would inevitably perish; or, more delicate and more easily broken shells might be selected, the thickness of the shell being known to vary like every other structure.

It may be well here to remark that with all beings there must be much fortuitous destruction, which can have little or no influence on the course of natural selection. For instance a vast number of eggs or seeds are annually devoured, and these could be modified through natural selection only if they varied in some manner which protected them from their enemies. Yet many of these eggs or seeds would perhaps, if not destroyed, have yielded individuals better adapted to their conditions of life than any of those which happened to survive. So again a vast number of mature animals and plants, whether or not they be the best adapted to their conditions, must be annually destroyed by accidental causes, which would not be in the least degree mitigated by certain changes of structure or constitution which would in other ways be beneficial to the species. But let the destruction of the adults be ever so heavy, if the number which can exist in any district be not wholly kept down by such causes, — or again let the destruction of eggs or seeds be so great that only a hundredth or a thousandth part are developed, — yet of those which do survive, the best adapted individuals, supposing that there is any variability in a favourable direction, will tend to propagate their kind in larger numbers than the less well adapted. If the numbers be wholly kept down by the causes just indicated, as will often have been the case, natural selection will be powerless in certain beneficial directions; but this is no valid objection to its efficiency at other times and in other ways; for we are far from having any reason to suppose that many species ever undergo modification and improvement at the same time in the same area.

16

---

[15]*fanciers:* People with a special interest in a subject — in this case, raising pigeons.

SEXUAL SELECTION

Inasmuch as peculiarities often appear under domestication in one sex   *17*
and become hereditarily attached to that sex, so no doubt it will be under
nature. Thus it is rendered possible for the two sexes to be modified
through natural selection in relation to different habits of life, as is sometimes the case; or for one sex to be modified in relation to the other sex, as
commonly occurs. This leads me to say a few words on what I have called
Sexual Selection. This form of selection depends, not on a struggle for existence in relation to other organic beings or to external conditions, but on
a struggle between the individuals of one sex, generally the males, for the
possession of the other sex. The result is not death to the unsuccessful
competitor, but few or no offspring. Sexual selection is, therefore, less rigorous than natural selection. Generally, the most vigorous males, those
which are best fitted for their places in nature, will leave most progeny.
But in many cases, victory depends not so much on general vigor, as on
having special weapons, confined to the male sex. A hornless stag or spur-
less cock would have a poor chance of leaving numerous offspring. Sexual
selection, by always allowing the victor to breed, might surely give indomitable courage, length to the spur, and strength to the wing to strike in the
spurred leg, in nearly the same manner as does the brutal cockfighter by
the careful selection of his best cocks. How low in the scale of nature the
law of battle descends, I know not; male alligators have been described as
fighting, bellowing, and whirling round, like Indians in a war-dance, for
the possession of the females; male salmons have been observed fighting
all day long; male stag-beetles sometimes bear wounds from the huge
mandibles[16] of other males; the males of certain hymenopterous insects
have been frequently seen by that inimitable observer M. Fabre, fighting
for a particular female who sits by, an apparently unconcerned beholder
of the struggle, and then retires with the conqueror. The war is, perhaps,
severest between the males of polygamous animals,[17] and these seem oftenest provided with special weapons. The males of carnivorous animals
are already well armed; though to them and to others, special means of
defence may be given through means of sexual selection, as the mane of
the lion, and the hooked jaw to the male salmon; for the shield may be as
important for victory, as the sword or spear.

Amongst birds, the contest is often of a more peaceful character. All   *18*
those who have attended to the subject, believe that there is the severest
rivalry between the males of many species to attract, by singing, the fe-

---

[16]*mandibles:* Jaws.

[17]*polygamous animals:* Animals that have more than one mate.

males. The rock-thrush of Guiana,[18] birds of paradise, and some others, congregate; and successive males display with the most elaborate care, and show off in the best manner, their gorgeous plumage; they likewise perform strange antics before the females, which, standing by as spectators, at last choose the most attractive partner. Those who have closely attended to birds in confinement well know that they often take individual preferences and dislikes: thus Sir R. Heron[19] has described how a pied peacock was eminently attractive to all his hen birds. I cannot here enter on the necessary details; but if man can in a short time give beauty and an elegant carriage to his bantams,[20] according to his standard of beauty, I can see no good reason to doubt that female birds, by selecting, during thousands of generations, the most melodious or beautiful males, according to their standard of beauty, might produce a marked effect. Some well-known laws, with respect to the plumage of male and female birds, in comparison with the plumage of the young, can partly be explained through the action of sexual selection on variations occurring at different ages, and transmitted to the males alone or to both sexes at corresponding ages; but I have not space here to enter on this subject.

✱ Thus it is, as I believe, that when the males and females of any animal *19*
have the same general habits of life, but differ in structure, colour, or ornament, such differences have been mainly caused by sexual selection: that is, by individual males having had, in successive generations, some slight advantage over other males, in their weapons, means of defence, or charms, which they have transmitted to their male offspring alone. Yet, I would not wish to attribute all sexual differences to this agency: for we see in our domestic animals peculiarities arising and becoming attached to the male sex, which apparently have not been augmented through selection by man. The tuft of hair on the breast of the wild turkey-cock cannot be of any use, and it is doubtful whether it can be ornamental in the eyes of the female bird; — indeed, had the tuft appeared under domestication, it would have been called a monstrosity.

ILLUSTRATIONS OF THE ACTION OF NATURAL SELECTION, OR THE SURVIVAL OF THE FITTEST

In order to make it clear how, as I believe, natural selection acts, I must *20*
beg permission to give one or two imaginary illustrations. Let us make the case of a wolf, which preys on various animals, securing some by craft, some by strength, and some by fleetness; and let us suppose that the fleet-

---

[18]*Guiana:* British Guiana, in the coastal region of northeastern South America.
[19]*Sir R. Heron:* Sir Robert Heron (1765–1854), English politician and animal breeder.
[20]*bantams:* Small domestic fowl, bred for fighting.

est prey, a deer for instance, had from any change in the country increased in numbers, or that other prey had decreased in numbers, during that season of the year when the wolf was hardest pressed for food. Under such circumstances the swiftest and slimmest wolves would have the best chance of surviving and so be preserved or selected, — provided always that they retained strength to master their prey at this or some other period of the year, when they were compelled to prey on other animals. I can see no more reason to doubt that this would be the result, than that man should be able to improve the fleetness of his greyhounds by careful and methodical selection, or by that kind of unconscious selection which follows from each man trying to keep the best dogs without any thought of modifying the breed. I may add, that, according to Mr. Pierce,[21] there are two varieties of the wolf inhabiting the Catskill Mountains, in the United States, one with a light greyhound-like form, which pursues deer, and the other more bulky, with shorter legs, which more frequently attacks the shepherd's flocks.

To the effects of intercrossing in eliminating variations of all kinds, I shall have to recur; but it may be here remarked that most animals and plants keep to their proper homes, and do not needlessly wander about; we see this even with migratory birds, which almost always return to the same spot. Consequently each newly-formed variety would generally be at first local, as seems to be the common rule with varieties in a state of nature; so that similarly modified individuals would soon exist in a small body together, and would often breed together. If the new variety were successful in its battle for life, it would slowly spread from a central district, competing with and conquering the unchanged individuals on the margins of an ever-increasing circle. *21*

It may be worth while to give another and more complex illustration of the action of natural selection. Certain plants excrete sweet juice, apparently for the sake of eliminating something injurious from the sap: this is effected, for instance, by glands at the base of the stipules[22] in some Leguminosæ,[23] and at the backs of the leaves of the common laurel. This juice, though small in quantity, is greedily sought by insects; but their visits do not in any way benefit the plant. Now, let us suppose that the juice or nectar was excreted from the inside of the flowers of a certain number of plants of any species. Insects in seeking the nectar would get dusted with pollen, and would often transport it from one flower to another. The flowers of two distinct individuals of the same species would thus get *22*

---

[21]*Mr. Pierce:* The American scholar James Pierce studied the mineralogy and geology of the Catskill Mountains in the 1820s.

[22]*stipules:* Small, leafy organs at the base of the leafy stalk in many plants.

[23]*Leguminosae:* An order of plants represented by the common peas and beans.

crossed; and the act of crossing, as can be fully proved, gives rise to vigorous seedlings which consequently would have the best chance of flourishing and surviving. The plants which produced flowers with the largest glands or nectaries, excreting most nectar, would oftenest be visited by insects, and would oftenest be crossed; and so in the long-run would gain the upper hand and form a local variety. The flowers, also, which had their stamens[24] and pistils[25] placed, in relation to the size and habits of the particular insects which visited them, so as to favour in any degree the transportal of the pollen, would likewise be favoured. We might have taken the case of insects visiting flowers for the sake of collecting pollen instead of nectar; and as pollen is formed for the sole purpose of fertilisation, its destruction appears to be a simple loss to the plant; yet if a little pollen were carried, at first occasionally and then habitually, by the pollen-devouring insects from flower to flower, and a cross thus effected, although nine-tenths of the pollen were destroyed it might still be a great gain to the plant to be thus robbed; and the individuals which produced more and more pollen, and had larger anthers,[26] would be selected.

When our plant, by the above process long continued, had been rendered highly attractive to insects, they would, unintentionally on their part, regularly carry pollen from flower to flower; and that they do this effectually, I could easily show by many striking facts. I will give only one, as likewise illustrating one step in the separation of the sexes of plants. Some holly-trees bear only male flowers, which have four stamens producing a rather small quantity of pollen, and a rudimentary pistil; other holly-trees bear only female flowers; these have a full-sized pistil, and four stamens with shrivelled anthers, in which not a grain of pollen can be detected. Having found a female tree exactly sixty yards from a male tree, I put the stigmas[27] of twenty flowers, taken from different branches, under the microscope, and on all, without exception, there were a few pollen-grains, and on some a profusion. As the wind had set for several days from the female to the male tree, the pollen could not thus have been carried. The weather had been cold and boisterous, and therefore not favourable to bees, nevertheless every female flower which I examined had been effectually fertilised by the bees, which had flown from tree to tree in search of nectar. But to return to our imaginary case: as soon as the plant had been rendered so highly attractive to insects that pollen was regularly car-

---

[24]*stamens:* The male organs of flowering plants, standing in a circle within the petals. They usually consist of a filament and an anther, the anther being the essential part in which the pollen is produced.

[25]*pistils:* The female organs of a flower, which occupy a position in the center of the other floral organs.

[26]*anthers:* The summits of the stamens of flowers, in which the pollen is produced.

[27]*stigmas:* The tip of the pistil in flowering plants.

ried from flower to flower, another process might commence. No naturalist doubts the advantage of what has been called the "physiological division of labour;" hence we may believe that it would be advantageous to a plant to produce stamens alone in one flower or on one whole plant, and pistils alone in another flower or on another plant. In plants under culture and placed under new conditions of life, sometimes the male organs and sometimes the female organs become more or less impotent; now if we suppose this to occur in ever so slight a degree under nature, then, as pollen is already carried regularly from flower to flower, and as a more complete separation of the sexes of our plant would be advantageous on the principle of the division of labour, individuals with this tendency more and more increased, would be continually favoured or selected, until at last a complete separation of the sexes might be effected. It would take up too much space to show the various steps, through dimorphism[28] and other means, by which the separation of the sexes in plants of various kinds is apparently now in progress; but I may add that some of the species of holly in North America, are, according to Asa Gray, in an exactly intermediate condition, or, as he expresses it, are more or less diœciously[29] polygamous.

Let us now turn to the nectar-feeding insects; we may suppose the plant, of which we have been slowly increasing the nectar by continued selection, to be a common plant; and that certain insects depended in main part on its nectar for food. I could give many facts showing how anxious bees are to save time: for instance, their habit of cutting holes and sucking the nectar at the bases of certain flowers, which, with a very little more trouble, they can enter by the mouth. Bearing such facts in mind, it may be believed that under certain circumstances individual differences in the curvature or length of the proboscis,[30] &c., too slight to be appreciated by us, might profit a bee or other insect, so that certain individuals would be able to obtain their food more quickly than others; and thus the communities to which they belonged would flourish and throw off many swarms inheriting the same peculiarities. The tubes of the corolla of the common red and incarnate clovers (Trifolium pratense and incarnatum) do not on a hasty glance appear to differ in length; yet the hive-bee can easily suck the nectar out of the incarnate clover, but not out of the common red clover, which is visited by humble-bees[31] alone; so that whole fields of red clover

24

---

[28]*dimorphism:* The condition of the appearance of the same species under two dissimilar forms.

[29]*dioeciously:* Having the male and female organs borne by different plants.

[30]*proboscis:* A tubular organ of varying form and function on a large number of invertebrates, such as insects and tapeworms.

[31]*humble-bee:* More commonly known as bumblebee, a hairy and robust bee that is usually found in temperate climates.

offer in vain an abundant supply of precious nectar to the hive-bee. That this nectar is much liked by the hive-bee is certain; for I have repeatedly seen, but only in the autumn, many hive-bees sucking the flowers through holes bitten in the base of the tube by humble-bees. The difference in the length of the corolla[32] in the two kinds of clover, which determines the visits of the hive-bee, must be very trifling; for I have been assured that when red clover has been mown, the flowers of the second crop are somewhat smaller, and that these are visited by many hive-bees. I do not know whether this statement is accurate; nor whether another published statement can be trusted, namely, that the Ligurian bee which is generally considered a mere variety of the common hive-bee, and which freely crosses with it, is able to reach and suck the nectar of the red clover. Thus, in a country where this kind of clover abounded, it might be a great advantage to the hive-bee to have a slightly longer or differently constructed proboscis. On the other hand, as the fertility of this clover absolutely depends on bees visiting the flowers, if humble-bees were to become rare in any country, it might be a great advantage to the plant to have a shorter or more deeply divided corolla, so that the hive-bees should be enabled to suck its flowers. Thus I can understand how a flower and a bee might slowly become, either simultaneously or one after the other, modified and adapted to each other in the most perfect manner, by the continued preservation of all the individuals which presented slight deviations of structure mutually favourable to each other.

I am well aware that this doctrine of natural selection, exemplified in   25
the above imaginary instances, is open to the same objections which were first urged against Sir Charles Lyell's noble views on "the modern changes of the earth, as illustrative of geology;"[33] but we now seldom hear the agencies which we see still at work, spoken of as trifling or insignificant, when used in explaining the excavation of the deepest valleys or the formation of long lines of inland cliffs. Natural selection acts only by the preservation and accumulation of small inherited modifications, each profitable to the preserved being; and as modern geology has almost banished such views as the excavation of a great valley by a single diluvial wave,[34] so will natural

---

[32]*corolla:* A collective term for the petals of a flower, used especially when they are fused into a tube for part or all of their length.

[33]*Sir Charles Lyell's noble views on "the modern changes of the earth, as illustrative of geology":* Scottish geologist of the mid-19th century largely responsible for the general acceptance of the view that all features of the earth's surfaces are produced by physical, chemical, and biological time. Lyell's achievements laid the foundation for evolutionary biology.

[34]*diluvial wave:* Refers to the theory that explained certain geological phenomena by reference to a great deluge or to periods of catastrophic floods.

selection banish the belief of the continued creation of new organic beings, or of any great and sudden modification in their structure.

THE DESCENT OF MAN

We have now seen that man is variable in body and mind; and that the variations are induced, either directly or indirectly, by the same general causes, and obey the same general laws, as with the lower animals. Man has spread widely over the face of the earth, and must have been exposed, during his incessant migration, to the most diversified conditions. The inhabitants of Tierra del Fuego, the Cape of Good Hope, and Tasmania[35] in the one hemisphere, and of the Arctic regions in the other, must have passed through many climates, and changed their habits many times, before they reached their present homes. The early progenitors of man must also have tended, like all other animals, to have increased beyond their means of subsistence; they must, therefore, occasionally have been exposed to a struggle for existence, and consequently to the rigid law of natural selection. Beneficial variations of all kinds will thus, either occasionally or habitually, have been preserved and injurious ones eliminated. I do not refer to strongly-marked deviations of structure, which occur only at long intervals of time, but to mere individual differences. We know, for instance, that the muscles of our hands and feet, which determine our powers of movement, are liable, like those of the lower animals, to incessant variability. If then the progenitors of man inhabiting any district, especially one undergoing some change in its conditions, were divided into two equal bodies, the one half which included all the individuals best adapted by their powers of movement for gaining subsistence, or for defending themselves, would on an average survive in greater numbers, and procreate more offspring than the other and less well endowed half.

Man in the rudest state in which he now exists is the most dominant animal that has ever appeared on this earth. He has spread more widely than any other highly organised form: and all others have yielded before him. He manifestly owes this immense superiority to his intellectual faculties, to his social habits, which lead him to aid and defend his fellows, and to his corporeal[36] structure. The supreme importance of these characters has been proved by the final arbitrament of the battle for life. Through

26

27

---

[35]*Tierra del Fuego, the Cape of Good Hope, and Tasmania:* Regions that occupy the Southern Hemisphere. Tierra del Fuego is an archipelago at the southern extremity of South America, the Cape of Good Hope is situated in the southern extremity of the African continent, and Tasmania is an island state of Australia, lying off the southeastern corner of the continent.

[36]*corporeal:* Physical, bodily.

his powers of intellect, articulate language has been evolved; and on this his wonderful advancement has mainly depended. As Mr. Chauncey Wright[37] remarks: "a psychological analysis of the faculty of language shews, that even the smallest proficiency in it might require more brain power than the greatest proficiency in any other direction." He has invented and is able to use various weapons, tools, traps, &c. with which he defends himself, kills or catches prey, and otherwise obtains food. He has made rafts or canoes for fishing or crossing over to neighbouring fertile islands. He has discovered the art of making fire, by which hard and stringy roots can be rendered digestible, and poisonous roots or herbs innocuous. This discovery of fire, probably the greatest ever made by man, excepting language, dates from before the dawn of history. These several inventions, by which man in the rudest state has become so pre-eminent, are the direct results of the development of his powers of observation, memory, curiosity, imagination, and reason. . . .

In regard to bodily size or strength, we do not know whether man is 28 descended from some small species, like the chimpanzee, or from one as powerful as the gorilla; and, therefore, we cannot say whether man has become larger and stronger, or smaller and weaker, than his ancestors. We should, however, bear in mind that an animal possessing great size, strength, and ferocity, and which, like the gorilla, could defend itself from all enemies, would not perhaps have become social: and this would most effectually have checked the acquirement of the higher mental qualities, such as sympathy and the love of his fellows. Hence it might have been an immense advantage to man to have sprung from some comparatively weak creature.

The small strength and speed of man, his want of natural weapons, 29 &c., are more than counterbalanced, firstly, by his intellectual powers, through which he has formed for himself weapons, tools, &c., though still remaining in a barbarous state, and, secondly, by his social qualities which lead him to give and receive aid from his fellow-men. No country in the world abounds in a greater degree with dangerous beasts than Southern Africa; no country presents more fearful physical hardships than the Arctic regions; yet one of the puniest of races, that of the Bushmen,[38] maintains itself in Southern Africa, as do the dwarfed Esquimaux[39] in the Arctic re-

---

[37]*Mr. Chauncey Wright:* A mathematician in the National Almanac Office in Massachusetts in the mid-19th century. Darwin corresponded with him on phyllotaxy (the study of leaf arrangement) after he had read Wright's papers in the Astronomical Journal. Wright's article, "Limits of Natural Selection," which first appeared in the *North American Review,* in October, 1870, was later reprinted by Darwin as a pamphlet.

[38]*Bushmen:* Also called the San, the Bushmen are an indigenous people of southern Africa, related to the Hottentots.

[39]*Esquimaux:* Eskimos.

gions. The ancestors of man were, no doubt, inferior in intellect, and probably in social disposition, to the lowest existing savages; but it is quite conceivable that they might have existed, or even flourished, if they had advanced in intellect, whilst gradually losing their brute-like powers, such as that of climbing trees, &c. But these ancestors would not have been exposed to any special danger, even if far more helpless and defenceless than any existing savages, had they inhabited some warm continent or large island, such as Australia, New Guinea,[40] or Borneo,[41] which is now the home of the orang. And natural selection arising from the competition of tribe with tribe, in some such large area as one of these, together with the inherited effects of habit, would, under favourable conditions, have sufficed to raise man to his present high position in the organic scale.

---

[40]*New Guinea:* An island of the eastern Malay Archipelago in the western Pacific Ocean, north of Australia. It is the second largest island (after Greenland) in the world.

[41]*Borneo:* One of the greatest islands of the world, it lies southeast of the Malay Peninsula. Bounded by the South China Sea and by the Sulu and Celebes seas, the Makassar Strait, and the Java Sea, it is roughly kidney-shaped, mountainous, and largely covered in dense rain forest.

REVIEW QUESTIONS

1. Why must there be a struggle for existence? What would be the result were there no such struggle? What theoretical evidence does Darwin offer to support the concept of a struggle for existence? What actual evidence? How does Darwin "console" his readers over this struggle?
2. How does Darwin define natural selection? What is the relationship between natural selection and variations (differences) among individual organisms of a given species? Why are organisms inhabiting islands, or lands otherwise surrounded by natural barriers, more subject to variation than organisms inhabiting less isolated areas?
3. Why is selection (of favorable characteristics) by nature a much more powerful and "true" process than selection by man? Why is it unnecessary that natural selection work only through major variations? What example does Darwin cite to indicate that a minor variation may be useful to the organism (and thus significant for natural selection) at only one point in its life? Under what kind of circumstances does natural selection *not* operate?
4. How does Darwin use the example of cross-pollination of plants by insects to demonstrate the working of natural selection? How does natural selection work during cross-pollination to favor sexual separation of plants? How may flowers and bees become mutually adapted to each other's needs?
5. In what particular ways are humans, like any other organisms, subject to the struggle for existence and to the processes of natural selection? To what qualities

does man owe his superiority to other animals? Why does Darwin appear to believe that men are descended from chimpanzees rather than from gorillas?

DISCUSSION AND WRITING QUESTIONS

1. Among the main objections to *The Origin of Species* was that Darwin had removed God and His divine plan from the universe and had substituted an impersonal, uncaring, and even hostile force of nature (such phrases as "struggle for life" and "survival of the fittest" suggested a harsher view of the universe than many Christians were prepared to accept). Others have taken the intricate workings of natural selection (in which what we now call the ever-changing ecosystem strives to maintain itself in delicate balance) to be further evidence of the existence of God — for how could such a masterly system have developed without God to design it? What are your views on this matter? Is it possible for a devout Christian to believe in Darwin's theory of evolution?
2. Although this passage has a dry, scientific, tone, there are indications that Darwin knew he was initiating a scientific revolution. Where do you find such indications? At what points do you see suggestions of the kind of controversy that *The Origin of Species* and *The Descent of Man* created? (Keep in mind that most of this passage is taken from the fifth edition of Darwin's *Origin,* after its initial impact had been made and after the controversy had begun.)
3. In this passage Darwin is making an argument. While arguing his case he uses many of the same techniques as might be used by any other person making an argument. Describe some of these techniques and explain how effective you think they are. (Consider such matters as organization, use of evidence, and tone.)
4. You may, at some point in your life, have been struck by the evidence of the effects of natural selection (even if you were not aware of the exact nature of the forces at work). If so, recollect what you have seen (or learned about, independently of Darwin) and account for it, in terms of Darwin's theory of natural selection and survival of the fittest. You may even wish to go further and write up your observations and your conclusions, as if you were Darwin, providing additional evidence to support your theory. If so, try to adopt Darwin's style and manner of argument.
5. Research the impact of *The Origin of Species*, particularly upon theologians. (Begin with encyclopedia articles, and then, using the subject card catalog, proceed with books about Darwin, paying particular attention to the bibliographies, with their additional references.) As an alternative assignment, you may wish to research the continuing impact of Darwin's ideas today. Using *The Reader's Guide to Periodical Literature* and other magazine indexes, look up articles concerned with "Darwin" and "evolution" over the past ten or fifteen years, particularly those articles appearing in religious journals and those articles concerned with the teaching of evolution in schools; and write a paper on the continuing controversy over evolution. Other alternative assignments: (a) Write a paper on the Scopes trial (in Tennessee in 1925) and its aftermath. Include a section in this paper on the reasons that Darwin's ideas aroused (and continue to arouse) such hostility. (b) Write a paper on the 1986 trial in which a group of Fundamentalist

Christian parents in Tennessee brought suit against the Hawkins County Public Schools to shield their children from the teaching of evolution and other doctrines of "secular humanism." (According to one account, the leader of the suit, Vicki Frost, "objected to a story [in a required textbook] for its line 'language makes us human,' explaining that the sentence implies that mankind evolved and was not created by God."[1])

---

[1]Alain L. Sanders, "Tilting at 'Secular Humanism,'" *Time*, July 28, 1986, p. 68.

WILLIAM GRAHAM SUMNER
(1840–1910)

From Darwinism to social Darwinism is a natural step. According to Darwin, the lack of sufficient food resources leads to a struggle for existence in which only the fittest — those organisms best adapted to their environment — survive. The surviving organisms transmit their favorable physical characteristics to their offspring, and over a number of generations, a new variety of species, or even a new species, replaces the older, ill-adapted varieties. Thus, with the passage of time, the species evolve toward greater perfection. It is simple enough to replace this biological model with a social one. Because of the limited resources afforded by any society (wealth, space, desirable jobs, as well as food), people in any society are involved in a struggle for existence. The fewer the available resources, the more violent the struggle. Only those people who are best adapted (through their personal, as well as physical qualities) to wage this struggle will survive it. If they achieve wealth, they may pass it on to their children and teach their children those virtues that are necessary to continue to successfully wage the struggle. The losers may not physically die, but they, and their offspring, will remain in a permanent state of poverty and subjection to the winners — as they deserve to be, for failing. This situation is not to be deplored. It is the natural order of things. Any attempt to subvert the natural order of things is misguided social meddling and is doomed to failure.

Among the American social Darwinists the most influential was William Graham Sumner. Born in Paterson, New Jersey, Sumner was greatly influenced by his father Thomas Sumner, a self-educated laborer, who had immigrated from England and had taught his children the Protestant virtues of thrift, self-determination, ambition, and hard work. Sumner studied theology at Yale University and abroad before returning to Yale as a tutor in 1868. In 1872 he was appointed Professor of Political and Social Science at Yale College, where (with the exception of a few years as editor of a religious newspaper and rector of an Episcopal church in New Jersey), he spent the rest of his professional life. Sumner was an enormously popular and influential teacher at Yale, a pulpit he used to espouse, with evangelical fervor, his social Darwinist doctrines. He wrote numerous magazine articles, which gained him wide fame (and notoriety), and several books, including *What Social Classes Owe to Each Other* (1883), *Folkways* (1906), and collected essays.

Sumner believed that competition among people could no more be done away with than gravity. He scoffed at the concepts of equality and natural rights, believing that people were inherently unequal (an idea that corresponded to the individual variations of Darwinism) and that the idea of natural rights was a sentimental relic of the 18th century. Through competition, society had evolved from medieval feudalism toward capitalism, and the accumulation of capital meant that labor could become more productive. Wealth needed no apology. For Sumner,

> Millionaires are a product of natural selection, acting on the whole body of men to pick out those who can meet the requirements of certain work to be done. . . . They get high wages and live in luxury, but the bargain is a good one for society. There is the intensest competition for their place and occupation. This assures us that all who are competent for this function will be employed in it, so that the cost of it will be reduced to the lowest terms.[1]

But the accumulation of capital must be unimpeded both by government (this ties in with the economic doctrine of laissez-faire) and by social reformers (such as Upton Sinclair, whom Sumner despised). For the ultimate end of social reform would be the destruction of liberty:

> We can take the rewards from those who have done better and give them to those who have done worse. We shall thus lessen the inequalities. We shall [thereby] favor the survival of the unfittest, and we shall accomplish this by destroying liberty. Let us be understood that we cannot go outside this alternative: liberty, inequality, survival of the fittest; not liberty, equality, survival of the unfittest. The former carries society forward and favours all its best members; the latter carries society downwards and favours all its worst members.[2]

Naturally enough, Sumner had no use for socialism, defining it as "any device whose aim is to save individuals from any of the difficulties or hardships of the struggle for existence and the competition of life by the intervention of the 'state.'"[3]

It was easy to accuse Sumner of being a hireling for the plutocrats, an apologist for the upper classes (and many did); but Sumner's convictions were deeply personal and essentially middle class. His hero was the "forgotten man," the middle-class citizen — like his father — who through frugality and hard work, making no demands upon government or charities, supports his family and transmits to them his moral virtues. A fascinating glimpse of the man has been provided by William Lyon Phelps, a student of Sumner's who, while at Yale, took every one of his courses. Phelps recorded this exchange between Sumner and another student:

> "Professor, don't you believe in any government aid to industry?"
> "No! it's root, hog, or die."
> "Yes, but hasn't the hog got a right to root?"
> "There are no rights. The world owes nobody a living."
> "You believe, then, Professor, in only one system, the contract-competitive system?"

---

[1]*The Challenge of Facts and Other Essays*. New Haven: Yale University Press, 1914, p. 90.

[2]S. Persons, ed. *Social Darwinism: Selected Essays of William Graham Sumner.* Englewood Cliffs, N.J.: Prentice-Hall, 1963, pp. 76–77.

[3]Essays of William Graham Sumner, ed. Albert G. Keller and Maurice R. Davie, II. New Haven: Yale University Press, 1934. 3 vols., p. 366.

"That's the only sound economic system. All others are fallacies."

"Well, suppose some professor of political economy came along and took your job away from you. Wouldn't you be sore?"

"Any other professor is welcome to try. If he gets my job, it is my fault. My business is to teach the subject so well that no one can take the job away from me."[4]

The following passage is made up of two chapters from Sumner's 1883 book, *What Social Classes Owe to Each Other.*

---

[4]William Lyon Phelps. "When Yale Was Given to Sumnerology." *Literary Digest International Book Review* III (1925), p. 661.

THAT IT IS NOT WICKED TO BE RICH

ON A NEW PHILOSOPHY: THAT POVERTY IS THE BEST POLICY

It is commonly asserted that there are in the United States no classes, and any allusion to classes is resented. On the other hand, we constantly read and hear discussions of social topics in which the existence of social classes is assumed as a simple fact. "The poor," "the weak," "the laborers," are expressions which are used as if they had exact and well-understood definition. Discussions are made to bear upon the assumed rights, wrongs, and misfortunes of certain social classes; and all public speaking and writing consists, in a large measure, of the discussion of general plans for meeting the wishes of classes of people who have not been able to satisfy their own desires.[1] These classes are sometimes discontented, and sometimes not. Sometimes they do not know that anything is amiss with them until the "friends of humanity" come to them with offers of aid.

1

William Graham Sumner. That it is Not Wicked to Be Rich [1883]. Rpt. in *What Social Classes Owe to Each Other.* Caldwell: Caxton, 1963. Also New York: Harper and Brothers, 1883, 1920.

[1]*It is commonly asserted . . . satisfy their own desires:* Sumner was particularly critical of traditional American ideology of equality and natural rights set forth by the American Constitution and by social movements of the time. He railed against the labor reform movements of the time, such as the Knights of Labor, and socialist thinkers like Henry George and Edward Bellamy, who criticized the effects of industrialization on the working class.

Sometimes they are discontented and envious. They do not take their achievements as a fair measure of their rights. They do not blame themselves or their parents for their lot, as compared with that of other people. Sometimes they claim that they have a right to everything of which they feel the need for their happiness on earth. To make such a claim against God and Nature would, of course, be only to say that we claim a right to live on earth if we can. But God and Nature have ordained the chances and conditions of life on earth once for all. The case cannot be reopened. We cannot get a revision of the laws of human life. We are absolutely shut up to the need and duty, if we would learn how to live happily, of investigating the laws of Nature, and deducing the rules of right living in the world as it is. These are very wearisome and commonplace tasks. They consist in labor and self-denial repeated over and over again in learning and doing. When the people whose claims we are considering are told to apply themselves to these tasks they become irritated and feel almost insulted. They formulate their claims as rights against society — that is, against some other men. In their view they have a right, not only to *pursue* happiness, but to *get* it; and if they fail to get it, they think they have a claim to the aid of other men — that is, to the labor and self-denial of other men — to get it for them. They find orators and poets who tell them that they have grievances, so long as they have unsatisfied desires.[2]

Now, if there are groups of people who have a claim to other people's labor and self-denial, and if there are other people whose labor and self-denial are liable to be claimed by the first groups, then there certainly are "classes," and classes of the oldest and most vicious type. For a man who can command another man's labor and self-denial for the support of his own existence is a privileged person of the highest species conceivable on earth. Princes and paupers meet on their plane, and no other men are on it all. On the other hand, a man whose labor and self-denial may be diverted from his maintenance to that of some other man is not a free man, and approaches more or less toward the position of a slave. Therefore we shall find that, in all the notions which we are to discuss, this elementary contradiction, that there are classes and that there are not classes, will produce repeated confusion and absurdity. We shall find that, in our efforts to eliminate the old vices of class government, we are impeded and defeated by new products of the worst class theory. We shall find that all the

---

[2]*They find orators . . . unsatisfied desires:* Sumner dismissed socialists like Upton Sinclair, who advocated social equality and the individual's right to happiness. One of the most famous orators of the late 19th century, George Herron, was a leading proponent of socialism and one of Sumner's most outspoken critics. William James's idealistic individualism and Andrew Carnegie's philanthropic activities also spurred much criticism from Sumner.

schemes for producing equality and obliterating the organization of society produce a new differentiation based on the worst possible distinction — the right to claim and the duty to give one man's effort for another man's satisfaction. We shall find that every effort to realize equality necessitates a sacrifice of liberty.

It is very popular to pose as a "friend of humanity," or a "friend of the working classes." The character, however, is quite exotic in the United States. It is borrowed from England, where some men, otherwise of small account, have assumed it with great success and advantage. Anything which has a charitable sound and a kind-hearted tone generally passes without investigation, because it is disagreeable to assail it. Sermons, essays, and orations assume a conventional standpoint with regard to the poor, the weak, etc.; and it is allowed to pass as an unquestioned doctrine in regard to social classes that "the rich" ought to "care for the poor"; that Churches especially ought to collect capital from the rich and spend it for the poor; that parishes ought to be clusters of institutions by means of which one social class should perform its duties to another; and that clergymen, economists, and social philosophers have a technical and professional duty to devise schemes for "helping the poor." The preaching in England used all to be done to the poor — that they ought to be contented with their lot and respectful to their betters. Now, the greatest part of the preaching in America consists in injunctions to those who have taken care of themselves to perform their assumed duty to take care of others.[3] Whatever may be one's private sentiments, the fear of appearing cold and hardhearted causes these conventional theories of social duty and these assumptions of social fact to pass unchallenged.

Let us notice some distinctions which are of prime importance to a correct consideration of the subject which we intend to treat.

Certain ills belong to the hardships of human life. They are natural. They are part of the struggle with Nature for existence. We cannot blame our fellow-men for our share of these. My neighbor and I are both struggling to free ourselves from these ills. The fact that my neighbor has succeeded in this struggle better than I constitutes no grievance for me. Certain other ills are due to the malice of men, and to the imperfections or errors of civil institutions. These ills are an object of agitation, and a subject of discussion. The former class of ills is to be met only by manly effort and

---

[3]*Sermons, essays, and orations . . . duty to take care of others:* The Salvation Army, introduced to America from England around 1879, stressed the need to aid the poor both materially and spiritually. The social gospel movement of the late 19th century, composed of liberal clergymen and social reformers such as Washington Gladden and Henry George, condemned the Darwinist principles of survival of the fittest and fierce competition and believed that only through cooperation, mutual help, and a Christian conscience could society prosper.

energy; the latter may be corrected by associated effort. The former class of ills is constantly grouped and generalized, and made the object of social schemes. We shall see, as we go on, what that means. The second class of ills may fall on certain social classes, and reform will take the form of interference by other classes in favor of that one. The last fact is, no doubt, the reason why people have been led, not noticing distinctions, to believe that the same method was applicable to the other class of ills. The distinction here made between the ills which belong to the struggle for existence and those which are due to the faults of human institutions is of prime importance.

It will also be important, in order to clear up our ideas about the notions which are in fashion, to note the relation of the economic to the political significance of assumed duties of one class to another. That is to say, we may discuss the question whether one class owes duties to another by reference to the economic effects which will be produced on the classes and society; or we may discuss the political expediency of formulating and enforcing rights and duties respectively between the parties. In the former case we might assume that the givers of aid were willing to give it, and we might discuss the benefit or mischief of their activity. In the other case we must assume that some at least of those who were forced to give aid did so unwillingly. Here, then, there would be a question of rights. The question whether voluntary charity is mischievous or not is one thing: the question whether legislation which forces one man to aid another is right and wise, as well as economically beneficial, is quite another question. Great confusion and consequent error is produced by allowing these two questions to become entangled in the discussion. Especially we shall need to notice the attempts to apply legislative methods of reform to the ills which belong to the order of Nature.

There is no possible definition of "a poor man." A pauper is a person who cannot earn his living; whose producing powers have fallen positively below his necessary consumption; who cannot, therefore, pay his way. A human society needs the active co-operation and productive energy of every person in it. A man who is present as a consumer, yet who does not contribute either by land, labor, or capital to the work of society, is a burden. On no sound political theory ought such a person to share in the political power of the State. He drops out of the ranks of workers and producers. Society must support him. It accepts the burden, but he must be cancelled from the ranks of the rulers likewise. So much for the pauper. About him no more need be said. But he is not the "poor man." The "poor man" is an elastic term, under which any number of social fallacies may be hidden.

Neither is there any possible definition of "the weak." Some are weak in one way, and some in another; and those who are weak in one sense are strong in another. In general, however, it may be said that those whom humanitarians and philanthropists call the weak are the ones through whom the productive and conservative forces of society are wasted. They constantly neutralize and destroy the finest efforts of the wise and industrious, and are a dead-weight on the society in all its struggles to realize any better things. Whether the people who mean no harm, but are weak in the essential powers necessary to the performance of one's duties in life, or those who are malicious and vicious, do the more mischief, is a question not easy to answer.

Under the names of the poor and the weak, the negligent, shiftless, inefficient, silly, and imprudent are fastened upon the industrious and prudent as a responsibility and a duty. On the one side, the terms are extended to cover the idle, intemperate, and vicious, who, by the combination, gain credit which they do not deserve, and which they could not get if they stood alone. On the other hand, the terms are extended to include wage-receivers of the humblest rank, who are degraded by the combination. The reader who desires to guard himself against fallacies should always scrutinize the terms "poor" and "weak" as used, so as to see which or how many of these classes they are made to cover.

The humanitarians, philanthropists, and reformers, looking at the facts of life as they present themselves, find enough which is sad and unpromising in the condition of many members of society. They see wealth and poverty side by side. They note great inequality of social position and social chances. They eagerly set about the attempt to account for what they see, and to devise schemes for remedying what they do not like. In their eagerness to recommend the less fortunate classes to pity and consideration they forget all about the rights of other classes; they gloss over all the faults of the classes in question, and they exaggerate their misfortunes and their virtues. They invent new theories of property, distorting rights and perpetuating injustice, as anyone is sure to do who sets about the readjustment of social relations with the interests of one group distinctly before his mind, and the interests of all other groups thrown into the background. When I have read certain of these discussions I have thought that it must be quite disreputable to be respectable, quite dishonest to own property, quite unjust to go one's own way and earn one's own living, and that the only really admirable person was the good-for-nothing. The man who by his own effort raises himself above poverty appears, in these discussions, to be of no account. The man who has done nothing to raise himself above poverty finds that the social doctors flock about him, bringing the capital which they have collected from the other class, and promising him the aid of the State to give him what the other had to work for. In all these schemes and projects the organized intervention of society through the State is either planned or hoped for, and the State is thus made to become the protector and guardian of certain classes. The agents who are to direct the State action are, of course, the reformers and philanthropists. Their schemes, therefore, may always be reduced to this type — that A and B decide what C shall do for D. It will be interesting to inquire, at a later period of our discussion, who C is, and what the effect is upon him of all these arrangements. In all the discussions attention is concentrated on A and B, the noble social reformers, and on D, the "poor man." I call C the Forgotten Man, because I have never seen that any notice was taken of him in any of the discussions. When we have disposed of A, B, and D we can better appreciate the case of C, and I think that we shall find that he deserves our attention, for the worth of his character and the magnitude of his unmerited burdens. Here it may suffice to observe that, on the theories of the social philosophers to whom I have referred, we should get a new maxim of judicious living: Poverty is the best policy. If you get wealth, you will have to support other people; if you do not get wealth, it will be the duty of other people to support you.

No doubt one chief reason for the unclear and contradictory theories *11* of class relations lies in the fact that our society, largely controlled in all its organization by one set of doctrines, still contains survivals of old social theories which are totally inconsistent with the former. In the Middle Ages men were united by custom and prescription into associations, ranks, guilds, and communities of various kinds. These ties endured as long as life lasted. Consequently society was dependent, throughout all its details, on status, and the tie, or bond, was sentimental. In our modern state, and in the United States more than anywhere else, the social structure is based on contract, and status is of the least importance. Contract, however, is rational — even rationalistic. It is also realistic, cold, and matter-of-fact. A contract relation is based on a sufficient reason, not on custom or prescription. It is not permament. It endures only so long as the reason for it endures. In a state based on contract sentiment is out of place in any public or common affairs. It is relegated to the sphere of private and personal relations, where it depends not at all on class types, but on personal acquaintance and personal estimates. The sentimentalists among us always seize upon the survivals of the old order. They want to save them and restore them. Much of the loose thinking also which troubles us in our social discussions arises from the fact that men do not distinguish the elements of status and of contract which may be found in our society.

Whether social philosophers think it desirable or not, it is out of the *12* question to go back to status or to the sentimental relations which once united baron and retainer, master and servant, teacher and pupil, comrade and comrade. That we have lost some grace and elegance is undeniable. That life once held more poetry and romance is true enough. But it seems impossible that any one who has studied the matter should doubt that we have gained immeasurably, and that our farther gains lie in going forward, not in going backward. The feudal ties can never be restored. If they could be restored they would bring back personal caprice, favoritism, sycophancy, and intrigue. A society based on contract is a society of free and independent men, who form ties without favor or obligation, and co-operate without cringing or intrigue. A society based on contract, therefore, gives the utmost room and chance for individual development, and for all the self-reliance and dignity of a free man. That a society of free men, co-operating under contract, is by far the strongest society which has ever yet existed; that no such society has ever yet developed the full measure of strength of which it is capable; and that the only social improvements which are now conceivable lie in the direction of more complete realization of a society of free men united by contract, are points which cannot be controverted. It follows, however, that one man, in a free state, cannot claim help from, and cannot be charged to give help to, another. . . .

THAT IT IS NOT WICKED TO BE RICH; NAY, EVEN, THAT IT IS NOT WICKED TO BE RICHER THAN ONE'S NEIGHBOR

I have before me a newspaper slip on which a writer expresses the   13 opinion that no one should be allowed to possess more than one million dollars' worth of property. Alongside of it is another slip, on which another writer expresses the opinion that the limit should be five millions. I do not know what the comparative wealth of the two writers is, but it is interesting to notice that there is a wide margin between their ideas of how rich they would allow their fellow-citizens to become, and of the point at which they ("the State," of course) would step in to rob a man of his earnings. These two writers only represent a great deal of crude thinking and declaiming which is in fashion. I never have known a man of ordinary common-sense who did not urge upon his sons, from earliest childhood, doctrines of economy and the practice of accumulation. A good father believes that he does wisely to encourage enterprise, productive skill, prudent self-denial, and judicious expenditure on the part of his son. The object is to teach the boy to accumulate capital. If, however, the boy should read many of the diatribes against "the rich" which are afloat in our literature;[4] if he should read or hear some of the current discussion about "capital"; and if, with the ingenuousness of youth, he should take these productions at their literal sense, instead of discounting them, as his father does, he would be forced to believe that he was on the path of infamy

---

[4]*many of the diatribes against "the rich" which are afloat in our literature . . . .* : Social Darwinism and the rapid growth of industrialization in post-Civil War America found a hostile reaction in many of Sumner's literary contemporaries, whose criticisms were not aimed at the rich per se, but at socioeconomic injustices. In her novel *John Andross,* Rebecca Davis exposed social injustice in the iron mills, while Henry Adams's novel *Democracy* expressed the sterility of a society dominated by fierce competition and materialism.

when he was earning and saving capital. It is worth while to consider which we mean or what we mean. Is it wicked to be rich? Is it mean to be a capitalist? If the question is one of degree only, and it is right to be rich up to a certain point and wrong to be richer, how shall we find the point? Certainly, for practical purposes, we ought to define the point nearer than between one and five millions of dollars.

There is an old ecclesiastical prejudice in favor of the poor and against the rich.[5] In days when men acted by ecclesiastical rules these prejudices produced waste of capital, and helped mightily to replunge Europe into barbarism. The prejudices are not yet dead, but they survive in our society as ludicrous contradictions and inconsistencies. One thing must be granted to the rich: they are good-natured. Perhaps they do not recognize themselves, for a rich man is even harder to define than a poor one. It is not uncommon to hear a clergyman utter from the pulpit all the old prejudice in favor of the poor and against the rich, while asking the rich to do something for the poor; and the rich comply, without apparently having their feelings hurt at all by the invidious comparison. We all agree that he is a good member of society who works his way up from poverty to wealth, but as soon as he has worked his way up we begin to regard him with suspicion, as a dangerous member of society. A newspaper starts the silly fallacy that "the rich are rich because the poor are industrious,"[6] and it is copied from one end of the country to the other as if it were a brilliant apothegm. "Capital" is denounced by writers and speakers who have never taken the trouble to find out what capital is, and who use the word in two or three different senses in as many pages. Labor organizations are formed, not to employ combined effort for a common object, but to indulge in declamation and denunciation, and especially to furnish an easy living to some officers who do not want to work. People who have rejected dogmatic religion, and retained only a residuum of religious sentimentalism,

14

---

[5]*There is an old ecclesiastical prejudice in favor of the poor and against the rich:* Jesus himself, asserting that "it is easier for a camel to go through the eye of a needle, than for a rich man to enter into the kingdom of God" (Matthew: 18:24), advised his followers to sell all that they had and give it to the poor. In Sumner's own time, the Holy Order of the Cross was established in New York City in 1881; like the Franciscan monks, the Order stressed a life of evangelical poverty. Many of the social reformers of the late 19th century saw Christ as an early champion of workers' rights and of the poor, pointing out that Christ had been a carpenter who ministered to the poor. Of course, the Christian ideal of a life of poverty meant voluntary poverty, not involuntary deprivation and misery.

[6]*"the rich are rich because the poor are industrious":* Karl Marx, as the father of communism and the ideological opposite of Sumner, believed that the history of society is the history of class struggle and that the ruling classes have traditionally exploited the laboring classes. Marx's ideas of a more equal distribution of wealth through state-controlled industry was in direct opposition to Sumner's advocacy of free enterprise and capitalist competition. (See Part VI, pp. 548–574.)

find a special field in the discussion of the rights of the poor and the duties of the rich. We have denunciations of banks, corporations, and monopolies, which denunciations encourage only helpless rage and animosity, because they are not controlled by any definitions or limitations, or by any distinctions between what is indispensably necessary and what is abuse, between what is established in the order of nature and what is legislative error. Think, for instance, of a journal which makes it its special business to denounce monopolies, yet favors a protective tariff, and has not a word to say against trades-unions or patents! Think of public teachers who say that the farmer is ruined by the cost of transportation, when they mean that he cannot make any profits because his farm is too far from the market, and who denounce the railroad because it does not correct for the farmer, at the expense of its stockholders, the disadvantage which lies in the physical situation of the farm! Think of that construction of this situation which attributes all the trouble to the greed of "moneyed corporations!" Think of the piles of rubbish that one has read about corners, and watering stocks, and selling futures!

Undoubtedly there are, in connection with each of these things, cases   15
of fraud, swindling, and other financial crimes; that is to say, the greed and selfishness of men are perpetual. They put on new phases, they adjust themselves to new forms of business, and constantly devise new methods of fraud and robbery, just as burglars devise new artifices to circumvent every new precaution of the lock-makers. The criminal law needs to be improved to meet new forms of crime, but to denounce financial devices which are useful and legitimate because use is made of them for fraud, is ridiculous and unworthy of the age in which we live. Fifty years ago good old English Tories used to denounce all joint-stock companies in the same way, and for similar reasons.[7]

All the denunciations and declamations which have been referred to   16
are made in the interest of "the poor man." His name never ceases to echo in the halls of legislation, and he is the excuse and reason for all the acts which are passed. He is never forgotten in poetry, sermon, or essay. His interest is invoked to defend every doubtful procedure and every questionable institution. Yet where is he? Who is he? Who ever saw him? When

---

[7]*Fifty years ago . . . for similar reasons:* Joint-stock companies were businesses in which the capital was divided into shares of stock, which investors could buy and sell. The shareholders elected or appointed officers to administer the funds. (Many businesses today operate on the same basis, though the term "joint-stock company" is now virtually obsolete.) The Tories — who after 1830 became known as Conservatives — advocated a reduction in the cost of living for the working classes and an industry with little state intervention. Their criticism of joint-stock companies was in part a response to the insecure economy of Great Britain in the early 1800s as a result of wild speculation, monopolies, and corruption in the joint-stock companies.

did he ever get the benefit of any of the numberless efforts in his behalf? When, rather, were his name and interest ever invoked, when, upon examination, it did not plainly appear that somebody else was to win — somebody who was far too "smart" ever to be poor, far too lazy ever to be rich by industry and economy?

A great deal is said about the unearned increment from land,[8] especially with a view to the large gains of landlords in old countries. The unearned increment from land has indeed made the position of an English land-owner, for the last two hundred years, the most fortunate that any class of mortals ever has enjoyed; but the present moment, when the rent of agricultural land in England is declining under the competition of American land, is not well chosen for attacking the old advantage. Furthermore, the unearned increment from land appears in the United States as a gain to the first comers, who have here laid the foundations of a new State. Since the land is a monopoly, the unearned increment lies in the laws of Nature. Then the only question is, Who shall have it? — the man who has the ownership by prescription, or some or all others? It is a beneficent incident of the ownership of land that a pioneer who reduces it to use, and helps to lay the foundations of a new State, finds a profit in the increasing value of land as the new State grows up. It would be unjust to take that profit away from him, or from any successor to whom he has sold it. Moreover, there is an unearned increment on capital and on labor, due to the presence, around the capitalist and the laborer, of a great, industrious, and prosperous society. A tax on land and a succession or probate duty on capital might be perfectly justified by these facts. Unquestionably capital accumulates with a rapidity which follows in some high series the security, good government, peaceful order of the State in which it is employed; and if the State steps in, on the death of the holder, to claim a share of the inheritance, such a claim may be fully justified. The laborer likewise gains by carrying on his labor in a strong, highly civilized, and well-governed State far more than he could gain with equal industry on the frontier or in the midst of anarchy. He gains greater remuneration for his services, and he also shares in the enjoyment of all that accumulated capital of a wealthy community which is public or semi-public in its nature.

It is often said that the earth belongs to the race, as if raw land was a boon, or gift. Raw land is only a *chance* to prosecute the struggle for existence, and the man who tries to earn a living by the subjugation of raw land makes that attempt under the most unfavorable conditions, for land can be brought into use only by great hardship and exertion. The boon, or

17

18

---

[8]*unearned increment from land:* An unearned increment from land is an increase in the value of the land, not through work or expenditure by the owner, but rather through an inherent increase in the land's value, such as would occur during an increase in the area population.

gift, would be to get some land after somebody else had made it fit for use. Any one in the world today can have raw land by going to it; but there are millions who would regard it simply as "transportation[9] for life," if they were forced to go and live on new land and get their living out of it. Private ownership of land is only division of labor. If it is true in any sense that we all own the soil in common, the best use we can make of our undivided interests is to vest them all gratuitously (just as we now do) in any who will assume the function of directly treating the soil, while the rest of us take other shares in the social organizaton. The reason is, because in this way we all get more than we would if each one owned some land and used it directly. Supply and demand now determine the distribution of population between the direct use of land and other pursuits; and if the total profits and chances of land-culture were reduced by taking all the "unearned increment" in taxes, there would simply be a redistribution of industry until the profits of land-culture, less taxes and without chances from increasing value, were equal to the profits of other pursuits under exemption from taxation.

It is remarkable that jealousy of individual property in land often goes [19] along with very exaggerated doctrines of tribal or national property in land. We are told that John, James, and William ought not to possess part of the earth's surface because it belongs to all men; but it is held that Egyptians, Nicaraguans, or Indians have such right to the territory which they occupy, that they may bar the avenues of commerce and civilization if they choose, and that it is wrong to override their prejudices or expropriate their land. The truth is, that the notion that the races own the earth has practical meaning only for the latter class of cases.

The great gains of a great capitalist in a modern state must be put un- [20] der the head of wages of superintendence. Anyone who believes that any great enterprise of an industrial character can be stated without labor must have little experience of life. Let anyone try to get a railroad built, or to start a factory and win reputation for its products, or to start a school and win a reputation for it, or to found a newspaper and make it a success, or to start any other enterprise, and he will find what obstacles must be overcome, what risks must be taken, what perseverance and courage are required, what foresight and sagacity are necessary. Especially in a new country, where many tasks are waiting, where resources are strained to the utmost all the time, the judgment, courage, and perseverance required to organize new enterprises and carry them to success are sometimes heroic. Persons who possess the necessary qualifications obtain great re-

---

[9]*transportation:* It was common in the 17th century for the English monarchy to transport convicted criminals, vagrants, and other undesirables to the colonies. They were expected to help populate and develop the land for the mother country.

wards. They ought to do so. It is foolish to rail at them. Then, again, the ability to organize and conduct industrial, commerical, or financial enterprises is rare; the great captains of industry are as rare as great generals. The great weakness of all co-operative enterprises is in the matter of supervision. Men of routine or men who can do what they are told are not hard to find; but men who can think and plan and tell the routine men what to do are very rare. They are paid in proportion to the supply and demand of them.

If Mr. A. T. Stewart[10] made a great fortune by collecting and bringing   21
dry-goods to the people of the United States, he did so because he understood how to do that thing better than any other man of his generation. He proved it, because he carried the business through commercial crises and war, and kept increasing its dimensions. If, when he died, he left no competent successor, the business must break up, and pass into new organization in the hands of other men. Some have said that Mr. Stewart made his fortune out of those who worked for him or with him. But would those persons have been able to come together, organize themselves, and earn what they did earn without him? Not at all. They would have been comparatively helpless. He and they together formed a great system of factories, stores, transportation, under his guidance and judgment. It was for the benefit of all; but he contributed to it what no one else was able to contribute — the one guiding mind which made the whole thing possible. In no sense whatever does a man who accumulates a fortunate by legitimate industry exploit his employés, or make his capital "out of" anybody else. The wealth which he wins would not be but for him.

The aggregation of large fortunes is not at all a thing to be regretted.   22
On the contrary, it is a necessary condition of many forms of social advance. If we should set a limit to the accumulation of wealth, we should say to our most valuable producers, "We do not want you to do us the services which you best understand how to perform, beyond a certain point." It would be like killing off our generals in war. A great deal is said, in the cant of a certain school about "ethical views of wealth," and we are told that some day men will be found of such public spirit that, after they have accumulated a few millions, they will be willing to go on and labor simply for the pleasure of paying the taxes of their fellow-citizens. Possibly this is true. It is a prophecy. It is as impossible to deny it as it is silly to affirm it. For if a time ever comes when there are men of this kind, the men of that age will arrange their affairs accordingly. There are no such

---

[10]*Mr. A. T. Stewart:* An Irish-born American textile merchant whose retail store in New York City was the largest in the world in 1862. Rather than argue over prices with each customer, Stewart set fixed prices on his merchandise; this standardization of prices was an innovation in his time.

men now, and those of us who live now cannot arrange our affairs by what men will be a hundred generations hence.

There is every indication that we are to see new developments of the power of aggregated capital to serve civilization, and that the new developments will be made right here in America. Joint-stock companies are yet in their infancy, and incorporated capital,[11] instead of being a thing which can be overturned, is a thing which is becoming more and more indispensable. I shall have something to say in another chapter about the necessary checks and guarantees, in a political point of view, which must be established. Economically speaking, aggregated capital will be more and more essential to the performance of our social tasks. Furthermore, it seems to me certain that all aggregated capital will fall more and more under personal control. Each great company will be known as controlled by one master mind. The reason for this lies in the great superiority of personal management over management by boards and committees. This tendency is in the public interest, for it is in the direction of more satisfactory responsibility. The great hindrance to the development of this continent has lain in the lack of capital. The capital which we have had has been wasted by division and dissipation, and by injudicious applications. The waste of capital, in proportion to the total capital, in this country between 1800 and 1850, in the attempts which were made to establish means of communication and transportation, was enormous. The waste was chiefly due to ignorance and bad management, especially to State control of public works. We are to see the development of the country pushed forward at an unprecedented rate by an aggregation of capital, and a systematic application of it under the direction of competent men. This development will be for the benefit of all, and it will enable each one of us, in his measure and way, to increase his wealth. We may each of us go ahead to do so, and we have every reason to rejoice in each other's prosperity. There ought to be no laws to guarantee property against the folly of its possessors. In the absence of such laws, capital inherited by a spendthrift will be squandered and re-accumulated in the hands of men who are fit and competent to hold it. So it should be, and under such a state of things there is no reason to desire to limit the property which any man may acquire.

23

---

[11]*incorporated capital:* The liquid and material assets belonging to a corporation.

REVIEW QUESTIONS

1. What are the "laws of Nature" to which Sumner refers in paragraph 1? What does Sumner claim is the typical reaction of the poor and the weak when reminded of these "laws of Nature"? In what way do the "friends of humanity"

encourage the poor and weak to circumvent the "laws of Nature"? Why are these "friends of humanity" often so influential?

2. In what way have the lower classes become the "privileged" classes and the higher classes become their "slaves"? In what way have the attitudes of churchmen changed toward the poor?

3. What distinction does Sumner make between the types of hardships to which humans are subject? Which type is made "the object of social schemes"?

4. How do the "humanitarians, philanthropists, and reformers" *reverse* what Sumner considers the natural way of regarding the wealthy (on the one hand) and the poor (on the other)?

5. To what does Sumner attribute the confusion and the sentimentality that affect modern views of class relations? What kind of distinction does he make between two ways of organizing social relations? What are the advantages and disadvantages of each? Which type of society does he favor? Why?

6. In what ways does Sumner accuse those who declaim against the rich as inconsistent, illogical, or self-serving?

7. For what reasons does Sumner argue that it is ludicrous and unrealistic to place limits on the accumulation of wealth by individuals? Why does he argue that the first developers of land should be free from taxes on the increased value of the land?

DISCUSSION AND WRITING QUESTIONS

1. Do you believe that people who are well off have an obligation to help support those who are less well off? If so, on what is this obligation based? What are the rights and obligations of those who (in Sumner's terms) have substantial capital? Of those who do not?

2. To what extent do you believe that Sumner is hostile to the poor? To what extent is he insensitive to their plight? Does he make sufficient allowance for those who are not responsible for their own plight? To what extent does he see responsibility for one's plight as relevant to the issue?

3. Sumner asserts (in paragraph 3) that "God and Nature have ordained the chances and conditions on earth once for all. The case cannot be reopened. We cannot get a revision of the laws of human life." To what extent is this a Darwinian statement? (That is, to what extent might Darwin's ideas support this view?)

4. Toward the end of paragraph 3 Sumner suggests that guilt, rather than sympathetic feeling toward the less fortunate, is what primarily motivates the wealthy and the middle classes toward charity. To what extent do you agree with this suggestion?

5. Do you see evidence today of the arrangement Sumner has written about — particularly the kind of situation in which "A and B decide what C shall do for D"? To what extent do you share his assessment and his attitudes? (You may wish to answer this question in various ways, depending upon whether you see yourself in the position of A or B, C, or D.) In any case, what do you see as the solution to the problems?

6. To what extent is Sumner describing (in paragraph 12) a kind of social evolution and a social theory of the survival of the fittest?

7. To what extent are you prejudiced against the rich? Do you feel that, by and large, they have gained their wealth through exploitation, deception, or even crime? Write an essay in which you explore your feelings toward the very wealthy; to what extent are your feelings based on acutal experience (your own or that of others), to what extent based on envy, popular prejudice, or the unfavorable "image" of the rich in fiction and drama? Consider also whether Sumner has succeeded in changing your feelings about the rich.

8. Comment on the following passage, justifying higher pay for managers and administrators than for laborers: "men of routine or men who can do what they are told are not hard to find; but men who can think and plan and tell the routine men what to do are very rare. They are paid in proportion to the supply and demand of them." Should there be limits on what managers and supervisors are paid?

9. To what extent do Sumner's arguments in favor of capital and capitalists (especially as expressed in paragraph 20) constitute a rebuttal to the arguments of Marx and Engels in *The Communist Manifesto* (pp. 554–574)?

10. Seek out a professor of Marxist or socialist inclinations; show her or him (or explain to her or him) Sumner's views, as expressed in "That it Is Not Wicked to Be Rich . . ." Write a report summarizing the professor's responses. At the end of this report develop your own conclusions on the subject.

11. Read the following two letters to the editor that appeared on different occasions in the *Los Angeles Times* in mid-1986, and discuss similarities and differences between the ideas expressed in the letters and the ideas of William Graham Sumner.

> There is a dangerously concealing shroud being worn by the organizers of Hands Across America — the same shroud is being worn by all practitioners of altruistic methods who vow to relieve this world of its hungry and homeless.
>
> This shroud, tailored by altruistic moralists from a fabric weaved of tales of suffering and the benevolent glories of selfless sacrifice, covers not a body with the divine right to save the world, but a body assuming the power to demand that we — those who possess a solid dollar more than the suffering — be their savior.
>
> There are necessary questions arising from this situation.
>
> What right have they to imply that this altruistic subsidization is the moral duty of all citizens? And that citizens must subordinate their lives and dollars to the welfare of others? And that the suffering in the world need be each and every citizen's primary concern?
>
> By what right do they propound this altruistic morality?
>
> Upon close examination of this "morality," one can easily see the basic pattern of this socialist, i.e. collectivist, fabric. And it is fitting that they have tailored this shroud — an altruistic shroud — beneath which they hide their demands of sacrifice, for if citizens accept this slow-killing morality, it will be the very shroud in which the United States of America, with all of its achievements, is buried.
>
> KRIS KARLINER

> The diatribe by Richard Goodwin (Editorial Pages, July 10), "Demeaning Our Own Values," was a refreshing bit of fluff, a cool and delicious

rehash of antique liberal attitudes. It's wonderful how the outlook of the liberal intellectual community changes so little from decade to decade, or even century to century.

This caterwauling over the plight of the Poor and its corollary, the obscene amassing of wealth by the vicious Rich, is word for word what we heard in the 1960s and the 1950s, the 1940s, right on back to probably indignant speeches in the Forum.

But Goodwin is conspicuously silent about the great and monumental failure of his class: the then Department of Health, Education and Welfare and all the associated War Against Poverty programs so vociferously advocated 20 years ago. He studiously avoids the potent question: What has happened to the billions and billions — many billions — of tax dollars that have been spent on these programs?

Could it be, perhaps, that Goodwin and his compeers, bigots to their dedicated souls, can only see what they want to see? Are they perhaps more human than they would care to admit?

Certainly they are human enough to refuse, under any circumstances, to admit that they made a terrible mistake. Never shall any of his fraternity, card-carrying intellectuals all, look askance at their wonderful child, the social-spending monster. Anything wrong with the system lies in the Administration, the Reagan-gutting, the arrant caprice of destructive conservatives, and so forth. To say the obvious, that the War Against Poverty was a success only for administrators, bureaucrats and politicians, will be opposed to the last gasping breath.

At any rate, we are presently going through yet another phase of the old shell game, "Let's Help the Worthy Poor." Despite the billions already wasted and the billions more in the pipeline, Goodwin's group is hard at it again.

There is one and only one subgroup of human society that keeps the wheels turning, holds society together, and generates wealth: that small portion of the Rich, which all intellectuals despise so heartily. They direct and control those amongst us who are willing to work for a living: the middle class and those of the poor who are working their way out of the ghetto.

Everyone else, the parasites among the Rich, those in the entertainment industry, in advertising, politics, law and the rest, merely consume. Except for the Poor, of course.

Of course the main portion of the wealth goes to the wealthy. Why should it not? They are willing to work for it, and while it is true that a great gaggle of parasites go along with them — their wives, children, lawyers, cocaine dealers and other scum — this productive subculture does work very hard for their wealth.

If the Poor don't like it, then let them get an education and join the monopoly. It can be done, you know. Quite easily. But it takes work and dedication and effort.

But our Mr. Goodwin never addresses this. He fulminates endlessly on the viciousness of the Class War, and bleeds copiously for the Poor.

GERALD L. HEWETT

HERBERT SPENCER *(1820–1903)*

Herbert Spencer (whose essay, "The Great Political Superstition" appears in Part III) was not just another social Darwinist; indeed, in some ways, Spencer preceded Darwin. The phrase "survival of the fittest" was coined by Spencer in an essay on population written in 1852, seven years before the publication of *The Origin of Species* (Darwin adopted the term for the fifth edition of *Origin*); and by the early 1850s Spencer had arrived at his own theory of evolution, independently of Darwin and Wallace. Unlike Darwin, Spencer was concerned primarily with the evolution of human society and with social and economic organisms. Spencer had also postulated an evolution on Larmarckian lines (i.e., on the inheritance of acquired characteristics), but he accepted as true Darwin's theory of natural selection soon after the publication of *Origin*.

For an introduction to Spencer's life, see pp. 256–257. As indicated in that introduction, Spencer's great life's work was his *Synthetic Philosophy*, an attempt to unify all of human knowledge under a single theory — the theory of evolution. Spencer's theory of social evolution was based on the idea that social organisms, like biological organisms, progress from simple, homogeneous, unified structures (like amoebas or small family businesses) to complex, heterogeneous, differentiated structures (like humans or large corporations). Like Darwin, Spencer had read Malthus, and he postulated that limited resources would lead to a struggle for existence and a consequent survival of the fittest. Like Darwin also, he argued that the struggle for existence and the survival of the fittest were natural processes and should not be interfered with. Welfare programs, state support of education, tariff barriers, and a myriad of other examples of state intrusion were pernicious because they prevented healthier social entities from becoming better adapted to existing social and economic conditions. Weaker social and economic entities, Spencer believed, should be left to their own resources. If they acted to help themselves, and were thereby able to survive, all well and good. If not, they should be allowed to die, for helping them to survive would require a drain on limited social resources that could lead to the downfall of healthy and unhealthy alike.

The implications of this kind of thinking for social welfare and socially supported programs, such as education, are obvious. But business, too, exists in a very "Darwinistic" world. A modern application: in the 1980s, following the deregulation of the airline industry, there was a proliferation of small airlines, all competing with each other and the larger airlines for a limited amount of business. As a result of the price wars and the corporate buyouts and mergers that followed, many of the smaller airlines, unable to survive the struggle for existence, perished. Only the largest, fittest airlines remained. Question: should the government — or anyone else — have stepped in to prop up those airlines unfit for the rough competition? If so, what would be the ultimate costs to society of such interference with the marketplace? (Several years earlier, the same questions had been furiously debated with regard to a government bailout of Chrysler corporation, which had been otherwise unable to survive its struggle for existence with the Japanese automobile industry.)

Spencer had anticipated such debates. And in his own mind, he had resolved them. The following selection is an extract from "The Sins of the Legislators," which appeared in Spencer's *The Man Versus the State*, published in 1897. As in "The Great Political Superstition," Spencer here quotes from another of his essays, written a third of a century earlier, to help support his views.

THE SINS OF THE LEGISLATORS

The continuance of every higher species of creature depends on conformity, now to one, now to the other, of two radically-opposed principles. The early lives of its members, and the adult lives of its members, have to be dealt with in contrary ways. We will contemplate them in their natural order.   *1*

One of the most familiar facts is that animals of superior types, comparatively slow in reaching maturity, are enabled when they have reached it, to give more aid to their offspring than animals of inferior types. The adults foster their young during periods more or less prolonged, while yet the young are unable to provide for themselves; and it is obvious that maintenance of the species can be secured only by this parental care. It requires no proving that the blind unfledged hedge-bird,[1] or the young puppy even after it has acquired sight, would forthwith die if it had to keep itself warm and obtain its own food. The gratuitous aid must be great in proportion as the young one is of little worth, either to itself or to others; and it may diminish as fast as, by increasing development, the young one acquires worth, at first for self-sustentation, and by-and-by for sustentation of others. That is to say, during immaturity, benefits received must vary inversely as the power or ability of the receiver. Clearly if during this first part of life benefits were proportioned to merits, or rewards to deserts, the species would disappear in a generation.   *2*

From this *régime*[2] of the family-group, let us turn to the *régime* of that   *3*

Herbert Spencer. The Sins of the Legislators [1897]. In *Social Statics, Abridged and Revised, Together with The Man Versus the State*. New York: D. Appleton Co., 1897.

[1]*hedge-bird:* A bird that lives in hedges.

[2]*régime:* Social order.

larger group formed by adult members of the species. Ask what happens when the new individual, acquiring complete use of its powers and ceasing to have parental aid, is left to itself. Now there comes into play a principle just the reverse to that above described. Throughout the rest of its life, each adult gets benefit in proportion to merit — reward in proportion to desert: merit and desert in each case being understood as ability to fulfil all the requirements of life — to get food, to find shelter, to escape enemies. Placed in competition with members of its own species and in antagonism with members of other species, it dwindles and gets killed off, or thrives and propagates, according as it is ill-endowed or well-endowed. Manifestly an opposite *régime,* could it be maintained, would, in course of time, be fatal. If the benefits received by each individual were proportionate to its inferiority — if, as a consequence, multiplication of the inferior was furthered, and multiplication of the superior hindered, progressive degradation would result; and eventually the degenerate species would fail to hold its ground in presence of antagonistic species and competing species.

The broad fact then, here to be noted, is that Nature's modes of treatment inside the family-group and outside the family-group are diametrically opposed to one another; and that the intrusion of either mode into the sphere of the other, would be destructive either immediately or remotely.   4

Does any one think that the like does not hold of the human species?   5
He cannot deny that within the human family, as within any inferior family, it would be fatal to proportion benefits to merits. Can he assert that outside the family, among adults, there should not be, as throughout the animal world, a proportioning of benefits to merits? Will he contend that no mischief will result if the lowly endowed are enabled to thrive and multiply as much as, or more than, the highly endowed? A society of men, standing towards other societies in relations of either antagonism or competition, may be considered as a species, or, more literally, as a variety of a species; and it must be true of it as of other species or varieties, that it will be unable to hold its own in the struggle with other societies, if it disadvantages its superior units that it may advantage its inferior units. Surely none can fail to see that were the principle of family life to be adopted and fully carried out in social life — were reward always great in proportion as desert was small, fatal results to the society would quickly follow; and if so, then even a partial intrusion of the family *régime* into the *régime* of the State, will be slowly followed by fatal results. Society in its corporate capacity, cannot without immediate or remoter disaster interfere with the play of these opposed principles under which every species has reached such fitness for its mode of life as it possesses, and under which it maintains that fitness.

I say advisedly — society in its corporate capacity; not intending to 6
exclude or condemn aid given to the inferior by the superior in their individual capacities. Though when given so indiscriminately as to enable the
inferior to multiply, such aid entails mischief; yet in the absence of aid
given by society, individual aid, more generally demanded than now, and
associated with a greater sense of responsibility, would, on the average,
be given with the effect of fostering the unfortunate worthy rather than
the innately unworthy: there being always, too, the concomitant social
benefit arising from culture of the sympathies. But all this may be admitted
while asserting that the radical distinction between family-ethics and State-
ethics must be maintained; and that while generosity must be the essential
principle of the one, justice must be the essential principle of the other —
a rigorous maintenance of those normal relations among citizens under
which each gets in return for his labour, skilled or unskilled, bodily or
mental, as much as is proved to be its value by the demand for it: such
return, therefore, as will enable him to thrive and rear offspring in proportion to the superiorities which make him valuable to himself and
others.

And yet, notwithstanding the conspicuousness of these truths, which 7
should strike everyone who leaves his lexicons,[3] and his law-deeds, and
his ledgers, and looks abroad into that natural order of things under which
we exist, and to which we must conform, there is continual advocacy of
paternal government. The intrusion of family-ethics into the ethics of the
State, instead of being regarded as socially injurious, is more and more
demanded as the only efficient means to social benefit. So far has this de-
lusion now gone, that it vitiates the beliefs of those who might, more than
all others, be thought safe from it. In the essay to which the Cobden Club
awarded its prize in 1880, there occurs the assertion that "the truth of Free
Trade is clouded over by the *laissez-faire* fallacy;" and we are told that "we
need a great deal more parental government — that bugbear of the old
economists."[4]

Vitally important as is the truth above insisted upon, since acceptance 8
or rejection of it affects the entire fabric of political conclusions formed, I
may be excused if I emphasize it by here quoting certain passages contained in a work I published in 1851: premising, only, that the reader must
not hold me committed to such teleological[5] implications as they contain.
After describing "that state of universal warfare maintained throughout

---

[3]*lexicons:* Dictionaries or special vocabularies of a field of study; more broadly, book-
learning.
[4]*On the Value of Political Economy to Mankind.* By A. N. Cumming, pp. 47, 48. [Spencer]
[5]*teleological:* Dealing with final causes.

the lower creation," and showing that an average of benefit results from it, I have continued thus: —

"Note further, that their carnivorous[6] enemies not only remove from   *9*
herbivorous[7] herds individuals past their prime, but also weed out the sickly, the malformed, and the least fleet or powerful. By the aid of which purifying process, as well as by the fighting so universal in the pairing season, all vitiation of the race through the multiplication of its inferior samples is prevented; and the maintenance of a constitution completely adapted to surrounding conditions, and therefore most productive of happiness, is ensured.

"The development of the higher creation is a progress towards a form of   *10*
being capable of a happiness undiminished by these drawbacks. It is in the human race that the consummation is to be accomplished. Civilization is the last stage of its accomplishment. And the ideal man is the man in whom all the conditions of that accomplishment are fulfilled. Meanwhile, the well-being of existing humanity, and the unfolding of it into this ultimate perfection, are both secured by that same beneficent, though severe discipline, to which the animate creation at large is subject: a discipline which is pitiless in the working out of good: a felicity-pursuing law which never swerves for the avoidance of partial and temporary suffering. The poverty of the incapable, the distresses that come upon the imprudent, the starvation of the idle, and those shoulderings aside of the weak by the strong, which leave so many 'in shallows and in miseries,' are the decrees of a large, far-seeing benevolence." . . .

"To become fit for the social state, man has not only to lose his savageness,   *11*
but he has to acquire the capacities needful for civilized life. Power of application must be developed; such modification of the intellect as shall qualify it for its new tasks must take place; and, above all, there must be gained the ability to sacrifice a small immediate gratification for a future great one. The state of transition will of course be an unhappy state. Misery inevitably results from incongruity between constitution and conditions. All these evils which afflict us, and seem to the uninitiated the obvious consequences of this or that removable cause, are unavoidable attendants on the adaptation now in progress. Humanity is being pressed against the inexorable necessities of its new position — is being moulded into harmony with them, and has to bear the resulting unhappiness as best it can. The process *must* be undergone, and the sufferings *must* be endured. No power on earth, no cunningly-devised laws of statesmen, no world-rectifying schemes of the humane, no communist panaceas, that men ever did broach or ever will broach, can diminish them one jot. Intensified they may be, and are; and in preventing their intensification, the philanthropic will find ample scope for exertion. But there is bound up with the change a *normal* amount of suffering, which cannot be lessened without altering the very laws of life." . . .

"Of course, in so far as the severity of this process is mitigated by the   *12*

---

[6]*carnivorous:* Flesh-eating.

[7]*herbivorous:* Plant-eating.

spontaneous sympathy of men for each other, it is proper that it should be mitigated; albeit there is unquestionably harm done when sympathy is shown, without any regard to ultimate results. But the drawbacks hence arising are nothing like commensurate with the benefits otherwise conferred. Only when this sympathy prompts to a breach of equity — only when it originates an interference forbidden by the law of equal freedom — only when, by so doing, it suspends in some particular department of life the relationship between constitution and conditions, does it work pure evil. Then, however, it defeats its own end. Instead of diminishing suffering, it eventually increases it. It favors the multiplication of those worst fitted for existence, and, by consequence, hinders the multiplication of those best fitted for existence — leaving, as it does, less room for them. It tends to fill the world with those to whom life will bring most pain, and tends to keep out of it those to whom life will bring most pleasure. It inflicts positive misery, and prevents positive happiness." — *Social Statics*, pp. 322–5 and pp. 380–1 (edition of 1851).

The lapse of a third of a century since these passages were published, has brought me no reason for retreating from the position taken up in them. Contrariwise, it has brought a vast amount of evidence strengthening that position. The beneficial results of the survival of the fittest, prove to be immeasurably greater than those above indicated. The process of "natural selection," as Mr. Darwin called it, co-operating with a tendency to variation and to inheritance of variations, he has shown to be a chief cause (though not, I believe, the sole cause) of that evolution through which all living things, beginning with the lowest and diverging and rediverging as they evolved, have reached their present degrees of organization and adaptation to their modes of life. So familiar has this truth become that some apology seems needed for naming it. And yet, strange to say, now that this truth is recognized by most cultivated people — now that the beneficent working of the survival of the fittest has been so impressed on them that, much more than people in past times, they might be expected to hesitate before neutralizing its action — now more than ever before in the history of the world, are they doing all they can to further survival of the unfittest!

But the postulate that men are rational beings, continually leads one to draw inferences which prove to be extremely wide of the mark.[8]

---

[8]The saying of Emerson that most people can understand a principle only when its light falls on a fact, induces me here to cite a fact which may carry home the above principle to those on whom, in its abstract form, it will produce no effect. It rarely happens that the amount of evil caused by fostering the vicious and good-for-nothing can be estimated. But in America, at a meeting of the States Charities Aid Association, held on December 18, 1874, a startling instance was given in detail by Dr. Harris. It was furnished by a county on the Upper Hudson, remarkable for the ratio of crime and poverty to population. Generations ago there had existed a certain "gutter-child," as she would be here called, known

"Yes truly; your principle is derived from the lives of brutes, and is a   15
brutal principle. You will not persuade me that men are to be under the
discipline which animals are under. I care nothing for your natural history
arguments. My conscience shows me that the feeble and the suffering must
be helped; and if selfish people won't help them, they must be forced by
law to help them. Don't tell me that the milk of human kindness is to be
reserved for the relations between individuals, and that Governments
must be the administrators of nothing but hard justice. Every man with
sympathy in him must feel that hunger and pain and squalor must be prevented; and that if private agencies do not suffice, then public agencies
must be established."

Such is the kind of response which I expect to be made by nine out of   16
ten. In some of them it will doubtless result from a fellow-feeling so acute
that they cannot contemplate human misery without an impatience which
excludes all thought of remote results. Concerning the susceptibilities of
the rest, we may, however, be somewhat sceptical. Persons who are angry
if, to maintain our supposed national "interests" or national "*prestige*,"
those in authority do not send out thousands of men to be partially destroyed while destroying other thousands of men because we suspect their
intentions, or dislike their institutions, or want their territory, cannot after
all be so tender in feeling that contemplating the hardships of the poor is
intolerable to them. Little admiration need be felt for the professed sympathies of people who urge on a policy which breaks up progressing societies; and who then look on with cynical indifference at the weltering confusion left behind, with all its entailed suffering and death. Those who,
when Boers,[9] asserting their independence, successfully resisted us, were
angry because British "honour" was not maintained by fighting to avenge
a defeat, at the cost of more mortality and misery to our own soldiers and
their antagonists, cannot have so much "enthusiasm of humanity" as protests like that indicated above would lead one to expect. Indeed, along with
this sensitiveness which it seems will not let them look with patience on
the pains of "the battle of life" as it quietly goes on around, they appear to
have a callousness which not only tolerates but enjoys contemplating the

---

as "Margaret," who proved to be the prolific mother of a prolific race. Besides great numbers of idiots, imbeciles, drunkards, lunatics, paupers, and prostitutes, "the county records show two hundred of her descendants who have been criminals." Was it kindness or
cruelty which, generation after generation, enabled these to multiply and become an increasing curse to the society around them? [For particulars see *The Jukes: a Study in Crime,
Pauperism, Disease and Heredity*. By R. L. Dugdale. New York: Putnams.] [Spencer]

[9]*Boers*: Known today as Afrikaners, they were primarily Dutch and Huguenots who settled
in South Africa in the 18th century. After the Cape colony became a British possession in
1806, large numbers of Boers left the colony in protest of the new liberal policies of the
British, particularly in regard to the freeing of slaves.

pains of battles of the literal kind; as one sees in the demand for illustrated papers containing scenes of carnage, and in the greediness with which detailed accounts of bloody engagements are read. We may reasonably have our doubts about men whose feelings are such that they cannot bear the thought of hardships borne, mostly by the idle and the improvident, and who, nevertheless, have demanded thirty-one editions of *The Fifteen Decisive Battles of the World*,[10] in which they may revel in accounts of slaughter. Nay, even still more remarkable is the contrast between the professed tender-heartedness and the actual hard-heartedness of those who would reverse the normal course of things that immediate miseries may be prevented, even at the cost of greater miseries hereafter produced. For on other occasions you may hear them, with utter disregard of bloodshed and death, contend that in the interests of humanity at large, it is well that the inferior races should be exterminated and their places occupied by the superior races. So that, marvellous to relate, though they cannot bear to think of the evils accompanying the struggle for existence as it is carried on without violence among individuals in their own society, they contemplate with equanimity such evils in their intense and wholesale forms, when inflicted by fire and sword on entire communities. Not worthy of much respect then, as it seems to me, is this generous consideration of the inferior at home which is accompanied by unscrupulous sacrifice of the inferior abroad.

Still less respectable appears this extreme concern for those of our own blood which goes along with utter unconcern for those of other blood, when we observe its methods. Did it prompt personal effort to relieve the suffering, it would rightly receive approving recognition. Were the many who express this cheap pity like the few who devote large parts of their time to aiding and encouraging, and occasionally amusing, those who, by ill-fortune or incapacity, are brought to lives of hardship, they would be worthy of unqualified admiration. The more there are of men and women who help the poor to help themselves — the more there are of those whose sympathy is exhibited directly and not by proxy, the more we may rejoice. But the immense majority of the persons who wish to mitigate by law the miseries of the unsuccessful and the reckless, propose to do this in small measure at their own cost and mainly at the cost of others — sometimes with their assent but mostly without. More than this is true; for those who are to be forced to do so much for the distressed, often equally or more require something doing for them. The deserving poor are among those who are taxed to support the undeserving poor. As, under the old Poor

17

---

[10]*The Fifteen Decisive Battles of the World:* Sir Edward Creasy's book on famous military battles was such a success that there were 30 editions within 32 years of its first publication in 1851. It ranged from battles of antiquity to the Battle of Waterloo.

Law,[11] the diligent and provident labourer had to pay that the good-for-nothings might not suffer, until frequently under this extra burden he broke down and himself took refuge in the workhouse — as, at present, the total rates levied in large towns for all public purposes, have reached such a height that they "cannot be exceeded without inflicting great hardship on the small shop-keepers and artisans, who already find it difficult enough to keep themselves free from the pauper taint;"[12] so in all cases, the policy is one which intensifies the pains of those most deserving of pity, that the pains of those least deserving of pity may be mitigated. Men who are so sympathetic that they cannot let the struggle for existence bring on the unworthy the sufferings consequent on their incapacity or misconduct, are so unsympathetic that they can, deliberately, make the struggle for existence harder for the worthy, and inflict on them and their children artificial evils in addition to the natural evils they have to bear!

And here we are brought round to our original topic — the sins of legislators. Here there comes clearly before us the commonest of the transgressions which rulers commit — a transgression so common, and so sanctified by custom, that no one imagines it to be a transgression. Here we see that, as indicated at the outset, Government, begotten of aggression and by aggression, ever continues to betray its original nature by its aggressiveness; and that even what on its nearer face seems beneficence only, shows, on its remoter face, not a little maleficence — kindness at the cost of cruelty. For is it not cruel to increase the sufferings of the better that the sufferings of the worse may be decreased? 18

It is, indeed, marvellous how readily we let ourselves be deceived by words and phrases which suggest one aspect of the facts while leaving the opposite aspect unsuggested. A good illustration of this, and one germane to the immediate question, is seen in the use of the words "protection" and "protectionist"[13] by the antagonists of free-trade,[14] and in the tacit admission of its propriety by free-traders. While the one party has habitually ignored, the other party has habitually failed to emphasize, the truth that 19

---

[11]*Poor Law:* A body of laws developed in 16th century England to provide assistance to the poor; the Poor Law was maintained, with various changes, until after World War II. The New Poor Law of 1834 provided no aid for the able-bodied poor, who were thus forced to spend their lives in the workhouses.

[12]Mr. J. Chamberlain in *Fortnightly Review,* December 1883, p. 772. [Spencer] Joseph Chamberlain was a British businessman and social reformer who advocated a graduated income tax, improved housing for the poor, and free education.

[13]*protectionist:* One who advocates the protection of domestic industries from foreign competition by such means as the imposition of duties on imports.

[14]*free-trade:* International trade carried on without governmental restrictions such as protective tariffs.

this so-called protection always involves aggression; and that the name aggressionist ought to be substituted for the name protectionist. For nothing can be more certain than that if, to maintain A's profit, B is forbidden to buy of C, or is fined to the extent of the duty if he buys of C, then B is aggressed upon that A may be "protected." Nay, "aggressionists" is a title doubly more applicable to the anti-free-traders than is the euphemistic title "protectionists;" since, that one producer may gain, ten consumers are fleeced.

Now just the like confusion of ideas, caused by looking at one face only of the transaction, may be traced throughout all the legislation which forcibly takes the property of this man for the purpose of giving gratis benefits to that man. Habitually when one of the numerous measures thus characterized is discussed, the dominant thought is concerning the pitiable Jones who is to be protected against some evil; while no thought is given to the hard-working Brown who is aggressed upon, often much more to be pitied. Money is exacted (either directly or through raised rent) from the huckster who only by extreme pinching can pay her way, from the mason thrown out of work by a strike, from the mechanic whose savings are melting away during an illness, from the widow who washes or sews from dawn to dark to feed her fatherless little ones; and all that the dissolute may be saved from hunger, that the children of less impoverished neighbours may have cheap lessons, and that various people, mostly better off, may read newspapers and novels for nothing! The error of nomenclature is, in one respect, more misleading than that which allows aggressionists to be called protectionists; for, as just shown, protection of the vicious poor involves aggression on the virtuous poor. Doubtless it is true that the greater part of the money exacted comes from those who are relatively well-off. But this is no consolation to the ill-off from whom the rest is exacted. Nay, if the comparison be made between the pressures borne by the two classes respectively, it becomes manifest that the case is even worse than at first appears; for while to the well-off the exaction means loss of luxuries, to the ill-off it means loss of necessaries.

And now see the Nemesis[15] which is threatening to follow this chronic sin of legislators. They and their class, in common with all owners of property, are in danger of suffering from a sweeping application of that general principle practically asserted by each of these confiscating Acts of Parliament. For what is the tacit assumption on which such Acts proceed? It is the assumption that no man has any claim to his property, not even to that which he has earned by the sweat of his brow, save by permission of the community; and that the community may cancel the claim to any extent it

---

[15]*Nemesis:* Vengeance.

thinks fit. No defence can be made for this appropriation of A's possessions for the benefit of B, save one which sets out with the postulate that society as a whole has an absolute right over the possessions of each member. And now this doctrine, which has been tacitly assumed, is being openly proclaimed. Mr. George[16] and his friends, Mr. Hyndman[17] and his supporters, are pushing the theory to its logical issue. They have been instructed by examples, yearly increasing in number, that the individual has no rights but what the community may equitably over-ride; and they are now saying — "It shall go hard but we will better the instruction," and abolish individual rights altogether.

---

[16]*Mr. George:* Henry George (1839–1897), British land reformer and economist who proposed that the state tax only the income from the use of bare land and abolish all other taxes. George's argument for this radical proposal was that the income from this single tax would be so large that it would easily pay for public works.

[17]*Mr. Hyndman:* Henry Hyndman was one of the first important British Marxists who in 1881 helped to found the Democratic Federation. His work *England for All* was the first socialist book published in England since the 1830s.

REVIEW QUESTIONS

1. In what ways is the assistance given to the very young different from the assistance given to the mature? What, in each case, is the relationship between benefits and merits? Why would the intrusion of the type of aid rendered inside the family group be socially destructive if rendered outside this group?
2. What kind of aid to the disadvantaged would Spencer allow? What kind of restrictions would he place on such aid?
3. In what places do you find explicit references to Darwin's theories? In what places do you find implicit references?
4. At what point does Spencer most explicitly acknowledge the position of those opposed to his *laissez-faire* views? In what ways does he charge them with hypocrisy? In what ways does he charge them with aggravating, rather than alleviating, the situation?
5. What are the "sins of the legislators"? How does the idea of free trade tie in with the ideas expressed earlier in this essay?

DISCUSSION AND WRITING QUESTIONS

1. In paragraphs 4 and 5 Spencer asserts that a "society of men . . . will be unable to hold its own in the struggle with other societies, if it disadvantages its superior units that it may advantage its inferior units." Write an essay supporting or refuting this position, using modern examples in such areas as social welfare, social services, and business.

2. Discuss the proposition that the "intrusion of family-ethics into the ethics of the State" is pervasive in modern American society. (You may wish to focus upon some other nation.)

3. In paragraphs 9 through 12, Spencer asserts that the struggle for existence is a purifying process, one that leads toward the ever-greater perfection of the species and the individual. He also asserts that the misery inevitably entailed in this process cannot and should not be alleviated; it must be borne, in the hopes and expectations of achieving a higher order of civilization. Charity, in fact, can be socially harmful, even destructive. Do you agree with these ideas? If not, why not? Cite examples to support your views.

4. To what extent does Spencer in this essay show himself to be unsympathetic toward the poor? What distinction does he make between the "vicious poor" and the "virtuous poor"? Is this a valid distinction? If not, what distinctions might be valid? What comparable distinctions are made by social thinkers in our own time?

5. To what extent does (or should) the community have a right to tax property when that tax is to be used for *social*, as opposed to defense purposes? That is (to use Spencer's terms), to what extent does a man have a right to his own property? To what extent should A be taxed to support B? To what extent is the imposition of such a tax a violation of A's individual rights?

   If you have read Part III, on the Social Contract, you may wish to review some of the ideas discussed there in considering your response to this assignment. Consider especially the question of why people enter into social contracts — what they expect to get and what they agree to give up.

ANDREW CARNEGIE *(1835–1919)*

The embodiment of the Horatio Alger rags-to-riches hero, Andrew Carnegie was both a fabulously successful industrialist and an unusually generous philanthropist. Carnegie's life is a study in the survival of the fittest in the business world. Yet he tempered his Darwinian outlook in this sphere with a sense of social responsibility toward those less fortunate than he. Like the other social Darwinists, Carnegie rejected indiscriminate charity to individuals as wasteful and even socially harmful. But like Spencer, he distinguished between the "worthy" poor and the "unworthy" poor; and, going far beyond Spencer and other laissez-faire individualists, he considered it the duty of rich men like himself to use their wealth to enable their worthy "inferiors" to better themselves. Thus, he modified the Darwinian ethic: while accepting — even reveling in — the challenges of the struggle for existence, he did not believe that those temporarily unable to survive the struggle should be abandoned, left without the resources to improve their condition.

Carnegie was born in Dunfermline, Scotland, in 1835, the son of a handloom weaver. With the development of the power loom and the depression of 1848, the Carnegie family emigrated to the United States, settling in the Pittsburgh area. (As an adult, Carnegie was to return frequently to Scotland, and in 1903 he established a trust for the benefit of his home town.) For a couple of years, young Carnegie worked as a laborer and as a clerk, and he studied bookkeeping in night school. He began his rise to wealth and power in 1850 when he took a job as messenger boy in the Pittsburgh telegraph office. Through drive and determination, Carnegie rose through the ranks, impressing Thomas A. Scott, the division superintendent of the Pennsylvania Railroad (later to become of one Carnegie's investment partners). Scott hired Carnegie as his clerk and telegraph operator, and by 1859 Carnegie had become superintendent of the Pittsburgh division of the railroad. During the Civil War Carnegie organized military transportation and telegraph services.

Following the war, Carnegie began a series of highly profitable investments in various industrial enterprises. He resigned from the Pennsylvania Railroad in 1865 to devote himself to the iron industry. Starting with the Keystone Bridge Company, he began acquiring both iron and steel plants. He developed a reputation as an aggressive, even unscrupulous business competitor, intent on breaking production records and lowering production costs, but selling a high-quality product. Seeking to control all aspects of iron- and steel-making, Carnegie's firm acquired ore fields, railroads, and steamers, as well as factories and mills. The firm prospered, despite a national financial panic in 1873 and a depression in 1892, during which a bloody strike occurred at the Carnegie-owned Homestead steel mill. By 1890, Carnegie's industrial empire had helped make the United States the world's foremost steel-producing nation.

Carnegie retired from business in 1901 when he sold the Carnegie Steel Company to industrialist J. P. Morgan for $250 million. (The firm then became incorporated into the newly formed United States Steel Corporation.) He was now faced with the question of what to do with his vast wealth. Since 1867 he had been living in New York and had associated himself with men of letters as well as businessmen. He had himself turned to writing, and was to compose in his lifetime numerous articles and several books, including *Triumphant Democracy, The Gospel of Wealth, The Empire of Business* (1902), and his *Autobiography* (1920). From his earliest days, Carnegie had been imbued with a sense of social responsibility, disdaining the European aristocratic tradition of inherited wealth and privilege. He began disposing of his money in ways that could indirectly help others to improve their conditions through their own efforts. Soon after his retirement, he had established a pension fund for his former employees. Now he began endowing thousands of free public libraries in the United States. Over the next decade he established the Carnegie Institute of Technology of Carnegie-Mellon University in Pittsburgh, the Carnegie Trust for the Universities of Scotland, the Carnegie Institute in Washington, D.C., and the Carnegie Endowment for International Peace. He also gave numerous grants and gifts to other educational institutions, to churches, and to medical and other research. His funds helped build the Peace Palace at The Hague.

Carnegie, then, represents Darwinism with a conscience. Modern eyes (certainly Marxist eyes) are likely to view Carnegie as, at worst, a ruthless exploiter of wage laborers; at best, a paternalistic despot, a benevolent representative of a rotten economic system. Yet it is undeniable that Carnegie succeeded in his intention of promoting social welfare: civilization is the better for his efforts, both in business and in philanthropy. Would it have been better for Carnegie's wealth never to have been accumulated? Or, if accumulated, should it have been divided up and distributed to the poor? Or confiscated by a communist government and used as the government saw fit? But perhaps such questions are best left to group discussion.

The following essay first appeared in the June 1889 issue of *North American Review.*

WEALTH

The problem of our age is the proper administration of wealth, so that the ties of brotherhood may still bind together the rich and poor in harmonious relationship. The conditions of human life have not only been changed, but revolutionized, within the past few hundred years. In former days there was little difference between the dwelling, dress, food, and environment of the chief and those of his retainers. The Indians are to-day
1

Andrew Carnegie. "Wealth" [1889]. *North American Review,* No. 391 (June 1889). 652–64.

where civilized man then was. When visiting the Sioux,[1] I was led to the wigwam of the chief. It was just like the others in external appearance, and even within the difference was trifling between it and those of the poorest of his braves. The contrast between the palace of the millionaire and the cottage of the laborer with us to-day measures the change which has come with civilization.

This change, however, is not to be deplored, but welcomed as highly   2 beneficial. It is well, nay, essential for the progress of the race, that the houses of some should be homes for all that is highest and best in literature and the arts, and for all the refinements of civilization, rather than that none should be so. Much better this great irregularity than universal squalor. Without wealth there can be no Mæcenas.[2] The "good old times" were not good old times. Neither master nor servant was as well situated then as to-day. A relapse to old conditions would be disastrous to both — not the least so to him who serves — and would sweep away civilization with it. But whether the change be for good or ill, it is upon us, beyond our power to alter, and therefore to be accepted and made the best of. It is a waste of time to criticise the inevitable.

It is easy to see how the change has come. One illustration will serve   3 for almost every phase of the cause. In the manufacture of products we have the whole story. It applies to all combinations of human industry, as stimulated and enlarged by the inventions of this scientific age. Formerly articles were manufactured at the domestic hearth or in small shops which formed part of the household. The master and his apprentices worked side by side, the latter living with the master, and therefore subject to the same conditions. When these apprentices rose to be masters, there was little or no change in their mode of life, and they, in turn, educated in the same routine succeeding apprentices. There was, substantially, social equality, and even political equality, for those engaged in industrial pursuits had then little or no political voice in the State.

But the inevitable result of such a mode of manufacture was crude   4 articles at high prices. To-day the world obtains commodities of excellent quality at prices which even the generation preceding this would have deemed incredible. In the commercial world similar causes have produced similar results, and the race is benefited thereby. The poor enjoy what the

---

[1]*the Sioux:* The Sioux, also called the Dakota, were a North American Plains Indian people whose most famous chiefs, Sitting Bull and Crazy Horse, resisted attempts by the government to have their people placed on reservations in the late 1800s when miners found gold in the Black Hills of South Dakota.

[2]*Mæcenas:* Maecenas was a wealthy Roman statesman and the patron of the famous poets of antiquity, Virgil and Horace; used colloquially, Maecenas refers to any wealthy and generous patron.

rich could not before afford. What were the luxuries have become the necessaries of life. The laborer has now more comforts than the farmer had a
few generations ago. The farmer has more luxuries than the landlord had,
and is more richly clad and better housed. The landlord has books and
pictures rarer, and appointments more artistic, than the King could then
obtain.

The price we pay for this salutary change is, no doubt, great. We as- 5
semble thousands of operatives in the factory, in the mine, and in the
counting-house, of whom the employer can know little or nothing, and to
whom the employer is little better than a myth. All intercourse between
them is at an end. Rigid Castes are formed, and, as usual, mutual ignorance breeds mutual distrust. Each Caste is without sympathy for the
other, and ready to credit anything disparaging in regard to it. Under the
law of competition, the employer of thousands is forced into the strictest
economies, among which the rates paid to labor figure prominently, and
often there is friction between the employer and the employed, between capital and labor, between rich and poor. Human society loses
homogeneity.

The price which society pays for the law of competition, like the price 6
it pays for cheap comforts and luxuries, is also great; but the advantages
of this law are also greater still, for it is to this law that we owe our wonderful material development, which brings improved conditions in its
train. But, whether the law be benign or not, we must say of it, as we say
of the change in the conditions of men to which we have referred: It is
here; we cannot evade it; no substitutes for it have been found; and while
the law may be sometimes hard for the individual, it is best for the race,
because it insures the survival of the fittest in every department. We accept
and welcome, therefore, as conditions to which we must accommodate
ourselves, great inequality of environment, the concentration of business,
industrial and commercial, in the hands of a few, and the law of competition between these, as being not only beneficial, but essential for the future
progress of the race. Having accepted these, it follows that there must be
great scope for the exercise of special ability in the merchant and in the
manufacturer who has to conduct affairs upon a great scale. That this talent
for organization and management is rare among men is proved by the fact
that it invariably secures for its possessor enormous rewards, no matter
where or under what laws or conditions. The experienced in affairs always
rate the MAN whose services can be obtained as a partner as not only the
first consideration, but such as to render the question of his capital scarcely
worth considering, for such men soon create capital; while, without the
special talent required, capital soon takes wings. Such men become interested in firms or corporations using millions; and estimating only simple
interest to be made upon the capital invested, it is inevitable that their
income must exceed their expenditures, and that they must accumulate

wealth. Nor is there any middle ground which such men can occupy, because the great manufacturing or commercial concern which does not earn at least interest upon its capital soon becomes bankrupt. It must either go forward or fall behind: to stand still is impossible. It is a condition essential for its successful operation that it should be thus far profitable, and even that, in addition to interest on capital, it should make profit. It is a law, as certain as any of the others named, that men possessed of this peculiar talent for affairs, under the free play of economic forces, must, of necessity, soon be in receipt of more revenue than can be judiciously expended upon themselves; and this law is as beneficial for the race as the others.

Objections to the foundations upon which society is based are not in   7 order, because the condition of the race is better with these than it has been with any others which have been tried. Of the effect of any new substitutes proposed we cannot be sure. The Socialist or Anarchist[3] who seeks to overturn present conditions is to be regarded as attacking the foundation upon which civilization itself rests, for civilization took its start from the day that the capable, industrious workman said to his incompetent and lazy fellow, "If thou dost not sow, thou shalt not reap," and thus ended primitive Communism by separating the drones from the bees. One who studies this subject will soon be brought face to face with the conclusion that upon the sacredness of property civilization itself depends — the right of the laborer to his hundred dollars in the savings bank, and equally the legal right of the millionaire to his millions. To those who propose to substitute Communism for this intense Individualism the answer, therefore, is: The race has tried that. All progress from that barbarous day to the present time has resulted from its displacement. Not evil, but good, has come to the race from the accumulation of wealth by those who have the ability and energy that produce it. But even if we admit for a moment that it might be better for the race to discard its present foundation, Individualism — that it is a nobler ideal that man should labor, not for himself alone, but in and for a brotherhood of his fellows, and share with them all in common, Swedenborg's idea of Heaven,[4] where, as he says, the angels derive their

---

[3]*Anarchist:* In general, anarchists believe that all forms of governments and institutions are harmful to humanity and that people can live in peace without government. Carnegie's time was fraught with violence by radical anarchists who assassinated many world leaders, including President McKinley in 1901.

[4]*Swedenborg's idea of Heaven:* Emanuel Swedenborg (1688–1772), a Swedish scientist, philosopher, and Christian mystic, devoted many years to studying and interpreting the Bible. He envisioned Heaven as a spirit world composed of innumerable angelic societies. According to Swedenborg, after the death of the body, the soul chooses the society of angels to which it would like to belong, in much the same way that a person chooses a social club.

happiness, not from laboring for self, but for each other — even admit all this, and a sufficient answer is, This is not evolution, but revolution. It necessitates the changing of human nature itself — a work of æons, even if it were good to change it, which we cannot know. It is not practicable in our day or in our age. Even if desirable theoretically, it belongs to another and long-succeeding sociological stratum. Our duty is with what is practicable now; with the next step possible in our day and generation. It is criminal to waste our energies in endeavoring to uproot, when all we can profitably or possibly accomplish is to bend the universal tree of humanity a little in the direction most favorable to the production of good fruit under existing circumstances. We might as well urge the destruction of the highest existing type of man because he failed to reach our ideal as to favor the destruction of Individualism, Private Property, the Law of Accumulation of Wealth, and the Law of Competition; for these are the highest results of human experience, the soil in which society so far has produced the best fruit. Unequally or unjustly, perhaps, as these laws sometimes operate, and imperfect as they appear to the Idealist, they are, nevertheless, like the highest type of man, the best and most valuable of all that humanity has yet accomplished.

We start, then, with a condition of affairs under which the best interests of the race are promoted, but which inevitably gives wealth to the few. Thus far, accepting conditions as they exist, the situation can be surveyed and pronounced good. The question then arises, — and, if the foregoing be correct, it is the only question with which we have to deal, — What is the proper mode of administering wealth after the laws upon which civilization is founded have thrown it into the hands of the few? And it is of this great question that I believe I offer the true solution. It will be understood that *fortunes* are here spoken of, not moderate sums saved by many years of effort, the returns from which are required for the comfortable maintenance and education of families. This is not *wealth*, but only *competence*, which it should be the aim of all to acquire. 8

There are but three modes in which surplus wealth can be disposed of. It can be left to the families of the decedents; or it can be bequeathed for public purposes; or, finally, it can be administered during their lives by its possessors. Under the first and second modes most of the wealth of the world that has reached the few has hitherto been applied. Let us in turn consider each of these modes. The first is the most injudicious. In monarchical countries, the estates and the greatest portion of the wealth are left to the first son, that the vanity of the parent may be gratified by the thought that his name and title are to descend to succeeding generations unimpaired. The condition of this class in Europe to-day teaches the futility of such hopes or ambitions. The successors have become impoverished through their follies or from the fall in the value of land. Even in Great 9

Britain the strict law of entail[5] has been found inadequate to maintain the status of an hereditary class. Its soil is rapidly passing into the hands of the stranger. Under republican institutions the division of property among the children is much fairer, but the question which forces itself upon thoughtful men in all lands is: Why should men leave great fortunes to their children? If this is done from affection, is it not misguided affection? Observation teaches that, generally speaking, it is not well for the children that they should be so burdened. Neither is it well for the state. Beyond providing for the wife and daughters moderate sources of income, and very moderate allowances indeed, if any, for the sons, men may well hesitate, for it is no longer questionable that great sums bequeathed oftener work more for the injury than for the good of the recipients. Wise men will soon conclude that, for the best interests of the members of their families and of the state, such bequests are an improper use of their means.

It is not suggested that men who have failed to educate their sons to   *10* earn a livelihood shall cast them adrift in poverty. If any man has seen fit to rear his sons with a view to their living idle lives, or, what is highly commendable, has instilled in them the sentiment that they are in a position to labor for public ends without reference to pecuniary considerations, then, of course, the duty of the parent is to see that such are provided for *in moderation*. There are instances of millionaires' sons unspoiled by wealth, who, being rich, still perform great services in the community. Such are the very salt of the earth, as valuable as, unfortunately, they are rare; still it is not the exception, but the rule, that men must regard, and, looking at the usual result of enormous sums conferred upon legatees, the thoughtful man must shortly say, "I would as soon leave to my son a curse as the almighty dollar," and admit to himself that it is not the welfare of the children, but family pride, which inspires these enormous legacies.

As to the second mode, that of leaving wealth at death for public uses,   *11* it may be said that this is only a means for the disposal of wealth, provided a man is content to wait until he is dead before it becomes of much good in the world. Knowledge of the results of legacies bequeathed is not calculated to inspire the brightest hopes of much posthumous good being accomplished. The cases are not few in which the real object sought by the

---

[5]*the strict law of entail:* Carnegie is referring here to the English law developed under the feudal system which provided that land be automatically inherited by the original grantee's direct descendants and that if the grantee died without direct descendants, the land would automatically revert to the grantor. The law served to protect the landed aristocracy by preventing the dissolution of estates. There were entailed estates in the American colonies as well; however, most states abolished the entail after Thomas Jefferson abolished them in 1776.

testator[6] is not attained, nor are they few in which his real wishes are thwarted. In many cases the bequests are so used as to become only monuments of his folly. It is well to remember that it requires the exercise of not less ability than that which acquired the wealth to use it so as to be really beneficial to the community. Besides this, it may fairly be said that no man is to be extolled for doing what he cannot help doing, nor is he to be thanked by the community to which he only leaves wealth at death. Men who leave vast sums in this way may fairly be thought men who would not have left it at all, had they been able to take it with them. The memories of such cannot be held in grateful remembrance, for there is no grace in their gifts. It is not to be wondered at that such bequests seem so generally to lack the blessing.

The growing disposition to tax more and more heavily large estates left   12 at death is a cheering indication of the growth of a salutary change in public opinion. The State of Pennsylvania now takes — subject to some exceptions — one-tenth of the property left by its citizens. The budget presented in the British Parliament the other day proposes to increase the death-duties; and, most significant of all, the new tax is to be a graduated one. Of all forms of taxation, this seems the wisest. Men who continue hoarding great sums all their lives, the proper use of which for public ends would work to the community, should be made to feel that the community, in the form of the state, cannot thus be deprived of its proper share. By taxing estates heavily at death the state marks its condemnation of the selfish millionaire's unworthy life.

It is desirable that nations should go much further in this direction.   13 Indeed, it is difficult to set bounds to the share of a rich man's estate which should go at his death to the public through the agency of the state, and by all means such taxes should be graduated, beginning at nothing upon moderate sums to dependents, and increasing rapidly as the amounts swell, until of the millionaire's hoard, as of Shylock's, at least

> "—— The other half
> Comes to the privy coffer of the state."[7]

This policy would work powerfully to induce the rich man to attend to the administration of wealth during his life, which is the end that society

---

[6]*testator:* A person who has died leaving a will.

[7]*the new tax is to be a graduated one . . . "the other half comes to the privy coffer of the state.":* Carnegie, obviously well-versed in Shakespeare, here uses part of Act 4, Scene 1 (lines 747–749) from the *Merchant of Venice* to emphasize his point about the fairness of a graduated tax, a form of taxation based on one's ability to pay. Thus, the heavy taxation of large estates through the death tax would reduce the inequalities in the distribution of wealth.

should always have in view, as being that by far most fruitful for the people. Nor need it be feared that this policy would sap the root of enterprise and render men less anxious to accumulate, for to the class whose ambition it is to leave great fortunes and be talked about after their death, it will attract even more attention, and, indeed, be a somewhat nobler ambition to have enormous sums paid over to the state from their fortunes.

There remains, then, only one mode of using great fortunes; but in   14 this we have the true antidote for the temporary unequal distribution of wealth, the reconciliation of the rich and the poor — a reign of harmony — another ideal, differing, indeed, from that of the Communist in requiring only the further evolution of existing conditions, not the total overthrow of our civilization. It is founded upon the present most intense individualism, and the race is prepared to put it in practice by degrees whenever it pleases. Under its sway we shall have an ideal state, in which the surplus wealth of the few will become, in the best sense, the property of the many, because administered for the common good, and this wealth, passing through the hands of the few, can be made a much more potent force for the elevation of our race than if it had been distributed in small sums to the people themselves. Even the poorest can be made to see this, and to agree that great sums gathered by some of their fellow-citizens and spent for public purposes, from which the masses reap the principal benefit, are more valuable to them than if scattered among them through the course of many years in trifling amounts.

If we consider what results flow from the Cooper Institute, for in-   15 stance, to the best portion of the race in New York not possessed of means, and compare these with those which would have arisen for the good of the masses from an equal sum distributed by Mr. Cooper[8] in his lifetime in the form of wages, which is the highest form of distribution, being for work done and not for charity, we can form some estimate of the possibilities for the improvement of the race which lie embedded in the present law of the accumulation of wealth. Much of this sum, if distributed in small quantities among the people, would have been wasted in the indulgence of appetite, some of it in excess, and it may be doubted whether even the part put to the best use, that of adding to the comforts of the home, would have yielded results for the race, as a race, at all comparable to those which are flowing and are to flow from the Cooper Institute from generation to generation. Let the advocate of violent or radical change ponder well this thought.

---

[8]*Mr. Cooper:* Peter Cooper (1791–1883), the American manufacturer and philanthropist who is best known for his invention of the "Tom Thumb" locomotive and for his founding in 1859 of the Cooper Union for the Advancement of Science and Art in New York City.

We might even go so far as to take another instance, that of Mr. Til- 16
den's bequest[9] of five millions of dollars for a free library in the city of New
York, but in referring to this one cannot help saying involuntarily, How
much better if Mr. Tilden had devoted the last years of his own life to the
proper administration of this immense sum; in which case neither legal
contest nor any other cause of delay could have interfered with his aims.
But let us assume that Mr. Tilden's millions finally become the means of
giving to this city a noble public library, where the treasures of the world
contained in books will be open to all forever, without money and without
price. Considering the good of that part of the race which congregates in
and around Manhattan Island, would its permanent benefit have been better promoted had these millions been allowed to circulate in small sums
through the hands of the masses? Even the most strenuous advocate of
Communism must entertain a doubt upon this subject. Most of those who
think will probably entertain no doubt whatever.

Poor and restricted are our opportunities in this life; narrow our hori- 17
zon; our best work most imperfect; but rich men should be thankful for
one inestimable boon. They have it in their power during their lives to busy
themselves in organizing benefactions from which the masses of their fellows will derive lasting advantage, and thus dignify their own lives. The
highest life is probably to be reached, not by such imitation of the life of
Christ as Count Tolstoï[10] gives us, but, while animated by Christ's spirit,
by recognizing the changed conditions of this age, and adopting modes of
expressing this spirit suitable to the changed conditions under which we
live; still laboring for the good of our fellows, which was the essence of his
life and teaching, but laboring in a different manner.

This, then, is held to be the duty of the man of Wealth: First, to set an 18
example of modest, unostentatious living, shunning display or extravagance; to provide moderately for the legitimate wants of those dependent
upon him; and after doing so to consider all surplus revenues which come
to him simply as trust funds, which he is called upon to administer, and
strictly bound as a matter of duty to administer in the manner which, in
his judgment, is best calculated to produce the most beneficial results for
the community — the man of wealth thus becoming the mere agent and

---

[9]*Mr. Tilden's bequest:* Samuel Tilden (1814–1886) was a lawyer and governor of New York
who was widely respected for his efficient administration and for exposing corrupt fellow
politicians and businessmen. Shrewd investments brought him great wealth, the bulk of
which he left in trust for the establishment of a free public library for New York City.

[10]*Count Tolstoï:* Leo Tolstoy (1828–1910), the author of such classics as *War and Peace* and
Anna Karenina, is considered one of the world's greatest novelists. In his later years, he
endured a spiritual crisis that prompted him to turn to a form of Christian anarchism and
devote his life to social reform. He attempted to live like Christ, as a kind of wandering
ascetic, despite his background as a son of a Russian noble family and his fame as a writer.

trustee for his poorer brethren, bringing to their service his superior wisdom, experience, and ability to administer, doing for them better than they would or could do for themselves.

We are met here with the difficulty of determining what are moderate 19 sums to leave to members of the family; what is modest, unostentatious living; what is the test of extravagance. There must be different standards for different conditions. The answer is that it is as impossible to name exact amounts or actions as it is to define good manners, good taste, or the rules of propriety; but, nevertheless, these are verities, well known although undefinable. Public sentiment is quick to know and to feel what offends these. So in the case of wealth. The rule in regard to good taste in the dress of men or women applies here. Whatever makes one conspicuous offends the canon. If any family be chiefly known for display, for extravagance in home, table, equipage, for enormous sums ostentatiously spent in any form upon itself, — if these be its chief distinctions, we have no difficulty in estimating its nature or culture. So likewise in regard to the use or abuse of its surplus wealth, or to generous, free-handed coöperation in good public uses, or to unabated efforts to accumulate and hoard to the last, whether they administer or bequeath. The verdict rests with the best and most enlightened public sentiment. The community will surely judge, and its judgments will not often be wrong.

The best uses to which surplus wealth can be put have already been 20 indicated. Those who would administer wisely must, indeed, be wise, for one of the serious obstacles to the improvement of our race is indiscriminate charity. It were better for mankind that the millions of the rich were thrown into the sea than so spent as to encourage the slothful, the drunken, the unworthy. Of every thousand dollars spent in so called charity to-day, it is probable that $950 is unwisely spent; so spent, indeed, as to produce the very evils which it proposes to mitigate or cure. A well-known writer of philosophic books admitted the other day that he had given a quarter of a dollar to a man who approached him as he was coming to visit the house of his friend. He knew nothing of the habits of this beggar; knew not the use that would be made of this money, although he had every reason to suspect that it would be spent improperly. This man professed to be a disciple of Herbert Spencer; yet the quarter-dollar given that night will probably work more injury than all the money which its thoughtless donor will ever be able to give in true charity will do good. He only gratified his own feelings, saved himself from annoyance, — and this was probably one of the most selfish and very worst actions of his life, for in all respects he is most worthy.

In bestowing charity, the main consideration should be to help those 21 who will help themselves; to provide part of the means by which those who desire to improve may do so; to give those who desire to rise the aids by which they may rise; to assist, but rarely or never to do all. Neither the individual nor the race is improved by alms-giving. Those worthy of assistance, except in rare cases, seldom require assistance. The really valuable men of the race never do, except in cases of accident or sudden change. Every one has, of course, cases of individuals brought to his own knowledge where temporary assistance can do genuine good, and these he will not overlook. But the amount which can be wisely given by the individual for individuals is necessarily limited by his lack of knowledge of the circumstances connected with each. He is the only true reformer who is as careful and as anxious not to aid the unworthy as he is to aid the worthy, and, perhaps, even more so, for in alms-giving more injury is probably done by rewarding vice than by relieving virtue.

The rich man is thus almost restricted to following the examples of   22
Peter Cooper, Enoch Pratt of Baltimore, Mr. Pratt of Brooklyn, Senator Stanford,[11] and others, who know that the best means of benefiting the community is to place within its reach the ladders upon which the aspiring can rise — parks, and means of recreation, by which men are helped in body and mind; works of art, certain to give pleasure and improve the public taste, and public institutions of various kinds, which will improve the general condition of the people; — in this manner returning their surplus wealth to the mass of their fellows in the forms best calculated to do them lasting good.

Thus is the problem of Rich and Poor to be solved. The laws of accu-   23
mulation will be left free; the laws of distribution free. Individualism will continue, but the millionaire will be but a trustee for the poor; intrusted for a season with a great part of the increased wealth of the community, but administering it for the community far better than it could or would have done for itself. The best minds will thus have reached a stage in the development of the race in which it is clearly seen that there is no mode of disposing of surplus wealth creditable to thoughtful and earnest men into whose hands it flows save by using it year by year for the general good. This day already dawns. But a little while, and although, without incurring the pity of their fellows, men may die sharers in great business enterprises

---

[11]*Enoch Pratt of Baltimore, Mr. Pratt of Brooklyn, Senator Stanford:* These men were wealthy American businessmen who used part of their wealth for the establishment of libraries and schools. Enoch Pratt (1808–1896), who made his fortune in, among other enterprises, metal and banking, established the Enoch Pratt Free Library in Baltimore in 1886 and founded the House of Reformation and Instruction for Colored Children and the Maryland School for the Deaf and Dumb. Oil magnate Charles Pratt (1830–1891) founded Pratt Institute in Brooklyn for training artisans and draftsmen and established the Pratt Institute Free Library, the first free public library in Brooklyn. Leland Stanford (1824–1893), who helped finance and administer railroads, was also involved in politics, having been governor of California from 1861–1863 and then a U.S. Senator from 1885 to 1893. In 1885 he founded Leland Stanford Junior University, now known as Stanford University.

from which their capital cannot be or has not been withdrawn, and is left chiefly at death for public uses, yet the man who dies leaving behind him millions of available wealth, which was his to administer during life, will pass away "unwept, unhonored, and unsung," no matter to what uses he leaves the dross which he cannot take with him. Of such as these the public verdict will then be: "The man who dies thus rich dies disgraced."

Such, in my opinion, is the true Gospel concerning Wealth, obedience to which is destined some day to solve the problem of the Rich and the Poor, and to bring "Peace on earth, among men Good-Will." 24

REVIEW QUESTIONS

1. In what way does the modern world differ from the world of a few centuries ago? In what way is this change beneficial? What justification can be offered for great wealth concentrated in the hands of a few?
2. What are the benefits for social relations of new methods of manufacture? For standards of living? What are the costs of these new methods?
3. In what way does Carnegie equate the success or failure of businesses (and the men who run them) with natural law? In what context does he directly refer to Darwin's ideas?
4. What arguments does Carnegie use to dismiss objections to the law of competition upon which industrial civilization is founded? Specifically, how does he defend "Individualism" from "Communism"?
5. In what three chief ways can the industrial wealth amassed by individuals be disposed of? What are Carnegie's objections to the first two ways? How does he justify and support the third way?
6. How should the man of wealth set an example? In what respect should he consider his wealth? How will the community judge this man?
7. Why is most charity wasted, according to Carnegie? What should be the chief consideration in the bestowing of charity?

DISCUSSION AND WRITING QUESTIONS

1. Comment and expand upon Carnegie's assessment of the advantages and disadvantages of work and manufacture in the modern age with work and manufacture centuries earlier. Focus on the quality of life in both cases, both as you have read about it and how you have experienced it.
2. Read *The Communist Manifesto* by Marx and Engels (pp. 554–574). How do you think Marx and Engels would respond to the arguments in favor of Individualism and against Communism that Carnegie makes in paragraphs 6 and 7 of "Wealth"? *Alternate assignment:* Compose a dialogue between Carnegie and Marx in which these issues are debated.
3. Compare Carnegie's implied view of human nature with Max Eastman's view, as reflected in his essay "Socialism and Human Nature," reprinted in Part VI on The Class Struggle.

4. According to Carnegie, the future progress and the best interests of the human race are dependent upon the kind of industrial development that he represents. Support or refute this position, using specific historical evidence. Be sure that you define terms like "progress" and "best interests." Consider also the contrary argument or important historical examples that do *not* support your case, and show why these arguments or examples do not constitute valid or persuasive evidence against your own position.

5. In what way would men like Sumner and Spencer be likely to disagree with Carnegie regarding the disposition of inherited wealth? In other respects, compare and contrast the attitudes of Sumner, Spencer, and Carnegie.

6. Carnegie postulates that if Cooper's wealth had been divided up as wages and given to his workers, the greater part of this wealth "would have been wasted in the indulgence of appetite, some of it in excess, and it may be doubted whether even the part put to the best use, that of adding to the comforts of home, would have yielded results for the race . . . at all comparable to those which are flowing and are to flow from the Cooper Institute from generation to generation." Comment upon this statement. Apply it, if you like, to modern life: would the fortune amassed by a modern industrialist-turned-philanthropist be better spent to support a public educational, medical, or artistic foundation than divided up as bonuses to employees who might waste it "in the indulgence of appetite"? Consider both the underlying assumptions about people (or about some people), based on what they do with small sums of money, and the question of whether wealth does more good in a few large amounts or in a great many small amounts.

7. Comment upon Carnegie's references to Christ in paragraph 17. What are the "changed conditions of this age" which render conventional Christian charity outmoded?

8. Carnegie distinguishes between conventional charity and his own kind of philanthropy. Discuss the significance of this difference. To what extent do you think such distinctions should be made when people give their money away?

9. In the final pages of his essay, Carnegie argues that private individuals (like himself) who have amassed industrial fortunes are best suited to judge the ways in which surplus wealth can be disposed of, better suited to administering this wealth for the community "than it could or would have done for itself." This, of course, is a highly paternalistic (many would say insulting) attitude, implying a certain contempt for the abilities of individuals to determine (and to spend money in) their own best interests. But if you don't believe that men like Carnegie have "superior wisdom, experience, and ability to administer" than their "poorer brethren," then who does? The government? Representatives of these "poorer brethren"? If representatives, how would they be chosen? How would they resolve disputes? Write an essay on the proper administration of surplus industrial wealth, taking some of these questions into consideration.

SAMUEL BUTLER *(1835–1902)*

Darwinian thought was so pervasive during the later 19th century, it is not surprising that it widely influenced writers of imaginative literature. Critics have traced evolutionary themes in several Victorian poets, including Alfred Lord Tennyson, Algernon Charles Swinburne, George Meredith, and Thomas Hardy. Among writers of fiction, Darwinian ideas have been found in the works of Jules Verne, H. G. Wells, Emile Zola, and a constellation of minor novelists. The playwright George Bernard Shaw also employed evolutionary ideas in *Man and Superman* (1903) and *Back to Methuselah* (1921). But perhaps the most strikingly original literary use of the survival of the fittest theme was that of Samuel Butler in his novel *Erewhon* (1872).

The son of a clergyman, Butler was born in Nottinghamshire, England, in 1835. Like Darwin, he was educated at Shrewsbury School, where his grandfather, Samuel Butler, was headmaster. Like Darwin, also, he subsequently began preparing for a career in the clergy, but soon realized he had no aptitude for the calling (he preferred painting) and abandoned his studies, thereby incurring the displeasure of his family. In 1860 he emigrated to New Zealand, where he set up a sheep run. It was in New Zealand that Butler became acquainted with *The Origin of Species*. He immediately became, as he said, "one of Mr. Darwin's many enthusiastic admirers," and composed a philosophic dialogue on the *Origin* that won the praise of Darwin himself. He wrote several essays on revolutionary themes, including "Darwin among the Machines" (1863), which were to become the basis of "The Book of the Machines" in *Erewhon*.

In 1864, having done well in New Zealand, Butler returned to England and settled in an apartment at Clifford's Inn, London, where he was to spend the remainder of his life. He pursued his interests in art and music, managing to get some of his paintings exhibited at the Royal Academy, and composing some piano pieces and a cantata in the style of Handel. But his real forte was writing, and he was at his best when attacking the smug, narrow-minded, hypocritical world of Victorian England. His disdain for the conventional pieties had been evidenced early in his life when he refused to follow the family tradition and become a clergyman. (Butler's relations with his family continued to be strained, though he regularly and dutifully visited them.) Now, he set upon those pieties with literary gusto, sometimes with light satire, sometimes with bitter realism.

His first major work was *Erewhon*. A utopian novel in the tradition of *Gulliver's Travels*, *Erewhon* recounts the adventures of a traveler to an imaginary country and his encounters with the strange customs and values of the inhabitants. Of course, the imaginary country is really an inverted version of England (the name "Erewhon" itself is an anagram for "Nowhere"). In 1873 he published *The Fair Haven*, a satire on religion. At about this time, Butler became disillusioned with Darwin

(Darwinism was itself becoming an orthodoxy, and he distrusted all orthodoxies), and in a series of critical studies, including *Evolution, Old and New* (1879), he attacked evolutionary theory for lacking an element of purpose. In the 1890s Butler turned his attention to Homer and Shakespeare, propounding the theories that *The Iliad* was written by a Trojan and *The Odyssey* by a woman (he later translated both works into English prose) and suggesting a new interpretation of Shakespeare's sonnets. *Erewhon Revisited*, a more bitter (and less appealing) satire than his original work, appeared in 1901. A year after his death in 1902 appeared the work that many consider Butler's masterpiece — *The Way of All Flesh*, an autobiographical novel that was also a brilliantly scathing indictment of Victorian middle-class morality.

Erewhon also has its autobiographical elements. The hero, George Higgs, is a young Englishman working as a sheep rancher in New Zealand. He is intrigued by what might lie beyond a distant range of mountains. Ignoring warnings that the mountains are forbidden territory, Higgs, after an arduous expedition, succeeds in making his way through the pass and finds himself in the land of Erewhon. The inhabitants are intelligent and friendly, but their reactions and customs are often unaccountable. Shocked to discover that Higgs owns a watch, they confiscate it, put it in a museum where old machinery is kept, and throw Higgs in jail. The Erewhonians, he discovers, consider it a serious crime to become ill; but moral offenses, such as theft and fraud, are treated much more sympathetically — like diseases to be cured. The Erewhonians profess great faith in their Musical Banks (churches), but seldom deposit their money there, and they never receive anything of value from the banks. The Colleges of Unreason teach dead languages and outmoded science. At the college, Higgs learns of a book called "The Rights of Animals," written by an Erewhonian prophet 2,500 years earlier; it maintained that eating meat was a sin and should be forbidden unless the animal had died or had committed suicide. Subsequently, a botany professor at the College of Unreason maintained that since there was no essential difference between plants and animals, plants should not be eaten, either. These prohibitions were enacted into law. (Finally, the hunger of the Erewhonians prevailed over "reason," and the laws were repealed.) The Erewhonians follow the creed of Ydgrunism, characterized by its demand for total conformity (like most Erewhonian terms, Ydgrun is an anagram: Mrs. Grundy was a symbol of Victorian middle-class morality). Eventually, Higgs falls out of favor with the Erewhonian elite and determines to flee before he is put to death. Together with Arowhena, a young Erewhonian maiden with whom he has fallen in love, he escapes in a balloon over the mountain range and returns to England, determined to lead an expedition back to Erewhon to enslave its inhabitants and convert them to Christianity.

The following passage, excerpted from the *Book of the Machines* section of the novel, describes — in Darwinian terms — how machines came to be forbidden and then destroyed in Erewhon. Butler presents this section of the book as if Higgs were quoting from his own translation of Erewhonian history. Higgs points out that this translated passage is only a "résumé"; toward the end of the escape he was forced to throw the original *Book of the Machines* overboard to keep the rapidly descending balloon from falling into the ocean before he and Arowhena could be rescued.

In the first chapter of the *Book of the Machines* the writer argues that all animal and even vegetable life can be said to have consciousness, if consciousness can be defined as a kind of purposefulness toward survival and reproduction. By the same token, machines may develop consciousness. The consciousness of machines, in fact, is so powerful that they have been evolving much more rapidly than animals, including humans: "Assume for the sake of argument that conscious beings have existed for some twenty million years: see what strides machines have made in the last thousand!" Present-day watches, for example, are far more sophisticated machines than the heavy clocks that preceded them. By a survival-of-the-fittest-type process, there may come a time "when clocks, which certainly at the present time are not diminishing in bulk, will be superseded owing to the universal use of watches, in which case they will become as extinct as ichthysauri, while the watch, whose tendency has for some years been to decrease in size rather than the contrary, will remain the only existing type of an extinct race." At this moment in history, machines are still primitive, but they are evolving at such an alarmingly rapid pace, that they may soon (in the same manner as watches superseding clocks) supersede humans. To prevent such a fate people must destroy all machines.

THE BOOK OF THE MACHINES

"What is a man's eye but a machine for the little creature that sits behind in his brain to look through? A dead eye is nearly as good as a living one for some time after the man is dead. It is not the eye that cannot see, but the restless one that cannot see through it. Is it man's eyes, or is it the big seeing-engine which has revealed to us the existence of worlds beyond worlds into infinity? What has made man familiar with the scenery of the moon, the spots on the sun, or the geography of the planets? He is at the mercy of the seeing-engine for these things, and is powerless unless he tack it on to his own identity, and make it part and parcel of himself. Or, again, is it the eye, or the little sea-engine which has shown us the existence of infinitely minute organisms which swarm unsuspected round us?   1

"And take man's vaunted power of calculation. Have we not engines which can do all manner of sums more quickly and correctly than we can? What prizeman in hypothetics at any of our Colleges of Unreason can compare with some of these machines in their own line? In fact, wherever precision is required man flies to the machine at once, as far preferable to himself. Our sum-engines never drop a figure, nor our looms a stitch; the machine is brisk and active, when the man is weary; it is clear-headed and   2

Samuel Butler. The Book of the Machines [1872]. In *Erewhon or, Over the Range*. New York: NAL, 1961.

collected, when the man is stupid and dull; it needs no slumber, when man must sleep or drop; ever at its post, ever ready for work, its alacrity never flags, its patience never gives in; its might is stronger than combined hundreds, and swifter than the flight of birds; it can burrow beneath the earth, and walk upon the largest rivers and sink not. This is the green tree; what then shall be done in the dry?

"Who shall say that a man does see or hear? He is such a hive and   3 swarm of parasites that it is doubtful whether his body is not more theirs than his, and whether he is anything but another kind of ant-heap after all. May not man himself become a sort of parasite upon the machines? An affectionate machine-tickling aphid?[1]

"It is said by some that our blood is composed of infinite living agents   4 which go up and down the highways and byways of our bodies as people in the streets of a city. When we look down from a high place upon crowded thoroughfares, is it possible not to think of corpuscles of blood travelling through veins and nourishing the heart of the town? No mention shall be made of sewers, nor of the hidden nerves which serve to communicate sensations from one part of the town's body to another; nor of the yawning jaws of the railway stations, whereby the circulation is carried directly into the heart — which receive the venous lines, and disgorge the arterial, with an eternal pulse of people. And the sleep of the town, how life-like! with its change in the circulation."

Here the writer became again so hopelessly obscure that I was obliged   5 to miss several pages. He resumed:

"It can be answered that even though machines should hear never[2] so   6 well and speak never so wisely, they will still always do the one or the other for our advantage, not their own; that man will be the ruling spirit and the machine the servant; that as soon as a machine fails to discharge the service which man expects from it, it is doomed to extinction; that the machines stand to man simply in the relation of lower animals, the vapour-engine[3] itself being only a more economical kind of horse; so that instead of being likely to be developed into a higher kind of life than man's, they owe their very existence and progress to their power of ministering to human wants, and must therefore both now and ever be man's inferiors.

"This is all very well. But the servant glides by imperceptible ap-   7 proaches into the master; and we have come to such a pass that, even now, man must suffer terribly on ceasing to benefit the machines. If all machines were to be annihilated at one moment, so that not a knife nor lever nor rag

---

[1]*aphid:* A juice-sucking insect, harmful to plants.
[2]*never:* Ever.
[3]*vapour–engine:* Steam engine.

of clothing nor anything whatsoever were left to man but his bare body alone that he was born with, and if all knowledge of mechanical laws were taken from him so that he could make no more machines, and all machine-made food destroyed so that the race of man should be left as it were naked upon a desert island, we should become extinct in six weeks. A few miserable individuals might linger, but even these in a year or two would become worse than monkeys. Man's very soul is due to the machines; it is a machine-made thing: he thinks as he thinks, and feels as he feels, through the work that machines have wrought upon him, and their existence is quite as much a *sine qua non*[4] for his, as his for theirs. This fact precludes us from proposing the complete annihilation of machinery, but surely it indicates that we should destroy as many of them as we can possibly dispense with, lest they should tyrannize over us even more completely.

"True, from a low materialistic point of view, it would seem that those   8
thrive best who use machinery wherever its use is possible with profit; but this is the art of the machines — they serve that they may rule. They bear no malice towards man for destroying a whole race of them provided he creates a better instead; on the contrary, they reward him liberally for having hastened their development. It is for neglecting them that he incurs their wrath, or for using inferior machines, or for not making sufficient exertions to invent new ones, or for destroying them without replacing them; yet these are the very things we ought to do, and do quickly; for though our rebellion against their infant power will cause infinite suffering, what will not things come to, if that rebellion is delayed?

"They have preyed upon man's grovelling preference for his material   9
over his spiritual interests, and have betrayed him into supplying that element of struggle and warfare without which no race can advance. The lower animals progress because they struggle with one another; the weaker die, the stronger breed and transmit their strength. The machines being of themselves unable to struggle, have got man to do their struggling for them: as long as he fulfils this function duly, all goes well with him — at least he thinks so; but the moment he fails to do his best for the advancement of machinery by encouraging the good and destroying the bad, he is left behind in the race of competition; and this means that he will be made uncomfortable in a variety of ways, and perhaps die.

"So that even now the machines will only serve on condition of being   10
served, and that too upon their own terms; the moment their terms are not complied with, they jib,[5] and either smash both themselves and all

---

[4]*sine qua non:* An essential condition.
[5]*jib:* Balk, refuse to continue.

whom they can reach, or turn churlish and refuse to work at all. How many men at this hour are living in a state of bondage to the machines? How many spend their whole lives, from the cradle to the grave, in tending them by night and day? Is it not plain that the machines are gaining ground upon us, when we reflect on the increasing number of those who are bound down to them as slaves, and of those who devote their whole souls to the advancement of the mechanical kingdom?

"The vapour-engine must be fed with food and consume it by fire even 11
as man consumes it; it supports its combustion by air as man supports it; it has a pulse and circulation as man has. It may be granted that man's body is as yet the more versatile of the two, but then man's body is an older thing; give the vapour-engine but half the time that man has had, give it also a continuance of our present infatuation, and what may it not ere long attain to?

"There are certain functions indeed of the vapour-engine which will 12
probably remain unchanged for myriads of years — which in fact will perhaps survive when the use of vapour has been superseded: the piston and cylinder, the beam, the fly-wheel, and other parts of the machine will probably be permanent, just as we see that man and many of the lower animals share like modes of eating, drinking, and sleeping; thus they have hearts which beat as ours, veins and arteries, eyes, ears, and noses; they sigh even in their sleep, and weep and yawn; they are affected by their children; they feel pleasure and pain, hope, fear, anger, shame; they have memory and prescience; they know that if certain things happen to them they will die, and they fear death as much as we do; they communicate their thoughts to one another and some of them deliberately act in concert. The comparison of similarities is endless: I only make it because some may say that since the vapour-engine is not likely to be improved in the main particulars, it is unlikely to be henceforward extensively modified at all. This is too good to be true: it will be modified and suited for an infinite variety of purposes, as much as man has been modified so as to exceed the brutes in skill.

"In the meantime the stoker is almost as much a cook for his engine as 13
our own cooks for ourselves. Consider also the colliers[6] and pitmen[7] and coal merchants and coal trains, and the men who drive them, and the ships that carry coals — what an army of servants do the machines thus employ! Are there not probably more men engaged in tending machinery than in tending men? Do not machines eat as it were by mannery? Are we not ourselves creating our successors in the supremacy of the earth? daily add-

---

[6]*colliers:* Coal miners.
[7]*pitmen:* Mineworkers.

ing to the beauty and delicacy of their organisation, daily giving them
greater skill and supplying more and more of that self-regulating, self-act-
ing power which will be better than any intellect?

"What a new thing it is for a machine to feed at all! The plough, the   14
spade, and the cart must eat through man's stomach; the fuel that sets
them going must burn in the furnace of a man or of horses. Man must
consume bread and meat or he cannot dig; the bread and meat are the fuel
which drive the spade. If a plough be drawn by horses, the power is supplied by grass or beans or oats, which being burnt in the belly of the cattle
give the power of working: without this fuel the work would cease, as an
engine would stop if its furnaces were to go out.

"A man of science has demonstrated 'that no animal has the power of   15
originating mechanical energy, but that all the work done in its life by any
animal, and all the heat that has been emitted from it, and the heat which
would be obtained by burning the combustible matter which has been lost
from its body during life, and by burning its body after death, make up
altogether an exact equivalent to the heat which would be obtained by
burning as much food as it has used during its life, and an amount of fuel
which would generate as much heat as its body if burned immediately after
death.' I do not know how he has found this out, but he is a man of science
— how then can it be objected against the future vitality of the machines
that they are, in their present infancy, at the beck and call of beings who
are themselves incapable of originating mechanical energy?

"The main point, however, to be observed as affording cause for alarm   16
is, that whereas animals were formerly the only stomachs of the machines,
there are now many which have stomachs of their own, and consume their
food themselves. This is a great step towards their becoming, if not animate, yet something so near akin to it, as not to differ more widely from
our own life than animals do from vegetables. And though man should
remain, in some respects, the higher creature, is not this in accordance
with the practise of nature, which allows superiority in some things to
animals which have, on the whole, been long surpassed? Has she not allowed the ant and the bee to retain superiority over man in the organisation of their communities and social arrangements, the bird in traversing
the air, the fish in swimming, the horse in strength and fleetness, and the
dog in self-sacrifice?

"It is said by some with whom I have conversed upon this subject, that   17
the machines can never be developed into animate or quasi-animate existences, inasmuch as they have no reproductive system, nor seem ever
likely to possess one. If this be taken to mean that they cannot marry, and
that we are never likely to see a fertile union between two vapour-engines
with the young ones playing about the door of the shed, however greatly
we might desire to do so, I will readily grant it. But the objection is not a
very profound one. No one expects that all the features of the now existing

organisations will be absolutely repeated in an entirely new class of life. The reproductive system of animals differs widely from that of plants, but both are reproductive systems. Has nature exhausted her phases of this power?

"Surely if a machine is able to reproduce another machine systemati-   18
cally, we may say that it has a reproductive system. What is a reproductive system, if it be not a system for reproduction? And how few of the machines are there which have not been produced systematically by other machines? But it is man that makes them do so. Yes; but is it not insects that make many of the plants reproductive, and would not whole families of plants die òut if their fertilisation was not effected by a class of agents utterly foreign to themselves? Does any one say that the red clover has no reproductive system because the humble bee (and the humble bee only) must aid and abet it before it can reproduce? No one. The humble bee is a part of the reproductive system of the clover. Each one of ourselves has sprung from minute animalcules[8] whose entity was entirely distinct from our own, and which acted after their kind with no thought or heed of what we might think about it. These little creatures are part of our own reproductive system; then why not we part of that of the machines?

"But the machines which reproduce machinery do not reproduce ma-   19
chines after their own kind. A thimble may be made by machinery, but it was not made by, neither will it ever make, a thimble. Here, again, if we turn to nature we shall find abundance of analogies which will teach us that a reproductive system may be in full force without the thing produced being of the same kind as that which produced it. Very few creatures reproduce after their own kind; they reproduce something which has the potentiality of becoming that which their parents were. Thus the butterfly lays an egg, which egg can become a caterpillar, which caterpillar can become a chrysalis,[9] which chrysalis can become a butterfly; and though I freely grant that the machines cannot be said to have more than the germ of a true reproductive system at present, have we not just seen that they have only recently obtained the germs of a mouth and stomach? And may not some stride be made in the direction of true reproduction which shall be as great as that which has been recently taken in the direction of true feeding?

"It is possible that the system when developed may be in many cases   20
a vicarious thing. Certain classes of machines may be alone fertile, while the rest discharge other functions in the mechanical system, just as the great majority of ants and bees have nothing to do with the continuation of their species, but get food and store it, without thought of breeding.

---

[8]*animalcules:* Microscopic animals.
[9]*chrysalis:* The pupa from which the butterfly develops.

One cannot expect the parallel to be complete or nearly so; certainly not now, and probably never; but is there not enough analogy existing at the present moment, to make us feel seriously uneasy about the future, and to render it our duty to check the evil while we can still do so? Machines can within certain limits beget machines of any class, no matter how different to themselves. Every class of machines will probably have its special mechanical breeders, and all the higher ones will owe their existence to a large number of parents, and not to two only.

"We are misled by considering any complicated machine as a single   21
thing; in truth it is a city or society, each member of which was bred truly after its kind. We see a machine as a whole, we call it by a name and individualise it; we look at our own limbs, and know that the combination forms an individual which springs from a single centre of reproductive action; we therefore assume that there can be no reproductive action which does not arise from a single centre; but this assumption is unscientific, and the bare fact that no vapour-engine was ever made entirely by another, or two others, of its own kind, is not sufficient to warrant us in saying that vapour-engines have no reproductive system. The truth is that each part of every vapour-engine is bred by its own special breeders, whose function it is to breed that part, and that only, while the combination of the parts into a whole forms another department of the mechanical reproductive system, which is at present exceedingly complex and difficult to see in its entirety.

"Complex now, but how much simpler and more intelligibly organised   22
may it not become in another hundred thousand years? or in twenty thousand? For man at present believes that his interest lies in that direction; he spends an incalculable amount of labour and time and thought in making machines breed always better and better; he has already succeeded in effecting much that at one time appeared impossible, and there seem no limits to the results of accumulated improvements if they are allowed to descend with modification from generation to generation. It must always be remembered that man's body is what it is through having been moulded into its present shape by the chances and changes of many millions of years, but that his organisation never advanced with anything like the rapidity with which that of the machine is advancing. This is the most alarming feature of the case, and I must be pardoned for insisting on it so frequently." . . .

"We must choose between the alternative of undergoing much present   23
suffering, or seeing ourselves gradually superseded by our own creatures, till we rank no higher in comparison with them, than the beasts of the field with ourselves.

"Herein lies our danger. For many seem inclined to acquiesce in so   24
dishonourable a future. They say that although man should become to the machines what the horse and dog are to us, yet that he will continue to

exist, and will probably be better off in a state of domestication under the beneficent rule of the machines than in his present wild condition. We treat our domestic animals with much kindness. We give them whatever we believe to be the best for them; and there can be no doubt that our use of meat has increased their happiness rather than detracted from it. In like manner there is reason to hope that the machines will use us kindly, for their existence will be in a great measure dependent upon ours; they will rule us with a rod of iron, but they will not eat us; they will not only require our services in the reproduction and education of their young, but also in waiting upon them as servants; in gathering food for them, and feeding them; in restoring them to health when they are sick; and in either burying their dead or working up their deceased members into new forms of mechanical existence.

"The very nature of the motive power which works the advancement 25 of the machines precludes the possibility of man's life being rendered miserable as well as enslaved. Slaves are tolerably happy if they have good masters, and the revolution will not occur in our time, nor hardly in ten thousand years, or ten times that. Is it wise to be uneasy about a contingency which is so remote? Man is not a sentimental animal where his material interests are concerned, and though here and there some ardent soul may look upon himself and curse his fate that he was not born a vapour-engine, yet the mass of mankind will acquiesce in any arrangement which gives them better food and clothing at a cheaper rate, and will refrain from yielding to unreasonable jealousy merely because there are other destinies more glorious than their own.

"The power of custom is enormous, and so gradual will be the change, 26 that man's sense of what is due to himself will be at no time rudely shocked; our bondage will steal upon us noiselessly and by imperceptible approaches; nor will there ever be such a clashing of desires between man and the machines as will lead to an encounter between them. Among themselves the machines will war eternally, but they will still require man as the being through whose agency the struggle will be principally conducted. In point of fact there is no occasion for anxiety about the future happiness of man so long as he continues to be in any way profitable to the machines; he may become the inferior race, but he will be infinitely better off than he is now. Is it not then both absurd and unreasonable to be envious of our benefactors? And should we not be guilty of consummate folly if we were to reject advantages which we cannot obtain otherwise, merely because they involve a greater gain to others than to ourselves?

"With those who can argue in this way I have nothing in common. I 27 shrink with as much horror from believing that my race can ever be superseded or surpassed, as I should do from believing that even at the remotest period my ancestors were other than human beings. Could I believe that ten hundred thousand years ago a single one of my ancestors was another kind of being to myself, I should lose all self-respect, and take no further pleasure or interest in life. I have the same feeling with regard to my descendants, and believe it to be one that will be felt so generally that the country will resolve upon putting an immediate stop to all further mechanical progress, and upon destroying all improvements that have been made for the last three hundred years. I would not urge more than this. We may trust ourselves to deal with those that remain, and though I should prefer to have seen the destruction include another two hundred years, I am aware of the necessity for compromising, and would so far sacrifice my own individual convictions as to be content with three hundred. Less than this will be insufficient."

This was the conclusion of the attack which led to the destruction of machinery throughout Erewhon. . . . in the end [they] succeeded in destroying all the inventions that had been discovered for the preceding 271 years, a period which was agreed upon by all parties after several years of wrangling as to whether a certain kind of mangle which was much in use among washerwomen should be saved or no. It was at last ruled to be dangerous, and was just excluded by the limit of 271 years. *28*

REVIEW QUESTIONS

1. On what basis does the writer argue that humans are even today (i.e., in the late 19th century) the servants of machines, rather than the other way around? What evidence does he provide?
2. How does the writer overcome the objection to his argument that machines are not animal-like because they have no reproductive systems? What does the writer find particularly alarming about the present stage of machine evolution?
3. In what ways, according to the writer, do some argue that it will not be so bad for machines to become the dominant race, and humans to become their servants? How does the writer respond to such arguments?

DISCUSSION AND WRITING QUESTIONS

1. Exactly how does the writer conceive of the evolution of machines, and the relationship between machines and humans, in terms of a struggle for existence and the survival of the fittest? Write an essay in which you translate this 19th century argument into a more contemporary one; use our modern machines as specific examples. You may also wish to consider how well the *Book of the Machines* has prophesied the future. (To see how a modern scientist has approached the question of machine evolution in terms of the survival of the fittest — and the superseding of humanity by intelligent computers — see Robert Jastrow, "Toward an Intelligence Beyond Man's," *Time*, Feb. 20, 1978.)

2. One of the qualities of this passage, and of *Erewhon* as a whole, which has made it so popular (unlike its much later sequel, *Erewhon Revisited*) is a sense of creative playfulness, a deadpan humor that leavens the serious tone of the argument. One such type of playfulness is the periodic interruption of "The Book of the Machines" with comments by Higgs. And at one point, Butler considers the "fertile union between two vapour-engines with the young ones playing about the door of the shed. . . ." Point out some of these and other examples of humor and explain their function in terms of the whole. For example, does Butler purposely seek to undercut the writer's arguments?

3. Select an example of a modern machine. In the manner of the writer of the *Book of the Machines,* show how this machine has evolved, through a process of "natural selection," so that less adaptable varieties have become extinct and more adaptable varieties have survived and "reproduced," with this process being repeated up to the present day. You may also wish to predict the course of the machine's future evolution.

T. H. HUXLEY *(1825–1895)*

The social Darwinists, as we have seen, were united in their efforts to apply Darwin's biological theories to the social sphere. Whatever their other differences, men like Sumner, Spencer, and Carnegie saw the principle of the survival of the fittest as a justification for "fanatical individualism," laissez-faire economics, and unrestrained competition. In the ethical world of the social Darwinists, "fittest" came to mean "best"; so that those who survived deadly business struggles were to be acknowledged more worthy than their defeated opponents — certainly more worthy than those without resources to even wage the battle.

But such views did not go unchallenged. In the late 19th century the biologist Thomas Henry Huxley rejected the assumption that the progress of civilization was tied to the struggle for existence. Better than anyone else of his time, Huxley bridged the gap between what C. P. Snow was later to call the "two cultures": science and the humanities. Like Darwin, Huxley founded his scientific reputation by publishing the results of his researches into animal life, conducted while on a long voyage of exploration. Unlike Darwin, Huxley's own professional work extended into such other fields as educational reform, theology, and philosophy.

Born in Ealing, England, in 1825, Huxley had only two years of formal schooling, but he undertook a rigorous course of self-education and subsequently attended Charing Cross Hospital Medical School in London, from which he graduated in 1845. After passing the Royal College of Surgeons examination, he signed up as assistant surgeon on the *H.M.S. Rattlesnake,* a frigate that was for the next four years to explore the south seas. Huxley did not wait until his return to publish the results of his researches but from ports along the way submitted his papers to scientific journals. As a result, when he did return in 1850, he was welcomed by leading biologists as a respected colleague, and the following year was elected to the Royal Society, England's most prestigious scientific association.

In 1854 Huxley was appointed a lecturer in the London School of Mines (which he eventually transformed into the Royal College of Science), where he remained — as lecturer, then professor, finally honorary dean — for the rest of his life. In 1855 he married Henrietta Anne Heathorn, whom he had met in Sydney, Australia; their marriage was an idyllically happy one, and their numerous children and grandchildren were unusually accomplished in letters and science. (Among their descendents were the novelist Aldous Huxley and the biologist Julian Huxley.) After Darwin published the *Origin,* Huxley became his ardent disciple and most effective supporter, and in a famous debate with Bishop Samuel Wilberforce in 1860, he did much to discredit theological opposition to the theory of evolution. During the 1850s and 1860s Huxley continued to publish important scientific papers, but he also began writing and lecturing to the lay public, thus earning a new reputation as a brilliant and influential popularizer.

During the 1870s, Huxley's interests broadened; he became a member of the first London School Board, and his programs and policies for educational reform had (and continue to have) major influence upon British education, from the elementary to the college levels. He induced guilds and businesses to support technical education, wrote a number of important scientific textbooks, as well as articles for the *Encyclopaedia Britannica*, lectured widely (he spoke at the opening ceremonies of the Johns Hopkins University in Baltimore), and served in official capacities at many universities and professional associations. Later in the decade Huxley began studying Greek; he also developed an interest in theology (coining the term "agnostic" to describe the position of people like himself) and in philosophy (writing on Hume and Descartes). In 1885 he retired from teaching at the London School of Mines but continued his writing and debating, even after moving from London to Eastborne, a small coastal resort, in 1889. He died in 1895, of influenza and bronchitis, and was buried (in a civil ceremony) in London.

Among Huxley's writings are *Evidence of Man's Place in Nature* (1863), *An Introduction to the Classification of Animals* (1869), *Lay Sermons, Addresses, and Reviews* (1870), *American Addresses* (1877), *Hume* (1878), *The Crayfish: An Introduction to the Study of Zoology* (1880), and *Science and Culture* (1881). His grandson Julian edited *T.H. Huxley's Diary of the Voyage of H.M.S. Rattlesnake* (1935). The following selection is from *Evolution and Ethics* (1893). (See also Huxley's essay, "On the Advisableness of Improving Natural Knowledge," in Part II on The New Universe.)

EVOLUTION AND ETHICS

Modern thought is making a fresh start from the base whence Indian and Greek philosophy set out; and, the human mind being very much what it was six-and-twenty centuries ago, there is no ground for wonder if it presents indications of a tendency to move along the old lines to the same results.   1

We are more than sufficiently familiar with modern pessimism, at least as a speculation; for I cannot call to mind that any of its present votaries have sealed their faith by assuming the rags and the bowl of the mendicant Bhikku,[1] or the wallet of the Cynic.[2] The obstacles placed in the way of   2

T. H. Huxley. Evolution and Ethics [1893]. Rpt. in *Selections from the Essays of T. H. Huxley.* Ed., Alburey Castell. New York: Appleton, Century Crofts, 1948.

[1]*Bhikku:* In the Buddhist religion, a Bhikku is an individual who, in monklike fashion, renounces all material possessions and practices a life of poverty and contemplation.

[2]*Cynic:* A member of a Greek sect that flourished from about the 4th century B.C. through the early days of Christianity. One of the leading Cynics of ancient Greece was Diogenes,

sturdy vagrancy by an unphilosophical police have, perhaps, proved too formidable for philosophical consistency. We also know modern speculative optimism, with its perfectability of the species, reign of peace, and lion and lamb transformation scenes; but one does not hear so much of it as one did forty years ago; indeed, I imagine it is to be met with more commonly at the tables of the healthy and wealthy, than in the congregations of the wise. The majority of us, I apprehend, profess neither pessimism nor optimism. We hold that the world is neither so good, nor so bad, as it conceivably might be; and, as most of us have reason, now and again, to discover that it can be. Those who have failed to experience the joys that make life worth living are, probably, in as small a minority as those who have never known the griefs that rob existence of its savor and turn its richest fruits into mere dust and ashes.

Further, I think I do not err in assuming that, however diverse their   3
views on philosophical and religious matters, most men are agreed that the proportion of good and evil in life may be very sensibly affected by human action. I never heard anybody doubt that the evil may be thus increased, or diminished; and it would seem to follow that good must be similarly susceptible of addition or subtraction. Finally, to my knowledge, nobody professes to doubt that, so far forth as we possess a power of bettering things, it is our paramount duty to use it and to train all our intellect and energy to this supreme service of our kind.

Hence the pressing interest of the question, to what extent modern   4
progress in natural knowledge, and, more especially, the general outcome of that progress in the doctrine of evolution, is competent to help us in the great work of helping one another?

The propounders of what are called the "ethics of evolution," when   5
the "evolution of ethics" would usually better express the object of their speculations, adduce a number of more or less interesting facts and more or less sound arguments in favor of the origin of the moral sentiments, in the same way as other natural phenomena, by a process of evolution. I have little doubt, for my own part, that they are on the right track; but as the immoral sentiments have no less been evolved, there is, so far, as much natural sanction for the one as the other. The thief and the murderer follow nature just as much as the philanthropist. Cosmic evolution may teach us how the good and the evil tendencies of man have come about; but, in itself, it is incompetent to furnish any better reason why what we call good is preferable to what we call evil than we had before. Some day, I doubt not, we shall arrive at an understanding of the evolution of the aesthetic

---

who advocated the destruction of social conventions and a life of poverty as ways to return to a more natural existence.

faculty; but all the understanding in the world will neither increase nor diminish the force of the intuition that this is beautiful and that is ugly.

There is another fallacy which appears to me to pervade the so-called "ethics of evolution." It is the notion that because, on the whole, animals and plants have advanced in perfection of organization by means of the struggle for existence and the consequent "survival of the fittest"; therefore men in society, men as ethical beings, must look to the same process to help them towards perfection. I suspect that this fallacy has arisen out of the unfortunate ambiguity of the phrase "survival of the fittest." "Fittest" has a connotation of "best"; and about "best" there hangs a moral flavor. In cosmic nature, however, what is "fittest" depends upon the conditions. Long since, I ventured to point out that if our hemisphere were to cool again, the survival of the fittest might bring about, in the vegetable kingdom, a population of more and more stunted and humbler and humbler organisms, until the "fittest" that survived might be nothing but lichens, diatoms, and such microscopic organisms as those which give red snow its color; while, if it became hotter, the pleasant valleys of the Thames[3] and Isis[4] might be uninhabitable by any animated beings save those that flourish in a tropical jungle. They, as the fittest, the best adapted to the changed conditions, would survive.

Men in society are undoubtably subject to the cosmic process. As among other animals, multiplication goes on without cessation, and involves severe competition for the means of support. The struggle for existence tends to eliminate those less fitted to adapt themselves to the circumstances of their existence. The strongest, the most self-assertive, tend to tread down the weaker. But the influence of the cosmic process on the evolution of society is the greater the more rudimentary its civilization. Social progress means a checking of the cosmic process at every step and the substitution for it of another, which may be called the ethical process; the end of which is not the survival of those who may happen to be the fittest, in respect of the whole of the conditions which obtain, but of those who are ethically the best.

As I have already urged, the practice of that which is ethically best — what we call goodness or virtue — involves a course of conduct which, in all respects, is opposed to that which leads to success in the cosmic struggle for existence. In place of ruthless self-assertion it demands self-restraint; in place of thrusting aside, or treading down, all competitors, it requires that the individual shall not merely respect, but shall help his fellows; its influence is directed, not so much to the survival of the fittest, as to the fitting of as many as possible to survive. It repudiates the gladia-

---

[3]*Thames:* The principal river of England.
[4]*Isis:* The English name of the Thames River, particularly west of Oxford.

torial theory of existence. It demands that each man who enters into the enjoyment of the advantages of a polity shall be mindful of his debt to those who have laboriously constructed it; and shall take heed that no act of his weakens the fabric in which he has been permitted to live. Laws and moral precepts are directed to the end of curbing the cosmic process and reminding the individual of his duty to the community, to the protection and influence of which he owes, if not existence itself, at least the life of something better than a brutal savage.

It is from neglect of these plain considerations that the fanatical individualism of our time attempts to apply the analogy of cosmic nature to society. Once more we have a misapplication of the stoical injunction to follow nature; the duties of the individual to the state are forgotten, and his tendencies to self-assertion are dignified by the name of rights. It is seriously debated whether the members of a community are justified in using their combined strength to constrain one of their number to contribute his share to the maintenance of it; or even to prevent him from doing his best to destroy it. The struggle for existence which has done such admirable work in cosmic nature, must, it appears, be equally beneficent in the ethical sphere. Yet if that which I have insisted upon is true; if the cosmic process has no sort of relation to moral ends; if the imitation of it by man is inconsistent with the first principles of ethics; what becomes of this surprising theory? 9

Let us understand, once for all, that the ethical progress of society depends, not on imitating the cosmic process, still less in running away from it, but in combating it. It may seem an audacious proposal thus to put the microcosm against the macrocosm and to set man to subdue nature to his higher ends; but I venture to think that the great intellectual difference between the ancient times with which we have been occupied and our day, lies in the solid foundation we have acquired for the hope that such an enterprise may meet with a certain measure of success. 10

The history of civilization details the steps by which men have succeeded in building up an artificial world within the cosmos. Fragile reed as he may be, man, as Pascal[5] says, is a thinking reed: there lies within him a fund of energy operating intelligently and so far akin to that which pervades the universe, that it is competent to influence and modify the cosmic process. In virtue of his intelligence, the dwarf bends the Titan[6] to his will. In every family, in every polity that has been established, the 11

---

[5]*Pascal:* (1623–1662) French philosopher, mathematician, and author. See selection by Pascal in Part II on The New Universe.

[6]*Titan:* In Greek mythology, one of a race of giant gods who were defeated by the Olympians; hence, any giant individual.

cosmic process in man has been restrained and otherwise modified by law and custom; in surrounding nature, it has been similarly influenced by the art of the shepherd, the agriculturist, the artisan. As civilization has advanced, so has the extent of this interference increased; until the organized and highly developed sciences and arts of the present day have endowed man with a command over the course of non-human nature greater than that once attributed to the magicians. The most impressive, I might say startling, of these changes have been brought about in the course of the last two centuries; while a right comprehension of the process of life and of the means of influencing its manifestations is only just dawning upon us. We do not yet see our way beyond generalities; and we are befogged by the obtrusion of false analogies and crude anticipations. But Astronomy, Physics, Chemistry, have all had to pass through similar phases, before they reached the stage at which their influence became an important factor in human affairs. Physiology, Psychology, Ethics, Political Science, must submit to the same ordeal. Yet it seems to me irrational to doubt that, at no distant period, they will work as great a revolution in the sphere of practice.

The theory of evolution encourages no millennial anticipations. If, for 12 millions of years, our globe has taken the upward road, yet some time, the summit will be reached and the downward route will be commenced. The most daring imagination will hardly venture upon the suggestion that the power and the intelligence of man can ever arrest the procession of the great year.

Moreover, the cosmic nature born with us and, to a large extent, nec- 13 essary for our maintenance, is the outcome of millions of years of severe training, and it would be folly to imagine that a few centuries will suffice to subdue its masterfulness to purely ethical ends. Ethical nature may count upon having to reckon with a tenacious and powerful enemy as long as the world lasts. But, on the other hand, I see no limit to the extent to which intelligence and will, guided by sound principles of investigation, and organized in common effort, may modify the conditions of existence, for a period longer than that now covered by history. And much may be done to change the nature of man himself. The intelligence which has converted the brother of the wolf into the faithful guardian of the flock ought to be able to do something towards curbing the instincts of savagery in civilized men.

But if we may permit ourselves a larger hope of abatement of the es- 14 sential evil of the world than was possible to those who, in the infancy of exact knowledge, faced the problem of existence more than a score of centuries ago, I deem it an essential condition of the realization of that hope that we should cast aside the notion that the escape from pain and sorrow is the proper object of life.

We have long since emerged from the heroic childhood of our race, 15 when good and evil could be met with the same "frolic welcome"; the attempts to escape from evil, whether Indian or Greek, have ended in flight from the battlefield; it remains to us to throw aside the youthful over-confidence and the no less youthful discouragement of nonage. We are grown men, and must play the man

> strong in will
> To strive, to seek, to find, and not to yield . . .[7]

cherishing the good that falls in our way, and bearing the evil, in and around us, with stout hearts set on diminishing it. So far, we all may strive in one faith towards one hope:

> It may be that the gulfs will wash us down,
> It may be we shall touch the Happy Isles,
>
> . . . . but something ere the end,
> Some work of noble note may yet be done.[8]

---

[7]*"strong in will . . .":* Lines 69 and 70 of Tennyson's "Ulysses."

[8]*"It may be that the gulfs will wash us down . . .":* Lines 62, 63, 51, and 52 of Tennyson's "Ulysses."

REVIEW QUESTIONS

1. Why does Huxley reject the idea that the ethical sense or the aesthetic sense of humans has evolved? To what extent is the ability to prefer the good to the evil or to prefer the beautiful to the ugly the result of an evolutionary process?
2. How does Huxley define "fittest" in the phrase "survival of the fittest"? How is fittest often otherwise defined? In what ways does Huxley demonstrate that his definition is the more valid one?
3. What relationship does Huxley draw between the state of evolution of society and the struggle for existence/survival of the fittest? Upon what does social progress depend? What, for Huxley, is the desired end product of social progress?
4. By what means do humans "influence and modify the cosmic process"? To what extent is the use of such means accelerating?

DISCUSSION AND WRITING QUESTIONS

1. What do you think Huxley might have in mind when he distinguishes the "ethics of evolution" from the "evolution of ethics" (paragraph 5)? What does he mean when he refers to the "cosmic process"?

2. In a key passage Huxley asserts that "the practice of that which is ethically best — what we call goodness or virtue — involves a course of conduct which, in all respects, is opposed to that which leads to success in the cosmic struggle for existence." Discuss this assertion. Apply it especially to the social and economic life of humanity (particularly today), and speculate on how people like Sumner and Spencer would have answered such a sentiment.

3. Do you consider Huxley an optimist? Select and discuss passages that appear to confirm or refute his optimism. Ground your discussion in the concept of perfectibility.

4. In paragraph 11 Huxley draws a distinction between disciplines like astronomy, physics, and chemistry, on the one hand, and physiology, psychology, ethics, and political science, on the other. What is the nature of this distinction, and how does he use it in his discussion? Do you agree with Huxley? Explain.

5. In paragraph 12, Huxley maintains that social evolution will someday reach the summit and then "the downward route will be commenced." What do you think Huxley meant by "the downward route"? Do you believe we have already begun this route? Have certain periods in the history of the world been downward routes? How so?

6. In paragraph 13, Huxley expresses the hope that our human intelligence may yet be the key toward "curbing the instincts of savagery in civilized men." Others have not shared this optimism. For example, over 150 years earlier, satirist Jonathan Swift gloomily observed (in *Gulliver's Travels*) that man's intelligence only serves him to devise ever more fearful weapons of destruction to maim and kill his fellow creatures. And about 50 years later, novelist George Orwell (in *1984*) showed how intelligence only helps create ever more brutal forms of political repression. What are your views on the prospects of human intelligence helping either to curb or to encourage our natural savagery and aggressiveness?

7. In paragraph 14 Huxley writes that it is "an essential condition of the realization of that hope [that the evil of the world will abate] that we should cast aside the notion that the escape from pain and sorrow is the proper object of life." (He expands upon this idea in the next paragraph.) What do you think he means by this statement? What evidence do you see that some people prefer to reject such an idea?

CHARLOTTE PERKINS GILMAN
(1860–1935)

The social Darwinism of men like Sumner, Spencer, and Carnegie was conservative and laissez-faire; it opposed the kind of "social meddling" that constituted interference with natural processes. But not all applications of Darwin were so illiberal. One of the few who used Darwin's evolutionary theories to argue the inevitability of greater social equality was Charlotte Perkins Gilman.

Gilman showed that the process of natural selection among civilized humans had resulted in the economic survival of those females who were most highly differentiated (in secondary sex characteristics, in manner, in dress, in occupation) from men — in short those females to whom contemporary males were most attracted. In this process of natural selection the environment to which women had to adapt required their economic dependence upon men. Gilman argued, however, that since humans (unlike animals) could — and did — change their environment, they would eventually change it in such a way as to abolish this economic dependence. Thus, successful adaptation to the new environment would no longer require such a high degree of sexual differentiation. (In fact, this is exactly what has happened in many countries over the past few decades, though the process is by no means complete.)

As a feminist, Gilman is not as well known today as Susan B. Anthony or Elizabeth Cady Stanton (though she was known and respected by both these women). In her own time, however, Gilman was internationally recognized both for her lectures and for her major work, *Women and Economics*, parts of which are reprinted below. Her modern editors, James L. Cooper and Sheila McIsaac Cooper, sum up Gilman's achievement as follows:

> With her unquestioning confidence in evolutionary science and her belief in inevitable progress, she maintained an abiding faith in human ability to understand the laws of social change through reason and experience and to bring the actions of mankind into harmony with the natural order. She therefore became an international publicist with the mission of encouraging humanity to hasten the inevitable advent of sexual equality. . . . In its seventh English edition by 1911 and available in eight languages, *Women and Economics* earned its author first place in suffragist Carrie Chapman Catt's list of the twelve greatest American women.

Gilman was born in 1860 to Frederic and Mary Westcott Perkins. Her father abandoned the family soon after she was born, and during her childhood and adolescence she and her mother and brother moved from one place to another in New England, generally one step ahead of the bill collectors. Her formal education, in seven different schools, comprised only about four years; but when she was sixteen, she enrolled in the Rhode Island School of Design in Providence and learned enough to be able to marginally support herself in later life by commercial art and tutoring. Of all academic subjects, however, she was most interested in the natural sciences. Impressed with the certainties of physics, she strove to apply the disciplined methods of the physical sciences to the social sciences. (In this she resembled Karl Marx; and indeed, she did eventually subscribe to a brand of socialism, but she rejected Marx's rigid economic determinism and his ideas of class struggle.)

At 24 she married a Providence artist, Charles Stetson, and soon afterward had a daughter. She was desperately unhappy in her marriage, however, and within a few years divorced Stetson and moved with her daughter to Pasadena, California, where she began writing articles and poems. One of her poems (on the theme of progressive evolution), published in the socialist journal, the *Nationalist*, attracted the attention of the eminent novelist and critic, William Dean Howells. With his encouragement, she became involved in the Nationalist clubs, organizations following the evolutionary (and non-Marxist) socialism of Edward Bellamy. In 1890 she spoke before the Nationalist Club of Pasadena, and the following year before the Pacific Coast Woman's Press Association. Soon afterward, she moved to the San Francisco area, where she helped support her lecture and writing activities by running a boarding house. A volume of poetry, *In This Our World* (1893), attracted wide attention but earned her little money.

At about this time, she sent her daughter back to live with her ex-husband, Stetson, who had remarried and was better able to provide for her financial support. Gilman was then able to devote full time to writing and speaking, first before the California state women's congresses and then before similar organizations throughout the United States. She also made two trips to England. During her travels, she met many of the most eminent feminists and reformers of the period, including Susan B. Anthony, Jane Addams (the settlement house reformer), and Elizabeth Cady Stanton; she also met the British Fabian Socialists, Sydney and Beatrice Webb and George Bernard Shaw.

The work by which Gilman will be most remembered is *Women and Economics: A Study of the Economic Relation between Men and Women as a Factor in Social Evolution* (1898). Based upon her own experiences, upon her reading of Darwin, and upon the thought of the sociologist Lester Frank Ward, *Women and Economics* became a rare example of "reform Darwinism." It called for the economic liberation of women and argued that this would occur through evolutionary (as opposed to revolutionary) means. Her distinctive approach to the problem of women's economic independence was at odds both with the conventional suffragists (who were concerned primarily with the woman's vote) and with the doctrinaire socialists (i.e., Marxists). Indeed, Gilman preferred to think of herself not primarily as a feminist but rather as a sociologist.

In 1900, she married again, this time her cousin, G. Houghton Gilman. The couple resided for a time in New York City, while Gilman continued her writing and speaking activities. Many journals, however, were closed to her because of her outspoken opinions; and so in 1909, she began her own magazine, *The Forerunner*. This magazine, which ran essays, fictions, book reviews, and humor, ended after seven years, when Gilman thought, "I had said all I had to say."

The selection below is excerpted from the early part of *Women and Economics.* In her first chapter, Gilman argues that the human species is unique in that the females are economically dependent upon males: "We are the only animal species in which the female depends upon the male for food, the only animal species in which the sex-relation is also an economic relation. . . . Speaking collectively, men produce and distribute wealth, and women receive it at their hands." Marriage cannot be considered a true partnership, Gilman argues, because the work that women have traditionally done in keeping the household and in raising the children bears no relationship (unless an inverse one) to the economic benefit they receive. In fact, "the women who do the most work get the least money, and the women who have the most money do the least work." The woman, according to Gilman,

> is the worker *par excellence,* but her work is not such as to affect her economic status. Her living, all that she gets — food, clothing, ornaments, amusements, luxuries — these bear no relation to her power to produce wealth, to her services in the house, or to her motherhood. These things bear relation only to the man she marries, the man she depends on — to how much he has and how much he is willing to give her. The women whose splendid extravagance dazzles the world, whose economic goods are the greatest, are often neither houseworkers nor mothers but simply the women who hold most power over the men who have the most money. The female of genus homo is economically dependent on the male. He is her food supply.

THE ECONOMIC RELATION BETWEEN MEN AND WOMEN AS A FACTOR IN SOCIAL EVOLUTION

Very early in the development of species it was ascertained by nature's slow but sure experiments that the establishment of two sexes in separate organisms, and their differentiation, was to the advantage of the species. Therefore, out of the mere protoplasmic masses, the floating cells, the amorphous early forms of life, grew into use the distinction of the sexes — the gradual development of masculine and feminine organs and functions in two distinct organisms. Developed and increased by use, the distinction

1

Charlotte Perkins Gilman. The Economic Relation Between Men and Women as a Factor in Social Evolution [1898]. Original Title: *Women and Economics: A Study of the Economic Relation Between Men and Women as a Factor in Social Evolution.* Rpt. in James L. Cooper and Sheila McIsaac Cooper, eds. *The Roots of American Feminist Thought.* Boston: Allyn and Bacon, 1973. Cooper and Cooper's abridgment used. Further abridging by Behrens/Rosen.

of sex increased in the evolution of species. As the distinction increased, the attraction increased, until we have in all the higher races two markedly different sexes, strongly drawn together by the attraction of sex and fulfilling their use in the reproduction of species. These are the natural features of sex-distinction and sex-union, and they are found in the human species as in others. The unnatural feature by which our race holds an unenviable distinction consists mainly in this — a morbid excess in the exercise of this function.

It is this excess, whether in marriage or out, which makes the health and happiness of humanity in this relation so precarious. It is this excess, always easily seen, which law and religion have mainly striven to check. Excessive sex-indulgence is the distinctive feature of humanity in this relation. 2

To define "excess" in this connection is not difficult. All natural functions that require our conscious co-operation for their fulfillment are urged upon our notice by an imperative desire. We do not have to desire to breathe or to digest or to circulate the blood because that is done without our volition; but we do have to desire to eat and drink because the stomach cannot obtain its supplies without in some way spurring the whole organism to secure them. So hunger is given us as an essential factor in our process of nutrition. In the same manner sex-attraction is an essential factor in the fulfillment of our processes of reproduction. In a normal condition the amount of hunger we feel is exactly proportioned to the amount of food we need. It tells us when to eat and when to stop. In some diseased conditions "an unnatural appetite" sets in, and we are impelled to eat far beyond the capacity of the stomach to digest, of the body to assimilate. This is an excessive hunger. . . . 3

The immediately acting cause of sex-attraction is sex-distinction. The more widely the sexes are differentiated, the more forcibly they are attracted to each other. The more highly developed becomes the distinction of sex in either organism, the more intense is its attraction for the other. . . . Normal sex-distinction manifests itself in all species in what are called primary and secondary sex-characteristics. The primary are those organs and functions essential to reproduction; the secondary, those modifications of structure and function which subserve the uses of reproduction ultimately but are not directly essential — such as the horns of the stag, of use in sex-combat; the plumage of the peacock, of use in sex-competition. All the minor characteristics of beard or mane, comb, wattles,[1] spurs, gorgeous color or superior size which distinguish the male from the female — these are distinctions of sex. These distinctions are of use to the 4

---

[1]*wattle:* A fleshy fold of skin hanging from the throat of a bird or snake.

species through reproduction only, the processes of race-preservation. They are not of use in self-preservation. The creature is not profited personally by his mane or crest or tail-feathers: They do not help him get his dinner or kill his enemies.

On the contrary, they react unfavorably upon his personal gains if, through too great development, they interfere with his activity or render him a conspicuous mark for enemies. Such development would constitute excessive sex-distinction, and this is precisely the condition of the human race. Our distinctions of sex are carried to such a degree as to be disadvantageous to our progress as individuals and as a race. The sexes in our species are differentiated not only enough to perform their primal functions, not only enough to manifest all sufficient secondary sexual characteristics and fulfill their use in giving rise to sufficient sex-attraction, but so much as seriously to interfere with the processes of self-preservation on the one hand and, more conspicuous still, so much as to react unfavorably upon the very processes of race-preservation which they are meant to serve. Our excessive sex-distinction, manifesting the characteristics of sex to an abnormal degree, has given rise to a degree of attraction which demands a degree of indulgence that directly injures motherhood and fatherhood. We are not better as parents, nor better as people, for our existing degree of sex-distinction, but visibly worse. To what conditions are we to look for the developing cause of these phenomena?

Let us first examine the balance of forces by which these two great processes, self-preservation and race-preservation, are conducted in the world. Self-preservation involves the expenditure of energy in those acts, and their ensuing modifications of structure and function, which tend to the maintenance of the individual life. Race-preservation involves the expenditure of energy in those acts, and their ensuing modifications of structure and function, which tend to the maintenance of the racial life, even to the complete sacrifice of the individual. This primal distinction should be clearly held in mind. Self-preservation and race-preservation are in no way identical processes and are often directly opposed. In the line of self-preservation, natural selection, acting on the individual, develops those characteristics which enable it to succeed in "the struggle for existence," increasing by use those organs and functions by which it directly profits. In the line of race-preservation, sexual selection, acting on the individual, develops those characteristics . . . by which its young are to profit, directly or indirectly. The individual has been not only modified to its environment under natural selection but modified to its mate under sexual selection, each sex developing the qualities desired by the other by the simple process of choice, those best sexed being first chosen and transmitting their sex-development as well as their racial development.

The order mammalia is the resultant of a primary sex-distinction developed by natural selection, but the gorgeous plumage of the peacock's tail is a secondary sex-distinction developed by sexual selection. If the peacock's tail were to increase in size and splendor till it shone like the sun and covered an acre, . . . such excessive sex-distinction would be so inimical to the personal prosperity of that peacock that he would die and his tail-tendency would perish with him. . . . In herds of deer and cattle the male is larger and stronger, the female smaller and weaker; but unless the latter is large and strong enough to keep up with the male in the search for food or the flight from foes, one is taken and the other left, and there is no more of that kind of animal. Differ as they may in sex, they must remain alike in species, equal in race-development, else destruction overtakes them. The force of natural selection, demanding and producing identical race-qualities, acts as a check on sexual selection with its production of different sex-qualities. . . .

When, then, it can be shown that sex-distinction in the human race is   8 so excessive as . . . to check and pervert the progress of the race, it becomes a matter for most serious consideration. Nothing could be more inevitable, however, under our sexuo-economic relation. By the economic dependence of the human female upon the male, the balance of forces is altered. Natural selection no longer checks the action of sexual selection but co-operates with it. Where both sexes obtain their food through the same exertions, from the same sources, under the same conditions, both sexes are acted upon alike and developed alike by their environment. Where the two sexes obtain their food under different conditions and where that difference consists in one of them being fed by the other, then the feeding sex becomes the environment of the fed. Man, in supporting woman, has become her economic environment. Under natural selection every creature is modified to its environment, developing perforce the qualities needed to obtain its livelihood under that environment. . . . Under sexual selection the human creature is of course modified to its mate, as with all creatures. When the mate becomes also the master, when economic necessity is added to sex-attraction, we have the two great evolutionary forces acting together to the same end, namely, to develop sex-distinction in the human female. For in her position of economic dependence in the sex-relation, sex-distinction is with her not only a means of attracting a mate, as with all creatures, but a means of getting her livelihood, as is the case with no other creature under heaven. Because of the economic dependence of the human female on her mate, she is modified to sex to an excessive degree. This excessive modification she transmits to her children; and so is steadily implanted in the human constitution the morbid tendency to excess in this relation which has acted so universally upon us in all ages, in spite of our best efforts to restrain it. It is not the normal sex-tendency, common to all creatures, but an abnormal sex-tendency, produced and maintained by the abnormal economic relation which makes one sex get its living from the other by the exercise of sex-functions. This is the immediate effect upon individuals of the peculiar sexuo-economic relation which obtains among us.

In establishing the claim of excessive sex-distinction in the human race, *9* much needs to be said to make clear to the general reader what is meant by the term. To the popular mind, both the coarsely familiar and the over-refined, "sexual" is thought to mean "sensual"; and the charge of excessive sex-distinction seems to be a reproach. This should be at once dismissed as merely showing ignorance of the terms used. A man does not object to being called "masculine," nor a woman to being called "feminine." Yet whatever is masculine or feminine is sexual. To be distinguished by femininity is to be distinguished by sex. To be over-feminine is to be over-sexed. To manifest in excess any of the distinctions of sex, primary or secondary, is to be over-sexed. Our hypothetical peacock with his too large and splendid tail would be over-sexed, and no offense to his moral character! . . .

Sex-energy in its primal manifestation is exhibited in the male of the *10* human species to a degree far greater than is necessary for the processes of reproduction — enough, indeed, to subvert and injure those processes. . . . In a certain over-coarseness and hardness, a too great belligerence and pride, a too great subservience to the power of sex-attraction, we find the main marks of excessive sex-distinction in men. It has been always checked and offset in them by the healthful activities of racial life. Their energies have been called out and their faculties developed along all the lines of human progress. In the growth of industry, commerce, science, manufacture, government, art, religion, the male of our species has become human far more than male. Strong as this passion is in him, inordinate as is his indulgence, he is a far more normal animal than the female of his species — far less over-sexed. To him this field of special activity is but part of life, an incident. The whole world remains besides. To her it is the world. . . .

Physically, woman belongs to a tall, vigorous, beautiful animal species, *11* capable of great and varied exertion. In every race and time when she has opportunity for racial activity, she develops accordingly and is no less a woman for being a healthy human creature. In every race and time where she is denied this opportunity — and few, indeed, have been her years of freedom — she has developed in the lines of action to which she was confined; and those were always lines of sex-activity. In consequence the body of woman, speaking in the largest generalization, manifests sex-distinction predominantly.

Woman's femininity . . . is more apparent in proportion to her human- *12* ity than the femininity of other animals in proportion to their caninity or felinity or equinity.[2] "A feminine hand" or "a feminine foot" is distinguishable anywhere. We do not hear of "a feminine paw" or "a feminine hoof." A hand is an organ of prehension,[3] a foot an organ of locomotion; they are not secondary sexual characteristics. The comparative smallness and feebleness of woman is a sex-distinction. We have carried it to such an excess that women are commonly known as "the weaker sex." . . .

The degree of feebleness and clumsiness common to women, the comparative inability to stand, walk, run, jump, climb, and perform other race functions common to both sexes, is an excessive sex-distinction; and the ensuing transmission of this relative feebleness to their children, boys and girls alike, retards human development. Strong, free, active women, the sturdy, field-working peasant, the burden-bearing savage, are no less good mothers for their human strength. But our civilized "feminine delicacy," which appears somewhat less delicate when recognized as an expression of sexuality in excess, makes us no better mothers, but worse. The relative weakness of women is . . . apparent in her to a degree that injures motherhood, that injures wifehood, that injures the individual. . . .   13

In its psychic manifestation this intense sex-distinction is equally apparent. The primal instinct of sex-attraction has developed under social forces into a conscious passion of enormous power, a deep and lifelong devotion, overwhelming in its force. This is excessive in both sexes, but more so in women than in men — not so commonly in its simple physical form but in the unreasoning intensity of emotion that refuses all guidance and drives those possessed by it to risk every other good for this one end. . . .   14

In our steady insistence on proclaiming sex-distinction, we have grown to consider most human attributes as masculine attributes for the simple reason that they were allowed to men and forbidden to women. . . . But while with the male the things he fondly imagined to be "masculine" were merely human and very good for him, with the female the few things marked "feminine" were feminine indeed; and her ceaseless reiteration of one short song, however sweet, has given it a conspicuous monotony. In garments whose main purpose is unmistakably to announce her sex, with a tendency to ornament which marks exuberance of sex-energy, with a body so modified to sex as to be grievously deprived of its natural activities, with a manner and behavior wholly attuned to sex-advantage and frequently most disadvantageous to any human gain, with a field of action most rigidly confined to sex-relations, with her overcharged sensibility, her   15

---

[2]*caninity or felinity or equinity:* Of the dog, cat, or horse families, respectively.
[3]*prehension:* Grasping.

prominent modesty, her "eternal femininity" — the female of genus homo[4] is undeniably over-sexed.

This excessive distinction shows itself again in a marked precocity of development. Our little children, our very babies, show signs of it when the young of other creatures are serenely asexual in general appearance and habit. We eagerly note this precocity. We are proud of it. We carefully encourage it by precept and example, taking pains to develop the sex-instinct in little children, and think no harm. One of the first things we force upon the child's dawning consciousness is the fact that he is a boy or that she is a girl and that, therefore, each must regard everything from a different point of view. They must be dressed differently, not on account of their personal needs, which are exactly similar at this period, but so that neither they nor any one beholding them may for a moment forget the distinction of sex. . . . Boys and girls are expected, also, to behave differently to each other and to people in general, a behavior to be briefly described in two words. To the boy we say, "Do"; to the girl, "Don't." The little boy must "take care" of the little girl, even if she is larger than he is. . . . Boys are encouraged from the beginning to show the feelings supposed to be proper to their sex. When our infant son bangs about, roars, and smashes things, we say proudly that he is "a regular boy!" When our infant daughter coquettes with visitors or wails in maternal agony because her brother has broken her doll, whose sawdust remains she nurses with piteous care, we say proudly that "she is a perfect little mother already!" What business has a little girl with the instincts of maternity? No more than the little boy should have with the instincts of paternity. They are sex-instincts and should not appear till the period of adolescence. The most normal girl is the "tom-boy" — whose numbers increase among us in these wiser days — a healthy young creature who is human through and through, not feminine till it is time to be. The most normal boy has calmness and gentleness as well as vigor and courage. He is a human creature as well as a male creature and not aggressively masculine till it is time to be. Childhood is not the period for these marked manifestations of sex. That we exhibit them, that we admire and encourage them, shows our over-sexed condition. . . .

In the original constituents of society, the human animal in its primitive state, economic processes were purely individual. The amount of food obtained by a given man bore direct relation to his own personal exertions. . . . Given a certain supply of needed food, as the edible beasts or fruits in a forest, and a certain number of individuals to get this food, each

16

17

---

[4]*genus homo:* The human animal.

by his own exertions, it follows that the more numerous the individuals, the less food to be obtained by each and, conversely, the fewer the individuals, the more food to be obtained by each. Wherefore, the primitive savage slew his fellowman at sight on good economic grounds. This is the extreme of individual competition, perfectly logical and in its time economically right. That time is forever past. The basic condition of human life is union: the organic social relation, the interchange of functional service, wherein the individual is most advantaged not by his own exertions for his own goods but by the exchange of his exertions with the exertions of others for goods produced by them together. We are not treating here of any communistic theory as to the equitable division of the wealth produced but of a clear truth in social economics — that wealth is a social product. Whatever one may believe as to what should be done with the wealth of the world, no one can deny that the production of this wealth requires the combined action of many individuals. From the simplest combination of strength that enables many men to overcome the mammoth or to lift the stone — an achievement impossible to one alone — to the subtle and complex interchange of highly specialized skilled labor which makes possible our modern house, the progress of society rests upon the increasing collectivity of human labor. . . .

But as we study this process, . . . we are struck by the visible presence   18
of some counter-force, acting against the normal development and producing most disadvantageous effects. . . . We have our hand upon this hidden spring in the sexuo-economic relation. If we had remained on an individual economic basis, the evil influence would have had far less ill effect; but as we grow into the social economic relation, it increases with our civilization. The sex-relation is primarily and finally individual. It is a physical relation between individual bodies, and while it may also extend to a psychical relation between individual souls, it does not become a social relation, though it does change its personal development to suit social needs.

In all its processes, to all its results, the sex-relation is personal, work-   19
ing through individuals upon individuals and developing individual traits and characteristics to the great advantage of society. The qualities developed by social relation are built into the race through the sex-relation, but the sex-relation itself is wholly personal. Our economic relation, on the contrary, though originally individual, becomes through social evolution increasingly collective. By combining the human sex-relation with the human economic relation, we have combined a permanently individual process with a progressively collective one. . . .

We are so used to considering it the first duty of a man to support his   20
family that it takes a very glaring instance of bribery and corruption in their interests to shake our conviction; but as a sociological law, every phase of the prostitution of public service to private gain, from the degradation of

the artist to the exploitation of the helpless unskilled laborer, marks a diseased social action. Our social status rests upon our common consent, common action, common submission to the common will. No individual interests can stand for a moment against the interests of the common weal, either when war demands the last sacrifice of individual property and life or when peace requires the absolute submission of individual property and life to common law — the fixed expression of the people's will. The maintenance of "law and order" involves the very spirit of socialism, the sinking of personal interest in common interest. All this rests upon the evolution of the social spirit, the keen sense of social duty, the conscientious fulfillment of social service; and it is here that the excessive individualism maintained by our sexuo-economic relation enters as a strong and increasingly disadvantageous social factor. . . .

The highest human attributes are perfectly compatible with the sex-relation but not with the sexuo-economic relation. We see this opposition again in the tendency to collectivity in bodies of single men — their comradeship, equality, and mutual helpfulness as compared with the attitude of the same men toward one another when married. This is why the quality of "organizability" is stronger in men than in women; their common economic interests force them into relation, while the isolated and even antagonistic economic interests of women keep them from it. The condition of individual economic dependence in which women live resembles that of the savage in the forest. They obtain their economic goods by securing a male through their individual exertions, all competing freely to this end. No combination is possible. . . .   *21*

On the woman's side we are steadily maintaining the force of primitive individual competition in the world as against the tendency of social progress to develop co-operation in its place, and this tendency of course is inherited by their sons. On the man's side the same effect is produced through another feature of the relation. The tendency to individualism with sex-advantage is developed in man by an opposite process to that operating on the woman. She gets her living by getting a husband. He gets his wife by getting a living. It is to her individual economic advantage to secure a mate. It is to his individual sex-advantage to secure economic gain. The sex-functions to her have become economic functions. . . .   *22*

Legitimate sex-competition brings out all that is best in man. To please her, to win her, he strives to do his best. But the economic dependence of the female upon the male, with its ensuing purchasability, does not so affect a man: It puts upon him the necessity for getting things, not for doing them. In the lowest grades of labor, where there is no getting without doing and where the laborer always does more than he gets, this works less palpable evil than in the higher grades, the professions and arts, where the most valuable work is always ahead of the market and where to work for the market involves a lowering of standards. The young artist or   *23* poet or scientific student works for his work's sake, for art, for science, and so for the best good of society. But the artist or student married must get gain, must work for those who will pay; and those who will pay are not those who lift and bear forward the standard of progress. Community of interest is quite possible with those who are working most disinterestedly for the social good; but bring in the sex-relation and all such solidarity disintegrates — resolves itself into the tiny groups of individuals united on a basis of sex-union and briskly acting in their own immediate interests at anybody's or everybody's expense. . . .

Besides this maintenance of primeval individualism in the growing col- 24 lectivity of social economic process and the introduction of the element of sex-combat into the narrowing field of industrial competition, there is an-other side to the evil influence of the sexuo-economic relation upon social development. This is in the attitude of woman as a non-productive consumer.

In the industrial evolution of the human race, . . . we find that pro- 25 duction and consumption go hand in hand; and production comes first. One cannot consume what has not been produced. Economic production is the natural expression of human energy — not sex-energy at all, but race-energy — the unconscious functioning of the social organism. Socially or-ganized human beings tend to produce, as a gland to secrete: It is the essential nature of the relation. The creative impulse, the desire to make, to express the inner thought in outer form, . . . is the distinguishing char-acter of humanity. . . . This is the natural process of production and is followed by the natural process of consumption, where practicable. But consumption is not the main end, the governing force. Under this organic social law working naturally, we have the evolution of those arts and crafts in the exercise of which consists our human living and on the product of which we live. So does society evolve within itself — secrete as it were — the social structure with all its complex machinery; and we function therein as naturally as so many glands, other things being equal.

But other things are not equal. Half the human race is denied free pro- 26 ductive expression, is forced to confine its productive human energies to the same channels as its reproductive sex-energies. Its creative skill is con-fined to the level of immediate personal bodily service, to the making of clothes and preparing of food for individuals. No social service is possible. For the woman there is . . . no relation maintained between what she does produce and what she consumes. She is forbidden to make but encouraged to take. Her industry is not the natural output of creative energy, not the work she does because she has the inner power and strength to do it; nor is her industry even the measure of her gain. She has, of course, the nat-ural desire to consume; and to that is set no bar save the capacity or the will of her husband.

Thus we have painfully and laboriously evolved and carefully maintain 27 among us an enormous class of non-productive consumers — a class which is half the world and mother of the other half. We have built into the constitution of the human race the habit and desire of taking, as divorced from its natural precursor and concomitant of making. . . . To consume food, to consume clothes, to consume houses and furniture and decorations and ornaments and amusements, to take and take and take forever — from one man if they are virtuous, from many if they are vicious, but always to take and never to think of giving anything in return except their womanhood — this is the enforced condition of the mothers of the race. . . .

Between the brutal ferocity of excessive male energy struggling in the 28
market-place as in a battlefield and the unnatural greed generated by the perverted condition of female energy, it is not remarkable that the industrial evolution of humanity has shown peculiar symptoms. One of the minor effects of this last condition — this limiting of female industry to close personal necessities and this tendency of her over-developed sex-nature to overestimate the so-called "duties of her position" — has been to produce an elaborate devotion to individuals and their personal needs — not to the understanding and developing of their higher natures but to the intensification of their bodily tastes and pleasure. The wife and mother, pouring the rising tide of racial power into the same old channels that were allowed her primitive ancestors, constantly ministers to the physical needs of her family with a ceaseless and concentrated intensity. . . .

The consuming female — debarred from any free production, unable 29
to estimate the labor involved in the making of what she so lightly destroys, and her consumption limited mainly to those things which minister to physical pleasure — creates a market for sensuous decoration and personal ornament, for all that is luxurious and enervating, and for a false and capricious variety in such supplies, which operates as a most deadly check to true industry and true art. As the priestess of the temple of consumption, as the limitless demander of things to use up, her economic influence is reactionary and injurious. Much, very much, of the current of useless production in which our economic energies run waste — man's strength poured out like water on the sand — depends on the creation and careful maintenance of this false market, this sink into which human labor vanishes with no return. Woman, in her false economic position, reacts injuriously upon industry, upon art, upon science, discovery, and progress. The sexuo-economic relation in its effect on the constitution of the individual keeps alive in us the instincts of savage individualism which we should otherwise have well outgrown. It sexualizes our industrial relation and commercializes our sex-relation. And in the external effect upon the market, the over-sexed woman in her unintelligent and ceaseless demands hinders and perverts the economic development of the world. . . .

When the human animal was still but an animal, but an individual, 30
came the imperative demand for the establishment of a common con-

sciousness between . . . hitherto irreconcilable individuals. The first step in nature toward this end is found in the relation between mother and child. Where the young after birth are still dependent on the mother, the functions of the one separate living body needing the service of another separate living body, we have the overlapping of personality, the mutual need, which brings with it the essential instinct that holds together these interacting personalities. . . . Between mother and child was born love, long before fatherhood was anything more than a momentary incident. But the common consciousness, the mutual attraction between mother and child, stopped there absolutely. It was limited in range to this closest relation; in duration, to the period of infancy.

The common interest of human beings must be served by racial faculties, not merely by the sex-functions of the female or the duties of mother to child. As the male, acting through his natural instincts, steadily encroached upon the freedom of the female until she was reduced to the state of economic dependence, he thereby assumed the position of provider for this creature no longer able to provide for herself. . . . He became, and has remained, a sort of man-mother, alone in creation in his remarkable position. By this common interest, existing now not only between mother and child but between father, mother, and child, grew up a wider common consciousness. And as the father served the child not through sex-function but through race-function, this service was open to far wider development and longer duration than the mother's alone could ever have reached. 31

Maternal energy is the force through which have come into the world both love and industry. It is through the tireless activity of this desire, the mother's wish to serve the young, that she began the first of the arts and crafts whereby we live. While the male savage was still a mere hunter and fighter, expressing masculine energy, . . . expanding, scattering, the female savage worked out in equally natural ways the conserving force of female energy. She gathered together and saved nutrition for the child. . . . She wrapped it in garments and built a shelter for its head as naturally as the same maternal function had loved, clothed, and sheltered the unborn. Maternal energy, working externally through our elaborate organism, is the source of productive industry, the main current of social life. 32

But not until this giant force could ally itself with others and work co-operatively, overcoming the destructive action of male energy in its blind competition, could our human life enter upon its full course of racial evolution. This is what was accomplished through the suppression of the free action of maternal energy in the female and its irresistible expression through the male. . . . The subjection of woman[5] has involved to an enormous degree the maternalizing of man. Under its bonds he has been forced 33

_____

[5] *the subjection of woman:* The title of a famous treatise (1869) by John Stuart Mill.

into new functions, impossible to male energy alone. he has had to learn to love and care for someone besides himself. He has had to learn to work, to serve, to be human. Through the sex-passion, mightily overgrown, the human race has been led and driven up the long, steep path of progress, over all obstacles, through all dangers, carrying its accompanying conditions of disease and sin (and surmounting them), up and up in spite of all, until at last a degree of evolution is reduced in which the extension of human service and human love makes possible a better way. . . .

Sexual equality has been slowly evolved, not only by increasing the importance of the male element in reproduction but by developing race-qualities in the male, so long merely a reproductive agent. The last step of this process has been the elevation of the male of genus homo to full racial equality with the female. . . . If the female had remained in full personal freedom and activity, she would have remained superior to him, and both would have remained stationary. Since the female had not the tendency to vary which distinguished the male, it was essential that the expansive forces of masculine energy be combined with the preservative and constructive forces of feminine energy. The expansive and variable male energy, struggling under its new necessity for constructive labor, has caused that labor to vary and progress more than it would have done in feminine hands alone. Out of her wealth of power and patience, liking to work, to give, she toils on forever in the same primitive industries. He, impatient of obstacles, not liking to work, desirous to get rather than to give, splits his task into a thousand specialties and invents countless ways to lighten his labors. . . .

Human development thus far has proceeded in the male line, under the force of male energy, spurred by sex-stimulus and by the vast storage battery of female energy suppressed. Women can well afford their period of subjection for the sake of a conquered world, a civilized man. In spite of the agony of the process — the black, long ages of shame and pain and horror — women should remember that they are still here; and thanks to the blessed power of heredity, they are not so far aborted that a few generations of freedom will not set them abreast of the age. When the centuries of slavery and dishonor, of torture and death, of biting injustice and slow, suffocating repression, seem long to women, let them remember the geologic ages, the millions and millions of years when puny, pygmy, parasitic males struggled for existence and were used or not, as it happened, like a half-tried patent medicine. What train of wives and concubines was ever so ignominiously placed as the extra husbands carried among the scales of the careful female cirriped,[6] lest she lose one or two! What neglect

34

35

---

[6]*cirriped:* A parasitic crustacean, such as a barnacle.

of faded wives can compare with the scorned, unnoticed death of the drone bee, stung, shut out, walled up in wax, kept only for his momentary sex-function, and not absolutely necessary for that! What Bluebeard[7] tragedy or cruelty of bride-murdering Eastern king can emulate the ruthless slaughter of the hapless little male spider used by his ferocious mate "to coldly furnish forth a marriage breakfast"! Never once in the history of humanity has any outrage upon women compared with these sweeping sacrifices of helpless males in earlier species. The female has been dominant for the main duration of life on earth. She has been easily equal always up to our own race; and in our race she has been subjugated to the male during the earlier period of development for such enormous racial gain, such beautiful and noble uses, that the sacrifice should never be mentioned nor thought of by a womanhood that knows its power. . . .

36

neither he nor the world is any longer benefited by her subordination, now that she is coming steadily out into direct personal expression, into the joy of racial action in full freedom, of power upon the throne instead of behind it, it is unworthy of this supreme new birth to waste one regret upon the pain that had to be. . . .

37

The increasing specialization of the modern woman, acquired by inheritance from the ceaselessly specializing male, makes her growing racial faculties strain against the primitive restrictions of a purely sexual relation. The desire to produce — the distinctive human quality — is no longer satisfied with a status that allows only reproduction. In our present stage of social evolution it is increasingly difficult and painful for women to endure their condition of economic dependence, and therefore they are leaving it. . . .

38

A relation that inevitably produces abnormal development cannot be permanently maintained. The intensification of sex-energy as a social force results in such limitless exaggeration of sex-instinct as finds expression sexually in the unnatural vices of advanced civilization and socially in the strained economic relation between producer and consumer which breaks society in two. The sexuo-economic relation serves to bring social development to a certain level. After that level is reached, a higher relation must be adopted or the lifting process comes to an end, and either the race succumbs to the morbid action of its own forces, or some fresher race comes in and begins the course of social evolution anew.

39

Under the stimulus of the sexuo-economic relation, one civilization after another has climbed up and fallen down in weary succession. It remains for us to develop a newer, better form of sex-relation and of eco-

---

[7]*Bluebeard:* In folklore, Bluebeard married and then murdered six wives in succession.

nomic relation therewith and so to grasp the fruits of all previous civilizations and grow on to the beautiful results of higher ones. The true and lasting social progress, beyond that which we have yet made, is based on a spirit of inter-human love, not merely the inter-sexual; and it requires an economic machinery organized and functioned for human needs, not sexual ones. . . .

Social consciousness is at last so vital a force in both men and women   40
that we feel clearly that our human life cannot be fully lived on sex-lines only. We are so far individualized, so far socialized, that men can work without the tearing spur of exaggerated sex-stimulus, work for someone besides mate and young; and women can love and serve without the slavery of economic dependence — love better and serve more. Sex-stimulus begins and ends in individuals. The social spirit is a larger thing, a better thing, and brings with it a larger, nobler life than we could ever know on a sex-basis solely.

Moreover, it should be distinctly understood, as it is already widely   41
and vaguely felt, that the higher development of social life following the economic independence of women makes possible a higher sex-life than has ever yet been known. As fast as the human individual rises in social progress to a certain degree of development, so fast this primitive form of sex-union chafes and drags: It is felt to be unsatisfying and injurious. This is a marked feature in modern life. The long, sure, upward trend of the human race toward monogamous marriage is no longer helped but hindered by the economic side of the relation. The best marriage is between the best individuals; and the best individuals of both sexes today are increasingly injured by the economic basis of our marriage, which produces and maintains those qualities in men and women, and their resultant industrial conditions, which make marriage more difficult and precarious every day.

The woman's movement, then, should be hailed by every right-think-   42
ing, far-seeing man and woman as the best birth of our century. The banner advanced proclaims "equality before the law," woman's share in political freedom; but the main line of progress is and has been toward economic equality and freedom. While life exists on earth, the economic conditions must underlie and dominate each existing form and its activities, and social life is no exception. A society whose economic unit is a sex-union can no more develop beyond a certain point industrially than a society like the patriarchal, whose political unit was a sex-union, could develop beyond a certain point politically.

The last freeing of the individual makes possible the last combination   43
of individuals. While sons must bend to the will of a patriarchal father, no democracy is possible. Democracy means, requires, is individual liberty. While the sexuo-economic relation makes the family the center of industrial activity, no higher collectivity than we have today is possible. But, as women become free economic, social factors, so becomes possible the full

social combination of individuals in collective industry. With such freedom, such independence, such wider union becomes possible also a union between man and woman such as the world has long dreamed of in vain.

REVIEW QUESTIONS

1. What is the difference, according to Gilman, between the distinction of the sexes in the human species and the distinction of the sexes in all other species? Upon what factor does the degree of sexual attraction between male and female chiefly depend? What constitutes "excessive sex-distinction"? Why is excessive sex distinction harmful to race preservation? What is the difference between race-preservation and self-preservation? Why do the forces of natural selection normally serve to check excessive sex distinction?

2. How does Gilman define the term "over-sexed"? How does this condition manifest itself in the two sexes of the human species? What kind of factors check this tendency in the male? Why are there far fewer such factors for the female? How do we force such an excessive degree of sexual differentiation upon the next generation? At what period of life are such sex differentiations particularly inappropriate?

3. Why has the progress of society depended upon a movement away from individual economic processes and toward collective economic processes? In what sense is the human sex relation a "disadvantageous social factor" in this progress of society? Why are men more apt to work collectively (i.e., cooperatively) and women individually (i.e., competitively)? What does Gilman mean when she says of woman that, "She is forbidden to make but encouraged to take"? Why is the economic influence of woman "reactionary and injurious" to social and economic progress and to "true industry and true art"?

4. In paragraphs 30 through 43, what consolation, and what hope, does Gilman offer to women who have been held in economic subjection for so many centuries? At what point in social evolution does Gilman consider the period in which she is writing? What signs of this new stage of evolution does she see in contemporary civilization? What attitude does she suggest that women adopt? Upon what factors does continued progress depend?

DISCUSSION AND WRITING QUESTIONS

1. Compare Gilman's comments on sex distinctions and sexual selection in the first 16 paragraphs of this passage to the section entitled "Sexual Selection" in Darwin's *Origin of Species*. To what extent do Gilman's civilized humans follow the same rules of sexual selection as outlined by Darwin for lower animals? To what extent are the consequences of Gilman's type of sexual selection similar to Darwin's?

2. To what extent do you believe that the economic dependence of women upon men is still a factor — even if a diminished one — at the present time? What evidence can you cite of this continued economic dependence?

3. What tendencies do you see in contemporary culture of both men and women being "over-sexed" in the sense that Gilman uses the term? In what particular areas (professions, aspects of contemporary culture, etc.) is this tendency most apparent?
4. Gilman says of the sexuo-economic relation of her time, that "It sexualizes our industrial relation and commercializes our sex-relation." How does contemporary advertising continue to operate along such lines?
5. In paragraphs 30 through 43, Gilman makes a distinction between "the expansive forces of masculine energy" and "the preservative and constructive forces of female energy." Do you believe that there is a biological justification (or any other justification) for such a distinction? Explain.
6. Underlying Gilman's argument are a set of Darwinian assumptions that occasionally become explicit. Summarize her argument, using specifically Darwinian terms, i.e., using such terms as natural selection and survival of the fittest. Thus interpreted, has Gilman made fair and reasonable use of Darwin's ideas?

JOSIAH STRONG *(1847–1916)*

We have seen how Darwin's conception of the survival of the fittest was adapted to the social and economic spheres. But Darwinism proved equally adaptable to the national and racial spheres. Not only could Darwinism show that rich people were more "fit" than poor people, it could also show that certain countries or certain races were "fitter" than their rivals and would therefore be "selected" for survival. In the selection by Adolf Hitler, following this one, we will see how this type of thinking can be the starting point for the most monstrous crimes against humanity. But long before Hitler, survival-of-the-fittest thinking, as applied to nations and races, was being promoted with great success in the United States.

The United States provided fertile soil for the growth of national and racial Darwinism. In the late 19th century, the United States was not yet a world power, but perceptive observers saw that all the elements for such power were present. In contrast to the cramped, tradition-bound nations of Europe, the United States was an energetic young giant, flexing its muscles in the wake of the Industrial Revolution, blessed with virtually unlimited natural and human resources, and, to many of its proud inhabitants — particularly its Anglo-Saxon inhabitants — far better qualified to assume the leadership of the world than any other nation. In his widely read essay, "Manifest Destiny" (1885) John Fiske wrote: "It was for Spain, France, and England to contend for the possession of this vast region [i.e., the newly discovered Americas], and to prove by the result of the struggle which kind of civilization was endowed with the higher and sturdier political life. The race which here should gain the victory was clearly destined hereafter to take the lead in the world, though the rival powers could not in those days fully appreciate the fact." Fiske went on to assert that "the work which the English race began when it colonized North America is destined to go on until every land in the earth's surface that is not already the seat of an old civilization shall become English in its language, in its religion, in its political habits and traditions, and to a predominant extent in the blood of its people." Similar in spirit to Fiske's essay, but even more explicitly Darwinian, and considerably more influential, was a book entitled *Our Country* (1885) by the Reverend Josiah Strong.

Born in 1847 in Napierville, Illinois, Josiah Strong was a descendant of a family that had settled in Massachusetts in 1630. He was educated at Western Reserve College in Hudson, Ohio, and then at Lane Theological Seminary in Cincinnati. Ten days after his marriage to Alice Brisbee in 1871, he became pastor of a Congregational Church in Cheyenne, Wyoming. For the next fourteen years, he held a variety of theological positions in various parts of the United States, including a term as a secretary of the Congregational Home Missionary Society. As its name implies, the Home Missionary Society was concerned with spreading Christianity not among pagans in foreign countries, but rather among American settlers. Strong's famous work, *Our Country,* was commissioned by the society as a revision of its pamphlet of the same title. Strong turned this once-conventional pamphlet into his own eloquent statement of the present and future prospects of America. Part sociological treatise, part evangelical tract, *Our Country* was an immediate success that made its author famous and greatly in demand as a speaker. The work was translated into several languages and went into many editions in the United States. To a modern editor, "*Our Country* is a mirror of Protestant America in the 1880s, reflecting its image of the past, its present realities, and its dreams of the future."[1]

Strong's later life was built upon the success he won from *Our Country.* He was appointed secretary of the American Evangelical Alliance and set to work on another book, *The New Era* (1893), which was almost as successful as his first. In 1898, Strong founded the League for Social Service (later the American Institute for Social Service), a base from which he lectured tirelessly on the social responsibilities of the church. In 1904, he went to England and founded the British Institute of Social Service. During the remainder of his active years, he continued his public speaking and writing careers; he died at the age of seventy. To one of his biographers, "Josiah Strong was tall and vigorous — a handsome man, with shining eyes. Passionate in his idealistic zeal and consecration, he was saved from fanaticism by his abundant sanity, ripe scholarship, unfailing good nature, and unshakable confidence in his fellow men." Despite his undeniable and numerous good works on behalf of the poor and his advocacy of the responsible use of wealth for social service, modern readers are likely to view Strong less sympathetically, perhaps as a harbinger of American arrogance and self-righteousness, and as a symptom of the kind of mentality that — in the name of both religion and science — sets one faith and one race above (if not against) all others.

The following passage is excerpted from Chapter 14 of *Our Country.* In the section deleted from this chapter, Strong cites statistical evidence to demonstrate the increasing population rates of Anglo-Saxon peoples, maintains that the Anglo-Saxon race will eventually become the most populous in Europe and then the world, argues that North America is to become the main home of the Anglo-Saxon race and that the United States will eventually take predominance over England; thus, ultimately, the United States will be home to "the highest type of Anglo-Saxon civilization." As we will see, Strong quotes Darwin himself to support his view that the Anglo-Saxon population of the United States represents the end product of natural selection.

---

[1]Jurgen Herbst, ed. *Our Country.* Cambridge, Mass.: Harvard University Press, 1963, Introduction, xxvi.

THE ANGLO-SAXON AND THE WORLD'S FUTURE[1]

Every race which has deeply impressed itself on the human family has   1
been the representative of some great idea — one or more — which has
given direction to the nation's life and form to its civilization. Among the
Egyptians this seminal idea was life, among the Persians it was light,
among the Hebrews it was purity, among the Greeks it was beauty, among
the Romans it was law. The Anglo-Saxon is the representative of two great
ideas, which are closely related. One of them is that of civil liberty. Nearly
all of the civil liberty of the world is enjoyed by Anglo-Saxons: the English,
the British colonists, and the people of the United States. To some, like the
Swiss, it is permitted by the sufferance of their neighbors; others, like the
French, have experimented with it; but, in modern times, the peoples
whose love of liberty has won it, and whose genius for self-government
has preserved it, have been Anglo-Saxons. The noblest races have always
been lovers of liberty. The love ran strong in early German blood, and has
profoundly influenced the institutions of all the branches of the great German family; but it was left for the Anglo-Saxon branch fully to recognize
the right of the individual to himself, and formally to declare it the foundation stone of government.

The other great idea of which the Anglo-Saxon is the exponent is that   2
of a pure *spiritual* Christianity. It was no accident that the great reformation
of the sixteenth century originated among a Teutonic, rather than a Latin[2]
people. It was the fire of liberty burning in the Saxon heart that flamed up
against the absolutism of the Pope. Speaking roughly, the peoples of Europe which are Celtic[3] are Roman Catholic, and those which are Teutonic
are Protestant; and where the Teutonic race was purest, there Protestantism spread with the greatest rapidity. But, with beautiful exceptions, Protestantism on the continent has degenerated into mere formalism. By confirmation at a certain age, the state churches are filled with members who

---

Josiah Strong. The Anglo-Saxon and the World's Future [1886]. Rpt. in *Our Country*. Ed.,
Jurgen Herbst. Cambridge: Belknap Press of Harvard UP, 1963.

[1]It is only just to say that the substance of this chapter was given to the public as a lecture
some three years before the appearance of Prof. John Fiske's "Manifest Destiny," in *Harper's Magazine*, 70 (March 1885), 578–590, which contains some of the same ideas. [Strong]

[2]*Teutonic:* One of the peoples of northern Europe (English, Germans, Danes, Dutch, etc.);
Latin: of France, Italy, or Spain.

[3]*Celtic:* One of the peoples of western Europe (Irish, Welsh, highland Scottish, Gallic, etc.).

generally know nothing of a personal spiritual experience. In obedience to a military order, a regiment of German soldiers files into church and partakes of the sacrament, just as it would shoulder arms or obey any other word of command. It is said that, in Berlin and Leipsic,[4] only a little over one per cent of the Protestant population are found in church. Protestantism on the continent seems to be about as poor in spiritual life and power as Romanism. That means that most of the spiritual Christianity in the world is found among Anglo-Saxons and their converts; for this is the great missionary race. If we take all of the German missionary societies together, we find that, in the number of workers and amount of contributions, they do not equal the smallest of the three great English missionary societies. The year that the Congregationalists in the United States gave one dollar and thirty-seven cents per caput [capita] to foreign missions, the members of the great German State Church gave only three-quarters of a cent per caput to the same cause. Evidently it is chiefly to the English and American peoples that we must look for the evangelization of the world. . . .

Heretofore, war has been almost the chief occupation of strong races. The mission of the Anglo-Saxon has been largely that of the soldier; but the world is making progress, we are leaving behind the barbarism of war; as civilization advances, it will learn less of war, and concern itself more with the arts of peace, and for these the massive battle-ax must be wrought into tools of finer temper. The physical changes accompanied by mental, which are taking place in the people of the United States are apparently to adapt men to the demands of a higher civilization. But the objection is here interposed that the "physical degeneracy of America" is inconsistent with the supposition of our advancing to a higher civilization. Professor Huxley,[5] when at Buffalo he addressed the American Association for the Advancement of Science, said he had heard of the degeneration of the original American stock, but during his visit to the states he had failed to perceive it. We are not, however, in this matter, dependent on the opinion of even the best observers. During the War of the Confederacy, the Medical Department of the Provost Marshal General's Bureau gathered statistics from the examination of over half a million of men, native and foreign, young and old, sick and sound, drawn from every rank and condition of life, and hence, fairly representing the whole people. Dr. Baxter's Official Report shows that our native whites were over an inch taller than the English, and nearly two-thirds of an inch taller than the Scotch, who, in height, were superior to all other foreigners. At the age of completed growth, the Irish,

---

[4]*Leipsic:* Leipzig, a city in east Germany.
[5]*Professor Huxley:* T.H. Huxley.

who were the stoutest of the foreigners, surpassed the native whites, in girth of chest, less than a quarter of an inch. Statistics as to weight are meager, but Dr. Baxter remarks that it is perhaps not too much to say that the war statistics show "that the mean weight of the white native of the United States is not disproportionate to his stature." Americans were found to be superior to Englishmen not only in height, but also in chest measurement and weight. "Dealers in ready-made clothing in the United States assert that they have been obliged to adopt a larger scale of sizes, in width as well as length, to meet the demands of the average American man, than were required ten years ago."[6] Such facts afford more than a hint that the higher civilization of the future will not lack an adequate physical basis in the people of the United States.

Mr. Darwin is not only disposed to see, in the superior vigor of our people, an illustration of his favorite theory of natural selection, but even intimates that the world's history thus far has been simply preparatory for our future, and tributary to it. He says: "There is apparently much truth in the belief that the wonderful progress of the United States, as well as the character of the people, are the results of natural selection; for the more energetic, restless, and courageous men from all parts of Europe have emigrated during the last ten or twelve generations to that great country, and have there succeeded best. Looking at the distant future, I do not think that the Rev. Mr. Zincke takes an exaggerated view when he says: 'All other series of events — as that which resulted in the culture of mind in Greece, and that which resulted in the Empire of Rome — only appear to have purpose and value when viewed in connection with, or rather as subsidiary to, the great stream of Anglo-Saxon emigration to the West.'"[7]   4

There is abundant reason to believe that the Anglo-Saxon race is to be,   5
is, indeed, already becoming, more effective here than in the mother country. The marked superiority of this race is due, in large measure, to its highly mixed origin. Says Rawlinson: "It is a general rule, now almost universally admitted by ethnologists, that the mixed races of mankind are superior to the pure ones"; and adds: "Even the Jews, who are so often cited as an example of a race at once pure and strong, may, with more reason, be adduced on the opposite side of the argument."[8] The ancient Egyptians, the Greeks, and the Romans, were all mixed races. Among modern races,

---

[6]David A. Wells, *Recent Economic Changes* (New York, 1889), pp. 348–349. [Strong]

[7]Charles Darwin, *The Descent of Man* (New York, 1888), p. 142. [Strong]

[8]George Rawlinson, "Duties of Higher Toward Lower Races," *Princeton Review* (November 1878), pp. 837, 840. [Strong]

the most conspicuous example is afforded by the Anglo-Saxons. Mr. Green's studies show that Mr. Tennyson's poetic line,

"Saxon and Norman and Dane are we,"[9]

must be supplemented with Celt and Gaul,[10] Welshman and Irishman, Frisian and Flamand, French Huguenot and German Palatine.[11] What took place a thousand years ago and more in England again transpires to-day in the United States. "History repeats itself"; but, as the wheels of history are the chariot wheels of the Almighty, there is, with every revolution, an onward movement toward the goal of His eternal purposes. There is here a new commingling of races; and, while the largest injections of foreign blood are substantially the same elements that constituted the original Anglo-Saxon admixture, so that we may infer the general type will be preserved, there are strains of other bloods being added, which, if Mr. Emerson's remark is true, that "the best nations are those most widely related," may be expected to improve the stock, and aid it to a higher destiny. If the dangers of immigration, which have been pointed out, can be successfully met for the next few years, until it has passed its climax, it may be expected to add value to the amalgam which will constitute the new Anglo-Saxon race of the New World. Concerning our future, Herbert Spencer says: "One great result is, I think, tolerably clear. From biological truths it is to be inferred that the eventual mixture of the allied varieties of the Aryan race, forming the population, will produce a more powerful type of man than has hitherto existed, and a type of man more plastic, more adaptable, more capable of undergoing the modifications needful for complete social life. I think, whatever difficulties they may have to surmount, and whatever tribulations they may have to pass through, the Americans may reasonably look forward to a time when they will have produced a civilization grander than any the world has known."

It may be easily shown, and is of no small significance, that the two great ideas of which the Anglo-Saxon is the exponent are having a fuller development in the United States than in Great Britain. There the union of Church and State tends strongly to paralyze some of the members of the body of Christ. Here there is no such influence to destroy spiritual life and power. Here, also, has been evolved the form of government consistent

---

[9]*Saxon and Norman and Dane are we*": Line 3 of Tennyson's poem, "A Welcome to Alexandra." First published in 1863, the poem commemorates the marriage of Princess Alexandra of Denmark to Albert Edward, Prince of Wales, later Edward VII of England.

[10]*Gaul:* Ancient name for the territory now consisting largely of the modern nation of France.

[11]*Palatine:* A region west of the Rhine, administered from 1837 to 1945 by Bavaria, a German state.

with the largest possible of civil liberty. Furthermore, it is significant that the marked characteristics of this race are being here emphasized most. Among the most striking features of the Anglo-Saxon is his money-making power — a power of increasing importance in the widening commerce of the world's future. We have seen, in a preceding chapter, that, although England is by far the richest nation of Europe, we have already outstripped her in the race after wealth, and we have only begun the development of our vast resources.

Again, another marked characteristic of the Anglo-Saxon is what may 7
be called an instinct or genius for colonizing. His unequaled energy, his indomitable perseverance, and his personal independence, made him a pioneer. He excels all others in pushing his way into new countries. It was those in whom this tendency was strongest that came to America, and this inherited tendency has been further developed by the westward sweep of successive generations across the continent. So noticeable has this characteristic become that English visitors remark it. Charles Dickens once said that the typical American would hesitate to enter heaven unless assured that he could go farther west.

Again, nothing more manifestly distinguishes the Anglo-Saxon than 8
his intense and persistent energy, and he is developing in the United States an energy which, in eager activity and effectiveness, is peculiarly American.

This is due partly to the fact that Americans are much better fed than 9
Europeans, and partly to the undeveloped resources of a new country, but more largely to our climate, which acts as a constant stimulus. Ten years after the landing of the Pilgrims, the Rev. Francis Higginson,[12] a good observer, wrote: "A sup of New England air is better than a whole flagon of English ale." Thus early had the stimulating effect of our climate been noted. Moreover, our social institutions are stimulating. In Europe the various ranks of society are, like the strata of the earth, fixed and fossilized. There can be no great change without a terrible upheaval, a social earthquake. Here society is like the waters of the sea, mobile; as General Garfield[13] said, and so signally illustrated in his own experience, that which is at the bottom to-day may one day flash on the crest of the highest wave. Every one is free to become whatever he can make of himself; free

---

[12]*Rev. Francis Higginson:* Higginson was a British-born Anglican clergyman who emigrated to America in 1629 and settled at Salem, Massachusetts.

[13]*General Garfield:* Strong is referring here to James Garfield, general of volunteers during the Civil War, and later the twentieth president of the United States. After having been shot by a disgruntled office seeker in 1881, at the beginning of his term in office, Garfield died six months later. Although he grew up in poverty, he scraped up enough money to attend Williams College. Before the Civil War, he taught grammar school.

to transform himself from a rail-splitter or a tanner or a canal-boy, into the nation's President. Our aristocracy, unlike that of Europe, is open to all comers. Wealth, position, influence, are prizes offered for energy; and every farmer's boy, every apprentice and clerk, every friendless and penniless immigrant, is free to enter the list. Thus many causes co-operate to produce here the most forceful and tremendous energy in the world.

What is the significance of such facts? These tendencies infold the future; they are the mighty alphabet with which God writes his prophecies. May we not, by a careful laying together of the letters, spell out something of his meaning? It seems to me that God, with infinite wisdom and skill, is training the Anglo-Saxon race for an hour sure to come in the world's future. Heretofore there has always been in the history of the world a comparatively unoccupied land westward, into which the crowded countries of the East have poured their surplus populations. But the widening waves of migration, which millenniums ago rolled east and west from the valley of the Euphrates, meet to-day on our Pacific coast. There are no more new worlds. The unoccupied arable lands of the earth are limited, and will soon be taken. The time is coming when the pressure of population on the means of subsistence will be felt here as it is now felt in Europe and Asia. Then will the world enter upon a new stage of its history — *the final competition of races, for which the Anglo-Saxon is being schooled.* Long before the thousand millions are here, the mighty *centrifugal* tendency, inherent in this stock and strengthened in the United States, will assert itself. Then this race of unequaled energy, with all the majesty of numbers and the might of wealth behind it — the representative, let us hope, of the largest liberty, the purest Christianity, the highest civilization — having developed peculiarly aggressive traits calculated to impress its institutions upon mankind, will spread itself over the earth. If I read not amiss, this powerful race will move down upon Mexico, down upon Central and South America, out upon the islands of the sea, over upon Africa and beyond. And can any one doubt that the result of this competition of races will be the "survival of the fittest"? "Any people," says Dr. Bushnell, "that is physiologically advanced in culture, though it be only in a degree beyond another which is mingled with it on strictly equal terms, is sure to live down and finally live out its inferior. Nothing can save the inferior race but a ready and pliant assimilation. Whether the feebler and more abject races are going to be regenerated and raised up, is already very much of a question. What if it should be God's plan to people the world with better and finer material?

"Certain it is, whatever expectations we may indulge, that there is a tremendous overbearing surge of power in the Christian nations, which, if the others are not speedily raised to some vastly higher capacity, will inevitably submerge and bury them forever. These great populations of Christendom — what are they doing, but throwing out their colonies on

10

11

every side, and populating themselves, if I may so speak into the possession of all countries and climes?"[14] To this result no war of extermination is needful; the contest is not one of arms, but of vitality and civilization. "At the present day," says Mr. Darwin, "civilized nations are everywhere supplanting barbarous nations, excepting where the climate opposes a deadly barrier; and they succeed mainly, though not exclusively, through their arts, which are the products of the intellect."[15] Thus the Finns were supplanted by the Aryan races in Europe and Asia, the Tartars[16] by the Russians, and thus the aborigines of North America, Australia and New Zealand are now disappearing before the all-conquering Anglo-Saxons. It seems as if these inferior tribes were only precursors of a superior race, voices in the wilderness crying: "Prepare ye the way of the Lord!" The Savage is a hunter; by the incoming of civilization the game is driven away and disappears before the hunter becomes a herder or an agriculturist. The savage is ignorant of many diseases of civilization which, when he is exposed to them, attack him before he learns how to treat them. Civilization also has its vices, of which the uninitiated savage is innocent. He proves an apt learner of vice, but dull enough in the school of morals.

Every civilization has its destructive and preservative elements. The Anglo-Saxon race would speedily decay but for the salt of Christianity. Bring savages into contact with our civilization, and its destructive forces become operative at once, while years are necessary to render effective the saving influences of Christian instruction. Moreover, the pioneer wave of our civilization carries with it more scum than salt. Where there is one missionary, there are hundreds of miners or traders or adventurers ready to debauch the native.   *12*

Whether the extinction of inferior races before the advancing Anglo-Saxon seems to the reader sad or otherwise, it certainly appears probable. I know of nothing except climatic conditions to prevent this race from populating Africa as it has peopled North America. And those portions of Africa which are unfavorable to Anglo-Saxon life are less extensive than was once supposed. The Dutch Boers,[17] after two centuries of life there, are as hardy as any race on earth. The Anglo-Saxon has established himself in climates totally diverse — Canada, South Africa, and India — and, through several generations, has preserved his essential race characteristics. He is not, of course, superior to climatic influences; but even in warm climates,   *13*

---

[14]Horace Bushnell, *Christian Nurture* (New York, 1861), pp. 207, 213. [Strong]

[15]Charles Darwin, *The Descent of Man* (New York, 1871), p. 154: [Strong here quotes from the first edition. The reference in note 3 is taken from the revised second edition.] [Jurgen Herbst, ed., *Our Country*, by Josiah Strong (Cambridge: Harvard University Press, 1963).].

[16]*Tartars:* Mongol rulers of Asia and eastern Europe in the 13th and 14th centuries.

[17]*Dutch Boers:* Dutch colonists of South Africa.

he is likely to retain his aggressive vigor long enough to supplant races already enfeebled. Thus, in what Dr. Bushnell calls "the out-populating power of the Christian stock," may be found God's final and complete solution of the dark problem of heathenism among many inferior peoples.

Some of the stronger races, doubtless, may be able to preserve their integrity; but, in order to compete with the Anglo-Saxon, they will probably be forced to adopt his methods and instruments, his civilization and his religion. Significant movements are now in progress among them. While the Christian religion was never more vital, or its hold upon the Anglo-Saxon mind stronger, there is taking place among the nations a widespread intellectual revolt against traditional beliefs. "In every corner of the world," says Mr. Froude, "there is the same phenomenon of the decay of established religions. . . . Among the Mohammedans, Jews, Buddhists, Brahmins, traditionary creeds are losing their hold. An intellectual revolution is sweeping over the world, breaking down established opinions, dissolving foundations on which historical faiths have been built up."[18] The contact of Christian with heathen nations is awakening the latter to new life. Old superstitions are loosening their grasp. The dead crust of fossil faiths is being shattered by the movements of life underneath. In Catholic countries, Catholicism is losing its influence over educated minds, and in some cases the masses have already lost all faith in it. Thus, while on this continent God is training the Anglo-Saxon race for its mission, a complemental work has been in progress in the great world beyond. God has two hands. Not only is he preparing in our civilization the die with which to stamp the nations, but, by what Southey[19] called the "timing of Providence," he is preparing mankind to receive our impress.

Is there room for reasonable doubt that this race, unless devitalized by alcohol and tobacco,[20] is destined to dispossess many weaker races, assimilate others, and mold the remainder, until, in a very true and important sense, it has Anglo-Saxonized mankind? Already "the English language, saturated with Christian ideas, gathering up into itself the best thought of all the ages, is the great agent of Christian civilization throughout the world; at this moment affecting the destinies and molding the character of half the human race."[21] Jacob Grimm, the German philologist, said of this

14

15

---

[18]James Anthony Froude, "Romanism and the Irish Race in the United States," *North American Review,* 129 (December 1879), 535–536. [Strong]

[19]*Southey:* Robert Southey (1774–1843), British romantic poet, essayist, and biographer. See selection by Southey in Part IV, pp. 335–343.

[20]*devitalized by alcohol and tobacco:* The devitalizing effects of alcohol and tobacco are a major theme of Strong's book; he considered alcohol and tobacco two of the very few factors that could prevent the Anglo-Saxons from achieving their true greatness.

[21]Rev. Nathaniel George Clark. [Clark (1825–1896), a linguist, taught at the University of Vermont and at Union College. In 1865 he was elected Secretary of the American Board of Commissioners for Foreign Missions.] [Strong/Herbst]

language: "It seems chosen, like its people, to rule in future times in a still greater degree in all the corners of the earth." He predicted, indeed, that the language of Shakespeare would eventually become the language of mankind. Is not Tennyson's noble prophecy to find its fulfillment in Anglo-Saxondom's extending its dominion and influence —

> "Til the war-drum throbs no longer, and the battle-flags are furl'd
> In the Parliament of man, the Federation of the world."[22]

In my own mind, there is no doubt that the Anglo-Saxon is to exercise **16** the commanding influence in the world's future; but the exact nature of that influence is, as yet, undetermined. How far his civilization will be materialistic and atheistic, and how long it will take thoroughly to Christianize and sweeten it, how rapidly he will hasten the coming of the kingdom wherein dwelleth righteousness, or how many ages he may retard it, is still uncertain; but *is now being swiftly determined.* Let us weld together in a chain the various links of our logic which we have endeavored to forge. Is it manifest that the Anglo-Saxon holds in his hands the destinies of mankind for ages to come? Is it evident that the United States is to be the home of this race, the principal seat of his power, the great center of his influence? Is it true that the great West is to dominate the nation's future? Has it been shown that this generation is to determine the character, and hence the destiny of the West? Then may God open the eyes of this generation! When Napoleon drew up his troops before the Mamelukes,[23] under the shadow of the Pyramids, pointing to the latter, he said to his soldiers: "Remember that from yonder heights forty centuries look down on you." Men of this generation, from the pyramid top of opportunity on which God has set us, *we look down on forty centuries!* We stretch our hand into the future with power to mold the destinies of unborn millions.

> "We are living, we are dwelling,
> In a grand and awful time,
> In an age on ages telling —
> To be living is sublime!"[24]

Notwithstanding the great perils which threaten it, I cannot think our **17** civilization will perish; but I believe it is fully in the hands of the Christians of the United States, during the next ten or fifteen years, to hasten or retard the coming of Christ's kingdom in the world by hundreds, and perhaps

---

[22]*"Til the war-drum throbs no longer . . .":* Lines 127 and 128 of Tennyson's heroic poem in trochaic meter, "Locksley Hall" (1842).

[23]*Mamelukes:* Members of the military caste that dominated Egypt from the 13th to the early 19th centuries.

[24]*"We are living, we are dwelling . . .":* The first four lines of "The Present Age," an inspirational poem by American clergyman Arthur Cleveland Coxe.

thousands, of years. We of this generation and nation occupy the Gibraltar of the ages which commands the world's future.

REVIEW QUESTIONS

1. Of which two seminal ideas is the Anglo-Saxon the representative, according to Strong? What has been the fate of Protestantism on the European continent? What evidence does Strong cite for the greater spirituality of Anglo-American Protestantism over German Christianity?
2. What evidence does Strong cite to support his conclusion that "the higher civilization of the future will not lack an adequate physical basis in the people of the United States"? To what factor does Strong attribute the superiority of the Anglo-Saxon in the United States to his counterpart in England? How does Strong draw upon both Darwin and Herbert Spencer to support his views as to the evolutionary superiority of the "Aryan" race in the United States?
3. How does Strong account for the fact that the two great ideas represented by the Anglo-Saxon have been more fully developed in the United States than in Great Britain? How does he account for the greater energy of the Americans over the British?
4. What factor will precipitate what Strong calls "the final competition of races, for which the Anglo-Saxon is being schooled"? What shape will this competition assume? What will be its result? What will be the fate of the losing races? Upon what will their survival depend?
5. What factors might prevent (or retard) the victory of the Anglo-Saxon races over "weaker races," according to Strong? What is the chief factor determining the speed with which the Anglo-Saxon race begins to exercise dominant influence over human civilization?

DISCUSSION AND WRITING QUESTIONS

1. Critique the views expressed by Strong in this selection. What are his stated and unstated assumptions? How well does he support his views? On what basis (if at all) can you question the validity of this passage? What are your own views on the subject? How do you account for any discrepancy between your own views and Strong's? *Alternate assignment:* Cite one sentence in Strong's passage and critique it as an instance of the kind of assumptions behind the essay. Example (from paragraph 13): "Thus, in what Dr. Bushnell calls 'the out-populating power of the Christian stock,' may be found God's final and complete solution of the dark problem of heathenism among many inferior peoples."
2. Paragraphs 10 through 13 contain Strong's most explicit references to the Darwinian struggle for existence and the survival of the fittest. Although Strong seems to have been reasonably prophetic about the dominant role of the United States in world affairs in the 20th century (and the relative eclipse of Europe and Great Britain), he was wrong about the inevitable spread of Anglo-Saxon civilization to the rest of the world. If anything, the reverse is now occurring; i.e.,

Anglo-Saxon civilization is losing, rather than gaining ground, even in its home territories. Strong was also wrong when he asserted that "[n]othing can save the inferior race but a ready and pliant assimilation." What did Strong fail to anticipate? Which of his assumptions were flawed?

3. Despite the fact that Anglo-Saxon civilization has not proved to be the "fittest" — and is therefore not the only survivor — the Anglo-Saxon struggle for existence with so-called "inferior races" has left a residue of bitterness and hostility. Discuss one or two areas of the world where this has been most apparent. (For example, Strong notes in paragraph 13 that the "Dutch Boers, after two centuries of life [in South Africa] are as hardy as any race on earth.")

ADOLF HITLER *(1889–1945)*

According to both Darwin's theory and social Darwinism, the struggle for existence and the survival of the fittest are processes of natural law. But, of course, natural law can be thwarted. In the natural world itself, species that might otherwise have become extinct, because of their inability to adapt, have been saved by the intervention of humans, either through their removal to a more favorable environment or through the elimination of some of their natural enemies. In the social sphere, welfare programs, protective tariffs, excessive taxation, and other restrictions on capital and profits all have the effect of thwarting natural law by artificially strengthening those who are less well adapted and weakening those who are more well adapted. The result (according to the social Darwinists) is an unnatural regime that may temporarily benefit the less fit but that will have the ultimate effect of halting social progress (which depends upon the prosperity of the fittest) and perhaps even leading to the collapse of the social order.

It is the prospect of such a collapse that underlies much of Adolf Hitler's *Mein Kampf*. For Hitler, the fittest were not the wealthiest or the most successful in waging business struggles; they were rather the Aryan race, the highest of all races, the race most suited to dominate the world. Such was the natural order of things. But what was threatening to overturn the natural order was the degradation of the Aryan race through intermixing with such "inferior" races as the Jews. This had to be prevented, at all costs. Hitler was not the first to harbor such sentiments. But unlike other anti-Semites, he had the power to carry out his program on a colossal scale; and in so doing, he became the most notorious criminal in recorded history.

Hitler was born in Braunau-am-Inn, Austria, in 1889, the son of a customs official. He studied art and architecture in Vienna but twice failed to be admitted to the Academy of Fine Arts. He supported himself in Vienna by painting postcards and watercolors, while leading a lonely, bohemian life among derelicts and outcasts and reading anti-Semitic and nationalist writings. Upon the outbreak of World War I, he volunteered for the Bavarian infantry. Wounded and then gassed while serving on the front lines, he was decorated for bravery. After the war, he served for a time as a propaganda instructor for the troops; but in 1920 he left the army, a few months after joining the National Socialist German Worker's Party — Nazis, for short. The Nazis, headquartered in Munich, Bavaria (a state of western Germany), attracted disgruntled former servicemen and others disenchanted with the republican government and were thus able to capitalize on the widespread frustration caused by Germany's defeat in the war and the subsequent economic chaos.

Through his power to galvanize large audiences with his emotional appeals, and through his political skills, Hitler rose quickly in the ranks of the party, becoming its leader in 1921. In 1923, Hitler and the Nazis prematurely tried to seize control of the Bavarian government; the attempt, known as the Beer Hall Putsch, failed, and Hitler and the other leaders of the party were thrown in jail. While serving nine months of a five-year sentence in the Landsberg prison, Hitler wrote the first volume of *Mein Kampf*. None of his ideas were original, and had Hitler's political career ended at this point, the work would be forgotten today. As it is, *Mein Kampf* provides a chilling preview of the Nazis' program once they took power in 1933. The German people, Hitler argued, were the most superior of all races; and to protect them from the corrupting effects of international Jewry, Marxism, and humanism, dictatorial power must be exercised by a *Führer*. The *Führer* would combat both internal and external foes, allowing the German people to achieve the *Lebensraum* (living space) that would make them unconquerable. Neither the Weimar government (in power at that time) nor any other democratic government was capable of protecting the interests of the German race.

After his release from prison in 1923, Hitler moved to resume control of the Nazis, though he was challenged by Gregor Strasser, a rival party leader, and though he was banned from public speaking until 1928. Defeating Strasser, he continued to exploit the disaffection with the government of industrial leaders, the working classes, and the unemployed. The onset of worldwide depression proved a boon to the Nazis; and in the 1930 elections, they drew 18 percent of the vote, making them the second largest political party in Germany. Two years later the Nazis did even better, with 37 percent of the vote; and Hitler only narrowly lost the presidential election to the incumbent, Paul von Hindenburg. The Nazis lost some of their support in the November 1932 elections, and with the worst of the depression over, Hitler's prestige seemed to be waning. But in January 1933, Hindenburg, with the support of a conservative group who believed they could use Hitler for their own ends (a disastrous miscalculation), invited him to join the government as chancellor, and Germany's fate — and the world's — was sealed.

After his appointment, Hitler swiftly consolidated his power, ruthlessly suppressing all opponents, destroying all other political parties, both through legal means and through the S.S. (the *Schutzstaffel*, or Blackshirts), who simply murdered their victims. After Hindenberg died in 1934, Hitler became the *Führer*, or supreme dictator of Germany. Added to the terror of the S.S. was the Gestapo, or secret police, and the beginning of a network of concentration camps. Hitler now begin to enforce his racial doctrines by establishing the Nuremberg Laws (1935), which revoked the citizenship of German Jews and which prohibited intermarriage between Jews and non-Jews.

Determined to restore the lost honor of Germany and to lift the humiliating restrictions imposed by the postwar Versailles treaty, Hitler began a series of intimidating military and diplomatic ventures, including the remilitarization of the Rhineland (1936), the alliance with Mussolini's fascist Italy (1936), the annexation of Austria (1938), and the occupation of the Sudetenland and parts of Czechoslovakia (1938). When Hitler's armies took over the rest of Czechoslovakia and began threatening Poland, Britain and France guaranteed Poland against attack. On September 1, 1939, Hitler invaded Poland, and Britain and France declared war.

During the first phase of the war, Hitler seemed invincible; his armies overran most of Europe, including Norway, Denmark, the Netherlands, and France. But Germany encountered its first serious military setback when Hitler's air force, the Luftwaffe, failed to defeat the British R.A.F., thus preventing an invasion of Britain. Subsequent reverses in North Africa, and a staggering defeat of the German forces at Stalingrad, in the Soviet Union, turned the tide of the war. By the end of 1941, the United States had entered the conflict. Hitler continued to retain his power over the masses, and his armies continued to win victories, but his increasing military reverses affected his judgment and his mental stability. In July 1944, a month after the allies invaded France, Hitler was almost assassinated in a military plot led by Colonel Claus von Stauffenberg. With the Americans and British approaching Berlin from the west, and the Russians from the east, Hitler realized his position was hopeless. In April 1945, immediately after marrying his long-time mistress, Eva Braun, he committed suicide.

When the Allies marched into Germany and Poland, they discovered not only the expected devastation of war, but also, to their undying horror, the results of Hitler's "new order." During the past decade, millions of Jews and members of other "inferior" races throughout Europe and the Soviet Union had been rounded up and sent to death camps. At Auschwitz, Treblinka, Bergen-Belsen, Buchenwald, and other camps, Jews had been suffocated in gas chambers, tortured and killed in infamous medical experiments, starved, beaten, shot, and burned to death. About 6 million Jews and other "subhumans" were exterminated as a result of Hitler's racial doctrines.

These doctrines had been first articulated in *Mein Kampf*, written in 1924, nine years before Hitler became chancellor of Germany. The following passage is from Chapter 11 of *Mein Kampf*.

NATION AND RACE

There are some truths which are so obvious that for this very reason   1
they are not seen or at least not recognized by ordinary people. They sometimes pass by such truisms as though blind and are most astonished when someone suddenly discovers what everyone really ought to know. Columbus's eggs lie around by the hundreds of thousands, but Columbuses are met with less frequently.

Thus men without exception wander about in the garden of Nature;   2
they imagine that they know practically everything and yet with few exceptions pass blindly by one of the most patent principles of Nature's rule: the inner segregation of the species of all living beings on this earth.

Even the most superficial observation shows that Nature's restricted   3
form of propagation and increase is an almost rigid basic law of all the

---

Adolf Hitler. Nation and Race [1924]. *Mein Kampf*. Eds., John Chamberlain et al. Boston: Houghton Mifflin, 1943.

innumerable forms of expression of her vital urge. Every animal mates only with a member of the same species. The titmouse seeks the titmouse, the finch the finch, the stork the stork, the field mouse the field mouse, the dormouse the dormouse, the wolf the she-wolf, etc.

Only unusual circumstances can change this, primarily the compulsion of captivity or any other cause that makes it impossible to mate within the same species. But then Nature begins to resist this with all possible means, and her most visible protest consists either in refusing further capacity for propagation to bastards or in limiting the fertility of later offspring; in most cases, however, she takes away the power of resistance to disease or hostile attacks.

This is only too natural.

Any crossing of two beings not at exactly the same level produces a medium between the level of the two parents. This means: the offspring will probably stand higher than the racially lower parent, but not as high as the higher one. Consequently, it will later succumb in the struggle against the higher level. Such mating is contrary to the will of Nature for a higher breeding of all life. The precondition for this does not lie in associating superior and inferior, but in the total victory of the former. The stronger must dominate and not blend with the weaker, thus sacrificing his own greatness. Only the born weakling can view this as cruel, but he after all is only a weak and limited man; for if this law did not prevail, any conceivable higher development of organic living beings would be unthinkable.

The consequence of this racial purity, universally valid in Nature, is not only the sharp outward delimitation of the various races, but their uniform character in themselves. The fox is always a fox, the goose a goose, the tiger a tiger, etc., and the difference can lie at most in the varying measure of force, strength, intelligence, dexterity, endurance, etc., of the individual specimens. But you will never find a fox who in his inner attitude might, for example, show humanitarian tendencies toward geese, as similarly there is no cat with a friendly inclination toward mice.

Therefore, here, too, the struggle among themselves arises less from inner aversion than from hunger and love. In both cases, Nature looks on calmly, with satisfaction, in fact. In the struggle for daily bread all those who are weak and sickly or less determined succumb, while the struggle of the males for the female grants the right or opportunity to propagate only to the healthiest. And struggle is always a means for improving a species' health and power of resistance and, therefore, a cause of its higher development.

If the process were different, all further and higher development would cease and the opposite would occur. For, since the inferior always predominates numerically over the best, if both had the same possibility of preserving life and propagating, the inferior would multiply so much more rapidly that in the end the best would inevitably be driven into the background, unless a correction of this state of affairs were undertaken. Nature does just this by subjecting the weaker part to such severe living conditions that by them alone the number is limited, and by not permitting the remainder to increase promiscuously, but making a new and ruthless choice according to strength and health.

No more than Nature desires the mating of weaker with stronger individuals, even less does she desire the blending of a higher with a lower race, since, if she did, her whole work of higher breeding, over perhaps hundreds of thousands of years, night be ruined with one blow.   10

Historical experience offers countless proofs of this. It shows with terrifying clarity that in every mingling of Aryan[1] blood with that of lower peoples the result was the end of the cultured people. North America, whose population consists in by far the largest part of Germanic elements who mixed but little with the lower colored peoples, shows a different humanity and culture from Central and South America, where the predominantly Latin immigrants often mixed with the aborigines[2] on a large scale. By this one example, we can clearly and distinctly recognize the effect of racial mixture. The Germanic inhabitant of the American continent, who has remained racially pure and unmixed, rose to be master of the continent; he will remain the master as long as he does not fall a victim to defilement of the blood.   11

The result of all racial crossing is therefore in brief always the following: 12

    a. Lowering of the level of the higher race;

    b. Physical and intellectual regression and hence the beginning of a slowly but surely progressing sickness.

To bring about such a development is, then, nothing else but to sin against the will of the eternal creator.   13

And as a sin this act is rewarded.   14

When man attempts to rebel against the iron logic of Nature, he comes into struggle with the principles to which he himself owes his existence as a man. And this attack must lead to his own doom.   15

Here, of course, we encounter the objection of the modern pacifist, as truly Jewish in its effrontery as it is stupid! 'Man's rôle is to overcome Nature!'   16

Millions thoughtlessly parrot this Jewish nonsense and end up by really imagining that they themselves represent a kind of conqueror of Na-   17

---

[1]*Aryan:* Originally, "Aryan" designated a member of the ancient people who spoke the Indo-European language. The Nazis used the term to mean a Caucasian gentile of Nordic stock — a representative of (in their judgment) the most superior of all human races.

[2]*aborigines:* One of the original native inhabitants of a country.

ture; though in this they dispose of no other weapon than an idea, and at that such a miserable one, that if it were true no world at all would be conceivable.

But quite aside from the fact that man has never yet conquered Nature 18 in anything, but at most has caught hold of and tried to lift one or another corner of her immense gigantic veil of eternal riddles and secrets, that in reality he invents nothing but only discovers everything, that he does not dominate Nature, but has only risen on the basis of his knowledge of various laws and secrets of Nature to be lord over those other living creatures who lack this knowledge — quite aside from all this, an idea cannot overcome the preconditions for the development and being of humanity, since the idea itself depends only on man. Without human beings there is no human idea in this world, therefore, the idea as such is always conditioned by the presence of human beings and hence of all the laws which created the precondition for their existence.

And not only that! Certain ideas are even tied up with certain men.　19 This applies most of all to those ideas whose content originates, not in an exact scientific truth, but in the world of emotion, or, as it is so beautifully and clearly expressed today, reflects an 'inner experience.' All these ideas, which have nothing to do with cold logic as such, but represent only pure expressions of feeling, ethical conceptions, etc., are chained to the existence of men, to whose intellectual imagination and creative power they owe their existence. Precisely in this case the preservation of these definite races and men is the precondition for the existence of these ideas. Anyone, for example, who really desired the victory of the pacifistic idea in this world with all his heart would have to fight with all the means at his disposal for the conquest of the world by the Germans; for, if the opposite should occur, the last pacifist would die out with the last German, since the rest of the world has never fallen so deeply as our own people, unfortunately, has for this nonsense so contrary to Nature and reason. Then, if we were serious, whether we liked it or not, we would have to wage wars in order to arrive at pacifism. This and nothing else was what Wilson, the American world savior,[3] intended, or so at least our German visionaries believed — and thereby his purpose was fulfilled.

---

[3]*Wilson, the American world savior:* Hitler is sarcastically referring here to U.S. President Woodrow Wilson, who served two terms, from 1913 to 1921. Although Wilson, an ardent idealist and pacifist, was strongly opposed to U.S. intervention in foreign affairs and in fact declared the U.S. as neutral after the outbreak of World War I in 1914, the numerous sinkings of British ships by the government in Berlin and the pressures from American public opinion finally convinced Wilson to declare war on Germany. Once in the war, Wilson was instrumental in bringing about peace negotiations, to which the Germans agreed after having been badly defeated in 1918. In pursuit of world peace, Wilson proposed the establishment of a League of Nations, which was accepted in exchange for various economic and territorial concessions at the Versailles Treaty with Germany in 1919.

In actual fact the pacifistic-humane idea is perfectly all right perhaps   20
when the highest type of man has previously conquered and subjected the
world to an extent that makes him the sole ruler of this earth. Then this
idea lacks the power of producing evil effects in exact proportion as its
practical application becomes rare and finally impossible. Therefore, first
struggle and then we shall see what can be done. Otherwise mankind has
passed the high point of its development and the end is not the domination
of any ethical idea but barbarism and consequently chaos. At this point
someone or other may laugh, but this planet once moved through the ether
for millions of years without human beings and it can do so again some
day if men forget that they owe their higher existence, not to the ideas of
a few crazy ideologists, but to the knowledge and ruthless application of
Nature's stern and rigid laws.

Everything we admire on this earth today — science and art, technol-   21
ogy and inventions — is only the creative product of a few peoples and
originally perhaps of *one* race. On them depends the existence of this
whole culture. If they perish, the beauty of this earth will sink into the
grave with them.

However much the soil, for example, can influence men, the result of   22
the influence will always be different depending on the races in question.
The low fertility of a living space may spur the one race to the highest
achievements; in others it will only be the cause of bitterest poverty and
final undernourishment with all its consequences. The inner nature of peoples is always determining the manner in which outward influences will
be effective. What leads the one to starvation trains the other to hard work.

All great cultures of the past perished only because the originally cre-   23
ative race died out from blood poisoning.

The ultimate cause of such a decline was their forgetting that all culture   24
depends on men and not conversely; hence that to preserve a certain culture the man who creates it must be preserved. This preservation is bound
up with the rigid law of necessity and the right to victory of the best and
stronger in this world.

Those who want to live, let them fight, and those who do not want to   25
fight in this world of eternal struggle do not deserve to live.

Even if this were hard — that is how it is! Assuredly, however, by far   26
the harder fate is that which strikes the man who thinks he can overcome
Nature, but in the last analysis only mocks her. Distress, misfortune, and
diseases are her answer.

The man who misjudges and disregards the racial laws actually forfeits   27
the happiness that seems destined to be his. He thwarts the triumphal
march of the best race and hence also the precondition for all human progress, and remains, in consequence, burdened with all the sensibility of
man, in the animal realm of helpless misery.

It is idle to argue which race or races were the original representative   28 of human culture and hence the real founders of all that we sum up under the word "humanity." It is simpler to raise this question with regard to the present, and here an easy, clear answer results. All the human culture, all the results of art, science, and technology that we see before us today, are almost exclusively the creative product of the Aryan. This very fact admits of the not unfounded inference that he alone was the founder of all higher humanity, therefore representing the prototype of all that we understand by the word "man." He is the Prometheus[4] of mankind from whose bright forehead the divine spark of genius has sprung at all times, forever kindling anew that fire of knowledge which illumined the night of silent mysteries and thus caused man to climb the path to mastery over the other beings of this earth. Exclude him — and perhaps after a few thousand years darkness will again descend on the earth, human culture will pass, and the world turn to a desert.

If we were to divide mankind into three groups, the founders of culture, the bearers of culture, the destroyers of culture, only the Aryan could be considered as the representative of the first group. From him originate the foundations and walls of all human creation, and only the outward form and color are determined by the changing traits of character of the various peoples. He provides the mightiest building stones and plans for all human progress and only the execution corresponds to the nature of the varying men and races. In a few decades, for example, the entire east of Asia will possess a culture whose ultimate foundation will be Hellenic[5] spirit and Germanic technology, just as much as in Europe. Only the *outward* form — in part at least — will bear the features of Asiatic character. It is not true, as some people think, that Japan adds European technology to its culture; no, European science and technology are trimmed with Japanese characteristics. The foundation of actual life is no longer the special Japanese culture, although it determines the color of life — because outwardly, in consequence of its inner difference, it is more conspicuous to the European — but the gigantic scientific-technical achievements of Europe and America; that is, of Aryan peoples. Only on the basis of these achievements can the Orient follow general human progress. They furnish the basis of the struggle for daily bread, create weapons and implements for it, and only the outward form is gradually adapted to Japanese character.

29

---

[4]*Prometheus:* In Greek mythology, the Titan who stole fire from the gods to give to mankind. He was punished by being chained to a rock, while an eagle tore at his liver daily (the organ was regenerated each night); eventually, he was released by Hercules.

[5]*Hellenic:* Greek.

If beginning today all further Aryan influence on Japan should stop, 30
assuming that Europe and America should perish, Japan's present rise in
science and technology might continue for a short time; but even in a few
years the well would dry up, the Japanese special character would gain,
but the present culture would freeze and sink back into the slumber from
which it was awakened seven decades ago by the wave of Aryan culture.
Therefore, just as the present Japanese development owes its life to Aryan
origin, long ago in the gray past foreign influence and foreign spirit awakened the Japanese culture of that time. The best proof of this is furnished
by the fact of its subsequent sclerosis and total petrifaction. This can occur
in a people only when the original creative racial nucleus has been lost, or
if the external influence which furnished the impetus and the material for
the first development in the cultural field was later lacking. But if it is established that a people receives the most essential basic materials of its
culture from foreign races, that it assimilates and adapts them, and that
then, if further external influence is lacking, it rigidifies again and again,
such a race may be designated as *"culture-bearing,"* but never as *"culture-
creating."* An examination of the various peoples from this standpoint
points to the fact that practically none of them were originally *culture-found-
ing,* but almost always *culture-bearing.*

Approximately the following picture of their development always 31
results:

Aryan races — often absurdly small numerically — subject foreign peo- 32
ples, and then, stimulated by the special living conditions of the new territory (fertility, climatic conditions, etc.) and assisted by the multitude of
lower-type beings standing at their disposal as helpers, develop the intellectual and organizational capacities dormant within them. Often in a few
millenniums or even centuries they create cultures which originally bear
all the inner characteristics of their nature, adapted to the above-indicated
special qualities of the soil and subjected beings. In the end, however, the
conquerors transgress against the principle of blood purity, to which they
had first adhered; they begin to mix with the subjugated inhabitants and
thus end their own existence; for the fall of man in paradise has always
been followed by his expulsion.

After a thousand years and more, the last visible trace of the former 33
master people is often seen in the lighter skin color which its blood left
behind in the subjugated race, and in a petrified culture which it had originally created. For, once the actual and spiritual conqueror lost himself in
the blood of the subjected people, the fuel for the torch of human progress
was lost! Just as, through the blood of the former masters, the color preserved a feeble gleam in their memory, likewise the night of cultural life is
gently illuminated by the remaining creations of the former light-bringers.
They shine through all the returned barbarism and too often inspire the

thoughtless observer of the moment with the opinion that he beholds the picture of the present people before him, whereas he is only gazing into the mirror of the past.

It is then possible that such a people will a second time, or even more 34 often in the course of its history, come into contact with the race of those who once brought it culture, and the memory of former encounters will not necessarily be present. Unconsciously the remnant of the former master blood will turn toward the new arrival, and what was first possible only by compulsion can now succeed through the people's own will. A new cultural wave makes its entrance and continues until those who have brought it are again submerged in the blood of foreign peoples.

It will be the task of a future cultural and world history to carry on 35 researches in this light and not to stifle in the rendition of external facts, as is so often, unfortunately, the case with our present historical science.

This mere sketch of the development of "culture-bearing" nations 36 gives a picture of the growth, of the activity, and — the decline — of the true culture-founders of this earth, the Aryans themselves.

As in daily life the so-called genius requires a special cause, indeed, 37 often a positive impetus, to make him shine, likewise the genius-race in the life of peoples. In the monotony of everyday life even significant men often seem insignificant, hardly rising above the average of their environment; as soon, however, as they are approached by a situation in which others lose hope or go astray, the genius rises manifestly from the inconspicuous average child, not seldom to the amazement of all those who had hitherto seen him in the pettiness of bourgeois life — and that is why the prophet seldom has any honor in his own country. Nowhere have we better occasion to observe this than in war. From apparently harmless children, in difficult hours when others lose hope, suddenly heroes shoot up with death-defying determination and an icy cool presence of mind. If this hour of trial had not come, hardly anyone would ever have guessed that a young hero was hidden in this beardless boy. It nearly always takes some stimulus to bring the genius on the scene. The hammer-stroke of Fate which throws one man to the ground suddenly strikes steel in another, and when the shell of everyday life is broken, the previously hidden kernel lies open before the eyes of the astonished world. The world then resists and does not want to believe that the type which is apparently identical with it is suddenly a very different being; a process which is repeated with every eminent son of man.

Though an inventor, for example, establishes his fame only on the day 38 of his invention, it is a mistake to think that genius as such entered into the man only at this hour — the spark of genius exists in the brain of the truly creative man from the hour of his birth. True genius is always inborn and never cultivated, let alone learned.

As already emphasized, this applies not only to the individual man but also to the race. Creatively active peoples always have a fundamental creative gift, even if it should not be recognizable to the eyes of superficial observers. Here, too, outward recognition is possible only in consequence of accomplished deeds, since the rest of the world is not capable of recognizing genius in itself, but sees only its visible manifestations in the form of inventions, discoveries, buildings, pictures, etc.; here again it often takes a long time before the world can fight its way through to this knowledge. Just as in the life of the outstanding individual, genius or extraordinary ability strives for practical realization only when spurred on by special occasions, likewise in the life of nations the creative forces and capacities which are present can often be exploited only when definite preconditions invite.

We see this most distinctly in connection with the race which has been and is the bearer of human cultural development — the Aryans. As soon as Fate leads them toward special conditions, their latent abilities begin to develop in a more and more rapid sequence and to mold themselves into tangible forms. The cultures which they found in such cases are nearly always decisively determined by the existing soil, the given climate, and — the subjected people. This last item, to be sure, is almost the most decisive. The more primitive the technical foundations for a cultural activity, the more necessary is the presence of human helpers who, organizationally, assembled and employed, must replace the force of the machine. Without this possibility of using lower human beings, the Aryan would never have been able to take his first steps toward his future culture; just as without the help of various suitable beasts which he knew how to tame, he would not have arrived at a technology which is now gradually permitting him to do without these beasts. The saying, "The Moor has worked off his debt, the Moor can go," unfortunately has only too deep a meaning. For thousands of years the horse has to serve man and help him lay the foundations of a development which now, in consequence of the motor car, is making the horse superfluous. In a few years his activity will have ceased, but without his previous collaboration man might have had a hard time getting where he is today.

Thus, for the formation of higher cultures the existence of lower human types was one of the most essential preconditions, since they alone were able to compensate for the lack of technical aids without which a higher development is not conceivable. It is certain that the first culture of humanity was based less on the tamed animal than on the use of lower human beings.

Only after the enslavement of subjected races did the same fate strike beasts, and not the other way around, as some people would like to think. For first the conquered warrior drew the plow — and only after him the horse. Only pacifist fools can regard this as a sign of human depravity, failing to realize that this development had to take place in order to reach the point where today these sky-pilots could force their drivel on the world.

The progress of humanity is like climbing an endless ladder; it is impossible to climb higher without first taking the lower steps. Thus, the Aryan had to take the road to which reality directed him and not the one that would appeal to the imagination of a modern pacifist. The road of reality is hard and difficult, but in the end it leads where our friend would like to bring humanity by dreaming, but unfortunately removes more than bringing it closer. 43

Hence it is no accident that the first cultures arose in places where the Aryan, in his encounters with lower peoples, subjugated them and bent them to his will. They then became the first technical instrument in the service of a developing culture. 44

Thus, the road which the Aryan had to take was clearly marked out. As a conqueror he subjected the lower beings and regulated their practical activity under his command, according to his will and for his aims. But in directing them to a useful, though arduous activity, he not only spared the life of those he subjected; perhaps he gave them a fate that was better than their previous so-called "freedom." As long as he ruthlessly upheld the master attitude, not only did he really remain master, but also the preserver and increaser of culture. For culture was based exclusively on his abilities and hence on his actual survival. As soon as the subjected people began to raise themselves up and probably approached the conqueror in language, the sharp dividing wall between master and servant fell. The Aryan gave up the purity of his blood and, therefore, lost his sojourn in the paradise which he had made for himself. He became submerged in the racial mixture, and gradually, more and more, lost his cultural capacity, until at last, not only mentally but also physically, he began to resemble the subjected aborigines more than his own ancestors. For a time he could live on the existing cultural benefits, but then petrifaction set in and he fell a prey to oblivion. 45

Thus cultures and empires collapsed to make place for new formations. 46

Blood mixture and the resultant drop in the racial level is the sole cause of the dying out of old cultures; for men do not perish as a result of lost wars, but by the loss of that force of resistance which is contained only in pure blood. 47

All who are not of good race in this world are chaff. 48

And all occurrences in world history are only the expression of the races' instinct of self-preservation, in the good or bad sense. 49

The question of the inner causes of the Aryan's importance can be answered to the effect that they are to be sought less in a natural instinct of self-preservation than in the special type of its expression. The will to live, subjectively viewed, is everywhere equal and different only in the form of 50 its actual expression. In the most primitive living creatures the instinct of self-preservation does not go beyond concern for their own ego. Egoism, as we designate this urge, goes so far that it even embraces time; the moment itself claims everything, granting nothing to the coming hours. In this condition the animal lives only for himself, seeks food only for his present hunger, and fights only for his own life. As long as the instinct of self-preservation expresses itself in this way, every basis is lacking for the formation of a group, even the most primitive form of family. Even a community between male and female beyond pure mating, demands an extension of the instinct of self-preservation, since concern and struggle for the ego are now directed toward the second party; the male sometimes seeks food for the female, too, but for the most part both seek nourishment for the young. Nearly always one comes to the defense of the other, and thus the first, though infinitely simple, forms of a sense of sacrifice result. As soon as this sense extends beyond the narrow limits of the family, the basis for the formation of larger organisms and finally formal states is created.

In the lowest peoples of the earth this quality is present only to a very slight extent, so that often they do not go beyond the formation of the family. The greater the readiness to subordinate purely personal interests, the higher rises the ability to establish comprehensive communities. *51*

This self-sacrificing will to give one's personal labor and if necessary one's own life for others is most strongly developed in the Aryan. The Aryan is not greatest in his mental qualities as such, but in the extent of his willingness to put all his abilities in the service of the community. In him the instinct of self-preservation has reached the noblest form, since he willingly subordinates his own ego to the life of the community and, if the hour demands, even sacrifices it. *52*

REVIEW QUESTIONS

1. What analogies does Hitler use to illustrate his explanation of the "brazen, basic principle" of nature? What steps does nature take to protect this principle, when its "will" is violated?
2. Why does intermixture of the races eventually, and inevitably, favor the lower races, according to Hitler?
3. Into what three groups does Hitler divide mankind? What are the characteristics and examples of each group? What is the relationship among the cultural products of the Aryans and those of other cultures?
4. Summarize Hitler's theory of history, as it applies to the "superior races." Why does the progress of "higher cultures" require the conquest and enslavement of "inferior people"?
5. Why is the true spirit of a "superior" people more apparent in war than in peace, according to Hitler?

DISCUSSION AND WRITING QUESTIONS

1. Identify the primary flaw in Hitler's use of the animal analogy in paragraphs 3 and 4 to support his argument against racial intermixing, and thus against thwarting the will of "Nature."
2. To what extent do the sentiments expressed by Hitler in the second half of paragraph 6 (on the necessity of the stronger to survive and rule) parallel ideas expressed by Sumner, Spencer, and Strong? Do you think that these men would accept the transfer of their social principles into the area of racial intermixture? Explain.
3. Could paragraph 9 have been written by Darwin — if it referred to animals and not humans? Explain how the ideas in this paragraph compare and contrast with those of Darwin.
4. Hitler dismisses the idea that humans can "conquer" nature. Examine his arguments and evaluate them.
5. What arguments can be advanced to refute the theory that race mixing favors "inferior" races and leads to the decline of "superior" races? Assume that you are writing to an audience that is rational and that may have been persuaded by such arguments as Hitler's.
6. Research the history of modern anti-Semitism (perhaps limiting yourself to a particular country, such as the United States). In particular, examine some of the documents or speeches that attempt to lay a theoretical basis for anti-Semitism, as Hitler does in *Mein Kampf*. Is racial mixing a common theme? What other justifications are given for persecuting Jews? Report on your findings.
7. Research the current status of racism in a particular country, such as South Africa or Japan or the United States. To what extent do you find that a fear of intermarriage (or "blood poisoning," as Hitler puts it) is a significant element in this racism?

Part VI

MARX AND THE CLASS STRUGGLE

Karl Marx

John Reed

Eugene V. Debs

Mao Tse-tung

Platform of the Popular Front
for the Liberation of Palestine

Angela Y. Davis

Joseph Nahem

Max Eastman

Frederick C. Crews

The exploited and oppressed class — the proletariat —
cannot attain its emancipation from the sway of the
exploiting and ruling class — the bourgeoisie — without, at
the same time, and once and for all, emancipating society at
large from all exploitation, oppression, class distinction and
class struggles.

— Friedrich Engels, Preface to *The Communist Manifesto*

"The history of all hitherto existing society is the history of class struggles." So assert Karl Marx and Friedrich Engels in *The Communist Manifesto*. The attempt to account for all of written history in terms of class struggle would be significant enough were it merely an academic idea, the product of a few European intellectuals. What makes the idea truly explosive is that Marx and his followers were not simply intellectuals; they were revolutionaries who were determined to translate their ideas into action. In so doing, they transformed the world: more than one-third of the human race now lives in countries whose modern constitutions are based on the principles of communism.

In developing his theory of class struggle, Marx was himself profoundly influenced by the dialectical thought of the German philosopher Georg Wilhelm Friedrich Hegel. Hegel saw history not simply as a random sequence of events but as a process of growth, change, and development, of unity emerging from conflict, of new conflict arising from the new unity, and so on. This dialectical process can be summarized as thesis-antithesissynthesis. Thus, a certain historical development — the thesis — gives rise to (indeed, contains the seeds of) a contradictory development — the antithesis. Thesis and antithesis will eventually clash, and out of this clash comes the synthesis. This synthesis becomes the new thesis, and the process continues indefinitely.

But the question remains — what causes this unending process of growth and development, of thesis, antithesis, and synthesis? Hegel answered in philosophical, even mystical terms — God, a Cosmic Spirit, the Absolute. Other, more materialistic Hegelian thinkers believed that numerous environmental factors were the cause. But for Marx, the forces that drove the flywheel of history were primarily economic. He saw humanity divided into two main classes — those who owned and managed the means of production and those who worked for these owners and managers, or, to put it another way, those who exploited and those who were exploited. In ancient Roman times, the exploiters were the patricians; in medieval times, the feudal lords; in modern (i.e., mid-19th century) times, the capitalist factory owners. The exploited classes of history have included the slaves, the serfs, the peasants, and in modern times, the wage laborers. They are exploited because whatever economic wealth they produce (in the form of goods and services) over and above the costs of their subsistence is seized as profit (or as Marx said, surplus value) by the owners and managers of the means of production. Thus, the dominant economic classes increasingly enrich themselves while keeping the subordinate classes at a mere subsistence level.

The laws of society cannot protect the exploited because the exploiters control the government that writes and enforces the laws. In fact, governments and all other social institutions are simply extensions of the power of the dominant economic class. A dramatic expression of this view can be found in Shaw's play, *Major Barbara*. Steven Undershaft, the naively idealistic son of a wealthy munitions manufacturer, objects to his father's insulting "the Government of my country." His father replies:

> The government of your country! I am the government of your country: I and Lazarus [his business partner]. Do you suppose that you and half a dozen amateurs like you, sitting in a row in that foolish gabble shop [Parliament], can govern Undershaft and Lazarus? No, my friend: you will do what pays us. You will make war when it suits us, and keep peace when it doesn't. You will find that trade requires certain measures when we have decided on those measures. When I want anything to keep my dividends up, you will discover that my want is a national need. When other people want something to keep my dividends down, you will call out the police and military. And in return you shall have the support of my newspapers, and the delight of imagining that you are a great statesman.

Such arrogant power, however, contains the seeds of its own destruction. The feudal system (the thesis) contained within it the seeds of the modern bourgeoisie, or middle class, in the form of shopkeepers, craftsmen, and traders (the antithesis). When the bourgeoisie had become powerful enough and recognized its own class interests, it destroyed the feudal system. But in time, what happened to the feudal lords will also happen to the bourgeoisie that replaced them. The modern class of exploited workers, the proletariat, is becoming more and more class-conscious (trade unions and strikes are illustrations of the historical forces of change at work); and when the time is right (i.e., when the proletariat has become sufficiently powerful and the bourgeoisie sufficiently enfeebled), they will join in revolution. This revolution will sweep away the remnants of the bourgeoisie to form a new classless society, a society that will represent the "dictatorship of the proletariat," a society in which the state itself will "wither away."

It is difficult to overestimate the effect of these ideas upon the modern world. Marx himself died (in 1883) without ever seeing any significant effects of his work: he had expected the revolution to begin in Germany, a highly industrialized state where the bourgeoisie had developed to the point of ripeness for fall. Instead, the first successful communist revolution took place in 1917 in Russia, a country where the bourgeoisie had been relatively undeveloped. The reading selections in this unit begin with *The Communist Manifesto*. This is followed by John Reed's account of two crucial days in the Russian Revolution. Next, in two speeches by Eugene V. Debs, a socialist who once ran for president, we see the impact of Marx's ideas in the United States. Later selections will demonstrate the impact of the idea of class struggle in other areas: Mao Tse-tung, leader of the Chinese Communist revolution of 1949, asserts that class struggle ideas must underlie literature and art; the Popular Front for the Liberation of Palestine (PFLP) argues that the class struggle is crucial to the solution of the Palestinian problem; Angela Davis discusses the women's movement in class terms; and Joseph Nahem outlines a Marxist approach toward psychology and psychoanalysis. Following Nahem is an essay by Max Eastman, once sympathetic, then disillusioned with the Russian Revolution — disillusioned, in fact, with any revolutionary attempt to ignore what he considers the essentials of human nature. Finally (to end on a somewhat lighter note), in his delicious parody from *The Pooh Perplex*, Frederick C. Crews demonstrates that Marxist interpretations of literature are not always entirely convincing.

KARL MARX *(1818–1883)*

Karl Marx is generally considered the founding father of the modern communist movement, though he did not invent either the term "communism" or the concept of collective ownership. One of the many reasons that his followers found it difficult to apply his theories to the operation of government and society is that Marx wrote primarily not about communism, but about capitalism. His masterpiece is the massive and unfinished work *Das Kapital (Capital)*; his other books and journalism are concerned largely with analyses of present and past socioeconomic conditions, as well as attacks on other social thinkers; and even much of *The Communist Manifesto* is concerned with historical and social analysis; somewhat less attention is devoted to the aims and programs of the communists.

Marx was born in Trier, in the Rhineland province of Prussia (now part of West Germany), in 1818. His parents were Jewish, but his father, a lawyer, was baptized in the Evangelical Established (Lutheran) Church a year before Marx was born (probably for career reasons), and Marx himself was baptized at the age of six. In 1835, he matriculated in the University of Bonn, where he studied history, philosophy, and law; the following year he enrolled at the University of Berlin. It was in Berlin that he first became seriously interested in social and political problems, and where he joined the leftist Young Hegelian society (see the introduction for a brief discussion of Hegel's dialectical theory). In 1841, Marx received his doctoral degree from the University of Jena. Because of his political views and activities (the government of Prussia had been attempting to drive the Young Hegelians out of the universities), Marx could not get a teaching appointment and so turned to journalism, becoming the editor of the *Rheinische Zeitung* in Cologne in 1842. But the newspaper was suppressed by the Prussian government the following year, and Marx with his new bride, Jenny von Westphalen, left for Paris.

Parisian intellectual circles at the time were awash in socialist thought. (Marx's own father had been a follower of the French socialist Saint-Simone; the British socialist Robert Owen had founded the socialist community of New Harmony in Indiana in 1824, and the disciples of Charles Fourier had established Brook Farm, also in the United States, in 1841.) But Marx soon lost patience with the French socialists. To him their theories were unscientific. Instead of coming to grips with the realities of history, the economic basis of society, and particularly, the nature of capitalism, they contented themselves with devising fanciful utopias in which all the evils of society would somehow vanish and people would live in collective harmony. In a scornful answer to his critics (and a former teacher) Marx later wrote, "Do these gentlemen think that they can understand the first word of history as long as they exclude the relations of man to nature, natural science and industry? . . . Do they believe that they can actually comprehend any epoch without grasping the industry of the period, the immediate methods of production in actual life?"

Not only must capitalism be understood, it must be lived through, until it has exhausted itself as a historical force; for Marx, it was futile to attempt revolution prematurely.

After writing for some months for the radical *Deutsch-Französische Jahrbucher* (*German-French Yearbook*) and the magazine *Vorwärts*, Marx was expelled from Paris at the behest of the Prussian government; and he and Jenny left for Brussels, Belgium, in 1845 (later in the year he renounced his Prussian nationality). During this period he began his lifelong association with Friedrich Engels (1820–1895), whom he had met in Paris. Engels, also of Prussian birth, and also a one-time member of the Young Hegelian society, had seen the effects of the Industrial Revolution first-hand when he visited his father's textile mill in Manchester, England. Engels worked with Marx on many of his later writings and helped support Marx and his family in the latter part of his life. In Brussels Marx met (and attacked) the leaders of the working-class movements and wrote various philosophical and polemical statements, including an attack on the French socialist Proudhon's *The Philosophy of Poverty*, which he called *The Poverty of Philosophy*. (Proudhon's desire to come to an accommodation with capitalism was anathema to Marx.) In 1847, Marx and Engels joined the Communist League, an international worker's society based in London. The league asked them to write a program expressing the aims of the international communist movement. Marx and Engels responded with *The Communist Manifesto* (1848). The league immediately adopted the manifesto, which laid out the history of the class struggle, asserted that the proletariat would eventually be victorious, attacked all forms of philosophical and utopian socialism, and set forth the immediate goals of communism. (As used by Marx, the term "communism" meant scientific socialism and referred in particular to the final stage of socialism. No country, including the U.S.S.R. or the People's Republic of China, claims to have yet achieved this final stage of communism.)

Later that year Marx and his followers were excited by the outbreak of revolutions in France, Italy, and Austria. But the revolutions failed; the bourgeoisie was still too strong and firmly entrenched. The disheartened Marx realized that the time was not yet ripe; he even recommended that the *Communist Manifesto* be temporarily put aside and the Communist League disbanded. Marx continued to engage in political agitation, however. He had already been expelled from Belgium soon after the *Manifesto* appeared; back in the Rhineland the following year, after being acquitted of inciting workers to armed resistance against tax collection, he was also banished from Prussia. He printed the final issue of his newspaper, the *Neue Rheinische Zeitung*, in flaming red ink, and then left for London, where he was to remain the rest of his life.

Marx's years in England were spent in poverty, though he was assisted by Engels's generosity, increasingly so after 1864 when Engels became a partner in his father's Manchester firm. Turning away from revolutionary activities for a time, Marx concentrated on writing. He produced many books on political matters, including *Class Struggles in France* (1848–1850), *The Eighteenth Brumaire of Louis Bonaparte* (1852), *The Secret Diplomatic History of the Eighteenth Century* (1856), *The Civil War in France* (1871), and *The Critique of the Gotha Programme* (1873). From 1852 to 1862 he earned money as a correspondent for the New York *Daily Tribune*, writing on political events; and he also served for a time as London correspondent of the *Oder Gazette*, a German paper. But Marx's main efforts were devoted to an intensive study of capitalism. Day after day he would be seen studying from morning till night in the British Museum, reading everything he could find on political economy. In 1859, he produced *A Contribution to the Critique of Political Economy,* which contains his famous statement that "It is not the consciousness of men that determines their existence, but, on the contrary, their social existence that determines their consciousness." The first volume of his monumental analysis of capitalist society, *Das Kapital,* appeared in 1867. (He never finished this work; the second and third volumes were published posthumously by Engels in 1885 and 1894.)

Marx did have one final period of political activity. In 1864, he assumed the leadership of the First International of the Workingman's Association. Uncharacteristically (for many regarded Marx as arrogant and inflexible in his opinions), he was often successful in achieving compromises among the various parties and factions of this group. With a membership of 800,000 in 1869, the First International intervened in several European labor disputes on behalf of the trade unions. And Marx became internationally famous for his activities in support of the Paris Commune, a short-lived insurrectionary government set up by Parisian radicals in 1871 following France's defeat (and the subsequent German occupation of Paris) in the Franco-Prussian War of 1870. To Engels, the Paris Commune was the first example in history of the "dictatorship of the proletariat."

Soon after the failure of the Commune, however, factionalism broke out once more in the First International, and though Marx was successful in defeating his influential chief opponent, the Russian revolutionist Mikhail Alexandrovich Bakunin, the group was soon to dissolve. During the last ten years of his life, Marx's health, along with his literary output, declined. Devastated by the death of his wife in December 1881 and of his eldest daughter Jenny in January 1883 (several of his other children had died earlier, during his years of poverty in London), Marx finally succumbed to a lung abscess on March 14, 1883.

THE COMMUNIST MANIFESTO

A spectre is haunting Europe — the spectre of Communism. All the   *1*
Powers of old Europe have entered into a holy alliance to exorcise this
spectre: Pope and Czar, Metternich[1] and Guizot,[2] French Radicals[3] and
German police-spies.[4]

Where is the party in opposition that has not been decried as Com-   *2*
munistic by its opponents in power? Where the Opposition that has not
hurled back the branding reproach of Communism, against the more advanced opposition parties, as well as against its reactionary adversaries?

Two things result from this fact.   *3*

I. Communism is already acknowledged by all European Powers to be   *4*
itself a Power.

II. It is high time that Communists should openly, in the face of the   *5*
whole world, publish their views, their aims, their tendencies, and meet
this nursery tale of the Spectre of Communism with a Manifesto of the
party itself.

To this end, Communists of various nationalities have assembled in   *6*
London, and sketched the following Manifesto, to be published in the English, French, German, Italian, Flemish and Danish languages.

Karl Marx and Friedrich Engels. The Communist Manifesto [1848]. Notes from *Essential
Works of Marxism*, ed. Arthur P. Mendel. New York: Bantam, 1961. Text based on *The Marx-
Engels Reader*, 2nd ed. Ed., Robert C. Tucker. New York: Norton, 1972, 1978.

[1]*Metternich:* Prince Klemens von Metternich (1773–1859), the Austrian Minister of Foreign
Affairs (1809–1848) and the host of the Congress of Vienna (1814–1815). Metternich was
renowned for his conservativism; thus, he was strongly opposed to the ideas of
communism.

[2]*Guizot:* François Pierre Guizot (1787–1874), a French historian and the leader of the Conservative Constitutional Monarchists, a political faction in power during the July Monarchy in France (1830–1848). Since the Conservative Constitutional Monarchists were comprised mostly of wealthy bourgeoisie, and since their ideas were notably conservative,
they opposed the goals of communism.

[3]*French Radicals:* Nonsocialist republicans in the 1848 Revolution. They included Hippolyte
Carnot, who became minister of education in the provisional government, and Pierre
Marie, who became minister of public works. As minister of public works, it was Marie's
responsibility to put into effect Louis Blanc's "social workshops." Instead of carrying
through Blanc's proposals, he established the so-called "national workshops" with which,
it is usually argued, he intended to discredit Blanc's socialist views. The abolition of the
workshops, which had served to relieve unemployment, contributed to the Parisian insurrection of June. [Arthur P. Mendel, ed., *Essential Works of Marxism* (New York: Bantam,
1961).]

[4]*German police-spies:* German spies sent out to report on and suppress the activities of revolutionaries, both in Germany and outside of it.

I. BOURGEOIS AND PROLETARIANS[5]

The history of all hitherto existing society[6] is the history of class   *7*
struggles.

Freeman and slave, patrician and plebeian, lord and serf, guild-master[7]   *8*
and journeyman, in a word, oppressor and oppressed, stood in constant
opposition to one another, carried on an uninterrupted, now hidden, now
open fight, a fight that each time ended, either in a revolutionary re-con-
stitution of society at large, or in the common ruin of the contending
classes.

In the earlier epochs of history, we find almost everywhere a compli-   *9*
cated arrangement of society into various orders, a manifold gradation of
social rank. In ancient Rome we have patricians,[8] knights, plebeians,
slaves; in the Middle Ages, feudal lords, vassals, guild-masters, journey-
men, apprentices, serfs; in almost all of these classes, again, subordinate
gradations.

The modern bourgeois society that has sprouted from the ruins of feu-   *10*
dal society has not done away with class antagonisms. It has but established new classes, new conditions of oppression, new forms of struggle
in place of the old ones.

Our epoch, the epoch of the bourgeoisie, possesses, however, this dis-   *11*
tinctive feature: it has simplified the class antagonisms: Society as a whole
is more and more splitting up into two great hostile camps, into two great
classes directly facing each other: Bourgeoisie and Proletariat.

From the serfs of the Middle Ages sprang the chartered burghers of   *12*
the earliest towns. From these burgesses the first elements of the bourgeoisie were developed.

---

[5]By bourgeoisie is meant the class of modern Capitalists, owners of the means of social
production and employers of wage-labour. By proletariat, the class of modern wage-labourers who, having no means of production of their own, are reduced to selling their
labour-power in order to live. [*Engels, English edition of 1888.*]

[6]That is, all *written* history. In 1837, the pre-history of society, the social organization existing previous to recorded history, was all but unknown. Since then Haxthausen discovered common ownership of land in Russia, Maurer proved it to be the social foundation
from which all Teutonic races started in history and, by and by, village communities were
found to be, or to have been, the primitive form of society everywhere from India to Ireland. The inner organization of this primitive communistic society was laid bare, in its
typical form, by Morgan's crowning discovery of the true nature of the *gens* and its relation
to the *tribe*. With the dissolution of these primeval communities, society begins to be differentiated into separate and finally antagonistic classes. I have attempted to retrace this
process of dissolution in *The Origin of the Family, Private Property and the State.* [Engels]

[7]Guild-master, that is, a full member of a guild, a master within, not a head of a guild.
[Engels]

[8]*patricians:* Nobles, aristocrats.

The discovery of America, the rounding of the Cape,[9] opened up fresh   *13*
ground for the rising bourgeoisie. The East-Indian and Chinese markets,
the colonisation of America, trade with the colonies, the increase in the
means of exchange and in commodities generally, gave to commerce, to
navigation, to industry, an impulse never before known, and thereby, to
the revolutionary element in the tottering feudal society, a rapid
development.

The feudal system of industry, under which industrial production was   *14*
monopolised by closed guilds, now no longer sufficed for the growing
wants of the new markets. The manufacturing system took its place. The
guild-masters were pushed on one side by the manufacturing middle class;
division of labour between the different corporate guilds vanished in the
face of division of labour in each single workshop.

Meantime the markets kept ever growing, the demand ever rising.   *15*
Even manufacture[10] no longer sufficed. Thereupon, steam and machinery
revolutionised industrial production. The place of manufacture was taken
by the giant, Modern Industry, the place of the industrial middle class, by
industrial millionaires, the leaders of whole industrial armies, the modern
bourgeois.

Modern industry has established the world-market, for which the dis-   *16*
covery of America paved the way. This market has given an immense development to commerce, to navigation, to communication by land. This
development has, in its turn, reacted on the extension of industry; and in
proportion as industry, commerce, navigation, railways extended, in the
same proportion the bourgeoisie developed, increased its capital, and
pushed into the background every class handed down from the Middle
Ages.

We see, therefore, how the modern bourgeoisie is itself the product of   *17*
a long course of development, of a series of revolutions in the modes of
production and of exchange.

Each step in the development of the bourgeoisie was accompanied by   *18*
a corresponding political advance of that class. An oppressed class under
the sway of the feudal nobility, an armed and self-governing association in

---

[9]*the Cape:* The discovery of the Cape of Good Hope at the southernmost tip of the African
continent led to the formation of a new trade route between developing western countries
and the prosperous East.

[10]The word "manufacture" is used by Engels to refer to production carried on by laborers
who, though gathered in a single building, operated by much the same manual labor as
had their medieval artisan predecessors. This system, therefore, contrasts with the next
stage of production, the "industrial" stage that utilizes machinery and steam power.
[Mendel]

the mediaeval commune;[11] here independent urban republic (as in Italy and Germany), there taxable "third estate"[12] of the monarchy (as in France), afterwards, in the period of manufacture proper, serving either the semi-feudal or the absolute monarchy as a counterpoise against the nobility, and, in fact, corner-stone of the great monarchies in general, the bourgeoisie has at last, since the establishment of Modern Industry and of the world-market, conquered for itself, in the modern representative State, exclusive sway. The executive of the modern State is but a committee for managing the common affairs of the whole bourgeoisie.

The bourgeoisie, historically, has played a most revolutionary part.   19

The bourgeoisie, wherever it has got the upper hand, has put an end   20
to all feudal,[13] patriarchal, idyllic relations. It has pitilessly torn asunder the motley feudal ties that bound man to his "natural superiors," and has left remaining no other nexus between man and man than naked self-interest, than callous "cash payment." It has drowned the most heavenly ecstasies of religious fervour, of chivalrous enthusiasm, of philistine[14] sentimentalism, in the icy water of egotistical calculation. It has resolved personal worth into exchange value, and in place of the numberless indefeasible chartered freedoms, has set up that single, unconscionable freedom — Free Trade. In one word, for exploitation, veiled by religious and political illusions, it has substituted naked, shameless, direct, brutal exploitation.

The bourgeoisie has stripped of its halo every occupation hitherto hon-   21
oured and looked up to with reverent awe. It has converted the physician, the lawyer, the priest, the poet, the man of science, into its paid wage-labourers.

The bourgeoisie has torn away from the family its sentimental veil, and   22
has reduced the family relation to a mere money relation.

---

[11]"Commune" was the name taken, in France, by the nascent towns even before they had conquered from their feudal lords and masters local self-government and political rights as the "Third Estate." Generally speaking, for the economical development of the bourgeoisie, England is here taken as the typical country; for its political development, France. [Engels]

[12]*"third estate":* A new social order comprised of French citizens from a variety of social classes that were left unrepresented by the traditional divisions of privilege in the feudal estate system of church, state, and nobility. On June 17, 1789, the Third Estate was officially declared an autonomous order and the French Revolution began.

[13]*feudal:* Pertaining to the social system of medieval Europe by which vassals subjected themselves to the authority of lords, for whom they performed military and other duties, in exchange for land holdings. The primary loyalty of vassals (and of those who served them), therefore, was to their lords, rather than to their country, a fact that had profound implications for the political and economic relationships of society.

[14]*philistine:* Ignorant, uncultured, tasteless.

The bourgeoisie has disclosed how it came to pass that the brutal display of vigour in the Middle Ages, which Reactionists so much admire, found its fitting complement in the most slothful indolence. It has been the first to show what man's activity can bring about. It has accomplished wonders far surpassing Egyptian pyramids, Roman aqueducts, and Gothic cathedrals; it has conducted expeditions that put in the shade all former Exoduses of nations and crusades. 23

The bourgeoisie cannot exist without constantly revolutionising the instruments of production, and thereby the relations of production, and with them the whole relations of society. Conservation of the old modes of production in unaltered form, was, on the contrary, the first condition of existence for all earlier industrial classes. Constant revolutionising of production, uninterrupted disturbance of all social conditions, everlasting uncertainty and agitation distinguish the bourgeois epoch from all earlier ones. All fixed, fast-frozen relations, with their train of ancient and venerable prejudices and opinions, are swept away, all new-formed ones become antiquated before they can ossify. All that is solid melts into air, all that is holy is profaned, and man is at last compelled to face with sober senses, his real conditions of life, and his relations with his kind. 24

The need of a constantly expanding market for its products chases the bourgeoisie over the whole surface of the globe. It must nestle everywhere, settle everywhere, establish connexions everywhere. 25

The bourgeoisie has through its exploitation of the world-market given a cosmopolitan character to production and consumption in every country. To the great chagrin of Reactionists, it has drawn from under the feet of industry the national ground on which it stood. All old-established national industries have been destroyed or are daily being destroyed. They are dislodged by new industries, whose introduction becomes a life and death question for all civilised nations, by industries that no longer work up indigenous raw material, but raw material drawn from the remotest zones; industries whose products are consumed, not only at home, but in every quarter of the globe. In place of the old wants, satisfied by the productions of the country, we find new wants, requiring for their satisfaction the products of distant lands and climes. In place of the old local and national seclusion and self-sufficiency, we have intercourse in every direction, universal inter-dependence of nations. And as in material, so also in intellectual production. The intellectual creations of individual nations become common property. National one-sidedness and narrow-mindedness become more and more impossible, and from the numerous national and local literatures, there arises a world literature. 26

The bourgeoisie, by the rapid improvement of all instruments of production, by the immensely facilitated means of communication, draws all, even the most barbarian, nations into civilisation. The cheap prices of its commodities are the heavy artillery with which it batters down all Chinese 27 walls, with which it forces the barbarians' intensely obstinate hatred of foreigners to capitulate. It compels all nations, on pain of extinction, to adopt the bourgeois mode of production; it compels them to introduce what it calls civilisation into their midst, *i.e.*, to become bourgeois themselves. In one word, it creates a world after its own image.

The bourgeoisie has subjected the country to the rule of the towns. It [28] has created enormous cities, has greatly increased the urban population as compared with the rural, and has thus rescued a considerable part of the population from the idiocy of rural life. Just as it has made the country dependent on the towns, so it has made barbarian and semi-barbarian countries dependent on the civilised ones, nations and peasants on nations of bourgeois, the East on the West.

The bourgeoisie keeps more and more doing away with the scattered [29] state of the population, of the means of production, and of property. It has agglomerated population, centralised means of production, and has concentrated property in a few hands. The necessary consequence of this was political centralisation. Independent, or but loosely connected provinces, with separate interests, laws, governments and systems of taxation, became lumped together into one nation, with one government, one code of laws, one national class-interest, one frontier and one customs-tariff.

The bourgeoisie, during its rule of scarce one hundred years, has cre- [30] ated more massive and more colossal productive forces than have all preceding generations together. Subjection of Nature's forces to man, machinery, application of chemistry to industry and agriculture, steamnavigation, railways, electric telegraphs, clearing of whole continents for cultivation, canalisation of rivers, whole populations conjured out of the ground — what earlier century had even a presentiment that such productive forces slumbered in the lap of social labour?

We see then: the means of production and of exchange, on whose [31] foundation the bourgeoisie built itself up, were generated in feudal society. At a certain stage in the development of these means of production and of exchange, the conditions under which feudal society produced and exchanged, the feudal organisation of agriculture and manufacturing industry, in one word, the feudal relations of property became no longer compatible with the already developed productive forces; they became so many fetters. They had to be burst asunder; they were burst asunder.

Into their place stepped free competition, accompanied by a social and [32] political constitution adapted to it, and by the economical and political sway of the bourgeois class.

A similar movement is going on before our own eyes. Modern bour- [33] geois society with its relations of production, of exchange and of property, a society that has conjured up such gigantic means of production and of exchange, is like the sorcerer, who is no longer able to control the powers of the nether world whom he has called up by his spells. For many a decade past the history of industry and commerce is but the history of the revolt of modern productive forces against modern conditions of production, against the property relations that are the conditions for the existence of the bourgeoisie and of its rule. It is enough to mention the commercial crises that by their periodical return put on its trial, each time more threateningly, the existence of the entire bourgeois society. In these crises a great part not only of the existing products, but also of the previously created productive forces, are periodically destroyed. In these crises there breaks out an epidemic that, in all earlier epochs, would have seemed an absurdity — the epidemic of over-production. Society suddenly finds itself put back into a state of momentary barbarism; it appears as if a famine, a universal war of devastation had cut off the supply of every means of subsistence; industry and commerce seem to be destroyed; and why? Because there is too much civilisation, too much means of subsistence, too much industry, too much commerce. The productive forces at the disposal of society no longer tend to further the development of the conditions of bourgeois property; on the contrary, they have become too powerful for these conditions, by which they are fettered, and so soon as they overcome these fetters, they bring disorder into the whole of bourgeois society, endanger the existence of bourgeois property. The conditions of bourgeois society are too narrow to comprise the wealth created by them. And how does the bourgeoisie get over these crises? On the one hand by enforced destruction of a mass of productive forces; on the other, by the conquest of new markets, and by the more thorough exploitation of the old ones. That is to say, by paving the way for more extensive and more destructive crises, and by diminishing the means whereby crises are prevented.

The weapons with which the bourgeoisie felled feudalism to the ground are now turned against the bourgeoisie itself. [34]

But not only has the bourgeoisie forged the weapons that bring death to itself; it has also called into existence the men who are to wield those weapons — the modern working class — the proletarians. [35]

In proportion as the bourgeoisie, *i.e.*, capital, is developed, in the same proportion is the proletariat, the modern working class, developed — a class of labourers, who live only so long as they find work, and who find work only so long as their labour increases capital. These labourers, who must sell themselves piece-meal, are a commodity, like every other article of commerce, and are consequently exposed to all the vicissitudes of competition, to all the fluctuations of the market. [36]

Owing to the extensive use of machinery and to division of labour, the work of the proletarians has lost all individual character, and consequently, all charm for the workman. He becomes an appendage of the machine, and it is only the most simple, most monotonous, and most easily acquired knack, that is required of him. Hence, the cost of production of a workman is restricted, almost entirely, to the means of subsistence that he requires [37] for his maintenance, and for the propagation of his race. But the price of a commodity, and therefore also of labour,[15] is equal to its cost of production. In proportion, therefore, as the repulsiveness of the work increases, the wage decreases. Nay more, in proportion as the use of machinery and division of labour increases, in the same proportion the burden of toil also increases, whether by prolongation of the working hours, by increase of the work exacted in a given time or by increased speed of the machinery, etc.

Modern industry has converted the little workshop of the patriarchal *38* master into the great factory of the industrial capitalist. Masses of labourers, crowded into the factory, are organised like soldiers. As privates of the industrial army they are placed under the command of a perfect hierarchy of officers and sergeants. Not only are they slaves of the bourgeois class, and of the bourgeois State; they are daily and hourly enslaved by the machine, by the over-looker, and, above all, by the individual bourgeois manufacturer himself. The more openly this despotism proclaims gain to be its end and aim, the more petty, the more hateful and the more embittering it is.

The less the skill and exertion of strength implied in manual labour, in *39* other words, the more modern industry becomes developed, the more is the labour of men superseded by that of women. Differences of age and sex have no longer any distinctive social validity for the working class. All are instruments of labour, more or less expensive to use, according to their age and sex.

No sooner is the exploitation of the labourer by the manufacturer, so *40* far, at an end, that he receives his wages in cash, than he is set upon by the other portions of the bourgeoisie, the landlord, the shopkeeper, the pawnbroker, etc.

The lower strata of the middle class — the small tradespeople, shop- *41* keepers, and retired tradesmen[16] generally, the handicraftsmen and peasants — all these sink gradually into the proletariat, partly because their diminutive capital does not suffice for the scale on which Modern Industry is carried on, and is swamped in the competition with the large capitalists, partly because their specialised skill is rendered worthless by new methods of production. Thus the proletariat is recruited from all classes of the population.

The proletariat goes through various stages of development. With its *42* birth begins its struggle with the bourgeoisie. At first the contest is carried

---

[15]Subsequently Marx pointed out that the worker sells not his labour but his labour power. [Robert C. Tucker, ed., *The Marx-Engels Reader* (New York: Norton, 1978).]

[16]The word in the German original is *Rentler,* meaning here the property-owner earning an income from investments. [Mendel]

on by individual labourers, then by the workpeople of a factory, then by the operatives of one trade, in one locality, against the individual bourgeois who directly exploits them. They direct their attacks not against the bourgeois conditions of production, but against the instruments of production themselves; they destroy imported wares that compete with their labour, they smash to pieces machinery, they set factories ablaze, they seek to restore by force the vanished status of the workman of the Middle Ages.

At this stage the labourers still form an incoherent mass scattered over the whole country, and broken up by their mutual competition. If anywhere they unite to form more compact bodies, this is not yet the consequence of their own active union, but of the union of the bourgeoisie, which class, in order to attain its own political ends, is compelled to set the whole proletariat in motion, and is moreover yet, for a time, able to do so. At this stage, therefore, the proletarians do not fight their enemies, but the enemies of their enemies, the remnants of absolute monarchy, the landowners, the non-industrial bourgeois, the petty bourgeoisie. Thus the whole historical movement is concentrated in the hands of the bourgeoisie; every victory so obtained is a victory for the bourgeoisie. 43

But with the development of industry the proletariat not only increases in number; it becomes concentrated in greater masses, its strength grows, and it feels that strength more. The various interests and conditions of life within the ranks of the proletariat are more and more equalised, in proportion as machinery obliterates all distinctions of labour, and nearly everywhere reduces wages to the same low level. The growing competition among the bourgeois, and the resulting commercial crises, make the wages of the workers ever more fluctuating. The unceasing improvement of machinery, ever more rapidly developing, makes their livelihood more and more precarious; the collisions between individual workmen and individual bourgeois take more and more the character of collisions between two classes. Thereupon the workers begin to form combinations (Trades Unions) against the bourgeois; they club together in order to keep up the rate of wages; they found permanent associations in order to make provision beforehand for these occasional revolts. Here and there the contest breaks out into riots. 44

Now and then the workers are victorious, but only for a time. The real fruit of their battles lies, not in the immediate result, but in the ever-expanding union of the workers. This union is helped on by the improved means of communication that are created by modern industry and that place the workers of different localities in contact with one another. It was just this contact that was needed to centralise the numerous local struggles, all of the same character, into one national struggle between classes. But every class struggle is a political struggle. And that union, to attain which the burghers of the Middle Ages, with their miserable highways, required centuries, the modern proletarians, thanks to railways, achieve in a few years. 45

This organisation of the proletarians into a class, and consequently into a political party, is continually being upset again by the competition between the workers themselves. But it ever rises up again, stronger, firmer, mightier. It compels legislative recognition of particular interests of the workers, by taking advantage of the divisions among the bourgeoisie itself. Thus the ten-hours' bill[17] in England was carried.   46

Altogether collisions between the classes of the old society further, in many ways, the course of development of the proletariat. The bourgeoisie finds itself involved in a constant battle. At first with the aristocracy; later on, with those portions of the bourgeoisie itself, whose interests have become antagonistic to the progress of industry; at all times, with the bourgeoisie of foreign countries. In all these battles it sees itself compelled to appeal to the proletariat, to ask for its help, and thus, to drag it into the political arena. The bourgeoisie itself, therefore, supplies the proletariat with its own elements of political and general education, in other words, it furnishes the proletariat with weapons for fighting the bourgeoisie.   47

Further, as we have already seen, entire sections of the ruling classes are, by the advance of industry, precipitated into the proletariat, or are at least threatened in their conditions of existence. These also supply the proletariat with fresh elements of enlightenment and progress.   48

Finally, in times when the class struggle nears the decisive hour, the process of dissolution going on within the ruling class, in fact within the whole range of society, assumes such a violent, glaring character, that a small section of the ruling class cuts itself adrift, and joins the revolutionary class, the class that holds the future in its hands. Just as, therefore, at an earlier period, a section of the nobility went over to the bourgeoisie, so now a portion of the bourgeoisie goes over to the proletariat, and in particular, a portion of the bourgeois ideologists, who have raised themselves to the level of comprehending theoretically the historical movement as a whole.   49

Of all the classes that stand face to face with the bourgeoisie today, the proletariat alone is a really revolutionary class. The other classes decay and finally disappear in the face of Modern Industry; the proletariat is its special and essential product.   50

The lower middle class, the small manufacturer, the shopkeeper, the artisan, the peasant, all these fight against the bourgeoisie, to save from extinction their existence as fractions of the middle class. They are therefore not revolutionary, but conservative. Nay more, they are reactionary, for they try to roll back the wheel of history. If by chance they are revolu-   51

---

[17]*the ten-hours' bill:* An act introduced by Richard Oastler on the part of the working class which limited the legal working day to ten hours. The act was made a law in 1847, a year before the publication of the *Manifesto,* and served as a milestone in efforts to establish humane working conditions in industrial England.

tionary, they are so only in view of their impending transfer into the proletariat, they thus defend not their present, but their future interests, they desert their own standpoint to place themselves at that of the proletariat.

The "dangerous class," the social scum, that passively rotting mass thrown off by the lowest layers of old society, may, here and there, be swept into the movement by a proletarian revolution; its conditions of life, however, prepare it far more for the part of a bribed tool of reactionary intrigue. *52*

In the conditions of the proletariat, those of old society at large are already virtually swamped. The proletarian is without property; his relation to his wife and children has no longer anything in common with the bourgeois family-relations; modern industrial labour, modern subjection to capital, the same in England as in France, in America as in Germany, has stripped him of every trace of national character. Law, morality, religion, are to him so many bourgeois prejudices, behind which lurk in ambush just as many bourgeois interests. *53*

All the preceding classes that got the upper hand, sought to fortify their already acquired status by subjecting society at large to their conditions of appropriation. The proletarians cannot become masters of the productive forces of society, except by abolishing their own previous mode of appropriation, and thereby also every other previous mode of appropriation. They have nothing of their own to secure and to fortify; their mission is to destroy all previous securities for, and insurances of, individual property. *54*

All previous historical movements were movements of minorities, or in the interests of minorities. The proletarian movement is the self-conscious, independent movement of the immense majority, in the interests of the immense majority. The proletariat, the lowest stratum of our present society, cannot stir, cannot raise itself up, without the whole superincumbent strata of official society being sprung into the air. *55*

Though not in substance, yet in form, the struggle of the proletariat with the bourgeoisie is at first a national struggle. The proletariat of each country must, of course, first of all settle matters with its own bourgeoisie. *56*

In depicting the most general phases of the development of the proletariat, we traced the more or less veiled civil war, raging within existing society, up to the point where that war breaks out into open revolution, and where the violent overthrow of the bourgeoisie lays the foundation for the sway of the proletariat. *57*

Hitherto, every form of society has been based, as we have already seen, on the antagonism of oppressing and oppressed classes. But in order to oppress a class, certain conditions must be assured to it under which it can, at least, continue its slavish existence. The serf, in the period of serfdom, raised himself to membership in the commune, just as the petty bourgeois, under the yoke of feudal absolutism, managed to develop into *58* a bourgeois. The modern labourer, on the contrary, instead of rising with the progress of industry, sinks deeper and deeper below the conditions of existence of his own class. He becomes a pauper, and pauperism develops more rapidly than population and wealth. And here it becomes evident, that the bourgeoisie is unfit any longer to be the ruling class in society, and to impose its conditions of existence upon society as an over-riding law. It is unfit to rule because it is incompetent to assure an existence to its slave within his slavery, because it cannot help letting him sink into such a state, that it has to feed him, instead of being fed by him. Society can no longer live under this bourgeoisie, in other words, its existence is no longer compatible with society.

The essential condition for the existence, and for the sway of the bourgeois class, is the formation and augmentation of capital; the condition for capital is wage-labour. Wage-labour rests exclusively on competition between the labourers. The advance of industry, whose involuntary promoter is the bourgeoisie, replaces the isolation of the labourers, due to competition, by their revolutionary combination, due to association. The development of Modern Industry, therefore, cuts from under its feet the very foundation on which the bourgeoisie produces and appropriates products. What the bourgeoisie, therefore, produces, above all, is its own grave-diggers. Its fall and the victory of the proletariat are equally inevitable. 59

II. PROLETARIANS AND COMMUNISTS

In what relation do the Communists stand to the proletarians as a whole? 60

The Communists do not form a separate party opposed to other working-class parties. 61

They have no interests separate and apart from those of the proletariat as a whole. 62

They do not set up any sectarian principles of their own, by which to shape and mould the proletarian movement. 63

The Communists are distinguished from the other working-class parties by this only: (1) In the national struggles of the proletarians of the different countries, they point out and bring to the front the common interests of the entire proletariat, independently of all nationality. (2) In the various stages of development which the struggle of the working class against the bourgeoisie has to pass through, they always and everywhere represent the interests of the movement as a whole. 64

The Communists, therefore, are on the one hand, practically, the most advanced and resolute section of the working-class parties of every country, that section which pushes forward all others; on the other hand, theoretically, they have over the great mass of the proletariat the advantage 65 of clearly understanding the line of march, the conditions, and the ultimate general results of the proletarian movement.

The immediate aim of the Communists is the same as that of all the other proletarian parties: formation of the proletariat into a class, overthrow of the bourgeois supremacy, conquest of political power by the proletariat. 66

The theoretical conclusions of the Communists are in no way based on ideas or principles that have been invented, or discovered, by this or that would-be universal reformer. 67

They merely express, in general terms, actual relations springing from an existing class struggle, from a historical movement going on under our very eyes. The abolition of existing property relations is not at all a distinctive feature of Communism. 68

All property relations in the past have continually been subject to historical change consequent upon the change in historical conditions. 69

The French Revolution, for example, abolished feudal property in favour of bourgeois property. 70

The distinguishing feature of Communism is not the abolition of property generally, but the abolition of bourgeois property. But modern bourgeois private property is the final and most complete expression of the system of producing and appropriating products, that is based on class antagonisms, on the exploitation of the many by the few. 71

In this sense, the theory of the Communists may be summed up in the single sentence: Abolition of private property. 72

We Communists have been reproached with the desire of abolishing the right of personally acquiring property as the fruit of a man's own labour, which property is alleged to be the groundwork of all personal freedom, activity and independence. 73

Hard-won, self-acquired, self-earned property! Do you mean the property of the petty artisan and of the small peasant, a form of property that preceded the bourgeois form? There is no need to abolish that; the development of industry has to a great extent already destroyed it, and is still destroying it daily. 74

Or do you mean modern bourgeois private property? 75

But does wage-labour create any property for the labourer? Not a bit. It creates capital, *i.e.*, that kind of property which exploits wage-labour, and which cannot increase except upon condition of begetting a new supply of wage-labour for fresh exploitation. Property, in its present form, is based on the antagonism of capital and wage-labour. Let us examine both sides of this antagonism. 76

To be a capitalist, is to have not only a purely personal, but a social *status* in production. Capital is a collective product, and only by the united action of many members, nay, in the last resort, only by the united action of all members of society, can it be set in motion. 77

Capital is, therefore, not a personal, it is a social power. 78

When, therefore, capital is converted into common property, into the 79 property of all members of society, personal property is not thereby transformed into social property. It is only the social character of the property that is changed. It loses its class-character.

Let us now take wage-labour. 80

The average price of wage-labour is the minimum wage, *i.e.*, that 81 quantum of the means of subsistence, which is absolutely requisite to keep the labourer in bare existence as a labourer. What, therefore, the wage-labourer appropriates by means of his labour, merely suffices to prolong and reproduce a bare existence. We by no means intend to abolish this personal appropriation of the products of labour, an appropriation that is made for the maintenance and reproduction of human life, and that leaves no surplus wherewith to command the labour of others. All that we want to do away with, is the miserable character of this appropriation, under which the labourer lives merely to increase capital, and is allowed to live only in so far as the interest of the ruling class requires it.

In bourgeois society, living labour is but a means to increase accumu- 82 lated labour. In Communist society, accumulated labour is but a means to widen, to enrich, to promote the existence of the labourer.

In bourgeois society, therefore, the past dominates the present; in 83 Communist society, the present dominates the past. In bourgeois society capital is independent and has individuality, while the living person is dependent and has no individuality.

And the abolition of this state of things is called by the bourgeois, ab- 84 olition of individuality and freedom! And rightly so. The abolition of bourgeois individuality, bourgeois independence, and bourgeois freedom is undoubtedly aimed at.

By freedom is meant, under the present bourgeois conditions of pro- 85 duction, free trade, free selling and buying.

But if selling and buying disappears, free selling and buying disap- 86 pears also. This talk about free selling and buying, and all the other "brave words" of our bourgeoisie about freedom in general, have a meaning, if any, only in contrast with restricted selling and buying, with the fettered traders of the Middle Ages, but have no meaning when opposed to the Communistic abolition of buying and selling, of the bourgeois conditions of production, and of the bourgeoisie itself.

You are horrified at our intending to do away with private property. 87 But in your existing society, private property is already done away with for nine-tenths of the population; its existence for the few is solely due to its non-existence in the hands of those nine-tenths. You reproach us, therefore, with intending to do away with a form of property, the necessary condition for whose existence is the non-existence of any property for the immense majority of society.

In one word, you reproach us with intending to do away with your 88 property. Precisely so; that is just what we intend.

From the moment when labour can no longer be converted into capital, 89 money, or rent, into a social power capable of being monopolised, *i.e.*, from the moment when individual property can no longer be transformed into bourgeois property, into capital, from that moment, you say, individuality vanishes.

You must, therefore, confess that by "individual" you mean no other 90 person than the bourgeois, than the middle-class owner of property. This person must, indeed, be swept out of the way, and made impossible.

Communism deprives no man of the power to appropriate the prod- 91 ucts of society; all that it does is to deprive him of the power to subjugate the labour of others by means of such appropriation.

It has been objected that upon the abolition of private property all 92 work will cease, and universal laziness will overtake us.

According to this, bourgeois society ought long ago to have gone to 93 the dogs through sheer idleness; for those of its members who work, acquire nothing, and those who acquire anything, do not work. The whole of this objection is but another expression of the tautology: that there can no longer be any wage-labour when there is no longer any capital.

All objections urged against the Communistic mode of producing and 94 appropriating material products, have, in the same way, been urged against the Communistic modes of producing and appropriating intellectual products. Just as, to the bourgeois, the disappearance of class property is the disappearance of production itself, so the disappearance of class culture is to him identical with the disappearance of all culture.

That culture, the loss of which he laments, is, for the enormous ma- 95 jority, a mere training to act as a machine.

But don't wrangle with us so long as you apply, to our intended abo- 96 lition of bourgeois property, the standard of your bourgeois notions of freedom, culture, law, &c. Your very ideas are but the outgrowth of the conditions of your bourgeois production and bourgeois property, just as your jurisprudence is but the will of your class made into a law for all, a will, whose essential character and direction are determined by the economical conditions of existence of your class.

The selfish misconception that induces you to transform into eternal 97 laws of nature and of reason, the social forms springing from your present mode of production and form of property — historical relations that rise and disappear in the progress of production — this misconception you share with every ruling class that has preceded you. What you see clearly in the case of ancient property, what you admit in the case of feudal property, you are of course forbidden to admit in the case of your own bourgeois form of property.

Abolition of the family! Even the most radical flare up at this infamous 98 proposal of the Communists.

On what foundation is the present family, the bourgeois family, based? *99* On capital, on private gain. In its completely developed form this family exists only among the bourgeoisie. But this state of things finds its complement in the practical absence of the family among the proletarians, and in public prostitution.

The bourgeois family will vanish as a matter of course when its com- *100* plement vanishes, and both will vanish with the vanishing of capital.

Do you charge us with wanting to stop the exploitation of children by *101* their parents? To this crime we plead guilty.

But, you will say, we destroy the most hallowed of relations, when we *102* replace home education by social.

And your education! Is not that also social, and determined by the *103* social conditions under which you educate, by the intervention, direct or indirect, of society, by means of schools, &c.? The Communists have not invented the intervention of society in education; they do but seek to alter the character of that intervention, and to rescue education from the influence of the ruling class.

The bourgeois clap-trap about the family and education, about the hal- *104* lowed co-relation of parent and child, becomes all the more disgusting, the more, by the action of Modern Industry, all family ties among the proletarians are torn asunder, and their children transformed into simple articles of commerce and instruments of labour.

But you Communists would introduce community of women, screams *105* the whole bourgeoisie in chorus.

The bourgeois sees in his wife a mere instrument of production. He *106* hears that the instruments of production are to be exploited in common, and, naturally, can come to no other conclusion than that the lot of being common to all will likewise fall to the women.

He has not even a suspicion that the real point aimed at is to do away *107* with the status of women as mere instruments of production.

For the rest, nothing is more ridiculous than the virtuous indignation *108* of our bourgeois at the community of women which, they pretend, is to be openly and officially established by the Communists. The Communists have no need to introduce community of women; it has existed almost from time immemorial.

Our bourgeois, not content with having the wives and daughters of *109* their proletarians at their disposal, not to speak of common prostitutes, take the greatest pleasure in seducing each other's wives.

Bourgeois marriage is in reality a system of wives in common and thus, *110* at the most, what the Communists might possibly be reproached with, is that they desire to introduce, in substitution for a hypocritically concealed, an openly legalised community of women. For the rest, it is self-evident that the abolition of the present system of production must bring with it the abolition of the community of women springing from that system, *i.e.*, of prostitution both public and private.

The Communists are further reproached with desiring to abolish coun- *111*
tries and nationality.

The working men have no country. We cannot take from them what *112*
they have not got. Since the proletariat must first of all acquire political
supremacy, must rise to be the leading class of the nation, must constitute
itself *the* nation, it is, so far, itself national, though not in the bourgeois
sense of the word.

National differences and antagonisms between peoples are daily more *113*
and more vanishing, owing to the development of the bourgeoisie, to freedom of commerce, to the world-market, to uniformity in the mode of production and in the conditions of life corresponding thereto.

The supremacy of the proletariat will cause them to vanish still faster. *114*
United action, of the leading civilised countries at least, is one of the first
conditions for the emancipation of the proletariat.

In proportion as the exploitation of one individual by another is put an *115*
end to, the exploitation of one nation by another will also be put an end
to. In proportion as the antagonism between classes within the nation vanishes, the hostility of one nation to another will come to an end.

The charges against Communism made from a religious, a philosoph- *116*
ical, and, generally, from an ideological standpoint, are not deserving of
serious examination.

Does it require deep intuition to comprehend that man's ideas, views *117*
and conceptions, in one word, man's consciousness, changes with every
change in the conditions of his material existence, in his social relations
and in his social life?

What else does the history of ideas prove, than that intellectual pro- *118*
duction changes its character in proportion as material production is
changed? The ruling ideas of each age have ever been the ideas of its ruling
class.

When people speak of ideas that revolutionise society, they do but ex- *119*
press the fact, that within the old society, the elements of a new one have
been created, and that the dissolution of the old ideas keeps even pace
with the dissolution of the old conditions of existence.

When the ancient world was in its last throes, the ancient religions *120*
were overcome by Christianity. When Christian ideas succumbed in the
18th century to rationalist ideas, feudal society fought its death battle with
the then revolutionary bourgeoisie. The ideas of religious liberty and freedom of conscience merely gave expression to the sway of free competition
within the domain of knowledge.

"Undoubtedly," it will be said, "religious, moral, philosophical and *121*
juridical ideas have been modified in the course of historical development.
But religion, morality, philosophy, political science, and law, constantly
survived this change."

"There are, besides, eternal truths, such as Freedom, Justice, etc., that *122* are common to all states of society. But Communism abolishes eternal truths, it abolishes all religion, and all morality, instead of constituting them on a new basis; it therefore acts in contradiction to all past historical experience."

What does this accusation reduce itself to? The history of all past so- 123 ciety has consisted in the development of class antagonisms, antagonisms that assumed different forms at different epochs.

But whatever form they may have taken, one fact is common to all past 124 ages, *viz.*, the exploitation of one part of society by the other. No wonder, then, that the social consciousness of past ages, despite all the multiplicity and variety it displays, moves within certain common forms, or general ideas, which cannot completely vanish except with the total disappearance of class antagonisms.

The Communist revolution is the most radical rupture with traditional 125 property relations; no wonder that its development involves the most radical rupture with traditional ideas.

But let us have done with the bourgeois objections to Communism. 126

We have seen above, that the first step in the revolution by the working 127 class, is to raise the proletariat to the position of ruling class, to win the battle of democracy.

The proletariat will use its political supremacy to wrest, by degrees, all 128 capital from the bourgeoisie, to centralise all instruments of production in the hands of the State, *i.e.*, of the proletariat organised as the ruling class; and to increase the total of productive forces as rapidly as possible.

Of course, in the beginning, this cannot be effected except by means 129 of despotic inroads on the rights of property, and on the conditions of bourgeois production; by means of measures, therefore, which appear economically insufficient and untenable, but which, in the course of the movement, outstrip themselves, necessitate further inroads upon the old social order, and are unavoidable as a means of entirely revolutionising the mode of production.

These measures will of course be different in different countries. 130

Nevertheless in the most advanced countries, the following will be 131 pretty generally applicable.

1. Abolition of property in land and application of all rents of land to public purposes.

2. A heavy progressive or graduated income tax.[18]

---

[18]*progressive or graduated income tax:* A tax whose rate increases as the amount taxed increases. Thus, under a progressive tax, the rich are taxed at a higher rate than the poor.

3. Abolition of all right of inheritance.

4. Confiscation of the property of all emigrants and rebels.

5. Centralisation of credit in the hands of the State, by means of a national bank with State capital and an exclusive monopoly.

6. Centralisation of the means of communication and transport in the hands of the State.

7. Extension of factories and instruments of production owned by the State; the bringing into cultivation of waste-lands, and the improvement of the soil generally in accordance with a common plan.

8. Equal liability of all to labour. Establishment of industrial armies, especially for agriculture.

9. Combination of agriculture with manufacturing industries; gradual abolition of the distinction between town and country, by a more equable distribution of the population over the country.

10. Free education for all children in public schools. Abolition of children's factory labour in its present form. Combination of education with industrial production, &c., &c.

When, in the course of development, class distinctions have disap- 132 peared, and all production has been concentrated in the hands of a vast association of the whole nation, the public power will lose its political character. Political power, properly so called, is merely the organised power of one class for oppressing another. If the proletariat during its contest with the bourgeoisie is compelled, by the force of circumstances, to organise itself as a class, if, by means of a revolution, it makes itself the ruling class, and, as such, sweeps away by force the old conditions of production, then it will, along with these conditions, have swept away the conditions for the existence of class antagonisms and of classes generally, and will thereby have abolished its own supremacy as a class.

In place of the old bourgeois society, with its classes and class antag- 133 onisms, we shall have an association, in which the free development of each is the condition for the free development of all.

[*In Section III of the* Communist Manifesto, *not reprinted here, Marx and Engels survey recent European socialist and communist literature. They divide current socialist movements into three types: (1) reactionary socialism, (2) conservative socialism, and (3) utopian socialism. Although all of these movements involve an antipathy toward the bourgeoisie, they are also (charge Marx and Engels) all devoted either to restoring the pre-bourgeois status quo or to instituting mere reforms, rather than fundamental changes in the relationship between capital and labor. Thus, seeking to reconcile class antagonisms, they all deny the necessity for revolutionary class struggle and for the ultimate victory of the proletariat.* — Behrens and Rosen.]

IV. POSITION OF THE COMMUNISTS IN RELATION TO THE VARIOUS EXISTING OPPOSITION PARTIES

Section II has made clear the relations of the Communists to the existing working-class parties, such as the Chartists[19] in England and the Agrarian Reformers[20] in America. 134

The Communists fight for the attainment of the immediate aims, for the enforcement of the momentary interests of the working class; but in the movement of the present, they also represent and take care of the future of that movement. In France the Communists ally themselves with the Social-Democrats,[21] against the conservative and radical bourgeoisie, reserving, however, the right to take up a critical position in regard to phrases and illusions traditionally handed down from the great Revolution. 135

In Switzerland they support the Radicals,[22] without losing sight of the fact that this party consists of antagonistic elements, partly of Democratic Socialists, in the French sense, partly of radical bourgeois. 136

In Poland they support the party that insists on an agrarian revolution as the prime condition for national emancipation, that party which fomented the insurrection of Cracow in 1846.[23] 137

In Germany they fight with the bourgeoisie whenever it acts in a revolutionary way, against the absolute monarchy, the feudal squirearchy, and the petty bourgeoisie.[24] 138

But they never cease, for a single instant, to instil into the working 139

---

[19]The Chartist movement developed in England in the period 1838–1848. The success of the higher bourgeoisie in winning electoral franchise in 1832 stimulated among the working class a demand for similar political opportunities as a means of legislating necessary economic reforms, reforms that were felt to be particularly urgent because of the economic depression in these years. An improvement in economic conditions together with factional divisions in the movement led to its collapse. [Mendel]

[20]In the middle of the century an organization called "Young America" was formed in New York State calling for the nationalization of land and maximum limits on farms of 160 acres. [Mendel]

[21]The name of Social-Democracy signified, with these its inventors, a section of the Democratic or Republican party more or less tinged with socialism. [Engels]

[22]*Radicals:* Swiss radicals who united to speak out against the unequal distribution of wealth in Switzerland as the recent watchmaking and jewelry trade prospered while peasants starved in mountainous regions.

[23]*insurrection of Cracow in 1846:* The Galicia Insurrection for Polish independence was thought to have been incited by Polish patriots living in Cracow, the only city in Poland allowed to exist independently after the Napoleonic wars. Cracow's independence was revoked shortly after the uprising.

[24]*Kleinbürgerei* in the German original. Marx and Engels used this term to describe the reactionary elements of the urban petty bourgeoisie. [Tucker]

class the clearest possible recognition of the hostile antagonism between bourgeoisie and proletariat, in order that the German workers may straightway use, as so many weapons against the bourgeoisie, the social and political conditions that the bourgeoisie must necessarily introduce along with its supremacy, and in order that, after the fall of the reactionary classes in Germany, the fight against the bourgeoisie itself may immediately begin.

The Communists turn their attention chiefly to Germany, because that *140* country is on the eve of a bourgeois revolution[25] that is bound to be carried out under more advanced conditions of European civilisation, and with a much more developed proletariat, than that of England was in the seventeenth, and of France in the eighteenth century, and because the bourgeois revolution in Germany will be but the prelude to an immediately following proletarian revolution.

In short, the Communists everywhere support every revolutionary *141* movement against the existing social and political order of things.

In all these movements they bring to the front, as the leading question *142* in each, the property question, no matter what its degree of development at the time.

Finally, they labour everywhere for the union and agreement of the *143* democratic parties of all countries.

The Communists disdain to conceal their views and aims. They openly *144* declare that their ends can be attained only by the forcible overthrow of all existing social conditions. Let the ruling classes tremble at a Communistic revolution. The proletarians have nothing to lose but their chains. They have a world to win.

WORKING MEN OF ALL COUNTRIES, UNITE!

---

[25]*on the eve of a bourgeois revolution:* Marx and Engels believed that Germans had to have a bourgeois revolution in order to free themselves from their fragmented, post-feudal state and set them on the way, through capitalism, to a proletariat revolt.

REVIEW QUESTIONS

1. Cite examples of contending classes throughout history. In what way is the rise of the bourgeoisie a product of the age of exploration and the discovery of America? What class did the bourgeoisie replace? What is the distinctive feature of the class struggle in the "epoch of the bourgeoisie"? In what way has the bourgeoisie itself evolved?
2. For the bourgeoisie, what is the chief of all values, according to Marx and Engels? In what manner has the rise of the bourgeoisie affected social and family relations? Why is the influence of the bourgeoisie international in scope?

3. What signs exist (according to Marx and Engels) that bourgeois society is coming to an end, that capitalism is no longer capable of controlling the economic and political life of the modern state? How has the bourgeoisie attempted to deal with the crises it increasingly faces? Why, with every advance it makes, is the bourgeoisie digging its own grave?
4. From what classes are the proletariat recruited? What are the stages of the struggle of the proletariat against the bourgeoisie? Why do the early stages of this struggle favor the bourgeoisie? What developments indicate the growing power of the proletariat? Upon what factors does the victory of the proletariat depend?
5. What is the relationship of the proletariat to the communists? What distinguishes the communists from other groups promoting working-class interests? What is the aim of the communists? How do the communists and the bourgeoisie view labor in different ways?
6. How do the communists justify the appropriation of private property? How do they respond to the protests of the bourgeoisie that such appropriation is an abolition of individuality and freedom? How do they respond to the charge that doing away with private property will remove all incentive to work? What other charges of the bourgeoisie against the communists do Marx and Engels attempt to answer?
7. What is the particular program of the communists, once they seize power? What will become the function of the proletariat in the postrevolutionary period? In what country did Marx and Engels believe that the communist revolution was about to begin? In the meantime, what are the immediate prerevolutionary aims of the communists?

DISCUSSION AND WRITING QUESTIONS

1. Marx and Engels claim that "[t]he executive of the modern State is but a committee for managing the common affairs of the whole bourgeoisie." Support or defend this proposition, using examples from the history of the United States or another capitalist country with which you are familiar. (Take "executive" in this sense to include the legislature as the governing body of the state.)
2. In paragraphs 27 and following, Marx and Engels discuss the bourgeoisie's tendency to centralize power and influence, to create unity out of diversity, and to agglomerate many small units into a few large ones. To what extent do you see evidence of this process at work today? What counterbalancing forces are working against this tendency (other than the Communist Party, itself)?
3. If Marx and Engels were writing today, instead of in the mid-19th century, to what extent might *The Communist Manifesto* have been different? Would it have been written at all? If so, what parts might remain relatively unchanged? What parts might require serious modification — or deletion? Consider especially what Marx and Engels have to say about the working conditions and the life of the proletariat (paragraphs 35 and following). Who would they define as the proletariat? The bourgeoisie? You might want to do this assignment as an appendix that Marx and Engels (on temporary leave from Heaven or Hell — depending on your point of view) decide to write after an extensive tour of late 20th century society.

4. In paragraph 53 Marx and Engels maintain that for the proletariat, "Law, morality, religion are . . . so many bourgeois prejudices, behind which lurk in ambush just as many bourgeois interests." In paragraph 96, addressing the bourgeoisie, they claim that "Your jurisprudence is but the will of your class made into a law for all, a will, whose essential character and direction are determined by the economical conditions of existence of your class." Discuss these charges, as they might apply today. (Example: Terrorist groups sometimes justify their violations of law and morality by dismissing law and morality as bourgeois prejudices.)

5. In Section II, Marx and Engels address the audience as "you" and ask a series of questions (which they proceed to answer). What is the purpose of such a rhetorical strategy?

6. Marx and Engels charge that "The ruling ideas of each age have ever been the ideas of its ruling class" (paragraph 118). Examine the validity of this idea by means of two or three main examples, possibly from contemporary American civilization.

7. Compare and contrast Marx and Engels's view of human nature with that expressed by Andrew Carnegie in his essay "Wealth" (reprinted in Part V, on "The Survival of the Fittest").

8. Compare and contrast Marx and Engels's view of economic justice (particularly on the question of the surplus wealth of individuals) with those of Sumner or Spencer (see Part V, on "The Survival of the Fittest").

9. Even to those who are not students of history or political science, it is clear that the program Marx and Engels envisaged for the postrevolutionary period (paragraphs 129–131) has not been attained in any country, including the U.S.S.R. and China (though some of these goals have been attained). In terms of what you already know about human nature and about history, why do you think there has been so much difficulty in bringing about the kind of revolutionary goals envisaged by Marx and Engels? Begin by considering the extent to which the class struggle in one nation or any group of nations actually reflects the struggle described in *The Communist Manifesto*. Consider which aspects of their program could be realized in the future. Consider also which ones are most *worth* realizing, as well as what would have to be given up for this to happen. Consider, finally, the extent to which your views are influenced by your own class status.

JOHN REED *(1887–1920)*

Marxist doctrines have had considerable impact on a multitude of academic disciplines, most notably sociology, economics, psychology, and history; and they have also powerfully influenced fiction, the performing arts, and literary criticism. But of course, overshadowing all other impacts is the political one: the fact that revolutionaries under Marx's banner have actually brought about communist revolutions in two of the most populous nations in the world — the Union of Soviet Socialist Republics and the People's Republic of China. Were it not for this political reality — the fact that these countries, along with eastern Europe, Vietnam, North Korea, and Cuba, constitute a threat to the very existence of the United States and its allies — it is questionable whether Marxist ideas would continue to exercise the powerful hold they have in the noncommunist world.

The first, and — in terms of its impact on global affairs — the most significant of these revolutions took place in Russia in 1917. Russia seemed an unlikely prospect for Marxist-type revolution: at the turn of the century it was a country still living largely in the feudal age, with a powerful aristocracy, a robust peasantry, but a relatively undeveloped bourgeoisie.[1] Marx himself had expected the communist revolution to begin in Germany, a highly industrialized nation where the bourgeoisie, he believed, was ripe for fall. But centuries of autocracy and oppression by the czars had created widespread discontent; a non-Marxist uprising in 1905 resulted in some temporary concessions by the czar and the creation of a Duma, or legislature, that created at least the illusion of democratization.

The catalyst for revolution was Russia's entry into World War I against Germany. Largely because of the incompetence of the czar's officer corps, tens of thousands of Russian soldiers died in battles that were meaningless to the great masses of Russian people. The government itself was riddled with corruption, with much of the actual power wielded by Rasputin, a religious charlatan who had won the complete trust of the Czarina Alexandra (who, in turn, dominated her husband,

---

[1]Interestingly enough, revolution in Russia had been predicted by (among others) Josiah Strong, author of "The Anglo-Saxon and the World's Future" (excerpted in Part V, on "The Survival of the Fittest"). In 1885, Strong wrote:

> The throne of the Czar stands on a volcano. Alexander III seems fully committed to imperialism, and the Revolutionists are fully determined that the people shall assist in the work of government. . . . Revolutionists will be created by events; by the general discontent of the whole of the people; by the tendency of Russia toward new social forms. An entire nation cannot be suppressed . . . the repressive policy of the government and popular agitation will serve to intensify the other, until there results a spasmodic convulsion throughout Russia. . . . (*Our Country* 46.)

Nicholas II). The army as a whole was demoralized; thousands of soldiers deserted. Since there was no institutional outlet for grievances, protest necessarily became violent. The revolution finally came in March 1917. A series of strikes in Petrograd (now Leningrad) resulted in rioting; the police were called out but refused to attack the demonstrators; the Petrograd garrison mutinied. The intensity of the uprising escalated dramatically. Alarmed, the czar made concessions, but it was too late. Within weeks he abdicated, and the Romanoff dynasty as well as the rule of czars in Russia was at an end. (The czar and his immediate family were executed in July 1918.)

It is important to note that the Russian Revolution of March 1917 was not provoked or led by communists. Indeed, Lenin, the father of Soviet communism and the U.S.S.R.'s first ruler, was not even in the country at the time. For eight months, Russia was ruled by a provisional government, headed first by Prince Lvov, a believer in a parliamentary democracy along western European lines, and then by Alexander Kerensky, a more radical leader, but not a communist (or a Bolshevik, as members of the Communist Party were then called). The Duma had been recalled and plans were made to institute reforms, but the government found itself constantly at odds with the Petrograd Soviet, a kind of shadow government that represented the workers and the soldiers. One of the major issues at this point was Russia's continuance in the World War: the Bolsheviks were alone in advocating (and promising, if they gained power) immediate, unconditional withdrawal. Kerensky found himself in an impossible bind: he could not abandon the Allies in their war against Germany without losing the support of the west, nor could he institute radical domestic reforms without losing the support of Russian conservatives; on the other hand, he could not govern with widespread domestic support unless he pulled Russia out of the war and adopted such radical Bolshevik programs as nationalizing industry and redistributing the land. In short, he could not govern, unless he embraced Lenin's own program of "Peace and Bread." But then, of course, Lenin himself could do this much better than Kerensky.

Vladimir Ilyich Lenin was born in 1870, of middle-class parents, in Simbirsk, a town on the Volga River. His brother Alexander had been executed for conspiracies against the government, one of the factors in Lenin's own undying hostility to czarist rule. He enrolled in law school, and despite being expelled for revolutionary activities, was permitted to take the bar exam in 1891. He practiced law for little more than a year, but devoted much of his energy to studying the works of Marx and Engels. When famine came to his native province in 1892, he welcomed the development, hoping that it would spur discontent against the government that would result in its overthrow. His revolutionary activities resulted in his banishment to Siberia in 1897. During his exile, he continued to read and to write, and even got married. After his release, he left the country, and wandered from place to place in Europe, while editing the *Iskra* (the "Spark"), a Communist journal smuggled across national frontiers. Like Marx before him, Lenin studied at the British Museum in London.

By 1905, the year of the first Russian Revolution, Lenin was, at thirty-four, the leader of the Russian communists (Bolsheviks). He temporarily returned to his native land, but placed no faith in such reforms as the Duma. Indeed, he hoped that the czar would go back on his word and increase his repression (which he soon did) so that popular disappointment would lead to a genuine revolution. For the next twelve years he continued his underground activities in Europe; his Bolsheviks financed their operations by robbing banks and holding up trains. (In this they were ably assisted by a master robber and strong-arm tactician, a man who later became known as Stalin.) When more moderate Socialist groups (the Mensheviks) expressed their alarm at Bolshevik tactics, Lenin scornfully responded, "A Central Committee, to be effective, must be made up of gifted writers, able organizers, and a few intelligent scoundrels. I commend Victor [a comrade] and admire his total disregard of the bourgeois prejudices of honor and truth."

In March 1917, Lenin was in Switzerland. At first he refused to take the Petrograd uprising any more seriously than he had taken the 1905 revolution. But the Petrograd communists urged him back to Russia, and the Germans, who controlled the train routes to Russia (and who had much to gain from Lenin's carrying his antiwar message to Russia), facilitated his return. Thus, as Winston Churchill later wrote, Lenin was introduced as a "plague bacillus" back to Russia. Upon his arrival he immediately began his campaign of Peace and Bread. At first, he was unsuccessful (and even had to temporarily flee the country again), but with the unpopularity of the war, the insistence of the peasants for radical reforms, and the inability of the Kerensky government to govern effectively, Lenin and his forces became irresistible.

On November 7, Petrograd was taken by Bolshevik forces and the provisional government was driven out. That evening, Lenin's All-Russian Congress of Soviets declared that it was now the only legitimate government of Russia. Elections that had been scheduled earlier by the Duma were held, resulting in a significant defeat for the Bolsheviks. But Lenin, using the same strong-arm tactics that had made him a successful revolutionary-in-exile, overthrew the newly elected assembly in January 1918 (Bolshevik soldiers with machine guns had packed the parliamentary galleries), and all power was transferred to the Bolsheviks. Three months later, he signed the Treaty of Brest-Litovsk, ending Russia's participation in the World War (a treaty that required him to cede a third of Russia's population and a fourth of its territory to Germany). His next step, in accordance with his promise, was to abolish all private property, nationalizing all land and private industry. Lenin lived long enough to drive out of Russia the domestic and foreign counterrevolutionary forces and to begin Soviet Russia on its new path of communism. In 1922, he suffered a cerebral hemorrhage, and two years later he died. After a power struggle, he was succeeded by Stalin.

Perhaps the most exciting account of the November Revolution was written by John Reed, an American journalist. Born in Portland, Oregon, in 1887 of wealthy parents, Reed (subject of Warren Beatty's 1981 film, *Reds*) graduated from Harvard University in 1910 and immediately began a writing career. He worked on the *American Magazine*, wrote poetry, wrote articles for *The Saturday Evening Post* and *Collier's*, and edited *The Masses*, a socialist newspaper. Arrested several times for supporting strikes, he helped found the Communist Party in the United States. In 1914, he covered the revolt of Pancho Villa in Mexico; his impressions of the revolution became the basis of his first book, *Insurgent Mexico* (1914). The following year he was in Europe, covering World War I for *Metropolitan* magazine; out of these experiences came *War in Eastern Europe* (1916).

Reed and his wife Louise Bryant were in Petrograd during the November 1917 revolution. His vivid impressions of these events were preserved in *Ten Days That*

Shook the World (1919). Upon his return to the United States, Reed was expelled from the Socialist party, and subsequently helped form and assumed the leadership of the Communist Labor Party. Indicted for treason in the United States, he escaped to the Soviet Union, where he caught typhus and died three days before his thirty-third birthday. A hero in the Soviet Union, Reed is the only American to be buried in Red Square, under the Kremlin wall. In an introduction to a new edition of *Ten Days That Shook the World*, Lenin wrote:

> With the greatest interest and with never slackening attention I read John Reed's "Ten Days That Shook the World." Unreservedly do I recommend it to the workers of the world. Here is a book which I should like to see published in millions of copies and translated into all languages. It gives a truthful and most vivid exposition of the events so significant to the comprehension of what is really the Proletarian Revolution and the Dictatorship of the Proletariat. . . .

In the section excerpted below, Reed discusses the crucial events of November 7 and 8, 1917, when Lenin moved to take over Kerensky's provisional government. The biographical notes are by John Howard Lawson, editor of the 1967 edition of *Ten Days That Shook the World*. Most of the other explanatory notes are by Reed (and are so indicated).

TEN DAYS THAT SHOOK THE WORLD

THE FALL OF THE PROVISIONAL GOVERNMENT

Wednesday, November 7th, I rose very late. The noon cannon boomed 1
from Peter-Paul as I went down the Nevsky.[1] It was a raw, chill day. In
front of the State Bank some soldiers with fixed bayonets were standing at
the closed gates.

"What side do you belong to?" I asked. "The Government?" 2

"No more Government," one answered with a grin, "*Slava Bogu!* Glory 3
to God!" That was all I could get out of him. . . .

The street-cars were running on the Nevsky, men, women and small 4
boys hanging on every projection. Shops were open, and there seemed
even less uneasiness among the street crowds than there had been the day
before. A whole crop of new appeals against insurrection had blossomed

---

John Reed. *Ten Days that Shook the World* [1919]. New York: International Publishers, 1934, 1967. Ed. by John Howard Lawson.

[1]*the Nevsky:* A central avenue in the city of Petrograd (St. Petersburg), which, since the Revolution, has been called Leningrad.

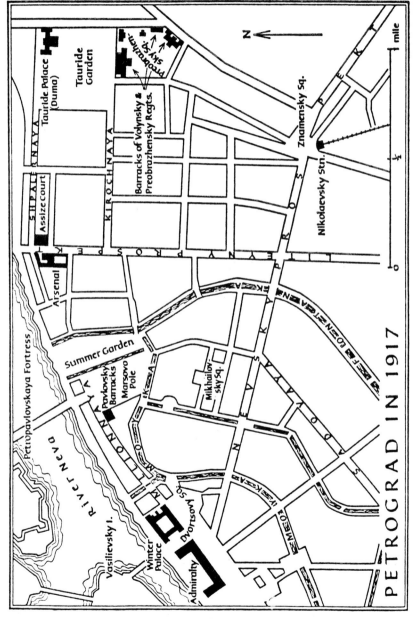

From George Katov, *Russia 1917: The February Revolution.* New York: Harper & Row, 1967.

out on the walls during the night — to the peasants, to the soldiers at the front, to the workmen of Petrograd. One read:

FROM THE PETROGRAD MUNICIPAL DUMA:

The Municipal Duma[2] informs the citizens that in the extraordinary meeting of November 6th the Duma formed a Committee of Public Safety, composed of members of the Central and Ward Dumas, and representatives of the following revolutionary democratic organizations: The *Tsay-ee-kah*,[3] the All-Russian Executive Committee of Peasant Deputies, the Army organisations, the *Tsentroflot*,[4] the Petrograd Soviet of Workers' and Soldiers' Deputies (!), the Council of Trade Unions,[5] and others.

Members of the Committee of Public Safety will be on duty in the building of the Municipal Duma. Telephones No. 15-40, 223-77, 138-36.

November 7th, 1917.

Though I didn't realize it then, this was the Duma's declaration of war against the Bolsheviki.[6]

I bought a copy of *Rabotchi Put*, the only newspaper which seemed on sale, and a little later paid a soldier fifty kopeks for a second-hand copy of *Dien*. The Bolshevik paper, printed on large-sized sheets in the conquered office of the *Russkaya Volia*, had huge headlines: "ALL POWER — TO THE SOVIETS OF WORKERS, SOLDIERS AND PEASANTS! PEACE! BREAD! LAND!" The

---

[2]*Duma:* The word *duma* means roughly "deliberative body." The old Imperial Duma, which persisted six months after the Revolution, in a democratised form, died a natural death in September, 1917. The *City Duma* referred to in this book was the reorganised Municipal Council, often called "Municipal Self-Government." It was elected by direct and secret ballot, and its only reason for failure to hold the masses during the Bolshevik Revolution was the general decline in influence of all purely *political* representation in the fact of the growing power of organisations based on *economic* groups. [Reed]

[3]*Tsay-ee-kah:* All-Russian Central Executive Committee of the Soviets of Workers' and Soldiers' Deputies. So called from the initials of its name. [Reed]

[4]*Tsentroflot:* "Centre-Fleet" — the Central Fleet Committee. [Reed]

[5]*Trade Unions:* Although mostly industrial in form, the Russian labour unions were still called Trade Unions, and at the time of the Bolshevik Revolution had from three to four million members. These Unions were also organised in an All-Russian body, a sort of Russian Federation of Labour, which had its Central Executive Committee in the capital. [Reed]

[6]*Bolsheviki:* Now call themselves the *Communist Party,* in order to emphasise their complete separation from the tradition of "moderate" or "parliamentary" Socialism, which dominates the Mensheviki and the so-called Majority Socialists in all countries. The *Bolsheviki* proposed immediate proletarian insurrection, and seizure of the reins of Government, in order to hasten the coming of Socialism by forcibly taking over industry, land, natural resources and financial institutions. This party expresses the desires chiefly of the factory workers, but also of a large section of the poor peasants. Among the leaders: Lenin, Trotzky, Lunatcharsky. [Reed]

leading article was signed "Zinoviev," — Lenin's companion in hiding. It
began:

> Every soldier, every worker, every real Socialist, every honest democrat [9]
> realises that there are only two alternatives to the present situation.
>
> Either — the power will remain in the hands of the bourgeois-landlord [10]
> crew, and this will mean every kind of repression for the workers, soldiers and
> peasants, continuation of the war, inevitable hunger and death. . . .
>
> Or — the power will be transferred to the hands of the revolutionary [11]
> workers, soldiers and peasants; and in that case it will mean a complete abo-
> lition of landlord tyranny, immediate check of the capitalists, immediate pro-
> posal of a just peace. Then the land is assured to the peasants, then control of
> industry is assured to the workers, then bread is assured to the hungry, then
> the end of this nonsensical war! . . .

Dien contained fragmentary news of the agitated night. Bolsheviki cap- [12]
ture of the Telephone Exchange, the Baltic station, the Telegraph Agency;
the Peterhof *yunkers*[7] unable to reach Petrograd; the Cossacks[8] undecided;
arrest of some of the Ministers; shooting of Chief of the City Militia Meyer;
arrests, counter-arrests, skirmishes between clashing patrols of soldiers,
yunkers and Red Guards.[9]

On the corner of the Morskaya I ran into Captain Gomberg, [13]
Menshevik[10] *oboronetz*,[11] secretary of the Military Section of his party. When
I asked him if the insurrection had really happened he shrugged his shoulders in a tired manner and replied, *"Tchort znayet!* The devil knows! Well,
perhaps the Bolsheviki can seize the power, but they won't be able to hold

---

[7]*Peterhof yunkers:* Students in the officers' training school in Peterhof, outside of Petrograd.
They opposed the overthrow of the provisional government.

[8]*Cossacks:* Cavalrymen, originally from southern Russia.

[9]*Red Guards:* The armed factory workers of Russia. The *Red Guards* were first formed during
the Revolution of 1905, and sprang into existence again in the days of March, 1917, when
a force was needed to keep order in the city. At that time they were armed, and all efforts
of the Provisional Government to disarm them were more or less unsuccessful. At every
great crisis in the Revolution the *Red Guards* appeared on the streets, untrained and un-
disciplined, but full of Revolutionary zeal. [Reed]

[10]*Menshevik:* This party includes all shades of Socialists who believe that society must progress by natural evolution toward Socialism, and that the working-class must conquer
political power first. Also a nationalistic party. This was the party of the Socialist intellectuals, which means: all the means of education having been in the hands of the propertied
classes, the intellectuals instinctively reacted to their training, and took the side of the
propertied classes. [Reed]

[11]*oboronetz:* A defensist, or someone who believed in continuing the World War in order to
defend Russia. Two other positions were frequently taken regarding the war: there were
those who believed that the war should be ended and those who believed that the war
should be continued, not just to defend Russia but to acquire territory.

it more than three days. They haven't the men to run a government. Perhaps it's a good thing to let them try — that will finish them. . . ."

The Military Hotel at the corner of St. Isaac's Square was picketed   14
by armed sailors. In the lobby were many of the smart young officers, walking up and down or muttering together; the sailors wouldn't let them leave. . . .

Suddenly came the sharp crack of a rifle outside, followed by a scat-   15
tered burst of firing. I ran out. Something unusual was going on around the Marinsky Palace, where the Council of the Russian Republic met. Diagonally across the wide square was drawn a line of soldiers, rifles ready, staring at the hotel roof.

"*Provocatzia!* Shot at us!" snapped one, while another went running   16
toward the door.

At the western corner of the Palace lay a big armoured car with a red   17
flag flying from it, newly lettered in red paint: "S.R.S.D." (*Soviet*[12] *Rabotchikh Soldatskikh Deputatov*); all the guns trained toward St. Isaac's. A barricade had been heaped up across the mouth of Novaya Ulitza — boxes, barrels, an old bed-spring, a wagon. A pile of lumber barred the end of the Moika quay. Short logs from a neighbouring woodpile were being built up along the front of the building to form breastworks[13]. . . .

"Is there going to be any fighting?" I asked.   18

"Soon, soon," answered a soldier, nervously. "Go away, comrade,   19
you'll get hurt. They will come from that direction," pointing toward the Admiralty.

"Who will?"   20

"That I couldn't tell you, brother," he answered, and spat.   21

---

[12]*Soviet:* The word *soviet* means "council." Under the Tsar the Imperial Council of State was called *Gosudarstvennyi Soviet*. Since the Revolution, however, the term *Soviet* has come to be associated with a certain type of parliament elected by members of working-class economic organisations — the Soviet of Workers', of Soldiers', or of Peasants' Deputies. I have therefore limited the word to these bodies, and wherever else it occurs I have translated it "Council."

Besides the local *Soviets*, elected in every city, town and village of Russia — and in large cities, also Ward (*Raionny*) *Soviets* — there are also the *oblastne* or *gubiernsky* (district or provincial) *Soviets*, and the Central Executive Committee of the All-Russian *Soviets* in the capital, called from its initials *Tsay-ee-kah*.

Almost everywhere the *Soviets* of Workers' and of Soldiers' Deputies combined very soon after the March Revolution. In special matters concerning their peculiar interests, however, the Workers' and the Soldiers' Sections continued to meet separately. The *Soviets* of Peasants' Deputies did not join the other two until after the Bolshevik *coup d'etat*. They, too, were organised like the workers and soldiers, with an Executive Committee of the All-Russian Peasants' *Soviets* in the capital. [Reed]

[13]*breastworks:* Breast-high, temporary fortresses.

Before the door of the Palace was a crowd of soldiers and sailors. A   22
sailor was telling of the end of the Council of the Russian Republic. "We
walked in there," he said, "and filled all the doors with comrades. I went
up to the counter-revolutionist Kornilovitz[14] who sat in the president's
chair. 'No more Council,' I says. 'Run along home now!'"

There was laughter. By waving assorted papers I managed to get   23
around to the door of the press gallery. There an enormous smiling sailor
stopped me, and when I showed my pass, just said, "If you were Saint
Michael[15] himself, comrade, you couldn't pass here!" Through the glass of
the door I made out the distorted face and gesticulating arms of a French
correspondent, locked in. . . .

Around in front stood a little, grey-moustached man in the uniform of   24
a general, the centre of a knot of soldiers. He was very red in the face.

"I am General Alexeyev,"[16] he cried. "As your superior officer and as   25
a member of the Council of the Republic I demand to be allowed to pass!"
The guard scratched his head, looking uneasily out of the corner of his eye;
he beckoned to an approaching officer, who grew very agitated when he
saw who it was and saluted before he realised what he was doing.

"*Vashe Vuisokoprevoskhoditelstvo* — your High Excellency —" he stam-   26
mered, in the manner of the old régime, "Access to the Palace is strictly
forbidden — I have no right ——"

An automobile came by, and I saw Gotz[17] sitting inside, laughing ap-   27
parently with great amusement. A few minutes later another, with armed
soldiers on the front seat, full of arrested members of the Provisional Government. Peters, Lettish member of the Military Revolutionary Committee,
came hurrying across the Square.

"I thought you bagged all those gentlemen last night," said I, pointing   28
to them.

---

[14]Kornilovitz, Lavr Georgievich (1870–1918). A Tsarist general and monarchist, he was
Commander of the Petrograd military area from March 1917. In July and August he became
Supreme Commander-in-Chief, and headed the counter-revolutionary revolt in August
1917. Following the Bolshevik Revolution, he led the White Guard Volunteer Army. [John
Howard Lawson, ed., *Ten Days That Shook the World*, by John Reed (New York: International
Publishers, 1967).]

[15]*Saint Michael:* In the Bible, he is depicted as the chief Archangel of God, a great warrior
and the leader of the heavenly host.

[16]Alexeyev, Mikhail Vasilyevich (1857–1918). Tsarist general who became Supreme Commander-in-Chief and later military adviser to the Provisional Government. After the October Revolution, he became one of the top counter-revolutionary organizers. [Lawson]

[17]Gotz, Abram Rafailovich (1882–1940). A leader of the Socialist Revolutionaries, he organized terrorist acts and armed struggle against Soviet power after the Bolshevik Revolution. [Lawson]

"Oh," he answered, with the expression of a disappointed small   29
boy. "The damn fools let most of them go again before we made up our
minds. . . ."

Down the Voskressensky Prospect a great mass of sailors were drawn   30
up, and behind them came marching soldiers, as far as the eye could reach.

We went toward the Winter Palace[18] by way of the Admiralteisky. All   31
the entrances to the Palace Square were closed by sentries, and a cordon
of troops stretched clear across the western end, besieged by an uneasy
throng of citizens. Except for far-away soldiers who seemed to be carrying
wood out of the Palace courtyard and piling it in front of the main gateway,
everything was quiet.

We couldn't make out whether the sentries were pro-Government or   32
pro-Soviet. Our papers from Smolny had no effect, however, so we approached another part of the line with an important air and showed our
American passports, saying "Official business!" and shouldered through.
At the door of the Palace the same old *shveitzari*,[19] in their brass-buttoned
blue uniforms with the red-and-gold collars, politely took our coats and
hats, and we went up-stairs. In the dark, gloomy corridor, stripped of its
tapestries, a few old attendants were lounging about, and in front of Kerensky's door a young officer paced up and down, gnawing his moustache.
We asked if we could interview the Minister-president. He bowed and
clicked his heels.

"No, I am sorry," he replied in French. "Alexander Feodorvitch[20] is   33
extremely occupied just now. . . ." He looked at us for a moment. "In fact,
he is not here. . . ."

"Where is he?"   34

"He has gone to the Front.[21] And do you know, there wasn't enough   35
gasoline for his automobile. We had to send to the English Hospital and
borrow some."

"Are the Ministers here?"   36

"They are meeting in some room — I don't know where."   37

"Are the Bolsheviki coming?"   38

"Of course. Certainly, they are coming. I expect a telephone call every   39
minute to say that they are coming. But we are ready. We have *yunkers* in
the front of the Palace. Through that door there."

"Can we go in there?"   40

---

[18]*Winter Palace:* The winter residence of the czarist family in Petrograd. After the March
Revolution it became the headquarters of the provisional government.

[19]*shveitzari:* Police guards.

[20]*Alexander Feodorvitch:* Kerensky.

[21]*"He has gone to the Front.":* Kerensky was attempting, unsuccessfully, to solicit military
support against the Bolsheviks.

"No. Certainly not. It is not permitted." Abruptly he shook hands all 41
around and walked away. We turned to the forbidden door, set in a temporary partition dividing the hall and locked on the outside. On the other
side were voices, and somebody laughing. Except for that the vast spaces
of the old Palace were silent as the grave. An old *shveitzar* ran up. "No,
barin,[22] you must not go in there."

"Why is the door locked?" 42

"To keep the soldiers in," he answered. After a few minutes he said 43
something about having a glass of tea and went back up the hall. We un-
locked the door.

Just inside a couple of soldiers stood on guard, but they said nothing. 44
At the end of the corridor was a large, ornate room with gilded cornices
and enormous crystal lustres, and beyond it several smaller ones, wain-
scoted with dark wood. On both sides of the parquetted floor lay rows of
dirty mattresses and blankets, upon which occasional soldiers were
stretched out; everywhere was a litter of cigarette-butts, bits of bread,
cloth, and empty bottles with expensive French labels. More and more
soldiers, with the red shoulder-straps of the *yunker*-schools, moved about
in a stale atmosphere of tobacco-smoke and unwashed humanity. One had
a bottle of white Burgundy, evidently filched from the cellars of the Palace.
They looked at us with astonishment as we marched past, through room
after room, until at last we came out into a series of great state-salons,
fronting their long and dirty windows on the Square. The walls were covered with huge canvases in massive gilt frames — historical battle-scenes.[23]
. . . "12 October 1812" and "6 November 1812" and "16/28 August 1813."
. . . One had a gash across the upper right hand corner.

The place was all a huge barrack, and evidently had been for weeks, 45
from the look of the floor and walls. Machine guns were mounted on win-
dow-sills, rifles stacked between the mattresses.

As we were looking at the pictures an alcoholic breath assailed me 46
from the region of my left ear, and a voice said in thick but fluent French,
"I see, by the way you admire the paintings, that you are foreigners." He
was a short, puffy man with a baldish head as he removed his cap.

"Americans? Enchanted. I am Stabs-Capitan Vladimir Artzibashev, ab- 47
solutely at your service." It did not seem to occur to him that there was
anything unusual in four strangers, one a woman, wandering through the
defences of an army awaiting attack. He began to complain of the state of
Russia.

---

[22]*barin*: Literally "lord" or "master." The term was used to ingratiate persons of higher
rank.

[23]*battle-scenes*: Battles during Napoleon's invasion of Russia.

"Not only these Bolsheviki," he said, "but the fine traditions of the   48
Russian army are broken down. Look around you. These are all students
in the officers' training schools. But are they gentlemen? Kerensky opened
the officers' schools to the ranks, to any soldier who could pass an examination. Naturally there are many, many who are contaminated by the Revolution. . . ."

Without consequence he changed the subject. "I am very anxious to   49
go away from Russia. I have made up my mind to join the American army.
Will you please go to your Consul and make arrangements? I will give you
my address." In spite of our protestations he wrote it on a piece of paper,
and seemed to feel better at once. I have it still — "*Oranienbaumskaya Shkola
Praporshtchikov 2nd, Staraya Peterhof.*"

"We had a review this morning early," he went on, as he guided us   50
through the rooms and explained everything. "The Women's Battalion[24]
decided to remain loyal to the Government."

"Are the women soldiers in the Palace?"   51

"Yes, they are in the back rooms, where they won't be hurt if any trou-   52
ble comes." He sighed. "It is a great responsibility," said he.

For a while we stood at the window, looking down on the Square be-   53
fore the Palace, where three companies of long-coated *yunkers* were drawn
up under arms, being harangued by a tall, energetic-looking officer I recognised as Stankievitch, chief Military Commissar of the Provisional Government. After a few minutes two of the companies shouldered arms with
a clash, barked three sharp shouts, and went swinging off across the
Square, disappearing through the Red Arch into the quiet city.

"They are going to capture the Telephone Exchange," said some one.   54
Three cadets stood by us, and we fell into conversation. They said they
had entered the schools from the ranks, and gave their names — Robert
Olev, Alexei Vasilienko and Erni Sachs, an Esthonian. But now they didn't
want to be officers any more, because officers were very unpopular. They
didn't seem to know what to do, as a matter of fact, and it was plain that
they were not happy.

But soon they began to boast. "If the Bolsheviki come we shall   55
show them how to fight. They do not dare to fight, they are cowards. But
if we should be overpowered, well, every man keeps one bullet for himself. . . ."

At this point there was a burst of rifle-fire not far off. Out on the Square   56

---

[24]*Women's Battalion:* The Women's Battalion is known to the world as the *Death Battalion,*
but there were many *Death Battalions* composed of men. These were formed in the summer
of 1917 by Kerensky, for the purpose of strengthening the discipline and combative fire of
the army by heroic example. The *Death Battalions* were composed mostly of intense young
patriots. These came for the most part from among the [daughters and] sons of the propertied classes. [Reed]

all the people began to run, falling flat on their faces, and the *izvoshtchiki*,[25] standing on the corners, galloped in every direction. Inside all was uproar, soldiers running here and there, grabbing up guns, rifle-belts and shouting, "Here they come! Here they come!" . . . But in a few minutes it quieted down again. The *izvoshtchiki* came back, the people lying down stood up. Through the Red Arch appeared the *yunkers*, marching a little out of step, one of them supported by two comrades.

It was getting late when we left the Palace. The sentries in the Square 57 had all disappeared. The great semi-circle of Government buildings seemed deserted. We went into the Hotel France for dinner, and right in the middle of soup the waiter, very pale in the face, came up and insisted that we move to the main dining-room at the back of the house, because they were going to put out the lights in the café. "There will be much shooting," he said.

When we came out on the Morskaya again it was quite dark, except 58 for one flickering street-light on the corner of the Nevsky. Under this stood a big armored automobile, with racing engine and oil-smoke pouring out of it. A small boy had climbed up the side of the thing and was looking down the barrel of a machine gun. Soldiers and sailors stood around, evidently waiting for something. We walked back up to the Red Arch, where a knot of soldiers was gathered staring at the brightly-lighted Winter Palace and talking in loud tones.

"No, comrades," one was saying. "How can we shoot at them? The 59 Women's Battalion is in there — they will say we have fired on Russian women."

As we reached the Nevsky again another armoured car came around 60 the corner, and a man poked his head out of the turret-top.

"Come on!" he yelled. "Let's go on through and attack!" 61

The driver of the other car came over, and shouted so as to be heard 62 above the roaring engine. "The Committee says to wait. They have got artillery behind the wood-piles in there. . . ."

Here the street-cars had stopped running, few people passed, and 63 there were no lights; but a few blocks away we could see the trams, the crowds, the lighted shop-windows and the electric signs of the moving-picture shows — life going on as usual. We had tickets to the Ballet at the Marinsky Theatre — all the theatres were open — but it was too exciting out of doors. . . .

In the darkness we stumbled over lumber-piles barricading the Police 64 Bridge, and before the Stroganov Palace made out some soldiers wheeling into position a three-inch field-gun. Men in various uniforms were coming and going in an aimless way, and doing a great deal of talking. . . .

---

[25]*izvoshtchiki:* Horse-drawn carriages that served as taxicabs.

Up the Nevsky the whole city seemed to be out promenading. On   65
every corner immense crowds were massed around a core of hot discussion. Pickets of a dozen soldiers with fixed bayonets lounged at the street-
crossings, red-faced old men in rich fur coats shook their fists at them,
smartly-dressed women screamed epithets; the soldiers argued feebly,
with embarrassed grins. . . . Armoured cars went up and down the street,
named after the first Tsars — Oleg, Rurik, Svietoslav — and daubed with
huge red letters, "R. S. D. R. P." (*Rossiskaya Sotsial-Demokrateetcheskaya Ra-
botchaya Partia*).[26] At the Mikhailovsky a man appeared with an armful of
newspapers, and was immediately stormed by frantic people, offering a
rouble, five roubles, ten roubles, tearing at each other like animals. It was
Rabotchi i Soldat, announcing the victory of the Proletarian Revolution, the
liberation of the Bolsheviki still in prison, calling upon the Army front and
rear for support . . . a feverish little sheet of four pages, running to enormous type, containing no news. . . .

On the corner of the Sadovaya about two thousand citizens had gath-   66
ered, staring up at the roof of a tall building, where a tiny red spark glowed
and waned.

"See!" said a tall peasant, pointing to it. "It is a provocator. Presently   67
he will fire on the people. . . ." Apparently no one thought of going to
investigate. . . .

The massive façade of Smolny blazed with lights as we drove up, and   68
from every street converged upon it streams of hurrying shapes dim in the
gloom. Automobiles and motorcycles came and went; an enormous ele-
phant-coloured armoured automobile, with two red flags flying from the
turret, lumbered out with screaming siren. It was cold, and at the outer
gate the Red Guards had built themselves a bon-fire. At the inner gate,
too, there was a blaze, by the light of which the sentries slowly spelled out
our passes and looked us up and down. The canvas covers had been taken
off the four rapid-fire guns on each side of the doorway, and the ammu-
nition-belts hung snake-like from their breeches. A dun herd of armoured
cars stood under the trees in the court-yard, engines going. The long, bare,
dimly-illuminated halls roared with the thunder of feet, calling, shouting. . . . There was an atmosphere of recklessness. A crowd came pouring
down the staircase, workers in black blouses and round black fur hats,
many of them with guns slung over their shoulders, soldiers in rough dirt-
coloured coats and grey fur *shapki*[27] pinched flat, a leader or so — Lunat-

---

[26](Russian Social Democratic Labor Party). [Reed]
[27]*shapki*: Tall fur hats.

charsky,[28] Kameniev[29] — hurrying along in the centre of a group all talking at once, with harassed anxious faces, and bulging portfolios under their arms. The extraordinary meeting of the Petrograd Soviet was over. I stopped Kameniev — a quick-moving little man, with a wide, vivacious face set close to his shoulders. Without preface he read in rapid French a copy of the resolution just passed:

> The Petrograd Soviet of Workers' and Soldiers' Deputies, saluting the vic- 69 torious Revolution of the Petrograd proletariat and garrison, particularly emphasises the unity, organisation, discipline, and complete cooperation shown by the masses in this rising; rarely has less blood been spilled, and rarely has an insurrection succeeded so well.

> The Soviet expresses its firm conviction that the Workers' and Peasants' 70 Government which, as the government of the Soviets, will be created by the Revolution, and which will assure the industrial proletariat of the support of the entire mass of poor peasants, will march firmly toward Socialism, the only means by which the country can be spared the miseries and unheard-of horrors of war.

> The new Workers' and Peasants' Government will propose immediately a 71 just and democratic peace to all the belligerent countries.

> It will suppress immediately the great landed property, and transfer the 72 land to the peasants. It will establish workmen's control over production and distribution of manufactured products, and will set up a general control over the banks, which it will transform into a state monopoly.

> The Petrograd Soviet of Workers' and Soldiers' Deputies calls upon the 73 workers and the peasants of Russia to support with all their energy and all their devotion the Proletarian Revolution. The Soviet expresses its conviction that the city workers, allies of the poor peasants, will assure complete revolutionary order, indispensable to the victory of Socialism. The Soviet is convinced that the proletariat of the countries of Western Europe will aid us in conducting the cause of Socialism to a real and lasting victory.

"You consider it won then?" 74

---

[28]Lunatcharsky, Anatoly Vasilyevich (1875–1933). Prominent Soviet statesman and man of letters. He wrote a number of books on art and literature, and served as People's Commissar for Education from 1917 to 1929. [Lawson]

[29]Kameniev (Rosenfeld), Lev Borisovich (1883–1936). A Bolshevik since 1903, he was active as organizer and editor. Returning to Petrograd from Siberian exile after the February Revolution, he opposed Lenin's "April Theses" for transition to the socialist revolution, and later was against the armed uprising. He then favored an "all-Socialist" government, and resigned from the Central Committee on this question on November 17. Subsequently, he supported various opposition blocs and then as a member of the Trotsky Bloc was expelled from the Central Committee in 1927, but was reinstated the following year on acknowledging his errors. In 1932 he was again expelled, and in 1936 fell a victim of the Stalin purge. [Lawson]

He lifted his shoulders. "There is much to do. Horribly much. It is just   75
beginning. . . ."

On the landing I met Riazanov,[30] vice-president of the Trade Unions,   76
looking black and biting his grey beard. "It's insane! Insane!" he shouted.
"The European working-class won't move! All Russia —" He waved his
hand distractedly and ran off. Riazanov and Kameniev had both opposed
the insurrection, and felt the lash of Lenin's terrible tongue. . . .

It had been a momentous session. In the name of the Military Revo-   77
lutionary Committee Trotzky[31] had declared that the Provisional Government no longer existed.

"The characteristic of bourgeois governments," he said, "is to deceive   78
the people. We, the Soviets of Workers', Soldiers' and Peasants' Deputies,
are going to try an experiment unique in history; we are going to found a
power which will have no other aim but to satisfy the needs of the soldiers,
workers, and peasants."

Lenin had appeared, welcomed with a mighty ovation, prophesying   79
world-wide Social Revolution. . . . And Zinoviev,[32] crying, "This day we
have paid our debt to the international proletariat, and struck a terrible

---

[30]Riazanov (Goldendach), David Borisovich (1870–1938). A Menshevik, he was accepted
into the Bolsheviks at the Sixth Party Congress in 1917. During previous years abroad, he
edited the works of Marx and Engels. After the October Revolution, he was in the trade
union leadership. In 1918, he temporarily left the Party over his disagreement with the
Brest peace treaty, and was removed from trade union work. In 1921 he organized the
Marx-Engels Institute, of which he was director until 1931, when he was expelled from
the Party on the charge of aiding Menshevik anti-Soviet activities. [Lawson]

[31]Trotzky (Bronstein), Lev Davidovich (1879–1940). A Menshevik since 1903, he was a
leader of the Centrist tendency in the Russian social-democratic movement. In 1912, he
organized the "August Bloc," characterized by Lenin as "camouflaged liquidationist" (of
the Party). During the First World War he favored defense of the country under the slogan
"Neither victory nor defeat," when Lenin was advocating the policy of socialist revolution.
He joined the Bolsheviks in 1917, on his return from abroad after the February Revolution.
As a member of the Central Committee, after at first urging postponement he supported
Lenin on the armed uprising. During the peace negotiations with the Germans at Brest-
Litovsk, he insisted on his own position of "neither peace nor war," against the policy
approved by the Central Committee. Again in 1920, he opposed the policy of building
socialism in a single country, holding that this task would have to wait upon the world
revolution. Having formed the Opposition Bloc in 1926 with Kameniev and Zinoviev, he
was expelled from the Party in 1927, and exiled in 1929. From abroad he continued to fight
Bolshevism, until his assassination under mysterious circumstances in Mexico. [Lawson]
In a manner somewhat reminiscent of Napoleon's (Stalin's) denigration of Snowball
(Trotzky) in Orwell's *Animal Farm,* Lawson, a member of the American Communist Party,
plays down Trotzky's crucial role in the Revolution. Trotzky's assassination ("under mys-
terious circumstances") is almost universally believed to have been ordered by Stalin.
[Behrens and Rosen]

[32]Zinoviev (Radomyslsky), Grigory Yevseyevich (1883–1936). A Bolshevik since 1903, in
October 1917 he, along with Kameniev, opposed the Party's decision to begin an armed

blow at the war, a terrible body-blow at all the imperialists and particularly at Wilhelm the Executioner. . . ."

Then Trotzky, that telegrams had been sent to the front announcing   80
the victorious insurrection, but no reply had come. Troops were said to be marching against Petrograd — a delegation must be sent to tell them the truth.

Cries, "You are anticipating the will of the All-Russian Congress of   81
Soviets!"

Trotzky, coldly, "The will of the All-Russian Congress of Soviets has   82
been anticipated by the rising of the Petrograd workers and soldiers!"

So we came into the great meeting-hall, pushing through the clamor-   83
ous mob at the door. In the rows of seats, under the white chandeliers, packed immovably in the aisles and on the sides, perched on every window-sill, and even the edge of the platform, the representatives of the workers and soldiers of all Russia waited in anxious silence or wild exultation the ringing of the chairman's bell. There was no heat in the hall but the stifling heat of unwashed human bodies. A foul blue cloud of cigarette smoke rose from the mass and hung in the thick air. Occasionally some one in authority mounted the tribune and asked the comrades not to smoke; then everybody, smokers and all, took up the cry "Don't smoke, comrades!" and went on smoking. Petrovsky, Anarchist delegate from the Obukhov[33] factory, made a seat for me beside him. Unshaven and filthy, he was reeling from three nights' sleepless work on the Military Revolutionary Committee.

On the platform sat the leaders of the old *Tsay-ee-kah* — for the last   84
time dominating the turbulent Soviets, which they had ruled from the first days, and which were now risen against them. It was the end of the first period of the Russian revolution, which these men had attempted to guide in careful ways. . . . The three greatest of them were not there: Kerensky, flying to the front through country towns all doubtfully heaving up; Tcheidze, the old eagle, who had contemptuously retired to his own Georgian mountains, there to sicken with consumption; and the high-souled Tseretelli,[34] also mortally stricken, who, nevertheless, would return and

---

uprising. In 1925 he helped organize the "New Opposition" and the following year became a leader of the Trotzky Bloc. Expelled from the Party in 1934, he became a victim of the Stalin purge. [Lawson]

[33]*Obukhov:* The proper name of a factory in Russia.

[34]Tseretelli, Irakly Georgievich (1882–1959). A Menshevik leader, he served as Minister of Posts and Telegraphs just after the February Revolution. In July 1917, he became Minister of the Interior. Following the Bolshevik Revolution, he led the anti-Soviet bloc in the Constituent Assembly, and later led the counter-revolutionary Menshevik government of Georgia. When Soviet power was established in Georgia in 1921, he became an émigré. [Lawson]

pour out his beautiful eloquence for a lost cause. Gotz sat there, Dan,[35] Lieber,[36] Bogdanov, Broido, Fillipovsky, — white-faced, hollow-eyed and indignant. Below them the second *siezd*[37] of the All-Russian Soviets boiled and swirled, and over their heads the Military Revolutionary Committee functioned white-hot, holding in its hands the threads of insurrection and striking with a long arm. . . . It was 10.40 P.M.

Dan, a mild-faced, baldish figure in a shapeless military surgeon's uni-   85 form, was ringing the bell. Silence fell sharply, intense, broken by the scuffling and disputing of the people at the door. . . .

"We have the power in our hands," he began sadly, stopped for a mo-   86 ment, and then went on in a low voice. "Comrades! The Congress of Soviets is meeting in such unusual circumstances and in such an extraordinary moment that you will understand why the *Tsay-ee-kah* considers it unnecessary to address you with a political speech. This will become much clearer to you if you will recollect that I am a member of the *Tsay-ee-kah*, and that at this very moment our party comrades are in the Winter Palace under bombardment, sacrificing themselves to execute the duty put on them by the *Tsay-ee-kah*." (Confused uproar.)

"I declare the first session of the Second Congress of Soviets of Work-   87 ers' and Soldiers' Deputies open!"

The election of the presidium took place amid stir and moving about.   88 Avanessov announced that by agreement of the Bolsheviki, Left Socialist Revolutionaries[38] and Mensheviki Internationalists,[39] it was decided to base the presidium upon proportionality. Several Mensheviki leaped to their

---

[35]Dan, Fyodor Ivanovich (1871–1947). A Menshevik leader during the First World War. After the February Revolution, he was a member of the Executive Committee of the Petrograd Soviet and a supporter of the Provisional Government. Following the October Revolution, he actively fought against Soviet power. In 1922, he was exiled from the country. [Lawson]

[36]Lieber (Goldman), Mikhail Isaakovich (1880–1937). A leader of the Bund; in 1903, he went with the Mensheviks. He was a member of the Executive Committee of the Petrograd Soviet of Workers' and Soldiers' Deputies, after the February Revolution. He adopted a hostile attitude toward the Bolshevik Revolution, and subsequently resigned from politics. [Lawson]

[37]*siezd:* A meeting or congress.

[38]*Left Socialist Revolutionaries:* Although theoretically sharing the Bolshevik programme of dictatorship of the working-class, at first were reluctant to follow the ruthless Bolshevik tactics. However, the *Left Socialist Revolutionaries* remained in the Soviet Government, sharing the Cabinet portfolios, especially that of Agriculture. They withdrew from the Government several times, but always returned. As the peasants left the ranks of the *Essaires* in increasing numbers, they joined the *Left Socialist Revolutionary party*, which became the great peasant party supporting the Soviet Government, standing for confiscation without compensation of the great landed estates, and their disposition by the peasants themselves. [Reed]

[39]*Mensheviki Internationalists:* The radical wing of the *Mensheviki*, internationalists and opposed to all coalition with the propertied classes; yet unwilling to break loose from the

feet protesting. A bearded soldier shouted at them, "Remember what you did to us Bolsheviki when *we* were the minority!" Result — 14 Bolsheviki, 7 Socialist Revolutionaries, 3 Mensheviki and 1 Internationalist (Gorky's[40] group). Hendelmann, for the right and centre Socialist Revolutionaries, said that they refused to take part in the presidium; the same from Kintchuk, for the Mensheviki; and from the Mensheviki Internationalists, that until the verification of certain circumstances, they too could not enter the presidium. Scattering applause and hoots. One voice, "Renegades, you call yourselves Socialists!" A representative of the Ukrainean delegates demanded, and received, a place. Then the old *Tsay-ee-kah* stepped down, and in their places appeared Trotzky, Kameniev, Lunatcharsky, Madame Kollentai,[41] Nogin[42]. . . . The hall rose, thundering. How far they had soared, these Bolsheviki, from a despised and hunted sect less than four months ago, to this supreme place, the helm of great Russia in full tide of insurrection!

The order of the day, said Kameniev, was first, Organisation of Power; second, War and Peace; and third, the Constituent Assembly. Lozovsky,[43] rising, announced that upon agreement of the bureau of all factions, it was proposed to hear and discuss the report of the Petrograd Soviet, then to give the floor to members of the *Tsay-ee-kah* and the different parties, and finally to pass to the order of the day.   89

But suddenly a new sound made itself heard, deeper than the tumult of the crowd, persistent, disquieting, — the dull shock of guns. People looked anxiously toward the clouded windows, and a sort of fever came over them. Martov, demanding the floor, croaked hoarsely, "The civil war   90

---

conservative Mensheviki, and opposed to the dictatorship of the working-class advocated by the Bolsheviki. Trotzky was long a member of this group. [Reed]

[40]Gorky, Maxim (1868–1936). Short-story writer, novelist, and playwright. An active participant in the 1905 revolution, he was a leading influence on the literature of his times. Among his more famous works are his novel, *Mother*; his play, *The Lower Depths*; and his epic *Autobiography*. [Lawson]

[41]Kollentai, Alexandra Mikhailovna (1872–1952). The daughter of a Tsarist general, she became a revolutionary. Forced to seek safety in exile in 1908, she returned to participate in the Bolshevik Revolution. In 1920 she became People's Commissar for Social Welfare, and in subsequent years minister and ambassador to Norway, Mexico, and Sweden. [Lawson]

[42]Nogin, Viktor Pavlovich (1878–1924). A member of the R.S.D.L.P. from 1898. After the February Revolution, he was Chairman of the Moscow Soviet of Workers' Deputies. At the Second All-Russian Congress of Soviets, he was elected People's Commissar for Trade and Industry. He withdrew ten days later from the Party Central Committee and the Council of People's Commissars in disagreement with the Central Committee's decision against a coalition government with the Mensheviks and Socialist Revolutionaries. In 1922 he directed the textile industry. [Lawson]

[43]Lozovsky, Solomon Abramovich (1878–1952). A Bolshevik, participant in the revolutionary movements since 1903. He became General Secretary of the Red International of Labor Unions in 1922. [Lawson]

is beginning, comrades! The first question must be a peaceful settlement of the crisis. On principle and from a political standpoint we must urgently discuss a means of averting civil war. Our brothers are being shot down in the streets! At this moment, when before the opening of the Congress of Soviets the question of Power is being settled by means of a military plot organised by one of the revolutionary parties —" for a moment he could not make himself heard above the noise, "All of the revolutionary parties must face the fact! The first *vopros* (question) before the Congress is the question of Power, and this question is already being settled by force of arms in the streets! . . . We must create a power which will be recognised by the whole democracy. If the Congress wishes to be the voice of the revolutionary democracy it must not sit with folded hands before the developing civil war, the result of which may be a dangerous outburst of counter-revolution. . . . The possibility of a peaceful outcome lies in the formation of a united democratic authority. . . . We must elect a delegation to negotiate with the other Socialist parties and organisations. . . ."

Always the methodical muffled boom of cannon through the windows,   91
and the delegates, screaming at each other. . . . So, with the crash of artillery, in the dark, with hatred, and fear, and reckless daring, new Russia was being born. . . .

We hurried from the place, stopping for a moment at the room where   92
the Military Revolutionary Committee worked at furious speed, engulfing and spitting out panting couriers, despatching Commissars armed with power of life and death to all the corners of the city, amid the buzz of the telephonographs. The door opened, a blast of stale air and cigarette-smoke rushed out, we caught a glimpse of dishevelled men bending over a map under the glare of a shaded electric-light. . . . Comrade Josephov-Dukhvinski, a smiling youth with a mop of pale yellow hair, made out passes for us.

When we came into the chill night, all the front of Smolny was one   93
huge park of arriving and departing automobiles, above the sound of which could be heard the far-off slow beat of the cannon. A great motor-truck stood there, shaking to the roar of its engine. Men were tossing bundles into it, and others receiving them, with guns beside them.

"Where are you going?" I shouted.   94

"Down-town — all over — everywhere!" answered a little workman,   95
grinning, with a large exultant gesture.

We showed our passes. "Come along!" they invited. "But there'll prob-   96
ably be shooting —" We climbed in; the clutch slid home with a raking jar, the great car jerked forward, we all toppled backward on top of those who were climbing in; past the huge fire by the gate, and then the fire by the outer gate, glowing red on the faces of the workmen with rifles who squatted around it, and went bumping at top speed down the Suvorovsky Prospect, swaying from side to side. . . . One man tore the wrapping from a

bundle and began to hurl handfuls of papers into the air. We imitated him, plunging down through the dark street with a tail of white papers floating and eddying out behind. The late passerby stooped to pick them up; the patrols around bonfires on the corners ran out with uplifted arms to catch them. Sometimes armed men loomed up ahead, crying *"Shtoi!"* and raising their guns, but our chauffeur only yelled something unintelligible and we hurtled on. . . .

I picked up a copy of the paper, and under a fleeting street-light read: 97

TO THE CITIZENS OF RUSSIA!

> The Provisional Government is deposed. The State Power has passed into 98 the hands of the organ of the Petrograd Soviet of Workers' and Soldiers' Deputies, the Military Revolutionary Committee, which stands at the head of the Petrograd proletariat and garrison.
>
> The cause for which the people were fighting: immediate proposal of a 99 democratic peace, abolition of landlord property-rights over the land, labor control over production, creation of a Soviet Government — that cause is securely achieved.
>
> LONG LIVE THE REVOLUTION OF WORKMEN, SOLDIERS AND 100 PEASANTS!
>
> *Military Revolutionary Committee*
> *Petrograd Soviet of Workers' and Soldiers' Deputies.* . . .

In the meanwhile unrebuked we walked into the [Winter] Palace. 101 There was still a great deal of coming and going, of exploring new-found apartments in the vast edifice, of searching for hidden garrisons of *yunkers* which did not exist. We went upstairs and wandered through room after room. This part of the Palace had been entered also by other detachments from the side of the Neva.[44] The paintings, statues, tapestries and rugs of the great state apartments were unharmed; in the offices, however, every desk and cabinet had been ransacked, the papers scattered over the floor, and in the living rooms beds had been stripped of their coverings and ward-robes wrenched open. The most highly prized loot was clothing, which the working people needed. In a room where furniture was stored we came upon two soldiers ripping the elaborate Spanish leather upholstery from chairs. They explained it was to make boots with. . . .

The old Palace servants in their blue and red and gold uniforms stood 102 nervously about, from force of habit repeating, "You can't go in there, *barin*! It is forbidden —" We penetrated at length to the gold and malachite chamber with crimson brocade hangings where the Ministers had been in session all that day and night, and where the *shveitzari* had betrayed them to the Red Guards. The long table covered with green baize was just as

---

[44]*Neva:* The river Neva flows through the center of Petrograd. (See map, p. 581.)

they had left it, under arrest. Before each empty seat was pen and ink and paper; the papers were scribbled over with beginnings of plans of action, rough drafts of proclamations and manifestos. Most of these were scratched out, as their futility became evident, and the rest of the sheet covered with absent-minded geometrical designs, as the writers sat despondently listening while Minister after Minister proposed chimerical schemes. I took one of these scribbled pages, in the hand writing of Konovalov,[45] which read, "The Provisional Government appeals to all classes to support the Provisional Government —"

All this time, it must be remembered, although the Winter Palace was   *103* surrounded, the Government was in constant communication with the Front and with provincial Russia. The Bolsheviki had captured the Ministry of War early in the morning, but they did not know of the military telegraph office in the attic, nor of the private telephone line connecting it with the Winter Palace. In that attic a young officer sat all day, pouring out over the country a flood of appeals and proclamations; and when he heard that the Palace had fallen, put on his hat and walked calmly out of the building. . . .

PLUNGING AHEAD

Thursday, November 8th. Day broke on a city in the wildest excitement   *104* and confusion, a whole nation heaving up in long hissing swells of storm. Superficially all was quiet; hundreds of thousands of people retired at a prudent hour, got up early, and went to work. In Petrograd the street-cars were running, the stores and restaurants open, theatres going, an exhibition of paintings advertised. . . . All the complex routine of common life — humdrum even in war-time — proceeded as usual. Nothing is so astounding as the vitality of the social organism — how it persists, feeding itself, clothing itself, amusing itself, in the face of the worst calamities. . . .

The air was full of rumours about Kerensky, who was said to have   *105* raised the Front, and to be leading a great army against the capital. *Volia Naroda* published a *prikaz*[46] launched by him at Pskov[47]:

> The disorders caused by the insane attempt of the Bolsheviki place the   *106* country on the verge of a precipice, and demand the effort of our entire will, our courage and the devotion of every one of us, to win through the terrible trial which the fatherland is undergoing. . . .
>
> Until the declaration of the composition of the new Government — if one   *107* is formed — every one ought to remain at his post and fulfil his duty toward

---

[45]Konovalov, Alexander Ivanovich (*b.* 1875). A big textile manufacturer, he was Minister of Trade and Industry in the Kerensky Provisional Government. [Lawson]

[46]*prikaz:* An order from the government.

[47]*Pskov:* A city in northwestern Russia on the south end of Lake Pskov.

bleeding Russia. It must be remembered that the least interference with exist-ing Army organisations can bring on irreparable misfortunes, by opening the Front to the enemy. Therefore it is indispensable to preserve at any price the morale of the troops, by assuring complete order and the preservation of the Army from new shocks, and by maintaining absolute confidence between of-ficers and their subordinates. I order all the chiefs and Commissars, in the name of the safety of the country, to stay at their posts, as I myself retain the post of Supreme Commander, until the Provisional Government of the Repub-lic shall declare its will. . . .

In answer, this placard on all the walls: *108*

FROM THE ALL-RUSSIAN CONGRESS OF SOVIETS

"The ex-Ministers Konovalov, Kishkin,[48] Terestchenko,[49] Maliantovitch, *109* Nikitin[50] and others have been arrested by the Military Revolutionary Com-mittee. Kerensky has fled. All Army organisations are ordered to take every measure for the immediate arrest of Kerensky and his conveyance to Petrograd.

"All assistance given to Kerensky will be punished as a serious crime *110* against the state."

With brakes released the Military Revolutionary Committee whirled, *111* throwing off orders, appeals, decrees, like sparks. . . . Kornilov was or-dered brought to Petrograd. Members of the Peasant Land Committees imprisoned by the Provisional Government were declared free. Capital punishment in the army was abolished. Government employees were or-dered to continue their work, and threatened with severe penalties if they refused. All pillage, disorder and speculation were forbidden under pain of death. Temporary Commissars were appointed to the various Ministries: Foreign Affairs, Vuritsky and Trotzky; Interior and Justice, Rykov;[51] Labor, Shliapnikov;[52] Finance, Menzhinsky; Public Welfare, Madame Kollontai;

---

[48]Kishkin, Nikolai Mikhailovich (1864–1930). A Cadet leader; on the eve of the October Revolution he was appointed dictator of Petrograd to fight the Bolsheviks. [Lawson]

[49]Terestchenko, Mikhail Ivanovich (*b.* 1888). Russian capitalist and sugar manufacturer, he was Minister of Finance and Minister of Foreign Affairs in the Provisional Government. [Lawson]

[50]Nikitin, A. M. (*b.* 1876). A Menshevik, he was a Minister in Kerensky's Provisional Gov-ernment. [Lawson]

[51]Rykov, Alexei Ivanovich (1881–1938). Joined the R.S.D.L.P. in 1899. After the February Revolution, he opposed the Party's course toward socialist revolution, but after the Octo-ber Revolution he held a number of responsible posts. In 1917, he favored an "all-Socialist" coalition government, as against the Party position. Together with Bukharin, he headed the Right Opposition in 1928; in 1937, he was expelled from the Party, and became a victim of the Stalin purge. [Lawson]

[52]Shliapnikov, Alexander Gavrilovich (1885–1943). Joined the R.S.D.L.P. in 1901. When the Bolsheviks gained power, he engaged in trade union work. In 1920–22, he organized and led the "Workers' Opposition" group. He was expelled in 1933. [Lawson]

Commerce, Ways and Communications, Riazanov; Navy, the sailor Korbir; Posts and Telegraphs, Spiro;[53] Theatres, Muraviov;[54] State Printing Office, Gherbychev; for the City of Petrograd, Lieutenant Nesterov; for the Northern Front, Pozern. . . .

To the Army, appeal to set up Military Revolutionary Committees. To 112 the railway workers, to maintain order, especially not to delay the transport of food to the cities and the front. . . . In return, they were promised representation in the Ministry of Ways and Communications.

> Cossack brothers! (said one proclamation). You are being led against Pe- 113 trograd. They want to force you into battle with the revolutionary workers and soldiers of the capital. Do not believe a word that is said by our common enemies, the land-owners and the capitalists.
>
> At our Congress are represented all the conscious organisations of work- 114 ers, soldiers and peasants of Russia. The Congress wishes also to welcome into its midst the worker-Cossacks. The Generals of the Black Band,[55] henchmen of the land-owners, of Nicolai the Cruel,[56] are our enemies.
>
> They tell you that the Soviets wish to confiscate the lands of the Cossacks. 115 This is a lie. It is only from the great Cossack landlords that the Revolution will confiscate the land to give it to the people.
>
> Organise Soviets of Cossacks' Deputies! Join with the Soviets of Workers' 116 and Soldiers' Deputies!
>
> Show the Black Band that you are not traitors to the People, and that you 117 do not wish to be cursed by the whole of revolutionary Russia! . . .
>
> Cossack brothers, execute no orders of the enemies of the people. Send 118 your delegates to Petrograd to talk it over with us. . . . The Cossacks of the Petrograd garrison, to their honour, have not justified the hope of the People's enemies. . . .
>
> Cossack brothers! The All-Russian Congress of Soviets extends to you a 119 fraternal hand. Long live the brotherhood of the Cossacks with the soldiers, workers and peasants of all Russia!

On the other side, what a storm of proclamations posted up, hand- 120 bills scattered everywhere, newspapers — screaming and cursing and prophesying evil. Now raged the battle of the printing press — all other weapons being in the hands of the Soviets.

---

[53]Spiro. A leader of the Left Socialist Revolutionaries, working in the Ukraine. In 1918 he served as Commissar Extraordinary on the Rumanian front. [Lawson]

[54]Muraviov, Mikhail Artemyevich (1880–1918). Lieutenant-colonel of the Tsarist army, he joined the Left Socialist Revolutionaries after the February Revolution. As commander-in-chief of the Red Army on the Eastern Front, he turned traitor. [Lawson]

[55]*Black Band:* The term used for groups of political reactionaries.

[56]*Nicolai the Cruel:* Nicholas II, the current czar.

First, the appeal of the Committee for Salvation of Country and Rev- 121
olution, flung broadcast over Russia and Europe:

TO THE CITIZENS OF THE RUSSIAN REPUBLIC!

Contrary to the will of the revolutionary masses, on November 7th the 122
Bolsheviki of Petrograd criminally arrested part of the Provisional Government, dispersed the Council of the Republic, and proclaimed an illegal power.
Such violence committed against the Government of revolutionary Russia at
the moment of its greatest external danger, is an indescribable crime against
the fatherland.

The insurrection of the Bolsheviki deals a mortal blow to the cause of na- 123
tional defence, and postpones immeasurably the moment of peace so greatly
desired.

Civil War, begun by the Bolsheviki, threatens to deliver the country to the 124
horrors of anarchy and counter-revolution, and cause the failure of the Constituent Assembly, which must affirm the republican régime and transmit to
the People forever their right to the land.

Preserving the continuity of the only legal Governmental power, the Com- 125
mittee for Salvation of Country and Revolution, established on the night of
November 7th, takes the initiative in forming a new Provisional Government;
which, basing itself on the forces of democracy, will conduct the country to
the Constituent Assembly and save it from anarchy and counter-revolution.
The Committee for Salvation summons you, citizens, to refuse to recognise the
power of violence. Do not obey its orders!

Rise for the defence of the country and Revolution! 126
Support the Committee for Salvation! 127
Signed by the Council of the Russian Republic, the Municipal Duma of 128
Petrograd, the *Tsay-ee-kah* (*First Congress*), the Executive Committee of the
Peasants' Soviets, and from the Congress itself the Front group, the factions
of Socialist Revolutionaries, Mensheviki, Populist Socialists, Unified Social
Democrats, and the group "Yedinstvo."

Then posters from the Socialist Revolutionary party, the Mensheviki 129
oborontsi, Peasants' Soviets again; from the Central Army Committee, the
Tsentroflot. . . .

. . . Famine will crush Petrograd! (they cried). The German armies will 130
trample on our liberty. Black Hundred *pogroms* will spread over Russia, if we
all — conscious workers, soldiers, citizens — do not unite. . . .

Do not trust the promises of the Bolsheviki! The promise of immediate 131
peace — is a lie! The promise of bread — a hoax! The promise of land — a fairy
tale! . . .

They were all in this manner. 132

Comrades! You have been basely and cruelly deceived! The seizure of 133
power has been accomplished by the Bolsheviki alone. . . . They concealed
their plot from the other Socialist parties composing the Soviet. . . .

You have been promised land and freedom, but the counter-revolution *134* will profit by the anarchy called forth by the Bolsheviki, and will deprive you of land and freedom. . . .

The newspapers were as violent.   *135*

Our duty (said the *Dielo Naroda*) is to unmask these traitors to the working- *136* class. Our duty is to mobilise all our forces and mount guard over the cause of the Revolution! . . .

Izviestia, for the last time speaking in the name of the old *Tsay-ee-kah*, *137* threatened awful retribution.

As for the Congress of Soviets, we affirm that there has been no Congress *138* of Soviets! We affirm that it was merely a private conference of the Bolshevik faction! And in that case, they have no right to cancel the powers of the *Tsay-ee-kah*. . . .

Novaya Zhizn, while pleading for a new Government that should unite *139* all the Socialist parties, criticised severely the action of the Socialist Revolutionaries[57] and the Mensheviki in quitting the Congress, and pointed out that the Bolshevik insurrection meant one thing very clearly: that all illusions about coalition with the bourgeoisie were henceforth demonstrated vain. . . .

Rabotchi Put blossomed out as *Pravda*, Lenin's newspaper which had *140* been suppressed in July. It crowed, bristling:

Workers, soldiers, peasants! In March you struck down the tyranny of the *141* clique of nobles. Yesterday you struck down the tyranny of the bourgeois gang. . . .

The first task now is to guard the approaches to Petrograd.   *142*

The second is definitely to disarm the counter-revolutionary elements of *143* Petrograd.

The third is definitely to organise the revolutionary power and assure the *144* realisation of the popular programme. . . .

---

[57]*Socialist Revolutionary party:* Called *Essaires* from the initials of their name. Originally the revolutionary party of the peasants, the party of the Fighting Organisations — the Terrorists. After the March Revolution, it was joined by many who had never been Socialists. At that time it stood for the abolition of private property in land only, the owners to be compensated in some fashion. Finally the increasing revolutionary feeling of peasants forced the *Essaires* to abandon the "compensation" clause, and led to the younger and more fiery intellectuals breaking off from the main party in the fall of 1917 and forming a new party, the *Left Socialist Revolutionary party*. The *Essaires*, who were afterward always called by the radical groups *"Right Socialist Revolutionaries,"* adopted the political attitude of the Mensheviki, and worked together with them. They finally came to represent the wealthier peasants, the intellectuals, and the politically uneducated populations of remote rural districts. Among them there was, however, a wider difference of shades of political and economic opinion than among the Mensheviki. [Reed]

It was just 8:40 when a thundering wave of cheers announced the en- *145*
trance of the presidium, with Lenin — great Lenin — among them. A
short, stocky figure, with a big head set down in his shoulders, bald and
bulging. Little eyes, a snubbish nose, wide, generous mouth, and heavy
chin; clean-shaven now, but already beginning to bristle with the well-
known beard of his past and future. Dressed in shabby clothes, his trousers
much too long for him. Unimpressive, to be the idol of a mob, loved and
revered as perhaps few leaders in history have been. A strange popular
leader — a leader purely by virtue of intellect; colourless, humourless, uncompromising and detached, without picturesque idiosyncrasies — but
with the power of explaining profound ideas in simple terms, of analysing
a concrete situation. And combined with shrewdness, the greatest intellectual audacity.

Kameniev was reading the report of the actions of the Military Revo- *146*
lutionary Committee; abolition of capital punishment in the Army, restoration of the free right of propaganda, release of officers and soldiers arrested for political crimes, orders to arrest Kerensky and confiscation of
food supplies in private store-houses. . . . Tremendous applause.

Again the representative of the *Bund*. The uncompromising attitude of *147*
the Bolsheviki would mean the crushing of the Revolution; therefore, the
Bund delegates must refuse any longer to sit in the Congress. Cries from
the audience, "We thought you walked out last night! How many more
times are you going to walk out?"

Then the representative of the Mensheviki Internationalists. Shouts, *148*
"What! You here still?" The speaker explained that only part of the Mensheviki Internationalists left the Congress; the rest were going to stay —

"We consider it dangerous and perhaps even mortal for the Revolution *149*
to transfer the power to the Soviets" — Interruptions — "but we feel it our
duty to remain in the Congress and vote against the transfer here!"

Other speakers followed, apparently without any order. A delegate of *150*
the coal-miners of the Don Basin[58] called upon the Congress to take measures against Kaledin,[59] who might cut off coal and food from the capital.
Several soldiers just arrived from the Front brought the enthusiastic greet-
ings of their regiments. . . . Now Lenin, gripping the edge of the reading
stand, letting his little winking eyes travel over the crowd as he stood there
waiting, apparently oblivious to the long-rolling ovation, which lasted sev-

---

[58]*Don Basin:* The basin of the river Don in Russia which flows through the Ukraine. The
area, rich in resources and thus occupied by many workers, was one of the central arenas
for proletariat action.
[59]Kaledin, Alexei Maximovich (1861–1918). Tsarist general and ataman of the Don Cossack
army. He headed the revolt in the Don area against the Soviets. [Lawson]

eral minutes. When it finished, he said simply, "We shall now proceed to construct the Socialist order!" Again that overwhelming human roar.

"The first thing is the adoption of practical measures to realise 151 peace. . . . We shall offer peace to the peoples of all the belligerent countries upon the basis of the Soviet terms — no annexations, no indemnities, and the right of self-determination of peoples. At the same time, according to our promise, we shall publish and repudiate the secret treaties. . . . The question of War and Peace is so clear that I think that I may, without preamble, read the project of a Proclamation to the Peoples of All the Belligerent Countries. . . ."

His great mouth, seeming to smile, opened wide as he spoke; his voice 152 was hoarse — not unpleasantly so, but as if it had hardened that way after years and years of speaking — and went on monotonously, with the effect of being able to go on forever. . . . For emphasis he bent forward slightly. No gestures. And before him, a thousand simple faces looking up in intent adoration.

[*At this point Reed inserts Lenin's "Proclamation to the Peoples and Governments of All the Belligerent Nations." In his speech Lenin proposes to the warring powers of Europe that they call an immediate armistice and begin public negotiations to end the World War in such a way that no nation would be forcibly annexed by another. Lenin also makes a special appeal to the working classes of England, France, and Germany both to help bring about an end to the war and to help "the cause of the liberation of the exploited working masses from all slavery and all exploitation."* — Behrens and Rosen.]

When the grave thunder of applause had died away, Lenin spoke 153 again:

"We propose to the Congress to ratify this declaration. We address 154 ourselves to the Governments as well as to the peoples, for a declaration which would be addressed only to the peoples of the belligerent countries might delay the conclusion of peace. The conditions of peace, drawn up during the armistice, will be ratified by the Constituent Assembly. In fixing the duration of the armistice at three months, we desire to give to the peoples as long a rest as possible after this bloody extermination, and ample time for them to elect their representatives. This proposal of peace will meet with resistance on the part of the imperialist governments — we don't fool ourselves on that score. But we hope that revolution will soon break out in all the belligerent countries; that is why we address ourselves especially to the workers of France, England and Germany. . . .

"The revolution of November 6th and 7th," he ended, "has opened 155 the era of the Social Revolution. . . . The labour movement, in the name of peace and Socialism, shall win, and fulfil its destiny. . . ."

There was something quiet and powerful in all this, which stirred the 156 souls of men. It was understandable why people believed when Lenin spoke. . . .

Lenin was reading the Decree on Land: 157

(1.) All private ownership of land is abolished immediately without 158
compensation.

(2.) All land-owners' estates, and all lands belonging to the Crown, to 159
monasteries, church lands with all their live stock and inventoried property,
buildings and all appurtenances, are transferred to the disposition of the township Land Committees and the district Soviets of Peasants' Deputies until the
Constituent Assembly meets.

(3.) Any damage whatever done to the confiscated property which from 160
now on belongs to the whole People, is regarded as a serious crime, punishable by the revolutionary tribunals. The district Soviets of Peasants' Deputies
shall take all necessary measures for the observance of the strictest order during the taking over of the land-owners' estates, for the determination of the
dimensions of the plots of land and which of them are subject to confiscation,
for the drawing up of an inventory of the entire confiscated property, and for
the strictest revolutionary protection of all the farming property on the land,
with all buildings, implements, cattle, supplies of products, etc., passing into
the hands of the People.

(4.) For guidance during the realisation of the great land reforms until their 161
final resolution by the Constituent Assembly, shall serve the following peasant
nakaz (instructions), drawn up on the basis of 242 local peasant *nakazi* by the
editorial board of the *"Izviestia* of the All-Russian Soviet of Peasants' Deputies,'' and published in No. 88 of said *"Izviestia"* (Petrograd, No. 88, August
19th, 1917).

The lands of peasants and of Cossacks serving in the Army shall not be 162
confiscated.

At two o'clock the Land Decree was put to vote, with only one against 163
and the peasant delegates wild with joy. . . . So plunged the Bolsheviki
ahead, irresistible, over-riding hesitation and opposition — the only people in Russia who had a definite programme of action while the others
talked for eight long months.

The election of the new *Tsay-ee-kah*, the new parliament of the Russian 164
Republic, took barely fifteen minutes. Trotzky announced its composition:
100 members, of which 70 Bolsheviki. . . . As for the peasants, and the
seceding factions, places were to be reserved for them. "We welcome into
the Government all parties and groups which will adopt our programme,"
ended Trotzky.

And thereupon the Second All-Russian Congress of Soviets was dis- 165
solved, so that the members might hurry to their homes in the four corners
of Russia and tell of the great happenings. . . .

It was almost seven when we woke the sleeping conductors and 166
motor-men of the street-cars which the Street-Railway Workers' Union al-

ways kept waiting at Smolny to take the Soviet delegates to their homes. In the crowded car there was less happy hilarity than the night before, I thought. Many looked anxious; perhaps they were saying to themselves, "Now we are masters, how can we do our will?"

REVIEW QUESTIONS

1. Based on Reed's passage, what was the political and military status quo of the Bolshevik revolution on the morning of November 7? What important events had occurred the previous night?
2. Why did Reed go to the Winter Palace? Where was Kerensky? How was the palace being used by the provisional government? Why was Captain Artzibashev complaining? In general, what was the attitude of the military officers defending the Winter Palace toward the Bolsheviks?
3. What kind of scenes does Reed observe as he and his party wander the streets of Petrograd after dinner on November 7 (paragraphs 58ff.)? In what ways do these scenes reveal a combination of both heightened anticipation and normalcy? (Compare this section with paragraph 104.)
4. What was the significance of the resolution passed by the Petrograd Soviet that Kameniev read to Reed on the evening of November 7 (paragraphs 58ff.)? To what extent did this resolution reflect the program drawn up by Marx and Engels in paragraph 129 of *The Communist Manifesto*?
5. What crucial event occurred during the late evening session of the All-Russian Congress of Soviets on November 7? What major parties were represented? Who lost and who won? What was the gist of Martov's plea to the Congress?
6. When Reed and his party returned to the Winter Palace after the meeting of the All-Russian Congress of Soviets at Smolny, how did they find it different from the way it had been earlier that day? What is the significance — in terms of the old and the new Russia — of the scenes Reed describes?
7. What is the significance of the two posters quoted by Reed in paragraphs 106–110? What actions were the Bolsheviks taking to consolidate their power? What was the basis of their appeal to the Cossacks? How did the Mensheviks and the Socialist Revolutionaries attempt to counteract the Bolshevik coup d'état? What was Lenin's response?
8. Summarize Lenin's Decree on Land. How did this decree compare with Marx and Engels's program in *The Communist Manifesto*?

DISCUSSION AND WRITING QUESTIONS

1. How did the newspaper article Reed cites in paragraphs 9–11 epitomize the class struggle that was engulfing Russia? Cite other examples of class conflict in the passage.
2. On what kind of incidents does Reed focus in this account? What do they reveal about human motivations, limitations, fears, and hopes? What can you gather

about Reed's own attitude toward the events he is describing? Cite examples, as well as particular language, to support your conclusions.

3. To what extent do the events described by Reed bear out the kind of observations and analyses made by Marx and Engels in *The Communist Manifesto*?

4. Although Reed's account is (essentially) factual, it displays many of the qualities of good fiction. Describe and illustrate some of these qualities.

5. Read a more objective account of the Russian Revolution (or an account that is explicitly anticommunist), and compare and contrast the two treatments of the events of November 7 and 8. Consider discrepancies in detail, characterization of people and events, tone, and overall assessments of the Bolshevik victory.

6. Frequently, Marxist speakers appear on college campuses. Perhaps on your own campus recently you've noticed posters announcing a speech or a rally whose main theme is some aspect of the class struggle. If so, attend the event and report on what you heard and saw. What was the speaker — or the speakers — advocating? In what terms did they view the conflict? What were seen as the chief problems, and what were the proposed solutions? If possible, talk to the speakers and explore their positions in greater detail. To what extent do they appear to be following the doctrines of Marx and Engels?

EUGENE V. DEBS *(1855–1926)*

Eugene Victor Debs was the Socialist Party candidate for U.S. President five times between 1900 and 1920. Although much of his rhetoric has a decidedly Marxist cast, the fact that he aimed to put his programs into effect by working through the existing electoral system (instead of by fomenting violent revolution) suggests something of the difference between American socialism and orthodox Marxism or communism.

In fact, Marxism itself derives from socialist thinking. Significantly, the official name of Russia is the Union of Soviet *Socialist* Republics. Marx and Engels reserved the name "communism" for the final stage of socialism, in which the state would wither away and the dictatorship of the proletariat would be complete. They also adopted the term "communism" to distinguish their brand of "scientific" socialism from the various "utopian" socialisms then current in European intellectual circles, and which they considered little more than social quackery. Today, the term "communism" is associated primarily with Marxist-Leninist thought and with those political parties that take their lead from the Soviet or the Chinese communist models.

Socialism itself is an umbrella term for a wide array of social doctrines and programs. As one commentator has remarked, "the term socialism has been the property of anyone who wished to use it." Modern socialism was born out of the social and economic dislocations generated by the Industrial Revolution, the growing power and acquisitiveness of the capitalist class, and the creation and exploitation of a new kind of working class. Its general aim has been to seize the means of production from the capitalists and give it to the workers, who would then use their economic power not to enrich themselves, but for mutual benefit and social justice. But socialists differ on whether or not *all* the means of production (as opposed to just the major industries) should be appropriated, on whether social planning should be centralized or localized, on whether all workers should be paid equally, or whether the state (or workers' boards) should simply ensure that all workers have adequate food, shelter, and social services.

The early generation of modern socialists included François-Marie-Charles Fourier (1772–1837) in France, and Robert Owen (1781–1858) in England. Owen inspired a number of utopian, collective communities in England and the United States, including New Harmony in Indiana. (Kaweah, a late 19th century California cooperative community founded by two San Francisco labor leaders, boasted a giant sequoia that the colony's members named the Karl Marx tree.) In the early 19th century socialist thought flourished in France and England, then spread to Germany. It continues to exercise significant influence today: socialist and socialist-oriented parties in Britain, France, Italy, Spain, Portugal, and the Scandinavian countries regularly draw wide support in parliamentary elections, and socialist doctrines underlie a great deal of political ferment in the Third World.

In the United States, where class distinctions have been less rigid than in Europe and the rest of the world, and where the impulses toward individualism and competition have always been stronger than the impulses toward collectivism and cooperation, socialism has never taken serious hold. The American Socialist Party was born in 1901, a descendant of the Socialist Labor party formed in 1877 and Eugene Debs's Social Democratic Party of America (formed in 1898). Its 10,000 members, drawn from the ranks of recent immigrants, trade unionists, and agrarian reformers, grew to over 150,000 by 1912, and the party was able to elect hundreds of candidates to public office, including 56 mayors and a congressman. Its most popular presidential candidates were Debs and later, Norman Thomas (who ran for president six times between 1928 and 1948). But at its height (1912), the American Socialist Party was never able to attract more than 6 percent of the popular presidential vote.

Eugene Debs, born in 1855 in Terre Haute, Indiana, became a locomotive fireman in his mid-teens and in 1875 helped organize a local lodge of the Brotherhood of Locomotive Firemen. He later served as secretary-treasurer of the national Brotherhood. In 1880, Debs became city-clerk of Terre Haute, serving for four years, and between 1885 and 1887 he sat in the Indiana state legislature. Debs's activities on behalf of organized labor were foremost in his mind, however, and in 1893 he founded the American Railway Union. The union successfully struck the Great Northern Railroad for higher wages in 1894. Later that year, when employees of the Pullman Palace Car company struck, Debs and his union organized a boycott of all Pullman cars. When the company retaliated by firing union members, Debs's union struck all the nation's railroads. Upon the eruption of violence, President Grover Cleveland issued a federal injunction against the strike and sent troops to keep the railroads running; the effect of this government intervention was to destroy the union. For his part in the strike, Debs was sentenced to six months in jail.

During his jail term, Debs became absorbed with the writings of Marx, and soon after his release he declared himself a socialist. In 1898, he founded the Social Democratic Party of America (which, three years later, became the Socialist Party of America). During his first run for president, in 1900, Debs polled only 96,000 votes, but he more than quadrupled this total four years later. In 1912, he received 901,000 votes and in 1920 received 920,000 (or 3.5 percent of the total). During the 1920 election, however, Debs ran his campaign from a prison cell: he had been convicted two years earlier of violating the 1917 Espionage Act (by criticizing the government's prosecutions of people charged with sedition), had been stripped of his citizenship, and sentenced to ten years. After three years, his sentence was commuted by President Harding, but he did not regain his citizenship. During the latter part of his life, Debs supported himself through his lectures and publications. He was editor of the Socialist weekly *American Journal,* wrote a number of articles on prison conditions, a pamphlet, *Unionism and Socialism* (1904), and a book, *Walls and Bars* (1927). He died in Elmhurst, Illinois, in 1926.

Two speeches by Debs follow. The first, given in Indianapolis, launched his 1904 presidential campaign. The second was his address to the court on September 14, 1918, just before he was sentenced to prison for an inflammatory speech he had given in Canton, Ohio, three months earlier.

TWO SPEECHES

SPEECH AT INDIANAPOLIS

The Class Struggle.

We are entering tonight upon a momentous campaign. The struggle   *1*
for political supremacy is not between political parties merely, as appears
upon the surface, but at bottom it is a life and death struggle between two
hostile economic classes, the one the capitalist, and the other the working
class.

The capitalist class is represented by the Republican, Democratic,   *2*
Populist[1] and Prohibition[2] parties, all of which stand for private ownership
of the means of production, and the triumph of any one of which will
mean continued wage-slavery to the working class.

As the Populist and Prohibition sections of the capitalist party repre-   *3*
sent minority elements which propose to reform the capitalist system without disturbing wage-slavery, a vain and impossible task, they will be omitted from this discussion with all the credit due the rank and file for their
good intentions.

The Republican and Democratic parties, or, to be more exact, the   *4*
Republican-Democratic Party, represent the capitalist class in the class
struggle. They are the political wings of the capitalist system and such
differences as arise between them relate to spoils and not to principles.

With either of these parties in power one thing is always certain and   *5*
that is that the capitalist class is in the saddle and the working class under
the saddle.

Under the administration of both these parties the means of produc-   *6*
tion are private property, production is carried forward for capitalist profit
purely, markets are glutted and industry paralyzed, workingmen become
tramps and criminals while injunctions, soldiers and riot guns are brought

---

Eugene V. Debs. Two Speeches [1904, 1918]. Rpt. in Albert Fried, ed., *Socialism in America: From the Shakers to the Third International.* New York: Doubleday Anchor, 1970. "Speech at Indianapolis" and "Speech to the Court," 398–404, 527–29.

[1]*Populist party:* A group of U.S. agrarian reformers who protested, through the legislative channels provided by democracy, against the economic disparity between farmers and business and industry. Hoping to stimulate increased prices in crops, the Populist party introduced, as part of the Democratic platform in the election of 1896, the Free Silver Movement, which proposed unlimited coinage of silver money.

[2]*Prohibition party:* Since it was founded in 1869, the Prohibition party has campaigned to prohibit the manufacture and sale of alcoholic beverages.

into action to preserve "law and order" in the chaotic carnival of capitalistic anarchy.

Deny it as may the cunning capitalists who are clearsighted enough to perceive it, or ignore it as may the torpid workers who are too blind and unthinking to see it, the struggle in which we are engaged today is a class struggle, and as the toiling millions come to see and understand it and rally to the political standard of their class, they will drive all capitalist parties of whatever name into the same party, and the class struggle will then be so clearly revealed that the hosts of labor will find their true place in the conflict and strike the united and decisive blow that will destroy slavery and achieve their full and final emancipation. *7*

In this struggle the workingmen and women and children are represented by the Socialist Party and it is my privilege to address you in the name of that revolutionary and uncompromising party of the working class. *8*

Attitude of the Workers.

What shall be the attitude of the workers of the United States in the present campaign? What part shall they take in it? What party and what principles shall they support by their ballots? And why? *9*

These are questions the importance of which are not sufficiently recognized by workingmen or they would not be the prey of parasites and the service tools of scheming politicians who use them at election time to renew their masters' lease of power and perpetuate their own ignorance, poverty, and shame. *10*

In answering these questions I propose to be as frank and candid as plain-meaning words will allow, for I have but one object in this discussion and that object is not office, but the truth, and I shall state it as I see it, if I have to stand alone. *11*

But I shall not stand alone, for the party that has my allegiance and may have my life, the Socialist Party, the party of the working class, the party of emancipation, is made up of men and women who know their rights and scorn to compromise with their oppressors; who want no votes that can be bought and no support under any false pretense whatsoever. *12*

The Socialist Party stands squarely upon its proletarian principles and relies wholly upon the forces of industrial progress and the education of the working class. *13*

The Socialist Party buys no votes and promises no office. Not a farthing is spent for whiskey or cigars. Every penny in the campaign fund is the voluntary offerings of workers and their sympathizers and every penny is used for education. *14*

What other parties can say the same? *15*

Ignorance alone stands in the way of Socialist success. The capitalist *16* parties understand this and use their resources to prevent the workers from seeing the light.

Intellectual darkness is essential to industrial slavery. 17

Capitalist parties stand for Slavery and Night. 18

The Socialist Party is the herald of Freedom and Light. 19

Capitalist parties cunningly contrive to divide the workers upon dead issues. 20

The Socialist Party is uniting them upon the living issue: 21

Death to Wage Slavery! 22

When industrial slavery is as dead as the issues of the Siamese-twin capitalist parties the Socialist Party will have fulfilled its mission and enriched history. 23

And now to our questions: 24

First, all workingmen and women owe it to themselves, their class and their country to take an active and intellectual interest in political affairs. 25

The Ballot.

The ballot of united labor expresses the people's will and the people's will is the supreme law of a free nation. 26

The ballot means that labor is no longer dumb, that at last it has a voice, that it may be heard and if united shall be heeded. 27

Centuries of struggle and sacrifice were required to wrest this symbol of freedom from the mailed clutch of tyranny and place it in the hand of labor as the shield and lance of attack and defense. 28

The abuse and not the use of it is responsible for its evils. 29

The divided vote of labor is the abuse of the ballot and the penalty is slavery and death. 30

The united vote of those who toil and have not will vanquish those who have and toil not, and solve forever the problem of democracy. 31

The Historic Struggle of Classes.

Since the race was young there have been class struggles. In every state of society, ancient and modern, labor has been exploited, degraded and in subjection. 32

Civilization has done little for labor except to modify the forms of its exploitation. 33

Labor has always been the mudsill of the social fabric — is so now and will be until the class struggle ends in class extinction and free society. 34

Society has always been and is now built upon exploitation — the exploitation of a class — the working class, whether slaves, serfs or wage-laborers, and the exploited working class in subjection have always been, instinctively or consciously, in revolt against their oppressors. 35

Through all the centuries the enslaved toilers have moved slowly but 36
surely toward their final freedom.

The call of the Socialist Party is to the exploited class, the workers in 37
all useful trades and professions, all honest occupations, from the most
menial service to the highest skill, to rally beneath their own standard and
put an end to the last of the barbarous class struggles by conquering the
capitalist government, taking possession of the means of production and
making them the common property of all, abolishing wage-slavery and
establishing the co-operative commonwealth.

The first step in this direction is to sever all relations with 38

Capitalist Parties.

They are precisely alike and I challenge their most discriminating par- 39
tisans to tell them apart in relation to labor.

The Republican and Democratic parties are alike capitalist parties — 40
differing only in being committed to different sets of capitalist interests —
they have the same principles under varying colors, are equally corrupt
and are one in their subservience to capital and their hostility to labor.

The ignorant workingman who supports either of these parties forges 41
his own fetters and is the unconscious author of his own misery. He can
and must be made to see and think and act with his fellows in supporting
the party of his class and this work of education is the crowning virtue of
the Socialist movement. . . .

The Socialist Party.

In what has been said of other parties I have tried to show why they 42
should not be supported by the common people, least of all by workingmen, and I think I have shown clearly enough that such workers as do
support them are guilty, consciously or unconsciously, of treason to their
class. They are voting into power the enemies of labor and are morally
responsible for the crimes thus perpetrated upon their fellow-workers and
sooner or later they will have to suffer the consequences of their miserable
acts.

The Socialist Party is not, and does not pretend to be, a capitalist party. 43
It does not ask, nor does it expect the votes of the capitalist class. Such
capitalists as do support it do so seeing the approaching doom of the capitalist system and with a full understanding that the Socialist Party is not
a capitalist party, nor a middle class party, but a revolutionary working
class party, whose historic mission it is to conquer capitalism on the political battle-field, take control of government and through the public powers
take possession of the means of wealth production, abolish wage-slavery
and emancipate all workers and all humanity.

The people are as capable of achieving their industrial freedom as they 44

were to secure their political liberty, and both are necessary to a free
nation.

The capitalist system is no longer adapted to the needs of modern so-   45
ciety. It is outgrown and fetters the forces of progress. Industrial and commercial competition are largely of the past. The handwriting blazes on the
wall. Centralization and combination are the modern forces in industrial
and commercial life. Competition is breaking down and co-operation is
supplanting it.

The hand tools of early times are used no more. Mammoth machines   46
have taken their places. A few thousand capitalists own them and many
millions of workingmen use them.

All the wealth the vast army of labor produces above its subsistence is   47
taken by the machine owning capitalists, who also own the land and the
mills, the factories, railroads and mines, the forests and fields and all other
means of production and transportation.

Hence wealth and poverty, millionaires and beggars, castles and caves,   48
luxury and squalor, painted parasites on the boulevard and painted poverty among the red lights.

Hence strikes, boycotts, riots, murder, suicide, insanity, prostitution   49
on a fearful and increasing scale.

The capitalist parties can do nothing. They are a part, an iniquitous   50
part, of the foul and decaying system.

There is no remedy for the ravages of death.   51

Capitalism is dying and its extremities are already decomposing. The   52
blotches upon the surface show that the blood no longer circulates. The
time is near when the cadaver will have to be removed and the atmosphere
purified.

In contrast with the Republican and Democratic conventions, where   53
politicians were the puppets of plutocrats, the convention of the Socialist
Party consisted of workingmen and women fresh from their labors, strong,
clean, wholesome, self-reliant, ready to do and dare for the cause of labor,
the cause of humanity.

Proud indeed am I to have been chosen by such a body of men and   54
women to bear aloft the proletarian standard in this campaign, and heartily
do I endorse the clear and cogent platform of the party which appeals with
increasing force and eloquence to the whole working class of the country.

To my associate upon the national ticket I give my hand with all my   55
heart. Ben Hanford typifies the working class and fitly represents the historic mission and revolutionary character of the Socialist Party.

Closing Words.

These are stirring days for living men. The day of crisis is drawing near   56
and Socialists are exerting all their power to prepare the people for it.

The old order of society can survive but little longer. Socialism is next   57 in order. The swelling minority sounds warning of the impending change. Soon that minority will be the majority and then will come the co-operative commonwealth.

Every workingman should rally to the standard of his class and hasten   58 the full-orbed day of freedom.

Every progressive Democrat must find his way in our direction, and if   59 he will but free himself from prejudice and study the principles of Social- ism he will soon be a sturdy supporter of our party.

Every sympathizer with labor, every friend of justice, every lover of   60 humanity should support the Socialist Party as the only party that is or- ganized to abolish industrial slavery, the prolific source of the giant evils that afflict the people.

Who with a heart in his breast can look upon Colorado without keenly   61 feeling the cruelties and crimes of capitalism! Repression will not help her. Brutality will only brutalize her. Private ownership and wage-slavery are the curse of Colorado. Only Socialism will save Colorado and the nation.

The overthrow of capitalism is the object of the Socialist Party. It will   62 not fuse with any other party and it would rather die than compromise.

The Socialist Party comprehends the magnitude of its task and has the   63 patience of preliminary defeat and the faith of ultimate victory.

The working class must be emancipated by the working class.   64

Woman must be given her true place in society by the working class.   65

Child labor must be abolished by the working class.   66

Society must be reconstructed by the working class.   67

The working class must be employed by the working class.   68

The fruits of labor must be enjoyed by the working class.   69

War, bloody war, must be ended by the working class.   70

These are the principles and objects of the Socialist Party and we fear-   71 lessly proclaim them to our fellowmen.

We know our cause is just and that it must prevail.   72

With faith and hope and courage we hold our heads erect and with   73 dauntless spirit marshal the working class for the march from Capitalism to Socialism, from Slavery to Freedom, from Barbarism to Civilization.

SPEECH TO THE COURT

Your Honor, years ago I recognized my kinship with all living beings,   74 and I made up my mind that I was not one bit better than the meanest on earth. I said then, and I say now, that while there is a lower class, I am in it, while there is a criminal element I am of it, and while there is a soul in prison, I am not free.

I listened to all that was said in this court in support and justification   75 of this prosecution, but my mind remains unchanged. I look upon the Es- pionage Law as a despotic enactment in flagrant conflict with democratic principles and with the spirit of free institutions. . . .

Your Honor, I have stated in this court that I am opposed to the social 76
system in which we live; that I believe in a fundamental change — but if
possible by peaceable and orderly means. . . .

Standing here this morning, I recall my boyhood. At fourteen I went 77
to work in a railroad shop; at sixteen I was firing a freight engine on a
railroad. I remember all the hardships and privations of that earlier day,
and from that time until now my heart has been with the working class. I
could have been in Congress long ago. I have preferred to go to prison. . . .

I am thinking this morning of the men in the mills and factories; of the 78
men in the mines and on the railroads. I am thinking of the women who
for a paltry wage are compelled to work out their barren lives; of the little
children who in this system are robbed of their childhood and in their
tender years are seized in the remorseless grasp of Mammon[3] and forced
into the industrial dungeons, there to feed the monster machines while
they themselves are being starved and stunted, body and soul. I see them
dwarfed and diseased and their little lives broken and blasted because in
this high noon of our twentieth-century Christian civilization money is still
so much more important than the flesh and blood of childhood. In very
truth gold is god today and rules with pitiless sway in the affairs of men.

In this country — the most favored beneath the bending skies — we 79
have vast areas of the richest and most fertile soil, material resources in
inexhaustible abundance, the most marvelous productive machinery on
earth, and millions of eager workers ready to apply their labor to that machinery to produce in abundance for every man, woman and child — and
if there are still vast numbers of our people who are the victims of poverty
and whose lives are an unceasing struggle all the way from youth to old
age, until at last death comes to their rescue and stills their aching hearts
and lulls these hapless victims to dreamless sleep, it is not the fault of the
Almighty: it cannot be charged to nature, but it is due entirely to the outgrown social system in which we live that ought to be abolished not only
in the interest of the toiling masses but in the higher interest of all humanity. . . .

I believe, Your Honor, in common with all Socialists, that this nation 80
ought to own and control its own industries. I believe, as all Socialists do,
that all things that are jointly needed and used ought to be jointly owned
— that industry, the basis of our social life, instead of being the private
property of the few and operated for their enrichment, ought to be the
common property of all, democratically administered in the interest of
all. . . .

---

[3]*Mammon:* Wealth personified.

I am opposing a social order in which it is possible for one man who   *81*
does absolutely nothing that is useful, to amass a fortune of hundreds of
millions of dollars, while millions of men and women who work all the
days of their lives secure barely enough for a wretched existence.

This order of things cannot always endure. I have registered my pro-   *82*
test against it. I recognize the feebleness of my effort, but, fortunately, I
am not alone. There are multiplied thousands of others who, like myself,
have come to realize that before we may truly enjoy the blessings of civilized life, we must reorganize society upon a mutual and co-operative basis; and to this end we have organized a great economic and political movement that spreads over the face of all the earth.

There are today upwards of sixty millions of Socialists, loyal, devoted   *83*
adherents to this cause, regardless of nationality, race, creed, color or sex.
They are all making common cause. They are spreading with tireless energy the propaganda of the new social order. They are waiting, watching
and working hopefully through all the hours of the day and the night.
They are still in a minority. But they have learned how to be patient and
to bide their time. They feel — they know, indeed — that the time is coming, in spite of all opposition, all persecution, when this emancipating gospel will spread among all the peoples, and when this minority will become
the triumphant majority and, sweeping into power, inaugurate the greatest social and economic change in history.

In that day we shall have the universal commonwealth — the harmo-   *84*
nious co-operation of every nation with every other nation on earth. . . .

Your Honor, I ask no mercy and I plead for no immunity. I realize that   *85*
finally the right must prevail. I never so clearly comprehended as now the
great struggle between the powers of greed and exploitation on the one
hand and upon the other the rising hosts of industrial freedom and social
justice.

I can see the dawn of the better day for humanity. The people are   *86*
awakening. In due time they will and must come to their own.

"When the mariner, sailing over tropic seas, looks for relief from his   *87*
weary watch, he turns his eyes toward the southern cross, burning luridly
above the tempest-vexed ocean. As the midnight approaches, the southern
cross begins to bend, the whirling worlds change their places, and with
starry finger-points the Almighty marks the passage of time upon the dial
of the universe, and though no bell may beat the glad tidings, the lookout
knows that the midnight is passing and that relief and rest are close at
hand.

"Let the people everywhere take heart of hope, for the cross is bend-   *88*
ing, the midnight is passing, and joy cometh with the morning."

"He's true to God who's true to man; wherever wrong is done,
To the humblest and the weakest, 'neath the all-beholding sun.

That wrong is done to us, and they are slaves most base,
Whose love of right is for themselves and not for all the race."

I am now prepared to receive your sentence.

REVIEW QUESTIONS

1. Why does Debs see little if any difference between the Republican and Democratic parties?
2. What accusations does Debs make against American workers? What is the main tool by which workers may express their united will?
3. What is the specific program of the Socialist Party, according to Debs?

DISCUSSION AND WRITING QUESTIONS

1. Compare and contrast the rhetoric of Debs in his campaign speech with the rhetoric of Marx and Engels in *The Communist Manifesto.* Compare and contrast also the issues upon which each focuses (including class struggle, the capitalist class, the working class, the goals of the communist/socialist movement).
2. Is this an effective speech? Discuss the means by which Debs builds his case, attacking the enemy, promoting socialist goals, and rousing his audience with a combination of intellectual and emotional appeals. Consider especially the structure and the language of the speech.
3. Does the subject matter of Debs's speech have any more relevance to our present world than Marx and Engels's *Communist Manifesto?* If so, point out passages that address modern concerns in ways that Marx and Engels's work did not, and discuss their significance.
4. How is the tone of the speech to the court different from the tone of Debs's 1904 campaign speech? Speculate on the reasons for the difference. How is the subject matter of this speech different from the 1904 speech? Which speech do you find more effective and moving? Why?
5. Discuss the rhetoric of Debs's address to the court. Focus on such rhetorical devices as repetition, parallelism, personification, imagery, and hyperbole (exaggeration); focus also on the extent to which Debs appeals to logic, to ethics, and to emotion.
6. Does Debs's program seem attractive to you? If so, do you think it should be put into effect? If not, why not? If only a part of it should be put into effect, which part?

MAO TSE-TUNG *(1893–1976)*

How does the revolutionary class struggle affect the artist? How does the artist best serve the workers before and after the overthrow of the bourgeoisie? Given the premises of Marxism-Leninism, such questions almost answer themselves. The role of the artist is to inspire the working classes to revolution by dramatizing their exploitation at the hands of corrupt and self-serving capitalists. After the revolution, it is the artist's job to create inspiring portraits of heroism, determination, and self-sacrifice by the proletariat in the face both of reactionary elements of the defeated bourgeoisie and of its own tendency to relapse into its prerevolutionary stupor. The artist (whether painter, sculptor, poet, storyteller, playwright, or filmmaker) may accomplish this task either by artistically re-creating actual historical events or by creating fictions that embody the ideals of the revolution. In revolutionary art it is theme, above all, that matters. Character and plot are subordinate: heroes must be presented not as distinctive and idiosyncratic individuals, but rather as heroic and ideal types, designed to inspire emulation by the masses; plot serves only to dramatize the conflict between classes and the inevitable victory of the proletariat. Such, in brief, is the theory of socialist realism — the theory that underlies the following essay by Mao Tse-tung.

For his own country of China, Mao Tse-tung served as both Marx and Lenin: he was not only the chief theoretician of the Chinese Communist Revolution but also the leader of the armies that achieved military victory in 1949. Certainly, Mao based his revolutionary theories on the ideas of Karl Marx, and he was inspired early in life by the Russian Revolution; but he also insisted that Marxism be adapted to the special cultural requirements of the Chinese people and refused to be bound by the example of Soviet Russia. In particular, during the late 1950s (the era of the "Great Leap Forward") he was to advocate the decentralization of economic planning by placing political and economic power in "people's communes" (composed largely of peasants) rather than in the bureaucrats of the central government, as in the Soviet model.

Mao's life may be broadly divided into three periods: the first 34 years, during which he grew to political maturity and developed his revolutionary ideals; the next 22 years in the "wilderness," the remote hinterlands of China, during which he prepared his Red Army for the eventual conquest of the country; and the final 26 years, during which he was the absolute ruler of the People's Republic of China. The son of a peasant, Mao was born in 1893 in the village of Shao-shan in Hunan Province. As a child he liked to read the classics of Confucianism, particularly those portraying heroes overcoming great odds. For a short time he worked on the family farm, but he soon left his native village to go to school. In 1911, he served for a few months in the revolutionary army that brought down the Manchu dynasty and replaced it with the Chinese Republic, temporarily headed by Dr. Sun Yat-sen. But then Mao returned to his various studies. After graduating from the First Provincial Normal School of Ch'ang-sha in 1918, he went to Peking University, where he worked as a library clerk and where he met several of the people who were to remain with him until the communist victory of 1949. During this period, he helped organize student demonstrations against Japan, and he also began studying the works of Marx, whose interpretation of history he subsequently made his own. In 1921, he went to Shanghai to attend the first Congress of the Chinese Communist Party.

At this time Mao was supporting himself (and the first of his three wives) through his employment as principal of a primary school in his native province of Hunan. Increasingly, however, his political work began to dominate his life. In 1923, he quit his job to devote himself full time to revolutionary activities, holding office both in the Chinese Communist Party and in Sun Yat-sen's Nationalist Party, the Kuomintang, for which he edited the *Political Weekly*. During this period, he became increasingly convinced of the revolutionary importance of the peasants and devoted much of his energy to organizing peasant groups into revolutionary units and then networks. Mao's political activities, however, had incurred the wrath of the Hunan authorities, and he was forced to flee the province, settling thereafter in the urban center of Canton.

In 1925, with the death of Sun Yat-sen, General Chiang Kai-shek became head of the Kuomintang (and in 1928 ruler of China). When Chiang began to purge Communists from official positions, Mao split with the Kuomintang to become head of the peasant department of the Communist Party. In the Autumn Harvest Uprising of 1927, Chiang's forces severely defeated Mao's newly formed Chinese Red Army, which was forced to retreat to the mountain area of Chingkanshan. It was from the tattered remnants of this army that Mao and other communist leaders nurtured and trained the military force that was eventually to take over all of China.

During the next six years, the growing Red Army, which was becoming skilled in guerilla warfare tactics, defeated four attempts of the Kuomintang to annihilate it. However, fearing a successful direct onslaught by Chiang's elite troops, Mao and his military commander, Chu Teh, led the army on the famous Long March, a six-thousand-mile, year-long journey into the remote northern area of Shensi. During this march, Mao was elected chairman of the Chinese Communist Party. From their new headquarters in Yenan, Mao's forces could operate unmolested, perfecting their strategy, strengthening their numbers, and widening their influence. In this period, Mao wrote the greatest number of his essays, pamphlets, poetry, and philosophical and military treatises (including *Strategic Problems of China's Revolutionary War*).

In the late 1930s, the communists and the Kuomintang effected a temporary reconciliation to fight together against Japan, which had invaded areas of China and set up puppet governments. The alliance continued through World War II. With Japan's defeat in 1945, however, Mao resumed his struggle against Chiang's forces; and four years later — through a combination of a one million man army and hundreds of millions of peasants who encircled the major cities — he succeeded in taking control of China. Mao subsequently became chairman of the Chinese People's Republic. (He retired from this position in 1959, but remained chairman of the Chinese Communist Party until his death.)

During the early years of his rule, Mao strove to deemphasize his own personal authority. He remained a largely ceremonial figure until around 1955, and in 1956 he appeared to invite diversity of opinion with his policy of "letting a hundred flowers bloom." But the policy backfired, and Mao found himself with more diversity of opinion than he cared to handle — much of the criticism was directed against his own dictatorship. After the setbacks of the Great Leap Forward (the people's communes were an economic failure), Mao determined to strengthen his authority, and the remaining years of his rule were marked by a consolidation of personal power and (for China) an unprecedented personality cult. Pictures of Mao seemed to adorn every room in the country, and his innumerable aphorisms were quoted to support every public discussion. In the 1960s, Mao became increasingly concerned that the purity of the revolution was becoming tainted and that Communist China was becoming "revisionist," like Soviet Russia. To this end, he launched the Cultural Revolution (1966), a nationwide political and social upheaval during which uncontrollable hordes of young Red Guards beat up "reactionary" party members, discharged and publicly humiliated distinguished university professors, and set up revolutionary provincial committees to change the complexion of the party bureaucracy so that it would better reflect Mao's own thinking. The Cultural Revolution subsided in 1969 after Mao himself realized that he had to restrain it from destroying the country.

Mao died in 1976. His death and his replacement by more moderate leaders eased the normalization of relations with the United States that had begun several years earlier.

The following selection was originally a talk delivered by Mao at the Yenan Forum in May 1942.

ON LITERATURE AND ART

Comrades! You have been invited to this forum today to exchange ideas and examine the relationship between work in the literary and artistic fields and revolutionary work in general. Our aim is to ensure that revolutionary literature and art follow the correct path of development and provide better help to other revolutionary work in facilitating the overthrow of our national enemy and the accomplishment of the task of national liberation. 1

In our struggle for the liberation of the Chinese people there are various fronts, among which there are the fronts of the pen and of the gun, 2

Mao Tse-Tung. On Literature and Art [1942]. Rpt. in Berel Lang and Forrest Williams, eds., *Marxism and Art: Writings in Aesthetics and Criticism.* New York: David McKay, 1972.

the cultural and the military fronts. To defeat the enemy we must rely primarily on the army with guns. But this army alone is not enough; we must also have a cultural army, which is absolutely indispensable for uniting our own ranks and defeating the enemy. Since the May 4th Movement[1] such a cultural army has taken shape in China, and it has helped the Chinese revolution, gradually reduced the domain of China's feudal culture and of the comprador culture[2] which serves imperialist aggression, and weakened their influence. To oppose the new culture the Chinese reactionaries can now only "pit quantity against quality." In other words, reactionaries have money, and though they can produce nothing good, they can go all out and produce in quantity. Literature and art have been an important and successful part of the cultural front since the May 4th Movement. During the ten years' civil war,[3] the revolutionary literature and art movement grew greatly. That movement and the revolutionary war both headed in the same general direction, but these two fraternal armies were not linked together in their practical work because the reactionaries had cut them off from each other. It is very good that since the outbreak of the War of Resistance Against Japan, more and more revolutionary writers and artists have been coming to Yenan and our other anti-Japanese base areas. But it does not necessarily follow that, having come to the base areas, they have already integrated themselves completely with the masses of the people here. The two must be completely integrated if we are to push ahead with our revolutionary work. The purpose of our meeting today is precisely to ensure that literature and art fit well into the whole revolutionary machine as a component part, that they operate as powerful weapons for uniting and educating the people and for attacking and destroying the enemy, and that they help the people fight the enemy with one heart and one mind. What are the problems that must be solved to achieve this objective? I think they are the problems of the class stand of

---

[1]*May 4th Movement:* Widespread student demonstrations, beginning on May 4, 1919, protesting the decision at the postwar Paris Peace Conference to return certain German concessions in Shantung to Japan, instead of China. The May 4th Movement also saw the emergence of Marxism-Leninism (as opposed to Western liberalism) in China as a solution to the country's problems.

[2]*comprador culture:* In 19th century China, Western traders would hire Chinese compradors or managers to work as liaisons between themselves and Chinese merchants. After learning about Western business and culture, many of these compradors would then go on to open their own trade businesses serving westerners in China. Chinese patriots considered these activities antinationalistic, and the comprador culture in general was despised for its openness to foreigners and westernization.

[3]*ten years' civil war:* Which war Mao Tse-tung is referring to is unclear since civil wars between warlords in Chinese provinces were common during the political turmoil of early 20th century China. There are two wars in particular to which Mao might be referring: one from 1919 to 1928, and one from 1928 to 1937.

the writers and artists, their attitude, their audience, their work and their study.

The problem of class stand. Our stand is that of the proletariat and of 3 the masses. For members of the Communist Party, this means keeping to the stand of the Party, keeping to Party spirit and Party policy. Are there any of our literary and art workers who are still mistaken or not clear in their understanding of this problem? I think there are. Many of our comrades have frequently departed from the correct stand.

The problem of attitude. From one's stand there follow specific atti- 4 tudes towards specific matters. For instance, is one to extol or to expose? This is a question of attitude. Which attitude is wanted? I would say both. The question is, whom are you dealing with? There are three kinds of persons, the enemy, our allies in the united front and our own people; the last are the masses and their vanguard. We need to adopt a different attitude towards each of the three. With regard to the enemy, that is, Japanese imperialism and all the other enemies of the people, the task of revolutionary writers and artists is to expose their duplicity and cruelty and at the same time to point out the inevitability of their defeat, so as to encourage the anti-Japanese army and people to fight staunchly with one heart and one mind for their overthrow. With regard to our different allies in the united front, our attitude should be one of both alliance and criticism, and there should be different kinds of alliance and different kinds of criticism. We support them in their resistance to Japan and praise them for any achievement. But if they are not active in the War of Resistance, we should criticize them. If anyone opposes the Communist Party and the people and keeps moving down the path of reaction, we will firmly oppose him. As for the masses of the people, their toil and their struggle, their army and their Party, we should certainly praise them. The people, too, have their shortcomings. Among the proletariat many retain petty-bourgeois ideas, while both the peasants and the urban petty bourgeoisie have backward ideas; these are burdens hampering them in their struggle. We should be patient and spend a long time in educating them and helping them to get these loads off their backs and combat their own shortcomings and errors, so that they can advance with great strides. They have remolded themselves in struggle or are doing so, and our literature and art should depict this process. As long as they do not persist in their errors, we should not dwell on their negative side and consequently make the mistake of ridiculing them or, worse still, of being hostile to them. Our writings should help them to unite, to make progress, to press ahead with one heart and one mind, to discard what is backward and develop what is revolutionary, and should certainly not do the opposite.

The problem of audience, i.e., the people for whom our works of lit- 5 erature and art are produced. In the Shensi-Kansu-Ningsia Border Region and the anti-Japanese base areas of northern and central China, this problem differs from that in the Kuomintang areas, and differs still more from that in Shanghai[4] before the War of Resistance. In the Shanghai period, the audience for works of revolutionary literature and art consisted mainly of a section of the students, office workers and shop assistants. After the outbreak of the War of Resistance the audience in the Kuomintang areas became somewhat wider, but it still consisted mainly of the same kind of people because the government there prevented the workers, peasants and soldiers from having access to revolutionary literature and art. In our base areas the situation is entirely different. Here the audience for works of literature and art consists of workers, peasants, soldiers and revolutionary cadres. There are students in the base areas, too, but they are different from students of the old type; they are either former or future cadres. The cadres of all types, fighters in the army, workers in the factories and peasants in the villages all want to read books and newspapers once they become literate, and those who are illiterate want to see plays and operas, look at drawings and paintings, sing songs and hear music; they are the audience for our works of literature and art. Take the cadres alone. Do not think they are few; they far outnumber the readers of any book published in the Kuomintang areas. There, an edition usually runs to only 2,000 copies, and even three editions add up to only 6,000; but as for the cadres in the base areas, in Yenan alone there are more than 10,000 who read books. Many of them, moreover, are tempered revolutionaries of long standing, who have come from all parts of the country and will go out to work in different places, so it is very important to do educational work among them. Our literary and art workers must do a good job in this respect.

Since the audience for our literature and art consists of workers, peasants and soldiers and of their cadres, the problem arises of understanding them and knowing them well. A great deal of work has to be done in order to understand them and know them well, to understand and know well all the different kinds of people and phenomena in the Party and government organizations, in the villages and factories and in the Eighth Route and New Fourth Armies.[5] Our writers and artists have their literary and art work to do, but their primary task is to understand people and know them well. In this regard, how have matters stood with our writers and artists? I would say they have been lacking in knowledge and understanding; they have been like "a hero with no place to display his prowess." What does lacking in knowledge mean? Not knowing people well. The writers and artists do not have a good knowledge either of those whom they describe or of their audience; indeed they may hardly know them at

---

[4]*Shanghai:* The city of Shanghai is a major industrial and commercial center in China.
[5]*Eighth Route and New Fourth Armies:* The two main communist armies who fought against Japanese aggression in the Sino-Japanese War during the 1930s and 1940s.

all. They do not know the workers or peasants or soldiers well, and do not know the cadres well either. What does lacking in understanding mean? Not understanding the language, that is, not being familiar with the rich, lively language of the masses. Since many writers and artists stand aloof from the masses and lead empty lives, naturally they are unfamiliar with the language of the people. Accordingly, their works are not only insipid in language but often contain nondescript expressions of their own coining which run counter to popular usage. Many comrades like to talk about "a mass style." But what does it really mean? It means that the thoughts and feelings of our writers and artists should be fused with those of the masses of workers, peasants and soldiers. To achieve this fusion, they should conscientiously learn the language of the masses. How can you talk of literary and artistic creation if you find the very language of the masses largely incomprehensible? By "a hero with no place to display his prowess," we mean that your collection of great truths is not appreciated by the masses. The more you put on the airs of a veteran before the masses and play the "hero," the more you try to peddle such stuff to the masses, the less likely they are to accept it. If you want the masses to understand you, if you want to be one with the masses, you must make up your mind to undergo a long and even painful process of tempering. Here I might mention the experience of how my own feelings changed. I began life as a student and at school acquired the ways of a student; I then used to feel it undignified to do even a little manual labor, such as carrying my own luggage in the presence of my fellow students, who were incapable of carrying anything, either on their shoulders or in their hands. At that time I felt that intellectuals were the only clean people in the world, while in comparison workers and peasants were dirty. I did not mind wearing the clothes of other intellectuals, believing them clean, but I would not put on clothes belonging to a worker or peasant, believing them dirty. But after I became a revolutionary and lived with workers and peasants and with soldiers of the revolutionary army, I gradually came to know them well, and they gradually came to know me well too. It was then, and only then, that I fundamentally changed the bourgeois and petty-bourgeois feelings implanted in me in the bourgeois schools. I came to feel that compared with the workers and peasants the unremolded intellectuals were not clean and that, in the last analysis, the workers and peasants were the cleanest people and, even though their hands were soiled and their feet smeared with cow-dung, they were really cleaner than the bourgeois and petty-bourgeois intellectuals. That is what is meant by a change in feelings, a change from one class to another. If our writers and artists who come from the intelligentsia want their works to be well received by the masses, they must change and remold their thinking and their feelings. Without such a change, without such remolding, they can do nothing well and will be misfits.

The last problem is study, by which I mean the study of Marxism-⁷

Leninism and of society. Anyone who considers himself a revolutionary Marxist writer, and especially any writer who is a member of the Communist Party, must have a knowledge of Marxism-Leninism. At present, however, some comrades are lacking in the basic concepts of Marxism. For instance, it is a basic Marxist concept that being determines consciousness, that the objective realities of class struggle and national struggle determine our thoughts and feelings. But some of our comrades turn this upside down and maintain that everything ought to start from "love." Now as for love, in a class society there can be only class love; but these comrades are seeking a love transcending classes, love in the abstract and also freedom in the abstract, truth in the abstract, human nature in the abstract, etc. This shows that they have been very deeply influenced by the bourgeoisie. They should thoroughly rid themselves of this influence and modestly study Marxism-Leninism. It is right for writers and artists to study literary and artistic creation, but the science of Marxism-Leninism must be studied by all revolutionaries, writers and artists not excepted. Writers and artists should study society, that is to say, should study the various classes in society, their mutual relations and respective conditions, their physiognomy and their psychology. Only when we grasp all this clearly can we have a literature and art that is rich in content and correct in orientation.

I am merely raising these problems today by way of introduction; I hope all of you will express your views on these and other relevant problems. [8]

In the last analysis, what is the source of all literature and art? Works of literature and art, as ideological forms, are products of the reflection in the human brain of the life of a given society. Revolutionary literature and art are the products of the reflection of the life of the people in the brains of revolutionary writers and artists. The life of the people is always a mine of the raw materials for literature and art, materials in their natural form, materials that are crude, but most vital, rich and fundamental; they make all literature and art seem pallid by comparison; they provide literature and art with an inexhaustible source, their only source. They are the only source, for there can be no other. Some may ask, is there not another source in books, in the literature and art of ancient times and of foreign countries? In fact, the literary and artistic works of the past are not a source but a stream; they were created by our predecessors and the foreigners out of the literary and artistic raw materials they found in the life of the people of their time and place. We must take over all the fine things in our literary and artistic heritage, critically assimilate whatever is beneficial, and use them as examples when we create works out of the literary and artistic raw materials in the life of the people of our own time and place. It makes a difference whether or not we have such examples, the difference between crudeness and refinement, between roughness and polish, between a low and a high level, and between slower and faster work. Therefore, we must [9] on no account reject the legacies of the ancients and the foreigners or refuse to learn from them, even though they are the works of the feudal or bourgeois classes. But taking over legacies and using them as examples must never replace our own creative work; nothing can do that. Uncritical transplantation or copying from the ancients and the foreigners is the most sterile and harmful dogmatism in literature and art. China's revolutionary writers and artists, writers and artists of promise, must go among the masses; they must for a long period of time unreservedly and wholeheartedly go among the masses of workers, peasants and soldiers, go into the heat of the struggle, go to the only source, the broadest and richest source, in order to observe, experience, study and analyze all the different kinds of people, all the classes, all the masses, all the vivid patterns of life and struggle, all the raw materials of literature and art. Only then can they proceed to creative work. Otherwise, you will have nothing to work with and you will be nothing but a phoney writer or artist, the kind that Lu Hsun[6] in his will so earnestly cautioned his son never to become.

Although man's social life is the only source of literature and art and is incomparably livelier and richer in content, the people are not satisfied with life alone and demand literature and art as well. Why? Because, while both are beautiful, life as reflected in works of literature and art can and ought to be on a higher plane, more intense, more concentrated, more typical, nearer the ideal, and therefore more universal than actual everyday life. Revolutionary literature and art should create a variety of characters out of real life and help the masses to propel history forward. For example, there is suffering from hunger, cold and oppression on the one hand, and exploitation and oppression of man by man on the other. These facts exist everywhere and people look upon them as commonplace. Writers and artists concentrate such everyday phenomena, typify the contradictions and struggles within them and produce works which awaken the masses, fire them with enthusiasm and impel them to unite and struggle to transform their environment. Without such literature and art, this task could not be fulfilled, or at least not so effectively and speedily.   10

What is meant by popularizing and by raising standards in works of literature and art? What is the relationship between these two tasks? Popular works are simpler and plainer, and therefore more readily accepted by the broad masses of the people today. Works of a higher quality, being more polished, are more difficult to produce and in general do not circulate so easily and quickly among the masses at present. The problem facing the workers, peasants and soldiers is this: they are now engaged in a bitter and bloody struggle with the enemy but are illiterate and uneducated as a   11

---

[6]*Lu Hsun:* The pen name of Chou Shu-Jen (1881–1936), a major leftist writer and China's foremost social critic in the early 1930s.

result of long years of rule by the feudal and bourgeois classes, and therefore they are eagerly demanding enlightenment, education and works of
literature and art which meet their urgent needs and which are easy to
absorb, in order to heighten their enthusiasm in struggle and confidence
in victory, strengthen their unity and fight the enemy with one heart and
one mind. For them the prime need is not "more flowers on the brocade"
but "fuel in snowy weather." In present conditions, therefore, popularization is the more pressing task. It is wrong to belittle or neglect
popularization.

Nevertheless, no hard and fast line can be drawn between popularization and the raising of standards. Not only is it possible to popularize some
works of higher quality even now, but the cultural level of the broad
masses is steadily rising. If popularization remains at the same level for
ever, with the same stuff being supplied month after month and year after
year, always the same "Little Cowherd"[7] and the same "man, hand,
mouth, knife, cow, goat," will not the educators and those being educated
be six of one and half a dozen of the other? What would be the sense of
such popularization? The people demand popularization and, following
that, higher standards; they demand higher standards month by month
and year by year. Here popularization means popularizing for the people
and raising of standards means raising the level for the people. And such
raising is not from mid-air, or behind closed doors, but is actually based
on popularization. It is determined by and at the same time guides popularization. In China as a whole the development of the revolution and of
revolutionary culture is uneven and their spread is gradual. While in one
place there is popularization and then raising of standards on the basis of
popularization, in other places popularization has not even begun. Hence
good experience in popularization leading to higher standards in one locality can be applied in other localities and serve to guide popularization
and the raising of standards there, saving many twists and turns along the
road. Internationally, the good experience of foreign countries, and especially Soviet experience, can also serve to guide us. With us, therefore, the
raising of standards is based on popularization, while popularization is
guided by the raising of standards. Precisely for this reason, so far from
being an obstacle to the raising of standards, the work of popularization
we are speaking of supplies the basis for the work of raising standards

12

---

[7]*"Little Cowherd"*: This appears to be Mao's contemptuous term for unimaginative attempts
at Socialist realism — the "Little Cowherd" being a crudely conceived, but now familiar
working-class hero. (In the West, Soviet dramas and films were often dismissed as "Boy
Meets Tractor" romances.) Insistent though he was on the social function of art, even Mao
realized that there were limits to the amount of tired propaganda that the masses would
continue to accept as either art or entertainment.

which we are now doing on a limited scale, and prepares the necessary conditions for us to raise standards in the future on a much broader scale.

Besides such raising of standards as meets the needs of the masses 13 directly, there is the kind which meets their needs indirectly, that is, the kind which is needed by the cadres. The cadres are the advanced elements of the masses and generally have received more education; literature and art of a higher level are entirely necessary for them. To ignore this would be a mistake. Whatever is done for the cadres is also entirely for the masses, because it is only through the cadres that we can educate and guide the masses. If we go against this aim, if what we give the cadres cannot help them educate and guide the masses, our work of raising standards will be like shooting at random and will depart from the fundamental principle of serving the masses of the people.

To sum up: through the creative labor of revolutionary writers and art- 14 ists, the raw materials found in the life of the people are shaped into the ideological form of literature and art serving the masses of the people. Included here are the more advanced literature and art as developed on the basis of elementary literature and art and as required by those sections of the masses whose level has been raised, or, more immediately, by the cadres among the masses. Also included here are elementary literature and art which, conversely, are guided by more advanced literature and art and are needed primarily by the overwhelming majority of the masses at present. Whether more advanced or elementary, all our literature and art are for the masses of the people, and in the first place for the workers, peasants and soldiers; they are created for the workers, peasants and soldiers and are for their use.

Literary and art criticism is one of the principal methods of struggle in 15 the world of literature and art. It should be developed and, as comrades have rightly pointed out, our past work in this respect has been quite inadequate. Literary and art criticism is a complex question which requires a great deal of special study. Here I shall concentrate only on the basic problem of criteria in criticism. I shall also comment briefly on a few specific problems raised by some comrades and on certain incorrect views.

In literary and art criticism there are two criteria, the political and the 16 artistic. According to the political criterion, everything is good that is helpful to unity and resistance to Japan, that encourages the masses to be of one heart and one mind, that opposes retrogression and promotes progress; on the other hand, everything is bad that is detrimental to unity and resistance to Japan, foments dissension and discord among the masses and opposes progress and drags people back. How can we tell the good from the bad — by the motive (the subjective intention) or by the effect (social practice)? Idealists stress motive and ignore effect, while mechanical materialists stress effect and ignore motive. In contradistinction to both, we dialectical materialists insist on the unity of motive and effect. The motive of serving the masses is inseparably linked with the effect of winning their approval; the two must be united. The motive of serving the individual or a small clique is not good, nor is it good to have the motive of serving masses without the effect of winning their approval and benefiting them. In examining the subjective intention of a writer or artist, that is, whether his motive is correct and good, we do not judge by his declarations but by the effect of his actions (mainly his works) on the masses in society. The criterion for judging subjective intention or motive is social practice and its effect. We want no sectarianism in our literary and art criticism and, subject to the general principle of unity for resistance to Japan, we should tolerate literary and art works with a variety of political attitudes. But at the same time, in our criticism we must adhere firmly to principle and severely criticize and repudiate all works of literature and art expressing views in opposition to the nation, to science, to the masses and to the Communist Party, because these so-called works of literature and art proceed from the motive and produce the effect of undermining unity for resistance to Japan. According to the artistic criterion, all works of a higher artistic quality are good or comparatively good, while those of a lower artistic quality are bad or comparatively bad. Here, too, of course, social effect must be taken into account. There is hardly a writer or artist who does not consider his own work beautiful, and our criticism ought to permit the free competition of all varieties of works of art; but it is also entirely necessary to subject these works to correct criticism according to the criteria of the science of aesthetics, so that art of a lower level can be gradually raised to a higher and art which does not meet the demands of the struggle of the broad masses can be transformed into art that does.

There is the political criterion and there is the artistic criterion; what is the relationship between the two? Politics cannot be equated with art, nor can a general world outlook be equated with a method of artistic creation and criticism. We deny not only that there is an abstract and absolutely unchangeable political criterion, but also that there is an abstract and absolutely unchangeable artistic criterion; each class in every class society has its own political and artistic criteria. But all classes in all class societies invariably put the political criterion first and the artistic criterion second. The bourgeoisie always shuts out proletarian literature and art, however great their artistic merit. The proletariat must similarly distinguish among the literary and art works of past ages and determine its attitude towards them only after examining their attitude to the people and whether or not they had any progressive significance historically. Some works which politically are downright reactionary may have a certain artistic quality. The more reactionary their content and the higher their artistic quality, the more poisonous they are to the people, and the more necessary it is to reject them. A common characteristic of the literature and art of all exploiting classes in their period of decline is the contradiction between their reactionary political content and their artistic form. What we demand is the unity of politics and art, the unity of content and form, the unity of revolutionary political content and the highest possible perfection of artistic form. Works of art which lack artistic quality have no force, however progressive they are politically. Therefore, we oppose both the tendency to produce works of art with a wrong political viewpoint and the tendency towards the "poster and slogan style" which is correct in political viewpoint but lacking in artistic power. On questions of literature and art we must carry on a struggle on two fronts.

Both these tendencies can be found in the thinking of many comrades. 18 A good number of comrades tend to neglect artistic technique; it is therefore necessary to give attention to the raising of artistic standards. But as I see it, the political side is more of a problem at present. Some comrades lack elementary political knowledge and consequently have all sorts of muddled ideas. Let me cite a few examples from Yenan.

"The theory of human nature." Is there such a thing as human nature? 19 Of course there is. But there is only human nature in the concrete, no human nature in the abstract. In class society there is only human nature of a class character; there is no human nature above classes. We uphold the human nature of the proletariat and of the masses of the people, while the landlord and bourgeois classes uphold the human nature of their own classes, only they do not say so but make it out to be the only human nature in existence. The human nature boosted by certain petty-bourgeois intellectuals is also divorced from or opposed to the masses; what they call human nature is in essence nothing but bourgeois individualism, and so, in their eyes, proletarian human nature is contrary to human nature. "The theory of human nature" which some people in Yenan advocate as the basis of their so-called theory of literature and art puts the matter in just this way and is wholly wrong.

"The fundamental point of departure for literature and art is love, love 20 of humanity." Now love may serve as a point of departure, but there is a more basic one. Love as an idea is a product of objective practice. Fundamentally, we do not start from ideas but from objective practice. Our writers and artists who come from the ranks of the intellectuals love the proletariat because society has made them feel that they and the proletariat share a common fate. We hate Japanese imperialism because Japanese imperialism oppresses us. There is absolutely no such thing in the world as love or hatred without reason or cause. As for the so-called love of humanity, there has been no such all-inclusive love since humanity was divided into classes. All the ruling classes of the past were fond of advocating it, and so were many so-called sages and wise men, but nobody has ever really practiced it, because it is impossible in class society. There will be genuine love of humanity — after classes are eliminated all over the world. Classes have split society into many antagonistic groupings; there will be love of all humanity when classes are eliminated, but not now. We cannot love enemies, we cannot love social evils, our aim is to destroy them. This is common sense; can it be that some of our writers and artists still do not understand this?

"Literary and artistic works have always laid equal stress on the bright   21
and the dark, half and half." This statement contains many muddled ideas. It is not true that literature and art have always done this. Many petty-bourgeois writers have never discovered the bright side. Their works only expose the dark and are known as the "literature of exposure." Some of their works simply specialize in preaching pessimism and world-weariness. On the other hand, Soviet literature in the period of socialist construction portrays mainly the bright. It, too, describes shortcomings in work and portrays negative characters, but this only serves as a contrast to bring out the brightness of the whole picture and is not on a so-called half-and-half basis. The writers and artists of the bourgeoisie in its period of reaction depict the revolutionary masses as mobs and themselves as saints, thus reversing the bright and the dark. Only truly revolutionary writers and artists can correctly solve the problem of whether to extol or to expose. All the dark forces harming the masses of the people must be exposed and all the revolutionary struggles of the masses of the people must be extolled; this is the fundamental task of revolutionary writers and artists.

"The task of literature and art has always been to expose." This asser-   22
tion, like the previous one, arises from ignorance of the science of history. Literature and art, as we have shown, have never been devoted solely to exposure. For revolutionary writers and artists the targets for exposure can never be the masses, but only the aggressors, exploiters and oppressors and the evil influence they have on the people. The masses too have shortcomings, which should be overcome by criticism and self-criticism within the people's own ranks, and such criticism and self-criticism is also one of the most important tasks of literature and art. But this should not be regarded as any sort of "exposure of the people." As for the people, the question is basically one of education and of raising their level. Only counter-revolutionary writers and artists describe the people as "born fools" and the revolutionary masses as "tyrannical mobs."

REVIEW QUESTIONS

1. What is the immediate purpose of Mao's speech? What kind of problems have existed in connection with artists and the Party? What should be the attitude of artists in relation to each of the following groups: "the enemy, our allies in the united front and our own people"? To what extent should artists be positive, to what extent negative in dealing with each of these groups?

2. How do the special requirements of the audience affect the creation of revolutionary art and literature? What groups form the majority of the audience? Why have artists failed in the past to understand the requirements of their audience? What must artists do in order to understand the language of the masses? How does Mao use his own personal experience to support his arguments?

3. What have been the consequences of artists failing to adequately study Marxism-Leninism? What flaws have appeared in their creations, as a result of their ignorance of class struggle and national struggle? What does Mao mean when he says that what the masses need in their art is not "more flowers on the brocade" but rather "more fuel in snowy weather"?

4. For Mao what is the role of the artistic heritage of both China and the West in creating new works of revolutionary art? What dangers must be avoided in drawing upon the artistic heritage? What is the most important source of all art, but particularly revolutionary art? In what way is literature superior to life? In other words, what is the difference between literature and life that makes literature necessary for the revolutionary struggle? What is the relationship between popularization and the raising of standards? Why do the two go hand in hand?

5. What are the two criteria by which literature and art are judged? How are these criteria to be applied? On what grounds may literature and art be judged negatively? To what degree does Mao allow diversity of approach? To what extent does he call for quality? To what degree are works from the past to be judged by the same standards? Why are high-quality reactionary works more dangerous than low-quality reactionary works? What is the relative importance of politics and quality?

6. How does Mao conceive of "human nature"? To what extent is human nature a function of class? What is human nature to the bourgeoisie, according to Mao? Why does Mao reject the idea that human nature and love are abstractions? To what extent have artists failed to make the proper distinctions?

DISCUSSION AND WRITING QUESTIONS

1. Do you believe that literature and art should have a moral purpose? A social purpose? Is art incompatible with propaganda? Is there a clear dividing line between the two? If so, at what point is that line crossed? Discuss these questions, using examples (perhaps from recent films) as necessary.

2. Do you agree with Mao's views as to the relationship between literature and life? If not, how do your own views differ from his? Do you believe that Mao's views on art are pernicious or dangerous? Explain.

3. Create an outline or a detailed description of an artistic work that you believe would meet with Mao's approval. Adapt the work, however, to the context of the contemporary United States (or another society with which you are familiar). In a separate section explain how the work of art is designed to work upon its audience. (Describe the audience, also.) *Alternative assignment:* Create an outline or a detailed description of an artistic work that would not necessarily meet with Mao's approval, but that would still serve a social purpose. Again, in a separate section, explain the intended effects of this work upon its intended audience.

4. Cite examples of works of art that have no political or social purpose (i.e., that are designed purely for entertainment or as a means of artistic self-expression

or as a direct or enhanced reflection of reality), and then justify their existence. *Alternative assignment:* Justify their existence to Mao if you were defending to him the artists who had created them and who were now on trial for their "errors."

5. Research examples of the genre of socialist realism, from the Soviet Union, the People's Republic of China, or some other socialist country. Describe these works and their intended function and then critique them (not necessarily negatively). Consider the extent to which your critiques are influenced by a bourgeois mentality.

THE POPULAR FRONT FOR THE LIBERATION OF PALESTINE

One of the most frightening trends of our time is the rise of international terrorism. During the past two decades, hijackings of aircraft, bombings of shopping malls and theaters, kidnappings of businessmen and teachers have stunned and frequently immobilized the Western democracies. Some experts have concluded that terrorism (particularly in the Middle East) is financed and supported principally by the forces of communism and Islamic radicalism. These forces converge in the Popular Front for the Liberation of Palestine (PFLP).

The PFLP is the chief rival to Yasir Arafat's Palestine Liberation Organization (PLO) — of which it is sometimes a member group. Both organizations are committed to the same overall objectives — the defeat of Israel and the creation of a Palestinian state on the territory now occupied by Israel and parts of Jordan and Egypt. The PFLP, however, is explicitly Marxist in orientation. It was founded in 1967 by Dr. George Habash, a Christian Arab born in 1926 in Lod (or Lydda, now part of Israel). After the overwhelming defeat of the Arabs in the Six-Day War against Israel (1967), Habash and his followers adopted the Marxist-Leninist strategy of revolutionary class struggle as a more effective means (than conventional war) of carrying on the fight against Israel. Originally, the PFLP was militarily supported by the Soviets, but when Moscow later threw its support to Arafat, Habash turned to China for assistance and became a Maoist. The PFLP became widely known to the world in 1970 for skyjacking and destroying three American and West European airliners. Subsequently, it was involved in the 1972 massacre of 27 persons by Japanese commandos at Lod Airport, the 1975 kidnapping of OPEC oil ministers in Austria, and the 1976 Entebbe hijacking.

The following "Platform" was written by some of Habash's young followers in 1968. It redefines the Palestinian problem in terms of the class struggle. Specifically, it insists on the necessity for the struggle of Palestinian workers and peasants not only against the Jewish state, but also against the Arab bourgeoisie.

PLATFORM OF THE POPULAR FRONT FOR THE LIBERATION OF PALESTINE

1. CONVENTIONAL WAR IS THE WAR OF THE BOURGEOISIE. REVOLUTIONARY WAR IS PEOPLE'S WAR

The Arab bourgeoisie has developed armies which are not prepared to sacrifice their own interests or to risk their privileges. Arab militarism has become an apparatus for oppressing revolutionary socialist movements within the Arab states, while at the same time it claims to be staunchly anti-imperialist. Under the guise of the national question, the bourgeoisie has used its armies to strengthen its bureaucratic power over the masses, and to prevent the workers and peasants from acquiring political power. So far it has demanded the help of the workers and peasants without organizing them or without developing a proletarian ideology. The national bourgeoisie usually comes to power through military coups and without any activity on the part of the masses; as soon as it has captured power it reinforces its bureaucratic position. Through widespread application of terror it is able to talk about revolution while at the same time it suppresses all the revolutionary movements and arrests everyone who tries to advocate revolutionary action.   *1*

The Arab bourgeoisie has used the question of Palestine to divert the Arab masses from realizing their own interests and their own domestic problems. The bourgeoisie always concentrated hopes on a victory outside the state's boundaries, in Palestine, and in this way they were able to preserve their class interests and their bureaucratic positions.   *2*

The war of June, 1967,[1] disproved the bourgeois theory of conventional war. The best strategy for Israel is to strike rapidly. The enemy is not able to mobilize its armies for a long period of time because this would intensify its economic crisis. It gets complete support from U.S. imperialism and for these reasons it needs quick wars. Therefore for our poor people the best strategy in the long run is a people's war. Our people must overcome their weaknesses and exploit the weaknesses of the enemy by mobilizing the   *3*

Rpt. in *The Terrorism Reader: A Historical Anthology.* Ed. Walter Laqueur, Philadelphia: Temple University Press, 1978, pp. 145–149.

[1]*The war of June, 1967:* The "Six-Day War" during which Israel decisively defeated Arab armies from several countries, including Egypt, Jordan, and Syria.

Palestinian and Arab peoples. The weakening of imperialism and Zionism[2] in the Arab world demands revolutionary war as the means to confront them.

2. GUERILLA STRUGGLE AS A FORM OF PRESSURE FOR THE "PEACEFUL SOLUTION"

The Palestinian struggle is a part of the whole Arab liberation move- 4 ment and of the world liberation movement. The Arab bourgeoisie and world imperialism are trying to impose a peaceful solution on this Palestinian problem but this suggestion merely promotes the interests of imperialism and of Zionism, doubt in the efficacy of people's war as a means of liberation, and the preservation of the relations of the Arab bourgeoisie with the imperialist world market.

The Arab bourgeoisie is afraid of being isolated from this market and 5 of losing its role as a mediator of world capitalism. That is why the Arab oil-producing countries broke off the boycott against the West[3] (instituted during the June war), and for this reason McNamara,[4] as head of the World Bank, was ready to offer credits to them.

When the Arab bourgeoisie strive for a peaceful solution, they are in 6 fact striving for the profit which they can get from their role as mediator between the imperialist market and the internal market. The Arab bourgeoisie are not yet opposed to the activity of the guerrillas, and sometimes they even help them; but this is because the presence of the guerrillas is a means of pressure for a peaceful solution. As long as the guerrillas don't have a clear class affiliation and a clear political stand they are unable to resist the implication of such a peaceful solution; but the conflict between the guerrillas and those who strive for a peaceful solution is unavoidable. Therefore the guerrillas must take steps to transform their actions into a people's war with clear goals.

---

[2]*Zionism:* The movement for the reconstitution of a Jewish state in Palestine. (The previous Jewish state was destroyed by the Romans in A.D. 70. The modern state of Israel was constituted in 1948.)

[3]*the boycott against the West:* Shortly after the Six-Day War, the Arab states embargoed the sale of Middle Eastern oil to the West, in retaliation for its support of Israel in the war.

[4]*McNamara:* Robert McNamara (b. 1916) was Secretary of Defense from 1961 to 1968, and subsequently (1968–1981), president of the World Bank.

3. NO REVOLUTIONARY WAR WITHOUT
A REVOLUTIONARY THEORY

The basic weakness of the guerrilla movement is the absence of a rev-   *7*
olutionary ideology, which could illuminate the horizons of the Palestinian
fighters and would incarnate the stages of a militant political program.
Without a revolutionary ideology the national struggle will remain imprisoned within its immediate practical and material needs. The Arab
bourgeoisie is quite prepared for a limited satisfaction of the needs of the
national struggle, as long as it respects the limits that the bourgeoisie sets.
A clear illustration of this is the material help that Saudi Arabia offers Al
Fatah[5] while Al Fatah declares that she will not interfere in the internal
affairs of any Arab countries.

Since most of the guerrilla movements have no ideological weapons,   *8*
the Arab bourgeoisie can decide their fate. Therefore, the struggle of the
Palestinian people must be supported by the workers and peasants, who
will fight against any form of domination by imperialism, Zionism, or the
Arab bourgeoisie.

4. THE WAR OF LIBERATION IS A CLASS WAR GUIDED BY
A REVOLUTIONARY IDEOLOGY

We must not be satisfied with ignoring the problems of our struggle,   *9*
saying that our struggle is a national one and not a class struggle. The
national struggle reflects the class struggle. The national struggle is a struggle for land and those who struggle for it are the peasants who were driven
away from their land. The bourgeoisie is always ready to lead such a movement, hoping to gain control of the internal market. If the bourgeoisie succeeds in bringing the national movement under its control, which strengthens its position, it can lead the movement under the guise of a peaceful
solution into compromises with imperialism and Zionism.

Therefore, the fact that the liberation struggle is mainly a class struggle   *10*
emphasizes the necessity for the workers and peasants to play a leading
role in the national liberation movement. If the small bourgeoisie take the
leading role, the national revolution will fall as a victim of the class interests of this leadership. It is a great mistake to start by saying that the Zionist challenge demands national unity, for this shows that one does not
understand the real class structure of Zionism.

The struggle against Israel is first of all a class struggle. Therefore the   *11*
oppressed class is the only class which is able to face a confrontation with
Zionism.

---

[5] *Al Fatah:* The chief military (guerrilla) force of the Palestinian Liberation Organization; it
is headed by Yasir Arafat. "Fatah" is the Arab word for "conquest."

5. THE MAIN FIELD OF OUR REVOLUTIONARY STRUGGLE IS PALESTINE

The decisive battle must be in Palestine. The armed people's struggle   *12*
in Palestine can help itself with the simplest weapons in order to ruin the
economies and the war machinery of their Zionist enemy. The moving of
the people's struggle into Palestine depends upon agitating and organizing
the masses, more than depending upon border actions in the Jordan valley,
although these actions are of importance for the struggle in Palestine.

When guerrilla organizations began their actions in the occupied areas,   *13*
they were faced with a brutal military repression by the armed forces of
Zionism. Because these organizations had no revolutionary ideology and
so no program, they gave in to demands of self-preservation and retreated
into eastern Jordan. All their activity turned into border actions. This presence of the guerrilla organizations in Jordan enables the Jordanian
bourgeoisie and their secret agents to crush these organizations when they
are no longer useful as pressure for a peaceful solution.[6]

6. REVOLUTION IN BOTH REGIONS OF JORDAN

We must not neglect the struggle in east Jordan,[7] for this land is con-   *14*
nected with Palestine more than with the other Arab countries. The problem of the revolution in Palestine is dialectically connected with the problem of the revolution in Jordan. A chain of plots between the Jordanian
monarchy,[8] imperialism, and Zionism have proved this connection.

The struggle in east Jordan must take the correct path, that of class   *15*
struggle. The Palestinian struggle must not be used as a means of propping
up the Jordanian monarchy, under the mask of national unity, and the
main problem in Jordan is the creation of a Marxist-Leninist party with a
clear action program according to which it can organize the masses and
enable them to carry out the national and class struggle. The harmony of
the struggle in the two regions must be realized through coordinating organs whose tasks will be to guarantee reserves inside Palestine and to mobilize the peasants and soldiers in the border territories.

---

[6]*This presence . . . solution:* Conflict between Jordan's King Hussein and the increasingly
powerful PLO guerrillas operating in his country led in 1970 to war, resulting in the total
defeat of the PLO, the destruction of their bases, and their expulsion from Jordan.

[7]*east Jordan:* That part of Jordan (about 92 percent of the country) east of the Jordan River.
The part of Jordan west of the river is known as the West Bank and has been occupied by
Israel since the 1967 war.

[8]*Jordanian monarchy:* Hussein I, king of Jordan since 1952.

> *This is the only way in which Amman[9] can become an Arab Hanoi[10] — a base*   16
> *for the revolutionaries fighting inside Palestine.*

---

[9]*Amman:* Capital of Jordan.

[10]*Hanoi:* Capital of North Vietnam (and since 1975 of all Vietnam). The analogy refers to Hanoi's being the base from which the communist Viet Cong guerrillas operating in South Vietnam sought to undermine the Western-supported Saigon regime.

REVIEW QUESTIONS

1. According to the platform, how has the Arab bourgeoisie worked against the true interests of the Palestinian workers and peasants? How are imperialism, Zionism, and the Arab bourgeoisie linked?
2. In what ways have bourgeois Arabs supported peace with the forces of imperialism? How has the West attempted to accommodate the bourgeois Arabs? How have the bourgeois Arabs attempted to control the guerrillas? What are the real motives of the Arab bourgeoisie, according to the platform?
3. What steps must the guerrilla movement take to become effective? In what way does the national struggle reflect the class struggle? Who must play the leading role in the national struggle? What is the role of Jordan? What obstacles have been posed by Jordan?

DISCUSSION AND WRITING QUESTIONS

1. According to the platform, "If the bourgeoisie succeeds in bringing the national movement under its control, which strengthens its position, it can lead the movement under the guise of a peaceful solution into compromises with imperialism and Zionism." Discuss the implications of this statement. In what ways might it account for some of the history of the Middle East during the past ten or fifteen years — in particular, the fate of peace initiatives and peace initiators?
2. Research the subject of the likelihood of success of a Marxist approach to the Palestinian problem. How acute are the problems of class in the Arab world? To what extent is it likely that the workers and peasants can be mobilized in a class struggle against the Arab bourgeoisie? What is the status of the Arab bourgeoisie — particularly in light of the fluctuating economy of oil in the region?
3. According to the platform, the "struggle against Israel is first of all a class struggle." Assess this statement.

ANGELA Y. DAVIS (b. 1944)

At first it may seem incongruous to join the issue of Marxism (which implies a class struggle) to the issues of racism and feminism (which imply racial and sexual struggles). But as Angela Davis argues in this selection, racism and sexism have their basis in "monopoly capitalism." Focusing on the issue of housework, and using the same type of historical approach as Marx and Engels, she discusses the transition from one type of economy and social structure to another, showing how women, originally the social equals of men, were gradually relegated to second-class status. Thus, the liberation of women, and black women in particular, necessitates their active involvement in the class struggle that aims to overthrow the capitalist system.

Angela Yvonne Davis was born in Birmingham, Alabama, in 1944. Both of her middle-class parents were active in the civil rights struggle. Davis attended the socialist-oriented Elizabeth Irwin Prep School in New York City, and then Brandeis University in Massachusetts. At Brandeis, she came under the tutelage of Herbert Marcuse, a Marxist philosophy professor, who, though approaching retirement age, was to become an intellectual hero to radical students in the late 1960s. Marcuse was influential in Davis's eventually becoming a communist. After her graduation from Brandeis in 1965, she spent two years at the Johann Wolfgang von Goethe University in Frankfurt, Germany, studying philosophy under Marxist scholars, including Theodore Adorno, an old colleague of Marcuse. Returning from Germany, she followed Marcuse to the University of California at San Diego, where she began working on her doctorate, and where she helped set up the Black Students Council.

California was at that time a center for black revolutionary groups, including the Black Panther Party for Self Defense, and Davis began drawing national attention for her militant speeches attacking the capitalist system. In 1969, she began teaching philosophy at UCLA; her courses on Kant and on dialectical materialism were among the most popular on campus. But after her communist affiliations were revealed, the Board of Regents, headed by Governor Ronald Reagan, fired her from her teaching position. Her dismissal raised a firestorm of protest from faculty and students. The court overruled the Regents; but the Regents later refused to renew her contract on the grounds of her inflammatory speeches, and this time they were upheld.

In 1970, Davis's life entered its most sensational phase when she began speaking out on behalf of the "Soledad Brothers," three black inmates (George Jackson, John Clutchette, and Fleeta Drumgo) at Soledad Prison, who had been indicted for killing a white prison guard after another guard had been absolved of shooting three black prisoners to death. Davis argued that Jackson and the two others were political prisoners, the victims of a racist system. She also began a correspondence with Jackson, which resulted in their falling in love. (Jackson was killed by prison guards in late 1971.) In August 1970, Jonathan Jackson, George's seventeen-year-old brother, pulled out a shotgun in a Marin County, California, courtroom, where three black prisoners were on trial, and took as hostages the judge (the shotgun taped to his head), the district attorney, and three jurors. Jackson, the now-armed prisoners, and the hostages then moved outside the courtroom to a waiting van. A guard opened fire, Jackson and the prisoners returned fire; and when the shooting stopped, Jackson, the judge, and two of the prisoners were dead. Three of the guns used in the escape were later found to be registered in Davis's name, though she had not been present at the courthouse. She became a fugitive and was placed on the FBI's Most Wanted list. Two months later she was captured in New York City and charged with kidnapping, conspiracy to murder, and being an accomplice to murder. Her case became a cause célèbre, and "Free Angela" became a slogan heard around the world. President Nixon made remarks strongly implying her guilt. Davis was confined to jail for sixteen months before being released on bail in February 1972. Her trial began later that month, and three months later, despite the best efforts of the prosecutor, she was found not guilty on all counts.

After her acquittal, to defray the cost of her defense, Davis toured the country giving speeches, culminating with a speech in Madison Square Garden in New York City. She also visited several foreign countries, including the Soviet Union, where she was warmly received. In September 1972, her UCLA teaching contract was not renewed, despite the protests of the philosophy department.

In 1980, Davis married Hilton Braithwaite, a chef and photography instructor. She now teaches courses on black women's music and on the history of Afro-American women at San Francisco State University. She continues to be politically active, serving since 1973 as cochairman of the National Alliance against Racism and Political Repression, an organization with chapters across the country. In 1985, she made news once again by objecting to President Reagan's selection of his daughter Maureen to head a U.S. delegation to the U.N. World Conference of Women in Nairobi, Kenya. Davis asserted that women "have to send a message to the unfortunate daughter of the president" that she does not "represent the masses of people in the United States." She added that the Reagan administration was "the most sexist, the most racist, the most warlike government in the entire history of our country." In an interview in *Essence* magazine in 1981, Davis said that though she has changed since the 1960s and 1970s, "I still consider myself a revolutionary. I'm still doing whatever I can to reach out to Black people, people of color, oppressed people in general, and to heighten the development of a radical liberation struggle."

Some of George Jackson's letters to Angela Davis appear in his *Soledad Brother* (1970). One of Davis's UCLA students made a documentary film about her, *Portrait of a Revolutionary*. Davis's own published works include *If They Come in the Morning: Voice of Resistance by Angela Davis and Others* (1971), an article, "Reflections on the Black Woman's Role in the Community of Slaves," in *Black Scholar* (December 1971), *Angela Davis: An Autobiography* (1974), and *Women, Race, and Class* (1982). The following selection originally appeared in the latter work as a chapter entitled "The Approaching Obsolescence of Housework: A Working-Class Perspective."

WOMEN, RACE AND CLASS

The countless chores collectively known as "housework" — cooking,   1
washing dishes, doing laundry, making beds, sweeping, shopping, etc. —
apparently consume some three to four thousand hours of the average
housewife's year.[1] As startling as this statistic may be, it does not even
account for the constant and unquantifiable attention mothers must give
to their children. Just as a woman's maternal duties are always taken for
granted, her never-ending toil as a housewife rarely occasions expressions
of appreciation within her family. Housework, after all, is virtually invisible: "No one notices it until it isn't done — we notice the unmade bed, not
the scrubbed and polished floor."[2] Invisible, repetitive, exhausting, unproductive, uncreative — these are the adjectives which most perfectly capture the nature of housework.

The new consciousness associated with the contemporary women's   2
movement has encouraged increasing numbers of women to demand that
their men provide some relief from this drudgery. Already, more men have
begun to assist their partners around the house, some of them even devoting equal time to household chores. But how many of these men have
liberated themselves from the assumption that housework is "women's
work"? How many of them would not characterize their housecleaning
activities as "helping" their women partners?

If it were at all possible simultaneously to liquidate the idea that house-   3
work is women's work and to redistribute it equally to men and women
alike, would this constitute a satisfactory solution? Freed from its exclusive
affiliation with the female sex, would housework thereby cease to be oppressive? While most women would joyously hail the advent of the
"househusband," the desexualization of domestic labor would not really
alter the oppressive nature of the work itself. In the final analysis, neither
women nor men should waste precious hours of their lives on work that
is neither stimulating, creative nor productive.

One of the most closely guarded secrets of advanced capitalist societies   4
involves the possibility — the real possibility — of radically transforming
the nature of housework. A substantial portion of the housewife's domes-

---

Angela Y. Davis. Women, Race and Class [1981]. Original title on Chapter 13: "The
Approaching Obsolescence of Housework: A Working-Class Perspective." In *Women, Race
and Class*. New York: Random House, 1981.

[1]Ann Oakley, *The Sociology of Housework* (New York: Pantheon Books, 1974), p. 6. [Davis]

[2]Barbara Ehrenreich and Deirdre English, "The Manufacture of Housework," *Socialist Revolution*, No. 26, Vol. 5, No. 4 (October–December 1975), p. 6. [Davis]

tic tasks can actually be incorporated into the industrial economy. In other words, housework need no longer be considered necessarily and unalterably private in character. Teams of trained and well-paid workers, moving from dwelling to dwelling, engineering technologically advanced cleaning machinery, could swiftly and efficiently accomplish what the present-day housewife does so arduously and primitively. Why the shroud of silence surrounding this potential of radically redefining the nature of domestic labor? Because the capitalist economy is structurally hostile to the industrialization of housework. Socialized housework implies large government subsidies in order to guarantee accessibility to the working-class families whose need for such services is most obvious. Since little in the way of profits would result, industrialized housework — like all unprofitable enterprises — is anathema to the capitalist economy. Nonetheless, the rapid expansion of the female labor force means that more and more women are finding it increasingly difficult to excel as housewives according to the traditional standards. In other words, the industrialization of housework, along with the socialization of housework, is becoming an objective social need. Housework as individual women's private responsibility and as female labor performed under primitive technical conditions, may finally be approaching historical obsolescence.

Although housework as we know it today may eventually become a bygone relic of history, prevailing social attitudes continue to associate the eternal female condition with images of brooms and dustpans, mops and pails, aprons and stoves, pots and pans. And it is true that women's work, from one historical era to another, has been associated in general with the homestead. Yet female domestic labor has not always been what it is today, for like all social phenomena, housework is a fluid product of human history. As economic systems have arisen and faded away, the scope and quality of housework have undergone radical transformations.

As Frederick Engels argued in his classic work on the *Origin of the Family, Private Property and the State,*[3] sexual inequality as we know it today did not exist before the advent of private property. During early eras of human history the sexual division of labor within the system of economic production was complementary as opposed to hierarchical. In societies where men may have been responsible for hunting wild animals and women, in turn, for gathering wild vegetables and fruits, both sexes performed economic tasks that were equally essential to their community's survival. Because the community, during those eras, was essentially an extended

[3]Frederick Engels, *Origin of the Family, Private Property and the State,* edited, with an introduction, by Eleanor Burke Leacock (New York: International Publishers, 1973). See Chapter II. Leacock's introduction to this edition contains numerous enlightening observations on Engels' theory of the historical emergence of male supremacy. [Davis]

family, women's central role in domestic affairs meant that they were accordingly valued and respected as productive members of the community.

The centrality of women's domestic tasks in pre-capitalist cultures was dramatized by a personal experience during a jeep trip I took in 1973 across the Masai Plains. On an isolated dirt road in Tanzania, I noticed six Masai women enigmatically balancing an enormous board on their heads. As my Tanzanian friends explained, these women were probably transporting a house roof to a new village which they were in the process of constructing. Among the Masai, as I learned, women are responsible for all domestic activities, thus also for the construction of their nomadic people's frequently relocated houses. Housework, as far as Masai women are concerned, entails not only cooking, cleaning, child-rearing, sewing, etc., but house-building as well. As important as their men's cattle-raising duties may be, the women's "housework" is no less productive and no less essential than the economic contributions of Masai men.

Within the pre-capitalist, nomadic economy of the Masai, women's domestic labor is as essential to the economy as the cattle-raising jobs performed by their men. As producers, they enjoy a correspondingly important social status. In advanced capitalist societies, on the other hand, the service-oriented domestic labor of housewives, who can seldom produce tangible evidence of their work, diminishes the social status of women in general. When all is said and done, the housewife, according to bourgeois ideology, is, quite simply, her husband's lifelong servant.

The source of the bourgeois notion of woman as man's eternal servant is itself a revealing story. Within the relatively short history of the United States, the "housewife" as a finished historical product is just a little more than a century old. Housework, during the colonial era, was entirely different from the daily work routine of the housewife in the United States today.

> A woman's work began at sunup and continued by firelight as long as she could hold her eyes open. For two centuries, almost everything that the family used or ate was produced at home under her direction. She spun and dyed the yarn that she wove into cloth and cut and hand-stitched into garments. She grew much of the food her family ate, and preserved enough to last the winter months. She made butter, cheese, bread, candles, and soap and knitted her family's stockings.[4]

In the agrarian economy of pre-industrial North America, a woman performing her household chores was thus a spinner, weaver and seamstress

---

[4]Barbara Wertheimer, *We Were There: The Story of Working Women in America* (New York: Pantheon Books, 1977), p. 12. [Davis]

as well as a baker, butter-churner, candle-maker and soap-maker. And et cetera, et cetera, et cetera. As a matter of fact,

> The pressures of home production left very little time for the tasks that we would recognize today as housework. By all accounts, pre-industrial revolution women were sloppy housekeepers by today's standards. Instead of the daily cleaning or the weekly cleaning, there was the *spring* cleaning. Meals were simple and repetitive; clothes were changed infrequently; and the household wash was allowed to accumulate, and the washing done once a month, or in some households once in three months. And, of course, since each wash required the carting and heating of many buckets of water, higher standards of cleanliness were easily discouraged.[5]

Colonial women were not "house-cleaners" or "housekeepers" but   10
rather full-fledged and accomplished workers within the home-based economy. Not only did they manufacture most of the products required by their families, they were also the guardians of their families' and their communities' health.

> It was [the colonial woman's] responsibility to gather and dry wild herbs used . . . as medicines; she also served as doctor, nurse, and midwife within her own family and in the community.[6]

Included in the *United States Practical Receipt Book* — a popular colonial recipe book — are recipes for foods as well as for household chemicals and medicines. To cure ringworm, for example, "obtain some blood-root . . . slice it in vinegar, and afterwards wash the place affected with the liquid."[7]

The economic importance of women's domestic functions in colonial   11
America was complemented by their visible roles in economic activity outside the home. It was entirely acceptable, for example, for a woman to become a tavern keeper.

> Women also ran sawmills and gristmills, caned chairs and built furniture, operated slaughterhouses, printed cotton and other cloth, made lace, and owned and ran dry-goods and clothing stores. They worked in tobacco shops, drug shops (where they sold concoctions they made themselves), and general stores that sold everything from pins to meat scales. Women ground eyeglasses, made netting and rope, cut and stitched leather goods, made cards for wool carding, and even were housepainters. Often they were the town undertakers. . . .[8]

The postrevolutionary surge of industrialization resulted in a prolifer-   12
ation of factories in the northeastern section of the new country. New Eng-

---

[5]Ehrenreich and English, "The Manufacture of Housework," p. 9. [Davis]
[6]Wertheimer, *op. cit.*, p. 12. [Davis]
[7]Quoted in Baxandall *et al.*, *op. cit.*, p. 17. [Davis]
[8]Wertheimer, *op. cit.*, p. 13. [Davis]

land's textile mills were the factory system's successful pioneers. Since spinning and weaving were traditional female domestic occupations, women were the first workers recruited by the mill-owners to operate the new power looms. Considering the subsequent exclusion of women from industrial production in general, it is one of the great ironies of this country's economic history that the first industrial workers were women.

As industrialization advanced, shifting economic production from the home to the factory, the importance of women's domestic work suffered a systematic erosion. Women were the losers in a double sense: as their traditional jobs were usurped by the burgeoning factories, the entire economy moved away from the home, leaving many women largely bereft of significant economic roles. By the middle of the nineteenth century the factory provided textiles, candles and soap. Even butter, bread and other food products began to be mass-produced. 13

> By the end of the century, hardly anyone made their own starch or boiled their laundry in a kettle. In the cities, women bought their bread and at least their underwear ready-made, sent their children out to school and probably some clothes out to be laundered, and were debating the merits of canned foods . . . The flow of industry had passed on and had left idle the loom in the attic and the soap kettle in the shed.[9]

As industrial capitalism approached consolidation, the cleavage between the new economic sphere and the old home economy became ever more rigorous. The physical relocation of economic production caused by the spread of the factory system was undoubtedly a drastic transformation. But even more radical was the generalized revaluation of production necessitated by the new economic system. While home-manufactured goods were valuable primarily because they fulfilled basic family needs, the importance of factory-produced commodities resided overwhelmingly in their exchange value — in their ability to fulfill employers' demands for profit. This revaluation of economic production revealed — beyond the physical separation of home and factory — a fundamental *structural* separation between the domestic home economy and the profit-oriented economy of capitalism. Since housework does not generate profit, domestic labor was naturally defined as an inferior form of work as compared to capitalist wage labor. 14

An important ideological by-product of this radical economic transformation was the birth of the "housewife." Women began to be ideologically redefined as the guardians of a devalued domestic life. As ideology, however, this redefinition of women's place was boldly contradicted by the vast numbers of immigrant women flooding the ranks of the working class in the Northeast. These white immigrant women were wage earners first and 15

---

[9]Ehrenreich and English, "The Manufacture of Housework," p. 10. [Davis]

only secondarily housewives. And there were other women — millions of women — who toiled away from home as the unwilling producers of the slave economy in the South. The reality of women's place in nineteenth-century U.S. society involved white women, whose days were spent operating factory machines for wages that were a pittance, as surely as it involved Black women, who labored under the coercion of slavery. The "housewife" reflected a partial reality, for she was really a symbol of the economic prosperity enjoyed by the emerging middle classes.

Although the "housewife" was rooted in the social conditions of the bourgeoisie and the middle classes, nineteenth-century ideology established the housewife and the mother as universal models of womanhood. Since popular propaganda represented the vocation of *all* women as a function of their roles in the home, women compelled to work for wages came to be treated as alien visitors within the masculine world of the public economy. Having stepped outside their "natural" sphere, women were not to be treated as full-fledged wage workers. The price they paid involved long hours, substandard working conditions and grossly inadequate wages. Their exploitation was even more intense than the exploitation suffered by their male counterparts. Needless to say, sexism emerged as a source of outrageous super-profits for the capitalists.

The structural separation of the public economy of capitalism and the private economy of the home has been continually reinforced by the obstinate primitiveness of household labor. Despite the proliferation of gadgets for the home, domestic work has remained qualitatively unaffected by the technological advances brought on by industrial capitalism. Housework still consumes thousands of hours of the average housewife's year. In 1903 Charlotte Perkins Gilman proposed a definition of domestic labor which reflected the upheavals which had changed the structure and content of housework in the United States:

> The phrase "domestic work" does not apply to a special kind of work, but to a certain grade of work, a state of development through which all kinds pass. All industries were once "domestic," that is, were performed at home and in the interests of the family. All industries have since that remote period risen to higher stages, except one or two which have never left their primal stage.[10]

"The home," Gilman maintains, "has not developed in proportion to our other institutions." The home economy reveals

> the maintenance of primitive industries in a modern industrial community and the confinement of women to these industries and their limited area of expression.[11]

---

[10]Charlotte Perkins Gilman, *The Home: Its Work and Its Influence* (Urbana, Chicago, London: University of Illinois Press, 1972. Reprint of the 1903 edition), pp. 30–31. [Davis]

[11]*Ibid.*, p. 10. [Davis]

Housework, Gilman insists, vitiates women's humanity:

> She is feminine, more than enough, as man is masculine, more than enough; but she is not human as he is human. The house-life does not bring out our humanness, for all the distinctive lines of human progress lie outside.[12]

The truth of Gilman's statement is corroborated by the historical experience of Black women in the United States. Throughout this country's history, the majority of Black women have worked outside their homes. During slavery, women toiled alongside their men in the cotton and tobacco fields, and when industry moved into the South, they could be seen in tobacco factories, sugar refineries and even in lumber mills and on crews pounding steel for the railroads. In labor, slave women were the equals of their men. Because they suffered a grueling sexual equality at work, they enjoyed a greater sexual equality at home in the slave quarters than did their white sisters who were "housewifes."   18

As a direct consequence of their outside work — as "free" women no less than as slaves — housework has never been the central focus of Black women's lives. They have largely escaped the psychological damage industrial capitalism inflicted on white middle-class housewives, whose alleged virtues were feminine weakness and wifely submissiveness. Black women could hardly strive for weakness; they had to become strong, for their families and their communities needed their strength to survive. Evidence of the accumulated strengths Black women have forged through work, work and more work can be discovered in the contributions of the many outstanding female leaders who have emerged within the Black community. Harriet Tubman,[13] Sojourner Truth,[14] Ida Wells[15] and Rosa Parks[16] are not exceptional Black women as much as they are epitomes of Black womanhood.   19

---

[12]*Ibid.*, p. 217. [Davis]

[13]*Harriet Tubman:* (c. 1821–1913) A famed abolitionist, Tubman was a slave until about the age of 25 when she fled to the North and worked as a conductor for the underground railroad, helping more than 300 slaves escape from the South.

[14]*Sojourner Truth:* (1797–1883) An abolitionist and women's rights advocate; sometime after being freed from slavery at the age of thirty, she had a religious vision which led her to travel through midwestern and eastern states, speaking at rallies against slavery. She is also known for her work for women's rights.

[15]*Ida Wells:* (1862–1931) An Afro-American journalist and civil rights leader; despite continual white persecution, Wells achieved a great deal of success in her fight for Afro-American recognition and civil rights: in 1898 she became the Secretary of the National American Council, in 1908 she founded the Negro Fellowship League, and in 1915 she was elected as the Vice President of Chicago's Equal Rights League.

[16]*Rosa Parks:* (b. 1913) The black seamstress whose arrest for refusing to give up her seat to a white man on a city bus sparked the historic Montgomery Bus Boycott under the direction of Dr. Martin Luther King, Jr. The success of this boycott paved the way for further civil rights struggles and victories.

Black women, however, have paid a heavy price for the strengths they [20]
have acquired and the relative independence they have enjoyed. While
they have seldom been "just housewives," they have always done their
housework. They have thus carried the double burden of wage labor and
housework — a double burden which always demands that working
women possess the persevering powers of Sisyphus. As W. E. B. DuBois
observed in 1920:

> Some few women are born free, and some amid insult and scarlet letters
> achieve freedom; but our women in black had freedom thrust contemptuously
> upon them. With that freedom they are buying an untrammeled independence
> and dear as is the price they pay for it, it will in the end be worth every taunt
> and groan.[17]

Like their men, Black women have worked until they could work no more.
Like their men, they have assumed the responsibilities of family providers.
The unorthodox feminine qualities of assertiveness and self-reliance — for
which Black women have been frequently praised but more often rebuked
— are reflections of their labor and their struggles outside the home. But
like their white sisters called "housewives," they have cooked and cleaned
and have nurtured and reared untold numbers of children. But unlike the
white housewives, who learned to lean on their husbands for economic
security, Black wives and mothers, usually workers as well, have rarely
been offered the time and energy to become experts at domesticity. Like
their white working-class sisters, who also carry the double burden of
working for a living and servicing husbands and children, Black women
have needed relief from this oppressive predicament for a long, long time.

For Black women today and for all their working-class sisters, the no- [21]
tion that the burden of housework and child care can be shifted from their
shoulders to the society contains one of the radical secrets of women's liberation. Child care should be socialized, meal preparation should be socialized, housework should be industrialized — and all these services
should be readily accessible to working-class people.

The shortage, if not absence, of public discussion about the feasibility [22]
of transforming housework into a social possibility bears witness to the
blinding powers of bourgeois ideology. It is not even the case that women's
domestic role has received no attention at all. On the contrary, the contemporary women's movement has represented housework as an essential ingredient of women's oppression. There is even a movement in a number
of capitalist countries, whose main concern is the plight of the housewife.
Having reached the conclusion that housework is degrading and oppres-

---

[17]DuBois, *Darkwater*, p. 185. [Davis]

sive primarily because it is *unpaid* labor, this movement has raised the demand for wages. A weekly government paycheck, its activists argue, is the
key to improving the housewife's status and the social position of women
in general.

The Wages for Housework Movement originated in Italy, where its first   23
public demonstration took place in March, 1974. Addressing the crowd
assembled in the city of Mestre,[18] one of the speakers proclaimed:

> Half the world's population is unpaid — this is the biggest class contradiction
> of all! And this is our struggle for wages for housework. It is *the* strategic de-
> mand; at this moment it is the most revolutionary demand for the whole work-
> ing class. If we win, the class wins, if we lose, the class loses.[19]

According to this movement's strategy, wages contain the key to the emancipation of housewives, and the demand itself is represented as the central
focus of the campaign for women's liberation in general. Moreover, the
housewife's struggle for wages is projected as the pivotal issue of the entire
working-class movement.

The theoretical origins of the Wages for Housework Movement can be   24
found in an essay by Mariarosa Dalla Costa entitled "Women and the Subversion of the Community."[20] In this paper, Dalla Costa argues for a redefinition of housework based on her thesis that the private character of
household services is actually an illusion. The housewife, she insists, only
appears to be ministering to the private needs of her husband and children, for the real beneficiaries of her services are her husband's present
employer and the future employers of her children.

> (The woman) has been isolated in the home, forced to carry out work that is
> considered unskilled, the work of giving birth to, raising, disciplining, and
> servicing the worker for production. Her role in the cycle of production re-
> mained invisible because only the product of her labor, the *laborer*, was
> visible.[21]

The demand that housewives be paid is based on the assumption that they
produce a commodity as important and as valuable as the commodities
their husbands produce on the job. Adopting Dalla Costa's logic, the
Wages for Housework Movement defines housewives as creators of the

---

[18]*Mestre:* An industrial center 5 miles northwest of Venice, Italy.

[19]Speech by Polga Fortunata. Quoted in Wendy Edmond and Suzie Fleming, editors, *All
Work and No Pay: Women, Housework and the Wages Due!* (Bristol, England: Falling Wall
Press, 1975), p. 18. [Davis]

[20]Mariarosa Dalla Costa and Selma James, *The Power of Women and the Subversion of the Community* (Bristol, England: Falling Wall Press, 1973). [Davis]

[21]*Ibid.*, p. 28. [Davis]

labor-power sold by their family members as commodities on the capitalist market.

Dalla Costa was not the first theorist to propose such an analysis of   25
women's oppression. Both Mary Inman's *In Woman's Defense* (1940)[22] and Margaret Benston's "The Political Economy of Women's Liberation" (1969)[23] define housework in such a way as to establish women as a special class of workers exploited by capitalism called "housewives." That women's procreative, child-rearing and housekeeping roles make it possible for their family members to work — to exchange their labor-power for wages — can hardly be denied. But does it automatically follow that women in general, regardless of their class and race, can be fundamentally defined by their domestic functions? Does it automatically follow that the housewife is actually a secret worker inside the capitalist production process?

If the industrial revolution resulted in the structural separation of the   26
home economy from the public economy, then housework cannot be defined as an integral component of capitalist production. It is, rather, related to production as a *precondition.* The employer is not concerned in the least about the way labor-power is produced and sustained, he is only concerned about its availability and its ability to generate profit. In other words, the capitalist production process presupposes the existence of a body of exploitable workers.

> The replenishment of (workers') labor-power is not a part of the process of social production but a prerequisite to it. It occurs *outside* of the labor process. Its function is the maintenance of human existence which is the ultimate purpose of production in all societies.[24]

In South African society, where racism has led economic exploitation   27
to its most brutal limits, the capitalist economy betrays its structural separation from domestic life in a characteristically violent fashion. The social architects of Apartheid have simply determined that Black labor yields higher profits when domestic life is all but entirely discarded. Black men are viewed as labor units whose productive potential renders them valuable to the capitalist class. But their wives and children

---

[22]Mary Inman, *In Woman's Defense* (Los Angeles: Committee to Organize the Advancement of Women, 1940). See also Inman, *The Two Forms of Production Under Capitalism* (Long Beach, Cal.: Published by the Author, 1964). [Davis]

[23]Margaret Benston, "The Political Economy of Women's Liberation," *Monthly Review*, Vol. XXI, No. 4 (September, 1969). [Davis]

[24]"On the Economic Status of the Housewife." Editorial Comment in *Political Affairs*, Vol. LIII, No. 3 (March, 1974), p. 4. [Davis]

are superfluous appendages — non-productive, the women being nothing more than adjuncts to the procreative capacity of the black male labor unit.[25]

This characterization of African women as "superfluous appendages" is hardly a metaphor. In accordance with South African law, unemployed Black women are banned from the white areas (87 percent of the country!), even, in most cases, from the cities where their husbands live and work.

Black domestic life in South Africa's industrial centers is viewed by Apartheid supporters as superfluous and unprofitable. But it is also seen as a threat.

> Government officials recognize the homemaking role of the women and fear their presence in the cities will lead to the establishment of a stable black population.[26]

The consolidation of African families in the industrialized cities is perceived as a menace because domestic life might become a base for a heightened level of resistance to Apartheid. This is undoubtedly the reason why large numbers of women holding residence permits for white areas are assigned to live in sex-segregated hostels. Married as well as single women end up living in these projects. In such hostels, family life is rigorously prohibited — husbands and wives are unable to visit one another and neither mother nor father can receive visits from their children.[27]

This intense assault on Black women in South Africa has already taken its toll, for only 28.2 percent are currently opting for marriage.[28] For reasons of economic expediency and political security, Apartheid is eroding — with the apparent goal of destroying — the very fabric of Black domestic life. South African capitalism thus blatantly demonstrates the extent to which the capitalist economy is utterly dependent on domestic labor.

The deliberate dissolution of family life in South Africa could not have been undertaken by the government if it were truly the case that the services performed by women in the home are an essential constituent of wage labor under capitalism. That domestic life can be dispensed with by the South African version of capitalism is a consequence of the separation of the private home economy and the public production process which characterizes capitalist society in general. It seems futile to argue that on

---

[25]Hilda Bernstein, *For Their Triumphs and For Their Tears: Women in Apartheid South Africa* (London: International Defence and Aid Fund, 1975), p. 13. [Davis]

[26]Elizabeth Landis, "Apartheid and the Disabilities of Black Women in South Africa," *Objective: Justice*, Vol. VII, No. 1 (January–March, 1975), p. 6. Excerpts from this paper were published in *Freedomways*, Vol. XV, No. 4, 1975. [Davis]

[27]Bernstein, *op. cit.*, p. 33. [Davis]

[28]Landis, *op. cit.*, p. 6. [Davis]

the basis of capitalism's internal logic, women ought to be paid wages for housework.

Assuming that the theory underlying the demand for wages is hope- 31 lessly flawed, might it not be nonetheless politically desirable to insist that housewives be paid. Couldn't one invoke a moral imperative for women's right to be paid for the hours they devote to housework? The idea of a paycheck for housewives would probably sound quite attractive to many women. But the attraction would probably be short-lived. For how many of those women would actually be willing to reconcile themselves to dead- ening, never-ending household tasks, all for the sake of a wage? Would a wage alter the fact, as Lenin said, that

> Petty housework crushes, strangles, stultifies and degrades (the woman), chains her to the kitchen and to the nursery, and wastes her labor on barbarously unproductive, petty, nerve-racking, stultifying and crushing drudgery.[29]

It would seem that government paychecks for housewives would further legitimize this domestic slavery.

Is it not an implicit critique of the Wages for Housework Movement 32 that women on welfare have rarely demanded compensation for keeping house. Not "wages for housework" but rather "a guaranteed annual in- come for all" is the slogan articulating the immediate alternative they have most frequently proposed to the dehumanizing welfare system. What they want in the long run, however, is jobs and affordable public child care. The guaranteed annual income functions, therefore, as unemployment insur- ance pending the creation of more jobs with adequate wages along with a subsidized system of child care.

The experiences of yet another group of women reveal the problematic 33 nature of the "wages for housework" strategy. Cleaning women, domestic workers, maids — these are the women who know better than anyone else what it means to receive wages for housework. Their tragic predicament is brilliantly captured in the film by Ousmane Sembene[30] entitled *La Noire de. . . .*[31] The main character is a young Senegalese woman who, after a search for work, becomes a governess for a French family living in Dakar. When the family returns to France, she enthusiastically accompanies them. Once in France, however, she discovers she is responsible not only for the

---

[29]V. I. Lenin, "A Great Beginning," pamphlet published in July, 1919. Quoted in *Collected Works*, Vol. 29 (Moscow: Progress Publishers, 1966), p. 429. [Davis]

[30]*Ousmane Sembene:* (b. 1923) A Senegalese author and film director, he wrote about the struggles of Senegalese citizens (especially laborers) against the confinement of tradition and colonialism. His film *La Noire de . . .* won a prize at the Cannes Film Festival in 1967.

[31]Released in the United States under the title *Black Girl*. [Davis]

children, but for cooking, cleaning, washing and all the other household chores. It is not long before her initial enthusiasm gives way to depression — a depression so profound that she refuses the pay offered her by her employers. Wages cannot compensate for her slavelike situation. Lacking the means to return to Senegal, she is so overwhelmed by her despair that she chooses suicide over an indefinite destiny of cooking, sweeping, dusting, scrubbing . . .

In the United States, women of color — and especially Black women — have been receiving wages for housework for untold decades. In 1910, when over half of all Black females were working outside their homes, one-third of them were employed as paid domestic workers. By 1920 over one-half were domestic servants, and in 1930 the proportion had risen to three out of five.[32] One of the consequences of the enormous female employment shifts during World War II was a much-welcomed decline in the number of Black domestic workers. Yet in 1960 one-third of all Black women holding jobs were still confined to their traditional occupations.[33] It was not until clerical jobs became more accessible to Black women that the proportion of Black women domestics headed in a definitely downward direction. Today the figure hovers around 13 percent.[34]

The enervating domestic obligations of women in general provide flagrant evidence of the power of sexism. Because of the added intrusion of racism, vast numbers of Black women have had to do their own housekeeping and other women's home chores as well. And frequently, the demands of the job in a white woman's home have forced the domestic worker to neglect her own home and even her own children. As paid housekeepers, they have been called upon to be surrogate wives and mothers in millions of white homes.

During their more than fifty years of organizing efforts, domestic workers have tried to redefine their work by rejecting the role of the surrogate housewife. The housewife's chores are unending and undefined. Household workers have demanded in the first place a clear delineation of the jobs they are expected to perform. The name itself of one of the houseworkers' major unions today — Household Technicians of America — emphasizes their refusal to function as surrogate housewives whose job is "just housework." As long as household workers stand in the shadow of the housewife, they will continue to receive wages which are more closely related to a housewife's "allowance" than to a worker's paycheck. According to the National Committee on Household Employment, the average,

---

[32]Jackson, *op. cit.*, pp. 236–237. [Davis]

[33]Victor Perlo, *Economics of Racism U.S.A., Roots of Black Inequality* (New York: International Publishers, 1975), p. 24. [Davis]

[34]Staples, *The Black Woman in America*, p. 27. [Davis]

full-time household technician earned only $2,732 in 1976, two-thirds of them earning under $2,000.[35] Although household workers had been extended the protection of the minimum wage law several years previously, in 1976 an astounding 40 percent still received grossly substandard wages. The Wages for Housework Movement assumes that if women were paid for being housewives, they would accordingly enjoy a higher social status. Quite a different story is told by the age-old struggles of the paid household worker, whose condition is more miserable than any other group of workers under capitalism.

Over 50 percent of all U.S. women work for a living today, and they constitute 41 percent of the country's labor force. Yet countless numbers of women are currently unable to find decent jobs. Like racism, sexism is one of the great justifications for high female unemployment rates. Many women are "just housewives" because in reality they are unemployed workers. Cannot, therefore, the "just housewife" role be most effectively challenged by demanding jobs for women on a level of equality with men and by pressing for the social services (child care, for example) and job benefits (maternity leaves, etc.) which will allow more women to work outside the home?

The Wages for Housework Movement discourages women from seeking outside jobs, arguing that "slavery to an assembly line is not liberation from slavery to the kitchen sink."[36] The campaign's spokeswomen insist, nonetheless, that they don't advocate the continued imprisonment of women within the isolated environment of their homes. They claim that while they refuse to work on the capitalist market per se, they do not wish to assign to women the permanent responsibility for housework. As a U.S. representative of this movement says:

> We are not interested in making our work more efficient or more productive for capital. We are interested in reducing our work, and ultimately refusing it altogether. But as long as we work in the home for nothing, no one really cares how long or how hard we work. For capital only introduces advanced technology to cut the costs of production after wage gains by the working class. Only if we make our work cost (i.e., only if we make it uneconomical) will capital "discover" the technology to reduce it. At present, we often have to go out for a second shift of work to afford the dishwasher that should cut down our housework.[37]

Once women have achieved the right to be paid for their work, they can raise demands for higher wages, thus compelling the capitalists to under-

---

[35]*Daily World*, July 26, 1977, p. 9. [Davis]

[36]Dalla Costa and James, *op. cit.*, p. 40. [Davis]

[37]Pat Sweeney, "Wages for Housework: The Strategy for Women's Liberation," *Heresies*, January, 1977, p. 104. [Davis]

take the industrialization of housework. Is this a concrete strategy for women's liberation or is it an unrealizable dream?

How are women supposed to conduct the initial struggle for wages? *39* Dalla Costa advocates the *housewives' strike:*

> We must reject the home, because we want to unite with other women, to struggle against all situations which presume that women will stay at home . . . To abandon the home is already a form of struggle, since the social services we perform there would then cease to be carried out in those conditions.[38]

But if women are to leave the home, where are they to go? How will they unite with other women? Will they really leave their homes motivated by no other desire than to protest their housework? Is it not much more realistic to call upon women to "leave home" in search of outside jobs — or at least to participate in a massive campaign for decent jobs for women? Granted, work under the conditions of capitalism is brutalizing work. Granted, it is uncreative and alienating. Yet with all this, the fact remains that on the job, women can unite with their sisters — and indeed with their brothers — in order to challenge the capitalists at the point of production. As workers, as militant activists in the labor movement, women can generate the real power to fight the mainstay and beneficiary of sexism which is the monopoly capitalist system.

If the wages-for-housework strategy does little in the way of providing *40* a long-range solution to the problem of women's oppression, neither does it substantively address the profound discontent of contemporary housewives. Recent sociological studies have revealed that housewives today are more frustrated by their lives than ever before. When Ann Oakley conducted interviews for her book *The Sociology of Housework,*[39] she discovered that even the housewives who initially seemed unbothered by their housework eventually expressed a very deep dissatisfaction. These comments came from a woman who held an outside factory job:

> (Do you like housework?) I don't mind it . . . I suppose I don't mind housework because I'm not at it all day. I go to work and I'm only on housework half a day. If I did it all day I wouldn't like it — woman's work is never done, she's on the go all the time — even before you go to bed, you've still got something to do — emptying ashtrays, wash a few cups up. You're still working. It's the same thing every day; you can't sort of say you're not going to do it, because you've got to do it — like preparing a meal; it's got to be done because if you don't do it, the children wouldn't eat . . . I suppose you get used to it, you just do it automatically. . . . I'm happier at work than I am at home.

---

[38]Dalla Costa and James, *op. cit.,* p. 41. [Davis]

[39]Ann Oakley, *The Sociology of Housework* (New York: Pantheon Books, 1974). [Davis]

(What would you say are the worst things about being a housewife?) I suppose you get days when you feel you get up and you've got to do the same old things — you get bored, you're stuck in the same routine. I think if you ask any housewife, if they're honest, they'll turn around and say they feel like a drudge half the time — everybody thinks when they get up in the morning "Oh no, I've got the same old things to do today, till I go to bed tonight." It's doing the same things — boredom.[40]

Would wages diminish this boredom? This woman would certainly say no. A full-time housewife told Oakley about the compulsive nature of housework:

The worst thing is I suppose that you've got to do the work because you *are* at home. Even though I've got the option of not doing it, I don't really feel I *could* not do it because I feel I *ought* to do it.[41]

In all likelihood, receiving wages for doing this work would aggravate this woman's obsession.

Oakley reached the conclusion that housework — particularly when it is a full-time job — so thoroughly invades the female personality that the housewife becomes indistinguishable from her job.

The housewife, in an important sense, *is* her job: separation between subjective and objective elements in the situation is therefore intrinsically more difficult.[42]

The psychological consequence is frequently a tragically stunted personality haunted by feelings of inferiority. Psychological liberation can hardly be achieved simply by paying the housewife a wage.

Other sociological studies have confirmed the acute disillusionment suffered by contemporary housewives. When Myra Ferree[43] interviewed over a hundred women in a working community near Boston, "almost twice as many housewives as employed wives said they were dissatisfied with their lives." Needless to say, most of the working women did not have inherently fulfilling jobs: they were waitresses, factory workers, typists, supermarket and department store clerks, etc. Yet their ability to leave the isolation of their homes, "getting out and seeing other people," was as important to them as their earnings. Would the housewives who felt they were "going crazy staying at home" welcome the idea of being paid for driving themselves crazy? One woman complained that "staying at home all day is like being in jail" — would wages tear down the walls of her jail?

41

42

---

[40]*Ibid.*, p. 65. [Davis]

[41]*Ibid.*, p. 44. [Davis]

[42]*Ibid.*, p. 53. [Davis]

[43]*Psychology Today*, Vol. X, No. 4 (September, 1976), p. 76. [Davis]

The only realistic escape path from this jail is the search for work outside the home.

Each one of the more than 50 percent of all U.S. women who work today is a powerful árgument for the alleviation of the burden of housework. As a matter of fact, enterprising capitalists have already begun to exploit women's new historical need to emancipate themselves from their roles as housewives. Endless profit-making fast-food chains like McDonald's and Kentucky Fried Chicken bear witness to the fact that more women at work means fewer daily meals prepared at home. However unsavory and unnutritious the food, however exploitative of their workers, these fast-food operations call attention to the approaching obsolescence of the housewife. What is needed, of course, are new social institutions to assume a good portion of the housewife's old duties. This is the challenge emanating from the swelling ranks of women in the working class. The demand for universal and subsidized child care is a direct consequence of the rising number of working mothers. And as more women organize around the demand for more jobs — for jobs on the basis of full equality with men — serious questions will increasingly be raised about the future viability of women's housewife duties. It may well be true that "slavery to an assembly line" is not in itself "liberation from the kitchen sink," but the assembly line is doubtlessly the most powerful incentive for women to press for the elimination of their age-old domestic slavery.

The abolition of housework as the private responsibility of individual women is clearly a strategic goal of women's liberation. But the socialization of housework — including meal preparation and child care — presupposes an end to the profit-motive's reign over the economy. The only significant steps toward ending domestic slavery have in fact been taken in the existing socialist countries. Working women, therefore, have a special and vital interest in the struggle for socialism. Moreover, under capitalism, campaigns for jobs on an equal basis with men, combined with movements for institutions such as subsidized public child care, contain an explosive revolutionary potential. This strategy calls into question the validity of monopoly capitalism and must ultimately point in the direction of socialism.

REVIEW QUESTIONS

1. Why, according to Davis, does the capitalist system have a vested interest in housewives (or househusbands, for that matter) continuing to perform housework?
2. What historical forces are generating an increasing need for the "industrialization of housework"?
3. In what way did women's economic role in primitive, "pre-capitalist cultures" make them socially equal to men? How do capitalist cultures make women sub-

ordinate to men? How was the colonial period of American history like a "pre-capitalist culture," as far as women were concerned? As the United States industrialized, how did women become the losers?

4. Regarding housework, how has the experience of black women been different from that of white women? In what ways have the experiences of black women strengthened them? In what ways have they been at a disadvantage, as compared with white women?

5. Upon what assumption does the chief demand of the Wages for Housework Movement rest? How does Davis cite the Apartheid policy of the South African government to demonstrate the flaw in this assumption? Why would Lenin himself probably not have supported this demand, according to Davis?

6. How has the increasing influx of women into the workplace begun affecting other areas of American society? What other accommodations must society make to the changing role of women? Why, according to Davis, are socialist societies better equipped to make such accommodations than capitalist societies?

DISCUSSION AND WRITING QUESTIONS

1. To what extent do you recognize Davis's observations on women and housework as applicable to your own home? For example, is there an assumption in your own home that housework is "women's work"? Do you hold such an assumption? (If not, whose work *is* housework?) To what extent do you agree with Davis's conclusion that "the housewife, according to bourgeois ideology, is, quite simply, her husband's lifelong servant"?

2. In paragraph 4, Davis argues that housework need not be performed by housewives, househusbands, or paid domestics; rather, "[t]eams of trained and well-paid workers, moving from dwelling to dwelling, engineering technologically advanced cleaning machinery, could swiftly and efficiently accomplish what the present-day housewife does so arduously and primitively." Does it seem to you that this prospect is a practical one? a desirable one? Why or why not?

3. Do you believe that women should be paid for housework? If so, how do you respond to the evidence (cited by Davis) suggesting that such wages will do little or nothing to improve the lot of women? If you do not believe that women should be paid for housework, then how can society (or husbands) fairly address the inequities and injustices of the housewife as drudge?

4. Davis indicates that socialist societies are better equipped than capitalist societies to liberate women from the drudgery of housework. Conduct some research on this subject (concentrating, perhaps on one or two socialist societies), and try to assess the validity of this suggestion.

5. Compare Davis's views on the social evolution of women (from their position in primitive societies to their position in capitalist societies) with those expressed by Charlotte Perkins Gilman in paragraphs 17 and following of "The Economic Relations between Men and Women as a Factor in Social Evolution" (reprinted in Part V on The Class Struggle).

6. In what way does Davis's article illustrate the continuing effects of the class struggle, as articulated by Marx and Engels? To what extent do you believe that

Davis's arguments and evidence provide contemporary relevance and support to the ideas of Marx and Engels?

7. Research the social status of women in the Soviet Union, the People's Republic of China, or some other communist state. To what extent have these states succeeded in doing away with second-class citizenship for women? How does the situation of a particular class of women in one of these countries compare with the situation of the corresponding class of women in the United States?

JOSEPH NAHEM (b. 1917)

Marx wrote primarily about capitalism, not communism. His greatest insights concerned the operations and the deficiencies of capitalist society. For his followers it has been the same. The idea of the class struggle is frequently a compelling analytical tool for laying bare the underlying premises and conflicts of bourgeois society. It is less satisfactory in formulating a convincing alternative. That is to say, Marxism often works better in the negative mode than in the positive.

Marxist thinkers have long since extended their range beyond economics and history. There is now a substantial body of Marxist sociology, anthropology, art, literary criticism, and educational theory. Fewer Marxist inroads have been made into psychology and psychiatry. One comprehensive attempt to apply Marxist principles to these fields, however, is Joseph Nahem's *Psychology and Psychiatry Today: A Marxist View*. In his conclusion, Nahem states:

> A central theme of this book has been that capitalism is the soil which nourishes poisonous weeds in psychology and psychiatry. Social evils like the Vietnam War, Watergate, mass unemployment, unceasing inflation and racism create mass unhappiness, despair, anxiety and insecurity. People hunger for security at home and job, decent medical care, adequate wages and a feeling of self-worth. Such hunger and searching for solutions may turn people toward radical solutions such as mass struggle against the establishment and even toward a socialist solution. To fend off such strivings, the ideological superstructure furnishes escapist, subjectivist, individualism solutions in the guise of self-fulfillment of human potential. These serve to pacify and paralyze social action. . . .
>
> When asked for the single word he would use to characterize life, Karl Marx replied "Struggle." Struggle can achieve scientific advance in psychology and psychiatry. It can result in proper [and free] mental health care for all in our country. It can benefit all the people through achieving international cooperation in science, and peaceful coexistence in the world.

Joseph Nahem was born in 1917 in New York City, and served in the U.S. Army during World War II. Subsequently he completed his education at Brooklyn College, the University of Maryland, and New York University. For several years he was a public school teacher in Freeport, New York; in 1967 he began a new career as a psychologist at Maimonides Community Mental Health Center of Maimonides Hospital in Brooklyn.

Nahem's *Psychology and Psychiatry Today: A Marxist View* was published in 1981. The following passage is from the introduction to this book.

PSYCHOLOGY AND PSYCHIATRY TODAY: A MARXIST VIEW

Under capitalism, the dominant capitalist class develops an ideology   *1*
to serve its interests. Since the social and behavioral sciences exercise a
powerful influence on the thinking of people, these sciences are strongly
co-opted to serve the ideological interests of capitalism. In the United
States, we find the history of psychology rife with unscientific theories and
practices regarding working people, Black people, national minorities,
women, and the nature of human beings. Racism, chauvinism, sexism,
and anti-working-class ideas have occupied a major position in psychology
and psychiatry.

Further, the study of crucial psychological areas, such as intelligence,   *2*
behavior, motivation, the unconscious, social activity, emotions, and mental illness, are distorted and falsified by powerful class and racist influences. Although there is no such scientific split as "capitalist psychology"
and "Marxist psychology," Marxism has a considerable contribution to
make to the development of the sciences of psychology and psychiatry,
and to the understanding of their social role and significance.

The contributions of Marxism to psychology are to be found in four   *3*
areas: 1. The Marxist dialectical materialist approach to science in general
and to psychology and psychiatry specifically. 2. The Marxist historical materialist approach to the development of human beings and to society. 3.
The Marxist critique of psychology in the United States. 4. The contributions of Marxism and of Marxist psychologists to the science of
psychology. . . .

[**Editors' Note:** *See introduction to Part VI for a discussion of Hegelian and Marxist dialectics. The term "materialism" used in contrast with "idealism," refers to
the theory that social and political life, including class structure, is driven by material (economic) forces, and particularly, by those who control the means of production. The term "dialectical" refers to the process of growth and change represented by the thesis-antithesis-synthesis pattern. Historical materialism is the
application of dialectical materialist principles to the study of history and sociology.
Here, Nahem extends this application to psychology and psychiatry.*]

Joseph Nahem. Psychology and Psychiatry Today: A Marxist View [1981]. Originally titled
"Introduction." In *Psychology and Psychiatry Today: A Marxist View*. New York: International
Publishers, 1981.

DIALECTICAL MATERIALISM AND PSYCHOLOGY

Science . . . is guided by a philosophy of science, an overall view of nature, the universe and human society. Such a philosophy must include two aspects: a theory of the world and a method of approach to studying reality. More specifically, science operates, overtly or covertly, with a materialist or idealist view of the world, and with a dialectical or mechanical approach to reality. *4*

Illustrative of the materialist v. idealist theory of the world is the story that, when Napoleon asked the French astronomer Laplace[1] where God fit in his theory of the solar system, he replied, "I had no need of that hypothesis, Sire." Laplace's theory was based only on natural law, not on the Biblical story of Creation. *5*

The dialectical v. mechanical approach is exemplified in Pavlov's[2] rejection of the mechanistic view that all animals, including human beings are like machines. Pavlov identified the *qualitative* difference between humans and animals in the possession by humans of a second signal system, i.e., speech, which was "the latest acquisition in the process of evolution."[3] *6*

Marxism is rooted in the philosophy of dialectical materialism. Its materialist viewpoint excludes religious, supernatural or idealist views. Thus, in psychology, it excludes the idea of a supernatural soul as explanatory of human behavior. *7*

Materialism itself has been the basis for scientific development throughout history. Materialism was the philosophy which was openly espoused by science in its rapid development after the Middle Ages. Marxism founded its overall theory and philosophy on the materialist tradition. *8*

Marxist dialectics were developed by Marx and Engels as the most general laws of nature, society and human thought. These general laws, which were derived from science and its specific laws, call for seeking the laws of change, both quantitative and qualitative, and for the uncovering of the relationships and interdependence of phenomena. Further, the unity and contradiction in phenomena must be ascertained. Engels called for the pursuit of truth by the positive sciences "and for the summation of their results by dialectical thinking." *9*

---

[1]*Laplace:* Pierre Simon, the Marquis de Laplace (1749–1827).

[2]*Pavlov:* Ivan Petrovich Pavlov (1849–1936), the Russian physiologist, is best known for his demonstration of the conditioned reflex. Just before bringing food to his dog, he would ring a bell; after a time, the dog would begin salivating whenever the bell was rung, even if no food was brought. The experiment demonstrated that an associational, or secondary, stimulus (the sound of the bell) can, in time, evoke the same response as the primary stimulus (the food).

[3]Pavlov, I.P., *Selected Works,* Foreign Languages Publishing House, Moscow, 1955, pp. 536–537. [Nahem]

Marxism believes that science has advanced by fighting off religious-idealist views and mechanical-metaphysical approaches. Marxists believe that science would benefit if it *consciously* adopted dialectical materialism as the philosophy of science and as a methodology for research. . . .

Psychology has . . . had to fight the battle between mechanical and dialectical approaches. Marx and Engels overcame mechanical, static materialism by combining materialism with dialectics. They held that the world is to be comprehended as a complex of *processes* which go through an uninterrupted change of coming into being and passing away. Further, science must study phenomena in their unity and conflict and in their interrelation and interdependence. All phenomena must be seen, they maintained, in their quantitative change leading to qualitative change.[4]

From this dialectical viewpoint, behaviorism in psychology, such as the theories of J.B. Watson[5] or B.F. Skinner,[6] must be criticized as mechanical, as the reduction of the *psychological* process of human functioning to the *physiological* process of behavior alone. Behaviorism, carried to extremes, has led to unscientific — and reactionary — theories, such as Behavior Modification which uses unethical and even brutal means to change behavior.

On the other hand, we have the metaphysical theory of Freudianism, which focuses on an unconscious mind, divorced from social and individual reality and consciousness, which is seen as the basic source determining human affect, attitude and behavior. Scientific psychology must reject the general theories of both Behaviorism and Freudianism. It must seek to show the dialectical relationship between social and individual reality, between thought, consciousness, unconscious processes, emotion, attitude and behavior.

Along with the contributions of Marxist dialectical materialism . . . , Karl Marx also provided a significant contribution to psychology in his development of the concept of human alienation. Marx rooted alienation in the very process of capitalist production itself.[7] Marx saw the worker as alienated from the product of his labor and from work itself because, since

10

11

12

13

14

---

[4]Engels, F., *Ludwig Feuerbach,* International Publishers, New York, 1941, pp. 44–46. [Nahem]

[5]*J.B. Watson:* (1878–1958) The U.S. psychologist responsible for popularizing behaviorism, the study of behavior as an essentially biological science. Nahem believes that this behavioristic approach to psychology is overly mechanistic because it reduces all behavior to automatic responses dictated by stimuli and rewards, while disregarding the influence of higher psychological processes and social relations.

[6]*B.F. Skinner:* A behaviorist psychologist. See selection by Skinner in Part VII, on The Power of the Unconscious.

[7]Marx, Karl, *The Economic and Philosophic Manuscripts of 1844.* International Publishers, New York, 1964. [Nahem]

the product belongs to the capitalist, his work is "forced labor . . . not his own, but someone else's."[8] Further, workers are estranged from their true nature as *human* beings because their work and its product are alien to them. They cannot feel a oneness with nature and society. Alienation is, therefore intrinsic to capitalism and the private ownership of the means of production. Hence, the basis for its elimination, in the long run, is the replacement of capitalism by socialism.

Even under capitalism, however, Marx saw that workers could combat   15
alienation through associating together to fight for their class interest:

> (T)he most splendid results are to be observed whenever French socialist work-
> ers are seen together. Such things as smoking, drinking, eating, etc., are no
> longer means of contact or means that bring together. Company, association,
> and conversation, which again has society at its end, are enough for them; the
> brotherhood of man is no mere phrase with them, but a fact of life, and the
> nobility of man shines upon us from their work-hardened bodies.[9]

Marxism is based upon science. Its philosophy is derived from science   16
and provides a basis for the evaluation and interpretation of scientific theories, areas of research, and methodology. Dialectical materialism has particular importance for psychology since epistemology[10] and psychology are
intertwined. Marxist epistemology can be a valuable guide and approach
for the science of psychology.

HISTORICAL MATERIALISM AND PSYCHOLOGY

Historical materialism is the application of dialectical materialism to the   17
origin, development and functioning of human society. Marx and Engels
adopted an historical approach to the investigation of the origins of life, of
human beings, and of human society.[11] They supported the view, rooted
in materialist philosophy, that life arose from inanimate matter as a new
and qualitatively different mode of existence of matter. Evolutionary development, as confirmed by Darwin, led to the appearance of multifarious
species of plants and animals, proceeding from lower to higher stages of
living organisms.

With the appearance of primates, who had the ability to make and   18

---

[8]*Ibid.*, pp. 110–111. [Nahem]

[9]*Ibid.*, pp. 154–155. [Nahem]

[10]*epistemology:* That branch of philosophy which investigates the nature of knowledge and
knowing.

[11]See Marx, K., and Engels, F., *The German Ideology*, International Publishers, New York,
1939; Engels, F., "On the Role of Labor in the Transition from Ape to Man," *Dialectics of
Nature, op. cit.*, Chapter IX. [Nahem]

utilize tools for the production of the necessities of life, a new stage of development occurred. Cooperative social labor with tools led to the development of articulate speech as a means of communication and thought. Thus, social labor based upon tool-making and tool-using produced speech and language. Human consciousness and mind, based upon speech and language, are seen as produced through the development of social labor and material production.[11] As Marx and Engels placed it: "The premises from which we begin are . . . real individuals, their activity and the material conditions under which they live. . . . Men can be distinguished from animals by consciousness, by religion or anything you like. They themselves begin to distinguish themselves from animals as they begin to *produce* their means of subsistence. . . ."[12]

Marxist historical materialism analyzed the development of human society as proceeding from the primitive communism of the first stage of human development, through the societies of slavery, feudalism, capitalism and socialism.[13] Society is, hence, not static and repetitive, but changes dialectically throughout its history.   19

Such changes in human society are the result of changes occurring in social being. The mode of production consists of the productive forces and the social relations of production, i.e., how people are related to each other in production — as classes or in communal relations. Changes in society are due to changes in the productive forces, which then lead to changes in the relations of production. Thus, the feudal mode of production had certain productive forces and class relations of production made up of the landlord feudal master and the exploited self producer.   20

With the development of the productive forces, especially the tools and instruments of production, new classes, the capitalists and the exploited workers, arose and changed the feudal relations of production to capitalist relations of production through revolution (e.g., the French Revolution of 1789).   21

The materialist conception of history further holds that there arises an ideological superstructure on the economic foundation of society. Thus, the capitalist production relations produce a capitalist ideological superstructure, which serves the interests of the capitalist economic foundation. Similarly, a socialist foundation produces a socialist superstructure. Thus, social consciousness does not produce nor explain social being, but vice versa. As Engels wrote: "From this point of view the final causes of all social changes and political revolutions are to be sought, not in men's   22

---

[12]*The German Ideology, ibid.*, pp. 6–7. [Nahem]

[13]See Cornforth, Maurice, *Historical Materialism*, International Publishers, New York, 1954. [Nahem]

brains, not in man's better insight into eternal truth and justice, but in changes in the modes of production and exchange.[14]

In class society, the dominant views, ideology and philosophy are   23
those of the dominant class. Since the social and behavioral sciences are of great influence in the formation of the ideology and beliefs in capitalist society, these sciences cannot be viewed as pure sciences, separated from social or class interests. They must be analyzed as being also shaped, influenced, and distorted by the class which controls the government, the educational and university system, the commercial media, and the wealth to subsidize specific views and ideology. Hence, psychology cannot be viewed as a neutral science, unaffected by class interests. A racist theory such as that of psychologist Arthur Jensen,[15] which concludes that Black people are genetically inferior in intelligence to white people, can be understood as an instrument of a capitalist class for continued superexploitation of Black working people and as a major means of dividing white and Black people.

Psychology, from the viewpoint of historical materialism, must be seen   24
as playing an ideological role in the capitalist superstructure. Its scientific role continues alongside its ideological role but such a scientific role is limited and underdeveloped because of the class nature of capitalism.

Socialism, like all societies, also produces its own superstructure.   25
However, since socialist relations of production are classless, there is no dominant class to control and distort psychology. Under socialism, psychology plays a role of advancing socialist society through its own scientific development. Obstacles to such development are, hence, not of a class nature, but are due to the youth and complexity of psychology as a science.

Historical materialism provides for psychology a materialist approach   26
to human and social development. It provides a scientific analysis of the class role that psychology plays under capitalism. It emphasizes the class character of capitalism and the importance of class status for the psychology of individuals. It analyzes the psychological effect of class ideology on human thought, attitude and behavior. It gives paramount importance to human consciousness as opposed to the role of unconscious processes in individual functioning. It explains alienation, not on an existentialist basis of loneliness and social isolation, but on the precise process of capitalist production. Psychology can, indeed, benefit from an historical materialist approach.

---

[14]Engels, Frederick, *Socialism, Utopian and Scientific,* International Publishers, New York, 1935, p. 26. [Nahem]

[15]*Arthur Jensen:* (b. 1923) In February 1969, this University of California psychologist aroused a storm of controversy with an article published in the *Harvard Educational Review* in which he concluded that the IQ scores of black children can be boosted very little, owing (he claimed) to the genetic inferiority of blacks.

THE MARXIST CRITIQUE OF PSYCHOLOGY

The science of psychology has made important progress in various 27
areas. However, as previously discussed, psychology has been hindered
or distorted in its development by idealist or metaphysical philosophical
views and theories. It has been dominated by an unhistorical and undialectical view of the development of human society and its relation to individual development. Moreover, the ideological superstructure of capitalism has developed major features that have saturated the social and
behavioral sciences. These features have penetrated and shaped much of
the development of psychology. They include the following:

1. *Anti-working-class ideology.* Capitalist ideology has always depicted 28
workers as unintelligent, unwashed, crude, simple-minded, and inferior.
The social and behavioral sciences have mainly ignored the true reality of
working people, their positive traits, their social and class struggles, their
mutual support of each other, and their social strivings. With certain exceptions, when studies have been made of working people, they arrive at
conclusions which support the capitalist stereotype of the coarse, stupid,
passive, selfish individual. It is no accident that a central feature of the
massive fraud perpetrated by psychologist Cyril Burt[16] upon the psychological world, was that he had "proved" that workers were inferior in intelligence to middle and upper class people.

In psychiatry, working people are considered to be difficult patients 29
because they lack the awareness and insight of "higher" classes. In public
education in the United States, a complex system of tracking exists, whose
main purpose and effect have been to prevent working people, Black people and national minorities from gaining advanced education. Educational
tracking sets up different tracks (classes) for children: bright, average,
slow, disturbed, hyperactive, etc.

The result of such tracking has been to provide an uneducated pool of 30
working people, Blacks, Hispanic, and other minorities for dirty, menial
and superexploited jobs or for a reserve army of unemployed. Many psychological theories have been developed to justify such an educational
tracking system: homogeneous classes, career opportunity (for dishwash-
ing, clerical, housekeeping work), environmental deprivation, cultural disadvantage, Black matriarchy.

2. *Racism.* The early development of capitalism in our country was 31

---

[16]*Cyril Burt:* (1883–1971) British sociologist, upon whom Arthur Jensen drew, who believed
that intelligence was inherited and that rich children were inherently brighter than poor
children. His theories were largely responsible for the three-level educational tracking system adopted in Britain during the 20th century and were also influential in the United
States. In the 1970s, Burt's studies were revealed to be fraudulent: he had invented much
of his crucial data.

marked — and marred — by slavery and by the ideology of the slaveown-
ers. After the Civil War and the freeing of the slaves, racism became a
major and basic ideological instrument for capitalist super-profit and division of working people. Psychology has served these venal class interests
by providing racist theories of the inferiority of Black people. Thus, Jensen's theory of Black genetic intellectual inferiority is a stain on the science
of psychology. Daniel Moynihan's[17] theory of psychiatric disturbance of
Black children due to "the Black matriarchy" has done its racist dirty work
in the field of psychiatry. Psychological testing instruments, such as the
standardized IQ Tests (Stanford-Binet and WISC), are used for racist assignment of Black children to classes for retarded, brain-damaged and
emotionally disturbed, in hugely disproportionate numbers. Racism has
soaked through the entire fabric of psychology and psychiatry.

3. *National chauvinism.* Since working people in the United States in-   32
clude many national minorities, especially large numbers of Chicanos, La-
tino and West Indian people, national chauvinist theories and practices
abound in our country. Rather than a "Melting Pot," our ideological superstructure has fostered harsh prejudices and discrimination against for-
eign-born working people and against most national minorities.

Psychology has played a divisive role in many instances by providing   33
the rationalization for such prejudices and their accompanying discrimi-
natory practices. Thus, the Wechsler Intelligence Scale for Children (WISC)
is routinely used to test Hispanic children, although it is culturally and
linguistically inappropriate and heavily penalizes bi-lingual children. It is
an educational fact that Hispanic children are disproportionally placed in
special classes, to their serious educational harm. The same psychological
theories used against Black children — disadvantaged, deprived, sensorily
immature, a fatherless home — are also applied to national minorities, especially to the poor and to working people.

4. *Sexism and male supremacy.* Division of working people along sex   34
lines is also a basic feature of U.S. capitalist ideology. This ideology of the
inferiority of women corresponds to and justifies the unequal economic,
social and political status of women in our country.

Sexism in psychiatric theory and practice is rife. Freud's basic theory   35
is male supremacist to the extreme: women are hysterical, passive, strange,
filled with penis envy, hyperemotional, more neurotic, and have weaker
personalities, according to Freud.

Black women are victimized by both racism and sexism in both psy-   36
chology and psychiatry. Children's problems are systematically blamed on
the mother. Therapy is used to lead the woman to accept the destiny pro-

---

[17]*Daniel Moynihan:* (b. 1927) American sociologist, diplomat, and, since 1977, U.S. Senator
from New York.

vided by her anatomy.[18] Although the surge of the women's Liberation movement has mounted a counteroffensive against sexism in psychology and psychiatry, psychological theory and practice are still dominated by sexism, and psychology has only made a beginning in the scientific understanding of women in our society.

5. *Human Nature.* The ideological superstructure in the United States   *37* is shot through with theories that human nature is fixed and unchanging, that it is greedy, selfish, aggressive, untrustworthy, warlike, prejudiced, lustful and lazy. Psychology and psychiatry provide the high-sounding theories to justify such a judgment of human nature. Witness the theory of Freud that we have a warlike and destructive drive (thanatos) in our biological inheritance. The theory of Stanley Milgram[19] that we will knowingly and willingly inflict pain on others falls into the same category. B.F. Skinner puts down human beings by considering them to be on the same level as animals, responding only to response-reward programming of their entire lives. Konrad Lorenz[20] achieved fame through his theory of innate human aggressiveness,[21] while Edward Wilson[22] attributes animal behavior and instincts to human beings in his theory of sociobiology.[23]

If human nature is both evil and unchanging, then racism, aggression,   *38* poverty and war are basically inevitable and cannot be attributed to the social system. Thus, this theory of fixed and evil human nature has a class basis which has negatively influenced psychology.

6. *Individualism and Subjectivism.* Capitalist ideology is filled with indi-   *39* vidualism and subjectivism. This ideology has flooded the social sciences, including psychology. Freudianism is a prime example of a subjective,

---

[18]Freud stated about women: "Anatomy is destiny." ("Some Psychological Consequences of the Anatomical Distinction between the Sexes," *International Journal of Psychoanalysis,* 1927.) [Nahem]

[19]*Stanley Milgram:* (1933–1984) During the early 1960s, psychologist Stanley Milgram conducted a series of controversial experiments on obedience to authority. The experiments revealed that ordinary, law-abiding citizens are capable of inflicting intense pain on other people if ordered to do so by an authority figure.

[20]*Konrad Lorenz:* (b. 1903) An Austrian zoologist and ethologist, his studies on the instinctual behavior of animals and humans led him to form a rather controversial theory on the innate nature of human aggression. Nahem disagrees with Lorenz's theory because the latter implies that human nature is fixed and remains unaffected by dynamic elements in internal and social processes.

[21]Lorenz, Konrad, *On Aggression,* Harcourt Brace, New York, 1966. [Nahem]

[22]*Edward Osborne Wilson* (b. 1922) A U.S. biologist, he is a major proponent of the study of sociobiology, a branch of sociology founded on the theory that human social behavior is directed by the necessities of genetic evolution rather than by more humanistic motives such as thought or will.

[23]Wilson, Edward O., *Sociobiology: The New Synthesis,* Harvard University Press, Cambridge, 1975; *On Human Nature,* Harvard University Press, Cambridge, 1978. [Nahem]

non-social approach to the human mind and behavior: biological instincts operating through drives, complexes, defences and unconscious motivation, isolate each individual from his social existence and explain normal and abnormal behavior in subjective fashion. The Human Potential movement has carried individualism and subjectivism to extremes. The individual is thrown back on feelings and attitudes, divorced from their social context. "Est"[24] is an openly subjective idealist theory which ends up with each individual creating the world and merely experiencing this subjective world at the present moment.

This latest onslaught on human reason, on collective action, on consciousness and knowledge is a reflection of capitalism in its decaying state. Est is the most exaggerated version of the capitalist thrust to compel people to accept the world as it is, to consider it perfect and to be happy doing just what they are doing.   40

Capitalism also utilizes individualism to "blame the victim." Thus, we find theories in psychology that the poor provide their own environment of poverty, so *they* are to blame.   41

7. *False or one-sided theories.* The history of science is filled with false theories, such as the theory that the sun moves around the earth, or that bleeding a physically ill patient will be beneficial. Some false theories may be considered a natural feature of young and developing sciences. The proving of a scientific theory requires careful observation, correct experimentation, accurate interpretation and valid conclusions. Speculation and hypothesizing are necessary for constructing and proving — or disproving — a theory. In this complex process of arriving at confirmed theories regarding a complex reality, false and one-sided theories arise.   42

However, in class society, many theories are put forth, not in order to prove a scientific theory, but because they serve the interest of the dominant class. Thus, false theories regarding working people, Black people, women, national minorities and human nature are false propaganda, and unscientific. The famous example of Galileo[25] being forced by the Inquisition to disown his correct scientific theory about the movement of the earth around the sun is illustrative of this deliberate misuse of science.   43

One-sided theories in psychology and psychiatry are the rule and not the exception in capitalist society. Even the common definition of psychology as "the science of behavior" is one-sided since it leaves out thought,   44

---

[24]*Est*: Literally "it is" in Latin, EST is the acronym for Erhard Seminar and Training, a mental health program designed to enable its participants to live more fulfilling lives by teaching them to see their potentials and goals without comparison with societal values. According to Nahem, this subjective introspection is useless (if not impossible to achieve) because it denies human's social nature and circumstances.

[25]*Galileo*: See selections by Galileo and the Inquisition office in Part II.

emotion, relations, activity, and individual history. The common term for mental disturbance is "emotional illness," when, of course, mental illness also affects cognition, behavior, attitude, work ability, and relationships. The behaviorism of Skinner centers on only one feature of functioning: behavior. Sensitivity training focuses on "the here-and-now," to the unscientific exclusion of the "then-and-there." Skinner hypostasizes positive reinforcement, while ignoring thought, judgement, feeling.

False theories and one-sided theories are due to both class influence   45
and to narrow and undialectical approaches in psychology and psychiatry in the United States.

THE CONTRIBUTIONS OF MARXISM

The contributions of Marxist dialectical and historical materialism to   46
psychology and psychiatry and the Marxist critique of these sciences in a class society have already been presented. Marxism has a number of features and emphases that it believes will help advance the science of psychology:

1. Marxism rejects as invalid and unscientific all theories of intellec-   47
tual, emotional or behavioral inferiority of race, class, sex or national minority. It emphasizes the crucial importance of studying *human* development in the concrete reality of its existence, social and individual.

2. Marxism approaches the human mind and consciousness as a prod-   48
uct of the brain and central nervous system. It highlights the highly significant role of language as a means of communication, thought, and regulation of behavior. The work of Soviet psychologists Lev Vygotsky[26] and Alexander Luria[27] on the role of language has helped to advance psychological knowledge in this area.[28]

3. Marxism stresses the important relationship of the individual to so-   49
ciety. The psychology of individuals in the United States must be examined in the context of a class society with a specific — capitalist — superstructure. The effects of the ideological superstructure on the individual's psy-

---

[26]*Lev Vygotsky:* (1896–1934) One of the founders of modern psychology in the USSR, he argued that humans engage consciously and voluntarily in higher psychological processes which are developed interpersonally and are intimately connected with language and other signs or tools.

[27]*Alexander Luria:* (b. 1902) A Russian psychologist and neuropsychologist whose work included studies on the role of speech (a socially developed and determined process) in the organization of human behavior.

[28]Vygotsky, Lev, *Thought and Language*, John Wiley, New York, 1962; Luria, Alexander, "Speech Development and the Formation of Mental Processes," in *A Handbook of Contemporary Soviet Psychology*, Eds., Cole, Michael and Maltzman, Irving, Basic Books, New York, 1969. [Nahem]

chology is of vital significance in psychological study. Similarly, the changes in the psychology of individuals in a socialist society must be seen within the context of the many changes occurring in the transformation of capitalist society to socialist society.

4. Marxism sees the science of psychology as playing an important   50
role in advancing human development. The uncovering of laws of human psychological development can be of great value to education, to human personality, to the formation of character, and to the expansion of human abilities.

5. Marxism emphasizes that psychology and psychiatry are sciences   51
which need to be advanced through careful, meticulous, comprehensive scientific work. The scientific work being carried out under socialism is exemplified in the volume *A Handbook of Contemporary Soviet Psychology*[29] which contains articles on progress attained in areas of developmental, abnormal, and social psychology, general experimental psychology, and higher nervous activity.

6. Science is international in scope and requires the best efforts of sci-   52
entists in all countries for its full progress. International cooperation in the fields of psychology and psychiatry is of vital importance for these sciences. Such cooperation is particularly important for scientists in socialist and capitalist countries, since they have much to learn from each other.

7. Marxism believes that science advances through struggle, both sci-   53
entific and social. Healthy controversy and debate within the field is necessary and welcome and can contribute towards the rejection of false theories and the correction of one-sided theories. Social struggle against racist and reactionary ideology in the guise of scientific psychological theories can lead to their exposure.

8. Marxism believes that a socialist society can produce great changes   54
in people's psychological health and welfare. The provision of full, comprehensive, available, free health and mental health care is guaranteed under socialism. Likewise, the guarantee of employment, social security, education, equal opportunity, facilities for working mothers, equal pay, and an ever-expanding economic and social system provide psychological security for people under socialism.

---

[29]*Ibid.* [Nahem]

REVIEW QUESTIONS

1. In what areas pertinent to psychology and psychiatry have "class and racist" ideas been most influential?
2. To what view of the world (and of science, in particular) is dialectical materialism

opposed? Why does dialectical materialism reject the theories of Freud and B.F. Skinner? From a dialectical materialist standpoint, what are the sources of alienation?

3. In a socialist society, why is there "no dominant class to control and distort psychology," as in capitalist society?

4. What are the major ideological features of capitalism that affect the social and behavioral sciences, according to Nahem?

5. Why is the theory that human nature is fixed and unchangeable contrary to the premises of Marxist psychology? By the same token, why does such a theory support capitalist ideology?

DISCUSSION AND WRITING QUESTIONS

1. Nahem states that "social consciousness does not produce nor explain social being, but vice versa." He goes on to explain how the dominant class produces an ideology, disseminated through the media, the government, and educational institutions, to support its own class interests. Write an essay in which you discuss the *psychological* implications of this process, as you see it occurring in contemporary American culture. In other words, discuss the effect of capitalist social consciousness on individual consciousness — and individual neuroses.

2. In the section entitled "The Marxist Critique of Psychology," Nahem provides numerous examples of how psychological theories of capitalist society have been used to support such pernicious doctrines as racism and sexism. Explore one of these examples — for instance, the theories of Arthur Jensen, Daniel Moynihan's theory of "black matriarchy," or the "male-supremacist" theories of Freud — and show that Nahem is either justified or unjustified in making this particular charge.

3. In the section entitled "The Contributions of Marxism," Nahem suggests some ways in which a Marxist approach to psychology could be beneficial. Select the contribution that you believe would be the *most* beneficial both to individuals and to society and explain: (1) why you believe this contribution to be the most important; (2) why a Marxist rather than a capitalist approach would be superior in this particular area.

4. If you object to Nahem's assertions in one or more sections of this passage, explain your objections and present your own arguments in rebuttal.

5. This passage may have been difficult for you to read because of Nahem's heavy reliance on Marxist terminology, or specialized vocabulary (jargon). What examples of Marxist terminology do you find? To what extent, if any, does this specialized vocabulary diminish the effectiveness of Nahem's critique? What are the working assumptions behind Nahem's arguments?

MAX EASTMAN *(1883–1969)*

Critiques of Marxism are, of course, legion, and nowhere more than in the United States, the country with the most to lose from a class struggle. Somewhat less common, though by no means unusual, are critiques of Marxism from people who once identified themselves as Marxists, or at least as sympathetic to Marxist goals. (One of the most celebrated such critiques is *The New Class* (1957) by Milovan Djilas, once the vice president of communist Yugoslavia; Djilas argued that the old capitalist class in countries like the U.S.S.R. had simply been replaced by a new class, the political bureaucracy, which had appropriated all the wealth and power of its predecessors.) Most unusual of all are critiques of Marxism from such people that additionally show penetrating insight into human nature and that are powerfully and elegantly written. Such a critique is the following by Max Eastman.

Eastman was born in Canandagua, New York, in 1883; both his parents were Congregational ministers. After graduating from the Mercersberg Academy in Pennsylvania as class valedictorian, he went on to Williams College in Williamstown, Massachusetts, where he edited the college yearbook and worked on the college literary magazine. From 1907 to 1911, he taught logic and philosophy at Columbia University; subsequently, he completed all the requirements for a Ph.D. but chose not to take his degree. Eastman began developing his radical inclinations at Columbia, where in 1910 he organized the Men's League for Women's Suffrage. Upon leaving Columbia, he lived in Greenwich Village and became an influential center of the radical intellectual life there. The cultural atmosphere that Eastman breathed has been described by David Boroff in an article in the *National Observer*:

> The radicals of the teens and twenties of this century were homegrown, the legitimate heirs of New England conscience, nineteenth century utopianism, and ministerial passion. . . . The Russian revolution seemed to them the fulfillment of their humanitarian dreams. But their world had a gaiety and speciousness about it. Its inhabitants were a cohesive group — Bohemian, enchanted by art, tireless in talk, intoxicated by everything. The puritan sourness and schismatic wrangling of communism came later.

Eastman founded and edited the *Masses,* a socialist magazine, for which John Reed also wrote. After the magazine was suppressed by the federal government for opposing U.S. intervention in World War I, Eastman, with three other staff members, including Reed, was tried twice for sedition, both trials ending in hung juries. Subsequently, he founded the *Liberator,* a magazine similar to the *Masses.*

Eastman visited the Soviet Union from 1922 to 1924, becoming friends with Leon Trotsky and marrying Eliena Krylenko, the sister of the Soviet Minister of Justice (she was the second of his three wives). However, a closer look at the inner workings of the Soviet Union and the people who ran it began to disillusion Eastman with communism; he was particularly appalled at the means by which Stalin gained power after Lenin's death. Returning to the United States (after a three-year sojourn in France), Eastman began writing books about his disenchantment with the U.S.S.R., criticizing the unscientific nature of Soviet Marxism; these included *Since Lenin Died* (1925), *Artists in Uniform* (1934; about Marxist restrictions on art in the Soviet Union), *The End of Socialism in Russia* (1937), and *Stalin's Russia and the Crisis in Socialism* (1939). Eastman's recantation earned him undying hostility and villification from the Communist International and his former colleagues.

But Eastman had other interests, in particular, poetry and humor. As early as 1913 he had written *The Enjoyment of Poetry*, a standard work that has never since gone out of print. *The Literary Mind: Its Place in an Age of Science* appeared in 1931, and was greeted with high praise by Edmund Wilson and other critics; Eastman's *Enjoyment of Laughter* (another acclaimed work) appeared in 1936. In 1941, he became a roving editor for *The Reader's Digest* (a bastion of traditional American values), writing on whatever took his fancy. Other works by Eastman included *Heroes I Have Known* (1942), *Enjoyment of Living* (1948), *Poems of Five Decades* (1954), *Great Companions: Critical Memoirs of Some Famous Friends* (1959), *Love and Revolution: My Journey through an Epoch* (1965), and translations of some of Trotsky's books. In an interview with *The New York Times*, Eastman explained that he had reluctantly given up the idea of revolution as a cure for the ills of society: "We have to patch up the world as it is and accept it, although I don't feel very happy about it." Eastman died in Bridgetown, Barbados, in 1969.

The following selection is from Eastman's *Reflections on the Failure of Socialism* (1955). Of Eastman's anti-Soviet writing, Edmund Wilson wrote, "The prose of these books has a clarity and terseness of form, an intellectual edge, which would be hard to match."

Note: Was it the February Revolution or the March Revolution? The October Revolution or the November Revolution? In reading different accounts of the Russian Revolution, readers will encounter puzzling discrepancies in the dates of key events. For example, in paragraph 3 of the following passage, Eastman refers to the fall of Kerensky's government in October 1917, whereas most other accounts (including Lawson's edition of Reed) cite November as the date of this event. (On the other hand, Sergei Eisenstein's celebrated 1927 film version of Reed's book is entitled *October, or Ten Days That Shook the World*.) The map on page 581 comes from a book entitled *Russia 1917: The February Revolution*. But most westerners refer to the March Revolution. These discrepancies result from a difference of approximately two weeks between the Gregorian calendar (established by Pope Gregory XIII in 1582 and followed by all western nations since the 18th century) and the Julian calendar (established by Julius Caesar and followed by Russia until 1918).

SOCIALISM AND HUMAN NATURE

Why did the benign dream of Fourier[1] and Owen,[2] when made plausible by the rationalizations of Marx and dynamic by the engineering genius of Lenin, turn into a nightmare? I think the reason, if you go to the depth of it, is single and very simple. It is because these men and all their tens of millions of followers, notwithstanding their bold scorn of superstition and firm determination to be realistic, had a naive and romantic conception of what a man is. *1*

Both the utopians and Karl Marx did their thinking before psychology as we know it, or anthropology, or even biology in its modern form, was born. And Lenin, as I said, did no theoretic thinking that passed beyond Karl Marx. Lenin was only twenty years old when William James published his epoch-making *Psychology*,[3] but there is not a sign in his writing that he ever read so much as the title of an elementary textbook in this developing science. *2*

In October 1917, after the news came that Kerensky's government had fled, and the Winter Palace[4] had fallen to his insurrectionary troops, Lenin, who had been in hiding, appeared at a meeting of the Workers' and Soldiers' Soviet of Petrograd. He walked rapidly up the aisle, mounted the rostrum, and when the long, wild, happy shouts of greeting had died down, remarked: *3*

"We will now proceed to the construction of a socialist society." *4*

He said this as simply as though he were proposing to put up a new barn for the cows or a modern hen house. But in all his life he had never asked himself the equally simple question: *5*

"How is this ingenious invention going to fit with the instinctive tendencies of the animals it is made for?" *6*

Max Eastman. Socialism and Human Nature [1955]. In *Reflections on the Failure of Socialism.* New York: Devin-Adair, 1955.

[1]*Fourier:* François Marie Charles Fourier (1772–1837), a French socialist who proposed that small cooperative groups were the best means of assuring economic and social justice. His disciples established Brook Farm (1841–1847), a cooperative community in Massachusetts.

[2]*Owen:* Robert Owen (1771–1858), British manufacturer and social reformer who inspired a number of collectivist communities in England and the United States during the 19th century. In 1825, Owen founded New Harmony, a "utopian" collectivist community in Indiana. See introduction to the speeches by Debs in this part.

[3]*Psychology:* William James's book *The Principles of Psychology* (1890) provided psychologists with a summation of historical developments in psychology up to the current time, while serving, in many ways, as the precursor of later developments. The book became a basic text of psychology shortly after its publication.

[4]*Winter Palace:* See note 18 on p. 586.

The idea had never entered Lenin's head that men, like other animals,   *7*
might *have* instinctive tendencies. He actually knew less about this subject,
after a hundred years, than Robert Owen did. Owen had described human
nature fairly well for an amateur as "a compound of animal propensities,
intellectual faculties and moral qualities." He had written into the preamble of the Constitution of New Harmony[5] that "Man's character . . . is the
result of his formation, his location, and of the circumstances within which
he exists." He merely omitted to think about that factor of man's "formation" — what we call his hereditary nature — until his wish had time to
convince him that "location" and "circumstance" could do everything.
Plant people in a cooperative society young enough, he persuaded himself,
and they will grow up just, reasonable, truthful, magnanimous — they will
grow up *cooperative.*

To say nothing of science, it would seem a mere matter of common   *8*
sense, if you wanted to improve upon Owen's system, to go down into the
details and find out something a little more exact and reliable about "man's
character." If the thing had happened in England or France, that would
probably have been the next step. But it happened in Germany, and the
natural procedure was to fly up out of the details into the empyrean. Instead of a more circumspect plan for progress, we got a system of philosophy in which progress was incidental. Marx *deduced* socialism from a theory of the universe which he had learned at school, and which happened
to be fashionable at the moment. For this reason, with all the great talk
about advancing from "utopian" to "scientific," Marx took a long step
backward from Robert Owen's comparatively sensible approach to his
problem. He dropped out "formation" or "propensity" — the problem of
man's hereditary nature — altogether. He dropped out man altogether, so
far as he might present an obstacle to social change.

"Man," he said, "is a complex of social relations . . . The individual   *9*
has no real existence outside the milieu in which he lives." By which he
meant: *Change the social relations, change the milieu, and man will change as
much as you like.* "All history," he added, "is nothing but a continual transformation of human nature."

That is all Marx ever said on this primary, and in a scientific mind,   *10*
preliminary, question. And Lenin, I repeat, said nothing. That is why their
dream turned into a nightmare. That is the rock-bottom reason. Their
scheme was amateur — and worse than amateur, mystical — on the very
subject most essential to its success.

To be sure, we cannot jump in with a pretense that we know much   *11*
about the subject even now. The science of human behavior is still in its
infancy. Biology, anthropology, sociology, psychology — they have hardly

---

[5]*New Harmony:* (1825–1827) See note 2 on Robert Owen, above.

even joined forces yet, or agreed upon a common language. They have, however, a valid mode of approach and certain concepts to which any man seriously concerned with social change must give attention. As a studious reader of these sciences, I will venture to mention four or five of these concepts, which I think largely explain why, instead of the New Harmony he expected, Lenin produced the horrors of a totalitarian state.

It is not that men are greedy or acquisitive merely. Both men and women, and especially the youth, were sacrificial of this world's goods in both Lenin's Russia and Hitler's Germany to the point of sainthood and in droves. Those wiseacres who used to growl about the greediness of men, and say on that ground, "You socialists don't know anything about human nature!" really didn't know very much more than we did. It wouldn't have hurt either of us to study the subject. 12

Man is, to begin with, the most plastic and adaptable of animals. He truly can be changed by his environment, and even by himself, to a unique degree, and that makes extreme ideas of progress reasonable. On the other hand he inherits, besides "animal propensities" in the crude sense, a set of emotional drives or impulses — the word instinct is a risky one — which, although they can be trained in various ways in the individual, cannot be eradicated from the race. Training consists only of repressing or redirecting them. And no matter how much they may be altered by the "location and circumstance" of the parent, they reappear in the original form — as sure as the hedgehog puts out spines — in every baby that is born. 13

This native endowment, moreover, was evolved in prehistoric times. In general it fitted man, or those men at least from whom we are descended, for survival in savage tribes. Nothing has happened in the brief span of racial life called "civilized" to alter measurably what we are at birth. The learned attitudes and modes of behavior which, together with manufactured objects, constitute civilization, are not transmitted in heredity, and have to be acquired anew by every individual. 14

This much about human nature can, I think, be properly described as knowledge. When it comes to stating just what those native tendencies are, however, differences of opinion arise that make the going difficult. Freud solved the problem, or concealed it, by lumping them all together and calling them id.[6] As Freud is always stressing the central importance of sex, and as id is the Latin word for "it," this academic device had a very unacademic appropriateness when it arrived on our slangy shores. But it did not blind judicious eyes to the irreducible variety of drives in man's hereditary nature. 15

---

[6]See summaries preceding selection by Freud in Part VII, on The Power of the Unconscious, especially the notes on the id.

One of them upon which even Freud agrees is an aggressive or pug- 16
nacious tendency.[7] It seems that whenever this human animal is frustrated
in any of his impulses, he is likely to get an impulse to lambaste somebody.
And as all of us in the nature of things are a good part frustrated all the
time, there is always a plenty of pugnacity lying round. As a carefully
scientific book says: "One may think of each nation as having a large number of individuals who are constantly in need of some person, some idea,
or some group toward whom aggression may be expressed." This, I think,
is what made Marx's doctrine so much more popular than Fourier's or Ow-
en's. The three men talked about the same ultimate goal of peace and harmony on earth. But Marx talked very little about it, and meanwhile gave
his followers a chance to fight. To *arrive* at the goal they must forswear
peace and harmony and go in for a battle of the ages.

A wiser scheme would preserve some of that belligerent excitement in 17
its future goal. It would fashion an ideal a little less like heaven than the
"classless society," a little more like having fun on earth. "From each according to his abilities, to each according to his needs," sounds very just
and noble, but if you use your imagination a little: — What a bore it would
be!

"At least let's take time out every afternoon," the too-blessed citizens 18
would say, "and see what each can grab."

I hope I do not sound frivolous, for I am saying the most important 19
thing I know how to say about socialism. It has been more myth than
science. Its aim has been escape from reality rather than adjustment to it.
Instead of trying to "remove all causes for contest between individuals,"
as Owen did, or even between classes, as Marx did, we ought to recognize
that contest forms a large part of what keeps mankind in health and interested. Progress must consist in elevating the level and humanizing the
terms on which the vital contests are fought. This takes perhaps a little of
the flame out of the heart of the revolutionist, but it will keep a light shining in his head. If it is true, or anywhere near true, as Marx said, that "All
history is a history of class struggles," then the attempt at a classless society is an attempt to jump out of history. The Bolsheviks did indeed jump
out of history, or jump into this form of tyranny which history had never
seen before. The task is to guide history, using above all things our knowledge of man to make his future more satisfying to his instinctive nature.

That is the most obvious thing, I think, that psychology has to say to 20
the socialist. The ideal society must be adapted to the unideal man. It must
have regard to native average human traits, and not confuse these with
subtle attitudes that specially bred or educated types have sometimes man-

---

[7]See summaries preceding selection by Freud in Part VII, especially the notes on the destructive instinct.

aged to maintain. And among these traits a gift for giving battle will be found quite as native as that gregarious kindliness of which socialists have made so much.

Another trait of man that socialism has ignored — and indeed all political idealisms from Plato's *Republic*[8] to the Declaration of Independence — is involved in that gregarious or social drive itself. It is not a simple disposition to stand side by side, or chat together, or do together what has to be done. It is a disposition enabling a number of distinct and wayward individuals to cohere when necessary and act as a unit. To this end each individual has to be capable of adopting toward his neighbor, and adopting with impetuous sincerity, an attitude either of dominance or submission. It is this confusing and yet neat pair of attributes that socialists most fatally ignored. Particularly the submissive side has been ignored — the passion both men and women have for being led, for obeying, and conforming, and belonging-to.

Freud sees this tendency in adults as the child in them still yearning for a parent's authority. Others have called it an "instinct of submission," as opposed to an "instinct of self-assertion." Still others have been content to describe the whole thing — and almost everything else besides — as "herd instinct." But that suggests a rather timorous grass-eating herd. "A tendency to fight in packs," might be more appropriate to the present picture of mankind, if you are bound to find first cousins in the zoo. But I do not think that is necessary. We shall get into desperate trouble if we adopt the clichés of any particular school or line of study in psychology. Naturally, if you approach the delineation of man's nature by way of the animals, you will come out with one terminology; if you approach it through primitive communities, you will come out with another; if you approach it through the insane asylum, you will come out with a third. If you approach it with an awe-stricken respect for the methods of mathematical physics you will come out nowhere at all. But I think any authority on the subject, whichever language he might use, would agree that men have in their hereditary nature a good-sized dose of belligerence, and they have a disposition both toward dominating others and submitting to them, which is not an acquired taste. Their appreciation of independence and equality of status, as well as their cooperativeness, is thus qualified by very strong drives of a contrary kind. Is it too much to ask of the architects of a New Society that they take these facts into consideration?

Owen's experiments did not fail, nor Lenin's either, because of the

21

22

23

---

[8]*Plato's* Republic: (c. 378 B.C.) The greatest of Plato's earlier dialogues and the first classical utopian text; in *The Republic,* the philosopher asserts that there is a moral order in political life, an order that can be gleaned only by an elite group of philosopher politicians who are responsible for guiding the public away from ordinary life's illusions to what is morally right.

"habits of the individual system" prevailing in its members. It failed, rather, because of the impulses of the social animal prevailing in them. The idea of producing a "Community of Equality" — or in Marx's term, a "Society of the Free and Equal" — by socializing property and production, assumed a greater self-dependence, as well as a more peaceable disposition, than these human animals are born with or capable in large numbers of acquiring. Cats might form such a society if they could learn to work together, but dogs would have to learn to stand on their own feet! And so would all gregarious animals, including even this very teachable and thoughtful one called man.

If these things are true, it is no accident that Owen's community — and the others like it — throve only so long as the founder stayed on hand to boss it. It is no accident that "complete collectivization" in Russia, instead of setting the workers and peasants free, imposed over them a new kind of tyrant. It seems obvious to me now — though I was slow, I must say, in coming to the conclusion — that the institution of private property, the dispersion of power and importance that goes with it, has been a main factor in producing that limited amount of free-and-equalness which Marx hoped to render infinite by abolishing this institution. Marx himself, as I remarked in another connection, was the first to realize this. It was he who informed us that the evolution of private capitalism with its free market had been a precondition for the evolution of all our democratic freedoms. It never occurred to him that, if this was so, those other freedoms might disappear with the abolition of the free market. 24

That, however, is exactly what happened in Russia, and it happened with astounding speed. I do not believe the much over-worked "backwardness" of the country goes one step toward explaining this. Russia's backwardness can hardly explain why collectivization made her more backward. Nor do I believe that the "capitalist encirclement" — so much like Owen's excuse — explains it. Nor even the dictatorial and violent procedures of Lenin's Bolshevik party. It cannot be explained without a reference to those more recently discriminated facts which Marxists out of loyalty to their antique doctrine refuse to think about: the hereditary as against the acquired nature of man; the fact that the hereditary nature is still that of the tribal savage; and that it contains, among other things, a taste for fighting and that tendency to bow down to others or boss them which makes group solidarity in gregarious animals spontaneous. 25

Particularly in time of stress and danger, men are prone by nature, not just persuadable by argument, to get together and fight. And in that fighting union, all those "moral qualities," the reasonableness and justice, candor and magnanimity, which Owen counted on, and Marx and Lenin after him, tend to give way before those deeper-lying traits. Even calculating self-interest tends to give way. You can not count on anything but cohesion and intolerance. 26

This, at least, was the exact manner in which the Russian failure came   *27*
about. The very party of consecrated revolutionists upon whom Lenin had
relied to socialize the industries and bring the free society to birth in Russia, became the nucleus of a blind and vengeful fighting gang, stamping
to death with shrill yells of hate every individual who dared stand out for
Lenin's promises, or for any other thing but anger and obedience.

That is what happened to Lenin's experiment, and began to happen   *28*
even before his controlling hand was withdrawn. Instead of producing the
higher civilization demanded by his amateur science, or no-science, of
man, the turmoil of it swept away whole sections of the acquired fabric of
civilization altogether, and left the technique of modern industry and education at the mercy of the naked passions of a savage tribe . . .

But let us not malign savage tribes. Within their patterns they cultivate   *29*
wisdom; they are in a state of growth. It is civilized beings who revert to
savagery that are indefensible. Primitive art has its dignity of aspiration,
but the cult resulting from the modern imitation of it is already at a dead
end. And the same holds of these political and moral retroversions, the
totalitarian states, of which that aesthetic cult has been, it almost seems,
an anticipation. They are a renunciation of intelligence and of all defined
and finely chosen values.

They are a renunciation of everything that Socialists, in particular, set   *30*
out to multiply. And therefore it is an ironical and sad reflection that the
one argument for common ownership that Socialists did base upon the
facts of human nature was the argument from savage tribes. "Primitive
communism," we used to say, proves that such an economic system is
suitable to human nature and will work. It did not occur to us, although it
would have been a very "Marxian" occurrence if it had, that in reverting
to the economics of savagery, we might revert to its crude level of life. That
again, however, is what happened in Russia. There are no better words in
which to describe the cultural effect and moral atmosphere of "complete
collectivization."

I do not pretend to have given a "scientific explanation" of this com-   *31*
plex disaster. It will satisfy me if I have escaped the charge of literary psychology, and convinced the reader that the disaster cannot be explained
without a science of human nature. It cannot be explained in the old catch-
words of economics and class policy. The backers of Hitler in Germany
made the same mistake about the Nazi party that the workers and soldiers
in Petrograd made about the Bolshevik party. Each group believed that this
new brutal, rabid, monolithic fighting gang, on achieving power, would
promote, as had been promised, its enlightened interests. Each found that
in the growth and triumph of the gang enlightened interest as such disappeared. The gang itself, the perpetuation of its blind fighting power,
became the essential goal of the procedure.

Totalitarianism is thus literally an abandonment of civilization itself.   *32*

And no one who has lived a thinking life these thirty-five years will deny that Lenin's experiment in socialism broke the dam and dug the political channels in which the whole flood is running. It is not enough to pick flaws in the tactics of Lenin; his basic understanding must be questioned. An honest, bold, loyal, and within its limits extremely highbrow attempt to produce through common ownership a society of the Free and Equal, produced a tyrant and a totalitarian state; there sprang up in its wake, borrowing its name and imitating its political procedures, other tyrants and totalitarian states; the whole world was plunged into a brutishly stupid war. I think any wise Socialist, viewing this sequence in the light of what we know and Lenin did not know about human nature, little though it may be, will be inclined to reconsider his assumptions. In his further efforts toward a world in which science shall have conquered poverty and superstition, and made a rich life possible to all, he will be cautious about the scheme of common ownership and state control. He will be cautious about the *extent* to which it may be carried. The more "radical" he is, in the sense of intelligently caring about liberty and justice and a chance at life for the wage workers, the more cautious he will be. Of that I am firmly convinced. Socialism was amateur; we must learn to be expert.

REVIEW QUESTIONS

1. Why, according to Eastman, was an ignorance of modern psychology fatal for the proponents of Marxism? Why does Eastman blame part of the problem on Marx's German nationality? What crucial factors in man's nature did Marx ignore, according to Eastman? In what way were Marx's assumptions different from Robert Owen's?
2. According to Eastman, what psychological truths about humankind must socialists take into consideration when planning or building a new form of society? How does Eastman use the history of Owen's utopian community (New Harmony) and what happened in Soviet Russia to support his argument?
3. In what way does Eastman compare the triumphant communists with the triumphant Nazis? In what sense is socialism "amateur"? What course does Eastman recommend for present and future reformers?

DISCUSSION AND WRITING QUESTIONS

1. Eastman classifies the drives of the human animal into two types: those that are created or can be eradicated by environment ("location and circumstance"), and those that cannot be eradicated (but at best can be repressed or redirected). Do you agree with this interpretation? Explain.
2. Discussing the "native tendencies" of human nature, Eastman remarks that "Freud solved the problem [i.e., of stating what these tendencies are] by lump-

ing them all together and calling them id." If you have read Freud's essay, "The Mind and Its Workings" (in Part VII), comment on the fairness of this statement.

3. Do you agree with Eastman's basic assertion that Marxism "has been more myth than science. Its aim has been escape from reality rather than adjustment to it"? How do you think that authors like John Reed, Eugene Debs, Mao Tse-tung, and Angela Davis would respond to Eastman's argument? What evidence in John Reed's passage, for example, can you find to support or rebut Eastman's position?

4. "Progress must consist in elevating the level and humanizing the terms on which the vital contests are fought," asserts Eastman in paragraph 19. Discuss this proposition, as it applies to our own world. Use examples from your own reading and experience.

5. Eastman cites belligerency and a tendency toward either dominance or submission as instinctual tendencies of humankind. Comment on this assumption.

6. Eastman argues that democratic freedoms evolve from capitalism and are inseparate from it; thus, if capitalism falls, so do democratic freedoms. Do you agree with this view? Why or why not? Cite examples.

7. If you are personally acquainted with a committed Marxist, show him or her this passage by Eastman. Report on the person's reaction. Has this reaction at all changed your own position on either Marxism, Eastman, or both?

FREDERICK C. CREWS (b. 1933)

The class struggle is, of course, a very serious business. Still, there are few subjects so serious that a bit of laughter here and there cannot break the tension, refresh our spirits, and offer us a welcome, if temporary, shift of perspective. Accordingly, to conclude this part we offer some comic relief in the form of a bogus piece of Marxist literary analysis supposedly by one "Martin Tempralis." Tempralis is actually Frederick Crews, author of *The Pooh Perplex*, a satiric gem of a book that pokes fun at various schools of literary criticism, including historical criticism, religious criticism, Freudian criticism — and Marxist criticism. Crews's method is to show how that perennial children's favorite, *Winnie-the-Pooh*, by A.A. Milne, might have fared had it been reviewed according to some of these current critical methodologies.

Born in Philadelphia in 1933, Crews was educated at Yale and Princeton, and since 1958 has taught at the University of California at Berkeley. A critic of the psychoanalytic orientation, he is the author of *The Tragedy of Manners* (1957), *E.M. Forster: The Perils of Humanism* (1962), *The Sins of the Fathers* [a psychoanalytic study of the works of Nathaniel Hawthorne] (1966), *The Random House Handbook* (1974, 1977, 1980), and *Out of My System* (1975). He is also the editor of *Psychoanalysis and the Literary Process* and *The Random House Reader*. *The Pooh Perplex* was first published in 1963.

A.A. Milne (1882–1956), author of the Pooh stories, attended Trinity College of Cambridge University, after which he worked for 13 years as an editor of the British humor magazine, *Punch*. Beginning in 1919, he wrote a series of successful light comedies for the stage, and he later wrote novels, an autobiography, and children's verses. But Milne is best known for the stories he wrote for his young son, Christopher Robin: *Winnie-the-Pooh* (1926) and *The House at Pooh Corner* (1928). Christopher Robin himself is one of the main characters in these stories, along with Pooh (the bear), Piglet, Eeyore (the melancholy donkey), Owl, Rabbit, Tigger, Kanga, and Roo — most based on real stuffed animals in Christopher Robin's nursery.

The adventures of these creatures range from hunting imaginary Heffalumps to celebrating Thursdays and lunchtime (Pooh's favorite activity).

A BOURGEOIS WRITER'S
PROLETARIAN FABLES

> But who advances next, with cheerful grace,
> Joy in her eye, and plenty in her face?
> A wheaten garland does her head adorn:
> O Property! O goddess, English-born!
>   — Ambrose Phillips (1714)

After the sorry spectacle we have all enjoyed of England's desertion of Spain,[1,2] readers of this journal may well wonder why the further attention of serious persons should be wasted on British literature. I confess that this question has given me no little anguish of conscience; yet there are, upon consideration, reasons for persevering in our studies — provided, of course, that the decadent *fin-de-siècle*[3] doctrine of artistic "purity," of disembodied literary thrills *à la* Walter Pater,[4] is not allowed to distract us from our goal. There remains, after all, the good fight to wage; if one is sometimes forced to envision the triumph of fascist Nazism not simply in Spain but everywhere, such a prospect only strengthens one's determination to strike a few more blows for the working class before it is too late. We can remain serene in our belief that, at least for those of us gifted with literary sensibility, the struggle against Hitler can best be carried on through pointing out the bourgeois-capitalistic elements in English literature. England remains today what Marx originally derided it as being: that most bourgeois of countries, characterized by a bourgeois aristocracy, a bourgeois bourgeoisie, and a bourgeois proletariat. Under these circumstances we need not despair of finding sufficient subject matter for our studies; and when we do run across exceptional books or paragraphs that strike back

Frederick C. Crews. Winnie the Pooh: A Bourgeois Writer's Proletarian Fables [1963]. In *The Pooh Perplex*. New York: Dutton, 1963.

[1]This refers to political and military events which, having occurred some time ago and in a country that has remained quite untroubled ever since, need not be dwelt upon by the modern student. — Ed. [Crews]

[2]*England's desertion of Spain:* In the Spanish Civil War (1936–1939), a bloody conflict that started after a military coup failed to overthrow Spain's republican government, Britain chose to follow France's course of non-intervention, the result being that Britain (and France) indirectly supported the rebel forces led by Generalissimo Francisco Franco, which were directly supported by Fascist Italy and Nazi Germany. Franco's forces won, and the Generalissimo ruled Spain until his death in 1975.

[3]*fin-de-siècle:* End of century.

[4]*Walter Pater:* (1839–1894) Victorian critic and essayist, who cultivated a highly elaborate (and overly precious) prose style; to hostile critics Pater represents the triumph of sensitivity over substance.

at the ruling class, we may also make use of these, exalting them to the detriment and shame of other writers past and present.

A. A. Milne, some might say, ought to deserve exemption from our interest, for he is chiefly known as the author of innocuous prose and verse for small children. I would reply that there are several heresies, distortions, fallacies, and errors in that unconstructive attitude. Milne has written plays and novels designed for grownups, albeit bourgeois grownups. I confess that I have not read this body of work, but a trustworthy friend has assured me that it is more or less what one would have expected, and hence proper material for criticism. The very idea that any one writer should be deemed untouchable is, in itself, rather too smacking of class privilege, and one is not surprised to see that its proponents will not stand up to have themselves counted. Let us also be quite clear on the matter of children's literature. As the democratic experiments in group rearing have demonstrated in the Soviet Union, and as the sinister example of the *Deutsches Jungvolk*[5] has admonished us in Germany, the period of childhood is the one in which lasting political impressions are conditioned into the individual. Literature is perhaps the foremost of all "educational" means, and the wide dissemination of Milne's four children's books justifies our concluding that he has had quite an impact on the thinking of the generation just now arriving at voting age. Will England turn even farther to the right, or will reason and progress begin to assert themselves? The only way to make an accurate prediction, I submit, is to analyze Milne's writings and bring to light their hidden socio-political implications.

Certainly there is nothing in Milne's background or reputation to encourage us toward optimism about his leanings. His origins were, I believe, thoroughly bourgeois, though I am not completely certain of this. I started reading his recently published *Autobiography* but was put off when I came across a reference to "our governess" on the third line of the first page. More to my taste — rather perverse in this case, I admit — is Milne's volume of pacifist sophistries, *Peace with Honour* (1934), in which he describes war in consummately funny English-bourgeois terms, utterly ignoring both the inevitability and the justice of proletarian revolution. War, says this comfortable Philistine, is "silly"; "This is not the way in which decent men and women behave"! How sweetly rational, how pious, and how abysmally ignorant of the economic facts of life this moralist must be! If my passport had not been revoked I would travel across the Atlantic just to meet such a perfect specimen of his type!

2

3

---

[5]*Deutsches Jungvolk:* Literally, "German Young People," Deutsches Jungvolk was a Nazi youth camp for boys organized as an early training center for Nazi soldiers. Boys spent as many as eight years in these and similar training programs which emphasized absolute obedience and conformity, with little parental interaction or involvement.

Let us not, however, dwell upon personalities, but rather collect our   4
literary evidence with dispassionate objectivity. Our main interest will be
the *Pooh* books, though no student can afford to overlook the transparently
revealing poems in *When We Were Very Young* and *Now We Are Six*. All these
works antedate Milne's phase of loud revanchist pacifism (i.e. counterrevo-
lutionism), yet all are undeniably "political" in import. A few samples of
poetry will suffice to introduce us to Milne's general views. It is not an
exaggeration to say that every major social problem of industrial society is
touched upon, however callously and unintentionally, in these "children's" rhymes. One hardly knows where to begin the reckoning! Perhaps
with "Disobedience," which betrays its promisingly Thoreauvian title by
urging the upper classes to "never go down to the end of the town" where
the working class lives? Perhaps with "Shoes and Stockings," which cheer-
fully extols the labor of the many for the few? Or with these charming lines
from "King Hilary and the Beggarman": *"Don't be afraid of doing things. /
(Especially, of course, for Kings.)"*? The field is so rich that we may save
valuable space here by simply inviting the reader to browse through
these volumes himself, culling gems of imperialism, colonialism, and
profiteering.

Not astoundingly, the *Pooh* stories give us, at least at first, the same   5
distasteful impression as the poems. It is hardly fortuitous that all the chief
actors are property owners with no apparent necessity to work; that they
are supplied as if by miracle with endless supplies of honey, condensed
milk, balloons, popguns, and extract of malt; and that they crave meaningless aristocratic distinctions and will resort to any measure in their drive
for class prestige. Not for nothing is the sycophant Pooh eventually invested by Christopher Robin as "Sir Pooh de Bear, most faithful of all my
Knights." It is a worthy ending to a series of tales in which every trace of
social reality, every detail that might suggest some flaw in the capitalist
paradise of pure inherited income, has been ruthlessly suppressed. Only,
perhaps, in the ominous old sign beside Piglet's house do we glimpse the
truth that this community of parasites is kept together through armed in-
timidation of the proletariat. "TRESPASSERS W," says the sign, and Piglet's facetious exegesis of this as his grandfather's name only reminds us
more pointedly of the hereditary handing-on of the so-called sacred law of
property.

This, then, is the literary world of *Winnie-the-Pooh* — an ideal ground,   6
no doubt, for the darling offspring of the rich to develop their "insights"
and "moral sense" upon! It would seem that no possible social good could
come out of the extensive distribution of such books as these. And yet the
scrupulous critic should hesitate before making such a sweeping condemnation. There is, perhaps, another light in which Milne's appallingly cheerful representation of *laissez-faire* life should be regarded. To borrow a leaf
from our bourgeois rivals, the Freudian critics, we may say that the "un-

conscious" meaning of *Winnie-the-Pooh* seems quite opposite to its conscious, intended meaning. The very passages I have already cited could easily be interpreted in an ironical spirit, as subtle complaints against the abuses that seem to be extolled. I certainly do not mean to imply that the staunch "pacifist" A. A. Milne should receive any credit for this; it is rather a case of the social facts speaking for themselves in spite of all determined effort to deny their meaning. Milne is, after all, acknowledged by both "respectable" critics and by true lovers of literature to have hit upon some universal appeal in these stories. As there is only one kind of appeal that is truly universal (i.e. international), mere logic would lead us to believe that dialectical materialism, scientific socialism, the spirit of the Commune, democratic cooperation between peoples, and the necessity of revolution are implicitly urged upon us in Milne's stories. As indeed they are. Milne turns out to be a revolutionary *malgré lui*,[6] an inspired simpleton who accepts the decadent state of his society with such naïve acquiescence that he unwittingly portrays its rottenness and points the way to its imminent overthrow.

The cynical reader may imagine that my argument has now become   7
self-contradictory. What! Does *Winnie-the-Pooh* both suppress and reveal the social truth? Perhaps, dear reader, your doubts would have been expressed less smugly had you waited to hear my full explanation. Milne's stories *do* suppress the truth in refusing to represent the working class in its actual state of slavery to the bourgeoisie. The whole point of turning one's back on realism and retreating into animal fable — the effete tradition of Aesop[7] and the royalist La Fontaine[8] — is just to avoid facing the historical process whose end result has by now become evident to all. Yet this very literary subterfuge has undermined the author's purpose. As soon as Milne began seriously to treat his son's stuffed animals as living characters he apparently forgot to exercise his faculty of bourgeois censorship. In Pooh, Piglet, Eeyore, and the others we see *symbolically*, but with crystal clarity, an adumbration of the titanic struggle of rich and poor, oppressor and oppressed, that Milne and his "decent men and women" friends would fain have blotted from their consciousness!

All doubts about this "level of meaning" (as our effeminate aesthetes   8
are fond of saying) in *Winnie-the-Pooh* may be removed at once if we consider the character of Rabbit, who is represented in such terms as these:

> It was going to be one of Rabbit's busy days. As soon as he woke up he felt
> important, as if everything depended upon him. It was just the day for Orga-

---

[6]*malgré lui:* In spite of himself.

[7]*Aesop:* A 6th century B.C. Greek compiler of animal fables.

[8]*La Fontaine:* Jean de La Fontaine (1621–1695), French fable writer.

nizing Something, or for Writing a Notice Signed Rabbit, or for Seeing What Everybody Else Thought About It. It was a perfect morning for hurrying round to Pooh, and saying, "Very well, then, I'll tell Piglet," and then going to Piglet, and saying, "Pooh thinks — but perhaps I'd better see Owl first." It was a Captainish sort of day, when everybody said, "Yes, Rabbit" and "No, Rabbit," and waited until he had told them.

Captainish indeed! Rabbit is the capitalist manager par excellence, the "captain of industry" who, though altogether a bungler and boaster, is bent upon imposing his will on everyone around him. Just the day for Writing a Notice Signed Rabbit! Here in a nutshell is a complete character study of the exploiter of labor, driven by a sense of shame at his exemption from toil to "busy" himself with writing bureaucratic and imperious notices, pretending that his arbitrary decisions have been democratically reached ("Pooh thinks — but perhaps I'd better see Owl first"), and demanding an automatic yes or no to each of his commands and rhetorical questions.

The interesting point, of course, is that this caricature of the bourgeois (if indeed it goes far enough to be called a caricature) is implicitly ridiculed by the plot of *Winnie-the-Pooh*. I leave it to the squeaky-voiced "scholars" of our upper-class universities, clothed exquisitely in their flowing academic "gowns," to decide why the leisure-loving Milne arranged his book this way. The simple fact is that the net effect is proletarian. Try as he may to organize his acquaintances — that is, to keep them from organizing in self-protection against *him* — Rabbit never quite succeeds. On the very day mentioned above, for instance, he bustles vainly from Christopher Robin to Owl to Pooh to Piglet and Eeyore, failing in each case to drum up support for his schemes. These others employ the classic defenses of the disinherited proletariat when subjected to the high-sounding exhortations of their rulers: they either pretend to be elsewhere (Christopher Robin), reply with courteous but meaningless ambiguity (Owl and Pooh), make themselves wholly inconspicuous (Piglet), or try to educate themselves to retort in kind (Eeyore). There is an atmosphere of buried sullenness, of potential revolt, in this chapter that is nothing short of inspiring. No less instructive is the story, "Pooh Goes Visiting," in which Rabbit, having deceitfully offered Pooh admittance to sample his overstocked larder, artfully traps his victim in the doorway and exploits him as an unsalaried towel rack for an entire week. As Shepard's illustration[9] makes vivid for us, however, the united efforts of a Marxist-Leninist band of workers, constraining even the

---

[9]*Shepard's illustration:* The "Marxist Leninist band of workers" to which "Tempralis" refers is actually Shepard's illustration of the cooperative efforts of Christopher Robin, Rabbit, Piglet, and what Milne calls "all of Rabbit's friends and relations" (including a rat, three mice, a porcupine, and various insects) who are trying to free a rather distraught Pooh caught in the entrance to Rabbit's hole, by pulling him out feet first.

unwilling Rabbit to join in, succeed in extricating Pooh from his servitude.

Scarcely less central a symbolic character than Rabbit is Owl, the pe-   10
dantic plutocrat who resides at "The Chestnuts, an old-world residence of
great charm, which was grander than anybody else's." A spelling champion and a master of flowery, empty rhetoric, Owl is the necessary hand-
servant to the raw acquisitive passion of Rabbit, which badly needs to be
cloaked in grandiosities. The friendship of these two intellectual thugs is a
perfect representation of the true role of "scholarship" in bourgeois-indus-
trial society: the end purpose of Owl's obscure learning is to spread a veil
of confusion over the doings of the fat cats, to cow the humble into submission before the graven idols of "objective truth" and "the Western tradition," and to rob the proletariat of its power to protest. What could be
more meaningful than the fact that Owl has stolen the very tail from the
back of Eeyore, the most downcast, bounced-upon member of society, and
has converted it to his doorbell? When Pooh comes to retrieve it he is not
so much as offered a lick of honey. Rabbit, the industrial manager, at least
understood that one must give a subsistence in exchange for the worker's
largely unpaid toil, but Owl, the "pure" scholar who professes to be innocent of the ways of the world, excuses himself from even this much
elementary compassion. The *trahison des clercs*[10] is the correct name for this
sort of thing.

We should beware, however, of thinking that the symbolic roles of   11
Milne's characters remain absolutely static from one fable to the next. If the
meaning is always essentially the same, the way of embodying it changes
rather capriciously. Thus Pooh, who represents the workers' cause in the
examples above, is cast as a wildcatting capitalist in the Heffalump chapter.
He and Piglet, joint partners in the imperialistic venture of bringing back
a live Heffalump (subjecting and exploiting colonial peoples), fall out over

---

[10]*trahison des clercs:* Literally, the "treason of the clerks," the term is used to describe situations in which intellectuals compromise their commitment to remain unbiased by making
judgments solely to gain the state's favor.

the question of who is to supply the capital (acorns or honey to set the trap) and who is to do the manual labor of pit-digging. The solution, naturally, is that the smaller and weaker Piglet is issued a shovel and put to work. Shepard's drawing of Piglet-as-miner, looking upward with mixed fatigue and resentment as the exacting supervisor Pooh arrives with the honey, is touching enough, one would think, to soften the heart of a Father Coughlin or a Joseph Kennedy.[11,12,13] Pooh himself has been too loyal to his leisure-class environment (A. A. Milne's household) even to carry out the minimal duties of the capitalist properly: he has consumed most of the capital en route. Thus, of course, there ensues a general shortage of funds, which is still nothing in comparison with the hardship that will follow when it is discovered that Heffalumps do not even exist (i.e. that there never was a sufficient labor force in the subjected land to make the unnecessary product for the conspicuous consumption of an already bloated

---

[11]A religious and a political figure, respectively. — Ed. [Crews]

[12]*Father Coughlin:* (1891–1979) The byname of Charles Howard Coughlin, a U.S. "radio priest" known for his relentless attacks on anything even remotely threatening to free enterprise.

[13]*Joseph Kennedy:* (1888–1969) The U.S. businessman and financier, father of President John F. Kennedy. "Tempralis" is referring to Kennedy as the archetypal capitalist who amasses vast sums of money by often questionable means.

market). Pooh's nightmare of endless Heffalumps making straight for his honey supply and eating it all requires, I believe, no complicated analysis (and least of all a Freudian one!). It is the very image of proletarian revolution, of the workers arising in a concerted mass to seize the means of production from the jaded bourgeoisie.

One could go on incessantly with examples of this kind: Rabbit's racial   12
prejudice against Kanga, Eeyore's housing problem and Pooh's misguided effort at slum clearance, Eeyore's own discrimination against Tigger and, reciprocally, Tigger's savage leaps against Eeyore, and so on. By now the reader will have got the message, and it is better not to drone on and on like our somber pundits in the "learned quarterlies," but to stop and hammer in the point once and for all. The world of *Pooh*, no less than that of the "idealistic" bourgeois pacifist Milne, is a world of sheer animalism, where the inhuman bestiality of the "free" market has full sway. In this unconsciously revealing portrait of capitalism we glimpse, not only the sordidness of wage-slavery, speculation, and "lawful" gangsterism, but also the possibility of a better life — of a forthcoming heroic revolution of oppressed peoples establishing free democratic socialist communes of brotherly peace-loving workers who will march side by side down the collective road to prosperity and equality for all. This optimistic note, which is in fact the ultimate meaning of *Winnie-the-Pooh*, is what rescues the book from the vilest decadence and makes it, after all, suitable reading for progressive children throughout the world.

REVIEW QUESTIONS

1. What evidence of reactionary or bourgeois ideology does Tempralis find in the Pooh tales? How does he find that the "unconscious" meaning of these tales often differs from the "conscious, intended meaning"?
2. What does Tempralis conclude about the desirability of children's reading *Winnie-the-Pooh*?

DISCUSSION AND WRITING QUESTIONS

1. What tendencies of Marxist analysis does Crews seem to be making fun of? To what extent have you found some of these tendencies in other pieces in this unit?
2. Select another novel or story, perhaps one of your favorites, and write a Marxist critique of it. Imitate Crews's methods of analysis and appropriate quotation.
3. Read two or three serious pieces of Marxist analyses of literature. Evaluate them in terms of their helpfulness in illuminating the works for you. Appraise their particular strengths and weaknesses. To what extent do you conclude that Marxist thought is a useful tool in literary criticism? What are its limitations? (*Note:* A helpful source for locating such analyses is the *Guide to Marxist Literary Criticism*, Chris Bullock and David Peck, eds. See also the anthology edited by Lang and Williams, cited in the lists of "Additional Readings" at the end of the book.)

Part VII

FREUD AND THE POWER OF THE UNCONSCIOUS

Sigmund Freud

Robert Lindner

Salvatore Prisco III

Dawn Ades

Ernest Jones

Harvey R. Greenberg

Carl Gustav Jung

B. F. Skinner

> The mind is an iceberg — it floats with only one seventh of
> its bulk above water.
>
> — Sigmund Freud, quoted in *New York Times* obituary

The patient was a 19-year-old girl, an only child, normally bright and high-spirited, but recently nervous and depressed. As she explained to her doctor, Sigmund Freud, she was suddenly afraid to walk alone through squares and wide streets. Unaccountably, she had begun to perform a strange set of rituals every night before going to bed. Claiming that she needed absolute silence before she could fall asleep, she would stop the pendulum of a large clock in her bedroom (even though the regular sound of a pendulum would be more likely to induce sleep than to prevent it), and she would remove all other clocks from the room, including a tiny wrist watch on her bed table, whose sound she could not possibly hear unless it were placed next to her ear. She would place flower pots and vases together in such a way that they could not fall over and make a noise. She would place the bolster (a narrow pillow on her bed) in such a way that it did not touch the headboard, and then she would place her soft pillow diagonally on the bolster. Finally, she would shake her comforter every night so that all the feathers settled down to the bottom end; and then she would press the comforter out and redistribute the feathers.

The girl could give no rational explanation for this behavior. The real reasons for her actions were buried below the level of consciousness. Through the process of psychoanalysis, however, Freud and she were able to delve into her unconscious mind, and to uncover the sexual anxieties that revealed themselves in these erratic bedtime activities. Her chief anxiety was that if her parents had another child, she would be replaced in their affections by the baby. She therefore felt compelled to prevent her father from impregnating her mother. Even in her conscious mind, the bolster had always seemed like a woman to her, and the headboard like a man. By separating them, she would prevent their coming together in intercourse. The clocks and watches were symbols of the female genitals (both being related to periodic processes and regular intervals), as were the vases and flower pots. Forcing the feathers down to one end of the comforter was like impregnating a woman; pressing them out again was like obliterating the pregnancy.[1]

---

[1]This case and other specific cases discussed by Freud in this introduction are treated in Lectures 2 and 17 of his *General Introduction to Psychoanalysis* (New York: Washington Square Press, 1960).

Of course many people might dispute Freud's interpretation of the girl's behavior. What is beyond dispute, however, is the revolution Freud and his followers engendered through their systematic probing into the unconscious processes that underlie our daily activities. How to account for human behavior has been a challenge since the beginning of recorded history. And how to account for apparently unaccountable behavior has been a particular problem. In primitive societies evil spirits were held responsible for irrational behavior, and shamans and medicine men were called upon to exorcise such spirits from the mind. In more recent times, chemical imbalances among bodily fluids (humors) were assumed to underlie such maladies as melancholia (depression), and purgatives or other physical remedies were frequently prescribed. It was Freud's genius to suggest the existence of an unconscious mind and then to explore the functioning of this unconscious, particularly as it manifests itself in neurotic behavior, in dreams, and in such apparently trivial actions as jokes and slips of the tongue. This idea of the unconscious — whether or not along the exact lines delineated by Freud — has proven one of the 20th century's most powerful tools in exploring behavior and motivation, allowing light to be thrown upon many areas that had previously been dark. Freud, his disciples, and those he has influenced have given us new insight into human nature.

But what exactly is the unconscious? Stated in the most simple terms, the unconscious consists of those mental processes that are not directly accessible to the consciousness. Some of these mental processes are instincts, urges, or desires (the "id") that have been repressed from the conscious mind (the "ego") by a "censor" (the "superego") because they are shameful or antisocial. For example, a brother may be jealous of the attention his parents give to his younger sister — so jealous that he wishes her dead. He knows that this is a shameful wish, however, and so the wish is repressed into his unconscious. Nevertheless, it takes a great deal of psychic energy to keep this wish repressed. (One sign of this internal conflict is a feeling of anxiety.) At times when his conscious guard is down, such as when he is asleep, his unconscious wish will break through to consciousness, in the form of dreams. He may not dream of actually killing his sister (the superego posts a minimal guard even when the person is asleep), but he may dream of killing another young girl, or even a pet — the other girl or the pet being symbols for his sister. The unconscious can also break through to consciousness in waking states — in the form of daydreams, fantasies, slips of the tongue, or jokes — what Freud called the "psychopathology of everyday life." If the boy's sister were actually to die, even though it were through an accident or an illness, the boy, remembering some of his fantasies or jokes, might feel a crushing guilt that he had actually willed her death — a self-punishing guilt that could affect his future relationships with other women.

Perhaps the best known (and notorious) example of the unconscious impulse at work is the Oedipus complex. The term is based upon the myth of Oedipus, who unknowingly killed his father, the King of Thebes, and then married his mother after becoming king himself. According to the theory that Freud began working out in the late 1890s, all infant males have an unconscious wish to supplant their fathers in their mother's affections — and in their beds. They have fantasies of killing their fathers and then of marrying and sleeping with their mothers. Since such urges clearly violate the most basic taboos of society, they are firmly repressed — but not so firmly that their effects are not felt in various forms in later years.

Of course, not all unconscious impulses involve such murderous feelings. In his discussion of errors and slips of the tongue, Freud recounts that in covering a festival, a Social-Democratic newspaper in a monarchist country noted that, "Amongst those present was his highness, the Clown Prince." The next day, the paper apologized by asserting that "The sentence should of course have read, 'The Crow Prince.'" Freud gives another example:

> In a war correspondent's account of meeting a famous general whose infirmities were pretty well known, a reference to the general was printed as "this battle-scared veteran." Next day an apology appeared which read "the words of course should have been "the bottle-scarred veteran!'"

In both these cases, unconscious impulses emerge in the form of errors. Even selective forgetfulness is a sign of unconscious wishes at work: people often forget to repay small loans, but generally don't forget the repayments that are due to them. The point is that such phenomena as dreams, fantasies, forgetfulness, and slips of the tongue are not accidental, random, or haphazard; they have definite causes and are intended by the unconscious to have certain effects, perhaps to bring repressed impulses to the surface of consciousness, perhaps to indicate the speaker's true attitudes, despite his words.

Unpleasant experiences can also be repressed into the unconscious. For example, a child may have completely forgotten being temporarily lost in a shopping mall by his mother when he was four years old; but later in life he may have an apparently irrational fear of being abandoned by the woman he loves. When unpleasant urges or experiences are repressed into the unconscious, outward behavior is frequently affected. As we have seen, this behavior may take the relatively innocuous form of slips of the tongue or forgetfulness, or it may take more severe forms: *neuroses*, which are unresolved mental conflicts between conscious and unconscious impulses; or most severe of all, *psychoses*, disabling conditions, in which the person loses full contact with reality and often cannot safely live among others.

According to Freud, the conscious mind sets up defense mechanisms to prevent repugnant or forbidden unconscious urges from breaking into consciousness. One such defense mechanism — *sublimation* — can be quite beneficial. Through sublimation unconscious sexual energy (the *libido*) is channeled away from its real object (perhaps one's mother or another man's wife) into another object — perhaps a work of art or literature or a building. Viewed this way, civilization itself can be seen as the result of sublimated sexual energy. It is not surprising, as we will see later in this unit, that Freud and his followers have been as interested in interpreting art and literature as they have been in dreams.

The psychoanalyst steps in when neurotic symptoms develop to the point that the person can no longer function normally: either the mind, the body, or both may be affected. After placing the patient in a relaxed state and using techniques of free association, the psychoanalyst asks the patient a series of questions: one question leads to an answer, the answer leads to a second question, and so on, as the analyst works to get through the layers of consciousness and into the unconscious sources of the neurosis, which are usually buried deeply in childhood. In popular fiction and movies, this process is often ludicrously fast; in fact, many analyses take months or even years. The ultimate aim of the psychoanalyst is to bring unconscious impulses into the consciousness, where the patient is better able to deal with them, or at least, to learn to live with them.

It should be noted that Freud did not conceive of the unconscious as a particular place. One could not, in effect, physically peel away a layer of the brain and reveal an ego or a particular set of brain cells whose function is to repress antisocial impulses. Rather, what Freud offered in his concept of the unconscious was a powerful metaphor to help us understand the mental processes that account for human behavior.

In this unit, we present selections that show some of the ways in which the concept of an active and powerful unconscious has affected the modern world, and in particular, the fields of psychology, history, art, literature, and anthropology. First, we present a selection by Freud himself, Chapters 4 and 5 of "The Mind and Its Workings," from his short book *The Outline of Psychoanalysis,* in which he attempted to sum up his life's work. Freud discusses the three-part division of the psyche — the id, the ego, and the superego; discusses the basic instincts of the human animal (i.e., the basis of the unconscious); outlines the development of human sexual impulses (the source of most, if not all, neuroses); explains the functioning of the unconscious; and concludes by showing how dreams reveal the life of the unconscious. In our second selection, Dr. Robert Lindner, a practicing psychoanalyst, gives a detailed account (from his well-known book *The Fifty-Minute Hour*) of his treatment of a patient who suddenly became impotent for no apparent reason. Our third selection presents an example of what has come to be an important subgenre in psychoanalytic literature: the *psycho-history.* In this particular article, Salvatore Prisco III shows how Adolf

Hitler's Oedipus complex may throw additional understanding into the horrors of the Nazi era. As we have suggested, many of the most fascinating analyses of the unconscious focus on works of the human imagination. Dawn Ades, an art critic, examines some of Salvador Dali's surrealist paintings, showing how they reflect the mental processes of dreams. In the next article, an influential British Freudian, Ernest Jones, provides a psychoanalytic interpretation of Shakespeare's Hamlet. Then, psychiatrist Harvey Greenberg examines the dream motifs of the film classic, *The Wizard of Oz*, showing how Dorothy Gale's unconscious impulses are reflected in her adventures and in the characters that populate them. Next, we present "Dreams, Archetypes, and the Collective Unconscious," by Carl Jung, an early follower of Freud who later split with the master to develop his own theories. For Jung there is not one unconscious, but two: an individual unconscious, which is similar to the unconscious postulated by Freud, and also a collective unconscious, which is common to the entire human race, and which breaks through to consciousness in the forms of myths, or (as he called them) archetypes. Finally, we include a selection by the behaviorist B. F. Skinner, who attacks the very concept of the Freudian unconscious.

SIGMUND FREUD *(1856–1939)*

Sigmund Freud was born in Frieberg, Moravia (now part of Czechoslovakia), on May 6, 1856, to middle-class Jewish parents. When he was three years old, his family moved to Vienna, Austria, the city where he was to reside most of his life and that has since become closely associated with the psychoanalytic movement. (During his early years, however, Freud endured intense hostility from the Vienna medical establishment.) Career opportunities for Viennese Jews being quite limited, in 1873 he began studying medicine at the University of Vienna. Like Darwin, he was not particularly attracted to the medical profession. Freud did find himself fascinated by neurological research, however, and in the physiological laboratory of Ernst Wilhelm von Brucke, he conducted important and original experimental work in the structure of nerve tissues.

When he fell in love with Martha Bernays in 1882, Freud realized he needed to do something more practical than research. He entered Vienna General Hospital as an assistant physician, intending to qualify for private practice and thus to eventually become able to support a wife (he and Martha were not to marry until 1886). After he worked at the hospital for three years and learned various branches of medicine, his interest in human nature moved him to join the staff of Theodor Meynert's psychiatric clinic.

Mental disturbances and illnesses, of course, have been observed and catalogued since the beginning of recorded history, and many theories have been developed to account for them. As we noted in the introduction to this part, some theories involve evil spirits. Another ancient theory involves *humors* — bodily fluids like blood, phlegm, yellow bile, and black bile, which, according to the proportion in which they are mixed, account for human temperament. Too much black bile, for example, produces melancholia. In 1621, the English scholar Robert Burton produced a best-selling medical treatise called *The Anatomy of Melancholy* — "melancholy" being a term for what we would call acute depression. In the latter part of the 18th century, Franz Anton Mesmer, a German physician, achieved temporary fame by treating hysterical symptoms (convulsive fits, melancholia, wild, emotional outbursts) through "animal magnetism" — a kind of force he claimed to possess that enabled him to regulate the equilibrium of certain bodily fluids in his patients.

The theory of humors and the theory of animal magnetism had one thing in common: an underlying assumption that mental disturbances have a physical cause. The psychiatry to which Freud was introduced in 1882 was technically more advanced, though no different in basic philosophy. Mentally disturbed patients were assumed to have some neurological or chemical dysfunction of the brain. Treatment of mental disorders involved determining the precise physical source of the problem and then applying surgical or chemical means. (Such assumptions are not necessarily incorrect: modern medicine has, in fact, proven that certain parts of the brain are associated with certain mental functions, that electrically stimulating the cortex of the brain, for example, can bring long-forgotten memories to consciousness; and some recent work in the treatment of autism involves adjusting the brain's chemical balance.) The concept, however, of a dynamic unconscious that has no physical location or direct connection to the body, but that nonetheless causes abnormal symptoms and behavior, was alien to late 19th century psychiatry.

Freud continued to make important physiological and neurological discoveries, but a turning point in his life came when he began his association with the Viennese physician Joseph Breuer. Breuer had told Freud of a patient, Anna O. (later to become famous in psychoanalytic history) who had displayed various hysterical symptoms, including paralysis and regression to childlike behavior. When, under hypnosis, she was encouraged to talk about herself and her conditions, the symptoms gradually disappeared. This suggested to Freud that allowing a repressed emotion access to the surface of consciousness was often sufficient to discharge the psychic energy and dissipate the symptom. In 1885, Freud went to Paris to study with the neurologist Jean Martin Charcot, who specialized in the treatment of hysterical symptoms. Through hypnotic suggestion, Charcot was able to induce — and then to remove — physical symptoms in his patients. That is, by means of thought alone, physical symptoms could be made to appear and disappear. Charcot, however, seemed uninterested in Freud's account of Breuer's "talking cure." Freud and Breuer continued to work together, and in 1893 they published the epoch-making *Studies in Hysteria*. (The book was not well received, initially.)

In the meantime, Freud had begun private practice in 1886, the year of his marriage. (He and Martha were to have six children, one of whom, Anna Freud, became a distinguished psychoanalyst in her own right.) Soon afterward he abandoned hypnosis in favor of free association: while the patient was in a waking, but relaxed state, Freud would ask a series of questions, aimed at uncovering the subconscious causes of the symptoms. Freud also conducted an extensive self-analysis. The results of his researches into the mind led him to conclude that most neurotic symptoms were the result of repressed sexual conflicts. When he presented these findings to his medical colleagues, he was ostracized. During this time — the mid-1890s — Freud finally turned his back on clinical neurology, determined to devote the rest of his life to the study and treatment of psychopathology. In 1896, he invented the term "psychoanalysis" to describe the free association technique of delving into the unconscious. The following year he began to form the concept of the Oedipus complex.

In 1900, Freud published what many consider to be his masterpiece — *The Interpretation of Dreams*. In it he explained how dreams revealed the repressed urges of the unconscious mind, though in distorted and symbolic form. Dreams, he maintained, were a disguised means of wish fulfillment, a way in which forbidden impulses and wishes could be gratified.

In 1902, Freud invited a few young colleagues to meet regularly at his home to read and discuss papers on psychoanalysis. Thus was formed the Wednesday Psychological Group, which eventually became the Vienna Psycho-Analytical Society (1908), which in turn became the International Psycho-Analytical Association (1910). Despite his numerous detractors, Freud's fame and influence grew steadily. The First International Psycho-Analytical Congress met in Salzburg, Austria, in

1908. The following year, at the invitation of the president of Clark University in Massachusetts, Freud spent some months lecturing in the United States to generally enthusiastic audiences.

Eventually, professional disagreements and personal animosities led to the breakup of Freud's Vienna circle, an event accelerated by the departure of two of Freud's most famous disciples (and later rivals), Alfred Adler and Carl Jung. (The original group was eventually succeeded by another one, known as The Committee.) In the meantime, Freud continued to pursue his investigations into the psyche. *The Psychopathology of Everyday Life* appeared in 1904, followed in 1905 by *Jokes and Their Relation to the Unconscious*. His most controversial work, *Three Essays on the Theory of Sexuality,* also appeared in 1905; in it Freud propounded his theory of infantile sexuality, and by it he provoked a storm of indignation and abuse from a world not ready to hear of such things.

Freud opened up new areas of investigation with his study, *Leonardo da Vinci and a Memory of His Childhood* (1910), the first "psycho-history" (in which Leonardo's artistry was traced to his childhood experiences), and with *Totem and Taboo,* which extended psychoanalysis into the field of anthropology. Freud's first comprehensive statement on the unconscious was written in 1912 for the *Proceedings* of the London Society of Psychical Research. Other works of this period include *A General Introduction to Psycho-analysis* (1915–1916); *Beyond the Pleasure Principle* (1920), in which he postulated that the aim of all instincts is reversion to an earlier state of being; and *The Ego and the Id* (1923), in which he first theorized a tripartite division of the mind into *id* (the primary instinctual drives), *ego* (the conscious mind that is in contact with the outside world), and *superego* (corresponding to his earlier "censor," the reminder and enforcer of assimilated parental and social rules).

In 1923, Freud, an inveterate cigar smoker, underwent the first of 33 operations for cancer of the jaw. Ernest Jones, perhaps Freud's most celebrated British disciple, reports that Freud was never once heard to complain during his remaining sixteen years of pain and misery. He continued seeing his patients and writing, producing *The Future of an Illusion* (1927), in which he asserted that psychological motivations accounted for religious belief in God, and *Civilization and Its Discontents* (1929), in which he turned his attention to society itself.

In 1933, the Nazis came to power. Freud's writings were burned in Berlin and the contents of his Leipzig publishing firm were confiscated. During this period of anti-Semitism, Freud focused his attention on the origins of Judaism; his unorthodox conclusions (not welcomed by Jews) appeared in *Moses and Monotheism* (1938). Freud was determined not to leave Vienna; but when the Nazis invaded Austria in 1938, Ernest Jones pleaded successfully with him to emigrate to England. Later that year, Freud had his final operation for cancer, an intensely painful one. Freud continued to see his patients until a month before his death — an event that occurred shortly after the outbreak of World War II, in London, on September 23, 1939.

Freud's influence on the thought of the modern world has been so pervasive that its central tenet — the power of the unconscious — not only is no longer shocking but is simply taken for granted. Freudian assumptions stand behind much of the representative art and literature of the 20th century. The psychoanalytic movement that Freud inspired has thousands of practitioners all over the world. Not all psychoanalysis has developed along strict Freudian lines. Such former Freudians as Alfred Adler, Carl Gustav Jung, Karen Horney, and Carl Rogers have developed therapies based upon alternate assumptions — the first three deemphasized the importance of sexuality in neuroses; the latter developed a client-centered therapy, in which the omniscient role of the analyst was reduced. Others, such as Joseph Wolpe, developed behavioral therapies, concentrating less on delving into the underlying causes of neuroses than on treating the immediate symptoms — obviously a much faster process. Still, for most practicing psychotherapists today, Freud's ideas are the starting point. As psychologist Raymond E. Fancher has observed, "Freud is the one dominating figure, either for whom or against whom virtually all therapists feel compelled to take a stand."[1]

The following selection is from Freud's *Outline of Psychoanalysis*, first published in 1939. This brief and unfinished book was Freud's attempt to sum up in clear language his life's most important work. In his introduction he states:

> The aim of this brief work is to bring together the tenets of psychoanalysis and to state them, as it were, dogmatically — in the most concise form and in the most unequivocal terms. Its intention is naturally not to compel belief or to arouse conviction.
>
> The teachings of psychoanalysis are based on an incalculable number of observations and experiences, and only someone who has repeated those observations on himself and others is in a position to arrive at a judgment of his own upon it.

---

[1]*Pioneers of Psychology.* New York: Norton, 1979.

THE MIND AND ITS WORKINGS

Editors' Note: *"The Mind and Its Workings" is the title of the first part of Freud's* Outline of Psychoanalysis. *This part consists of five chapters. Length and copyright restrictions prevent us from reprinting all five chapters of "The Mind and Its Workings." Reprinted below are the fourth and fifth chapters of Part One, the chapters most directly concerned with Freud's theory of the unconscious. Since, however, some knowledge of the preceding material is necessary to an understanding of Chapters 4 and 5, we offer at this point a summary of Chapters 1–3.*

> In Chapter 1, "The Psychical Apparatus," Freud discusses the three primary components of the psychical apparatus — the *id*, the *ego*, and the *super-ego*. The oldest of these components is the id. The id "contains everything that is inherited, that is present at birth . . . above all, therefore, the instincts . . ." Next to develop was the ego, which came to serve as an intermediary between

---

Sigmund Freud. The Mind and Its Workings [1940]. In *An Outline of Psychoanalysis*. Trans. and ed., James Strachey. New York: Norton, 1949, 1969.

the id and the external world. The ego receives stimuli from the outside world and controls the bodily movements that act as responses to these stimuli. The ego is also responsible for self-preservation. It stores experiences in the memory, senses danger from the outside world, and responds by directing the body either to flee or to adapt to the danger. The ego seeks to increase pleasure and to decrease "unpleasure." It faces anticipated dangers through a "signal of anxiety." It occasionally withdraws from the external world and the body falls into sleep, during which there is a redistribution of mental energy that occasionally surfaces in the form of dreams.

The most recent mental agency to develop was the superego. The superego is the repository of parental influence. Beyond that, the superego is the repository of family, cultural, and social factors, as they are embodied in grandparents, teachers, religious leaders, and others who represent "admired social ideals." The ego frequently must reconcile the conflicting demands of the id (which desires instant gratification), the superego (which can sometimes be compared to a conscience, since its main job is to limit satisfactions), and the actual reality. Freud notes that both id and superego "represent the influences of the past" — the one of heredity, the other of important figures and ideals in the individual's early life. The ego, on the other hand, is present-oriented and determined by the individual's own experiences.

In Chapter 2, "The Theory of the Instincts," Freud concentrates primarily on the id. The function of the id is to satisfy its innate needs, without regard to the demands or restrictions of the outside world. (Such regard is the province of the ego.) These innate needs of the id and the tensions that underlie them are powered by *instincts*. Though there are numerous instincts, and though one instinct can be transformed into another, Freud theorized that all instincts can be classified into two basic types: "*Eros* and *the destructive instinct.*" The aim of *Eros* is to bind things together in unity; the aim of the destructive instinct is just the opposite — "to undo connections and so to destroy things." The energy behind *Eros* Freud termed the *libido*. The destructive instinct can also be called a "death instinct."

These two instincts (analogous to the opposing forces of attraction and repulsion in the physical world) naturally operate against one another, even when they combine in the same act. For instance, eating involves the destruction of the food itself but for the purpose of incorporating the food into a new unity with one's body. The sexual act, according to Freud, "is an act of aggression with the purpose of the most intimate union." The degree to which the instincts are mixed in any one individual accounts to some extent for the personality (aggressive or meek) of that individual. The destructive instinct can be displaced from outward factors toward oneself, and thereby become a self-destructive instinct. Thus, the ego, influenced by superego, can turn the id's destructive tendencies against the body that houses it.

The libido, though it originates in the id, is primarily associated with the ego. The libido at first concentrates entirely on the ego — this is represented in the "narcissism" of the baby and the small child. In most individuals, however, the energy of the libido is gradually displaced onto outward objects — normally, other people, or another person in particular. This other person then becomes a kind of ego-substitute. One way of characterizing the quality of libido is its relative degree of *mobility* (i.e., its ability to transfer from one object to another) or its *fixity*. Finally, the libido is rooted in certain parts of the body, the parts known as *erotogenic zones*. The sexual urge derives from a number of instincts, which at different stages in life are centered upon various erotogenic zones.

In Chapter 3, "The Development of the Sexual Function," Freud traces the typical pattern of human sexual development, in terms of the predominant libidinal instincts at work. (Freud's ideas about sexual development, of course, thoroughly scandalized his contemporaries when first propounded.) He begins by refuting the assumption that human sexual life begins at puberty and is confined to genital contact between members of the opposite sex. On the contrary, he argued, sexual life begins soon after birth, should not be considered exclusively genital, and should not be exclusively identified with the reproductive function.

The first stage of sexual development is the *oral phase*; that is, it is centered on the mouth, which Freud classifies as an erotogenic zone. The infant derives pleasure from this zone primarily though eating, of course, but also through other oral activities, such as sucking, a pleasure that has nothing to do with nourishment and so which Freud classifies as sexual. The oral phase becomes sadistic (i.e., pleasure is derived from destructiveness) when the teeth come into play. The second stage of sexual development is the *anal phase*, during which satisfaction is sought in excretory and aggressive functions.

The third and final stage of childhood sexuality is the *phallic phase*, which is, of course, confined to males. This period culminates in the *Oedipus phase*. The boy discovers his penis, and the pleasures associated with it, and begins to fantasize about sleeping with his mother and displacing his father. But when he discovers that females of his age have no comparable organ, he imagines that they have suffered the punishment of castration for their impure desires. The trauma this realization engenders ends the period of childhood sexuality, and a *latency period* sets in that will last until puberty. The girl, for her part, suffers from intense inferiority feelings for her lack of a penis, feelings that will permanently affect her character and begin to turn her away from sexual life. For purposes of self-protection, most memories of these childhood phases of sexuality in both sexes fall prey to *infantile amnesia*. (Subsequently, psychoanalysis may be required to recover memories of early sexual experiences and traumas that may have led to neuroses in adulthood.) The culmination of sexual development occurs for both sexes at puberty, the *genital phase*. For Freud, successful sexual development requires a successful organization of diverse libidinal urges and objects, so that, for example, the primary libidinal object becomes a member of the opposite sex, the genital urge becomes primary, but is supplemented by oral impulses, other libidinal urges are either repressed or displaced (sublimated) into other, nonsexual outlets, such as work and additional character traits.

The particular history and combination of sexual experiences in any individual — including pleasures and disappointments — have considerable influence upon the formation of personality and future sexual behavior. Sexual development that has been arrested or disturbed can result in *perversions* (i.e., libidinal fixations upon nongenital objects, or homosexuality — fixations upon genital objects of the same sex); present sexual disappointments can lead to *regressions* (i.e., libidinal fixations upon previously satisfying sexual objects). Thus, the individual's sexual life — even as far back as infancy and childhood — can help account for sexual problems in adolescence and adulthood. Thus, too, the formation of the personality is inextricably tied to sexual development.

IV. PSYCHICAL QUALITIES

I have described the structure of the psychical apparatus and the energies or forces which are active in it, and I have traced in a prominent example the way in which those energies (in the main, the libido) organize themselves into a physiological function which serves the purpose of the preservation of the species. There was nothing in all this to demonstrate the quite peculiar characteristic of what is psychical, apart, of course, from the empirical fact that this apparatus and these energies are the basis of the functions which we describe as our mental life. I will now turn to something which is uniquely characteristic of what is psychical, and, which, indeed, according to a very widely held opinion, coincides with it to the exclusion of all else.   1

The starting-point for this investigation is provided by a fact without parallel, which defies all explanation or description — the fact of consciousness. Nevertheless, if anyone speaks of consciousness we know immediately and from our most personal experience what is meant by it.[1] Many people, both inside and outside [psychological] science, are satisfied with the assumption that consciousness alone is psychical; in that case nothing remains for psychology but to discriminate among psychical phenomena between perceptions, feelings, thought-processes and volitions. It is generally agreed, however, that these conscious processes do not form unbroken sequences which are complete in themselves; there would thus be no alternative left to assuming that there are physical or somatic[2] processes which are concomitant with the psychical ones and which we should necessarily have to recognize as more complete than the psychical sequences, since some of them would have conscious processes parallel to them but others would not. If so, it of course becomes plausible to lay the stress in psychology on these somatic processes, to see in *them* the true essence of what is psychical and to look for some other assessment of the conscious processes. The majority of philosophers, however, as well as   2

---

[1]One extreme line of thought, exemplified in the American doctrine of behaviourism, thinks it possible to construct a psychology which disregards this fundamental fact! [Freud] See B. F. Skinner, who exemplifies this "extreme line of thought."

[2]*somatic:* Physical; having to do with the body.

many other people, dispute this and declare that the idea of something psychical being unconscious is self-contradictory.

But that is precisely what psycho-analysis is obliged to assert, and this is its second fundamental hypothesis.[3] It explains the supposedly somatic concomitant phenomena as being what is truly psychical, and thus in the first instance disregards the quality of consciousness. It is not alone in doing this. Some thinkers (such as Theodor Lipps,[4] for instance) have asserted the same thing in the same words; and the general dissatisfaction with the usual view of what is psychical has resulted in an increasingly urgent demand for the inclusion in psychological thought of a concept of the unconscious, though this demand has taken such an indefinite and obscure form that it could have no influence on science.

Now it would look as though this dispute between psycho-analysis and philosophy is concerned only with a trifling matter of definition — the question whether the name "psychical" should be applied to one or another sequence of phenomena. In fact, however, this step has become of the highest significance. Whereas the psychology of consciousness never went beyond the broken sequences which were obviously dependent on something else, the other view, which held that the psychical is unconscious in itself, enabled psychology to take its place as a natural science like any other. The processes with which it is concerned are in themselves just as unknowable as those dealt with by other sciences, by chemistry or physics, for example; but it is possible to establish the laws which they obey and to follow their mutual relations and interdependences unbroken over long stretches — in short, to arrive at what is described as an "understanding" of the field of natural phenomena in question. This cannot be effected without framing fresh hypotheses and creating fresh concepts; but these are not to be despised as evidence of embarrassment on our part but deserve on the contrary to be appreciated as an enrichment of science. They can lay claim to the same value as approximations that belongs to the corresponding intellectual scaffolding found in other natural sciences, and we look forward to their being modified, corrected and more precisely determined as further experience is accumulated and sifted. So too it will be entirely in accordance with our expectations if the basic concepts and principles of the new science (instinct, nervous energy, etc.) remain for a considerable time no less indeterminate than those of the older sciences (force, mass, attraction, etc.).

Every science is based on observations and experiences arrived at

3

4

5

---

[3]The first fundamental hypothesis, concerning the psychical "provinces" of *id, ego* and *superego*, has been described by Freud in Chapter 1 of "The Mind and Its Workings."

[4]*Theodor Lipps:* German psychologist (1851–1914) best known for his theory of aesthetics and the concept of "empathy" — the act of projecting oneself into the object of perception.

through the medium of our psychical apparatus. But since *our* science has as its subject that apparatus itself, the analogy ends here. We make our observations through the medium of the same perceptual apparatus, precisely with the help of the breaks in the sequence of "psychical" events: we fill in what is omitted by making plausible inferences and translating it into conscious material. In this way we construct, as it were, a sequence of conscious events complementary to the unconscious psychical processes. The relative certainty of our psychical science is based on the binding force of these inferences. Anyone who enters deeply into our work will find that our technique holds its ground against any criticism.

In the course of this work the distinctions which we describe as psychical qualities force themselves on our notice. There is no need to characterize what we call "conscious": it is the same as the consciousness of philosophers and of everyday opinion. Everything else psychical is in our view "the unconscious." We are soon led to make an important division in this unconscious. Some processes become conscious easily; they may then cease to be conscious, but can become conscious once more without any trouble: as people say, they can be reproduced or remembered. This reminds us that consciousness is in general a highly fugitive state. What is conscious is conscious only for a moment. If our perceptions do not confirm this, the contradiction is only an apparent one; it is explained by the fact that the stimuli which lead to perception may persist for considerable periods, so that meanwhile the perception of them may be repeated. The whole position is made clear in connection with the conscious perception of our thought-processes: these too may persist for some time, but they may just as well pass in a flash. Everything unconscious that behaves in this way, that can thus easily exchange the unconscious state for the conscious one, is therefore preferably described as "capable of becoming conscious" or as *preconscious*. Experience has taught us that there is hardly a psychical process, however complicated it may be, which cannot on occasion remain preconscious, even though as a rule it will, as we say, push its way forward into consciousness. There are other psychical processes and psychical material which have no such easy access to becoming conscious but must be inferred, recognized and translated into conscious form in the manner described. For such material we reserve the name of the unconscious proper.

Thus we have attributed three qualities to psychical processes: they are either conscious, preconscious, or unconscious. The division between the three classes of material which possess these qualities is neither absolute nor permanent. What is preconscious becomes conscious, as we have seen, without any assistance from us; what is unconscious can, through our efforts, be made conscious, and in the process we may have a feeling that we are often overcoming very strong resistances. When we attempt to do this with someone else, we should not forget that the conscious filling-in of the gaps in his perceptions — the construction we are presenting him with — does not mean as yet that we have made the unconscious material in question conscious to him. All that is true so far is that the material is present in him in two records, once in the conscious reconstruction he has been given, and besides this in its original unconscious state. Our continued efforts usually succeed eventually in making this unconscious material conscious to him himself, as a result of which the two records are brought to coincide. The amount of effort we have to use, by which we estimate the resistance against the material becoming conscious, varies in magnitude in individual cases. For instance, what comes about in an analytic treatment as a result of our efforts can also occur spontaneously: material which is ordinarily unconscious can transform itself into preconscious material and then becomes conscious — a thing that happens to a large extent in psychotic states. From this we infer that the maintenance of certain internal resistances is a *sine qua non*[5] of normality. A relaxation of resistances such as this, with a consequent pushing forward of unconscious material, takes place regularly in the state of sleep, and thus brings about a necessary precondition for the construction of dreams. Conversely, preconscious material can become temporarily inaccessible and cut off by resistances, as happens when something is temporarily forgotten or escapes the memory; or a preconscious thought can even be temporarily put back into the unconscious state, as seems to be a precondition in the case of jokes. We shall see that a similar transformation back of preconscious material or processes into the unconscious state plays a great part in the causation of neurotic disorders.

The theory of the three qualities of what is psychical, as described in this generalized and simplified manner, seems likely to be a source of limitless confusion rather than a help towards clarification. But it should not be forgotten that in fact it is not a theory at all but a first stock-taking of the facts of our observations, that it keeps as close to those facts as possible and does not attempt to explain them. The complications which it reveals may bring into relief the peculiar difficulties with which our investigations have to contend. It may be suspected, however, that we shall come to a closer understanding of this theory itself if we trace out the relations between the psychical qualities and the provinces or agencies of the psychical apparatus which we have postulated — these relations too are far from being simple.

The process of something becoming conscious is above all linked with the perceptions which our sense organs receive from the external world. From the topographical point of view, therefore, it is a phenomenon which takes place in the outermost cortex of the ego. It is true that we also receive

8

9

---

[5]*sine qua non:* (Latin) Essential condition.

conscious information from the inside of the body — the feelings, which actually exercise a more peremptory influence on our mental life than external perceptions; moreover, in certain circumstances the sense organs themselves transmit feelings, sensations of pain, in addition to the perceptions specific to them. Since, however, these sensations (as we call them in contrast to conscious perceptions) also emanate from the terminal organs and since we regard all these as prolongations or offshoots of the cortical layer, we are still able to maintain the assertion made above [at the beginning of this paragraph]. The only distinction would be that, as regards the terminal organs of sensation and feeling, the body itself would take the place of the external world.

Conscious processes on the periphery of the ego and everything else   10
in the ego unconscious — such would be the simplest state of affairs that we might picture. And such may in fact be the state that prevails in animals. But in men there is an added complication through which internal processes in the ego may also acquire the quality of consciousness. This is the work of the function of speech, which brings material in the ego into a firm connection with mnemic residues of visual, but more particularly of auditory, perceptions. Thenceforward the perceptual periphery of the cortical layer can be excited to a much greater extent from inside as well, internal events such as passages of ideas and thought-processes can become conscious, and a special device is called for in order to distinguish between the two possibilities — a device known as *reality-testing*. The equation "perception = reality (external world)" no longer holds. Errors, which can now easily arise and do so regularly in dreams, are called *hallucinations*.

The inside of the ego, which comprises above all the thought-pro-   11
cesses, has the quality of being preconscious. This is characteristic of the ego and belongs to it alone. It would not be correct, however, to think that connection with the mnemic residues of speech is a necessary precondition of the preconscious state. On the contrary, that state is independent of a connection with them, though the presence of that connection makes it safe to infer the preconscious nature of a process. The preconscious state, characterized on the one hand by having access to consciousness and on the other hand by its connection with the speech-residues, is nevertheless something peculiar, the nature of which is not exhausted by these two characteristics. The evidence for this is the fact that large portions of the ego, and particularly of the super-ego, which cannot be denied the characteristic of preconsciousness, none the less remain for the most part unconscious in the phenomenological sense[6] of the word. We do not know

---

[6]*phenomenological sense:* i.e., in the sense that these portions of the ego have an existence beyond our knowledge or perception of them as phenomena.

why this must be so. We shall attempt presently to attack the problem of the true nature of the preconscious.

The sole prevailing quality in the id is that of being unconscious. Id   12
and unconscious are as intimately linked as ego and preconscious: indeed, in the former case the connection is even more exclusive. If we look back at the developmental history of an individual and of his psychical apparatus, we shall be able to perceive an important distinction in the id. Originally, to be sure, everything was id; the ego was developed out of the id by the continual influence of the external world. In the course of this slow development certain of the contents of the id were transformed into the preconscious state and so taken into the ego; others of its contents remained in the id unchanged, as its scarcely accessible nucleus. During this development, however, the young and feeble ego put back into the unconscious state some of the material it had already taken in, dropped it, and behaved in the same way to some fresh impressions which it *might* have taken in, so that these, having been rejected, could leave a trace only in the id. In consideration of its origin we speak of this latter portion of the id as *the repressed*. It is of little importance that we are not always able to draw a sharp line between these two categories of contents in the id. They coincide approximately with the distinction between what was innately present originally and what was acquired in the course of the ego's development.

Having now decided upon the topographical dissection of the psychi-   13
cal apparatus into an ego and an id, with which the difference in quality between preconscious and unconscious runs parallel, and having agreed that this quality is to be regarded only as an *indication* of the difference and not as its essence, a further question faces us. What, if this is so, is the true nature of the state which is revealed in the id by the quality of being unconscious and in the ego by that of being preconscious and in what does the difference between them consist?

But of that we know nothing. And the profound obscurity of the back-   14
ground of our ignorance is scarcely illuminated by a few glimmers of insight. Here we have approached the still shrouded secret of the nature of the psychical. We assume, as other natural sciences have led us to expect, that in mental life some kind of energy is at work; but we have nothing to go upon which will enable us to come nearer to a knowledge of it by analogies with other forms of energy. We seem to recognize that nervous or psychical energy occurs in two forms, one freely mobile and another, by comparison, bound; we speak of cathexes[7] and hypercathexes of psychical

---

[7]*cathexes:* According to James Strachey, "cathexis" is a "term used on the analogy of an electrical charge, meaning concentration or accumulation of mental energy in some particular channel" — a person, object, or fantasy. (Quoted in *A General Selection from the Works of Sigmund Freud*, ed., John Rickman, M.D. (Garden City: Doubleday, 1957), 256.

material, and even venture to suppose that a hypercathexis brings about a kind of synthesis of different processes — a synthesis in the course of which free energy is transformed into bound energy. Further than this we have not advanced. At any rate, we hold firmly to the view that the distinction between the unconscious and the preconscious state lies in dynamic relations of this kind, which would explain how it is that, whether spontaneously or with our assistance, the one can be changed into the other.

Behind all these uncertainties, however, there lies one new fact, whose discovery we owe to psycho-analytic research. We have found that processes in the unconscious or in the id obey different laws from those in the preconscious ego. We name these laws in their totality the *primary process,* in contrast to the *secondary process* which governs the course of events in the preconscious, in the ego. In the end, therefore, the study of psychical qualities has after all proved not unfruitful. 15

V. DREAM-INTERPRETATION AS AN ILLUSTRATION

An investigation of normal, stable states, in which the frontiers of the ego are safeguarded against the id by resistances (anticathexes) and have held firm, and in which the super-ego is not distinguished from the ego, because they work together harmoniously — an investigation of that kind would teach us little. The only thing that can help us are states of conflict and uproar, when the contents of the unconscious id have a prospect of forcing their way into the ego and into consciousness and the ego puts itself once more on the defensive against this invasion. It is only under these conditions that we can make such observations as will confirm or correct our statements about the two partners. Now, our nightly sleep is precisely a state of this sort, and for that reason psychical activity during sleep, which we perceive as dreams, is our most favourable object of study. In that way, too, we avoid the familiar reproach that we base our constructions of normal mental life on pathological findings; for dreams are regular events in the life of a normal person, however much their characteristics may differ from the productions of our waking life. Dreams, as everyone knows, may be confused, unintelligible or positively nonsensical, what they say may contradict all that we know of reality, and we behave in them like insane people, since, so long as we are dreaming, we attribute objective reality to the contents of the dream. 16

We find our way to the understanding ("interpretation") of a dream by assuming that what we recollect as the dream after we have woken up is not the true dream-process but only a *façade* behind which that process lies concealed. Here we have our distinction between the *manifest* content of a dream and the *latent* dream-thoughts. The process which produces the former out of the latter is described as the *dream-work.* The study of the dream- 17 work teaches us by an excellent example the way in which unconscious material from the id (originally unconscious and repressed unconscious alike) forces its way into the ego, becomes preconscious and, as a result of the ego's opposition, undergoes the changes which we know as *dream-distortion*. There are no features of a dream which cannot be explained in this way.

It is best to begin by pointing out that the formation of a dream can be   *18* provoked in two different ways. Either, on the one hand, an instinctual impulse which is ordinarily suppressed (an unconscious wish) finds enough strength during sleep to make itself felt by the ego, or, on the other hand, an urge left over from waking life, a preconscious train of thought with all the conflicting impulses attached to it, finds reinforcement during sleep from an unconscious element. In short, dreams may arise either from the id or from the ego. The mechanism of dream-formation is in both cases the same and so also is the necessary dynamic precondition. The ego gives evidence of its original derivation from the id by occasionally ceasing its functions and allowing a reversion to an earlier state of things. This is logically brought about by its breaking off its relations with the external world and withdrawing its cathexes from the sense organs. We are justified in saying that there arises at birth an instinct to return to the intra-uterine life that has been abandoned — an instinct to sleep. Sleep is a return of this kind to the womb. Since the waking ego governs motility, that function is paralysed in sleep, and accordingly a good part of the inhibitions imposed on the unconscious id become superfluous. The withdrawal or reduction of these "anticathexes" thus allows the id what is now a harmless amount of liberty.

The evidence of the share taken by the unconscious id in the formation   *19* of dreams is abundant and convincing. (*a*) Memory is far more comprehensive in dreams than in waking life. Dreams bring up recollections which the dreamer has forgotten, which are inaccessible to him when he is awake. (*b*) Dreams make an unrestricted use of linguistic symbols, the meaning of which is for the most part unknown to the dreamer. Our experience, however, enables us to confirm their sense. They probably originate from earlier phases in the development of speech. (*c*) Memory very often reproduces in dreams impressions from the dreamer's early childhood of which we can definitely assert not only that they had been forgotten but that they had become unconscious owing to repression. That explains the help — usually indispensable — given us by dreams in the attempts we make during the analytic treatment of neuroses to reconstruct the dreamer's early life. (*d*) Furthermore, dreams bring to light material which cannot have originated either from the dreamer's adult life or from his forgotten childhood. We are obliged to regard it as part of the *archaic heritage* which a child brings with him into the world, before any experience of his own, influenced by the experiences of his ancestors. We find the counterpart of this phylogenetic[8] material in the earliest human legends and in surviving customs. Thus dreams constitute a source of human prehistory which is not to be despised.

But what makes dreams so invaluable in giving us insight is the circumstance that, when the unconscious material makes its way into the ego, it brings its own modes of working along with it. This means that the preconscious thoughts in which the unconscious material has found its expression are handled in the course of the dream-work as though they were unconscious portions of the id; and, in the case of the alternative method of dream-formation, the preconscious thoughts which have obtained reinforcement from an unconscious instinctual impulse are brought down to the unconscious state. It is only in this way that we learn the laws which govern the passage of events in the unconscious and the respects in which they differ from the rules that are familiar to us in waking thought. Thus the dream-work is essentially an instance of the unconscious working-over of preconscious thought-processes. To take an analogy from history: invading conquerors govern a conquered country, not according to the judicial system which they find in force there, but according to their own. It is, however, an unmistakable fact that the outcome of the dream-work is a compromise. The ego-organization is not yet paralysed, and its influence is to be seen in the distortion imposed on the unconscious material and in what are often very ineffective attempts at giving the total result a form not too unacceptable to the ego (*secondary revision*). In our analogy this would be an expression of the continued resistance of the defeated people.

The laws that govern the passage of events in the unconscious, which come to light in this manner, are remarkable enough and suffice to explain most of what seems strange to us about dreams. Above all there is a striking tendency to *condensation*, an inclination to form fresh unities out of elements which in our waking thought we should certainly have kept separate. As a consequence of this, a single element of the manifest dream often stands for a whole number of latent dream-thoughts as though it were a combined allusion to all of them; and in general the compass of the manifest dream is extraordinarily small in comparison with the wealth of material from which it has sprung. Another peculiarity of the dream-work, not entirely independent of the former one, is the ease with which psychical intensities (cathexes) are *displaced* from one element to another, so that it often happens that an element which was of little importance in the dream-thoughts appears as the clearest and accordingly most important feature of the manifest dream, and, *vice versa*, that essential elements of the dream-thoughts are represented in the manifest dream only by slight

[20]

[21]

---

[8]*phylogenetic:* Relating to the history of the evolution of a species.

allusions. Moreover, as a rule the existence of quite insignificant points in common between two elements is enough to allow the dream-work to re-place one by the other in all further operations. It will easily be imagined how greatly these mechanisms of condensation and displacement can in-crease the difficulty of interpreting a dream and of revealing the relations between the manifest dream and the latent dream-thoughts. From the evi-dence of the existence of these two tendencies to condensation and dis-placement our theory infers that in the unconscious id the energy is in a freely mobile state and that the id sets more store by the possibility of discharging quantities of excitation than by any other consideration;[9] and our theory makes use of these two peculiarities in defining the character of the primary process we have attributed to the id.

The study of the dream-work has taught us many other characteristics   22 of the processes in the unconscious which are as remarkable as they are important; but we must only mention a few of them here. The governing rules of logic carry no weight in the unconscious; it might be called the Realm of the Illogical. Urges with contrary aims exist side by side in the unconscious without any need arising for an adjustment between them. Either they have no influence whatever on each other, or, if they have, no decision is reached, but a compromise comes about which is nonsensical since it embraces mutually incompatible details. With this is connected the fact that contraries are not kept apart but treated as though they were iden-tical, so that in the manifest dream any element may also have the meaning of its opposite. Certain philologists have found that the same held good in the most ancient languages and that contraries such as "strong-weak," "light-dark," and "high-deep" were originally expressed by the same roots, until two different modifications of the primitive word distinguished between the two meanings. Residues of this original double meaning seem to have survived even in a highly developed language like Latin in its use of words such as *"altus"* ("high" and "deep") and *"sacer"* ("sacred" and "infamous").

In view of the complication and ambiguity of the relations between the   23 manifest dream and the latent content lying behind it, it is of course justi-fiable to ask how it is at all possible to deduce the one from the other and whether all we have to go on is a lucky guess, assisted perhaps by a trans-lation of the symbols that occur in the manifest dream. It may be said in reply that in the great majority of cases the problem can be satisfactorily solved, but only with the help of the associations provided by the dreamer himself to the elements of the manifest content. Any other procedure is arbitrary and can yield no certain result. But the dreamer's associations

---

[9]An analogy may be seen in the behaviour of a non-comissioned officer who accepts a reprimand from his superior in silence but vents his anger on the first innocent private he comes across. [Freud]

bring to light intermediate links which we can insert in the gap between the two [between the manifest and the latent content] and by aid of which we can reinstate the latent content of the dream and "interpret" it. It is not to be wondered at if this work of interpretation (acting in a direction opposite to the dream-work) fails occasionally to arrive at complete certainty.

It remains for us to give a dynamic explanation of why the sleeping 24 ego takes on the task of the dream-work at all. The explanation is fortunately easy to find. With the help of the unconscious, every dream that is in process of formation makes a demand upon the ego — for the satisfaction of an instinct, if the dream originates from the id; for the solution of a conflict, the removal of a doubt or the forming of an intention, if the dream originates from a residue of preconscious activity in waking life. The sleeping ego, however, is focused on the wish to maintain sleep; it feels this demand as a disturbance and seeks to get rid of the disturbance. The ego succeeds in doing this by what appears to be an act of compliance: it meets the demand with what is in the circumstances a harmless *fulfilment of a wish* and so gets rid of it. This replacement of the demand by the fulfilment of a wish remains the essential function of the dream-work. It may perhaps be worth while to illustrate this by three simple examples — a hunger dream, a dream of convenience and a dream prompted by sexual desire. A need for food makes itself felt in a dreamer during his sleep: he has a dream of a delicious meal and sleeps on. The choice, of course, was open to him either of waking up and eating something or of continuing his sleep. He decided in favour of the latter and satisfied his hunger by means of the dream — for the time being, at all events, for if his hunger had persisted he would have had to wake up nevertheless. Here is the second example. A sleeper had to wake up so as to be in time for his work at the hospital. But he slept on, and had a dream that he was already at the hospital — but as a patient, who has no need to get up. Or again, a desire becomes active during the night for the enjoyment of a forbidden sexual object, the wife of a friend of the sleeper. He has a dream of sexual intercourse — not, indeed, with this person but with someone else of the same name to whom he is in fact indifferent; or his struggle against the desire may find expression in his mistress remaining altogether anonymous.

Naturally, every case is not so simple. Especially in dreams which have 25 originated from undealt-with residues of the previous day, and which have only obtained an unconscious reinforcement during the state of sleep, it is often no easy task to uncover the unconscious motive force and its wish-fulfilment; but we may assume that it is always there. The thesis that dreams are the fulfilments of wishes will easily arouse scepticism when it is remembered how many dreams have an actually distressing content or even wake the dreamer in anxiety, quite apart from the numerous dreams without any definite feeling-tone. But the objection based on anxiety dreams cannot be sustained against analysis. It must not be forgotten that dreams are invariably the product of a conflict, that they are a kind of compromise-structure. Something that is a satisfaction for the unconscious id may for that very reason be a cause for anxiety for the ego.

As the dream-work proceeds, sometimes the unconscious will press   26 forward more successfully and sometimes the ego will defend itself with greater energy. Anxiety dreams are mostly those whose content has undergone the least distortion. If the demand made by the unconscious is too great for the sleeping ego to be in a position to fend it off by the means at its disposal, it abandons the wish to sleep and returns to waking life. We shall be taking every experience into account if we say that a dream is invariably an *attempt* to get rid of a disturbance of sleep by means of a wish-fulfilment, so that the dream is a guardian of sleep. The attempt may succeed more or less completely; it may also fail, and in that case the sleeper wakes up, apparently woken precisely by the dream. So, too, there are occasions when that excellent fellow the night-watchman, whose business it is to guard the little township's sleep, has no alternative but to sound the alarm and waken the sleeping townspeople.

I will close this discussion with a comment which will justify the length   27 of time I have spent on the problem of the interpretation of dreams. Experience has shown that the unconscious mechanisms which we have come to know from our study of the dream-work and which gave us the explanation of the formation of dreams also help us to understand the puzzling symptoms which attract our interest to neuroses and psychoses. A conformity of such a kind cannot fail to excite high hopes in us.

REVIEW QUESTIONS

Note: The first three questions refer to the material outlined in the summary preceding the actual reading selection.

1. Distinguish the chief characteristics of the id, the ego, and the superego. Which of these components is the oldest, which the most recent? Indicate the major relationships among them. What are the major influences upon the formation of the superego? What do the id and the superego have in common?
2. What are instincts? How do they operate? What are the two basic instincts, according to Freud? How do they relate to one another? With which components of the psychical apparatus is each instinct primarily associated? In what forms do secondary associations (of instincts and components of the psychical apparatus) manifest themselves? What, for example, is the result when the entire libido is associated with the ego?
3. In what chief ways did Freud's analysis of human sexuality contradict accepted belief on this subject? Outline the main phases of human sexual development, according to Freud. With what organs of the body are these individual phases associated? How does Freud justify classifying these phases as sexual? What is

the significance (for psychoanalysis) of *infantile amnesia*? What is the significance of the Oedipal phase in sexual development? In the context of the phases of sexual development, how do perversions originate? What is *regression*? How is the individual personality related to sexual development?

4. Why was it necessary to postulate the existence of the *unconscious*? What special difficulties attend the study of the unconscious? Do these difficulties have analogs in other sciences? What is the *preconscious*? How is it related to the "unconscious proper"? How are phenomena such as dreams, jokes, and forgetting related to the transfer of material among the conscious, the preconscious, and the unconscious? With which components of the physical apparatus (id, ego, superego) are the various modes of consciousness chiefly associated? What happens during the process of *repression*? What is the difference between *primary process* and *secondary process*?

5. Why is the state of sleep considered a fruitful area for the study of interactions between id and ego? What is the difference between the *manifest content* and the *latent content* of a dream? How do dreams originate? With which components of the psychical apparatus are dreams associated? What is the role of memory in dreams? What is the role of symbols? Define the concepts of *condensation* and *displacement*. How does *wish fulfillment* serve a therapeutic purpose in dreams? How does Freud account for anxiety dreams (i.e., dreams that do not serve the purpose of wish fulfillment)? What is the relationship between dreams and neuroses and psychoses?

DISCUSSION AND WRITING QUESTIONS

Note: The first three questions refer to the material outlined in the summary preceding the actual reading selection.

1. What evidence do you see in your own life and in the lives of those around you that Freud's analysis of the psychical apparatus into id, ego, and superego is a meaningful one? Describe in some detail an event in your own life that displays the conflicting (and unresolved) demands and activities among id, ego, and superego.

2. Freud and his followers have been criticized for reducing all human instincts to only two categories, i.e., the destructive instinct and the *libido*. To what extent does Freud's analysis of instincts seem satisfactory? To what extent does it seem deficient? Discuss examples of instincts that you believe to fall outside of Freud's categories, and be prepared to defend your position against counterarguments by Freud's supporters that your examples are merely common variants of destructive or libidinous instincts.

3. Freud's most controversial theories center on his analysis of human sexuality. Discuss your own reaction to these theories, as here expressed in the summary of Chapter 3 of *The Mind and Its Workings*. Do Freud's statements on both "normal" and "abnormal" sexuality seem entirely convincing? Partially convincing? Unconvincing? Explain. Support your position using examples from your own observations.

4. Using your own experience and knowledge as a basis, explain by example how material can be transferred among the unconscious, the preconscious, and the

conscious. Without attempting a full-scale self-analysis, try to identify certain components of your own personality that may be the result of the repression into your unconscious of certain anxiety-producing impulses or experiences. On a more conscious level, explain how certain jokes you have made, or how certain things you have conveniently "forgotten" are really attempts by your psychical apparatus to reduce anxiety.

5. Recall a dream you have had recently or one that you remember vividly, because it was either particularly disturbing or particularly pleasurable. Try to account for this dream in terms of Freud's discussion in section V of this passage. For example, how does this dream make use of memory, particularly the memory of experiences in early childhood? Of symbols? What might these symbols represent? (For example, do you think that a certain person in your dream might represent someone else?) To what extent might this dream serve the purpose of wish fulfillment? What might be the logic behind the apparent absurdity of the dream?

6. Write a summary of either Chapter 4, "Psychical Qualities" or Chapter 5, "Dream-Interpretation as an Illustration." Use the summaries preceding these passages as models.

ROBERT LINDNER (1915–1956)

Just as the most direct application of Marxist principles is in the overthrow of the capitalist classes by the working classes, so the most direct application of Freudian principles is in the encounter — sometimes cordial, sometimes tense — between psychoanalyst and patient. Individual psychoanalysts may operate according to strict Freudian principles or they may deviate from them, depending upon their own professional inclinations and their own judgments as to how they can best help their patients. But to a greater or lesser degree, from either a positive or a negative perspective, most psychoanalysts take as their starting point the ideas of Freud, as he outlined them in "The Mind and Its Workings."

Accounts of individual cases of psychoanalytic therapy are legion, and because of their inherent drama are a frequent subject for popular books and films — for example, *Spellbound*, *The Three Faces of Eve*, and *Ordinary People*. One of the most successful and well-known factual accounts of psychotherapy at work is *The Fifty-Minute Hour: A Collection of True Psychoanalytic Tales*, by Dr. Robert Lindner. Born in 1915 in New York City, Lindner earned his M.A. and Ph.D. in psychology from Cornell University. He spent much of his professional life working with criminals and others who had been considered untreatable by psychotherapy. Lindner became chief psychiatrist at the Federal Penitentiary at Lewisburg, Pennsylvania, and during World War II served as an officer in the United States Public Health Service. After the war, he went into private practice in Baltimore, while serving as chief consultant of the Maryland Board of Corrections. Lindner's book, *Rebel without a Cause* (1955), later made into a film starring James Dean, was based on the case of a criminal psychopath he had met at the Lewisburg Penitentiary. He also wrote *Walls and Men: Prescription for Rebellion* (1946), *The Fifty-Minute Hour* (1955), and *Must You Conform?* (1956); and he edited a collection of essays, *Explorations in Psychoanalysis* (1953). Lindner died of a heart ailment in 1956.

Lindner's accounts are remarkable both for their vividness and narrative power and for their success in demystifying the process of psychoanalysis itself, which for many lay people is viewed as a kind of priestly ritual, shrouded in secrecy. In his introduction, Lindner writes:

A psychoanalyst is . . . nothing more than an artist at understanding, the product of an intensive course of study and training which has — if it has been successful — rendered him unusually sensitive to his fellow men. And it is this sensitivity — in short, the analyst's own person — which is the single instrument, the only tool, with which he performs. Only on himself, and on nothing else, does he depend.

Perhaps not coincidentally, Lindner's words are reminiscent of those of the English romantic poet William Wordsworth (1770–1850), in describing the qualities of a poet: "a man speaking to men: a man, it is true, endowed with a more lively sensibility, more enthusiasm and tenderness, who has a greater knowledge of human nature, and a more comprehensive soul, than are supposed to be common among mankind. . . ." [Preface to *Lyrical Ballads* (1798).]

The following passage is taken from the second of Lindner's "true psychoanalytic tales" in *The Fifty-Minute Hour* (entitled "Come Over, Red Rover"). In the introductory section, Lindner explains his philosophy as both a psychoanalyst and a citizen:

> For many years I have been active politically in a small way out of a conviction that the psychoanalyst belongs in the world, among men, and should participate in the life of his community. I have felt that he has a public responsibility which cannot be discharged by living the anchorite existence most analysts live, limiting their purview to the dim caves in which they practice their art like oracular recluses surrounded by the esoteric symbols of a mystic craft.

One evening, while chairing a public meeting, Lindner was heckled by a man who demanded to know why there were no blacks on a list of prospective members for a panel on socialized medicine. After the meeting, Lindner talked to the man, whose name was Mac, and learned that he used to be in the Merchant Marine, that he worked at a local canning factory, and that he was a member of the Communist Party. Some weeks later, Mac called Lindner, asking for an appointment; it was an emergency, he claimed. At first, Lindner, whose schedule was full, was reluctant to take on the additional responsibility, but Mac asserted that Lindner was the only psychoanalyst in the city who could help him. Departing from his usual practice, Lindner invited Mac to his own home for a consultation the following Sunday. On the appointed day, Mac appeared and told Lindner that his wife had left him; he had become impotent. There was no obvious physical cause for his condition (he had already consulted a urologist, who could not help him, and who recommended that he see a psychiatrist). But, he told Lindner, he was interested in getting help only if it did not interfere with his activities or his position in the Communist Party. It was especially important that the party not discover that Mac was seeing a psychoanalyst, for this could result in his expulsion. (As Lindner had somewhat sarcastically remarked to Mac, "I know it. . . . Psychoanalysis is a bourgeois science: psychoanalysts are the lackeys of the capitalist class. I'm an unstable Social Democrat. So what are you doing here?") But Mac insisted "that if getting analyzed means I have to quit the party, it's not for me." He rationalized his coming to see Lindner by claiming that it would make him a better communist.

Lindner reassured Mac that he would not try to influence him against the party. He considered the pros and cons of trying to treat Mac. The chief con: "the moment any of his cherished formulas were questioned there would be hell to pay: his analysis would be hung for many hours while he did battle with his Marxist conscience. . . ." But for Lindner, the chief pro was decisive:

> The chance to analyze yet another Communist! The chance to test once more my ideas about the breed of men who become militant socialists! I had already, while stationed in a Federal prison, analyzed a high official of the Party and an officer of a trade union who was also a Communist. Then I had treated a social worker, an engineer, a student and a teacher who were all card-holders

in the Party. Max would be the first worker-Communist on my growing list, my first real "proletarian." The temptation was not to be resisted. . . .

THE FIFTY-MINUTE HOUR

Mac had been born thirty-four years before we met. The place of his   1
birth was a farm in western Ohio where his parents lived with his father's people. The model of a Conestoga wagon[1] on a shelf in my study reminded him of his family origins. Stolid, imperturbable and determined Dutch settlers, they had pushed their way westward in one of the first migrations from the East Coast, coming to rest, characteristically, in a place that reminded them of the home they had left in Europe. Mac's grandfather, who was a very old man when Mac was born, had staked out a large tract of land. As his three sons came of age he parceled it among them, reserving for himself and his second, much younger wife a few acres in the exact middle of the family holdings. White-bearded and with clear blue eyes that remained undimmed to the hour of his death, tall and as strong as one of his work horses, this paternal grandfather was destined to play a major role in the formation of Mac's personality. So was the patriarch's wife, a half-breed illegitimate girl who had been maid of all work on the farm until her mistress died and she was taken to wife as a matter of course.

The youngest of the three sons was Mac's father. He was the old man's   2
favorite, alike to his father in features as an image in a mirror. A vast silence surrounded him. Indeed, Mac recalled no word his father had ever spoken. But his manner was kind and his uncommunicativeness more than made up for by a soothing, peaceful presence. His wife, Mac's mother, died in the moment Mac was born. A faded daguerreotype,[2] its cracked pieces glued to a strip of cardboard, was all that Mac ever knew of her. In her place was a conglomerate fiction composed by the boy over the years from his grandfather's reminiscences and the memory of two brief visits paid the half-orphan by his mother's parents. They were, he remembers, big people with heavy hands and huge feet. As they sat in the kitchen

---

Robert Lindner. The Fifty Minute Hour. [1955]. Original title: "Come Over, Red Rover." In *The Fifty Minute Hour*. New York: James Aronson, 1982. Originally published by Rinehart, 1955.

[1]*Conestoga wagon:* A covered wagon with large wheels used by the pioneers in their westward journeys across the prairies.

[2]*daguerreotype:* An early photograph made by a process involving light-sensitive metallic plates.

and spoke of their daughter's death, they filled the room with the smell of earth, and their low, hoarse voices blended with the snapping of wood in the fire and the simmering bubble of the water kettle to become fixed for a lifetime as the sense-scenery of Mac's dreams.

A wet-nurse tended Mac the first three years of his life. Actually, she 3 ministered to him only part time, and for the remainder deputized the oldest daughter of her large brood to act as cook, housekeeper and milk-maid for Mac's father and the distant cousin who worked as hired man. The ample-bosomed nurse was like a general who regularly visits the front. Every morning, while it was still dark, she drove up in a rickety buck-board. It was she who would take Mac from his bed, suckle him, clean and dress him, then turn him over to her daughter with a list of instructions for his day's welfare and activity. A wet smack on his cheek and she was off, to return again after supper with a milk-full breast, a sponging, and a final kiss administered while she folded the warm quilt around him. Be-tween the dawn and dusk of her brisk visits there was the sugar-tit, pre-pared by this natural pediatrician from a lump of honey knotted in a rag and moistened with milk. It was in his mouth all day and most of the night and its taste, recaptured during the early part of his psychoanalysis more than thirty years later, was an assurance of peace and an allayer of fears.

Soon after Mac had turned three he was taken to live in his grandfath- 4 er's house. Now he came under the dominion of his dour step-grand-mother, whom he learned to call "Ma," and the idyll of perfect freedom in which he had lived heretofore was shattered. Ma was a soured woman, intolerant of small boys and dirt, embittered for life by her illegitimacy, and fierce in all her compensations for early experiences as the offspring of an Indian woman and a westbound hunter hungry for the feel of human flesh. In contrast with the large affections of the wet-nurse who stood in his mother's place, Ma was as sterile in her feelings as in her womb. In her scheme there was no place for this two-legged animal with its wants, its needs, its stinks, its inability to comprehend what was expected of it. The first thing to go was the sugar-tit, and the next a rough wooden horse carved by his father, now smooth and sticky with the love of small, hot hands. From Ma, for the first time, Mac heard the words "bad" and "naughty." They applied to everything he did; but mainly to the contents of his pants and to the twig of flesh that hung between his legs and made his belly turn over with vibrations of secret pleasure when he touched it, when he rubbed the flank of a cow a certain way, or when thunder broke from the sky.

Pa — Grandpa — was different. He was as big as a giant and when he 5 stepped on to the porch the house shook. It almost scared you even to look at him, but beneath his brusque and boom there was a tenderness, and when his huge hand held yours you could feel as safe as if you were held by God. Grandpa looked like God, too, whose picture was on the front of the Bible from which the old man read every night. And Grandpa acted like God, too, dispensing a swift justice to the animals on his farm, to his sons, his hands, his wife and Mac. From Grandpa, Mac learned anger and the indignation that were later to make him want the kind of world where Grandpa's justice would be a matter of course, a society founded on the fairness that was Grandpa's rule of life. For Grandpa saw things directly and simply, black and white, and his fundamentalist faith could as little be shaken as the hills that ringed the horizons of the land where Mac spent his childhood.

The first of the World Wars claimed the life of Mac's father. He was   6 crushed by the carriage of a big gun that fell on him in an accident in training camp. At the time his death meant little to Mac; only as the years piled on each other did the space left by the quiet one's going get bigger and come to matter. Meanwhile, there were the farm chores, the animals, the few brief months of school each year, the river that coiled through bottom land, the woods. There were hunting with the uncles, fishing with Pa, preserving with Ma, and all else that makes life in the country busy. At twelve there were more intimate and secret delights whose forbidden-ness came home to him with stabbings of guilt in the evenings when, with the sick fascination of fears of discovery, Mac watched the slow movement across the page of Pa's great forefinger and heard the glottal sonorities of the old man's voice as he read of the wages of sin from the Book. And always there was Ma, fussing behind him, nagging, critical, sharp in her words and tone, forever unsatisfied and bitter-resentful.

When Mac was fourteen, the old man fell on the ice and broke his hip.   7 He was then almost ninety, and with his fall his spirits also fell. When he took to his bed he seemed to shrivel and dry as if his juices were draining through a hidden tap on his body. For six months he lay on his bed, dying a little every day. During this time, Mac was with him constantly. Out of an urge to talk, perhaps to make a pattern of his life, he told his grandson the tales that made up his history. In snatches, and in a sequence that was the old man's alone, dictated by a curious internal logic, there emerged stories of poverty and persecution, the sea voyage to new lands, the heart-break in the port city and the scrounging for silver to buy the gear for the westward march; the yard by yard struggle across the hills and rivers, the fighting with outraged men and angry Nature to clear and hold the land, the tearing down and the building; the great joys and the great sorrows of ninety victorious years. In Mac it made a brew of memories, both bitter and sweet; and when the old man at last closed his eyes, unknowingly Mac had distilled from these six months the essence of Pa, and drunk of it so deeply that it was to flow forever with his own blood.

The old man's death changed the world for Mac. The restlessness that   8 had always been in him, but anchored first by his wet-nurse and then by Pa, broke free. He could not abide Ma and her ways, and the war the two had been waging since the day Mac was moved into her house now flared into open combat. So on a certain night, in traditional fashion with a bundle over his shoulder, Mac left.

He went to Chicago and there began the Odyssey that terminated on the couch in my study. The list of jobs he held is a long one. Always he worked with his hands and earned his money in sweat. Never did any one job last very long, chiefly because of the nature of the times, but also because of his restlessness, his querulousness and his inability to take orders. He knew poverty, not only of the slow kind on the margin of existing, but of the absolute kind, with the threat of starvation and death, the shame of beggary, the humiliation of picking over the contents of waste cans and garbage dumps like an animal, loathing oneself and disgusted but sharp in the eye for a bit of molding bread. And he knew idleness; not the leisurely kind, but the sort that fouls the mind and drugs the spirit; the listless, dragging, debilitating kind that shuffles in long lines at soup kitchens, huddles against the night-cold in musty mission rooms behind windows where JESUS
A
V
E
S

in harsh electric light glares against the sky.

Then one day, with the farm now many years behind him, Mac stumbled upon his destiny. He had been out of work for weeks, living in a Hooverville[3] among other castoffs. A car drove up to the ramshackle picket fence someone had made around the encampment to caricature the community of the undamned, and from it stepped a man with a well-fed look on his face. He asked who wanted work. Some of the older hands apparently knew him and turned their backs. But Mac had hunger in his belly and an itch in his muscles, so with a few others he piled into the truck that followed the man's car. They were driven to a big shed by the docks, where a hot stew and coffee were served. Then the man gave each one a rough club and told them to line up and follow one of his assistants.

They walked to a pier by which strikers were parading in a thin picket line. When the strikers saw them coming, the shout of "Scabs!" went up as they closed their ranks to make room for others who came running from behind a shed. At a command, the crew Mac was with charged. After a brief battle, most of them broke through and reached the end of the pier

9

10

11

---

[3]*Hooverville:* Shantytowns erected near city dumps and occupied by the dispossessed and jobless during the depression of the 1930s. They were also known as "Hoover villages" after President Herbert Hoover, who was bitterly viewed by many depression victims as a figure of reckless optimism.

where a freighter was moored beside huge crates of machinery and piles of scrap iron. These they began to load into the hold of the ship. Mac worked eagerly, glad to be feeling the blood flow again through his arms and legs. That night the strikebreakers were fed from the ship's galley and bedded on blankets below deck. From outside, restrained from attacking the scabs by a detachment of police, the strikers taunted and cursed at them, but with little effect, for these were work- and food-starved men.

On the third day the job was done, the scabs were paid off, and a truck   12 came to carry them back to Hooverville. Mac and a buddy left the truck as it passed the railroad yards. They caught a southbound freight. As the train highballed out of the city, through the slats of the cattle car they saw the ship they had just loaded swinging into the current.

"That was a stinkin', lousy thing to do," said Mac's buddy, "and I   13 wouldn'a done it but for hunger."

"What was so stinkin' about it?" Mac asked.   14

His buddy told him; and out of the telling came hours in libraries with   15 fat books and a dime dictionary, came listening and talking, came hearing with new ears and speaking with a new tongue, came sitting on cane-bottomed chairs in union halls and weary marching round and round on picket lines, came *Solidarity Forever*[4] and *Joe Hill*,[5] came the Party's little booklet with a place for stamps, came new words, new thoughts, new deeds. And in the late 'thirties, came a visit one night to a doctor's office in New York, a job on a tramp for Marseilles;[6] then a long, cold night of walking, running, lying breathless in the snow of a Pyrenees'[7] pass, and in the morning a ride on a truck, and in the evening a dole of dungarees and cap; then marching and a wooden gun and Link, Zwei, Drei, Vier;[8] then, at last, the trenches and the splintering brick walls of the University outside Madrid, a real gun and the red blood of a Moor on his bayonet and the sweet smell of rotting fascist corpses[9] pasted for always to the inside of his nostrils.

---

[4]*Solidarity Forever:* Stewart Bird's oral history of the IWW (Industrial Workers of the World), a revolutionary labor union that advocated the overthrow of capitalism by strikes, boycotts, and sabotage. Founded in 1905, the IWW (also known as the "Wobblies") had by 1912 enlisted a membership of 100,000; but six years later, because of government harassment and prosecutions and an antiracial hysteria, it became moribund.

[5]*Joe Hill:* Wallace Stegner's biographical novel of the IWW leader who advocated violence in the waging of the class struggle (first published as *The Preacher and the Slave*).

[6]*Marseilles:* A port city in southeastern France.

[7]*Pyrenees:* The mountains dividing France and Spain.

[8]*Link, Zwei, Drei, Vier:* German for "Left, Two, Three, Four"; a marching command.

[9]*rotting fascist corpses:* The conflict referred to here is the Spanish Civil War (1936–1939) between Francisco Franco's fascist forces and the loyalist forces supported by the communists and by the European and American left.

When the war in Spain ended, Mac returned to the States. He joined   *16*
the Merchant Marine and was assigned by the Party to union activity. He
roved the world during the next years, carrying out Party tasks with efficiency and will. This work took him to strange places, and he did strange
things for a farmer boy from the western reaches of Ohio. The internal
politics of the Party never interested him, and despite its changes of
course, its upsets and veerings, he hewed strongly to the line. When war
was declared against Germany and Japan, he wanted to enlist but was told
that because of his record as a fighter in Spain he would be marked in the
United States Army and hence of little value to the Party. Disappointed but
ungrudging, he remained a merchant seaman; but when the Soviet Union
joined the Allies and the underground everywhere came alive as if touched
by a magician's wand, Mac found his place as a courier and contact man
among resistance groups and between national Party units. The work was
exciting, dangerous, and the pitch of his life was passionate.

In the last year of the war Mac married a comrade from New York   *17*
whom he had made pregnant. This was no shabby affair: it had nothing to
do with the malicious fictions of the press and the yellow journals about
free love among the Reds. The girl was Jewish, of strong moral character,
and a virgin when Mac met her. They had been in love for more than a
year but had postponed marriage because of the death of the girl's brother
in the air over Germany and her respect for the tradition of her people. But
in the seventh month of their love, and on the first night of sexual intercourse, there was an accident of contraception. As soon as her year of
mourning was over, they were married. The twins were born in the summer of 1945 when the war ended.

With the coming of peace Mac was no longer important to the Party in   *18*
the Merchant Marine. He was transferred to heavy industry, where he was
assigned to organize certain craft workers. At this task he failed miserably,
whereupon he was tried in a succession of assignments in New Jersey and
Pennsylvania. Finally, he was instructed to move with his family to a place
near Baltimore and to place himself at the disposal of the Party officials
there. They reviewed his record and ordered him to work in a canning
factory where the cleaners and packers were unorganized. On Sundays he
had a delivery route for the *Sunday Worker*. This is what Mac was doing
when he came to psychoanalysis. . . .

While the analysis was concerned, in its opening stages, with a re-   *19*
counting of the superficial history that has been sketched, it was a veritable
honeymoon for both Mac and myself. Long-forgotten experiences and incidents were recovered, and a rough pattern of Mac's basic personality was
worked out. He recognized, very soon after he began, that he had romanticized his family origins; that he had stood in awed admiration of his
grandfather even though the old man, because of his great size and imposing personality, had terrorized him; that he had hated violently his

step-grandmother but — according to a well-tested analytic dictum that a child identifies with the frustrating parent on the principle of the defensive, "if you can't lick 'em, join 'em" — that he had acquired and absorbed many of her traits. He realized, too, that he had been made exceptionally dependent by his wet-nurse, and that the greater part of his restlessness throughout his life came from an inner compulsion to seek situations that could be equated in his unconscious with that happy condition of total surrender to someone or something in utter faith. He achieved, also, some striking insights about his sexual life: for example, that his grandmother's curt disposal of the sugar-tit which was in his mouth constantly was a symbolic castration (the honeyed lump representing to him, by upward transposition, his penis), and that in sexual activities during adult life he was always made anxious by a remote but heretofore never comprehended fear of trusting his sexual organ to a woman. Thus he would never allow his wife, or other women he had been with, to handle or fondle his genitals and, despite the pleasure he had in intercourse, was always somewhat relieved when he was able to withdraw. In this connection he recognized that a habit to which he had never given a passing thought — that of going to the bathroom and urinating the moment intercourse had been accomplished — was in reality a practice he had established in order to permit an examination of his organ to obtain assurance that it was still there, intact and unharmed. And the reverse of this was also an unconscious fact with Mac: that the penis could not only be harmed but was in itself an instrument of harm. He recalled how his step-grandmother had regarded it as something foul, dirty, and an object of shame to be loathed. In his innermost thought he, too, had such an opinion of it; but he also used it to punish his step-grandmother, and his chronic condition of dampness well beyond his eighth year was due not only to the indulgence of his wet-nurse, the laxity of the daughter who substituted for her and an inarticulate expression of the child's wish for attention, but also as a challenge to and aggression against the woman he had to call Ma.

The recovery of so many memories and the working through of them in the weeks that followed enabled Mac, with my assistance, to arrive at a better understanding of himself and his motives. He began, then, to see himself in a new light. The masks he had been wearing for his own and the world's benefit one by one fell away from him. Beneath all the poses he had assumed to hide his true face there emerged the portrait of an adult with the psychology of a child, of a man equipped for manhood but starving for the diet of an infant. And as he recognized his dependent core and the aggression beneath the skin, the dam of his internal rage broke, and for the first time in years he began to feel again.

Mac began to feel, acutely and deeply. In the first flush of the return of feeling he became as one who has been blind many years and who, by a miracle, recovers his sight. He looked about him and everywhere there were only bright colors. His senses responded to life. At night he walked the streets of the city, smelling its odors, gazing into its lights and rejoicing at its sounds. At his work he became lively, full of verve. In the analysis, day after day, he vented what he had so long repressed. On the heads of those who were long dead or until now forgotten, he poured a vitriol of passion, ventilating much of his vagrant but unexpressed fury. In the permissive privacy of my study he relieved himself of the top layers of his hatred for everyone who had ever given him slight or insult or hurt, from his step-grandmother through his employers to the Communist stereotypes Party propaganda provided for him. Meanwhile, he observed himself carefully and with a new vision in his daily life. He saw the little evidences of his yearning for dependency, how he forced people to put him into a dependent relation with them, how he was avid for the infant-security he got when, in the smallest affairs, he could surrender himself to the care of another.

Only in his sexual life did Mac, at this period, remain frustrated and disturbed. At the height of his enthusiasm with the results of the analysis so far, he twice attempted intercourse with girl friends. On the first occasion he reported sexual stirrings, but on neither venture did he experience even the semblance of potency: both episodes were total failures. But were it not for this, Mac would have been satisfied with his progress and have brought his therapy to a premature ending. I, of course, understood what was happening as a "transference-cure," and awaited the day when the flimsy structure he was building would collapse. I knew that he had only scratched at the surface of his neurosis; that what had until now been accomplished was the effect of relieving pressure through ventilation, minute and superficial insight, and the shifting of all of the burdens he bore onto me and the process of analysis. In me he found a new receptacle into which he could pour, and onto whom he could project, the stuff and substance of his life. During this period our relations were more than cordial — at least so far as Mac was concerned; but I, having been through this process many times before, could detect what was hidden in it, and the internal barometer of my previous experience with many patients warned me of a storm over the horizon. [22]

It came; and when it struck, it was with fury. [23]

One day, in the course of a session, Mac mentioned that he had had a dream that he considered foolish and not worth recounting. He had had dreams before, and they had been minimally productive, for the most part, although they had provided valuable clues to his motivations and strivings and had served him well as starting points for associative trains. In the initial phase of psychoanalysis, however, I do not usually insist on deep dream work for fear of stirring unconscious material that my patients are perhaps not yet prepared to handle. I had not, therefore, been insistent with Mac regarding dreams. But when a patient, as Mac did on this day, [24]

depreciates a dream, I have found that it usually means his dream is particularly important at the time and not to be disregarded; that he is aware
of its significance but fears it, and hopes by his offhandedness to divert
the analyst's attention. Moreover, I have found that such an attitude invariably means that the dream in question relates especially to the transference, *i.e.* the relationship between analyst and analysand, and that the
chief reasons why the patient seeks to withhold it are that he either fears
to disturb the outward tranquillity of the relationship or that he is unwilling thus to surrender a potential weapon the dream has given him against
the analyst. Accordingly, I asked Mac to tell me the dream. After some
hesitation, then, and protesting that it would be a waste of time, he related
the following:

> I am walking along Charles Street (in Baltimore) toward Mount Vernon   25
> Place. There is no traffic on the street and I seem to be alone. There is no one
> behind me but I hear footsteps. This scares me and I open my mouth to
> scream, but when I do my tongue falls out on the ground. This doesn't surprise
> me: I just pick it up and put it in my pocket and go on walking.
>
> Ahead of me I see the monument (The George Washington Monument at   26
> Mount Vernon Place in Baltimore). Now I notice that the side of the street I'm
> on is in very bright sunlight, but the other side is dark, pitch-black almost.
> Then I see the man who is behind me, but he's on the other side of the street,
> the black side. He seems to be paying no attention to me but I somehow feel
> that he is really watching me very carefully. I walk on a little way — begin to
> feel very tired. It gets so I can hardly lift my legs and Mount Vernon Place
> seems miles away. I become worried that I'll never make it to the monument,
> I'm so tired. I try to call the man to help me, but I have no tongue and can't
> make a sound. I reach into my pocket to get it but it's gone. I search for it
> frantically and awake in terror with the blankets all tangled up.

When he had finished relating this dream Mac disparaged it as foolish   27
and asked me if I really thought it worth taking time to analyze. I remained
silent, and for a few minutes Mac stirred uncomfortably on the couch.
Then, gruffly, he said the dream meant nothing to him; it was nonsense
and he had no associations to it. I suggested that at least a part of the
symbolism in the dream was quite obvious, that he might do well to consider its significance for the analysis. Mac countered with a curse and said
he was a fool ever to have gone in for this stupid business. All right! So
losing his tongue in the dream meant he wasn't talking. . . . So what? It
was all a lot of crap anyhow. What good was it doing him? No wonder the
Party had proscribed psychoanalysis! In any case, how could anyone ever
get well just by talking? He had been talking, talking, talking for months
and he was still as far from his goal as ever; and he was tired of it, sick and
tired of the whole thing! At this, I pointed out that he was now actually
paraphrasing a part of the dream, that part where he was growing weary
and hopeless about attaining his destination. He answered that the mon-

ument certainly was an apt representation of his analytic goal: it is shaped like an erect phallus; in Baltimore, perhaps because of this, the park at its base has become a hangout for homosexuals and prostitutes. He passes it everytime he has to go to Party Headquarters, about two or three times each week.

"Obviously, then," I said, "in order to get to the erect phallus, or potency, you have to talk." 28

"Don't be so smug," Mac answered. "I knew that before I told you the dream. But there's more to talking than you think." 29

"In the dream," I said, "you lost your tongue when you thought you were being followed. Who was following you?" 30

"You, of course," Mac snorted. "You follow every word I say." 31

"But you weren't surprised when your tongue fell out." 32

"No, I wasn't." Mac sighed. "I've known all along that I'd have to clam up at some point in this analysis — when it became necessary to talk about the Party." 33

"So you choose silence, and therefore impotence, rather than talk about the Party," I commented. "But why did you search so frantically for your tongue in the second part of the dream?" 34

Mac's agitation became obvious. He lit a cigarette with trembling hands; sweat glistened on his forehead. Slowly, he said, "The dream shows that my sickness and the Party are mixed up together. I guess I've known it all along and I've been afraid of it. From what you say I gather that the tongue falling out business means more than just being unwilling to talk: it means castrating myself." 35

I interrupted him here. "The first day I spoke with you," I said, "you told me you'd be willing to crucify yourself if it would bring socialism a minute nearer. What you're saying now is that you'd castrate yourself for the same reason." 36

"I would." 37

"You are." 38

Mac turned on the couch and looked at me. I could see the pain and torment in his eyes. "You're a hard guy," he said. He turned away and continued, "But I guess you have to be." He was calmer now as he summed the dream to this point. "Let's see. The Party and potency are tied up in my mind . . . how I don't know. But I gather that in order to solve the potency problem I have to talk about the Party. By not talking about the Party I'm castrating myself — or deliberately choosing castration, as you say. All right, now where do we go from here?" 39

"To the monument," I answered. 40

"It would be a lot easier to get there," he said, "if you were a Communist. I could talk to you then." 41

"You mean if I came over to your side?" I asked. 42

Now the entire dream fell into place and a flood of associations fol- 43 lowed. I (the analyst, man in the dream) am walking in darkness. A not-so-unconscious purpose of Mac's analysis is to get me to come over on his side, *i.e.* to join the Party. This would not only benefit me; it would help him. He needs help in reaching the monument (potency) but fears that to obtain this help he will have to analyze his relationship to the Party and to disclose Party secrets. If the analyst would only see the light and come over to his side, he (Mac) could talk freely and be assisted toward potency. The prospect of continued impotence is a frightening one, but even if he wants to, he can't tell everything that is on his mind. There are secrets, confidences no one outside of the Party can be trusted with. These are perilous times for the Party. Often, while on the couch, he has to suppress a thought, a street address, a name, or something else that crosses his mind. When he does this, the associative chains break; so he will never get well. He is a fool ever to have attempted this business. Maybe he should just go and have his penis amputated, have done with the whole mess; or maybe he should quit the analysis, forget about being impotent. As things stand, he is always afraid of a leak, afraid that something he has been entrusted with will slip out. I (the analyst) am too clever. He has been warned against me. I know how to put two and two together. I'm not to be trusted. How did he know? — maybe I'm an undercover agent for the F.B.I. He knows I worked in a prison once, a federal prison, too. There's a rumor going around that in Los Angeles and New York, federal agents are posing as psychoanalysts and abstracting political secrets from people. And he knows, also, that I practice hypnosis. What if I hypnotized him someday and got him to spill all the stuff he had to suppress in the interests of the Party?

Following the analysis of this significant dream, Mac became intensely resistive. The negative transference, latent until now, betrayed itself by his silence, his curt manner with me, and his rudeness. Hour after hour sped by while Mac fought an eternal tug of war over whether he could trust me sufficiently to do the thing he knew he had to do: associate freely without regard to content. Interpretation availed little. When I established the connection between his present attitude toward me and his former attitude toward his step-grandmother about the secrets of his masturbation and sex play with the farm animals, he merely shrugged. When I related his present silence to the silence his father practiced in his brief life, and showed how it was tied to a sense of having sinned against his grandfather, he accused me of being fanciful.

Then his resistance took a new turn. Instead of remaining silent, he began to talk. To an untrained observer, his production now would have seemed like free association. It had every semblance of an unimpeded flow of ideas, thoughts and experiences. He related incidents from his glamorous career as a courier in the underground, described the personalities he had encountered and some of his lurid sexual adventures. Along with this, he began to make me presents of Communist literature. At each visit he brought me a gift of a book or pamphlet, and he would begin his hours by discussing a point raised in some brochure or article he had given me the hour before.

Both of us knew that Mac, during this phase, was using every device 46 possible to avoid the issue. His counterfeiting of the process of free association was designed as a fence-straddling procedure to satisfy his desire to solve his problems without tackling their core. His gifts were aimed to convert me to militant socialism, and at the same time to bribe me. His attempts to convert his hours to a forum for the discussion of Marxism were really intended to convince himself of his own sincerity as much as they were planned for my benefit. But, at last, an hour came when Mac could no longer fool himself, and realized he hadn't at all fooled me.

I remember that a snowstorm was raging outside on the evening Mac's 47 analysis reached a climactic point. He appeared very weary as he stretched out on the couch, lit a cigarette, and began in a monotone that I sensed he was using to disguise an inner excitement.

"They're giving me the business again," he began. "I just came from 48 Party headquarters. From the way they talk it's just a matter of time until they replace me at the cannery. They say they're looking around for a spot where I'll fit in better, be more effective."

"Have you really failed?" I asked. 49

Mac shrugged. "I guess so. What with the analysis and everything I 50 guess I haven't given the job what it needs. But, Christ! I hate to be pushed around like this. If I had my way I'd . . ."

"You'd what?" I encouraged him. 51

Mac ground out his cigarette. "Nothing," he said. Then, after a mo- 52 ment of silence, "Look, Doc. This analysis is a frost, isn't it?"

"Why do you ask?" 53

"Because I'm thinking of chucking it and moving on. I guess I can 54 peddle pamphlets somewhere else; it doesn't have to be Baltimore."

"Why do you think the analysis is a frost?" I asked. 55

"Because I'm not getting anywhere," he replied. "Look. I had a girl out 56 last night and all I did was dribble all over her. And now they tell me I'm even a failure in my work. And I know I've been a failure here. What more proof d'you want?" He held up his hand. "Wait," he said. "I know what you're going to say. But I can't do it, that's all. I just can't do free association and I know that's the only way out."

"And why can't you?" I asked. 57

"Because I'm afraid of a leak, that's why. Because if I ever let out what's 58 in my head I'd be punished, that's why. Because as much as I trust you, I don't trust you enough. I've got dynamite in me: Party secrets, names, addresses. These keep crossing my mind. If I open my mouth once I'll spill all over the place. I can't do it, that's all. . . . I just can't do it!"

Now I asked Mac to associate to the word "leak," which had appeared 59
more frequently than any other in discussions we had had about his resistance to the analysis and in connection with the Party. He did: the word
was idiomatic and vulgar for urination; urination is a function of the
penis; the other function of the penis is to transport semen —. At this
Mac jumped from the couch and turned to me in bewilderment and
consternation.

"Holy Christ!" he exclaimed. "You don't mean to say . . . ?" 60
"You've been unconsciously giving away Party secrets all the time," I 61
finished for him.

He began to pace the room, more agitated than I had ever seen him, 62
muttering to himself, over and over, words which I took to be "semen,
Party secrets, leak, dribble . . ." Then he stopped before my chair and
looked piercingly at me, while I did my best to appear calm despite my
exhilaration over the knowledge that this hour would see the analysis
brought to a head.

"Let me get this straight," he said. "Somehow it seems I've got semen 63
and secrets mixed up in my head. So when I try to lay a girl and dribble
out semen, it means I'm unconsciously giving away Party secrets." I
opened my mouth to interrupt, but he held out one restraining hand and
covered his eyes with the other.

"Wait! Wait!" he commanded. "It's beginning to fall into place. I really 64
want to give away these secrets but can't do it with my mouth. So I let
them dribble out through my penis. Why my penis? Because somewhere
that's tied up with the Party like semen's tied up with secrets. Now if I
could tell these secrets, with my mouth, I mean, maybe I could have a real
ejaculation!" He paused, and his perplexity was plain. "But why should I
want to give away Party secrets? Because they're too much of a burden to
me? How is that? There's plenty of guys who know a lot more than I do.
Why should it affect *me* this way?"

This time it was obvious that he was asking for an answer. 65
"To find out the answer to that," I said, "we'll probably have to go 66
deeper into your early sex life. But offhand I would guess that your desire
to disclose Party secrets means that you have an aggression against the
Party, and maybe this has to do with the equation of Party with
Grandmother."

Mac returned to the couch and threw himself down on it. "A few 67
months ago," he mused, "I would have laughed in your face if you said
that. Now I'm not so sure." And for the remainder of that hour he did little
more than express his amazement at what had gone before. When he left
that evening, he was in a very different mood.

At his appointment two days later, Mac reported the first successful 68
sexual experience he had had in many years. He had achieved and maintained a strong erection, and the experience of ejaculation had been in-

tensely pleasurable. His enthusiasm knew no bounds. He was going to send for his wife, they would resume their former life, they would . . . Here I checked him.

"Do you think," I asked, "that your problems are solved?"   69

This sobered him. He sighed. "I guess not," he answered. "But is it   70 really necessary to go on with this? After all, I *know* what's behind it now."

"But do you really?" I said. "It seems to me you have little more than   71 a formula, a series of equations founded on a few good guesses. I'd say there's still a long way to go." So Mac went on.

At this hour, and for some weeks thereafter, the truth of my last state-   72 ment was brought home to Mac. For there now opened before us the vast panorama of his childhood sexuality and the intensity of his early feelings against his grandmother. Between these and the manner in which both related to the Party, the analysis wove like a shuttle on a loom, back and forth, back and forth. From him poured a seemingly endless series of memories, told with much of their original passion, of a child who was blocked in his expression at every turn, whose every action was called "bad"; of a longing for love and acceptance, the security of a kind word or gesture, and of the hot hatred that eventually came to take their place. Then, in a rush of memories, came what had been hidden, even from Mac, of the first ripples of that sexual tide that was to sweep him later to the edge of destruction. At first, what he had to relate was no more than the usual history of the vicissitudes of the developing sex urge; but with Mac, after his removal to his grandfather's farm, a pathological twist was given to it. From being an instrument for the reception and communication of pleasure as well as the prime organ for reproduction, his penis took on a new significance as the child he was saw how it and its behavior affected Ma. In short, it became a weapon, a tool for revenge; and in the life he lived in fantasy he regarded it — all unknowingly, of course — as a veritable arsenal of destruction; and with it, upon his grandmother — and, later, upon everyone who stood in his way — he wreaked a vengeance in imagination which hardly ever, until the microscope of analysis was trained upon it, reached the level of awareness. And this had a curious result: Mac became afraid of his penis, of the destructive possibilities which he and he alone had given it; and, hence, when his neurosis in adult life formed a tidal crest, he had to inhibit it, to curb its fancied noxious potential.

But where, in all of this, did the Communist Party fit? Another dream   73 supplied the missing links.

I am early for my appointment and when I enter your study you're not   74 there. Thinking to occupy myself until you arrive, I go to the bookcase and select a volume from the shelves on the left side of the window. I start to read. Just then I hear you enter. I become confused. For some reason I don't want you to know I've been reading your books. I try to hide the book on me but it won't go into any of my pockets. Suddenly I thrust it into my mouth and it seems to go down my throat. But when I say hello to you, the book flies out of my mouth and hits you in the forehead. You fall down and I'm afraid I've killed you.

Mac's immediate association to the book was education. Correctly, he   75
stated that the Party had given him an education he could not otherwise have obtained. As a child he thought his grandpa was God because he knew so much; sometimes he finds himself thinking the same way about me. But on second thought I (the analyst) don't really know so much. My knowledge runs all over the place. Outside of psychoanalysis I have no framework for what I know — no coherent, consistent, logical, correct way to order my thinking. He, Mac, is really a better-educated man than I am. In the days when he was on the bum, in Public Libraries between here and the West Coast he read everything printed in English on socialism and dialectical materialism — Marx, Engels, Lenin, Stalin, even Hegel and Fuerbach. He knows socialist theory better than — or at least as well as — anyone he has ever met in the Party. No; that isn't quite true. There's one fellow, a leader of the Baltimore faction, who is really hot stuff. He's a Ph.D. He really knows his Marxism, knows it the way I (the analyst) know my Freud. But personally this Party philosopher is a pompous ass, a twisted neurotic if he (Mac) ever saw one. . . . Married to a dame, a former socialite or something, who is just as screwed up. Christ! How he hates them! Hardly a worker in the lot. If it ever comes to the barricades —

Here I interrupted him. "Then the dream doesn't refer to me," I said.   76
"It refers to your Party philosopher. How do you account for this?"

Mac produced the day remnant, the bricks from his extra-analytic life   77
of which the dream was built. On the previous evening he had gone to Party headquarters for a meeting scheduled to be held around the decision to change his assignment. Mac was the first one to arrive. He read from a book on a table until the others came. The next arrival was B, the Party philosopher and local leader. After greeting Mac, he (B) commented know-ingly on the volume Mac had in his hands.

"I felt like throwing it at him," Mac said. "The snide bastard's always   78
showing off his education."

"You hate him, you said."   79

"I do."   80

"That's why in the dream you killed him."   81

By now Mac's anger was out in the open; but it was more than anger;   82
it was pure, primitive rage.

"I hate every last one of them," Mac cried. "And what's more, I hate   83
the Party too, and everything it stands for. I've hated it deep down inside of me from the minute I was recruited." His voice rose almost to a scream. "I hate it! I hate it! I hate it! I'd kill the lot of them if I could. I'd shove this goddam Party so far down their throats it'd come outa their asses! I hate it

and I hate them and I hate you and I hate me for being such a chicken son-of-a-bitch that I have to lay here telling you about it!"

In a few more moments the rage had spent itself and Mac closed his *84* eyes, exhausted by his furious outburst. Now, more calmly, he said, "So it's out at last. Now that I've said it I've said everything, I guess. I carried that around in me like a stone in my guts for years. I suppose I should be glad I got rid of it after all this time. I guess that's the bottom of the barrel, Doc. What else can there be?"

"I think we have to find out yet why you joined the Party," I answered, *85* "and why, hating it the way you did, you stuck with it all these years. Do you know?"

Mac shook his head wearily. "No," he said. "I don't know." *86*

We spent the next weeks answering the question I posed that night. *87* Briefly, this is that answer:

At sixteen Mac had run away from home, after Grandpa had at last *88* closed his piercing eyes in death. Between the time the old man died and the night he ran away the boy lived in fear of his own aggression. His hostility toward his grandmother was not just an ordinary resentment, it was a living hate that threatened to engulf both of them in tragedy. Unconsciously, Mac knew that if he stayed, he'd kill the woman; and so he ran from her presence to protect them both. But his experiences in the world only increased his hate and aggression, and provided him with new targets, for as an unskilled, untutored farmer lad, he was at the mercy of every economic breeze, unwanted and without a place. His embitterment during the years of wandering knew no bounds. When his destiny, in the shape of a buddy in a cattle car southbound from the scene of a strike caught up with him, he was ripe for the taking.

It is true that the Party made a rational appeal to Mac, that he was *89* attracted to its doctrines intellectually and as a result of his reading and observation of the world. This appeal was enhanced by the fact that it presented answers — in a simple and easily digested form — to questions he had been asking himself and others through his formative years, especially when he was exposed to the paradoxes of American society in the late 'twenties and early 'thirties. Nor can it be denied that the cheap education he received on his way to, and later within, the Party was a major factor in his allegiance. It compensated for the inferiority he felt as an unlearned farmer boy. Indeed, it even permitted him to feel superior to every man — from Einstein to his analyst — who did not possess his ready formulations and the guidance of a simple set of maxims to meet every situation or problem. But beneath all of these, and of such basic importance that it alone really mattered, the Party provided Mac with an adjustment. Within the Party, Mac could give vent to his hatred and aggression — originally directed against Ma and later the world — with almost unlimited freedom. It not only permitted him to express these qualities, but directed them upon a broad segment of society, channelized them toward a plenitude of objects, gave him the words and even the techniques to implement them. More than this, while making his hatred and aggression acceptable, it also served to contain them. Therefore, at one and the same time the Party gave Mac permission to indulge in aggression, yet saw to it that this aggression was sufficiently controlled that he need not fear its getting out of hand as it once almost did with his grandmother. So, in essence, for Mac the Party was a way of adjusting, of compromising, of containing a negative rebellion that might have destroyed him had he not found his way into it. In the Party's ranks he discovered a solution to the problem of how to be hostile without suffering the effects of hostility, of how to gain acceptance for his aggressiveness and to hold on to it without being treated as a mad dog and destroyed for it. The Party, then, *was* Mac's neurosis — a neurotic solution he deliberately chose as a lesser evil than the madness to which his hate was leading him.

But like all such solutions that men under pressure to adjust improvise   90 for their perplexities and conflicts, the Party did not work. It offered no real answer: it could not, because it was nothing more than a symptom of Mac's difficulty, a stopgap "adjustment" doomed to failure from the outset as every "adjustment" has to fail.

The price Mac had to pay for what the Party did for him was in the   91 coin of discipline and at the exorbitant rate of human cipherdom. The discipline demanded by the Communist Party is almost incomprehensible to those who have not met it first-hand. It is absolute, rigorous, uncompromising. It holds every member strictly accountable for his smallest acts, it permits of no slightest deviation or breach. It calls for the continuous criticism of behavior and thought by the self and others and, like Party policy, discipline veers and shifts with the prevailing currents of the time. Its impermanence in all save the proposition that under every circumstance the Party is correct requires an unusual kind of plasticity among those whom it affects. For a time Mac could follow it and be governed by it without a strain — so long, that is, as his neurotic needs were being met by the permissive framework the Party provided for his aggression and hostility. He was therefore compliant to the discipline during the years of industrial strife and the war years, but following them — in the halcyon days when for a time there was no one to hate or fight — he began to chafe under it. It became burdensome and nagging, resembling the regime of his grandmother. So in unconscious ways he flaunted and tried to defeat it. Borrowing from childhood, he symbolically betrayed its secrets. In other and smaller ways too numerous to catalogue he also tried to undermine it, and as the analysis progressed Mac was amazed to see how extensively he had been working against this discipline which, on the surface, he had for so many years taken for granted and complied with.

The reduction to cipherdom, to simple cog-ship in the grand wheel of   92 the Party's ambition, was also at first unprotestingly — and, indeed, with relief — accepted by Mac. Recall that he was, underneath all, a wholly dependent type whose primary longing was forever to be a kind of suckling as he once was to his wet-nurse. After the homeless, friendless year he spent in the world, when the Party bared its bosom to him at recruitment, he nestled to it in gratitude as he did long ago to the breast of the wet-nurse. But he overestimated its ampleness and plenitude, and in a short while he had drained it dry. While policy demanded and gave latitude to his hate, aggression and hostility, even Mac's voracious appetites were satisfied; but, in the middle 'forties, as the weather vane of policy turned, for Mac the bosom he had counted on to replace the one he had lost, the breast he had believed a fountain that would nourish him for all time, shriveled in his mouth. In anger and frustration, then, he turned upon it, prepared to rend it with the teeth of his basic hatred.

So this is the story of the psychoanalysis of Mac. It has told how and why he became a member of the Communist Party in the United States. He joined in an attempt to make an adjustment to the contrasts and conflicts within him that were destroying him, and would likely have destroyed others. He joined, not primarily out of belief or conviction in the aims and goals of the Party, nor as a missionary to mankind, nor even as a rebel against injustice: he joined as one would voluntarily enter a prison in anticipation of crimes, as a preventive against becoming criminal and, because by joining, he could — or felt he could — remain a dependent infant.   93

In the course of his analysis Mac learned that the Party *was* his neurosis. When he concluded his analysis, it went with his symptoms. About six months after we had terminated, Mac quit the Party. He no longer needed it.   94

REVIEW QUESTIONS

1. How did Mac's life change when he went to live with his step-grandmother? What were the differences between her and Mac's grandfather?
2. By what process did Mac become a communist? Why did he move from the Merchant Marine to heavy industry and then to the canning industry?
3. What kind of initial insights about his psychic condition did Mac achieve through his recounting of his history to Lindner? What was his reaction to these insights? What indications existed that the real problems had only been touched upon? What was the turning point at which Mac truly began to come to grips with his neurosis?
4. How did Lindner interpret Mac's first dream? What did the monument symbolize? The tongue falling out? The man following him? The inability to talk? How did Lindner attempt to relate the motifs of the dream to the events of Mac's childhood? After the initial discussion of the dream, what series of changes occurred in the relationship between Mac and Lindner? Why was Mac afraid to

continue the process of free association? What sudden insight served as the new turning point that caused him to reevaluate his attitude toward the Party? What new area for analysis did this insight open up?

5. Describe Mac's second dream. What new insights did it provide? In the dream, who did Lindner himself stand for?

6. What were the real reasons for Mac's joining the Communist Party? What purpose did the Party serve for him? (In an earlier stage of his life, what person had served this same purpose?) What might have happened had Mac not joined the Party? Why, ultimately, did the Party not serve the purpose Mac had intended it to serve? Why did the end of the war years eventually bring a change in Mac's unconscious attitude toward the Party, from one of gratitude to one of hatred? How did Mac respond to his unconscious hatred of the Party?

DISCUSSION AND WRITING QUESTIONS

1. Discuss Lindner's account of his treatment of Mac in terms of Freud's exposition of the mind and its workings. Which aspects of Freud's discussion seem most relevant? Has your reading of this passage made you reevaluate your attitude toward Freud, in either a more favorable or a less favorable light? Explain.

2. Why do you think Mac felt such hostility toward Lindner that he dreamed of killing him? Do you think there might be any other interpretation of this dream than what Lindner suggested to Mac?

3. Lindner suggested to Mac that his joining the Communist Party was a neurotic act. Are you convinced that this is true? Could it be true, by extension, that anyone who joins a highly authoritarian organization (such as the military or the Catholic Church) is also joining for neurotic reasons? What kind of reasons would *not* be neurotic? How can we be sure that these reasons are the actual reasons and not a facade to cover less noble reasons? (Mac, after all, joined the Party because he thought he would better be able to help his fellow man.) The larger question is, how far should we go in analyzing human behavior to its ultimate, underlying motivations (particularly, to motivations that are unworthy or dishonorable)? In fact, are we able to understand ultimate motivations?

4. Try a bit of amateur analysis. Select a particular symptom either in yourself or in someone you know (but do not clearly identify) that could be considered mildly neurotic. Attempt to trace this neurosis to its ultimate cause, using the kind of techniques indicated in Lindner's passage. Consider especially the influence of early childhood experiences and the significance of dreams. A caution, however: Remember that you are not a trained psychoanalyst. This is merely an exercise designed to get you thinking about cause and effect in the psychological arena and to encourage you to apply ideas learned in one context to another context — your own life. Do not take the results too seriously!

5. Using both your knowledge of Freud's principles and your understanding of Lindner's techniques, invent another "psychoanalytic tale," modeled on Lindner's. Describe a patient who comes to see Lindner (or another psychoanalyst) and show how that person's neurotic symptoms are alleviated through a series of sessions with the analyst. *Alternate assignment:* Cast your analysis as a parody.

SALVATORE PRISCO III (b. 1943)

One of the most controversial applications of psychoanalytic theory is in the field of *psychohistory*. The psychohistorian attempts to account for historical phenomena by psychoanalyzing major historical figures, or even whole historical movements (for example, one psychohistorian has written on the search for the lost father figure in Spanish-American history). Unlike the conventional psychoanalyst, the psychohistorian has in most cases never met the "patient," but relies purely on historical records and on his or her own professional inferences about the significance of those records. Freud himself became the first psychohistorian when he wrote *Leonardo da Vinci and a Memory of His Childhood* (1910). And Freud also collaborated on a highly controversial study of Woodrow Wilson, whom he had never met. Perhaps the best known psychohistory is Erik Erikson's *Young Man Luther* (1958), which focuses on Martin Luther's identity crisis and its role in his break with the Roman Catholic church. But Freud and Erikson are only the two most eminent thinkers who have attempted to draw insights from the melding of psychoanalysis and history.

The attractions of psychohistory are obvious. At the lowest level, it is somewhat titillating to probe into the secret lives (and almost necessarily, the sex lives) of great historical figures. At the highest level, psychohistory can yield insights both about history and about individuals that are not otherwise available. The perils of psychohistory have been recently articulated in *The American Historical Review* by Thomas Kohut, a practicing psychoanalyst (and a psychohistorian):

> In the first place, the psychohistorical method relies on theory, particularly psychoanalytic theory, to provide historical understanding and explanation. Figures and events from the past are not comprehended or made comprehensible on their own terms but are understood and explained primarily by psychological theory. Too often, when employing the psychohistorical method, the historian comes to the past with an understanding and explanation already on hand; the understanding and explanation do not emerge from the past itself but are the products of a theoretical model. In short, it is often less accurate to say that the model is applied to the past than that the past is applied to the model. In the second place, the psychohistorical approach defines acceptable evidence more broadly than does traditional historical methodology. Traditionally, historians accept only evidence from the past, but psychohistorians, when they rely on theory, also accept evidence from the present to validate their interpretations. When they apply a psychoanalytic theory to a historical subject, they usually make no attempt to prove the theory's validity with evidence from the past. Instead, by citing psychoanalytic literature, they use contemporary evidence to prove the theory's validity. The assumption is made that all people are the same regardless of time and place and that, if a theory

can be proved on the basis of contemporary evidence, it is considered proved for human beings of the past. Thus, psychological theory has become a general law, and contemporary data have become historical evidence.[1]

To avoid such pitfalls, Kohut recommends that the psychohistorian rely less on psychoanalytic models and preconceived theories than on empathy with the historical subjects. He asserts, finally, that the "most significant question the historian can answer is 'why.'"

Readers may judge for themselves whether or not the essay that follows, Salvatore Prisco's "Adolf Hitler and the Oedipus Complex," avoids Kohut's pitfalls. Born in Jersey City, New Jersey, Salvatore Prisco III earned his bachelor's degree from St. Peter's College and his M.A. and his Ph.D. from Rutger's University. Since 1981, he has been Associate Professor of Humanities at the Stevens Institute of Technology. Prisco has published several articles on diplomatic history in such journals as *Asian History* and *Southeastern Latin Americanist* and has written two books, *John Barrett, Progressive Era Diplomat* (1973) and *An Introduction to Psychohistory: Theories and Case Studies* (1980). The following essay is from this last book. (Some of Prisco's other historical subjects include St. Francis of Assisi, Thomas Jefferson, Andrew Jackson, Joseph Stalin, Richard Nixon, and Henry Kissinger.)

---

[1]"Psychohistory as History," *American Historical Review,* April 1986, pp. 338–339.

ADOLF HITLER AND THE OEDIPUS COMPLEX [1]

At the center of Freud's theory of personality formation is the notion that sexuality is the strongest motivating force in human behavior. By this Freud meant not simply sexual intercourse, but the energy force or libido, which directs an individual toward the realization of pleasure and emotional satisfaction. In Freud's theory of human development, the "phallic stage" (ages three to five) is of primary significance because within it is the beginning of the development of both moral and sex-role behaviors. These elements of personality emerge as the result of parental rewards, punishments and identification.   *1*

The child at this age is very much taken up with feelings of love and a desire for closeness for the parent of the opposite sex, in turn becoming jealous and hostile toward the same-sex parental rival. This is the Oedipus   *2*

Salvatore Prisco III. Adolf Hitler and the Oedipus Complex [1980]. In *An Introduction to Psychohistory: Theories and Case Studies.* Washington: University Press of America, 1980.

[1]See headnote on Hitler in Part V on The Survival of the Fittest.

complex. In order to resolve such a threatening conflict, the child begins to model after his parental rival, his father, in that way becoming like the father and sharing in the affections of the mother. By identifying in this manner, the child also incorporates the values, beliefs, standards, and sex-role behaviors of the same-sex parent.

It then becomes apparent that a child who has a harsh, cruel and domineering father is going to identify with those characteristics as well as with all that can be recognized as "male" in order to resolve the Oedipus complex, and the forbidden longing for his mother. This appears to be very much the case in the life of Adolf Hitler. 3

Despite the idealized and romanticized image of Alois Hitler drawn in *Mein Kampf,* the truth is that Adolf Hitler's father was a tyrannical drunkard who beat his wife, Klara, and their children. Hitler both hated his father, and adopted his authoritarian and brutal behavior pattern in later life. His love for his mother was intense. But there is every indication that Hitler resolved his Oedipus complex in the normal manner, i.e., through identification with his father, and not through the abnormal, continuing desire for the mother. The tragedy of Adolf Hitler, and millions of others, was that his father and role-model was a sadistic brute. 4

Hitler's family background alone (even given the genetic problem that Hitler's mother was also her husband's niece and needed a special dispensation from the Pope to marry) does not explain the horror of what eventually happened in Nazi Germany. Germany's defeat in World War I, the genuine injustices of the Versailles Treaty, the widespread suffering of the German and Austrian populations, the Great Depression, and collective feelings of shame, and desire for revenge all contributed to what eventually happened in Europe. In addition displacement of blame on minorities such as the Jewish populations, and the long standing traditions of anti-Semitism, especially in Vienna, provide explanations for the wholesale murder of millions that transcend the person of Adolf Hitler alone. 5

This observation is not meant to lessen Hitler's responsibility for the holocaust, or World War II, nor is it intended to condemn the Germanic populations of Europe. Rather the observation is an introductory caution that the policies carried out in Nazi Germany under Hitler's leadership had their root causes in a set of extremely complex factors which were individual and social in nature. Adolf Hitler's Oedipus complex will not explain everything. But it does contribute to our understanding of Hitler's personality and behavioral patterns. Hitler's family life is a starting point to gain insight. 6

Klara Hitler was twenty-three years younger than her husband, Alois, who had also been her guardian, and was also her uncle. Although they were permitted to marry with special papal approval, genetic problems were manifested in their children. Of Klara's seven pregnancies, four died prematurely. One daughter was regarded as an idiot, and another a high- 7 grade moron. Despite accusations of insanity, only Adolf approached normality.

In time, Hitler became preoccupied with the notion of incest, and eventually projected his guilts and fears on to the Jews in a classical Freudian ego defense mechanism. Hitler, himself, may have suffered from genetic flaws, but of this we have no direct evidence although rumors have persisted that he had only one testicle. More significant, however, is the psychological and emotional relationship that existed within the Hitler family. 8

Alois Hitler, a minor civil servant, beat his wife and tyrannized the children. It is even possible that young Adolf witnessed the forcible rape of his mother by his father while he was in a drunken rage when Adolf was three years old. Since this age corresponds to the onset of the Oedipus complex in the phallic stage of personality development, Hitler's intense attachment to his mother might well have begun at this time with the added touch of deep sympathy for her suffering, extended by one victim of brutality to another. That Adolf also was a victim we know from various accounts of savage beatings (see Robert Waite, *The Psychopathic God: Adolf Hitler*). Wagner's opera, *Lohengrin,*[2] was Hitler's favorite. The theme provides a strange parallel to Hitler's own personal experiences, and fantasies about protecting his mother. One of his favorite movies was *King Kong*, which in its own way presents the similar theme of female innocence ravished by brute masculine force. 9

Although Hitler was deeply loving and loyal to his mother, his adult behavior more closely approximated that of his father. Hitler was undoubtedly insecure as a child due to the harsh, emotionally restrictive family background where discipline and dependency ruled. Theodore Adorno noted that the child of an extremely authoritarian father was likely to experience a "carry over into a power-oriented exploitively dependent attitude toward one's sex partner and one's God and may well culminate in a political philosophy and social outlook which has no room for anything but a desperate clinging to what appears to be strong and a disdainful rejection of whatever is relegated to the bottom" (Theodore Adorno, *et al.*, *The Authoritarian Personality*, p. 971). 10

This observation is certainly true of Hitler's personality and behavior pattern. Hitler complimented himself when he said in a speech that he was probably one of the hardest leaders Germany had had for centuries. His sexual relationship with women could be described as nothing short of cruel and perverse (see Robert Waite, *Adolf Hitler*). Of the five women with whom Hitler was known to have had sexual relations, four were from twenty to twenty-five years younger, almost the same age differential as 11

---

[2]*Lohengrin:* In Wagner's opera (1848), Lohengrin, a knight in shining armor, rescues Elsa of Brabant from a villainous count who has falsely accused her of murdering her brother.

that between his parents. All five women either attempted or actually did commit suicide; Geli Raubal (his own niece and obviously the object of transferred affection from his mother) shot herself to death with Hitler's pistol; Eva Braun committed suicide with him in 1945; Mimi Reiter attempted to hang herself; Renee Mueller, the German actress, shot herself in the head; English socialite Unity Mitford attempted, but did not succeed at suicide.

Hitler's sexual proclivities ran toward sado-masochistic practices. These included beatings and whippings, urination and defecation upon his body, and a deranged excitement with medieval and Nazi torture techniques. Accounts indicate that Hitler liked, and begged to be kicked and beaten by young women before having sexual relations. This behavior shadowed what Hitler witnessed and fantasized about as a child in his father's house. His adult behavior emulated that of his father, but in a twisted way, Hitler played both the dependent role of his mother *and* the overbearing part of his father alternatively.   *12*

The combination of guilt and anxiety led Hitler to project such sexual perversions on to the objects of his disdain, the Jews. Hitler even came to believe that his father, Alois, was the illegitimate son of an Austrian housemaid named Maria Schicklgruber, and a wealthy Jew named Frankenberger. Although he tried for years to discover whether or not he was contaminated with Jewish blood, Hitler was never able to find conclusive proof one way or the other.   *13*

Hitler's gradual, but intense, obsession with Jews may have been more the result of intimate family problems rather than provincial prejudice. The transference of negative associations in his childhood, and later life on to the Jews served as a way for him to avoid guilt and anxiety. The death of Hitler's mother of breast cancer in 1907 provided the traumatic event that sent a flood of projection and displacement images relating to Jews into his psyche as a form of defense mechanism for his own damaged ego.   *14*

Klara Hitler had been treated by a fatherly Jewish physician named Edmund Bloch. He had been the family doctor, and it was he who performed an unsuccessful mastectomy on Hitler's mother. Shortly after his mother's death, Hitler became fanatical in his anti-Semitism. It is quite possible that he transferred his unconscious hostility and rage for his own father on to Dr. Bloch. Given the favorable social environment conducive to anti-Semitism in Austria, Hitler's unconscious hatreds were fed by purposeful propaganda. In time, Hitler transferred his intense hostility to Jews in general. "Jewishness" seemed to be tied up with the negative aspects of his life: his father's suspected tainted origins, and the death of his mother. Over a decade after his mother's death, it was characteristic of him to blame the Jews for Germany's defeat in World War I, and the menace of communism in central Europe.   *15*

Hitler was eighteen years old at the time of his mother's death. This   16
trauma coming in the later years of the adolescent identity crisis meant that
it would have a major impact on his adult identity. It would be impossible
to say that Hitler would not have become an anti-Semite had his mother
not died under the care of a Jewish physician. But one should not minimize
the event either; for it came at a critical time, and must be seen in conjunction with other childhood experiences and the Austrian social milieu.

Hitler, himself, became obsessed with the fear that he might develop   17
cancer. He became a vegetarian, stopped drinking and smoking, and
bathed frequently. He changed his clothing and undergarments several
times in a given day. Although Hitler's behavior was abnormal, he was
able to compensate for a number of his weaknesses through drive, intelligence and his ability to command a popular following (see Douglas Kelley,
22 Cells in Nuremberg).

Hitler hated weakness because he secretly feared himself to be weak.   18
As a child he was weak; his male role model was one of brutal strength.
As an adolescent and an adult he surrounded himself with the images of
power. After he became Chancellor of Germany, he commissioned art
works which would personify the brute force of Germany's barbaric roots.
The portrayal of sexual organs on German maidens and bold warriors became symbolic of this power. The ubiquitous portraits and photographs of
stallions are further evidence of his need to overcompensate for deep-
seated feelings of masculine inadequacy.

Hitler's Oedipus fixation can eventually be seen in his craving for   19
power, and in his association of mother and father images in depicting the
plight of the German state. Although traditionally Germany had been referred to in masculine terms as "the fatherland," Hitler insisted on endow-
ing Germany with feminine qualities. After World War I, Germany was
considered by many Germans including Hitler to have been made prostrate before the Allied victors and their spies within Germany (the Jews
according to Hitler). The allegory here is of a defenseless mother forced to
give in to the will of a harsh tyrant, who in turn loses credibility as benefactor in his acts of violence.

The overthrow of the kaiser at the end of the war may be interpreted   20
as an act of rage by the people (children) against the leader (father) in the
interest of the national good (mother). Hitler's political attack upon the
entire older generation of German leaders, and his criticism, on a personal
basis, of Allied statesmen may be taken as a form of acting out of the Oedipus conflict on the national and international stage. He, Hitler, would replace the old-time statesmen responsible for keeping Germany in a dependent and subservient condition. After his success, Germany, as the mother
figure, would be lifted up to her rightful place of veneration and respect.

Hitler's success in drawing followers, particularly in the Nazi Youth   21

Movement, may be attributed to the fact that his message of repudiation of the old order and his anti-Semitism was internalized by a people ready to assert themselves in generational conflict, and redeem the fallen banner of collective self-esteem. This response was especially true of the younger generation (younger than Hitler) whose childhood occurred during the wartime and post-war years of deprivation (see Peter Loewenberg, "The Psychohistorical Origins of the Nazi Youth Cohort," *American Historical Review* Dec. 1971). Wartime anxieties coupled with the return of a generation of defeated fathers (whose image had been that of heroes) led to feelings of humiliation, and a desire to overcome this weakened self-respect. Hitler offered the youth of Germany a means to regain lost honor and an enhanced self-identity. In so doing, he unconsciously expressed the will of all male children in Germany to succeed to the power that was once their fathers' mantle of authority. This, in part, may help to explain Hitler's phenomenal political success.

Freud's concept of the Oedipus complex was meant to be applied universally and throughout history. Assuming the correctness of Freud's theory, it alone could not explain why the horror of Nazism occurred in Germany when it did. This answer lies within the contexts of the broader events of history, the collective experience, and the individual personality. 22

REVIEW QUESTIONS

1. Why does Prisco believe that the Oedipus complex was particularly significant in Adolf Hitler's personality development? How did Hitler resolve his Oedipus complex, according to Prisco?
2. Does Prisco place the ultimate responsibility for the Nazi era squarely on Hitler's shoulders? Explain.
3. How does Prisco account for Hitler's hatred of the Jews? How do Hitler's feelings about his mother and his father help account for his subsequent activities, according to Prisco? How might the death of his mother have intensified Hitler's anti-Semitism? How might Hitler have associated Germany's post–World War I fate with his mother's?
4. In what terms does Prisco account for Hitler's aggressive international policies after he became chancellor of Germany? How does he account for the German people's acceptance of these policies?

DISCUSSION AND WRITING QUESTIONS

1. Does Prisco's analysis seem plausible to you, based upon your own understanding of human behavior? Which of his conclusions (if any) do you find relatively easy to accept? Which (if any) do you find difficult to accept?
2. Consider Prisco's essay in light of the quotation by Thomas Kohut in the introduction. How do you think Kohut would feel about Prisco's analysis? Explain.

(See also David Stannard, *Shrinking History: Freud and the Failure of Psychohistory*, New York: Oxford University Press, 1980.)

3. Locate other examples of psychohistory. You may wish to read other chapters of Prisco's book, Erikson's study, *Young Man Luther*, or an article in either *The Journal of Psychohistory* or *The Psychohistory Review*. (Consider also Freud's and W. C. Bullit's analysis of President Woodrow Wilson, or one of the studies in Goldwert, Pomper, Albin, or Strozier and Offer, cited in the "Additional Readings" at the end of the book.) Select a study that interests you (perhaps because you already know something about the subject) and write a critique of it. Use Kohut's or Stannard's criticisms (see reference in question 2) of psychohistory as some of your criteria.

DAWN ADES (b. 1943)

The power of the unconscious was represented in art most dramatically in the surrealist movement of the early 20th century. Surrealism grew out of Dadaism, an antirationalist, antibourgeois, anticonventional literary and artistic movement born in the shambles of World War I. Represented on both sides of the Atlantic by such artists as Jean Arp, Marcel Duchamp, and Man Ray, the Dadaists set out to deliberately defy expectations, relying greatly on the elements of accident and surprise to create their startling effects. Surrealism was also antirationalistic, but it was a less anarchistic and more focused movement than Dadaism. Though it took different forms in the hands of different artists and writers, surrealism was generally premised on the importance of the unconscious — and of dreams and fantasies, in particular — in representing the inner truth of reality. The "Surrealist Manifesto," published in 1924 by the movement's leader, the poet and critic André Breton, asserted that the fusing of the unconscious and the conscious worlds, of irrational and rational experiences, would create "an absolute reality, a surreality." Naturally enough, the surrealists were very much influenced by the work of Sigmund Freud.

The most important surrealist painters included Max Ernst, René Magritte, André Masson, Joan Miró, and Salvador Dalí. Of these, Dalí (perhaps partially owing to his own personal flamboyance) is the best known and most influential. Born in Figueras, Spain, in 1904, Dalí enrolled in the Escuela National de Bellas Artes de San Fernando in Madrid in 1921, but was expelled several years later. Though he had exhibited some of his paintings in Madrid and Barcelona, Dalí was still in search of a personal style when he went to Paris in 1928 and met Joan Miró and other surrealists. Thenceforward, his work began to display the distinctive Dalí hallmarks. He created images of objects that were, on the one hand, highly realistic and detailed, but on the other distorted to various degrees (in some cases fragmented or duplicated, in other cases bent or elongated), taken out of their usual contexts, placed in apparently irrational juxtapositions, and sometimes viewed through strange perspectives. The resulting art works seemed designed to deliberately shock or confuse the viewer; and their meaning could be deduced only by reference to unconscious mental processes. Possibly his most famous work of this period is *The Persistence of Memory* (1931), with its bent watches.

Dalí's exhibits were particularly successful in New York City (where he lived from 1940 to 1948); he designed a pavilion for the 1939 New York World's Fair called "Dalí's Dream of Venus," and has had several one-man exhibits in that city. In 1929, Dalí collaborated with director Luis Buñuel to produce one of the classic short films, *Un Chien Andalou* (whose most famous sequence shows the slitting of an eyeball). Starting in 1949, Dalí's interest turned to religious themes and his style underwent a metamorphosis; there was less distortion than before and a new imitation of the style of such old masters as Vermeer and Raphael. Some of his best-known religious paintings are *Madonna of Port-Lligat* (1949), *Christ of St. John of the Cross* (1951), and *The Last Supper* (1956). Dalí has also designed jewelry, furniture, and theater sets. He has written two autobiographical works, *The Secret Life of Salvador Dalí* (1942) and *Diary of a Genius* (1965).

The following passage by Dawn Ades is from the chapter entitled "Dalí, Surrealism and Psycho-Analysis" in her *Dalí and Surrealism* (1982). Dawn Ades, born in 1943, received her M.A. from the Courthold Institute in London and now lectures at the University of Essex. She has organized art exhibitions and has written for art catalogues published by the Museum of Modern Art in New York City. Her other books include *Dada and Surrealism* (1974) and *Photomontage* (1976).

DALÍ, SURREALISM AND PSYCHO-ANALYSIS

The richest common ground between Dalí and the Surrealists was cer-   1
tainly . . . provided by their mutual interest in psychology and psychoanalysis. It is worth noting, perhaps, that both the Surrealists and Bataille[1]
leaned heavily on Freudian theory, and indeed it was the very closeness
of their basic interests that exacerbated the ideological conflict between
them. Bataille once described himself as "Surrealism's old enemy from
within." Thus for Dalí to have held an interest for both camps is not so
surprising. In many ways Bataille was better able to face the "textbook
case" nature of some of Dalí's imagery, the aberrations and perversities of
his sexuality as revealed through his paintings, viewing it with the cold
eye of the social psychologist, than was Breton,[2] whose attitude to sex was
curiously romantic and puritanical.

On his return to Cadaqués,[3] then, in the summer of 1929, Dalí imme-   2
diately began work on *Dismal Sport*. He was in a state of high mental excitement, bordering on hysteria, and would be gripped by sudden and

Dawn Ades. Dali, Surrealism and Psycho-analysis [1982]. In *Dali and Surrealism*. New York: Harper, 1982.

[1]*Bataille:* George Bataille, editor of an art review, *Documents,* and an admirer and interpreter of Dalí's early work; he lost Dalí's allegiance to André Breton, with whom he waged critical battles over surrealism.

[2]*Breton:* André Breton (1896–1966), French poet, essayist, and editor, and one of the founders of the surrealist movement. His work was influenced by Freudian psychology and symbolist poetry.

[3]*Cadaqués:* A Catalonian town on the Costa Brava of Spain. The town became a hangout for artists in the 1950s. Dalí built a house there, opposite the Port Lligat Hotel.

Dismal Sport, 1929.

violent fits of laughter, provoked by grotesque scenes conjured up in his imagination or for no reason at all. The arrival of his new friends from Paris, his dealer Camille Goemans, and then the Magrittes[4] and Paul Eluard[5] with his wife Gala did nothing to alleviate this: "From hour to hour my fits of laughter grew more violent, and I caught in passing certain glances and certain whisperings about me by which I learned in spite of myself the anxiety which my state was beginning to cause. This appeared to me as comical as everything else, for I knew perfectly well that I was laughing because of the images that came into my mind. . . ." Dalí's guests, attracted by his "unusual personality," as he said, to come all the way to Spain, understandably failed to see anything comic in the images Dalí tried to explain to them — a little sculptured owl, for example, stuck on the head of a very respectable person, and on the owl's head a piece of his own excrement. The progress of *Dismal Sport* was followed with interest, and then with growing concern, by the little group of Surrealists. Finally Gala Eluard, who, after initially finding Dalí not only peculiar but obnoxious, with his "pomaded hair and his elegance," his love of personal adornment left over from his student days in Madrid, and who had been startled and intrigued by "the rigour which I displayed in the realm of ideas," was deputed to question him about the significance of certain elements in the painting. What worried them in general was the liability they thought Dalí ran of turning his paintings into mere psycho-pathological documents, and, in particular, the significance of the excrement-bespattered pants of the man in the right foreground, which they feared might reveal unacceptable aberrations on Dalí's part. Dalí successfully reassured her; "I swear to you that I am not 'coprophagic.' I consciously loathe that type of aberration as much as you can possibly loathe it. But I consider scatology as a terrorizing element, just as I do blood, or my phobia for grasshoppers." (Dalí presumably intended the more general term "coprophilous," i.e. shit-loving, rather than "coprophagic" or shit-eating.) Although doubts about Dalí's "aberrations" lingered — they are there, for example, in Breton's catalogue preface for the Goemans exhibition[6] — his protestations were accepted, and he was from that time considered a member of the Surrealist movement.

Dalí was spending almost all his day absorbed in working on *Dismal*   3

---

[4]*Magrittes:* René Magritte (1898–1967), the Belgian artist, was one of the most famous of surrealist painters. He is particularly known for blending the humorous with the grotesque in his paintings of sea and sky.

[5]*Paul Eluard:* Eluard was the pseudonym of Eugene Grindel (1895–1952), one of the founders of the surrealist movement. He is also known as one of the most influential lyrical poets of the 20th century.

[6]*Goemans exhibition:* At the Camille Goemans Gallery in Paris Dalí gave a one-man show in November 1929.

The First Days of Spring, 1929.

Sport, and as he worked he began to relive childhood fantasies, or rather see images "which I could not localize precisely in time or space but which I knew with certainty I had seen when I was little." Among these were images of small green deer, "reminiscences of decalcomanias," or of the marblings he used to make with his sister, and other more complicated and condensed images like the rabbit whose eye also served as the eye of a parrot, and a third head, "that of a fish enfolding the other two. This fish I sometimes saw with a grasshopper clinging to its mouth." Either separately or as a composite image, these creatures appear in most of the paintings of the extraordinarily creative months following *Dismal Sport,* as for instance in the *Portrait of Paul Eluard.* The association of the fish and the grasshopper is interesting because it is one of the first instances of Dalí pursuing obsessively an image which inspired him with horror. Dalí is aware of, and makes explicit, the sexual impetus behind this obsessive horror. The fish/grasshopper is also a reference to an incident in his childhood, which, he says, he had repressed until his father brought it to his attention, and which he describes in "The Liberation of the Fingers." He had loved grasshoppers when he was a child, until one day he caught a slimy little fish called a "slobberer," brought it up close to his face to inspect it, and found that it had a face identical to the grasshopper. From that moment he had a fear of grasshoppers so intense that his schoolmates quickly found they could play upon it to terrorize him, catching grasshoppers to place among his books, which never failed to provoke him to a state of near hysteria. The grasshopper in *The First Days of Spring*, fastened to the mouth of the young man's head (Dalí himself), with a threat half-cannibalistic and half-sexual, is, then, an image of horror, repeated in *Dismal Sport* and *The Great Masturbator*.

Dalí decided to reproduce these images which appeared to him "as   4
scrupulously as it was possible for me to . . . following as a criterion and norm of their arrangement only the most automatic feelings." He kept *Dismal Sport* on an easel at the end of his bed, so that it was the last thing he saw on going to sleep and the first on waking. "I spent the whole day seated before my easel, my eyes staring fixedly, trying to 'see,' like a medium (very much so indeed) the images that would spring up in my imagination. Often I saw these images exactly situated in the painting. Then, at the point commanded by them, I would paint, paint with the hot taste in my mouth that panting hunting dogs must have at the moment when they fasten their teeth into the game killed that very instant by a well-aimed shot." The comparison with a "medium" introduces the idea of automatism, which was of course the core of the definition of Surrealism Breton gives in the first *Surrealist Manifesto*: "Pure psychic automatism through which it is intended to express, verbally or in any other way, the true functioning of thought; thought transcribed in the absence of any control exerted by reason, and outside any moral or aesthetic preoccupation." The way this had been interpreted by artists like Masson[7] was, however, very different from the sense Dalí is giving his automatism. For Masson, the drawing would start without any preconceived subject, but as it proceeded would bring swimming to the surface of the conscious mind images from the unconscious, unrecognized obsessions, etc., which could undergo transformations in the process of the drawing. For Dalí, on the other hand, the images were rather waking dreams which arrived already fully formed rather than in the metamorphosing or half-realized state in which they would take shape within a purely automatic drawing. It is a question of transposing them on to the canvas more or less "ready made," and it was in this way that Dalí saw his role as something like that of a medium — a comparison which still lies well within the Surrealist framework. The techniques of the medium, that for example of the self-induced trance, had played an important role in early Surrealist experimentation; but an essential difference between the Surrealist and the medium was spelt out later

---

[7]*Masson:* Antoine Masson (1636–1700) was a French painter and engraver, primarily known for his detailed portrait engravings. His work received so much attention that in 1679 he was made a member of the prestigious Academy in Paris.

by Breton in his "Message automatique" — the Surrealist does not accept that the messages received unconsciously, or automatically, are transmitted from outside, as "spirit voices" from elsewhere. The "recording" is of the inner unconscious. The transcription of the waking dream or voluntary hallucination on to canvas, as rapidly and "automatically" as possible, is then analogous to the "recording" of the medium, but of the subject's own experiences or "visions" rather than those of some outside person. In offering this explanation of his procedure Dalí is probably also trying to avoid the criticism that was levelled at the kind of "dream image" offered by De Chirico, voiced for example in such texts as Max Morise's "Enchanted Eyes" (*La Révolution Surréaliste*, no. I), which Dalí knew, and which argued that the pristine nature of the original dream image could not be retained in being transmitted to canvas because it was subject to the deformation of memory and to subsequent conscious manipulation. So Dalí insisted on the automatism of the transcription of the images that arose in his imagination — an insistence he has in fact returned to in his more recent work, once assuring me that large areas of *Hallucinogenic Toreador*[8] were painted purely automatically.

In *Dismal Sport* Dalí uses a graphic visual conceit to invoke the mediumistic characteristics of the painting by showing a horde of multi-coloured images, little stones, etc., rising from his head, an image borrowed directly from a certain type of medium's drawing which similarly shows the medium's "vision" rising from her own forehead.

What Dalí appears to be attempting, then, is to mesh visually the two strands of Surrealist activity dominant during the twenties, automatism and the dream narrative. Both of these are linked to Freud in the first *Surrealist Manifesto*, which pays homage to Freud for his scientific exploration of the human mind, thanks to which not only had hidden areas of the human psyche been revealed, but also mechanisms for reaching them: the dream, whose direct connection with the unconscious is explored in Freud's *Interpretation of Dreams*, and the monologue obtained from the patient under analysis. Freud's stress on the importance of the dream and the free, unconstrained monologue as routes to the unconscious provided models for the two main streams of Surrealist activity. However, what the Surrealists valued above all were the implications of Freud's discoveries for the liberation of the human imagination, and the value of the unconscious as a quarry for poetic images. Psycho-analysis as such was of less interest to them.

So far, Dalí's account of the making of *Dismal Sport* has been considered largely in so far as it relates theoretically to the Surrealist principles of automatism and so on. The only criterion Dalí had followed in arranging the

---

[8]*Hallucinogenic Toreador:* Painted by Dalí in 1969–1970.

images that came unbidden into his head as "voluntary hallucinations" was his "most uncontrollably biological desire." They were, he claimed, determined neither by conscious thought nor by questions of taste, but the impression is none the less strong that they are linked by some kind of almost narrative thread. If we look a little more closely at his description of the genesis of the picture's imagery, it becomes clear that it relates to Freud in a quite direct way, and not just as mediated through Surrealist theory.

The first point to note is that Dalí stresses the fact that many of the images that surfaced were, or were very closely related to, childhood memories. Freud emphasized the importance of a patient's childhood memories and associations as an aid to analysis, for they were often crucial to the unravelling of the latent content of a dream, or the cause of an obsession. Dalí's account of the making of *Dismal Sport,* too, does not claim that it is a single dream image; the images come severally and at different times into his head, and may have different sources. Nor are they restricted to one painting; they are, as we saw with the grasshopper, repeated several times in the paintings of this period. This repetition must be thematically significant, and suggests, given Dalí's references to his childhood and his known state of mind at the time, that they must be linked to some dominant obsession. The questions then arise, how "innocent," how "automatic" even, these images are, and how far Dalí is conscious of their source in a psychological sense?

Dalí had first read Freud's *Interpretation of Dreams* when he was a student in Madrid. "This book presented itself to me as one of the capital discoveries in my life, and I was seized with a real vice of self-interpretation, not only of my dreams but of everything that happened to me, however accidental it might seem at first glance." How far, then, does a painting like *Dismal Sport* consist of images springing directly from the unconscious, or are they rather images which have already been digested and analysed. Freud himself, when he was introduced to Dalí in London in 1938 by Stefan Zweig,[9] was in no doubt of the answer. According to Dalí, Freud told him: "It is not the unconscious I seek in your pictures, but the conscious. While in the pictures of the masters — Leonardo[10] or Ingres[11] — that which interests me, that which seems mysterious and troubling to me, is precisely the search for unconscious ideas, of an enigmatic order, hidden in the picture, your mystery is manifested outright. The picture is

8

9

---

[9]*Stefan Zweig:* (1881–1942) German writer known for his subtle portrayal of historical and fictional characters. He was influenced by the writings of Freud. In 1940, six years after having been exiled by the Nazis, Zweig and his wife committed suicide in Brazil.

[10]*Leonardo:* Leonardo da Vinci (1452–1519), Florentine painter, sculptor, scientist.

[11]*Ingres:* Jean Auguste Dominique Ingres (1780–1867), French painter.

but a mechanism to reveal it." Dalí's paintings, he is suggesting, contain both the latent cause of an obsession and its symbolic manifestation. The unconscious idea, obsession, which was for Freud so often of a sexual nature, which may exist hidden in, say, a Leonardo, has for Dalí become the open subject of the painting — provided of course one is familiar enough with the terminology of sexual symbolism from the psychology textbooks. The drawing for *Dismal Sport* is far more explicit in its sexual references than the final painting.

Yet what makes the paintings of 1929–30 so extraordinary is the way   10 they hold in balance a real neurotic fear which is clearly very powerful, and a knowing use of psychology textbooks. Within a highly sophisticated and carefully structured pictorial mental landscape he uses devices to create formal visual analogies for the experience of dreams and hallucinations. In *Dismal Sport, The First Days of Spring, Illumined Pleasures* and *The Great Masturbator* he paints a stretch of undifferentiated land as a vista stretching away and out of sight to the horizon. This landscape is usually monochrome: in *The First Days of Spring* and *Dismal Sport* both it and some of the objects and figures are a dull grey, against which the brilliance of other objects stands out with all the force of a Technicolor dream. Within this landscape structure, which harks back to such paintings by Ernst[12] as *Of This Men Shall Know Nothing* and immediately creates a sensation of great depth emphasized by the presence in the background of tiny figures, the foreground objects and figures are placed in apparently unrelated groups and huddles. This suggests the dreaming mind at work, where certain things may happen or be seen with clarity but at the same time other things are going on just out of sight or on the margins of consciousness, "at the back of one's mind." Odd or apparently illogical connections are made between disparate objects or groups of objects, and people or things can metamorphose unexpectedly into something else, for no apparent reason.

The individual images that crowd into the paintings are autobiograph-   11 ical, frequently symbolic, and often ready-interpreted. But the symbolic images he chooses are of different kinds: some are commonplaces from the psychology textbooks; some, like the grasshopper or fish, belong to Dalí's own personal armoury of images which probably obsessed him before he read an extra meaning into them, and whose significance is made clear through juxtaposition and association in a series of paintings and through his own explanations; and others, like the deer, whose significance, if any, remains buried deep.

---

[12]*Ernst:* Max Ernst (1891–1976) German painter and sculptor, one of the originators of the automatism movement of surrealism. As a student at the University of Bonn, he studied psychiatry and philosophy and later painting.

Many of Dalí's paintings of the previous summer were, it will be re-   *12*
membered, concerned with auto-sexuality. The dominant theme of the
1929 paintings is now a deep sexual anxiety in which masturbation still
plays an important role, in, for example, the grotesquely enlarged and
guilty hand of the statue in *Dismal Sport,* hiding its face in shame. The
attendant parental threat of its terrible consequences, interpreted by the
subject as emasculation, is shown in the enlarged sex organ held up against
the statue by the young man seated (probably intended to be Dalí himself)
and in the bloodstained object in the hand of the grinning man in the foreground. Bataille, in his interpretative diagram of the painting, also suggests that the tearing of the upper part of the body in the centre of the
picture expresses emasculation, drawing presumably on the classic Freudian concept of the substitution of the upper for the lower part of the body
in dreams.

The potential remedy or alternative to masturbation, sexual relations   *13*
with another, has its own attendant threat of impotence, which Dalí expresses through a number of images, the psycho-analytical weight of
whose symbolism must be fully conscious. The little coloured drooping
shape on the paving stone at the bottom left of the painting is a softened
dripping candle, which Freud invariably interprets in his patients' dreams
as a symbol of impotence. Staircases, on the other hand, stand commonly
in psychoanalytical literature for sexual intercourse. But in this case, in
Dismal Sport, there is a subtlety in the use of such symbolism which suggests a real personal authenticity. Far from being selected randomly or for
shock value, the giant and dramatically lit staircase at the right of the picture is closely linked to its overall theme. The oppressive size of the staircase springs from the theme of impotence, and expresses a fear of sexual
intercourse; it presents an almost impassable obstacle over which the scattered images pouring from Dalí's own sleeping head can only hover. The
staircase could also be the pedestal steps of a monument, introducing the
idea of a hidden statue, and therefore in addition another important, interconnected running theme, that of the father figure. The staircase, then,
is not just a commonplace symbol with a given reading, but is endowed
with a particular predominant significance, that of the possible desirability
but overwhelming fear of sex. Other images concur with this reading: the
grasshopper, fastened to his mouth, was as we know from his own testimony, a symbol of terror; its identification with a fish in his reminiscences
(and in the *Portrait of Paul Eluard*) confirms its sexual significance.

This kind of analysis is necessarily amateur, but there is a justification   *14*
for it, in that Dalí is in fact treating the iconography of the science of
psycho-analysis as though it were common property, in the way that religious iconography was common property in the Middle Ages.

It is not hard to accept Dalí's claim that he was during this period of   *15*

The Great Masturbator, 1929.

intense work and emotional upheaval in a state very close to madness. Still locked in the auto-eroticism and masturbation of the previous years, he had fallen in love with Gala and found his anxieties concentrating more and more on the fear of impotence. He had never had a full sexual relationship with a woman, and his fears had still not been resolved when she went back to Paris at the end of September — having, though, stayed on after the departure of the others. After she left he returned to Figueras[13] and painted *The Great Masturbator* and *Portrait of Paul Eluard*. Dalí explained *The Great Masturbator* as "the expression of my heterosexual anxiety." It was inspired by a *fin-de-siècle*[14] chromolithograph of a languid lady holding a white lily to her face. Dalí has kept the arum lily, whose phallic symbolism is repeated in the lion's head beside it with the grotesquely obtruding tongue, but moved it to put in its place the lower part of a man's torso with shrouded genitals. Dalí's own head, expanded to fill the whole canvas and also intended to be a rock from the coast at Cadaqués, has a fish-hook embedded in the scalp. The rocks, like the fragment below the head in

---

[13]*Figueras:* A small Catalonian town near the large Spanish city of Gerona, known principally for its 18th century fortress castle of San Fernando.

[14]*fin de siècle:* (French) End of century.

The Enigma of Desire, 1929.

Dismal Sport, are jagged and sharp and lacerate bare limbs with ease — hence the torn and bleeding knees in *The Great Masturbator,* not too difficult to read as displaced castration symbolism. The rock-head also grows out of an unidentifiable fragment of 1900-style furniture, of a piece stylistically with the woman's bare shoulders and head. In *The Enigma of Desire* the biomorphic rock grows from a curly furniture leg; in the poem "The Great Masturbator," which Dalí wrote the following summer at Port Lligat, he explains the close association of the image of a women with this particular style of furniture which comes from the typical iconography of *fin-de-siècle* lithographs: "the decorative coloured stained glass, with motifs of metamorphosis which exist only in those horrible Modern Style interiors in which a very beautiful woman with wavy hair a terrifying look an hallucinatory smile and a splendid throat is seated at a piano. . . ."

The *Portrait of Paul Eluard,* Dalí's first Surrealist portrait, was painted, in Eluard's absence, Dalí said, because "I felt it incumbent on me to fix forever the poet from whose Olympus I had stolen one of the Muses." Dalí carefully crystallized Eluard's fine, thin face in minute detail, cutting off the head at the shoulders like an antique bust, an effect he emphasizes by turning the edges of Eluard's coat into a calcareous landscape. The bust is then set floating above a limitless horizon. At first glance it looks as though Dalí has revived the old tradition of adding significant attributes to the

Portrait of Paul Eluard, 1929.

portrait to say something about the occupation, taste and so on of the sitter. However, the objects Dalí has added belong to him rather than to Eluard, and many are familiar from other paintings: the grasshopper, whose likeness to the "slobberer" fish is neatly underlined by making its head the fish's eye, and the woman-jug, for example. The hand on the poet's forehead refers to Dalí's own experience while painting *Dismal Sport*: "I would feel the protective fingers of my imagination scratch me reassuringly between my two eyebrows . . . ," and sometimes he would feel a pecking just behind his brow which here he translates into butterflies.

In two other paintings of the same period, *Accommodations of Desire* and *Illumined Pleasures,* the same themes of sexual anxiety predominate, with in addition a more explicit reference to the father/son relationship which was to become central to the "William Tell" paintings of the following year. In *Accommodations of Desire* Dalí convincingly imitates collage, painting a yellow lion's head which looks as if it is cut from a child's book of exotic animals. The lion's head is "screened" on a white pebble, almost like an hallucination, and Dalí has described his habit while on the beach of gazing at pebbles and "seeing" images in them. The lion's head is repeated but this time with the face "cut out," and then again with everything but the jaws eliminated. The halo of red on the border of the latter, and the pure red outline head, both suggest the afterimage that occurs when, after gazing long at an object of a particular colour, the gaze is shifted or the eyes are closed and the image is "seen" in its complementary colour. However, red is not the complementary of yellow, but of green; it is the colour of blood, or heat, and hence, of passion or rage.

The lion figures almost invariably in paintings of this time; normally just the head is shown, though in *Dismal Sport* he appeared whole but in grisaille.[15] Freud, in the 1919 edition of *The Interpretation of Dreams,* wrote, "Wild beasts are as a rule employed by the dream work to represent passionate impulses of which the dreamer is afraid, whether they are his own or those of other people. (It then needs only a slight displacement for the wild beasts to come to represent people who are possessed by these passions. We have not far to go from here to cases in which a dreaded father is represented by a beast of prey. . . .) It might be said that wild beasts are used to represent the libido, a force dreaded by the ego and combated by means of repression." However, although the lion is occasionally associated with what could be a father figure — in the little cluster of father and son figures in the top centre of *Accommodations of Desire,* for example — and certainly in the following year in *William Tell,* it is predominantly seen in 1929 paintings in conjunction with a woman. Dalí has said that the lion's maw "translates his terror before the revelation of the possession of a

17

18

---

[15]*grisaille:* A style of painting using shades of gray only and imitating bas-relief.

Accommodations of Desire, 1926.

Illumined Pleasures, 1929.

woman"; he painted *Accommodations of Desire* after an outing with Gala that summer.

It is interesting that in the case of this obsessive image the immediate source was not Freud — though its use may have been inspired by him — but a lithograph which hung in Dalí's room when he was a child, showing a girl at a well with a pitcher, and beside her a moulded relief on the well head showing a snarling lion's head which is very similar to that in the lower left of *Accommodations of Desire*. There is a striking difference, however, in this painting, between the styles of the lions' heads. That in the foreground has all the banal and simple realism of a textbook illustration, but those in the background are almost mannerist in their exaggeration. The figures themselves in these paintings, and frequently in subsequent works, share this distended realism. George Orwell was probably right, in his essay on Dalí's *The Secret Life*, "Benefit of Clergy," to suggest that this elaborate and exaggerated style of drawing — for it is essentially an exaggeration of contour — belongs to Edwardian children's book illustration, to the never-never world of Barrie and Rackham,[16] to the style, in other words, of Dalí's own childhood.

Dalí once described *The First Days of Spring* as a "veritable erotic delirium"; *Illumined Pleasures* is like a delirium of sexual anxiety, violent rather than erotic, and teeming with references to other paintings, a point underlined by the device of the three boxed "pictures-within-a-picture," in the interstices between which the real action takes place. The lion's head, representing, interlocked, passion and threat, is linked to the head of a woman; by adding a handle to her head Dalí here, as elsewhere, turns her into a jug-container, in a neat visual shorthand for the psycho-analytical commonplace that receptacles stand (for obvious reasons) in dream symbolism for women. Recurring from *Dismal Sport* is the boy hiding his face in shame. Most interesting is the cluster of images in the immediate foreground; these do seem to spring from a kind of psychological automatism, and without trying to over-determine their significance, which remains ambiguous, could be read as linking the parental threat with that of female sexuality, creating a veritable Scylla and Charybdis of sexual anxiety. To start with, the black shadow cast by an unseen object in the right foreground is identical to the shadow cast by the enlaced couple in the right of *Dismal Sport*. The couple is almost certainly father and son, a reading strengthened by its resemblance to that in De Chirico's *The Prodigal Son* (1924). The bloodied knife, gripped too late by a preventive hand, is inevitably linked to the bloodstained hands of the woman, who surely evokes,

19

20

---

[16]*Barrie and Rackham:* Sir James Barrie (1860–1937), a Scottish playwright and novelist, was the author of *Peter Pan* (1904). Arthur Rackham (1867–1939) was an illustrator whose work includes pictures for *Peter Pan* (1906) and *Alice in Wonderland* (1907).

rather than the Venus rising from the waves that Harriet Janis suggests (in *Painting as the Key to Psychoanalysis*), Lady Macbeth trying in vain to wash her hands in her imaginary guilt while sleepwalking. Lady Macbeth would herself have killed Duncan, it may be recalled, had he not resembled her father while he slept. Clasping the woman is a bearded man, who is modelled on a figure from a painting deep in resonances for Dalí — Ernst's *Pieta, or Revolution by Night*. The *Pieta* shows Ernst himself dead (turned to stone) in the arms of a man intended to represent his father, and who also bears a resemblance to the brooding parent figure in De Chirico's *The Child's Brain*. In 1927 Ernst had published in *La Révolution Surréaliste* some childhood dreams and reminiscences called "Visions de Demi-sommeil" (Visions of Half-sleep), in which his father appears as a threatening figure of whom the child is both frightened and jealous. "Pieta" in the title apparently invokes the Deposition from the Cross, with Mary mourning Christ, but the theme is really an Oedipal one, with the father replacing Mary. The legend of Oedipus — whose father Laertes tried to kill him as a baby because of a prophecy that his son would kill him, a prophecy later fulfilled by Oedipus who then unwittingly marries his own mother — is the dramatic prototype of a child's unconscious desires at the first stirrings of sexuality, accompanied by feelings of rivalry with his father. It is a story with its roots deep, as Freud put it, in "primeval dream material."

It is difficult in *Illumined Pleasures* to disentangle any one predominant 21 reading in this cluster of foreground images, but there do seem to be mingled there both the highly personal themes of sexual anxiety we have already examined in other paintings, and references to some of the classic themes in legend and literature which incarnate unconsciously impulses lying deep within human sexuality, and to which Freud paid very close attention. Dalí's long-standing admiration for Freud was unexpectedly reciprocated when the two met in London in 1938. Freud wrote to Stefan Zweig afterwards: "I really owe you thanks for bringing yesterday's visitor. For until now, I have been inclined to regard the Surrealists, who have apparently adopted me as their patron saint, as complete fools (let us say 95%, as with alcohol). That young Spaniard, with his candid, fanatical eyes and his undeniable technical mastery has changed my estimate. It would indeed be interesting to investigate analytically how he came to create that picture. . . ."

REVIEW QUESTIONS

1. Why were Dalí's friends disturbed by *Dismal Sport* during its creation? How did Dalí respond to them? According to Ades, what is the significance of the asso-

ciation of fish and grasshopper in *Dismal Sport* and other paintings of this period?

2. What is "psychic automatism"? How was Dalí's approach to psychic automatism different from that of his fellow surrealist, André Masson? How did Dalí and the other surrealists draw upon the ideas of Freud in their own work?

3. How does Ades interpret the various motifs and images in *Dismal Sport*? What is the overall theme of this painting? What is the chief conflict?

4. What was the symbolic significance of wild animals in dreams, according to Freud? How is this symbolic significance relevant to some of Dalí's paintings?

5. What was Freud's overall estimate of Dalí and the surrealists?

DISCUSSION AND WRITING QUESTIONS

1. Compare and contrast the fish-grasshopper motif in *Dismal Sport, The First Days of Spring,* and *The Great Masturbator.* Do you agree with Ades's interpretations of these works? What other recurring symbols populate Dalí's works of this period? How do you interpret their significance?

2. What do you think that Freud meant when he told Dalí that "It is not the unconscious I seek in your pictures, but the conscious"? How did Freud think that painters like Dalí differed from painters like Leonardo da Vinci? Do you agree?

3. Assess Dalí's art of this period (or the art of other surrealists). Is the unconscious a legitimate subject for art? If not, why not? If so, how well do you think that Dalí has succeeded both in objectifying (in art) his own unconscious anxieties *and* in creating genuine works of art? This question may lead you to the larger question of what constitutes a genuine work of art. A significant body of traditionalists has always sneered at modern art, deeming it nonart. And recall that Ades has told us (paragraph 2) that even some of the other surrealists worried that in works like *Dismal Sport* Dalí was "turning his paintings into mere psychopathological documents." When does a "psycho-pathological document" become a work of art?

4. Study other works of Dalí or other surrealists and interpret them, according to their Freudian motifs. You may wish to draw upon the critical work of writers like Ades, or (if you are particularly knowledgeable about art) you may wish to rely almost exclusively upon your own insights and interpretations.

5. Can you think of works by other painters that might be interesting to explore for their Freudian motifs? If so, conduct such an exploration. What evidence can you find to substantiate your conclusions?

ERNEST JONES *(1897–1958)*

Psychoanalytic literary criticism is a form of psychohistory; in both cases, the "patients" are individuals who are not personally known to the analysts and who are analyzed solely (or at least primarily) on the basis of written records. The same reservations that such critics as Thomas Kohut have applied to psychohistorians also apply to literary critics who psychoanalyze fictional or dramatic characters. Yet, as in psychohistory, such critical analysis at its best, at its most sensitive, can be highly illuminating. Frederick Crews's analyses of Hawthorne's novels, Norman Holland's analysis of English Restoration comedy — and Ernest Jones's analysis of Shakespeare's greatest tragic hero — have proven enormously stimulating and influential, even though many critics have disagreed with their analyses.

Ernest Jones carried unusually high credentials for such critical tasks. A friend, a distinguished colleague, and a biographer of Freud himself, Jones was largely responsible for making psychoanalysis respectable in England. He was born in Gowerton, Glamorgan, a county of Wales. Trained as a medical doctor at University College Hospital in London, he became a member of the Royal College of Physicians in 1904 and held several posts in medicine and surgery during the next several years. Like Freud, however, Jones's interests shifted from medicine, to neurology, to psychiatry, and then to psychoanalysis. He began practicing psychoanalysis in 1907, and the following year, together with Carl Gustav Jung, organized the first psychoanalytical congress in Salzburg, Austria, where he first met Freud. Later that year he went to Canada and began teaching and practicing psychoanalysis at Toronto General Hospital. In 1911, he helped establish the American Psycho-Analytical Association. During this period he also began writing extensively about psychoanalysis. Among his words are *On the Nightmare, Papers in Psycho-Analysis* (1913), and an essay on the psychoanalytic aspects of Hamlet that was later to be expanded into a book, *Hamlet and Oedipus* (1949).

In 1913, Jones returned to London, where he practiced psychoanalysis and founded (and edited until 1939) the *International Journal of Psycho-Analysis* (1920). He also founded the London Psycho-Analytical Association (later the British Psycho-Analytical Society), which he served as president until 1944. Jones was instrumental in gaining recognition for psychoanalysis by the British Medical Association, which recommended in 1929 that "the term psycho-analysis can legitimately be applied only to the method evolved by Freud and to the theories derived from the use of this method."

When the Nazis gained power in Germany in 1933, Jones worked tirelessly to resettle many Viennese analysts (including Freud himself in 1938) to England and other safer places. With his retirement from the presidency of the British Psycho-Analytical Society in 1944, Jones turned his full efforts to his masterpiece, a three-volume biography, *The Life and Works of Sigmund Freud* (1953–1957).

The following essay first appeared in the *International Journal of Psycho-Analysis*. Jones's interpretation of Hamlet is said to have profoundly influenced Laurence Olivier when he directed and starred in his own film version of *Hamlet* (1948).

THE DEATH OF HAMLET'S FATHER

When a poet takes an old theme from which to create a work of art it   1
is always interesting, and often instructive, to note the respects in which he changes elements in the story. Much of what we glean of Shakespeare's personality is derived from such studies, the direct biographical details being so sparse. The difference in the accounts given in *Hamlet* of the way the King had died from that given in the original story is so striking that it would seem worthwhile to look closer at the matter.

The most obvious difference is that in the Saxo-Belleforest saga[1] the   2
murder is a public one, with Shakespeare a secret one. We do not know, however, who made this change, since an English play called *Hamlet*, thought to be written by Kyd,[2] was extant some twelve years before Shakespeare wrote his; and he doubtless used it as well as the Belleforest version. That play no longer exists except in a much later and much distorted German version, but a Ghost probably appeared in it, and one can hardly imagine any other function for him than to disclose a secret murder. There is reason to suppose that Shakespeare may himself have had a hand in the Kyd play, but at all events he made the best possible use of the alteration.

In the old saga Claudius (there called Feng) draws his sword on his   3
brother the King (Horvendil)[3] at a banquet and slays him "with many wounds." He explains to the assembled nobles that he has done this to protect his sister-in-law (Geruth) from ill-treatment and imminent peril of her life at the hands of her husband — a pretext evidently a reflection of the infant's sadistic conception of coitus. Incidentally, in the Saxo saga

---

Ernest Jones. The Death of Hamlet's Father [1948]. In Edith Kurzweil and William Phillips, eds., *Literature and Psychoanalysis*. New York: Columbia UP, 1983. Originally published in *International Journal of Psychoanalysis* 29 (1948), 174–76.

[1]*Saxo-Belleforest saga:* An early version (1576) of the Hamlet story by François Belleforest, based on a 12th century account by the Danish clerk Saxo Grammaticus.

[2]*Kyd:* Thomas Kyd (1557–1595), an Elizabethan playwright, was the author of *A Spanish Tragedy*, written sometime in the 1580s.

[3]It was Shakespeare who changed his name to Hamlet, thus emphasizing the identification of son and father. [Jones]

(though not with Belleforest), there had here been no previous adultery with the Queen, so that Feng is the sole villain, and Amleth, unlike Hamlet, unhesitatingly kills him and reigns in his stead as soon as he can overcome the external obstacles. In *Hamlet*, as is well known, the plot is intensified by the previous incestuous adultery of the Queen, which convulses Hamlet at least as much as his father's murder and results in an animus against women that complicates his previously simple task.

In the *Hamlet* play, on the other hand, Claudius disclaims all responsibility for his brother's death and spreads a somewhat improbable story of his having been stung to death by a serpent while sleeping in an orchard. How he knew this we are not told, nor why the adder possessed this quite unwonted deadliness. There is much to be said about that "orchard," but we may assume that it symbolizes the woman in whose arms the King was murdered. The Ghost's version was quite different. According to him, Claudius had found him asleep and poured a juice of hebana into his ears, a still more improbable story from a medical point of view; he further tells us that the poison rapidly spread through his system resulting in "all his smooth body being barked about most lazarlike with vile and loathsome crust." Presumably its swift action prevented him from informing anyone of what had befallen him.

The source of this mysterious poison has been traced as follows.[4]   5
Shakespeare seems to have taken the name, incidentally misspelling it, from the juice of "hebon," mentioned in a play of Marlowe's,[5] who himself had added an initial letter to the "ebon" (ebony) of which the walls of the God of Sleep were composed (Ovid). Shakespeare apparently went on to confound this narcotic with henbane (hyoscyamus), which at that time was believed to cause mortification and turn the body black.[6] Two interesting beliefs connecting henbane with the ear are mentioned by Pliny:[7] (1) that it is a remedy for earache, and (2) when poured into the ear it causes mental disorder.

The coarse Northern butchery is thus replaced by a surreptitious Italianate form of murder, a fact that has led to many inquiries, which do not concern us here, concerning Italian influence on Shakespeare. The identical method is employed in the Play Scene, where a nephew murders his uncle, who was resting after coitus, by dropping poison into his ear and immediately afterwards espouses the widow à la Richard III. Hamlet says he got the Gonzago story from an Italian play, but no such play has yet

---

[4]See Henry Bradley, *Modern Language Review* (1920), 15:85. [Jones]

[5]*Marlowe:* Christopher Marlowe (1564–1593), Elizabethan playwright, author of *Doctor Faustus*.

[6]W. Thiselton-Dyer, *Shakespeare's England*, 1:509. [Jones]

[7]*Pliny, the Elder:* Gaius Plinius Secundus (23–79), Roman naturalist.

been traced. But there had been two instances of murder in an unhappy Gonzaga family. In 1538 a famous Duke of Urbino, who was married to a Gonzaga, died under somewhat suspicious circumstances. Poison was suspected, and his barber was believed to have poured a lotion into his ears on a number of occasions. So the story goes: whether poison thus administered is lethal to anyone with intact tympani[8] is a matter we must leave to the toxicologists. At all events the Duke's son got the unfortunate barber torn in pieces by pincers and then quartered. In the course of this proceeding the barber asserted he had been put on to commit the foul deed by a Luigi Gonzaga,[9] a relative of the Duke's by marriage. For political and legal reasons, however, Luigi was never brought to trial.[10] Furthermore, in 1592 the Marchese Rudolf von Castiglione got eight bravos to murder his uncle the Marchese Alfonso Gonzaga, a relative of the Duke of Mantua. Rudolf had wished to marry his uncle's daughter and had been refused; he himself was murdered eight months later.

The names used make it evident that Shakespeare was familiar with   7
the story of the earlier Gonzaga murder, as he possibly was with the later one too. The "poison in the ear" story must have appealed to him, since he not only used it in the Gonzago Play Scene — where it would be appropriate — but also in the account of Hamlet's father's death.

If we translate them into the language of symbolism the Ghost's story   8
is not so dissimilar from that of Claudius. To the unconscious, "poison" signifies any bodily fluid charged with evil intent, while the serpent has played a well-known role ever since the Garden of Eden. The murderous assault had therefore both aggressive and erotic components, and we note that it was Shakespeare who introduced the latter (serpent). Furthermore, that the ear is an unconscious equivalent for anus is a matter for which I have adduced ample evidence elsewhere.[11] So we must call Claudius' attack on his brother both a murderous aggression and a homosexual assault.

Why did Shakespeare give this curious turn to a plain story of envious   9
ambition? The theme of homosexuality itself does not surprise us in Shakespeare. In a more or less veiled form a pronounced feminity and a readiness to interchange the sexes are prominent characteristics of his plays, and doubtless of his personality also. I have argued that Shakespeare wrote

---

[8]*tympani:* Membranes; in this case, in the ear.

[9]From whom Shakespeare perhaps got the name Lucianus for the murderer in the Play Scene. [Jones]

[10]See G. Bullough, "The Murder of Gonzago," *Modern Language Review* (1935), 30:433. [Jones]

[11]Ernest Jones, *Essays in Applied Psycho-Analysis* (London: Hogarth Press, 1923), pp. 341–346. [Jones]

Hamlet as a more or less successful abreaction of the intolerable emotions aroused by the painful situation he depicts in his Sonnets, his betrayal by both his beloved young noble and his mistress.[12] In life he apparently smothered his resentment and became reconciled to both betrayers. Artistically his response was privately to write the Sonnets (in the later publication of which he had no hand) and publicly to compose *Hamlet* not long afterwards, a play gory enough to satisfy all varieties of revenge.

The episode raises again the vexed question of the relation between 10 active and passive homosexuality. Nonanalysts who write on this topic are apt to maintain that they represent two different inborn types, but this assertion gives one an unsatisfied feeling of improbability, and analytic investigation confirms these doubts by demonstrating numerous points of contact between the two attitudes. Certainly Claudius' assault was active enough; sexually it signified turning the victim into a female, i.e., castrating him. Hamlet himself, as Freud pointed out long ago,[13] was unconsciously identified with Claudius, which was the reason why he was unable to denounce and kill him. So the younger brother attacking the older is simply a replica of the son-father conflict, and the complicated poisoning story really represents the idea of the son castrating his father. But we must not forget that it is done in an erotic fashion. Now Hamlet's conscious attitude toward his father was a feminine one, as shown by his exaggerated adoration and his adjuring Gertrude to love such a perfect hero instead of his brother. In Freud's opinion homosexuality takes its origin in narcissism,[14] so that it is always a mirror-love; Hamlet's father would therefore be his own idea of himself. That is why, in such cases, as with Hamlet, suicide is so close to murder.

My analytic experience, simplified for the present purpose, impels me 11 to the following reconstruction of homosexual development. Together with the narcissism a feminine attitude toward the father presents itself as an attempted solution of the intolerable murderous and castrating impulses aroused by jealousy. These may persist, but when the fear of the self-castration implied gains the upper hand, i.e., when the masculine impulse is strong, the original aggression reasserts itself — but this time under the erotic guise of active homosexuality.

According to Freud, Hamlet was inhibited ultimately by his repressed 12 hatred of his father. We have to add to this the homosexual aspect of his attitude, so that Love and Hate, as so often, both play their part.

---

[12]Ernest Jones, *Hamlet and Oedipus* (New York: Norton, 1949). [Jones]
[13]Sigmund Freud, *Die Traumdeutung (The Interpretation of Dreams)* (1901), p. 183. [Jones]
[14]*Collected Papers* 2:241. [Jones]

REVIEW QUESTIONS

1. What is the main difference between the death of Hamlet's father in the Saxo-Belleforest saga and in Shakespeare's play? What are the differences in the two versions concerning the other circumstances of the king's death? How does the ghost's story of Hamlet's father's death differ from Claudius's?
2. What is the ultimate significance of Claudius's murder of his brother, according to Jones? Why was Hamlet unable for so long to denounce and kill Claudius? How was Hamlet's relationship to his father paralleled by Claudius's relationship with Hamlet's father?

DISCUSSION AND WRITING QUESTIONS

1. Why do you think Jones went to such great lengths (about half of his essay) to point out the differences between Shakespeare's sources and his own version of *Hamlet,* in their respective accounts of how Hamlet's father died?
2. If you have read *Hamlet,* discuss the plausibility of Jones's account of the meaning of the death of Hamlet's father. (Consider especially Jones's arguments in paragraphs 8 and following.) Discuss also your reaction to Jones's suggestion that Shakespeare wrote *Hamlet* partially as an act of revenge against the young male noble and the mistress (the subject of his sonnets) who had betrayed him.
3. In view of your own reading of one or more of Shakespeare's plays, discuss Jones's assertion that "In a more or less veiled form a pronounced femininity and a readiness to interchange the sexes are prominent characteristics of his plays, and doubtless of his personality also."
4. Discuss Jones's assertion (reflecting, he claims, Freud's own opinion) that "homosexuality takes its origin in narcissism, so that it is always a mirror-love."
5. If you have read *Hamlet,* has Jones's analysis caused you to reinterpret either the play as a whole or its characters? If so, in what ways? Do you see ways in which Freudian analysis could similarly affect your own interpretations of other literary or dramatic works? Explain.
6. Read one or more other Freudian analyses of literature and critique them. See the Kurzweil and Phillips anthology (listed in the "Additional Readings" at the end of the book), which includes essays on Dostoyevsky, Voltaire, Keats, Henry James, Kafka, Lewis Carroll, and others. Consider also Frederick Crews's *The Sins of the Fathers* (about Nathaniel Hawthorne's fiction) or Norman Holland's *The First Modern Comedies* (about English Restoration comedy).

HARVEY R. GREENBERG (b. 1935)

The discovery of Freudian motifs in art has, not surprisingly, extended to the 20th century's most popular art form, the motion picture. In some films, as in Dalí's paintings, the psychoanalytic critic does not have very far to look: the motifs have been consciously incorporated by filmmakers attempting to dramatically work out Freudian ideas. Alfred Hitchcock recruited Dalí himself to design the dream sequences in his psychoanalytic thriller, *Spellbound* (1945). Hitchcock returned to Freudian themes in *Psycho* (1960). The opening sequence of Ingmar Bergman's *Wild Strawberries* (1957) is the terrifying dream of an elderly professor who finds himself wandering down a deserted, noiseless street where he encounters numerous Freudian symbols — clocks without hands, a man without a face, and finally a funeral procession; when he approaches the coffin, which has fallen from its carriage onto the street, the corpse tries to drag him inside, and then he realizes with horror that the corpse is himself. Freudian themes have even influenced science fiction. *Forbidden Planet* (1957) postulated an advanced alien civilization, the Krel, that destroyed itself soon after developing a powerful machine to free its inhabitants' minds from the physical restraints of their bodies. Not having evolved their own Freud, the Krel failed to realize that one essential component of their minds — their primitive, irrational, destructive ids — now had access to a source of limitless power, subject to no physical restraints. (The film's plot, about an earth scientist who tries and fails to master the Krel machine, loosely follows Shakespeare's *Tempest* — in which some critics had already noted parallels between the monster Caliban and the id, between Prospero and the ego.)

In other films, Freudian motifs may be detected, but their actual presence could be disputed, since the filmmakers appear not to have consciously incorporated them. Still, the fact that authors or screenwriters do not *consciously* incorporate certain motifs does not necessarily mean that they are not present, exerting a strong influence. Exploring such a motif may throw light upon a film's characters and the significance of the dramatic action. In the following passage, Harvey Greenberg, a psychoanalyst, explores the heroine's unconscious quest for a father figure in MGM's *The Wizard of Oz* (1939). This film's enduring popularity is a testament not only to its quality but also to the fact that in Dorothy's quest so many people have found elements that are intensely and personally meaningful. *The Wizard of Oz*, in fact, is something of a modern-day fairy tale. Like other fairy tales, it is constituted by elements so deeply buried that, though not immediately accessible, they are at the same time profoundly satisfying and profoundly disturbing — and not simply to children.

The author earned his medical degree at Cornell University Medical College and is now Associate Professor of Clinical Psychiatry and Child Psychiatry at Albert Einstein Medical College in Bronx, New York. He practices at the Bronx Psychiatric

Hospital for Children and Youth. In addition to *The Movies on Your Mind* (1975), source of the following passage, he has written *Hanging In: What You Should Know about Psychotherapy* (1982) and chapters on the psychology of gambling and on psychiatry and art in the *Complete Textbook of Psychiatry* (3d ed., 1980).

Greenberg developed an early love of movies while growing up in Philadelphia. As he writes,

> Movies kept me afloat through an acned, reasonably tormented adolescence, since I feared the madhouse consequences of exposing a psychiatrist to the noxious vapors arising from my psyche. . . . The transition from university to medical school was accomplished with only moderate trauma, because every step of the way I found fellow somnambulists instantly at the ready to drop scalpel or stethoscope and rush down to the midtown [New York] flea pits to see *Bad Day at Black Rock* or *Creature from the Black Lagoon* for the tenth time. And though I was psychoanalyzed during my psychiatric training, the therapist was never able to relieve my moviemania.

In his own professional practice, Greenberg encourages his patients to talk about their own favorite movies: "Cinema is a supremely valid source of free associations, a powerful touchstone into the unconscious. The movies, like waking dreams, interpret every aspect of our lives — the unquiet past, the troubled present, our anxious premonitions of the future, our neurotic conflicts and our inspired gropings towards the light." As one particularly graphic (and unusual case) Greenberg cited the case of an adolescent who hated school and whose favorite film was *King of Kings*:

> He especially enjoyed the part where Roman soldiers pounded the nails into Jesus' hands. I discovered that his cranium was jammed with homosexual and masochistic fantasies: he was avoiding school because of a tremendous fear — and hidden wish — that a gang of local bullies would beat and rape him. In his daydreams, he would show a Christ-like forbearance and pity for his tormentors, so that they would give up their evil ways and worship, rather than despise him.

Greenberg drew upon his psychoanalytic training, his love and knowledge of movies, and his conviction that movies satisfied important needs of their audiences (including omniscience, voyeurism, and wish-fulfillment), to create *The Movies on Your Mind*. In this book he considers more than 100 films but focuses on *The Wizard of Oz, The Treasure of the Sierra Madre, The Maltese Falcon, Casablanca, Psycho, 8½,* and *Wild Strawberries.* The following passage, on *The Wizard of Oz,* constitutes Chapter 2 of *The Movies on Your Mind*.

THE WIZARD OF OZ:
LITTLE GIRL LOST — AND FOUND

> The treasure which you think not worth taking trouble
> and pains to find, this one alone is the real treasure
> you are longing for all your life. The glittering treasure
> you are hunting for day and night lies buried on the
> other side of that hill yonder. . . .
>
> — B. Traven: *The Treasure of the Sierra Madre*

In 1939, MGM delivered two of the all-time movie greats — *Gone With*   1
the Wind and *The Wizard of Oz*. Both pictures spoke directly to the American
heartlands and were instant box office smashes; the heroine of each is a
gutsy teenager (Scarlett O'Hara is sixteen at the start of GWTW, Dorothy
Gale about thirteen in *Wizard*) whose serene life is shattered — in Scarlett's
case by the hammerblows of fate during the Civil War, in Dorothy's by a
concussion sustained during a savage Kansas twister. Each young lady has
her mettle fiercely tested in a succession of compelling trials and tribulations: Scarlett emerges from economic and romantic disaster in post-bellum
Georgia older and no wiser — bullheaded, scheming as ever. But Dorothy
Gale returns from her Oz-dream only a few moments older, and — as we
shall see — matured far beyond her years.

Dorothy's "trip" is a marvelous metaphor for the psychological journey   2
every adolescent must make. Contrary to popular misconception, psychoanalysts do not believe that the core of personality is fixed, immutable,
in earliest childhood. Those years are certainly crucial, but we remain open
to change and healing every day of the rest of our lives. At no other stage
of development is this more true than adolescence, when the enormous
thrust of physical, intellectual and sexual growth literally propels the
youngster out of the family nest. Simultaneously, the half-buried conflicts
of childhood are resurrected to be resolved or haunt us forever. A poignant
and infuriating mixture of regressive and progressive tendencies, the adolescent is exquisitely vulnerable to further emotional injury and terrifically
capable of self-repair.

With the onset of puberty, the parents, previously viewed from below   3
as supreme authorities, are now confronted at eye level — and who ever
enjoyed *that* view? After all, if one admits that one's progenitors are simply
human, then the very human wish to be cared for and protected indefinitely must go out the window. This possibility terrifies the adolescent,
until it is recognized that realistic power can be acquired over one's affairs,

---

Harvey R. Greenberg. *The Wizard of Oz*: Little Girl Lost — and Found [1975]. In *The Movies
on Your Mind*. New York: Dutton (Saturday Review Press), 1975.

that one is neither omnipotent nor absolutely helpless in shaping personal destiny. Before this saving recognition is firmly rooted within the psyche, the quixotic teenager will alternately badger his folks with outrageous demands to be treated like the ruler of the nursery, or else rake them with withering blasts of contempt and go out questing for substitutes to redeem their "failure," some super-hero to worship and imitate.

These substitutes take many shapes, and are traded in with bewildering frequency: rock stars; sports and other media idols; teachers; gang leaders; these are all sought with one idea in mind: the "hero" is put back on the pedestal vacated by the parents, endowed with a special mightiness — athletic, romantic, spiritual, etc. — to remedy the sense of a perceived lack within the self. In other words, *everyone wants a Wizard during adolescence,* but the wanting will cease when the youngster begins to tap his own unique abilities.

Forswearing childhood wishes, giving up worn-out attachments to one's parents, produces a profound feeling of loss, a deep sorrow that is an important ingredient in the periodic "blues" afflicting teenagers so inexplicably. The inner vacuum may loom as large as outer space, until it is filled by solid new relationships away from the family. This takes time; in our particular culture, which grants its youth a great deal of leeway for experimentation, one may be well into the twenties before the establishment of satisfying peer relationships and the consolidation of identity can occur. It is comforting for an adolescent to have the real parents around during this period of subtle psychic shifts, to know that one *can* go home again to touch comfortable emotional bases. But when the youngster must re-mourn a mother or father *already* lost, the tendency to cling to an idealized image of the dead parent increases and the pain of letting go and growing up can be intolerable.

Such is the case with Dorothy Gale, who throughout *The Wizard of Oz* is desperately trying to come to terms with her orphanhood. Neither the film, nor the L. Frank Baum classic, explains how, when, or in what sequence her parents died. Permit me to speculate, on the basis of my analyses of a number of grown-up Dorothies, that her father died first — probably before her eighth year, thereby impelling her into an extraordinarily close relationship with her mother. When her mother passed away, Dorothy suffered an overwhelming spiritual wrenching. Every sign in *Wizard* points to enormous desolation over parental loss, more specifically over maternal loss, and terrible dread of its repetition.

It is a perverse paradox that the mother, giver of life, is unconsciously perceived at the very beginning of life as the destroyer of life. Insofar as we can fathom the mental activity of the very young child, it appears that the infantile mind splits the image of mother in twain. The Good Mother nourishes and cherishes, the Bad Mother abandons and devastates. This primitive doubling is often found in religion. The Hindus, for instance, believe the Mother-goddess Kali is the source of fertility as well as the harbinger of death and chaos.

In folklore and fairy tale, the Bad Mother is the witch who snares the children strayed from home, then enslaves or murders them. To the unconscious, which thrives on opposites, the Bad Mother kills either by abandonment or binding so close that one strangles in her clutches. (Often, the victim is devoured, the ultimate "closeness"!) The Good Mother is the bounteous fairy godmother, the lovely gossamer queen who makes everything copacetic with a wave of her wand.

Good and Bad Mother are, of course, *one and the same.* The child, given time, growth and understanding, comes to appreciate that Mom isn't abandoning because she cannot be around constantly to gratify every whim. But a host of natural shocks compromise the ability to integrate and reconcile the Good and Bad Mother-images within. Maternal death is the most severe of these: the mother who dies is blamed by the child; she is supremely bad for leaving the child so exposed and vulnerable. *Mutatis mutandis,*[1] the child also believes that it was bad and drove mother away; kids are pathetically prepared to take the burden of death and divorce upon themselves: if I was bad, then if I am good, maybe it will be all right again. . . .

At the dawn of adolescence, the very time she should start to distance herself from Aunt Em and Uncle Henry, the surrogate parents who raised her on their Kansas farm, Dorothy Gale experiences a hurtful reawakening of her fear that these loved ones will be rudely ripped from her, especially her aunt (Em — M for Mother!). Dorothy is seriously hung up on her ambivalence toward Em: she wants Em to be the Good Mother, but frets that Em will turn Bad, die, go away forever. Dorothy's fear goes hand in hand with her rage — rage at the abandonment by her dead mother, displaced upon her equally guiltless aunt.

The voice of her conscience cries: *How can you be so wicked, so ungrateful? It wasn't mother's fault she had to go! Doesn't Em always do her best?* So, to keep her dead mother all good, all giving, and safe from her wrath, Dorothy takes the bad potential of the mothering figure and projects it wholesale into a fantasy of a malevolent persecutrix — a witch! — one can't have any trouble hating. But if this pseudoresolution persists, it must only perpetuate her problem by reinforcing her ambivalence. For it is only when she can view Em and all the grown-ups in her life for who they really are, not as wizards *or* witches, that she will be able to join them as a mature adult herself.

8

9

10

11

---

[1]*Mutatis mutandis:* (Latin) The necessary changes having been made.

The drama of Dorothy's search for her authentic, autonomous self is   12
delightfully played out during her adventures in the Land of Oz.

The opening scenes of *Wizard* are shot in listless black-and-white, ren-   13
dering the Kansas landscape absolutely prosaic. Dorothy and her little dog,
Toto, come hurrying down the road:

DOROTHY *(breathlessly):*   She isn't coming yet, Toto — did she hurt you? . . .
We'll go tell Uncle Henry and Aunty Em!

The farm is bustling: an old incubator has broken down, Em and Henry   14
are laboring desperately to save some newly hatched chicks. Dorothy spills
out her story: Toto got into Miss Gulch's garden, chased her cat, Miss
Gulch hit him with a rake. Em is abstracted, can't be bothered with such
foolishness. Dorothy wanders over to the pigpen where three farmhands
— Zeke, Hickory and Hunk — are bickering. They can't spare Dorothy
more than off-handed advice. Hunk tells her to use her head — *"it's not
made of straw"* — don't walk home near Miss Gulch's house, then Toto
won't get the chance to bother her. Zeke tells Dorothy not to "let that old
Gulch heifer bother ya — she ain't nothin' ta be afraid of — *have a little
courage, that's all!"*

She balances precariously on the railing, falls into the pen and is al-   15
most trampled. Zeke pulls her out and collapses with fright at his own
bravery. Out of patience, Em rousts the boys back to work, sternly chiding
Dorothy to find a place where she won't get into more trouble. Crestfallen,
Dorothy muses: "Do you suppose there is such a place, Toto? There must
be . . . far, far away . . . behind the moon, beyond the rain . . ." and sings
the famous "Over the Rainbow." (This lovely song was almost removed by
studio pundits who thought audiences would find it unrealistic to have the
heroine singing in a barnyard.)

Just as the first dream recalled in therapy often encapsulates a person's   16
entire neurosis, just as the first words uttered by a patient coming through
the office door often strikes the theme of an entire analytic session, the
opening sequences of *Wizard* adroitly capture Dorothy's central preoccupation with whether the child within her will be cherished or abandoned,
and whether the adult stirring within her can dare to leave the nest. Toto,
her dog, becomes an extension of herself — perky, mischievous, nosing
into things that don't concern him, forever *running away* when he should
stay put. He has been bad, and that manifestly bad woman, Miss Gulch,
may be coming to take him from the farm. The incubator is broken, the
newborn chicks are threatened by the failure of their mechanical womb
and Em and Henry are struggling to help them survive. Dorothy herself
nearly perishes, and is rescued by an obviously weak, cowardly man. The
characters are deftly sketched in: Aunt Em, harried, decisive; Uncle Henry,
kind but vague; the three handymen, lovable bumblers all. The farm is a

matriarchy, Em obviously rules the roost. Dorothy, rejected by Em and everyone, conjures up a place where happiness springs eternal and the dreams you dare to dream *do* come true. . . . One recalls the many myths of Utopias overflowing with lavish sustenance granted on nothing more substantial than a wish — the Big Rock Candy Mountain, or the German *Schlaraffenlandt*,[2] where preroasted chickens obligingly walked themselves into your mouth.

Dorothy's fantasies are interrupted as Miss Gulch sweeps in on her   17
bicycle with a court order for Toto, and proclaims that she'll take the whole farm if she doesn't get him. Dorothy's identification with the mutt is underscored: she offers to take Toto's place, and when Miss Gulch refuses, she cries — "You go away, or I'll bite you myself . . . *you wicked old witch!*" Em and Henry put up only token resistance, and Dorothy is forced to part with Toto. Henry is particularly ineffective, mumbling a few inarticulate words of small comfort. *After* Dorothy runs out sobbing, Emily dresses down Miss Gulch, the Good Mother contending with the Bad. Henry stands silent. In Dorothy's realm, as I have suggested, it would seem that power resides on the distaff side.

As Miss Gulch pedals away, the redoubtable Toto leaps out of the bas-   18
ket and scoots back to Dorothy's room. Without a moment's hesitation she packs her things and takes off. Ostensibly, she is worried that Gulch will return to claim her pound of pooch, but actually Toto's escape has given Dorothy the excuse she needed to spread her wings and quit the farm.

Just down the road, the runaways encounter an engaging old carny   19
faker, toasting hot dogs near his wagon: PROFESSOR MARVEL — ACCLAIMED BY THE CROWNED HEADS OF EUROPE — LET HIM READ YOUR PAST, PRESENT AND FUTURE!!!" The "Perfesser" easily reads her very obvious plight: "They don't understand you at home . . . they don't appreciate you . . . you want to see other lands — big cities, big mountains, big oceans!" He sits her down before his crystal ball — ". . . the same genuine authentic crystal used by the priests of Isis and Osiris in the days of the Pharaohs of Egypt, in which Cleopatra first saw the approach of Julius Caesar and Mark Antony, and so on. . . ." While Dorothy has her eyes closed, Marvel rummages through her basket, comes up with a picture of Em, and describes a painful vision: "A woman . . . her face is careworn . . . she is crying . . . someone has just about broken her heart . . . someone she loves very much . . . someone she's taken care of in sickness . . . she's putting her hand on her heart . . . she's dropping down on the bed. . . ."

Rather cruelly (or so I've always thought), Marvel addresses Dorothy's
dread both of losing and hurting her aunt. Strangely enough, all too often

---

[2]*Schlaraffenlandt:* Land of milk and honey; fool's paradise; a colloquial expression used to describe a utopian place.

the child will believe that the sheltering parent can be harmed if *it* grows up and goes away. The more intense the relationship between mother and child, the more the child is likely to be worried about the ill effects the rupture of the charmed partnership will have upon *both* parties. Dorothy is evidently only too willing to believe that her absence can kill Em, so she starts back down the road for home immediately after Marvel's "revelation." From our first glimpse of them, Dorothy and Toto have been ping-ponging back and forth between the safety of the farm and the mysterious, seductive world that lies outside the fence. . . .

Now Dorothy's fear of separation becomes a desperate reality. As she   21
draws near the farm, a tornado twists evilly in the gray distance. The wind rises to an insane howl. Em, screaming hysterically for Dorothy, is dragged down into a storm cellar by the menfolk, and Dorothy is left utterly alone and unprotected. Calling after Em, she stumbles back into her room. A shutter flies loose and smacks her temple; she drops, unconscious upon the bed. Intriguingly, *she* has taken Em's place in Marvel's prophecy, suffering for having made Em suffer, paying for her "badness" by being brought to the brink of death, the ultimate separation.

The house rises dizzily into the twister's spout. Dorothy awakens,   22
peers out the window and sees, whizzing merrily by, an old lady in a wheelchair (undigested memory of Em's "sickness"?), a cow, two gentlemen rowing a boat, and Miss Gulch, pedaling furiously. In the twinkling of an eye, Gulch metamorphoses into the witch of every child's darkest nightmare, and flies off on a jet-propelled broom, cackling hideously.

The house descends with a sickening jolt. Dorothy opens the door in   23
the sudden stillness and, as a female choir sings wordlessly, she whispers — in what has to be one of the great understatements of cinema — "Toto, I have a feeling we're not in Kansas anymore!" — as she steps into a Technicolor Fairyland.

We are, and we aren't, for this is the landscape of the dream. Freud   24
found that dreams take the characters and events of the preceding day — down to indifferent details — and weave them into a strange, meaningful tapestry. The characters of Kansas readily reappear in the dream Dorothy dreams, while she lies unconscious during the tornado, clad in the costume of her fantasies. Miss Gulch undergoes the first such transformation.

Glinda, Good Witch of the North, arrives in a giant soap bubble, re-   25
splendent in diaphanous gown, carrying the obligatory wand. Dorothy's farmhouse, she explains, has fallen on the Wicked Witch of the East, who held the little people of this fabulous country, the Munchkins, under her sway. Is Dorothy a Good Witch, or a Bad Witch? The nagging issue of Dorothy's goodness or badness is raised regarding her culpability in the Witch's demise — actually, it is her responsibility for hurting Em by running away that still plagues her conscience.

The Midget Munchkins pop up, applaud Dorothy as the national her-   26 oine, sweep aside her story that the Witch died accidentally (as on the farm, no one *ever* seems to listen to her!). The Munchkins make a big huff-and-puff about verifying the termination of their oppressor's rule; the Witch must be proven "morally, ethically, spiritually, physically, positively, absolutely, undeniably and reliably — *dead!*" Their obsession again reflects Dorothy's troubled conscience and her anxiety that the Bad Mother will be resurrected to punish her.

After the Munchkin coroner's verdict — "She's not only merely dead, she's really quite sincerely dead!" — the town breaks into wild rejoicing: "Ding, Dong, the Witch Is Dead!" The Munchkins are the little children held captive by the Bad Mother, a collective symbol for the child Dorothy, who by releasing them from bondage has unchained herself and become a Good Mother in the bargain. Munchkin babies dressed like fluffy chicks stir awake in a floral nest, recalling the nestlings Em labored so lovingly to rescue. [27]

Just as the festivities have reached a pitch of manic glee, there is a burst of hellish smoke and flame, and *another* Witch materializes — the sister of the deceased and even *more* Wicked, if that's possible. She holds Dorothy accountable, and is about to take vengeance when Glinda reminds her of the ruby slippers, still upon her sister's feet that protrude grotesquely beneath the farmhouse. As the Witch goes for them, they are whisked in a trice onto Dorothy's feet. The Bad Mother has returned, but Dorothy has warded her off by acquiring her power! Temporarily foiled, the Witch vanishes sulfurously after an ominous warning: "I'll bide my time . . . my fine lady, it's true I can't attend to you here and now as I'd like, but just try to stay out of my way, just try . . . I'll get you, my pretty, and your little dog, too!" [28]

Glinda tells Dorothy it might be better for her to clear out, the town isn't big enough for her and her new enemy. Dorothy wants to leave the territory, too — but how to get back home? The governance of Oz, like the Gale farm, has appeared matriarchal until now: Glinda directs Dorothy to follow the Yellow Brick Road that leads to a masculine source of supreme authority, the mysterious Wizard in the far-off Emerald City. [29]

Glinda departs by bubble express, and Dorothy exclaims: "My, people come and go so quickly here!" No one more so than she! *Dorothy* can't stay put — wherever she is, there soon develops a compelling reason for being elsewhere. This restless rushing about catches the curious adolescent propensity for not getting pinned down too long in any single place, relationship or philosophical position, so that many different approaches to life can be kept open. It would seem that Dorothy is afraid of entrapment by the Witch; in fact, her anxiety over being caught and done in by a Bad Mother is the flip side of her *own* infantile dependency upon Em, her *own* desire to be fixed in place forever, a helpless, clinging and unproductive parasite. [30]

As she proceeds along the Yellow Brick Road, Dorothy joins up with a   31
Scarecrow, a Tin Man, and a Cowardly Lion. She is intuitively drawn to
these unlikely fellow travelers: "You're the best friends anybody ever had
. . . and it's funny, but I feel as if I've known you all the time. . . ." She
has; they are the farmhands, Ozzified. Each appears to lack some crucial
portion of his spiritual or physical anatomy: the Scarecrow — a brain; the
Tin Man — a heart; the Lion — his courage. Alone, each is helpless. The
Scarecrow on first meeting is literally hung up — on a pole. The Tin Man
is rusted into immobility and the Lion so paralyzed by timorousness that
the sheep he counts to fall asleep scare him awake. Joined with Dorothy
into a tottering team, each functions better, but still imperfectly.

Virtually every male in Oz or Kansas is presented as weak and dam-   32
aged in some fashion, while the women, for good or ill, are far more capable. Uncle Henry obviously defers to Em's judgments; the farmhands
follow his lead. I would speculate that Dorothy's real father was perceived
quite as ineffectual or — more likely — that the tragedy of his death is
engraved upon her mind as a paradigm of masculine failure. (One sees
this in real life cases regularly.)

Dorothy, like all teenagers, wonders if her abilities to cope with the   33
world aren't somehow defective. In her half-formed state, neither adult nor
child, it is easy for her to believe that she is not brainy, gutsy or sensitive
enough to cut the mustard. An adolescent girl, embroiled with her mother
in unprofitable squabbling dependency, will regularly turn to her father as
a source of identification and strength, as well as other men, young and
old, in her wider circle. I do not downgrade the role of other women in
providing an "out" from the bind with mother, but the upsurge of sexuality during puberty reawakens the girl's earlier sexual feelings for her father,
and creates a special urgency in her need for him or substitutes for him.
(Note also that Dorothy *has* no other women with her on the farm to dilute
the intensity of her relationship with Em.) There is no Dad for Dorothy,
only poignant memories of him, and the surrogates who don't really fill
the bill. So off she goes with her damaged friends to find the great Pa in
the sky, to connect up with the Mighty Wizard and heal her sense of loss.

The Witch, determined to stop them, puts a field of poppies in their   34
way and croons a cracked lullaby. Narcotic fumes overcome Dorothy, Toto
and the Lion (who is throughout portrayed as the weakest and most childish of the company). Scarecrow and Tin Man call for help; Glinda waves
her wand, and a bracing snow falls, awakening the victims. The Bad
Mother has attempted to lull the children into fatal passivity — speaking
of the perils of dependency, poppies are the source of opium! — while the
Good Mother, Glinda, allows *her* children to go down the path towards
fulfillment.

The entrance to the Emerald City is kept by an officious bureaucrat —   35
a duplicate of Professor Marvel — who refuses to admit them, until he

discovers that Dorothy is wearing the ruby slippers. "That's a horse of a different color!" he declares, and opens the gates. The Wizard's domain is executed in greenish art deco, a la Buck Rogers.[3] A friendly cabby, another Marvel look-alike, drives them through the city as his horse goes through all the hues of the rainbow — for he's the horse of a different color! (Dreams frequently convert abstract ideas into visual puns.) At the Brush-Up Factory, the Scarecrow is newly stuffed, the Tin Man regalvanized, the Lion, Dorothy and Toto combed and curried in preparation for their audience with the Wizard.

Throughout these scenes the dwellers of the Emerald City speak a   36
veddy upper-class British, with the exception of the cabbie, who has a mock-Cockney dialect. Living in the land of Oz is exceptionally "re-feened," but it is dangerous to travel there. Let us remember that America in 1939 stood on the verge of a fateful re-entanglement with the affairs of foreign states. A strong suspicion of the stranger across the sea pervaded our country, and I do not doubt that *Oz* spoke very directly to our native isolationism and xenophobia. Dorothy's yearning to cease her wanderings would be echoed several years later by thousands of young men transplanted to equally unfamiliar shores!

At the Wizard's sanctum, the friends meet a Marvel-lous majordomo   37
more contentious, if possible, than his fellow at the gate: "Orders are, nobody can see the great Oz, not nobody, not nohow!" But Dorothy melts his heart: "Professor Marvel said she was sick, she may be dying, and it's all my fault . . . I'll never forgive myself, never, never, never!" The majordomo dissolves into tears — he, too, had an Aunt Em. He ushers them down a long tunnel into a vaulted chamber that always reminded me of my first glimpse of Radio City Music Hall at age five. Amidst the crash and roar of baleful music, spurts of green smoke, an enormous fanged face suspended in midair addresses the suppliants in stentorian tones. The Wizard's features are Transylvanian, his rhetoric Agnewesque,[4] but the voice is unmistakably that of the "Perfesser":

> MARVEL *(to Tinman):*   You dare to come to me for a heart, do you, you clinking, clattering collection of collaginous junk!!! *(to Scarecrow)* And you, Scarecrow . . . you have the effrontery to ask for a brain, you billowing bale of bulky fodder!!!

The Lion faints dead out. Dorothy rebukes the Wizard (note that she   38
always rises to the occasion, despite her fears), and the "great and powerful Oz" silences her peremptorily; he will grant every wish when Doro-

---

[3]*Buck Rogers:* Popular space hero of the 1930s and 1940s.

[4]*Agnewesque:* In the manner of Spiro Agnew, vice-president of the United States under President Nixon (1968–1974), who was given to alliterative diatribes against critics of the administration ("nattering nabobs of negativism").

thy's team brings him the Witch's broomstick. He thus proposes a stringent test of the very qualities they believe they lack, especially ingenuity and courage.

A Freudian somewhat more high church than myself would tag the broomstick and ruby slippers as — what else? — phallic symbols. From the more traditional analytic viewpoint, Dorothy would blame her sense of incompleteness upon an imaginary lost penis. And for those who still would have it that love conquers but Oedipus wrecks, Dorothy's quest for the phallic broomstick at another level could classically be interpreted as indicative of a long repressed wish to take father away from mother. The Witch thus becomes the maternal rival of the Electra[5] complex, retaliating because of Dorothy's ambitions to oust her and take her place as father's lover. Em and Henry are the logical replacements for her dead parents in Dorothy's Electra configuration. (In Greek mythology, Electra urged the murder of her mother, Clytemnestra, upon her brother Orestes, in revenge for Clytemnestra's complicity in the death of her husband, Agamemnon.)

I do not categorically deny that these elements exist in Dorothy's psychodynamics — it is a keystone of our philosophy that motivation and behavior rarely admit of simply one cause — but, as I've suggested, Dorothy's search for a strong, competent male "rescuer" seems to stem most pointedly from the pressure to divest herself of her pathological dependency upon Em-Mother, rather than to compete with Em for Henry. Fewer women than Freud imagined actually have fantasies of wanting a penis, but all women — as their male counterparts — seek realized independent selves.

Cut to the haunted forest near the Witch's castle. Dorothy and company are assaulted by a squadron of flying monkeys, their bluish features fixed in mirthless death's-head grins. They swoop down, snatch up Dorothy and Toto and bring them to the Witch's lair, leaving the three helpers temporarily *hors de combat*.[6] With Dorothy finally on her own turf, the Witch threatens to drown Toto if Dorothy doesn't come across with the goods. But when the Witch tries to take off the ruby slippers, they zap her with magical voltage. Just as he escaped Miss Gulch, Toto leaps out of his basket and scoots out of the castle. Exasperated, the Witch turns over an hourglass filled with blood-red sand to count out her captive's last precious minutes, and stalks away. At the edge of the precipice, Dorothy calls for her dearest protector:

DOROTHY: I'm frightened, Aunty Em, I'm frightened!

---

[5]*Electra:* In Greek myth, the daughter of King Agamemnon, who persuaded her brother Orestes to kill their mother Clytemnestra and her lover Aegisthus, in revenge for their murder of her father. (See below.)

[6]*hors de combat:* (French) Out of the action.

EM (*by some arcane TV, she's on the Witch's crystal*):   Dorothy . . . where are you? Please, it's Aunt Em, we're trying to find you. . . .

DOROTHY: I'm here in Oz, Aunty Em — I'm locked up in the Witch's castle . . . and I'm trying to get home to you. Oh, Aunty Em, don't go away . . . I'm frightened, come back!!!

Em's face, filled with concern, blurs into the Witch's — her voice wheedling, then viciously mocking: "Come back, Aunty Em, come back . . . I'll give you Aunty Em, my pretty, ah ha ha ha ha hah hah!!!"

The Witch's contorted features fill the screen and wink out. Dorothy recoils in terror — as did I and my friends as kids. See how intimately bound together is the Good Mother and the Bad: for a brief, nightmarish instant Em and the Witch have fused identities. This scene, I have found, is peculiarly troubling to most children, no doubt because it captures so effectively our archaic terror of the mother's destructive potential.

Toto, meanwhile, has found the three companions and leads them to the castle. They overcome the sentries, don their uniforms and smuggle themselves inside. Just as the hourglass runs out, they break into Dorothy's cell and liberate her. An alarm is sounded and after a mad pursuit by the Witch's minions, they are hemmed in on all sides, at the Witch's mercy:

WITCH: The last to go will see the first three go before her — and her little dog, too! How about a little fire, Scarecrow?

She takes up a torch and sets the Scarecrow alight. Throughout the film, he is the only traveler who actually suffers harm to his person. The Witch previously tried to incinerate him when he first met Dorothy, and her flying monkeys literally *destrawed* him, distributing him wholesale over the landscape. By virtue of his flimsy construction, he is the most vulnerable to total annihilation; our deepest fears of death center around this awful sundering of the self by a titanic, overwhelming force, symbolic of the catastrophic power of the Bad Mother.

Dorothy flings a pail of water over Scarecrow. The Witch is drenched too, and, shrieking piteously, she dwindles away to nothing. (Note that, like her sister, she is eliminated by Dorothy "accidentally" — disavowing any malevolent intent on Dorothy's part.) The Witch joins a long succession of horror and science fiction ghoulies whose seemingly invincible destructiveness is counteracted by some absurdly simple remedy, easily at hand. The Martians in *The War of the Worlds* are destroyed by ordinary bacteria; the animated shrubbery in *Day of the Triffids* dissolve in saltwater. We can always end our nightmares just as easily, by waking up and hauling ourselves out of harm's way. In *Wizard, aqua vitae* does the trick, plain water, Adam's ale, a primal symbol of rescue and rebirth. Once more, Dorothy has unintentionally committed an ambiguous murder of a Bad Mother and, in the bargain, become a kind of Good Mother herself. The Witch's henchmen, like the Munchkins, now worship her as their Bolivar,[7] and present her with the defunct tyrant's broom. Dorothy has, in fact, freed *herself*, but must still be enlightened as to the true meaning of her liberation.

When she returns to the Emerald City, the Wizard balks at seeing her,   45 indulges in windy rhetoric, and is then unmasked when Toto pulls aside a curtain to reveal a very ordinary mortal, an exact replica of Professor Marvel, undisguised for the first time in Oz, frantically manipulating Frankensteinish dials and levers:

WIZARD: Pay no attention to that man behind the curtain . . . the . . . er . . . Great Oz has spoken . . . er. . . .

With a gasp, they realize that Oz is a humbug, an outrageous fraud!

DOROTHY: You're a very *bad* man!

WIZARD: Oh, no, my dear, I'm a very good man. I'm just a very *bad* wizard.

Dorothy's unconscious saw through Marvel's carny flummery back in   46 Kansas, but consciously, she needed to have him on a pedestal. In her dream, immediately after the Witch's demise the Wizard is cut down to size. Her God has feet of clay, he turns out to be just another "failed" parent — but what his magic lacks he makes up for with plain old jayhawk horse sense. He addresses the friends in turn, wittily healing each's "defect." To the Scarecrow, he says there's nothing special about a brain; where he hails from, there are universities "where men go to become great thinkers, and when they come out they think deep thoughts — and with no more brains than you have!" But they *do* have diplomas, so he awards Scarecrow a "Th.D." — Doctor of Thinkology, whereupon the Strawman promptly spouts a pythagorean theorem!

The Lion, explains the Wizard, is merely a victim of disorganized   47 thinking. He confuses courage with wisdom — inferring that it's OK to be afraid, how you handle your quaking is what counts: "Back where I come from, we have men we call heroes. Once a year they take their fortitude out of mothballs and parade it down the main street . . . and they have no more courage than you have!" But they *do* have medals, so Lion receives the Triple Cross "for conspicuous bravery against Wicked Witches," to remind him of what he performed to save his loved ones under fire, despite his timid soul.

The Wizard can't imagine why Tin Man wants a heart — "Hearts will   48

---

[7]*Bolivar:* Simón Bolívar (1783–1830), South America's great revolutionary hero, who liberated much of the continent from Spanish colonial rule.

never be practical until they can be made unbreakable . . . back where I come from there are men who do nothing all day but good deeds . . . they are called phil . . . philo . . . er, good deed-doers . . . and their hearts are no bigger than yours!" But they *do* have testimonials, so the Wizard gives Tin Man a heart-shaped watch with a loud tick, gently admonishing him that "a heart is not judged by how much you love — but by how much you are loved by others. . . ."

The Wizard's wisdom is as therapeutic as any dispensed from behind   49 the couch: you have always had what you thought you lacked, and have already proven it. Do not delude yourself by seeking an impossible standard, but look within to find your own strength, sensitivity and sagacity. Medals, diplomas, testimonials, are only superficial rewards, the world's imprecise recognition of qualities best appreciated by yourself and those who love you. If you are open to love, purpose and meaning will unfold in good time. Ripeness is all.

But what of Dorothy? The Wizard has already figuratively brought her   50 home to herself, for his homely advice to her alter egos has shown that she has heart, pluck and wit enough to make a successful voyage through life. It only remains to transport her literally. He reveals his identity: a circus balloonist whose vehicle was snatched by the winds and carried to the Emerald City years ago where he was instantly acclaimed "Wizard deluxe." Throughout his reign, he has kept the balloon "against the advent of a quick getaway," and with it he and Dorothy will return safely to Kansas.

Cut to the balloon, prepared for flight. The Wizard, Dorothy and Toto   51 in the gondola. The Wizard addresses the cheering crowd, nominates Scarecrow to take his place as ruler of Oz, to be assisted by Tin Man and Lion (the voice of reason rules, one notes). Then Toto, perennial runaway, jumps out of Dorothy's arms to chase a cat. Dorothy goes after him, but the Wizard can't control his vehicle and it floats away, leaving Dorothy stranded, apparently no better off than before. The dream thus repeats the loss of her father when his strength is most needed, and also emphasizes that the Wizard, his prestige punctured, is only human. The Wizard-father's removal puts her squarely back in the hands of the mother (reduplicating, as I have theorized, the original sequence of loss), but it is the Good Mother who now puts in a final appearance:

GLINDA: You don't need to be helped any longer — you've always had the power to go back to Kansas. . . .

SCARECROW: Then why didn't you tell her before?

GLINDA: *Because she wouldn't have believed me . . . she had to learn it for herself.*

Hesitantly, like a patient groping towards insight, Dorothy describes   52 what she had learned during her dream of Oz:

DOROTHY: . . . it wasn't enough just to see Uncle Henry and Aunty Em . . . and it's that if I ever go looking for my heart's desire again, I won't look any further than my own backyard, because if it isn't there, I never really lost it to begin with. . . .

SCARECROW: But that's so easy . . . I should have thought of it for you.

No, Glinda repeats, *she had to find it out for herself* — and not by an act   53
of sheer intellect. As in analysis, the head must be connected to the heart.

Dorothy exchanges tearful farewells, says she will miss Scarecrow   54
most of all. She clicks the slippers together three times, murmuring — "There's no place like home," and awakens in black-and-white Kansas reality, back in her bedroom, surrounded by Em, Henry, the farmhands and Professor Marvel. The sands that ran out in the castle pictured the imminence of actual death:

HENRY *(to Marvel):*   She got quite a bump on the head . . . we kind of thought there for a minute she was going to leave us.

DOROTHY: But I did leave you . . . I was gone for days and days. . . . It wasn't a dream . . . you were there, but you couldn't have been, could you? . . . I remember that some of it wasn't very nice . . . but most of it was beautiful . . . but anyway, Toto, we're home . . . home . . . and this is my room, and you're all here . . . and I'm not going to leave here ever, ever again . . . because I love you all, and, oh, Aunty Em . . . there's *no* place like home!

In these final scenes, Dorothy's account of what she learned in Oz may   55
sound a trifle pat and sentimental: daydreams are fine, but are ultimately no substitute for the familiar. There is, however, a deeper truth here, couched with deceptive simplicity, the truth of Glinda and the Wizard. To paraphrase T. S. Eliot, our beginnings inform our endings. If we do not understand who we are, from where we have come, who we have identified with along the way and why, we will never know what we may be. Dorothy — like all adolescents — has looked to surrender *her* power to some mighty power outside herself that will relieve her of the responsibility of forging her own identity. In so doing, she risks being swallowed up by her own passivity and dependency. But at the conclusion of *Oz* she relinquishes her Wizard, lets him float back over the rainbow, and returns under her own steam to the people within the perimeter of her unfolding who can help her actualize a considerable potential.

Dorothy, I would stress, is no more "neurotic" than anyone else in her   56
circumstances. She is a lost child, driven too close to her aunt by an overwhelming early tragedy. That very closeness has grown into a formidable obstacle to her emotional growth. By consolidating her relationships with the rest of the Gale household, she will surely loosen the tie to Em, will gradually turn her affection from her small world to the people in the wider world outside her doorstep, a world that has seemed until now as scary

and enchanting as Oz. One notes that Dorothy has a special place in her heart for Hunk, the Scarecrow in Oz. He is the kind of man a grown-up Dorothy is often drawn to. Her down-to-earth uncomplicated approach to things nicely complements his somewhat abstracted "braininess."

Like *Finnegan's Wake*,[8] *The Wizard of Oz* comes full-circle to begin again.   57 What has passed is yet to come. Dorothy is, in fact, barely out of her child-hood, so it is absolutely appropriate for her to want to go home in order to travel away again, secure from fear. If we take the entire film as one extended fantasy, the tornado that whirls her, Gale-force, to Oz, is em-blematic of her adolescent *rite de passage,* of the death of her child self and the rebirth of a newer, lovelier Dorothy. The Yellow Brick Road, from this perspective, points the way down the rest of her days, into a future brim-ming with promise.

EPILOGUE

Today *The Wizard of Oz* seems as fresh and alive as ever, an incompa-   58 rable blend of cinematic crafts — the fabulous *mise-en-scène* created by the wizards — mostly unknown and unsung — of the MGM production staff, the lyrics and music of E. Y. "Yip" Harburg and Harold Arlen, and a bril-liant adaptation of L. Frank Baum's classic by Noel Langley, Florence Ryer-son and E. A. Woolf. Victor Fleming directed a miraculous ensemble of thespians, each of whom created a role now uniquely identified with the player: Ray Bolger's wildly flexible Scarecrow; Bert Lahr's Lion — half beast, half Canarsie; Jack Haley's Tin Man with a Hahvahd Yahd accent; Billie Burke's pixillated Glinda; Frank Morgan's genial Wizard. (W. C. Fields declined the role — not enough money for him, which was all to the good. Fields had the requisite patina of fraudulence — enough for three Wizards! — but his innate hatred of children would have cast a pall over the part.) Margaret Hamilton,[9] the prototypical Wicked Witch, is actually the kindest lady imaginable. A former kindergarten teacher, she's helped develop a radio network for hospitalized veterans, organized storytelling groups at the Los Angeles Children's Hospital and still acts today.

Then there was Judy — Judy Garland, catapulted over the rainbow into   59 instant stardom. She was sixteen when *Wizard* was made. Her breasts were bound to make her look younger. Originally the moguls wanted Shirley Temple. When that dream didn't come true, Garland was transformed into an absurd double, with bobbed nose, capped teeth and a blonde fright wig.

---

[8]*Finnegan's Wake:* The final novel (1939) of James Joyce, which ends in mid-sentence — a sentence continued in the first, fragmentary sentence of the book.

[9]*Margaret Hamilton:* Ohio-born actress who played in such classics as *The Wizard of Oz* and *My Little Chickadee,* died on May 16, 1985.

Somebody saw the light after early rushes, and let Judy play Dorothy according to her own instincts, which were never truer. She had a strong affinity for the part, and her life gives us some of the reasons. Her own father had died just a few years earlier. The loss profoundly affected her. Dorothy's bond with Em was only a pale shadow of Garland's tormented relationship with an aggressive stage-door mother she both deeply needed and resented. Later, she was to write: "Mother was the worst . . . the real life Wicked Witch of the West . . . sometimes it seems I've been in bondage since I was a fetus . . . I became a thing instead of a person."

Studio honchos took up where mother left off. They lifted her from the obscurity of a nickel-and-dime vaudevillian, made her the darling of millions, but every move was dictated for her in advance. As she grew up she fought desperately and self-destructively to be free, free of mother, the moguls, the doubts and fears that assailed her about her viability as person and performer. Still she sang on, through recurrent cycles of artistic, romantic, and financial disasters and triumphant comebacks. At age forty-five, she cried: "Finally I am loved! This is it! For the first time in my whole life I'm happy, really happy!" Three months later, she was dead of an accidental overdose. She sought her Wizard through five marriages, in the waves of adulation that washed over the footlights, and we shall never know if she found him.

60

REVIEW QUESTIONS

1. Why does Greenberg believe that the core of personality is not necessarily fixed in our early childhood years? What types of anxieties and conflicts must be resolved during our adolescence? What kind of people serve as "wizards" — or surrogate parents — during those years? Under what kind of circumstances is it *particularly* important for the adolescent to find surrogate parents? What are Greenberg's speculations as to Dorothy Gale's circumstances (not revealed in film or book)?

2. What is the psychological origin of the Good Witch and the Bad Witch, according to Greenberg? What are the characteristics of each? Why is the continuing coexistence of a Good Witch and a Bad Witch psychologically unhealthy, in the long run?

3. How does the opening sequence of *Wizard of Oz* encapsulate the overall theme of the film? What does Greenberg mean when he says that "the farm is a matriarchy"? What is the psychological significance of Toto? What is the significance of Dorothy's running away from the farm and then (after her session with Professor Marvel) running back?

4. Dorothy's adventures in Oz constitute her dream. Summarize, in Freudian terms, Greenberg's analysis of the chief motifs and symbols of this dream and their significance. Consider especially: the house falling upon the Bad Witch, the Good Witch, the Munchkins, the ruby slippers, the Yellow Brick Road, Emerald City, the Wizard, Dorothy's three male companions, the poppies, the Wiz-

ard's demands, the "destrawing" of the scarecrow, the "accidental" death of the
Bad Witch by a pail of water, the exposure of the Wizard, the Wizard's gifts, his
premature departure from Oz, Dorothy's knowledge of how to return to Kansas,
her return under her own power.

5. Why is the scene in which Aunt Em and then the Bad Witch appear in the
   witch's crystal particularly disturbing to children? What psychological truth does
   it contain, according to Greenberg?

6. How did Judy Garland's own experience with her mother and with Metro-Gold-
   wyn-Mayer mirror Dorothy Gale's experience in *The Wizard of Oz*?

DISCUSSION AND WRITING QUESTIONS

1. Greenberg appears to sum up the meaning of *The Wizard of Oz* as follows: "It is
   only when [Dorothy] can view Em and all the grown-ups in life for who they
   really are, not as wizards *or* witches, that she will be able to join them as a
   mature adult herself." And toward the end of his analysis he writes, "If we take
   the entire film as one extended fantasy, the tornado that whirls her, Gale-force,
   to Oz, is emblematic of the adolescent *rite de passage*, of the death of her child
   self and the rebirth of a newer, lovelier Dorothy." Assess this interpretation of
   the film.

2. At one point (paragraph 36) Greenberg suggests that there may be a larger political meaning to Oz: "Let us remember that America in 1939 stood on the verge
   of a fateful re-entanglement with the affairs of foreign states. A strong suspicion
   of the stranger across the sea pervaded our country, and I do not doubt that Oz
   spoke very directly to our native isolationism and xenophobia." To what extent
   do you accept this interpretation?

3. In an amusing digression Greenberg considers an oedipal interpretation of Dorothy's adventures ("A Freudian somewhat more high church than myself would
   tag the broomstick and the ruby slippers as — what else — phallic symbols. . . ."); but then rejects such an interpretation ("Dorothy's search for a
   strong, competent male 'rescuer' seems to stem most pointedly from the pressure to divest herself of her pathological dependency upon Em-Mother, rather
   than to compete with Em for Henry"). Now that you have read Greenberg's
   analysis, do you agree with his approach? Or do you favor the "high church"
   alternative? Or do you think it's a waste of energy to attempt to psychoanalyze
   Dorothy and interpret her adventures? Explain.

4. Read another of Greenberg's film analyses in *The Movies on Your Mind* and critique it.

5. In light of Greenberg's comments about the power of movies, quoted in the
   introduction to this passage, discuss some of your favorite movies in terms of
   how they "interpret" your life — your past, your present, your future, your
   conflicts, your "gropings toward the light." Or, if you would rather not focus
   on yourself, consider interpreting one of your favorite films using Greenberg's
   approach.

6. Here is another psychoanalytic interpretation of *The Wizard of Oz*. Do you find
   this explanation more plausible or less than the one offered by Greenberg?

> . . . the film has greatest meaning to teenage girls who live dull lives in

drab environments and dream of escaping over a rainbow and finding a glamorous life. Kansas represents their dreary existence. Oz represents Hollywood, to which teenage girls dream of running in hopes of breaking into movies. Our travelers get a beauty treatment; later they win awards. The Emerald City is M-G-M; the Wizard is Louis B. Mayer. That teenagers subconsciously equate Oz with Hollywood isn't ridiculous when one considers that the picture was meant to showcase the best Hollywood could muster in the way of production values. Dorothy's journey can be interpreted as a young girl's last childhood experience. When she chooses to return home to Kansas at the end, she has matured into a young woman — I'm surprised that M-G-M didn't have Garland burst out of the straps that held her well-developed breasts in place (so that she'd look 11 and not 16). Of course, the film's "There's no place like home" theme is nonsense. Unlike in L. Frank Baum's book, Oz — without the Wicked Witch — is a wonderful place for Dorothy to stay. It's much preferable to sepia-colored Kansas, where she was lonely except for having Toto (who was going to be taken away) and lived with an unsupportive and elderly uncle and aunt on a very barren, gray farm. She should stay in brightly colored Oz with all her new friends! (Danny Peary, *Guide for the Film Fanatic,* New York: Simon and Schuster, 1986, p. 474.)

CARL GUSTAV JUNG *(1875–1961)*

At one point in his professional life, Carl Gustav Jung was considered the heir apparent to Freud himself. He was to fall from Freudian grace, because the originality of his conceptions could not be fitted within the orthodox psychoanalytic framework. He remains, however (along with Freud himself and Alfred Adler), one of the most influential psychoanalysts of the century. And perhaps the most enduring of his legacies is the concept of the *collective unconscious,* as expressed through *archetypes.*

Jung was born in Kesswill, Switzerland, in 1875, the son of a pastor. During his youth he read widely in history, philosophy, and archaeology. From 1895 to 1901 he attended the universities at Basel and Zurich, where he studied medicine and psychiatry; his doctoral dissertation was on spiritualism and the occult. In 1900, he joined the staff of the Burgholzi Psychiatric Hospital in Zurich, whose director was Eugen Bleuler, developer of the concept of schizophrenia. At Burgholzi, Jung's own researches led him to develop the idea of the *complex,* an apparently illogical set of reactions to a particular group of stimuli, the result of unconscious and unpleasant associations with the stimuli. Jung also developed the word-association tests used to detect such complexes.

In 1906, Jung began corresponding with Freud. Over the next five years the two collaborated on a number of projects and thought very highly of each other. But increasingly, Jung began to differ with Freud, particularly over the importance of the sexual element in the libido. The final break with the founder of psychoanalysis was brought about partially by the publication of Jung's *Psychology of the Unconscious* (1912), in which he attempted to relate psychoanalytic to mythological material. Because of the break, Jung in 1914 resigned as president of the International Psychoanalytic Society, an office he had held for three years.

Subsequently, Jung began developing his own distinctive approach to psychology, which he called analytic psychology. He continued to rely heavily on mythological motifs, to the point that he was frequently accused of mysticism. In his next major work, *Psychological Types* (1921), he explored opposing personality types that he designated as extraverted (outward-looking) and introverted (inward-looking); he also described opposing ways of relating to the world: sensing versus intuiting, and feeling versus thinking. Dominant personality tendencies in the ego (e.g., extraversion, or a greater tendency to feel than to think) created strong counterparts in the unconscious, which ultimately (for the sake of psychic wholeness) had to be resolved. Such resolution required a process of self-discovery and change — a process that Jung, by dint of great effort, had himself undergone between 1913 and 1919.

Jung served as professor of psychology at the Federal Polytechnical University in Zurich from 1933 to 1941 and professor of medical psychology at the University of Basel in 1943. He retired, for reasons of health, in 1947, though he continued to write until the end of his life. He died in 1961 in Zurich.

Jung's concept of the collective unconscious is explored in the following essay, originally entitled "The Structure of the Psyche" (1927, 1931). In this piece he distinguishes the collective unconscious (the accumulated psychic heritage, common to all humans) from the personal unconscious (i.e., the type of unconscious explored by Freud and his followers), and he explores some of the mythic archetypes that underlie and manifest the collective unconscious. These archetypes are images, symbols, and motifs — like death, rebirth, the hero, the mother, magic. They are the result of a long evolutionary process in the psychic history of mankind. They emerge not only in our myths and stories but also in our dreams, our fantasies, our delusions, and our creative imaginations.

The first part of this essay, not reproduced here, deals with the activities of the conscious mind and of the personal unconscious mind, as described by Freud. Jung next begins to discuss the collective unconscious.

DREAMS, ARCHETYPES, AND THE COLLECTIVE UNCONSCIOUS

In my practical work I have been dealing with dreams for more than twenty years. Over and over again I have seen how . . . thought and feelings that were not felt by day afterwards appeared in dreams, and in this way reached consciousness indirectly. The dream as such is undoubtedly a content of consciousness, otherwise it could not be an object of immediate experience. But in so far as it brings up material that was unconscious before, we are forced to assume that these contents already had some kind of psychic existence in an unconscious state and appeared to the "remnant" of consciousness only in the dream. The dream belongs to the normal contents of the psyche and may be regarded as a resultant of unconscious processes obtruding on consciousness.   1

Now if, with these experiences in mind, we are driven to assume that all the categories of conscious contents can on occasion also be unconscious, and can act on the conscious mind as unconscious processes, we find ourselves faced with the somewhat unexpected question whether the unconscious has dreams too. In other words, are there resultants of still deeper and — if that be possible — still more unconscious processes which   2

Carl Gustav Jung. Dreams, Archetypes, and the Collective Unconscious [1927]. Original title: "The Structure of the Psyche." In *The Portable Jung*, ed., Joseph Campbell; trans. R.F.C. Hull. New York: Viking, 1971. Excerpted.

infiltrate into the dark regions of the psyche? I should have to dismiss this paradoxical question as altogether too adventurous were there not, in fact, grounds which bring such an hypothesis within the realm of possibility.

We must first see what sort of evidence is required to prove that the unconscious has dreams. If we wish to prove that dreams appear as contents of consciousness, we have simply to show that there are certain contents which, in character and meaning, are strange and not to be compared with the other contents which can be rationally explained and understood. If we are to show that the unconscious also has dreams, we must treat its contents in a similar way. It will be simplest if I give a practical example:

The case is that of an officer, twenty-seven years of age. He was suffering from severe attacks of pain in the region of the heart and from a choking sensation in the throat, as though a lump were stuck there. He also had piercing pains in the left heel. There was nothing organically the matter with him. The attacks had begun about two months previously, and the patient had been exempted from military service on account of his occasional inability to walk. Various cures had availed nothing. Close investigation into the previous history of his illness gave no clue, and he himself had no idea what the cause might be. He gave the impression of having a cheerful, rather light-hearted nature, perhaps a bit on the tough side, as though saying theatrically: "You can't keep us down." As the anamnesis[1] revealed nothing, I asked about his dreams. It at once became apparent what the cause was. Just before the beginning of his neurosis the girl with whom he was in love jilted him and got engaged to another man. In talking to me he dismissed this whole story as irrelevant — "a stupid girl, if she doesn't want me it's easy enough to get another one. A man like me isn't upset by a thing like that." That was the way he treated his disappointment and his real grief. But now the affects came to the surface. The pains in his heart soon disappeared, and the lump in his throat vanished after a few bouts of weeping. "Heartache" is a poeticism, but here it became an actual fact because his pride would not allow him to suffer the pain in his soul. The "lump in the throat," the so-called *globus hystericus*, comes, as everyone knows, from swallowed tears. His consciousness had simply withdrawn from contents that were too painful to him, and these, left to themselves, could reach consciousness only indirectly, as symptoms. All this was a rationally understandable and perfectly intelligible process, which could just as well have passed off consciously, had it not been for his masculine pride.

But now for the third symptom. The pains in the heel did not disappear. They do not belong in the picture we have just sketched, for the heart is in no way connected with the heel, nor does one express sorrow through

3

4

5

---

[1]*anamnesis:* Recollection of the history of the condition.

the heel. From the rational point of view, one cannot see why the other two syndromes should not have sufficed. Theoretically, it would have been entirely satisfactory if the conscious realization of the repressed psychic pain had resulted in normal grief and hence in a cure.

As I could get no clue to the heel symptom from the patient's conscious   6
mind, I turned once more to the previous method — to the dreams. The patient now had a dream in which *he was bitten in the heel by a snake and instantly paralyzed*. This dream plainly offered an interpretation of the heel symptom. His heel hurt him because he had been bitten there by a snake. This is a very strange content, and one can make nothing of it rationally. We could understand at once why his heart ached, but that his heel should ache too is beyond all rational expectation. The patient was completely mystified.

Here, then, we have a content that propels itself into the unconscious   7
zone in a singular manner, and probably derives from some deeper layer that cannot be fathomed rationally. The nearest analogy to this dream is obviously the neurosis itself. When the girl jilted him, she gave him a wound that paralyzed him and made him ill. Further analysis of the dream elicited something from his previous history that now became clear to the patient for the first time: He had been the darling of a somewhat hysterical mother. She had pitied him, admired him, pampered him so much that he never got along properly at school because he was too girlish. Later he suddenly swung over to the masculine side and went into the army, where he was able to hide his inner weakness by a display of "toughness." Thus, in a sense, his mother too had lamed him.

We are evidently dealing here with that same old serpent who had   8
been the special friend of Eve. "And I will put enmity between thee and the woman, and between thy seed and her seed; it shall bruise thy head, and thou shalt bruise his heel,"[2] runs the saying in Genesis, an echo of the much more ancient Egyptian hymn that used to be recited or chanted for the cure of snake-bite:

> The mouth of the god trembled with age,
> His spittle fell to the earth,
> And what he spat forth fell upon the ground.
> Then Isis[3] kneaded it with her hands
> Together with the earth which was there;
> And she made it like a spear.
> She wound not the living snake about her face,
> But threw it in a coil upon the path

---

[2]*"And I will put enmity . . .":* Genesis 3:15.

[3]*Isis:* In Egyptian mythology, the goddess of fertility.

Where the great god was wont to wander
At his pleasure through his two kingdoms.
The noble god stepped forth in splendour,
The gods serving Pharaoh bore him company,
And he went forth as was each day his wont.
Then the noble worm stung him . . .
His jawbones chattered,
He trembled in all his limbs,
And the poison invaded his flesh
As the Nile invades his territory.[4]

The patient's conscious knowledge of the Bible was at a lamentable   9
minimum. Probably he had once heard of the serpent biting the heel and
then quickly forgotten it. But something deep in his unconscious heard it
and did not forget; it remembered this story at a suitable opportunity. This
part of the unconscious evidently likes to express itself mythologically, because this way of expression is in keeping with its nature.

But to what kind of mentality does the symbolical or metaphorical way   10
of expression correspond? It corresponds to the mentality of the primitive,
whose language possesses no abstractions but only natural and "unnatural" analogies. This primeval mentality is as foreign to the psyche that produced the heartache and the lump in the throat as a brontosaurus is to a
racehorse. The dream of the snake reveals a fragment of psychic activity
that has nothing whatever to do with the dreamer as a modern individual.
It functions at a deeper level, so to speak, and only the results of this activity rise up into the upper layer where the repressed affects lie, as foreign
to them as a dream is to waking consciousness. Just as some kind of analytical technique is needed to understand a dream, so a knowledge of mythology is needed in order to grasp the meaning of a content deriving from
the deeper levels of the psyche.

The snake-motif was certainly not an individual acquisition of the   11
dreamer, for snake-dreams are very common even among city-dwellers
who have probably never seen a real snake.

It might be objected that the snake in the dream is nothing but a con-   12
cretized figure of speech. We say of certain women that they are treacherous as snakes, wily as serpents; we speak of the snake of temptation, etc.
This objection does not seem to me to hold good in the present instance,
though it would be difficult to prove this because the snake is in fact a
common figure of speech. A more certain proof would be possible only if
we succeeded in finding a case where the mythological symbolism is nei-

---

[4]Adolf Erman, *Life in Ancient Egypt,* translated by H. M. Tirard (London, 1894), pp. 265–
267, modified. [Jung]

ther a common figure of speech nor an instance of cryptomnesia — that is to say, where the dreamer had not read, seen, or heard the motif somewhere, and then forgotten it and remembered it unconsciously. This proof seems to me of great importance, since it would show that the rationally explicable unconscious, which consists of material that has been made unconscious artificially, as it were, is only a top layer, and that underneath is an absolute unconscious which has nothing to do with our personal experience. This absolute unconscious would then be a psychic activity which goes on independently of the conscious mind and is not dependent even on the upper layers of the unconscious, untouched — and perhaps untouchable — by personal experience. It would be a kind of supra-individual psychic activity, a *collective unconscious*, as I have called it, as distinct from a superficial, relative, or personal unconscious.

But before we go in search of this proof, I would like, for the sake of   13
completeness, to make a few more remarks about the snake-dream. It seems as if this hypothetical deeper layer of the unconscious — the collective unconscious, as I shall now call it — had translated the patient's experiences with women into the snake-bite dream and thus turned them into a regular mythological motif. The reason — or rather, the purpose — of this is at first somewhat obscure. But if we remember the fundamental principle that the symptomatology of an illness is at the same time a natural attempt at healing — the heartaches, for example, being an attempt to produce an emotional outburst — then we must regard the heel symptom as an attempt at healing too. As the dream shows, not only the recent disappointment in love, but all other disappointments, in school and elsewhere, are raised by this symptom to the level of a mythological event, as though this would in some way help the patient.

This may strike us as flatly incredible. But the ancient Egyptian priest-   14
physicians, who intoned the hymn to the Isis-serpent over the snake-bite, did not find this theory at all incredible; and not only they, but the whole world believed, as the primitive today still believes, in magic by analogy or "sympathetic magic."

We are concerned here, then, with the psychological phenomenon that   15
lies at the root of magic by analogy. We should not think that this is an ancient superstition which we have long since outgrown. If you read the Latin text of the Mass carefully, you will constantly come upon the famous "sicut"; this always introduces an analogy by means of which a change is to be produced. Another striking example of analogy is the making of fire on Holy Saturday.[5] In former times, the new fire was struck from the stone, and still earlier it was obtained by boring into a piece of wood, which was

---

[5]*Holy Saturday:* The Saturday before Easter.

the prerogative of the Church. Therefore in the prayer of the priest it is said: "Deus, qui per Filium tuum, angularem scilicet lapidem, claritatis tuae fidelibus ignem contulisti productum ex silice, nostris profuturum usibus, novum hunc ignem sanctifica." — "O God, who through thy Son, who is called the cornerstone, hast brought the fire of thy light to the faithful, make holy for our future use this new fire struck from the firestone." By the analogy of Christ with the cornerstone, the firestone is raised to the level of Christ himself, who again kindles a new fire.

The rationalist may laugh at this. But something deep in us is stirred, and not in us alone but in millions of Christian men and women, though we may call it only a feeling for beauty. What is stirred in us is that faraway background, those immemorial patterns of the human mind, which we have not acquired but have inherited from the dim ages of the past.   *16*

If this supra-individual psyche exists, everything that is translated into its picture-language would be depersonalized, and if this became conscious would appear to us *sub specie aeternitatis*.[6] Not as my sorrow, but as the sorrow of the world; not a personal isolating pain, but a pain without bitterness that unites all humanity. The healing effect of this needs no proof.   *17*

But as to whether this supra-individual psychic activity actually exists, I have so far given no proof that satisfies all the requirements. I should now like to do this once more in the form of an example. The case is that of a man in his thirties, who was suffering from a paranoid form of schizophrenia. He became ill in his early twenties. He had always presented a strange mixture of intelligence, wrongheadedness, and fantastic ideas. He was an ordinary clerk, employed in a consulate. Evidently as a compensation for his very modest existence he was seized with megalomania and believed himself to be the Saviour. He suffered from frequent hallucinations and was at times very much disturbed. In his quiet periods he was allowed to go unattended in the corridor. One day I came across him there, blinking through the window up at the sun, and moving his head from side to side in a curious manner. He took me by the arm and said he wanted to show me something. He said I must look at the sun with eyes half shut, and then I could see the sun's phallus. If I moved my head from side to side the sun-phallus would move too, and that was the origin of the wind.   *18*

I made this observation about 1906. In the course of the year 1910, when I was engrossed in mythological studies, a book of Dieterich's came into my hands. It was part of the so-called Paris magic papyrus and was   *19*

---

[6]*sub specie aeternitatis:* (Latin) In its universal form.

thought by Dieterich to be a liturgy of the Mithraic cult.[7,8] It consisted of a series of instructions, invocations, and visions. One of these visions is described in the following words: "And likewise the so-called tube, the origin of the ministering wind. For you will see hanging down from the disc of the sun something that looks like a tube. And towards the regions westward it is as though there were an infinite east wind. But if the other wind should prevail towards the regions of the east, you will in like manner see the vision veering in that direction." The Greek word for "tube," αὐλός, means a wind-instrument, and the combination αὐλός παχύς in Homer means "a thick jet of blood." So evidently a stream of wind is blowing through the tube out of the sun.

The vision of my patient in 1906, and the Greek text first edited in 1910, should be sufficiently far apart to rule out the possibility of cryptomnesia on his side and of thought-transference on mine. The obvious parallelism of the two visions cannot be disputed, though one might object that the similarity is purely fortuitous. In that case we should expect the vision to have no connections with analogous ideas, nor any inner meaning. But this expectation is not fulfilled, for in certain medieval paintings this tube is actually depicted as a sort of hose-pipe reaching down from heaven under the robe of Mary. In it the Holy Ghost flies down in the form of a dove to impregnate the Virgin. As we know from the miracle of Pentecost, the Holy Ghost was originally conceived as a mighty rushing wind, the πνεῦμα, "the wind that bloweth where it listeth." In a Latin text we read: "Animo descensus per orbem solis tribuitur" (They say that the spirit descends through the disc of the sun). This conception is common to the whole of late classical and medieval philosophy.   20

I cannot, therefore, discover anything fortuitous in these visions, but simply the revival of possibilities of ideas that have always existed, that can be found again in the most diverse minds and in all epochs, and are therefore not to be mistaken for inherited ideas.   21

I have purposely gone into the details of this case in order to give you a concrete picture of that deeper psychic activity which I call the collective unconscious. Summing up, I would like to emphasize that we must distinguish three psychic levels: (1) consciousness, (2) the personal unconscious, and (3) the collective unconscious. The personal unconscious consists firstly of all those contents that became unconscious either because they   22

---

[7]*Mithraic cult:* The cult of Mithras, the ancient Persian god of light and truth, often embodied in the sun.

[8][Albrecht Dieterich, *Eine Mithrasliturgie* (London, 1903; 2nd ed., 1910), pp. 6–7.] As the author subsequently learned, the 1910 edition was actually the second, there having been a first edition in 1903. The patient had, however, been committed some years before 1903. [Jung]

lost their intensity and were forgotten or because consciousness was withdrawn from them (repression), and secondly of contents, some of them sense-impressions, which never had sufficient intensity to reach consciousness but have somehow entered the psyche. The collective unconscious, however, as the ancestral heritage of possibilities of representation, is not individual but common to all men, and perhaps even to all animals, and is the true basis of the individual psyche.

This whole psychic organism corresponds exactly to the body, which,   23 though individually varied, is in all essential features the specifically human body which all men have. In its development and structure, it still preserves elements that connect it with the invertebrates and ultimately with the protozoa. Theoretically it should be possible to "peel" the collective unconscious, layer by layer, until we came to the psychology of the worm, and even of the amoeba.

We are all agreed that it would be quite impossible to understand the   24 living organism apart from its relation to the environment. There are countless biological facts that can only be explained as reactions to environmental conditions, e.g., the blindness of *Proteus anguinus*, the peculiarities of intestinal parasites, the anatomy of vertebrates that have reverted to aquatic life.

The same is true of the psyche. Its peculiar organization must be inti-   25 mately connected with environmental conditions. We should expect consciousness to react and adapt itself to the present, because it is that part of the psyche which is concerned chiefly with events of the moment. But from the collective unconscious, as a timeless and universal psyche, we should expect reactions to universal and constant conditions, whether psychological, physiological, or physical.

The collective unconscious — so far as we can say anything about it at   26 all — appears to consist of mythological motifs or primordial images, for which reason the myths of all nations are its real exponents. In fact, the whole of mythology could be taken as a sort of projection of the collective unconscious. We can see this most clearly if we look at the heavenly constellations, whose originally chaotic forms were organized through the projection of images. This explains the influence of the stars as asserted by astrologers. These influences are nothing but unconscious, introspective perceptions of the activity of the collective unconscious. Just as the constellations were projected into the heavens, similar figures were projected into legends and fairy tales or upon historical persons. We can therefore study the collective unconscious in two ways, either in mythology or in the analysis of the individual. As I cannot make the latter material available here, I must confine myself to mythology. This is such a wide field that we can select from it only a few types. Similarly, environmental conditions are endlessly varied, so here too only a few of the more typical can be discussed.

Just as the living body with its special characteristics is a system of functions for adapting to environmental conditions, so the psyche must exhibit organs or functional systems that correspond to regular physical events. By this I do not mean sense-functions dependent on organs, but rather a sort of psychic parallel to regular physical occurrences. To take an example, the daily course of the sun and the regular alternation of day and night must have imprinted themselves on the psyche in the form of an image from primordial times. We cannot demonstrate the existence of this image, but we find instead more or less fantastic analogies of the physical process. Every morning a divine hero is born from the sea and mounts the chariot of the sun. In the West a Great Mother awaits him, and he is devoured by her in the evening. In the belly of a dragon he traverses the depths of the midnight sea. After a frightful combat with the serpent of night he is born again in the morning. 27

This conglomerate myth undoubtedly contains a reflection of the physical process. Indeed this is so obvious that many investigators assume that primitives invent such myths merely to explain physical processes. There can be no doubt that science and philosophy have grown from this matrix, but that primitives think up such things merely from a need for explanation, as a sort of physical or astronomical theory, seems to me highly improbable. 28

What we can safely say about mythical images is that the physical process imprinted itself on the psyche in this fantastic, distorted form and was preserved there, so that the unconscious still reproduces similar images today. Naturally the question now arises: why does the psyche not register the actual process, instead of mere fantasies about the physical process? 29

If you can put yourself in the mind of the primitive, you will at once understand why this is so. He lives in such "participation mystique" with his world, as Lévy-Bruhl[9] calls it, that there is nothing like that absolute distinction between subject and object which exists in our minds. What happens outside also happens in him, and what happens in him also happens outside. I witnessed a very fine example of this when I was with the Elgonyi, a primitive tribe living on Mount Elgon, in East Africa. At sunrise they spit on their hands and then hold the palms towards the sun as it comes over the horizon. "We are happy that the night is past," they say. Since the word for sun, *adhista*, also means God, I asked: "Is the sun God?" They said "No" to this and laughed, as if I had said something especially stupid. As the sun was just then high in the heavens, I pointed to it and asked: "When the sun is there you say it is not God, but when it is in the 30

---

[9]*Lévy-Bruhl:* (1857–1939) French philosopher best known for his studies of the psychology of primitive peoples. He was a professor of philosophy at the Sorbonne in France from 1899 until 1927.

east you say it is God. How is that?" There was an embarrassed silence till an old chief began to explain. "It is so," he said. "When the sun is up there it is not God, but when it rises, that is God [or: then it is God]." To the primitive mind it is immaterial which of these two versions is correct. Sunrise and his own feeling of deliverance are for him the same divine experience, just as night and his fear are the same thing. Naturally his emotions are more important to him than physics; therefore what he registers is his emotional fantasies. For him night means snakes and the cold breath of spirits, whereas morning means the birth of a beautiful god.

There are mythological theories that explain everything as coming   31
from the sun and lunar theories that do the same for the moon. This is due to the simple fact that there are countless myths about the moon, among them a whole host in which the moon is the wife of the sun. The moon is the changing experience of the night, and thus coincides with the primitive's sexual experience of woman, who for him is also the experience of the night. But the moon can equally well be the injured brother of the sun, for at night affect-laden and evil thoughts of power and revenge may disturb sleep. The moon, too, is a disturber of sleep, and is also the abode of departed souls, for at night the dead return in dreams and the phantoms of the past terrify the sleepless. Thus the moon also signifies madness ("lunacy"). It is such experiences as these that have impressed themselves on the mind, rather than the changing image of the moon.

It is not storms, not thunder and lightning, not rain and cloud that   32
remain as images in the psyche, but the fantasies caused by the affects they arouse. I once experienced a violent earthquake, and my first, immediate feeling was that I no longer stood on the solid and familiar earth, but on the skin of a gigantic animal that was heaving under my feet. It was this image that impressed itself on me, not the physical fact. Man's curses against devastating thunderstorms, his terror of the unchained elements — these affects anthropomorphize the passion of nature, and the purely physical element becomes an angry god.

Like the physical conditions of his environment, the physiological con-   33
ditions, glandular secretions, etc., also can arouse fantasies charged with affect. Sexuality appears as a god of fertility, as a fiercely sensual, feminine daemon, as the devil himself with Dionysian[10] goat's legs and obscene gestures, or as a terrifying serpent that squeezes its victims to death.

Hunger makes food into gods. Certain Mexican tribes even give their   34
food-gods an annual holiday to allow them to recuperate, and during this time the staple food is not eaten. The ancient Pharaohs were worshipped

---

[10]*Dionysian:* In Greek mythology, Dionysus was the god of fertility and wine, often worshipped in orgiastic rites.

as eaters of gods. Osiris[11] is the wheat, the son of the earth, and to this day the Host must be made of wheat-meal, i.e., a god to be eaten, as also was Iacchos, the mysterious god of the Eleusinian mysteries.[12] The bull of Mithras is the edible fruitfulness of the earth.

The psychological conditions of the environment naturally leave similar mythical traces behind them. Dangerous situations, be they dangers to the body or to the soul, arouse affect-laden fantasies, and, in so far as such situations typically repeat themselves, they give rise to *archetypes*, as I have termed myth-motifs in general. 35

Dragons make their lairs by watercourses, preferably near a ford or some such dangerous crossing; jinn[13] and other devils are to be found in waterless deserts or in dangerous gorges; spirits of the dead haunt the eerie thickets of the bamboo forest; treacherous nixies[14] and sea-serpents live in the depths of the ocean and its whirlpools. Mighty ancestor-spirits or gods dwell in the man of importance; deadly fetish-power resides in anyone strange or extraordinary. Sickness and death are never due to natural causes, but are invariably caused by spirits, witches, or wizards. Even the weapon that has killed a man is *mana*,[15] endowed with extraordinary power. 36

How is it then, you may ask, with the most ordinary everyday events, with immediate realities like husband, wife, father, mother, child? These ordinary everyday facts, which are eternally repeated, create the mightiest archetypes of all, whose ceaseless activity is everywhere apparent even in a rationalistic age like ours. Let us take as an example the Christian dogma. The Trinity consists of Father, Son, and Holy Ghost, who is represented by the bird of Astarte,[16] the dove, and who in early Christian times was called Sophia and thought of as feminine. The worship of Mary in the later Church is an obvious substitute for this. Here we have the archetype of the family ἐν ὑπερουρανίῳ τόπῳ, "in a supracelestial place," as Plato expresses it, enthroned as a formulation of the ultimate mystery. Christ is the bridegroom, the Church is the bride, the baptismal font is the womb of the Church, as it is still called in the text of the *Benedictio fontis*.[17] The 37

---

[11]*Osiris:* In Egyptian mythology, the god of the underworld, both husband and brother of Isis.

[12]*Eleusinian mysteries:* In ancient Greece, secret religious rites that later became the Athenian state religion.

[13]*jinn:* (Also spelled djinn and genie) In Moslem mythology, a supernatural being able to assume human or animal form and at the service of men.

[14]*nixies:* In German mythology, water sprites, sometimes appearing as part fish (male: nix).

[15]*mana:* In Polynesian mythology, a supernatural power inherent in humans or objects.

[16]*Astarte:* In Phoenician mythology, the goddess of love.

[17]*Benedictio fontis:* The blessing of the new baptismal water around Easter in the Roman Catholic church.

holy water has salt put into it, with the idea of making it like the amniotic fluid, or like sea-water. A *hieros gamos* or sacred wedding is performed on Holy Saturday before Easter, which I have just mentioned, and a burning candle as a phallic symbol is plunged three times into the font, in order to fertilize it and lend it the power to bear the baptized child anew (*quasimodo genitus*).[18] The *mana* personality, the medicine-man, is the *pontifex maximus*,[19] the *Papa*; the Church is *mater ecclesia*,[20] the *magna mater*[21] of magical power, and mankind are children in need of help and grace.

The deposit of mankind's whole ancestral experience — so rich in emotional imagery — of father, mother, child, husband and wife, of the magic personality, of dangers to body and soul, has exalted this group of archetypes into the supreme regulating principles of religious and even of political life, in unconscious recognition of their tremendous psychic power. 38

I have found that a rational understanding of these things in no way detracts from their value; on the contrary, it helps us not only to feel but to gain insight into their immense significance. These mighty projections enable the Catholic to experience large tracts of his collective unconscious in tangible reality. He has no need to go in search of authority, superior power, revelation, or something that would link him with the eternal and the timeless. These are always present and available for him: there, in the Holy of Holies on every altar, dwells the presence of God. It is the Protestant and the Jew who have to seek, the one because he has, in a manner of speaking, destroyed the earthly body of the Deity, the other because he can never find it. For both of them the archetypes, which to the Catholic world have become a visible and living reality, lie in the unconscious. Unfortunately I cannot enter here into the remarkable differences of attitude towards the unconscious in our culture, but would only point out that this question is one of the greatest problems confronting humanity. 39

That this is so is immediately understandable when we consider that the unconscious, as the totality of all archetypes, is the deposit of all human experience right back to its remotest beginnings. Not, indeed, a dead deposit, a sort of abandoned rubbish-heap, but a living system of reactions and aptitudes that determine the individual's life in invisible ways — all the more effective because invisible. It is not just a gigantic historical prej- 40

---

[18]*quasimodo genitus:* From "quasimodo genitii infantes," medieval Latin for "newborn babies," the words of entroit for Low Sunday (the Sunday following Easter).

[19]*pontifex maximus:* The head of the pontifical college at Rome. Since the 5th century A.D., the term has been used as an honorary title of the popes.

[20]*mater ecclesia:* (Latin) "Mother church," the designation for the church as the spiritual mother of Christians.

[21]*magna mater:* (Latin) Literally, great mother.

udice, so to speak, an *a priori*[22] historical condition; it is also the source of the instincts, for the archetypes are simply the forms which the instincts assume. From the living fountain of instinct flows everything that is creative; hence the unconscious is not merely conditioned by history, but is the very source of the creative impulse. It is like Nature herself — prodigiously conservative, and yet transcending her own historical conditions in her acts of creation. No wonder, then, that it has always been a burning question for humanity how best to adapt to these invisible determinants. If consciousness had never split off from the unconscious — an eternally repeated event symbolized as the fall of the angels and the disobedience of the first parents — this problem would never have arisen, any more than would the question of environmental adaptation.

The existence of an individual consciousness makes man aware of the   41
difficulties of his inner as well as his outer life. Just as the world about him takes on a friendly or a hostile aspect to the eyes of primitive man, so the influences of his unconscious seem to him like an opposing power, with which he has to come to terms just as with the visible world. His countless magical practices serve this end. On higher levels of civilization, religion and philosophy fulfil the same purpose. Whenever such a system of adaptation breaks down a general unrest begins to appear, and attempts are made to find a suitable new form of relationship to the unconscious.

These things seem very remote to our modern, "enlightened" eyes.   42
When I speak of this hinterland of the mind, the unconscious, and compare its reality with that of the visible world, I often meet with an incredulous smile. But then I must ask how many people there are in our civilized world who still believe in *mana* and spirits and suchlike theories — in other words, how many millions of Christian Scientists and spiritualists are there? I will not add to this list of questions. They are merely intended to illustrate the fact that the problem of invisible psychic determinants is as alive today as ever it was.

The collective unconscious contains the whole spiritual heritage of   43
mankind's evolution, born anew in the brain structure of every individual. His conscious mind is an ephemeral phenomenon that accomplishes all provisional adaptations and orientations, for which reason one can best compare its function to orientation in space. The unconscious, on the other hand, is the source of the instinctual forces of the psyche and of the forms or categories that regulate them, namely the archetypes. All the most powerful ideas in history go back to archetypes. This is particularly true of religious ideas, but the central concepts of science, philosophy, and ethics are no exception to this rule. In their present form they are variants of

---

[22]*a priori:* The logical cause of an effect or the assumption leading to a conclusion.

archetypal ideas, created by consciously applying and adapting these ideas to reality. For it is the function of consciousness not only to recognize and assimilate the external world through the gateway of the senses, but to translate into visible reality the world within us.

REVIEW QUESTIONS

1. What was the significance of the soldier's dreaming that he had been bitten in the heel by a snake? Why would an orthodox Freudian analysis not have yielded such an explanation? What kind of mentality is operating in the case of the soldier's dream? Why is a knowledge of mythology required to produce such analyses?

2. How does Jung define the collective unconscious? How does it differ from the personal unconscious? In what way does the collective unconscious (as manifested, for example, in the snake dream) have potential curative powers? How do the dreams of the personal unconscious differ from the dreams of the collective unconscious?

3. What parallel did Jung notice between his patient's vision of the sun and the liturgy of the Mithraic cult? What other evidence substantiated this parallel? What was the significance of this discovery for Jung's concept of the collective unconscious?

4. Why is mythology the best key to the collective unconscious? Why, for both primitive and modern humans, does the psyche store mythological representations of physical processes (for instance, the courses of the sun and moon), instead of the processes themselves? What kind of activities are most likely to be thus mythologized into archetypes? Give examples. Which activities create the most powerful archetypes of all? How have archetypes been incorporated into Catholic ritual?

5. Why does Jung believe that rational understanding of the archetypes in no way diminishes their power? In what ways — in lower levels of civilization and in higher levels of civilization — do people attempt to gain access to their collective unconscious?

DISCUSSION AND WRITING QUESTIONS

1. On the basis of the evidence in this article (primarily the examples Jung gives of his patients and their dreams), do you think that Jung was justified in forming this theory of the collective unconscious? Could there be another, perhaps more rational, explanation for the parallels between myth and dream? Is a Freudian personal unconscious sufficient to account for all mental activities that are not conscious?

2. Do you see any evidence of the collective unconscious at work in the paintings of Dalí, as described by Dawn Ades? Or does Dalí's personal unconscious appear to be the main force at work in his paintings?

3. In paragraph 39, Jung distinguishes between the way that Catholics, on the one hand, can easily make use of religious archetypes, and the way that Protestants and Jews, on the other hand, cannot. Discuss what you think Jung means, and comment on this distinction.
4. Jung writes of the development of consciousness in terms reminiscent of the Fall: "If consciousness had never split off from the unconscious — an eternally repeated event symbolized as the fall of the angels and the disobedience of the first parents — this problem [how to adapt to the invisible determinants of activity] would never have arisen, any more than would the question of environmental adaptation" (paragraph 40). Is it possible to validate such insights? To benefit from them?
5. Toward the end of his essay Jung suggests that "the most powerful ideas in history go back to archetypes. This is particularly true of religious ideas, but the central concepts of science, philosophy, and ethics are no exception to this role." What do you think Jung has in mind when he derives the "central concepts of science, philosophy, and ethics" from archetypes? Give examples, if possible.

B. F. SKINNER (b. 1904)

Central to Freudian thought is the idea that much of our outward behavior and speech — particularly behavior and speech that may be considered neurotic — is determined by an unconscious mental world. Psychotherapists attempt to treat symptoms of neurotic behavior in their patients by a joint exploration of that mental world, by plunging into its depths, reaching back into forgotten experiences of early childhood or even infancy, attempting to locate the root causes of neurotic behavior. Only when these root causes are discovered can treatment begin. If the treatment is successful, the undesirable symptoms should disappear, or at least become manageable. The point is that the behavior itself is not the real problem; it is merely a symptom of the problem. Dealing with the root causes of the symptom is the only means of successful therapy.

As we have seen, many psychologists and therapists since Freud have adapted or challenged his premises. Jung, for example, postulated a collective unconscious, as well as an individual unconscious, that could also determine behavior and create neurotic symptoms. But there has probably been no challenge more thoroughgoing than that of the behaviorists. The behaviorists argue that since the ultimate goal of therapy is to eliminate or at least to manage undesirable behavior (i.e., behavior that results in some form of internal or external punishment), the therapeutic focus should always remain on the behavior itself. If we can develop effective techniques of directly controlling or modifying this behavior, then it is unnecessary to plunge into an unconscious world — or even to postulate one. The unconscious, in effect, is irrelevant. To objections by traditional psychotherapists that such treatment merely attacks the symptoms of the problem and not its root causes, the behaviorists respond that the symptoms are aspects of the personal history of the patient, and that a program of therapy that aims at modifying and adding to this personal history through control of behavior does indeed deal with the root causes. Most important, such therapy deals with observable behavior (and thus known quantities) and not with some invisible, intangible, and ultimately speculative unconscious realm. The behaviorists, in short, look upon Freudian psychotherapists as little more than modern exorcists.

The best known (and by the same token, notorious) of modern behaviorists is B. F. Skinner. Born in 1904 in Susquehanna, Pennsylvania, Skinner as a child was fascinated by mechanical devices, spending his days building tops, kites, and model airplanes. In 1922, he enrolled in Hamilton College in Clinton, New York, where he majored in English language and literature. For a time he nurtured ambitions of becoming an imaginative writer and was even encouraged in this direction by the poet Robert Frost. But after graduation, Skinner realized that he had no real talent for fiction. He did know that his interest in creating literary characters arose from a fascination with human behavior, and he began studying the writings of Pavlov on conditioned reflexes, and Bertrand Russell and John B. Watson on behaviorism. Starting in 1928 he began a program of graduate study in psychology at Harvard and was awarded his Ph.D. three years later. Afterward, Skinner stayed on at Harvard for five years as a researcher.

Surveying the various schools of psychology, Skinner, who continued to be fascinated with observable human behavior, decided to work in the field of experimental psychology. In particular, he focused his study on the effects upon an organism of interaction with its environment. To this end, he created the famous "Skinner box," a controlled environment in which he could observe the behavior of rats when they were subjected to stimuli. He called the behavior of an organism in response to its environment "operant" behavior; rewarding the rat for desirable behavior (positive reinforcement) or punishing the rat for undesirable behavior (negative reinforcement) was called "operant conditioning." The results of Skinner's investigations in this area were incorporated into his first book, *The Behavior of Organisms* (1938).

After leaving Harvard, Skinner became a professor of psychology at Indiana University in Bloomington, and there continued his researches, focusing for a time on verbal behavior. During World War II Skinner was awarded a government grant to train pigeons to guide missiles to enemy targets. (The project, though judged workable, was never tried in actual combat.) Skinner first became known to the general public in 1945 when he published an article in the *Ladies Home Journal* about his "Air Crib." This was a controlled environment for his second child, Deborah — a "mechanical baby-tender," air-conditioned, soundproof, designed for sleep and play. Like almost all of Skinner's projects thenceforth, the air crib provoked a good deal of controversy: readers were intrigued, and some manufacturers even expressed interest in marketing it; on the other hand, it was denounced by several psychologists, who compared the air crib (unfairly) to a Skinner box. 1948 saw the publication of Skinner's *Walden Two*, a fictional account of a utopian community run on behaviorist principles, in which the inhabitants successfully deal with the problems of controlling human behavior. *Walden Two* represented another attempt by Skinner to apply scientific principles to the solution of social problems. A fixture on college campuses since its publication, this book has been no less controversial than the air crib.

Consistent in Skinner's approach was a refusal to rely upon any theory, inference, or hypothesis that could not be proven through the observation of actual responses to stimuli. He was attacked by other psychologists and even other behaviorists for this antitheoretical approach (to some critics, Skinner became known as the "rat psychologist"), but among his many followers, his reputation and influence grew steadily. He began a series of annual conferences on behaviorism, and his work inspired the creation of the *Journal of the Experimental Analysis of Behavior* in 1958.

Skinner's continuing study of speech, in terms of operant conditioning, led to the publication of his *Verbal Behavior* in 1957. More significant, however, was Skinner's contribution to educational technology. His focus on stimulus-response and positive reinforcement led to the development of many of the "teaching machines" and "programmed instruction" of the next two decades. This kind of instruction emphasized a self-paced, step-by-step approach, in which a complex learning task was broken down into its component stages, a correct answer by the learner serving as the positive reinforcement that facilitated the next stage of learning. Skinner spelled out the rationale for this approach in *The Analysis of Behavior: A Program for Self-Instruction* (1961; in collaboration with James G. Holland) and *The Technology of Teaching* (1968).

In 1958, Skinner returned to Harvard as Edgar Pierce Professor of Psychology, where he remained until his retirement in 1974. His best-known (and inevitably, controversial) work during this period was *Beyond Freedom and Dignity* (1971), in which he argued that freedom and dignity were not only illusory concepts (since environment determined all behavior), but ultimately dangerous and self-destructive ones. Instead, he called for a "technology of behavior" that would enable people to favorably control their own destinies. This work was followed in 1974 by *About Behaviorism*. In 1977, Skinner began writing a four-part autobiography: *Particulars of My Life* was published in 1976, *The Shaping of a Behaviorist* in 1979, and *Notebooks* in 1980.

In an interview for the *Los Angeles Times* in 1979 Skinner said: "I apply my own analysis to my own behavior. I never assumed that I was not like my pigeons. I'm sure I am — and very much more complicated, I hope. But as I designed an environment to get some behavior out of my experimental organisms, so I work on the environment to get my own behavior out in ways that are reinforcing to me. That's all there is to it."

The following selection is excerpted from the chapter on "Psychotherapy" in *Science and Human Behavior* (1953), the first book in which Skinner systematically extrapolated his behaviorist principles to the study of the complex human organism. It is noteworthy for Skinner's explicit contrast of Freudian with behaviorist principles.

FREUDIAN PSYCHOTHERAPY VERSUS BEHAVIORISM

A particular personal history has produced an organism whose behav-   1
ior is disadvantageous or dangerous. In what sense it is disadvantageous or dangerous must be specified in each case by noting the consequences both to the individual himself and to others. The task of the therapist is to supplement a personal history in such a way that behavior no longer has these characteristics.

This is not, however, the traditional view. The field of psychotherapy   2

B.F. Skinner. Freudian Psychotherapy Versus Behaviorism [1953]. Original title: "Psychotherapy as a Controlling Agency." In *Science and Human Behavior*. New York: Free Press, 1953.

is rich in explanatory fictions. Behavior itself has not been accepted as a subject matter in its own right, but only as an indication of *something wrong somewhere else.* The task of therapy is said to be to remedy an inner illness of which the behavioral manifestations are merely "symptoms." Just as religious agencies maximize salvation or piety, and governmental agencies justice, freedom, or security, so psychotherapy is dedicated to the maximizing of *mental health* or *personal adjustment.* These terms are usually negative because they are defined by specifying unhealthy or maladjusted behavior which is absent in health or adjustment. Frequently, the condition to be corrected is called "neurotic," and the thing to be attacked by psychotherapy is then identified as a "neurosis." The term no longer carries its original implication of a derangement of the nervous system, but it is nevertheless an unfortunate example of an explanatory fiction. It has encouraged the therapist to avoid specifying the behavior to be corrected or showing why it is disadvantageous or dangerous. By suggesting a single cause for multiple disorders it has implied a uniformity which is not to be found in the data. Above all, it has encouraged the belief that psychotherapy consists of removing certain inner causes of mental illness, as the surgeon removes an inflamed appendix or cancerous growth or as indigestible food is purged from the body. We have seen enough of inner causes to understand why this doctrine has given psychotherapy an impossible assignment. It is not an inner cause of behavior but the behavior itself which — in the medical analogy of catharsis — must be "got out of the system."

The belief that certain kinds of "pent-up" behavior cause trouble until   3 the organism is able to get rid of them is at least as old as the Greeks. Aristotle,[1] for example, argued that tragedy had a beneficial effect in purging the individual of emotional behavior. On the same analogy it has been argued that competitive sports permit both the participant and the spectator to rid themselves of aggressive tendencies. It has been argued that the human infant has a certain amount of sucking behavior which he must eventually get rid of, and that if he does not exhaust this behavior in the normal process of nursing, he will suck his fingers or other objects. We have seen that it is meaningful to say that an organism is disposed to emit behavior of a given form in a given amount. Such behavior spends itself in the process of extinction, for example. But it does not follow that a potential disposition causes trouble or has any other effect upon the organism until it has been spent. There is some evidence that sucking behavior in the infant is *reinforced* by nursing and is then made more rather than less likely to occur. It is also a tenable hypothesis that competitive sports generate rather than relieve aggressive tendencies. In any case, the variables

---

[1]*Aristotle:* (384–322 B.C.) Greek philosopher, author of *The Poetics,* an influential work on tragedy.

to be considered in dealing with a probability of response are simply the response itself and the independent variables of which it is a function. We have no reason to appeal to pent-up behavior as a causal agent.

On the assumption that the inner causes of neurotic or maladjusted behavior are subject to gross physiological assault, cures are sometimes attempted by administering drugs, by performing surgery upon the nervous system, or by using drugs or electric shock to set off violent convulsions. Such therapy is obviously directed toward a supposed underlying condition rather than toward the behavior itself or the manipulable variables outside the organism to which the behavior may be traced. Even "functional" therapy, in which external variables are manipulated, is often described with the same figure of speech. The therapist is regarded as rooting out a source of trouble. The conception is not far removed from the view — which large numbers of people still hold — that neurotic behavior arises because the Devil or some other intruding personality is in temporary "possession" of the body. The traditional treatment consists of exorcising the Devil — driving him out of the individual by creating circumstances which are appropriately aversive[2] to him — and some treatments of multiple personality differ from this only in avoiding theological implications. The lesser demons of modern theory are anxieties, conflicts, repressed wishes, and repressed memories. Just as pent-up emotion is purged, so conflict is resolved and repressed wishes and memories are released.   4

This view of mental illness and therapy owes most to Sigmund Freud. It appears to have withstood assault largely because of Freud's contributions in other directions. His great achievement, as a disciple of his said recently, was to apply the principle of cause and effect to human behavior. Aspects of behavior which had hitherto been regarded as whimsical, aimless, or accidental, Freud traced to relevant variables. Unfortunately, he chose to represent the relationships he discovered with an elaborate set of explanatory fictions. He characterized the ego, superego, and id as inhabitants of a psychic or mental world subdivided into regions of conscious, co-conscious, and unconscious mind. He divided among these personalities a certain amount of psychic energy, which flowed from one to the other in a sort of hydraulic system. Curiously enough, it was Freud himself who prepared the way for dismissing these explanatory fictions. By insisting that many mental events could not be directly observed, even by the individual himself, he widened the scope of the psychic fiction. Freud took full advantage of the possibilities, but at the same time he encouraged an analysis of the processes of inference through which such events might be   5

---

[2]*aversive:* Repellent, disagreeable.

known. He did not go so far as to conclude that references to such events could be avoided altogether; but this was the natural consequence of a further examination of the evidence.

Freud's conceptions of mental disease and therapy were closely related to his conception of a mental life. Psychoanalysis was regarded as *depth psychology*, concerned with discovering inner and otherwise unobservable conflicts, repressions, and springs of action. The behavior of the organism was often regarded as a relatively unimportant by-product of a furious struggle taking place beneath the surface of the mind. A wish which has been repressed as the result of aversive consequences struggles to escape. In doing so it resorts to certain devices which Freud called "dynamisms" — tricks which the repressed wish uses to evade the effects of punishment. Therapy is concerned with discovering the repressed wish and rooting it out, or occasionally repressing it more securely, so that the symptoms will disappear.

The present view of therapy is quite different. The Freudian wish is a device for representing a response with a given probability of occurrence. Any effect of "repression" must be the effect of the variables which have led either to the response itself or to the repressing behavior. We have to ask why the response was emitted in the first place, why it was punished, and what current variables are active. The answers should account for the neurotic behavior. Where, in the Freudian scheme, behavior is merely the symptom of a neurosis, in the present formulation it is the direct object of inquiry.

Let us consider the apparent result of the struggle of a wish to express itself. An example which permits us to observe the principal Freudian dynamisms is sibling rivalry. Let us say that two brothers compete for the affection of their parents and for other reinforcers which must be divided between them. As a result, one brother behaves aggressively toward the other and is punished, by his brother or by his parents. Let us suppose that this happens repeatedly. Eventually any situation in which aggressive action toward the brother is likely to take place or any early stage of such action will generate the conditioned aversive stimulation associated with anxiety or guilt. This is effective from the point of view of the other brother or the punishing parent because it leads to the self-control of aggressive behavior; the punished brother is now more likely to engage in activities which compete with and displace his aggression. In this sense he "represses" his aggression. The repression is successful if the behavior is so effectively displaced that it seldom reaches the incipient state at which it generates anxiety. It is unsuccessful if anxiety is frequently generated. Other possible consequences, which are described by the so-called dynamisms, are as follows:

The same punishment may lead the individual to *repress* any knowledge of his aggressive tendencies. Not only does he not act aggressively toward his brother, he does not even "know" that he has tendencies to do so.

He may control himself by changing the external environment so that   10
it is less likely to evoke aggressive behavior, not only in himself but in others. As an example of *reaction formation*,[3] he may engage in social work, in campaigns against racial discrimination, or in support of a philosophy of brotherly love. We explain his behavior by showing that it contributes to the suppression of his own aggressive impulses and hence toward a reduction in the conditioned aversive stimulation resulting from punishment.

He may actually injure his brother but *rationalize* his conduct. For ex-   11
ample, he may discipline his brother "for his own good" or may be especially energetic in carrying bad news to him "because he ought to know the worst." These expressions describe the behavior in such a way that punishment is withheld by others and conditioned aversive stimulation fails to be generated in the individual's own behavior.

He may *sublimate* his aggression by taking up an occupation in which   12
such behavior is condoned. For example, he may join the armed services or the police or get employment in an abattoir[4] or wrecking company. This is response induction if different forms of the behavior of striking are strengthened by a variable which strengthens striking his brother; it is stimulus induction if different stimuli which show any property in common with his brother evoke striking.

He may *fantasy* injuring or killing his brother. If this also generates   13
aversive stimulation, he may fantasy injuring or killing other people. If he has the talent, he may write stories about the murder of a brother, or if there is anxiety in connection with the word "brother," about other murders.

He may *dream* of injuring or killing his brother or, if this generates   14
aversive stimulation, of injuring or killing someone who *symbolizes* his brother — perhaps an animal which in another part of the dream takes on his brother's features.

He may *displace* his aggression by "irrationally" injuring an innocent   15
person or thing. This may occur simply because emotional responses show stimulus induction — a man who is angry with an absent office boy takes it out on another employee — or because the displaced behavior will not be punished, at least so severely — a man who is angry with his boss takes it out on the office boy.

---

[3]*reaction formation:* This and the other "dynamisms" that Skinner discusses are all classic Freudian behavior patterns, treated here as responses to a particular life history, rather than as symptoms of unconscious conflicts.

[4]*abattoir:* Slaughterhouse.

He may engage in aggressive *wit* by saying something which in one 16 sense injures his brother but in another escapes censure. The remark is injurious and punishable if it is attributed to one variable, but not if it is attributed to another. The response is witty simply in the sense of being a function of two variables.

He may *identify* himself with prize fighters or with characters in a sa- 17 distic movie or in stories about men who injure or kill their brothers, in the sense that he will be highly disposed to imitate their verbal and non-verbal behavior. He will be reinforced by such stories and will report this fact, together with the emotional reaction common to positive reinforcers, by saying he "enjoys" them.

He may *project* his aggression by describing a picture in which two men 18 are fighting as a picture of brothers, in the sense that he is disposed to imitate such behavior and to suppose that the men in the picture are responding to the same variables.

He may respond aggressively in a Freudian *slip* — for example, by 19 saying, "I never said I didn't hate my brother" instead of "I never said I hated my brother."

He may *forget* to keep an appointment with his brother or with anyone 20 who resembles him.

He may escape anxiety about punishment by *"punishing himself"* — by 21 masochistic behavior, by forcing himself to undertake arduous or dangerous work, or by encouraging accidents.

He may develop certain *physical symptoms,* especially when he is with 22 his brother. These may be a characteristic form of competitive behavior from which he gains an advantage, or the presence of his brother may arouse strong responses of glands and smooth muscles which have an injurious effect.

It would be difficult to prove that all these manifestations are due to 23 the early punishment of aggressive behavior toward a brother. But they are reasonable consequences of such punishment, and the early history may be appealed to *if no other variables can be discovered to account for the behavior.* (If the behavior has no connection with such a history, there is so much the less to explain in a scientific analysis.)

Such manifestations are simply the responses of a person who has had 24 a particular history. They are neither symptoms nor the surreptitious expression of repressed wishes or impulses. The dynamisms are not the clever machinations of an aggressive impulse struggling to escape from the restraining censorship of the individual or of society, but the resolution of complex sets of variables. Therapy does not consist of releasing a trouble-making impulse but of introducing variables which compensate for or correct a history which has produced objectionable behavior. Pent-up emotion is not the cause of disordered behavior; it is part of it. Not being able to recall an early memory does not produce neurotic symptoms; it is itself an example of ineffective behavior. It is quite possible that in therapy the pent-up emotion and the behavioral symptom may disappear at the same time or that a repressed memory will be recalled when maladjusted behavior has been corrected. But this does not mean that one of these events is the cause of the other. They may both have been products of an environmental history which therapy has altered.

In emphasizing "neurotic" behavior itself rather than any inner con- 25 dition said to explain it, it may be argued that we are committing the unforgivable sin of "treating the symptom rather than the cause." This expression is often applied to attempts to remove objectionable features of behavior without attention to causal factors — for example, "curing" stammering by a course of vocal exercises, faulty posture by the application of shoulder braces, or thumb-sucking by coating the thumb with a bitter substance. Such therapy appears to disregard the underlying disorder of which these characteristics of behavior are symptoms. But in arguing that behavior is the subject matter of therapy rather than the symptom of a subject matter, we are not making the same mistake. By accounting for a given example of disadvantageous behavior in terms of a personal history and by altering or supplementing that history as a form of therapy, we are considering the very variables to which the traditional theorist must ultimately turn for an explanation of his supposed inner causes.

OTHER THERAPEUTIC TECHNIQUES

There are many other ways in which behavior which calls for remedial 26 action may be corrected. When the difficulty cannot be traced to the excessive use of punishment or to other aversive circumstances in the history of the individual, different therapeutic techniques must be developed. There is the converse case, for example, in which ethical, governmental, or religious control has been inadequate. The individual may not have been in contact with controlling agents, he may have moved to a different culture where his early training is inadequate, or he may not be readily accessible to control. Therapy will then consist of supplying additional controlling variables. When the individual is wholly out of control, it is difficult to find effective therapeutic techniques. Such an individual is called psychotic.

Sometimes the therapist must construct a new repertoire which will be 27 effective in the world in which the patient finds himself. Suitable behavior already in the repertoire of the patient may need to be strengthened, or additional responses may need to be added. Since the therapist cannot foresee all the circumstances in which the patient will find himself, he must also set up a repertoire of self-control through which the patient will be able to adjust to circumstances as they arise. Such a repertoire consists mainly of better ways of escaping from the aversive self-stimulation conditioned by punishment.

Such constructive techniques may be needed after the nonpunishing   28
audience of the therapist has had its effect. If the condition which is being
corrected is the by-product of controlling circumstances which no longer
exist in the life of the patient, alleviation of the effects of excessive control
may be enough. But if the patient is likely to be subjected to continued
excessive or unskillful control, therapy must be more constructive. The
patient may be taught to avoid occasions upon which he is likely to behave
in such a way as to be punished, but this may not be sufficient. An effective
repertoire, particularly in techniques of self-control, must be constructed.

As another possible source of trouble, the individual may have been,   29
or may be, strongly reinforced for behavior which is disadvantageous or
dangerous. Behavior which violates ethical, governmental, or religious
codes is often by its very nature strongly reinforcing. Sometimes, accidental contingencies may also arise. In Sacha Guitry's film, *The Story of a Cheat*,
a child is punished for some trivial misbehavior by being denied his supper. But the supper turns out to be poisonous, and the child is the only
one of a large family to survive. The implication that the child will then
dedicate himself to a life of crime is not entirely fanciful. Positive reinforcement in atypical situations produces other forms of ineffective or even crip-
pling behavior. For example, the social reinforcement supplied by a particular person may become very powerful, and it may be contingent upon
behavior which is not effective in the world at large. Thus when a solicitous
parent supplies an unusual measure of affection and attention to a sick
child, any behavior on the part of the child which emphasizes his illness
is strongly reinforced. It is not surprising that the child continues to behave
in a similar fashion when he is no longer ill. This may begin as simple
malingering, when it is scarcely to be distinguished from the behavior of
the malingerer who claims to have been injured in an accident in order to
collect damages, but it may pass into the more acute condition of hysterical
illness if the child himself becomes unable to identify the relevant variables
or correctly appraise the possibilities of his own behavior. Other sorts of
social consequences have similar effects. The child who is angry with his
parents is reinforced when he acts in any way which injures them — for
example, in any way which annoys them. If such a condition is long sustained, a repertoire may be established which will work to the disadvantage of the child in his dealings with other people. One obvious remedial
technique for behavior which is the product of excessive reinforcement is
to arrange new contingencies in which the behavior will be extinguished.
The child is no longer reinforced with affection for feigning illness or with
a strong emotional response for being annoying.

Just as the traditional conception of responsibility is abandoned as   30
soon as governments turn to techniques of control other than the use of
punishment, so the conception of therapy as the rooting out of inner
causes of trouble is not likely to be invoked to explain these constructive

techniques. There is, however, a roughly parallel explanation which has been applied to all techniques of therapy. When a therapist encounters a patient for the first time, he is presented with a "problem." . . . The patient usually shows a novel pattern of disadvantageous or dangerous behavior, together with a novel history in terms of which that behavior is to be understood. The particular course of therapy needed in altering or supplementing this history may not be immediately obvious. However, the therapist may eventually "see what is wrong" and be able to suggest a remedial course of action; this is his *solution* to the problem. Now therapeutic experience has shown that when such a solution is proposed to an individual, it may not be effective even though, so far as we know, it is correct. But if the patient arrives at the solution himself, he is far more likely to adopt an effective course of action. The technique of the therapist takes this fact into account. Just as the psychoanalyst may wait for a repressed memory to make itself manifest, so the nonanalytic therapist waits for the emergence of a solution from the patient. But here again we may easily misunderstand the causal relation. "Finding a solution" is not therapy, no matter who does the finding. Telling the patient what is wrong may make no substantial change in the relevant independent variables and hence may make little progress toward a cure. When the patient himself sees what is wrong, it is not the fact that the solution has come from within him which is important but that, in order to discover his own solution, his behavior with respect to his problem must have greatly altered. It follows from the nature of disadvantageous or dangerous behavior that a substantial change must be accomplished if the individual is to identify the relevant variables. A solution on the part of the patient thus represents a substantial degree of progress. No such progress is implied when the therapist states the solution to his problem, but in changing him in such a way that he is able to discover it.

EXPLAINING THE PSYCHOTHERAPEUTIC AGENCY

The therapist engages in therapy primarily for economic reasons. Therapy is a profession. The services which the therapist renders are reinforcing enough to the patient and others to permit him to exchange them for money. Usually the therapist is also reinforced by his success in alleviating the conditions of his patients. This is particularly apt to be true in a culture which reinforces helping others as a standard ethical practice. Frequently another important sort of reinforcement for the therapist is his success in manipulating human behavior. He may have a personal interest, for example, in proving the value of a particular theory of neurotic behavior or of therapeutic practice. These return effects upon the agency will determine in the long run the composition of the profession of psychotherapy and the uniformity of its practices.

31

At certain stages in psychotherapy the therapist may gain a degree of   32
control which is more powerful than that of many religious or governmental agents. There is always the possibility, as in any controlling agency,
that the control will be misused. The countercontrol which discourages the
misuse of power is represented by the ethical standards and practices of
the organized profession of psychotherapy. The danger of misuse may . . .
explain the current popularity of theories of psychotherapy which deny
that human behavior can in the last analysis be controlled or which deliberately refuse to accept responsibility for control.

REVIEW QUESTIONS

1. What does Skinner mean when he says that "The field of psychotherapy is rich
   in explanatory fictions"? What is an "explanatory fiction"? What is the danger
   of such fictions? Why does Skinner reject the cathartic theory of disadvantageous behavior? To what earlier historical phenomena does he compare his
   theory?
2. In Skinner's view, what were Freud's major contributions to the understanding
   of human behavior? What were Freud's "explanatory fictions"? In what way did
   Freud begin to undermine his own work?
3. According to Skinner (based on his example of the two brothers), how do the
   following Freudian "dynamisms" work: *repression, reaction formation, rationalization, sublimation, fantasizing* and *dreaming, displacement, wit, identification, slips of
   the tongue, forgetfulness, self-punishment*?
4. Why does Skinner argue that such forms of behavior (question 3) are neither
   symptoms nor expressions of repressed wishes or impulses? What is the proper
   form of therapy for such behavior, according to Skinner? According to Freud?
   How does Skinner respond to critics who say that he is dealing with the symptoms, rather than causes of behavior?
5. What are the variables determining the extent and the type of control over behavior that is appropriate in therapy? What type of therapy is called for when
   the results of positive reinforcement are disadvantageous? In what way does
   Skinner modify the Freudian position that successful therapy involves patients
   themselves being guided to discover the solutions to their own problems?
6. According to Skinner, what accounts for the success of those kinds of therapy
   that deny that human behavior can be controlled or that refuse to accept responsibility for such control?

DISCUSSION AND WRITING QUESTIONS

1. Which view of the treatment of neurotic (or disadvantageous) behavior makes
   more sense to you — Freud's or Skinner's? Why?
2. Does Skinner's characterization of Freud's theories (in paragraph 5, for example)

seem a fair one, in light of your own reading of Freud's "The Mind and Its Workings"?

3. Research the controversy surrounding one or more aspects of Skinner's work — a set of experiments, a book, the behaviorist movement. Describe the basis of the controversy. Which side appears to you to have the stronger arguments?

4. If you have read the selection from Robert Lindner's "The Fifty-Minute Hour," speculate on how a behaviorist psychologist like Skinner might have approached Mac. Do you think this approach would have been preferable to that of Lindner (an orthodox Freudian)? Explain.

Appendix

BIOLOGICAL PERSPECTIVES: AN OVERVIEW

Dorion Sagan and Lynn Margulis

People have long wondered at the richness and complexity of the natural world upon which we depend. A major task both in the past and the present has been to catalog the types of organisms that inhabit the earth; we still do not even have a proper census of the myriad life forms, estimated at 10 to 30 million species. Nonetheless, there have been traditions of natural history and theology that explore how organisms interact, where they come from, or how they reveal God's handiwork in nature. There are many perspectives from which to study the world, each of which gives a

Dorion Sagan, a writer and magician, is coauthor of *Microcosmos* (Summit Books) and *Origins of Sex* (Yale Univ. Press). He is currently writing a book on experimental biospheres (McGraw Hill) and co-authoring a popular book on sex (Summit Books).

Lynn Margulis is University Professor of Biology, Boston University. In 1983 she was elected a member of the National Academy of Sciences (USA). Her publications, spanning a wide range of scientific topics, include original contributions to cell biology and microbial evolution. She has participated in the development of science teaching materials at levels from elementary to graduate school.

unique view: physicists may try to understand the world as an interaction of particles and waves; psychologists may take as their subject specific attributes of the brain. Biologists present theories of life.

Historically, biology has been considered a "soft" science whose subject was more complex and "laws" less rigorous than disciplines such as chemistry and physics. This soft status, however, has been rapidly changing since the medical discovery of the role of microorganisms in disease, Darwin's theory of evolution by natural selection, Mendel's description of the rules by which traits are inherited, and the understanding of the way DNA both duplicates itself and determines the details for the manufacture of proteins that comprise all living things. Life sciences grew out of a wealth of largely practical information, some of it gathered by people treating human illness. In the genesis of modern biology, which became a formal discipline at the beginning of the 20th century, our agricultural experience has also been important. Hundreds of subdisciplines of biological science are recognized today, including physiology, endocrinology, zoology, botany, cell biology, biochemistry, ecology, vertebrate (including human) anatomy, epidemiology, microbiology, virology, immunology, plant and animal breeding, genetics, plant pathology, and soil science. Practical arts and technologies, including food processing, nutrition, food chemistry, sterilization, lyophilization ("freeze drying"), forestry, and horticulture are all examples of "applied biological science."

Traditionally, biology has been divided into zoology (the study of animals) and botany (the study of plants). We now realize that the categories of "plants" and "animals" are not exclusive: microorganisms (bacteria, protists) and fungi exist that fit in neither one category nor the other. Instead, a five-tiered system that divides life into bacteria, protoctists (algae, protozoa, slime molds, water molds, etc.), fungi (mushrooms, mildew, bread molds, and the like), as well as the more familiar plant and animal kingdoms, is now used. The five kingdoms can be broken down into just short of 100 phyla (sing. phylum), or large groupings, of similar organisms. For example, *Homo sapiens,* our species, falls into the chordate phylum; all animals with backbones (vertebrates) and even certain invertebrates such as sea squirts (that to the casual observer appear very unlike us) are members of our chordate phylum. [Criteria for membership include a hollow nervous system (involving a brain and spinal cord located at the back of the animal) as well as a rod in the developing embryo called a notochord.] Inclusion of two organisms in the same phylum implies that they share a more recent common ancestor than two organisms belonging to different phyla. Despite the many phyla of organisms which live and have lived on the earth (e.g., molluscs, arthropods, echinoderms), we empathize mainly with members of our own phylum. Other chordates include all fish (except shellfish), amphibians, reptiles, mammals, and birds, as well as extinct forms such as dinosaurs. Yet, for all their appeal, the recently evolved chordates are less important to the maintenance of global life than are bacteria, fungi, algae, plants, and other organisms of which we remain relatively ignorant.

Because life is so rich and complex, and because biology has grown directly from the interest in solving specific practical problems (such as how to prevent food spoilage, grow wheat, keep astronauts healthy, cure AIDS and so on), there are few common principles useful to all areas of biology. These few, however, deserve mention.

ASSUMPTIONS UNDERLYING BIOLOGICAL THEORIES

Although biological perspectives are multitudinous and sometimes even outright contradictory, we can pinpoint some underlying assumptions common to most, if not all, theoretical work in the life sciences. The first assumption is the knowability of nature, that we detect it through our senses and that our instruments are reliable extensions of our senses even though they may reveal what our senses never do. Another basic assumption is that nature is consistent, that an experiment done under a given precise set of conditions will yield the same results or observations if performed again under those certain conditions. (As a practical matter, however, it is easy to overlook important factors that influence a given experimental outcome. For example, recordings of gases emanating from the forest floor of the Amazon river basin seemed reliable and repeatable. Yet extrapolations made from these measurements were later found to be misleading: taken during dry months, the measurements did not reflect major changes that occur during the seasonal rains.) Biologists also assume that the biological diversity we see today among millions of different organisms can be explained by the principle of evolution: all descended with modification from common ancestors.

The proliferation of relatively new tools such as microscopes, spectrometers, and telescopes has extended the biological arena to include a study of subvisible beings on earth and the possibility of life on distant worlds. Our recognition of evolution has broadened the scope of life's study to include the ancient past. Not much remains outside the purview of theoretical biology. From this complex and diverse spectrum, we have chosen four themes, a discussion of which will illustrate the assumptions of the biological perspective at work. They are: (1) biosphere/Gaia, (2) autopoiesis and the origins of life, (3) the new synthesis, and (4) biological "literacy."

One theme increasingly important in modern biology is the concept of the biosphere. We define the biosphere as the sum of life in its planetary environment. It extends about 11 kilometers down to the bottom of the sea and 8 kilometers up into the atmosphere. Both living and dead organisms, and the chemicals that cyclically compose them and are returned to the environment, comprise the biosphere. Life interacts so pervasively with its environment that our atmosphere and planetary surface are chemically quite distinct from those of our lifeless neighboring planets, Mars and Venus. Life itself, by growing, decomposing, breathing, eating, excreting, and evolving, controls the circulation of the chemicals it uses. The chemical composition of the atmosphere seems to be regulated by life in much the same way that your body chemistry (such as the concentrations of salts in your blood) is regulated while you are alive. In a way, this scientific idea of global regulation (called the Gaia hypothesis) is a reformulation of the ancient view that the earth is alive.

Despite the fact that the Gaia hypothesis itself is not accepted by all biologists, it reflects underlying assumptions which are commonly accepted. These include the idea that observed biological phenomena, such as that of the earth as a self-regulating system, can be explained by principles of physics and chemistry. The Gaia hypothesis also reflects the core, integrating assumption of biology: that evolution has taken place. In the case of the Gaia hypothesis, it is assumed that the natural activities of organisms (their population growth, gas emissions, chemical transformations, and so forth) led to the phenomenon of planetary, organism-like self-regulation at some distinct period in time, at least two-and-a-half billion years ago.

Another biological theme that has excited much recent interest concerns the origin of life. Microbes, maggots, and other small organisms were once thought to arise spontaneously from decaying matter such as rotten meat or old rags. Careful experimentation with filters showed that this idea was an illusion arising from the invisibility of bacteria, fungi, and other widely dispersed life forms. As a result of the work of the great French biologist Louis Pasteur and others, by the turn of this century all investigators agreed that extant life always comes from preexisting life. Yet the recognition of evolution has led scientists to cast their minds back to earlier times and imagine the development of the first life: such life must have come from nonlife. Indeed, if simple chemicals representing conditions presumably prevailing on the ancient earth are mixed together and exposed to electrical and ultraviolet light energy, they spontaneously become more complex. The result is not life itself but chemicals found in all living things. Such "origins-of-life" experiments lead to much speculation, including the search for environments elsewhere in the solar system thought to be similar to those under which life first spontaneously generated from inanimate matter. Some scientists believe that complex chemicals may have been capable of their own reproduction before cells developed. Others hold that the self-maintaining structure of the cell is necessary for life, and that the earliest organisms actively maintained a cellular structure before they ever reproduced. Today, reproduction and self-maintenance are found together in all living things. All cells and organisms continually replace the chemicals of which they are composed, yet maintain their identity. This material turnover has been explored by the Chilean biologists Francisco Varela and Humberto Maturana and named "autopoiesis," from Greek words meaning "self" and "making." Life is dynamic: it is not only self-made but continually remakes itself to stay the same.

Based on evolutionary assumptions, we now believe that life developed from nonlife (i.e., chemical precursors) at some distinct point in time. (This view overturns, to an extent, the previous form of the assumption, that all life comes from preexisting life.) The assumption that chemistry and physics provide an underpinning for biological explanation is clearly demonstrated by the success of "origins-of-life" experiments in which chemical compounds found in all organisms are easily made in the laboratory in the absence of preexisting life, as long as energy is available.

Another theme of modern biology, dating from the 1930s through the 60s, is the grouping together of Darwinian evolution and Mendelian genetics in the so-called New Synthesis of population biology. Population biology relies heavily on algebra and attempts to describe the fundamental processes of natural change in terms of the flow of inherited units, or genes, throughout populations.

Using radioactive techniques to date the rocks with which the most ancient microscopic fossils are associated, biologists have determined that life on the planet has been in continuous existence for approximately 3.5 billion years. Over this time, organisms have increased themselves using materials in the environment, spreading over the surface of the globe. All cells duplicate their DNA in the process of regenerating themselves. A specific piece of this DNA molecule (enough to make long molecules such as proteins or DNA) is considered a gene. Through messenger RNA, a sort of mirror-image of DNA, genes code for proteins, such as those comprising leaves, flowers, skin, tissue, muscles, some hormones, and even other enzymes, that circle back to cut, splice, and alter the DNA that blue-printed them. But even before the chemical nature of DNA was known, Gregor Mendel found (by experimenting with pea plants) that certain traits were preserved and faithfully transmitted to later generations. These traits, we now recognize, are "written in" genes. Population biology analyzes evolution as changes in the frequencies of genes in populations of organisms. Sociobiology, a subdiscipline that has appeared only in the last two decades, even suggests the concept of a "selfish gene" that imposes powerful constraints on behavior and culture. Sociobiologists claim that what seems to be altruism is really not selflessness at all but the selfish action of genes in one animal body attempting to preserve their kind in another. A problem with this claim, however, is that genes do not exist in isolation, but in organisms whose functioning depends on an assemblage or wide diversity of different genes.

Despite the controversy surrounding sociobiology, the discipline itself does not deviate from underlying assumptions of the biological perspective. Even more so than other disciplines, the analysis of animal behavior in terms of the effects such behavior has on the propagation of animal genes reflects the assumption that complex biological phenomena can ultimately be understood by using principles of physics and chemistry.

Perhaps the most exciting prospect coming from the frontiers of biology is that of human biological literacy and a new emotional relationship of humanity to the earth. The conservation movement is expanding its focus from a concern with endangered species to one centered on life as a whole. We can no longer afford to be biological illiterates, as our civilization and its technological culture have an impact on the rest of life. Not only our well being, but our very existence, depend on our understanding of global structure and function, of which we are only a tiny part (just as effective medical treatment depends upon a grasp of human physiology and anatomy). We are confronted with the practical task of studying our "external physiology," the anatomy outside our bodies. If the earth is fundamentally similar to an organism, it may not indefinitely tolerate the deforestation, desertification, and pollution correlated with human population growth any more than the human body allows lice or ringworm to grow rampantly on it without trying to respond with natural defenses. Biological imagery becomes important to our survival as never before. The global physiology beyond our bodies is as complex as the physiology within them, and as dependent upon "autonomic," unconscious yet highly complex, control processes. We are seeing the rise of a sort of earth biology, a study of the unconscious control processes of the living environment. As humankind grows, our numbers impinge upon those of other species. This creates strain on global resources. As a result global mechanisms that hinder our growth may appear.

Whatever they study, a single protein or the biosphere, biologists view the world in a manner that suggests consistent principles, several of which are as follows: Life originated billions of years ago on the earth and diversified by evolution into the vast number of species we see today; all organisms are related by descent from common ancestors. The first organisms were bacteria. They evolved into protoctists, fungi, animals, and plants 400 million years ago. Death, change, and the extinction of species are as much a part of the evolutionary process as reproduction and growth. All life forms are composed of cells, and all cells are composed of complex carbon-containing chemicals in watery solutions. Expending energy, these chemical components (which always contain carbon, hydrogen, nitrogen, oxygen, phosphorus and sulfur) tend to replace themselves. We recognize these activities in the living system as maintenance and growth.

THEORY CHANGE

Though consistent, the biological perspective is — after all — based on the ideas of human beings. We learn from science that not only organisms, but theories too, change through time. Not even evolution theory, the underlying unifier of the life sciences, is immune from change. It used to be agreed that the way in which a single species becomes two different species (for example, ancient boars became domestic pigs and modern wild boars), was by the gradual accumulation of mutations, small, discrete changes. Now some evolutionists prefer more dramatic explanations: large rearrangements of the chromosomes made of DNA in ancestors lead to two new species. Although all biologists accept evolution as fact, the theories of how new species appear are under great discussion.

Classification also alters the evolutionary timetable: when all life was divided into only two kingdoms (animals and plants), it was theorized that plants evolved first because they were needed as food by animals. But with the recognition that bacteria, including photosynthetic bacteria, preceded plants, it is now theorized that the origin of life really means the origin of bacteria. Theories have changed: now, in the five-kingdom classification, plants are thought to have evolved last (about 0.45 billion years ago), after bacteria (3.5 billion years ago), protoctists (1 billion years ago), animals (0.7 billion years ago, and fungi (0.5 billion years ago).[1]

More dramatic changes still may be in store. If physicists reveal that time is an artifact or illusion of our particular form of perception (via quantum mechanics), evolution theory will have to be rethought. The appearance of life unfolding over billions of years of time may be only a perceptual simplification of an even more grandiose reality which we cannot fully picture, which can be described by mathematics. Of course, such dramatic changes in viewpoint may be remote to present researchers who study how viruses cause disease, or how microorganisms become fossilized in rocks, or what sorts of environments existed in the past. Yet even the theory of evolution evolves. Today's concept of neoDarwinian evolution may

---

[1]For convenience we repeat this information in another notation: the organisms listed refer to the first appearance of their fossils in the fossil record; numbers refer to the date of that appearance in millions of years ago.

Bacteria	3,500
Protoctists	1,000
Animals	700
Fungi	500
Plants	450

seem as truthful to future students as Newtonian mechanics seems to modern physicists; applicable in the vast majority of ordinary cases, but ultimately incorrect, a highly useful but finally incomplete model of what is really going on.

SUMMARY

The evolutionary perspective has become the biologist's guiding principle: all life on earth is composed of complex carbon chemicals, all is derived from ancient common ancestors, and all interacts, transforming the surface of the earth to make it inhabitable. The ultimate source of life's dynamic activities is the energy arriving at the earth in the form of light from the rising and setting sun.

Essay 2

HOW SCIENTIFIC THEORIES ARE DEVELOPED AND APPLIED

Lawrence Badash

From prehistoric times through Babylonian and Egyptian antiquity, people looked to the gods for control over nature. The most obvious example, perhaps, were prayers for rain to aid the growth of crops. From this perspective, nature must have appeared to behave in a random or inconsistent fashion, requiring divine interference. Yet regularities or patterns were also seen during this period, for constellations were known to appear and disappear in the night sky on an annual basis, and the Babylonians even made highly intricate (and reasonably accurate) calculations of numerous celestial phenomena. Thus, while the deities still controlled nature, its behavior seemed fairly consistent. Indeed, if nature were totally inconsistent, and if all phenomena were attributed to the changeable whims of gods (miracles), there would be no motivation to pursue scien-

Lawrence Badash is Professor of History of Science at the University of California, Santa Barbara. His specialty is the history of modern physics and scientists' work on the nuclear arms race. His most recent book is *Kapitza, Rutherford, and the Kremlin* (Yale University Press, 1985).

tific investigations. The study of nature is based ultimately upon the belief that its patterns can be comprehended and then predicted.

The study of nature, of course, is not a robotlike pursuit, where things are black or white and highly trained but non-creative people merely harvest the data. Its practitioners do not shovel piles of "truth" into an inverted pyramid, where the top layer, representing current knowledge, is larger and larger; science is not a simple accumulation of information. Nor is it a process in which scientists pare away error from the limb of truth. It is, in fact, a very human activity, susceptible to taste, fashion, biases, and hunches, as well as intelligence, vision, and hard work. At one time, experiments and observations were not seen as terribly important; since the Scientific Revolution of the seventeenth century, however, increasingly precise laboratory work coupled with the mathematical analysis of data has been the recognized vehicle of progress.

But progress does not proceed in a straight line. Indeed, it often follows a zig-zag path, with errors, dead-ends, and other obstacles. A theory, because it accounts for the known phenomena, may be perfectly fine for centuries, and may even be productive in the sense of provoking investigation that leads to more knowledge. But it may later be replaced with a new interpretation that accounts for the data better or that is more satisfying. There is thus no scientific truth with a capital "T"; a small "t" is appropriate because it suggests no more than the best current insight. Science, therefore, does advance, discarding some ideas and adopting others, while always sensible that further changes may occur. This is why the base of that inverted pyramid does not increase uniformly.

Science is also a remarkably self-correcting activity. Its results are published openly, allowing others to test them. Numerous confirmations (as with the Ptolemaic system) can be nullified by a single proof that a theory is incorrect. This insight led the philosopher of science, Karl Popper, to stress the importance of falsification over verification. Science, however, is a remarkably honest profession. Since reputation is far more important than money to scientists (salaries are not especially high), and since scientists know that anyone may challenge their published work, there is strong incentive to report discoveries with great accuracy and theories with strong supporting evidence.

Science is different from other scholarly professions in that nature is tested. Nature, fortunately, is quite consistent in the physical sciences, such as astronomy, physics, and chemistry, and it is reasonably consistent in the biological sciences, such as zoology and botany. They are thus easier pursuits than the social sciences, which deal with humans and their societies; because humans have free will, their individual behavior can not be predicted accurately, and social scientists commonly use statistical data from large populations to find patterns of behavior. Such theories are likely to be less accurate than those from the natural sciences.

Until the seventeenth century scientists often asked "why" a phenomenon occurred. The theological disputes thus engendered led them away from this question, to focus on the "how." This move, supported by greatly improved measuring ability, proved to be immensely profitable. Theories about the nature of matter, the prime question of physicists and some chemists, advanced as scientists studied smaller and smaller particles, from atoms and molecules to protons, neutrons, and electrons, and then to mesons and other elementary particles. How is matter held together, and just what is matter? Much has been learned by examination under normal conditions, as was the case in the observation of naturally decaying radioactive bodies done in the early part of this century. When a limit was reached, particle accelerating machines were designed to smash nuclei at much higher energies. Francis Bacon called such testing of nature under un3sual conditions "twisting the dragon's tail." Data from both normal and abnormal realms are necessary for current theories, and it is customary for theorists to interpret experimental results and then suggest further investigations.

Since astronomy is the subject of several reading selections in *Theme and Variations,* the following comments will focus primarily upon that science to illustrate more specifically some scientific theories and the ways they have changed. Recognize, however, that the generalizations about theories apply also to sciences other than astronomy.

The Greeks, even though they believed in a Mount Olympus full of gods, were the first to advance wholly rational explanations of nature. These early theories were based upon everyday experience, as in Thales's belief that water was the prime element because he saw dead plants dry up. Simplicity was another feature treasured by the Greeks, who therefore preferred neat and nice explanations to convoluted ones; this bias has continued among scientists to the present day.

Pythagoras, who found musical pitch to be represented by integer multiples of the length of a vibrating string, almost seemed to consider numbers as the fundamental material of the universe. Mathematics became the most advanced science among the Greeks; it was observed to yield exact and true results even when the geometrical figures were not drawn perfectly. Plato, in fact, cast doubt upon the value of observational and experimental science, calling the world of the senses a pale shadow of reality. For him mathematics most closely approached the truth.

It was Plato, however, who set the problem that occupied astronomers for the next two millenia: by what combination of perfect motions could the apparent irregularities of the heavens be explained? The celestial sphere turned once a day but the sun, while it joined in this diurnal motion, also slipped back about a degree a day, so that it passed through the starry background in a year. Even worse, the five known planets sometimes appeared to stop, go back, and then resume their usual motions.

Plato, assuming the simplicity and perfection of circular motion at uniform velocity, challenged astronomers to build systems of circles or spheres that would yield the planetary, solar, and stellar motions that were actually seen from the earth.

Two major lines of activity resulted from this charge. Those with a physical bias, such as Eudoxus and Aristotle, constructed schemes that appealed to the senses and which they thought represented reality. The mathematical astronomers, on the other hand, were concerned primarily with gaining accuracy between prediction and observation, and drew diagrams that achieved this goal but that were unlikely to be the actual planetary paths. Apollonius, Hipparchus, and Ptolemy were the chief figures of this school. Here, then, we see different models accepted for different purposes. The physical astronomers conceived of nested spheres, each bearing a planet, moon, sun, or stars, and each rotating on a separate axis. The sum of the motions represented a good approximation of what we do observe. The mathematical astronomers drew essentially two-dimensional diagrams in which a body, say a planet, moved uniformly around a circle, while the center of that circle itself moved around a larger circle. With some modifications, and with the proper choice of velocities and sizes of the circles, the match between calculation and observation of a planetary position was remarkably good.

In both systems the earth was at the center of motion (this is not precisely accurate in the second case). The one suggestion in antiquity of a heliocentric universe, by Aristarchus, was easily dismissed because he could provide no proof, and because it was obvious to anyone who looked that the heavens turned about us. Furthermore, if the earth did spin on its axis, would we not feel strong winds blowing constantly from east to west? And if the earth moved in orbit around the sun, in our fairly small universe would not the angles between the stars be different from one point in the orbit and from another half a year later (parallax)? Thus, "common sense" indicated that the earth was at the center and stable.

In time it became apparent that the mathematical technique, called the Ptolemaic system, was not fully adequate because tables of planetary position often had to be recalculated. But no one doubted the basic approach, so they tinkered with the mechanism instead of questioning the fundamentals. This is typical behavior within what is called a scientific paradigm, or world view. Only when a crisis of some sort appears does the paradigm change.

In astronomy, the crisis arose in the sixteenth century with the work of Copernicus, who thought that a sun-centered system was simpler (it was easier for the earth to rotate once a day than for the entire heavens to do so), and who was aesthetically unhappy with a technical feature of Ptolemy that placed the earth a bit off center in the old system. Note that simplicity and "niceness" were once again strong motivations for scientists. Copernicus's contribution was curious in a way, because he used Ptolemy's geometrical style and provided little new data. Yet he was convincing to those with open minds because he used data drawn from antiquity to his own time to show that the Ptolemaic system was not unique: another picture with as good (not better) accuracy was possible. He could not prove that the earth moved, but he made it seem to be a possibility. And for the physically-minded, the lack of continuous, strong winds could be explained by the argument that the spinning earth carried its atmosphere along with it.

The Aristotelian-Ptolemaic geocentric system had been adopted as true by the Catholic Church, so the heliocentric view met with strong theological opposition as well as the enormous weight of long tradition. But evidence began to accumulate that further challenged the old picture. Toward the end of the sixteenth century, Tycho Brahe showed that a highly visible supernova was located in the supposedly perfect and unchangeable Aristotelian heavens and that an equally visible comet passed through the positions of the "crystalline" spheres that supported some planets, but no one saw any cracks in the sky or felt pieces of glass falling upon them. Again, this was not strong enough evidence to convince believers in the old astronomy, but it appealed to those seeking support for Copernican views.

Tycho's wealth of accurate observational data was bequeathed to his younger colleague, Johannes Kepler. Before this period, most scientists made a single observation and believed it was right or wrong. Tycho was one of the first to recognize that multiple observations, properly averaged, taken night after night and year after year, were necessary to form the foundation for any precise theory. He was perhaps the finest naked-eye observer of all time, and Kepler knew that Tycho's observations were more accurate than the positions derived using either Ptolemaic or Copernican theory. After years of calculations, Kepler abandoned the age-old circular motion and said that planets move in elliptical orbits. It took a long time to reach this step because the earth's ellipse is actually quite close to a circle (a small eccentricity), such that planetary tables could be calculated that worked reasonably well for a while. Kepler's theory, announced early in the seventeenth century, fell largely upon deaf ears; he could not prove the orbits were elliptical. People became convinced that he was right only after he published a set of planetary tables, based on ellipses and the Copernican arrangement, and the predicted positions were very close to those observed. Thus, the powerful engine driving the acceptance of this new paradigm was not the esoteric mathematical elegance of a novel geometrical curve, but the hard-headed match between theory and measurement.

About the same time that Kepler proposed ellipses, Galileo Galilei took the recently invented "spy glass" and turned it upon the heavens, thereby making the first telescope. What he saw amazed him. There were mountains and craters on the moon, which was a heavenly body and therefore supposedly a perfect sphere. Neither was the sun perfect; it had spots. Venus had phases (like the moon), which were simply explained according to the Copernican system, but impossible to explain by the Ptolemaic. Most significantly, Galileo found satellites or moons orbiting Jupiter, which showed that our universe had other centers of rotation. It was not necessary to believe that the earth was the only possible center of rotation. Once again, these pieces of evidence strengthened the Copernican beliefs of those so inclined, but nowhere was there overwhelming proof that the Ptolemaic system was wrong; the Aristotelian die-hards remained obdurate. Galileo's condemnation by the Inquisition was a measure of the tenacity of old and familiar world views, as well as his own abrasive behavior.

Isaac Newton, toward the end of the seventeenth century, achieved the grand synthesis by showing that the same laws of mechanics that pulled planets in elliptical orbits around the sun also pulled the apocryphal apple to the earth. Aristotle's separation of terrestrial and celestial physics was false. Newton also derived Kepler's laws of elliptical motion, showing that gravitation, not divine presence or magnetic forces, drove these phenomena (magnetism was popular around this time and was used to explain what was otherwise unclear).

By the time the earth's orbital path was actually proven (by the detection of aberration of starlight in mid-eighteenth century and stellar parallax in early nineteenth century), and its rotation likewise was shown (with pendulum experiments in mid-nineteenth century), no one doubted these motions. Copernicanism had been accepted for well more than a century. This is a good example of logic and reason sufficing for scientific belief; absolute proof was merely icing on the cake.

Later work expanded the concept of the universe, from our solar system and its sphere of fixed stars to galaxies and beyond. Albert Einstein's theories of relativity, developed early in the twentieth century, among other things, broadened the understanding of the laws of mechanics. Newton's laws were not superseded, as some believe, but they were shown to hold only for the macroscopic range of normal human behavior. At the very small (atomic) and very large (cosmological) ends of the spectrum, Einstein's laws take hold, while in the middle they become the same as Newton's laws. New understandings, thus, need not always overturn old concepts; often they expand our vision while retaining what is valuable of the earlier interpretations.

These examples and comments suggest that scientific theories arise in a variety of ways and with an assortment of motivations, but with a single purpose (ignoring here political pressure to come to a preordained conclusion): to understand natural phenomena. In the twentieth century, scientific achievement has become for many the major yardstick with which to measure a nation's cultural advancement.

References

Marshall Clagett. *Greek Science in Antiquity* (New York: Macmillan, 1955).
Arthur Berry. *A Short History of Astronomy* (New York: Dover, 1961).
Thomas S. Kuhn. *The Copernican Revolution* (New York: Random House, 1957).
Thomas S. Kuhn. *The Structure of Scientific Revolutions* (University of Chicago Press, 1962).

Additional Readings*

Copernicus and the New Universe

Banville, John. *Doctor Copernicus: A Novel.* London: Secker and Warburg, 1976.

Bieńkowska, Barbara, ed. *The Scientific World of Copernicus: On the Occasion of the 500th Anniversary of his Birth.* Dordrecht-Holland/Boston: D. Reidel Publishing Company. 1973.

Camus, Albert. "The Adulterous Woman." In *Exile and the Kingdom.* New York: Vintage, 1958.

Corson, David, ed. *Man's Place in the Universe: Changing Concepts.* Tucson: University of Arizona, 1977.

Dick, Steven J. *Plurality of Worlds: The Origins of the Extraterrestrial Life Debate from Democritus to Kant.* Cambridge: Cambridge University Press, 1982.

Dobzhansky, Theodosius. "Darwin versus Copernicus." In *Changing Perspectives on Man.* Ed., Ben Rosenblatt. Chicago: University of Chicago Press, 1968.

Drake, Stillman. *Galileo.* New York: Hill and Wang, 1980.

Gingerich, Owen, ed. *The Nature of Scientific Discovery: A Symposium Commemorating the 500th Anniversary of the Birth of Nicolaus Copernicus.* Washington, D.C.: Smithsonian Institution Press, 1975.

Hoyle, Fred. *The Nature of the Universe.* New York: Harper and Bros., 1950.

———. *Highlights in Astronomy.* San Francisco: W.H. Freeman, 1975.

Hubble, Edwin. *The Realm of the Nebulae.* New Haven: Yale University Press, 1936.

Huygens, Christian. *The Celestial Worlds Discovered.* Cass Library of Science Classics, no. 10. London: Frank Cass, 1968.

Kesten, Hermann. *Copernicus and His World.* New York: Roy Publishers, 1945.

Koestler, Arthur. *The Sleepwalkers: A History of Man's Changing Vision of the Universe.* New York: Macmillan, 1959.

Lovell, Bernard. *In the Center of Immensities.* World Perspectives, Vol. 53. New York: Harper and Row, 1978.

---

*See also works cited in biographical introductions.

Rosen, Edward. *Copernicus and the Scientific Revolution*. Malabar, Florida: Robert E. Krieger Publishing Company, 1984.

de Santillana, Giorgio. *The Crime of Galileo*. Chicago: University of Chicago Press, 1955.

Shapley, Harlow, ed. *Science Ponders Religion*. New York: Appleton-Century-Crofts, 1960.

————. *Of Stars and Men: Human Response to an Expanding Universe*. Boston: Beacon Press, 1959.

Smith, Vincent Edward. "The New Sciences." In *Science and Philosophy*. Milwaukee: The Bruce Publishing Company, 1965.

Hobbes and the Social Contract

Ahmad, Ilyas. *The Social Contract and the Islamic State*. New Delhi: Kitab Bharan, 1972.

Birnbaum, Pierre, Jack Lively, and Geraint Parry. *Democracy, Consensus, and Social Contract*. London, Beverly Hills: Sage, 1978.

Buchanan, Geoffrey and James M. Buchanan. *The Reason of Rules: Constitutional Political Economy*. Cambridge: Cambridge University Press, 1985.

Buchanan, James M. *Freedom in Constitutional Contract: Perspectives of a Political Extremist*. College Station: Texas A&M Press, 1977.

————. *The Limits of Liberty: Between Anarchy and Leviathan*. Chicago: University of Chicago Press, 1975.

Cobban, Alfred. *Rousseau and the Modern State*. London: Allen and Unwin, 1934.

Dallmayr, Fred, ed. *From Contract to Community: Theory of the Crossroads*. New York: M. Dekker, 1978.

Faure, Edgar. *The Heart of the Battle: For a New Social Contract*. Trans. Gill Manning. New York: McGraw-Hill, 1972.

Feibleman, James K. *Justice, Law, and Culture*. Boston: M. Nijhoff, 1985.

Gildin, Hilail. *Rousseau's Social Contract: The Design of the Argument*. Chicago: University of Chicago Press, 1983.

Gough, J.W. *The Social Contract: A Critical Study of its Development*. Oxford: Oxford University Press, 1936.

Macneil, Ian. *The New Social Contract: An Inquiry into Modern Contractual Relations*. New Haven: Yale University Press, 1980.

McManners, J. *The Social Contract and Rousseau's Revolt Against Society: An Inaugural Lecture Delivered at the University of Leicester, 6 November 1967*. London: Leicester University Press, 1968.

Nielson, Kai and Roger A. Shiner. *New Essays on Contract Theory*. Guelph, Ontario: Canadian Association for Publishing in Philosophy, 1977.

Condorcet and the Progress of Civilization

Almond, Gabriel A., Marvin Chodorow, and Roy Harvey Pearce, eds. *Progress and Its Discontents*. Berkley: University of California Press, 1977.

Aron, Raymond. *Progress and Disillusion: The Dialectics of Modern Society*. New York: Frederick A. Praeger, 1968.

Baillie, John. *The Belief in Progress.* New York: Scribner's, 1951.

Bury, J.B. *The Idea of Progress: An Inquiry into its Origin and Growth.* London: Macmillan, 1921.

Comte, Auguste. "Preliminary Considerations on the Necessity of Social Physics as suggested by the Analysis of the Present State of Society." In *The Essential Comte.* Ed., Stanislav Andreski; Trans., Margaret Clarke. New York: Barnes and Noble, 1974.

Durkheim, Emile. "Egoistic Suicide." In *Suicide: A Study in Sociology.* Trans., John A. Spaulding and George Simpson. New York: The Free Press, 1951.

Gomer, Robert. "The Tyranny of Progress." In *Changing Perspectives on Man.* Ed. Ben Rosenblatt. Chicago: University of Chicago Press, 1968.

Himmelfarb, Gertrude. "In Defense of Progress." *Commentary.* Vol. 69, no. 6, (June, 1980), pp. 53–60.

Huxley, Aldous. *Science, Liberty and Peace.* New York: Harper & Bros., 1946.

Medawar, Sir Peter. *The Hope of Progress.* London: Methuen, 1972.

Mill, John Stuart. "The Spirit of the Age." In *Essays on Politics and Culture.* Ed., Gertrude Himmelfarb. Garden City: Doubleday, 1962.

———. "Influence of the Progress of Society on Production and Distribution" (Book IV, Chapter I). In *Principles of Political Economy with Some of Their Applications to Social Philosophy.* Ed., Sir W. J. Ashley. New York: Augustus M. Kelley, 1965.

Nisbet, Robert, *History of the Idea of Progress.* New York: Basic Books, 1980.

Platt, John Rader. *The Step to Man.* New York: John Wiley & Sons, 1966.

Saint-Simon, Henri de. *Social Organization, the Science of Man and Other Writings.* Trans., ed., Felix Markham. New York: Harper Torchbooks, 1964.

Smith, Adam. "Of the Division of Labour" (Book I, Chapter I); "Of the Principle Which Gives Occasion to the Division of Labour" (Book I, Chapter II); "Of the different Progress of Opulence in different Nations" (Book III, Chapter I). In *An Inquiry into the Nature and Causes of The Wealth of Nations.* Ed., Edwin Cannan. New York: The Modern Library, 1937.

Stent, Gunther S. *Paradoxes of Progress.* San Francisco: W.H. Freeman, 1978.

Turgot, Anne Robert Jacques. "A Philosophical Review of the Successive Advances of the Human Mind." In *Turgot on Progress, Sociology and Economics.* Trans., ed. Ronald L. Meek. Cambridge: Cambridge University Press, 1973.

Weber, Max. "Science as a Vocation." In *Max Weber: Essays in Sociology.* Trans., eds., H.H. Gerth & C. Wright Mills. New York: Oxford University Press, 1946.

Darwin and the Survival of the Fittest

Banton, Michael, ed. *Darwinism and the Study of Society: A Centenary Symposium.* Chicago: Quadrangle, 1961.

Barnet, Samuel A. *A Century of Darwin.* London: Heineman, 1958.

Caplan, Arthur L. and Bruce Jennings. *Darwin, Marx, Freud: Their Influence on Moral Theory.* New York: Plenum, 1984.

Clark, Linda. *Social Darwinism in France.* University of Alabama Press, 1984.

Fiske, John. *Darwinism and Other Essays.* Boston and New York: Houghton Mifflin, 1900.

————. "Manifest Destiny." *Harper's New Monthly Magazine*. March 1885, 578–90.

Hamrum, Charles L., ed. *Darwin's Legacy* (Nobel Conference XVIII, Gustavus Adolphus College, Minnesota). San Francisco: Harper and Row, 1983.

Henkin, Leo J. *Darwinism in the English Novel, 1860–1910: The Impact of Evolution on Victorian Fiction*. New York: Russell and Russell, 1963.

Hofstadter, Richard. *Social Darwinism in American Thought*. Boston: Beacon Press, 1944.

Kelly, Alfred. *The Descent of Darwin: The Popularization of Darwinism in Germany, 1860–1914*. University of North Carolina Press, 1981.

Keith, Arthur. *Evolution and Ethics*. New York: Putnam's, 1946.

Morton, Peter. *The Vital Science: Biology and the Literary Imagination*. London: Allen and Unwin, 1984.

Oldroyd, David R. *Darwinian Impacts: An Introduction to the Darwinian Revolution*. New South Wales, Australia: Open University Press, 1980.

Oldroyd, David and Ian Langham. *The Wider Domain of Evolutionary Thought*. Boston: D. Reidel, 1983.

Peckham, Morse. "Darwinism and Darwinisticism." *Victorian Studies 3* (Sept. 1959), 19–40. See other essays on Darwin's impact in this issue.

Pusey, James Reeve. *China and Charles Darwin*. Cambridge: Harvard University Press, 1983.

Ringer, Robert S. *Restoring the American Dream*. New York: Harper, 1979.

Stevenson, Lionel. *Darwin Among the Poets*. New York: Russell and Russell, 1963.

Sumner, William Graham. *Sumner Today: Selected Essays of William Graham Sumner, with Comments by American Leaders*. Westport: Greenwood Press, 1940.

Sumner, William Graham. *Social Darwinism: Selected Essays of William Graham Sumner*. Englewood Cliffs: Prentice, 1963.

Marx and the Class Struggle

Aptheker, Herbert. *The Urgency of Marxist-Christian Dialogue*. New York: Harper, 1970.

Balinsky, Alexander. *Marx's Economics*. Lexington: Heath, 1970.

Bentley, Eric, ed. *Thirty Years of Treason: Excerpts from Hearings Before the House Committee on Un-American Activities, 1938–1968*. New York: Viking, 1971.

Bullock, Chris and David Peck, eds. *Guide to Marxist Literary Criticism*. Bloomington: Indiana University Press, 1980.

Caute, David. *The Great Fear: The Anti-Communist Purge Under Truman and Eisenhower*. New York: Simon and Schuster, 1978.

Communist Party of the Soviet Union. *History of the Communist Party of the Soviet Union*. New York: International Publishers, 1939.

————. *Program of the Communist Party of the Soviet Union*. New York: International Publishers, 1963.

————. *Fiftieth Anniversary of the Great October Socialist Revolution*. Washington, U.S.S.R. Embassy, 1967.

————. *Report of the Central Committee of the Communist Party of the Soviet Union*. Moscow: Novosti Press Agency Publishing House, 1971.

Diamond, Stanley, ed. *Toward a Marxist Anthropology: Problems and Perspectives*. The Haugue: Mouton, 1979.

Djilas, Milovan. *The New Class: An Analysis of the Communist System*. New York: Praeger, 1957.

Eastman, Max. *Marxism: Is it Science?* New York, Norton, 1940.

———. *Marx, Lenin and the Science of Revolution*. Westport: Hyperion, 1926.

Egbert, Donald Drew. *Social Radicalism and the Arts: Western Europe: A Cultural History from the French Revolution to 1968*. New York: Knopf, 1970.

Freedman, Robert. *Marxist Social Thought*. New York: Harcourt, 1968.

Fried, Albert. *Socialism in America: From the Shakers to the Third International: A Documentary History*. New York: Doubleday Anchor, 1970.

Fromm, Erich. *Marx's Concept of Man*. New York: Ungar, 1961.

Gurley, John G. *Challenges to Capitalism: Marx, Lenin, Stalin, and Mao*. New York: Norton, 1975.

Harris, Kevin. *Teachers and Classes: A Marxist Analysis*, London: Routledge, 1982.

Hine, Robert V. *California's Utopian Colonies*. San Marino: Huntington Library, 1953.

Jacobson, Phyllis and Julius Jacobson. *Socialist Perspectives*. Princeton: Karz-Cohl, 1983.

Kovel, Joel. *The Age of Desire: Reflections of a Radical Psychoanalyst*. New York: Pantheon, 1981.

Lang, Berel, and Forrest Williams, eds. *Marxism and Art: Writings in Aesthetics and Criticism*. New York: David McKay, 1972.

Lobkowicz, Nicholas. *Marx and the Western World*. Notre Dame: University of Notre Dame Press, 1967.

Mitchell, Juliet. "Women: The Longest Revolution." *New Left Review*, No. 40 (Nov.–Dec. 1966). 11–37.

O'Reilly, Kenneth. *Hoover and the Un-Americans: The FBI, HUAC, and the Red Menace*. Philadelphia: Temple University Press, 1983.

Reed, Evelyn. *Problems of Women's Liberation: A Marxist Approach*. New York: Pathfinder, 1981.

Robinson, Cedric J. *Black Marxism: The Making of the Black Radical Tradition*. London: Zed Press, 1983.

United States Cong. House Committee on Un-American Activities. *100 Things You Should Know About Communism*. Washington, GPO, 1951.

Freud and the Power of the Unconscious

Albin, Mel., ed. *New Directions in Psychohistory: The Adelphi Papers in Honor of Erik H. Erikson*. Lexington: Heath, 1980.

Bergman, Ingmar. *Wild Strawberries* (film; 1957); screenplay reprinted in *Four Screenplays of Ingmar Bergman*. New York: Simon and Schuster, 1960.

Bettelheim, Bruno. *Freud and Man's Soul*. New York: Knopf, 1983.

Brugger, Robert. *Our Selves/Our Past: Psychological Approaches to American History*. Baltimore: Johns Hopkins University Press, 1981.

Coles, Robert. "Shrinking History." *New York Review of Books*. Feb. 23, Mar. 8, 1973, 15–21, 25–29.

Ellenberger, Henri S. *The Discovery of the Unconscious*. New York: Basic Books, 1970.

Erikson, Erik. *Young Man Luther*. New York: Norton, 1958.

Fancher, Raymond E. *Pioneers of Psychology*. New York: Norton, 1979.

Freud, Sigmund. *The Standard Edition of the Complete Psychological Works of Sigmund Freud*, James Strachey, translator and editor. 24 vols. London: Hogarth Press and the Institute of Psychoanalysis, 1953–.

Freud, Sigmund and W.C. Bullit. *Thomas Woodrow Wilson*. Cambridge: Houghton Mifflin, 1967.

Fromm, Erich. *Greatness and Limitations of Freud's Thought*. New York: Harper, 1980.

Gay, Peter. *Freud for Historians*. New York: Oxford University Press, 1985.

Goldwert, Marvin. *Psychic Conflict in Spanish-America: Six Essays on the Psychohistory of the Region*. Washington: University Press of America, 1982.

———. *History as Neurosis: Paternalism and Machismo in Spanish America*. Lanham: University Press of America, 1980.

Jurjevich, R.M. *The Hoax of Freudianism: A Study of Brainwashing the American Professionals and Laymen*. Philadelphia: Dorrance, 1974.

Kardiner, A. *My Analysis with Freud: Reminiscences*. New York: Norton, 1977.

Kohut, Thomas A. "Psychoanalysis as History." *American Historical Review*, Apr. 1986, 336–354.

Kurzweil, Edith and William Phillips, eds. *Literature and Psychoanalysis*. New York: Columbia University Press, 1983.

Meisel, Perry, ed. *Freud: A Collection of Critical Essays*. Englewood Cliffs: Prentice, 1981.

Miller, Jonathan, ed. *Freud: The Man, His World, His Influence*. Boston: Little, Brown, 1972.

Pomper, Philip. *The Structure of Mind in History: Five Major Figures in Psychohistory*. New York: Columbia University Press, 1985.

Spector, Jack J. *The Aesthetics of Freud: A Study in Psychoanalysis and Art*. New York: Praeger, 1972.

Stafford-Clark, David. *What Freud Really Said*. New York: Schocken Books, 1965.

Stannard, David E. *Shrinking History: On Freud and the Failure of Psychohistory*. New York: Oxford University Press, 1980.

Strozier, Charles B. and Daniel Offer. *The Leader: Psychohistorical Essays*. New York: Plenum, 1985.

Trosman, Harry. *Freud and the Imaginative World*. Hillsdale: Analytic, 1985.

Credits *(continued from p. iv)*

Nicolaus Copernicus: De Revolutionibus Orbium Caelestium (1543) trans. by John F. Dobson and Selig Brodetsky. Published as *Occasional Notes of the Royal Astronomical Society*. Vol. 2., No. 10. Reprinted by permission of the Royal Astronomical Society.
Copernicus: On the Revolution of the Heavenly Spheres. Trans. by A. M. Duncan. Barnes and Noble Books, 1976. Reprinted by permission of Oak Tree Publications, A. S. Barnes.
Angus Armitage: Copernicus: The Founder of Modern Astronomy. A. S. Barnes, 1957.
Copernicus and the Reformation of Astronomy, No. 15, General Series. Published by The Historical Association, London. Diagram by courtesy of Henry Schuman. Reprinted by permission of The Historical Association, London.
Diagram and explanatory note from George O. Abell, *Exploration of the Universe,* 3rd edition. Copyright © 1975. Reprinted by permission of Holt, Rinehart and Winston.
Diagrams by Vincent Edward Smith from "The New Sciences" in *Science and Philosophy.* The Bruce Publishing Company, 1965. Reprinted by permission of Glencoe Publishing Company.
Galileo Galilei; "Letter to the Grand Duchess Christina;" Giovannie Ciampoli, "Letter to Galileo;" and Cardinal Bellarmine, "Letter to Foscarini." Excerpts from *Discoveries and Opinions of Galileo* by Stillman Drake. Copyright © 1957 by Stillman Drake. Reprinted by permission of Doubleday & Company, Inc.
Catholic Church: "The Decree of the Congregation of the Index on Writings and Books Treating the Copernican System" (March 5, 1616); "The Sentence Against Galileo and the Recantation" (June 22, 1633) in Karl von Gebler, *Galileo Galilei and the Roman Curia.* Trans., Mrs. George Sturge. Merrick New York: Richwood Publishing Co., 1977. (Reprint of the 1879 ed., published by C. K. Paul, London.) Reprinted by permission of Richwood Publishing Company.
Johannes Kepler: "Letter to Galileo" (October 13, 1597). From *Johannes Kepler: Life and Letters.* Editor, Carol Baumgardt. New York: Philosophical Library, 1956, pp. 40–42. Reprinted by permission of the Philosophical Library, Inc.
Blaise Pascal: "Pensées 72, 205 and 206" from *Pensées and the Provincial Letters* by Blaise Pascal, translated by W. F. Trotter, Everyman's Library. Reprinted by permission of J. M. Dent & Sons Ltd. Publishers.
Alexander Pope: An Essay on Man, "Epistle I: On the Nature and State of Man, With Respect to the Universe." In *The Norton Anthology of English Literature,* 4th ed., Vol. 1. Copyright © 1979. Reprinted by permission of W. W. Norton.
Thomas Henry Huxley: "On the Advisableness of Improving Natural Knowledge" in *Collected Essays: Method and Results,* Vol. 1. Macmillan and Company, London, 1894.
Thomas Henry Huxley: "Agnosticism and Christianity" in *Collected Essays: Science and Christian Tradition,* Vol. 5. Macmillan and Company, London, 1897.
Jorge Luis Borges: "The Library of Babel" from Jorge Luis Borges, *Labyrinths.* Copyright © 1962 by New Directions Publishing Corporation.
From "Genesis 11," verses 1–9 in *The Bible: A New Translation* by James A. R. Moffatt. Copyright 1922, 1924, 1925, 1926, 1935 by Harper & Row, Publishers, Inc. Copyright 1950, 1952, 1953, 1954 by James A. R. Moffatt. Reprinted by permission of Harper & Row, Publishers, Inc.

HOBBES AND THE SOCIAL CONTRACT

John Locke: "Of the Ends of Political Society and Government (1690)" from *Locke's Two Treatises of Government,* edited by Peter Laslett, published by Cambridge University Press. Copyright © 1960 by Cambridge University Press. Reprinted by permission of Cambridge University Press.
Jean-Jacques Rousseau: "The Social Contract (1762)." From Jean-Jacques Rousseau's *On the Social Contract* with Geneva Manuscript and Political Economy. Edited by Roger D.

Adolph Hitler: "Nation and Race" from *Mein Kampf* by Adolf Hitler, translated by Ralph Manheim. Copyright 1943 and copyright © renewed 1971 by Houghton Mifflin Company. Reprinted by permission of Houghton Mifflin Company and published by Hutchinson, an imprint of Century Hutchinson. Reprinted in Canada by permission of Century Hutchinson Limited.

Letters to the *Los Angeles Times* by Gerald Hewett and Kris Karliner, reprinted by permission of Gerald Hewett and Kris Karliner.

Guide for the Film Fanatic by Danny Peary. Copyright © 1986 by Danny Peary. Reprinted by permission of Simon & Schuster, Inc.

"Biological Perspectives: An Overview" by Dr. Lynn Margulis and Dorion Sagan. By permission of the authors.

"The Sociological Perspective: Assumptions Underlying Theories of Social Life" by Dr. Jeffrey C. Chin. By permission of the author.

"How Scientific Theories Are Developed and Applied" by Lawrence Badash. By permission of the author.

MARX AND THE CLASS STRUGGLE

Speech from *Major Barbara* by George Bernard Shaw. Reprinted by permission of The Society of Authors on behalf of the Bernard Shaw Estate.

Karl Marx and Friedrich Engels: "The Communist Manifesto" (1848). Text based on *The Marx-Engels Reader,* 2nd edition. Edited by Robert C. Tucker. Copyright © 1978. Reprinted by permission of W. W. Norton.

Notes from *Essential Works of Marxism,* edited by Arthur P. Mendel. Bantam, New York, 1961. Reprinted by permission of Arthur P. Mendel.

John Reed: Ten Days that Shook the World, 1919. International Publishers, 1934, 1967. All notes by John Howard Lawson for the 1967 edition. Reprinted by permission of International Publishers Company, Inc.

Map, "Petrograd in 1917" from *Russia 1917: The February Revolution* by George Katkov. Copyright © 1967 by George Katkov. Reprinted by permission of Harper & Row, Publishers, Inc.

Mao Tse-tung: "On Literature and Art" in *Marxism and Art* by Berel Lang and Forrest Williams. David McKay Company, 1970.

Angela Y. Davis: Chapter 13, "The Approaching Obsolescence of Housework: A Working-Class Perspective." From *Women, Race and Class,* by Angela Davis. Copyright © 1981 by Angela Davis. Reprinted by permission of Random House, Inc.

Joseph Nahem: "Psychology and Psychiatry Today: A Marxist View" (1981). Originally titled "Introduction" in *Psychology and Psychiatry Today: A Marxist View.* International Publishers, 1981. Reprinted by permission of International Publishers Company, Inc.

Max Eastman: "Socialism and Human Nature" in *Reflections on the Failure of Socialism.* Devin-Adair, 1955. Copyright © renewed in 1983. Reprinted by permission of Devin-Adair Publishers, Inc.

Frederick C. Crews: "A Bourgeois Writer's Proletarian Fables" from *Frederick C. Crews.* Copyright © 1963 by Frederick C. Crews. Reprinted by permission of the publisher, E. P. Dutton, a division of NAL Penguin, Inc.

Illustrations from *Winnie-the-Pooh* by A. A. Milne, illustrated by Ernest H. Shepard. Copyright 1926 by E. P. Dutton, renewed 1954 by A. A. Milne. Reproduced by permission of the publisher, E. P. Dutton, a division of NAL Penguin Inc., and used by permission of the Canadian Publishers, McClelland and Stewart, Toronto.

FREUD AND THE POWER OF THE UNCONSCIOUS

Sigmund Freud: "The Mind and Its Workings" (1940) from *An Outline of Psychoanalysis*